COWBOY

Boulder
Boulder
WE ARE COMING
GERONIMO INOSINCIO
YSIDORA ALCANTARA
FELIX ALCANTARA

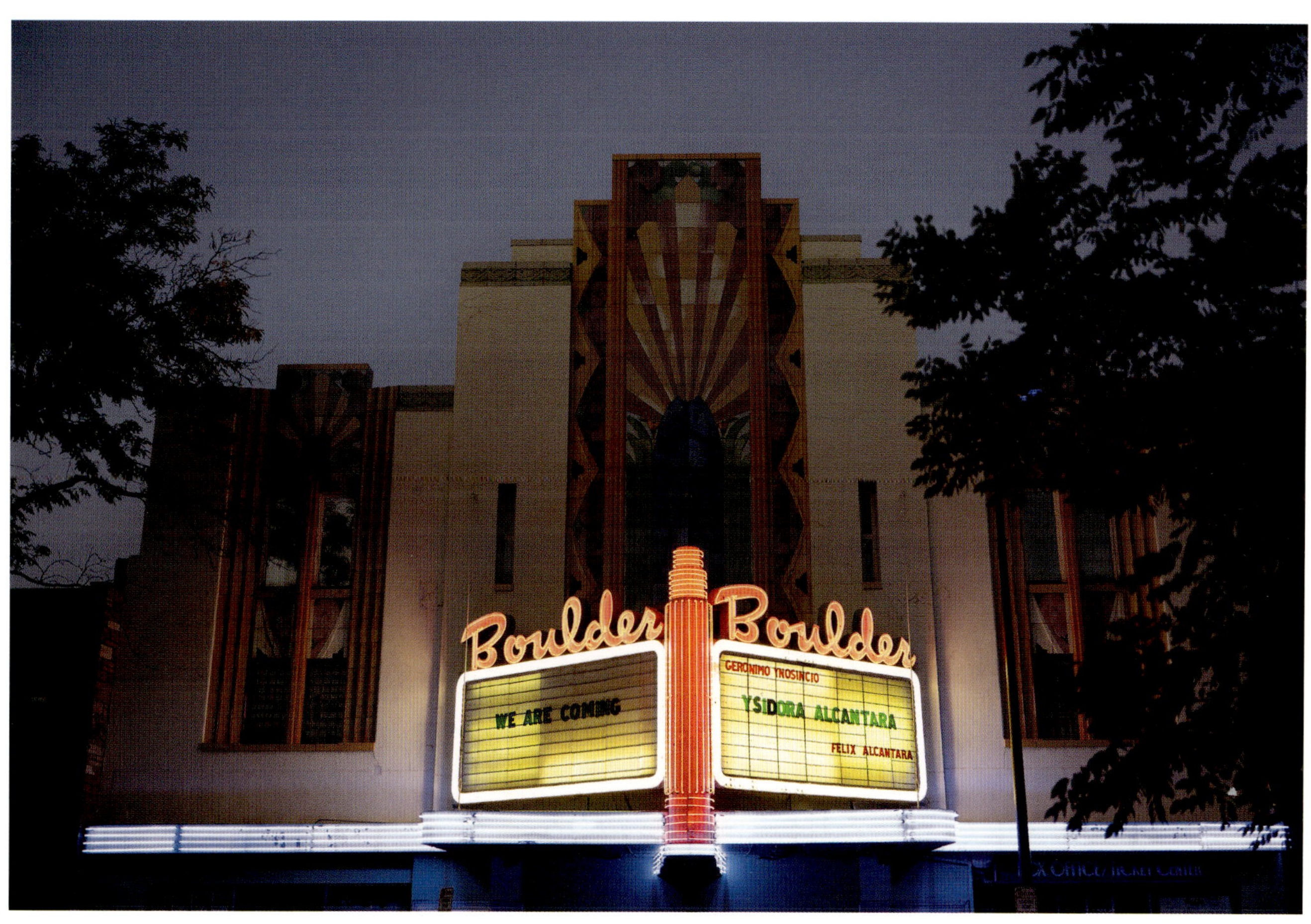

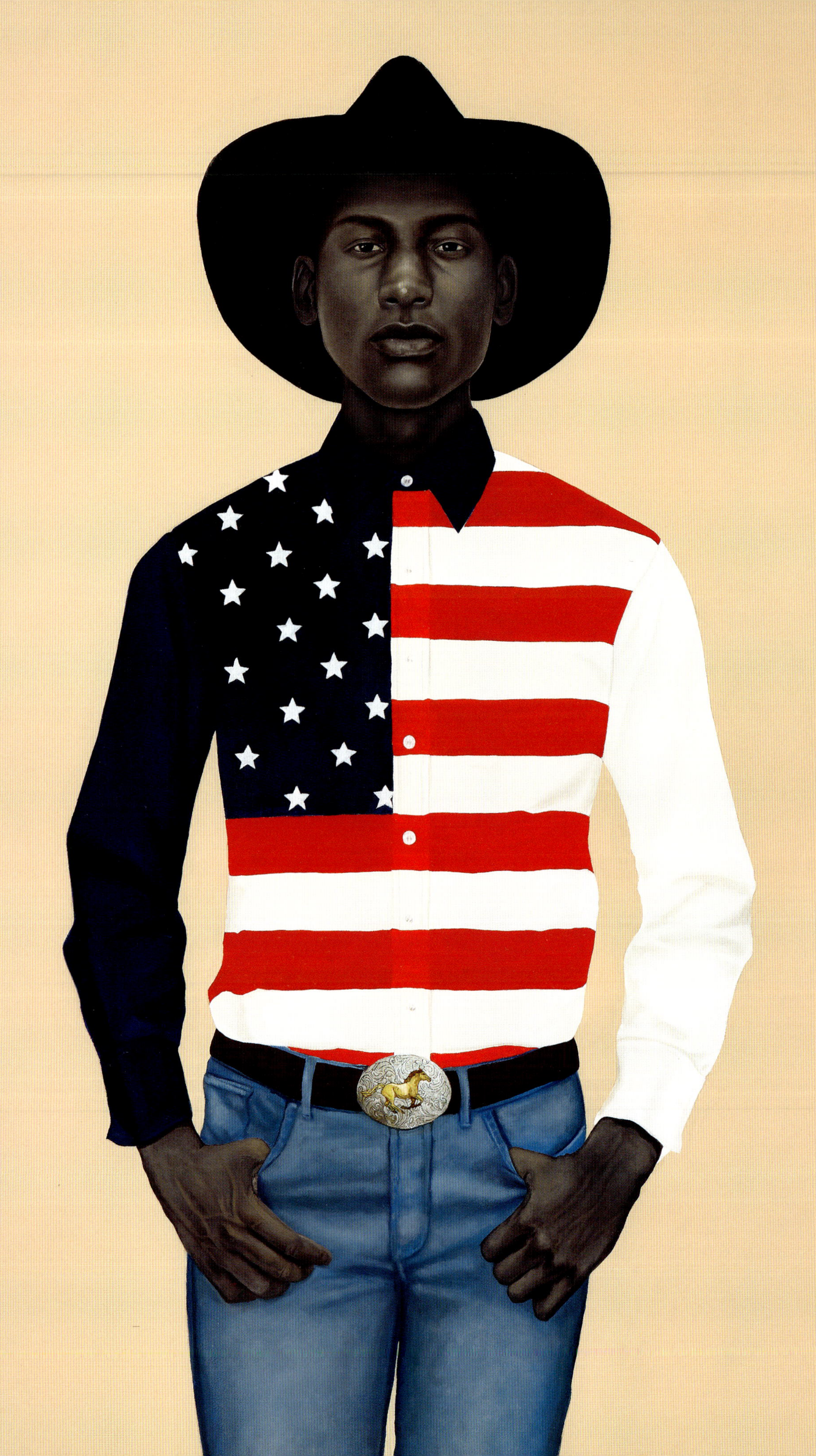

COWBOY

Rizzoli Electa

CONTENTS

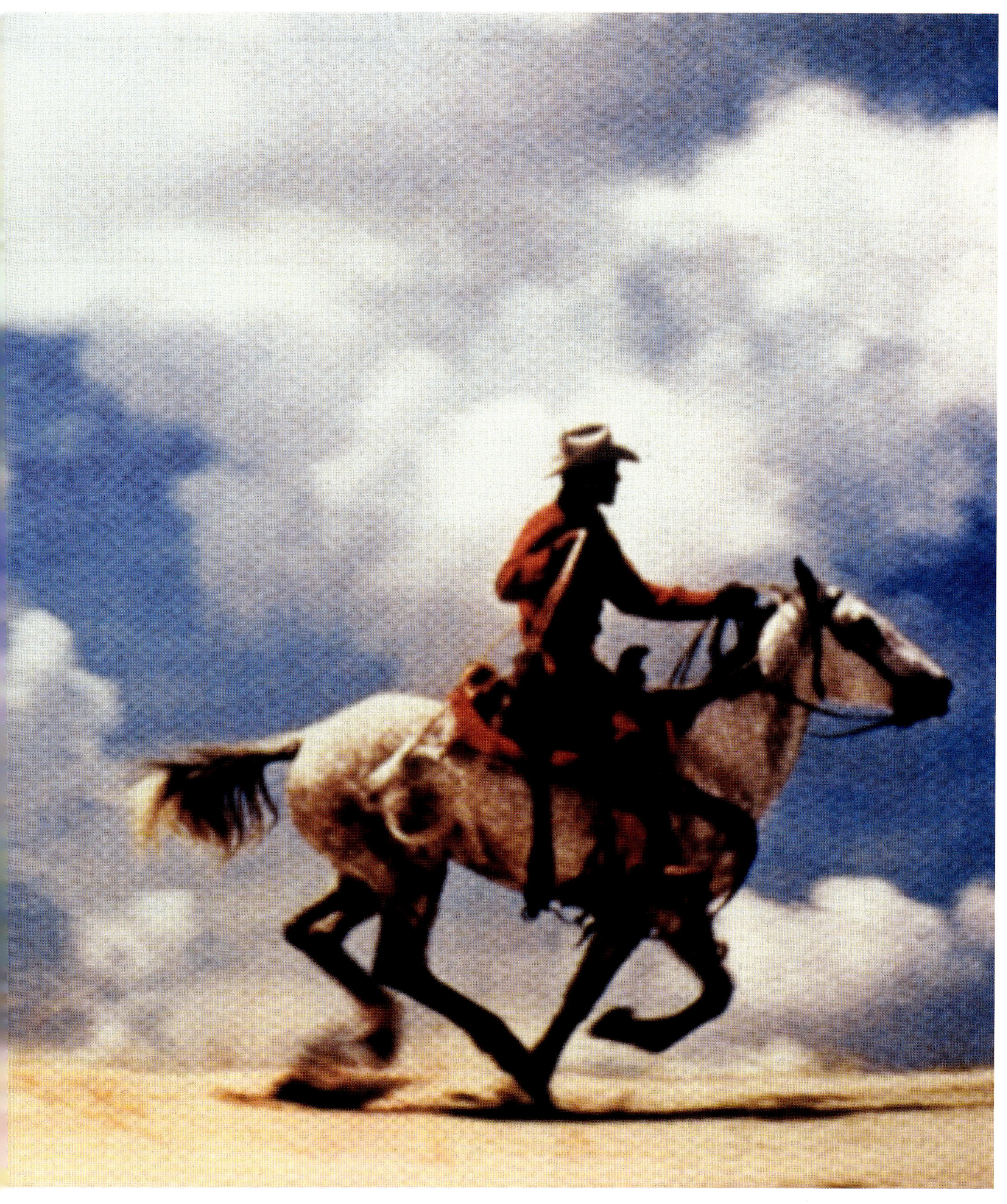

THERE ARE FEW ARCHETYPES THAT ELICIT AS STRONG OF A REACTION AS the cowboy. The mystique, the history, the staging, the representation, and above all, the resilience of his iconography all contribute to the popular enthrallment with this character.

Since the nineteenth century, the myth of the cowboy has been adopted in myriad forms as a profitable, attractive, and compelling tool for commercialization, political gain, the reinforcement of racial and gendered stereotypes, and as an idealized justification for American land appropriation and ambition. This myth materialized in popular culture but was also exploited as a tool for diplomacy, an idealization of American heroism, an archetype of masculinity, and an individualized model for taming the natural world.

MCA Denver committed to this project for a number of reasons, primarily for the opportunity to explore in depth a central figure who

DIRECTOR'S FOREWORD

Nora Burnett Abrams

contributed so profoundly to the development of the American West—either by fact or fictional representation. Fundamental to our curatorial approach is a focus on history and narratives that have inspired, shaped, and formed the region of the Mountains West and Colorado, specifically. To surface and interrogate the events and figures that collectively set the stage for where we find ourselves in the present day is a throughline of MCA Denver's exhibition platform and is brought to life by this project in particular.

The character of the American cowboy is a vehicle through which history can be reexamined as much as our present-day unpacked. There is no other figure in the American popular imagination who bears such weight, enigma, and adoration. To explore the history of the cowboy is to explore American history, and, in particular, the history of the American West, the vast diversity of its cowboy origins, its dependency on and exploitation of natural resources, and the counternarratives that challenge popular conceptions of the cowboy as an American (white, male) hero. To put forward the origins of this myth as well as a far-ranging counterpoint to such conceptions is to journey through the cultural history of the American West and to acknowledge, unpack, and explore the many forces that attempted to control and advance it.

Cowboy aims to complicate the durability of this mythic figure by presenting multifaceted approaches that reframe and resituate this icon in the present day. The guiding questions that drove our research focus on how the mythology of the cowboy exists today; how the cowboy as an archetype of masculinity shaped how we think about gender now; how the myth circulates and who controls that circulation; how elastic is the perception of the cowboy, and how has it veered from its nineteenth-century origins?

The contributors to this publication thoughtfully and creatively offer myriad responses to such questions. The challenge of addressing the cowboy mythology in the present tense is effectively met by a range of critical voices that focus on discrete aspects of historical and contemporary cowboy culture and practice. Myeshia C. Babers looks at the history of the Black rodeo cowboy and how this figure performs and functions today; co-curator Miranda Lash delves into artist rafa esparza's personal history and evolution of his practice in an enlightening interview; R. Alan Brooks conjures the history of Dearfield, Colorado, one of the earliest Black homesteading communities in the state, through a graphic, dream-like vision; and Jongwoo Jeremy Kim shares a comprehensive analysis of artist Kenneth Tam's practice and a deeper discussion of Asian American masculinity, sexuality, and how they have been and are permitted to be represented.

Amplifying the work presented in the exhibition, this publication avers wildly diverse manifestations of cowboy life and culture and, by doing so, illustrates how the history and lives of cowboys have always had and will continue to have a broader scope and more fluid identity than is represented in popular culture. To look at the evidentiary and fictional tropes, behaviors, cultural norms, and lifestyles associated with this figure is both to look at real, lived experience and to recognize the performative and artificial pretense that the cowboy encompasses. The American cowboy is a problematic figure not because it isn't real but because it is so vividly and persistently present in the popular mindset, as a character as much as a laborer.

Problematic and complex, this exhibition and accompanying catalogue engage with and provoke those who practice and perform, who expose and who expand our understanding of the cowboy and the enormity with which this figure has shaped the history of this region, as well as that of the country as a whole.

A PROJECT OF THIS SCALE AND SCOPE IS THE RESULT OF HUNDREDS OF conversations, the first of which began with the arrival of Miranda Lash at MCA Denver in the fall of 2020. As we Zoomed about exhibition ideas, artists we were curious about, and projects we wanted to bring to life, we connected deeply with the stories that related most intimately and expansively to the city and state in which we now both live. Inspired by the work of Amanda Hunt, Head of Public Engagement at the Walker Art Center who curated *Black Cowboy* at the Studio Museum in Harlem (2017), we wanted to unpack this icon further. Our desire to engage deeply with a figure of mythic proportions and also bring to bear the humility and tenderness of the cowboy's real, lived experience collectively launched us into this monumental project and continued to carry it forward over three years.

We gratefully acknowledge the many, many individuals and organizations whose support and contributions enabled this project to emerge, grow, and blossom into its fullest form. Generous support from the National Endowment for the Arts (NEA) was crucial to our mounting this exhibition at the vision and scale

ACKNOWLEDGMENTS

Nora Burnett Abrams
Miranda Lash

we imagined. The Blue Rider Group at Morgan Stanley also provided meaningful support for this publication, enabling the exhibition to live well beyond the walls of the museum.

We are honored to collaborate with the many artists, curators, writers, poets, musicians, and historians, as well as museums, galleries, and artists' estates to ensure both a sensitive and also radically reimagined interpretation of the cowboy figure in the present tense. We thank, first and foremost, the artists who share their work, their practice, and their critical lens on this subject through approaches ranging from the conceptual to the concrete: John Baldessari, R. Alan Brooks, Mel Chin, Gregg Deal, Angela Ellsworth, rafa esparza, Juan Fuentes, Fabian Guerrero, Karl Haendel, Luis Jiménez, Kahlil Joseph, Grace Kennison, Deana Lawson, Matthew J. Mahoney, Laurel Nakadate, Richard Prince, Otis Kwame Quaicoe, Akasha Rabut, Lucy Raven, Ken Taylor Reynaga, Jaye Rhee, Yumi Roth in collaboration with Emmanuel David, Ana Segovia, Amy Sherald, Stephanie Syjuco, Kenneth Tam, Andy Warhol, and Nathan Young.

We appreciate the support and commitment of those who have graciously agreed to lend their work to this exhibition and enabled the project to be both rigorous and expansive: the Andy Warhol Museum, the Bonnefanten Museum, Evan Boris and Monique Meloche, Matthew and Melanie Bronfman, Commonwealth and Council, Elizabeth Rooklidge, the Estate of John Baldessari, the Estate of Ann Harithas, Gerald Peters Gallery, Carlos Huber & Andrew Timberlake, Leslie Tonkonow Artworks + Projects, Devon Musgrave, Adam Schiffer, and Stefan Simchowitz.

The process of securing loans and new commissions required the generous support and coordination of many individuals: Ashley White at Almine Rech Gallery; Maggie Adler, Selena Capraro, and Kristen Gaylord at the Amon Carter Museum of American Art; Marissa Arndt and Greg Pierce at the Andy Warhol Museum; Charlotte Fijen, Charlotte Franzen, and Mirjam Meisen at Bonnefanten; Catharine Clark, Zoe Reinhardt, and Anton Stuebner at Catharine Clark Gallery; Maureen Chimento; Kibum Kim, Brenda Reyes-Chavez, Breanne Bradley, and Matt Town at Commonwealth and Council; Dzifah Danso and JR Henneman at the Denver Art Museum; Rocio Fernandez de Angulo; Julie Fitzgerald, Kathy Paciollo, Antwaun Sargent, and Diallo Simon-Ponte at Gagosian Gallery; Verónica Guerrero and Karen Huber at Galería Karen Huber; Alice Duncan at Gerald Peters Gallery; Yomahra Gonzalez at rafa esparza Studio; Hanna Soltys at the Library of Congress; Lisa Sette Gallery; Joel Draper at Lisson Gallery; Lori and Stephen Mahoney; Margaret Andrea at the Milwaukee Art Museum; Betty Moody at Moody Gallery; Heryte T. Tequame and Hai Zhang at the Queens Museum; Dave Austin and Matt Gaughan at Richard Prince Studio; Maurice Roberts; Jeff Bergman at Ryan Lee Gallery; Dylan Schwartz; José Carlos Diaz and Hannah Jirano at the Seattle Art Museum; Lisa Pomares and Celeste Reyes at Simchowitz Gallery; Marck Julián Elizalde Solis; Adél Erdei-Melis, Simone Manwarring, Claire de Dobey Rifelj, and Dionne de la Vega at Sprüth Magers; Patrick Hughes and Jeffery Kuiper at Turner Carroll Gallery; Star Castro, Matthew Lax, and Ariel Lauren Pittman at Vielmetter Los Angeles; Stefanie Haferbeck at WENTRUP; and David Clapp and Andrea R. Hanley at the Wheelwright Museum of the American Indian.

At MCA Denver, we recognize our fearless Board of Trustees whose support and counsel provide an exceptional foundation for experimentation and creativity. We also express our deepest thanks to the many colleagues who contributed to the development of this project: Rebecca Gates, Exhibitions Coordinator, who kept every detail straight, well-organized, and mercifully accurate; Leilani Lynch, Associate Curator, who ensured that this publication was completed on time and with great care; Anna Martin, Exhibitions Manager, who provided endless solutions to the many entanglements that installation planning can cause; our colleagues on the Development team, Lela Urquhart and Elizabeth Baribeau, who raised meaningful support to enable this project to come to life; to our Programs team, including Sarah Kate Baie and Christina Chambers, for their inspiring engagement with the themes of this exhibition; Florie Hutchinson and Courtney Law, Director of Communications, Partnerships, and Digital Initiatives, for their expert promotion of the show; and to the entire staff of MCA Denver who contributed behind the scenes, at the front of house, and everywhere in between to ensure a beautiful and lively exhibition production.

We are immensely grateful to all who contributed to the production of this publication, especially the brilliant and reflective writers and interlocutors: Myeshia C. Babers, R. Alan Brooks, rafa esparza, and Jongwoo Jeremy Kim. We also thank our partners at Rizzoli Electa, Isabel Venero, our rigorous and devoted editor, and Charles Miers, publisher, who has been an ardent champion of MCA Denver's programs.

We are honored to bring this exhibition and its accompanying publication to life, to realize long-simmering questions and to engage, provoke, and delight audiences and readers. To collaborate with each other on this project has been a gift and we are thrilled to be able to share it with the world.

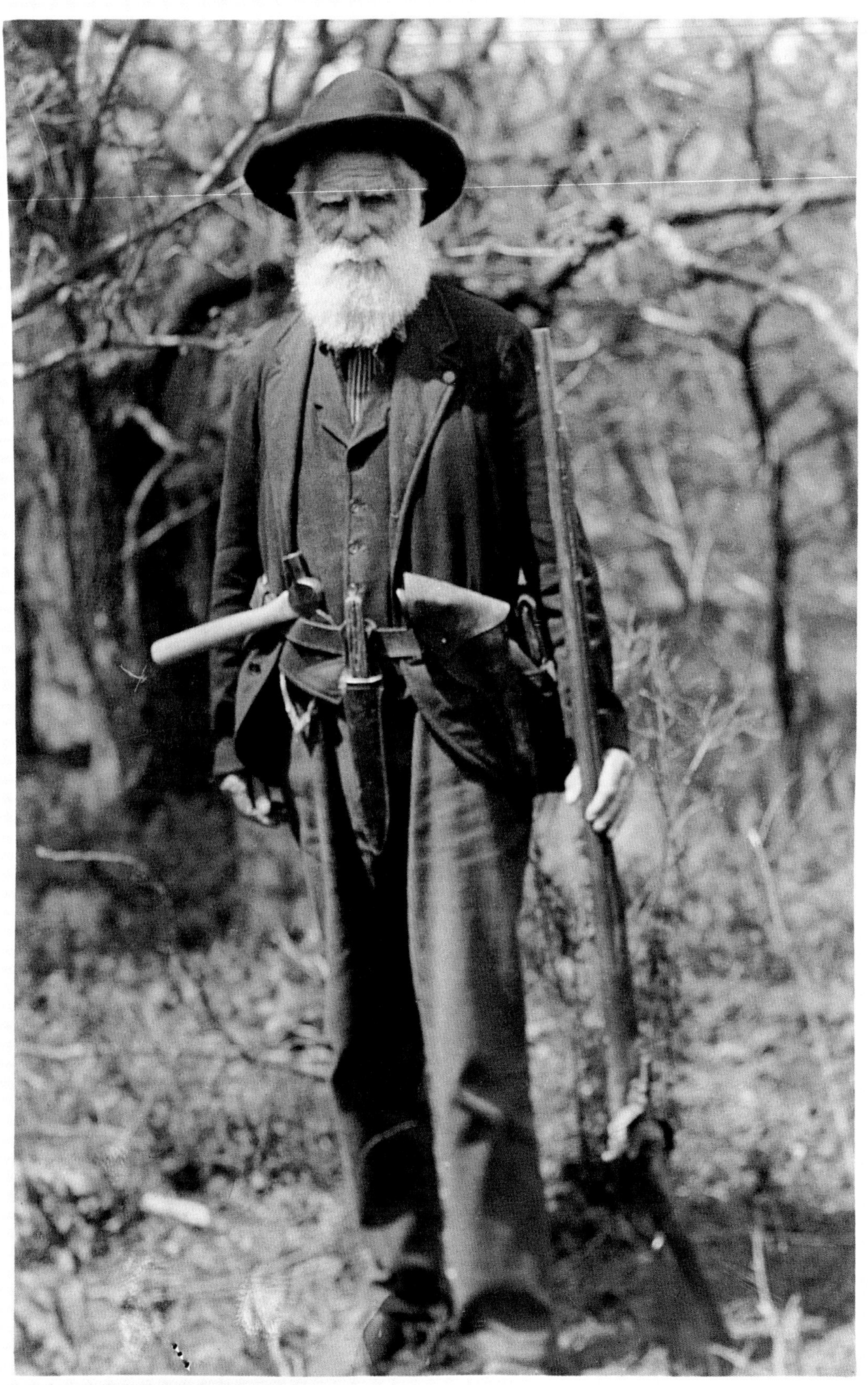

RICHARD PRINCE'S DEADPAN, CONCEPTUAL WORK OF 1989 IS A COPY (the photograph) of a copy (a Marlboro cigarette advertisement) of a myth (the cowboy) (pp. 4–5). It is, in fact, a copy of an idea—a copy of an invention. Its grainy texture suggests the fuzziness of memory or the haze of nostalgia. This signature image by Prince attests to how entrenched the image of the cowboy remains in the popular mindset as much as it affirms the free circulation of such tropes across popular media. The intention of a work like this is to highlight our belief in its mythology; it suggests that we *want* to be seduced by this scene, to believe that it *was* real, that it *did* exist, that the stirring of feeling from a man taming animals and nature and looking unafraid before a vast unknown is in fact honest and accurate.

FROM FACT TO MYTH AND BACK AGAIN: THE COWBOY AND CONTEMPORARY ART

Nora Burnett Abrams

But is it?

Popular notions of the cowboy comprise multiple strata of fact and fiction built up over centuries, the sum of which illustrates how this figure came to embody so decisively and persuasively a symbol of an American male hero. And, such an accumulation of narrative and history invites a deeper probe regarding the durability of this figure: is it imagined or honest, accurate or incomplete, more fiction than fact?

These questions inspired the exhibition *Cowboy* and this accompanying publication and, unsurprisingly, offered up new lines of inquiry into this ubiquitous figure. Character, icon, performer, yet also laborer, rancher, and animal caretaker, the cowboy is both an invention and a historical and contemporary reality. No other role features so prominently in the lexicon of American labor and imagination than that of the image incessantly perpetuated through popular media and culture. The facticity of the cowboy's representation is what this exhibition questions and readdresses: briefly tracing the historical events that gave rise to a cowboy figure and how that figure was plucked from reality and placed into a cinematic and literary spectacle is a flatly modern act of creativity and erasure. What this exhibition makes clear, however, is how contemporary artists have consistently disclosed this fiction and replaced it with historical evidence

Daniel Freeman standing, holding gun, with hatchet tucked in belt. Nebraska Beatrice, ca. 1904. Photograph

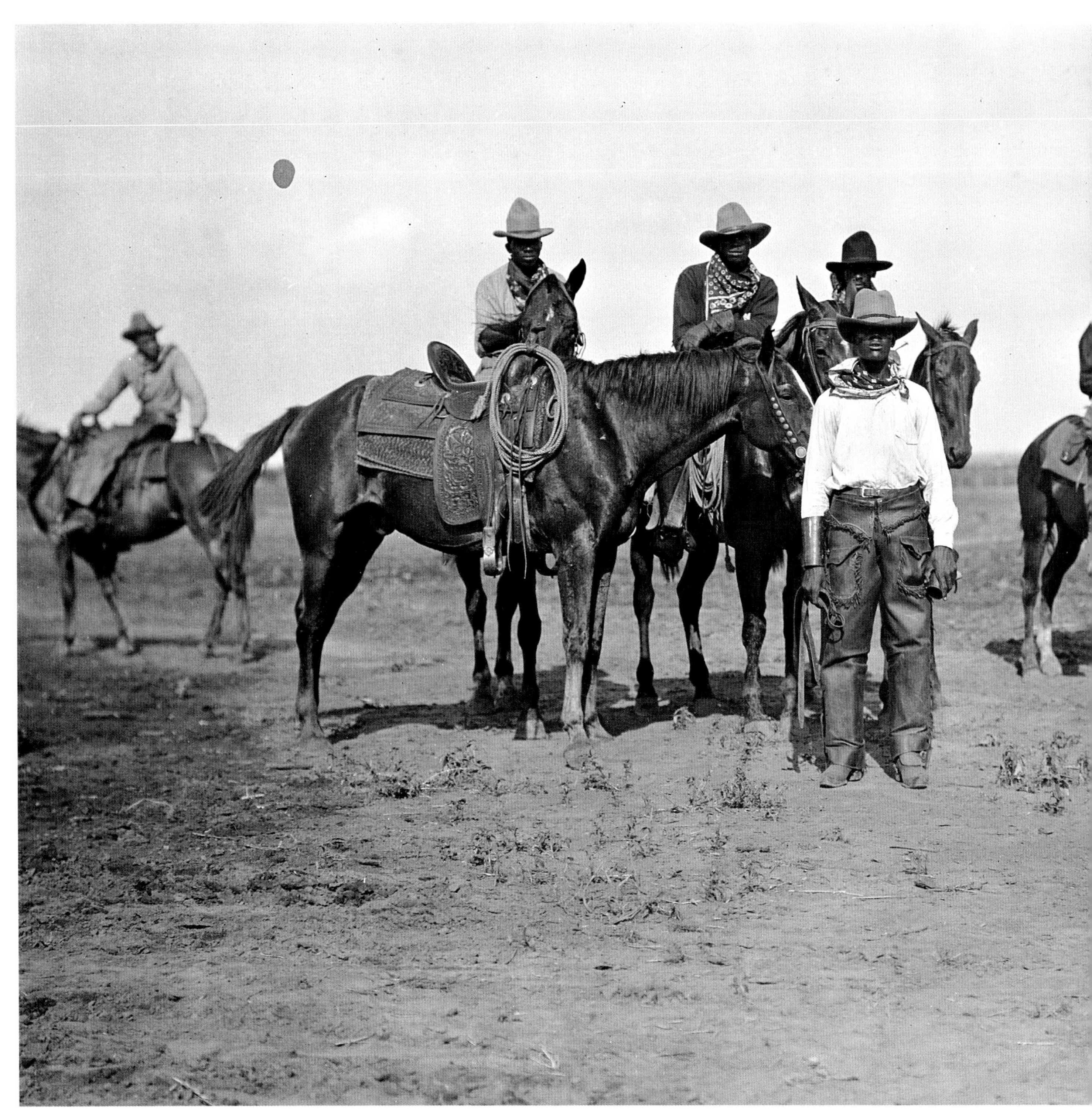

Erwin E. Smith, [AFRICAN-AMERICAN COWBOYS DURING THE NEGRO STATE FAIR, BONHAM, TEXAS], 1911. Nitrate negative. Erwin E. Smith Collection of the Library of Congress on Deposit at the Amon Carter Museum of American Art, Fort Worth, Texas. LC.S611.015

and narrative, using contemporary practices to deliver the truth that over a hundred years of mythmaking had expunged.

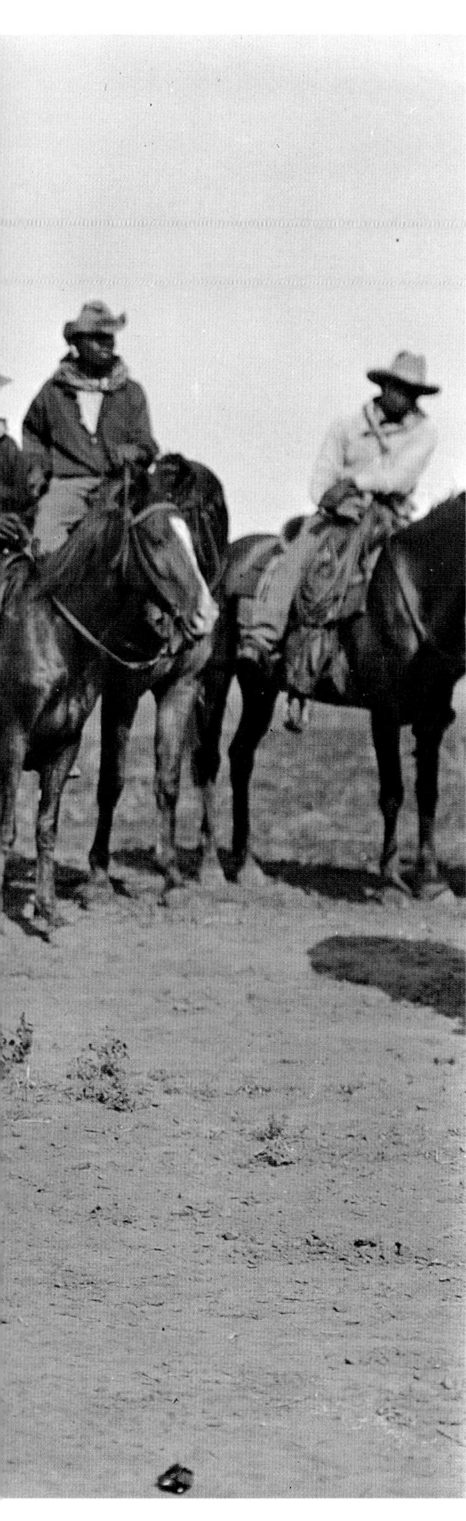

EARLY EXAMPLES

The functional role of a cowboy emerged primarily after the Civil War and was sparked by the cattle industry. In the years immediately following the Civil War, the idea—the possibility—of the West represented a new frontier, one vastly different from the devastation of the battlefields in the American South and the industrialization of the East coast. The cattle industry in the 1860s was largely unregulated and the landscape of the Midwest and Mountain West regions offered a perception of open spaces—the hundreds of thousands of Indigenous people and communities living in these territories were of little consequence to those engaged in moving cattle, specifically from Texas to the railroad cities that would send it all to the burgeoning urban centers in the Midwest and on the East Coast.

The big open spaces of Texas, the Midwest, and Mountain West regions required that cattle be accompanied, overseen, and corralled—tough, exhausting labor in extreme weather conditions along trails to marketplaces and railroad connections that were only in the process of being charted. It was, for the most part, isolating, lonely, grueling, and dangerous. These "range cowboys" herded cattle at roundups, branded them, and prepared them for sale for their owners (pp. 12–13).

The Homestead Act of 1862 granted land claims in thirty states (p. 10). These land claims were located on the traditional or treaty lands of many Native American tribes, forcing their removal and fueling a false notion of the West as a site of discovery, possibility, and economic opportunity. In the late nineteenth century, cattle could be sold for thirty to forty dollars a head,[1] highly incentivizing the cattle ranchers to seize more land and generate lucrative financial outcomes.

The ever-expanding open ranges for cattle grazing and the dubiously legal removal of Native tribes from their indigenous territory and onto reservations radically shifted the landscape. This restructuring of the landscape and, really, the restructuring of the natural order of the landscape, proved profitable for a select few businessmen, like Joseph McCoy,[2] and devastating for the animals, water, flora, and Native people who had historically occupied the land.

During the cattle industry's explosive growth in the twenty-five years after the Civil War, thousands of people of color (men and women) served as cowhands or laborers to service this growing market—and, notably, several economic drivers contributed to the diversification of the cowboy role. There was abundant opportunity to provide beef to the urban centers across the country that were themselves growing rapidly due to industrialization, immigration, and postwar rebuilding efforts. During this period, roughly 1868–95, of the nearly 35,000 cowboys who supported the ranching and cattle industry, over one-third of them were Black or Mexican (pp. 12 and 14).[3] The reality is that there was always racial diversity across cowboy culture, but the cowboy myths that concurrently, and subsequently, permeated popular culture did not reflect this fact.

For many cowboys, the skills and expertise that they were known for and utilized were learned from the Mexican vaqueros, who were especially known for their cattle roping and ranching expertise. The vaquero, from the Spanish *vaca* for cow, arrived in Spanish-controlled Texas in the eighteenth century (p. 15).[4] Demand for these skills contributed to the influx of Mexican laborers in "the cradle of the Western cattle business" in southwest Texas.[5] The growth of the Texas cattle industry in the early nineteenth century is largely due to the skills of these Mexican cowboys, mainly young and single men, who could handle the physical demands of the labor. Though the vaqueros were instrumental in creating the cattle industry, they were excluded from the economic boom to which their efforts contributed.[6]

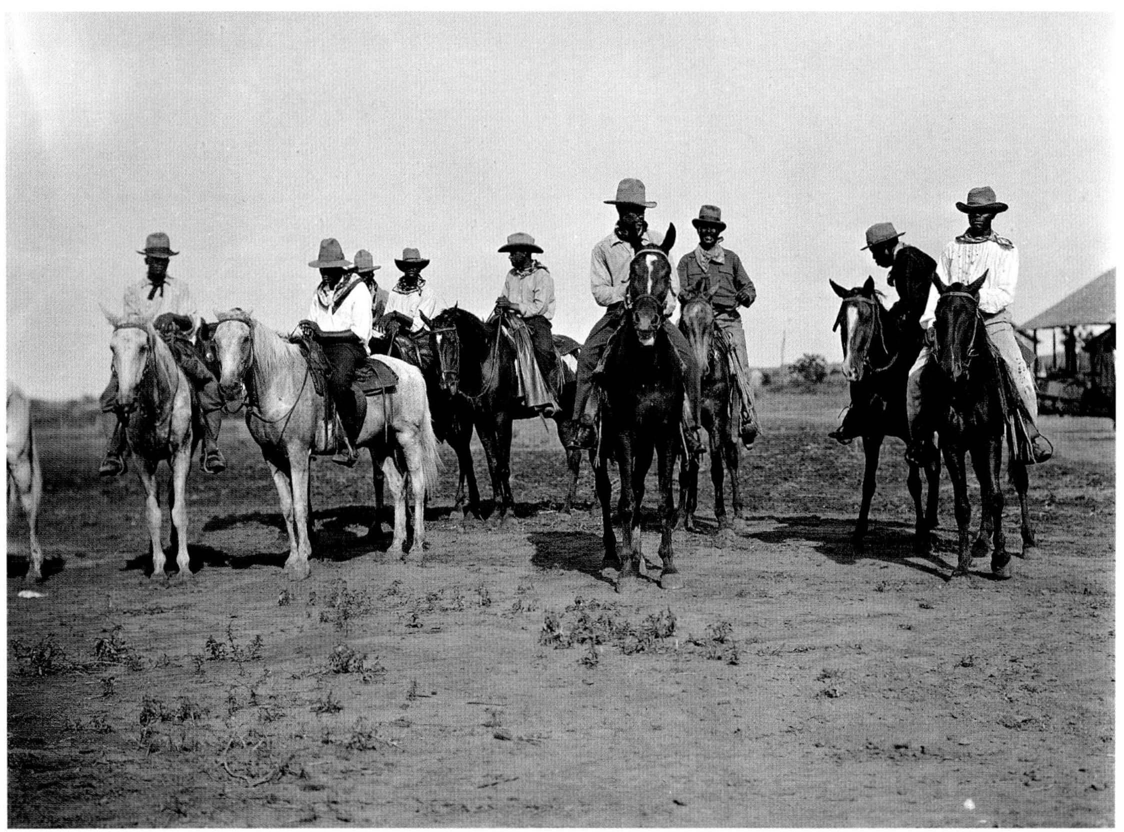

Erwin E. Smith, [AFRICAN-AMERICAN COWBOYS ON THEIR MOUNTS READY TO PARTICIPATE IN HORSE RACE DURING NEGRO STATE FAIR, BONHAM, TEXAS], 1911. Nitrate negative. Erwin E. Smith Collection of the Library of Congress on Deposit at the Amon Carter Museum of American Art, Fort Worth, Texas. LC.S611.016

In the years following the Civil War, demand for cattle accelerated across the Southwest and the Plains to such a degree that prohibitions on who could perform such labor were significantly reduced.[7] "And for African-Americans, the cattle industry offered one of the few chances for equal, exciting, labor in a country that increasingly closed doors to people of color."[8] Of the thousands of Black cowboys who took on this work in the nineteenth century, many had served as cattle herders during slavery, even attending to the cattle while their owners served in the Confederacy.[9] Their training for the role—even the origin of the term "cowboy," in part—has roots in and is inseparable from the economic system of slavery. As one scholar noted, "Cowhands were ordinary men who possessed outdoor skills and a strong love of horses and cattle. Daily life on the range was more often hard, tedious, and lonely than filled with high adventure."[10]

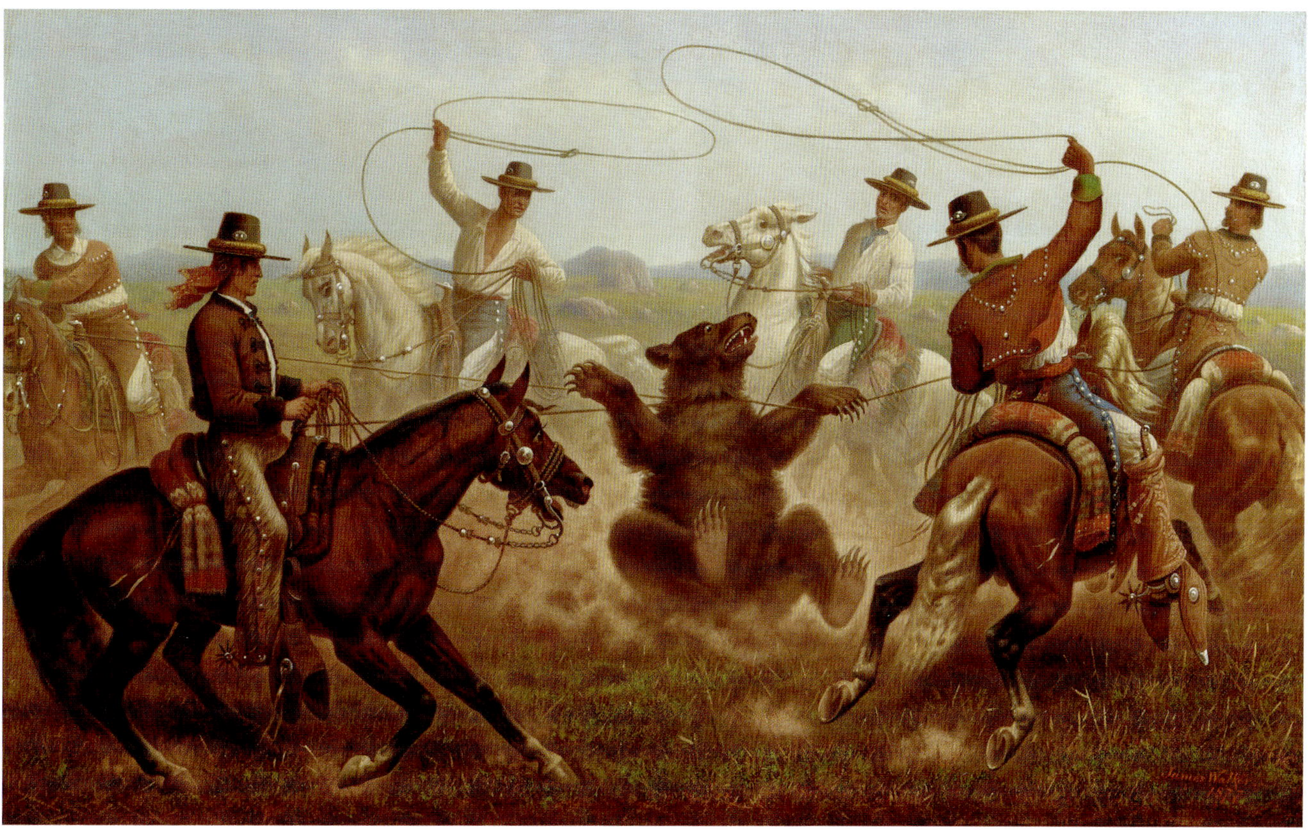

James Walker, COWBOYS ROPING A BEAR, ca. 1877. Denver Art Museum, Fred E. Gates Collection, 1955.87

While the growth and expansion of the cattle industry continued into the later nineteenth century, opportunities for the cowboy diminished significantly in the 1880s due to a few key developments: An increase in the privatization of land restricted the open spaces for cattle grazing. The introduction of barbed wire fencing reduced the need for oversight and corralling by cowboys. Several years of grueling winter weather in the late 1880s, and, significantly, immigration and an influx of new farmers who further privatized the open range, cumulatively negated the possibility of long cattle drives across states and territories.

FUELING A MYTH

What is so striking about the evolution of the cowboy figure is that his original context changed towards the end of the nineteenth century, but the ideas and values with which he was associated did not.

While the functional role of a cowboy persisted well through the twentieth century and into the present, the cultural context (via popular media) in which we more broadly consider who a cowboy is, what the role of a cowboy is, and how a cowboy interacts within an ecosystem of animals, landscape, and other laborers has not necessarily evolved over the last 140 years to reflect those changes. In many ways, the ideas surrounding the cowboy, which serve up one of the most powerful archetypes in modern history, remain fixed, seemingly impossible to dislodge from a collective or popular mindset.

Ironically, the mythology of the cowboy as a character emerged at the very moment that the reality of this role—as initially embodied and performed—was declining. By the end of the nineteenth century, instead of being seen as an Edenic escape from the devastation and brutality of the battlefield, the ideal had been reversed as settlers, ranchers, and opportunists colonized the West, violently and legislatively forced the removal of those living on Native lands, and now, functionally, occupied this "New Frontier." The limitless possibility that had been perceived as a driving force behind homesteading and cultivation of the Western landscape had been brutally contained.

The late nineteenth century also witnessed the industrialization and expansion of the railroad across the West and the western desert, foreclosing the notion of an uncharted territory to be discovered, seized, and repurposed for non-Indigenous settlers.

> *Ransom Stoddard: You're not going to use the story, Mr. Scott?*
> *Maxwell Scott: No, sir. This is the West, sir. When the legend becomes fact, print the legend."*
> —The Man Who Shot Liberty Valance, 1962[11]

And the main reason for that is the proliferation of vehicles that perpetuated what would become the key myths surrounding the cowboy: road shows, dime novels, and ultimately, Hollywood.

Why does this myth persist despite its factual lapses and cultural inaccuracies? The reasons are manifold: the need for a symbol of national identity, a spirit of unbridled courage and freedom at a moment when everything (culturally, politically, technologically) was changing and therefore destabilizing. To hearken to an idea of bravery or independence—however fraught that might be—was a salve to the changes wrought by industrialization, resource exploitation, and global colonization. To conceptualize the cowboy as one who could tame and bend an animal to his will is to metaphorically connect with a figure who is larger than life, and who can wrestle (literally) the broader, existential threats of the surrounding environment.

Forbes Co., Lithographer, and Paul Frenzeny, THE SCOUT BUFFALO BILL. HON. W.F. CODY, between 1872 and 1890. Forbes Co., Boston & N.Y. Color lithograph

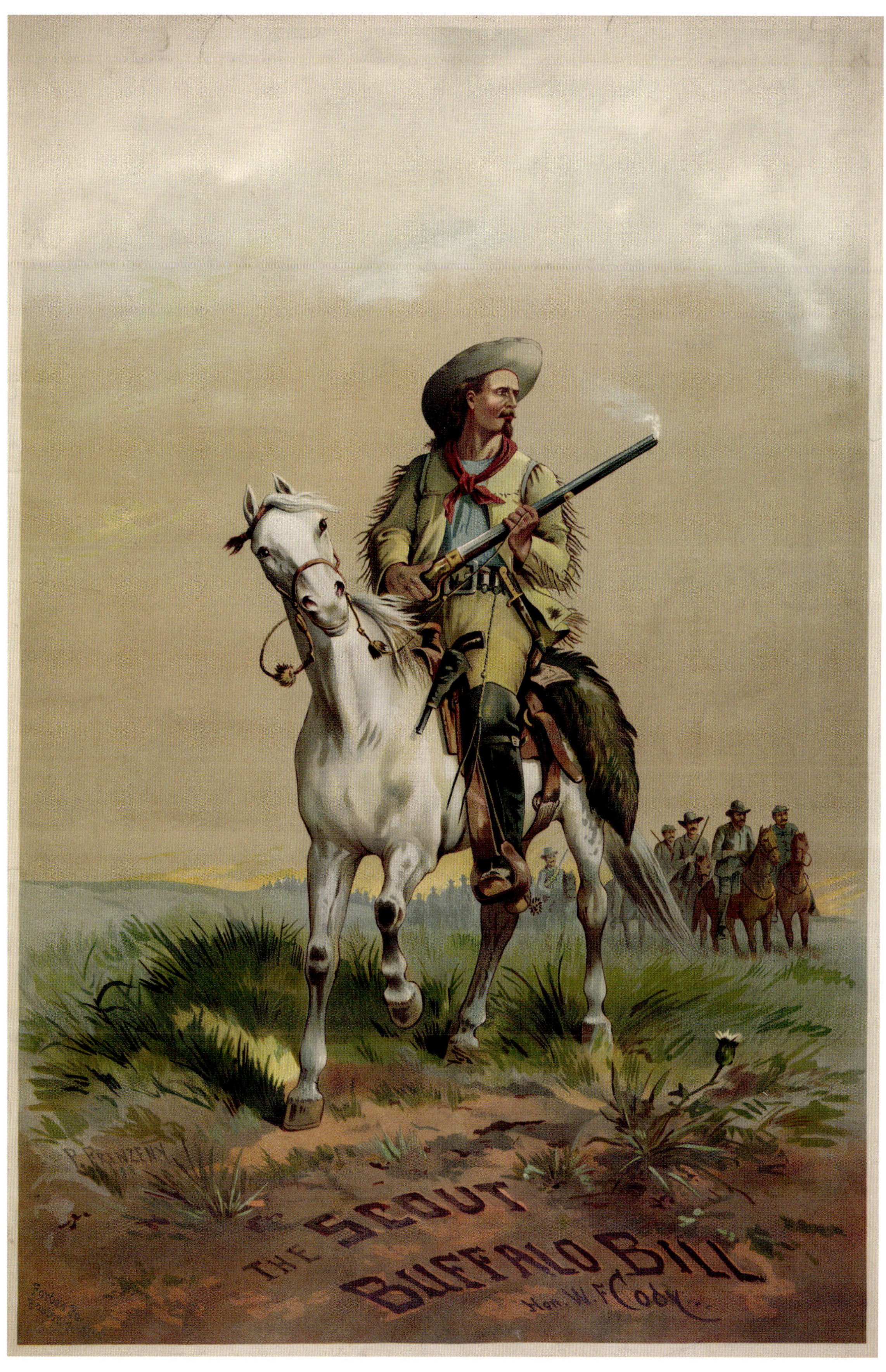
THE SCOUT
BUFFALO BILL
Hon. W. F. Cody

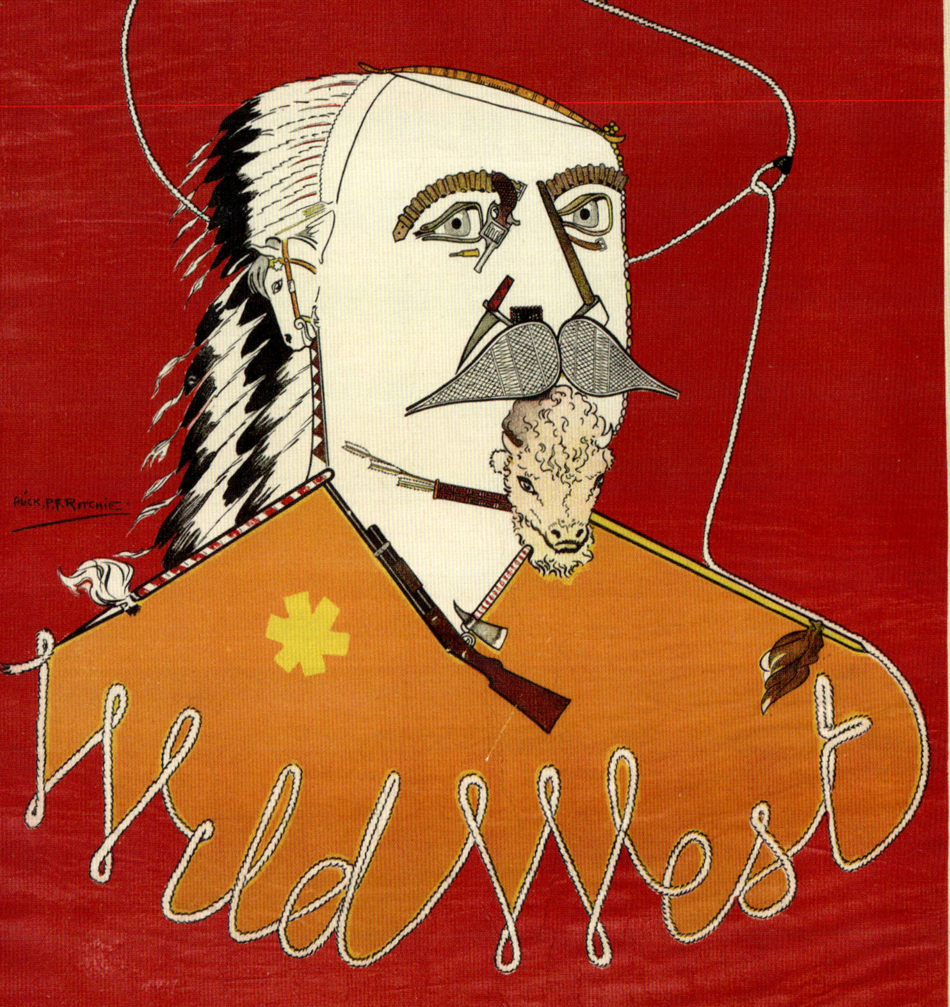
BUFFALO BILL'S
Dick. P.F. Ritchie
Wild West
COL. W. F. CODY.
WEINERS LTD LONDON

This was the purpose of cultural icons like Buffalo Bill Cody (p. 17), whose intention, through his elaborate "Wild West" performances and accompanying mythology, was to revive or rewrite the "imagery" of the West—to bring to life the concepts that were perpetuated and propagated through dime novels and periodicals, and to concretize these myths in his performances.

The dime novel (p. 18) emerged toward the end of the cowboy's prominence—in 1878, when Beadle and Adams launched their publishing business, which aimed at younger adult readers. Within the dime novel library, however, the cowboy didn't emerge as a subject until 1883, as the cowboy's role was fading.

Upon entering the popular mindset through the publication of the first novel about Buffalo Bill, the *story* of the cowboy—the *performance* of a cowboy—dislodged from fact and was replaced with fictitious tropes about cowboy culture and way of life. While Cody supposedly earned the nickname Buffalo Bill after killing over 4,000 buffalo in eight months, the fictionalizing of his adventures led the writer Ned Buntline to pen over 400 novels describing his escapades in the Western landscape.[12] As one scholar has noted, "Cody probably had a greater effect upon the American imagination than any other showman."[13] Buffalo Bill first appeared as a character featured in dime novels, and William F. Cody enacted the character of Buffalo Bill on stage. But it was the imagery and literature promoting his performances (left) that made Cody the actor and Buffalo Bill one and the same.

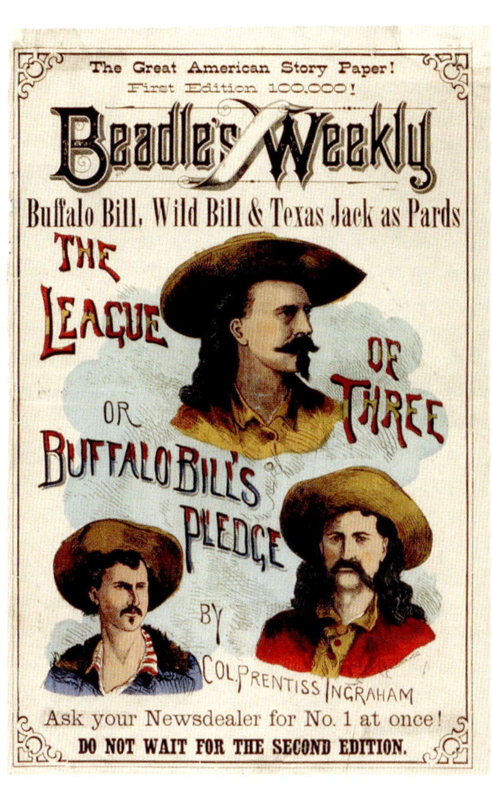

The overlapping influences of visual art, popular imagery, and the dime novel, all of which experienced growth in distribution at the end of the nineteenth century, accelerated the mythmaking of the cowboy.[14] And, this intersection of cheap, readily available visual material, such as posters and broadsides, pointedly generated a type or figure who was then brought to real life on the stage of the "Wild West" and in other entertainment productions. The inventions of Buffalo Bill during performances and throughout the literature made clear through repetition and powerful visual imagery certain fictional events that would, over time, circulate *as* fact. For example, the Deadwood stagecoach became the most recognizable object in the Wild West (p. 20). This scene of the stagecoach being attacked by Native Americans with Buffalo Bill leading the cavalry to the rescue was replayed at every performance of the Wild West show throughout its 30-year history.[15]

As one scholar has noted, "Perhaps the biggest discrepancy between the myth and the reality of cowboy legend was that the black cowboys [and all cowboys of color] were almost totally ignored by the mythmakers of the eastern publishing houses and the Hollywood movie sets."[16] The stereotyping of the cowboy through popular culture and entertainment extended to other racial and ethnic historical figures. For those Native Americans who participated in Buffalo Bill's Wild West

Opposite: **Alick P. F. Ritchie, BUFFALO BILL'S WILD WEST, COL. W.F. CODY, 1890. London: Weiners, Ltd. Color print**

Above: **BEADLE'S WEEKLY: THE LEAGUE OF THREE OR BUFFALO BILL'S PLEDGE BY COL. PRENTISS INGRAHAM. New York: Orr N. Co., 1880. Color print** productions—performing all over the country and across Europe—in a sense reinforced culturally specific archetypes and behaviors, and rigorously restrictive notions of how the Indigenous and white settlers clashed or cooperated.

While the imagery used to perpetuate these contrived relations only reinforced the artifice of the performance, there was also a subversiveness to the performance. Many of the non-white performers participated in the show in part to survive, to avoid being jailed or worse, but also to have an opportunity to "freely" practice their rituals, their traditions, and their culture—which was otherwise outlawed by the US government.[17]

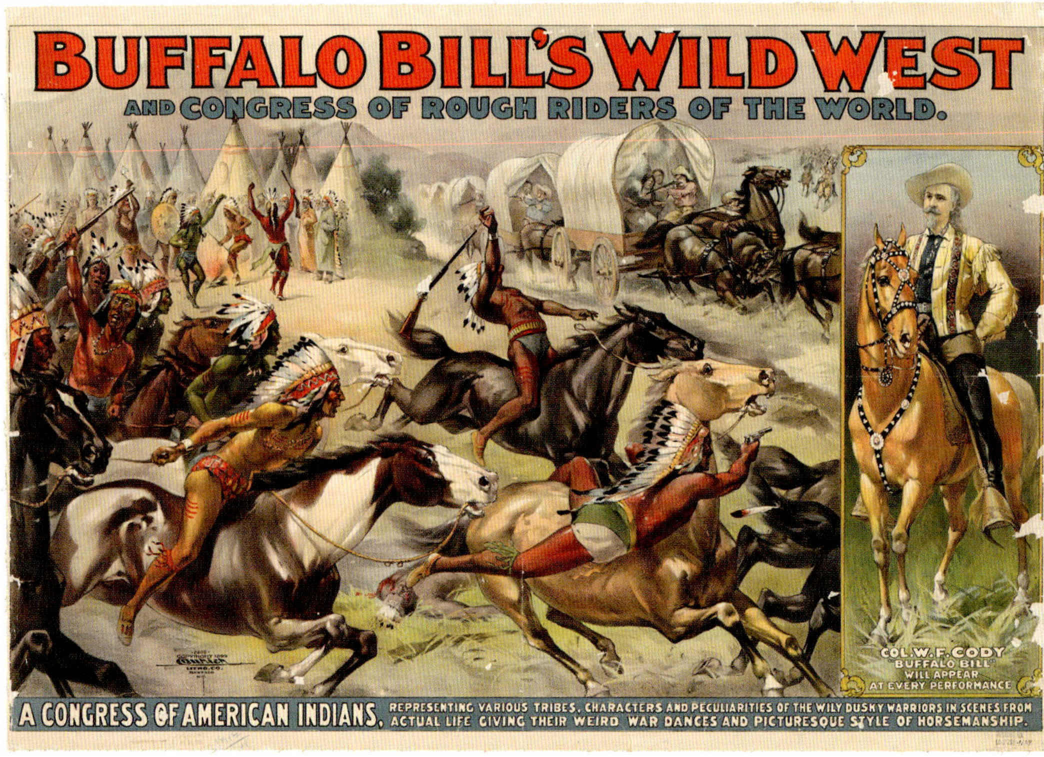

BUFFALO BILL'S WILD WEST AND CONGRESS OF ROUGH RIDERS OF THE WORLD. A CONGRESS OF AMERICAN INDIANS., ca. 1899. Buffalo, New York: Courier Litho. Co. Chromolithograph

The journey of Buffalo Bill's performances to the silver screen in the twentieth century amplified a single type of figure who could be described in a rather limited set of terms: He is always a HE; he is almost exclusively white and heterosexual; and he is unafraid, undaunted, and independent. This narrowly defined figure was reinforced through broadsides, magazines, novels, toys, games, and ultimately the entire entertainment industry, which filtered out much of the historically accurate details of who this figure had been and what he had contributed. The presentation of the cowboy in the twentieth century ultimately lionized a very different figure—one that emerged from a sense of nostalgia and anxiety as much as it did from fiction and imagination.

FROM MYTH BACK TO FACT

So, how does the mythic figure of the cowboy persist today? How are artists complicating and, in many cases, reinserting the historical record back into our notion of the cowboy? For those engaged creatively on this subject, the question is far more focused on how to honor a much broader and more diverse understanding of this role and its contribution to American history and the narratives that define and punctuate our country's development.

The work of Yumi Janairo Roth and Emmanuel David, for example, resurfaces the Filipino performers who were part of Buffalo Bill's Wild West production: Ysidora Alcantara, Felix Alcantara, and Geronimo

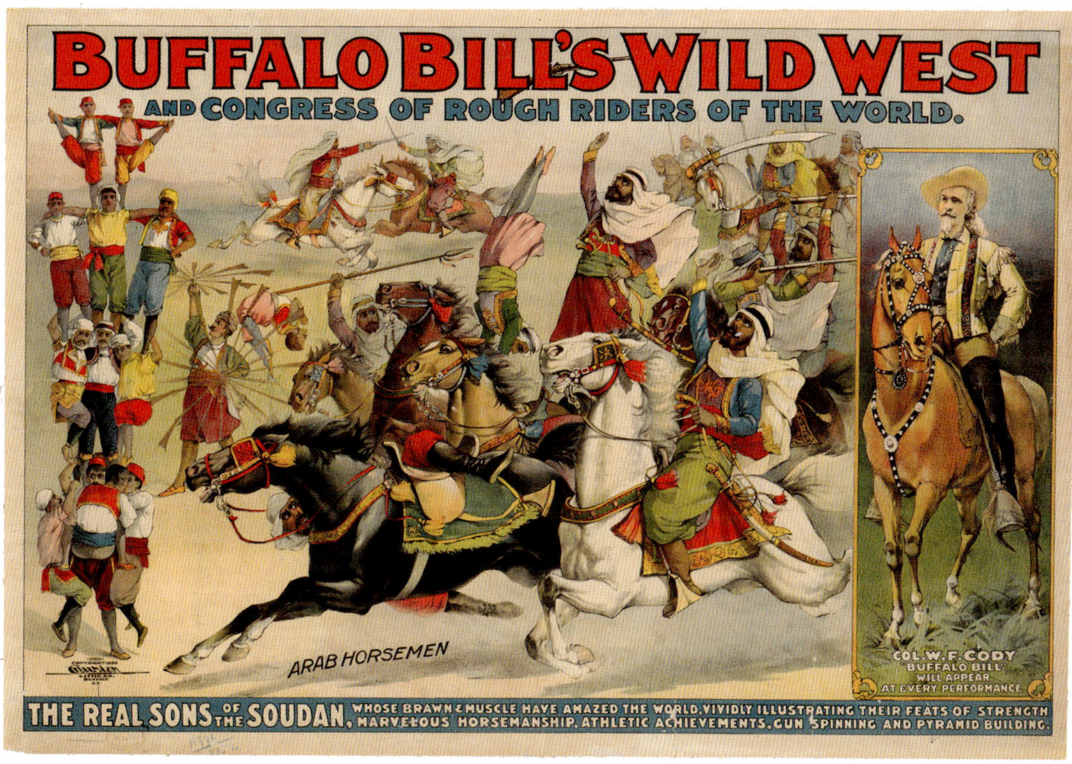

Ynosincio joined the troupe, the Congress of Rough Riders, in 1899 and toured the United States at the very moment of America's imperialist incursion into the Philippines. Left out of most accounts of Buffalo Bill's legacy, the role of these performers speaks to a far more diverse story of immigration, Western expansion, and, critically, the accuracy of the historical record. Through their project *We Are Coming* (pp. 174–77), Roth and David use the theatrical rendering and language of Buffalo Bill's show to announce not the singular cowboy figure's arrival but rather a collective, decentered presence of a different racial identity. Using the marquees of historical theaters in the towns and cities where Buffalo Bill's show traveled, Roth and David announce the arrival of the three Filipino actors and reinsert them into the discourse of the American West.

BUFFALO BILL'S WILD WEST AND CONGRESS OF ROUGH RIDERS OF THE WORLD. THE REAL SONS OF THE SOUDAN., ca. 1899. Buffalo: Courier Litho Co. Chromolithograph

Amy Sherald (p. 193) presents the cowboy here as a contemporary icon. The cowboy hat, denim jeans, and thick belt buckle featuring a galloping horse all signal the traditional details of a cowboy's attire. But it is the American flag shirt that both amplifies this traditional representation and simultaneously complicates it. Against the stark background, the familiar pattern of the Stars and Stripes carves the figure out and avers the American-ness of the figure. Sherald's cowboy and his "all-American" identity centers a person of color to wedge the fiction from the fact of who can claim the cowboy title and how it can be represented. To be "all-American" is to broaden and include the many different identities who embody this role, this labor, and this culture.

Kahlil Joseph combines visual art, fashion, and popular music to create films that challenge linear narratives. *Wildcat*, a black-and-white film (pp. 122–27), explores the past and present African American rodeo subculture in Grayson, Oklahoma, the town formerly known as Wildcat. The film weaves together the community and its traditions while including an homage to "Aunt Janet," who founded the town's rodeo. DJ and rapper Flying Lotus created the experimental score, inspired by the composition and performance of jazz music. The result is a dreamlike narrative, balanced between slow pans of the rodeo grounds, drives across the Southern landscape, and snapshots of those who have built up and continue to maintain the town. The combination of imagery and sound provides a window into the experience of Black cowboys in America.

While Joseph's work is set in the present, several artists are also reaching into the recesses of history to pull forward narratives, events, and specific histories that complicate the narrow vision of cowboy culture that Hollywood and popular culture have advanced for over a century. In his two-channel video, Kenneth Tam considers stereotypes of Asian men and how they compare to the cowboy as the definition of American masculinity. The video also explores Western expansion through the construction of the US transcontinental railroad (1863–69) and the labor strike organized by Chinese railroad workers in 1867. *Silent Spikes* (pp. 202–05) can be taken as a response not only to this history but also to centuries of stereotyped representation of the Asian male in media, particularly in Western-genre films. Inhabiting and adapting the archetype of the American cowboy, Tam aims to honor inherited struggles while centering vulnerability and connection as subtly radical forms of masculine identity.

The photographic work of both Juan Fuentes in Colorado and Akasha Rabut in New Orleans similarly probe the rich traditions and conventions of a subculture and the community that envelops it. Fuentes's direct and intimate images of the immigrant and Spanish-speaking populations of Bennett, Colorado, a rural town east of Boulder, focus on the quiet signifiers of daily life—the cowboy hats for sale in a local market, the animals who comprise the labor of the landscape, and the landmarks of the town itself (pp. 110–17). His series personalizes the issues of population growth, demographic shifts, and such impacts on a community through a poignant and humanizing depiction of the lived experiences of those within that locale. Similarly, Rabut's photographs of the Southern Riderz and urban cowboy clubs document the tenderness and intimacy between the riders and their animals, as well as the colorful and exuberant interventions that define the rituals and practices of these clubs (pp. 152–61). Collisions of context—riders on horses moving through a gas station, for example—anchor Rabut's work in the dialogue around contemporary cowboy culture and which groups and communities are recognized and portrayed within it. Like so many artists in this exhibition, Rabut makes clear that the history of the cowboy as laborer, as caretaker, and as celebrated hero, lives out today in ever more diverse and varied examples. Ultimately, by offering a broader scope of nuanced and bespoke traditions, Rabut shakes the foundation of the cowboy figure to allow for a far greater understanding of such an archetype.

The contribution of R. Alan Brooks, writer, graphic novelist, and artist, to this catalogue highlights the particular history of the Colorado ghost town Dearfield, which was the first Black homesteading community in the state (pp. 79–85). It was founded by Oliver Toussaint Jackson, who sought to establish an all-Black colony that could support and sustain itself. Brooks's vivid and surreal narrative identifies Dearfield as a space of possibility, only to be wiped out by the Dust Bowl of the 1930s. The glimmer of its potential, the opportunity to carve out a space for this community in this landscape is the spark of his provocation—as he concludes, the history of Dearfield is the "history of something great, and the hope of something more."

Moving from fact-based narratives toward a carefully constructed image, Deana Lawson's powerful photograph (pp. 130–31) disentangles the sexual allure of the cowboy from whiteness. Her photograph depicts two young men (and a third cropped at the far right) riding at night in Georgia. Captured on horseback and looking past the viewer, they are focused elsewhere. Empowered and engaging, the cowboys perform their roles as protectors of a community or cause. This fictionalized scene, which the artist tightly constructed through setting, lighting, and pose, reads as cinematic and stark. The legacy of the American cowboy perpetuates the figure as hero, and her resulting images celebrate Black bodies in a manner that is formally rigorous and riveting. Similarly, Otis Kwame Kye Quaicoe's paintings (pp. 144–51) of Black cowboys isolate boldly rendered, vibrantly hued figures, often against a spare background. The patterning of their clothing, the intensity of their gaze, and the skewed angles with which they are articulated formally center Black figures engaged in the rituals of the rodeo and bring the extensive history of Black cowboys to the surface.

rafa esparza investigates histories of Latinx and queer communities, power structures, relationships to land, and traditional practices such as adobe making, which he learned from his father. This work centers on an intimate scene of Latinx men dancing in a queer bar. The seamless intermingling of their bodies effectively and movingly disrupts the notion of the American cowboy as a heterosexual, Anglo figure.

Also fascinated by the limited role through which notions of the cowboy permeate contemporary culture, Ana Segovia explores the fraught and constrained portrayals of masculinity within the history of American and Mexican cinema. Her video work *Aunque Me Espine la Mano,* for example, questions the virile, stoic, and hyper-macho attributes associated with the *charro* figure in Mexican film (pp. 176–79). Since the mid-twentieth century, this figure has been used to convey a spirit of righteousness as much as desire; he is the one women want and the one men want to be—tough, distant, unafraid. Through the gestures and actions of the actors, the boldly lit production, and the flamboyant costumes, Segovia performs the performance of a *charro* and heightens the artifice, the theatricality, and the unreality of the archetype. Her work makes clear the construction of this identity, a parallel to the ways in which Hollywood and popular culture skirt the reality of the American cowboy and the actual elasticity of this figure.

In his multi-dimensional practice, Gregg Deal (Pyramid Lake Paiute Tribe) exposes the construct of the myth of the West and its present-day implications on Indigenous communities. A self-described disruptor, Deal uses performance, storytelling, painting, installation, music, and sculpture to upend erroneous and stereotypical representations of Native people and to recognize the ways in which such inaccuracies continue to circulate within popular culture (pp. 94–99). Past performances, such as *The Last American Indian on Earth* and *Invisible Series,* unequivocally interrupt this circulation of representation and instead enable viewers to engage directly with a shared responsibility for the erasure and suppression of a more accurate, nuanced, and culturally specific presence.

Karl Haendel began his series of female riders after visiting the Western Art collection of the Denver Art Museum (pp. 118–21). Struck by the dominance of male riders, cowboys, surveyors, and Western actors, he commenced a series of over a dozen, larger-than-life drawings of women on horses and in moments of exuberance, intense focus, and action. Haendel's portrayal of female cowboys and rodeo competitors captures the real-life experiences of many young women and girls who are as actively a part of the cowboy culture as their male counterparts. Reinserting those who have been underrepresented or represented in a narrow, often sexualized and passive manner, Haendel also celebrates their agency and active presence within this milieu. There are no men to control, limit, or tame them; they lead, direct, and, above all, experience the thrill of the ride.

The finger-print–covered photographs from Laurel Nakadate's *Lucky Tiger* series similarly explore gendered power dynamics within the context of cowboy culture (pp. 138–43). The series began with the scantily clad artist posing with horses and trucks in sweeping landscapes, in order to offer her body intentionally for the male gaze to behold and devour.

Conceptually experimenting with desire, longing, fantasy—and who gets to define and experience these behaviors—the artist invited random men (some found through Craigslist) to fondle and consume the prints of herself. Before the men handled the photographs, their hands were inked so that the residue of their touch remains on the photos. With each photograph handled in unpredictable ways, some photos are densely pocked with prints, others less so. Nakadate's project toys with the tropes of the cinematic Western and the ways in which women in this context are often portrayed as objects of desire rather than as agents of their own direction. By making her photographs a physical object to be touched, she makes explicit the gendered dynamic that tightly controls how, where, and why women are offered up for male consumption. She sets up and enacts this dynamic with strangers, and in so doing, reveals the persistence of such power relations.

Several artists engage with the signifiers of cowboy culture, rendering the familiar objects associated with working the land or engaging with animals highly surreal and problematic. Born in Houston, Texas, and raised in a Chinese American household, conceptual artist Mel Chin has for decades created works that advocate for social justice and an awareness of underrecognized narratives. In *Rough Rider*, Chin creates a roping saddle made of barbed wire to allude to the violence that took place during the colonization and settlement of Texas (pp. 92–93). The barbed wire evokes the Christian iconography of Jesus's crown of thorns as much as it references the introduction of barbed wire that transformed the ranching industry in the nineteenth century. The reference to Christian imagery deliberately connects with the colonization of Texas by the conquistadors and Catholic missionaries during the seventeenth and eighteenth centuries.

Luis Jiménez created prints, drawings, and sculptures that examined his heritage as a Hispanic American. Born in El Paso, Texas, his work often looks at life on the border, cultural assimilation, and our relationship to the natural landscape. Jiménez often utilized vibrant colors and gravity-defying compositions to bring a heightened dynamism and cinematic quality to his work. *Progress II* represents one of his earliest monumental works and features symbols of the American West. A vaquero on an electric blue mustang dives towards a leaping longhorn, dramatizing in exuberant fashion one of the key aspects of a cowboy's role in taming animals, and the interconnectedness of predator and prey.

Unpacking the weight of the cowboy mythology, John Baldessari's final series, from 2019, explores the ways in which simple elements can be read as the summation of a cowboy's identity. With *The Space Between Hat, Rock and Shadow.*, he offers the hints of a character, set against a stark white background, and invites the viewer to complete the picture (pp. 90–91). Having blotted out all other aspects of the photograph with white paint, Baldessari shares a sliver of a film still and adds text at the bottom to further clarify the parts that remain. How one might connect the disparate details he provides is precisely the type of engagement that Baldessari sought throughout his career. The provocation to the viewer is to question *why* the objects that remain compel a reading of the image as that of a cowboy; the association underscores the magnitude of Hollywood's role in the durability and persistence of this icon.

Angela Ellsworth and Ken Taylor Reynaga create surreal sculptures that transform common items into threatening objects. Ellsworth's *Seer Bonnets,* made of thousands of corsage pins, repel any functional role of shielding the nineteenth-century Mormon women for whom they were originally made (pp. 100–05). Instead, the elaborate designs on the outside of the bonnets seem to externalize the thoughts of the Mormon women who wore them yet were denied the opportunity to express them. Ellsworth's family history, which connects her to one of the founders of the Mormon church, in part inspires this ongoing series and drives her research into ways of giving voice to those who have been silenced—historically and in the present. Similarly, Reynaga's ceramic sculptures of cowboy hats draw in part from his own experience growing up in Bakersfield, California, a vital agrarian community where the cowboy hat is a highly functional item (pp. 164–73). Reynaga's oversized and subtly rendered ceramic sculptures reinterpret the cowboy through metaphor: by reimagining this most explicit signifier as colorful, supple, and outsized, he invites an expanded perspective of the figure who wears it.

Nathan Young's multifaceted practice furthers this expanded register of cowboy culture and its signifiers by placing many of these traditional objects within an Indigenous context and surfacing the stories and narratives that animate them (pp. 210–15). An enrolled member of the Delaware Tribe of Indians and a direct descendent of the Pawnee Nation and Kiowa Tribe, Young approaches all of his projects from a spiritual as well as conceptual framework. For his *Activation/Transformation II* installation in this exhibition, Young drew from his own family's collection of artifacts and artworks, as well as those of public and private Western art collections, to probe the practice of collecting. Arranging the objects to form new constellations of meaning by their adjacency, he foregrounds the connections between the cowboy figure and the practices of his community.

One of the ways in which artists are interrogating the figure of the cowboy and, specifically, the history of his representation is by demythologizing not only the embodiment of this icon but also the environment through which he moved. Lucy Raven and Stephanie Syjuco both explore the figure, in part, through his absence. Raven's *Untitled* shadowgrams examine sound waves, motion, and the ways in which images are constructed within the expansiveness of the arid Western landscape (New Mexico, specifically, in response to where the atomic bomb was created and tested) (pp. 162–63). She articulates a setting through which the cowboy comes alive, but also denies the figure's visibility. The movement of sound waves *as* light and image that she seductively employs in this work implies the disruption of the landscape by human intervention and suggests the horrific outcome of such actions. On the other hand, Syjuco, in her monumental installation *Double Vision,* initially commissioned by the Amon Carter Museum, reconstitutes the Western landscape as seen in canvases by the nineteenth-century painters (particularly Charles Russell and Frederic Remington) largely responsible for crafting a perception of the West as a site of open, lustrous expanse (pp. 194–201). Syjuco takes that context as her starting point and creates a vibrant, immersive environment inspired by paintings from the Amon Carter Museum's collection along with large-scale photographs of bronze sculptures from this same era. The photographs include details of the art preparators' gloves and tools, and collectively speak to the image-making of the institution. The West, Syjuco seems to argue, was invented not only by the artists but also by the structures and systems of the museums that commission, conserve, and collect their work.

Demythologizing the cowboy inevitably means teasing apart fiction from fact, a task borne out by artists whose emphasis on the mythical aspects of this figure speak to the larger myths that Hollywood depends upon. The series of drawings by Matthew J. Mahoney, for example, reads collectively as a deconstructed film strip, carrying the viewer through different scenes and events of a single cowboy figure (pp. 132–37). Inspired by Cormac McCarthy's character John Joel Glanton in *Blood Meridian,* Mahoney's cowboy is actively present on the paper. Simultaneously explosive and focused, Mahoney articulates different moments of solitude and drama with equal force and simplicity. Collectively, the works on paper from this series emerge from the artist's own questioning of the valor and heroicism with which cowboys have historically been treated without greater acknowledgment of the misogyny and violence that also characterize the figure throughout popular culture.

A similar re-evaluation of the cowboy is put forward in the large-scale paintings by the artist Grace Kennison (p. 128–29). Both inspired and provoked by traditional representations of the American West landscape, Kennison's paintings engage directly with the fictions embedded in those earlier representations. At times fantastical as well as critical, her paintings often center female protagonists in a moment of emotionally intense challenges or conflicts, infusing the work with a heightened sense of drama and tension. The depicted struggles attest to the artist's own questioning of how to achieve a sense of harmony within a contested landscape—such contestations over land, identity, representation, and other forms of authority abound in the history of the American West, and Kennison's female cowboys offer an alternative approach to engaging with such history.

Andy Warhol (p. 208–09) understood the power of an image and how it circulates in popular culture. He presciently recognized the vacuousness of Hollywood imagery, the flatness of fame, and also, its seductive power.

That he created this image in 1963 using a film still of Elvis Presley from the 1960 film *Flaming Star* comments on the fading stardom of the King of Rock 'n' Roll and invites a sense of nostalgia.[18] Some might read that as nostalgia for an earlier Hollywood era, but perhaps we can read it as nostalgic for the *conception* of a cowboy—a mournful farewell to another era—another era in filmmaking as much as an era of American history that frankly *never* existed as it had been portrayed in Hollywood.

On top of this silver image—another clear reference to the silver screens of the entertainment industry—Warhol asserts a new definition of the West: Southern California, the hub of popular culture and the fabricator of imagination. Not only was the pop culture figure of the cowboy never accurate, this new definition of the West itself was also radically different from its historic referent—it was now a soundstage with stage sets and props. The cowboy of this new West was a pop star with a fading fan base. Warhol's mournful treatment of Elvis seems to capture the waning of multiple myths while simultaneously acknowledging the power of those myths.

ENDNOTES

1 William Loren Katz, *The Black West: A Documentary and Pictorial History of the African American Role in the Westward Expansion of the United States* (Golden, Colorado: Fulcrum Publishing, 2019), 146.

2 Robert M. Seiler and Tamara P. Seiler, "The Social Construction of the Canadian Cowboy: Calgary Exhibition and Stampede Posters, 1952–1972," *Journal of Canadian Studies* 33, no. 3 (1998): 53.

3 Roger D. Hardaway, "African American Cowboys on the Western Frontier," *Negro History Bulletin* 64, no. 1/4 (January–December 2001): 28.

4 Jack Weston, *The Real American Cowboy* (New York: Schocken Books, 1985), 138–52.

5 Ibid., 139.

6 Ibid., 145.

7 Katz, 146.

8 Ibid.

9 Ibid.

10 Ibid., 149.

11 *The Man Who Shot Liberty Valance*, directed by John Ford, screenplay by James Warner Bellah and Willis Goldbeck (Paramount Pictures, 1962), 2 hr., 3 min.

12 Seiler and Seiler, 55.

13 Warren French, "The Cowboy in the Dime Novel," *The University of Texas Studies in English* 30 (1951): 221.

14 Selier and Seiler, 58.

15 Ibid., 57.

16 RD Hardaway, "African American Cowboys on the Western Frontier," *Negro History Bulletin* 64, no. 1/4 (January–December 2001): 27.

17 Christine Bold, "Performance: Print, and the Popularization of the Pre-cinematic American West" in Thomas Brent Smith and Mary-Dailey Desmarais, eds. *Once Upon a Time . . . The Western: A New Frontier in Art and Film* (Montreal: 5 Continents Editions, 2019), 54.

18 Stéphane Aquin, "Western Film and Contemporary Art: A Tale of Lost Innocence," in *Once Upon a Time . . .* , 248.

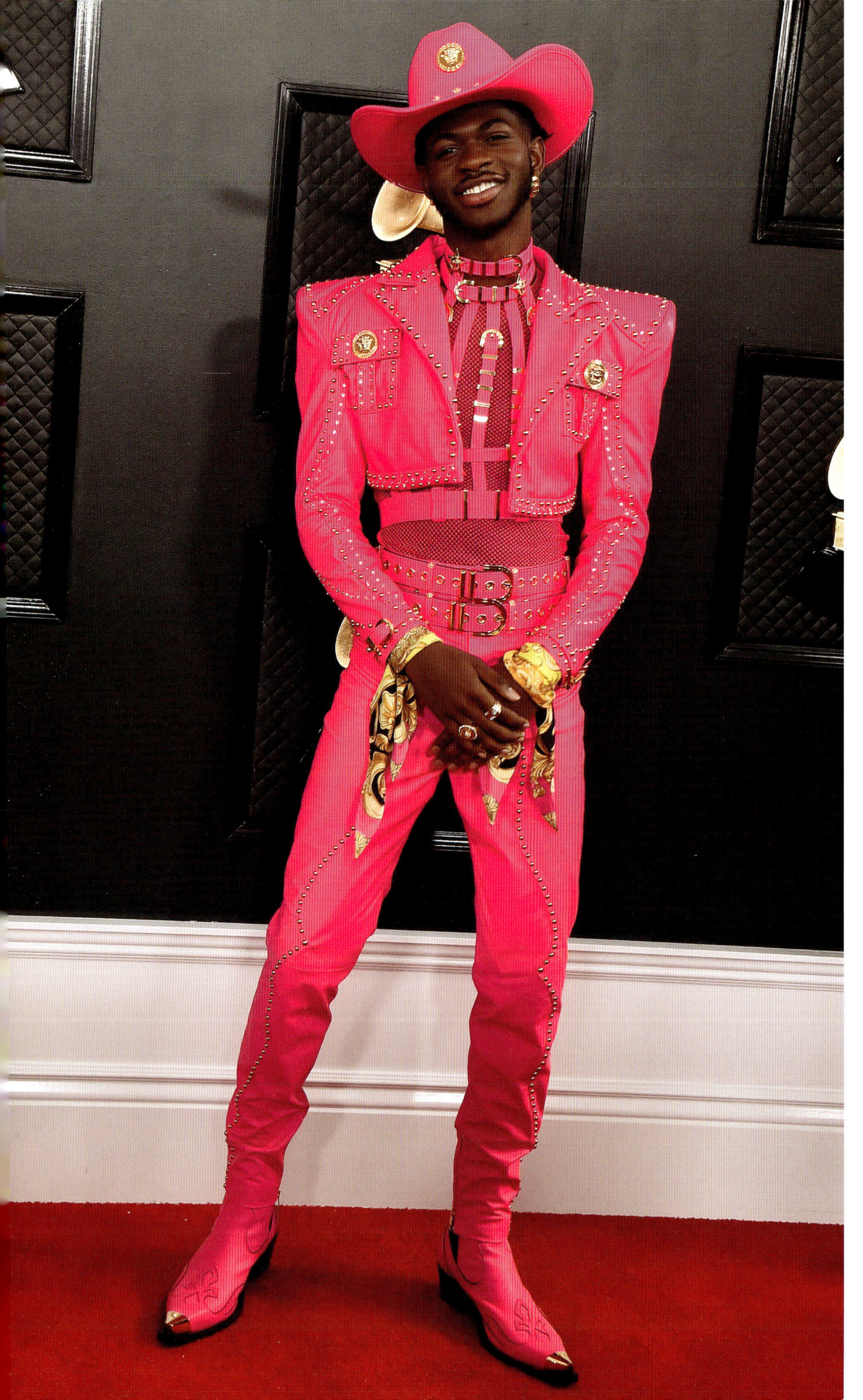

WHEN LIL NAS X RELEASED HIS HIT SONG "OLD TOWN ROAD" IN 2018, his likeness threatened the long-held image of the Western cowboy. The showmanship of Black artistry, coupled with the public's love for style, collided with the dusty seriousness of the version of the white cowboy unable to bend and adapt to change. As a result of this controversy, the reality and aesthetics of a Black cowboy were thrust into the spotlight. We may question Lil Nas X's authenticity as a cowboy in popular culture, but not because he is Black. Seeing Black cowboys and considering their experiences in American West history and culture creates an opportunity to reflect on what we are looking at and what we see.

In 2019, after facing backlash for "Old Town Road," Lil Nas X recorded a new version with Billy Ray Cyrus, a country music legend. But this did not protect his partnership with popular Western clothing brand

ALTERNATE HISTORIES OF THE COWBOY MYTH

Myeshia C. Babers, PhD

Wrangler from accusations of "cowboy" cultural appropriation, as fans of the genre took to social media to voice their outrage and threaten to boycott Wrangler. In response to the criticism, the song was removed from Billboard's country music charts.[1] Music critic Brittany Spanos describes how the musician, Lil Nax X, first gained popularity and acceptance on social media before entering mainstream popular culture.[2] Ideally, the country music canon allows us to trace and demonstrate cultural and musical influence rather than popularity determined by likes, shares, and views on social media, where the song was first released. The resistance Lil Nas X encountered in his desire to identify as a cowboy highlights our nation's overall lack of familiarity with the lives of Black cowboys.

Historical representations of the cowboy do not show how history has stripped Black people of their place in Western culture, then and now. In this essay, I will compare the archetypal definition of the cowboy, as put forward by Hollywood and other entertainment industries, with the modern Black rodeo cowboy, and what distinguishes the experiences of the white rodeo and Black rodeo today. I will explore the experiences of ordinary Black boys and men who live the cowboy lifestyle and whose identities are based on generational knowledge, history, and heritage passed down through their ancestors. Given that official archives and

Lil Nas X attending the GRAMMY Awards at Staples Center, Los Angeles, 2020 repertoires have undermined Black Western traditions through erasure and exclusion, I offer instead a discussion of Black cultural ideas formed around the family, interpersonal relationships, and specific definitions of masculinity.

For example, historian Jacqueline M. Moore says that "the masculine cowboy hero portrayed in film and literature is usually a figure straddling the frontier between civilization and the wilderness, sometimes siding with the townspeople against the wilderness and sometimes with the equally mythical, noble Indian savage against civilization."[3] Moore goes on to describe how "the [news] paper also participated in the cult of the cowboy hero, painting the men of the Wild West as manly heroes and perfect gentlemen." It's easy to wonder where the contemporary Black portrayal originates. We can trace the genealogy of modern Black cowboy culture to a distinctly Black American past.

During the second industrial revolution (1870–1914), also known as the technological revolution in the United States, many working cowboys were forced to leave their rural homes to perform as rodeo cowboys to financially provide for their family. Alternatively, some Black cowboys selected "civilized employment," such as train porters for the United States railroad system.[4] During this time, the American cowboy myth of masculinity was written down in dime novels, establishing as white the "the original cowboy."

Rodeos can be profitable, but they are expensive to enter and keep cowboys away from their families for a long time. Cowboys used to put on shows like steer wrestling, bulldogging, and other events to make money, and what started as a pastime among ranch hands became rodeo events. However, today most Black cowboys can't afford to be in the pro-rodeo world. Instead, they compete in Black rodeos or on the Black rodeo circuit, which has a lower payout and charges lower entry fees.[5] As part of the American tradition of erasing the contributions of Blacks throughout history, Black Western culture and cowboys have been mistaken as appropriations of white culture, from the look of the cowboy to the land he owns.[6] The biographies of famous African American cowboys Isom Dart and William "Bill" Pickett prove otherwise.

Isom Dart (né Ned Huddleston) was born enslaved in Arkansas in 1849. He earned the nicknames the "Black Fox" and "Calico Cowboy" for his riding, roping, and bronco-busting skills, which were undoubtedly helpful as a notorious outlaw in the Wyoming Territory. After the Civil War, Dart worked at a rodeo on the Texas-Mexico border, where he became a stunt rider and a master horseman. Around 1890, Dart started his ranch in Brown's Hole, Colorado. Local ranchers thought he stole cattle to grow his herd, and some hired range detective Tom Horn to remove Dart from the territory. On October 3, 1900, Horn fatally ambushed Isom Dart outside his cabin. Residents of Brown's Hole mourned Dart's death, claiming Horn killed him for his land and cattle. The residents' claim was highly probable, given Dart's positive reputation in town, and that Black landowners were frequently terrorized for their land.[7] However, others believed he kept rustling cattle and remained a threat.[8]

William "Bill" Pickett was an African American and Native cowboy. Pickett started roping, riding, and bulldogging in elementary school for donations. Soon after moving to Taylor, Texas, in 1888, he performed at the town's first fair and started working at Taylor's horse-breaking shop. The 101 Ranch hired him in 1905, and by 1907 he was a full-time employee. Later, he moved his family to Oklahoma. The 101 Ranch Wild West Show was a national attraction from 1905 to 1931. Pickett also invented the

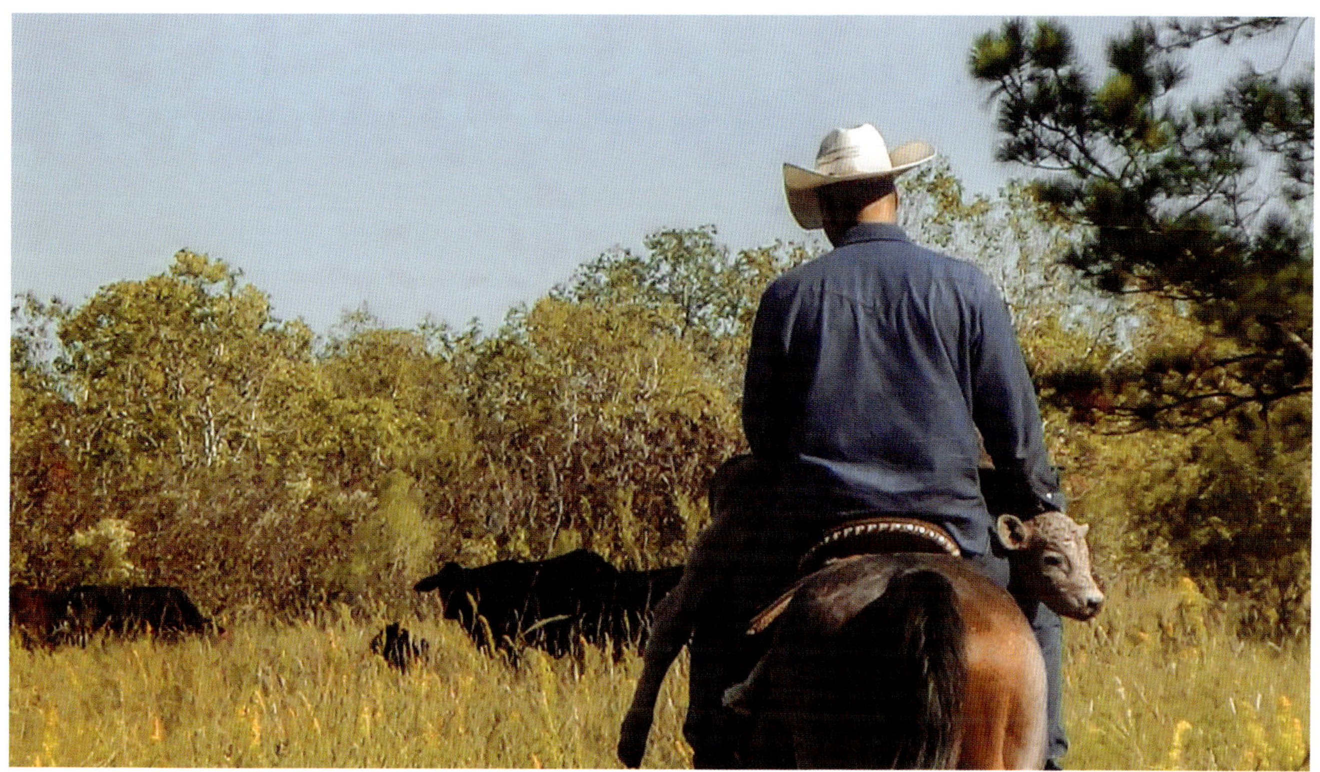

technique of bulldogging (rodeo steer wrestling), by twisting a steer's head and biting its upper lip to gain control[9]. He would go on to perform in South America, Mexico, Canada, and England. Pickett could have set a record in bulldogging if he'd competed against white rodeo competitors. He frequently emphasized his Native American heritage to compete in rodeo competitions where anti-Black racism would have prevented him from participating.[10]

Pickett was also the first Black cowboy movie star. Pickett's second acting role, in 1922, was in *The Crimson Skull*, which was filmed in the "All-Colored City" of Boley, Oklahoma, according to the Norman Film

Myeshia C. Babers, LOST LAMB, 2013. Photograph

Manufacturing Company pressbook. The pressbook also states that the film's "action and story [are] on a par with white productions with the drawing feature of a cast composed entirely of colored artists. (There is not a white character in it.) [It is] a story free from the usual mimicry of the colored man; free from 'race problems' that engender friction."[11]

Between what is real and what is for show, the cowboy on the frontier represented by Hollywood actors in movies typically depict generic white men with pistols carrying out their racist, sexist fetish for power over African Americans and the Indigenous population. The implications this has for the racial politics of cowboys of color are significant. Consequently, a response to these power dynamics are visible in the way Black cowboys rejected Hollywood and popular culture's mythology of the cowboy. Black cowboy cultures today are not recognizably "cowboy" when visually represented. Therefore, it is crucial to emphasize pictures and narratives that explicitly link the emergence of Black Western culture to a creative and aesthetic staging, since perceptions of what it means to be a "cowboy" vary greatly. This manifests in various ways for those who engage in Western cultural practices. The diverse subcultures Black cowboys occupy comprise overlapping areas of work and play, including entertainment, which is not too far removed from the farm, ranch, or trail ride. What we hang our hat on to define a real or authentic "cowboy" depends on the kind of work the cowboy performs. For example, rodeo is considered cowboy entertainment compared to farming and ranching. However, if we compare professional rodeo to trail riding (also known as pleasure riding), the rodeo cowboy is regarded as an authentic cowboy at work, in contrast to the latter's leisurely nature.

Even though their identities contradict what is often depicted of white men in the American West, Black cowboys have left us with stories of their own lives that teach us about what it means to be Black. Through their own experiences, myths, stories, and comedy, Black cowboys teach us what it means to be "Western" as a Black man. This form of folklore demonstrates that they know how preconceptions of Black masculinity collide with the archive and how they deal with these misconceptions. For example, Big Reach, a professional Black rodeo cowboy who travels and competes primarily in the United States, guided me through the professional rodeo world as he knows it. At the 2014 Houston Rodeo, I witnessed his interaction with an event staff member that demonstrated why one should not expect rodeo event staff to recognize a professional rodeo cowboy when they see one. When one of the rodeo workers, a white man, inquired how he was getting passes to enter the arena with the competitors every day, it became clear that Big Reach was not universally accepted as a professional rodeo cowboy. A white rodeo worker seemed astounded that a Black man could freely enter a space reserved for professional (read: white) rodeo contestants.

Big Reach's response made me laugh, but Zora Neal Hurston's study of Black people's reactions to white investigators who approach them and "get in their business" may also shed some light on it. What he said to the man was a creatively expressive Black way of saying "mind your own business." However, drawing attention to the situation's absurdity by exaggerating and fictionalizing his presence in a space he belongs in, more authentically than the staff member, only works some of the time. When it does, you can see the value of equity in representation.

We ate while watching tie down roping as competitors entered and exited the Houston Rodeo's hospitality area. The way white rodeo competitors interacted among themselves differed considerably from how they interacted with Big Reach. Their interactions were brief and impersonal; greetings were expressed with terse "hellos" or quick head nods, perhaps due to formality. But when Big Reach appeared, people smiled warmly and said: "What's up man?" "Hello, how are you?" "Where are you headed next?" or "Are you attending the calf roping or rodeo this weekend?" It appeared that the various (white) cowboys were genuinely interested in what Big Reach had to say or, at the very least, wanted to see and be seen with him. Considering these relationships in terms of actual versus imagined competition is another way to go about it. Although Big Reach wasn't a direct competitor then, the possibility of "meeting" or surpassing him soon was real.

If I thought he had been "disarmed," I would tease him, saying, "These white people love you." His mocking reply would be "girl, hush" or "I sware, some of them don't have any Black friends other than me." Another strange thing about these encounters was how they behaved differently once Big Reach, being the gregarious fellow he is, showed interest in or at least curiosity about the person and allowed them to ask him questions about a particular rodeo, a technique, or a critique of their ride. The subsequent inquiries were always about how Big Reach felt about their onstage performance. Big Reach knows that, despite being a talker and a charismatic businessman, someone can be your roping partner at one rodeo and your rival the next. Only a few of these cowboys could turn their small talk into a whole discussion because Big Reach saw them as genuine allies.

This story challenges notions that Black cowboys replicate mainstream culture representations. The Black cowboy—as a rancher and "hand," or all-around cowboy in the rodeo arena—is distinguished by the historical heritage of Afro-descendant enslaved people who broke horses and cared for ranch owners' cattle. When most people think of a cowboy, they envision someone who resembles John Wayne rather than Isom Dart or Bill Pickett. These ideologies and representations reflect and refract across space and time relate to their influence on boys dressing up and portraying a cowboy to the experiences of being a real cowboy and not seen as one because of their Blackness, when Big Reach says:

When we was little, everybody wanted to be a cowboy. When we was like 4 and 5 years old everybody was a cowboy, but when you got up to like middle school people got into like playing sports and other things and they left that culture alone. And through high school they left it alone. But I got friends that's 30 and 40 years old that's getting into roping right now and they've never even rode a horse before. And, you know, when I see 'em I laugh and they wonder why. I laugh because I'm like, what turned you into this? I swear I don't know. Roping . . . being country now [is] a fad to everybody.[12]

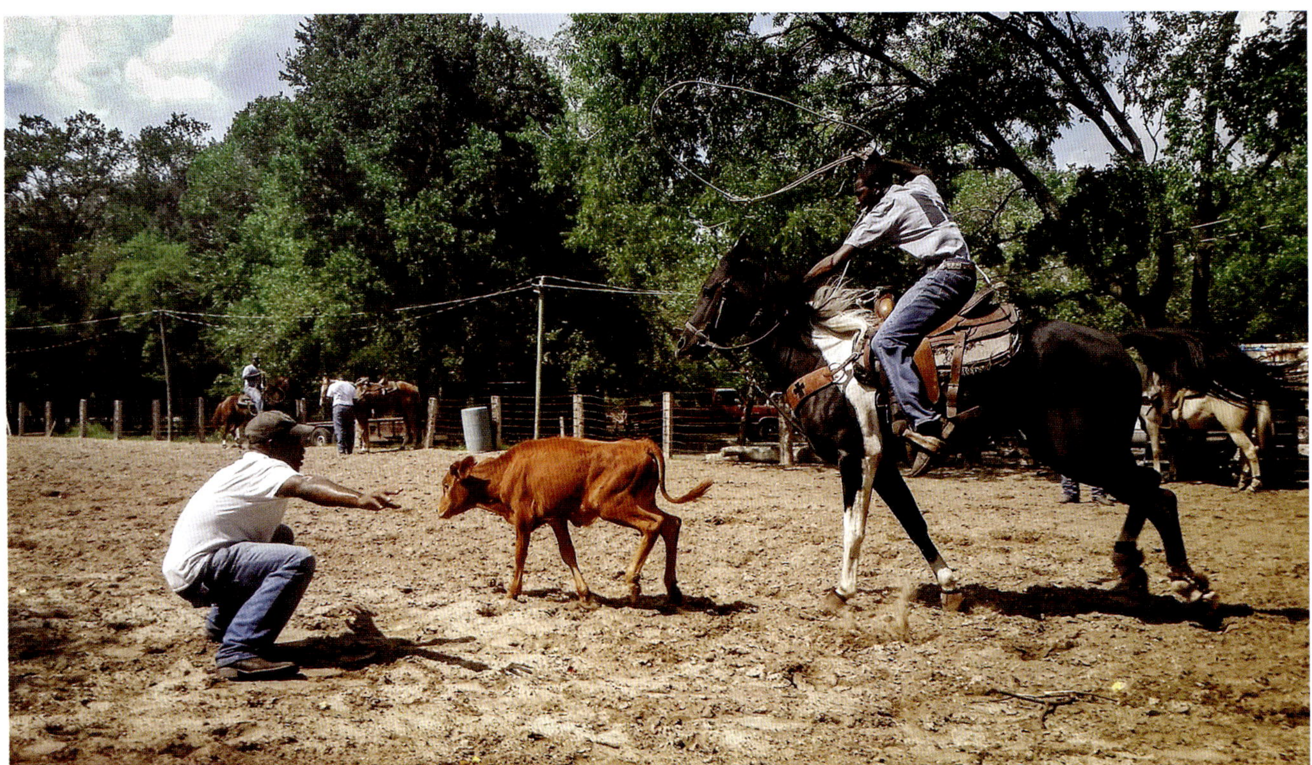

Myeshia C. Babers, ROPING PRACTICE, 2015. Photograph

In *Anthropology News*, I described the look of pride in a Black cowboy's posture when he is secure in the saddle and in command of his ranch's operation. The look of control can also take the form of attentiveness and care. I see the subtle shifts in the Black cowboy's ability to get, be, and maintain control of his environment in a way that is beautifully methodical.[13] I see this kind of methodical control extended to the way Big Reach plays with cowboy fashion and Black cultural aesthetic as he continues:

I used to wear them; you ever see them hats women wear like they sold last night? You see the hats they sellin'? Them Tim McGraw–lookin' hats? I used to wear one of them. . . . I used to draw so much attention

> *to myself at the rodeo the cowboys couldn't stand it. "Why you gotta wear that hat [Cam]? That's not a real cowboy hat." I don't give a fuck what they think, you know what I'm sayin'. But the media, the public, they dig that shit. I went to the rodeo in Ellensburg, [Washington], I had a hat on like that, and I won. They made the big[gest deal] . . . the people went crazy, das cause of the hat. They thought, like, "wow." But I let people know you don't have to look like a fuckin' John Wayne to be in the rodeo. You know what I'm sayin'? It's not the same you. I don't wanna be lookin' like everybody else. Hell naw! But the deal is though, let me tell you what's bad though and the thing that I do that's bad. In a way, I've done stuff to help me; I've done stuff to kill me.' Cause rodeo is a redneck world.*[14]

In my article "Cowboy Cool," I discuss attending to the materiality of doing Blackness—how race is a cultural artifact and political identity with observable traits that affect how it is used—to emphasize how Cam uses his ascribed racialized identity. Cam teaches us about the importance of Black bodily creative expression to gain visibility—using art as a means of Black expression—in response to being silenced and suppressed.[15]

> *Well, the deal is, in the rodeo world, 90 percent of the people wear the same thing. Like, you see how I wore them pants to the [Black] rodeo last night? In a white rodeo, I'da stopped the whole rodeo. They woulda had a media flash. They don't see that kind of stuff. They woulda made the biggest deal out of it on the loudspeaker you ever heard. The announcer woulda said, "Wow, did you see Big Reach's pants tonight?" They woulda made a big deal out of it because they don't see that. You go to a Black rodeo, hell, that's normal. "Nigga got on some goddamn fancy britches," you know what I'm sayin'? Oh, but white people, oh hell naw.*[16]

In response to the lack of space in professional rodeo for him to express his identity aesthetically and the idea of having to look like all other cowboys, except when it comes to his skin color, Cam continues:

> *Every white person that rodeo wear the exact same thing. They wear Wranglers with Wrangler shirts. They might have different patches on 'em, but they all got the exact same clothes on. Everybody.*[17]

Black aesthetic creativity would have us consider, as part of the cowboy aesthetic, a Black cowboy wearing bedazzled blue jeans, or an all-pink cowboy-inspired outfit complete with a pink cowboy hat instead of the traditional cowboy uniform worn for the practical purposes of work on the ranch. However, the posture of confidence in the Black cowboy's control over his ability to dictate his direction on the road remains weather he a cowboy in traditional cowboy spaces or Lil Nas X telling his cowboy story in a song. As a Black artist making country music and wearing Western-style clothing in such colors as pink, red and gold, and light blue with leopard print, Lil Nas X retains control over the optics of a Black artist who makes country music. In the rodeo, Black cowboys pay the same attention to their preparation and execution of control of their aesthetic and performance as they do when roping calves on a ranch. These visual representations of the Black cowboy, then and now, are significant because they are emotionally compelling, influential, and persuasive for how they clarify and distinguish reality from myth.

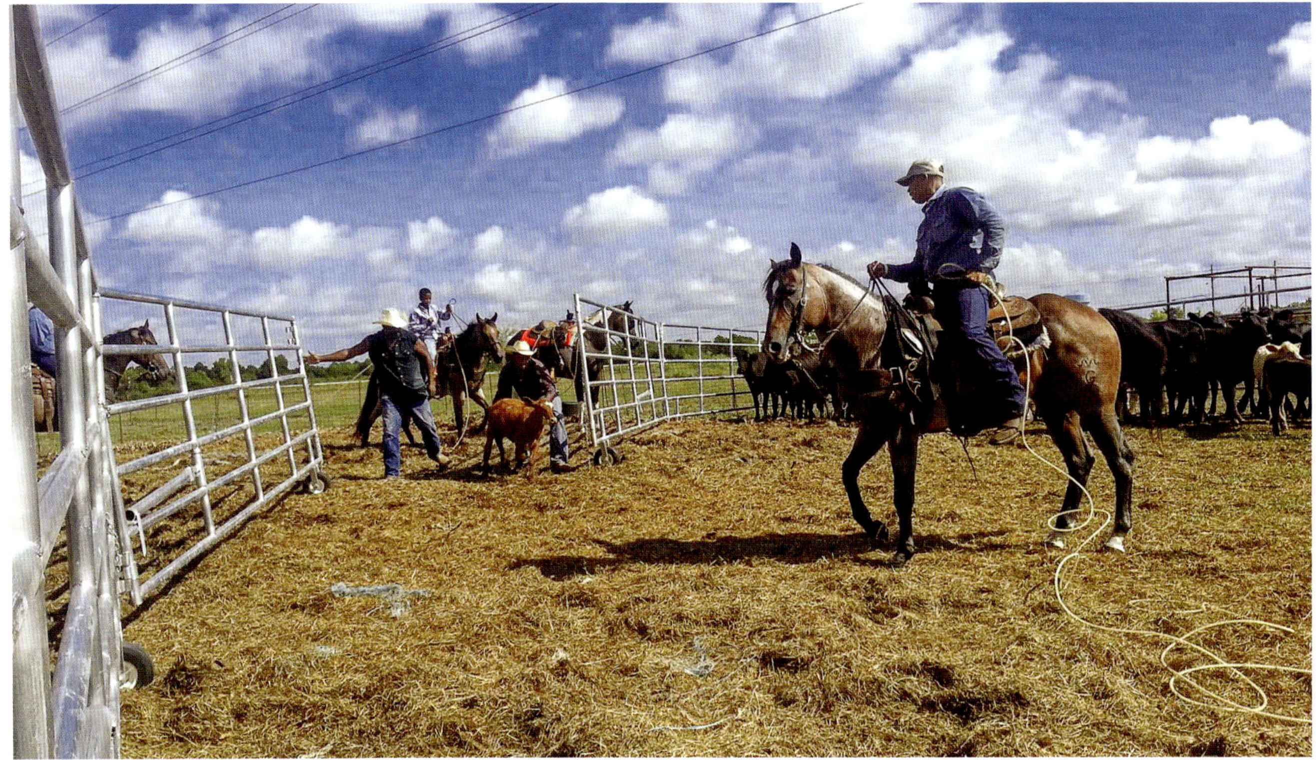

Myeshia C. Babers, ROUND UP, 2013. Photograph

ENDNOTES

1 Cydney Henderson, "Wrangler's Lil Nas X 'Old Town Road' Collection Slammed as Cowboy 'Cultural Appropriation,'" *USA Today*, May 24, 2019. https://www.usatoday.com/story/life/entertainthis/2019/05/23/wranglers-old-town-road-slammed-cowboy-cultural-appropriation/1214099001/.

2 Brittany Spanos, "How Lil Nas X and 'Old Town Road' Defy Categorization," *Smithsonian Magazine*, December 19, 2019. Accessed January 28, 2022. https://www.smithsonianmag.com/arts-culture/lil-nas-x-old-town-road-american-ingenuity-180973492/

3 Jacqueline M. Moore, *Cow Boys and Cattle Men: Class and Masculinities on the Texas Frontier, 1865–1900* (New York: New York University Press, 2009).

4 Katie Nodjimbadem, 2017. "The Lesser-Known History of African-American Cowboys | History | Smithsonian." February 13. Accessed July 2018, 2017. http://www.smithsonianmag.com/history/lesser-known-history-african-american-cowboys-180962144/

5 The rates of pay posted on the schedules for the ProRodeo versus the Black Professional Cowboys and Cowgirls Association can be found online at www.prorodeo.com/schedule and https://bpcca.com.

6 Julian Agyeman and Kofi Boone, "Land Loss Has Plagued Black America since Emancipation – Is It Time to Look Again at 'Black Commons' and Collective Ownership?" *The Conversation*. The Conversation US, October 19, 2022. https://theconversation.com/land-loss-has-plagued-black-america-since-emancipation-is-it-time-to-look-again-at-black-commons-and-collective-ownership-140514.

7 Ibid.

8 Tricia Martineau Wagner, 2007–2017. "Isom Dart (1849-1900)." Accessed October 24, 2017. http://www.blackpast.org/aaw/isom-dart-1849-1900

9 Bill Pickett - National Rodeo Hall of Fame - National Cowboy & Western Heritage Museum. (n.d.). National Cowboy & Western Heritage Museum. https://nationalcowboymuseum.org/collections/awards/rodeo-hall-of-fame/inductees/5074/

10 William Loren Katz, 2000–2013. "Bill Picket was a Cowboy Legend." Accessed October 24, 2017. https://aaregistry.org/story/bill-pickett-was-a-cowboy-legend/

11 "The Crimson Skull," Turner Classic Movies, https://www.tcm.com/tcmdb/title/579718/the-crimson-skull#notes.

12 Myeshia C. Babers, "Cowboy Cool: A Professional Black Cowboy's Perspective," *Transform Anthropology* 30 (2022): 157.

13 Myeshia C. Babers, "Controlling the Reins," *Anthropology News*, March 14, 2023. https://www.anthropology-news.org/articles/controlling-the-reins/.

14 Babers, "Cowboy Cool," 155.

15 Ibid., 150–64.

16 Ibid., 155.

17 Ibid., 155.

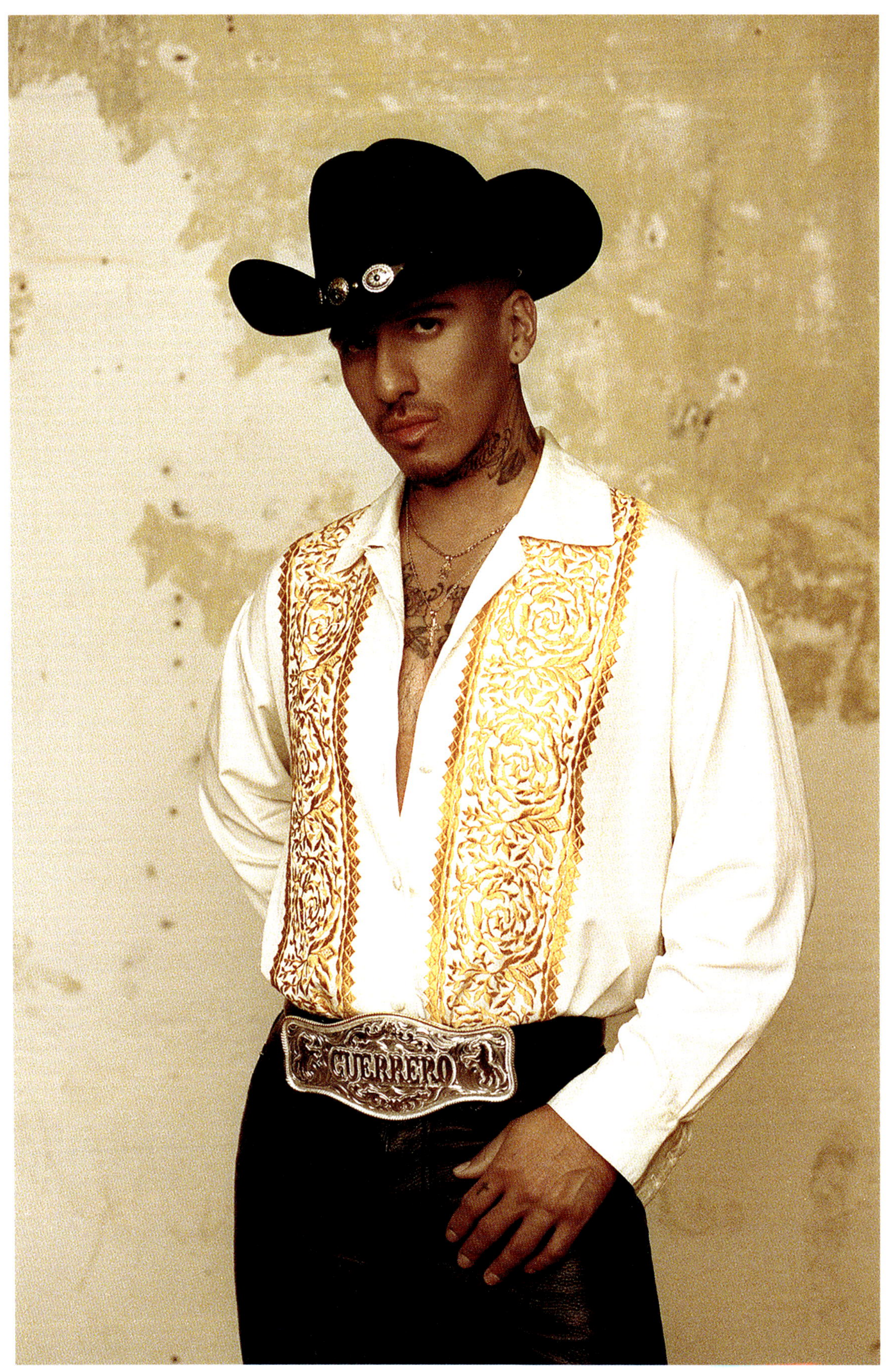
GUERRERO

IN FEBRUARY 2023, I INTERVIEWED ARTIST RAFA ESPARZA AT HIS STUDIO in Los Angeles about his love of Norteño music and culture. Norteño is a genre of music from Northern Mexico, known for its polka rhythms, vibrant accordions, and *bajo sextos*. It emerged in the late nineteenth century as a mix of regional Mexican music and the folk music of German, Polish, and Czech immigrants in Mexico. Today Norteño's popularity extends globally but is most prevalent in Texas (where its offshoot, Tejano music, reigns), California, and areas of the Southwest, where there are large populations of Mexican immigrants and their descendants.

Like esparza, I was raised in a Mexican American household in Los Angeles, and I recall attending extended family gatherings and church functions where Norteño *corridos* could be heard amid the laughter of

QUEER NORTEÑO AND THE VAQUERO AS "ANTI-COWBOY"

An interview with rafa esparza by Miranda Lash

cousins, aunts, and uncles. Norteño men's clothing in many ways resembles the attire typically associated with cowboys, including cowboy hats (a functional protection from the sun), leather boots, large belt buckles, and button-up shirts, which can be worn more formally to attend social functions and family events. Like cowboy culture, Norteño has a long history of rigidly prescribed gender roles and pervasive machismo. Until recently there has been little tolerance for overt expressions of queerness, particularly among men who desire men.

The Museum of Contemporary Art's *Cowboy* exhibition features esparza's *al Tempo,* a 2021 painting on adobe based on a photograph taken at Tempo, a queer club in West Hollywood that plays Norteño music. MCA Denver's *Cowboy* will also present the beginnings of a documentary esparza is developing with the photographer Fabian Guerrero. This film will focus on clubs like Tempo that foster a sense of community and belonging for queer Norteño fans. In this interview esparza describes his personal relationship with Norteño culture and his goals in creating this documentary.

Fabian Guerrero and Tony Alvarez, FABIAN GUERRERO, 2016, from the series QUEER BROWN RANCHERO. Photograph

MIRANDA LASH We are coming together to talk about Norteño culture in the context of MCA's *Cowboy*, which explores the stereotypes,

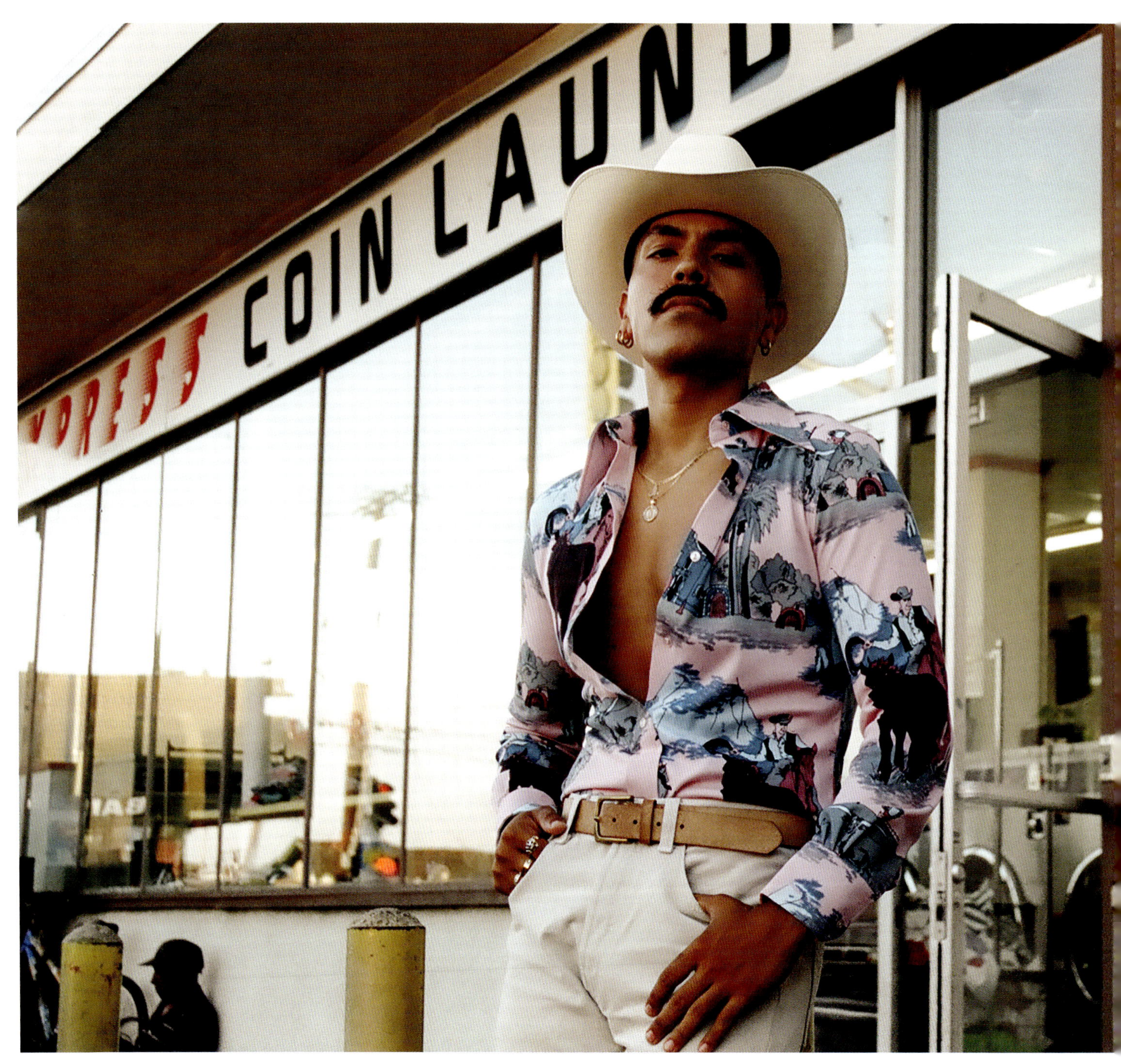

Fabian Guerrero, JOSE HERNANDEZ, LOS ANGELES, CA, 2017, from the series QUEER BROWN RANCHERO. Photograph

expectations, and desires surrounding the idea of the American cowboy. You've had an expansive career as a performance artist, and I know you've been thinking about Norteño culture for some time. Could you begin by sharing how you first encountered Norteño?

RAFA ESPARZA I grew up immersed in it. My folks are from a small pueblo that's called Ricardo Flores Magón. It's in Durango, in northern central Mexico, a very rural state. It was important for my folks to take me and my siblings to visit Mexico every summer, from when I was five years old up until I was a late teenager. I lived there for two years as a kid as well. The pueblo is still a very rural farming community with unpaved roads. You can see people riding around on horses and bicycles and you're surrounded by farmland. It was very common for me to see all the men in my family don the cowboy boots, jeans, leather goods, belt buckles, and the *tejanas* or cowboy hats.

I don't think I realized until I was in the first or second grade that this upbringing was different or not the norm in metropolitan communities like Los Angeles. I remember my dad used to send us to school in cowboy boots at a young age, and we hated it. We wanted to wear all the cool sneakers that everyone else was wearing. The boots made it hard to do things that the other kids were doing, like running around and playing kickball in P.E. [physical education class].

I remember my older brother and I (we are three years apart) pleading with my father: "Please let us wear tennis shoes, or any other shoes. Just please let us not wear boots to school." Thankfully my mom chimed in and he gave his permission. I grew up in a very social, but also a very rigid, macho-oriented, patriarchal family unit. My father eased up on the shoes, but it was such a battle growing up with him.

ML **Why do you think wearing boots was important to him?**

RE In the moment we just thought that my dad was being strict. Through the years, perhaps because I've always known that I'm gay and that I'm queer, the way that I view my family has been from this place of being part of the family but also feeling outside of it all the time. Now that I'm an adult and I have a different relationship with my parents, I can see aspects of his decision-making around how we dressed having to do with preserving his culture. He wanted to preserve a way of life that maintained for him a connection to *Mexicanidad*, which instilled the gender roles that he expected us to fulfill.

Aside from the formality of how we presented ourselves to the world, there were also chores that he made sure that we learned how to do. These chores were always enforced. I think my siblings and I can attribute the very strong work ethic that we've developed over the years to our upbringing and working with my father. I remember we had a small corn *milpa* in the backyard. I look back on that and think, "Oh my God. Dad was totally trying to recreate aspects of what he remembered growing up with, that felt important for him to preserve and for us to experience." Aside from the trips to Mexico, these were ways of reinforcing this relationship to Durango that he wanted us to have.

ML Could you describe your visits to Durango?

RE I remember from my first visit being afraid of animals, because you have *vacas* and *burros*, and they're just out roaming through the streets. We didn't go out for the first couple of days because we were terrified that they were going to eat us! I remember the sounds of pigs and roosters . . . I loved waking up in the morning and hearing the chattering of all the women in the house.

My mom's side of the family was very matriarchal. I have more *tías* than I do uncles. My grandmother had a strong presence in the way that the family was held together. I used to love waking up and going to the kitchen and having coffee with the grownups and listening to the gossip or the news of the day and then going to the *molino* to pick up tortillas. It felt really good to be in the warmth of that space in the house. I remember coming back into the States and continuing to want to be in that space with my *tías* that lived in the US, along with my mom and all of my *primas* and the women in my family.

I also remember very distinctly realizing the poverty that my family grew up in. I don't know if my parents felt that it was important for me and my brother to experience that, but I remember one of my grandmother's houses didn't have proper plumbing. The way that you showered and used the restroom was just out in the corral or in a bucket, in a big *cazo*, showering yourself with buckets of water.

In retrospect, visiting Durango was one of my most impactful experiences. Every time that we went back to Mexico and every time we came back to the States, it shaped our sense of this capitalist culture that we navigated as an immigrant family, as first-generation Mexican Americans. Knowing that we have a family that's very dear to us that we're also existing in this place for. There'd be moments when my siblings and I would complain about not having certain things, not being able to have the coolest clothes. But then every year around the time that it came for us to go back to Mexico, we would start to put together clothes and hand-me-downs that felt still okay to give away. I remember feeling a sense of responsibility of taking care of our shoes. It was just not so that they look good, but also, "Oh, maybe my cousin or my *tío* could have these when we go back." Everything was shared.

Both of my parents are from the same town. Most people in the pueblo work in farming and their relationship to land is nothing like I had ever experienced here in Pasadena, where I grew up. To this day, there isn't an irrigation system in the pueblo that waters the farmland. Their relationship to the land is also one that extends to nature. They're so dependent on rainwater, which makes life very difficult because there are moments of drought. I grew up hearing in my family, "as long as you have work, you're fine." These things come from my parents' upbringing as working class. They are very proud people, but I know that their childhood was devastated by poverty and inequality.

ML When you described how your father wanted you to dress, do you think it's connected to that sense of pride? My grandmother also came from a poor family in Mexico, but she would always stress, "Your clothes have to be ironed. You have to show up clean and well-dressed." She instilled a sense of pride through how we presented ourselves.

RE Oh my god, yes. I think along with the fashion that we were asked to wear, it was also about how you were styled. Your shirt had to always be tucked in. You always had to have a belt. The neatness of how you wore your clothes mattered as much as what you were wearing. There was a lot of pride in that kind of presentation. That's also part of why my father felt it was an important thing to pass down to us.

ML You have created several artworks with your father over the years, and your family is a huge source of influence to your practice. It's also clear that you've taken a great deal of initiative in defining how you approach your heritage. Could you talk about when you realized it was time for you "to take the reins" in terms of defining your own identity?

RE I feel like it was when most kids start to rebel, in their teenage years. It wasn't because I didn't like Norteño music, because I grew up with it and I love that music. What that music means to me now is so [entwined with] these family gatherings and how I carry memories of my family with me.

I think rebelling had more to do with taking control of what we were wearing and what we were listening to. My father forbade us from listening to hip hop, which was the sound and the music that we were creating as young, Black and brown kids in the barrios. That music felt so important to us as a way of participating in that culture. And we did it at the cost of sometimes getting some beatings, being scolded, having our boombox thrown away over and over again, and us having to hide these cassette tapes. But me and my older brother were like, "No, this is what we want to do and this is what we want to wear." But it was a battle. It was such a clash, always. We would sneak clothes into our backpacks. We were in middle school in the mid '90s, and we would switch our clothes on the way to school. My father forbade "*esa ropa de cholos*."

My family also used the words *nahuas* or *nahualon*. Nahua is an indigenous female. The clothes that many indigenous groups in northern Mexico, including the Nahuas, wore were flowy, blousy, billowing garments. I realized there was a gender critique or disdain within my family for something feminine that was also racialized at the same time.

ML So indigeneity was equated with being feminine?

RE Yeah. And the clothes that my siblings and I were wearing were these oversized khakis or jeans that were so flowy and very androgynous. Both boys and girls, men and women, were wearing the same oversized shirts and the same oversized pants. When he knew that these [oversized clothes] are here to stay, he said, "At least tuck in your shirts."

At the same time, when I was exploring different ways of wearing clothes, different hairdos, I was also listening to different music. Then I started to also consume different literature; books that were critical of Catholicism, of religion. I didn't read my first pure literature until I was in college, but I was paying attention to what was happening in the world, the Zapatista uprisings and what was happening in Chiapas, and how politics was also informing a counterculture in Los Angeles, and a lot of punk music. All of that was veering me far, far away from Norteño culture.

ML Were you still returning to Durango during this time?

RE I was. I remember every time that I would go back to the pueblo, Magón was the same. The roads are still unpaved. It's still largely a farming community. Our families have put in a lot of effort into resourcing our families in Mexico so that they have proper plumbing and lighting. But overall, it's remained the same. I remember going out to Magón and wearing these clothes that, when I think back now, were so extreme. No one was shaving their heads over there, no one was piercing. My ears were covered in piercings. I had an eyebrow piercing. I had a lip piercing. Then the extreme silhouettes of our baggy jeans, the jewelry that we wore, we were just weird. I remember when we were teenagers, my mom would try to shop for us because she was like, "I bought clothes for you guys to wear in Mexico."

But the family in Durango also knew that we're gringos and they thought, "*Así se visten allá,*" so maybe for the first few years our clothes seemed very different and new. But the pueblo eventually saw the fads on TV, and then it wasn't so weird. I'm so grateful for my parents and their willingness to see us and understand the culture that we were growing up in, and to also adapt themselves, which I know had to have been so challenging.

My parents came to the US when they were late teenagers. Their experience of us growing up here is probably so different from the expectations that they had. I don't think they ever imagined who we would become. It must have been hard for them to let go of some of these ideals and goals that they had for their children. The family unit is probably one of the most important things (along with labor) in my family. They really saw us evolve together. These expressions that we were exploring through fashion and music and the things that we wanted to do were so individualistic. That's what you do [as an artist]. You want to explore who you are. There's an aspect of the family unit becoming undone, maybe temporarily . . .

ML It's clear that you've folded your family into your process in a way that feels genuine to you and who you are. That said, to incorporate your family into your growth has got to be challenging.

RE It is hard. I feel like when I decided to move out and transfer from East LA College to UCLA, there were big shifts in the way that I related to my close friends and family, and my relationship with my father shifted drastically. We didn't speak for a couple of years. It was hard because I was going to school, doing all of this on my own. There were moments where I couldn't pay rent. Or I was in between living spaces, and feeling very unsupported and lost, quite frankly.

I was still heavily invested in school and performance and making art. I remember making a mold of an adobe brick for a sculpture class that Rodney McMillan was teaching in 2008. I talked about this object and about how traditionally adobe bricks require two people. The mold that I remember growing up seeing was a two-brick mold. I made a mold that was just one brick, and I was like, "I'd love to evolve this project to make a traditional mold and then invite people to make bricks with it." I thought, "I'm going to ask my dad if he'll teach me how to make bricks." I needed guidance. I needed to figure out how to find stability in my life. And I thought, "My dad was orphaned at a very young age and he had a tough upbringing. I know that he has so much knowledge he'll be able to tell me what I need to do."

It had been longer in between visits to my house because I had a partner. Every time that we walked into the room, my dad would leave. He wouldn't say hi. So, I had decided to stop visiting. I went by myself and I asked my dad if he would teach me how to make bricks. I had these ambitious ideas about conversations that we could have through that process, about him growing up, before he met my mom, about how he imagined his life. He agreed to teach me how to make the bricks. We spent an entire afternoon in his backyard making these tiny, red clay bricks. And it was nice. We didn't fight, we didn't argue. We hardly even spoke. Everything that we talked about was about making our little brick, the task at hand.

Then fast-forward to 2014, brickmaking was the first step in mending our relationship. I think it meant something for him to see me engage in an aspect of his childhood that he had held so close. We became friendly enough for me to feel comfortable to invite him to lead another red brick production that included the rest of my family. The project was called *building: a simulacrum of power*. It consisted of inviting my father to lead this team that included my five siblings, to make enough bricks that would cover the surface of an existing sculpture made by Michael Parker called *The Unfinished*.

I had done a lot of reflecting about my upbringing and my relationship to my dad, but also about how this family unit functioned as a team. I wanted to interrogate the roles that we all perform as siblings, as parents, as sons and daughters, and as women and men. Everyone participated in a different way and supported the process. I had some siblings that had other full-time jobs, but everyone always came by maybe once or twice a week. They would bring lunch and sit and have food with us. My brother would bring my nephews and nieces. All of those conversations with my dad that I was hoping for back in 2008 started happening organically when we were stomping in the big pile of mud. So many stories started with a brick, but then ended with my mom and dad's first date. These beautiful intimate stories all are so dear to me. I'll never forget them. We spent an entire summer making bricks. We made 1,400. It's backbreaking work. The bricks weigh about forty-five pounds each. We were lifting tons of material

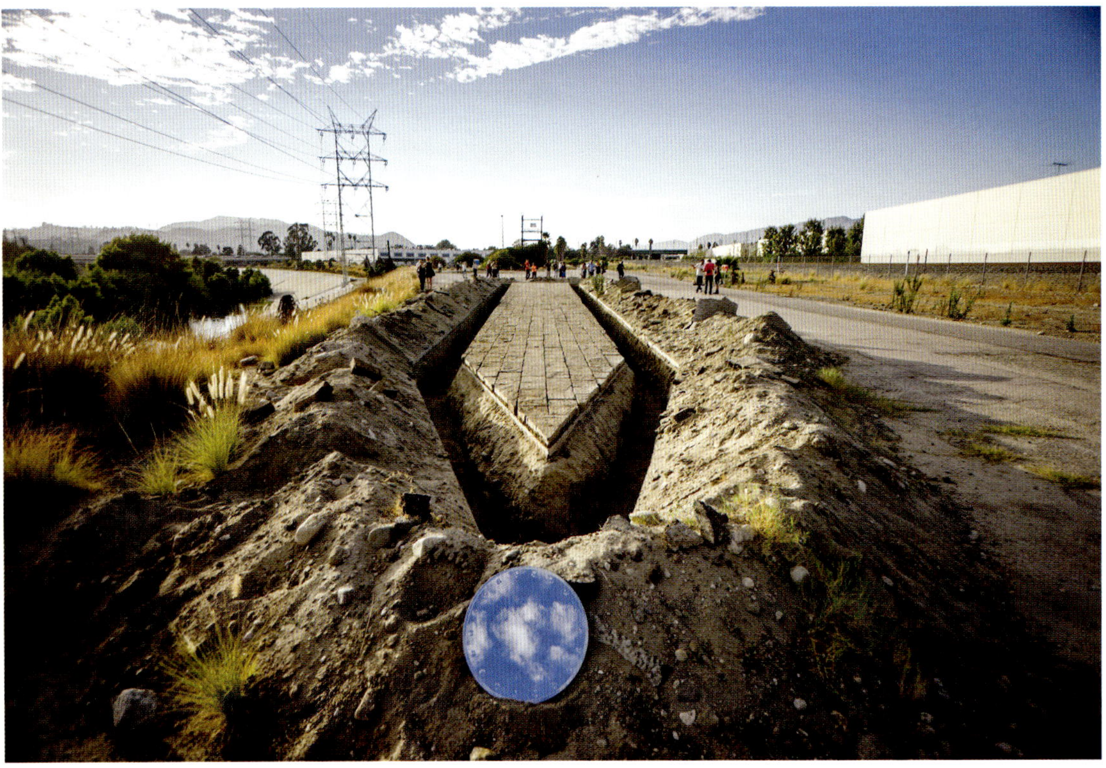

for weeks, paving the surface of the sculpture. The sculpture is an obelisk that's marked by a trench that surrounds the entire edifice. As we amassed bricks, this idea of the potentiality of what the space would be also grew. I ended up deciding to do a performance.

The performance [*building*] was in response to who I made these bricks with and who was going to be there to see this performance. There's honoring that happens in the performance because I've been doing Danza Azteca for fifteen years and this obelisk sat beside the LA River. So I did a water dance around the entire space. Then there's a shift in clothing that's also marked by a sexual act. I dragged myself across the entire surface

Above: **rafa esparza, BUILDING: A SIMULACRUM OF POWER, 2014. Site-specific performance**

Opposite: **rafa esparza, BUILDING: A SIMULACRUM OF POWER, 2014. Site-specific performance** of the bricks. I kept myself from walking on top of the bricks because we spent the entire summer shaping the adobe with our hands, picking it up, dropping to our knees. We had this very frontal, very specific movement in ways that we touched the bricks that I wanted to break out of. I wanted to have my entire body touch all of these bricks.

I approached moving through the space as if this obelisk were erect. I attempted to climb the obelisk while it's on the floor. So it looks like I'm dragging my body, but I'm climbing it at the same time. And when I get to the apex of this sculpture, I'm removing and leaving parts of my dance garments behind, until I'm bare-ass naked. I plant my ass at the tip of this

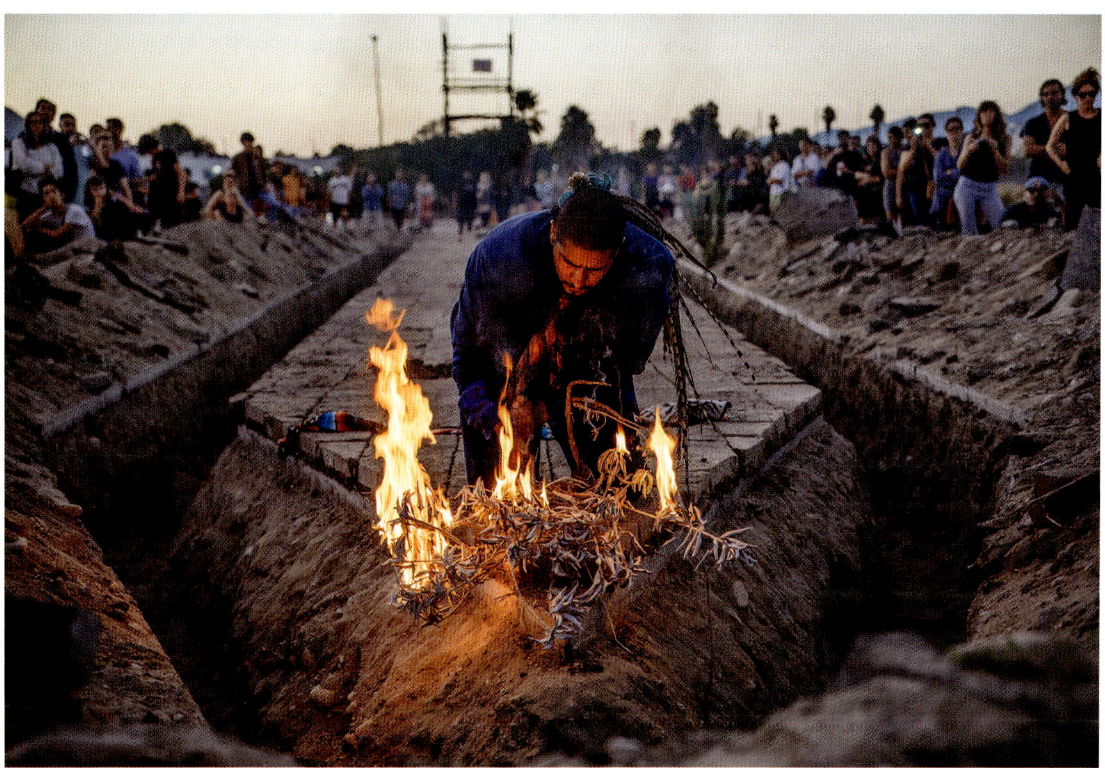

entire sculpture. Then I climb off and I change into a blue suit and tie, a very formal uniform. I walked back to the beginning of the sculpture and then I finally walk on top of the obelisk and I burn this sage bush that my father had found while we were working. There was that tension, that challenge to my family to see me in this way. Sure, there are art-historical references that we could talk about, like Ron Athey. But for me, the power of performance is the risk that people take to embody an action, a process, a character that's intended to be seen by an audience. And for me, my family is always at the helm of that audience. They're always a primary audience of sorts.

Something that I wanted to provoke [through my performance] was, "How are you going to hold this? How are you going to hold this image with you? Because I have to hold this body every day." But I knew that they could. My family has beyond exceeded my expectations of what they're able to do. And I think they've surprised themselves of what they're able to do.

ML **Because you have been on this journey of pulling away from your upbringing at intervals and engaging with your family over time, do you feel more comfortable exploring Norteño culture now than you would have, perhaps, ten years ago?**

RE Yeah. There's been explicit conversations about Norteño culture within my work . . . but I feel ready to have this conversation on a different scale. Some of it has had to do with the journey of coming out, obviously, and rebuilding with my family, growing with my family, but also having the distance that I needed to have from Norteño culture to be able to now appreciate it in a different way. That's not to say that my appreciation was never there, but my rebellion against Norteño culture relates to the place that it held in my family as this authoritative, patriarchal entity. I don't think, in years past, I was coveting Norteño culture in the way I am celebrating it and loving it now. It's a complicated thing to say, but I do love it. I do love the way that the music and the culture exists in my life, thanks to the queer spaces that allow us to have a relationship to the music and to the fashion outside of this [traditional] paradigm that's so toxic and so violent and unsafe for us.

ML **Do you want to talk about the club Tempo and queer spaces like that?**

RE I was just out on Sunday. Tempo is this magical queer haven that I was invited to before I even came out. I was going to clubs and partying kind of in secret, and I was invited by a friend. Tempo is situated in a shopping mall. It has multiple rooms. There's a room where they play a lot of *cumbia* and pop music, and then there's an upstairs where they have drag shows and they also play dance music. Directly across from that space is a patio where they make tacos and sell food. I remember walking into the bar. It was early and the door [to the downstairs] was closed. Then at some point people just started gravitating downstairs, and I remember following people down there, and I walk in, and there's a live Norteño band playing, and there's a plethora of mostly men, vaqueros, dancing with each other to this music that I grew up listening to.

I was, I think, in shock and awe . . . kind of stunned, because of the music and the attire . . . I just never imagined a queer possibility for all of that.

ML **Could you paint the picture a little? I imagine the accordions, the *bajo sexto* . . .**

RE Yeah, and you have a vocalist, you have the *baterísta*. This group had a saxophone player, a guitarist. They're also clad in vaquero wear from head to toe, button-up shirts, Wranglers, Levi's jeans, and pointy, pointy cowboy boots. Also very familiar clothes—very plain jeans and the plaid button-up Wrangler shirts. Then you have also these customized vaquero looks that have sequins, with designs or patterns on the shirts, tassels hanging from these shirts, jeans that have very beautiful stitching, and a lot more color. It was the first time I had seen [Norteño culture] queer. Again, I didn't even think it was possible. I'd been to the [club] Arena prior to that, where you see this kind of drag that people perform to attract the people that they want to leave the club with. I remember seeing cholos at Arena, or people that I thought were cholos, and then I talked to them and was like, "You're not a cholo at all." I remember seeing a few cowboys in that party, but not a whole room of vaqueros. It didn't feel like drag. It felt like everyone knew how to dance to the music.

ML It should be acknowledged that the dancing you're describing is couples dancing.

RE It's couples dancing. They knew what they were doing. This wasn't their first time. Growing up with a Norteño family, a Norteño community—dancing is a coming-of-age thing that you do. For young women, there's a certain age, maybe it's when you turn fifteen, that you're permitted to dance.

ML Post-quinceañera.

RE Post-quinceañera, exactly. Men have a lot more permission to do anything, in general, but when it came to comes to dancing, boys think, "I have to learn how to dance," because that's the first step in courting someone, is to take them out on a *baile*. When you see a couple that knows how to dance, you know that they've been [trained]. There's so many different puzzles to the different types of music that's being played. It takes growing up with it, or practicing that kind of dance for a while, to be considered a seasoned dancer.

ML I think too about how men are always expected to lead. How does it work when two Norteño men dance together?

RE Men lead and men follow. It's so beautiful to watch, to see a man follow. My first teachers were my *tías*. I had a very festive *tía* and she made it her thing to ensure that all of us knew how to dance. She would bring all of the kids and we would all join the crowd and dance and take turns dancing with her. We were eight or nine years old, so we grew up dancing to this music. I remember paying attention to the women and how they would dance, because I imagined myself dancing with a man in the future. I was like, "I'm not going to be able to practice this here, obviously." When I was in the room [at Tempo] . . . it transported me back to these family parties

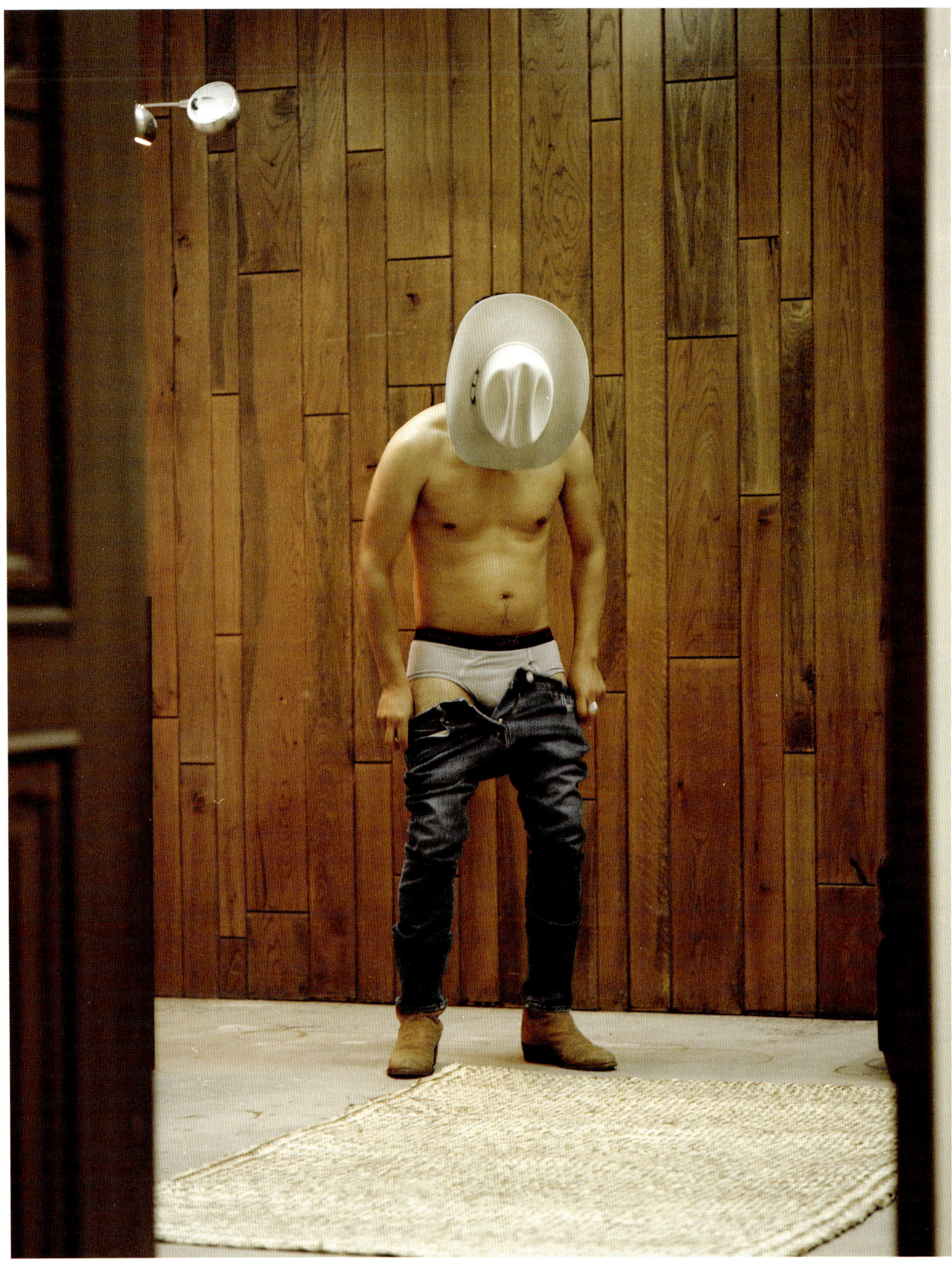

and studying the women in my family. Now, this future that I always imagined was here in front of my eyes, and the possibility of dancing and leading or following was real.

ML What year was this?

RE This was in 2001. It left a long-lasting impression me. I had to go back, and I did. I continue to go back as often as I can to this day. At some point, I became curious about whether there are other places like Tempo. It's the only one in Los Angeles, really.

ML That feels surprising for a city the size of LA.

RE It does, but when you think of Tempo's proximity to West Hollywood, it kind of makes sense that it's the only place, because it's still very challenging for us to create our own spaces. They're always very precarious. Many of us come to West Hollywood or to Hollywood to be in queer spaces, because there aren't enough in the Eastside, or hardly any. Beyond that, if you think about further east into San Bernardino, less so. Fabian Guerrero is finding out about this place in Arizona. I hope that our journey with the documentary allows us to learn of other spaces like it, because Tempo shouldn't be the only one.

ML No, it shouldn't. You mentioned a place in Dallas too . . .

RE Yes, and in this conversation with the owner of Club Los Rieles, Fabian learned of a bar in Arizona. Since then, I have seen, especially through social media, videos of queer people dancing to Norteño music in these massive rodeos. These rodeos happen maybe a few times a year. There's very little queer representation, but I think it's also due to how few [queer] spaces exist. Tempo remains to me like a gem. I've been to Mexico. I've been to Tijuana. I've been to Mexicali. I've been to Mexico City. Even in Durango itself, the capital [of Norteño culture], there isn't a place like this. I've thought about it a lot, and I feel like it makes sense that places like Tempo are in cities like Dallas and Los Angeles, where there are majority immigrant communities that are migrating up from northern Mexico. When they find that there are safe spaces, they seek them, or they make them.

ML Your performances often probe the boundaries of what is safe. You described to me a performance you did in Mexico, where you were dancing to Norteño music with a male collaborator outside of a club and just seeing what would happen. You were curious how the audience would react.

RE I think having had the relationship that I have with Tempo, I do want more. Tempo feels like it is a haven for a community that wants to listen to this music and dress up like a vaquero.

ML Do you think it's "dress-up"?

Fabian Guerrero, JOSE VILLANUEVA, FT. WORTH TX, 2022, from the series QUEER BROWN RANCHERO. Photograph

RE It's dress-up in the way that you would dress to go to a formal event, but it doesn't feel like drag. Like how I was describing the scenario at Arena, where in the nineties the cholo was sexualized and there were people performing this kind of gangster or cholo [aesthetic] to attract other cholos. Tempo has never ever felt that way. When you speak with people at Tempo, they don't sound like someone who decided, "Oh, I want to dress up like a cowboy and go and hook up with a cowboy," though I'm sure there is some of that. It really feels like people that have a longing for these spaces, and that have found a home.

ML We talked previously about the difference between vaqueros and cowboys. There's the obvious divide of the border and race that could be used to distinguish these identities, but I feel like you are pointing to more layered cultural distinctions relating to how brown people are perceived in the United States. Could you talk about why you use the word *vaquero*?

RE I feel like for migrating communities in Los Angeles, the markers of vaquero culture have to be left behind, or maybe kept private for a while, so that [these migrants] are able to blend in and assimilate enough to find a job. Markers [of vaquero culture] are still very present in stereotypes of immigrant communities, especially if it's a brown person wearing [the hat and the belt buckle]. Right? It's a marker of someone that doesn't belong.

ML Someone who is a new arrival.

RE A new arrival, a *paisa*. In the nineties, that word, *paisa,* was derogatory. I remember Chicanos using that word, *paisa*, or *paisita,* to refer to recent immigrants. It's diminutive. It's funny because now, in our generation, you start to see us own that word and hold it with a sense of pride. *Chuntaro* is another word. Spanish-speaking people would use that word to speak down to immigrants. When I think about a vaquero versus a cowboy . . . there's an ethnic difference for me, but I think it's also about access and mobility. A cowboy is associated with a history of colonization and with a person that takes up space. Their right to a kind of manifest destiny is embodied and personified through how a cowboy is expected to behave and the kind of man that a cowboy should be. In so many ways, the vaquero is the antithesis of that because, especially within the US and even in Mexico, vaqueros are so looked down upon.

ML They're seen as rural, the antithesis of a *chilango* [person from Mexico City].

RE Even within other bigger cities in Guadalajara or Monterrey, vaqueros are seen in a manner similar to the way city dwellers in the US look at rural Americans. Vaqueros are associated with poverty or the working class, or a type of work that is not modern. A vaquero is dated in the imaginary of the larger public, and even within families, because a vaquero represents someone that lives in Mexico. When you see families that are here for a generation or two, or even just one, and they're still dressed in the boots and the cowboy hat, you're like, "Why are you still dressing like that? "*Eso ya déjalo allá, eso no es de aqui*." Brown vaqueros, immigrant vaqueros are othered in ways that a cowboy isn't.

ML The cowboy is held up as a heroic figure in America. Meanwhile, the vaquero represents one of white America's greatest fears: the immigrant who cannot or will not assimilate.

RE Totally.

ML A takeover or "taking up space" in a very different way. I think about the role of nostalgia, too, which plays a large role within cowboy culture. I was at the National Cowboy Poetry Gathering in Elko, Nevada, this year.

RE Wow.

ML Yes, that was fascinating! Nostalgia was a huge theme within the Gathering's poetry and songs—a longing for a way of life that is disappearing or already gone and a relationship to the land that traces back to a very short-lived period in the United States, when free-range cattle were driven across vast expanses. Many of the cowboy poems described the experience of living close to the land and the tenderness found in working with animals. I heard poems about the birthing of calves, the bellowing of the animals sleeping outside, the seasonal changes in the trees and plants. There's danger in that nostalgia because it requires an amnesia regarding the traumas inflicted upon Native Americans. This nostalgia also pivots around a deeply entitled sense of individualism.

At the same time, I recognize that nostalgia also plays a strong role in Mexican immigrant culture and (for some) the longing for the *rancho* left behind. I think about that classic Mexican song (and film) *Allá en el Rancho Grande*. When my grandmother played that song, it reflected her nostalgia not just for a place but a way of life.

RE Nostalgia, I feel, is why Tempo exists. Or, maybe it's not nostalgia but longing. It's like in José Esteban Muñoz's *Cruising Utopia*—"the not yet queer." I think it's longing for both *allá, "el rancho donde vivía,"* but also this queer space. It can't be nostalgia because that space didn't exist.

ML Tempo doesn't exist back at the *rancho*. There is no *rancho* like Tempo.

RE Still, I think some of those dangerous aspects of nostalgia exist within vaquero culture as well. Indigenous people in Mexico continue to be the worst-treated, the most denigrated population.

ML So, let's talk about this project that you've been thinking about for MCA Denver, *Querías Norte*. You've done collaborations before with Fabian Guerrero.

RE I have. Fabian's such a talented artist. He works primarily with photography but has also been experimenting with film and performance. I met him here in Los Angeles. He had been living here for roughly six or eight years. He's always been a Tejano and very proud to have grown up in Tamaulipas, Mexico, and Dallas, Texas. When I had this idea for the project, I thought of Fabian because of portraits that he'd already been taking of queer Norteño subjects. I thought he could bring something really beautiful to this project because of his sensitive approach. He's part of a school of photographers that is not extracting images from our communities but making images with our communities. Our documentary tells a story of these queer spaces that Norteños have built and cultivated, including bars like Tempo and Los Reiles, and maybe some of the rodeos, and the places where immigrant communities from El Norte exist in the US. We want to show how queer people are navigating these new spaces in the US.

I'm thinking about informal communities that are supporting each other, but it's also a good time to think about Norteño culture and Norteño music and understand where it comes from. Then also be able to take a snapshot of how Norteño culture has pierced into global, mainstream pop music. You're starting to see queer expressions among some of these artists and musicians. Fabian and I want to learn about these spaces and to help tell a story. I hope that what we're able to show through this film, is that we have always been in these spaces.

ML You've said queer people have always been a part of Norteño culture.

RE We have. Maybe they haven't been in the most public and expressive ways, but we have been there, and there is music that shows you that we've been there. We have people like Chavela Vargas and Juan Gabriel, who are such important queer models for young, contemporary musicians. They're the referent for us. They made music within a landscape where people like them were not popular or supported.

ML We've talked about what it would mean to share images and information about these communities to the broader world, and to a world that might not have the context of how these spaces are formed.

RE I think to be able to have a document of us as a community, to have proof of our existence, is invaluable. We are moving with intention and with care for the future, and for the culture in its present moment. We hope that we could finally be seen by our Norteño community, and to acknowledge that we have been here and that we are here, and that we're also producing culture. I don't know if it's ambitious to think of acceptance as being one of the outcomes, but I'm sure it's on Fabian's mind. It's definitely on my mind. There are personal stakes for me and Fabian. We both have talked about not growing up with a blueprint of how to be a man. There have been ways that men in our lives have wanted to instill what being a

Fabian Guerrero, JAIME RODRIGUEZ, LOS ANGELES, CA, 2018, from the series QUEER BROWN RANCHERO. Photograph

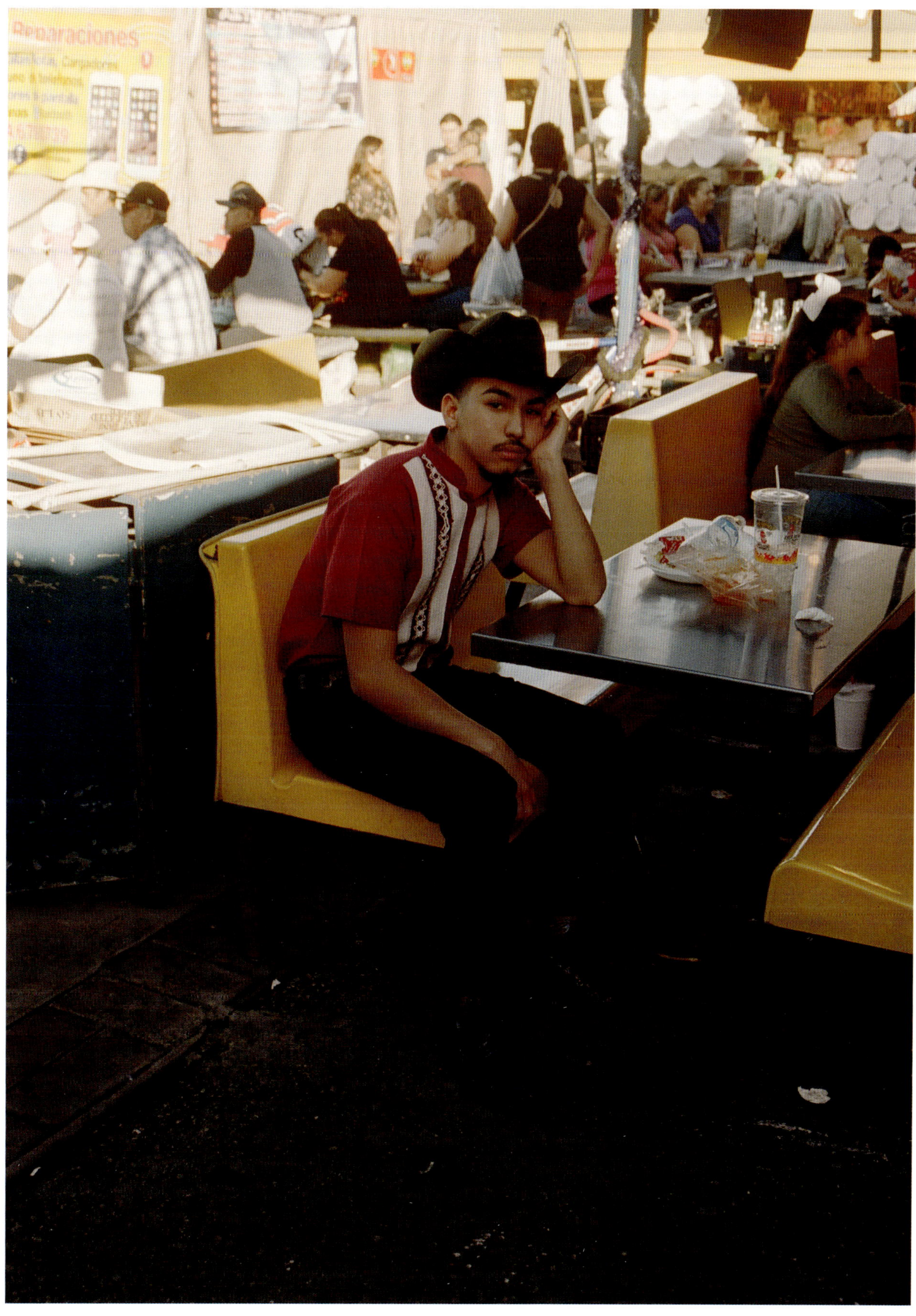
Reparaciones

man looks like, but it's so fraught. It leaves you not being able to even really be a human.

ML You've also shared, and I've seen within my own experience, that within Latinx clubs there is more permission for women to dance with women than men dance with men.

RE I feel like two men dancing presents so much fear for [traditional Norteño men]. Especially in a culture where so much is taboo, there's so much fear that your friend might be a gay man that desires you. There are all these negative connotations associated with being feminine, being weak. A lot of queer men bring women into dance clubs to help us be safe. We went to a straight bar, and I wanted to dance. We saw a couple of queer folks there, but in mixed-gender groups. I thought, "Oh, yeah, of course we're here, but we're not here with other gay men. We're here with our friends that are women."

ML So you feel that the culture is evolving?

RE Yes. I recently experienced going to a club in Los Angeles that I'd been to maybe fifteen years ago and danced for the first time ever with another guy. No one seemed to be bothered. I feel like that's a good sign of change in the culture and in the bar itself. That wouldn't have happened fifteen years ago.

What we get to do as queer people and what all people should be able to do is chart their own growth for themselves. You interrogate what masculinity has been projected and imposed onto you, and you shape what that could look like. I hope that this upcoming documentary does some of that as well. I feel like we're holding up a mirror for a greater public to be able to see themselves, not just this group of queer Norteños, but see themselves, because we all listen to this music. We all dance to this music.

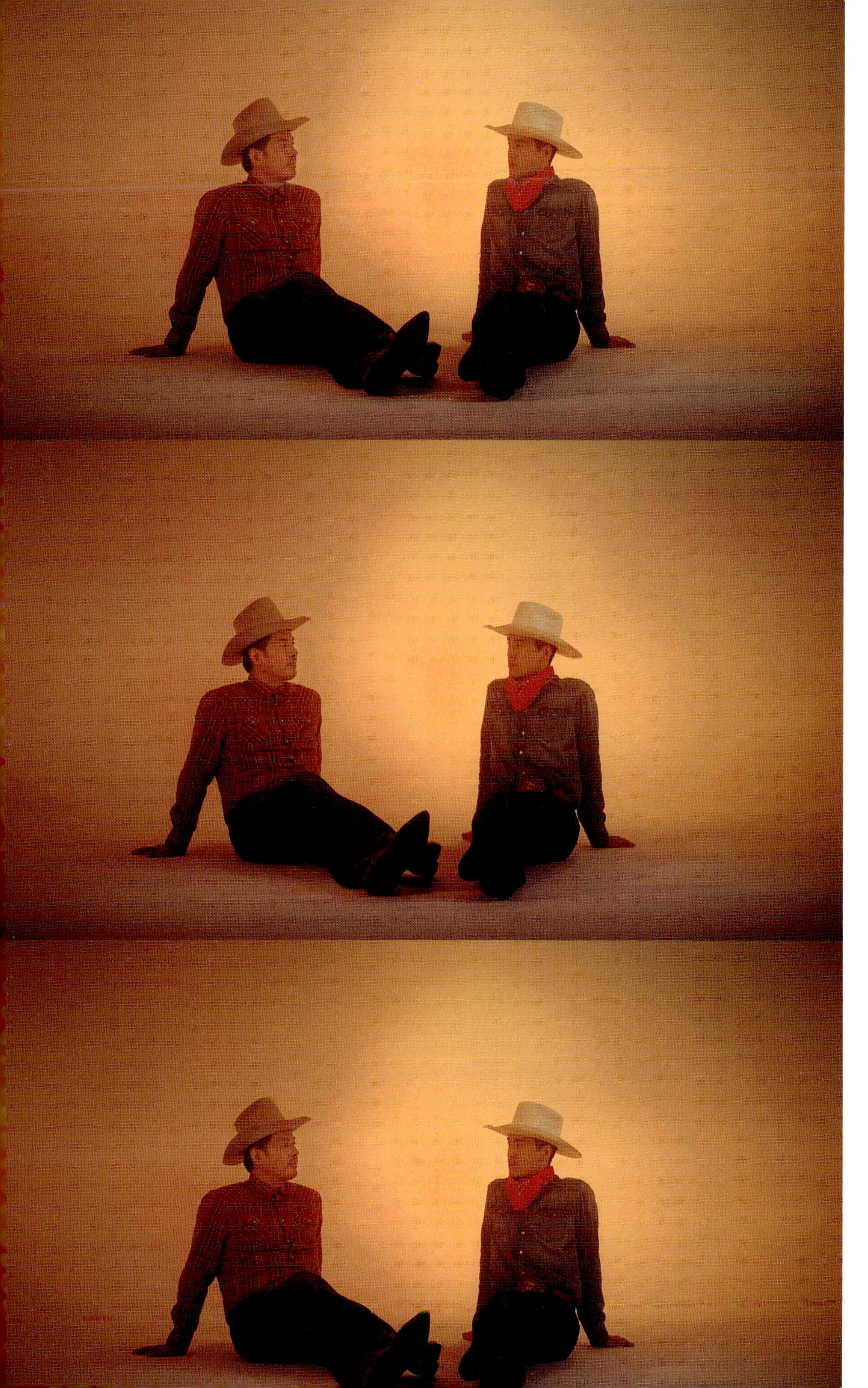

KENNETH TAM COMPLICATES OUR UNDERSTANDING OF WHAT IT IS LIKE TO be a man—or what it means to act like a man. Stating that masculinity is "a concept learned," Tam investigates the bond between men within peer groups and patriarchal hierarchies.[1] In his explorations through video, sculpture, performance, installation, and other media spanning more than a decade, he studies and challenges the vernacular customs in the preserve of the male sex, heuristically intersecting with the racial history of the United States. Tam's 2021 two-channel video installation *Silent Spikes* (20 min, 29 sec) should be placed in this vein but beware: *Silent Spikes* is a deceptively complex work, with its meaning decentered and cleverly elusive.[2] About sixteen minutes into the work, one of the performers, off-screen, asks nine questions in succession[3]:

KENNETH TAM'S WILD WEST: FABULATIONS FOR JOHN CHINAMAN

Jongwoo Jeremy Kim

> *Do you think that you are an individual?*
> *Do you feel that you have to hide yourself?*
> *Do you think that you have to be somebody else to live your life?*
> *How do you think your father sees you?*
> *Do you like to be with other people?*
> *Are you happy with the way your life turned out right now?*
> *Have you ever experienced discrimination?*
> *Do you feel that you have to straddle two different worlds, and you have to assimilate?*
> *Do you feel that you have to compromise yourself to get what you want out of life here?*

It isn't so much that *Silent Spikes* systematically answers these questions as the amalgam of these questions discourages reading the work as merely a fantasy about Asian American cowboys, an investigation into the history of Chinese railroad workers in the US, or an intersectional challenge against racial capitalism and patriarchy. *Silent Spikes* contains elements pertaining to all three of these priorities, but at the same time it feels there is something else held back, just beyond our reach. The work adumbrates many contours of half-shared meaning, past and present—as if to mimic

Opposite and pages 62–66, 70–71, 73, 75: **Kenneth Tam, stills from SILENT SPIKES, 2021. Two channel video with sound. Duration: 20:29 minutes. Commissioned by the Queens Museum with support from the Asian Art Circle of the Guggenheim Museum** the protean waves of the Pacific that tens of thousands of Cantonese men would have witnessed in their migration to the American West in the nineteenth century. (The word protean comes from Proteus, the "minor sea god who had the power of prophecy but who would assume different shapes to avoid answering questions"—like an oracular theater of Proteus, Tam's video does not offer any definite answers.[4])

The nine questions are posed in *Silent Spikes* just as an Asian man starts dancing on the left screen to the sound of an Eastern string instrument. He wears cowboy attire—a brown cattleman hat; a sandy, wild rag around his neck; a russet shirt with single-point pockets, yokes, and three-snap barrel cuffs; and the rest of Western sartorial clichés like the chaps

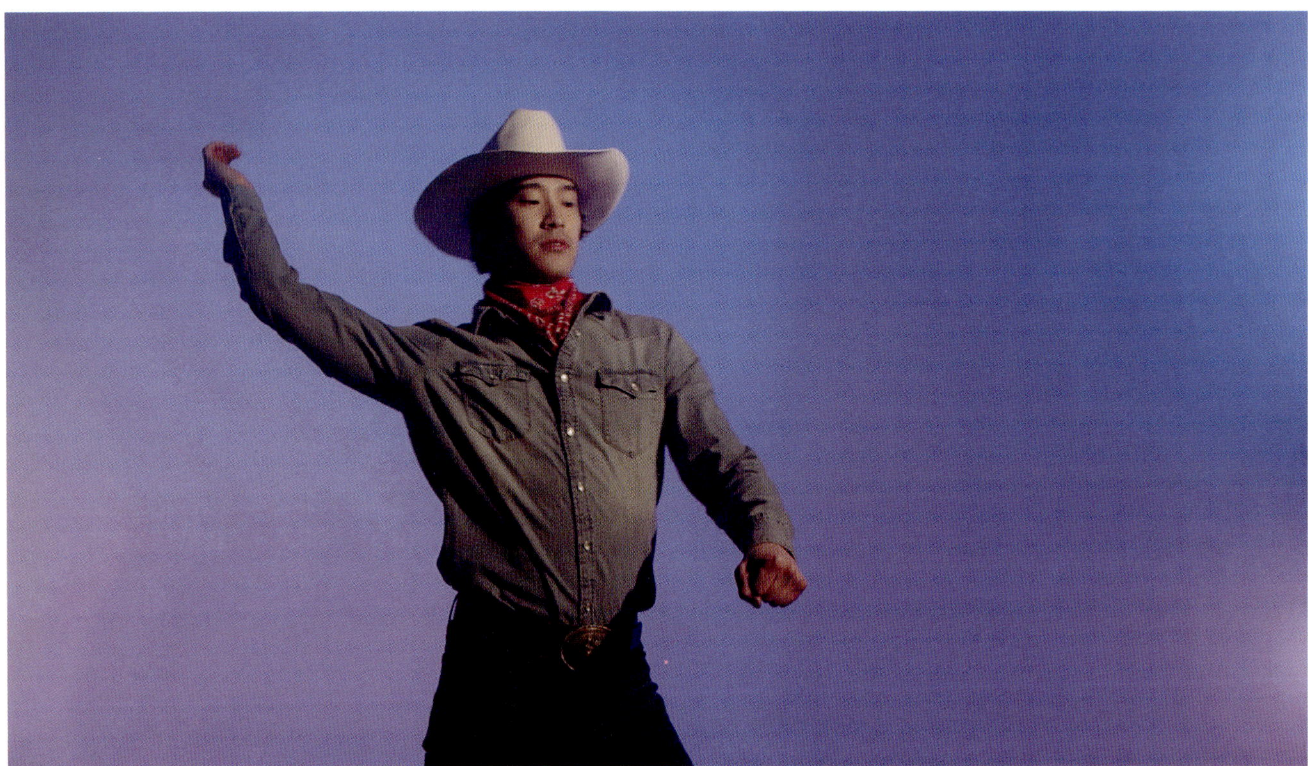

over his jeans. As if called forth by this costume dance, another cowboy, also Asian, appears on the right screen for a pas de deux (p. 62–63). He joins the pageantry wearing a bolo tie and a caramel-toned leather vest along with a cowboy hat. Then, the first one suddenly disappears, leaving the left screen black. A few seconds later a different Asian cowboy pops up on the left, wearing an off-white hat, a red kerchief, and a blue denim Western shirt. The two cowboys, contained in their own separate screens, appear to dance in coordinated movements until the man on the right vanishes and the screen goes dark. The whole choreography lasts a little less than one minute thirty seconds, but the motions of the three men are in a slo-mo sequence, as if they are moving underwater—making time malleable. Like in a strange dream, these attractive men play-act in an interpretive mimesis of a masculine ritual, in the sense that they move as though they were on broncos or bulls in a rodeo when in fact they stand on their two feet in a completely empty, interior space with studio lighting of lulling blue and purple. Their male bodies languidly jerk and gyrate to achieve a time-warped spectacle, accentuating unexpectedly sensuous arcs of torsos and thrusts of studly hips. One arm swings into the air, shoves forward, shakes downward, pretending to sustain balance atop an unseen, violent animal while the dominant hand feigns to grip the riggin' or the rein. Because all these bodily movements are represented in the speed slower than they would transpire in real life, viewers experience a curious

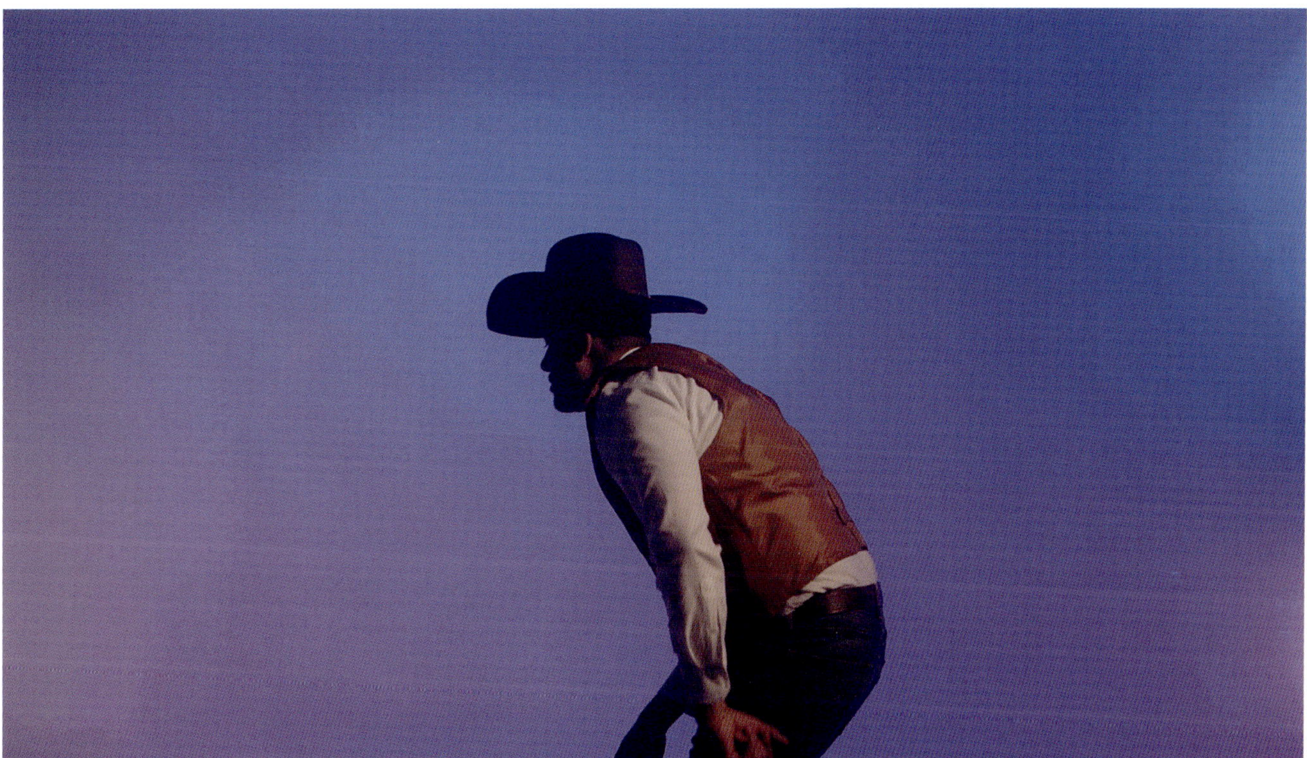

feeling of preternaturally scrutinizing each split second of the incredible tension and release, roll and bounce, whip and hit, spin and drop, scoop and shoot, and bodacious swags of sexy bodies arrested in the blissful, camp eternity of the Wild West—a male burlesque with an Eastern twist.

In what ways do the overlapped solo-dances of Asian *twunks* respond to the narration of the nine questions about individuality, dissemblance of the true self in society, code-switching and passing, discrimination and success, paternal approval and disapproval, alienation, assimilation, and compromise? Disconnectedly, at best. The rodeo ballet thus feels like a visual taunt, a sardonic misdirection, and a cinema of fuck-you, less than/other than an earnest celebration of—or a creative inquiry into—an American ideal of the masculine, which comprises ridiculously white-centric stereotypes like the Marlboro Man, after all. Not only are the wild bulls, half-tamed horses, cheering crowd, and dust clouds kicked up from the ground missing in *Silent Spikes* but also the honky-tonks of country-music guitars is replaced by the twang of *erhus*, *guzhengs*, *gayageums*, and similar Eastern instruments.[5] The impeccably dressed Western men are not so many copies of John Wayne per se but variations of John Chinaman. *Silent Spikes* depicts not so much immigrant pathos lingering in successful assimilation—or an easy banality of the melting pot—as the sublimated bathos of Asian American masculinity, or the unhurried, salty joy of recognizing the historical arc from the naive multiculturalism of earlier decades' immigration—as famously encapsulated

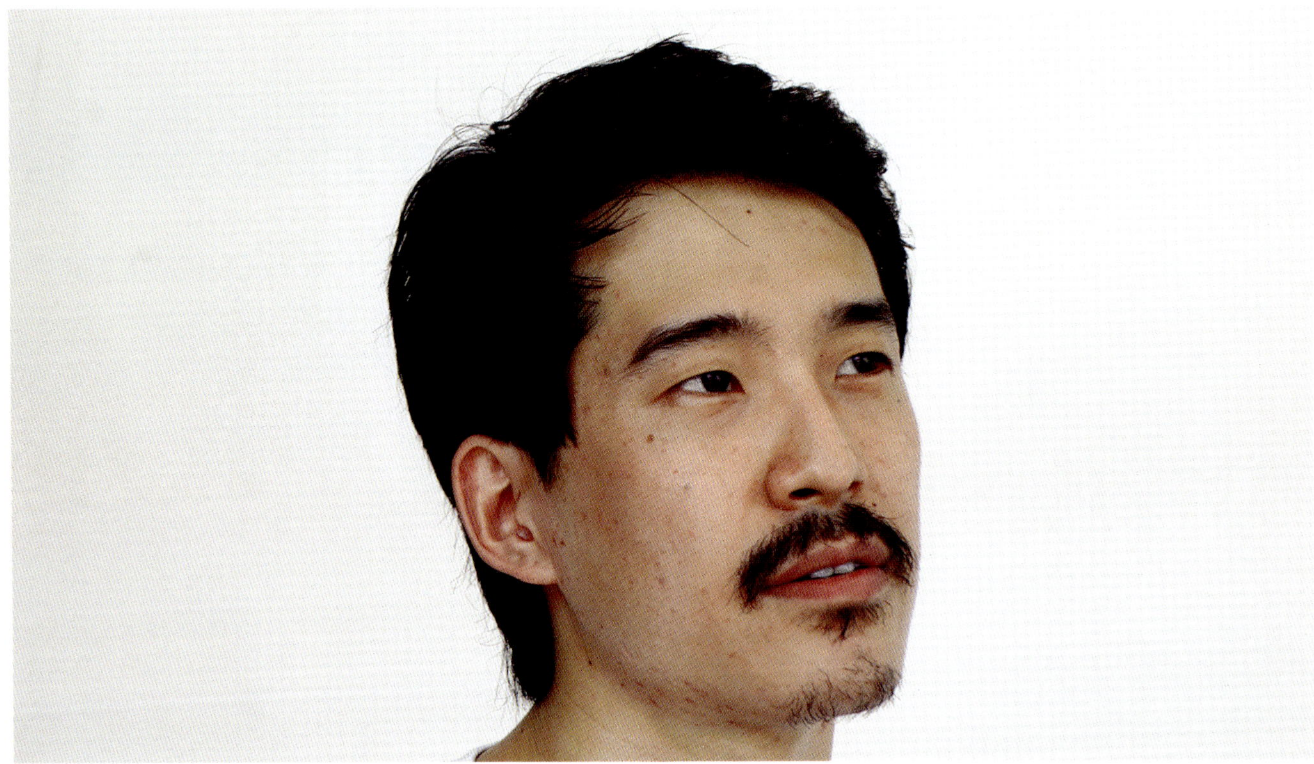

in Rodgers & Hammerstein's number *Chop-Suey* in the 1961 film *Flower Drum Song*—to the kind of demented intelligence and "minor feelings" in immigrant communities that would produce films like last year's *Everything Everywhere All at Once*.[6] The bottom line here is that Asian American masculinity still feels like a studio production, a make-believe, as in Tam's cowboy dance cycle. So, the succession of the nine questions feels like an unending loop of conundrums about our selfhood in the US when our skin is not white—for Chinese speakers, the number nine sounds much like the character for "everlasting."

Other vignettes in *Silent Spikes* further complicate the way we may read Tam's portrayals of Asian American cowboys. In different segments of the video, three performers, again all Asian, sit for the camera in their everyday clothes as they try to explain what the word *sensuality* means to them. Early in the video, one performer defines the term in relation to haptic pleasure:

> *My hand just went into it . . . and there's a little . . . fir, fibers, . . . cotton, really soft and really smooth . . . sort of get that sensation sometimes when I . . . rub my arm up one way . . . my hair is pointing one way, and I rub it up in the other direction and then it just like all falls down . . . that similar feeling of building up tension and then releasing the tension . . . like a feeling like . . . softer textures of . . . fir, cotton . . . my hair. Sort of feels like, I guess, sensual.*

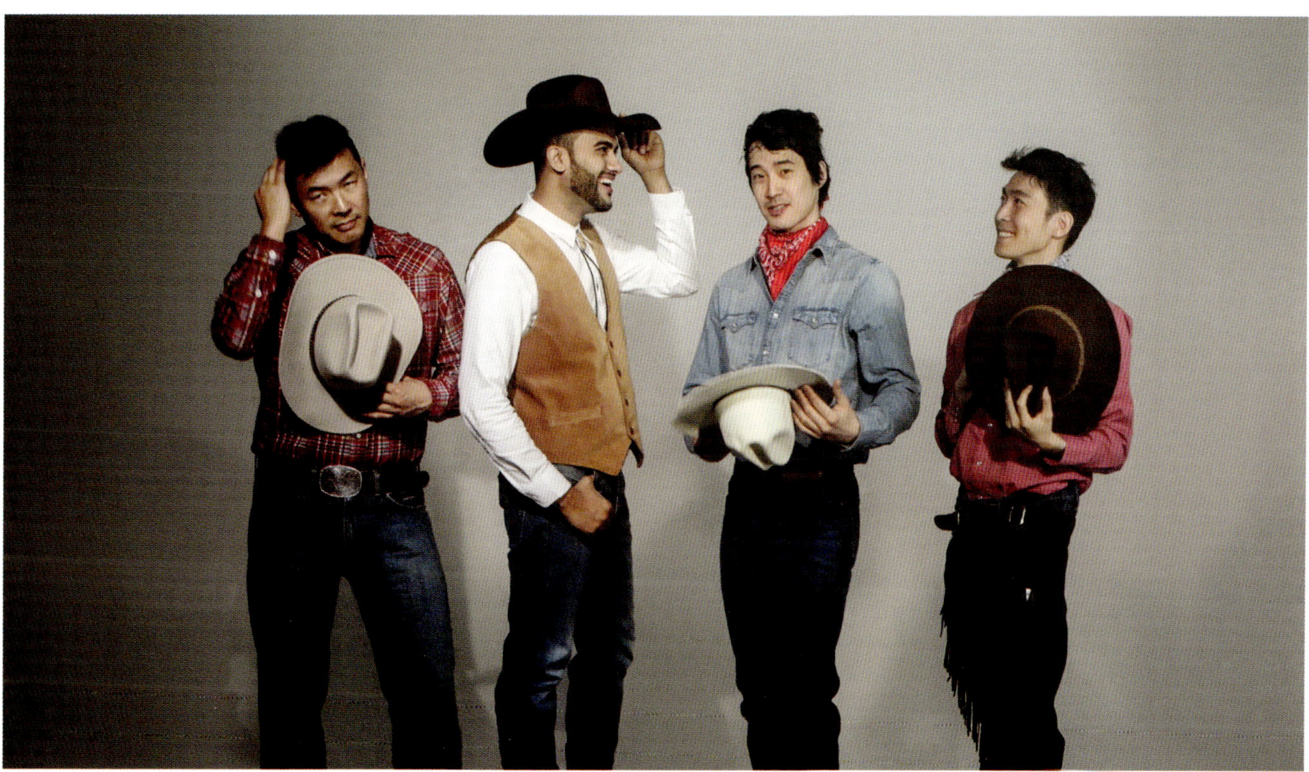

Another man (who performs as one of the dancing cowboys) considers the word sensuality in the context of his body configuring a song or a dance:

> *Sensuality is something that we can feel or that we can make someone feel about it. And could be . . . in any terms, like maybe sexually, maybe non-sexually as well. Could be through dancing, through singing. I think whatever you can sense or whatever you can make feel someone else. So, for example, if I am performing, you know, some kind of song where it has that kind of lyrics or that kind of mood, then my body automatically reacts but I'm like a little bit sensual or trying to do my sexy move and all that, so that is sensuality.*

Finally, halfway through the video, another performer (also a dancing cowboy, in the blue denim shirt) talks about his idea of sensuality in terms of post-coital bliss:

> *So, let's say . . . you see your lover after a long layover . . . say, you were out of town for work for a month and then you finally see them. You spend the night together. You make love and then the next morning they have to run off and do some chores or whatever it is for the day . . . They sort of give you a touch and a kiss, very light touching, a kiss that's not, you know, that's not sexual nature but very light and personal and sensual. That's what I would say is the example of, um, the definition that I was going for[.]*

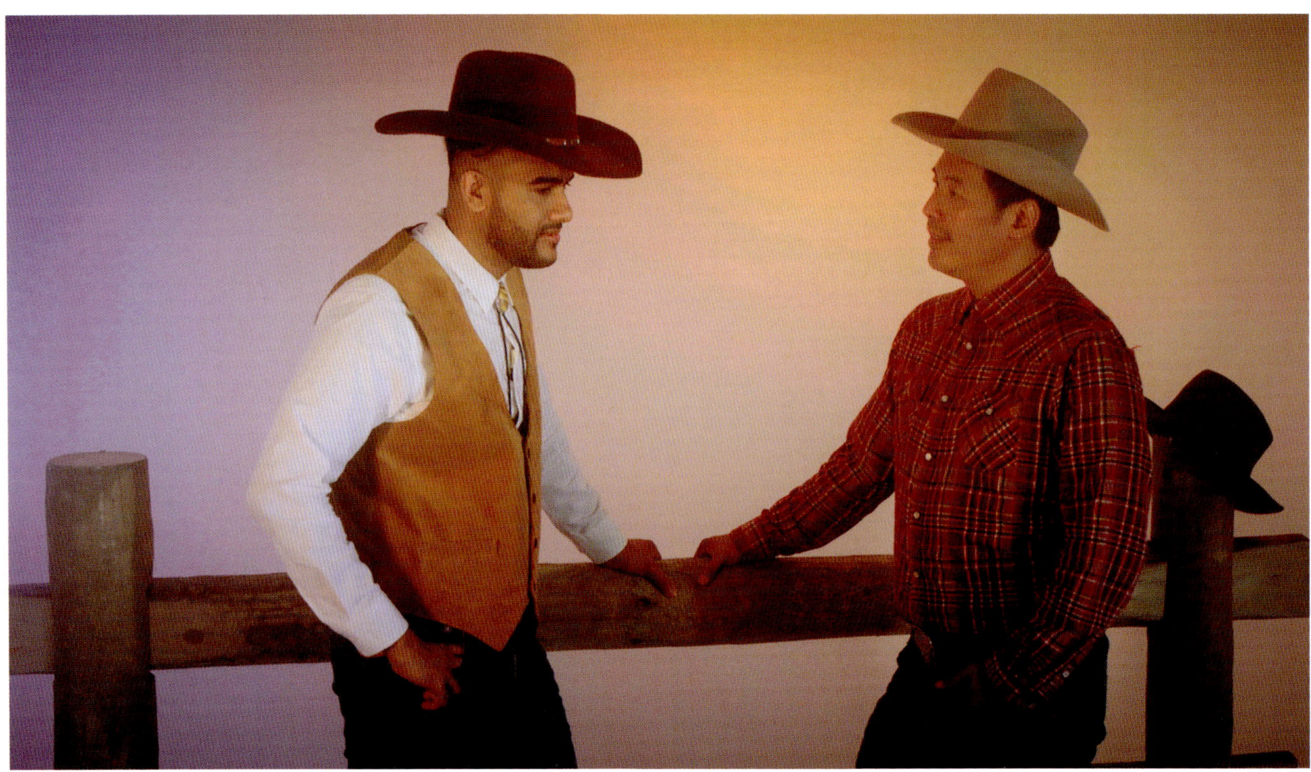

All three of them are asked to discuss exactly the kind of thing that falls into the purview of emotional intelligence, which stereotypical macho American men would avoid discussing in the company of their buddies lest they feel awkward and appear unmanly. Yet, these Asian men, whose sexual orientation is never disclosed—and the ambiguity germinates here—openly comment on their feelings without exhibiting the common fear of emasculation. The first man describes auto-sensuality in relation to hair, fiber, and the flesh. The second thinks about his body transforming to the suggestions of words and sounds despite himself. And the last man verbalizes the gentle glow of morning-after with a lover whose gender is kept in the neutrality of "they/them."

The spectrum of masculine sensibility thus becomes augmented and saturated in Tam's Wild West.[7] To even further nuance the masculine trope, particularly in the intersections of gender and race, the artist thrice pairs up Asian cowboys in different moments in *Silent Spikes*. About a quarter way through the video, two cowboys, one bearded and the other clean-shaven, stand by a split-rail fence (p. 66). Each of them holds the top rail with one hand and shoves the other hand into a jeans pocket. In their mirrored comportment, the man in the red plaid shirt speaks, looking into the face of his friend, who shyly keeps his gaze lowered:

> *I think that you are a very nice guy. Just like you treat people. How you speak to them. Very kind. I think you are very intelligent. Without intelligence I don't think you could have achieved what you've done so far, especially in the industry you are in. I also think that you are a very good-looking guy with great heights [sic]. I'm sometimes a little envious of the height. But I think that you have a lot going for you, positive things, great things. Well, overall, I think that you are a nice guy and an attractive guy.*

The situation between two cowboys takes on an oddly or uniquely romantic hue not only because they stand really close to each other without anyone else in sight but also because it takes place against the backdrop of pastel shades—a profusion of purple, lilac, and lavender, fading into mauve. It is also the way these words are delivered. In this economy of verbal and ocular courtship, the man who speaks probes his friend's face in patent admiration, complete and absorptive, and the other man simply, intently, and actively listens. This blush-worthy intimacy and tenderness exhibited on the screen explores the boundaries between male friendship and queer romance, redefining the limits of heteronormative masculinity. Many straight men are reluctant to comment on each other's physical traits and personality to each other's face, for such verbal gestures can too easily imply foreplay and eroticism.

Later, the same cowboy in the red plaid shirt sits on the ground, this time next to a different Asian man with a red bandana around his neck. Bathed in delicate gradations of peach-sunset light, their bodies are arranged in unison. Both are seated with their legs stretched out and crossed. Both lean back onto their arms, their palms pressed flat on the ground. The two hotties look each other directly in the eye. The man in the plaid shirt says:

> *I think there is a real cool factor about you. I think . . . you seem really relax [sic] in your skin and very chill. Very fun to be around, I think. I think people tend to like you for . . . um . . . I wanna say a little cavalier in a good way. You don't take life too seriously in a good way . . . I think you will be fun to hang around with, too, and I can learn a lot from you as well . . . just seeing how you live your life.*

A few minutes before the video ends—in a scene saturated by a burnt orange glow—the rapt listener in the first tête-à-tête scene now turns his adulation toward another cowboy friend, the one with a red wild rag. Their boots are touching:

> *You are a hard-working guy. You are positive, full of life, very enthusiastic. At the same time, I find you very cool and chill. You know, social, trying to interact with a lot of people, trying to, you know . . . achieve a lot of things in life. And you are definitely . . . putting all your efforts in whatever things you do, very hard-working, and so that's quite inspiring and I get inspired a lot from your day-to-day activities or, you know, all the projects you do. That's really good.*

Tam has previously explored the curious discomfort that arises when a man describes on the spot the physical characteristics of another man standing right next to him. Such verbal interaction appears in Tam's 2016 single-channel, 16-minute video *Breakfast in Bed*, in which social intimacy between frequently shirtless, under-groomed men is examined through team-building exercises and games. Yet, there is a marked difference between Tam's two works that are only five years apart. In *Silent Spikes*, all-male intimacy devoid of genital activities is predicated on the complete absence of a white man. In *Breakfast in Bed*, no verbal description of another man takes place without involving a white male, and the participants appear to be predominantly white—moreover, no Asian male body is featured in the work. The particular texture of affect arising from Asian same-sex affinity in *Silent Spikes* is thus markedly absent in *Breakfast in Bed*. Awkwardness commonly occurs in both works, but the difference is the effect of what Fred Moten and Stefano Harney call the undercommons, as opposed to the commons—a form of gathering, a *being-with* for all those who are oppressed—which too often devolves into another domain of white-settler culture.[8] According to Moten and Harney, we—Black, Indigenous, and people of color in the United States—only have "an illusory right to what we do not have," and that which we do not have is the commons; what we claim instead is the undercommons.[9] The undercommons is thus "an outside, a nonplace," the thought of which is precluded in the rational mind that is—by definition and in the colonial legacy of the Enlightenment—always structured through the rhetoric of whiteness and constituent racism.[10] Forming a lens-based undercommons, *Silent Spikes* shows male intimacy among racial others who resist, survive, and overcome white patriarchy.

Another recurring trope in Tam's oeuvre that fuels *Silent Spikes* may be the artist's relationship with the paternal in his personal life and, by extension, a racially differential patriarchy in America. In his 2015 single-channel video *sump* (7 min 32 sec), Tam tests the strain of his filial bond with his father and plumbs their wordless kinship that is distant and startlingly intimate at the same time. In an early part of the video, Tam—shirtless and toned—finger paints loops of continuing circles on his aging father's bare chest and large abdomen; the black ink evokes Chinese calligraphy but not only are these shapes childish and meaningless in his father's native tongue but also Tam's finger-work proceeds horizontally, left to right, in defiance of the traditional writing format in China. In another scene, the two Tam men take a shower together under the cover of a large, nearly transparent plastic bag. The water from the shower head only hits the exterior of the bag, leaving the Tams dry. Both men are shirtless, and forced by the bag to stand close to each other; the father's eyes are often peacefully closed while the son's eyes, wandering, wide open, or determinedly closed, perhaps to exhibit discomfort inadvertently. Then, the older Tam rides his son as if he were a horse: the artist crawls on all fours on the tiled floor, carrying his father who tries not to put all his weight on his son's back perhaps in parental care. Later in the video, both men, again shirtless and avoiding eye contact, are shown to pull on the waistband of each other's pants in the front.

Another Chinese American artist, Patty Chang, similarly explores kinship in Asian families and its impossible dictates of filial piety (demanding various forms of self-sacrifice that would seem excessive, even perverse in white America) with a sense of absurdity and humor. In her 2001 dual-channel video *In Love* (3 min 28 sec), Chang appears to deep-kiss an older woman in one frame and an older man in the other—all shedding tears as if overwhelmed by emotion: they are in fact taking nourishment (an onion) together, preposterously mouth-to-mouth, but the sequence is played in reverse so that action of eating is revealed only later. That delayed knowledge makes the viewer gasp at Chang's bravado mocking the division between kinship and eroticism, forming a strange extension of "Roman Charity" in the history of Western art: Chang in effect French-kisses her mother and father in *In Love*. American children of Asian immigrants might scrutinize the physical taboo in an attempt to overcompensate and force-connect with their authoritative, noncommunicative parents who have been often consumed, even defeated, by exigencies and discriminations in the foreign land to become unnoticed and silent.

In Tam's *sump,* the bizarre basement sequence of bonding exercises also straddles intergenerational (homo)eroticism and filial piety (Chang feeds her parents while Tam provides companionship to his graying father, treating him like his child at times). It feels important to remember that one of the unanswerable, nine questions in *Silent Spikes* is: *How do you think your father sees you?* The way he appears in the eyes of his father seems to be a distinct concern for Tam and any man like him who grew up in an immigrant family in which parents often sacrifice their lives to bring home the bacon—any recognition of the enormity of that sacrifice is always too much to bear for the children as well as the parents themselves, and often impossible to redress and honor.[11] Tam's sustained interest in his relationship with his father or fatherly proxies, the masculine vernacular, and the continuity and discontinuity of Asian patriarchy in the United States over a century might have led him to his research into Chinese migrant workers of the nineteenth century: all those men who struggled and perished laying down the transcontinental railroad are in many ways Tam's own paternal cyphers.

The aspect of minoritarian time-management/chronopolitics in Tam's work, or the blurring of historical fantasy and reality in the long temporal arc of the trans-Pacific passage terminating in the mountain range of the Wild West, is mulled over in the recurring tunnel sequence of *Silent Spikes*.[12] An archaeology of Eastern patriarchy in the American frontier emerges in fragments, in the deliberately disjunctive pastiche of Tam's diegesis. Almost seven minutes into the video, a deep and bodiless Cantonese voice narrates historical events of the railroad work:

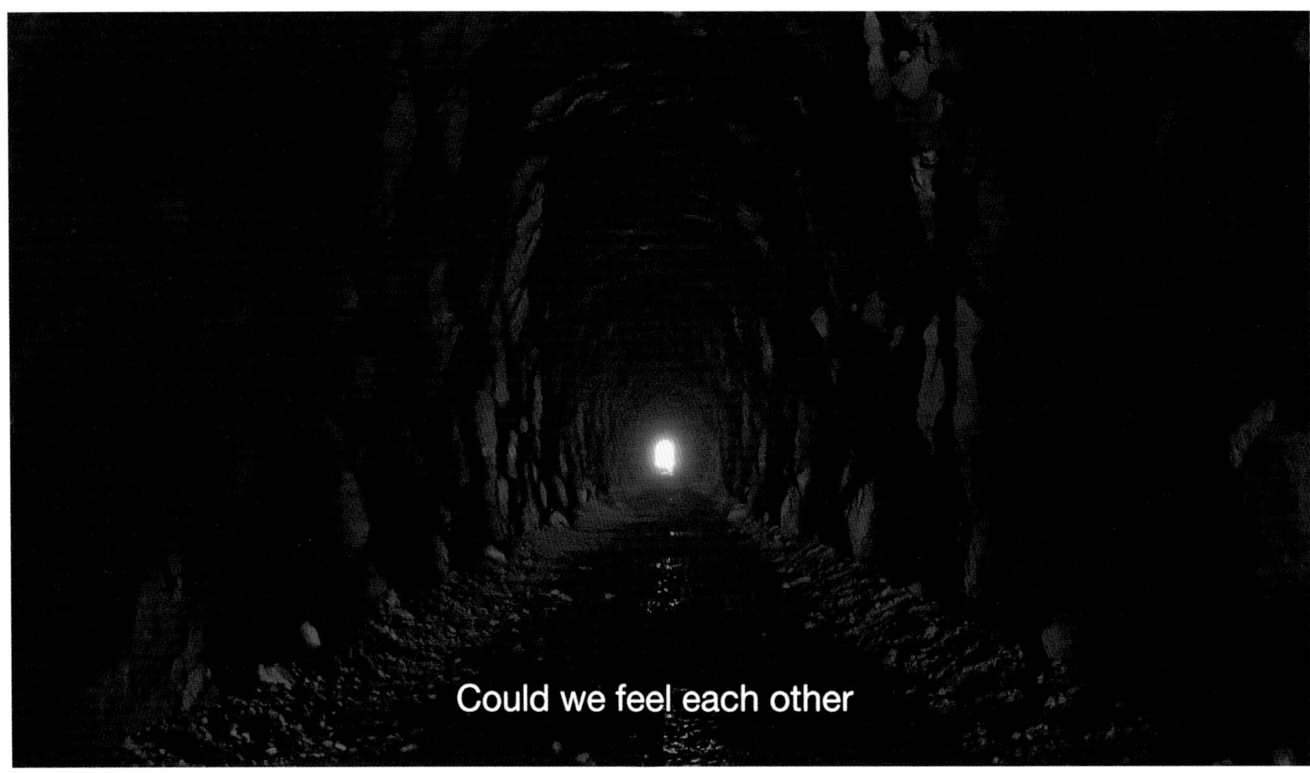

> *On June 24, 1867, the Year of the Rabbit, we laid down our tools and stopped working. From Cisco to Truckee, every man decided to strike. We demanded higher wages and shorter workdays like the white workers had. The bosses threatened to bring in other men: the Irish, freed slaves, the Japanese, and even more Chinese . . . It was later called one of the largest strikes ever known in this country. But I wouldn't know. I died before ever leaving Gold Mountain or the railroad.*

The narrator feels as though he speaks directly to the viewer in the present moment, sharing his recollections of past events that he lived through. An assumption that a diary of a railroad worker might have survived and that the artist had it read by a Cantonese speaker for *Silent Spikes* may be easy to make, but if such a diary truly exists, how could its writer know that at the time of writing, he would die "before ever leaving Gold Mountain or the railroad"?[13] The temporal anomaly is striking. Did the Chinese worker journal from the beyond, and does the film enact the voice of a ghost? The mesmerizing and vaguely ominous shots of a long Donner Summit tunnel in the Sierra Nevada mountains help distort a normative sense of time, memory, and fiction. Tam creates and lengthens an impossible passage between the past and present, which becomes the site of Tam's deathless diegesis.

Interspersed in the middle parts of *Silent Spikes*, one of the cowboy performers appears in a brown Tangzhuang with a mandarin collar and

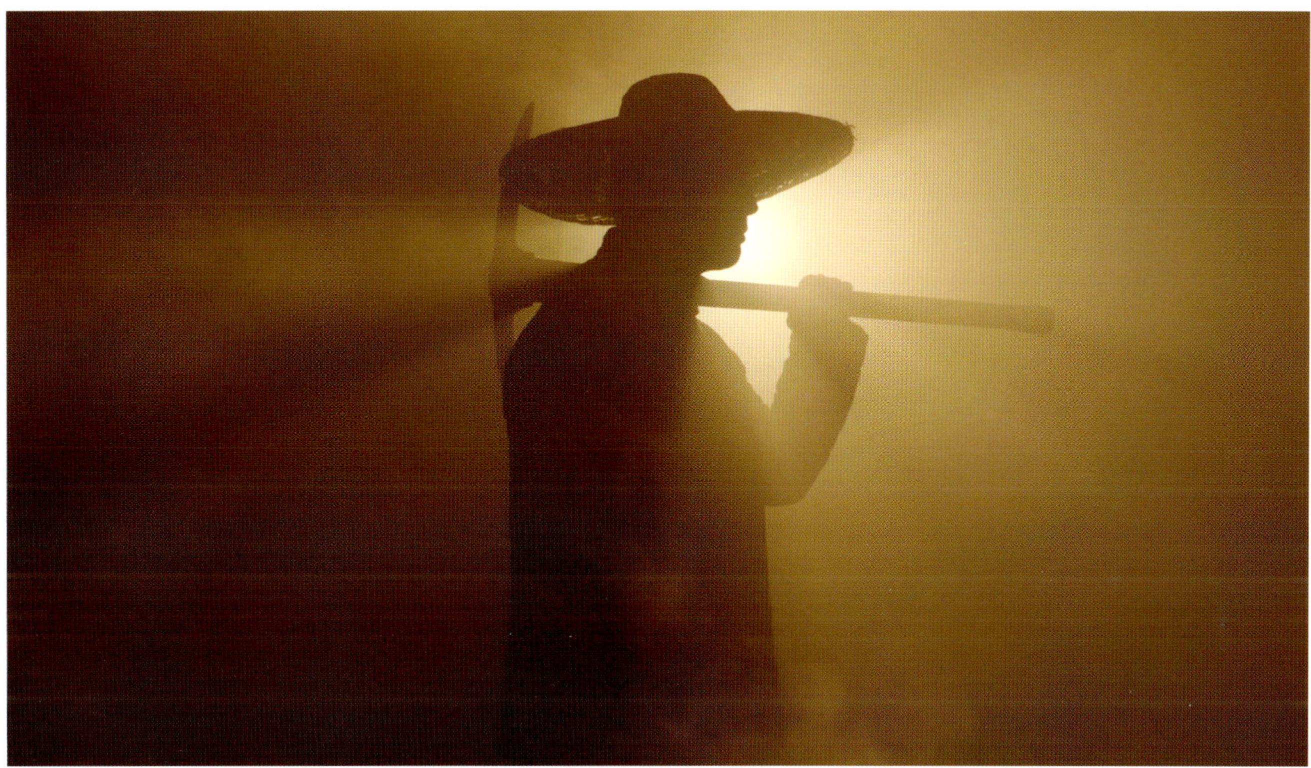

frog buttons, wearing a triaxial plaited hat and carrying a pickaxe; he appears in a yellow cloud of smoke and later, stands against the radiating, golden light (above). Toward the end of *Silent Spikes*, the voice-over solemnly recalls in Cantonese:

> *The bosses joked that we would dig ourselves back to China. There was some truth to that. With every piece of rock I chiseled, I felt I was one step closer to returning home. In the tunnels now I can travel across great lengths of time and space. They are portals to my past life and allow me to return to my home village . . . I often revisit myself at the docks where I boarded the ship that brought me to America. I try to warn*

> *myself that the path in front me is harsh and difficult and that I will never see my home village again. My younger self listens but decides to go anyway. Once I followed myself onto the ship wanting to see the ocean again. Crossing the Pacific once more I was overcome with emotion. The salt water tasted like tears and sweat and cut the inside of my mouth like sharp stone. Floating on an endless sea, I realized, actually, that I was still in the tunnels.*

Was the narrator hallucinating in hunger and fatigue? Or did the tunnels have magical properties allowing time travel to facilitate a wormhole conversation between the young worker embarking on the voyage and his future self on the other side of the ocean? In the diegesis of the phantom diary itself, and in its reiteration in Tam's video, such temporal wonder feels entirely possible, dismantling the boundaries between facts and fiction to recover truths. The first shots as well as the final shots of *Silent Spikes* are long takes of a roughly hewn granite tunnel that seems to go on forever. The fragmented diegesis Tam builds may be understood as events in an Asian man's subterranean dream—a cavernous tale that is neither factual nor falsified.

In the entirety of *Silent Spikes*, there are two bucking barrel sequences. In the first one, appearing a little after four minutes into the video, an Asian man moves up and down in apparent joy—almost simulating a sex act (opposite). The man behind him activates a bucking barrel by pushing the handle up and down, but the camera does not show the mechanism itself so as to render the action inexplicably titillating. When the second bucking barrel scene takes place, the contraption is fully visible. The self-satisfied expression of the rider straddling the fakery makes the whole scene farcical: he pretends to nonchalantly ride a horse when there is none. A bucking barrel is used to train riders for the rodeo, not for a leisurely horseback outing, yet that is exactly what this performer imitates. That these two Asian cowboys bestride invisible, non-existent animals or that they enjoy a bucking barrel is perhaps the point. All this cowboy choreography is a bit tongue-in-cheek. In fact, even the Chinese worker in the supposedly period attire in *Silent Spikes* seems to be hamming it up—not only does his pristine Tangzhuang lack verisimilitude but also the yellow smoke and the golden light surrounding him are too extravagant to be taken seriously. Viewers may wonder if the artist's seeming approach to the subject matter is less than uniform in tone because what Tam ostensibly covers in *Silent Spikes* is not exactly what the work achieves in its diegesis: historical authenticity and righteous recovery for the oppressed, exploited, and silenced may not be the primary or singular goal here. And yet, it is precisely this equivocation, diegetic disorientation, and ambiguity that make Tam's work gripping and mercurially complex. The absurdly loving way two cowboys pose for the camera to hold a green, plastic calf head (a "roping dummy" for rodeo practice) against their cheek in *Silent*

Spikes should also be thought in the same vein of potential parody and snarky wisdom, *torn between ways* (p. 75).[14] In the historical consciousness of Western iconography, such enamored gestures with the dummy recall two 1926 photographs by Man Ray, *Noire et blanche* (aka *Visage de nacre et masque de ébène* [mother of pearl face and ebony mask]) and *Noire et blanche (Kiki Holding African Mask)* (p. 74).[15] Tam's videography in effect replaces the pale-as-a-ghost face of French model Kiki de Montparnasse with a white man's bovine, Wild West paraphernalia while swapping out Man Ray's Baule mask from the Ivory Coast with the handsome faces of two Asian men, producing a sly, spicy critique on the racial rhetoric of beauty and its other in the Occidental imagination.

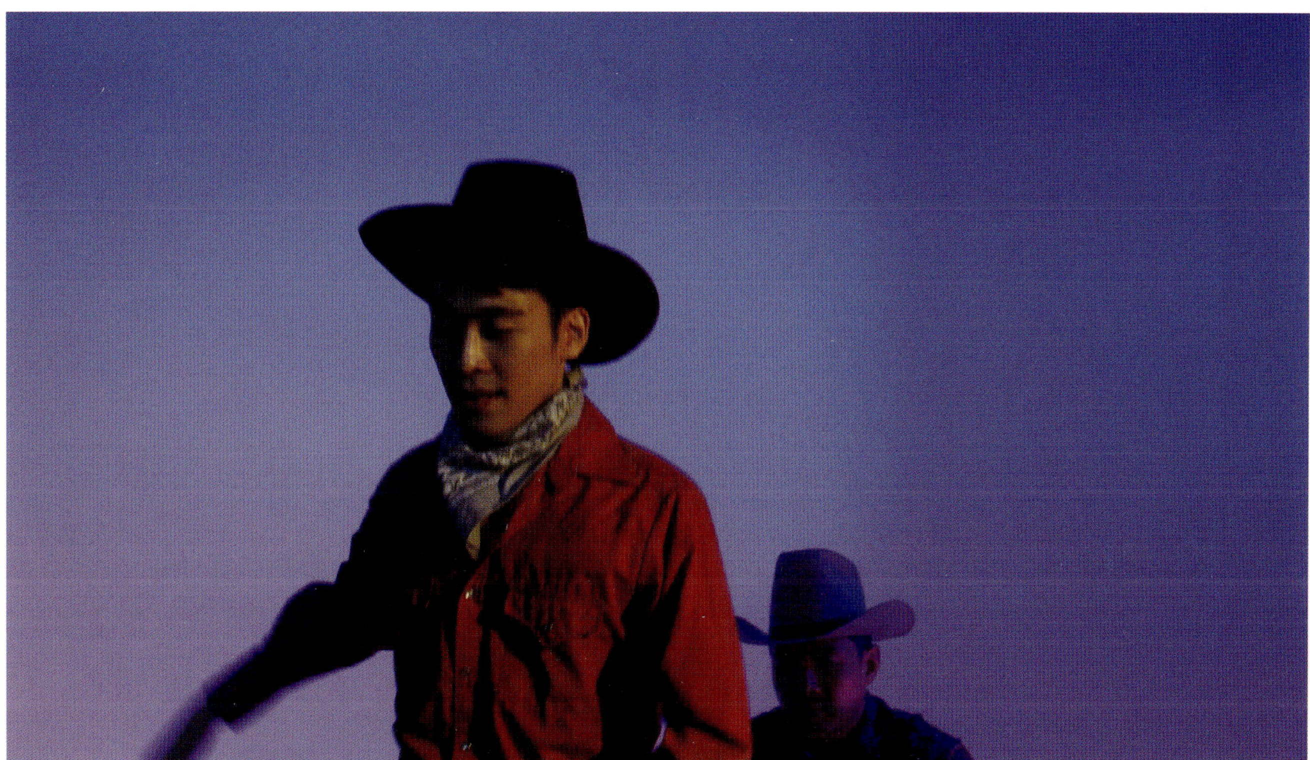

All four of the cowboy performers appear in contemporary clothes and dance to the sounds of Asian string music in fractured segments throughout *Silent Spikes*. In a pastiche of traditional Eastern music and modern Western dance, Tam's pan-Asian, all-male troupe commands the stage. One dancer's eyes are tightly shut in emotional distress, while another looks bewildered by his own fast-moving fingers. The next man swivels his hips, and a tall one repeatedly stretches his arms and retracts them as if in search of something unseen. Yet another dancer cradles an invisible object in his hands and inexplicably kicks the air. (There is even an additional dancer who does not participate in any of the cowboy sequences, but contorts and dances on an asphalt road against a backdrop of warehouses and other urban

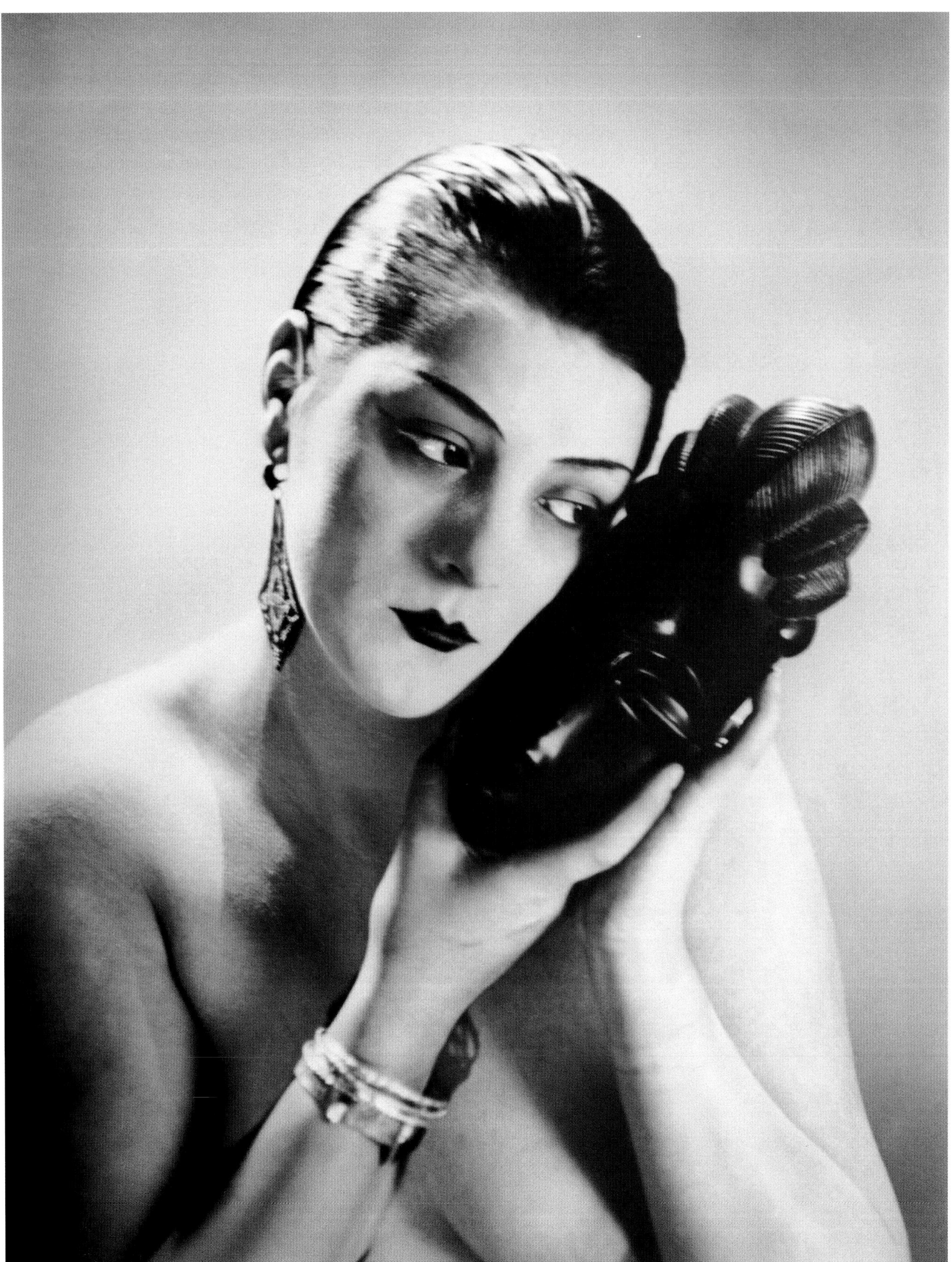

architecture.) The kaleidoscope of all these dispersed dances, conducted in T-shirts, hoodies, beanies, jeans, and whatnot, seems to function as an invocation set in contemporaneity for the spectral past—as though these bodily movements constitute a ritual, like prayers in flesh, to bring the tunnels to life, along with the spirits of the dead and the undead, so that Tam's camera may narrate the haunting story of Asian American cowboys that never were and Chinese railroad labor for the Pacific Railway that was made to feel as though it never was. About five minutes before *Silent Spikes* ends, the Cantonese narrator shares his desire for a community of the likeminded.

> *As we continued to dig, I imagined that the tunnel felt like a birth canal with us workers gestating inside. However, those that survived this long,*

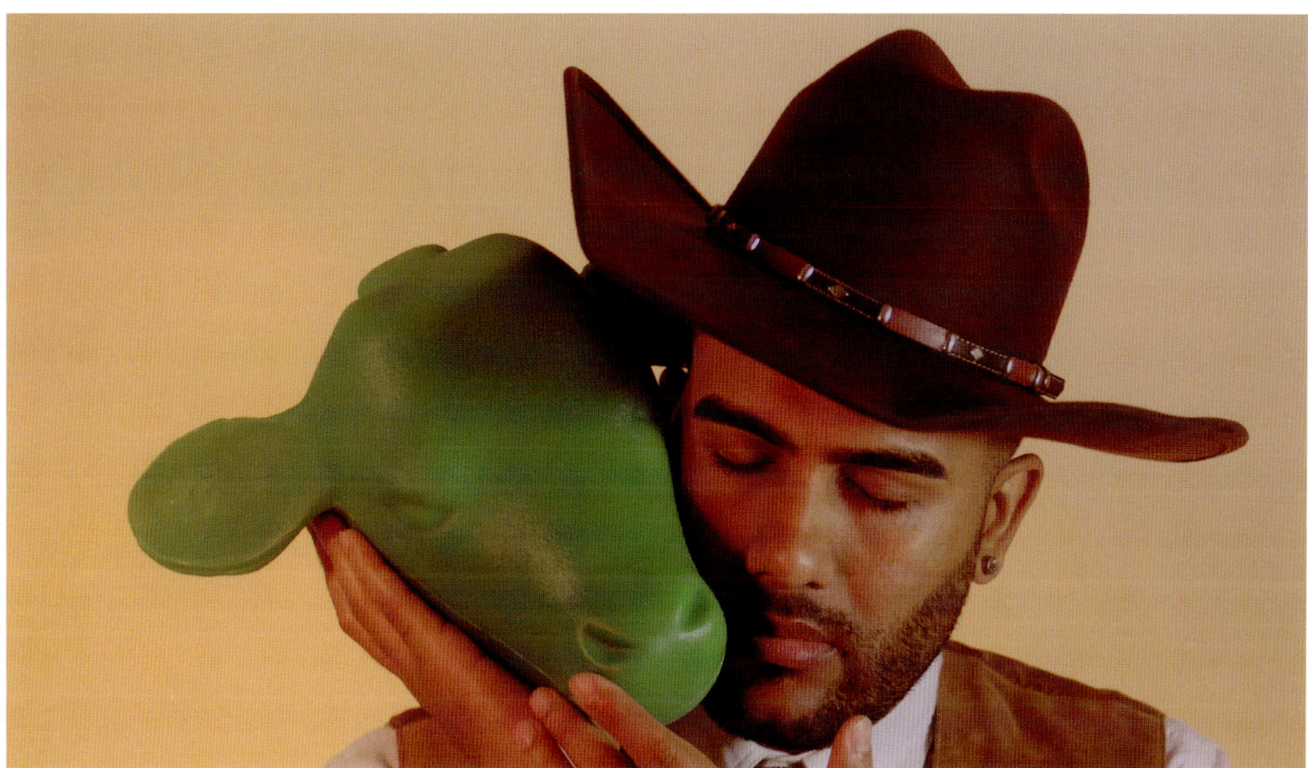

> *painful birth would come out as the children of this foreign land. While we would never be citizens of this country, we would claim part of this mountain as our birthright . . . [A]fter the strike, each one of us felt different. We were no longer simple peasants from Canton. While our demands were not met, the experience of having a common purpose brought us closer together . . . My heart aches for the companionship born from solidarity.*

Silent Spikes is an example of fabulation for pan-Asian communities in white America. "Neither true nor false," fabulation concerns a "mythmaking function": it constitutes a "shadow" which is "cast over the illuminated human centers of intelligence, imagination, and reason."

Opposite: Man Ray, NOIRE ET BLANCHE (VARIATION), 1926. Photograph

Tam messes with these "overarching metaphors" of Western civilization because they continue to reassert only the white "tradition as the locus of enunciation" and affirm the West as the authorized framework through which knowledge is put together into words.[16] Similarly, national history—a normalizing construct, an ideological apparatus for advantageous misperception for self-narrative—serves the "geopolitics of knowledge" that produce a genealogy of the Other in relation to *our* view as factual, *our* rhetoric as reasonable, and *our* experience as real.[17] Against the stale history of a nation aggrandizing Whiteness, Tam's fabulating video installation interpellates the Asian American, camp Western as the new "site of collective contestations, the point of departure for a set of historical reflections and futural imaginings."[18]

ENDNOTES

1 Jan Christian Bernabe, "Negotiating Desire and (Queer) Masculinity: An Interview with Kenneth Tam," in *Queer Contemporary Asian American Art*, ed. Laura Kina and Bernabe (Seattle: University of Washington Press, 2017), 97.

2 In *Ghost of Gold Mountain: the Epic Story of the Chinese Who Built the Transcontinental Railroad* (Boston: Mariner Books, 2019), 6, Gordon H. Chang explains: "Chinese railroad workers were acknowledged as ubiquitous and indispensable, but they were accorded no voice, literally and figuratively. We cannot hear what they said, thought, or felt. They were "silent spikes" or "nameless builders," evocative terms recently coined by scholars seeking to recover the experiences and identities of those Chinese who built the Transcontinental." The term "silent spikes" is defined as the "nameless Chinese builders of the North American railroads" in *The Silent Spikes: Chinese Laborers and the Construction of North American Railroads*, ed. Huang Annian, trans. Zhang Juguo (Beijing: China Intercontinental Press, 2006), 8.

3 The participants or performers in *Silent Spikes* are Tyler Chen, Theodore Lee, Virgo Raaz, Alfred Tom, and Ahnaf Zitou.

4 *Oxford English Dictionary*, s.v. "protean" and "Proteus."

5 When I asked Kenneth Tam about the Eastern string music in his work, he replied: "Yes, various East Asian string instruments are heard—erhus, guzhengs, gayageums. There might have been another. I chose them mainly because I felt they sounded similar to a classic Western film soundtrack, think Ennio Morricone by way of Asia. The tone is playful but occasionally mournful. Some of the pieces of music I used were also slightly manipulated, slowed down in some instances or even played backwards, a nod to the temporal dislocations in the video." Email messages between the author and the artist, February 20 and 21, 2023.

6 "Minor feelings" refers to a set of daily, icky affects people of color experience in a white-settler culture: often we are gaslighted to believe that these feelings are trivial, small-minded, and unconstructive, and that they are most likely results of our racial paranoia, always assuming the worst in our white other. These "negative" feelings, however, are real and powerful in their capacity to resist the tyranny of the white, majoritarian rhetoric in places like the United States, where nobody is truly *from here* except for Native Americans. See Cathy Park Hong, *Minor Feelings: An Asian American Reckoning* (New York: One World, 2020), 56.

7 In “Kenneth Tam Excavates the History of Chinese Labor in the American West,” Alyce Santorio comments on *Silent Spikes*: “Tam creates a space for intimacy between Asian American men without adverse conditions. In one segment, he splits them into pairs and has them compliment each other, permitting a rare and relieving opportunity to witness men concentrating on each other in a way that is not primarily sexual or laden with ulterior motives.” I disagree in that the point here is not about providing or finding relief in nonsexual, same-sex intimacy; rather *Silent Spikes* shows the easy passage from male friendship to homoeroticism—demonstrating how the spectrum of masculinity is inherently queer. See *Hyperallergic*, January 26, 2023, https://hyperallergic.com/776174/kenneth-tam-history-of-chinese-labor-american-west-ballroom-marfa/.

8 In “‘Gimme Gimme This . . . Gimme Gimme That’: Annihilation and Innovation in the Punk Rock Commons,” *Social Text* 31, no. 3 (2013), 99, José Esteban Muñoz explains that the commons is “a being-with, in which various disaffected, antisocial actants found networks of affiliation and belonging that allowed them to think and act otherwise, together, in a social field that was most interested in dismantling their desire for different relations with the social.” In *Vibrant Matter: A Political Ecology of Things* (Durham, NC: Duke University Press, 2010), viii, Jane Bennett defines an *actant* as “that which has efficacy, can *do* things, has sufficient coherence to make a difference, produce effects, alter the course of events.” The concept *actant* (or *actor*) is contextualized in Bruno Latour’s Actor-Network Theory (ANT); see Latour, “On Actor-Network Theory: A Few Clarifications,” *Soziale Welt 47* (1996): 370.

9 Stefano Harney and Fred Moten, *The Undercommons: Fugitive Planning & Black Study*, (Wivenhoe: Minor Compositions, 2013), 18.

10 Harney and Moten, *The Undercommons*, 39.

11 Tam comments on his “fraught relationship” with his father in Bernabe, “Negotiating Desire and (Queer) Masculinity,” 97.

12 About the notion of the majoritarian/minoritarian or minority/majority, see Gilles Deleuze and Félix Guattari, *A Thousand Plateaus: Capitalism and Schizophrenia*, trans. Brian Massumi (Minneapolis: University of Minnesota Press, 1987), 105–6: “The opposition between minority and majority is not simply quantitative. Majority implies a constant, of expression or content, serving as a standard measure by which to evaluate it. Let us suppose that the constant or standard is the average adult-white-heterosexual-European-male-speaking a standard language (Joyce’s or Ezra Pound’s *Ulysses*). It is obvious that ‘man’ holds the majority, even if he is less numerous than mosquitoes, children, women, blacks, peasants, homosexuals, etc . . . Majority assumes a state of power and domination, not the other way around. It assumes the standard measure, not the other way around . . . A determination different from that of the constant will therefore be considered minoritarian, by nature and regardless of number, in other words, a subsystem or an outsystem . . . There is no becoming-majoritarian; majority is never becoming. All becoming is minoritarian.”

13 When I asked Kenneth Tam, “What is the text that the voice-over in Cantonese narrates? Is it a fictional account based on historical facts?,” he explained: “Yes, the broad strokes of the narration conform to historical accounts of Chinese migration during that period, but the voice is entirely fictional.” Email messages between the author and the artist, February 20 and 21, 2023.

14 Gloria Anzaldúa, *Borderlands/*La Frontera*: The New Mestiza* (Aunt Lute Books, 1999), 100.

15 See Whitney Chadwick, “Fetishizing Fashion/Fetishizing Culture: Man Ray’s ‘Noire et blanche,’” *Oxford Art Journal* 18, no. 2 (1995): 3–17. On page 12, Chadwick explains, “What linked fashion’s ideal of female beauty and African sculpture like the Baule mask in the Paris of the 1920s may have had less to do with their formal resemblances than with the ways that these relationships reinforced unconscious processes of fetishization which . . . secured women and other people within systems of exchange produced and controlled by the institutions of capitalism and patriarchy.” Chadwick concludes, on page 15: the fetishistic “substitutions that take place within *Noire et blanche* work not because the images are equivalents, but because they participate in European systems of representation which commodify sexualized looking, and which reinforce dominant hierarchies of power and control over women and over other cultures.”

16 Tavia Nyong’o, *Afro-Fabulation: The Queer Drama of Black Life* (New York: New York University Press, 2019), 14–15. Walter D. Mignolo, *Local Histories/Global Designs: Coloniality, Subaltern Knowledges, and Border Thinking* (Princeton, NJ: Princeton University Press, 2000), 23 and 93.

17 Mignolo’s idea of “geopolitics of knowledge” highlights the fact that potency of any given knowledge is not universal but contingent on regions in which that knowledge is generated and practiced—just as it is influenced by those regions’ relationship with the neighboring territories of other political entities. Mignolo explains, “Postcoloniality (and its equivalents) is both a critical discourse that brings to the foreground the colonial side of the ‘modern world system’ and the coloniality of power imbedded in modernity itself, as well as a discourse that relocates the ratio between geohistorical locations (local histories) and knowledge production.” See Mignolo, *Local Histories/Global Designs*, 92–93.

18 Judith Butler, *Bodies That Matter: On Discursive Limits of “Sex”* (New York: Routledge, 1993), 228.

A DREAM TO DEARFIELD

R. Alan Brooks

IT'S BEEN OVER FOUR CENTURIES SINCE AMERICAN SLAVERY BEGAN, but just 55 years since Dr. Martin Luther King, Jr. was assassinated. My parents were young teenagers then, and when I talk with them, it reminds me that it wasn't that long ago.

One of the many notorious legacies of this oppression is the fact that Black history has been buried, denied and suppressed. Like seriously, I was raised with my parents proactively teaching me Black History—my mother baked a cake every year for MLK's birthday (before it was even a holiday), and my dad bought me Black History coloring books as a child.

And still, I'm surprised by how much Black History I don't know.

So, when I was asked by MCA Denver to write and draw a comic about Dearfield, the Colorado Black homesteading town, my first reaction was, "Wow. How much other Black History is there that I may never know?"

But my second reaction was happiness at the opportunity to honor the legacy of this beautiful Black town.

Dearfield, CO—the largest black homesteading settlement in the state, was located about 70 miles from Denver, near Greeley. Established by Oliver Toussaint Jackson in 1910, Dearfield was at its peak from 1917–21, when it housed nearly 300 residents, had lumber and coal yards, a boarding house, a store, a hotel, and at least two churches. Sadly, the Dust Bowl forced most Dearfield homesteaders out, and the town never recovered.

So, this story is an abstract exploration of that history. Thanks for taking the time to read it.

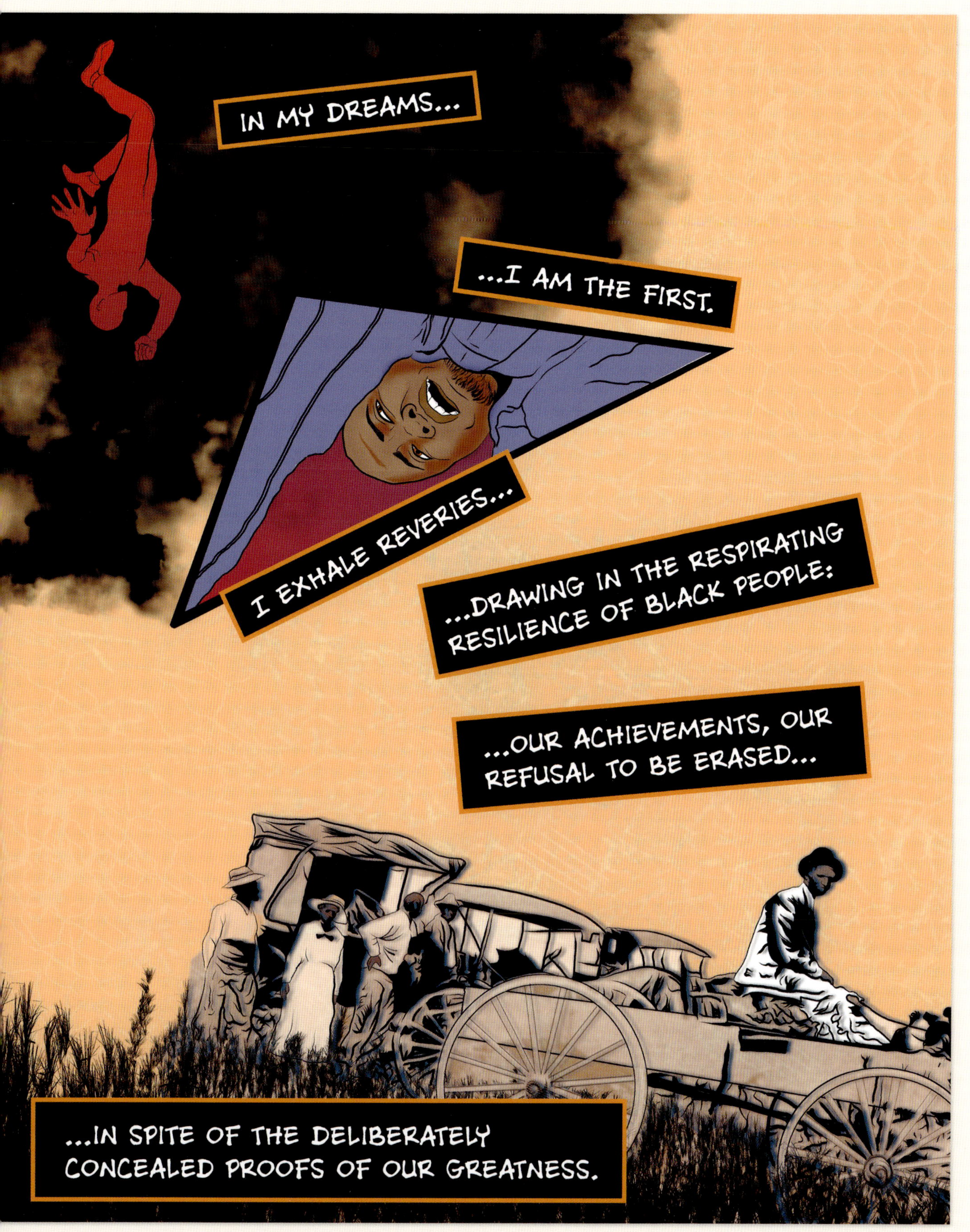
IN MY DREAMS...
...I AM THE FIRST.
I EXHALE REVERIES...
...DRAWING IN THE RESPIRATING RESILIENCE OF BLACK PEOPLE:
...OUR ACHIEVEMENTS, OUR REFUSAL TO BE ERASED...
...IN SPITE OF THE DELIBERATELY CONCEALED PROOFS OF OUR GREATNESS.

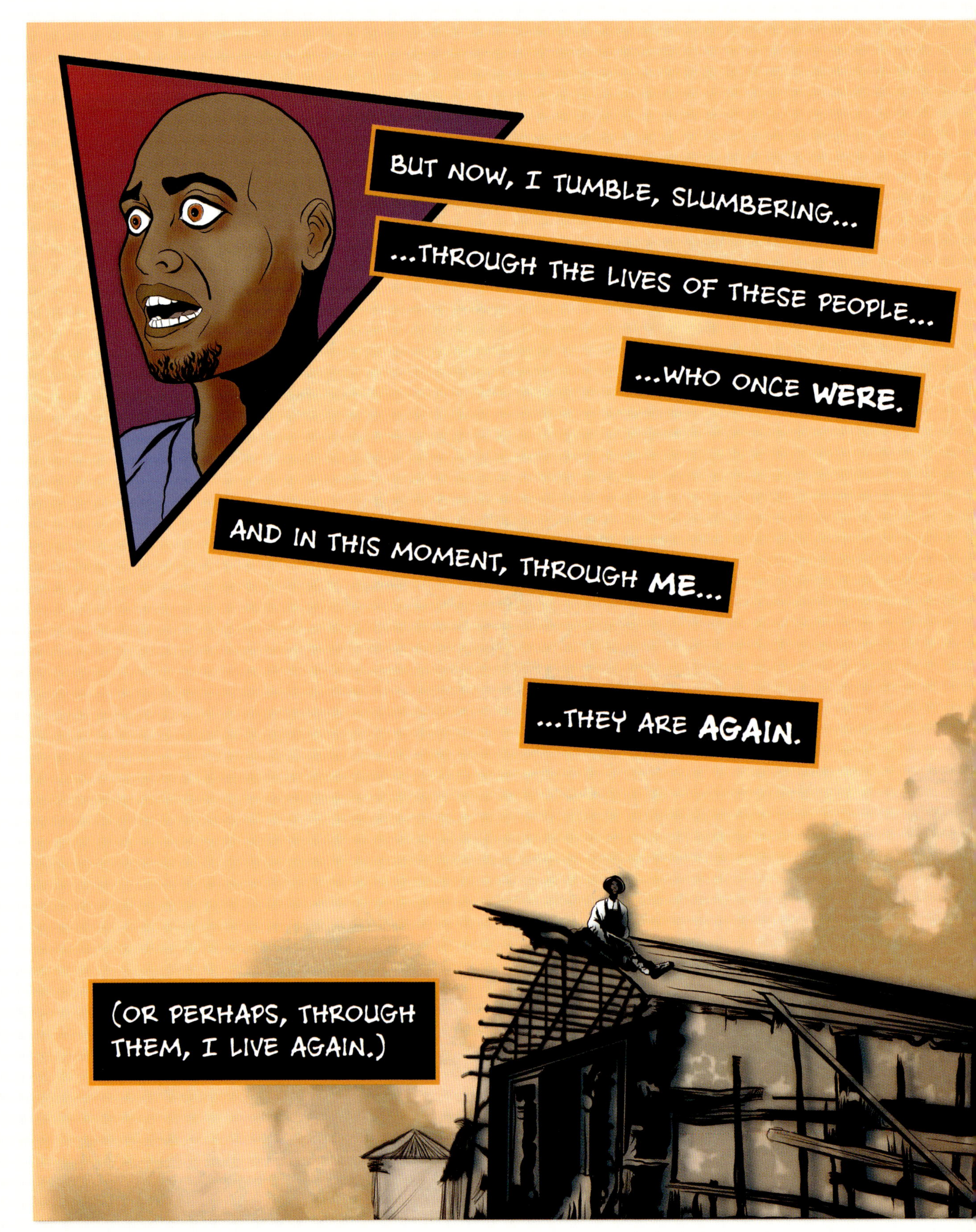
BUT NOW, I TUMBLE, SLUMBERING...
...THROUGH THE LIVES OF THESE PEOPLE...
...WHO ONCE WERE.
AND IN THIS MOMENT, THROUGH ME...
...THEY ARE AGAIN.
(OR PERHAPS, THROUGH THEM, I LIVE AGAIN.)

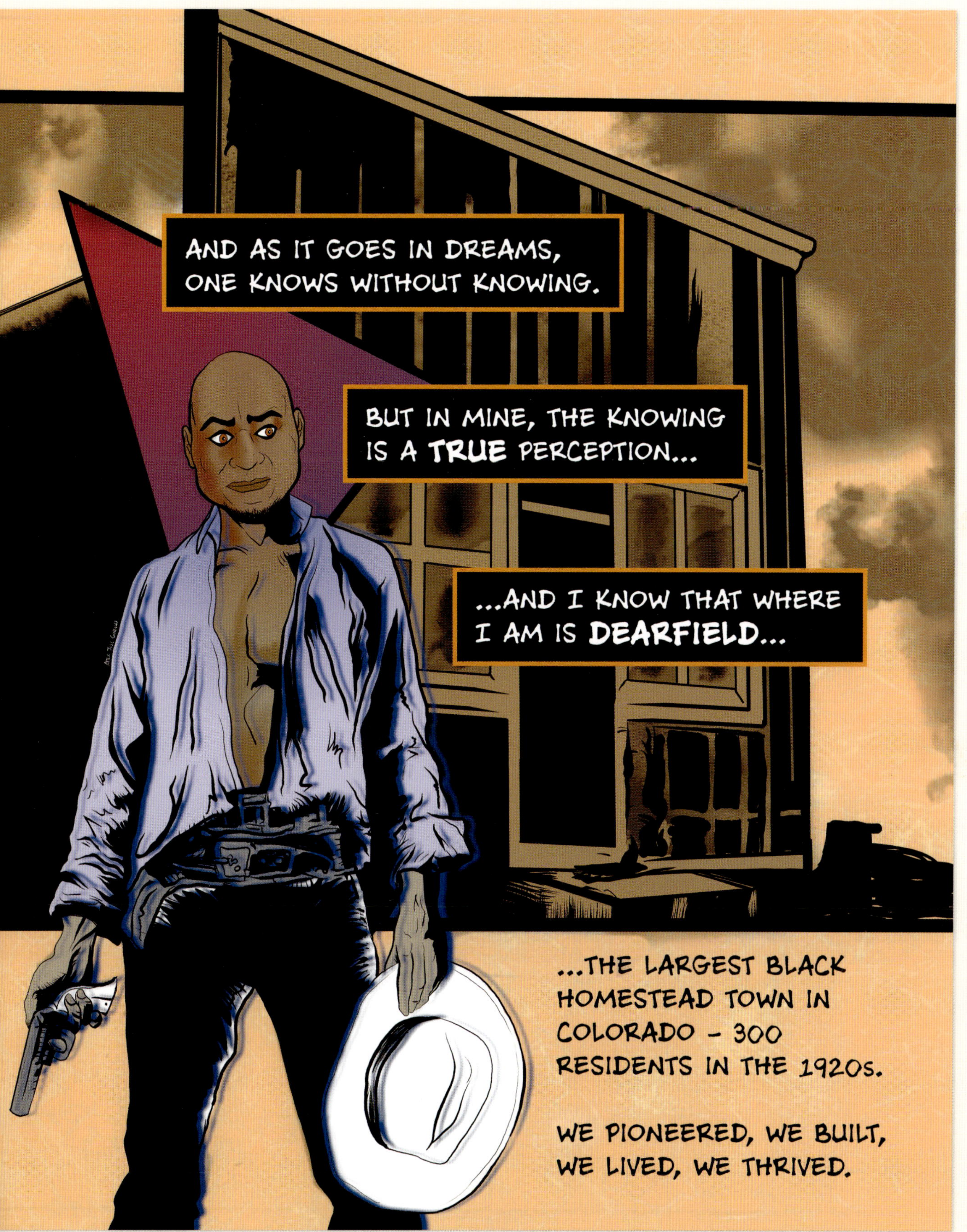
AND AS IT GOES IN DREAMS, ONE KNOWS WITHOUT KNOWING.
BUT IN MINE, THE KNOWING IS A TRUE PERCEPTION...
...AND I KNOW THAT WHERE I AM IS DEARFIELD...
...THE LARGEST BLACK HOMESTEAD TOWN IN COLORADO - 300 RESIDENTS IN THE 1920s.
WE PIONEERED, WE BUILT, WE LIVED, WE THRIVED.

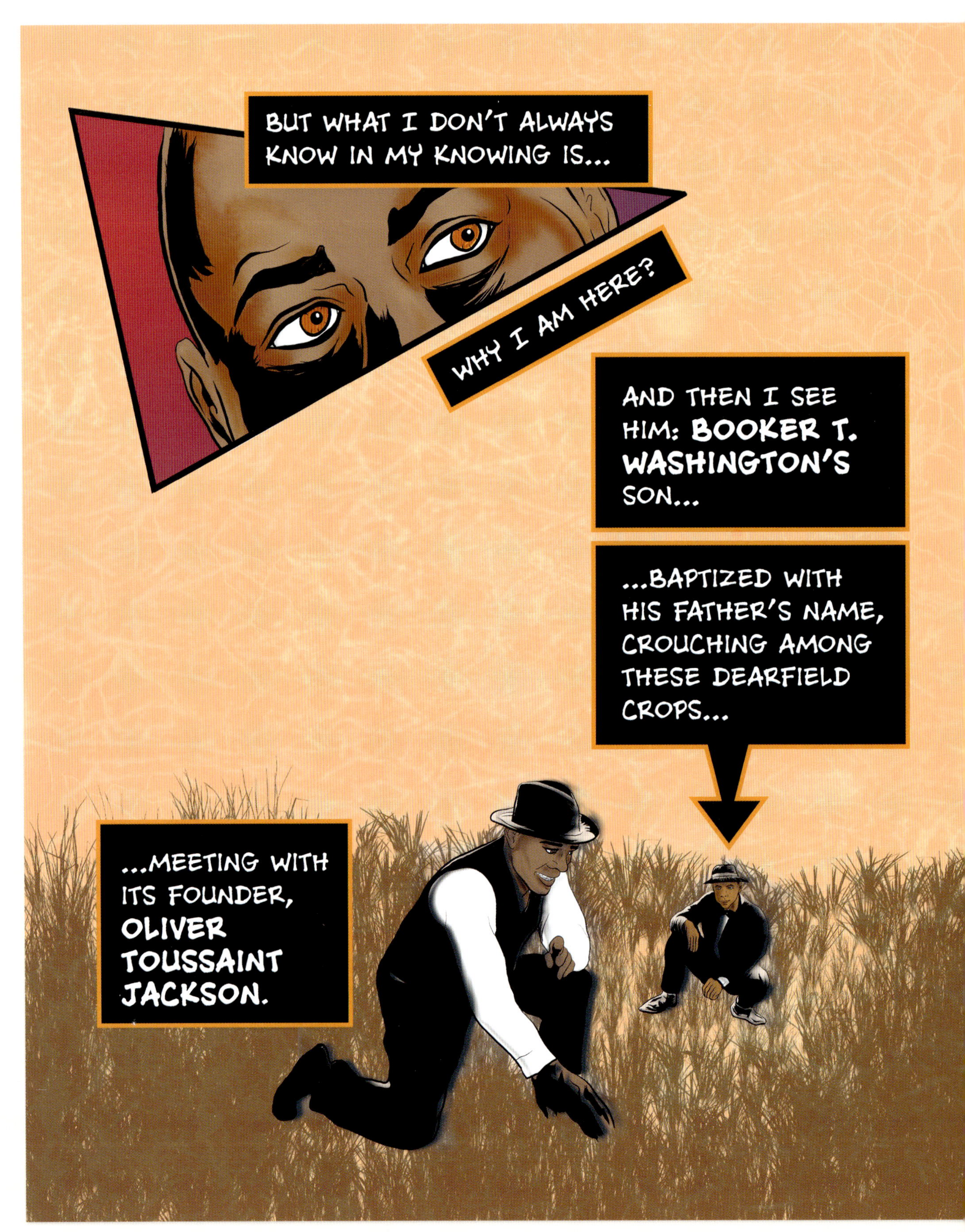
BUT WHAT I DON'T ALWAYS KNOW IN MY KNOWING IS...
WHY I AM HERE?
AND THEN I SEE HIM: BOOKER T. WASHINGTON'S SON...
...BAPTIZED WITH HIS FATHER'S NAME, CROUCHING AMONG THESE DEARFIELD CROPS...
...MEETING WITH ITS FOUNDER, OLIVER TOUSSAINT JACKSON.

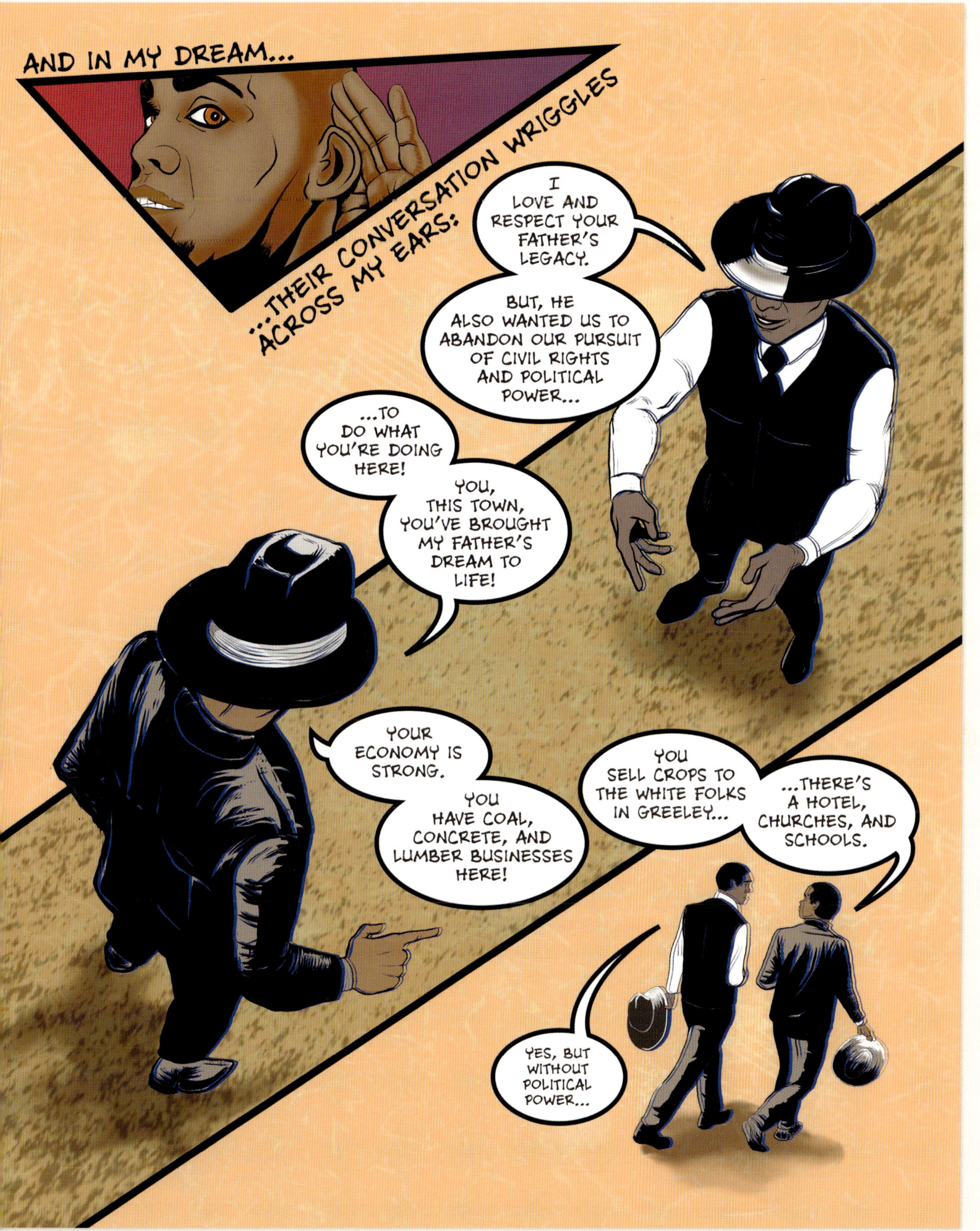
AND IN MY DREAM...
...THEIR CONVERSATION WRIGGLES ACROSS MY EARS:
I LOVE AND RESPECT YOUR FATHER'S LEGACY.
BUT, HE ALSO WANTED US TO ABANDON OUR PURSUIT OF CIVIL RIGHTS AND POLITICAL POWER...
...TO DO WHAT YOU'RE DOING HERE!
YOU, THIS TOWN, YOU'VE BROUGHT MY FATHER'S DREAM TO LIFE!
YOUR ECONOMY IS STRONG.
YOU HAVE COAL, CONCRETE, AND LUMBER BUSINESSES HERE!
YOU SELL CROPS TO THE WHITE FOLKS IN GREELEY...
...THERE'S A HOTEL, CHURCHES, AND SCHOOLS.
YES, BUT WITHOUT POLITICAL POWER...

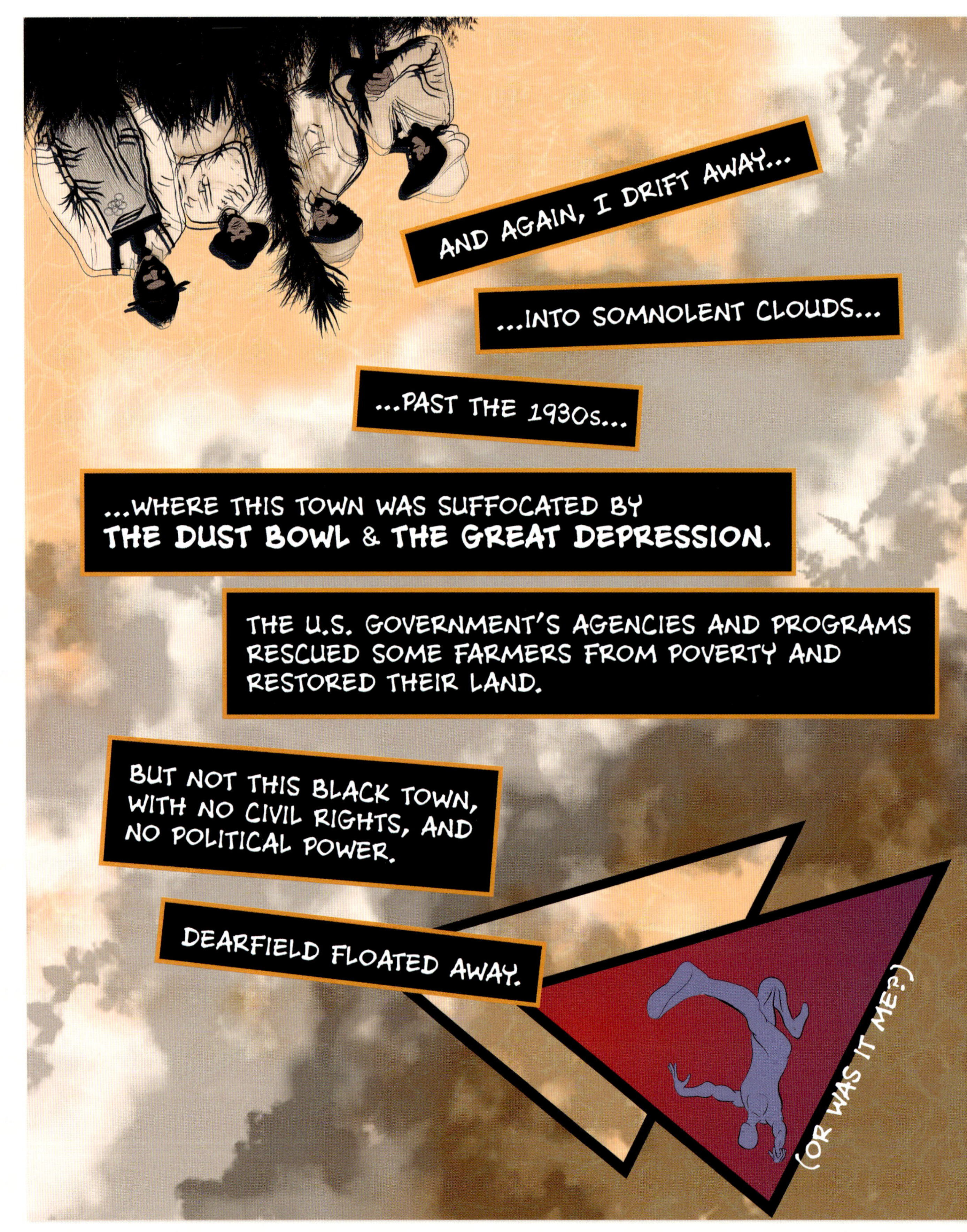
AND AGAIN, I DRIFT AWAY...
...INTO SOMNOLENT CLOUDS...
...PAST THE 1930s...
...WHERE THIS TOWN WAS SUFFOCATED BY THE DUST BOWL & THE GREAT DEPRESSION.
THE U.S. GOVERNMENT'S AGENCIES AND PROGRAMS RESCUED SOME FARMERS FROM POVERTY AND RESTORED THEIR LAND.
BUT NOT THIS BLACK TOWN, WITH NO CIVIL RIGHTS, AND NO POLITICAL POWER.
DEARFIELD FLOATED AWAY.
(OR WAS IT ME?)

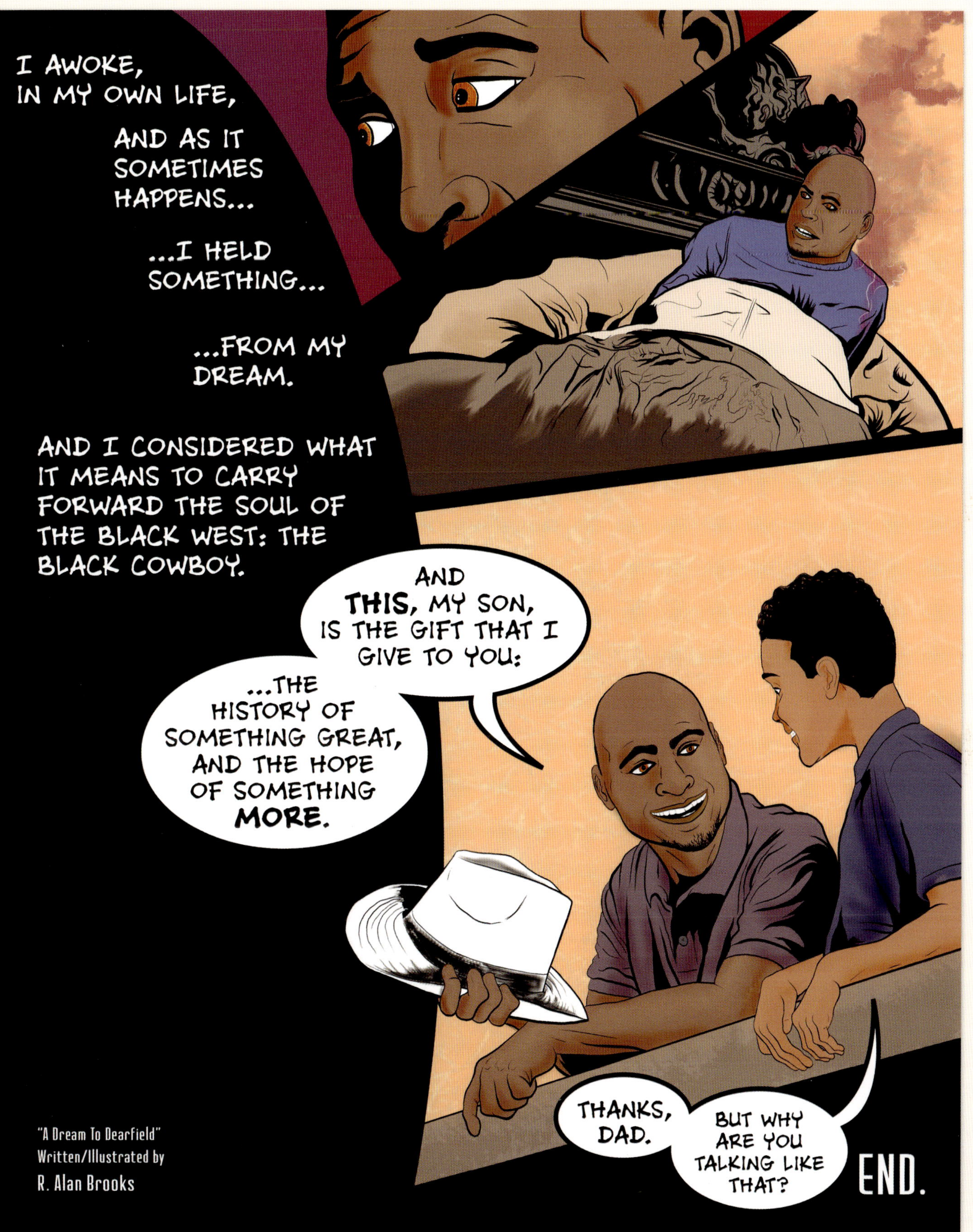
I AWOKE, IN MY OWN LIFE,
AND AS IT SOMETIMES HAPPENS...
...I HELD SOMETHING...
...FROM MY DREAM.
AND I CONSIDERED WHAT IT MEANS TO CARRY FORWARD THE SOUL OF THE BLACK WEST: THE BLACK COWBOY.
AND THIS, MY SON, IS THE GIFT THAT I GIVE TO YOU:
...THE HISTORY OF SOMETHING GREAT, AND THE HOPE OF SOMETHING MORE.
THANKS, DAD.
BUT WHY ARE YOU TALKING LIKE THAT?
END.
"A Dream To Dearfield"
Written/Illustrated by
R. Alan Brooks

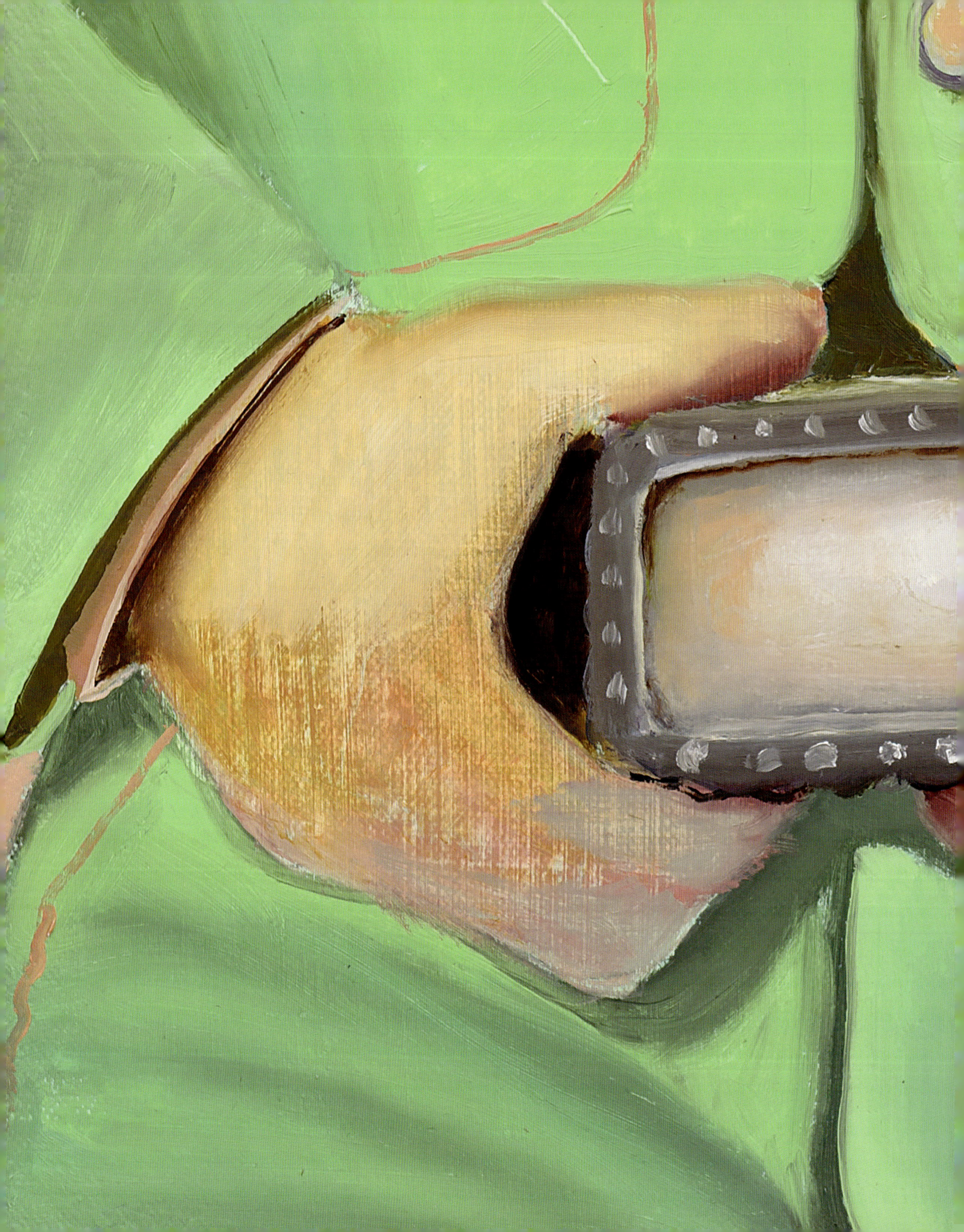

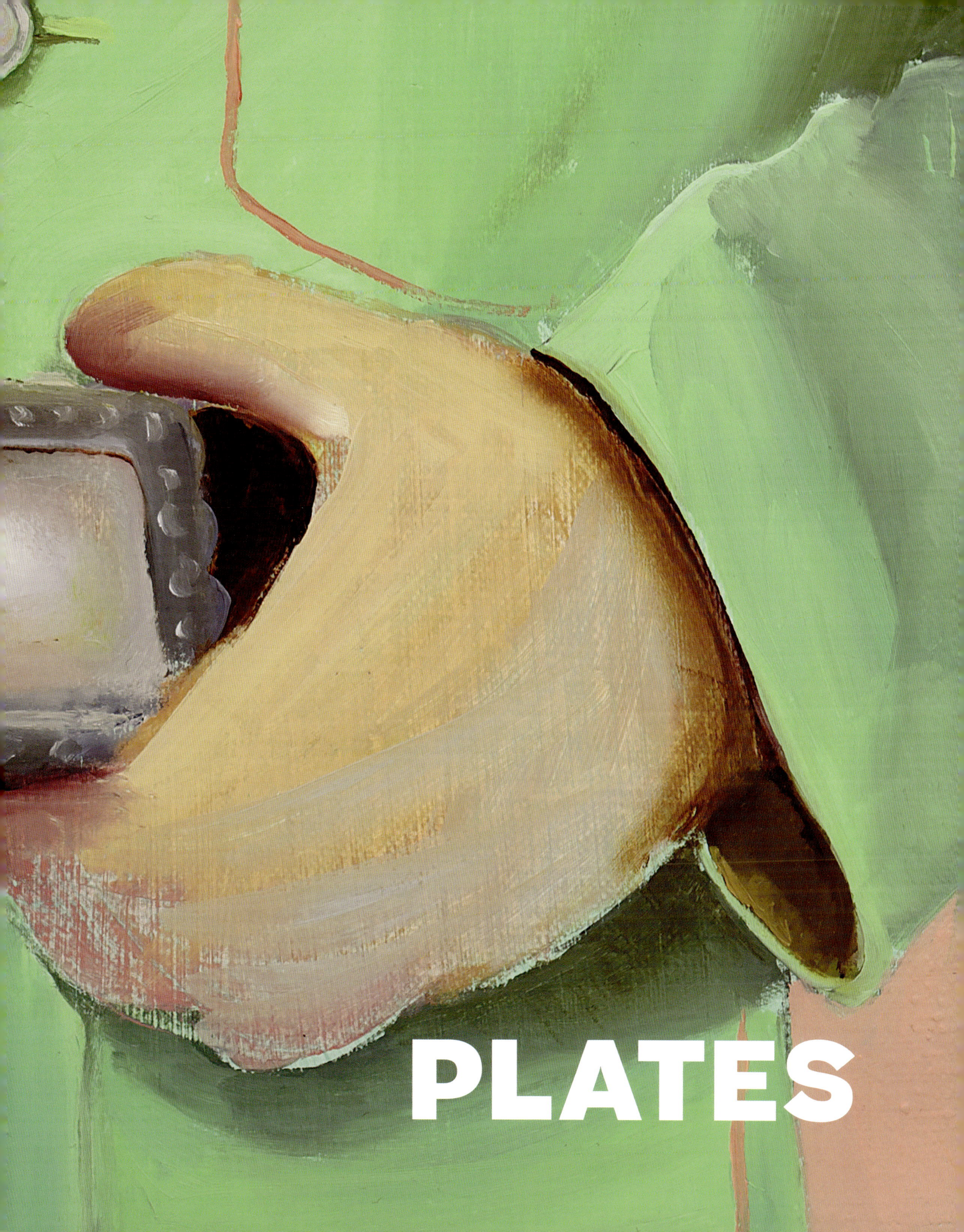

PLATES

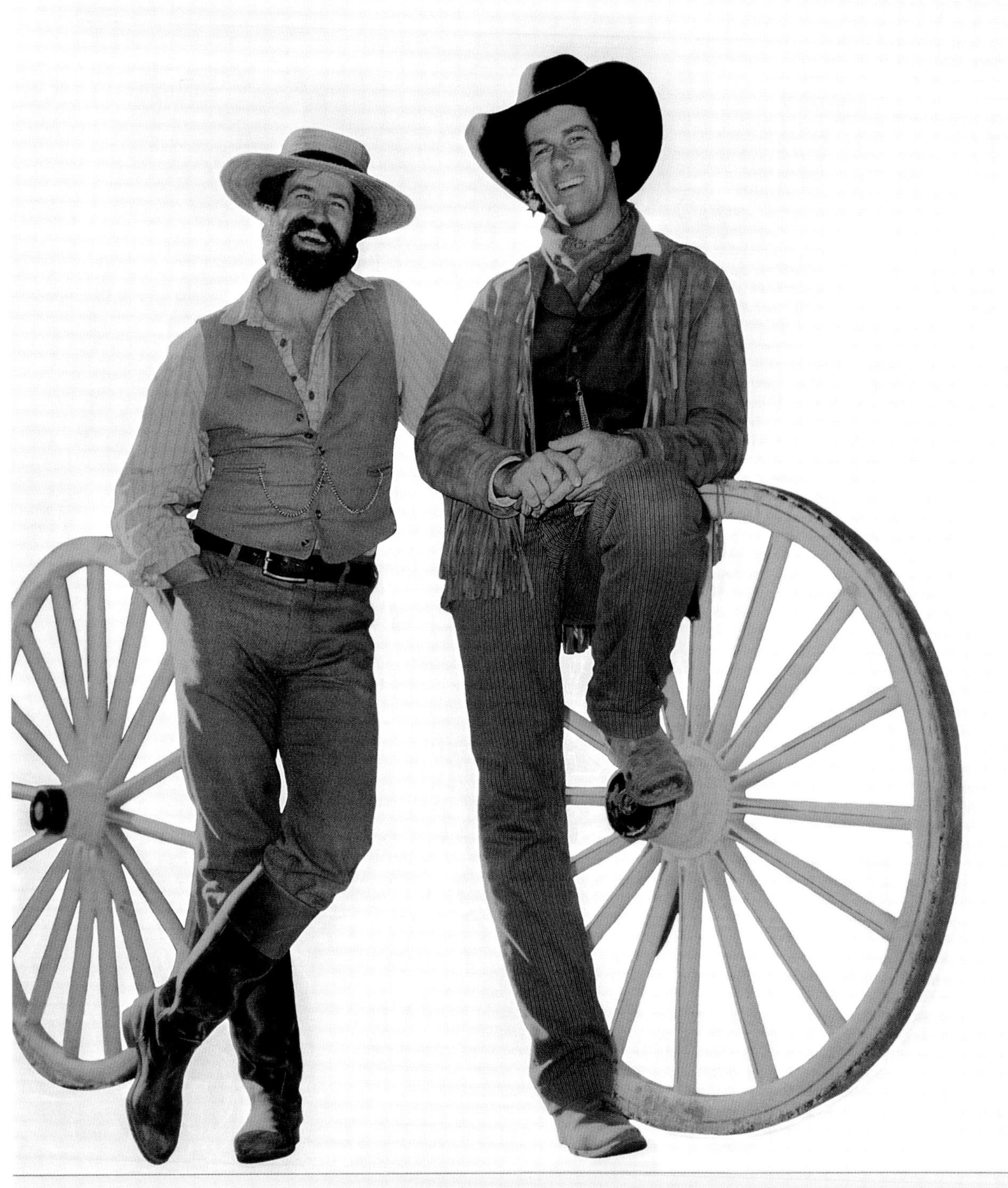

THE SPACE BETWEEN
TWO COWBOYS.

John Baldessari, THE SPACE BETWEEN TWO COWBOYS., 2019.
Varnished inkjet prints on canvas with acrylic paint. 54⅛ × 57⅝ × 1½ inches

John Baldessari, THE SPACE BETWEEN HAT, ROCK AND SHADOW., 2019.
Varnished inkjet prints on canvas with acrylic paint. 54⅛ × 57⅝ × 1½ inches

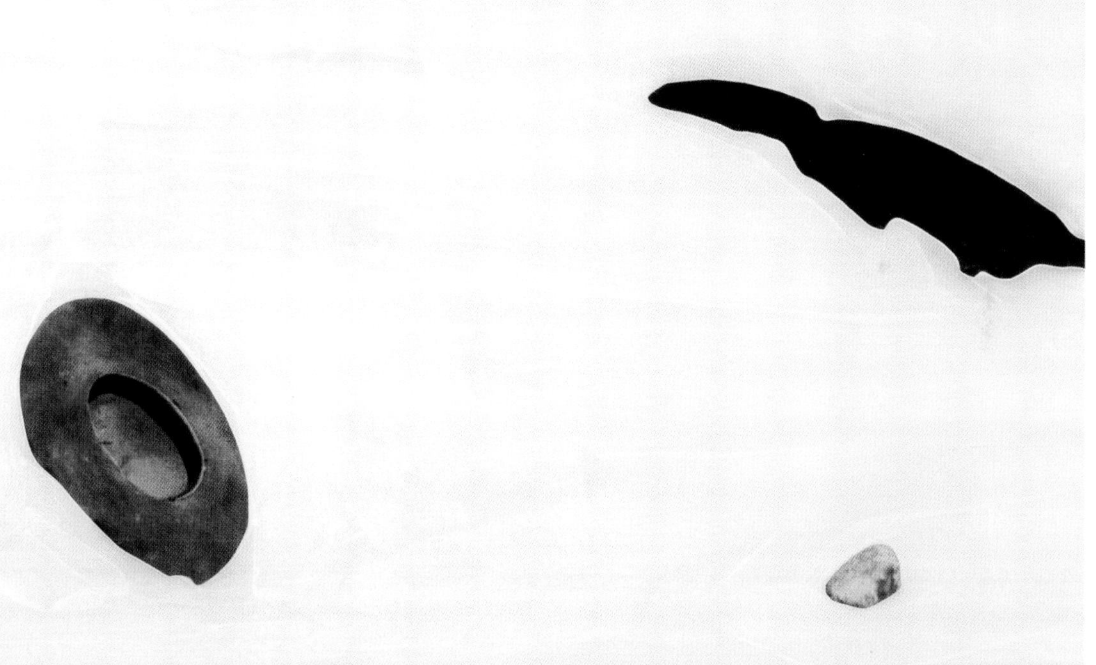

THE SPACE BETWEEN
HAT, ROCK AND SHADOW.

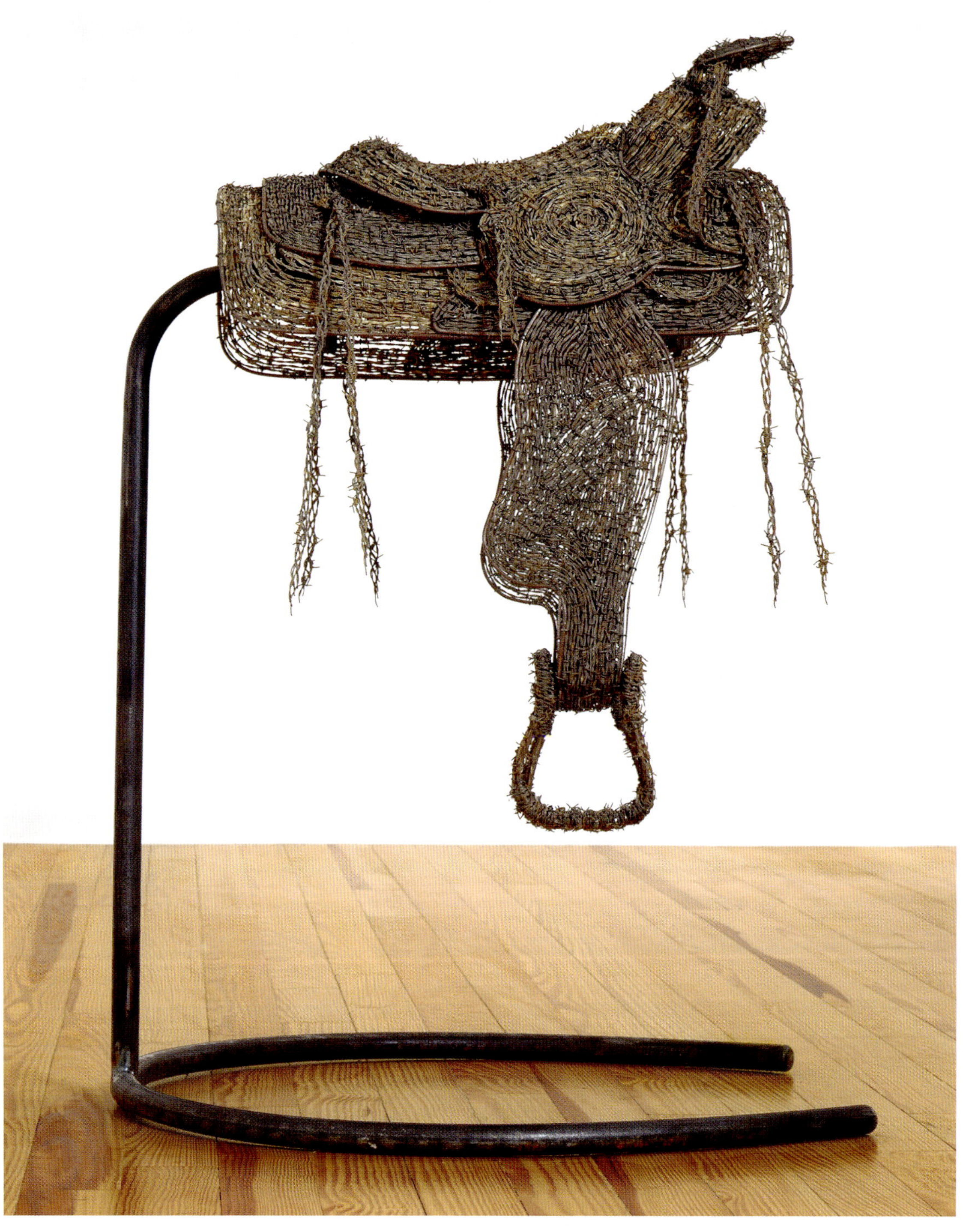

Above and detail opposite: Mel Chin, ROUGH RIDER, 2002.
Barbed wire and steel. 38 x 29 x 23 inches. Collection of the Estate of Ann Harithas

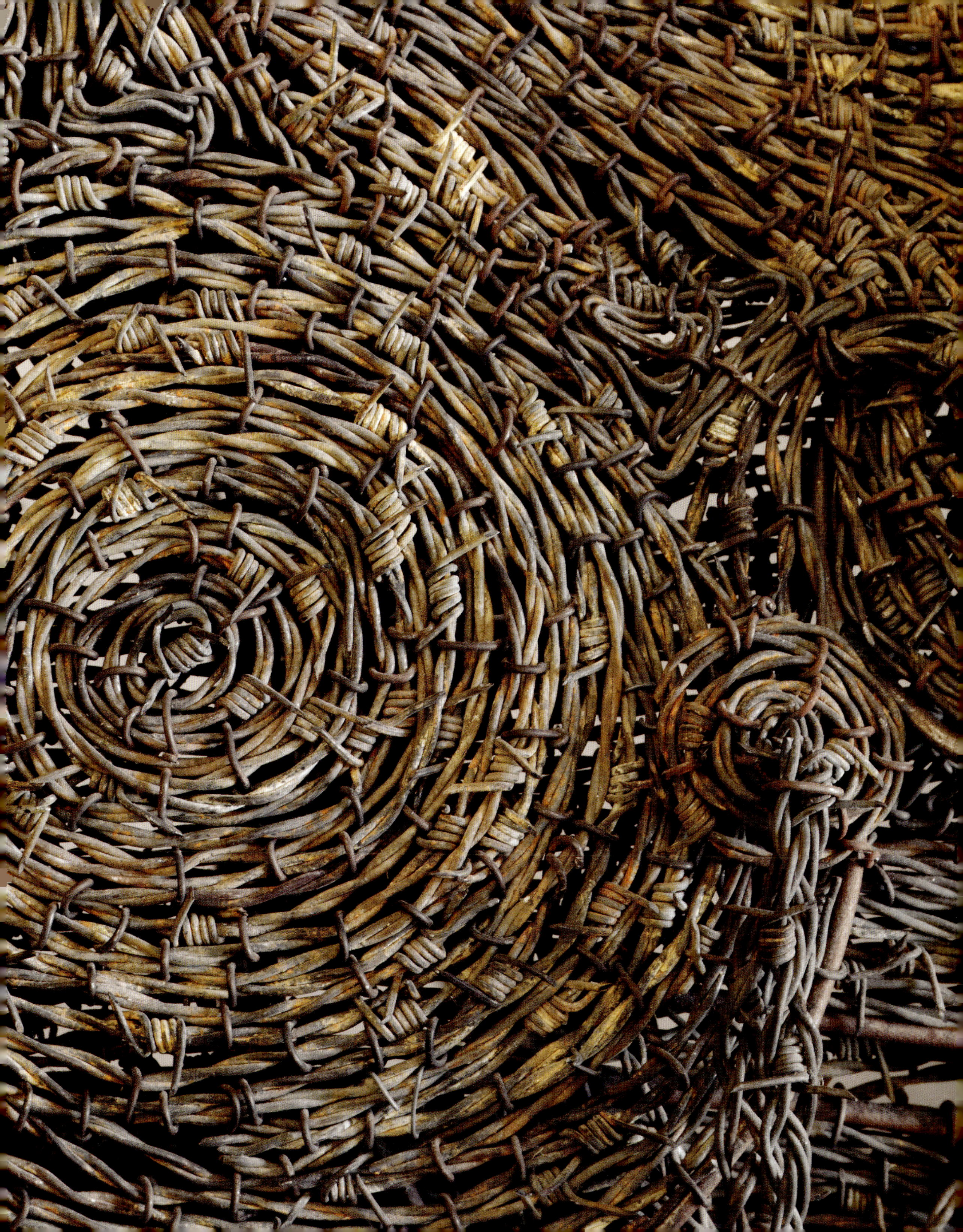

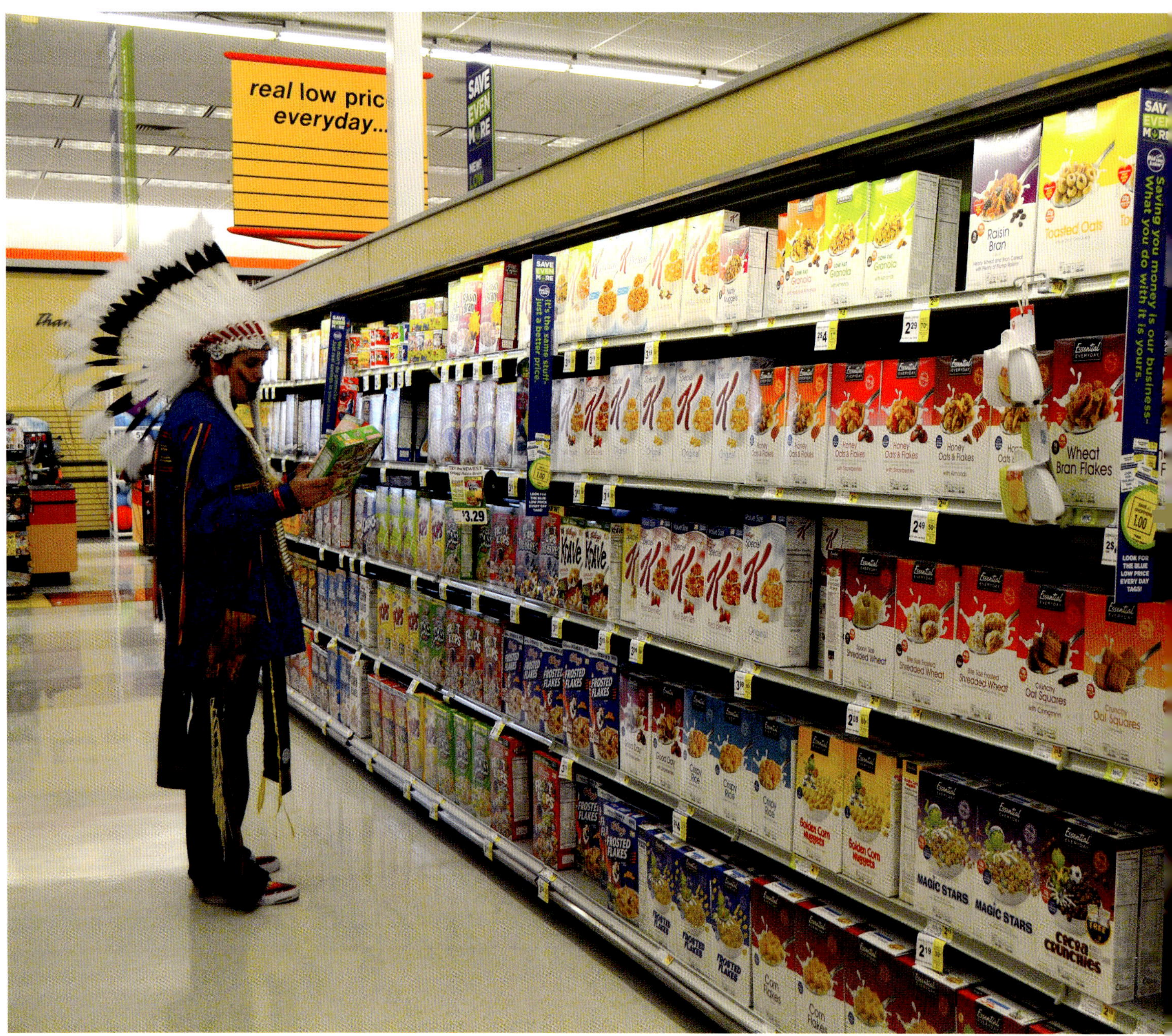
real low pric
everyday...
SAVE EVEN MORE
It's the same stuff–just a better price.
Saving you money is our business–What you do with it is yours.
Raisin Bran
Toasted Oats
Granola
Wheat Bran Flakes
Honey Oats & Flakes
Shredded Wheat
Oat Squares
FROSTED FLAKES
Crispy Rice
Golden Corn Nuggets
MAGIC STARS
Cocoa Crunchies
Corn Flakes
$3.29

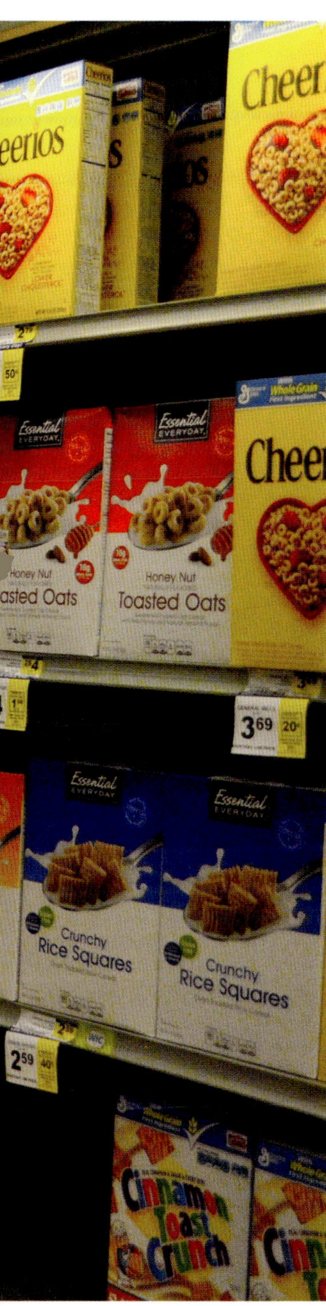

Gregg Deal, THE LAST AMERICAN INDIAN ON EARTH, 2013–14. Performance

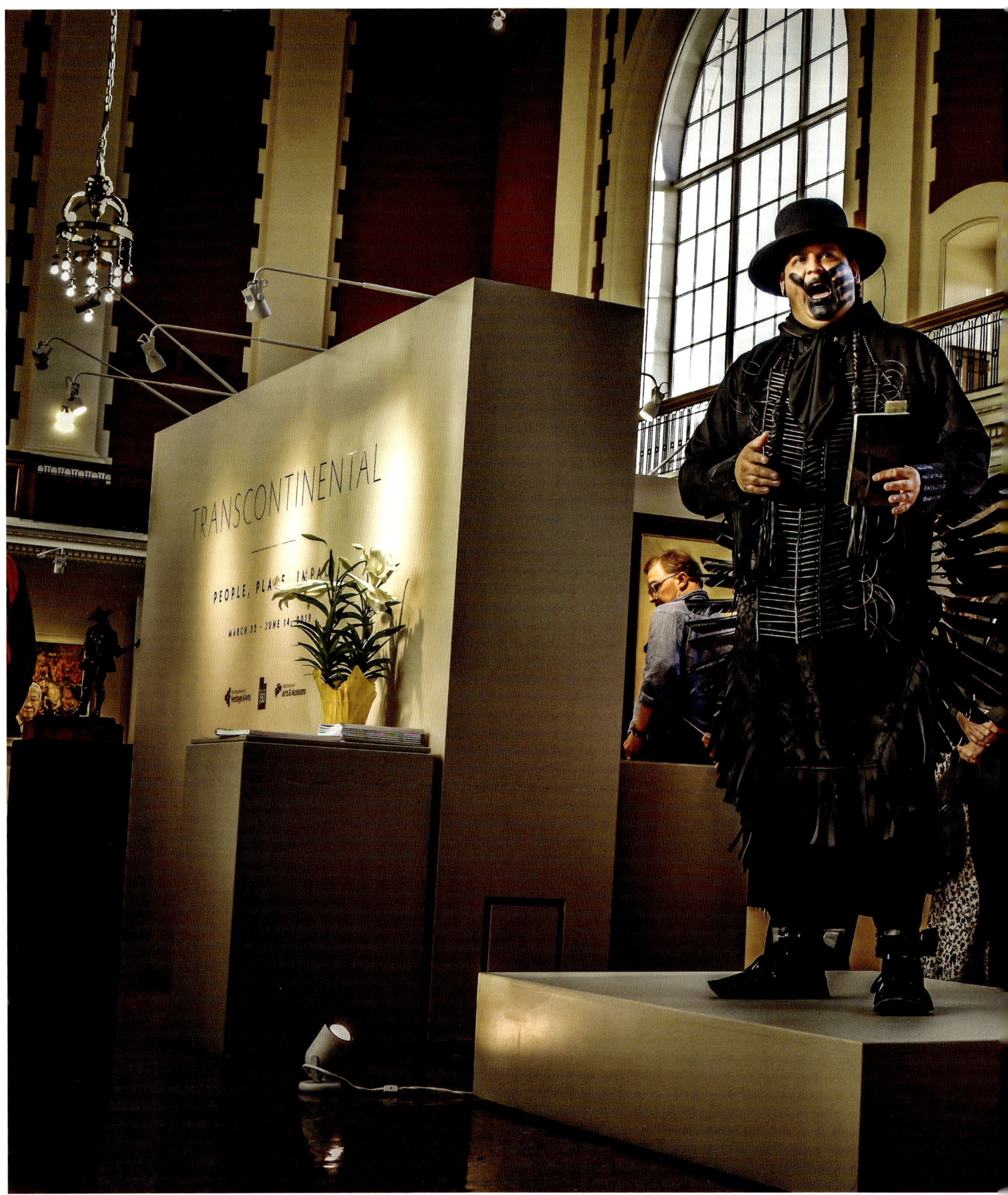
TRANSCONTINENTAL
PEOPLE,
MARCH 22 - JUNE 14,
Heritage & Arts
Arts & Museums

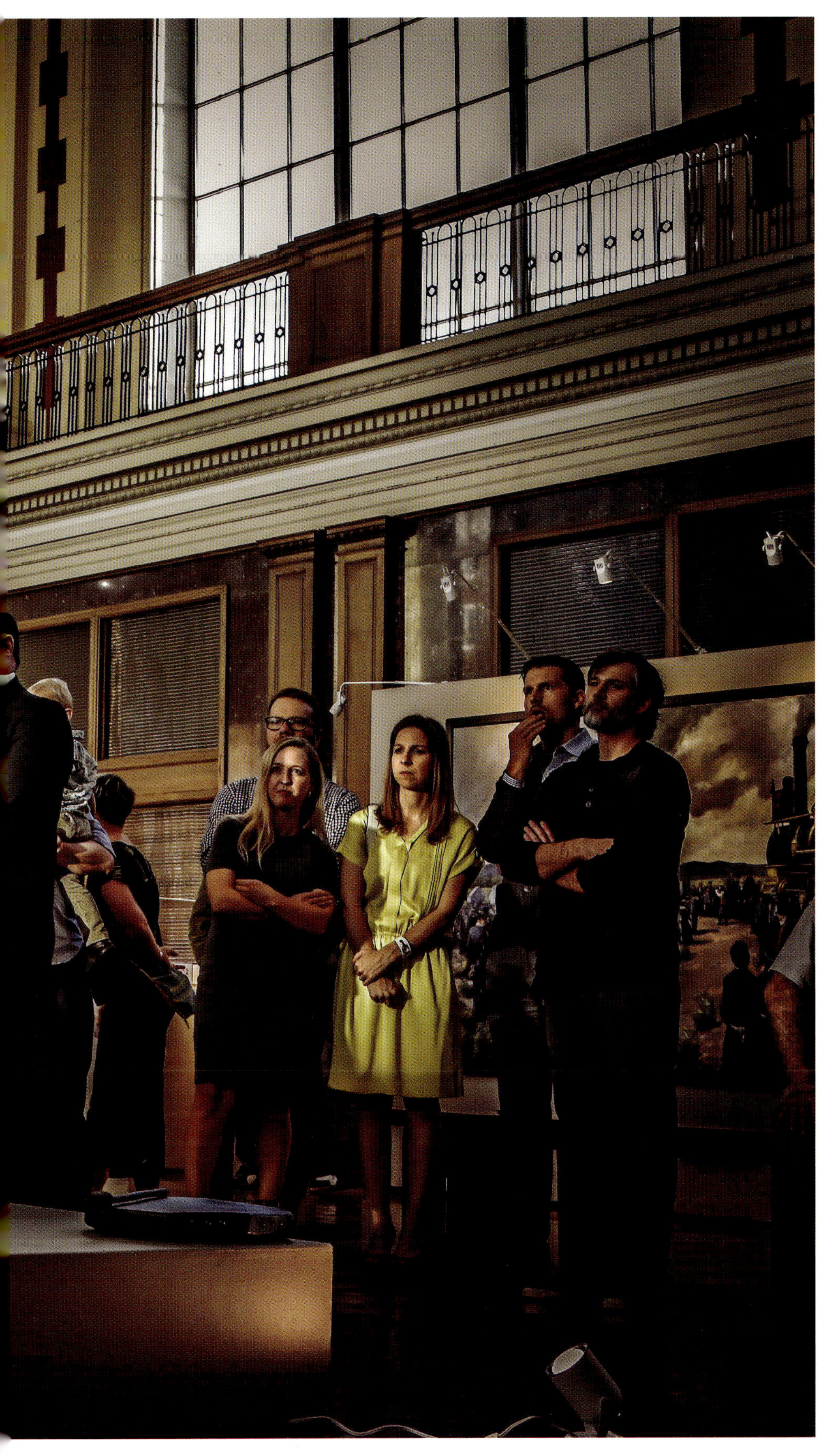

Left and pages 98–99:
Gregg Deal, INVISIBLE EULOGY, 2019. Performance

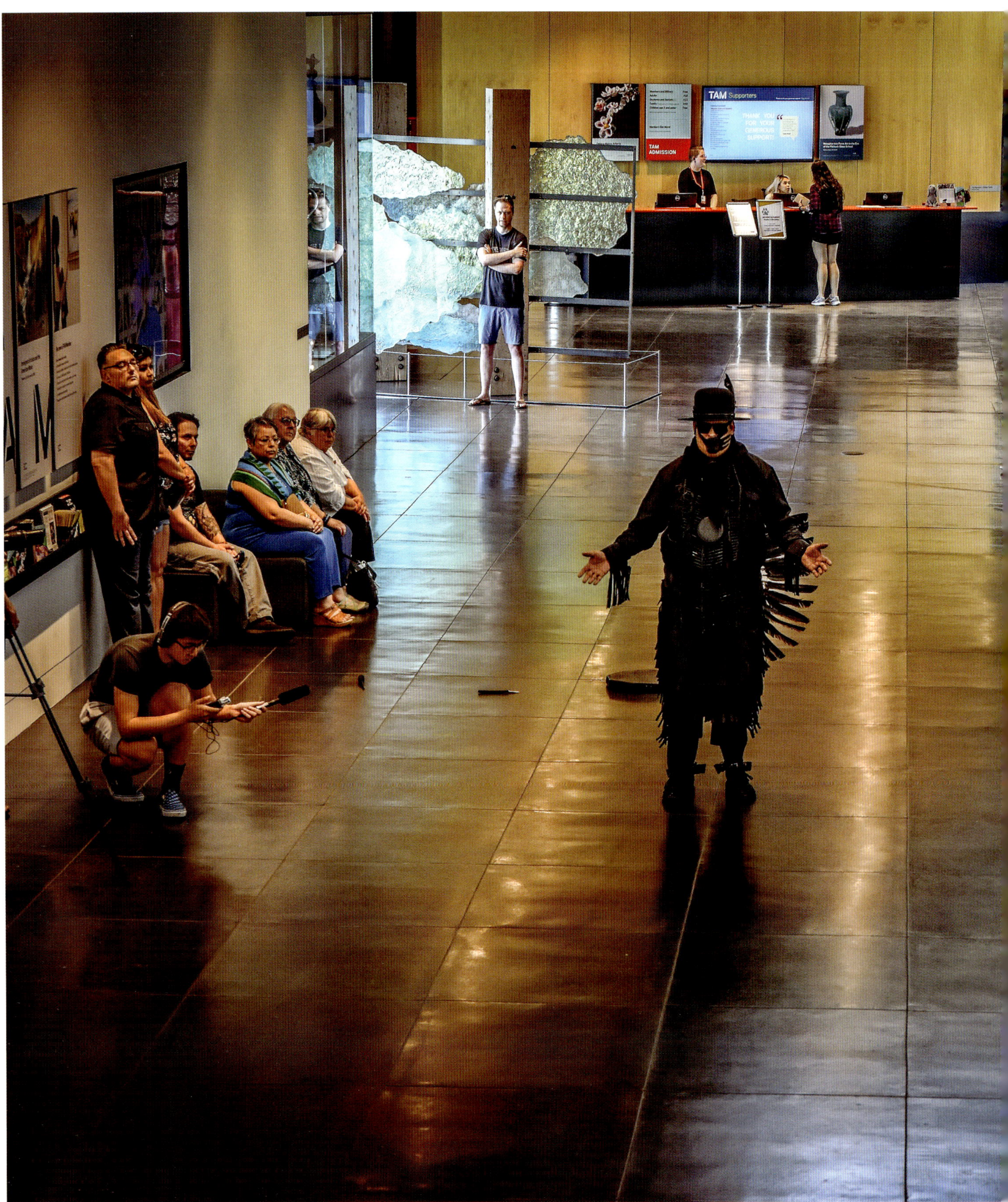
TAM ADMISSION
TAM Supporters
THANK YOU FOR YOUR GENEROUS SUPPORT!

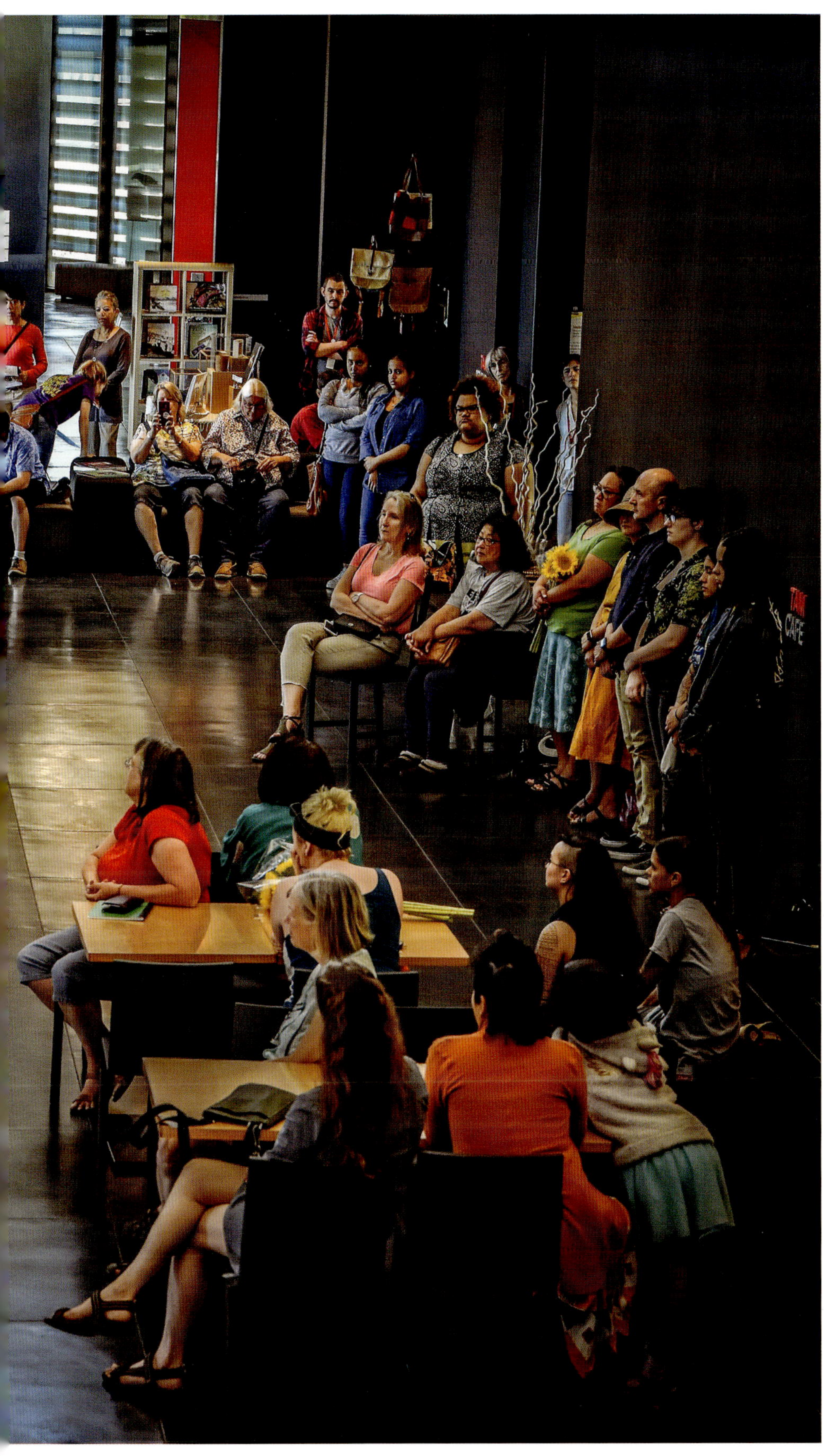
CAFE

Angela Ellsworth, IN MEMORY OF OUR SISTERS (detail), 2022. 13,758 black dress pins and boutonnière pins, wood, fabric, and steel. 24 x 13 x 15 inches

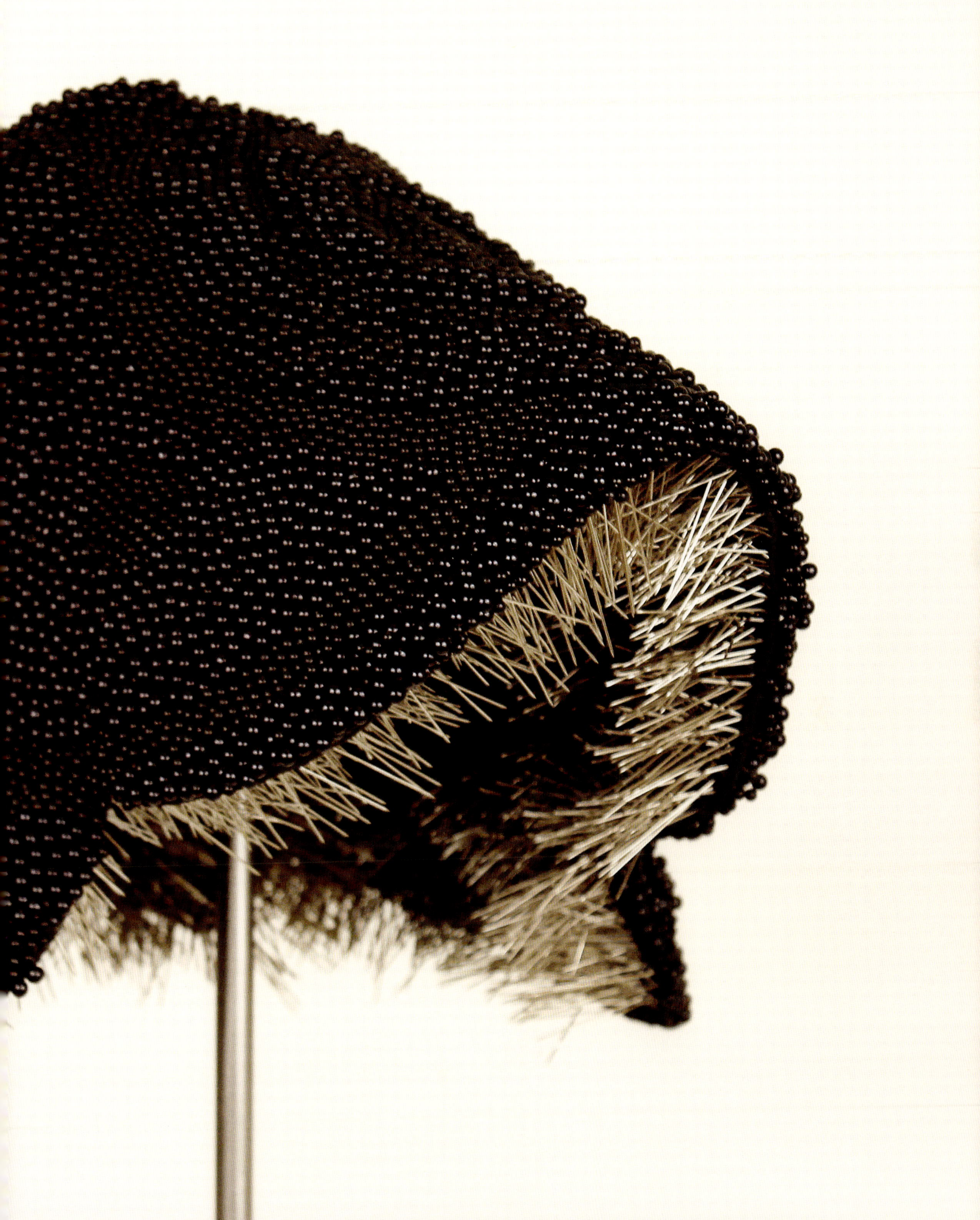

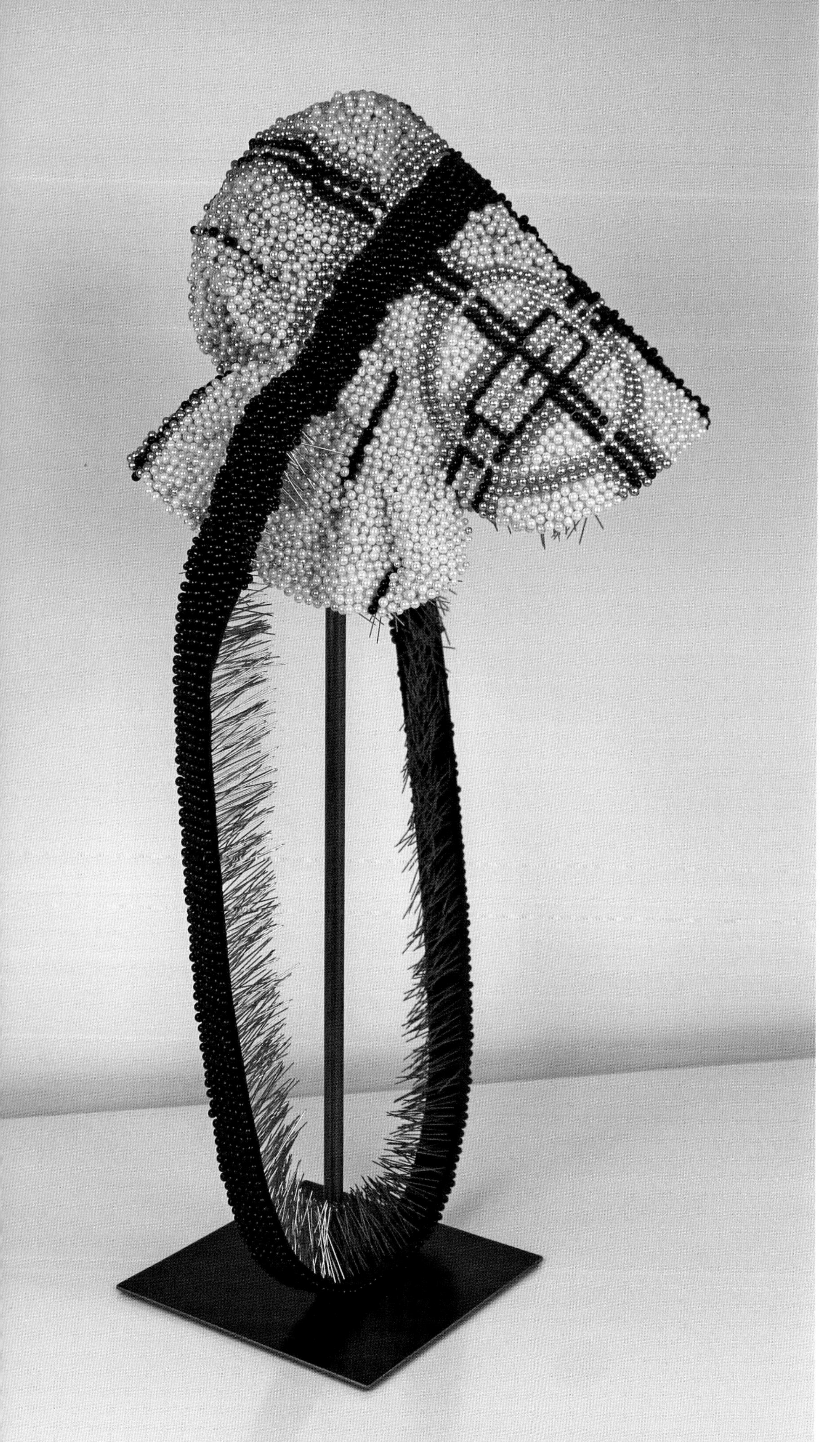

Angela Ellsworth,
IN ARMS I, 2023. 11,112 black and white dress pins / boutonnière pins, wood, fabric, and steel. 28½ x 12 x 13 inches

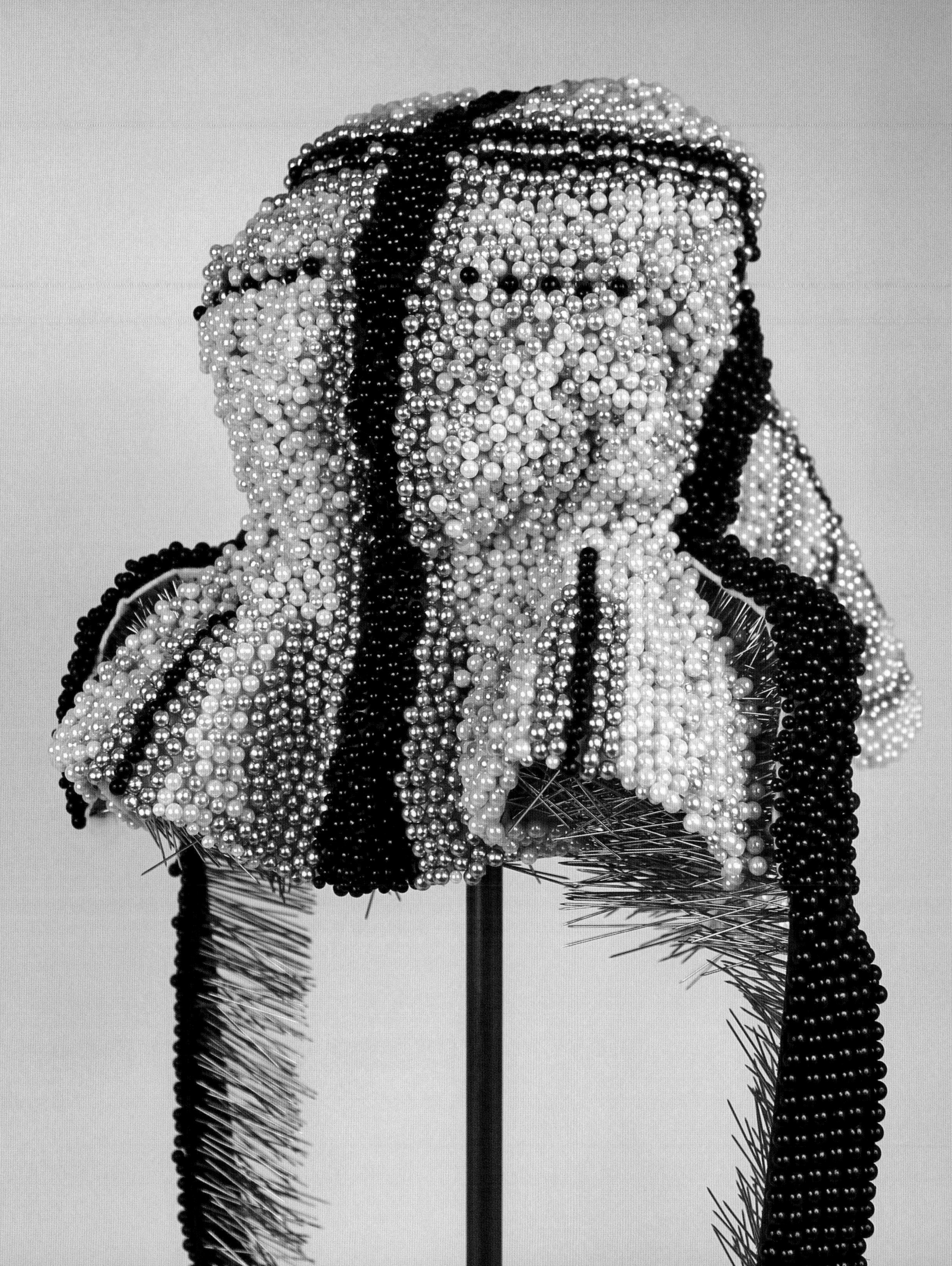

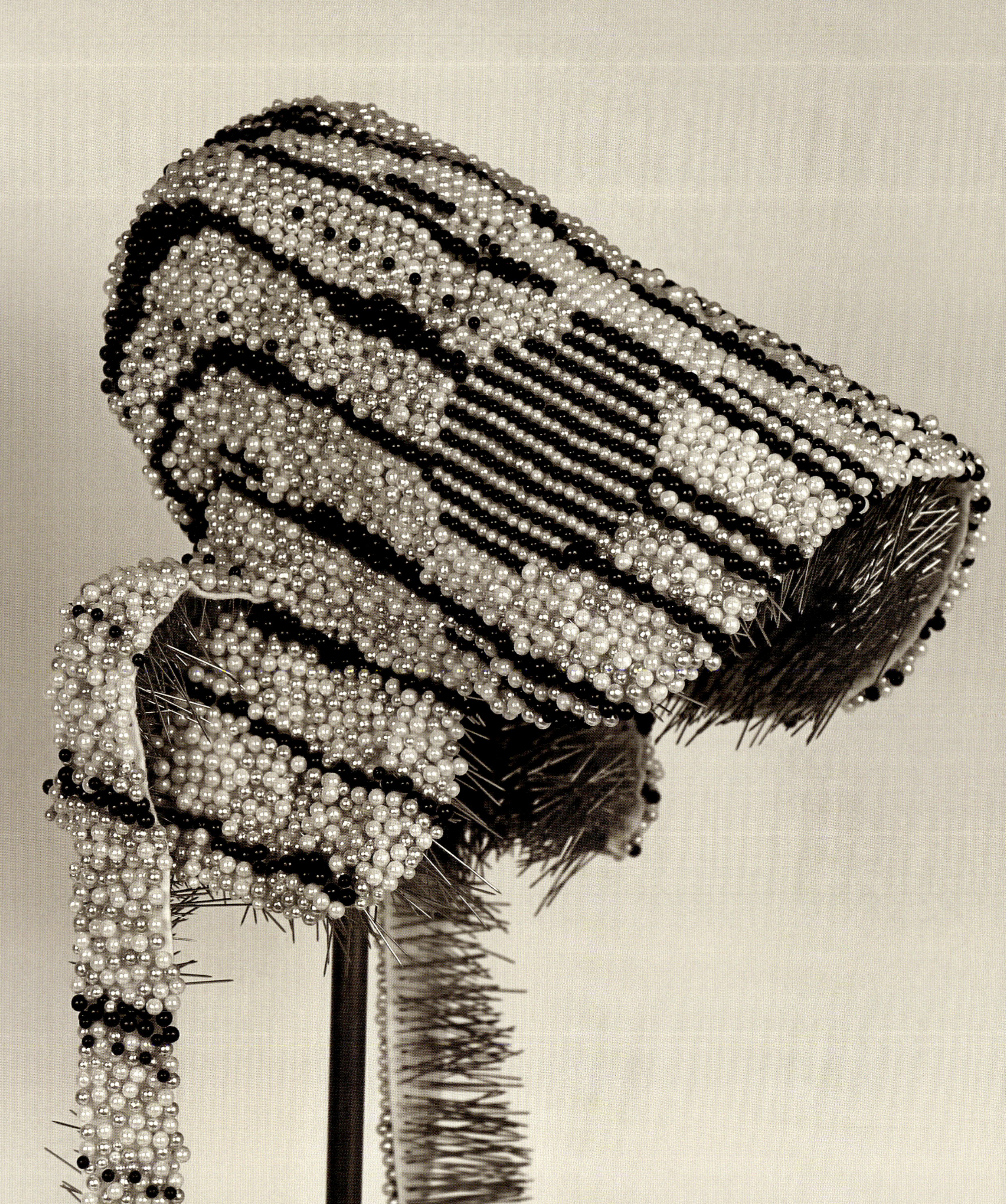

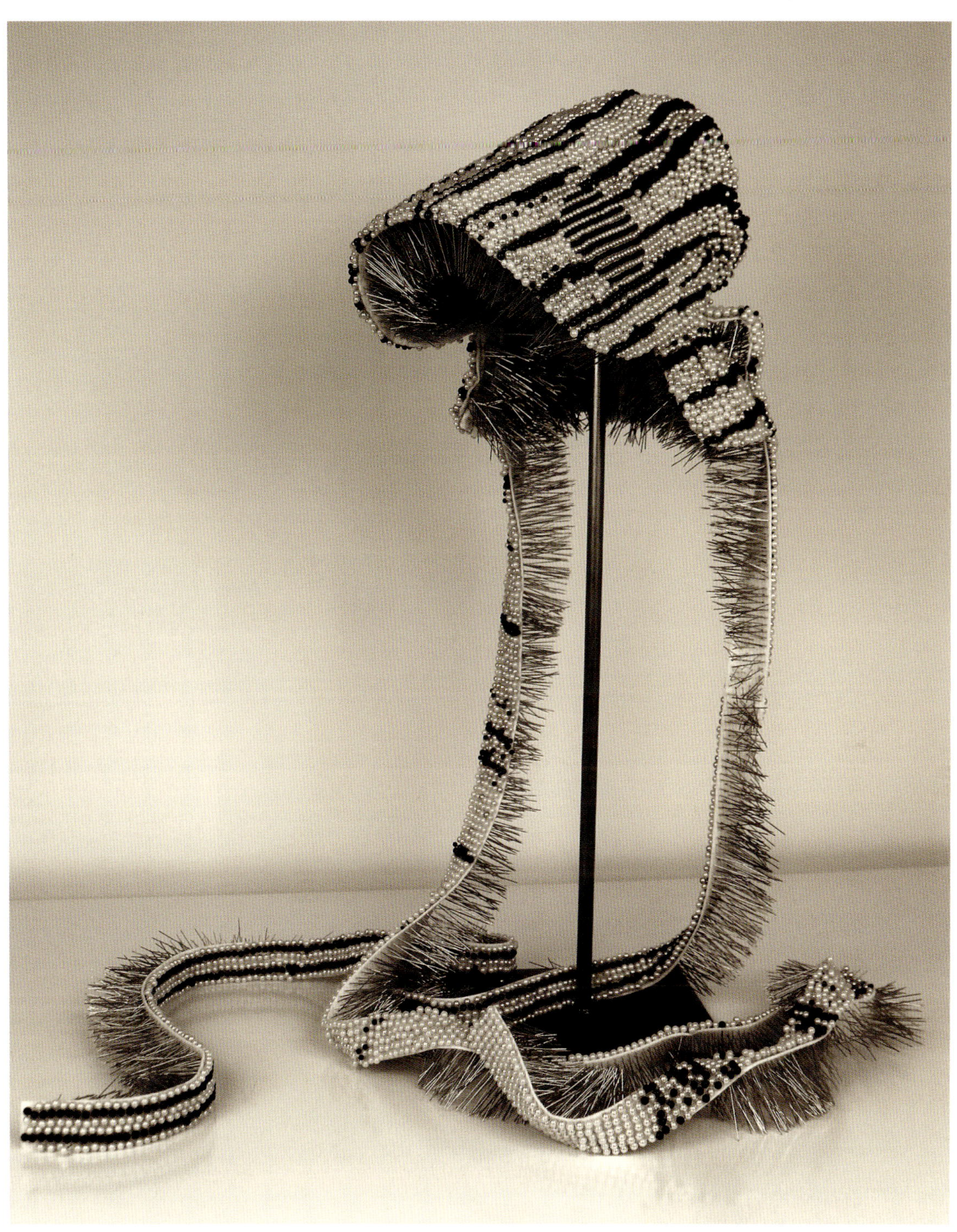

Angela Ellsworth, IN ARMS II, 2023. 12,248 black and white dress pins / boutonnière pins, wood, fabric, and steel. 28 x 10 x 13 inches

Opposite and detail following pages: rafa esparza, AL TEMPO, 2021.
Acrylic on adobe. 72 x 113½ x 2 inches (diptych)

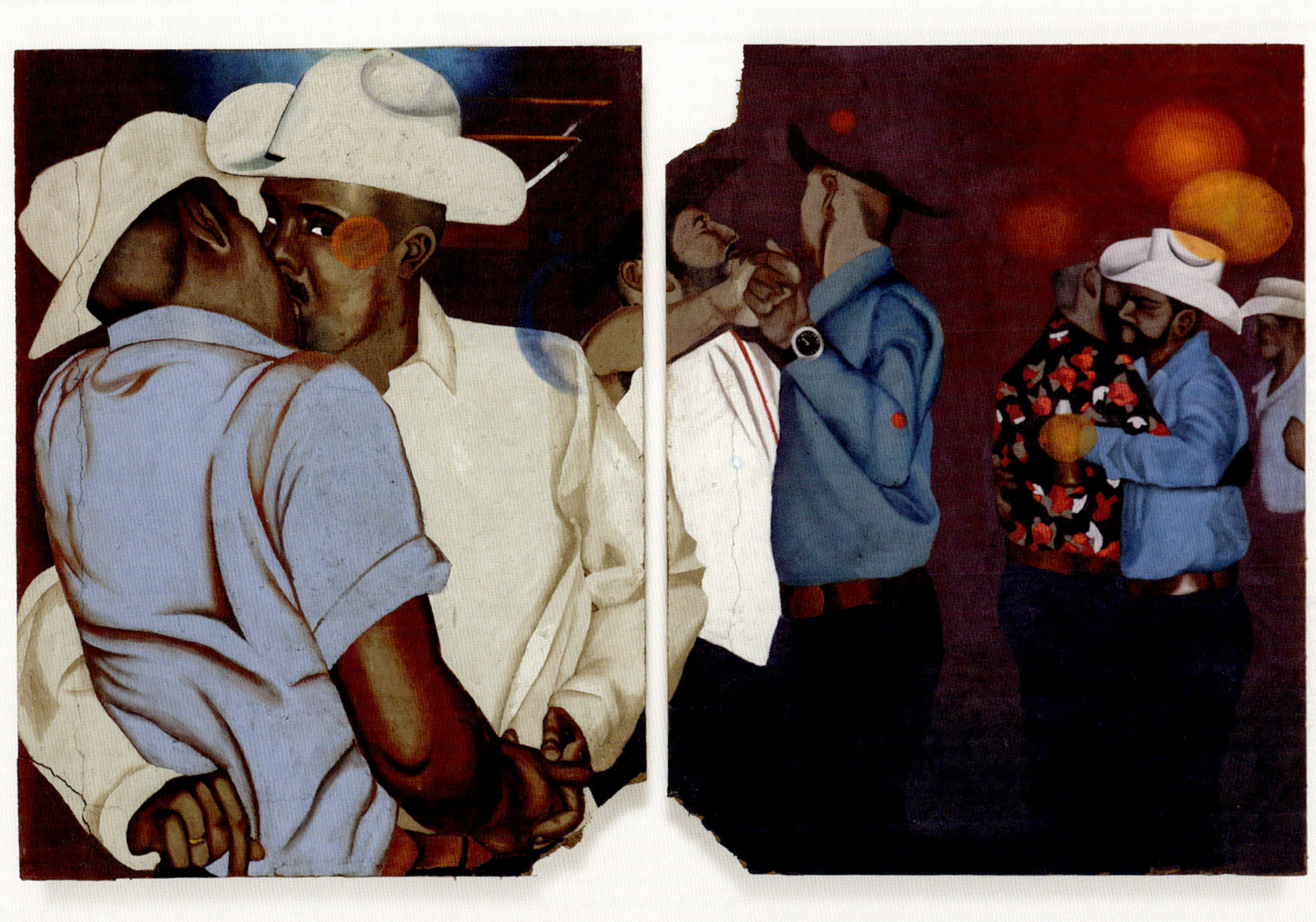

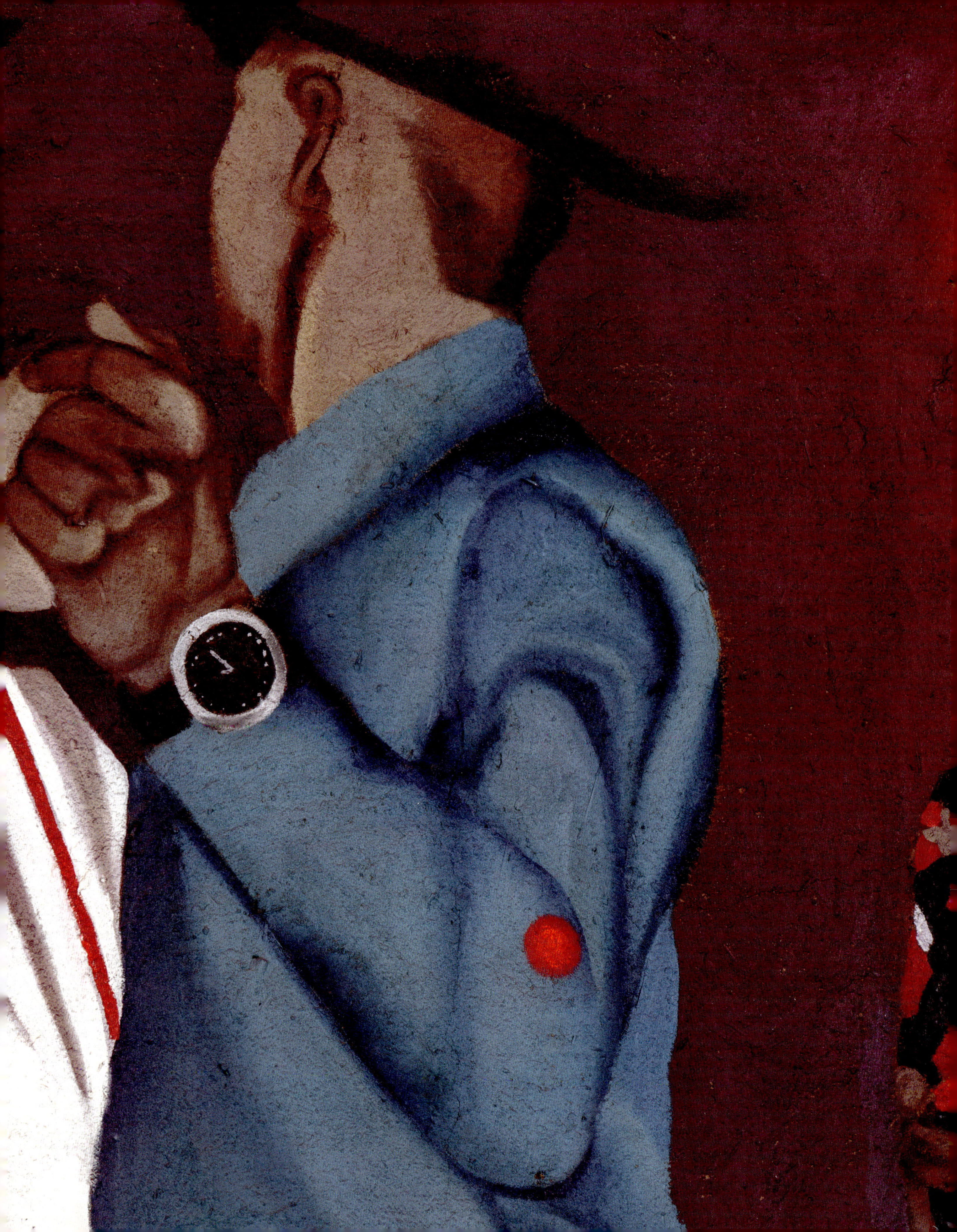

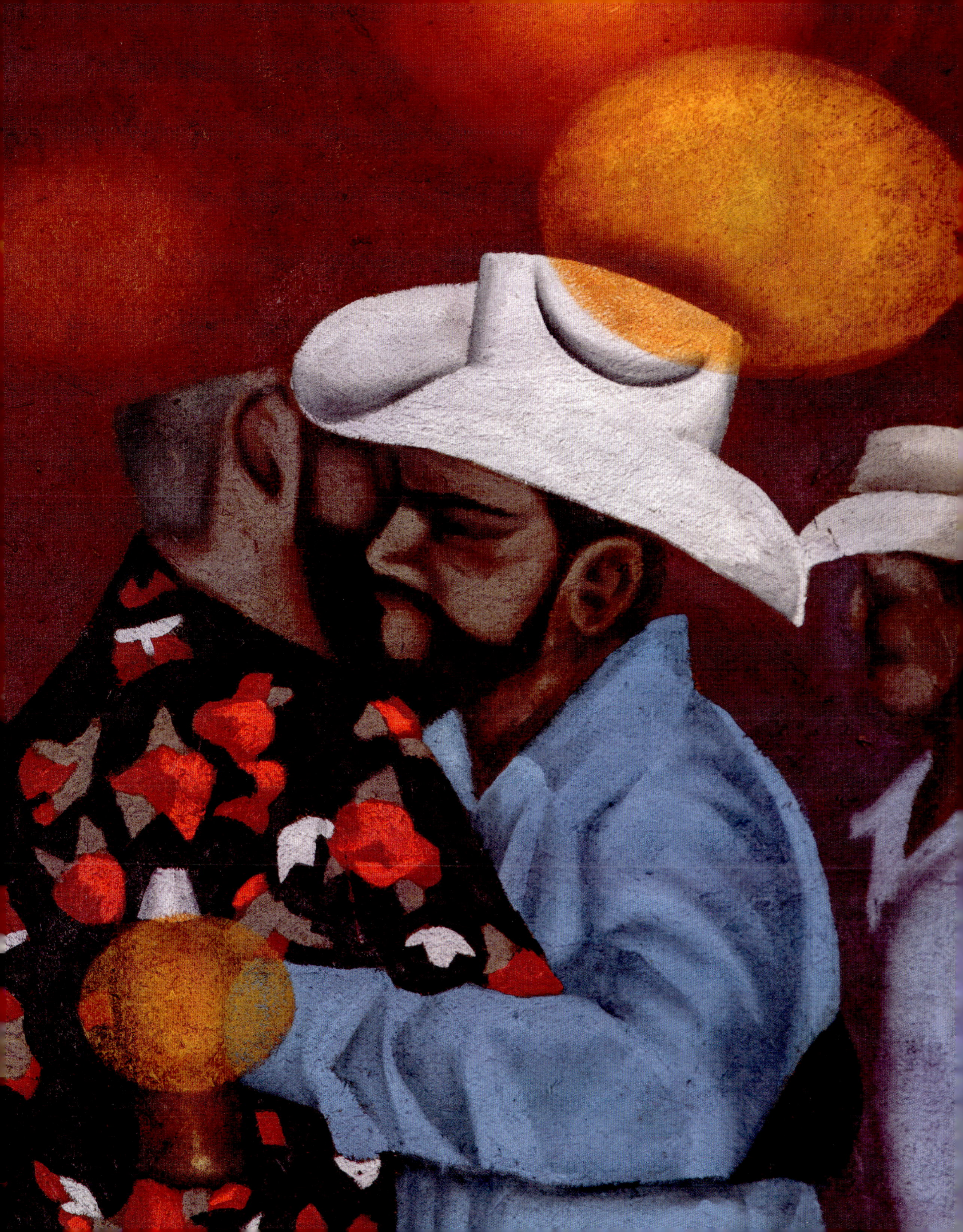

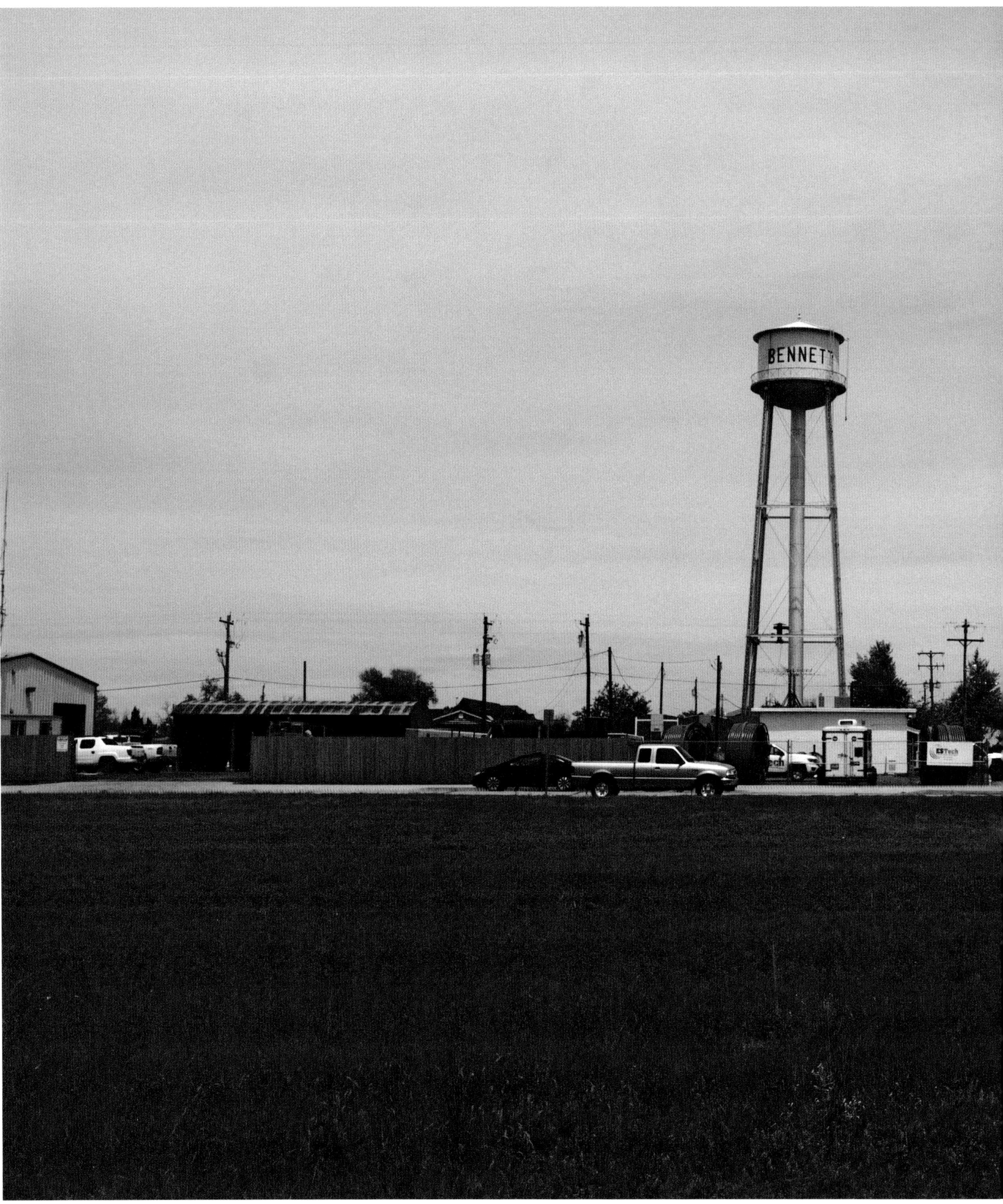
BENNETT
ESTech

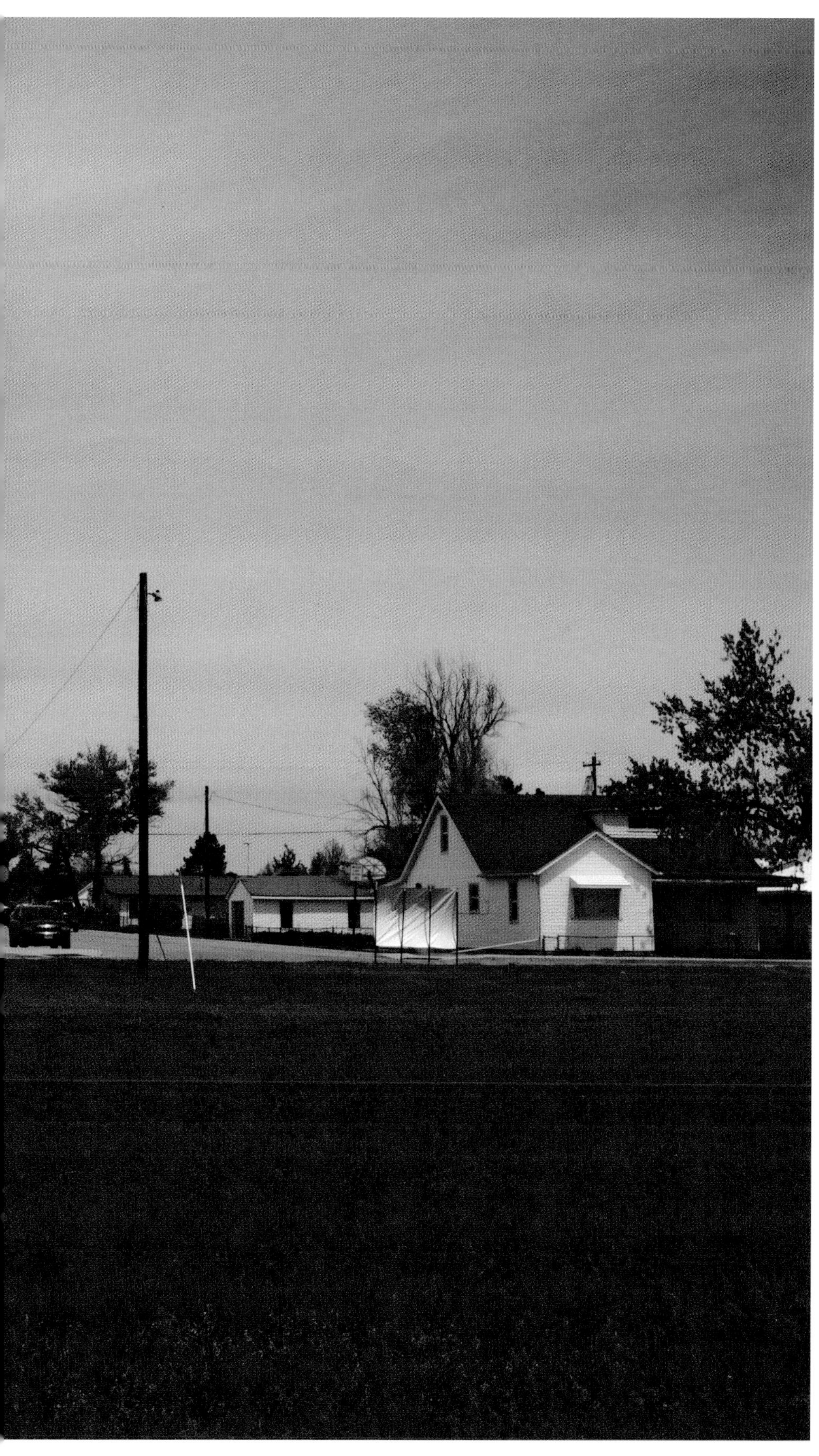

Juan Fuentes, UNTITLED, 2021,
from the series THIRTY-SIX
MILES EAST. Photograph

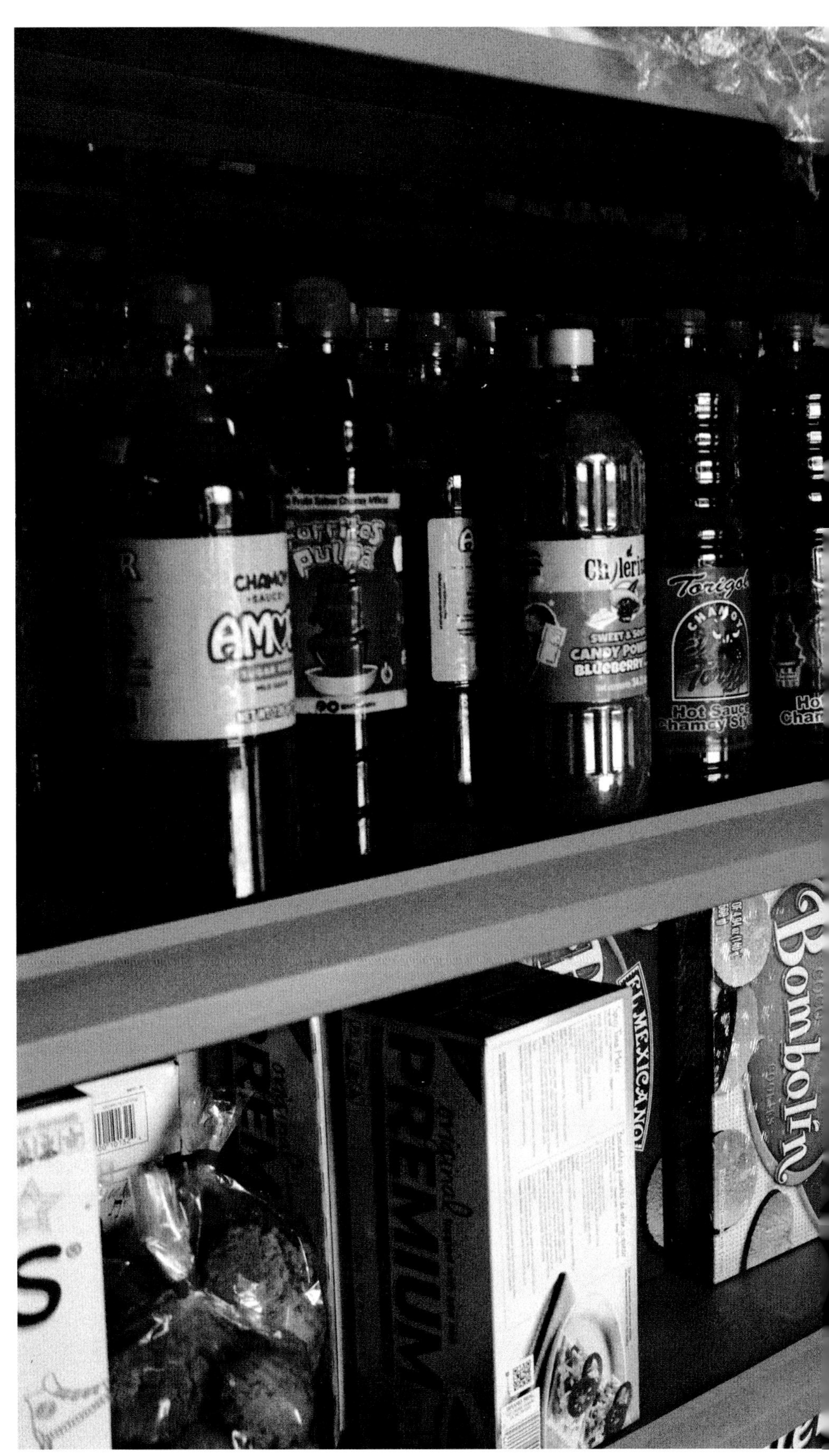

Juan Fuentes, UNTITLED, 2021, from the series THIRTY-SIX MILES EAST. Photograph

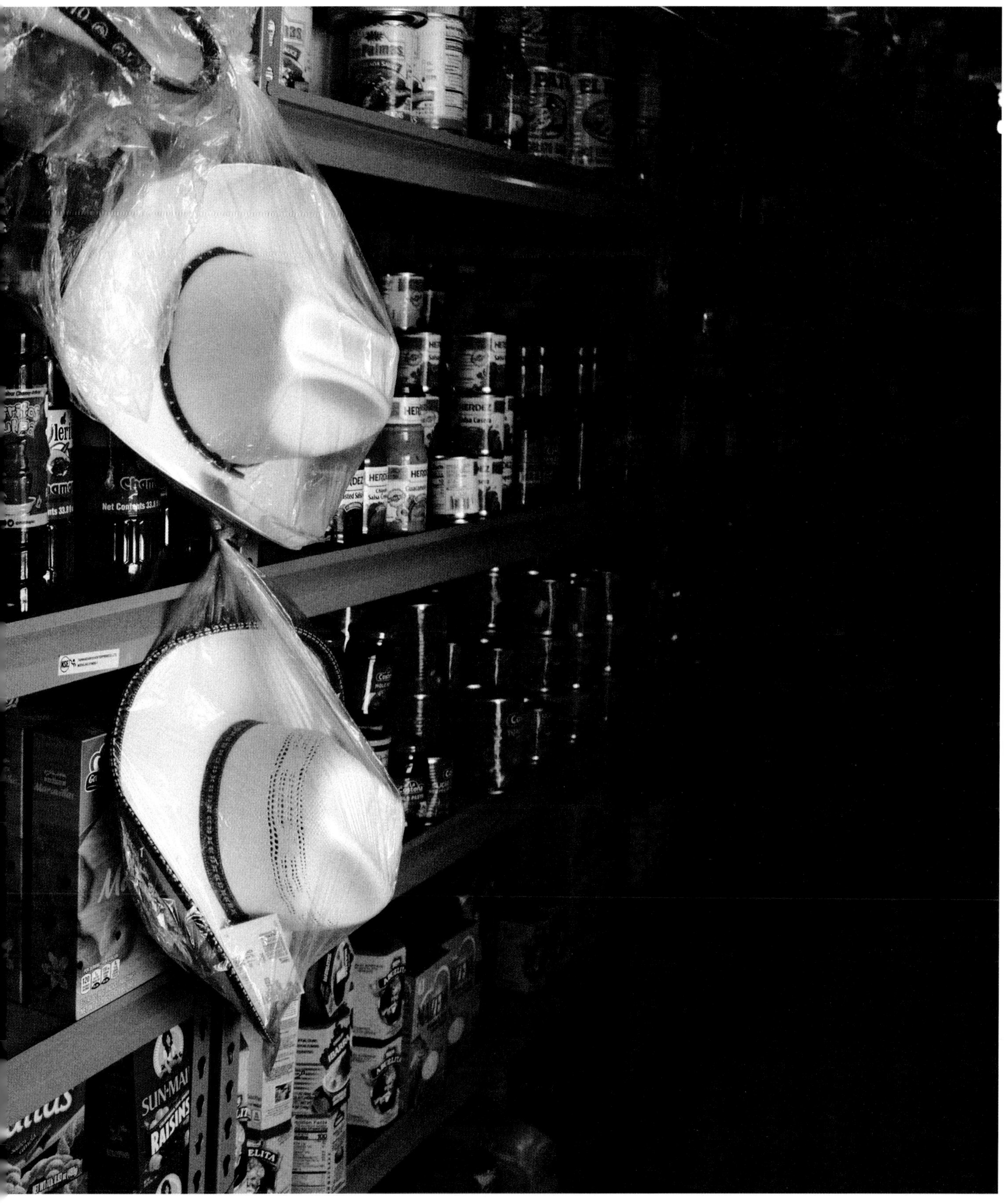
HERDEZ
SUN-MAID
RAISINS

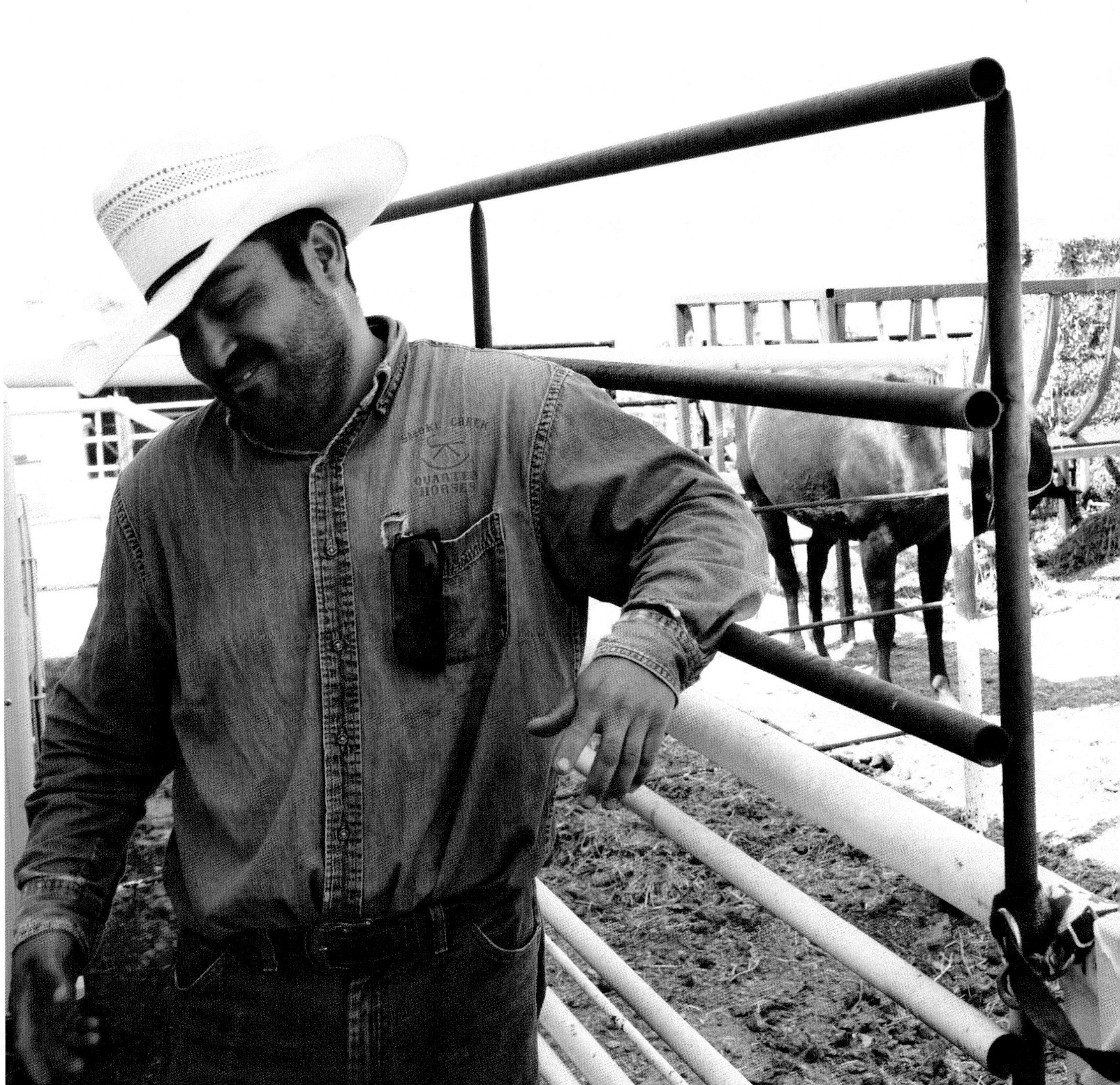
SMOKE CREEK
QUARTER HORSES

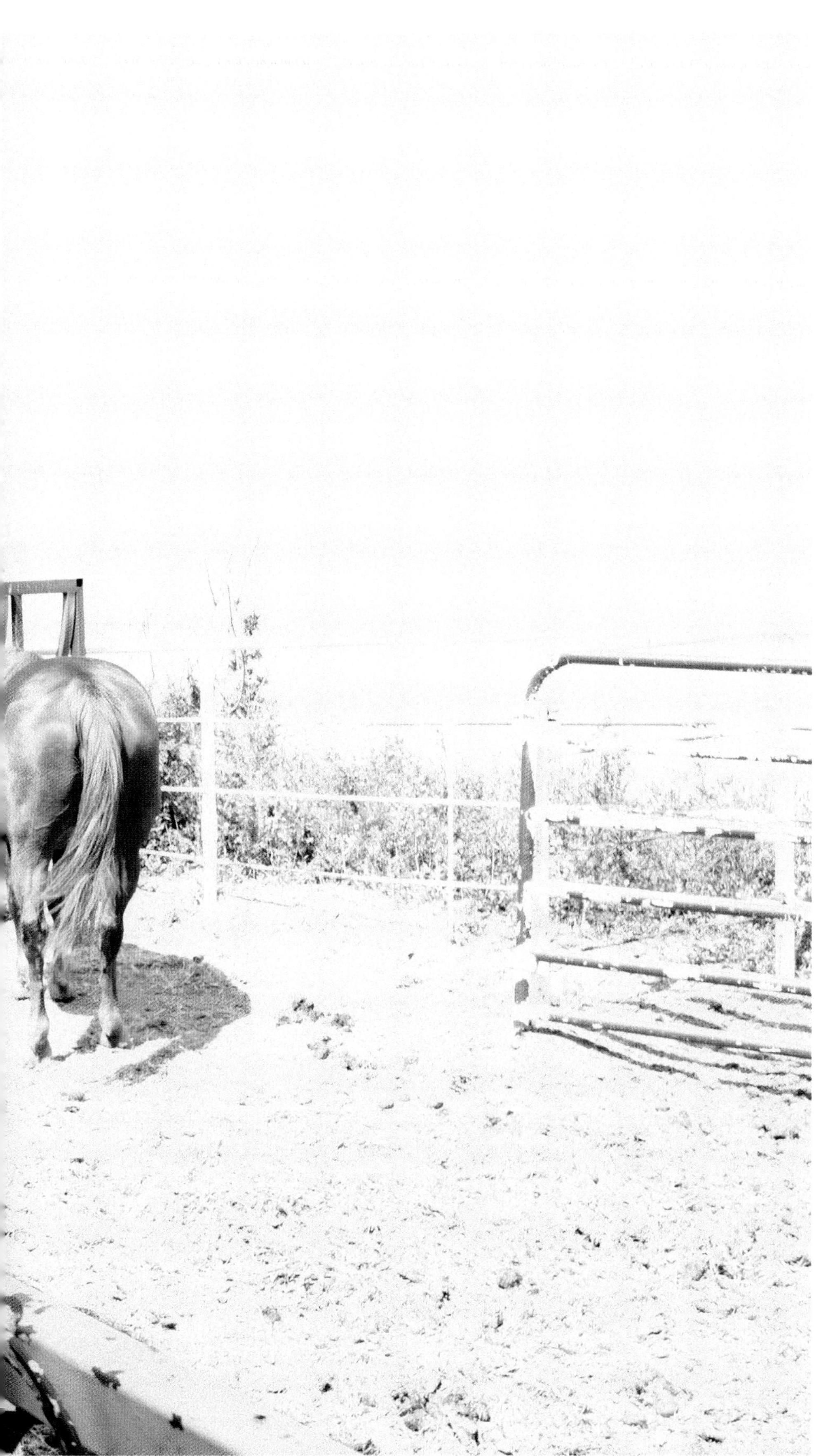

Juan Fuentes, UNTITLED, 2021, from the series THIRTY-SIX MILES EAST. Photograph

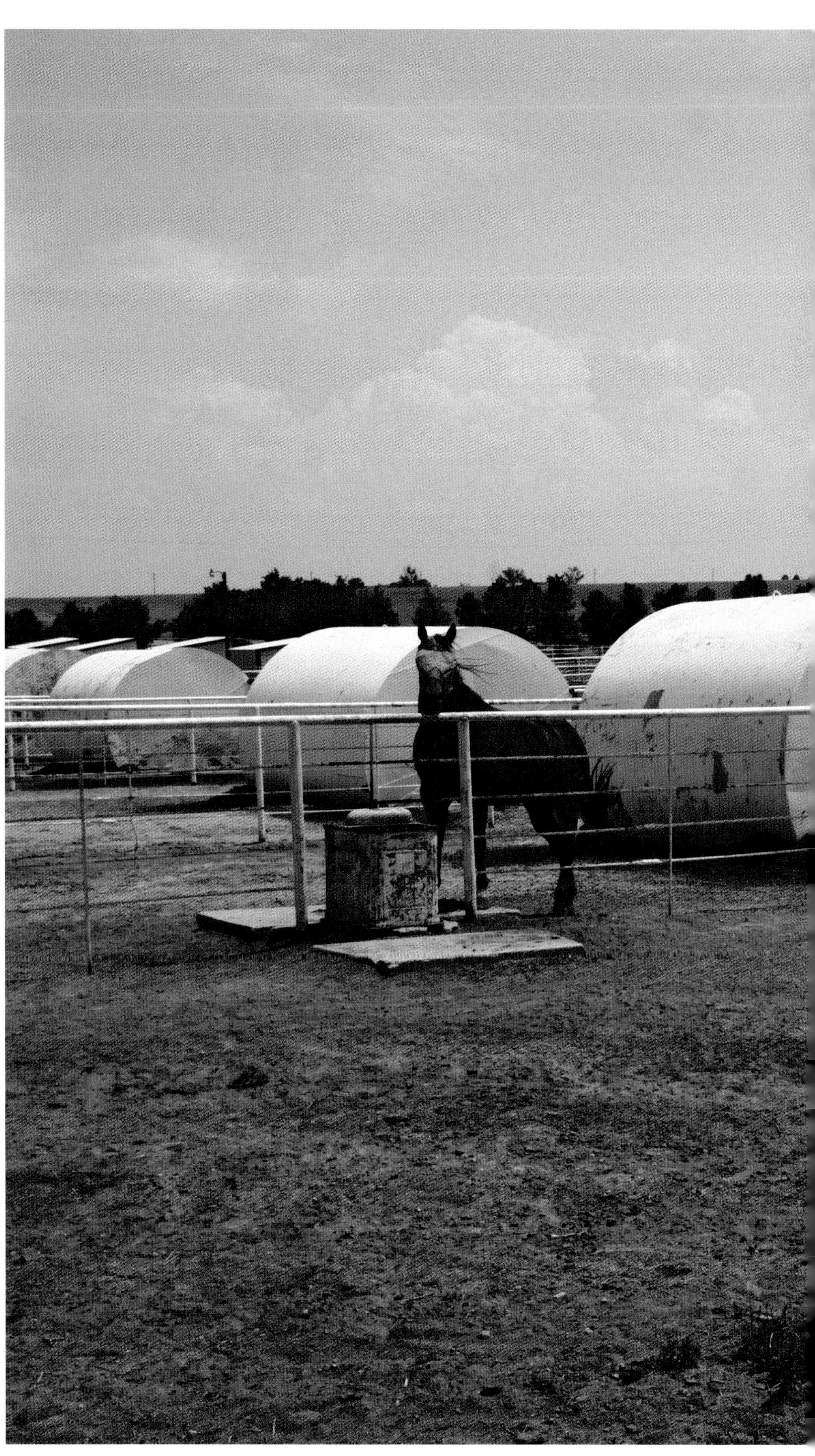

Juan Fuentes, UNTITLED, 2021, from the series THIRTY-SIX MILES EAST. Photograph

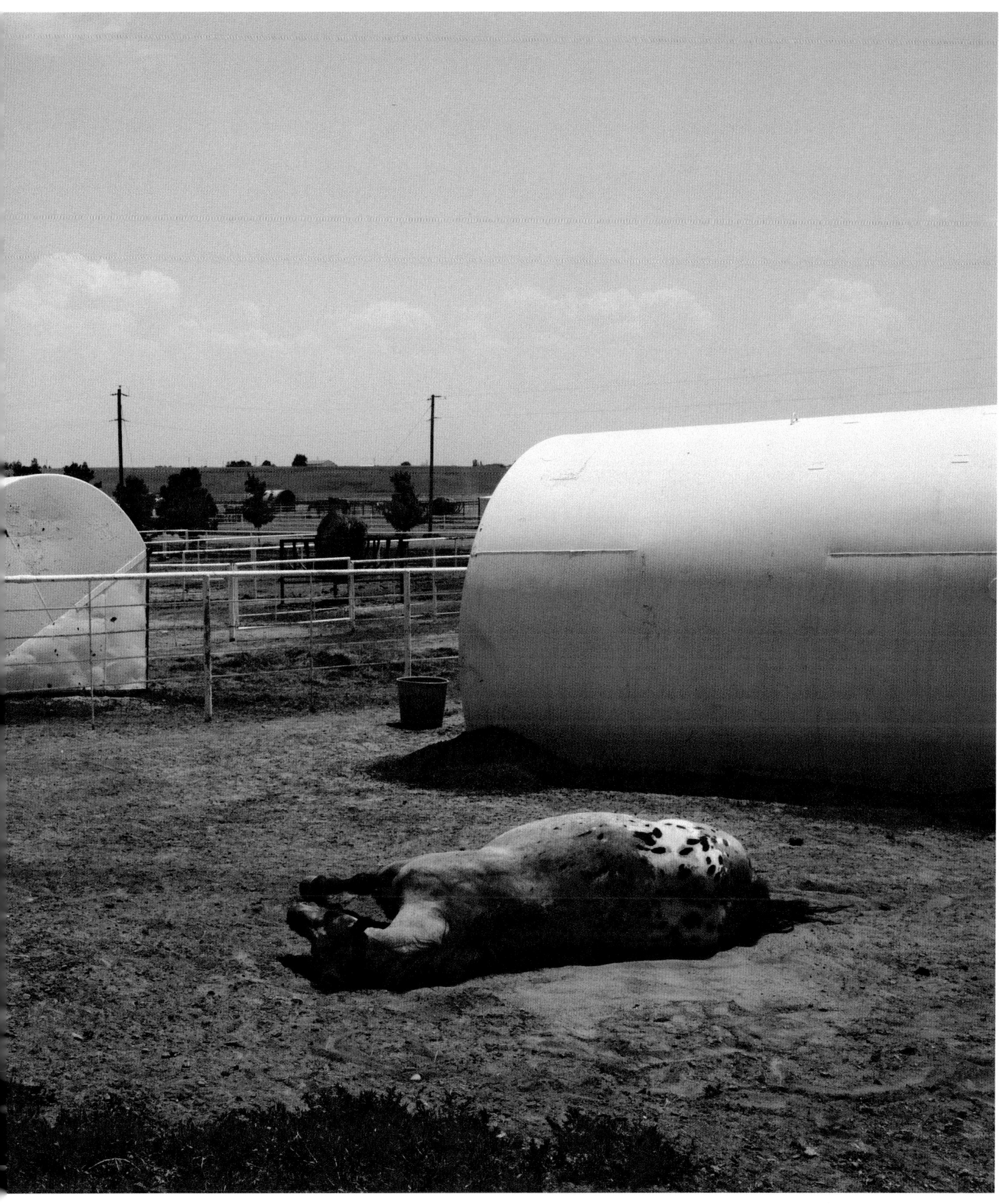

Opposite: Karl Haendel, RODEO 9, 2017.
Pencil and graphite powder on paper. 103 x 77 inches.
Private collection, Germany

Following pages: Karl Haendel, RODEO 8, 2016.
Pencil and graphite powder on paper. 103 x 84½ inches.
Private collection, Switzerland

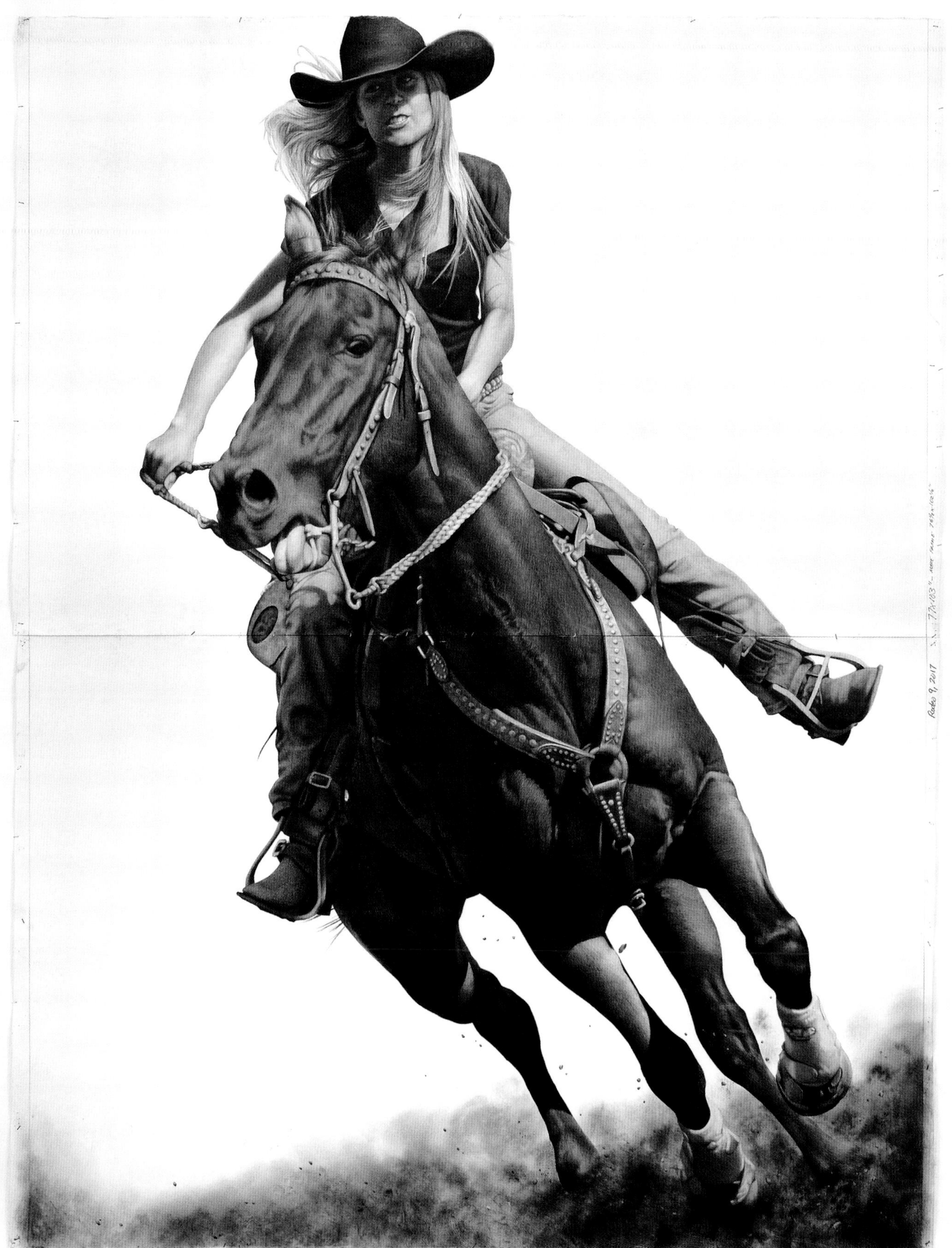

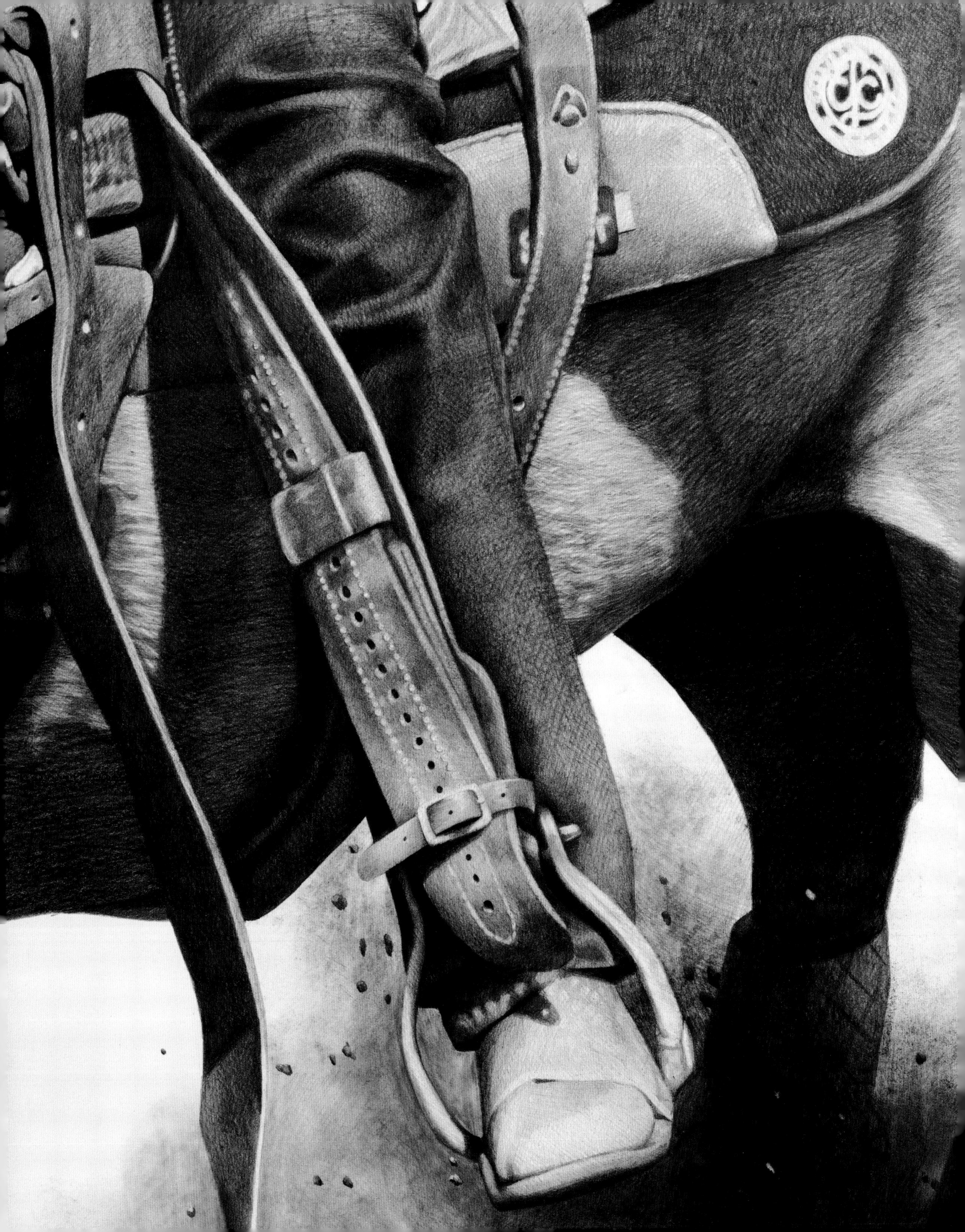

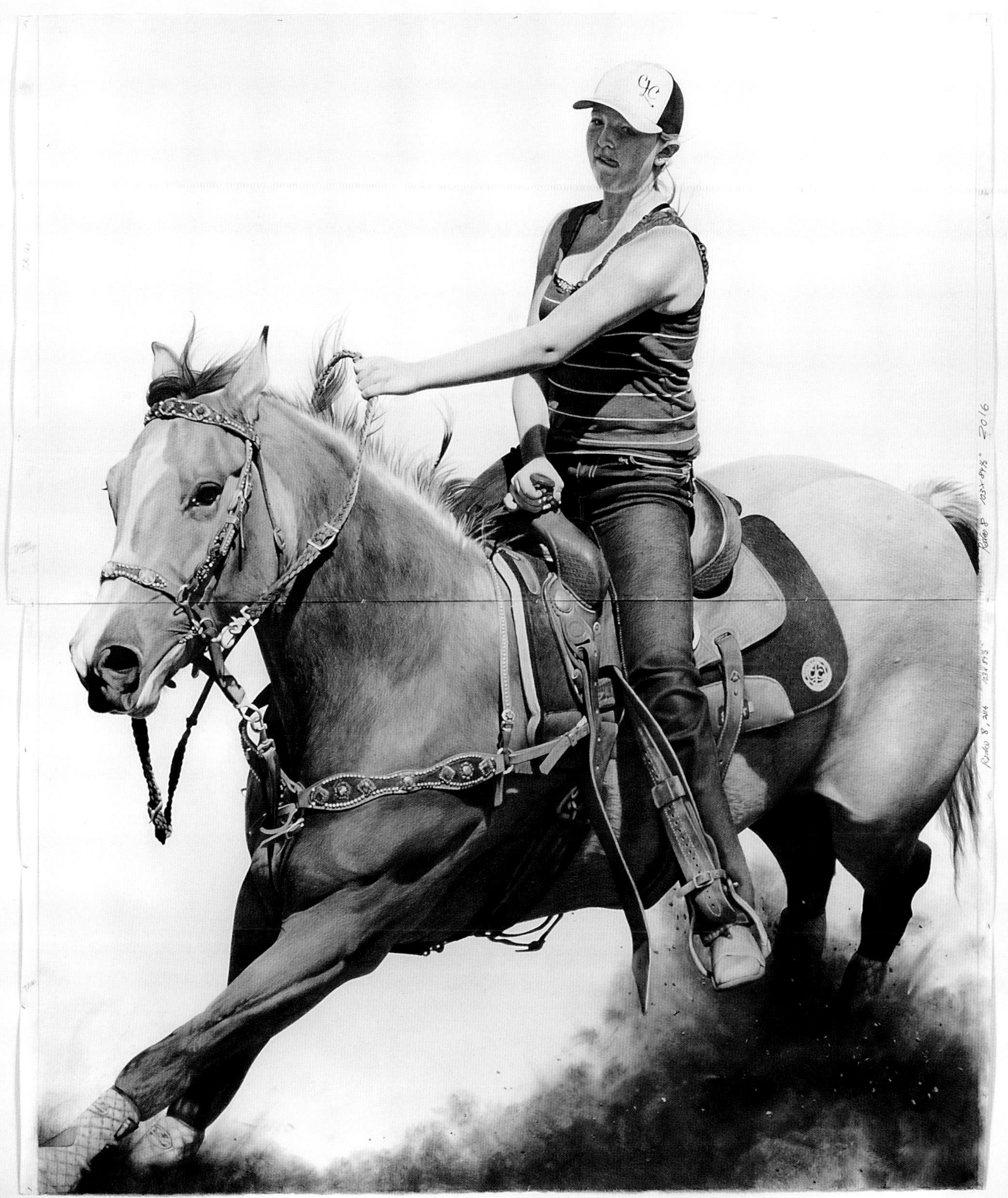

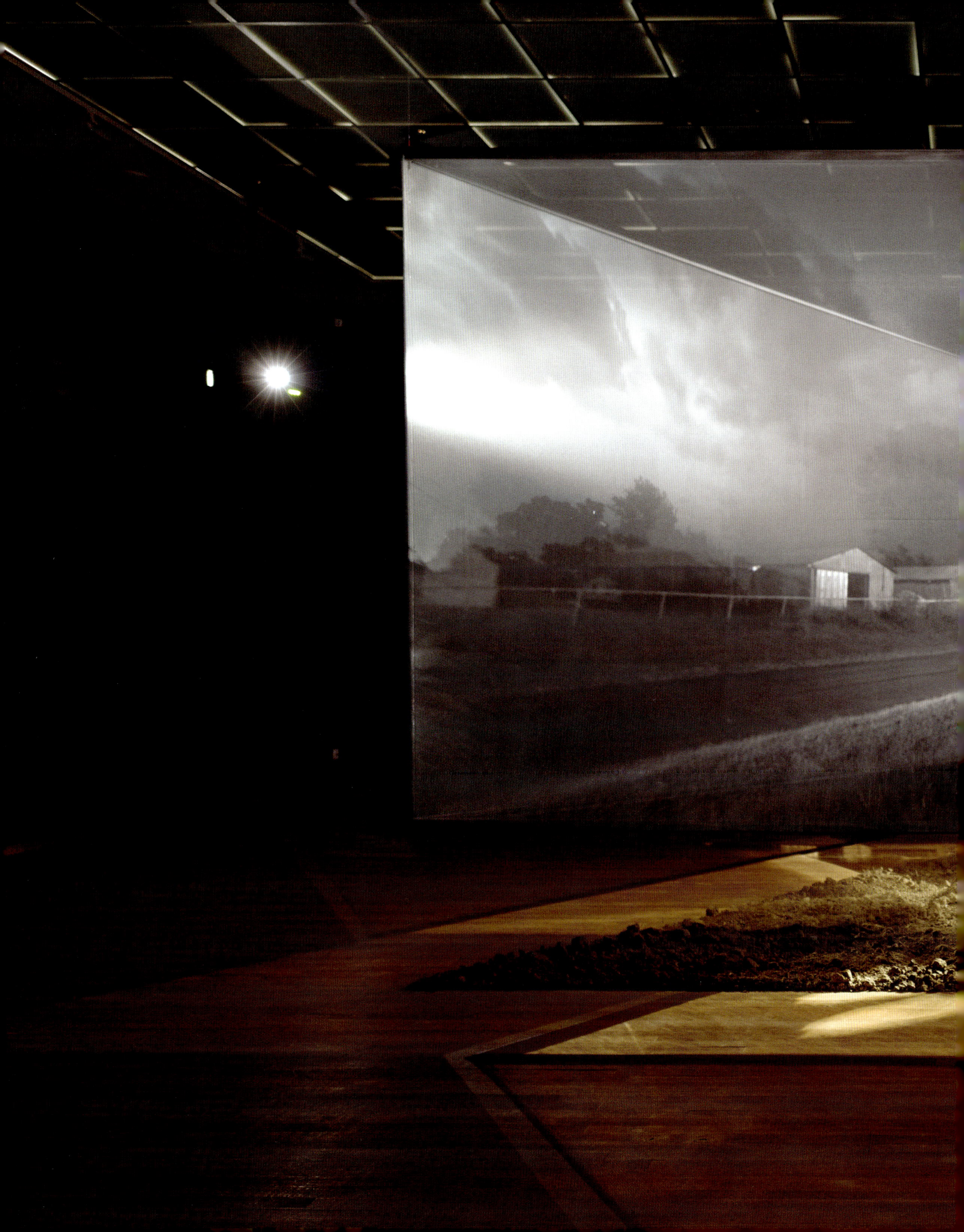

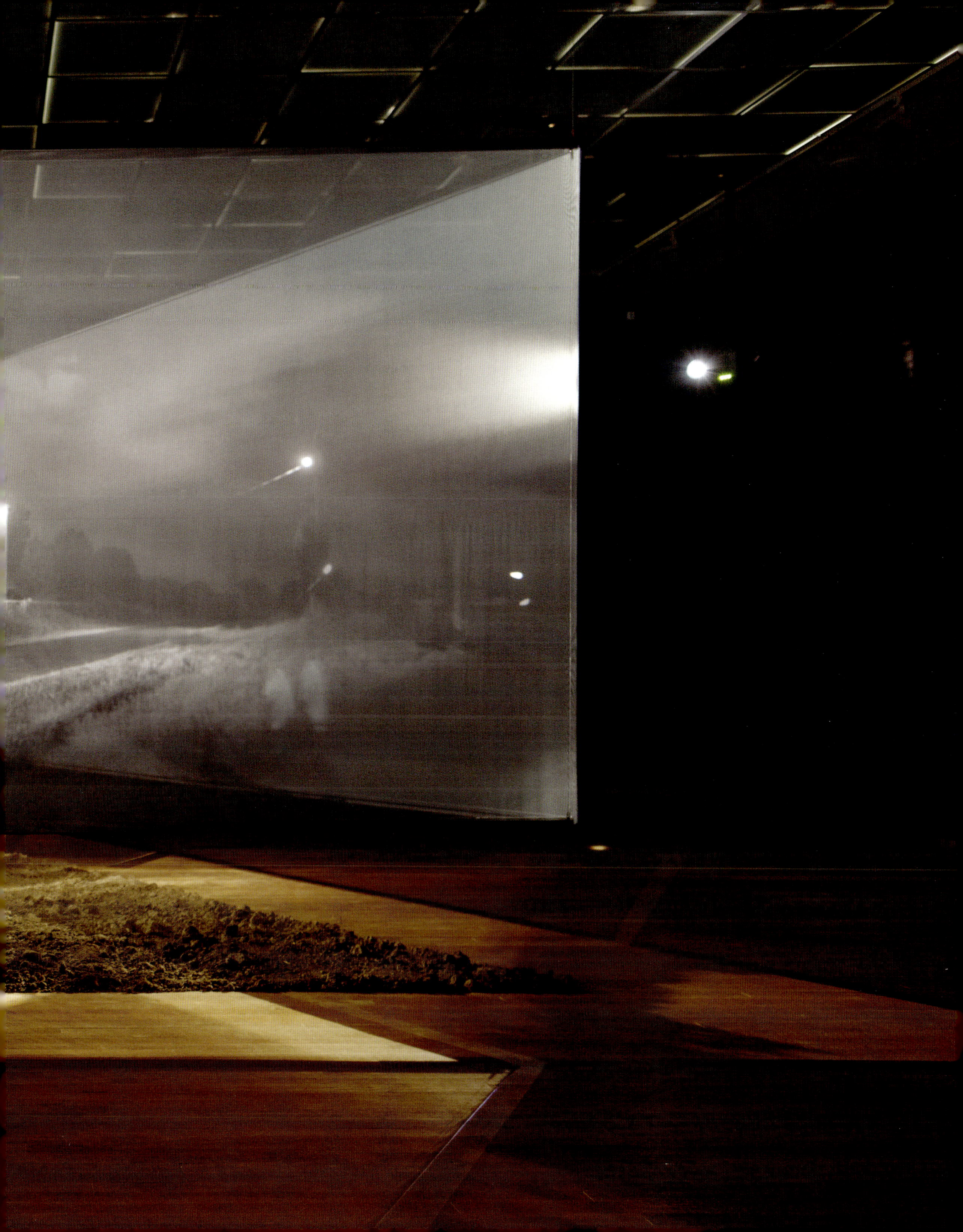

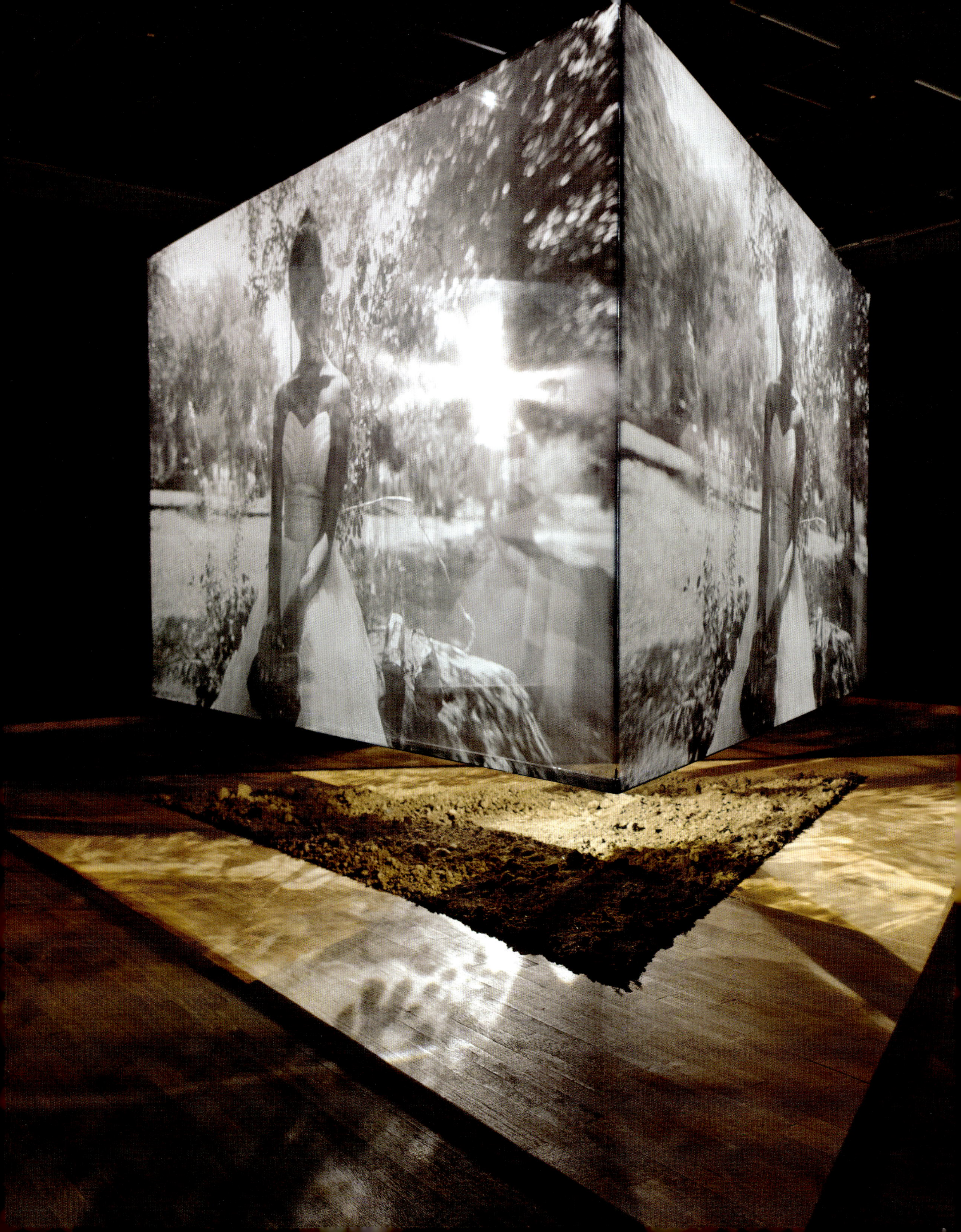

Previous pages, left, and following pages: Kahlil Joseph, WILD CAT (AUNT JANET), 2016. Installation view, The Bonnefanten, Maastricht. Three channel video. Duration: 7:53 minutes. Collection of the Bonnefanten

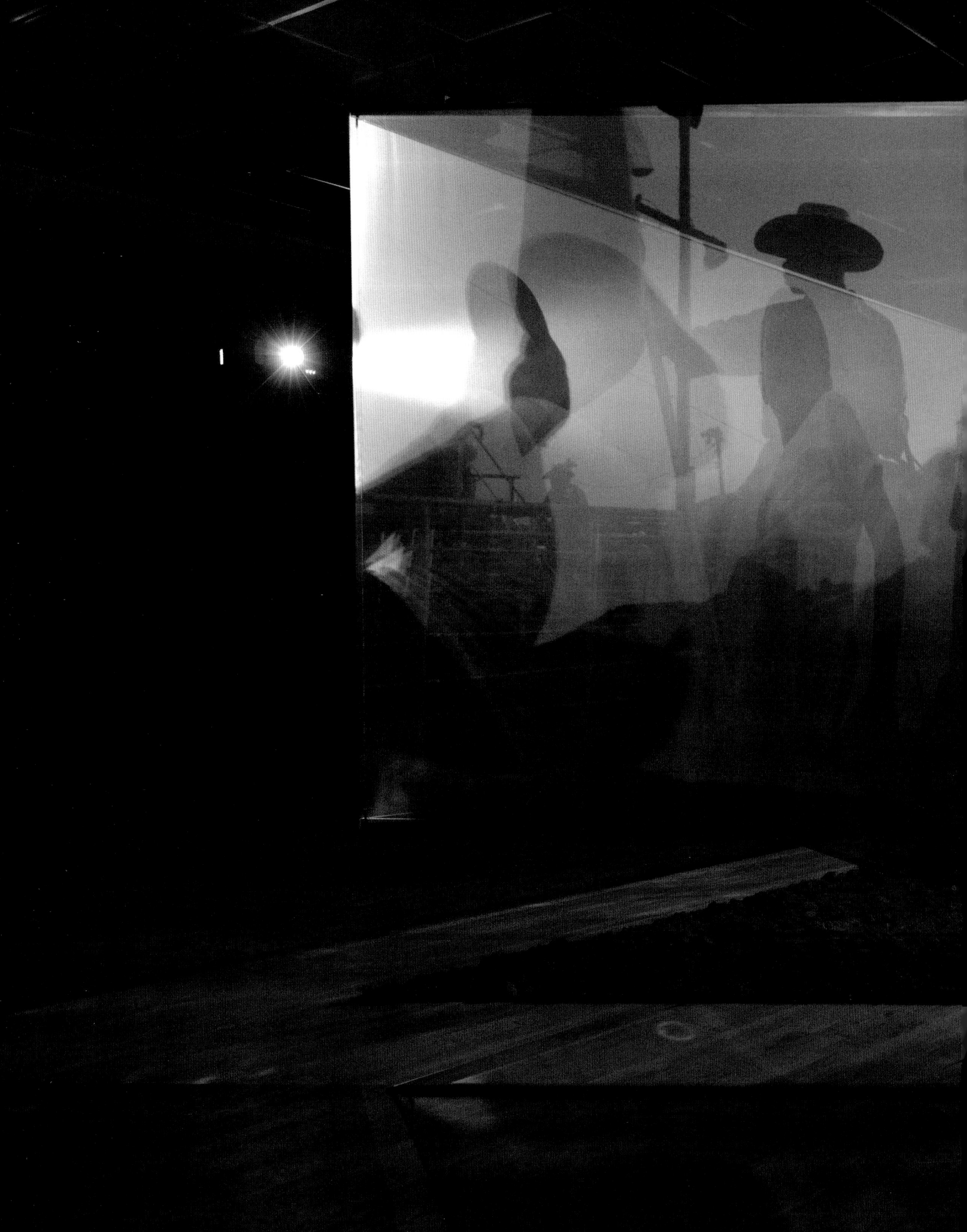

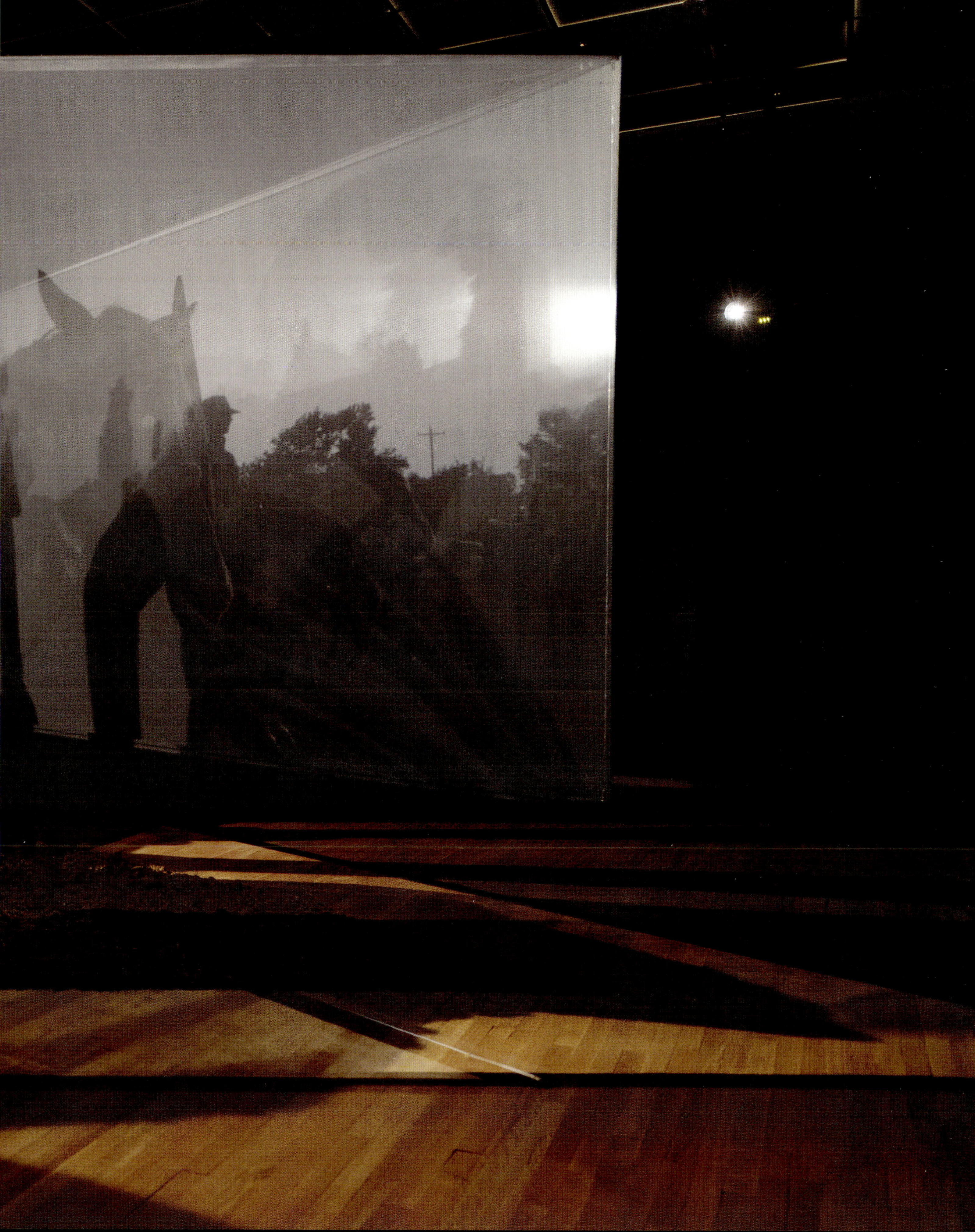

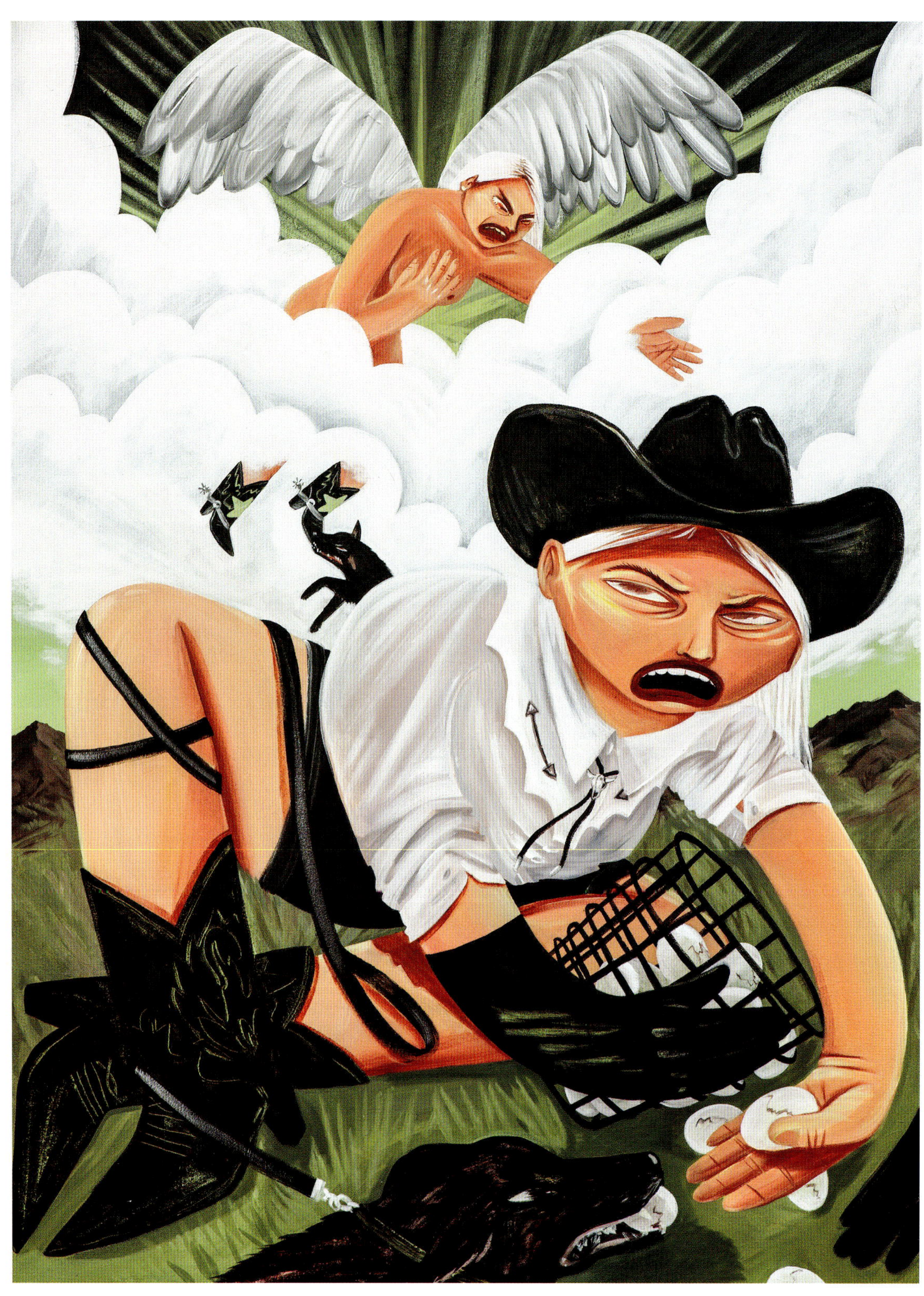

Grace Kennison, NO MEMORY IS EVER ALONE, 2021.
Acrylic on canvas. 48 x 36 inches. Collection of Junkuan Zhuang

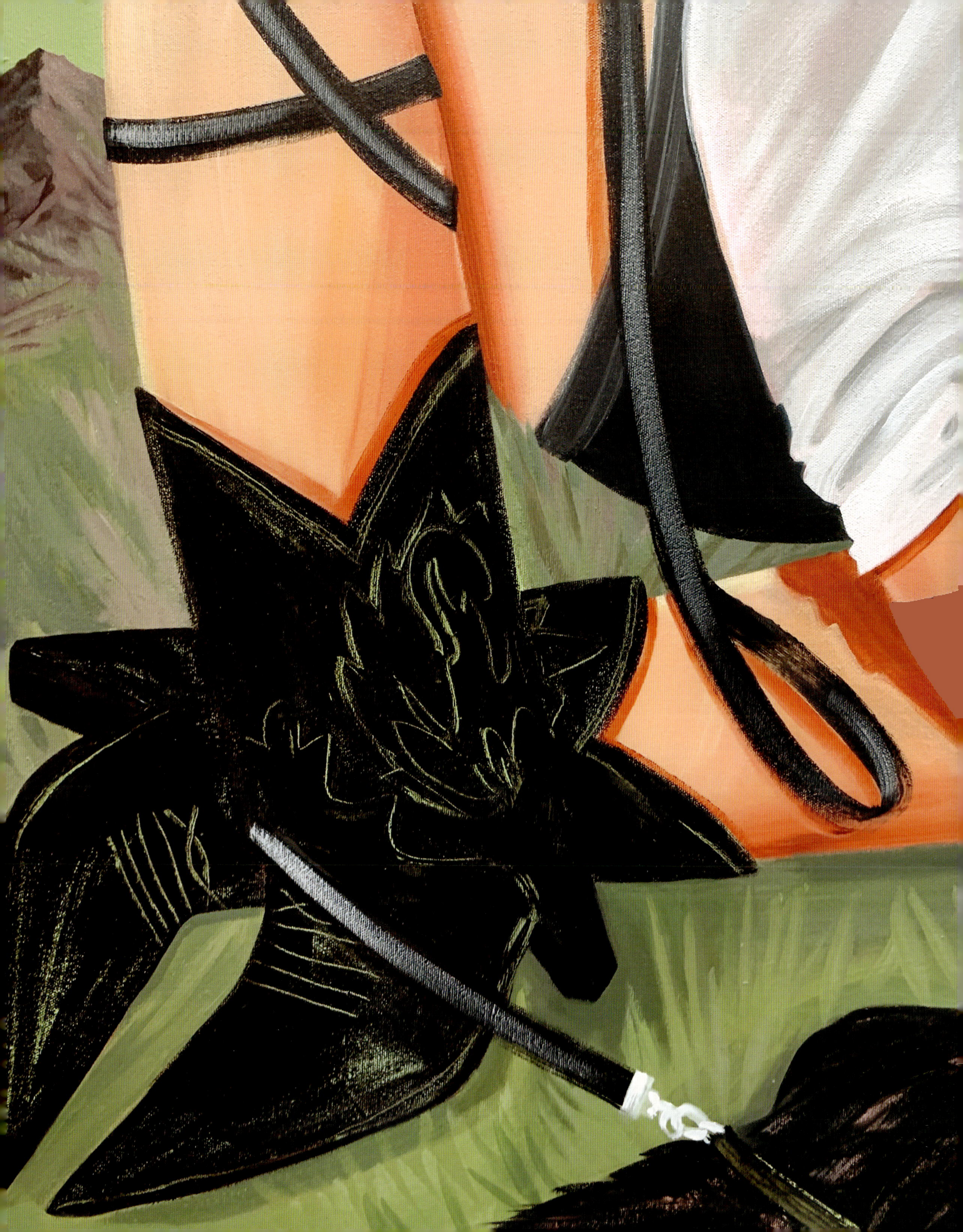

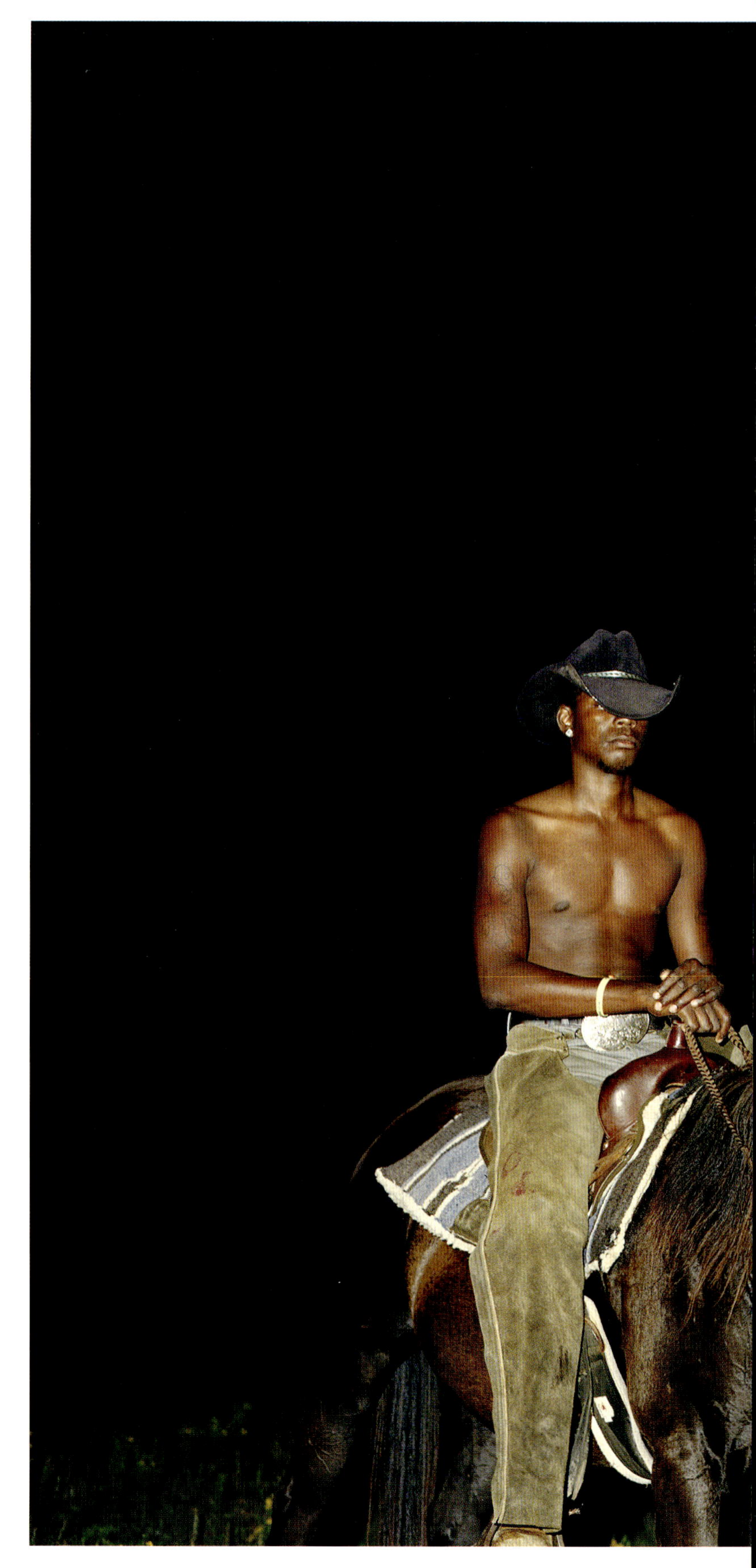

Deana Lawson, COWBOYS, 2014.
Pigment print. 40 x 50 inches

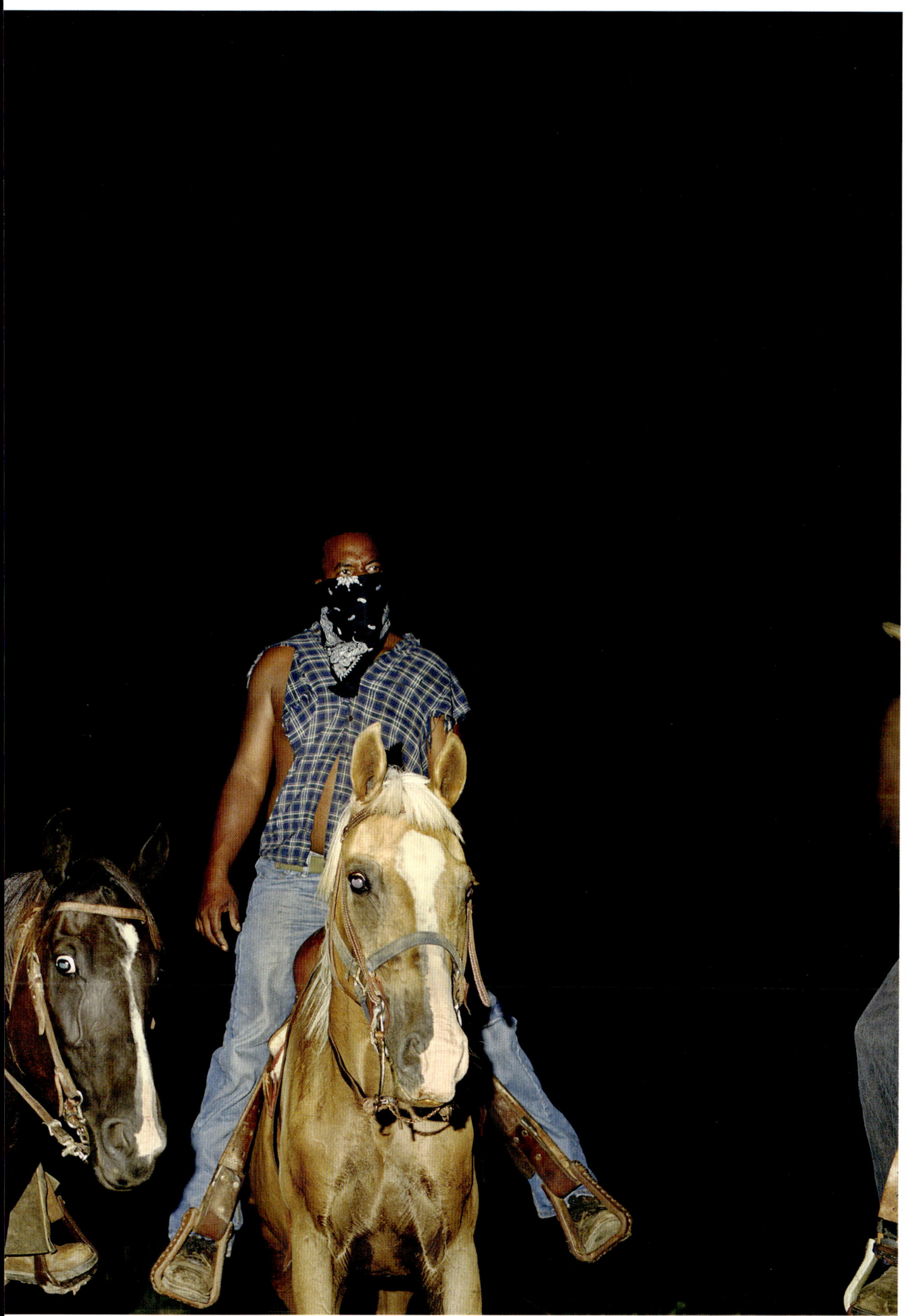

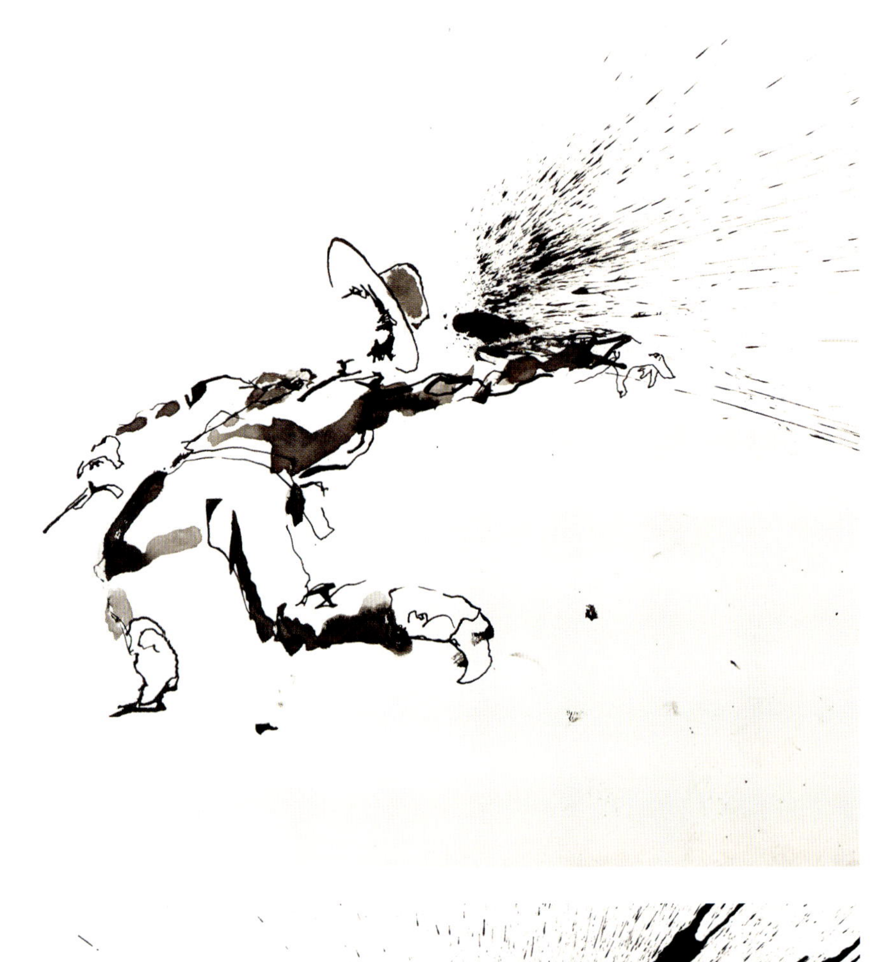

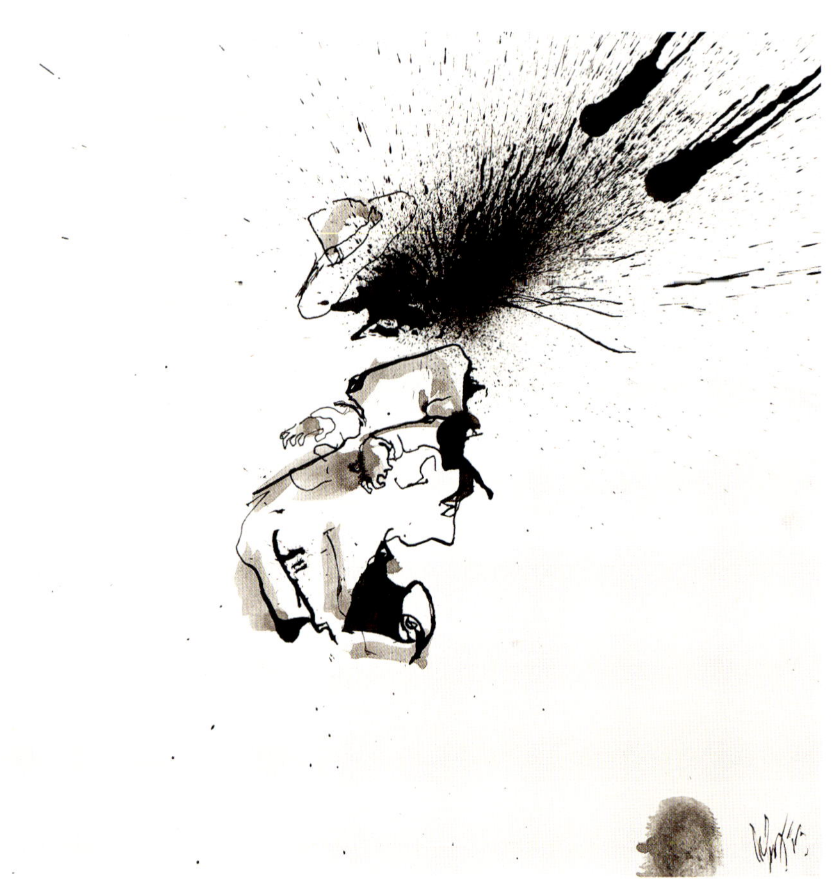

All works on pages 132–37: Matthew J. Mahoney, UNTITLED, 2013, from the series IN THE WAKE OF JOHN JOEL GLANTON. Ink on paper. 9 x 12 inches

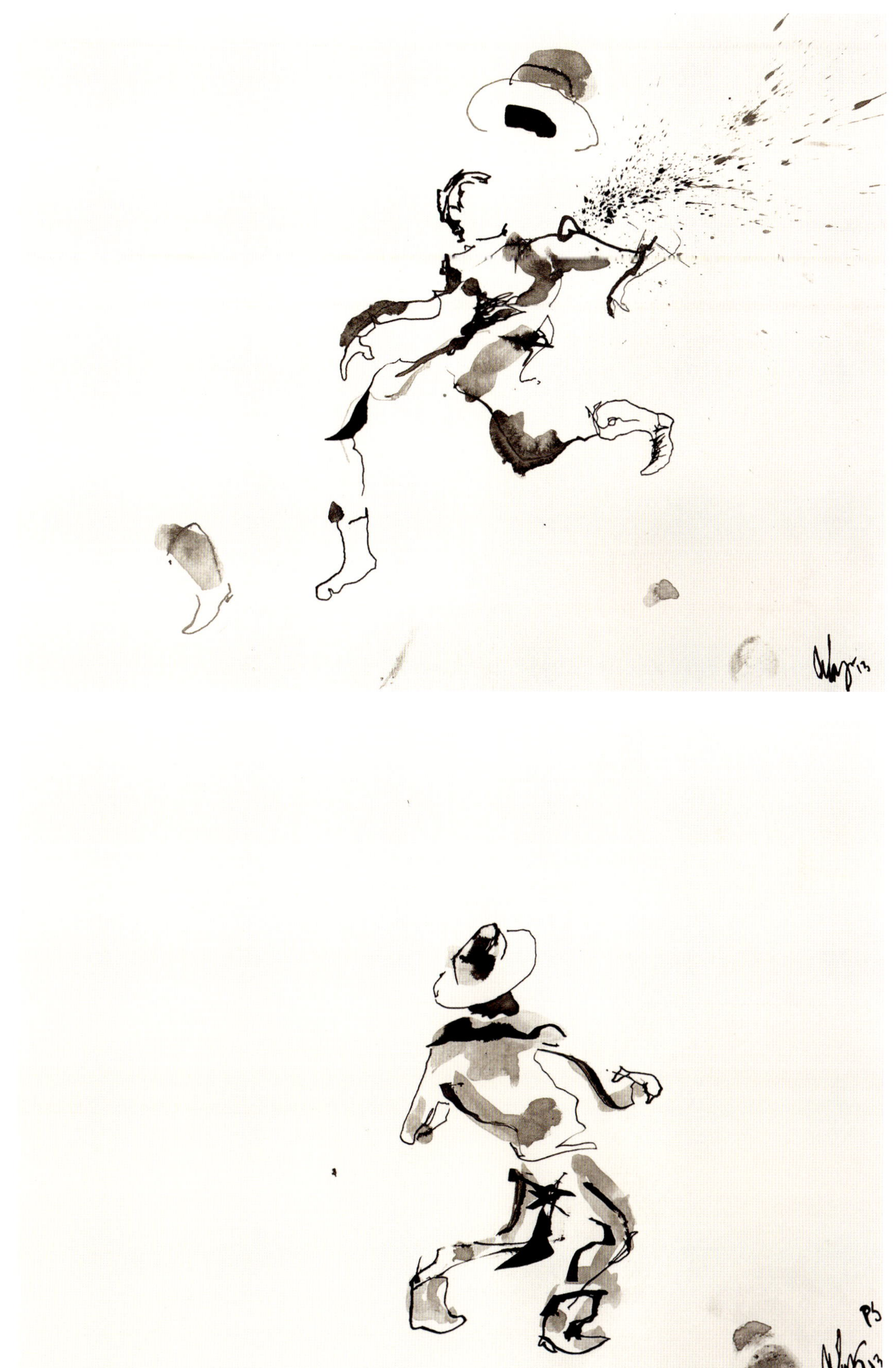

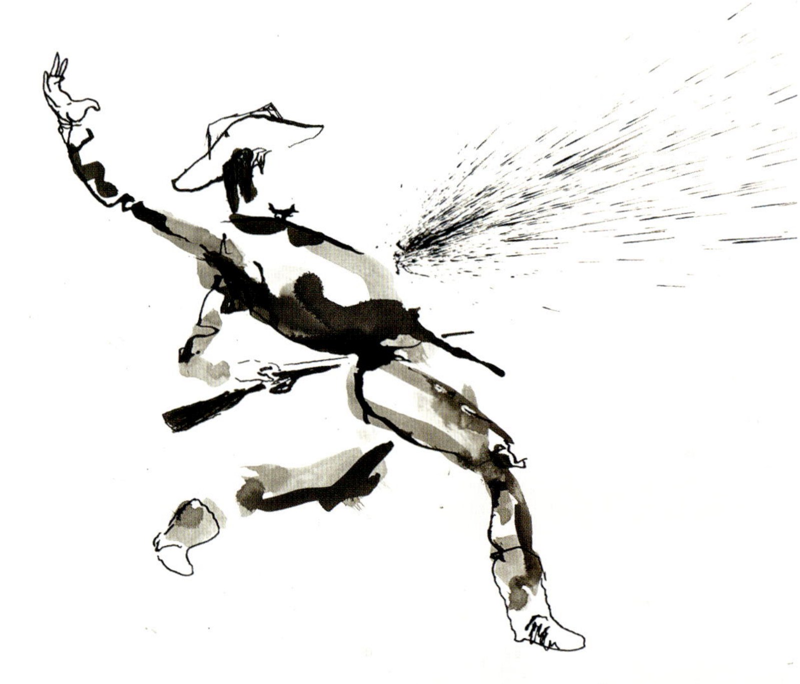

"In the Wake of John Joel Glanton"

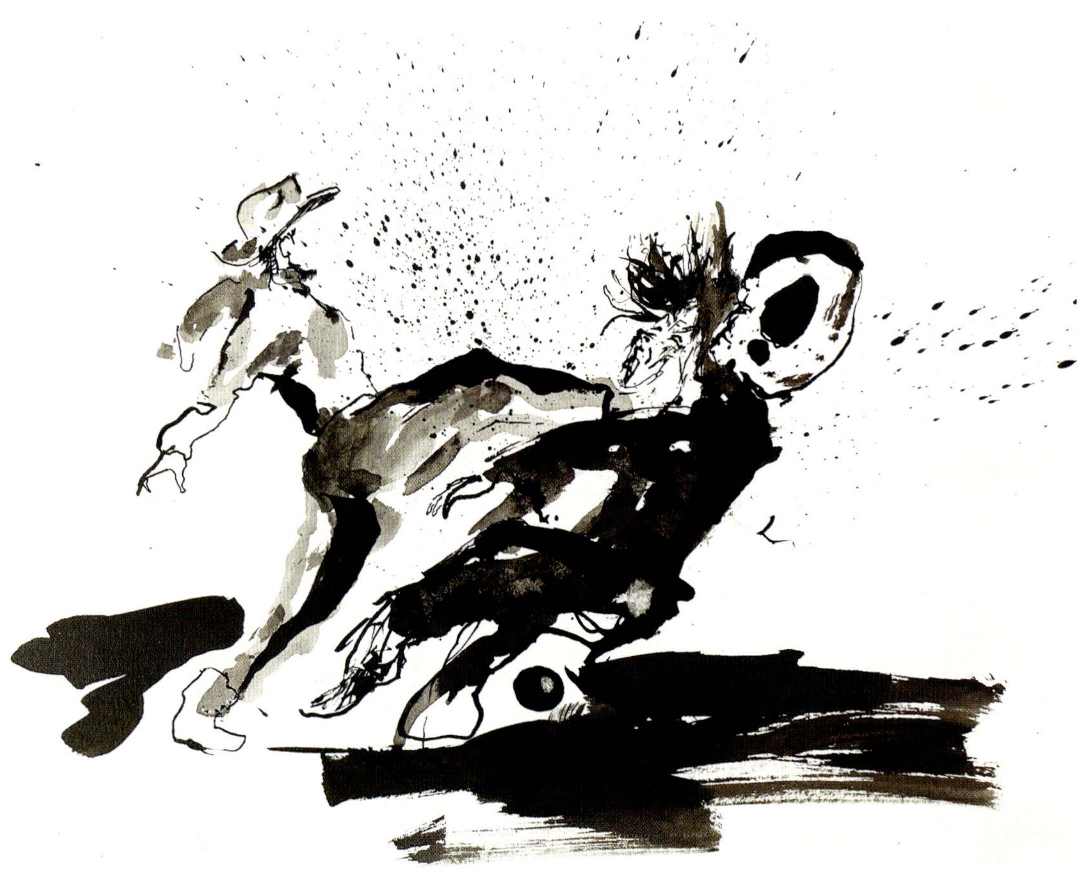

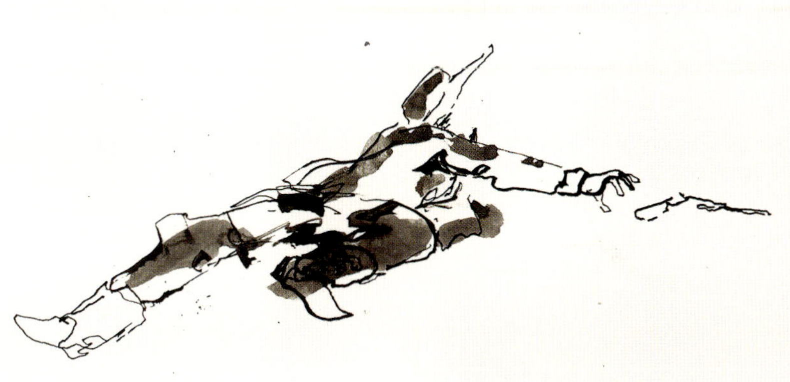

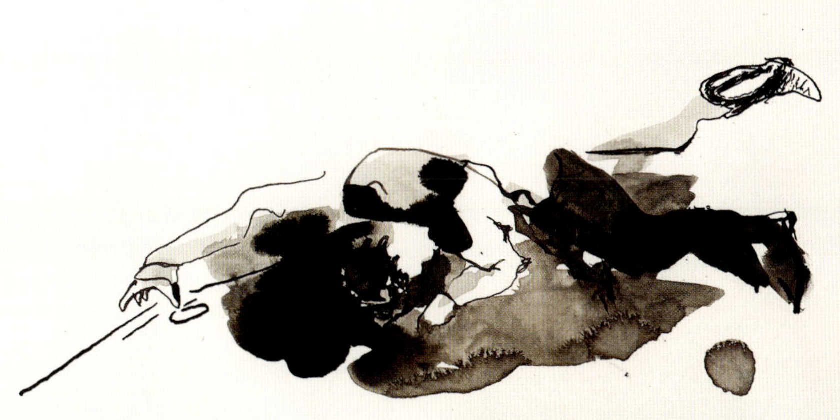

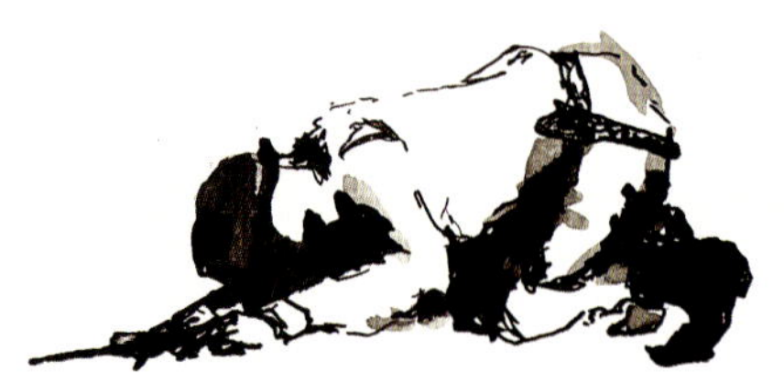

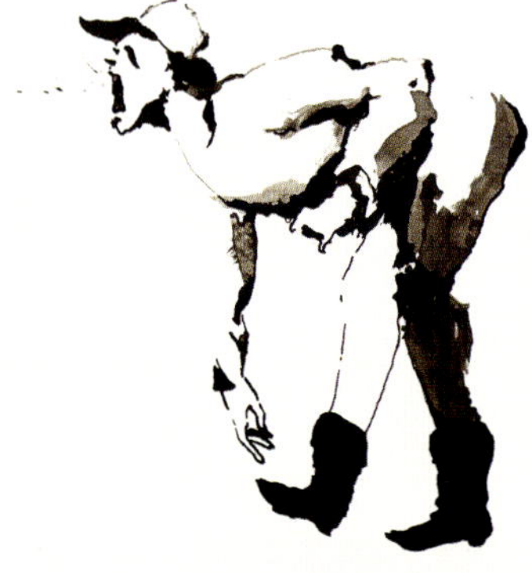

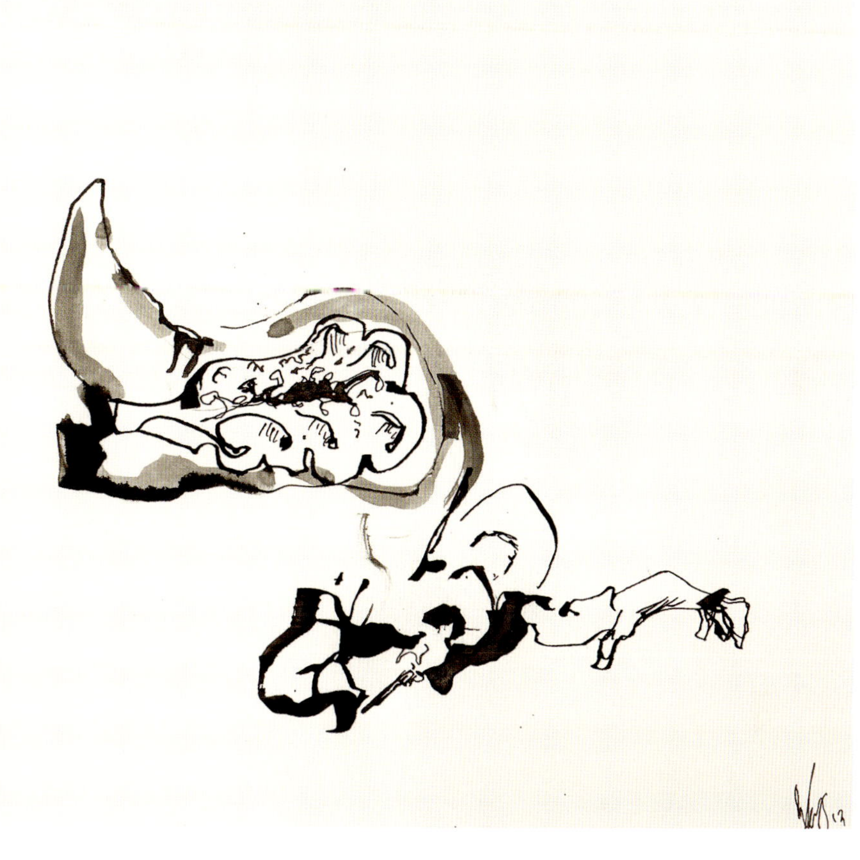

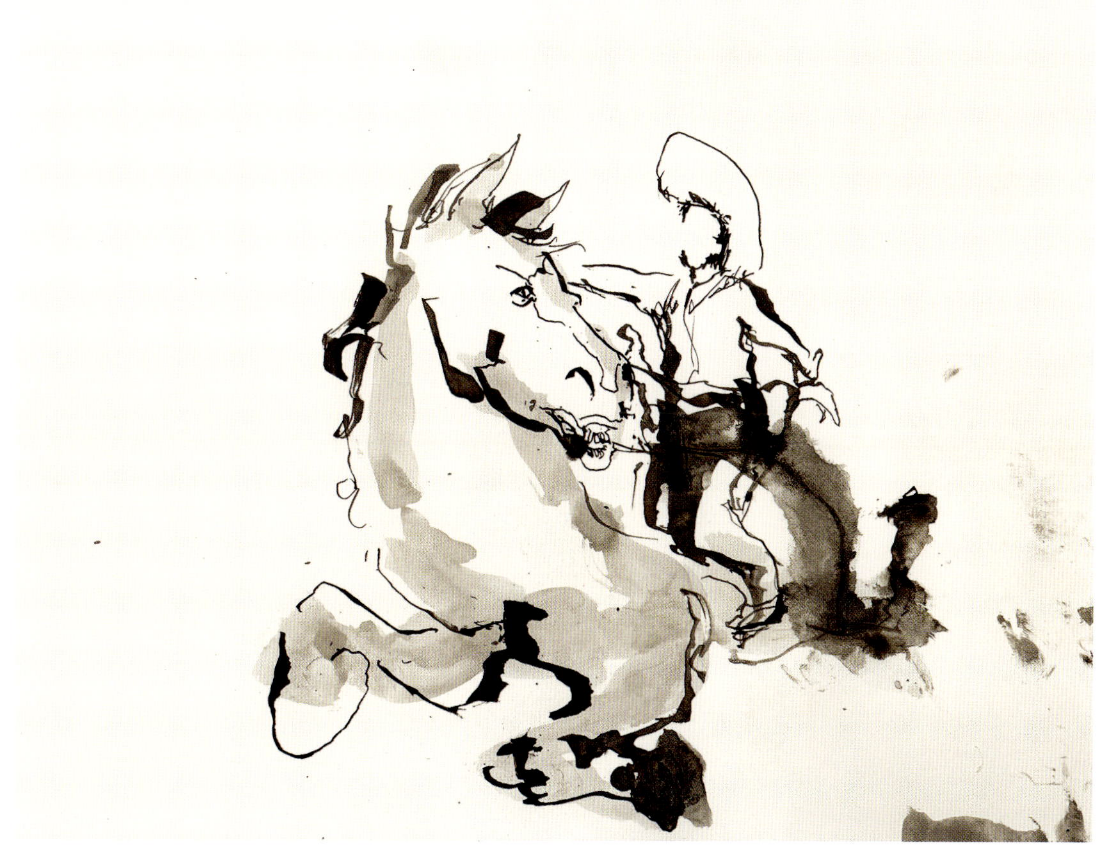

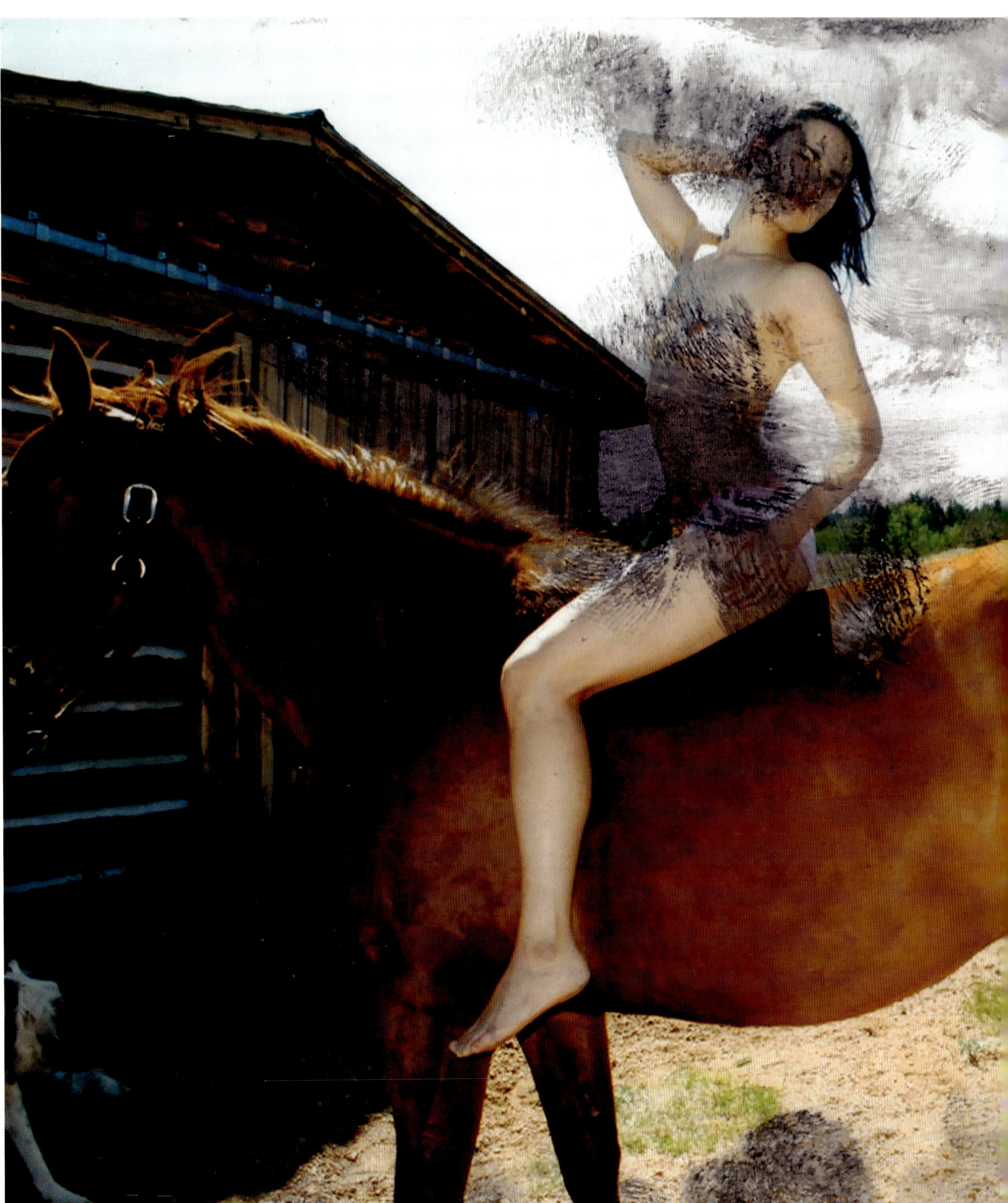

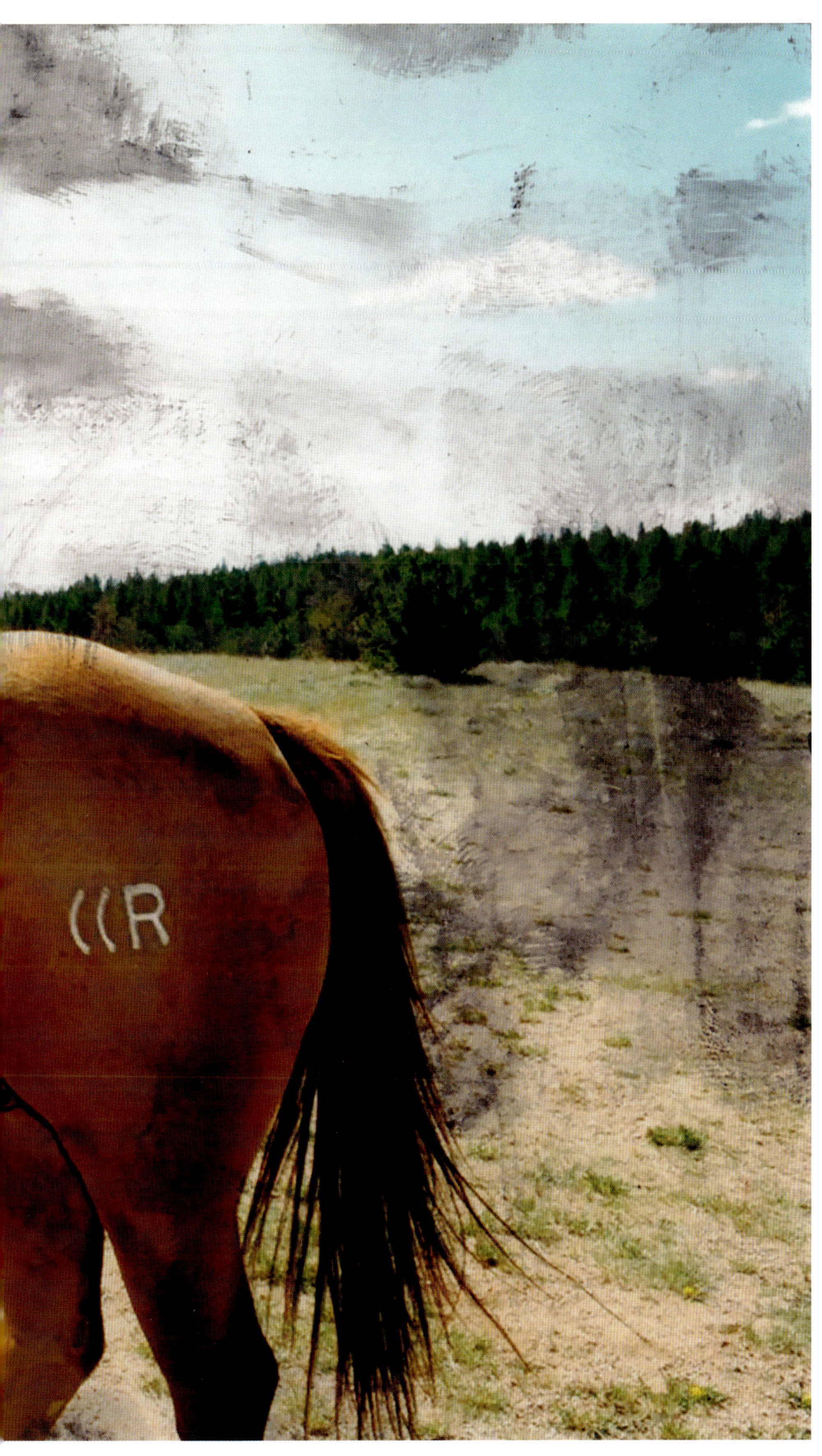

Laurel Nakadate,
LUCKY TIGER #47, 2009.
Type-C print and
fingerprinting ink.
4 x 6 inches

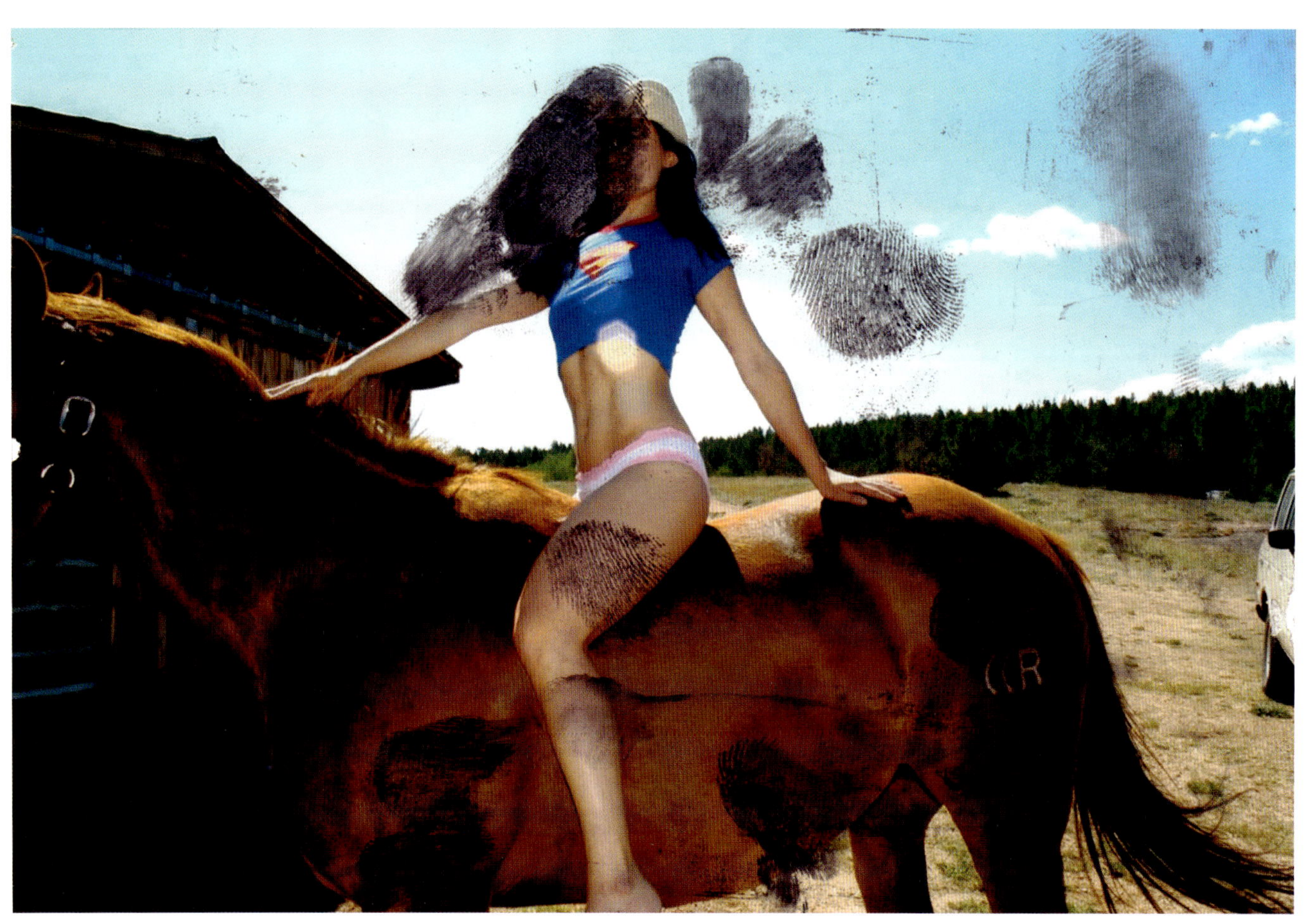

Laurel Nakadate, LUCKY TIGER #20, 2009.
Type-C print and fingerprinting ink. 4 x 6 inches

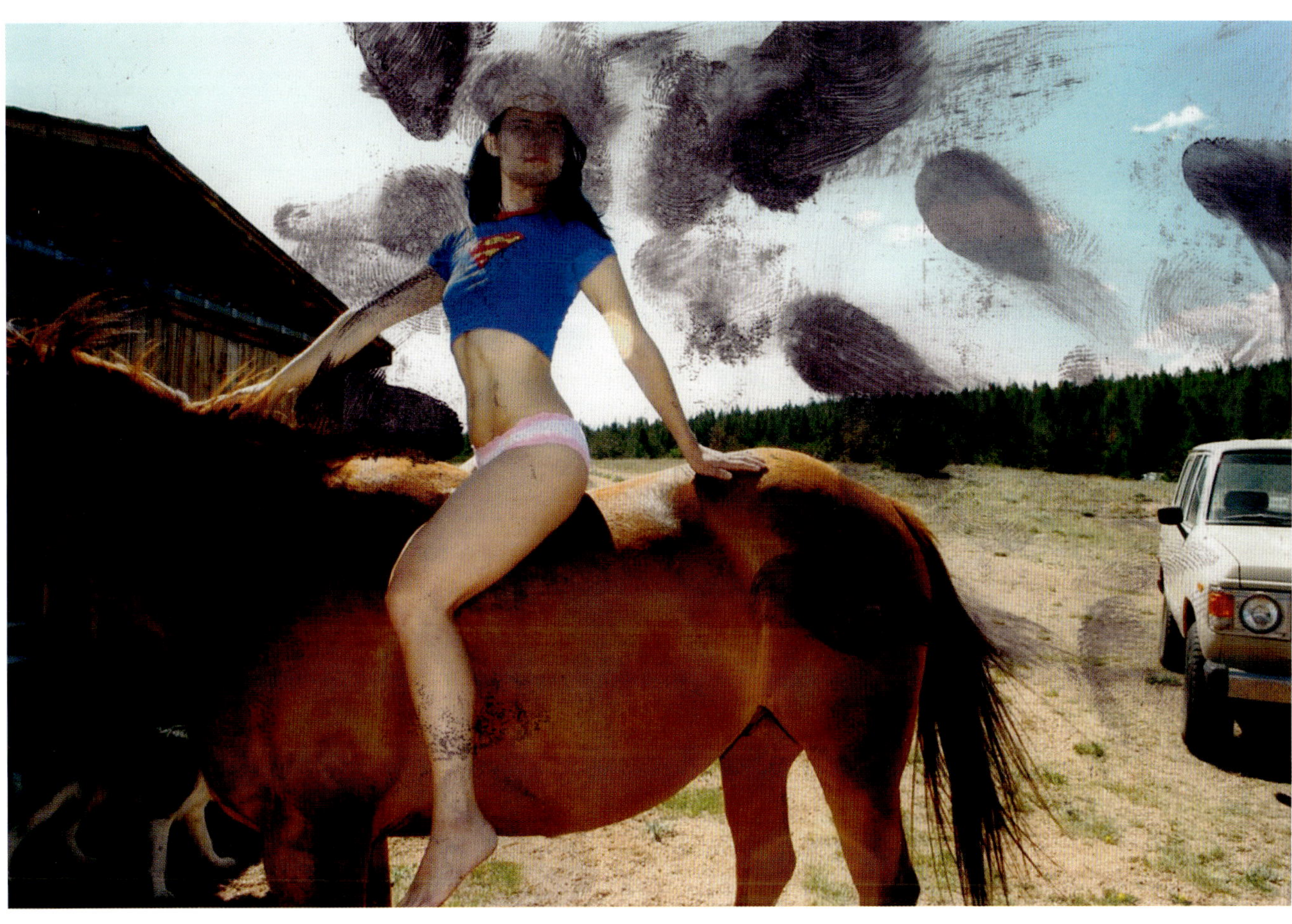

Laurel Nakadate, LUCKY TIGER #48, 2009.
Type-C print and fingerprinting ink. 4 x 6 inches

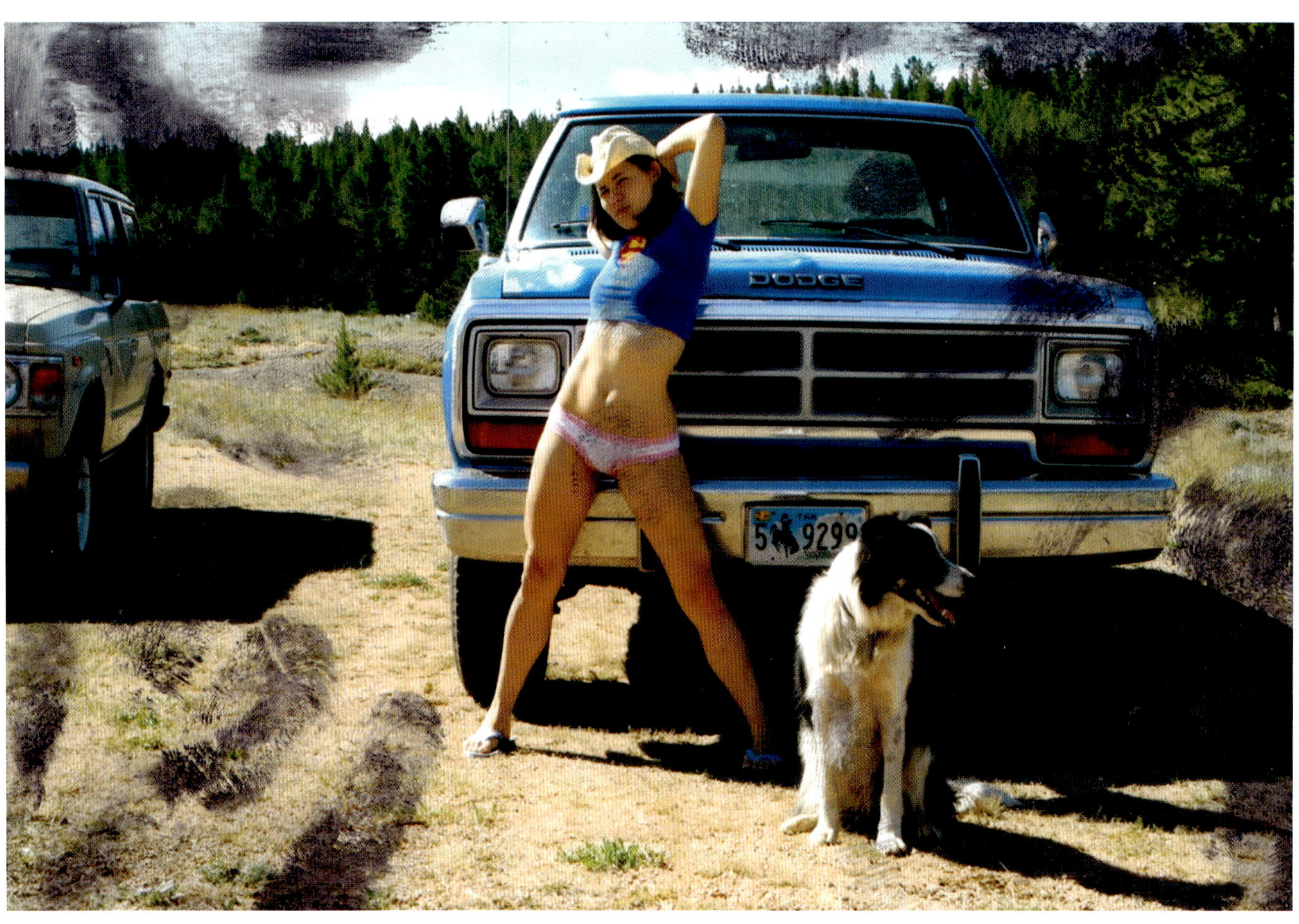

Laurel Nakadate, LUCKY TIGER #140, 2009.
Type-C print and fingerprinting ink. 4 x 6 inches.
Collection of Leslie Tonkonow and Klaus Ottmann

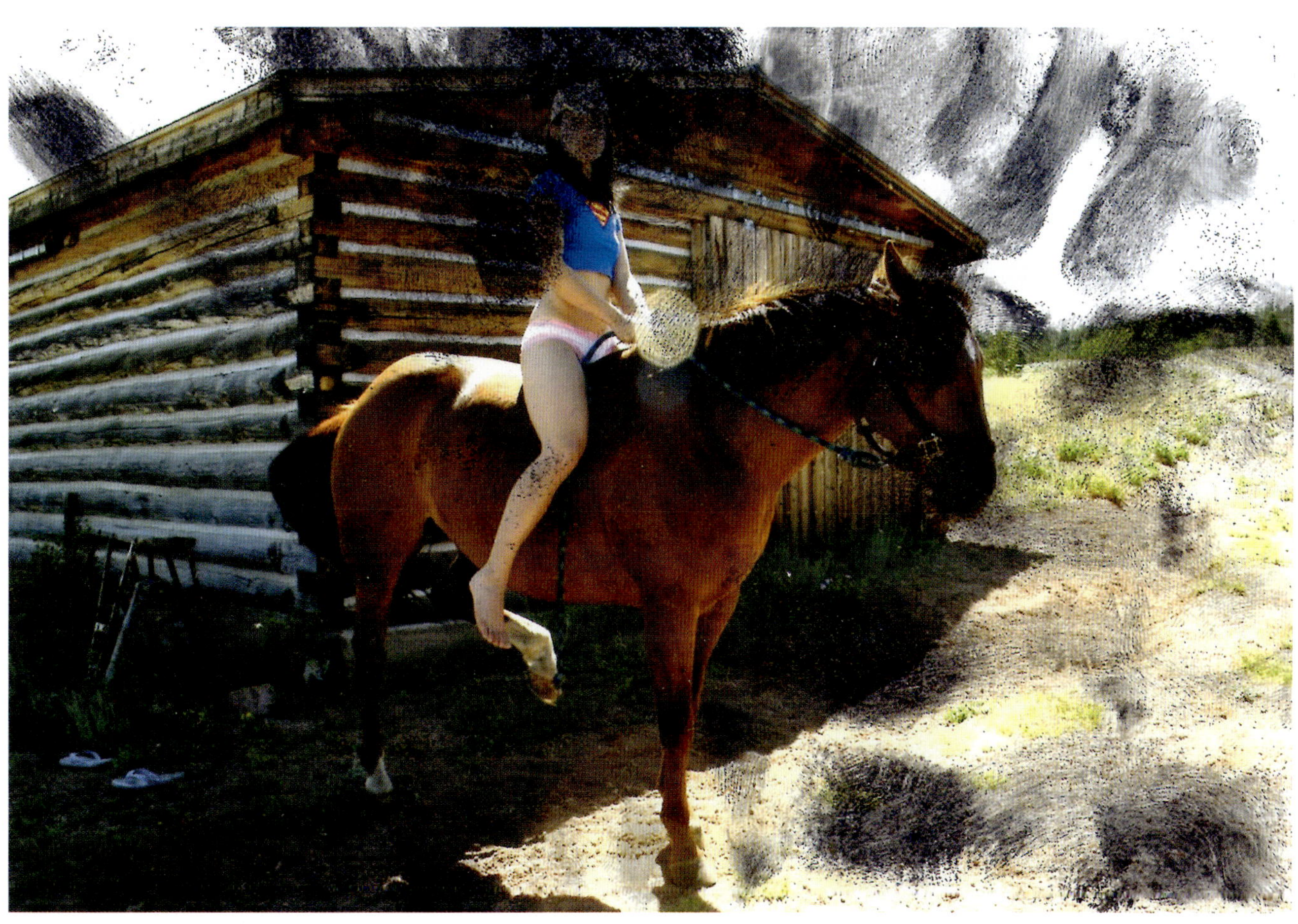

Laurel Nakadate, LUCKY TIGER #203, 2009.
Type-C print and fingerprinting ink. 4 x 6 inches

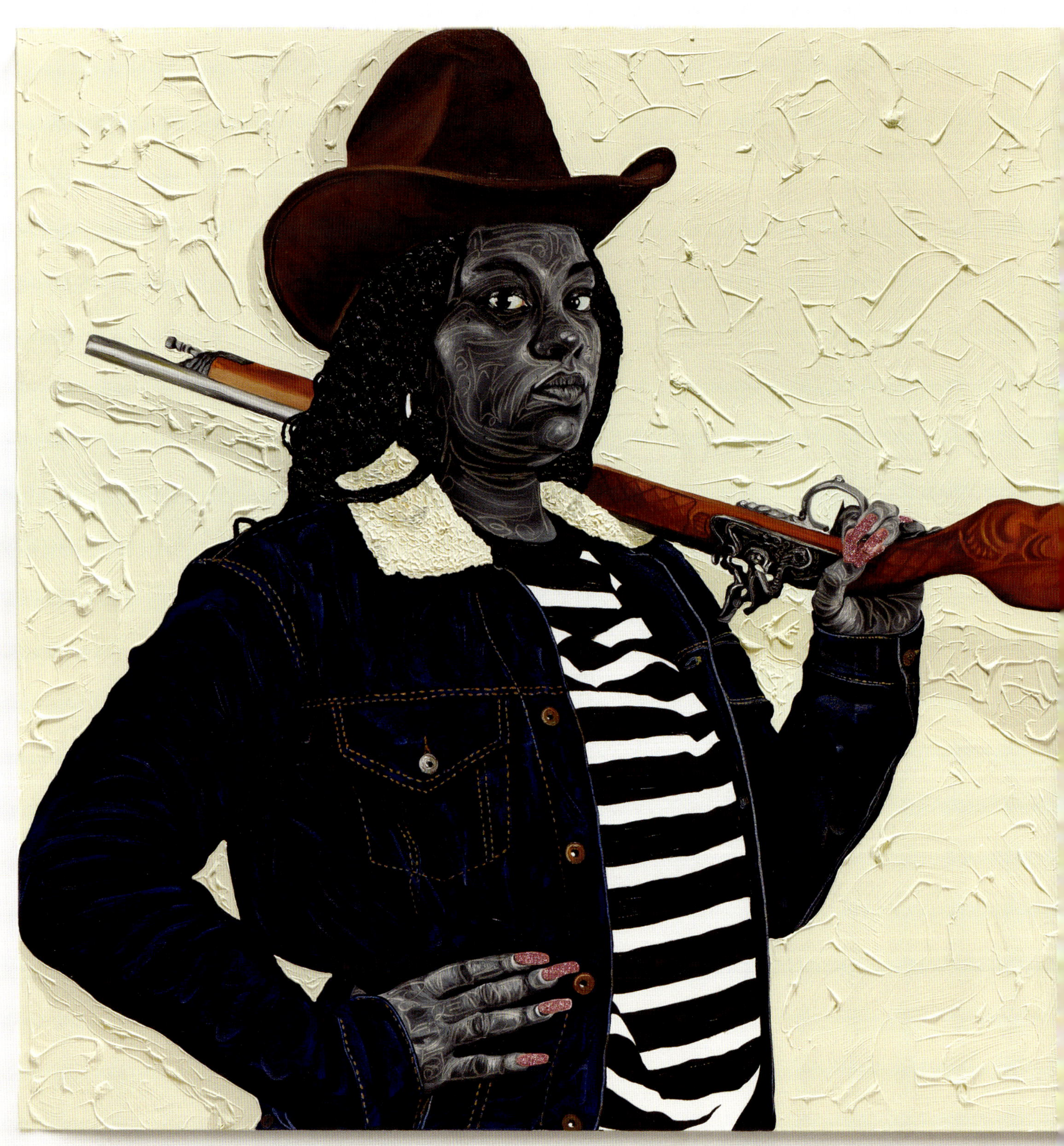

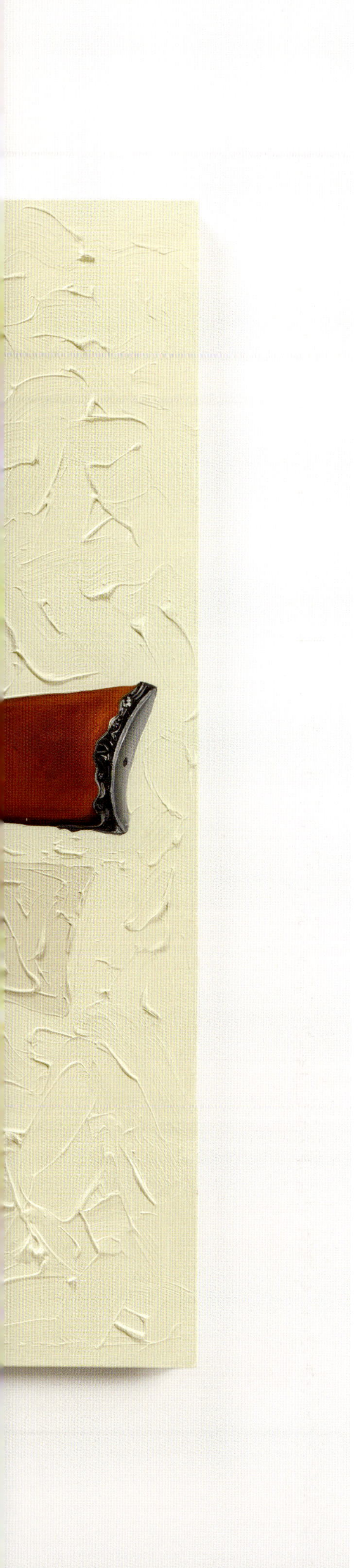

Opposite: Otis Kwame Quaicoe, OLIVIA, 2021.
Oil and glitter on canvas. 60 x 72 inches

Following pages: Otis Kwame Quaicoe, RODEO BOYS, 2022.
Oil and fabric appliqué on canvas. 84 x 54 inches.
Collection of Matthew and Melanie Bronfman

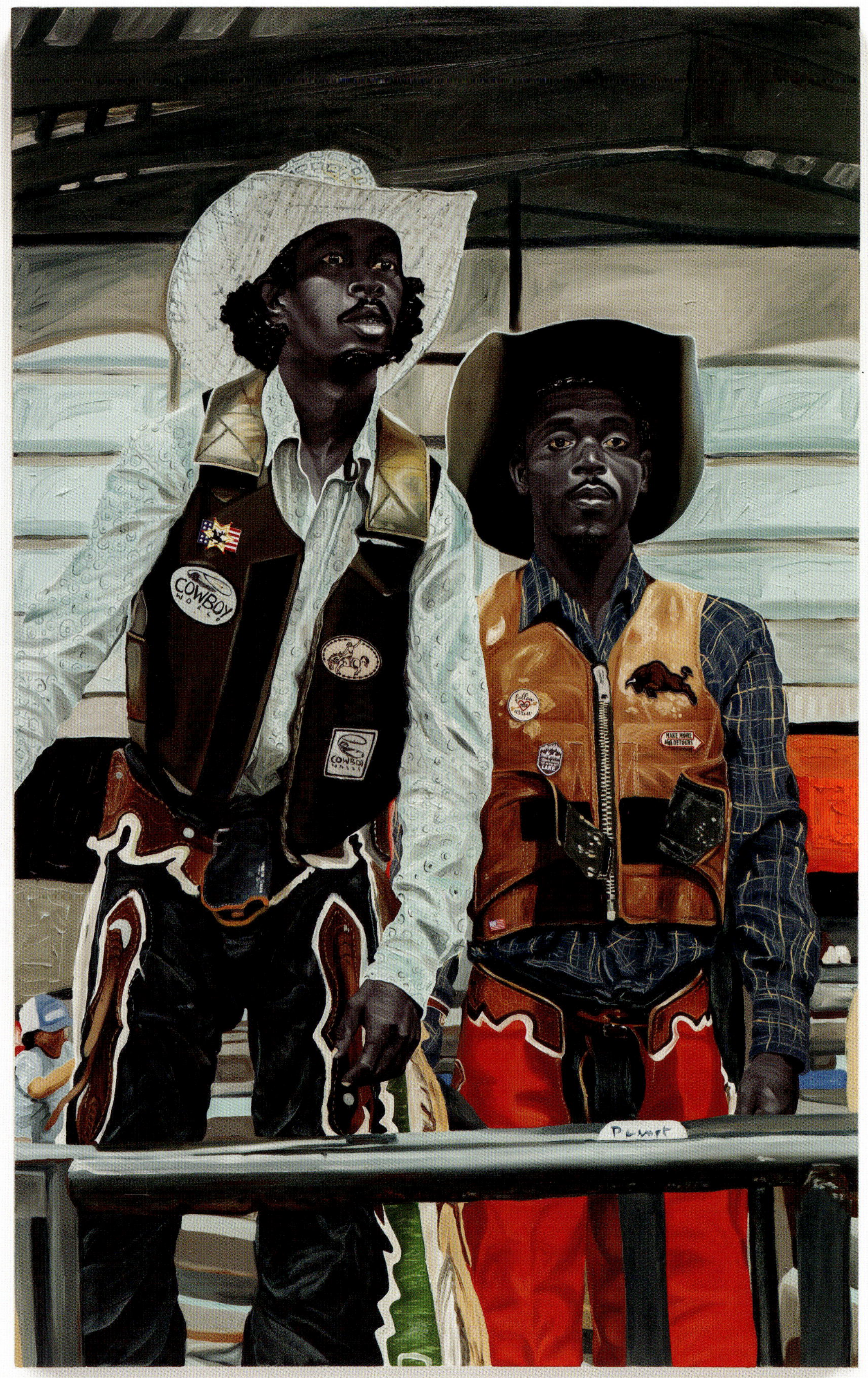
COWBOY

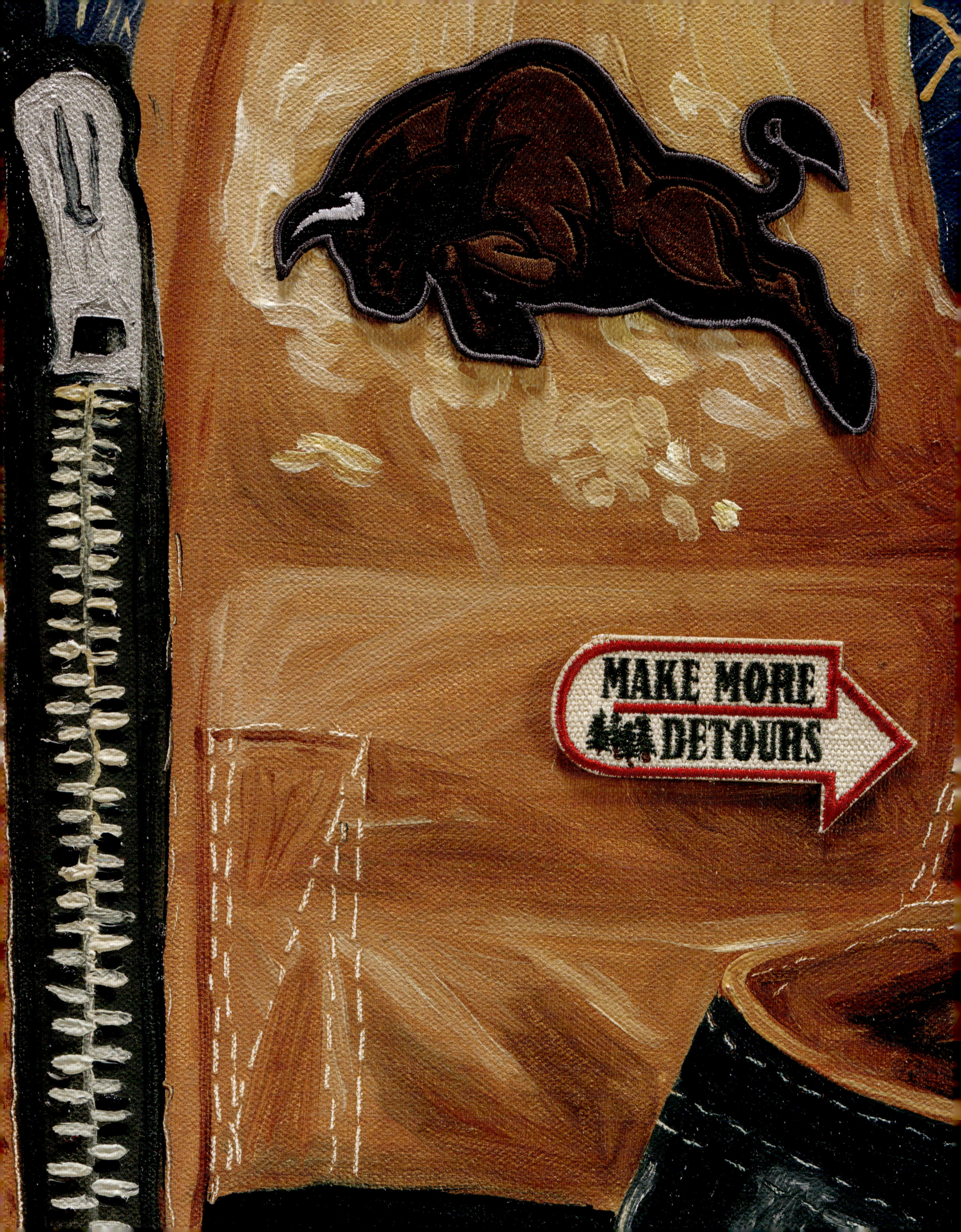
MAKE MORE
DETOURS

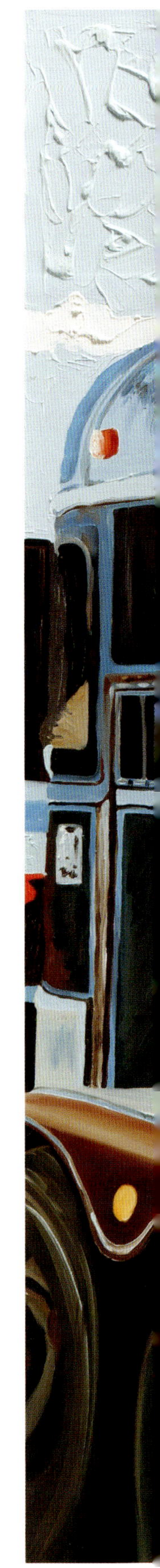

Otis Kwame Quaicoe, DJANGO, 2021.
Oil and fabric appliqué on canvas. 72 x 72 inches

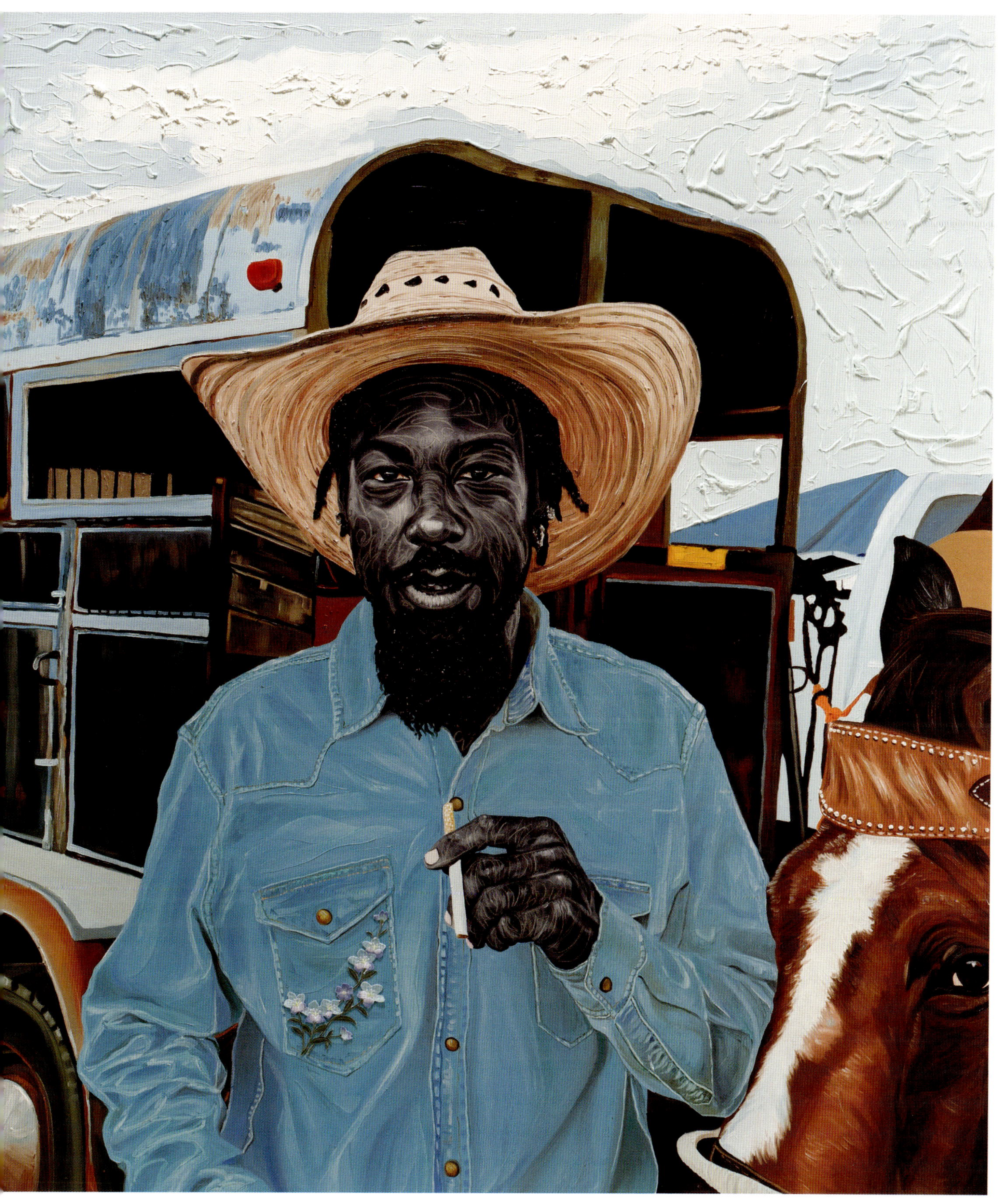

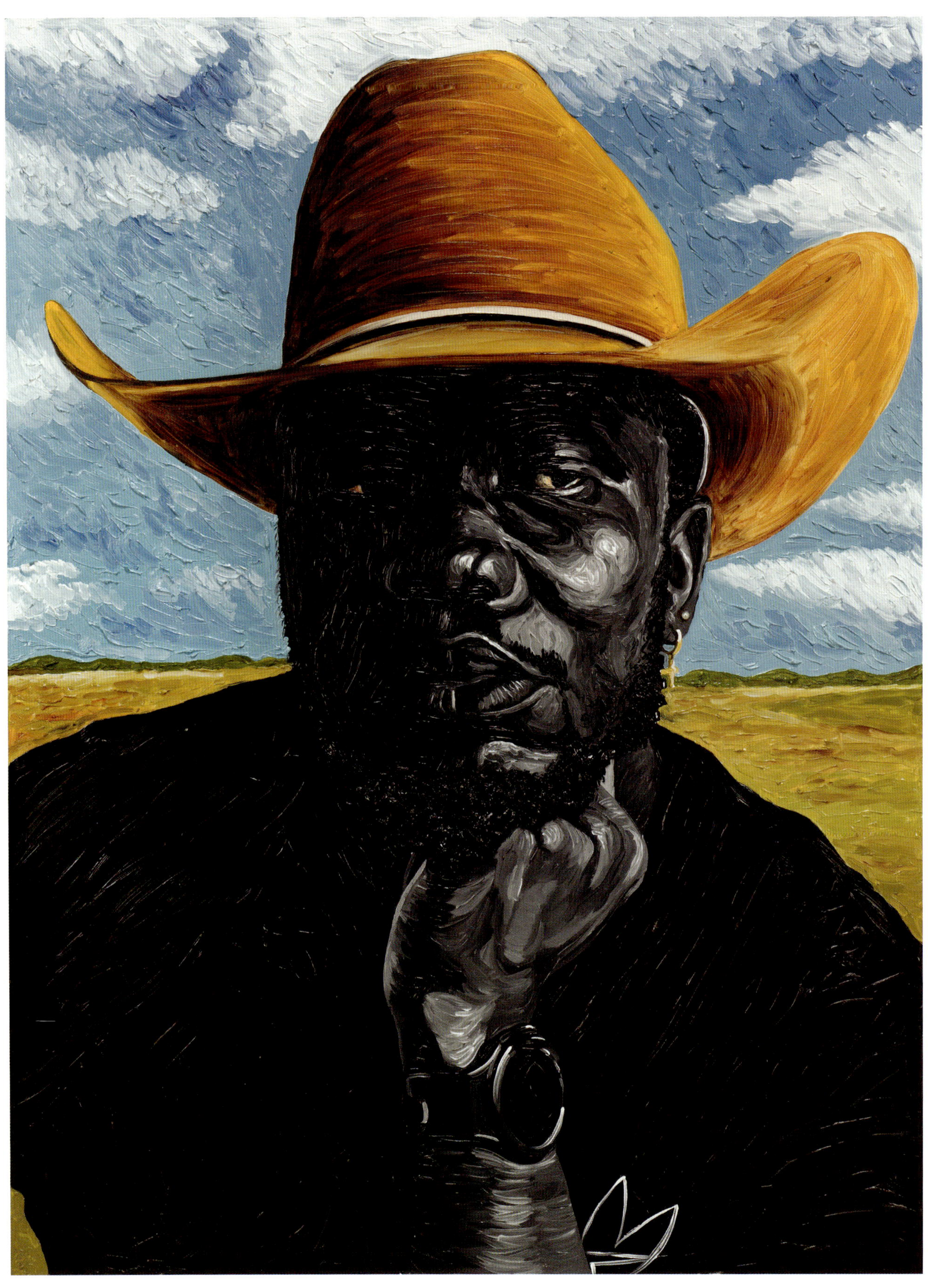

Otis Kwame Quaicoe, CAUGHT IN THE ACT, 2023.
Oil on wood panel. 48 x 36 Inches

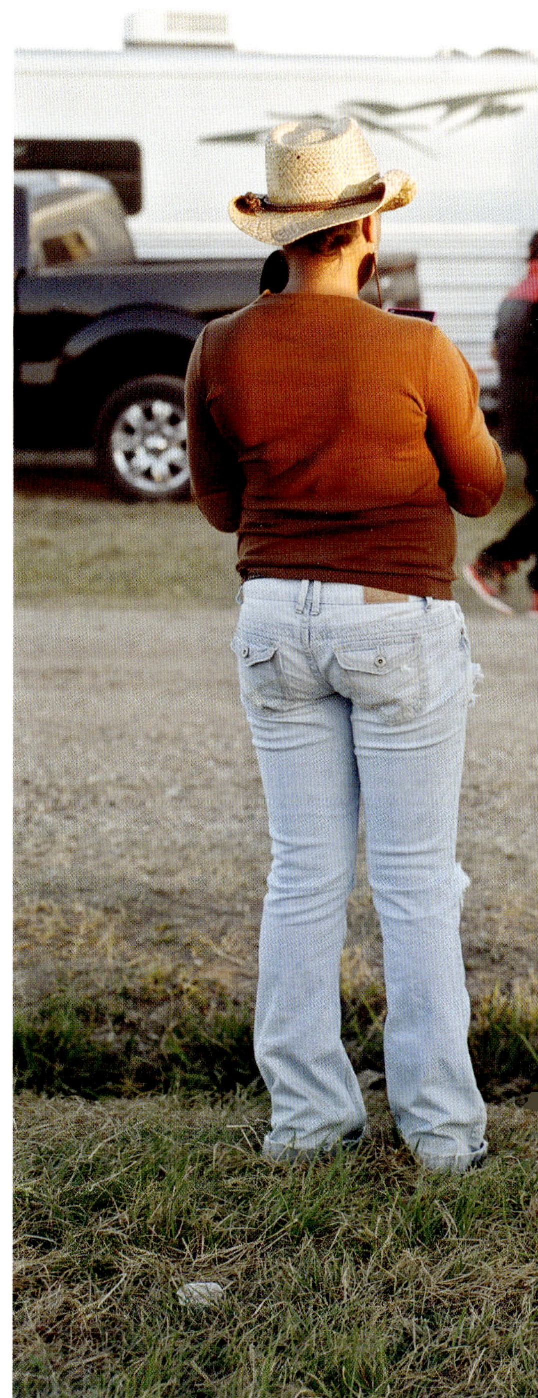

Akasha Rabut, WAITING AT SUNSET, 2014.
Archival digital print mounted to matboard. 24 x 28 inches

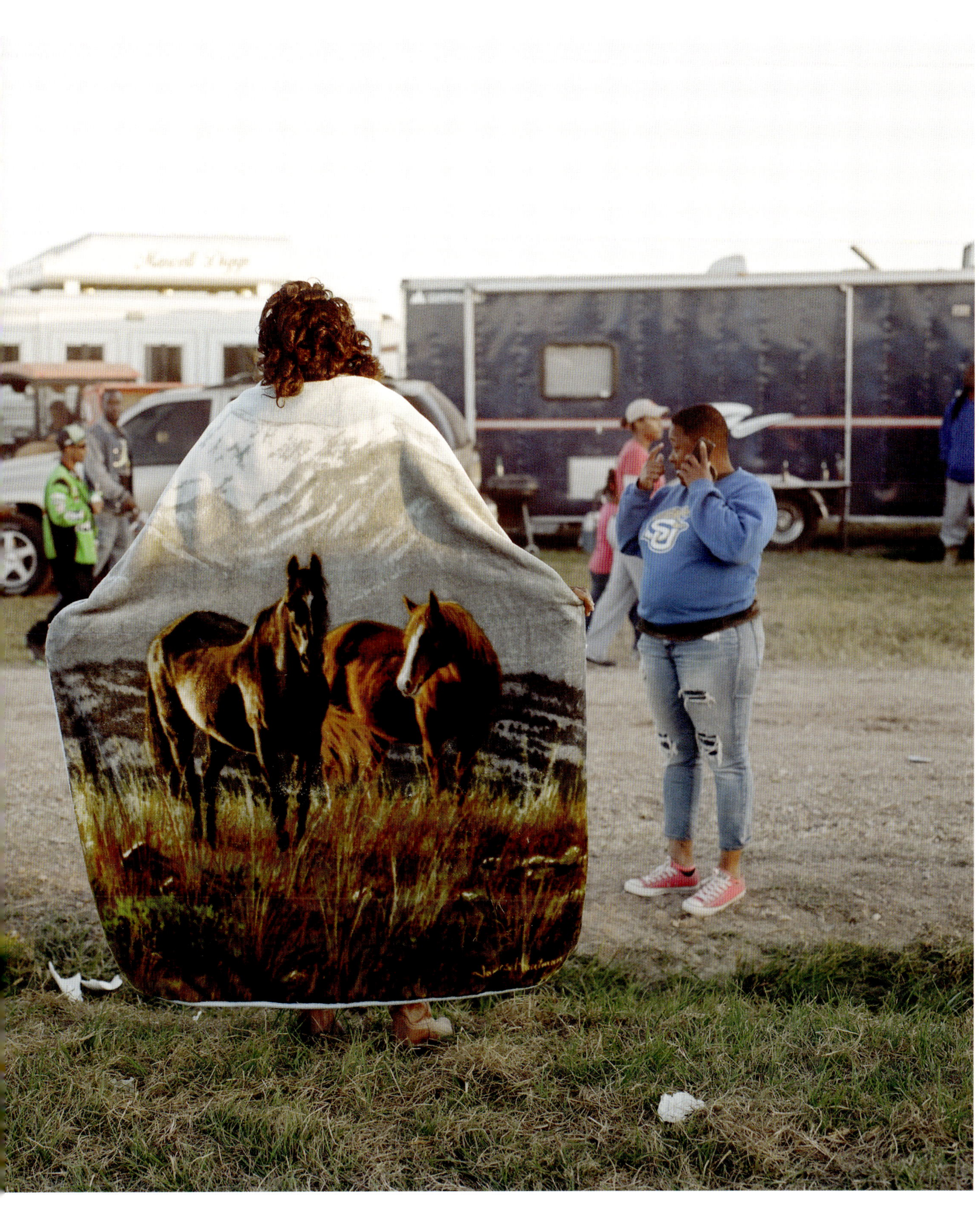

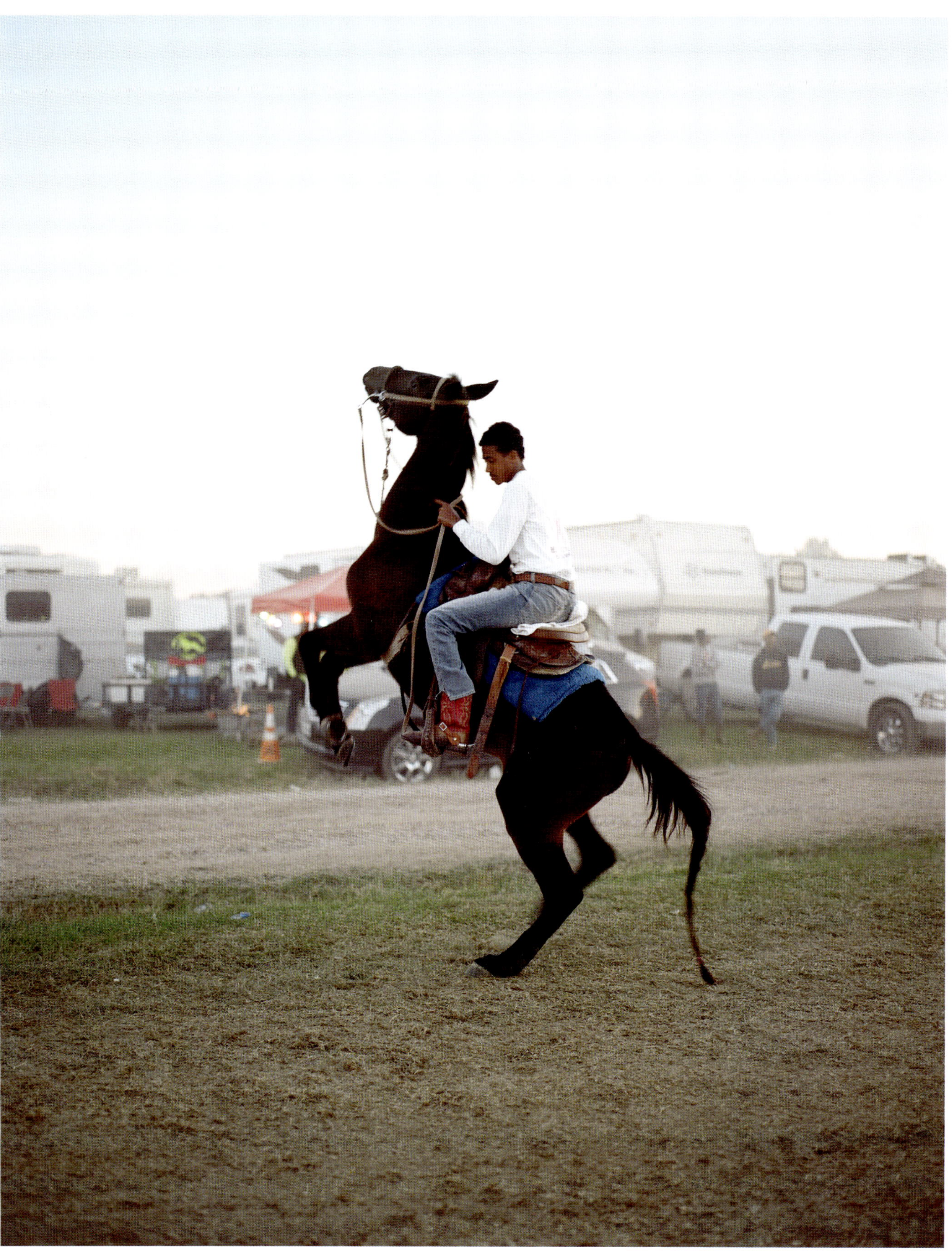

Akasha Rabut, TRAIL RIDER AT SUNSET, 2014.
Archival digital print mounted to matboard. 24 x 28 inches

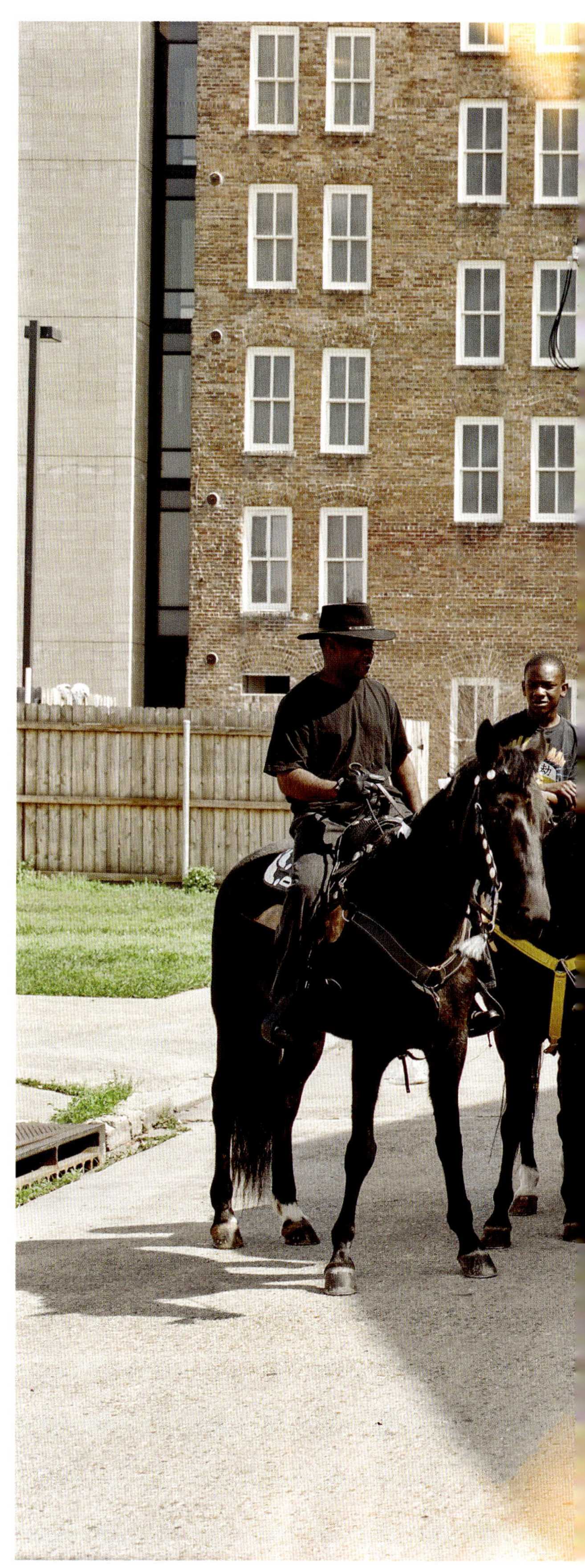

Akasha Rabut, UNTITLED (ARAB 0024), n.d.
Archival digital print mounted to matboard. 24 x 28 inches

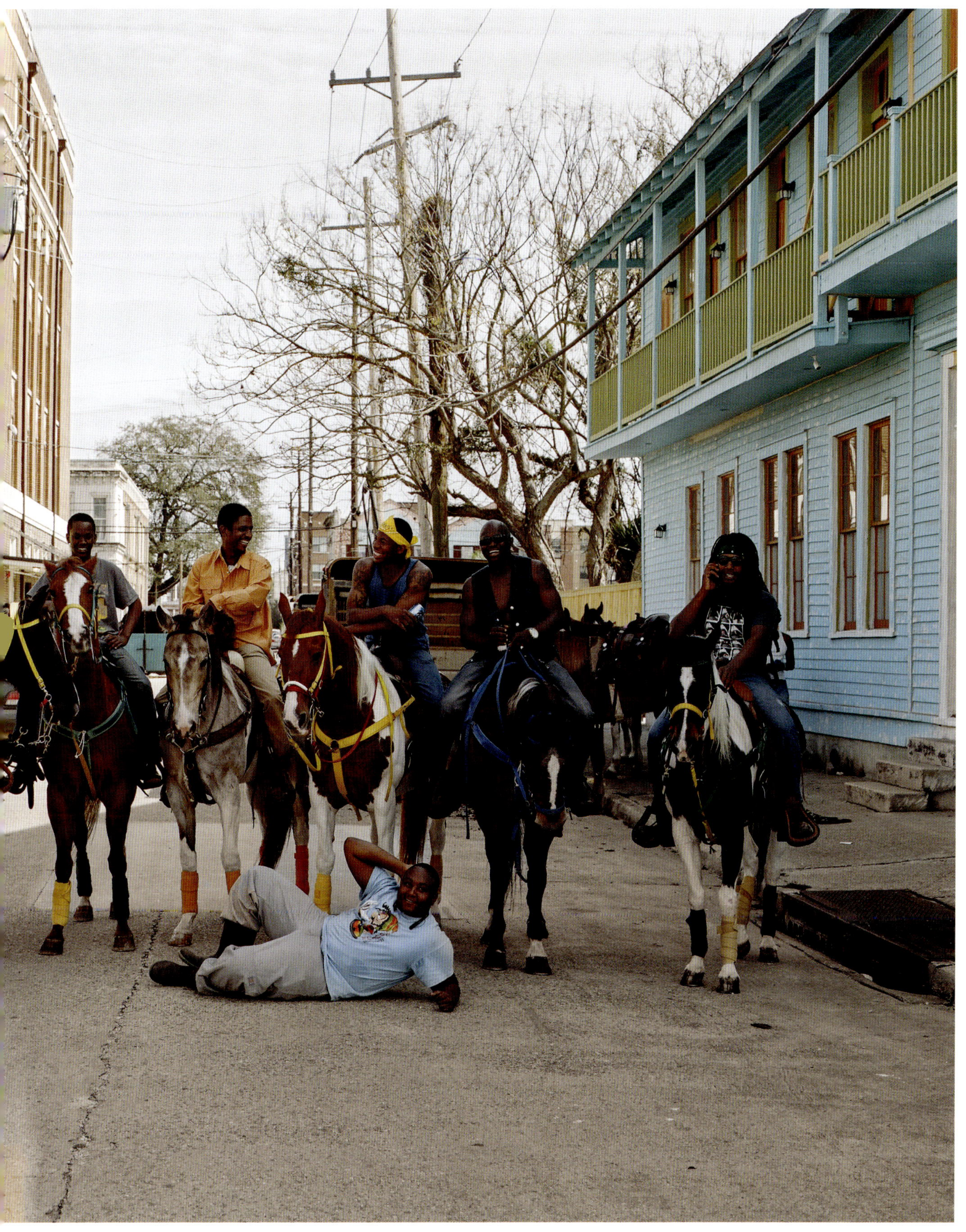

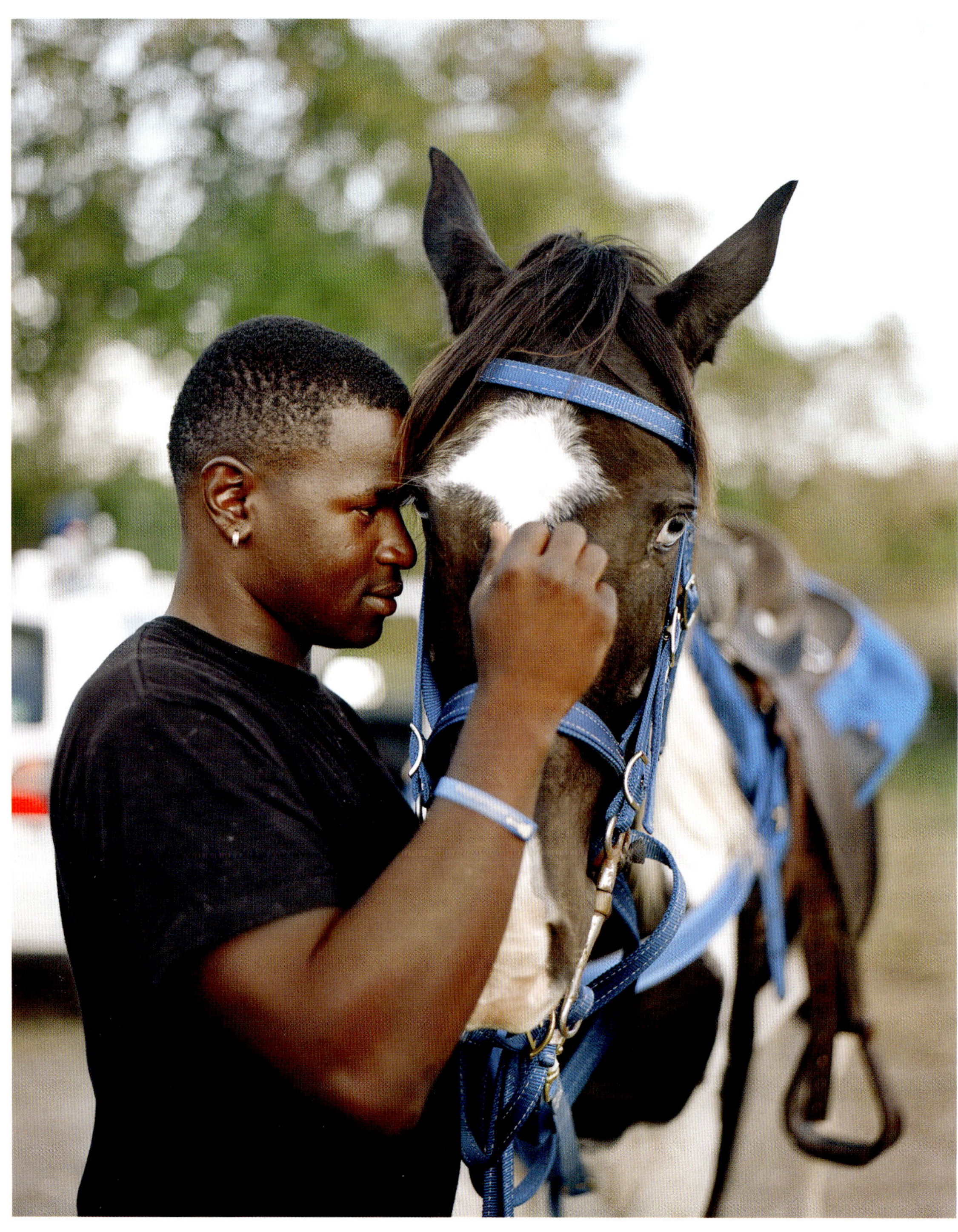

Akasha Rabut, JESSE MURDOCK, 2014.
Archival digital print mounted to matboard. 28 x 24 inches

Opposite: Akasha Rabut, KRISTIN LEWIS-HAMPTON AND DEVENCE HAMPTON, 2016.
Archival digital print mounted to matboard. 28 x 24 inches

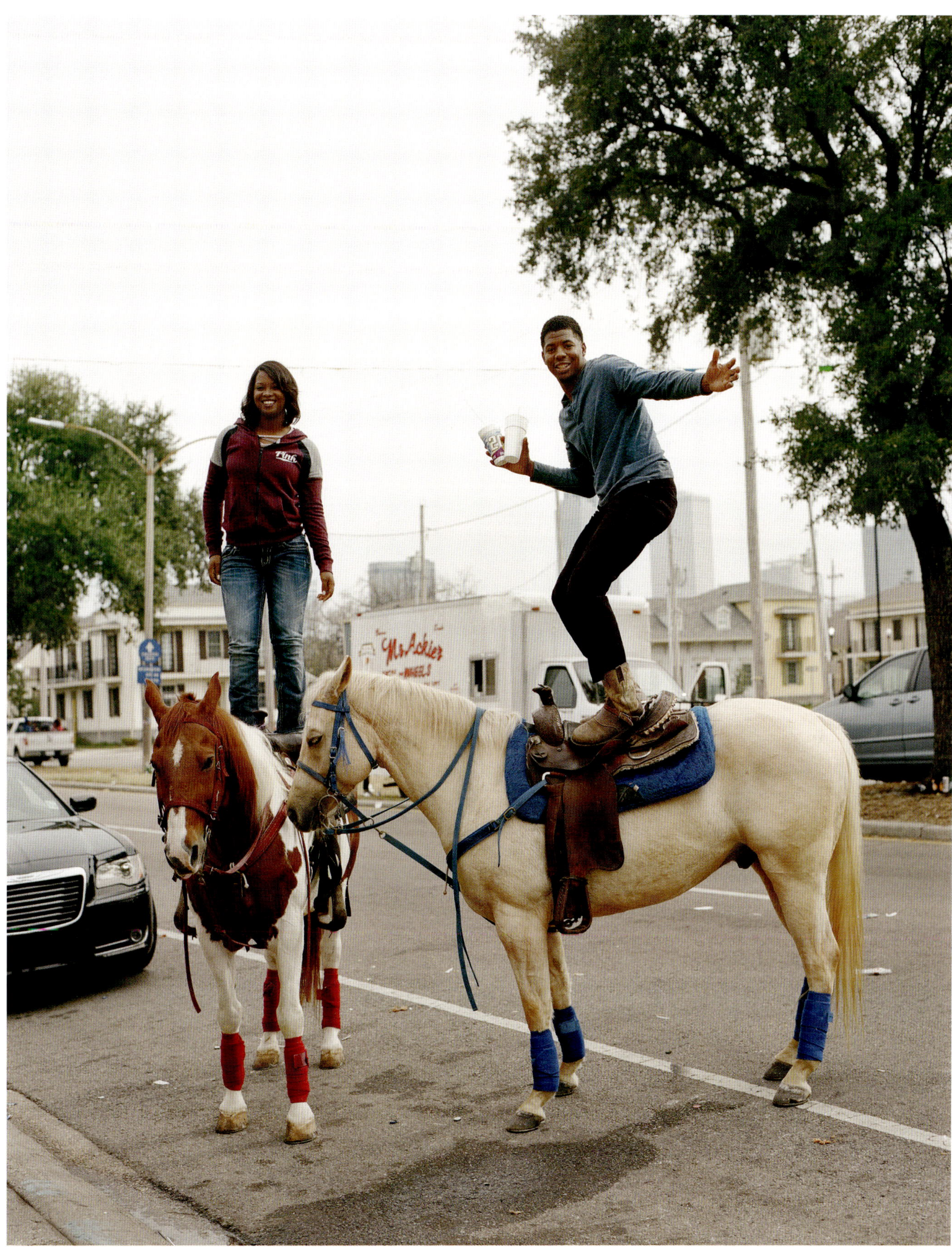
Pink

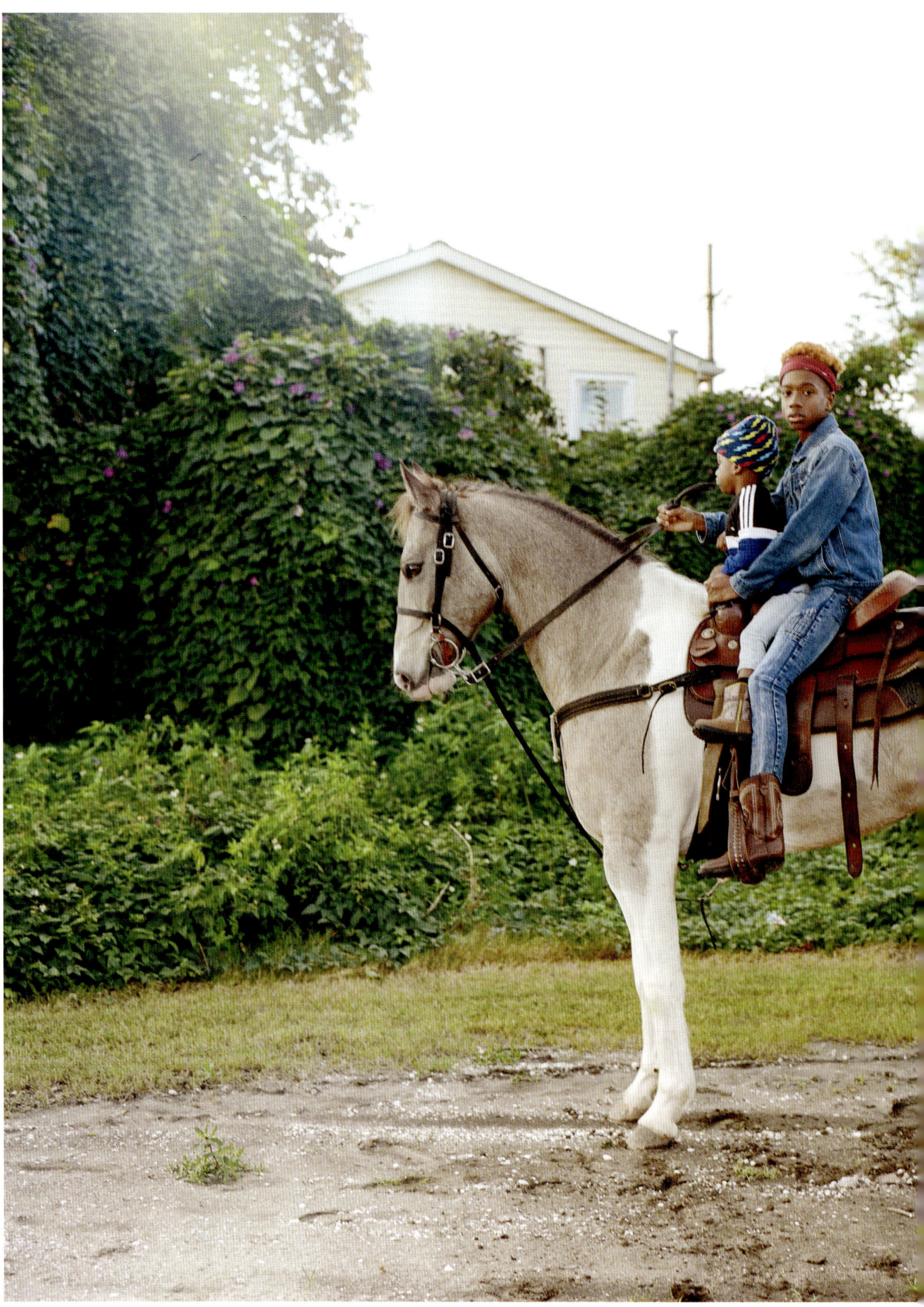

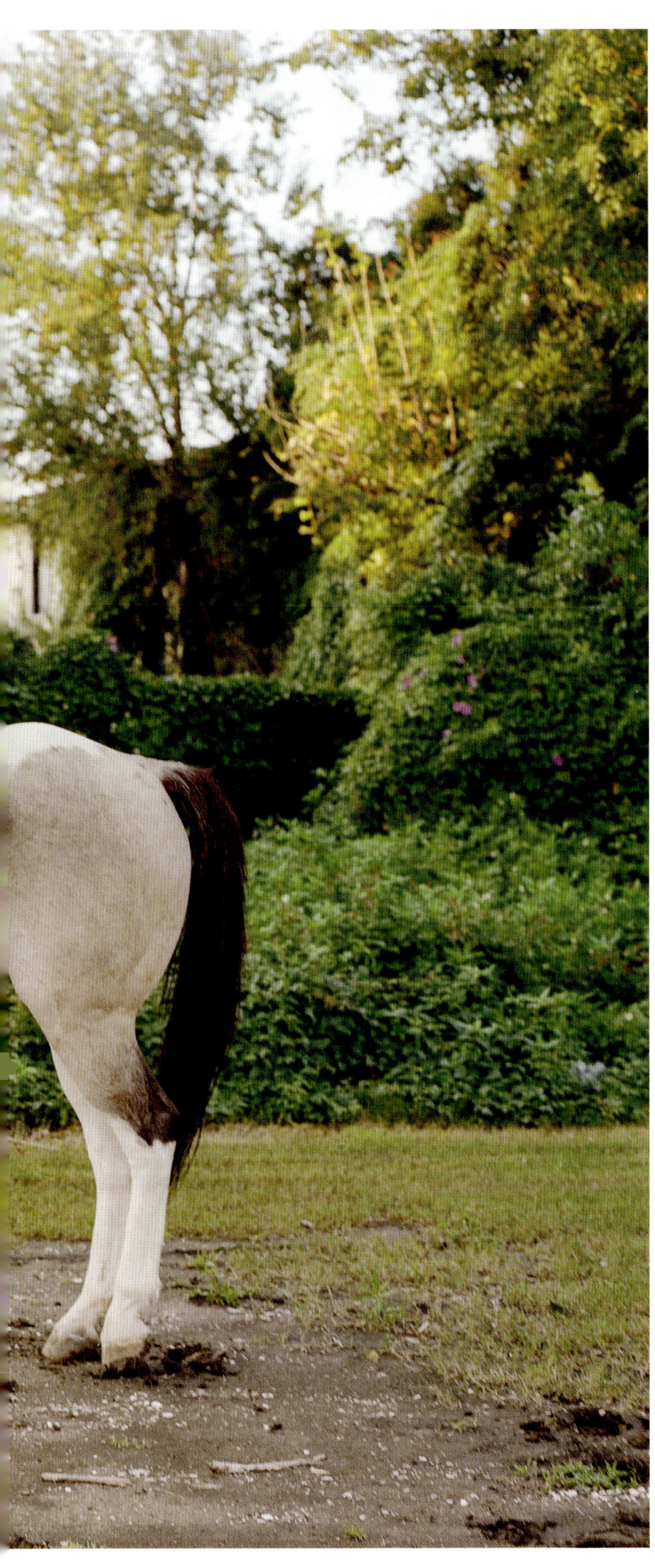

Akasha Rabut, SUNDAY AFTERNOON ON CLAIBORNE AVE, n.d. Archival digital print mounted to matboard. 24 x 28 inches

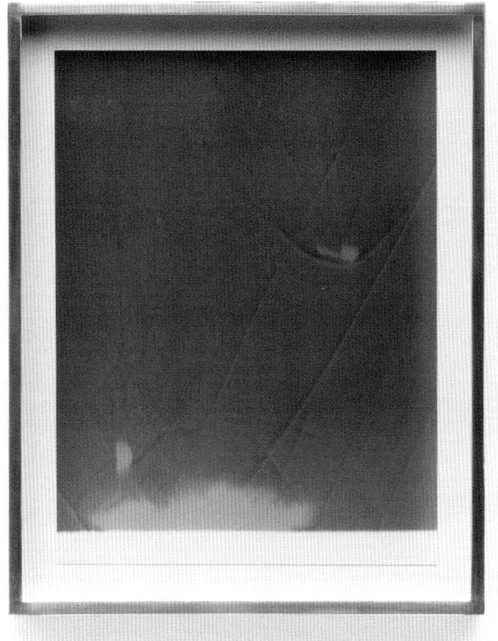

Lucy Raven, UNTITLED, 2021. Framed shadowgram; silver gelatin direct print. 14 x 11 inches

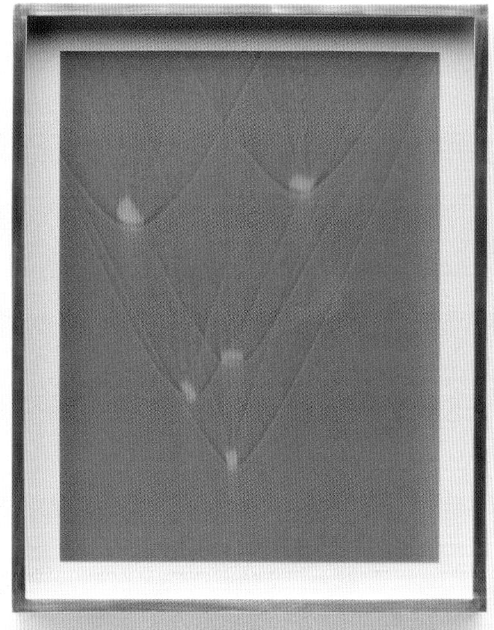

Lucy Raven, UNTITLED, 2021. Framed shadowgram; silver gelatin direct print. 14 x 11 inches

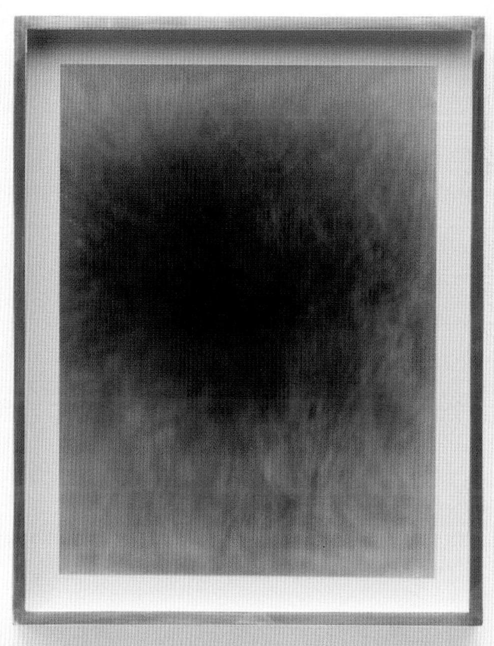

Lucy Raven, UNTITLED, 2021. Framed shadowgram; silver gelatin direct print. 14 x 11 inches

Lucy Raven, UNTITLED, 2021. Framed shadowgram; silver gelatin direct print. 14 x 11 inches

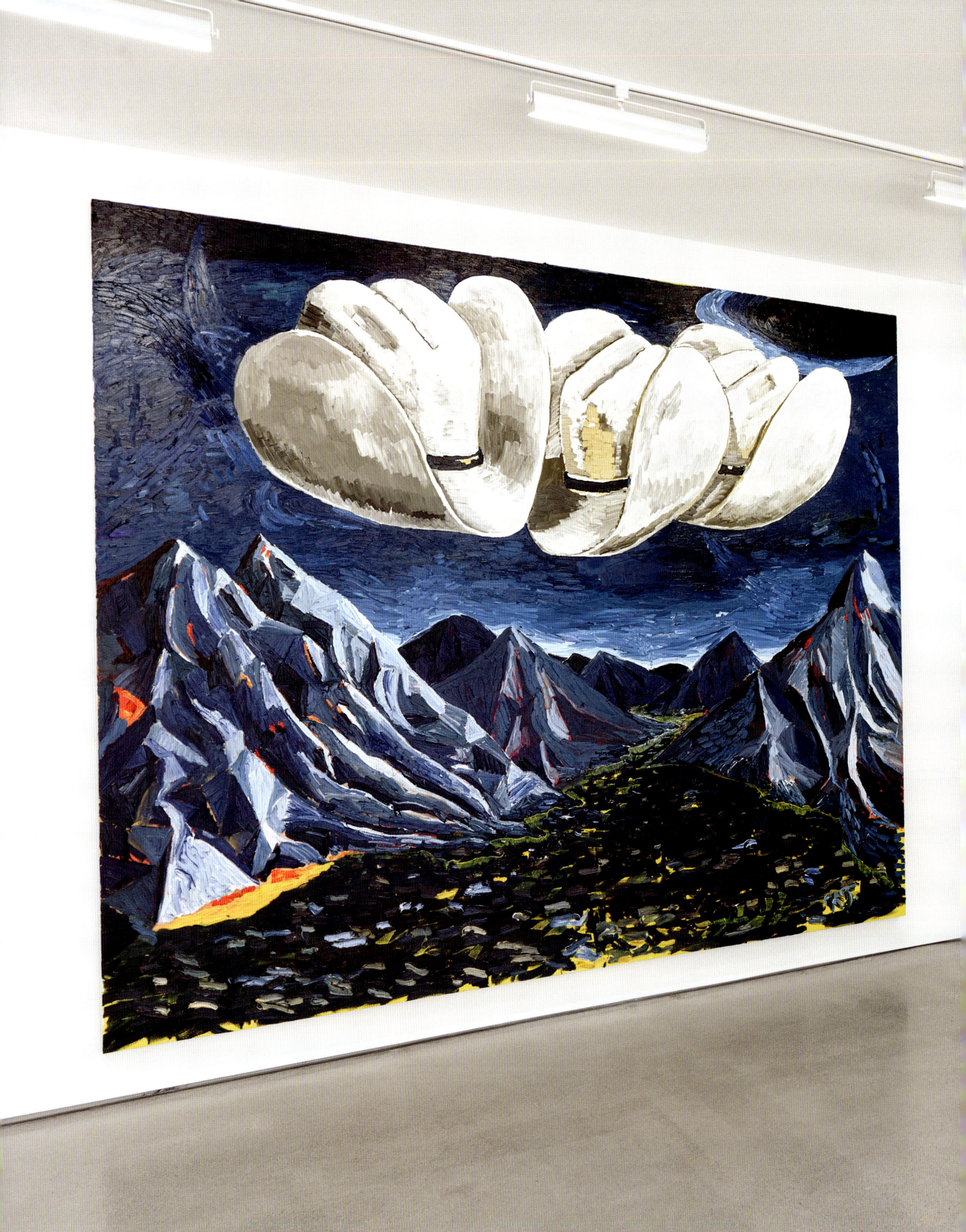

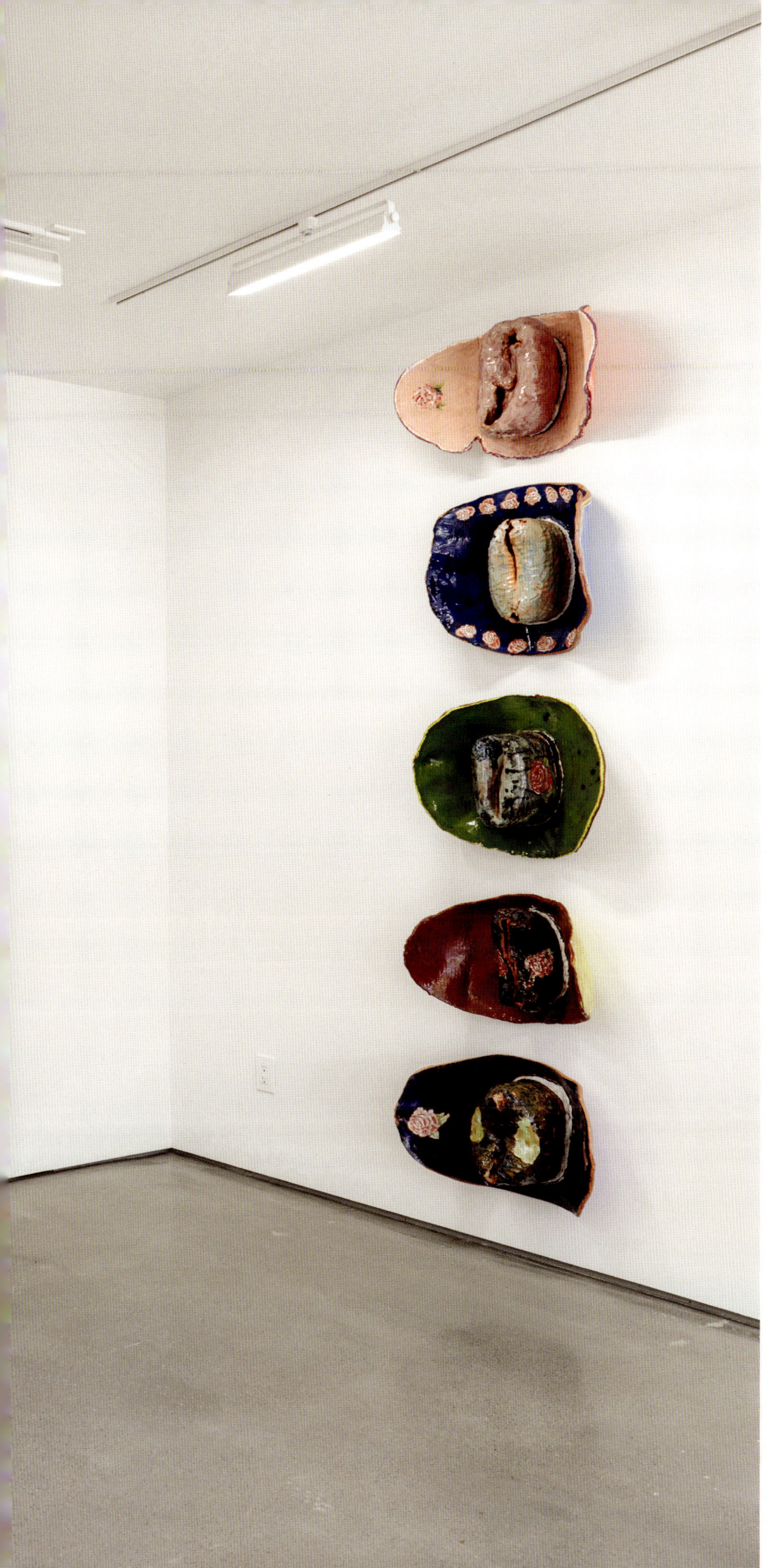

Left and following pages:
Ken Taylor Reynaga,
EL VALLE AT DUSK,
2020, and SOMBRERO
CERAMICS, 2021.
Installation views,
MOUNTAINS AND
ROSES, Simchowitz
Gallery, Los Angeles, 2021

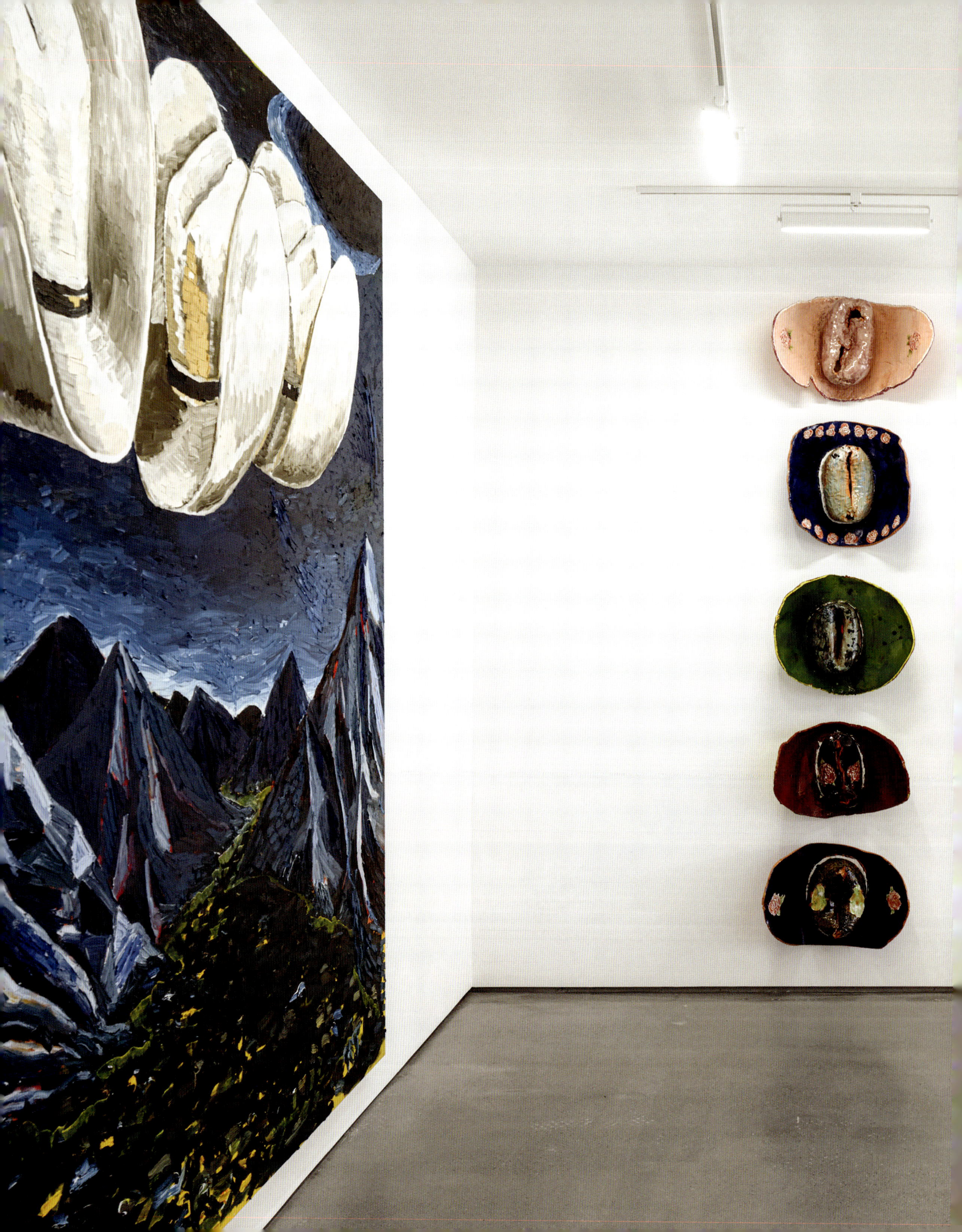

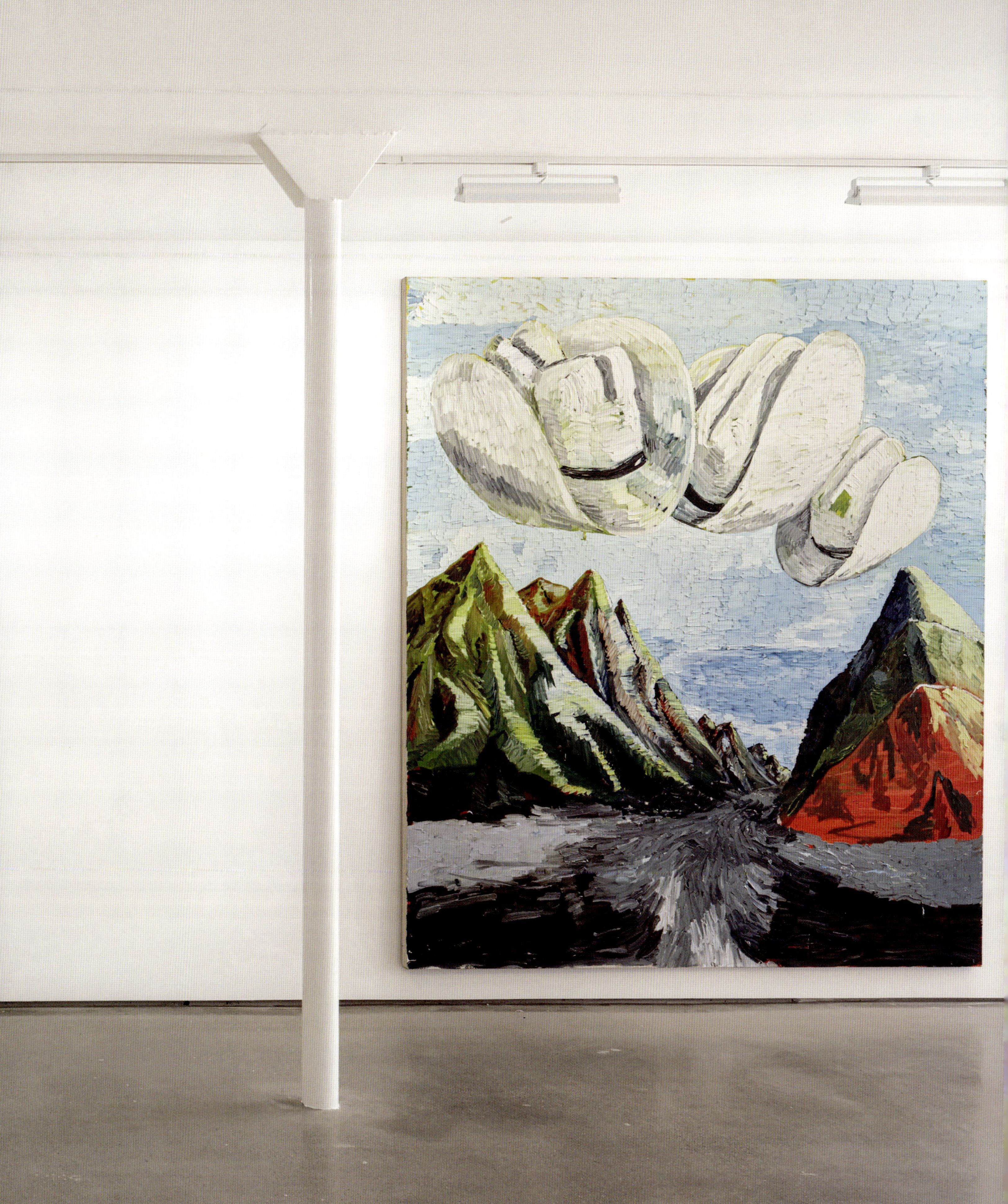

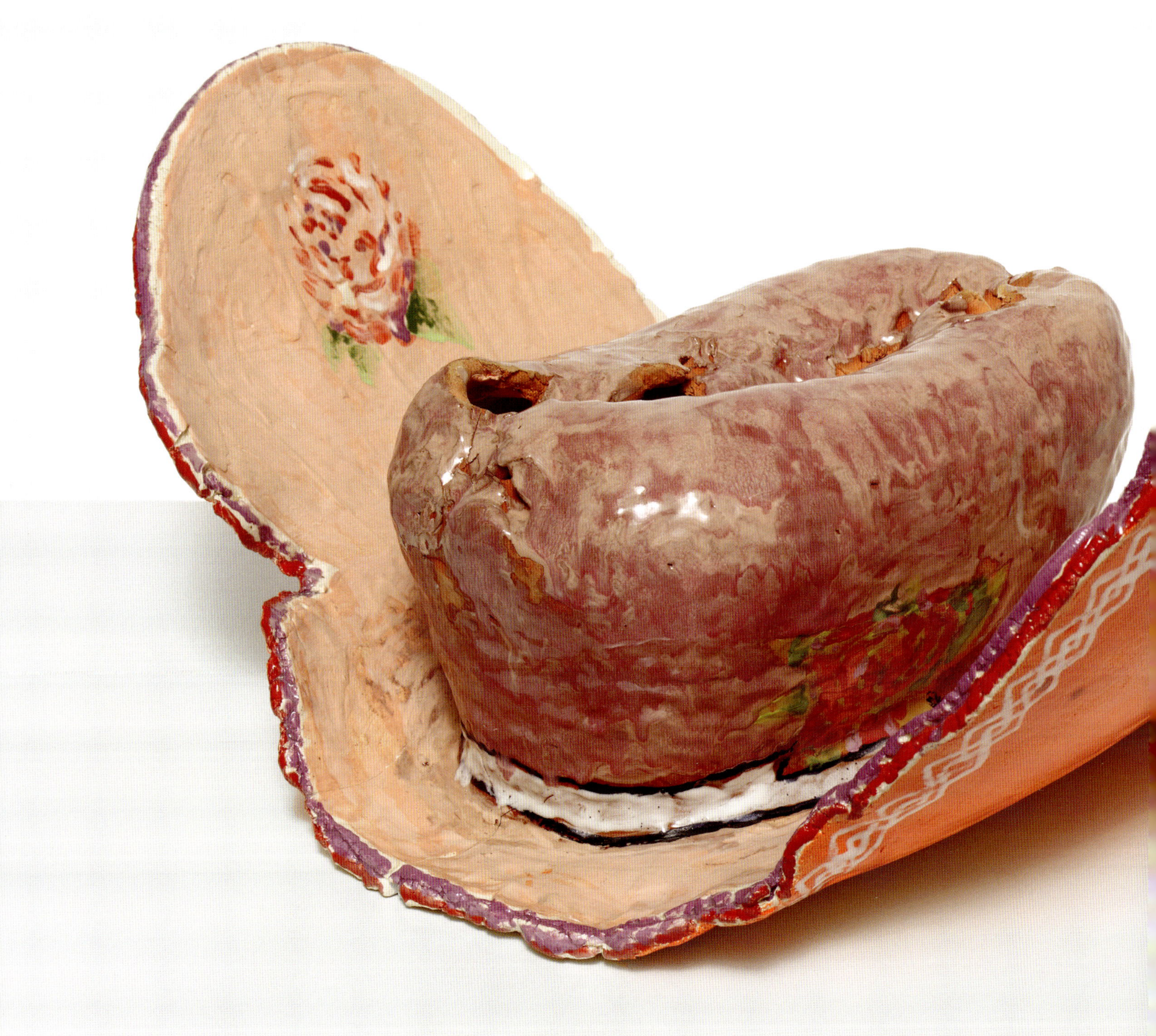

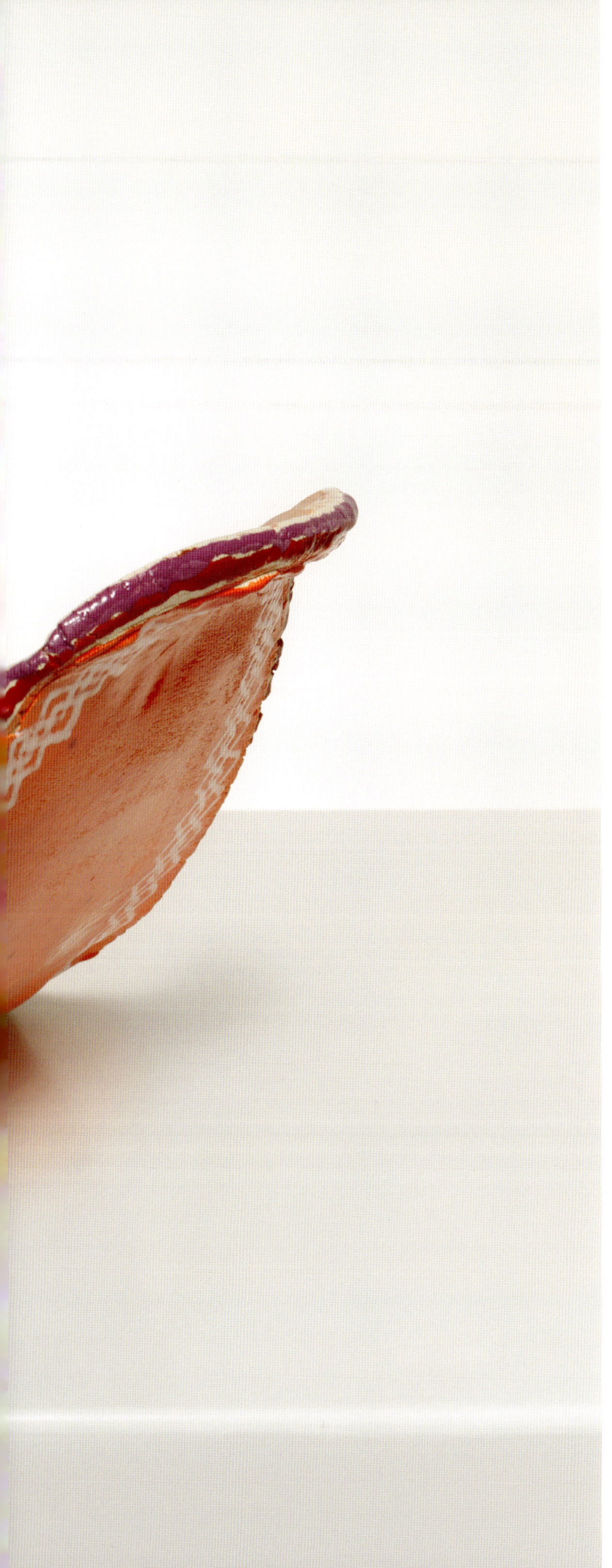

Ken Taylor Reynaga, SOMBRERO CERAMIC PINK,
2021. Glazed ceramic. 11 x 24¼ x 16 inches

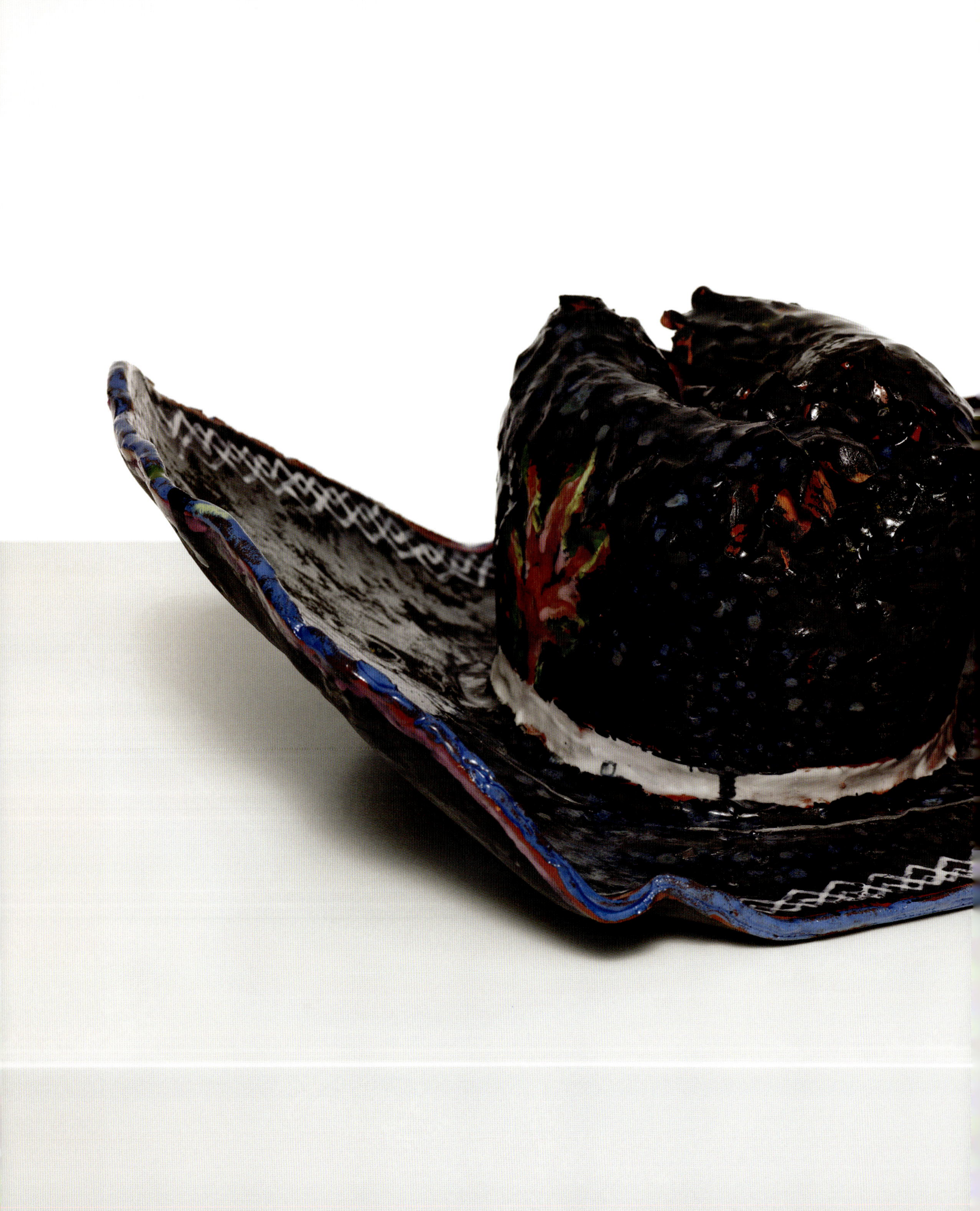

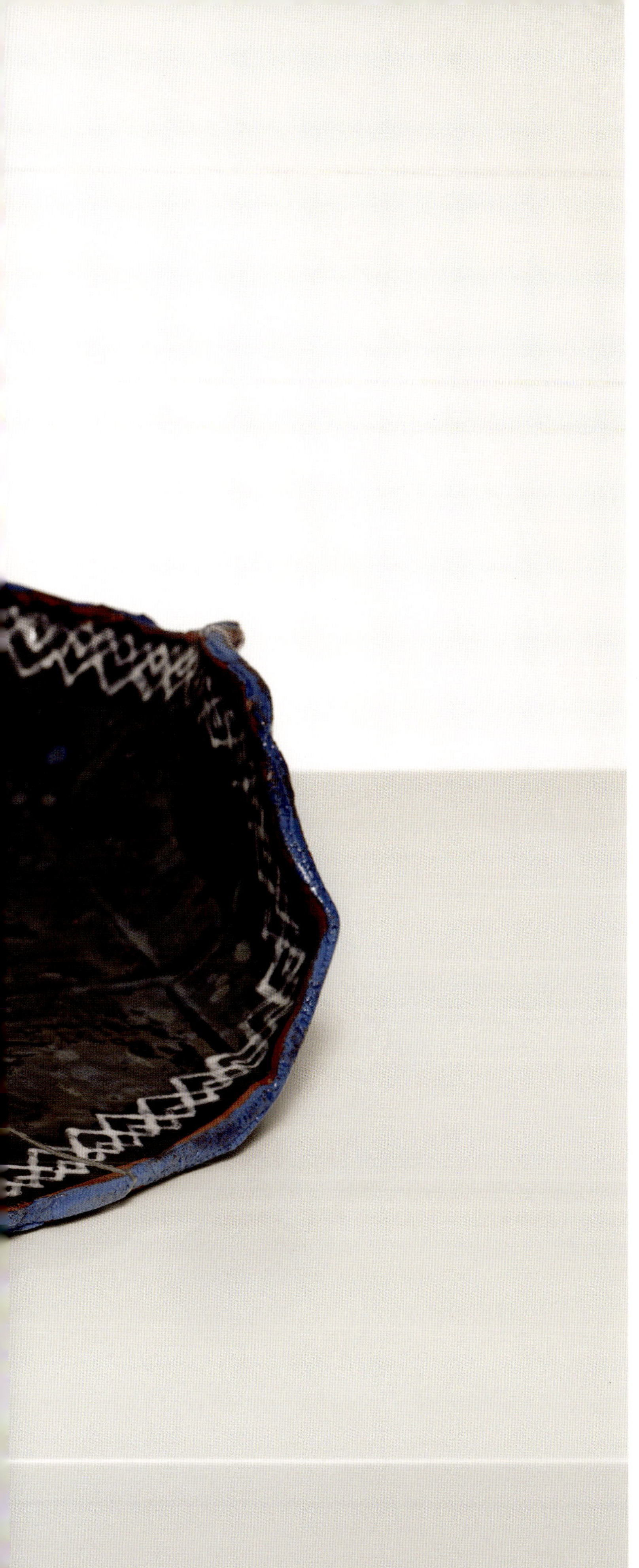

Ken Taylor Reynaga, SOMBRERO CERAMIC BLACK, 2021. Glazed ceramic. 6 x 19 x 16¼ inches

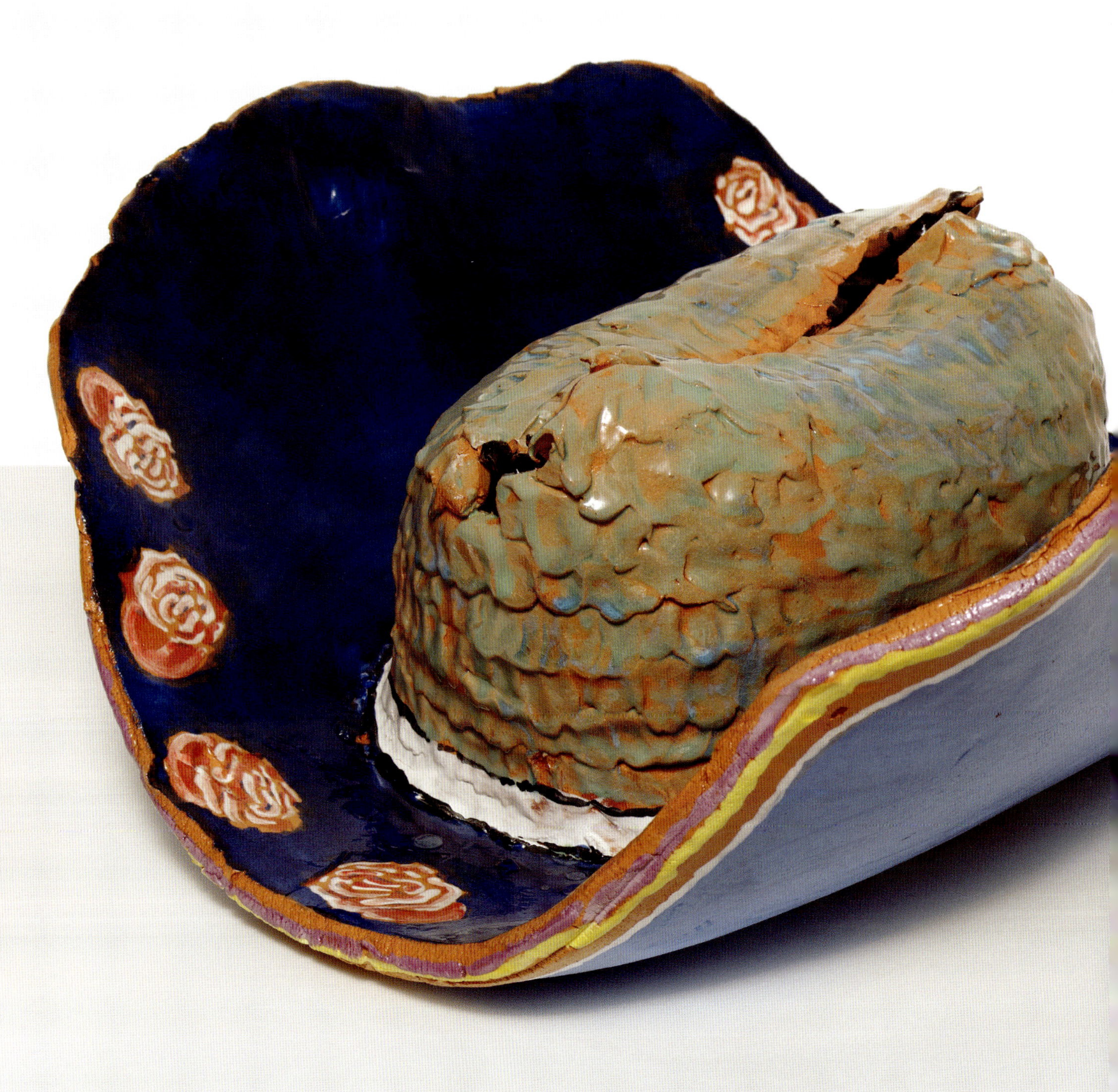

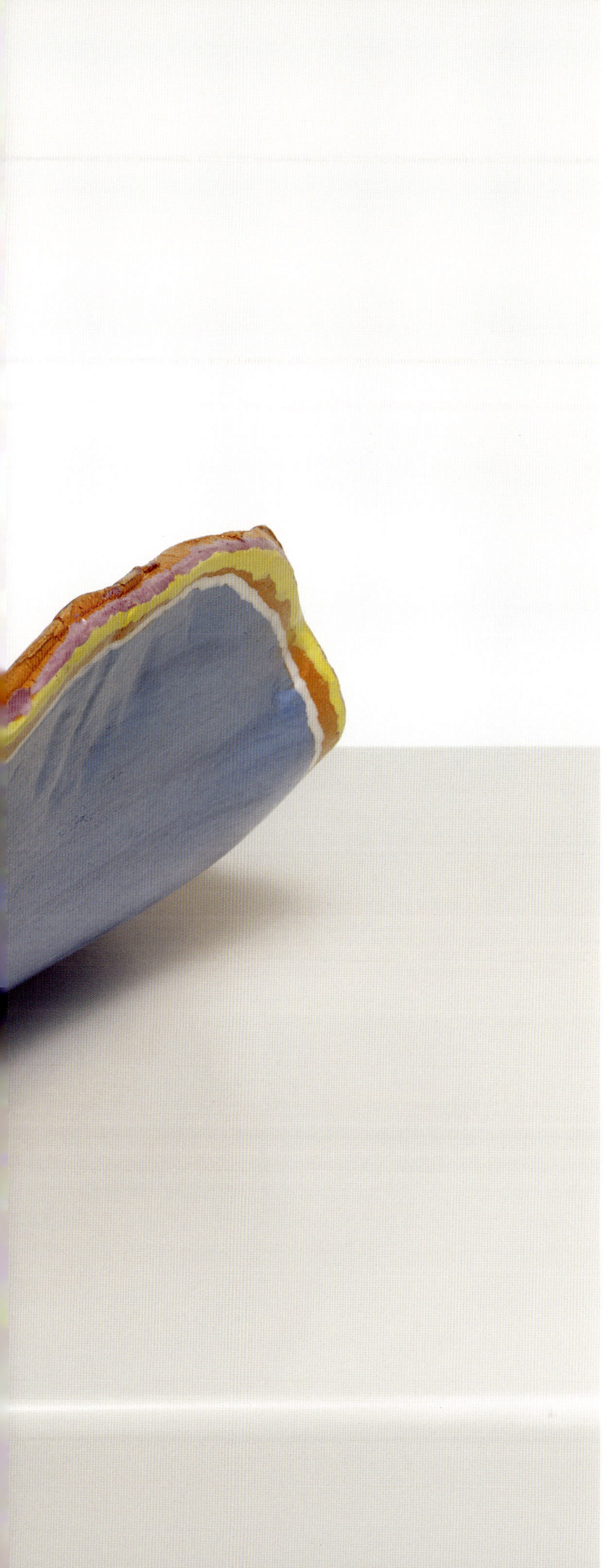

Ken Taylor Reynaga, SOMBRERO CERAMIC AQUA, 2021. Glazed ceramic. 8½ x 18¾ x 19¼ inches

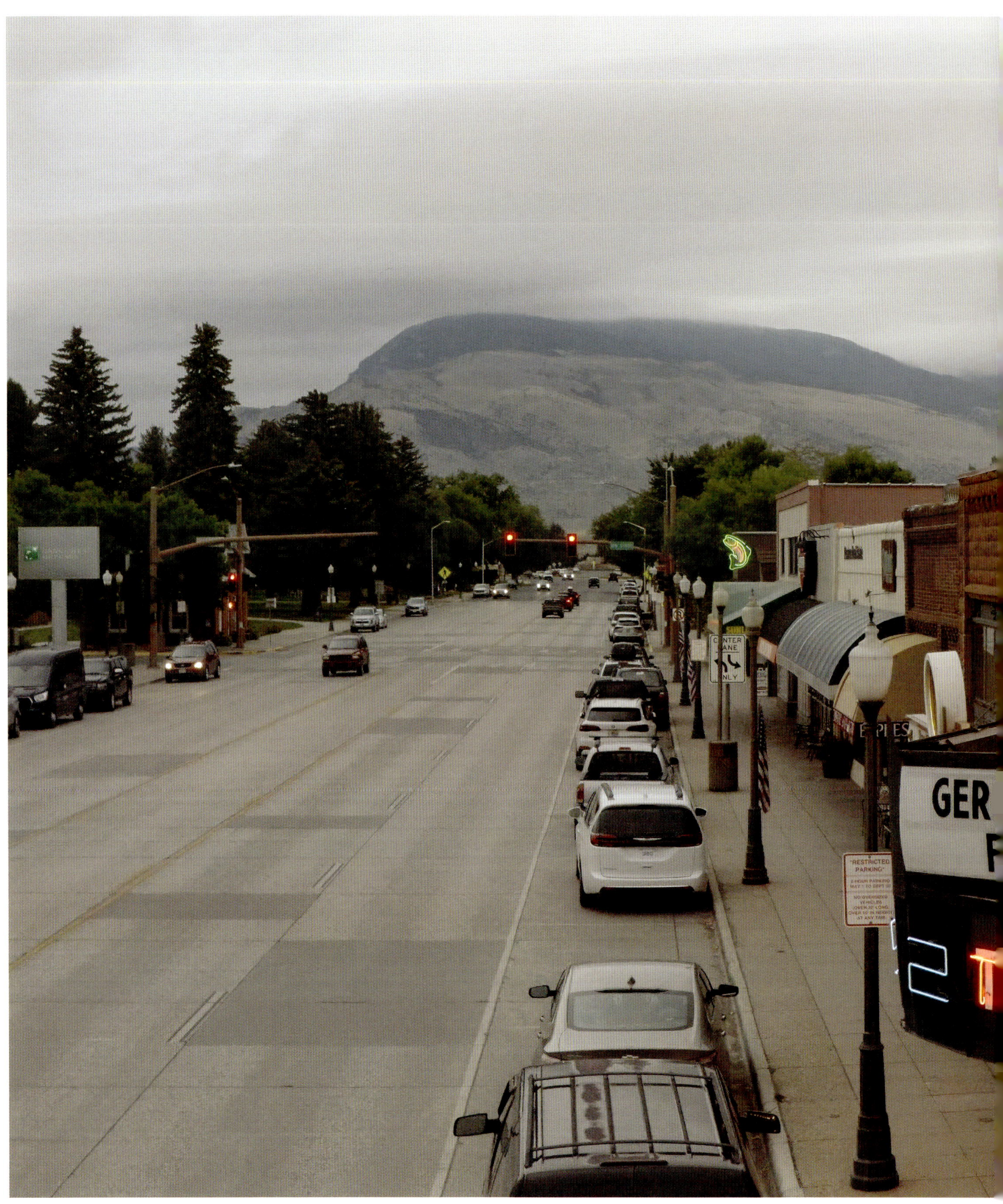
"RESTRICTED PARKING"
GER

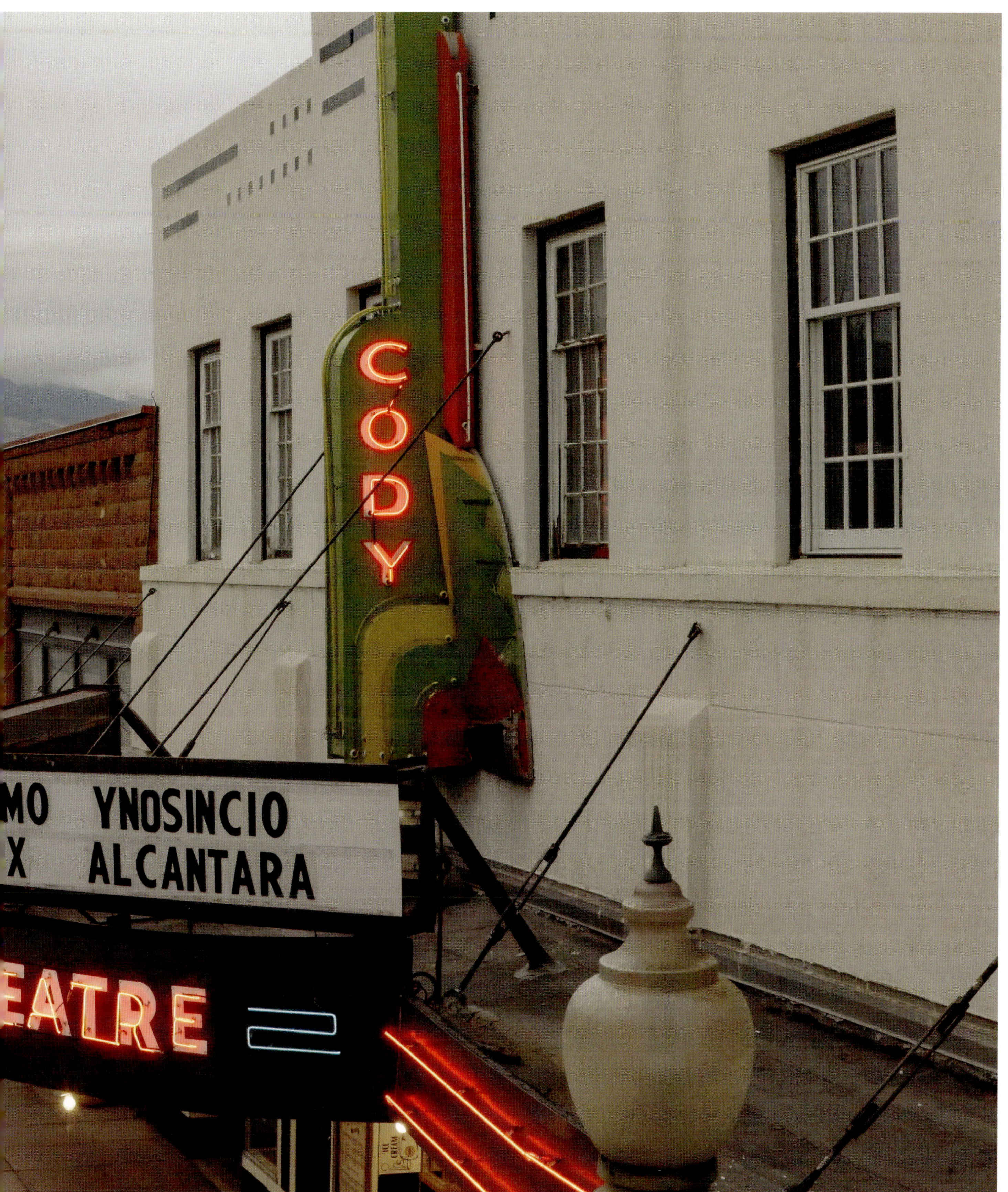
CODY
MO YNOSINCIO
X ALCANTARA
EATRE

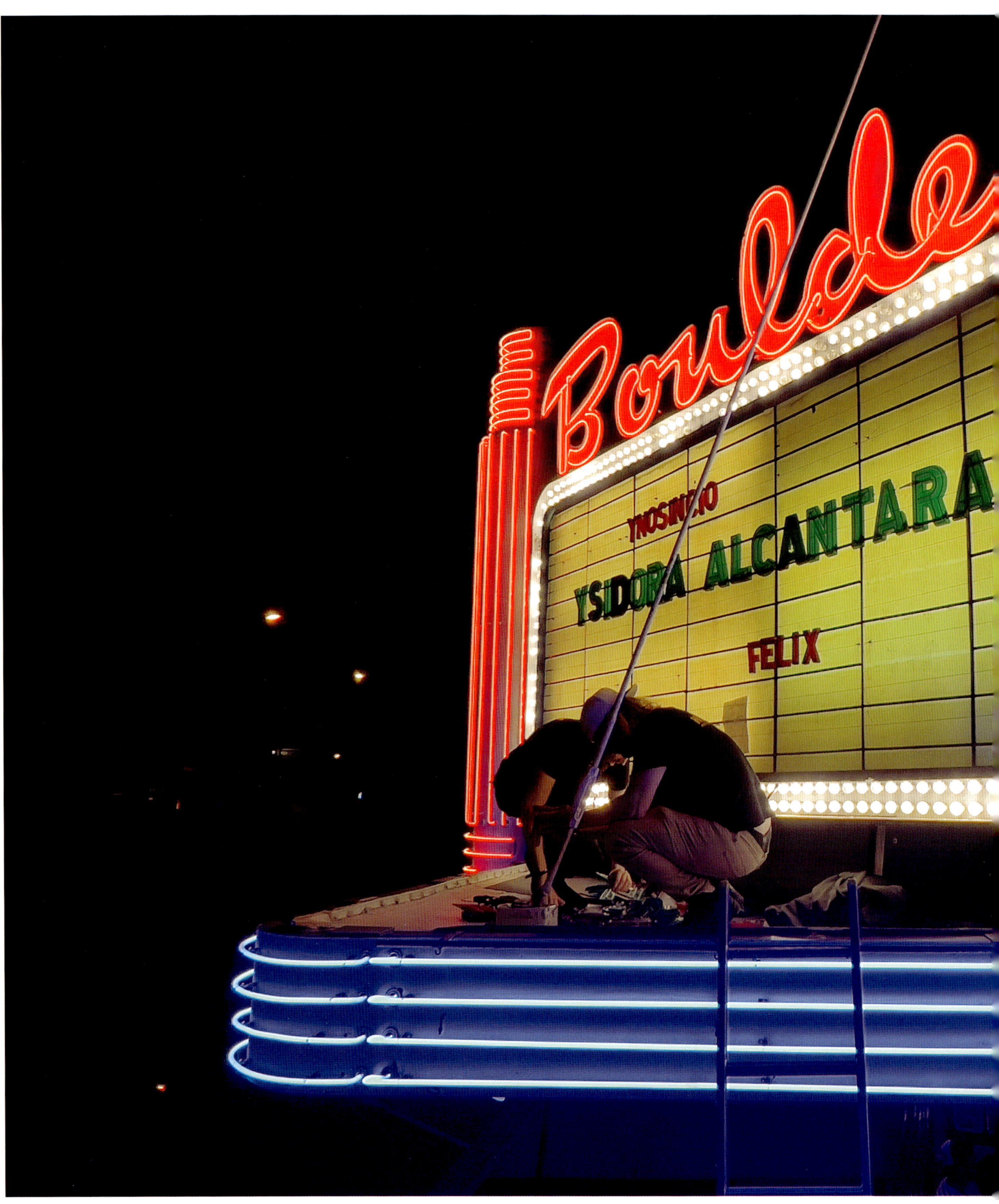
YSIDORA ALCANTARA
FELIX

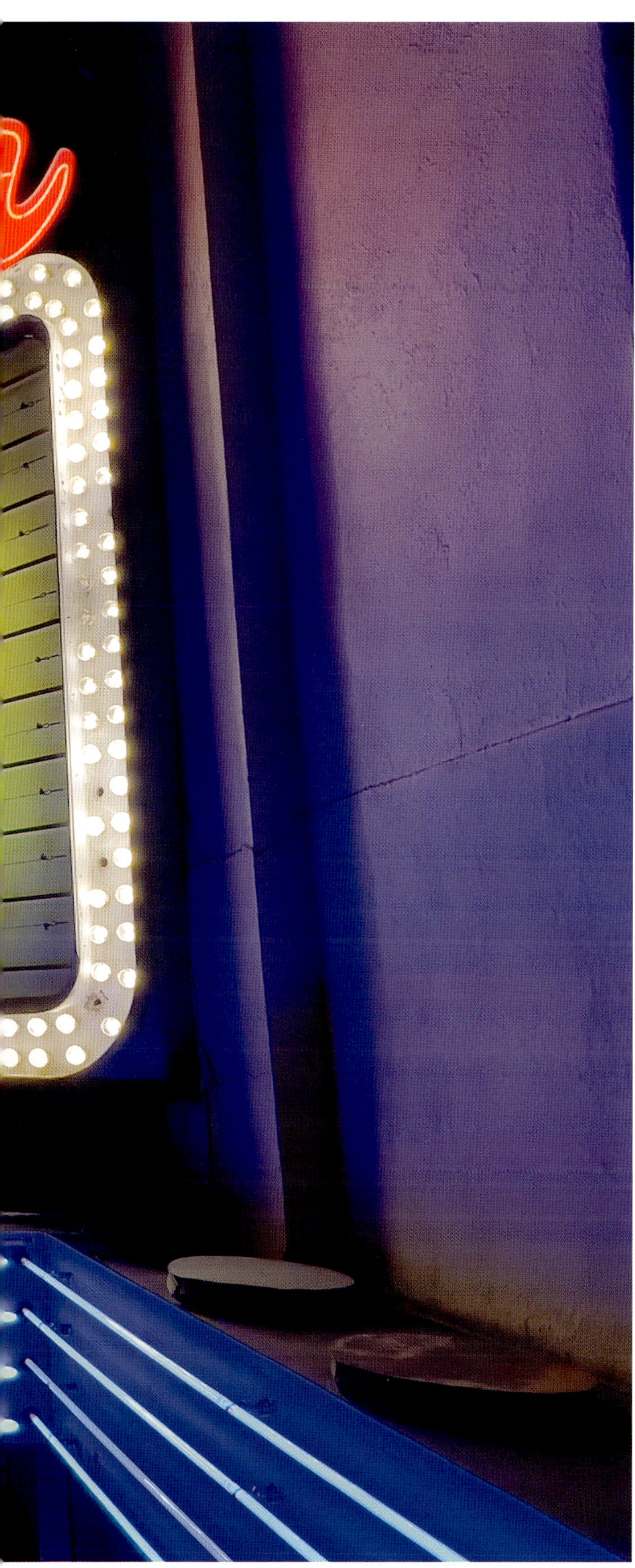

Previous pages: Yumi Janairo Roth and Emmanuel David, WE ARE COMING (THE CODY THEATRE, CODY, WY), 2022. Photograph.

Left: Yumi Janairo Roth and Emmanuel David, WE ARE COMING (BOULDER THEATER, BOULDER, CO), 2022. Photograph

Pages 178–185: Ana Segovia, stills from AUNQUE ME ESPINE LA MANO, 2018. Video. Duration: 5:35 minutes

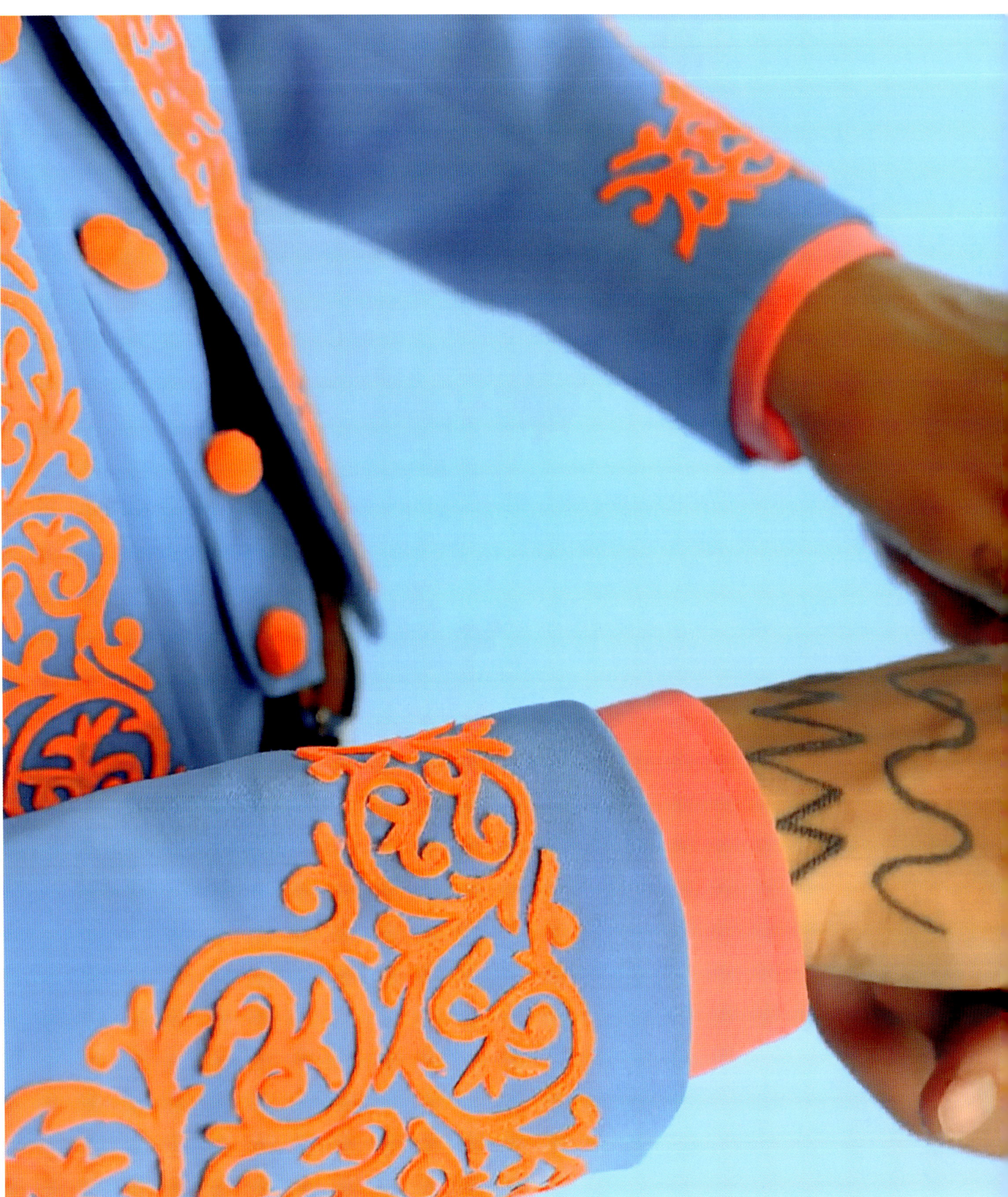

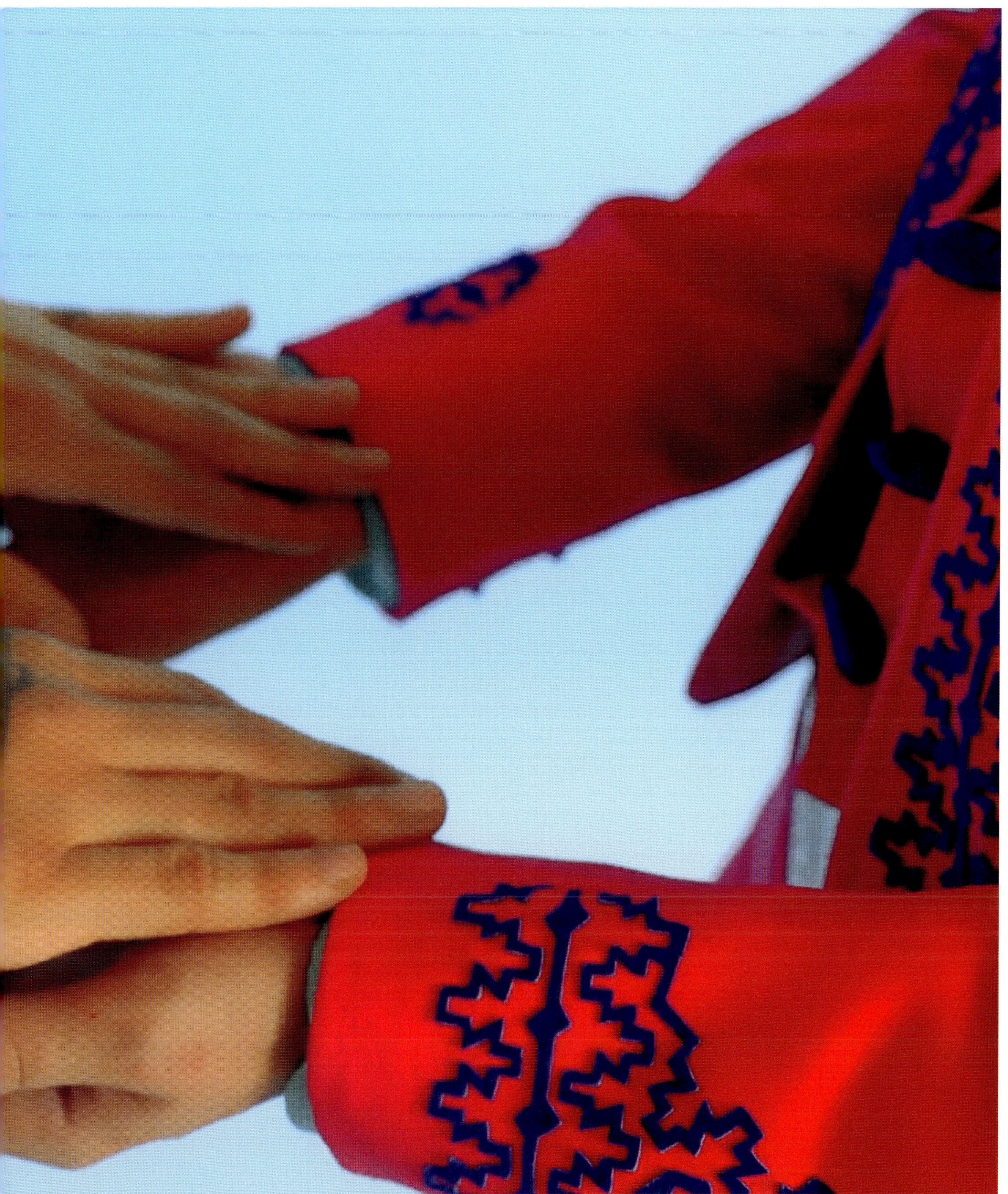

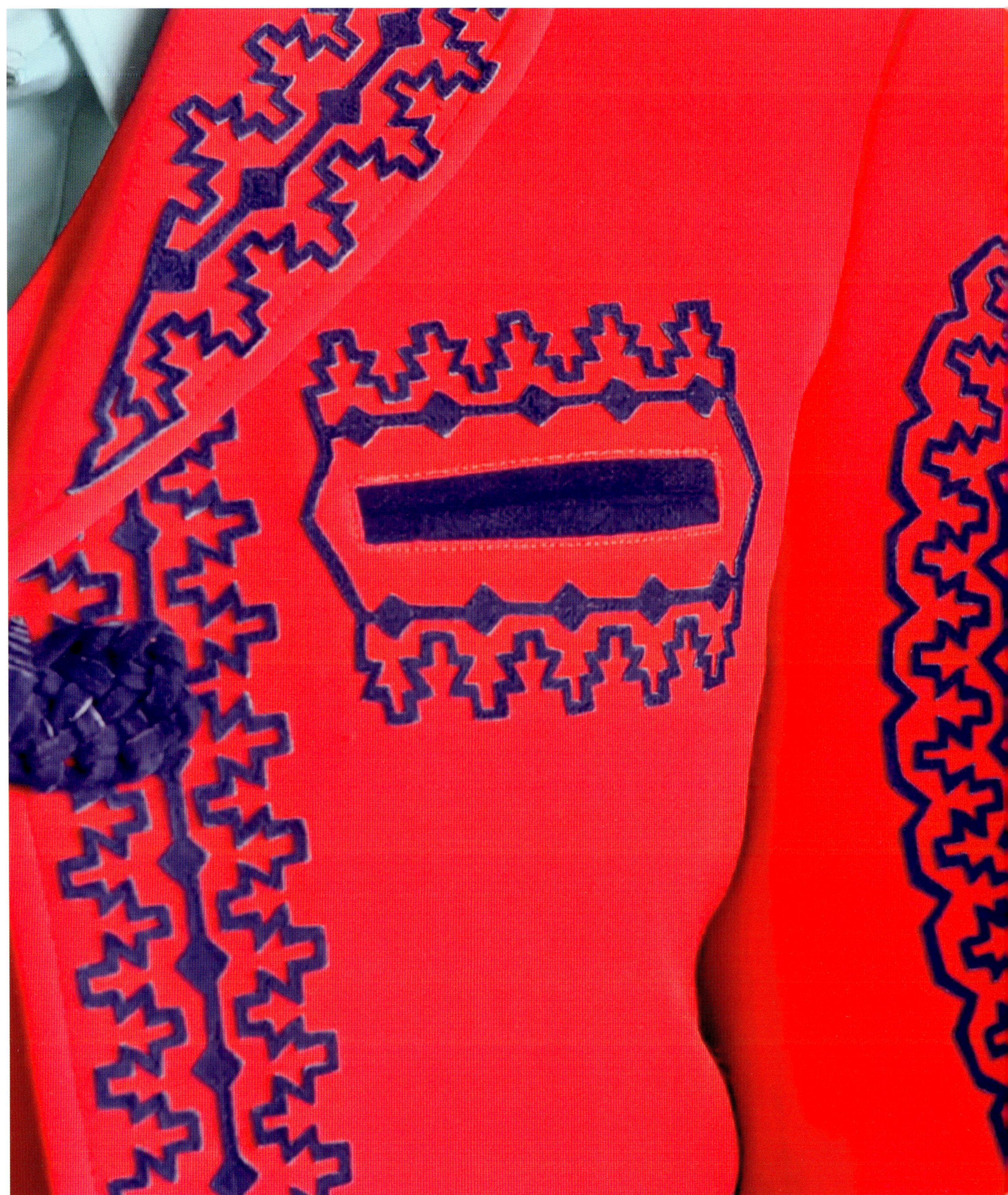

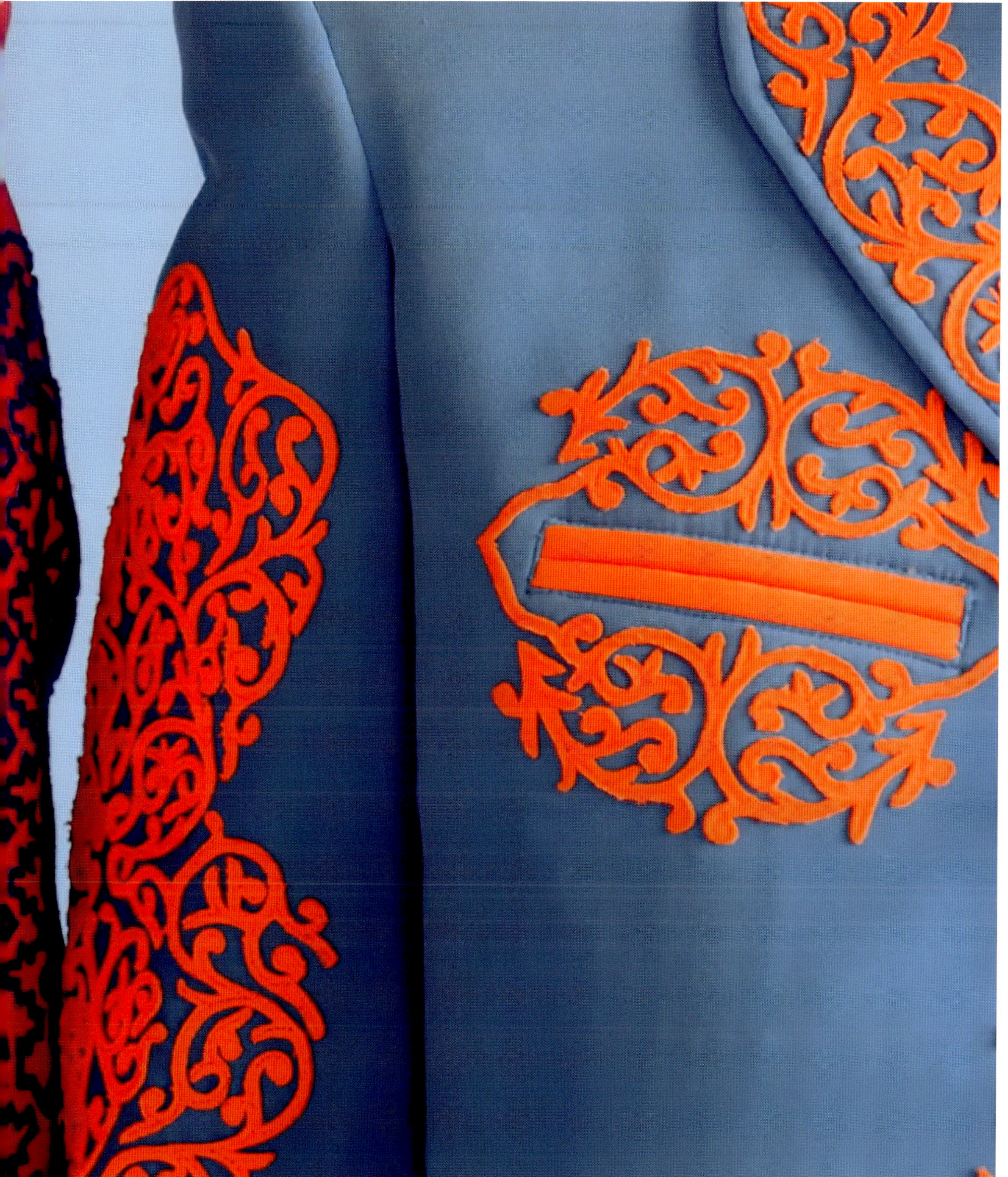

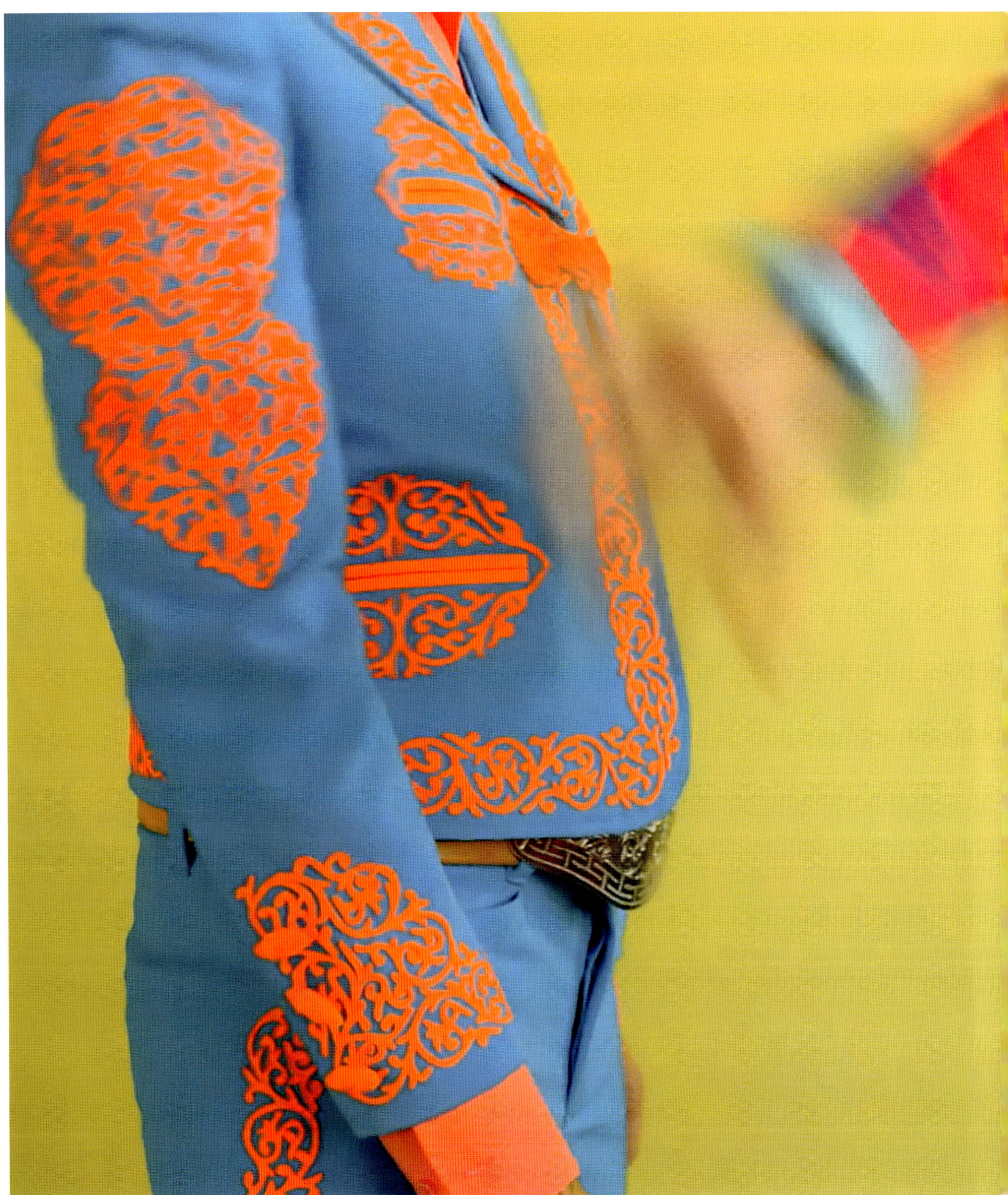

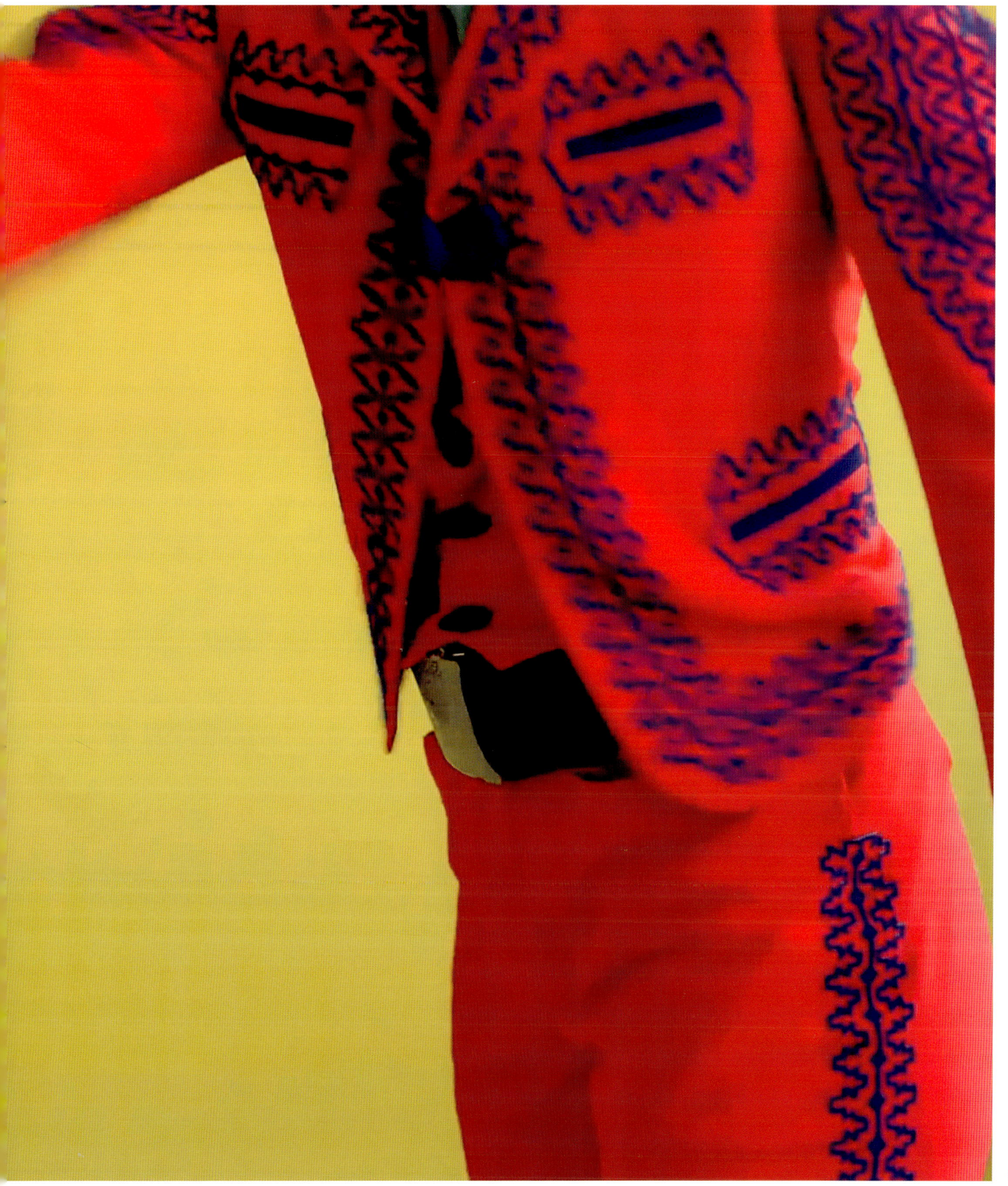

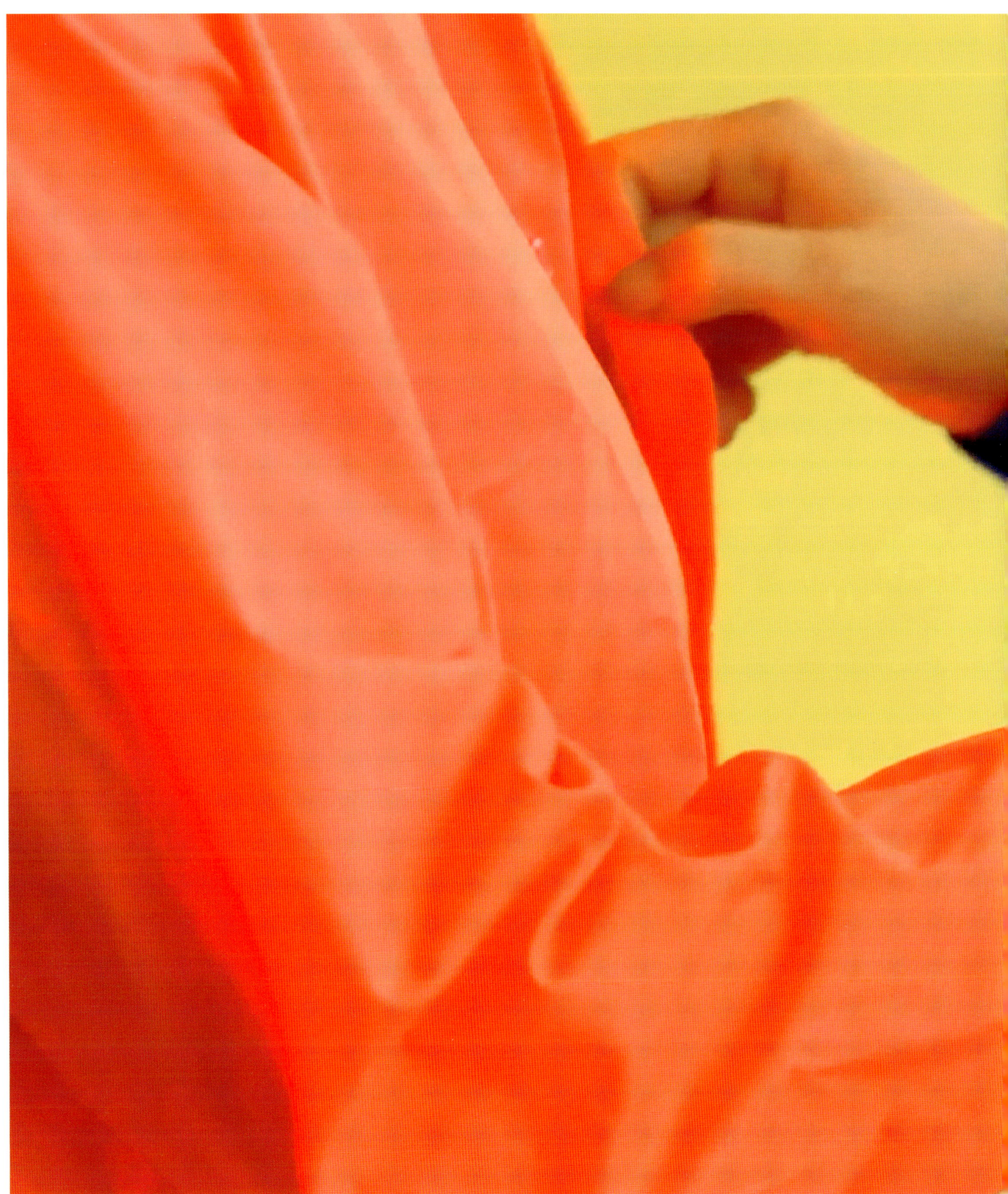

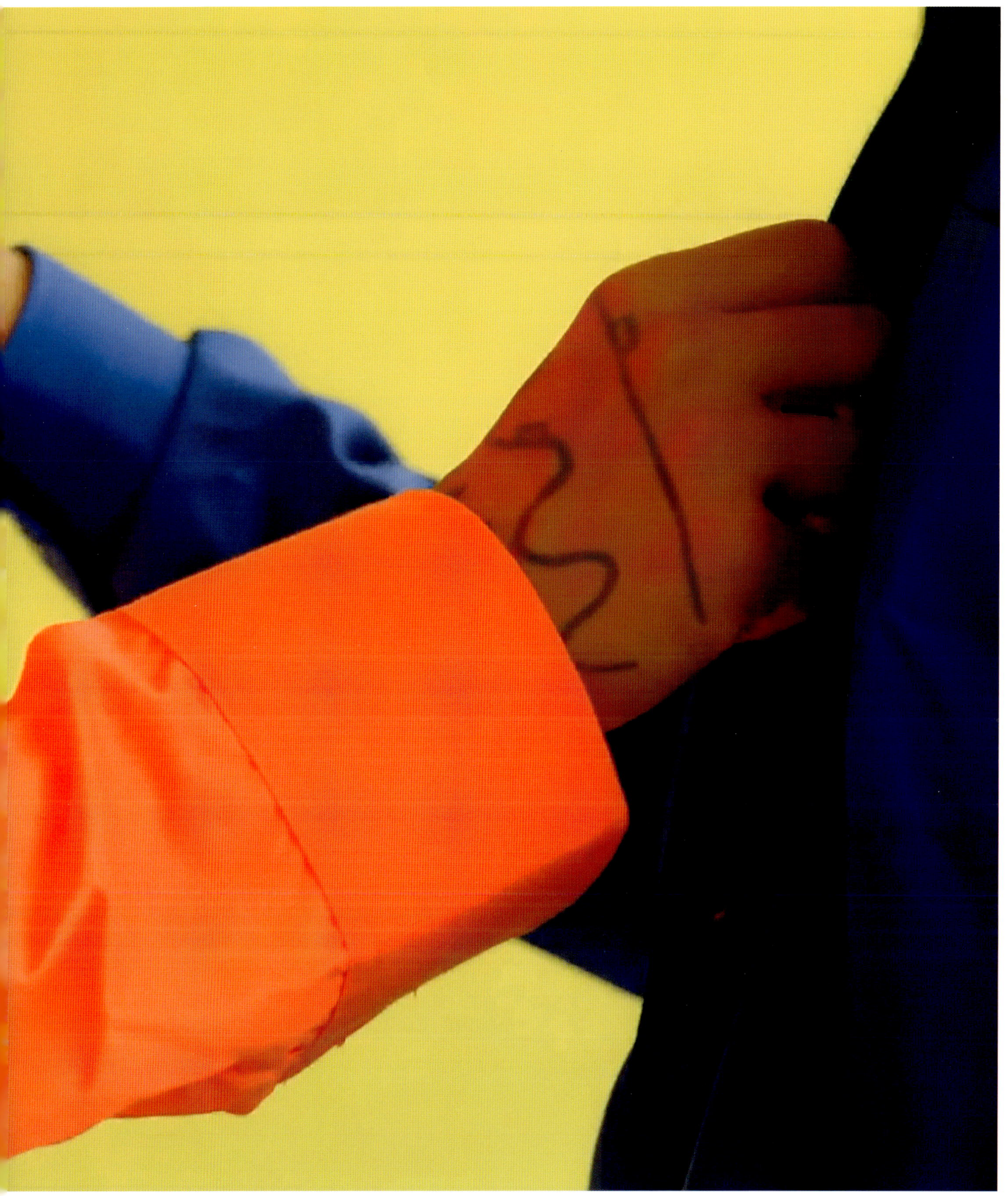

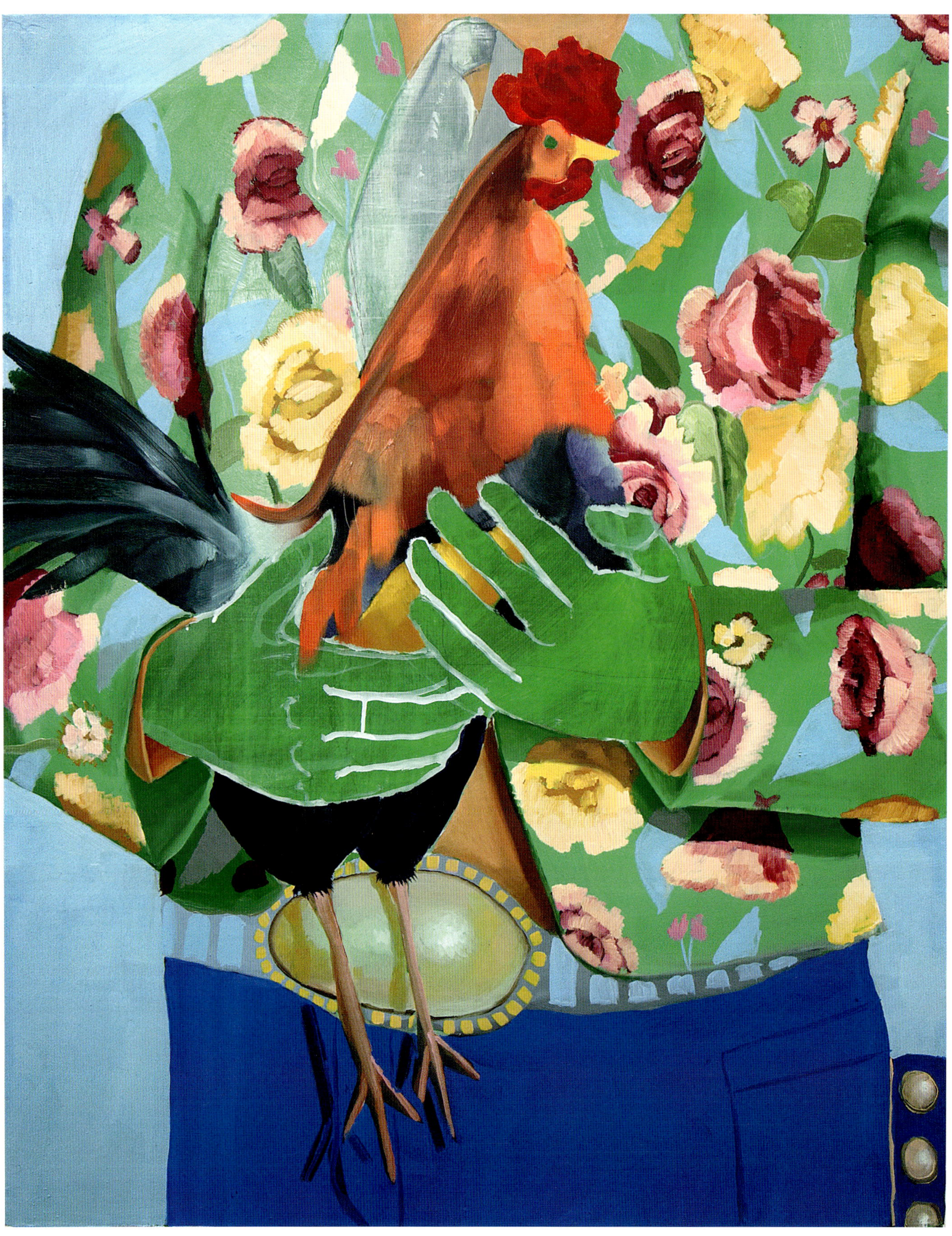

Ana Segovia, JORGE NEGRETE'S COCK, 2018.
Oil on linen. 24 x 30 inches. Private collection

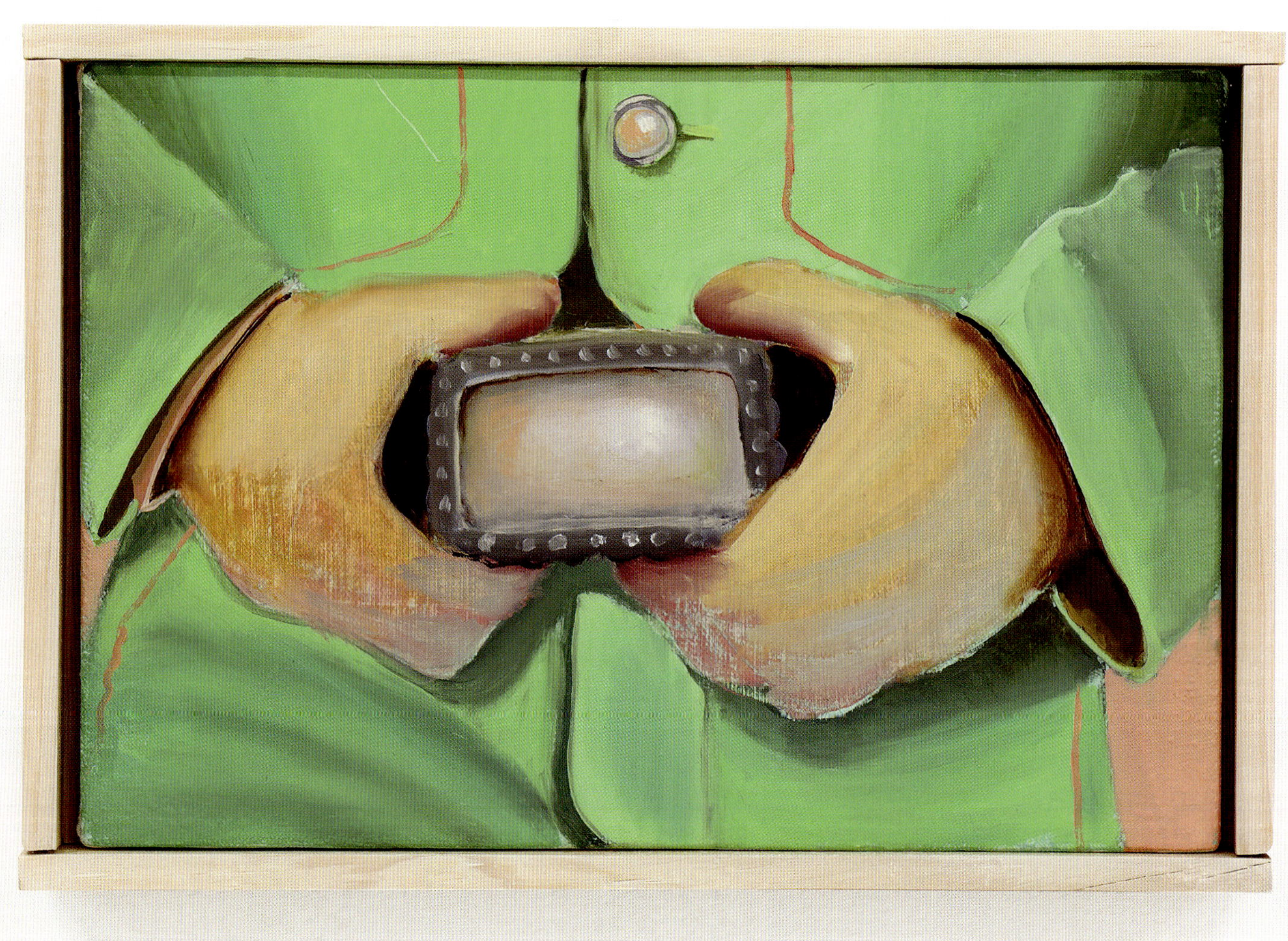

Ana Segovia, YOU LIKE IT HOW I LIKE IT – I, 2018.
Oil on canvas. 8¾ x 13½ inches. Private collection

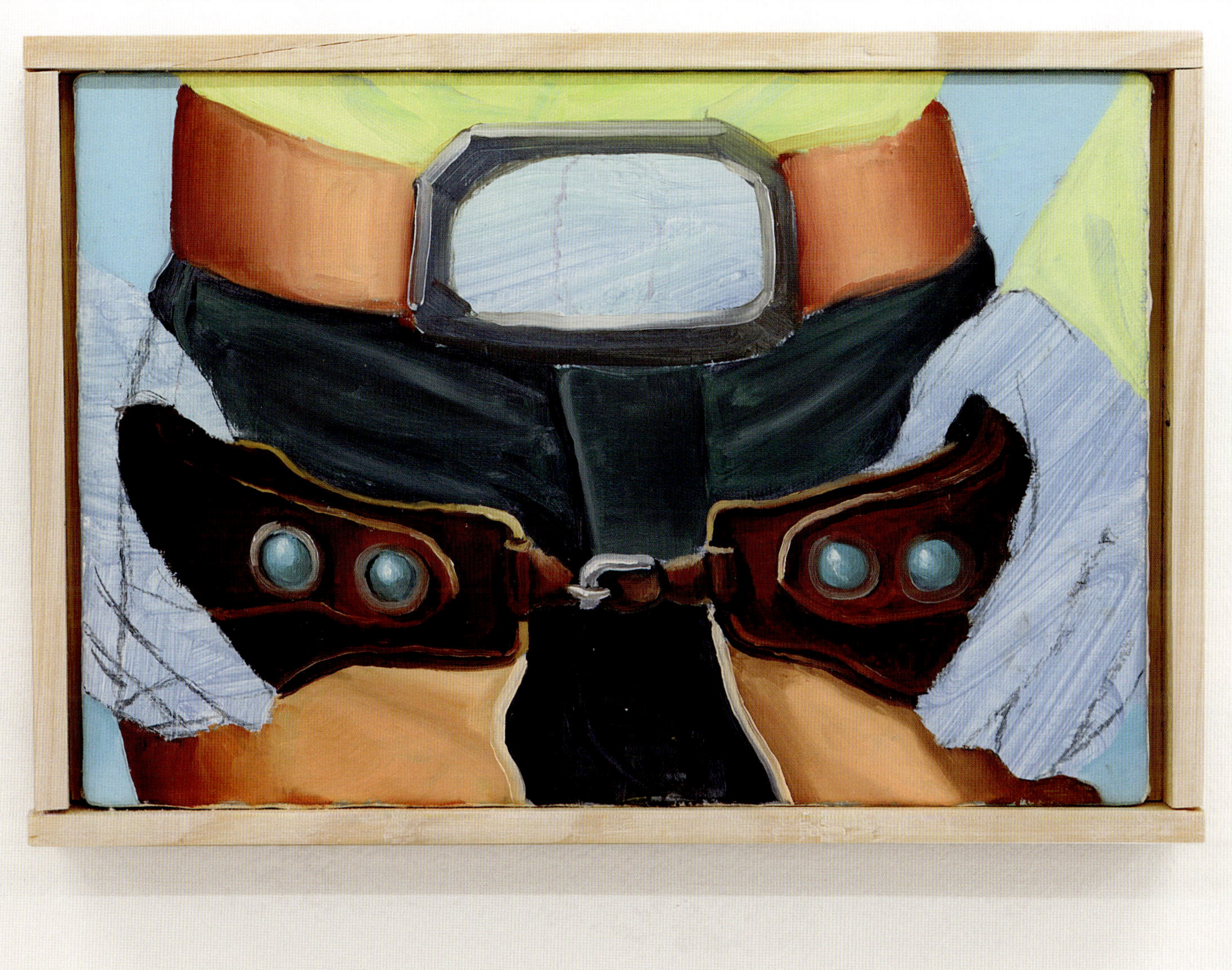

Ana Segovia, YOU LIKE IT HOW I LIKE IT – IV, 2018.
Oil on canvas. 8¾ x 13½ inches. Private collection

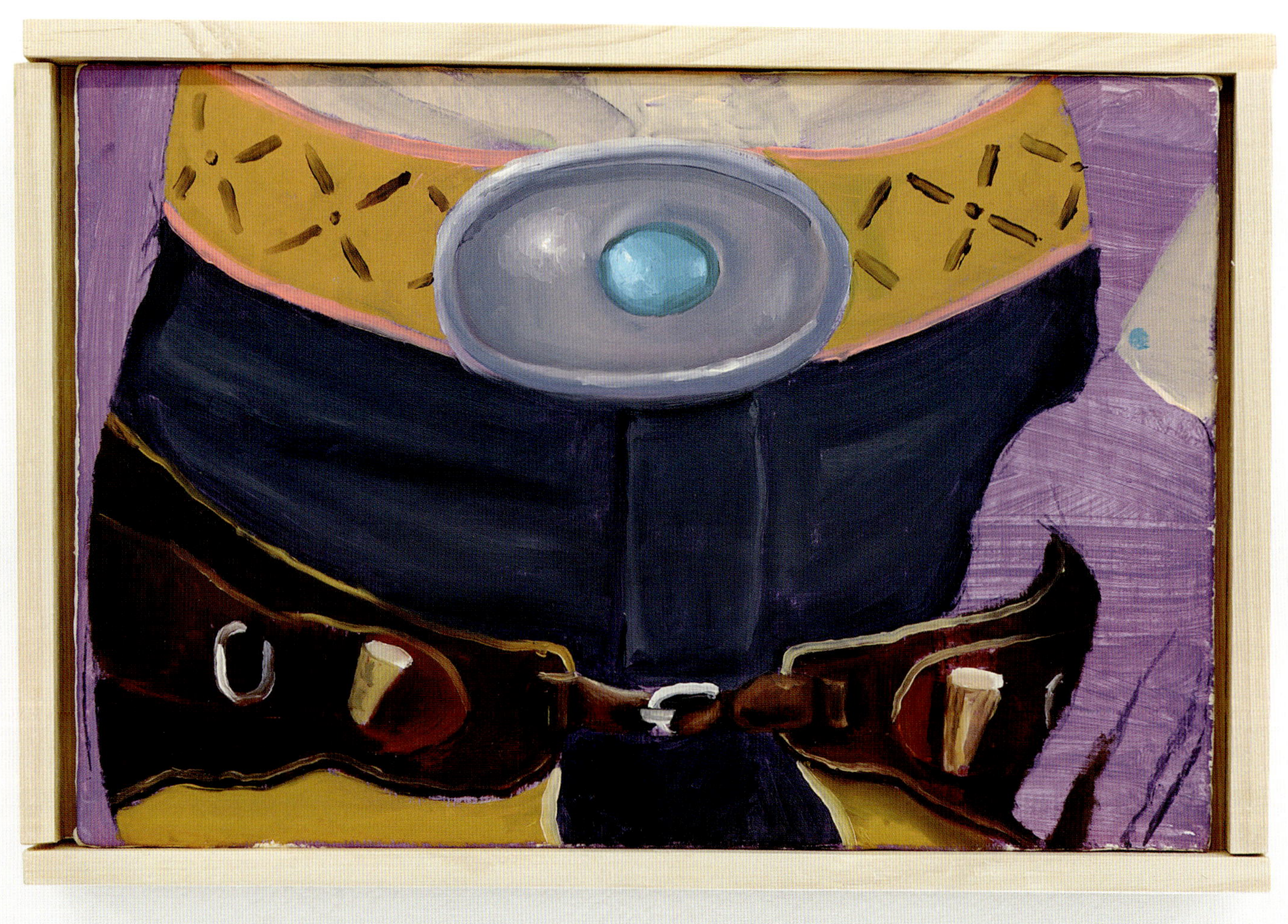

Ana Segovia, YOU LIKE IT HOW I LIKE IT – II, 2018.
Oil on canvas. 8¾ x 13½ inches. Private collection

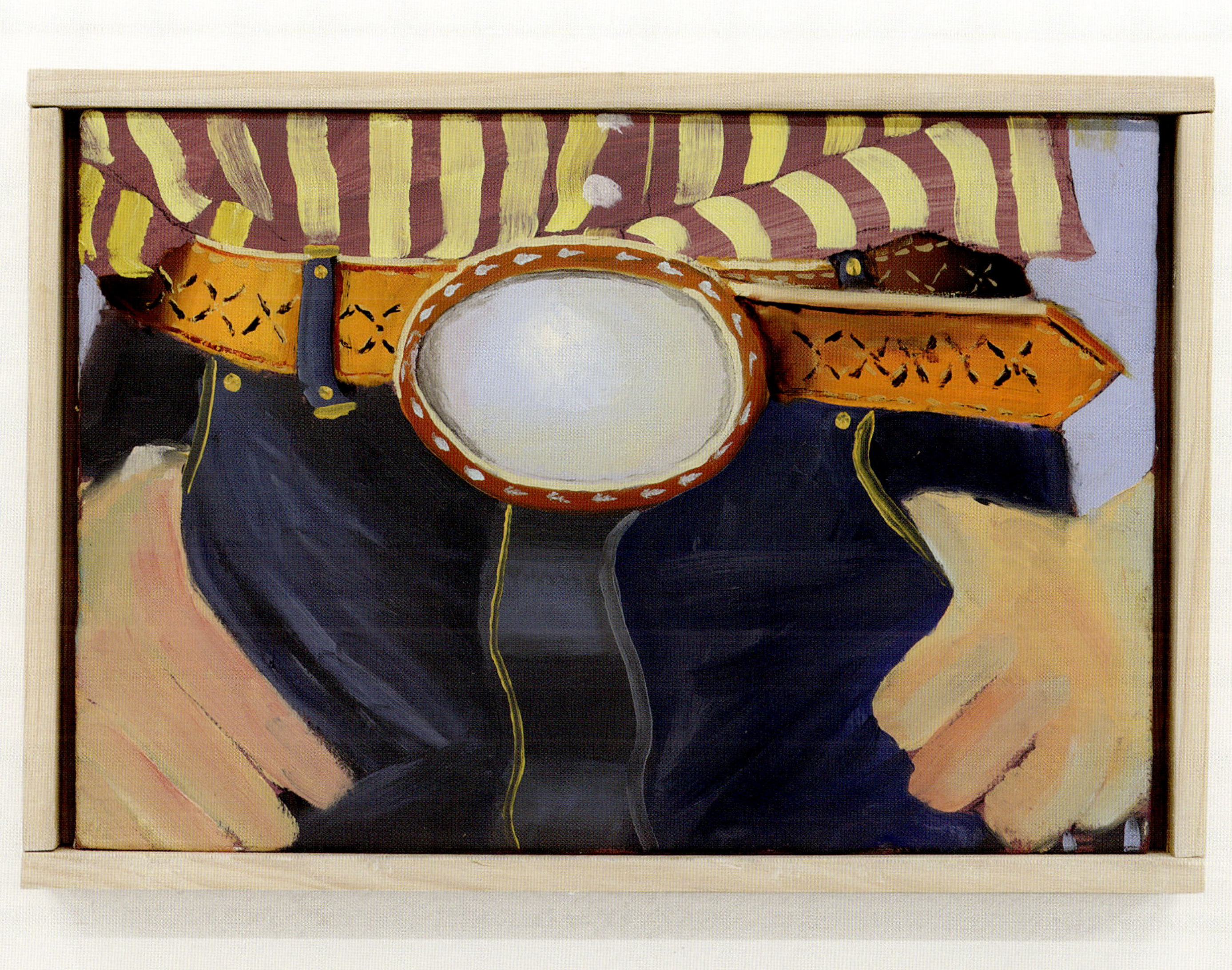

Ana Segovia, YOU LIKE IT HOW I LIKE IT – III, 2018.
Oil on canvas. 8¾ x 13½ inches. Private collection

Opposite: Amy Sherald, WHAT'S PRECIOUS INSIDE OF HIM DOES NOT CARE TO BE KNOWN BY THE MIND IN WAYS THAT DIMINISH ITS PRESENCE (ALL AMERICAN), 2017. Oil on canvas. 54 x 43 inches. Collection of Evan Boris and Monique Meloche

Following pages: Stephanie Syjuco, DOUBLE VISION, 2022. Digitally printed vinyl, 25 dye-sublimation prints on aluminum, 4 framed pigment prints, and digitally printed fabric panels. Installation view at the Amon Carter Museum of American Art, Fort Worth.

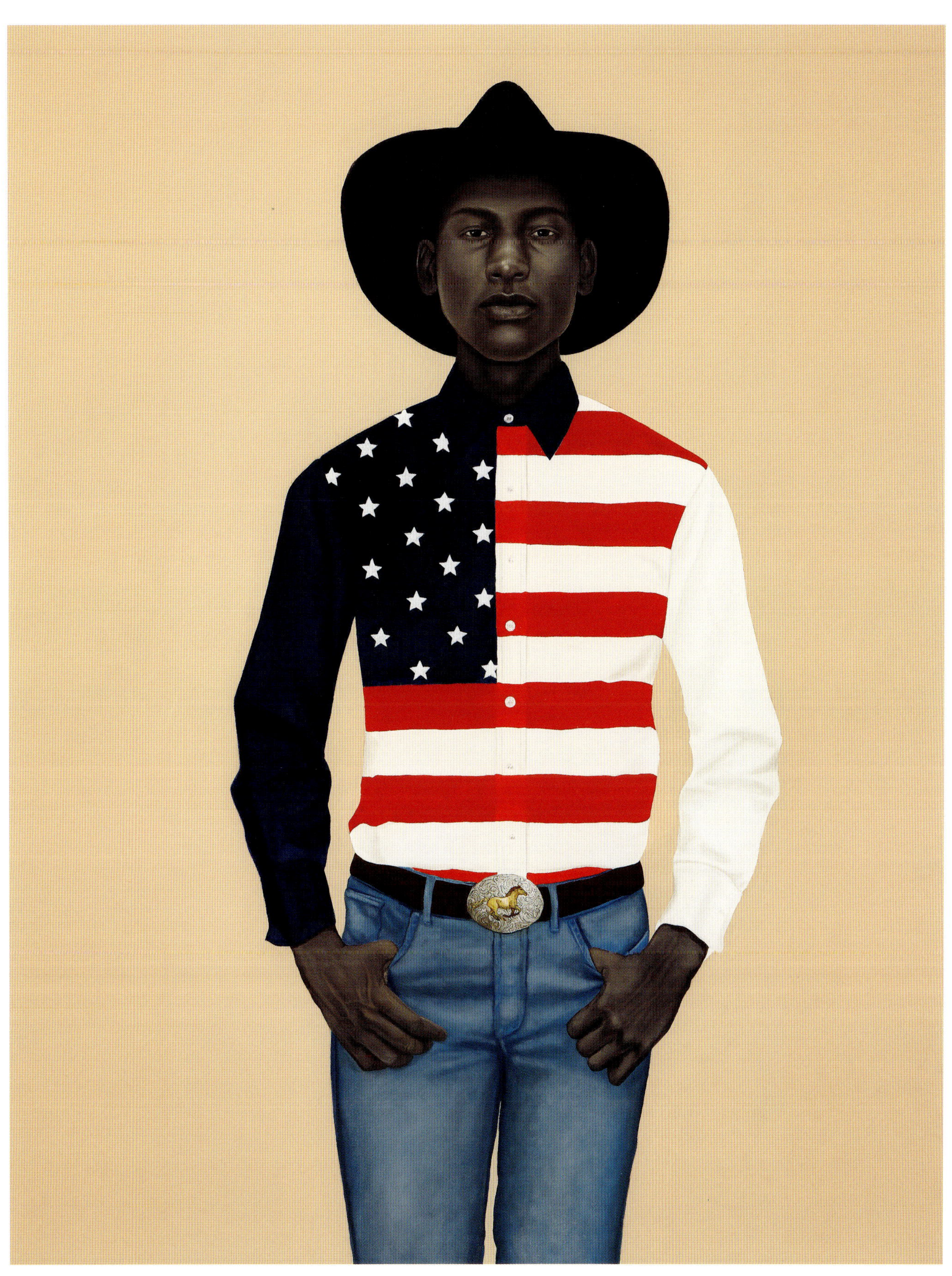

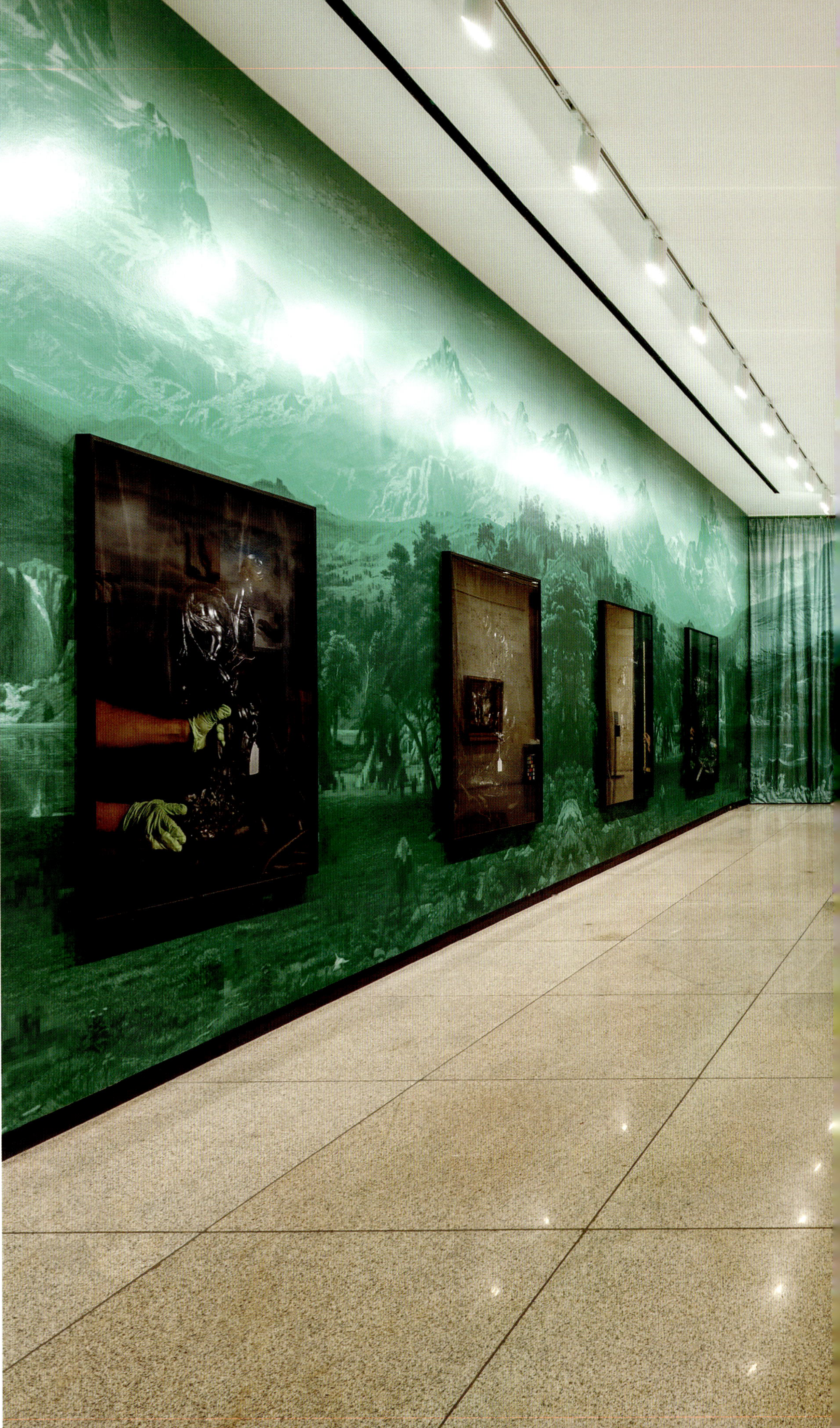

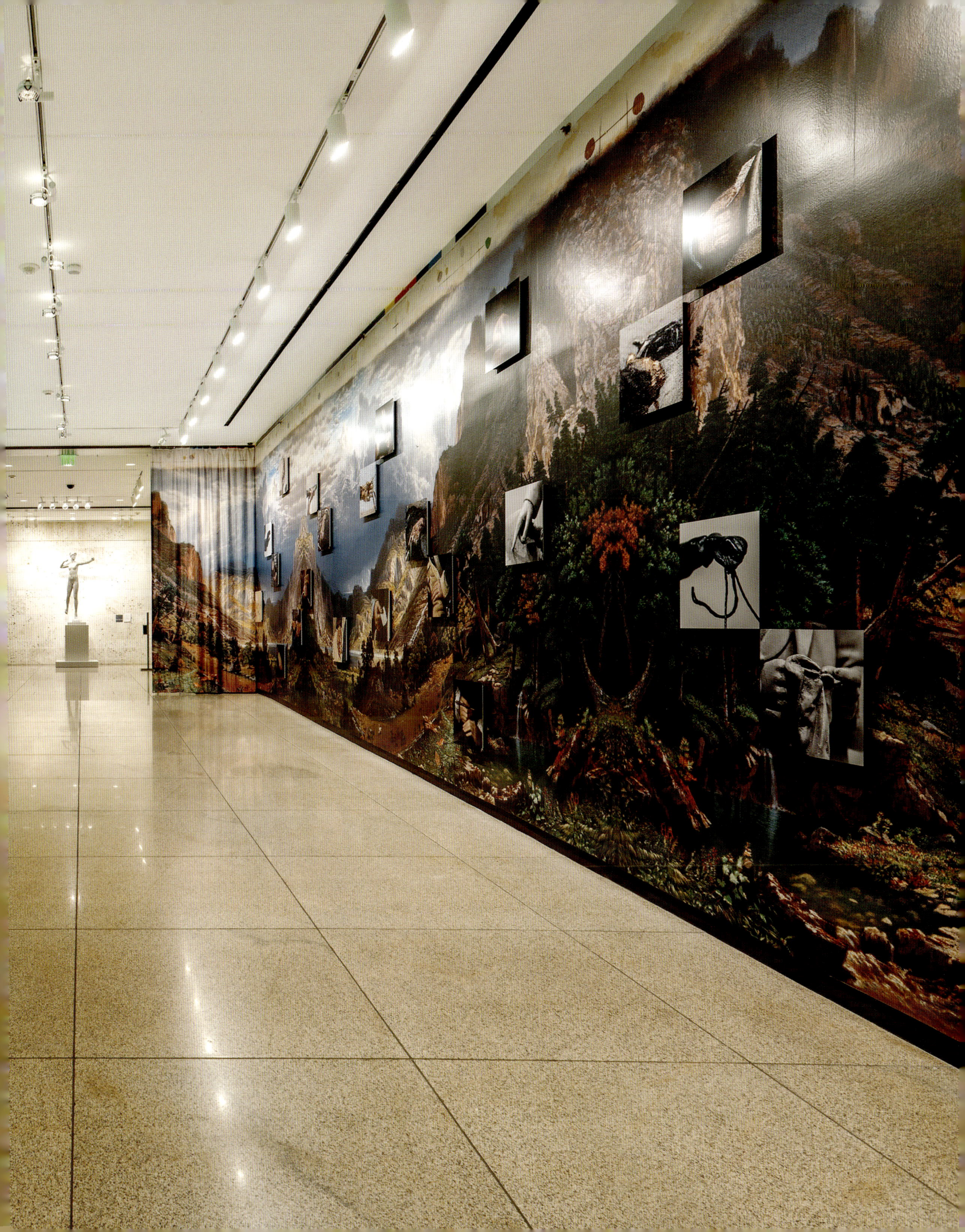

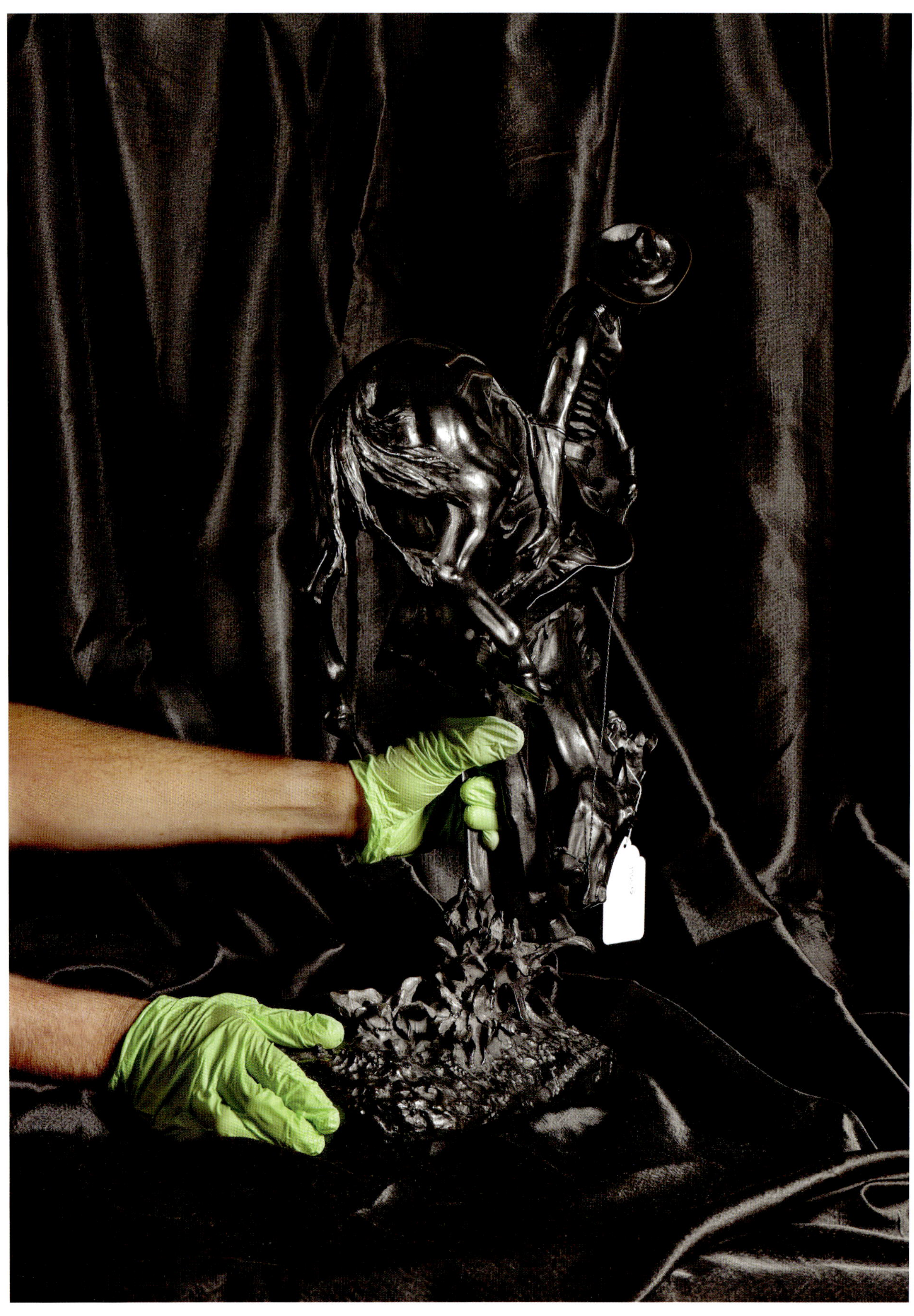

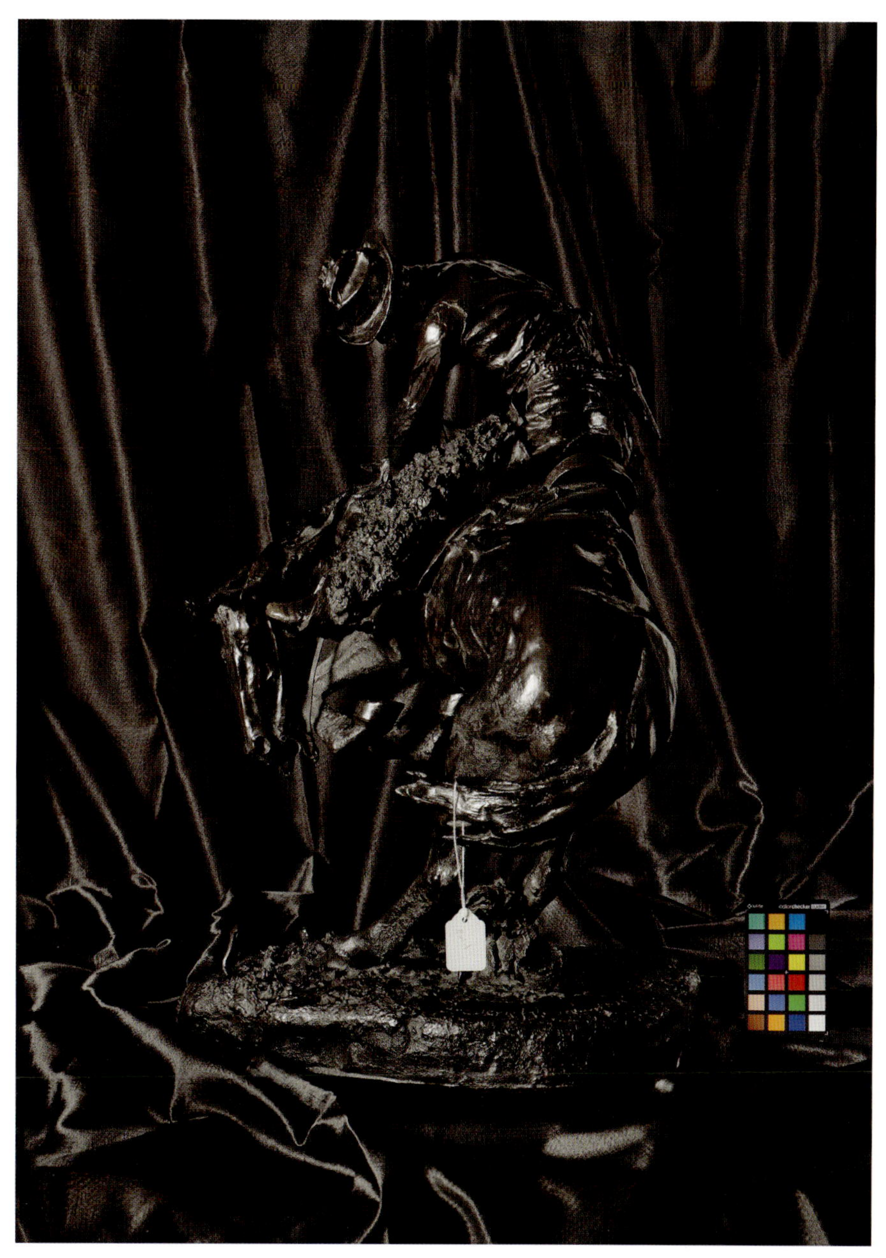

Opposite: Stephanie Syjuco, SET-UP (THE OUTLAW), 2022.
Archival pigment print. 72 x 52 inches, framed

Above: Stephanie Syjuco, SET-UP (THE RATTLESNAKE), 2022.
Archival pigment print. 72 x 52 inches, framed

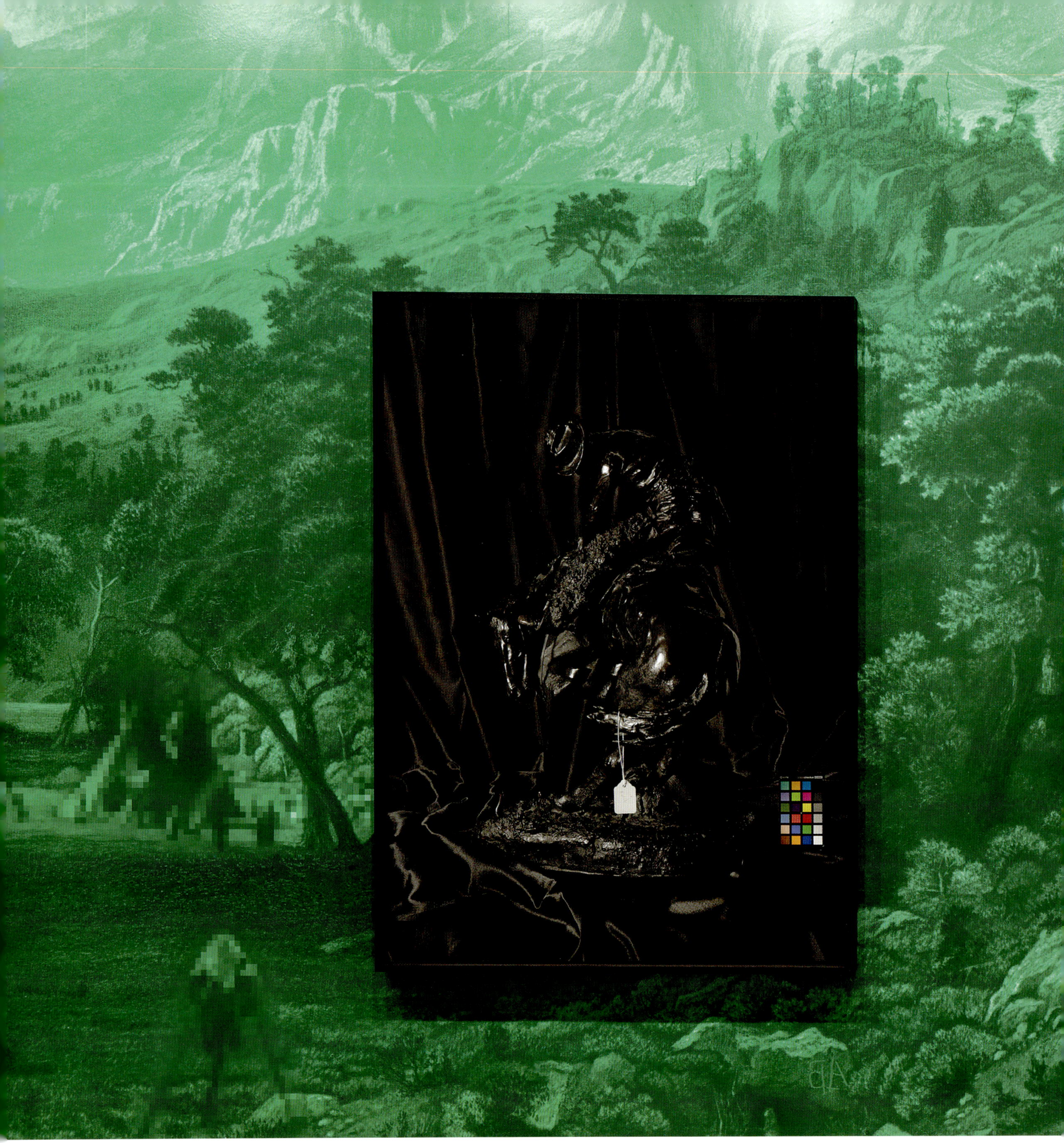

Stephanie Syjuco, DOUBLE VISION, 2022. Digitally printed vinyl, 25 dye-sublimation prints on aluminum, 4 framed pigment prints, and digitally printed fabric panels. Installation view at the Amon Carter Museum of American Art, Fort Worth

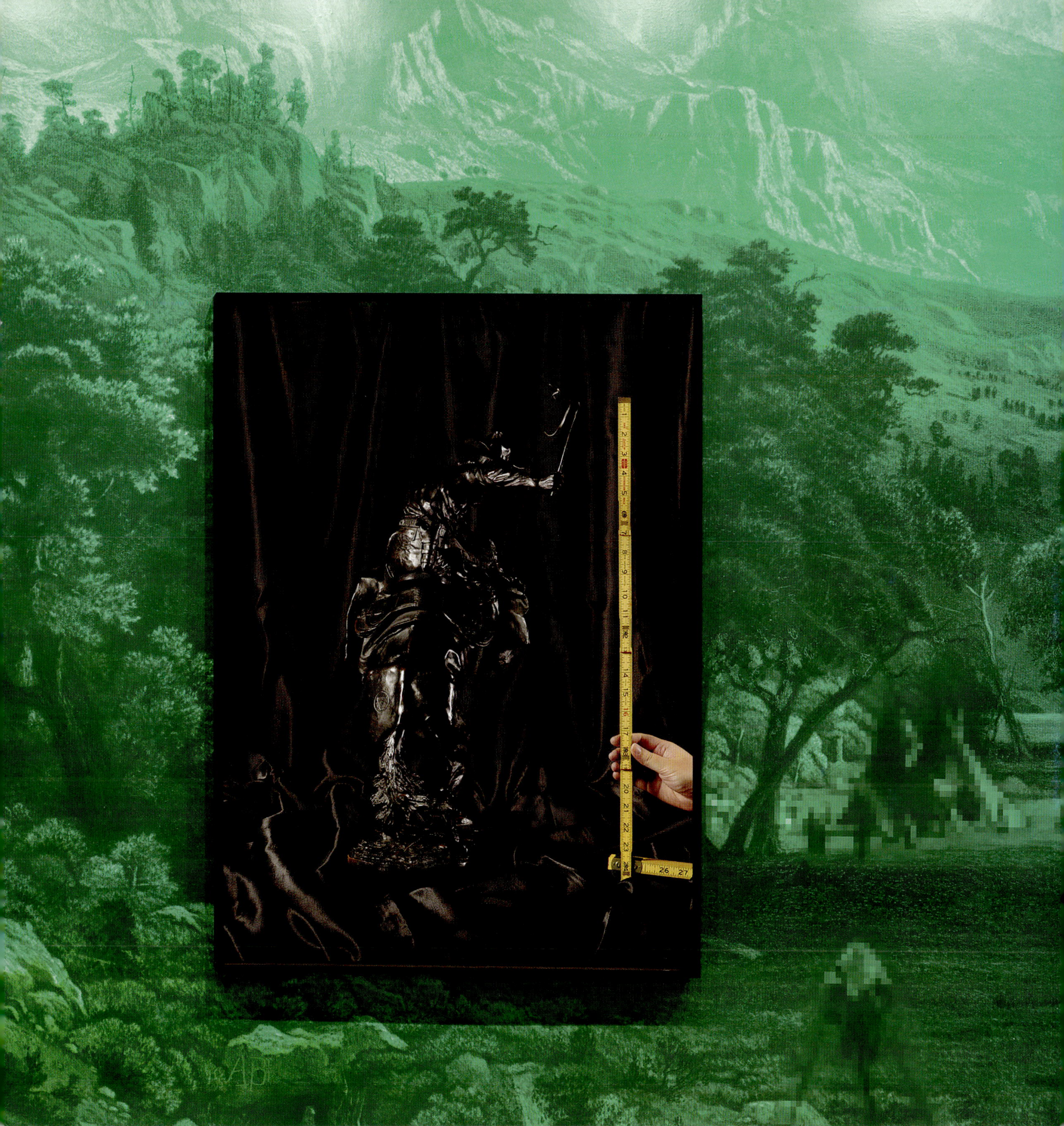

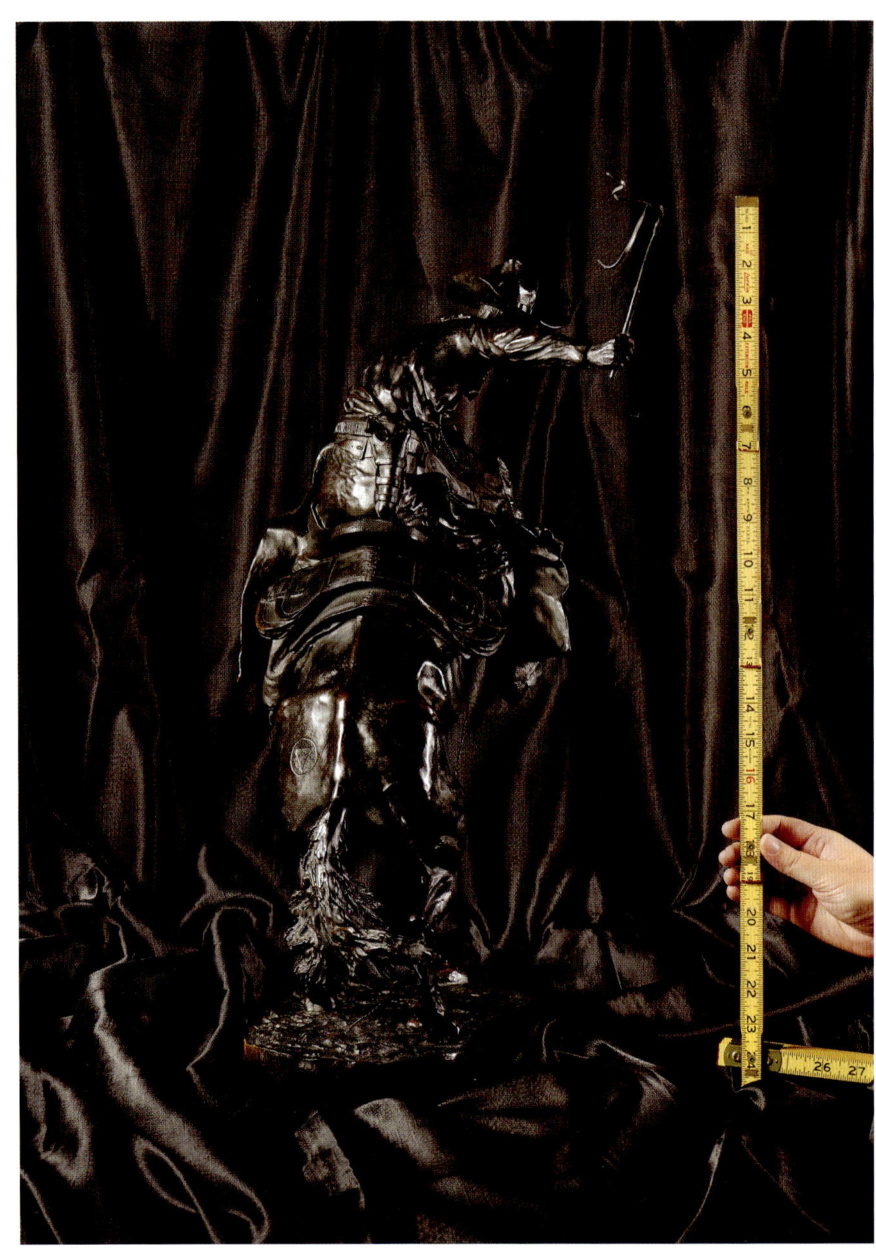

Above: **Stephanie Syjuco, SET-UP (THE BRONCHO BUSTER 1), 2022. Archival pigment print. 72 x 52 inches, framed**

Opposite: **Stephanie Syjuco, SET-UP (THE BRONCHO BUSTER 2), 2022. Archival pigment print. 72 x 52 inches, framed**

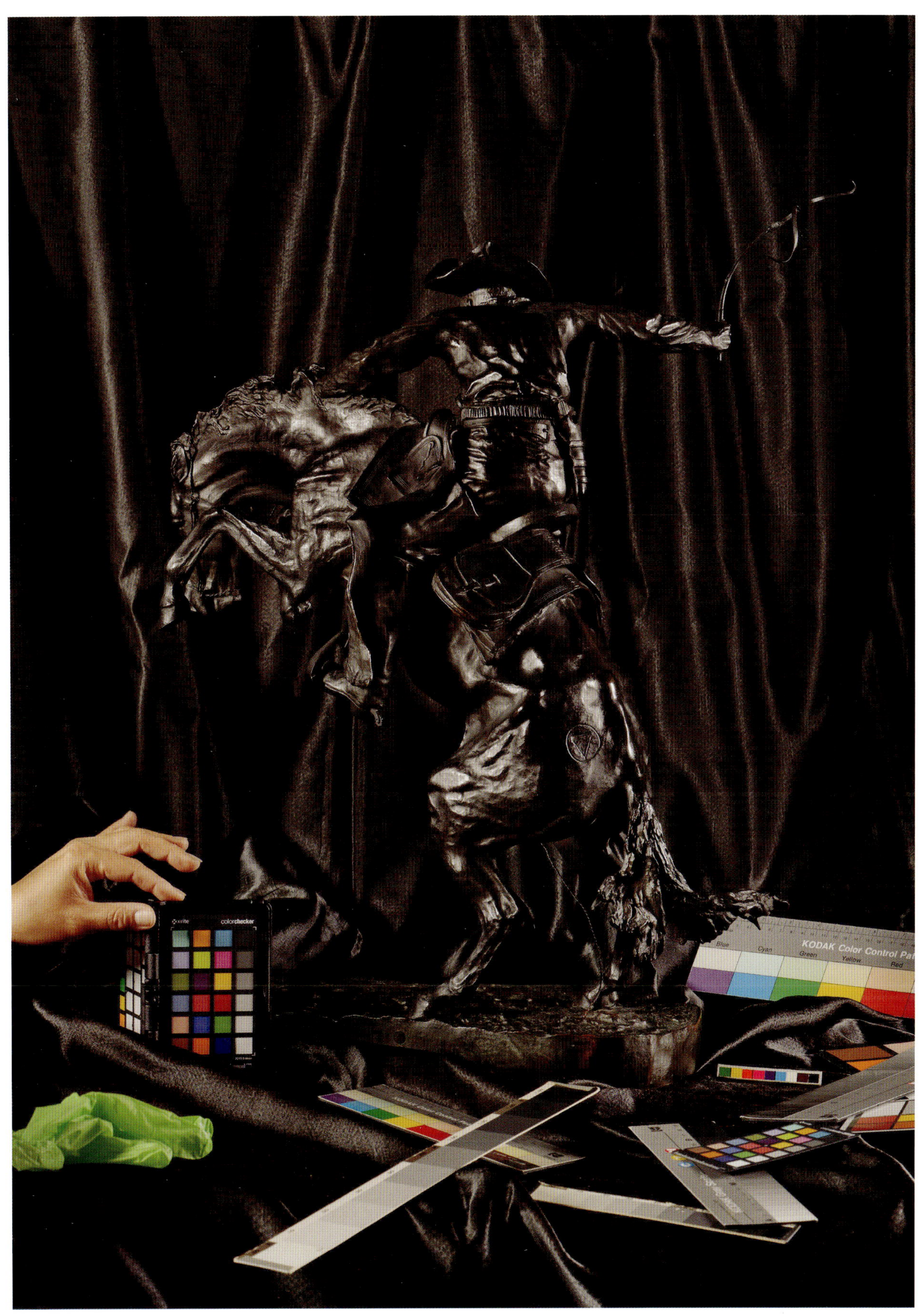
colorchecker
KODAK Color Control
Blue
Cyan
Green
Yellow
Red

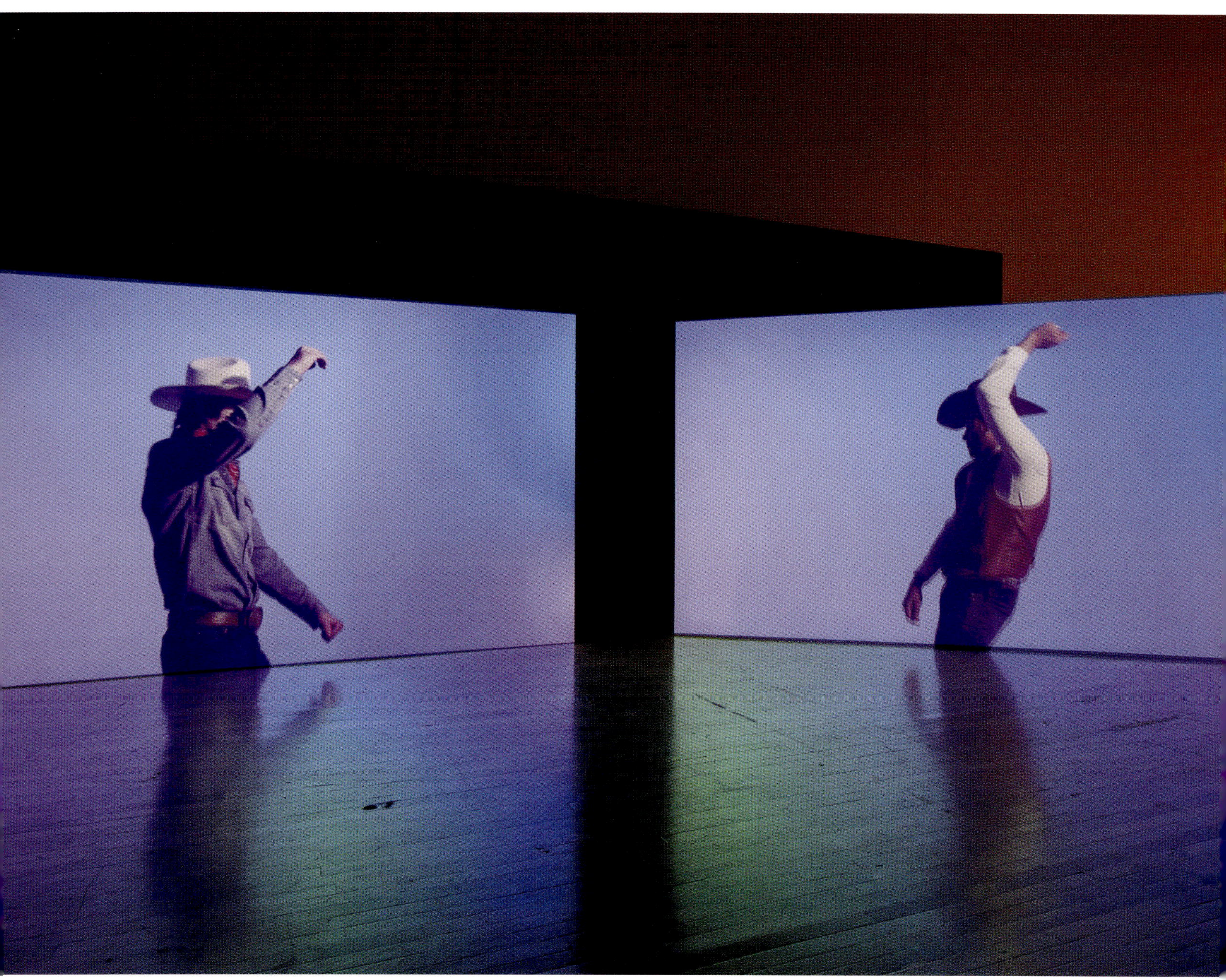

Pages 202–05: Kenneth Tam, SILENT SPIKES, 2021. Installation view, Queens Museum, New York. Two channel video with sound. Duration: 20:29 minutes. Commissioned by the Queens Museum with support from the Asian Art Circle of the Guggenheim Museum

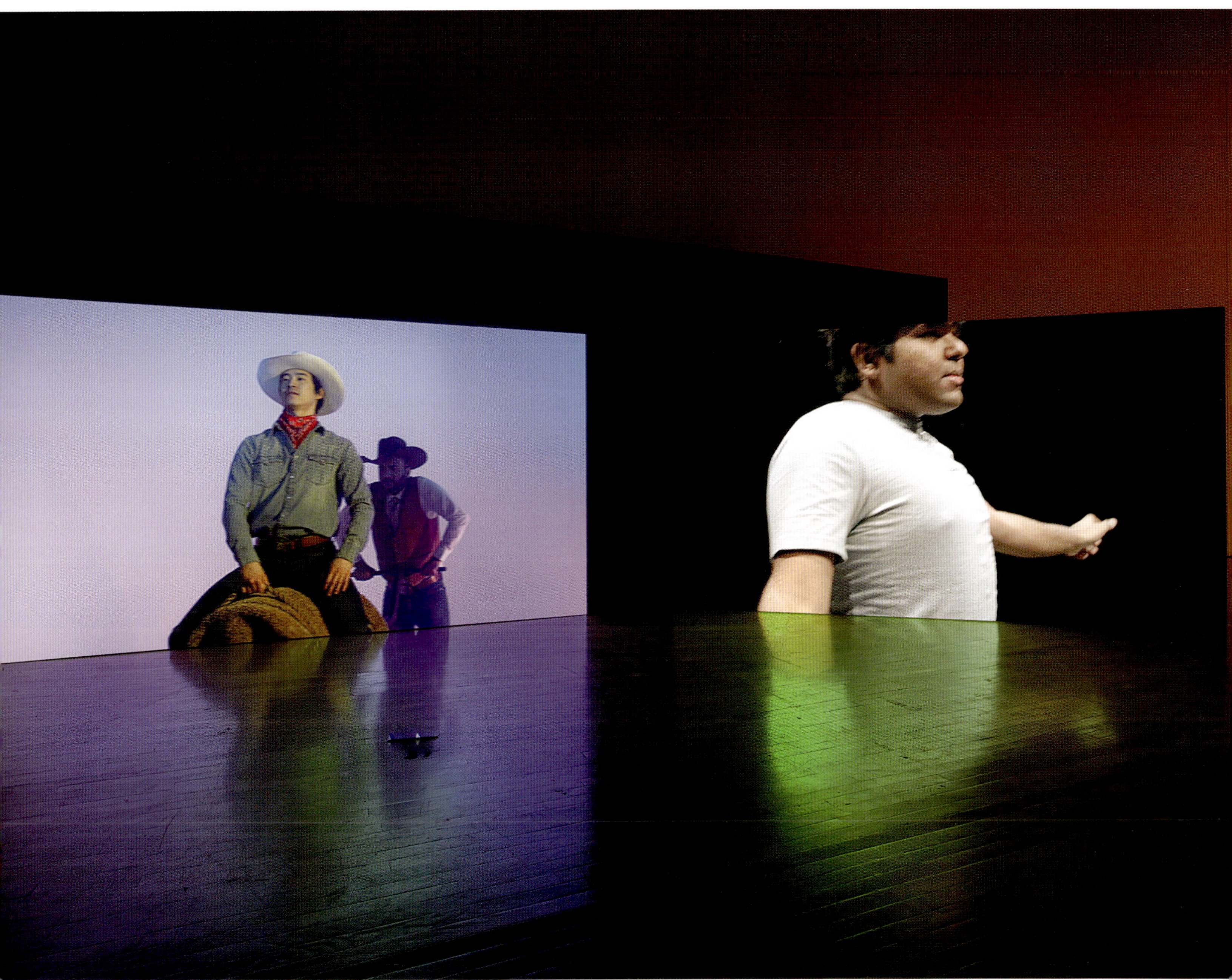

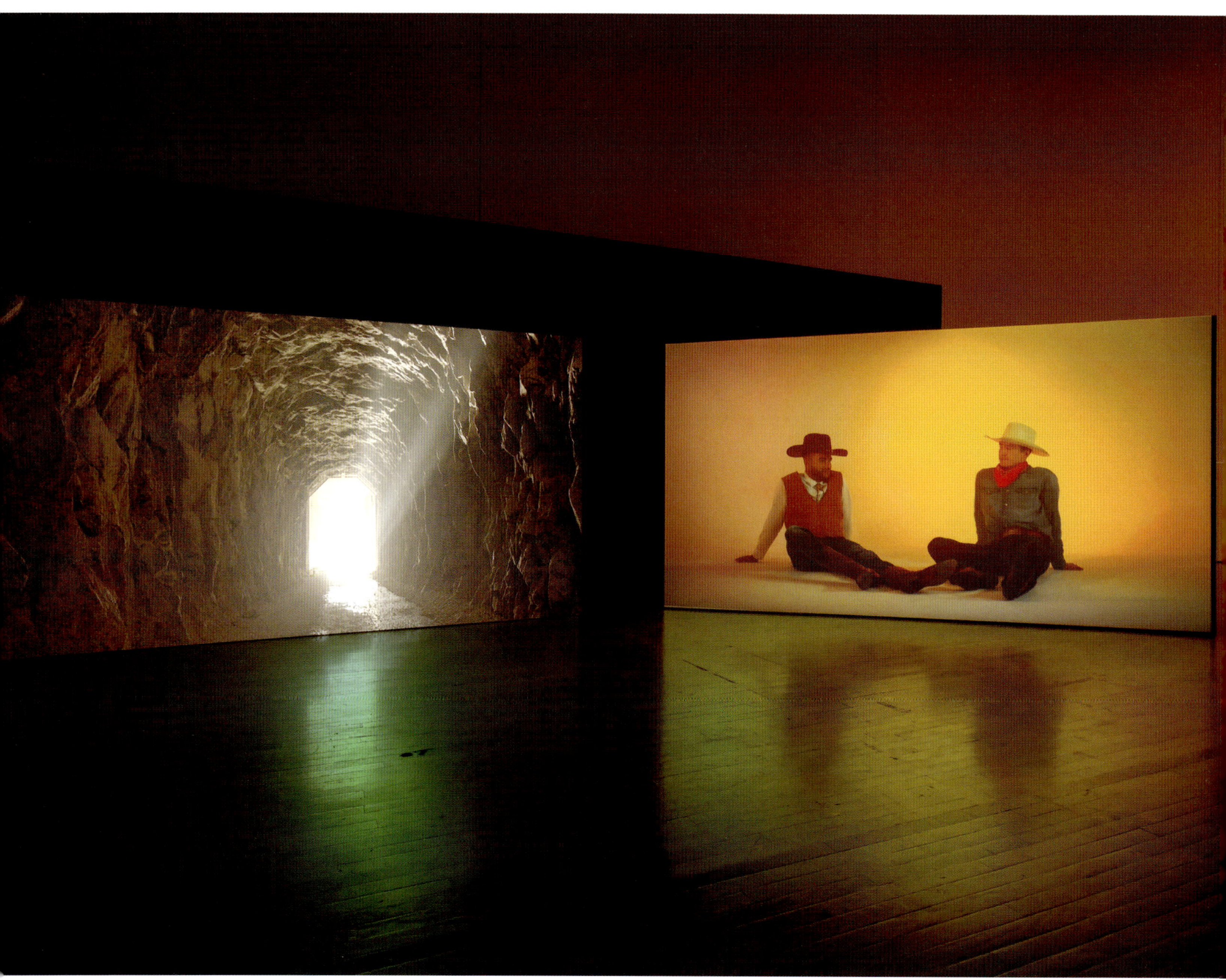

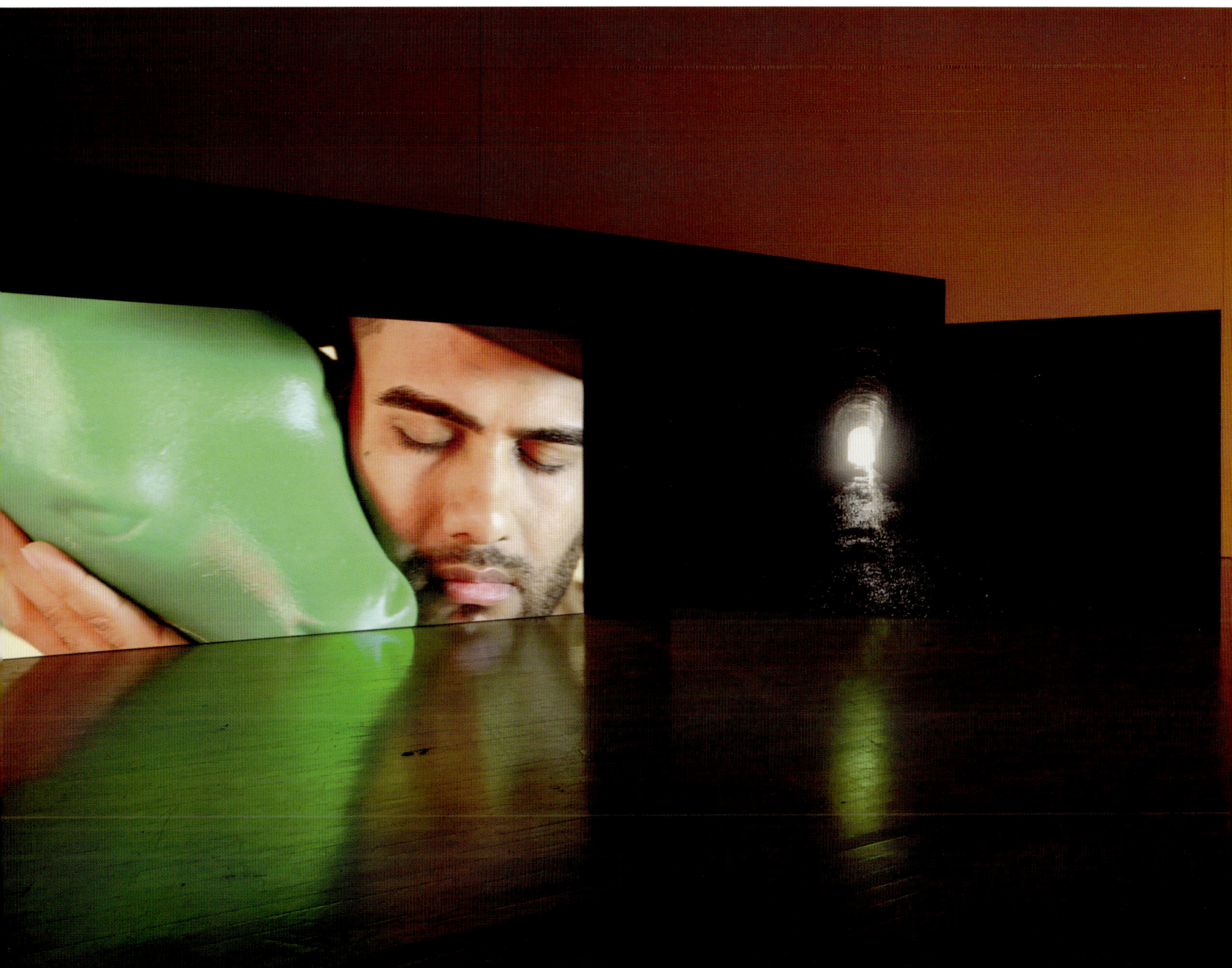

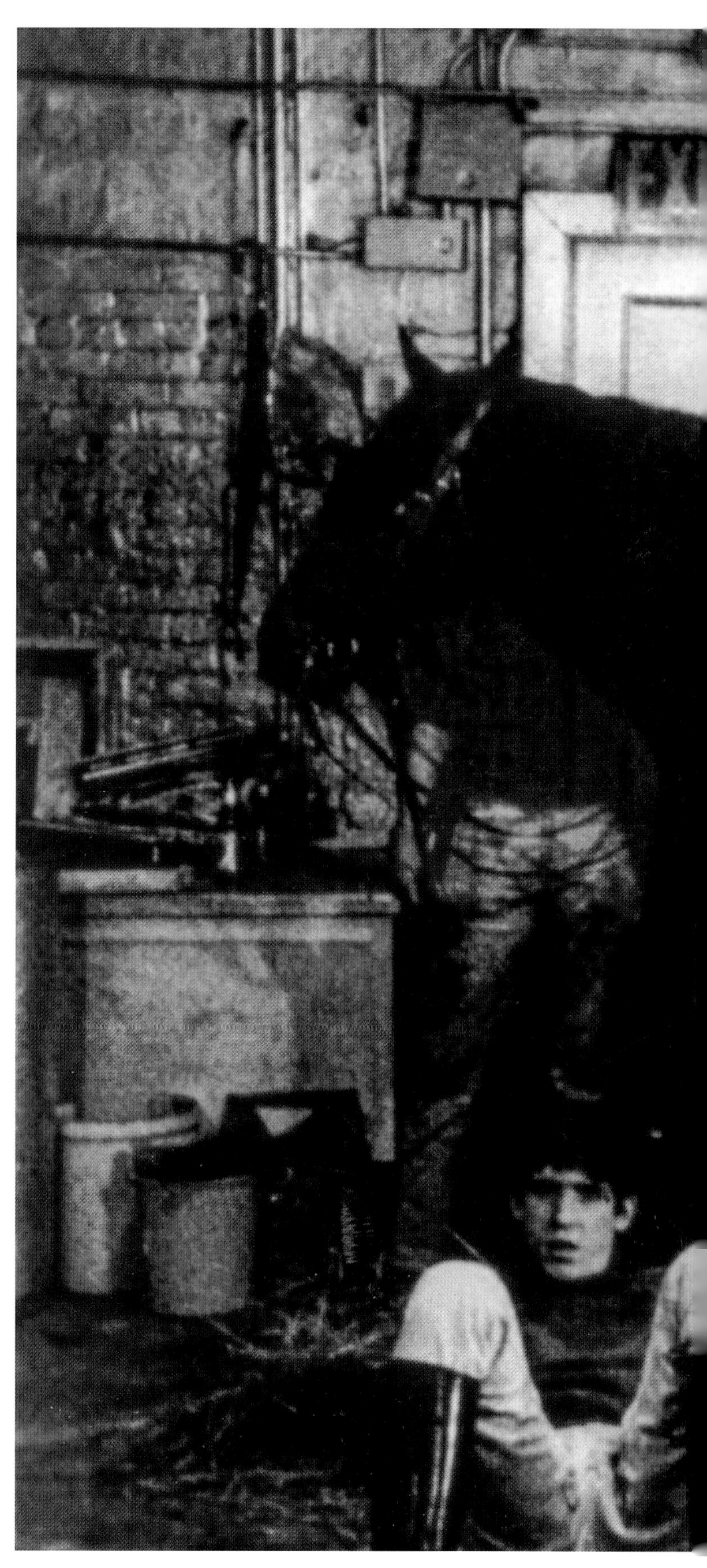

Andy Warhol, still from HORSE, 1965.
16mm black-and-white film, sound.
Duration: 66 minutes

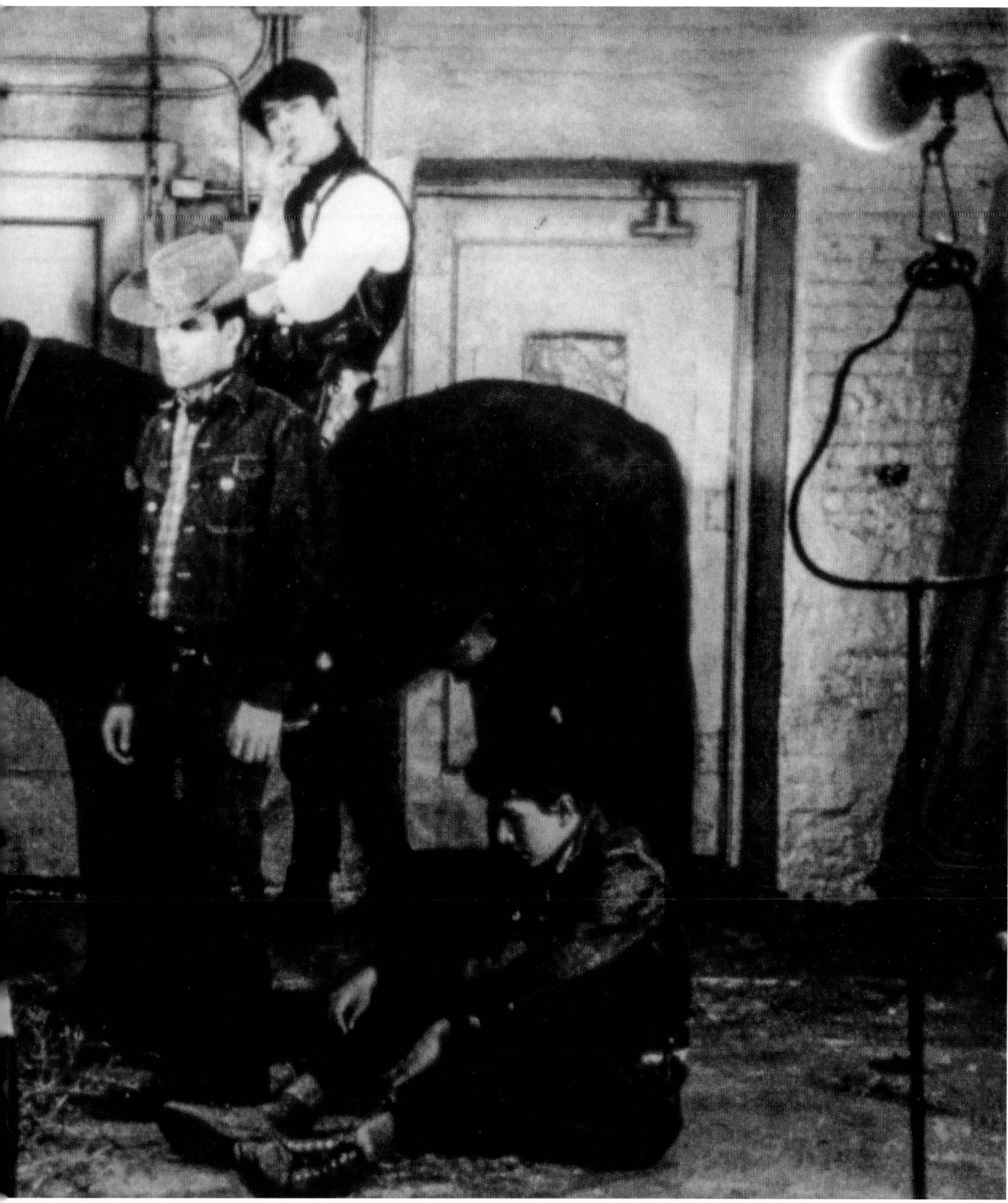

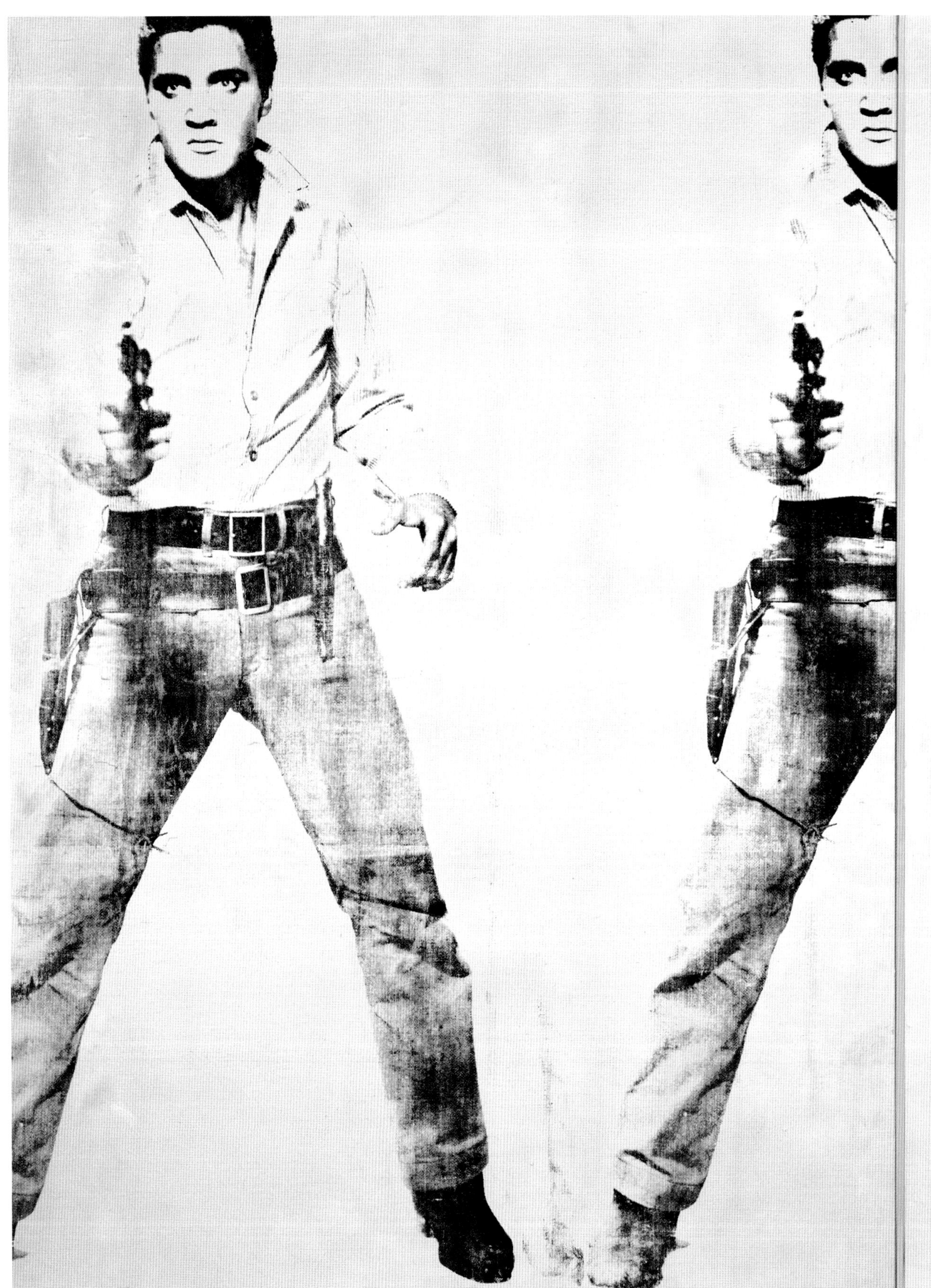

Andy Warhol, DOUBLE ELVIS, 1963/1976. Silkscreen ink and synthetic polymer paint on canvas. Each panel: 82¼ x 59⅛ inches. Collection of the Seattle Art Museum. Courtesy of the National Endowment for the Arts, PONCHO and the Seattle Art Museum Guild, 76.9. Photo: Paul Macapia.

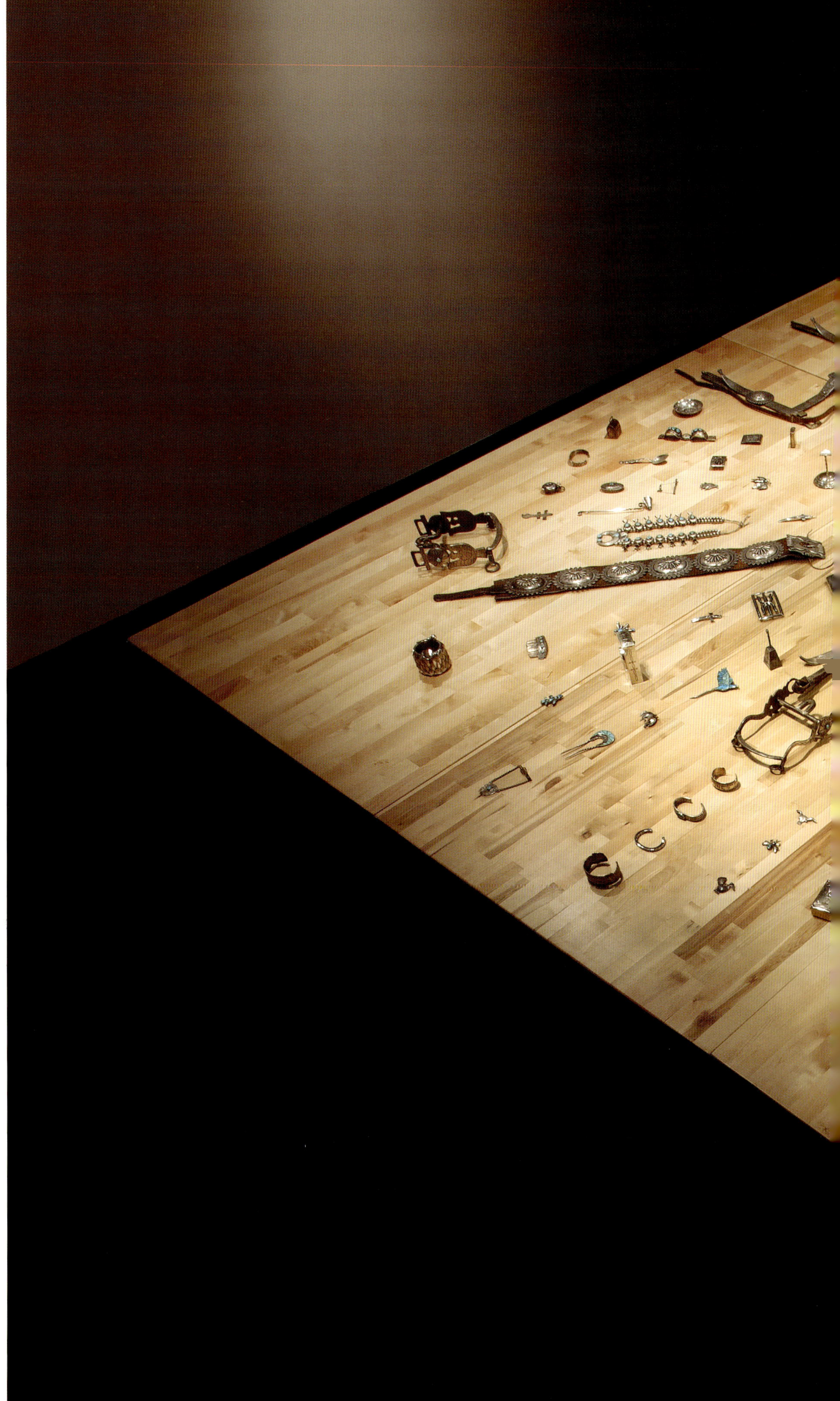

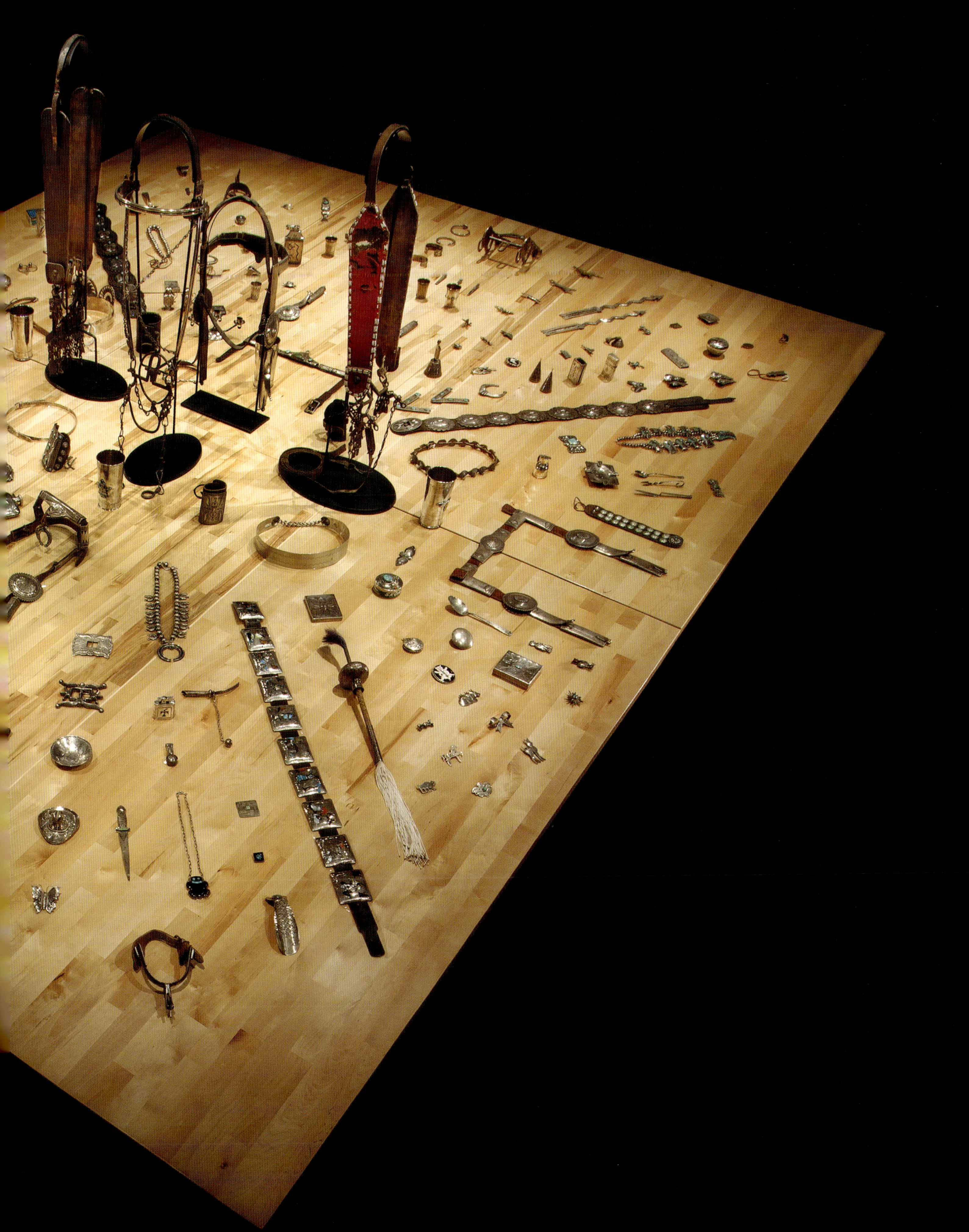

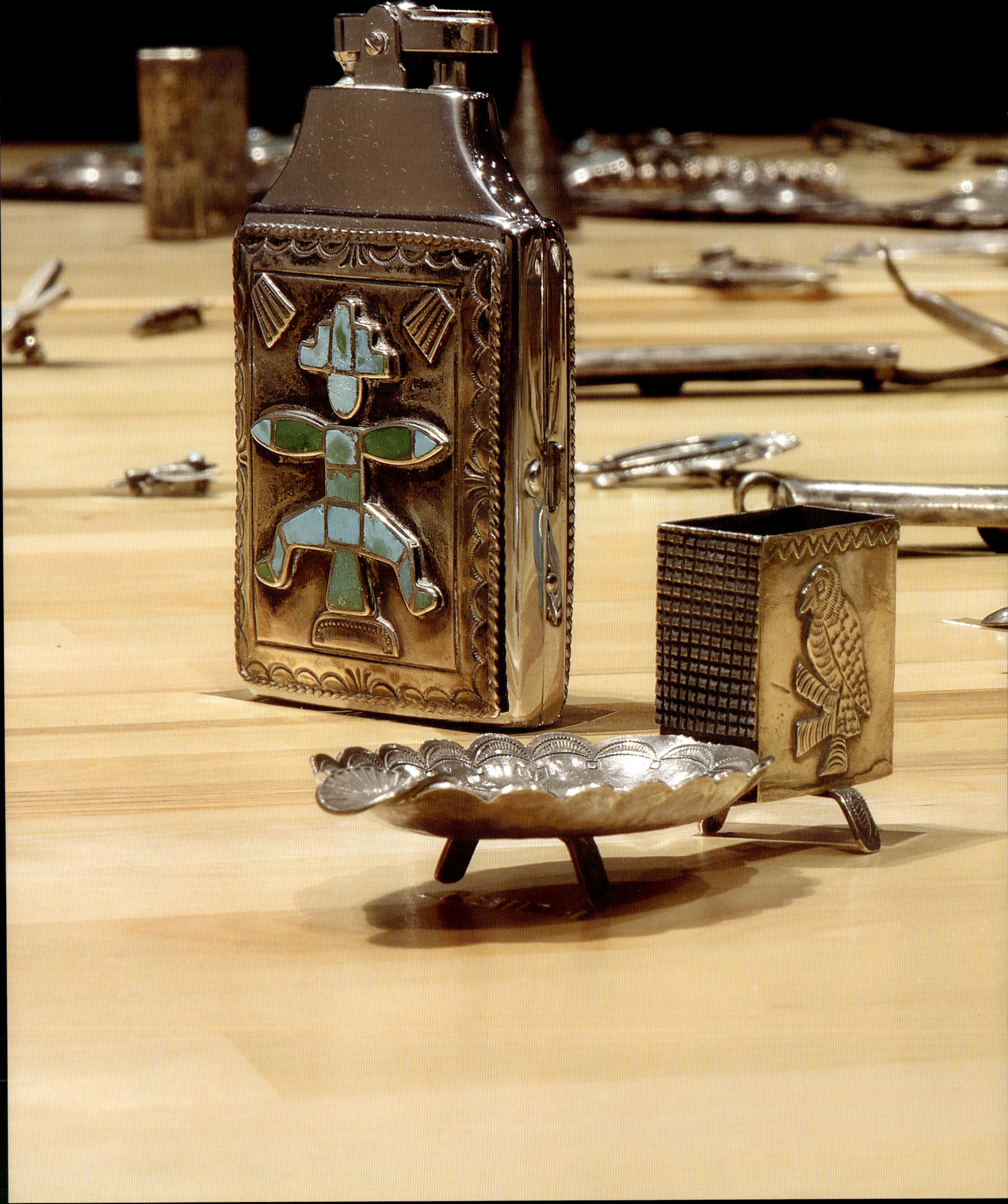

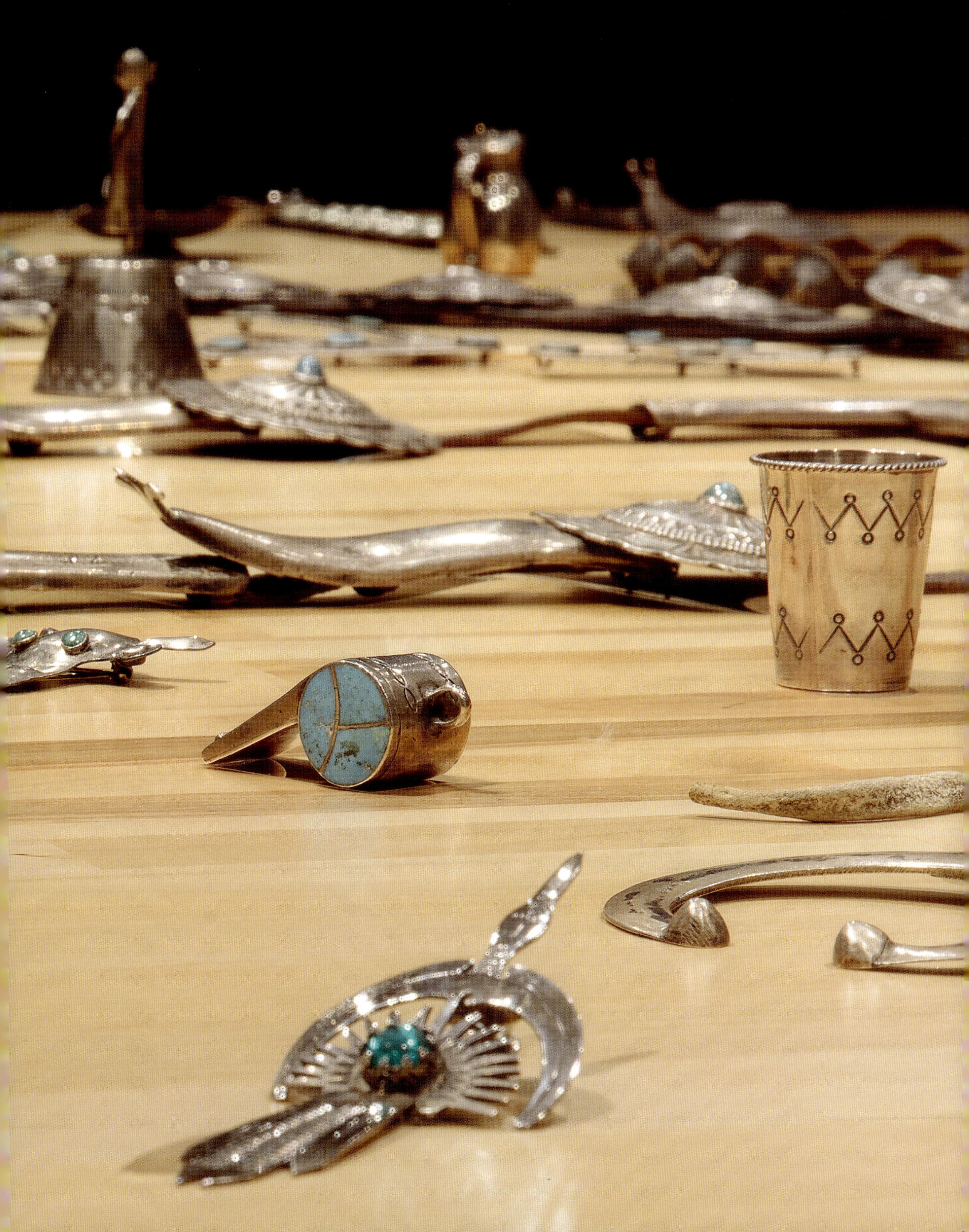

Pages 210–213: Nathan Young, ACTIVATION/TRANSFORMATION, 2021. Installation view, Wheelwright Museum, Sante Fe, 2021

Opposite: Nathan Young (Delaware/Kiowa/Pawnee) in the process of installing ACTIVATION/TRANSFORMATION, 2021

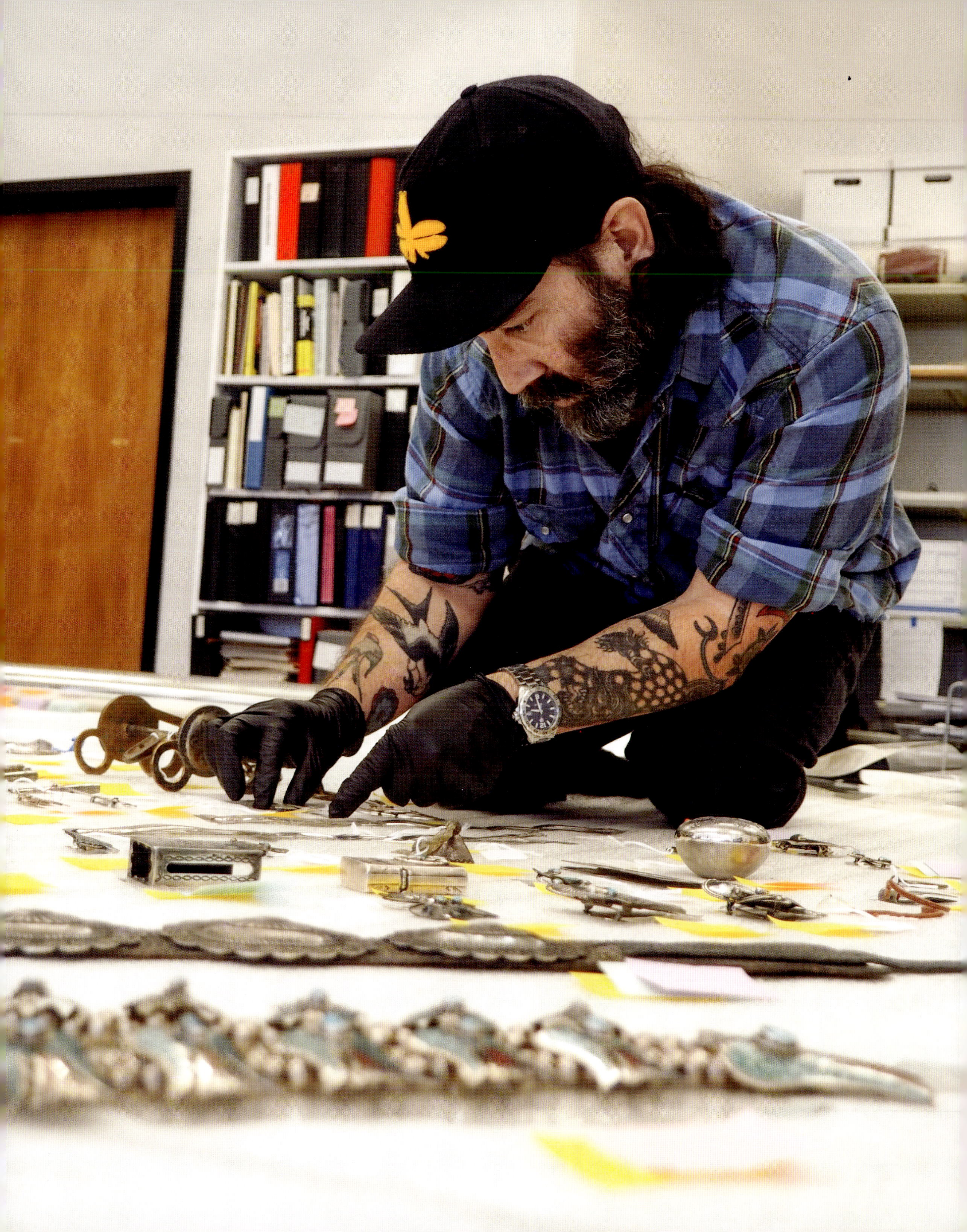

CHECKLIST

John Baldessari (1931–2020)
THE SPACE BETWEEN HAT, ROCK AND SHADOW., 2019
Varnished inkjet prints on canvas with acrylic paint
54⅛ × 57⅝ × 1½ inches
© John Baldessari 2019. Courtesy of the Estate of
John Baldessari © 2023. Courtesy of Sprüth Magers

R. Alan Brooks (b. 1975)
A DREAM TO DEARFIELD (Panels 1–7), 2023
Graphic novel
Courtesy of the artist

Mel Chin (b. 1951)
ROUGH RIDER, 2002
Barbed wire and steel
38 x 29 x 23 inches
Collection of the Estate of Ann Harithas

Gregg Deal (b. 1975)
TEEPUGOOBAKWAETU MODU
(ANIMALS THAT ROAM ON THE EARTH), 2023
Performance, mixed media
Courtesy of the artist

Angela Ellsworth (b. 1964)
IN ARMS I, 2023
11,112 black and white dress pins /
boutonnière pins, wood, fabric, and steel
28½ x 12 x 13 inches
Courtesy of the artist and Turner Carroll Gallery, Santa Fe

Angela Ellsworth (b. 1964)
IN ARMS II, 2023
12,248 black and white dress pins /
boutonnière pins, wood, fabric, and steel
28 x 10 x 13 inches
Courtesy of the artist and Turner Carroll Gallery, Santa Fe

Angela Ellsworth (b. 1964)
IN MEMORY OF OUR SISTERS II, 2023
Black and pewter dress pins / boutonnière pins,
wood, fabric, and steel
29 x 11½ x 13½ inches
Courtesy of the artist and Turner Carroll Gallery, Santa Fe

rafa esparza (b. 1981)
AL TEMPO, 2021
Acrylic on adobe
72 x 113½ x 2 inches (diptych)
Courtesy of the artist and Commonwealth and
Council, Los Angeles and Mexico City

rafa esparza (b. 1981), in collaboration with
Fabian Guerrero
QUERÍAS NORTE, 2023
Mixed media
Courtesy of the artists

Juan Fuentes (b. 1990)
UNTITLED, 2021, from the series
THIRTY-SIX MILES EAST
Photograph
11 x 14 inches
Courtesy of the artist

Juan Fuentes (b. 1990)
UNTITLED, 2021, from the series
THIRTY-SIX MILES EAST
Photograph
11 x 14 inches
Courtesy of the artist

Juan Fuentes (b. 1990)
UNTITLED, 2021, from the series
THIRTY-SIX MILES EAST
Photograph
11 x 14 inches
Courtesy of the artist

Juan Fuentes (b. 1990)
UNTITLED, 2021, from the series
THIRTY-SIX MILES EAST
Photograph
11 x 14 inches
Courtesy of the artist

Karl Haendel (b. 1976)
RODEO 10, 2023
Pencil and graphite on paper
103 x 84 inches
Courtesy of the artist and Vielmetter Los Angeles;
Mitchell-Innes & Nash, New York; and WENTRUP, Berlin

Karl Haendel (b. 1976)
RODEO 11, 2023
Pencil and graphite on paper
103 x 85 inches
Courtesy of the artist and Vielmetter Los Angeles;
Mitchell-Innes & Nash, New York; and WENTRUP, Berlin

Luis Jiménez (1940–2006)
RODEO QUEEN, 1972
Fiberglass and nylon "hair"
49 x 23 x 45 inches
Courtesy of Gerald Peters Gallery

Luis Jiménez (1940–2006)
STUDY PROGRESS II, 1974
Colored pencil on paper
39 x 111 inches
Collection of Adam Schiffer, Houston, TX

Kahlil Joseph (b. 1981)
WILDCAT (AUNT JANET), 2016
Three channel video
Duration: 7:53 minutes
Collection of the Bonnefanten
Copyright © Kahlil Joseph

Grace Kennison (b. 1995)
I REMEMBER BEING ALONE, 2023
Acrylic on canvas
63 x 40 inches
Courtesy of the artist

Deana Lawson (b. 1979)
COWBOYS, 2014
Pigment print
40 x 50 inches
Copyright © Deana Lawson Studio. Courtesy of the artist;
Gagosian, New York; David Kordansky Gallery, Los Angeles

Matthew J. Mahoney (1988–2017)
UNTITLED, 2013, from the series
IN THE WAKE OF JOHN JOEL GLANTON
Ink on paper
9 x 12 inches
Courtesy of the Estate of Matthew J. Mahoney

Matthew J. Mahoney (1988–2017)
UNTITLED, 2013, from the series
IN THE WAKE OF JOHN JOEL GLANTON
Ink on paper
9 x 12 inches
Courtesy of the Estate of Matthew J. Mahoney

Matthew J. Mahoney (1988–2017)
UNTITLED, 2013, from the series
IN THE WAKE OF JOHN JOEL GLANTON
Ink on paper
9 x 12 inches
Courtesy of the Estate of Matthew J. Mahoney

Matthew J. Mahoney (1988–2017)
UNTITLED, 2013, from the series
IN THE WAKE OF JOHN JOEL GLANTON
Ink on paper
9 x 12 inches
Courtesy of the Estate of Matthew J. Mahoney

Matthew J. Mahoney (1988–2017)
UNTITLED, 2013, from the series
IN THE WAKE OF JOHN JOEL GLANTON
Ink on paper
9 x 12 inches
Courtesy of the Estate of Matthew J. Mahoney

Matthew J. Mahoney (1988–2017)
UNTITLED, 2013, from the series
IN THE WAKE OF JOHN JOEL GLANTON
Ink on paper
9 x 12 inches
Courtesy of the Estate of Matthew J. Mahoney

Matthew J. Mahoney (1988–2017)
UNTITLED, 2013, from the series
IN THE WAKE OF JOHN JOEL GLANTON
Ink on paper
9 x 12 inches
Courtesy of the Estate of Matthew J. Mahoney

Matthew J. Mahoney (1988–2017)
UNTITLED, 2013, from the series
IN THE WAKE OF JOHN JOEL GLANTON
Ink on paper
9 x 12 inches
Courtesy of the Estate of Matthew J. Mahoney

Matthew J. Mahoney (1988–2017)
UNTITLED, 2013, from the series
IN THE WAKE OF JOHN JOEL GLANTON
Ink on paper
9 x 12 inches
Courtesy of the Estate of Matthew J. Mahoney

Matthew J. Mahoney (1988–2017)
UNTITLED, 2013, from the series
IN THE WAKE OF JOHN JOEL GLANTON
Ink on paper
9 x 12 inches
Courtesy of the Estate of Matthew J. Mahoney

Matthew J. Mahoney (1988–2017)
UNTITLED, 2013, from the series
IN THE WAKE OF JOHN JOEL GLANTON
Ink on paper
9 x 12 inches
Courtesy of the Estate of Matthew J. Mahoney

Matthew J. Mahoney (1988–2017)
UNTITLED, 2013, from the series
IN THE WAKE OF JOHN JOEL GLANTON
Ink on paper
9 x 12 inches
Courtesy of the Estate of Matthew J. Mahoney

Laurel Nakadate (b. 1975)
LUCKY TIGER #20, 2009
Type-C print and fingerprinting ink
4 x 6 inches
Courtesy of the artist and Leslie Tonkonow Artworks + Projects

Laurel Nakadate (b. 1975)
LUCKY TIGER #47, 2009
Type-C print and fingerprinting ink
4 x 6 inches
Courtesy the Artist and Leslie Tonkonow Artworks + Projects

Laurel Nakadate (b. 1975)
LUCKY TIGER #48, 2009
Type-C print and fingerprinting ink
4 x 6 inches
Courtesy of the artist and Leslie Tonkonow Artworks + Projects

Laurel Nakadate (b. 1975)
LUCKY TIGER #140, 2009
Type-C print and fingerprinting ink
4 x 6 inches
Collection of Leslie Tonkonow and Klaus Ottmann

Laurel Nakadate (b. 1975)
LUCKY TIGER #203, 2009.
Type-C print and fingerprinting ink
4 x 6 inches
Courtesy of the artist and Leslie Tonkonow Artworks + Projects

Richard Prince (b. 1949), UNTITLED (COWBOY), 1989
Chromogenic print
50 x 70 inches
Courtesy of Richard Prince Studio

Otis Kwame Quaicoe (b. 1988)
CAUGHT IN THE ACT, 2023
Oil on wood panel
48 x 36 Inches
Courtesy of the artist and Almine Rech
© Otis Kwame Qaicoe

Otis Kwame Quaicoe (b. 1988)
RODEO BOYS, 2022
Oil and fabric appliqué on canvas
84 x 54 inches
Collection of Matthew and Melanie Bronfman;
courtesy of the artist and Almine Rech
© Otis Kwame Qaicoe

Akasha Rabut (b. 1981)
SUNDAY AFTERNOON ON CLAIBORNE AVE, n.d.
Archival digital print mounted to matboard
24 x 28 inches
Courtesy of the artist

Akasha Rabut (b. 1981)
WAITING AT SUNSET, 2014
Archival digital print mounted to matboard
24 x 28 inches
Courtesy of the artist

Akasha Rabut (b. 1981)
JESSE MURDOCK, 2014
Archival digital print mounted to matboard
28 x 24 inches
Courtesy of the artist

Akasha Rabut (b. 1981)
UNTITLED (ARAB 0024), n.d.
Archival digital print mounted to matboard
24 x 28 inches
Courtesy of the artist

Akasha Rabut (b. 1981)
KRISTIN LEWIS-HAMPTON AND DEVENCE HAMPTON, 2016
Archival digital print mounted to matboard
28 x 24 inches
Courtesy of the artist

Akasha Rabut (b. 1981)
TRAIL RIDER AT SUNSET, 2014
Archival digital print mounted to matboard
28 x 24 inches
Courtesy of the artist

Lucy Raven (b. 1977)
UNTITLED, 2021
Framed shadowgram; silver gelatin contact print
19¼ x 23¾ inches
Courtesy of the artist and Lisson Gallery
© Lucy Raven

Lucy Raven (b. 1977)
UNTITLED, 2021
Framed shadowgram; silver gelatin contact print
19¼ x 23¾ inches
Courtesy of the artist and Lisson Gallery
© Lucy Raven

Lucy Raven (b. 1977)
UNTITLED, 2021
Framed shadowgram; silver gelatin direct print
20 x 16 inches
Courtesy of the artist and Lisson Gallery
© Lucy Raven

Lucy Raven (b. 1977)
UNTITLED, 2021
Framed shadowgram; silver gelatin direct print
20 x 16 inches
Courtesy of the artist and Lisson Gallery
© Lucy Raven

Lucy Raven (b. 1977)
UNTITLED, 2021
Framed shadowgram; silver gelatin direct print
14 x 11 inches
Courtesy of the artist and Lisson Gallery
© Lucy Raven

Ken Taylor Reynaga (b. 1990)
SOMBRERO CERAMIC AQUA, 2021
Glazed ceramic
8½ x 18¾ x 19¼ inches
Courtesy of Stefan of Simchowitz

Ken Taylor Reynaga (b. 1990)
SOMBRERO CERAMIC BLACK, 2021
Glazed ceramic
8½ x 18¾ x 19¼ inches
Courtesy of Stefan Simchowitz

Ken Taylor Reynaga (b. 1990)
SOMBRERO CERAMIC PINK, 2021
Glazed ceramic
11 x 24¼ x 16 inches
Courtesy of Stefan Simchowitz

Jaye Rhee (b. 1973)
ARIZONA COWBOY (as part of FAR WEST, SO CLOSE), 2023
Sound. Original song in 1955 composed by
Oh-Seung Jeon, lyrics by Bhu-Hae Kim,
arranged by BOHEME and produced by Jaye Rhee
Duration: 8:00 minutes
Courtesy of the artist

Yumi Janairo Roth (b. 1970) and Emmanuel David (b. 1980)
WE ARE COMING (BOULDER THEATER, BOULDER, CO), 2022
Photograph
Courtesy of the artists

Yumi Janairo Roth (b. 1970) and Emmanuel David (b. 1980)
WE ARE COMING (MINI MARQEE), 2023
Mixed media
Courtesy of the artists

Ana Segovia (b. 1991)
AUNQUE ME ESPINE LA MANO, 2018
Video
Duration: 5:35 minutes
Foley artists and sound design: Equipo Ruido (Maria Alejandra and Rojas Arantxa Oliver); Editing: Ricardo Martínez; Sound mixing: Arturo Salazar R.B. "Frosty"; Cinematography and editing: Josue Eber Morales; Charros suits: Dinastía Moralez (Javier); Production: Rocío Fernandez de Angulo
Courtesy of the artist

Ana Segovia (b. 1991)
REGAINING LOST CONFIDENCE, 2019
Oil on canvas
21 x 14¾ inches
Collection of Devon Musgrave

Ana Segovia (b. 1991)
CARNAGE, 2017
Oil on canvas
46 x 39½ inches
Huber & Timberlake Collection

Amy Sherald (b. 1973)
WHAT'S PRECIOUS INSIDE OF HIM DOES NOT CARE
TO BE KNOWN BY THE MIND IN WAYS THAT
DIMINISH ITS PRESENCE (ALL AMERICAN), 2017
Oil on canvas
54 x 43 inches
Collection of Evan Boris and Monique Meloche
Copyright © Amy Sherald

Stephanie Syjuco (b. 1974)
DOUBLE VISION, 2022
Site specific installation; dimensions variable
Courtesy of the artist; Catharine Clark Gallery, San Francisco; RYAN LEE Gallery, New York; and Silverlens, Manila

Stephanie Syjuco (b. 1974)
SET-UP (THE BRONCHO BUSTER 1), 2022
Archival pigment print
72 x 52 inches, framed
Courtesy of the artist; Catharine Clark Gallery, San Francisco; RYAN LEE Gallery, New York; and Silverlens, Manila

Stephanie Syjuco (b. 1974)
SET-UP (THE BRONCHO BUSTER 2), 2022
Archival pigment print
72 x 52 inches, framed
Courtesy of the artist; Catharine Clark Gallery, San Francisco; RYAN LEE Gallery, New York; and Silverlens, Manila

Stephanie Syjuco (b. 1974)
SET-UP (THE RATTLESNAKE), 2022
Archival pigment print
72 x 52 inches, framed
Courtesy of the artist; Catharine Clark Gallery, San Francisco; RYAN LEE Gallery, New York; and Silverlens, Manila

Stephanie Syjuco (b. 1974)
SET-UP (THE OUTLAW), 2022
Archival pigment print
72 x 52 inches, framed
Collection of the Amon Carter Museum of American Art

Kenneth Tam (b. 1982)
SILENT SPIKES, 2021
Two channel video with sound
Duration: 20:29 minutes
Commissioned by the Queens Museum with support from the Asian Art Circle of the Guggenheim Museum

Andy Warhol (1928–1987)
HORSE, 1965
Digital copy of 16mm film
Excerpted duration: 10 minutes. Total duration: 66 minutes
© The Andy Warhol Museum, Pittsburgh, PA,
a museum of Carnegie Institute. All rights reserved
Courtesy of The Andy Warhol Museum

Nathan Young (b. 1975)
ACTIVATION/TRANSFORMATION II, 2023
Installation, mixed media
Dimensions variable
Courtesy of the artist

CREDITS

2: Courtesy of the artist and Hauser & Wirth. Photo: Joseph Hyde. 10: Library of Congress. 15: Photography courtesy Denver Art Museum. 17–21: Library of Congress. 30: Image courtesy of AFF / Alamy Stock Photo. 33, 36, 38: Courtesy of the artist. 40: Courtesy of the artists; Photo: Tony Alvarez. 42–43: Courtesy of the artist. 48–49: Photos: Dylan Schwartz. 52, 57: Courtesy of the artist. 74: Banque d'Images, ADAGP / Art Resource, NY. Licensed by Artists Rights Society (ARS), New York. 88–91: © John Baldessari 2019. Courtesy of the Estate of John Baldessari © 2023, courtesy of Sprüth Magers; photos: Joshua White/ JWPictures. 92: Photo: John Lucas. 93: Photo: Maurice Roberts. 94–99: Courtesy of the artist. 100–01: Courtesy of the artist and Lisa Sette Gallery. 107–09: Photos: Joshua White, photos courtesy of Jeffrey Deitch, Los Angeles. 119: Courtesy of WENTRUP, Berlin; photo: Karl Haendel. 120–21: Courtesy of Vielmetter Los Angeles; photo: Jeff McLane. 122–27: Photos: Peter Cox. 128–29: Courtesy of the artist. 138–43: © Laurel Nakadate, courtesy of Leslie Tonkonow Artworks + Projects, NY. 144–45: Courtesy of the artist and Almine Rech; © Otis Kwame Qaicoe; photo: Hugard & Vanoverschelde. 146–47: Photos: Hugard & Vanoverschelde. 149: Courtesy of the artist and Almine Rech; © Otis Kwame Qaicoe; photo: Hugard & Vanoverschelde. 150: Photo: Mario Gallucci. 162–63: Courtesy Lisson Gallery; © Lucy Raven; photos: Mark Waldhauser. 164–67: Courtesy of the artist and Simchowitz Gallery. 174–75: Courtesy of the artists. 186, 188–91: Courtesy of the artist and Galería Karen Huber. 193: Courtesy of the artist and Hauser & Wirth. Photo: Joseph Hyde. 194–95, 198–99: Courtesy of the Amon Carter Museum of American Art, Fort Worth, TX. 202–05: Photos: Jason Madella. 206–07: © The Andy Warhol Museum, Pittsburgh, PA, a museum of Carnegie Institute. All rights reserved. Film still courtesy The Andy Warhol Museum. 210–13: Photos: Addison Doty. 215: Photo courtesy of the Wheelwright Museum

Nora Burnett Abrams

Nora Burnett Abrams is the Mark G. Falcone Director of the Museum of Contemporary Art Denver. Among the youngest museum directors in the country, Burnett Abrams moved into the Director role after nearly a decade as the Ellen Bruss Curator and Director of Planning. Her curatorial approach has been instrumental in making MCA Denver one of the most important cultural institutions in Colorado. Since arriving in Denver in 2010, she has organized more than forty exhibitions and authored or contributed to over a dozen accompanying publications. Recent projects highlighted unusual or little-known episodes in artists' careers, such as *Basquiat Before Basquiat* (2017), which traveled to three other venues. Her most recent projects include a retrospective of works by Tara Donovan (2018), which traveled to the Smart Museum at the University

AUTHORS' BIOGRAPHIES

of Chicago, and a focused presentation of never-before-seen photographs and ephemera by Francesca Woodman (2019). She has taught art history at New York University and lectured throughout the country on modern and contemporary art. She holds art history degrees from Stanford University (BA), Columbia University (MA), and a PhD from the Institute of Fine Arts at New York University.

Myeshia C. Babers, PhD, Cultural Anthropologist, Let's Dialogue, LLC

Myeshia C. Babers is a cultural translator specializing in the study of African American masculinity in 21st-century Western culture and a lecturer in the Africana Studies program at Texas A&M University. She is an outgoing educator dedicated to creating an environment that encourages open awareness and curiosity for learning cultural concepts. Babers focuses on the development and implementation of research and deep reflection to produce mindful scholars.

Miranda Lash

Miranda Lash is the Ellen Bruss Senior Curator at the Museum of Contemporary Art Denver and the Susan Brennan co-Artistic Director of the international art triennial *Prospect.6* in New Orleans, scheduled to open in fall 2024. Lash has organized numerous museum exhibitions, including *Tomashi Jackson: Across the Universe; Clarissa Tossin: Falling from Earth; Eamon Ore-Giron: Competing with Lighting / Rivalizando con el relampágo*; *Jason Moran: Bathing the Room with Blues*; the traveling retrospective *Mel Chin: Rematch*; *Camille Henrot: Cities of Ys*; and *Rashaad Newsome: King of Arms*. In 2016 Lash and Trevor Schoonmaker co-organized the acclaimed exhibition *Southern Accent: Seeking the American South in Contemporary Art*. From 2008 to 2014, Lash was the founding curator of modern and contemporary art at the New Orleans Museum of Art. She currently serves on the board of the Joan Mitchell Foundation and was a 2022 Fellow with the Center for Curatorial Leadership. She holds a BA with honors from Harvard University in the History of Art and Architecture and an MA from Williams College in the History of Art.

Jongwoo Jeremy Kim

Jongwoo Jeremy Kim is Associate Professor of Critical Studies, Art History and Theory in the School of Art at Carnegie Mellon University. He is the author of *Painted Men in Britain, 1868-1918: Royal Academicians and Masculinities*, as well as *Male Bodies Unmade: Picturing Queer Selfhood*, a book that explores white men's disunified physicality in modern and contemporary art while attending to erotic polysemy that questions the visual ethos of Occidental patriarchy. His approach is informed by his own status as an immigrant—a polyglot queen drawn to extravagant fantasies of misbehaving bodies that are in truth foreign territories, colonies of misbelief. After teaching in New York, Vermont, and Kentucky over the past two decades, Kim now lives in Pittsburgh with his husband Steven Paganelli.

R. Alan Brooks

R. Alan Brooks teaches graphic novel writing for Regis University's MFA program and at Lighthouse Writers Workshop. He's the author of *The Burning Metronome* and *Anguish Garden*—graphic novels featuring social commentary. His award-winning weekly comic for the *Colorado Sun*, "What'd I Miss?," has been praised for its direct engagement with social issues. His TED Talk on the importance of art reached a million views in two months. His graphic novel work is featured in the Denver Art Museum's renovated Western exhibit. He hosts the Museum of Contemporary Art Denver's "How Art Is Born" podcast, as well as his own "MotherF**ker In A Cape" comics podcast, and has written comic books for Pop Culture Classroom, Zenescope Entertainment, and more.

Published on the occasion of *Cowboy* at the Museum of Contemporary Art Denver, September 29, 2023–February 18, 2024

Exhibition and publication support generously provided by

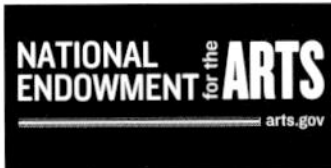

Blue Rider Group
MORGAN STANLEY PRIVATE WEALTH MANAGEMENT

First published in the United States of America in 2023 by
Rizzoli Electa, A Division of
Rizzoli International Publications, Inc.
300 Park Avenue South
New York, NY 10010
www.rizzoliusa.com

in association with

MCA Denver
1485 Delgany Street
Denver, CO 80202
mcadenver.org

Publisher: Charles Miers
Editor: Isabel Venero
Production Manager: Colin Hough-Trapp
Designer: Sarah Gifford

Printed in Hong Kong

2023 2024 2025 2026 / 10 9 8 7 6 5 4 3 2 1
ISBN: 978-0-8478-7375-3
Library of Congress Control Number on file

Visit us online:
Facebook.com/RizzoliNewYork
Twitter: @Rizzoli_Books
Instagram.com/RizzoliBooks
Pinterest.com/RizzoliBooks
Youtube.com/user/RizzoliNY

I wish to thank Miranda Lash for the incredible and collaborative adventure of bringing this project to life. I also wish to acknowledge my amazing family—Brian, Xander, and Knox—for their ongoing curiosity, humor, and love, which inspired my interest in delving more deeply into the history of this wondrous and complex corner of the world.

—NORA BURNETT ABRAMS

I wish to thank my co-curator Nora for inviting me on this ride and trusting me in sharing this vision. To my husband Jim Mulvihill and my boys Francis and Joseph, I love you more than words can say. To my family in Los Angeles, New Mexico, and New Orleans, thank you for being my strength and joy. I dedicate this to all the *tíos* and *primos* looking *guapísimo* in their cowboy hats.

—MIRANDA LASH

Page 1: Yumi Janairo Roth and Emmanuel David, WE ARE COMING (BOULDER THEATER, BOULDER, CO), 2022. Photograph

Page 2: Amy Sherald, WHAT'S PRECIOUS INSIDE OF HIM DOES NOT CARE TO BE KNOWN BY THE MIND IN WAYS THAT DIMINISH ITS PRESENCE (ALL AMERICAN), 2017. Oil on canvas. 54 x 43 inches. Collection of Evan Boris and Monique Meloche

Pages 4–5: Richard Prince, UNTITLED (COWBOY), 1989. Chromogenic print. 50 x 70 inches

Pages 86–87: Ana Segovia, YOU LIKE IT HOW I LIKE IT – I (DETAIL), 2018. Oil on canvas. 8¾ x 13½ inches. Private collection

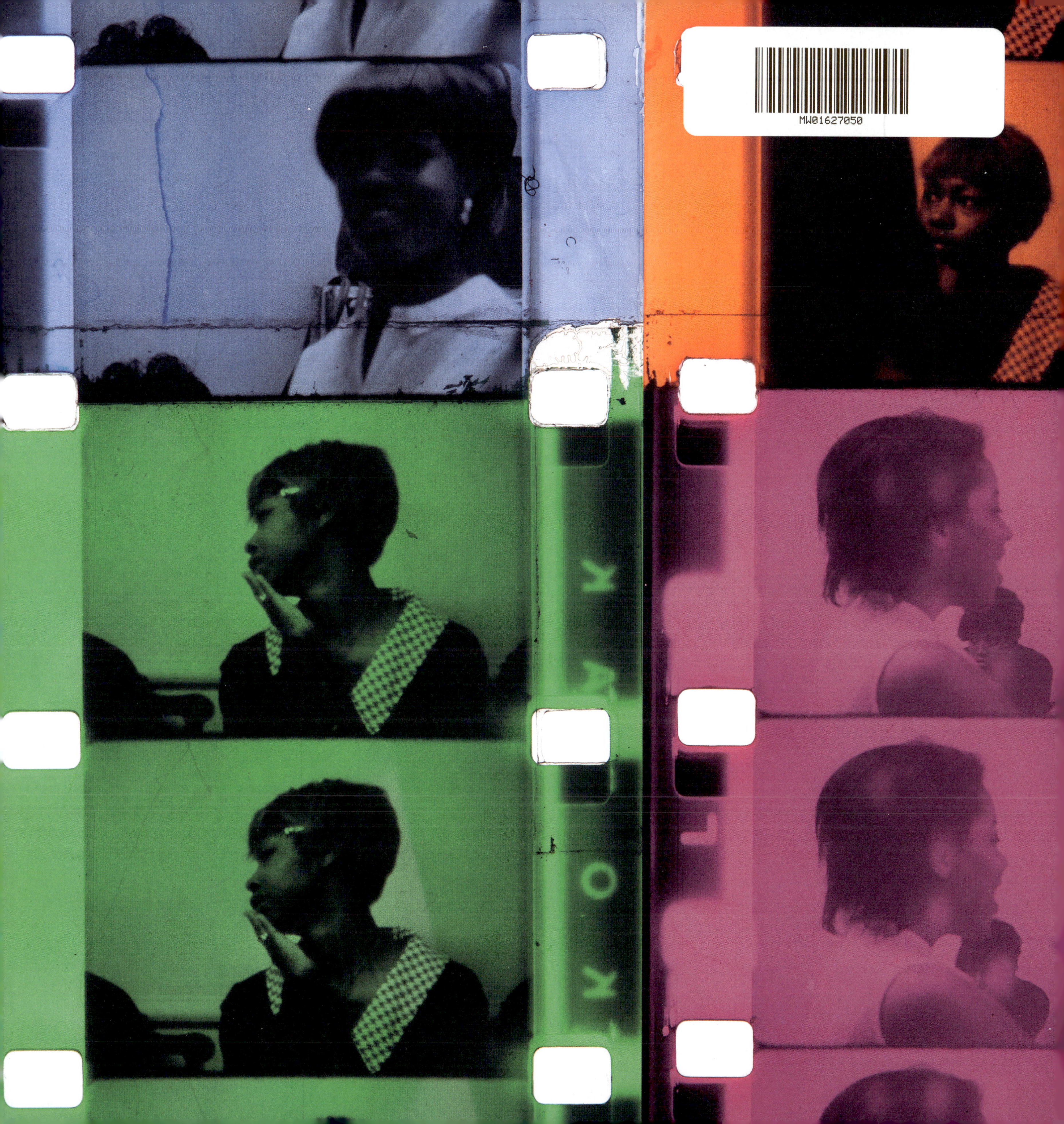
MW01627050

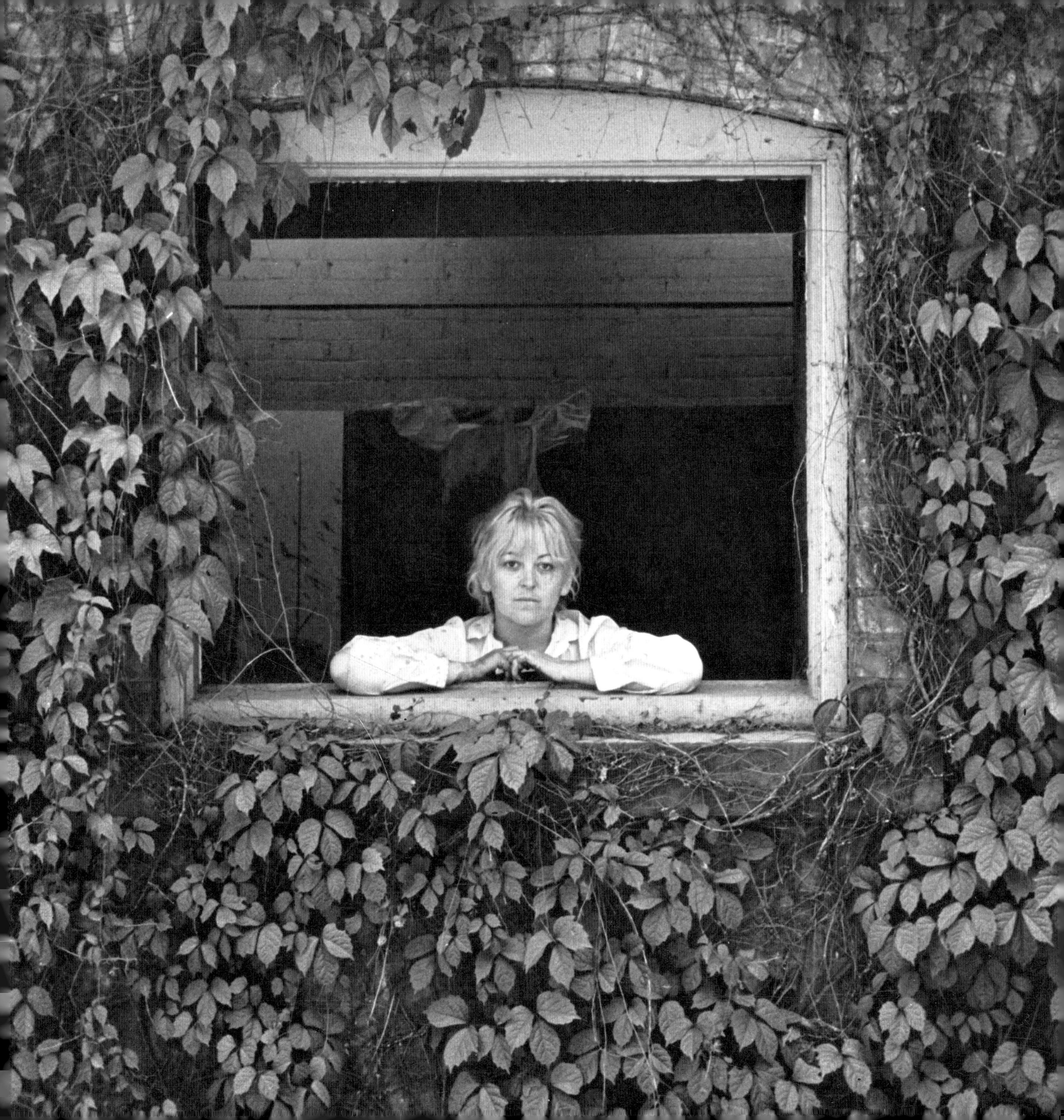

OYCE WIELAND RETROSPECTIVE AT GLENDON COLLEGE, IN THE ART GALLERY 2275 BAYVIEW AVE. OPENING 7 O'CLOCK 26 OF FEBRUARY, TO BE FOLLOWED BY FILMS (WIELAND) AT 8:30 in ROOM 204 GALLERY HOURS MON. THRU FRI. - 9:00-5:00 p.m. SAT. 1:00 P.M.-5:00 P.M. FOR INQUIRIES PHONE: 487-6107/8. BORN IN TORONTO STUDIED ART AT CENTRAL TECH WORKED IN ADVERTISING WORKED FOR GEORGE DUNNING (WHO DIRECTED THE YELLOW SUBMARINE) AS AN ANIMATOR FOR TWO YEARS .AT THE SAME TIME WORKING ON CANADA'S FIRST UNDERGROUND MOVIES LIKE 'ASSAULT IN THE PARK 'TEA IN THE GARDEN' WORKED AS A PAINTER AND COLLAGIST .... HAD SOME ONE WOMAN SHOWS ..... WENT TO LIVE IN NEW YORK IN '62 1. FOUR ONE WOMAN SHOWS AT THE ISAACS GALLERY 1958 to 1967 2. two retrospectives ONE AT LONDON ONTARIO AND ONE IN THE VANCOUVER ART GALLERY........GROUP SHOWS.... ALBRIGHT KNOX GALLERY BUFFALO.... J.B. SPEED MUSEUM ,LOUISVILLE KENTUCKY PHILADELPHIA MUSEUM OF ART MONTREAL MUSEUM NATIONAL GALLERY OTTAWA CANADA D'ART AUJOUD'HUI EUROPEAN SHOW CANADIAN GOVERNMENT PAVILLION EXPO VANCOUVER GALLERY UNIVERSITY OF WATERLOO WINNIPEG ART GALLERY HUDSON GALLERY DETROIT QUEEN'S UNIVERSITY CONFEDERATION MUSEUM P.E.I. COLLECTIONS OF MUSEUM OF MODERN ART PHILADELPHIA MUSEUM NATIONAL GALLERY VANCOUVER GALLERY CANADA COUNCIL ART GALLERY OF ONTARIO PRIVATE COLLECTION ...... MRS. JOHN DAVID EATON MR. AND MRS M. YOLLES MR. AND MRS. R.G.N. LAIDLAW PAUL BREAK MR. AND MRS. PERCY WAXER MR.AND MRS. G.H. MONTAGUE GRAEME FERGUSON MR. IRVING ROSSMAN RAYMOND JESSEL MR, AND MRS. G. RICHARDSON MARIE FLEMING ABRAHAM ROTSTEIN WILLIAM KILBOURN COMMISSIONS AND GRANTS, AWARDS. 1. CANADA COUNCIL GRANT FOR PAINTING 1966 1968 WON TWO PRIZES FOR FILM CALLED 'RAT LIFE AND DIET IN NORTH AMERICA AT AMERICAN THIRD INDEPENDENT FILMAKERS FESTIVAL IN NEW YORK CITY. camera WOMAN ON FILM CALLED 'HUNTINGTON' FOR THE JOB CORPS SPONSERED BY ZEROX. 1967 CAMERA WOMAN ON SHIRLEY CLARKES FILM ON ANDRE VOSNESENSKY 1967 CANADA COUNCIL GRANT FOR ART AND FILM 1968 COMMISIONED TO DESIGN TWO PRODUCTIONS OF MARY MITCHELL'S PLAY 'ENACTMENT..USING ELECTRONIC SOUND.FILMS LIVE MUSIC.. CONSIDERED BY PENNEBAKER TO BE THE FIRST MCLUHAN TYPE PERFORMED AT LA MAMA THEATRE NEW YORK '65 '67 COMMISSIONED TO MAKE ONE HOUR FILMED EXPANDED CINEMA PIECE .CALLED BILL'S HAT...1967 COMMISSIONED TO DO AN EXPANDED CINEMA VERSION OF THE SAME PIECE BY THE ART GALLERY OF ONTARIO.1968 .... CAMERA WOMAN ON FILM ABOUT PROBLEMS OF THE HARLEM HEAD START PROGRAM FOR THE HEAD START 1967 .... GROUP SHOWINGS OF FILMS .... HUNTER COLLEGE (THREE EVENINGS OF AMERICAN AVANT-GARDE CINEMA) BOSTON MUSEUM OF CONTEMPORARY ART 1967 ...... OESTERREICHES FILM MUSEUM ..VIENNA ..PROGRAM OF RENOIR SNOW, LUMIERE, MELIES, DREYER AND WIELAND .... THE JEWISH MUSEUM NEW YORK (THE PAINTER AS A FILMAKER) 1967 GROUP SHOW OF AMERICAN CINEMA YALE UNIVERSITY MUSEUM OF MODERN ART CINAPROBE SERIES FILM SHOWN ON TWO EVENINGS 1969 WASHINGTON D.C. (UNDERGROUND SERIES) HUNTINGTON HARTFORD MUSEUM RETOSPECTIVE OF JOYCE WIELAND FILMS 1969 FILMS IN THE COLLECTIONS OF FAIRLEIGH DICKENSON UNIVERSITY MUSEUM OF MODERN ART ROYAL BELGIUM FILM ARCHIVE NORDDEUTSCHEN RUNDFUNK, BAYERISCHEN RUDFUNK, HESSISCHEN RUDFUNK (WEST GERMAN TELEVISION STATIONS) THINGS PEOPLE SAY ABOUT HER WORK ..... P. ADAMS SITNEY FILM CULTURE MAGAZINE SAYS .... THE EMERGENCE OF AN AVANTGARDE CINEMA IN CANADA SINCE THE MIDDLE SIXTIES FAR OVERSHADOW ANY OTHER REGIONAL DEVELOPMENT IN THE FIELD. THOSE WHO ARE TRULY SIGNIFICANT AMONG THE CANADIANS, LIKE JOYCE WIELAND ARE AT THE VERY FRONTLINE OF THE WORLD CINEMA TODAY. HER FILMS ARE STRUCTURAL REVELATIONS; SIMPLE, REPETITIVE FILLED WITH CLARITY, THEY CAN TRAVEL ANYWHERE AS SIGNPOSTS OF THE CINEMA IN ITS MOST RADICAL DEVELOPMENT NOW. DESCRIPTION WOULD BE AN AFFRONT TO HER THREE SHORT FILMS, 1933, CATFOOD, SAILBOAT, SINCE IT WOULD PRESUME UPON THE ESSENCE OF THE WORKS, WHICH IS ALLOWED AFFIRMATION OF THE ELEMENTARY EVENT AS THE CRUX OF PERCEPTIONAND OF ART. HER LATEST FILM RAT LIFE AND DIET IN NORTH AMERICA IS UNIQUE, PAR EXCELLENCE CANADIAN FILM COME TO MATURITY. CARL ANDRE SAYS WHEN I WAS LITTLE I WAS TOLD THAT IF I STOOD IN THE BOTTOM OF A DEEP WELL AND LOOKED UP I COULD SEE THE STARS IN BROAD DAYLIGHT, I DO NOT KNOW IF THIS IS TRUE BUT THAT IS WHAT SEEING JOYCE SNOW'S MOVIES IS LIKE. JONAS MEKAS..THE VILLAGE VOICE SAYS LAST WEEKEND, I SAW FIVE FILMS OF JOYCE WIELAND'S. I AM HAPPY TO REPORT HERE THAT THE AVANT-GARDE HAS GAINED ONE MORE ARTIST WHOSE WORKS I HAVE NO DOUBT WILL TAKE A PERMANENT PLACE IN THE AVANT-GARDE FILM REPERTORY. I FIND IN JOYCE WIELAND'S WORK A CREATIVE SENSITIVITY AND INTELLIGENCE THAT IS NOT THAT OF THE EVERYDAY. CHARLOTTE MOORMAN SAYS THAT PAIK IS A FAN OF JOYCE'S QUILTS.... MARY MITCHELL SAYS IF PRIME MINISTER TRUDEAU REPRESENTS L'ESPRIT DU TEMPS IN WORLD POLITICS JOYCE WIELAND IS HIS RUNNING MATE IN THE WORLD OF ART, BARRY HALE, THE TELEGRAM....."SHE IS ALSO AN ARTIST, THE FINEST FEMALE ARTIST THIS COUNTRY HAS EVER PRODUCED (SORRY, EMILY), AND AS AN ARTIST, OFTEN AS A WOMAN TOO, SHE IS SPIKEY AS SHE IS WELL-ROUNDED. HARRY MALCOLMSON, THE TELEGRAM.."NO ONE ELSE COMES CLOSE TO WIELAND'S INNOCENCE, INFORMALITY AND JOY" HOLLIS FRAMPTON SAYS... HER ART IS MEANT TO NOURISH THE AFFECTIONS, AND HER SENSE OF ITS INTERNAL NECESSITIES IS TACTILE. JOYCE WIELAND'S ART IS , IN EXACT AND HUMANE SENSE, PERSONAL . SHIRLEY CLARKE SAYS... "IN THE LAST FIFTEEN YEARS IN THE WORLD CINEMA HAS PRODUCED A FEW WOMAN FILMAKERS WITH IMPORTANT THINGS TO SAY. FRANCE HAS GIVEN US AGNES

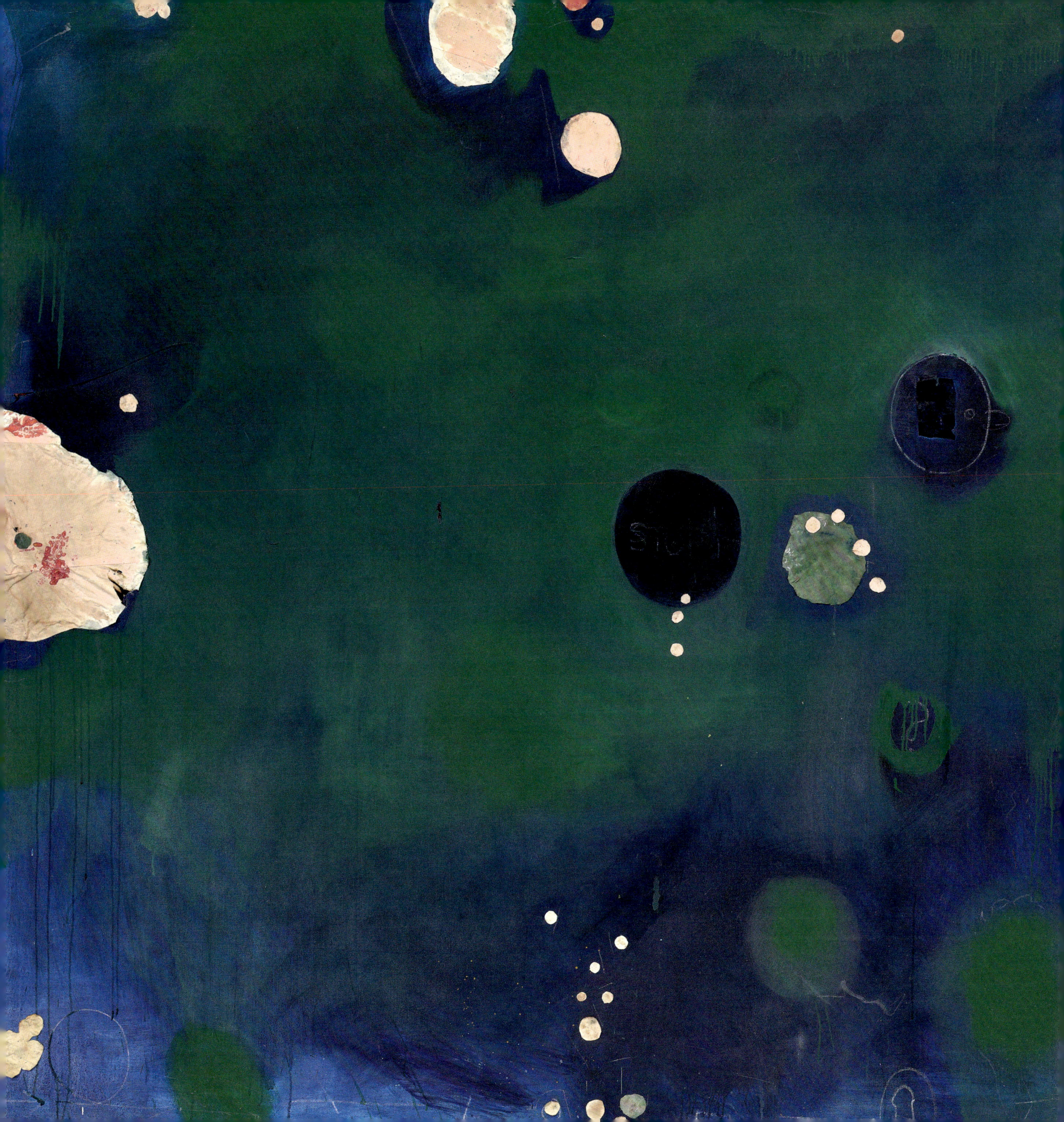

JOYCE WIELAND

EDITED BY Anne Grace + Georgiana Uhlyarik

HEART ON

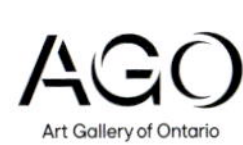

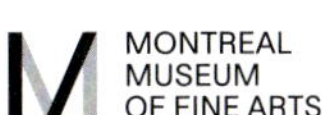

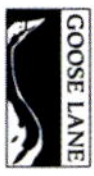

CONTENTS

DIRECTORS' FOREWORD

It is a great privilege to present this exhibition honouring the art of Joyce Wieland (1930–1998), a Canadian artist and filmmaker whose practice of five decades has only grown more relevant with time. Wieland's body of work—radical, playful, and politically engaged—demands to be rediscovered by new generations of museum visitors and re-examined by those already lucky enough to be familiar with her production. *Joyce Wieland: Heart On*, led by curators Anne Grace and Georgiana Uhlyarik, the first retrospective on her career in almost forty years, aspires to give this influential artist her rightful place on the international stage as a groundbreaking figure of twentieth-century art and film.

Convinced of the transformative power of art, Wieland developed a practice that delved into politics, feminism, social equity, and ecology. Her intelligence, wit, and audacity, along with her passion for history and literature, underpinned her artistic vision, allowing her, as the critic Susan Crean wrote, to take the serious lightly and the lighthearted seriously.

Wieland was a trailblazer who received considerable recognition in her time. When her experimental film *Rat Life and Diet in North America* was screened in New York in the 1960s, it was lauded by filmmaker Jonas Mekas as possibly "the best (or richest) political movie around." She became the first living woman artist to be given her own exhibition, *True Patriot Love*, at the National Gallery of Canada (NGC) in 1971. Her career retrospective at the Art Gallery of Ontario in 1987 marked the first time the institution ever dedicated such an exhibition to a living woman artist. Subsequent generations of artists undeniably felt the influence of Wieland's drawings, paintings, films, textiles, and prints, and the themes she explored, in addition to her unorthodox approach to materials, continue to resonate closely with contemporary art practices today.

It is fitting that *Joyce Wieland: Heart On* takes place in Toronto, where Wieland was born and spent most of her life, apart from the decade she lived in New York City with her then-husband, Michael Snow. The AGO provided early support to Wieland, acquiring important paintings as far back as 1966, collecting and screening her experimental films, and, more recently, bringing attention to her overlooked late paintings by highlighting them in its galleries. It is also fitting that this exhibition be held in Montreal as well. Although not as widely known to the Montreal public, Wieland had close friends and supporters in the city. She also had a great enthusiasm for Quebec culture and history. She once recalled that when she began her pioneering effort in art to seek out Canadian heroines, she found that "most of the women I admired were Québécoise." Inquisitive and deeply thoughtful about the complexities of "the two solitudes," she sought out dialogues between the two cultures in her film and textile works. The Montreal Museum of Fine Arts' former director Pierre Théberge was a staunch admirer of Wieland. He was instrumental in nurturing her career when he was a young curator at the NGC, organizing her *True Patriot Love* exhibition and acquiring major works for its collection, many of which are included in *Heart On*.

The AGO and MMFA curators, conservators, and exhibition teams have worked tirelessly to locate, examine, restore, research, and bring together nearly 150 works for this exhibition, a project never undertaken at this scale until now. We are grateful for the extraordinary support of the National Gallery of Canada, which generously restored and loaned a large number of works, and their Archival Research and Conservation team: Philip Dombowsky, Valérie Gauthier, Christine Lalonde, Geneviève Saulnier, and Ainsley Walton. Special thanks to Cinémathèque québécoise, custodians of Wieland's films, which undertook extensive archival research and overseeing digitization of key films in preparation for the exhibition.

We extend our gratitude to all other lenders: Agnes Etherington Art Centre, Queen's University; Barry Appleton; the Art Gallery of Guelph; the Art Gallery of Hamilton; the Art Gallery of York University; Art Windsor-Essex; Rachel Barney; the Beaverbrook Art Gallery; Katia and John Bianchini; Margaret J. Break; the Canada Council Art Bank; the City of Toronto and the Toronto Transit Commission; Christopher Cutts Gallery; Munro Ferguson; Lucas Ferguson-Sharp; Robert Fulford and Geraldine Sherman; Galeries Bellemare Lambert; Phyllis Lambert; Les G. Lawrence; the Leonard & Bina Ellen Art Gallery, Concordia University; the MacKenzie Art Gallery; the MacLaren Art Centre; Museum London; the National Gallery of Canada Library and Archives; the National Research Council Canada; Colette Perron-Sharp; Remai Modern; the Robert McLaughlin Gallery; Susan Rynard; the University of Lethbridge Art Collections; the Vancouver Art Gallery; Doug Watters; Sally Wright; Morden and Edie Yolles; and our anonymous lenders.

The AGO also extends its deep gratitude to the exhibition's Supporting Sponsor, Power Corporation of Canada; lead supporter the Volunteers of the AGO; Jamie & Patsy Anderson, The Birks Family Foundation, Dr. Ronald M. Haynes, Rosamond Ivey, J.S. McLean Fund, and the Women's Art Initiative for their generous support; Charles Brindamour & Josée Letarte for their additional support; the Canada Council for the Arts for supporting contemporary art programming at the AGO; and the Sorel Etrog Publication Fund for supporting this book. The MMFA gratefully acknowledges its Presenting Sponsor, Hatch; public partners Conséil des arts de Montreal and the Government of Quebec; and the Canada Council for the Arts for its financial support.

Thank you sincerely for helping us honour the legacy of Joyce Wieland.

STÉPHANE AQUIN
Director
Montreal Museum of Fine Arts

STEPHAN JOST
Michael and Sonja Koerner Director, and CEO
Art Gallery of Ontario

CURATORS' ACKNOWLEDGEMENTS

We owe our deep gratitude to the extraordinary *Joyce Wieland: Heart On* team, Renée van der Avoird, Chloé Martel, and Chloé Wittes, for their intelligence, commitment, and grace, as well as their immense patience and big hearts. We are grateful for the thoughtful and thorough research by Rhiannon Vogl (Mimi Fullerton AGO-UofT Art History Fellow), and Shannon Stride (Birks Family Foundation Internship Award at the MMFA). A very special thank-you to our diligent editor Kieran Grant, and to the team at Bla bla rédaction and our translators for conveying Wieland's playful use of language; to book designer Lara Minja, of Lime Design, who captured beautifully the artist's multifarious aesthetic in these pages; and to Robyn Lew, whose exceptional production skills made it seem effortless to bring this publication together. Jim Shedden has been our most steadfast and generous collaborator, offering his profound knowledge and deep appreciation of the artist.

Early in the preparation for the exhibition, fruitful conversations with Concordia University Professors Martha Langford and Johanne Sloan led to a series of study days. Those gathered included Wieland collaborators, along with artists, scholars, and curators. The first session, held in Montreal, was supported and hosted by the Jarislowsky Institute for Studies in Canadian Art. A second session united conservation teams from the Canadian Conservation Institute (CCI), the National Gallery of Canada, the Canada Council Art Bank, the Art Gallery of Ontario, and the Montreal Museum of Fine Arts to examine works in Ottawa. A very special thanks to Allison Kelley and Steven Leclair from the National Research Council Canada. The third gathering took place at the AGO, Toronto, and included talks, screenings, and visits to the Spadina TTC station and Grange Park. We are forever indebted to participants' generous contributions, insights, and reminiscences.

We felt the love for Wieland across the country. The variety of formats and the unconventional materials the artist used demanded a weighty commitment from our conservation teams. We are deeply appreciative of their curiosity, insights, and excellent care of Wieland's plastic works, in partnership with specialists from the CCI.

We are especially indebted to those close to Joyce Wieland, who conveyed to us what an exceptional artist she was, her sense of adventure, her wit, and her intelligence, namely Phyllis Lambert, Judy Steed, Leila Sujir, Irene Whittome, Michiko Gagnon, Munro Ferguson, and the late Betty Ferguson and Avrom Isaacs. Our enthusiasm for the project was buoyed by the warm reception we received in Berlin from Stefanie Schulte Strathaus,

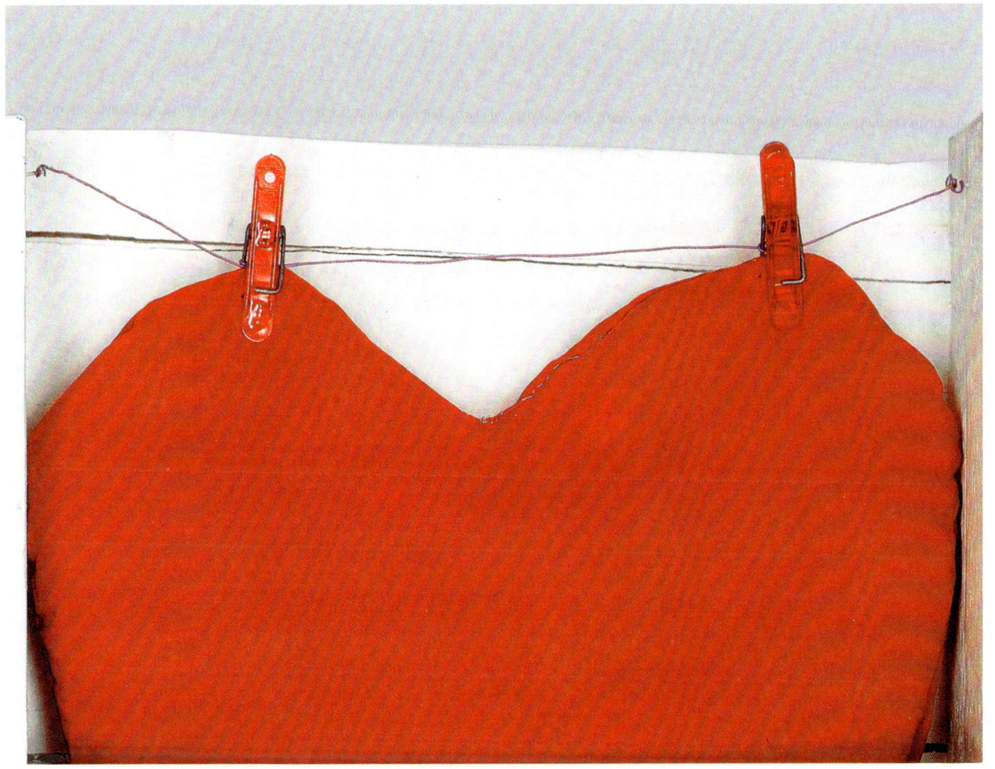

Cooling Room II (detail), 1964
Wood, paint, metal toy airplane, cloth, metal wire, plastic boat, paper collage, ceramic, cups with lipstick, spoon, mounted in painted wooden case
114.4 × 94 × 18.3 cm
National Gallery of Canada, Purchased 1971
16706
Photo: NGC

NEXT SPREAD
Handtinting (film print), 1967
Film, 16mm, colour, silent
6 min
Joyce Wieland fonds, Cinémathèque québécoise
Photo: Stéphanie Côté, courtesy of Cinémathèque québécoise

Bettina Ellerkamp, Jörg Heitmann, and Linda Winkler, and closer to home from Reesa Greenberg, Cynthia Hammond, and Joyce Zemans.

Along our many-year journey, we have received wonderful support and encouragement from AGO colleagues Jessica Bright, Theodora Doulamis, Laura Comerford, Julian Cox, and Adam Welch, and Mary-Dailey Desmarais, Richard Gagnier, Carolina Calle Sandoval, and Carolina Bassani at the MMFA.

We are inspired by Wieland's collaborative and generous spirit. We seek to foreground her voice, which figures prominently in this publication. The polyvalent nature of Wieland's practice guided us to include many authors from a variety of disciplines, who consider her work through many lenses. Our profound gratitude goes to all the contributors.

We are fortunate to have lifelong mentors, family, friends, and loved ones who have inspired and emboldened us. Most of all, we honour the extraordinary Joyce Wieland. Our work brought the two of us together as colleagues around a dinner table many years ago in New York City. This time spent working to celebrate the fierce vision and joy at the core of Wieland's art and life has transformed our lives forevermore. With her seductive wit and piecing intelligence, Joyce Wieland asks us all to do better, to care more.

Our hearts are full and forever in bloom,
ANNE GRACE + GEORGIANA UHLYARIK

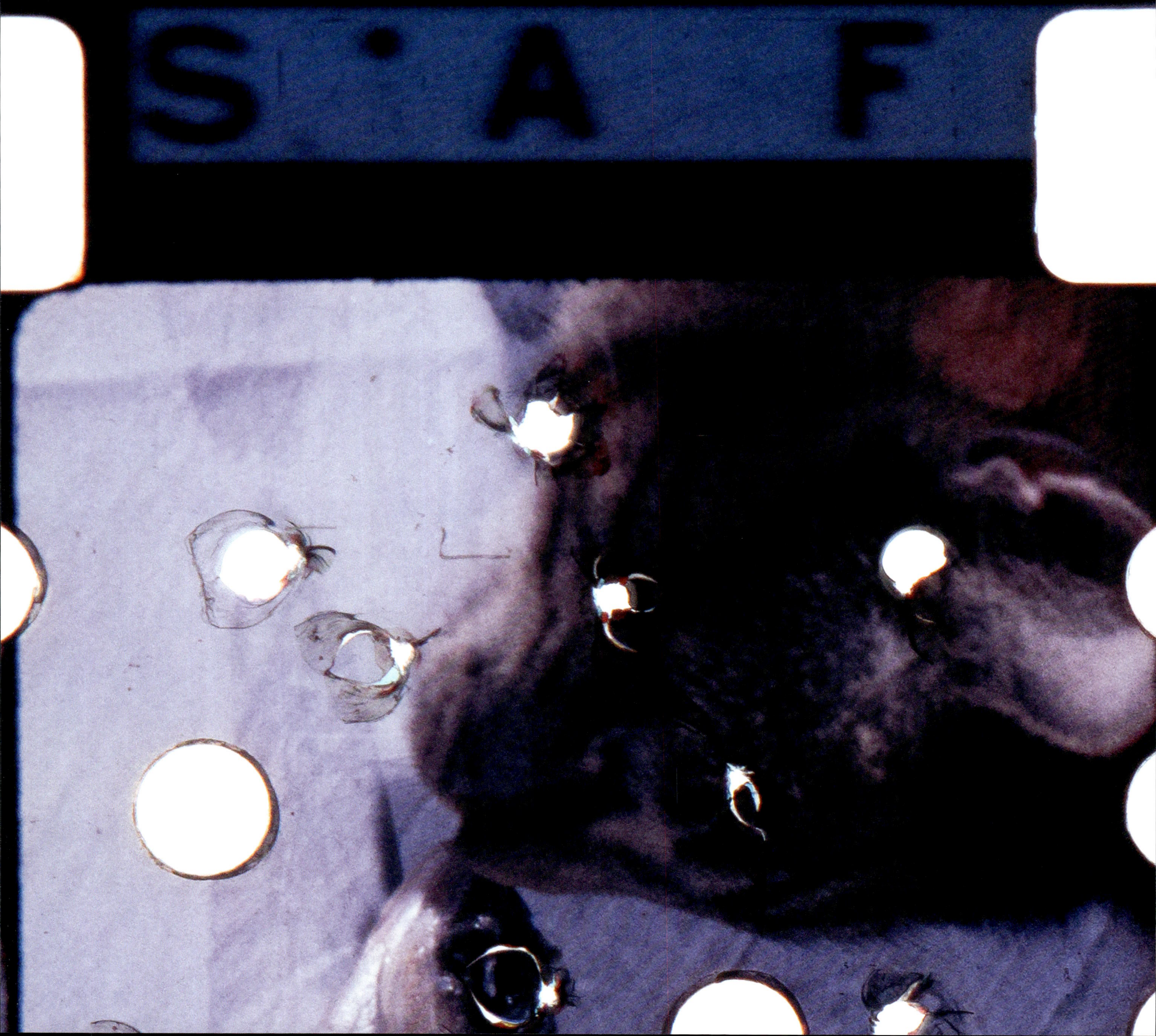
S • A • F

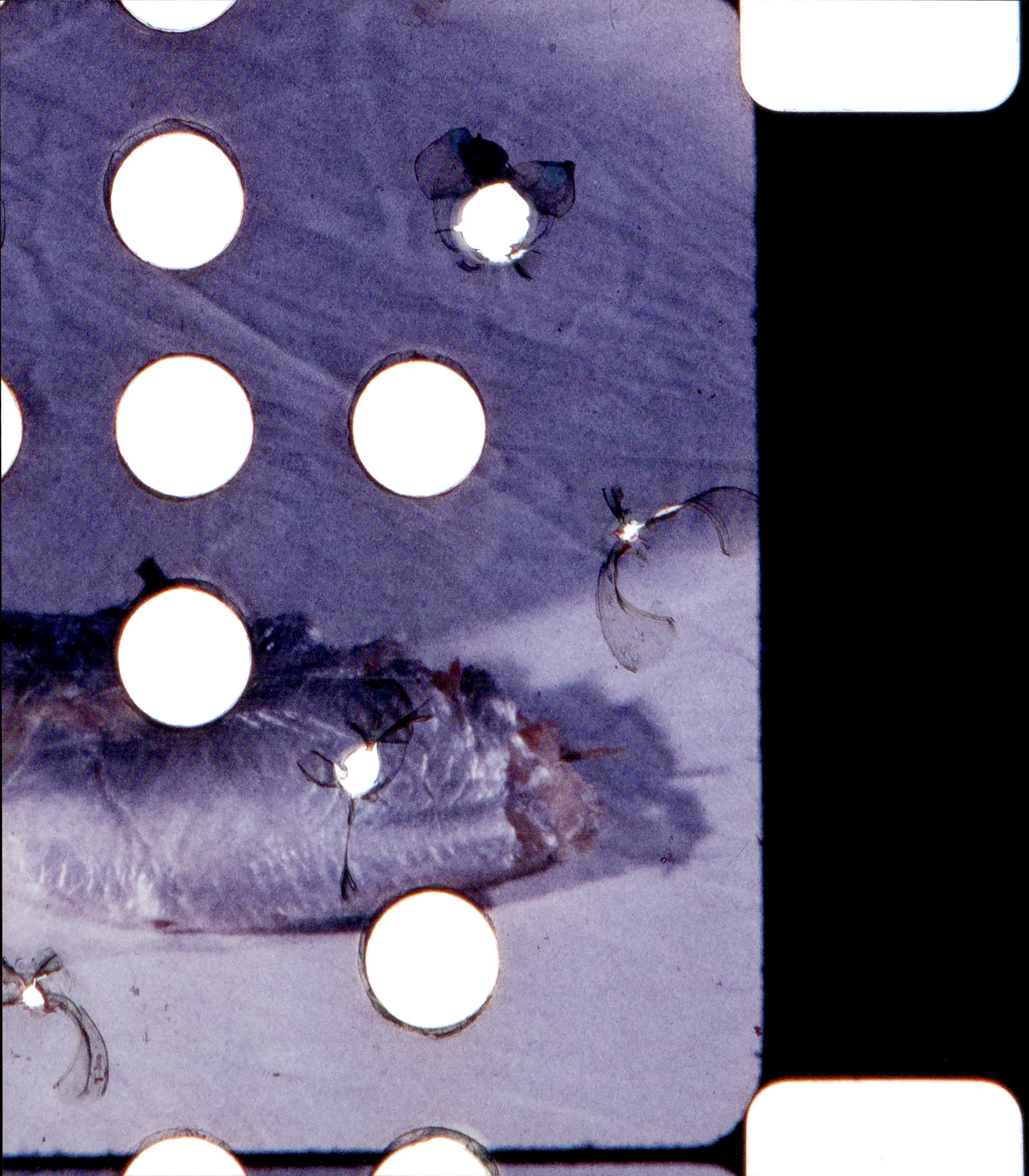

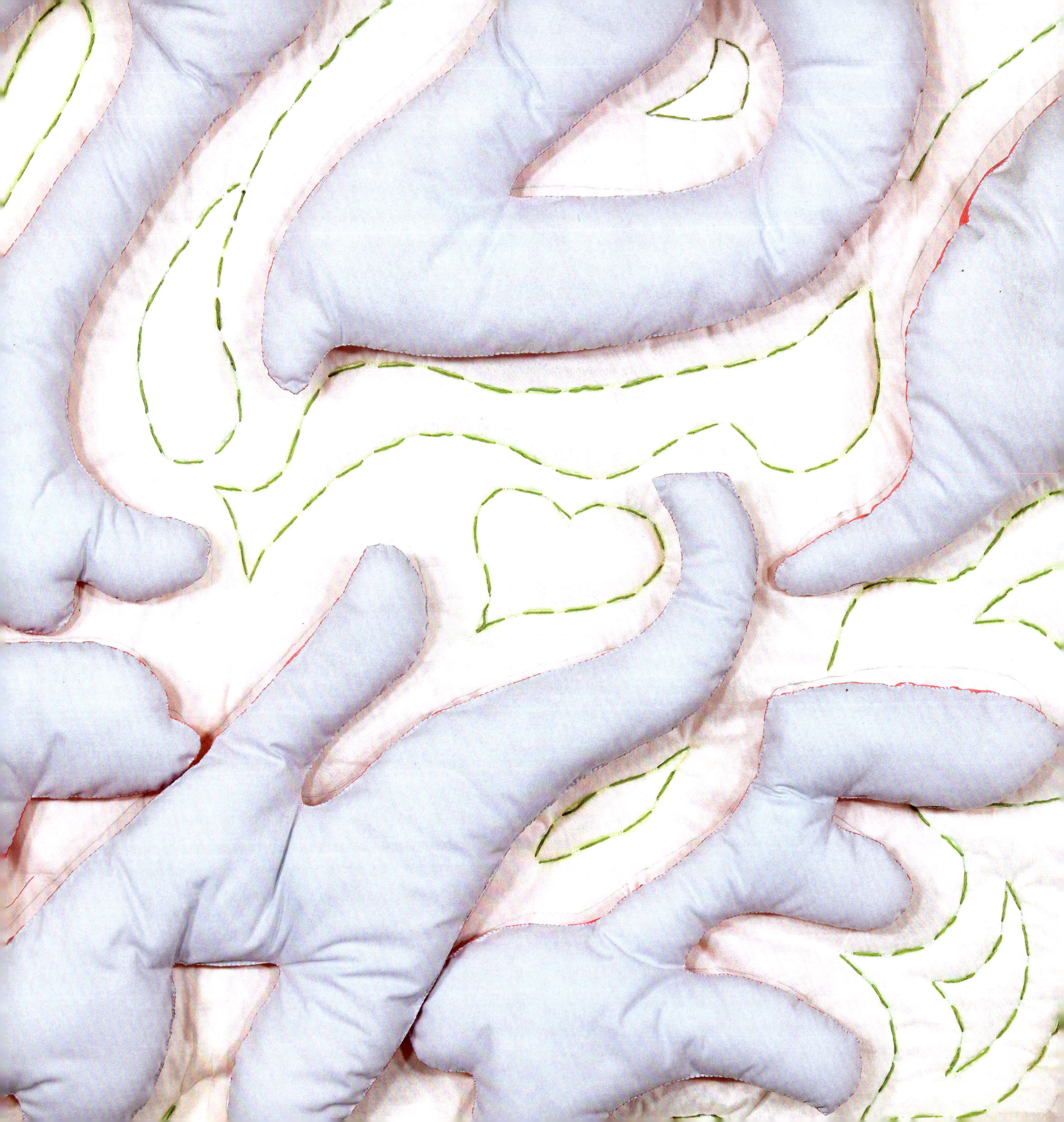

ACTIVISTE CULTURELLE

ANNE GRACE

When artists seek out that which is generative and hopeful and put ideas forward and images of the world as it might be otherwise, it can trigger the utopian imagination within both themselves and their audience. This is the care work of artists.[1]

In their 2021 book *Contemporary Art and Feminism*, which provides a radical re-reading of the contemporary moment, Jacqueline Millner and Catriona Moore respond to the need for a history of contemporary art that recognizes the critical role that "feminism has played in enabling current modes of artmaking, spectatorship and theoretical discourses."[2] Their investigation focusing on feminist art practices dating from the 1970s is at once revealing, frustrating, and promising, given the degree to which the paths taken half a century ago now coalesce. The authors' optimism lies in their assertion that "such approaches engage with notions such as leaving a light footprint, caring for country, relatedness, and the embrace of alterity; they move Western cultures beyond a respect for difference and the politics of witnessing, into complex affective territory more akin to love."[3] Millner and Moore come to the conclusion that "Ethics has once again become the touchstone of art; we see it in contemporary work that concerns itself with how to live sustainably, how to relate to oneself, others and the world, and how to align values to actions."[4] This recent scholarship informed by care ethics positions *art* at the forefront of forging alternative ethics in times of crisis.

During the 1960s and '70s, at the height of her recognition as a visual artist and an experimental filmmaker, Joyce Wieland often articulated the period in which she lived as one of crisis, both political and ecological: "There was a great urgency, I felt,

1 Kylie Banyard, "Remaining Alert to an Ethos of Care: The Responsiveness of Artistic Process," in *Care Ethics and Art*, ed. Jacqueline Millner and Gretchen Coombs (New York: Routledge, 2022), 94–95.

2 Jacqueline Millner and Catriona Moore, *Contemporary Art and Feminism* (New York: Routledge, 2022), 1.

3 Millner and Moore, *Contemporary Art and Feminism*, 1.

4 Millner and Moore, *Contemporary Art and Feminism*, 1.

PREVIOUS SPREAD
Defend the Earth (detail), 1972
Egyptian cotton, embroidery thread, thread, batting
193 × 716.3 × 12.7 cm
National Research Council Canada, Ottawa, ON, commissioned for the National Science Library
Photo: Rémi Thériault

basically in the terms: 'Is there going to be a country left.'"[5] She joined others of her generation in voicing a deep concern for the future of the planet. She was remarkably magnanimous in sharing the platform she had earned as an established artist in Canada to create art that celebrated craft and the handmade, inciting others to engage in driving political, social, and environmental change.

Wieland's practice forged connections of all kinds: temporal, material, technical, linguistic, social, and among flora and fauna. These connections shaped the direction of her practice but also point to the notion of care as a central impulse for her art. Her overarching capacity for care expanded her art-making from the exploration of radically new and experimental filmmaking to equally groundbreaking, polymorphous artworks that often integrated different craft-based techniques steeped in tradition. Her authentic voice—one that consistently strove to be inclusive—underpins this singular trajectory, accounting for the relevance of Wieland's art today.

Eventually, women's concerns and my own femininity became my artist's territory

Still, when I went out into the world I could see there were no women in art history so I looked to women writers as models. I chose Colette, George Sand and Katherine Mansfield.[6]

Wieland's love of drawing was foundational to her becoming an artist. It also prompted her older sister Joan, her guardian since she was orphaned around the age of ten, to enrol her at Toronto's Central Technical School rather than at a more conventionally gendered choice of high school for a young woman who would need to find a job to support herself in the early 1950s. Wieland's accomplished draftsmanship allowed her to find employment first at an advertising agency and later at an animation studio, Graphic Associates Film Production Ltd. Led by filmmaker and animator George Dunning (1920–1979), the studio was a hub of creative work, introducing Wieland to the works of directors such as Norman McLaren (1914–1987) and giving her the opportunity to meet others who shared her artistic aspirations. Her task painting cels (transparent celluloid used in animation works) gave her a sense of the tactility of film and instilled a desire to experiment with this medium. It was in this milieu that she met Michael Snow (1928–2023), whom she would marry in 1956, and alongside

5 Joyce Wieland interview by Barbara Stevenson, published in Kristy A. Holmes-Moss: "Joyce Wieland, Interview and Notes on *Reason over Passion* and *Pierre Vallières*," *Canadian Journal of Film Studies*, 15, no. 2 (Fall 2006): 117.

6 Wieland quoted in Susan M. Crean, "Notes from the Language of Emotion: A Conversation with Joyce Wieland," *Canadian Art* 4, no. 1 (Spring 1987): 64.

whom she would create some of her first films. It was not long before the couple distinguished themselves as part of a rising generation of Toronto artists. As Wieland established herself in the art world, her sharp wit found a place among those who embraced the language of Neo-Dada, and among other artists who also showed at the city's new Greenwich Gallery, soon to be renamed The Isaacs Gallery. Her ability to balance irony and sincerity became firmly ensconced in her work at this time, and continues to make her work both challenging and compelling.

As her artistic practice began to take hold, Wieland was deliberate in her search for her own voice. In an interview later in her life, she recalled the impetus for painting *War Memories* (1960) (p. 66) after a year of studying the work of Joan Miró (1893–1983). She described a "conscious decision to be influenced by someone other than the milieu that I was associated with, [most of whom] were men."[7] While this comment obliquely reveals the lack of women artists available as mentors, it also demonstrates how Miró may have inspired Wieland's impulse to move seamlessly from drawing to painting. As she observed: "It's drawing with a brush and it's oil on canvas."[8] The apparent ease with which Wieland brought one medium into another is manifest not only in how she handled the brush but also in the way she penetrated the painterly layer with chalkboard or graffiti-like markings.

Wieland's early search for authenticity took her from the deeply personal in *War Memories* (the painting references memories of her older brother's participation overseas in World War II) to a specifically female, feminine, and by extension Canadian subject matter.[9] Honouring a legendary figure from the War of 1812, the work *Laura Secord Saves Upper Canada* (1961) (p. 71) marks the beginning of Wieland's adoption of Canadian subject matter. In a battle fought by men, Laura Secord, a mother of seven children, demonstrated the acumen and bravery to travel over thirty kilometres to warn the British of an impending attack by US soldiers, thus ensuring victory in what would become known as the Battle of Beaver Dams.

The heroine of *Laura Secord Saves Upper Canada* is directly present only in its title. The symbol of the flag (Union Jack), a spiral, and hand-drawn numbers and arrows evoke the classroom context in which the artist first learned about Secord. This formal imagery is shared with the artists whom Wieland would have been familiar with already because of her frequent trips to New York City, where Robert Rauschenberg, Jasper Johns, and Claes Oldenburg were receiving increasing attention. She appropriates this vocabulary but adds a significant dimension by creating an inclusive and hopeful narrative and bringing a heroic woman into the fold. Aligned with contemporary feminist practices that forge connections to history, this type of artistic strategy also proposes, in Kylie Banyard's words, "hopeful narratives about the future with the aim of rekindling a sense of the utopian imagination."[10] This is an early manifestation of an act of care.

7 Transcript of Joyce Wieland artist's talk at the University of Lethbridge, 1985, 2 (edited quote from cassette tape "Joyce Wieland on Her Work"; transcript held at the University of Lethbridge Art Gallery, Alberta—hereafter cited as Wieland, Lethbridge transcript). A notable exception was Wieland's high-school teacher Doris McCarthy, whom she considered a mentor.

8 Wieland, Lethbridge transcript, 1.

9 By 1971, the two concepts converged for Wieland: "I think of Canada as female," she stated to the press on the occasion of her exhibition at the National Gallery of Canada. Johanne Sloan, "Key Works: O Canada," in *Joyce Wieland: Life & Work* (Toronto: Art Canada Institute), www.aci-iac.ca/art-books/joyce-wieland/.

10 Banyard, "Remaining Alert," 103.

A lot of things turned up from being and working at home

I knew [Judd] and I knew Andre very well and Andre liked my work. However, I did things my way and there was no way I could do things the way they were doing them. It didn't appeal to me. I knew it was good, and I knew it changed the tide of history for a while, but you know, big money changed that history. I mean the big galleries and the big bucks that went into the product [. . . .] When it was written down, that was the history, the official history.[11]

In early-1960s Toronto, Wieland produced some of the most stunningly beautiful and powerful paintings that would come out of Canada that decade. Access for the first time to a large studio allowed her to create the magnificent paintings *Time Machine Series* (p. 77) and *Hallucination* (pp. 74–75) (both 1971), consisting of canvases with saturated blues, turquoise, pink, and greens. The artist later remarked that these paintings "just came out."[12] Their sensual rhythms and generous brushwork suggest otherwise, placing them instead within the pedigree of her contemporary lyrical ink drawings.

Having completed this extraordinary body of paintings, earning recognition from major art Canadian institutions that began collecting and exhibiting her work, in 1962 she and Snow left Toronto to live in New York City. This ambitious move marked a decisive shift from the production of large-scale paintings to a focus on filmmaking, a medium Wieland had just begun to explore in Toronto. In addition to delving into this experimental media, she continued to produce markedly different paintings and extend the material base of her work to construct assemblages of mostly found objects, as well as to stuff and stitch plastic wall hangings and quilts.

The body of works produced during her almost decade-long stay in New York demonstrates how Wieland positioned herself outside the city's "mainstream" avant-garde visual art world, a stance affirmed by her active participation in the developing underground film scene. Employing innovative techniques, including using found footage as well as physically intervening on the film by dying and puncturing the celluloid with a sewing needle, expanded the possibilities of filmmaking. Wieland later expressed how she valued the open community that film scene offered: "It was what I believed about what artists should be, what I'd read in history, I was meeting it, and I was becoming part of it. But with the underground filmmakers, it was loose. You could make mistakes, and mistakes are part of film creation. I was terrified of the art scene, and something in me couldn't get it together to make anything for that scene. It turned my juice off. I just took what I could from it without losing sight of something in myself."[13]

11 Joyce Wieland, interview by Barbara Stevenson, October 8, 1986, quoted in Kristy A. Holmes-Moss, "Joyce Wieland: Interview and Notes on *Reason over Passion* and *Pierre Vallières*," *Canadian Journal of Film Studies* 15, no. 2 (Fall 2006): 115.

12 Wieland, Lethbridge transcript, 3.

13 Quoted in Lauren Rabinovitz, "An Interview with Joyce Wieland," *Afterimage* 8, no.10 (May 18): 9.

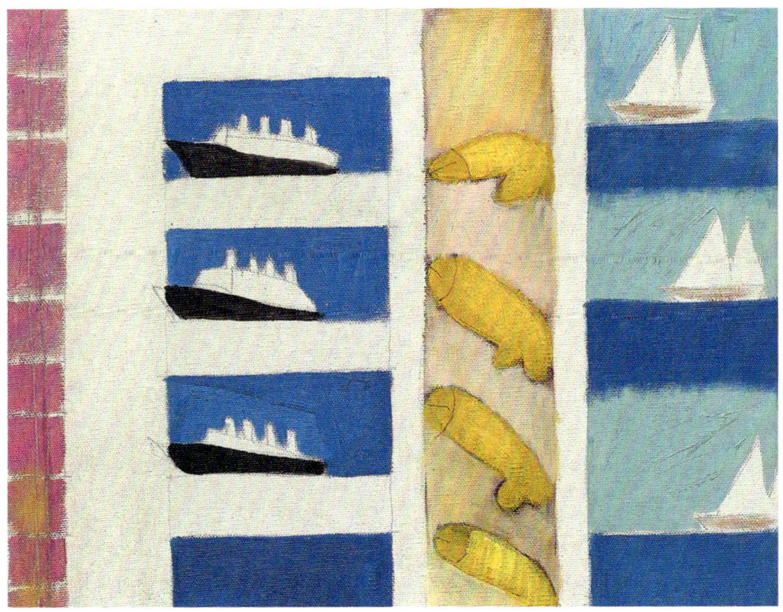

Flick Pics #4 (detail), 1963
Oil on canvas
106.6 × 40.8 cm
Art Gallery of Ontario, Gift of Morton and Carol Rapp, 2007
2007/429
Photo: AGO, Craig Boyko

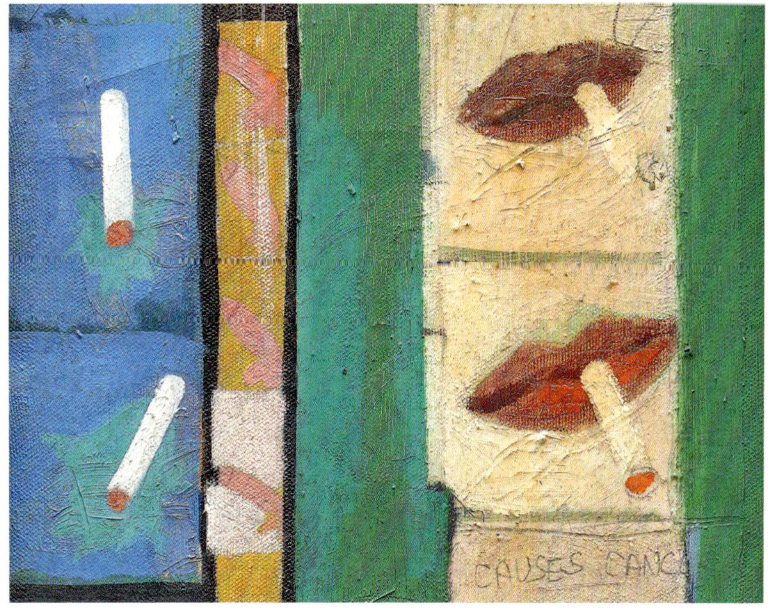

West 4th (detail), 1963
Oil on canvas
76.2 × 22.9 cm
Private Collection
Photo: AGO, Craig Boyko

When Wieland did produce paintings and assemblages during her New York years, which she showed in Canada only, the formal language of film structured their compositions. Among those works with the most pronounced references to the sequential format of film are *Flick Pics #4* (p. 82) and *West 4th* (p. 82), demonstrating how Wieland used humour to challenge dominant ideologies of the visual art scene she encountered in New York. As Lauren Rabinovitz has noted, Wieland utilized "existing avant-garde styles to celebrate female motifs, symbols, and experiences while satirizing phallic power."[14]

In *Flick Pics #4*, four vertical rows of images each suggest distinct filmstrips. Two of these are depictions of boats: one an ocean liner and the other a sailboat, painted floating in and out of view. Parallel to the frames showing the ocean liner floating—and sinking—is a series of thirteen penises that echo the buoyancy and sinking (fading into a blur) of the vessel. By deflating such a charged symbol of masculinity, Wieland responds to the macho art scene that encroached on her own world. *West 4th*, with its similar format, can be read as affirming her stance of resistance, undermining as it does the slick commercial and often gendered appeal of Pop art. In the narrow space between the two vertical rows of cigarettes—one shown amid expanding turquoise smoke, the other grasped between lips depicted increasingly in close-up—Wieland squeezes in the image of a sequence of pink penises. In the somewhat unkempt, painterly renditions of a mouth, as well as the equation of the cigarette and penis, she pokes fun at the detached cool of her contemporaries who usurp the female lips to create their chauvinistic brand of imagery. The cautionary "causes cancer," inscribed awkwardly in pencil, chastens the viewer, who indulges in the hedonistic, filmic allure of the images. Wieland's facetious public service announcement is offered to the careful observer.

14 Rabinovitz, "An Interview," 8.

OPPOSITE
Film Mandala (detail), 1966
Quilting by Joan Stewart and Gladys Chambers
Cloth, thread, batting
203 × 202 cm
Macdonald Stewart Art Centre Collection at the Art Gallery of Guelph, Gift of Doug MacPherson, 2006
MS2006.023
Photo: AGO, Craig Boyko

I wanted to elevate and honour craft

My sister, Joan Stewart, was making quilts all this time. She needed work. She didn't have any money, and I liked what she was doing. I thought maybe I could design a quilt about a person. So I designed one for a friend's son about his character and the things he liked at age five. I cut things out, basted the quilt, and my sister completed it.[15]

The two reasons stated by Wieland that prompted her to make her first quilt are aesthetics and care. The artist endeavoured to support Stewart in a time of need (no doubt she felt indebted to her for the care she provided Wieland as a child amid dire poverty); her offer to provide monetary compensation affirmed the worthiness of her sister's quilt work. Wieland's desire to closely collaborate with her sister, on this quilt and on the many others that followed over the next decade, unequivocally demonstrates how she valued the practice of quiltmaking, a medium not yet sanctioned by the art world.[16] It is significant that the first quilt the Wieland sisters created was a gift, one that could also be considered as a reciprocal act of generosity, as it was made for Michael, the son of Donna Montague, who had lent Wieland the coach house to use as a studio in Toronto.

Historically, the concept of gift is central to the quilt, resistant—in part, by necessity—to economic currency, and typically handed directly from maker or makers to the recipient. The quilts made by privation (from fabric remnants or repurposing cloth such as flour bags) are also a testament to ingenuity. Wieland's first quilt was conceptually closer to her own work in collage: she cut out the fabric shapes, worked out the composition, and basted them in place, and her sister took on the intensive skilled work to complete it, "sewing with the tiny perfect hand stitches of tradition."[17] The next quilts she and Joan created, destined for the art world, would purposefully honour the venerable artisanal practice.

Creating a three-way dialogue between craft, visual art, and film, *Film Mandala* (p. 138) and *The Camera's Eyes* (p. 137) mark a historically significant moment in Wieland's practice. In the red, square centre of *Film Mandala,* the outline of a film reel is sewn with red thread. The remaining composition consists of framing the square in quilted borders of larger, contiguous squares in white, blue, and grey similar to the "homage to the square" compositions of Josef Albers (1888–1976), within the yellow quilted border acting as a frame. A deliberate link with the German-born artist, settled by now in the United States, is conceivable if we consider that Wieland considered this quilt an "homage to film," and her reference to its "radiance": "Homage to film and particularly, to 8mm film and handling it a lot making 8mm films in New York . . . . The lights falls on all these lines which in a way are the proportion of 8mm film strips. It has to do with radiance."[18] This grey area, delineated with stitches that

15 Wieland quoted in Rabinovitz, "An Interview," 10.

16 Later, the milestone exhibition at the Whitney Museum of American Art, *Abstract Design in American Quilts*, curated by Jonathan Holstein and Gail van der Hoof, which opened on July 1, 1971 (the same day as Wieland's *True Patriot Love* exhibition opened at the National Gallery of Canada), provided recognition in the visual art world for quiltmaking. Holstein interviewed Wieland, along with other Canadian artists based in New York, for the article "New York's Vitality Tonic for Canadian Artists," published in *Canadian Art* 21. no. 5 (September/October 1964): 270–79.

17 Kat Kritzwiser, "A Record of the Sixties in Colourful Quilts," *The Globe and Mail*, March 25, 1967, 17.

18 Wieland, Lethbridge transcript, 3.

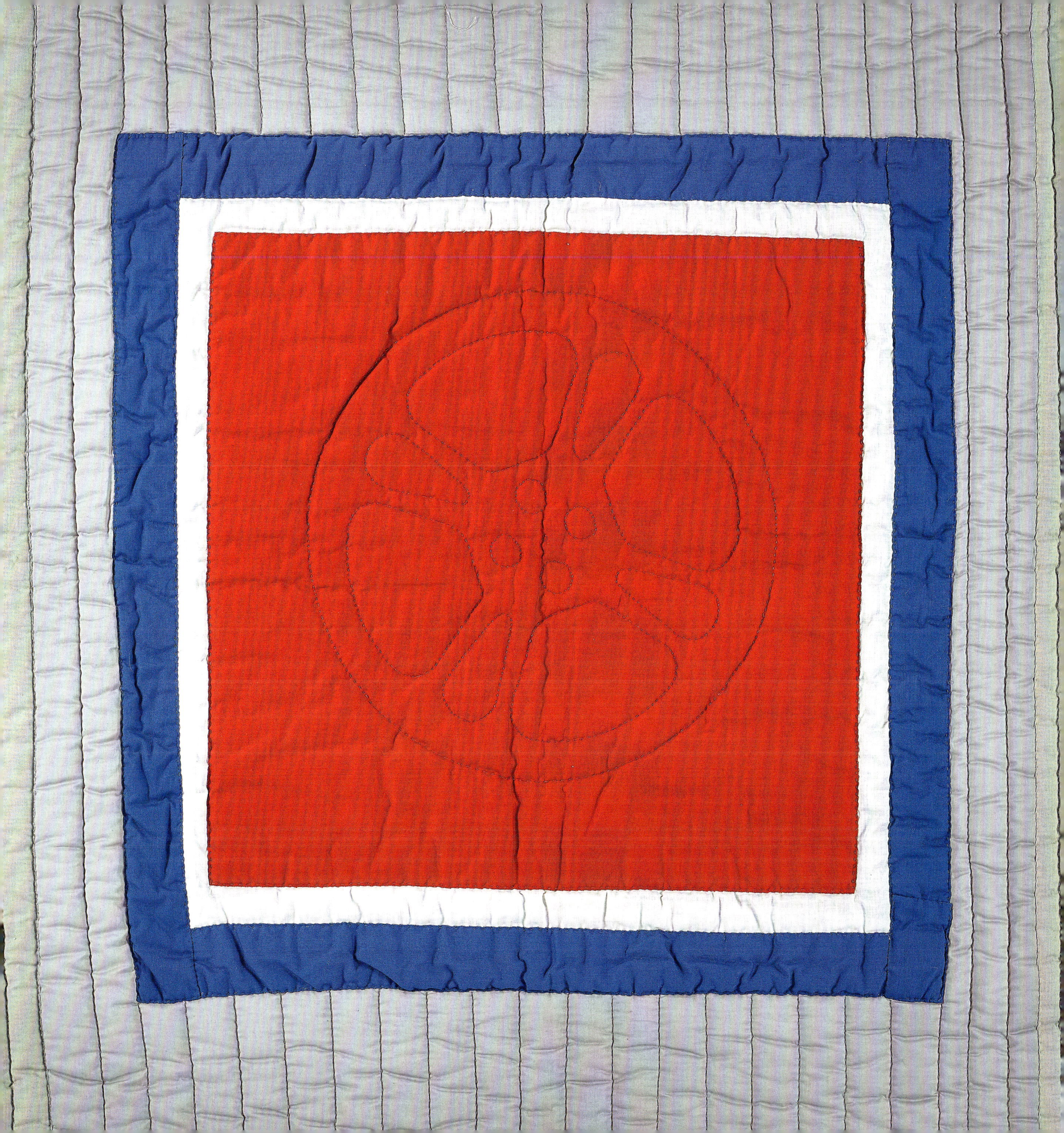

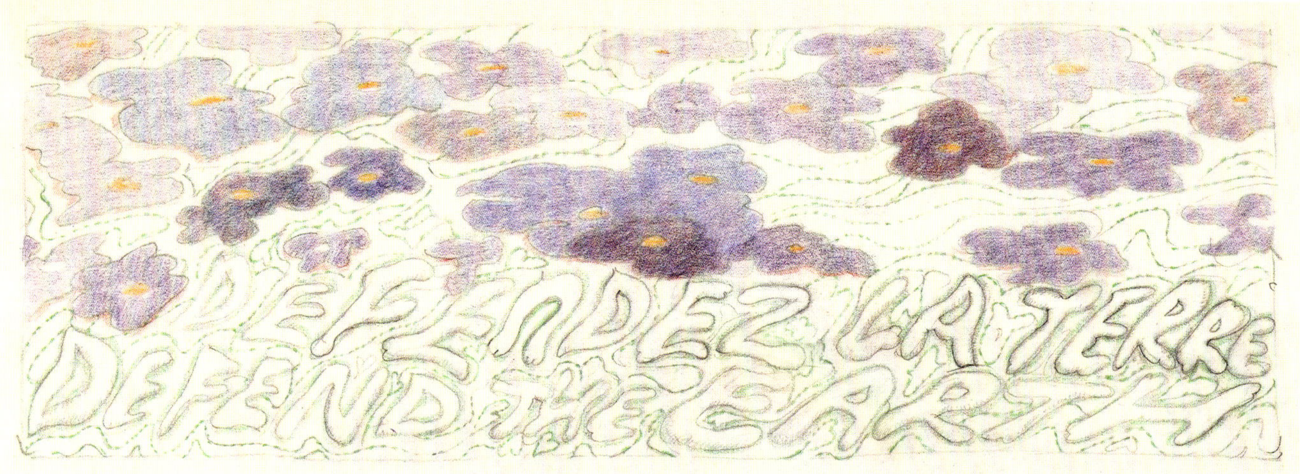

Preparatory sketch for *Defend the Earth* quilt, c. 1972
Graphite on tracing paper
22.3 × 30.1 cm
Joyce Wieland fonds, NGC Library and Archives
Photo: NGC

parallel the sequence and proportion of an 8mm filmstrip guide the viewer's attention to the "film mandala." The precise path of the cotton thread, as it weaves in and out of the layers of fabric and batting to outline the film reel, echoes the even cadence of a film projector, as the "film reel spins off dreams."[19]

The shape of the film reel is similar to the wagon wheel, a popular traditional quilt pattern. The title, *Film Mandala*, partakes in the quiltmaking custom of giving names to quilts, as it does for titles of artworks. The degree to which it embraces the quilting tradition so fully demonstrates Wieland's wholehearted respect of this time-honoured craft, an object of beauty made through love and labour to provide both warmth and comfort. Wieland considered the conventional use of her quilts in an interview: "Miss Wieland points out that the quilt can be washed by hand in cold water."[20]

When Wieland was offered a 1971 exhibition at the National Gallery of Canada—the first living woman artist to be honoured in this way—she invited other women to share the stage with her: "[T]he idea of involving women who did crafts in Canada was the basis of my National Gallery of Canada show, 'True Patriot Love/Véritable amour patriotique,' in 1971. I would look at maps thinking of regions, and when I taught in the Maritimes for three months in 1970, it was an opportunity to visit fairs and places like that and find women. I wanted to elevate and honor craft by joining women together in an exhibition where they would be united and proud of what they had done.... The embroideress Joan McGregor did the greatest embroideries called *Wolfe's Last Letter* and *Montcalm's Last Letter.* The letters were reproduced on linen-like photographic cotton, and then she had to embroider them, something that was quite difficult. She did an incredible job, and it was beautiful work."[21]

The exhibition also marked the artist's return to live in Toronto. *True Patriot Love* demonstrates how Wieland's love of history and beauty, respect for the handmade, as well as her magnanimity in choosing to use her platform to empower other women, speak to her force as an artist and the prescience of her art. Wieland fully understood the value of, and selflessly practised, what Betsy Greer, the sociologist and crafter who coined the term "craftivism" in 2003, would later write: "[T]he creation of things by hand leads to a better understanding of democracy, because it reminds us that we have power."[22]

19 Kritzwiser, "A Record," 17.

20 Kritzwiser, "A Record," 17.

21 Wieland quoted in Rabinovitz, "An Interview," 10.

22 This often-quoted phrase was first published in Betsy Greer's blog in 2002. The term "craftivism" was coined by Greer in 2003.

If we are going to save the planet, women are going to have to do it

I have been very aware of the fact that there is Art and there is Politics, and I have been working on putting them together in aesthetic terms for years. I think I am getting somewhere. I think one can have all the thrill of doing art as well as embedding the political thing in it—inside it.[23]

Defend the Earth (*Défendez la terre*) (pp. 202–203), a wondrous wall hanging that presents a blooming expanse of swelling mauve blooms, painstakingly stitched and stuffed, was the artist's first and only commission for the federal government's Department of Public Works (DPW). Installed in 1972 and still on display in the lobby of the National Research Council Canada's National Science Library in Ottawa, *Defend the Earth* is as untouched as its counterpart on the opposite wall by Vancouver artist Glenn Lewis (b. 1935), a mural composed of twelve rows of transparent acrylic boxes, each conceived as a time capsule whose contents were submitted by artists across the country. The sculptures by five other artists reveal an impressive array of materials such as living plants, textile banners, interactive fluorescent tubes, and Corten steel, and are a testament to how each artist responded to the NRC's major public art commission.[24] Wieland's "ecology quilt," as it was also known, stands out among these works in the directness of its message, with the artist urging the scientific community to "defend the earth."[25]

Wieland was inspired by her growing concern for the environment, returning to Canada in 1971, a year after the Quebec government announced its major James Bay hydroelectric project, which would involve the flooding of over ten thousand square kilometres of land in the north of the province. As an active member of Canadian Artists Representation (CAR), she was involved in the association's initiative to raise money for the Cree Nation by selling artists' prints to help finance legal proceedings to stop the project.[26] Wieland recalled that the experience galvanized her to start to "do more work that was centered on ecology."[27]

Thus, when she had the opportunity to create a large-scale work that once again had a national platform but this time could speak directly to Canadian scientists, she took responsibility. Surprisingly, perhaps, the straightforward words "Defend the Earth" were those she commissioned specifically for the project by her friend, the writer Sara Bowser (1927–2012). Wieland also took care to acknowledge the work of her sister by including Joan Stewart's name along with her own on the bronze plaque displayed on the wall beside the quilt.

23 Wieland quoted in Debbie Magidson and Judy Wright, "Interviews with Canadian Artists: Debbie Magidson and Judy Wright Interview Joyce Wieland," *Canadian Forum* 54 (May/June 1974), 61.

24 According to Douglas S. Richardson, the Department of Public Works' Fine Art program provided over $120,000 in commissions as part of an initiative that dedicated 1 percent of the building's construction budget to artworks. Douglas S. Richardson, "National Science Library: Art in Architecture," *artscanada*, no. 190–91 (Autumn 1974): 49.

25 Public Works Canada, unpaginated pamphlet published at the time of the inauguration of the National Research Council (NRC) art commissions for building m-55. The author is grateful to Steven Leclair, NRC archives officer, for providing archival documents as well as for being so responsive to requests about this overlooked commission.

26 Rabinovitz, "An Interview," 11.

27 Quoted in Rabinovitz, "An Interview," 11.

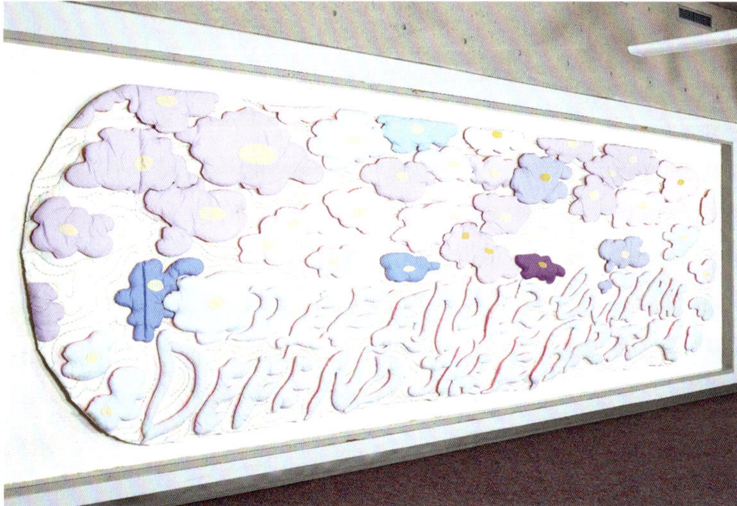

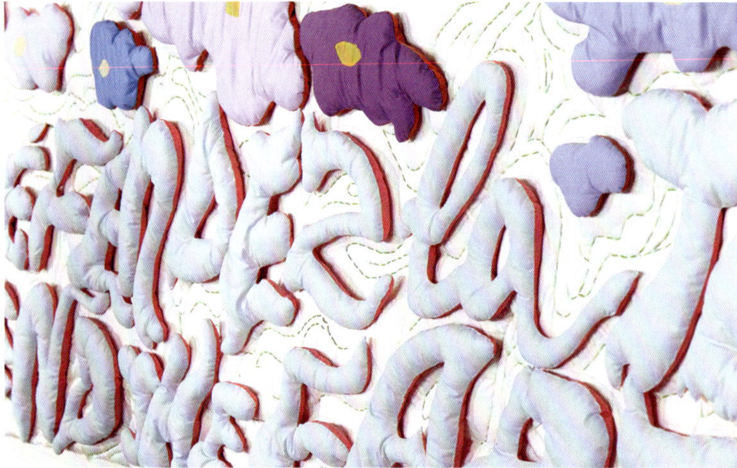

ABOVE
Installation view of
Defend the Earth, 1972
Photo: Rémi Thériault

BELOW
Defend the Earth (detail), 1972
Photo: Rémi Thériault

OPPOSITE
Defend the Earth (detail), 1972
Photo: Rémi Thériault

The bubble letters spelling "Defend the Earth" and "Défendez la terre" have lost their usual upright stance compared with the earlier text-based quilted works; here they appear windblown or imaginably anthropomorphized, hinting at a vulnerability, somewhat squished as they fit into the bottom of the composition, each language vying for space. Wieland, who by 1972 had already created bilingual quilted works, would certainly have made sure that her message to the scientific community, in her first public federal art commission, was written in both English and French. As an artist who shunned the elite, theoretical language of the art world and was committed to the accessibility of her art, she approached her commission generously as she delivered this urgent message for the sake of the planet. When the work was unveiled, the press release declared: "She is very happy with her work and believes people will readily understand the hanging and its message."[28]

Wieland's ecology quilt offers the antithesis of the cold, brutalist architecture of the NRC building for which it was made. Softness and puffiness is stitched into every component of the oversized, oblong quilt. Long green embroidery-thread stitches meander around the rounded curves of the flowers and the letters, hinting at the gentle hills of a meadow. Anyone who takes the time to look closely will discover that the outline of a heart is nestled in the abstract pattern, a Wieland leitmotif that discreetly heightens the emotional plea to the science community. The flowers, in shades of mauve, pink, and blue, have yellow centres, their petals overlapping or floating on their own above the meadow as if they are clouds in the sky. Their lightness and circular forms offer an opportunity to dream, as if Wieland hopes to channel thought bubbles to the scientists as a reminder of their role as guardians of the planet.

Wieland often created contrasting colour backings to her quilts and stuffed letters, in keeping with the tradition of a craft where, unlike painting, the recto and verso are both integral to the aesthetic of the object. The bright red backings of the letters provide a slight optical glow, heightening the luminosity of the work. The beauty, fragility, and temporality of Wieland's

28 Press release, Public Works Canada. See p. 201.

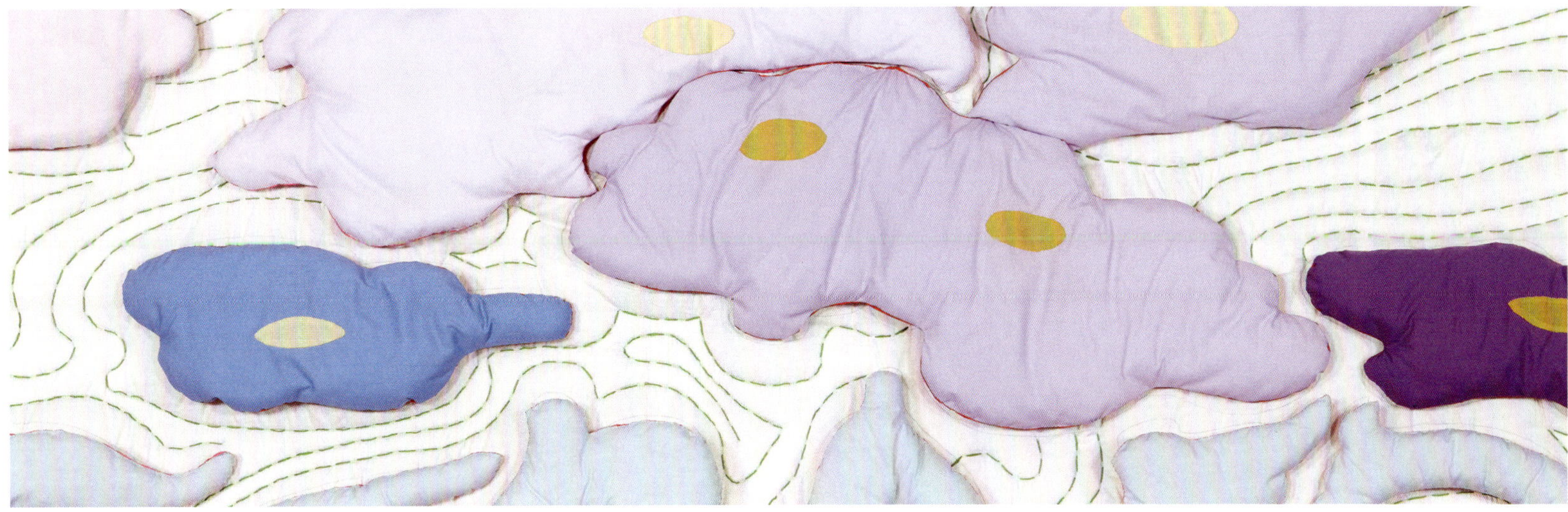

billowy flower meadow—soft in both colour and in texture—is in stark contrast to the bare concrete wall behind the work. The plexiglass that separates the quilt from the viewer frustrates the haptic experience but amplifies its billboard missive. Fortuitously, from an art-conservation viewpoint, the casing means that the quilt has remained remarkably in the same condition as it was when it was made more than fifty years ago. Although the colours have faded slightly with age, the message has only become more pressing. Wieland's anti-monumental public artwork, with its expansive horizontal format and warm, quilted layers and rounded edges, is an act of care, stirring the imagination and offering a protective blanket to planet Earth.

The way you make a future what you want is by paying attention to ecology

> *It seems to be easier for us today to imagine the throughgoing deterioration of the earth and nature than the breakdown of late capitalism; perhaps that is due to some weakness in our imaginations.*[29]
>
> —FREDERIC JAMESON, *The Seeds of Time*

As critic Susan Crean (b. 1945) noted in 1987, Wieland was unfairly excluded from much of the art-historical cannon because contemporary art theory was not adequate to fully capture the essence of her art: "In the sixties, as now, Wieland's work is not explained by the theory written by men. Then, the theory was all about form when Wieland's language derived from emotions."[30] With the relatively recent articulation of the theory of care, a theoretical underpinning has provided a new way to frame Wieland's practice. *The Care Manifesto*, written by the Care Collective in 2020, recognizes and embraces interdependencies and the importance of "the political, social, material, and emotional conditions that allow the vast majority of people and living creatures on this planet to thrive—along with the planet itself."[31] Their message echoes the sense of urgency that stirred Wieland, who described herself as an *activiste culturelle*, to find uncharted ways to create art that would put care at its core. ›››

29 Frederic Jameson, *The Seeds of Time* (New York: Columbia University Press, 1994), xii.

30 Susan Crean, "The Erotic Nationalism of Joyce Wieland," *This Magazine*, August/September 1987, 15. Crean credits Leila Sujir for this phrase.

31 The Care Collective (Andreas Chatzidakis, Jamie Hakim, Jo Littler, Catherine Rottenberg, and Lynne Segal), *The Care Manifesto: The Politics of Interdependence* (London: Verso, 2020), 5.

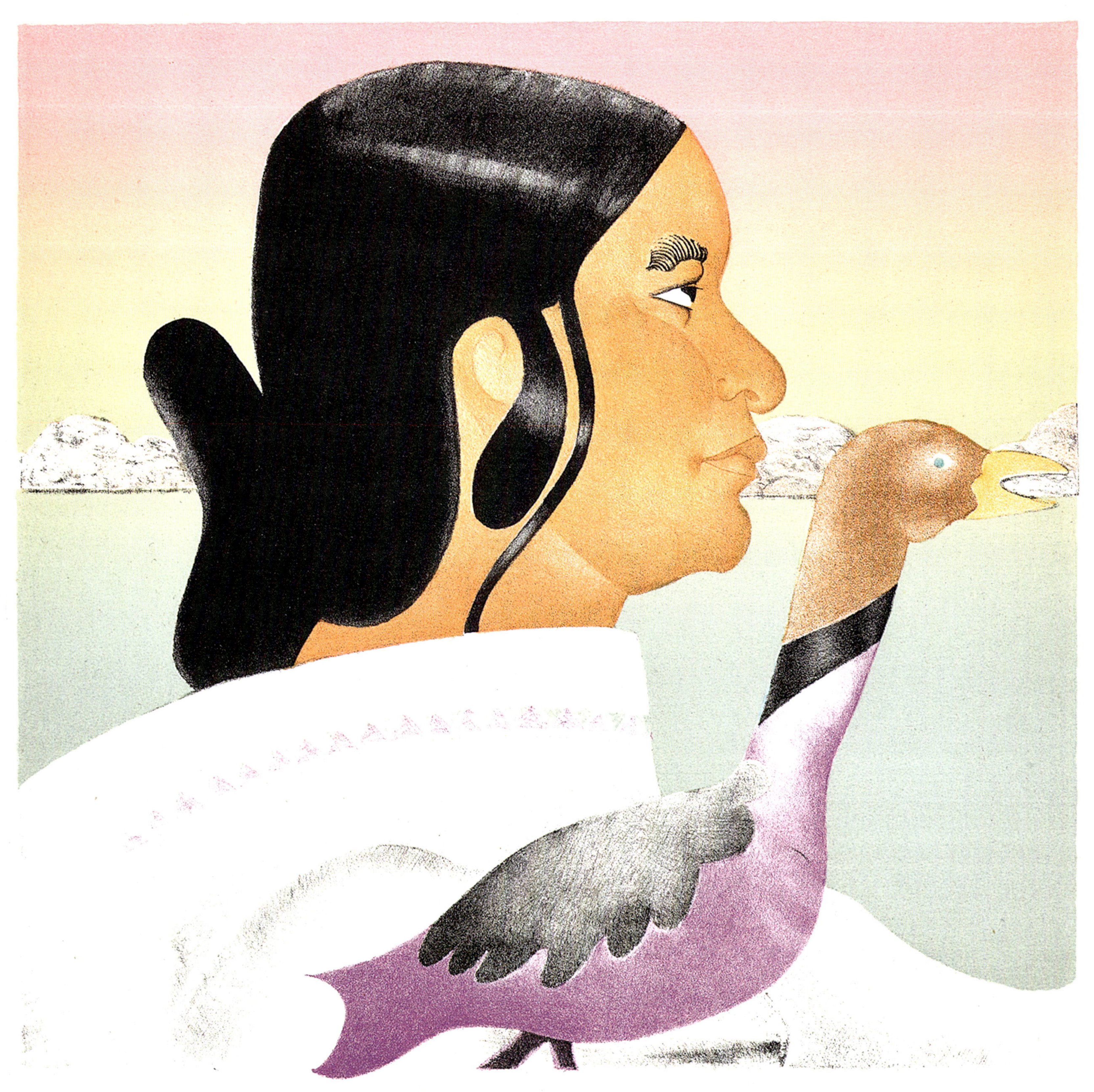
Soroseelutu, Artist of Cape Dorset
Joyce Wieland 20/50 1979

FACING NORTH

GEORGIANA UHLYARIK

Among the principal subjects in Joyce Wieland's work over her five-decade career, the least discussed is the Arctic.[1] The "North" is a subject she returned to repeatedly during the 1970s, in an impressive range of media, to create some of her most well-known and ambitious works. Yet she was rarely asked about it directly, and spoke of it only in passing a handful of times. There are scarce traces of the Arctic in her archives, making it difficult to understand her source materials, or to confirm when she visited Kinngait, Northwest Territories (now in Nunavut), and how many times. It is—perhaps as it should be—only through the works themselves that the Arctic reveals itself as an intricate, persistent, and powerful theme for Wieland. Her perspective is at once progressive and original, as well as complicated and limited by her position as an anglophone in southern Canada.

Wieland's notions about the region are shaped by a complicated love for her country. In her work, the Arctic of her imagination is bountiful, full of colour and life, and under attack.[2] She idealizes the Arctic as "the true north" symbol of Canada—and thus assimilated into Canada's national identity—yet her artistic contribution to "the idea of North" and its representation is far from a common stereotype. As cultural critic Susan Crean argues, "Wieland uses the trappings of Canadianism with unashamed love yet without sentimentality, as no one else has done."[3] The Arctic is a predominant theme in her landmark *True Patriot Love / Véritable amour patriotique* exhibition at the National Gallery of Canada (NGC) in the summer of 1971, with some aspect of the Arctic featured in nearly a quarter of the works included.[4]

1 There are two scholarly discussions: Kristy A. Holmes, "Imagining and Visualizing 'Indianness' in Trudeauvian Canada: Joyce Wieland's *The Far Shore* and *True Patriot Love*," *RACAR* 35, no. 2 (2010): 47–64, and Kristy A. Holmes, "Negotiating the Nation: The Work of Joyce Wieland, 1968–1976" (PhD diss., Queen's University, 2007); and Matthew Purvis, "John Boyle, Greg Curnoe and Joyce Wieland: Erotic Art and English Canadian Nationalism" (PhD diss., Carleton University, 2020).

2 According to Anne Montagnes, "Wieland stated that, far from disputing sentiment, her feeling for the Arctic was love—realistic love. Behind the adulation was the knowledge that the Arctic is being raped." Purvis, "John Boyle, Greg Curnoe and Joyce Wieland," 296.

3 Susan Crean, "The Erotic Nationalism of Joyce Wieland," *This Magazine*, August/September 1987, 17.

4 There were thirty-seven works on view: thirty-six works listed in Joyce Wieland, *True Patriot Love / Véritable amour patriotique* (Ottawa: National Gallery of Canada, 1971), plus Wieland's artist book, also included in the installation.

PREVIOUS SPREAD
Soroseelutu, Artist of Cape Dorset, 1979
Lithograph on paper
34.3 × 32.7 cm
Art Gallery of Ontario, Purchase 1987
86/283
Photo: AGO, Craig Boyko

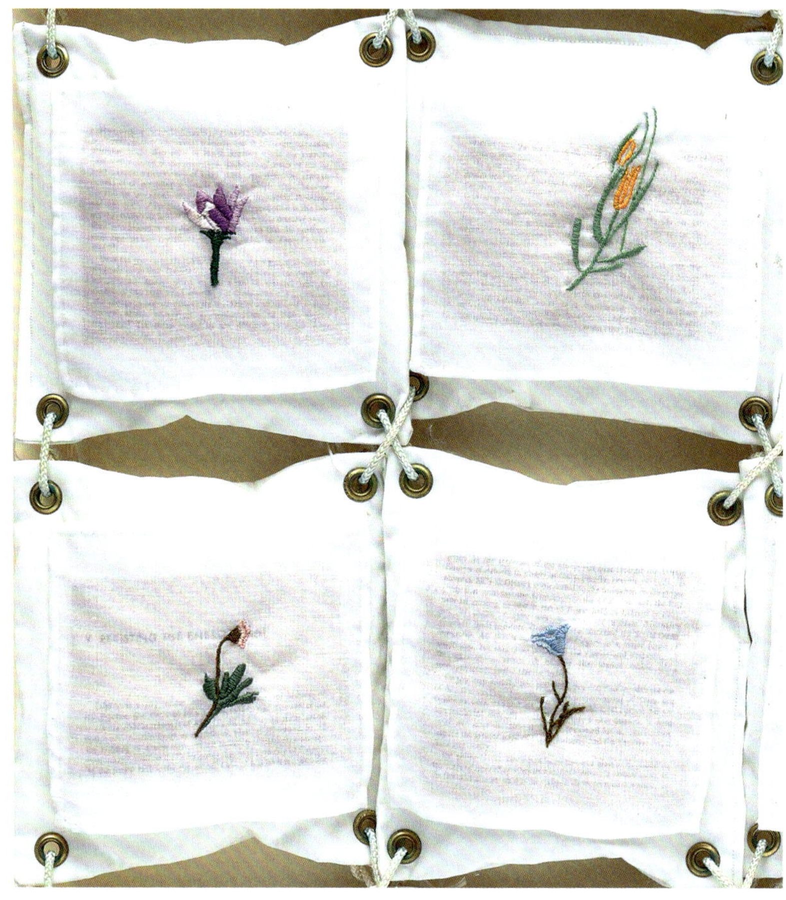

The Water Quilt (detail), 1970–1971
Embroidery by Joan Stewart
Cloth, embroidery thread, thread, metal grommets, braided rope, ink
121.9 × 121.9 cm
Art Gallery of Ontario, Purchase with assistance from Wintario, 1977
76/221
Photo: AGO, Craig Boyko

> 'Water' quilt, *1970–1971, contains and is composed of 60 pages from James Laxer's* The Energy Poker Game *photographed on cotton, mounted on 60 cotton pillows (with brass grommets in all 4 corners. Veiled by 60 Arctic flowers embroidered on cotton).*
> *"To believe in nature was to rebel"*
> *– Thoreau*[5]

This is how Wieland introduces one of her signature textiles in the artist book accompanying the exhibition. Further down the page she indicates that each six-by-six-inch "pillow" is to be "tied through" with "sailor's rope" in order "to hold 'Water' Quilt together." The final work is comprised of sixty-four rather than sixty "pillows" arranged in a square grid, framed, glazed, and hanging on brass hooks through the sixteen grommets at the top. Despite its title—the only one of Wieland's works to include the word "quilt"—it makes for a rather inadequate blanket, and there is no depiction of water, unless we imagine the plain white cotton support as snow.

The Water Quilt (p. 192) is a conceptually arranged field of delicately embroidered flowers: a composite arctic landscape, deceptively serene and disquietly indexical. Each cotton square is a portrait of an arctic flower and its leaves, small, expressive, and singular.[6] Wieland found them illustrated and described in a government-funded bulletin documenting "the 340 species and major geographical races of flowering plants and ferns that comprise the vascular flora as it is known at present of the Canadian Arctic Archipelago."[7] (This is the book she took apart, altered, and reassembled at her kitchen table in New York in order to create her exhibition publication.[8]) It includes black-and-white botanical drawings with scientific descriptions of each plant,

5 Wieland, *True Patriot Love*, 29. This text is handwritten in the top margin of the page. It is also written in French, in the right margin, perpendicular to the English.

6 Joan Stewart, her sister, embroidered the flowers.

7 A.E. Porsild, *Illustrated Flora of the Canadian Arctic Archipelago*, bulletin no. 146, Biological Series no. 50 (Ottawa: National Museum of Canada, 1964), 1. It was first published in 1957. Alf Erling Porsild was the chief curator of the National Herbarium of Canada from 1945 to 1967.

8 See maquette text in this publication, p. 194.

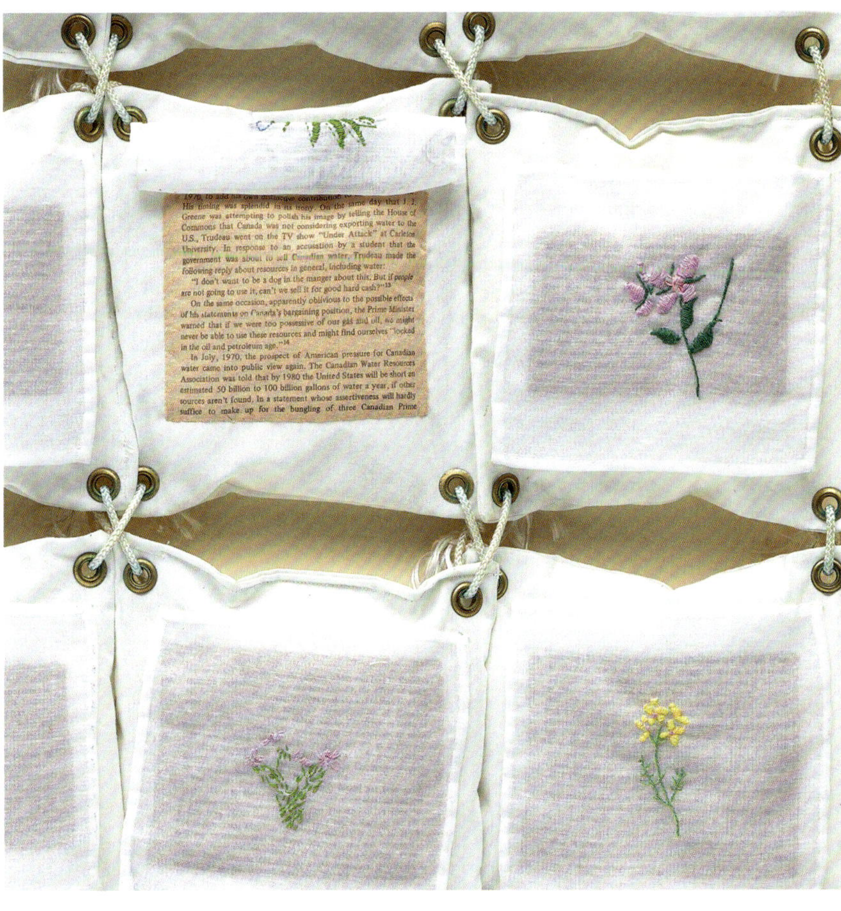

The Water Quilt (detail), 1970–1971
Photo: AGO, Craig Boyko

including the colour of the flowers and shape of leaves and stem. While the book is an empirical guide praised for advancing scientific knowledge of the archipelago, Wieland's composition frees the flora from the imposed botanical classification and instead presents the plants in a colourful array suggesting an alphabet of nature. The sixty-four flowers are an expression of the fertile and diverse vegetation of the Arctic, in extraordinary contrast with the common southern misconception that the region is barren, bleak, and inhospitable.

Wieland's intention is not to be descriptive or instructive. Rather, she seeks to create an aesthetically compelling vision out of very ordinary—"innocent"—themes, as she once described them.[9] In *The Water Quilt*, Wieland takes something as familiar and overlooked as an embroidered flower and imbues this traditionally decorative motif with agency and meaning. The flowers are small yet they spread into an immersive composition that draws in the viewer. Up close, the individuality of the careful stitching coveys the lively personality of each plant. These are no ordinary blossoms. Wieland's beautiful, graceful flowers thrive in the far north. Indeed, to believe in nature is to defy convention, to rebel.

Beneath this cover of resilient innocence is Wieland's active rebellion. "There is Art and there is Politics, and I have been working on putting them together in aesthetic terms for years," she said in 1974. "I think one can have all the thrill of doing art as well as embedding the political thing in it—inside it."[10] Veiled, yet noticeable under each flower, is a page from political economist, historian, and activist James Laxer's *The Energy Poker Game: The Politics of the Continental Resources Deal*, published in late 1970. "A beautiful way to hide something terrible," she said.[11] This is the anti-government "bulletin" Wieland favours and lists first in

9 Crean "The Erotic Nationalism of Joyce Wieland," 17.

10 Quoted in Debbie Magidson and Judy Wright, "Interviews with Canadian Artists: Debbie Magidson and Judy Wright Interview Joyce Wieland," *Canadian Forum* 54 (May/June 1974): 61.

11 Quoted in Harry Malcolmson, "True Patriot Love: Joyce Wieland's New Show," *Canadian Forum* 51 (June 1971): 17.

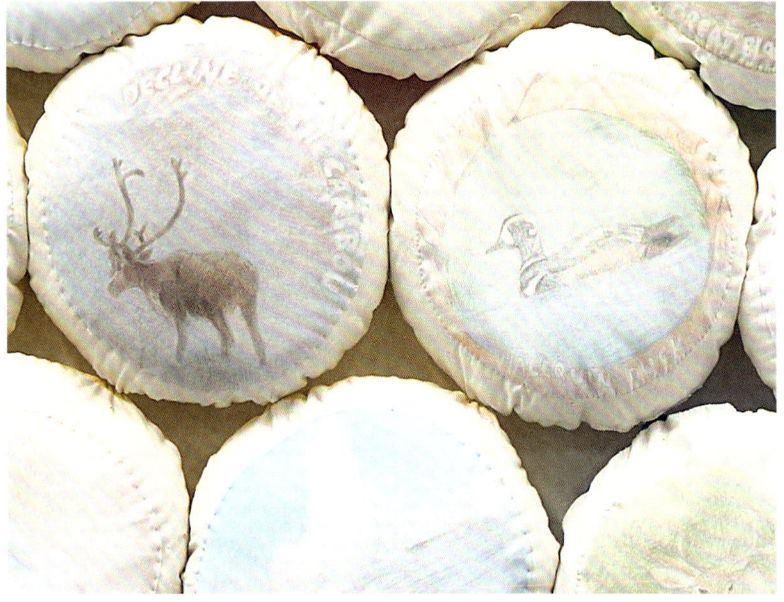

Arctic Day (detail), 1970–1971
Sewing assistance by Joyce Martin
Coloured pencil on cloth cushions, batting
248.6 cm diameter
National Gallery of Canada, Purchased 1971
16893
Photo: NGC

her description of *The Water Quilt*. Laxer's is a passionate and informed political guide raising awareness of the threat presented by the American "corporate and military empire" extending its reach to extract and deplete Canada's natural resources.[12] "There is little doubt that once the U.S. successfully gains access to our oil and natural gas on its terms, it will turn to our water," he writes in a chapter dedicated to water, "the ultimate energy resource."[13] Outlining the complicity of Canadian politicians (with then–prime minister Pierre Elliott Trudeau's face as the Joker on the cover), his book is an appeal to "resist the energy deal" as it was being negotiated at the time. *The Water Quilt* is Wieland's artistic response to Mel Watkins's call in the introduction: "We will be armed with this book. Read it and join us."[14] There is no comfort to be found in Wieland's "quilt." The sailor's rope that binds it can come undone. The threat of ecological devastation is imminent. She makes her call to action more explicit in the companion quilt, *Arctic Day* (1970–1971).

Nearly two-and-a-half metres in diameter, *Arctic Day* (p. 193) suggests a stylized view of the world from above the North Pole. Comprised of over 160 circular cushions of various sizes gathered together in a large round frame, this work implies a circumpolar view of the Earth as well as a magnified view of multiplying cells in a Petri dish: life![15] Wieland breathes vibrancy into this grand white tondo, imbuing it with an inner glow produced by the bright colour fabric sewn on the back of the cushions.[16] "I am trying to give the illusion of shadows on the snow with my *Arctic Day*," she declared while she was making it.[17]

Like *The Water Quilt*, it plays with scale and invites close looking. As the viewer draws near, *Arctic Day* reveals the diverse ecosystem of the region. With coloured pencils, Wieland has drawn individual portraits of arctic flowers, mammals, birds, and insects in their habitat, along with icebergs and the land. Each textile drawing is sewn to the front of a cushion. She identifies a few, such as the great black-backed gull and willow ptarmigan. Wieland conducted extensive research "about the animals, the insects, the flowers of the Arctic" to create these drawings.[18] Just off-centre and above is a caribou, with a warning over its majestic antlers. As though puffy clouds have aligned to deliver a message,

12 James Laxer, *The Energy Poker Game: The Politics of the Continental Resources Deal* (Toronto: New Press, 1970), 49.

13 Laxer, *The Energy Poker Game*, 35.

14 Mel Watkins, "Introduction" in Laxer, *The Energy Poker Game*, ii. Laxer and Watkins were leaders of the radical wing of the New Democratic Party, co-writing the *Waffle Manifesto: For an Independent Socialist Canada* in 1969. For a discussion of Wieland's own association with the Waffle Party, see Johanne Sloan, "Joyce Wieland at the Border: Nationalism, the New Left, and the Question of Political Art in Canada," *Journal of Canadian Art History* 26 (2005): 81–104.

15 A third of the pages of Porsild, *Illustrated Flora of the Canadian Arctic Archipelago*, feature maps geographically locating the distribution of the plants across the Arctic.

16 The backs of the cushions are in red, yellow, blue, green, and pink fabric. Wieland's description reads: "Arctic Day a quilt made of circular pillows (160 pillows in cotton) with coloured backing white tops—with drawings of Arctic animals, flowers, birds, insects—done with coloured pencils." Wieland, *True Patriot Love*, 160.

17 Quoted in Kay Kritzwiser, "A Woman's Work in the National Gallery," *The Globe and Mail*, February 19, 1971, 13.

18 Kritzwiser, "A Woman's Work," 13.

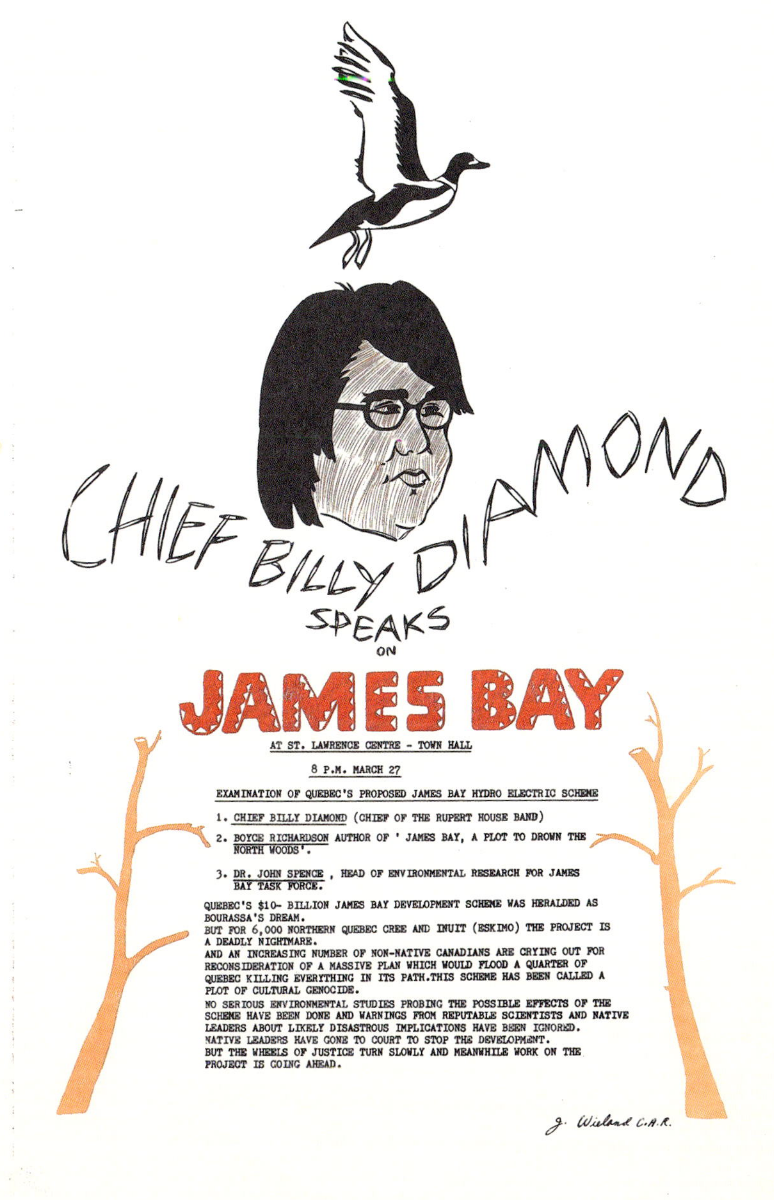

Chief Billy Diamond Speaks on James Bay poster, c. 1972
Print on paper
43.2 × 28 cm
Joyce Wieland fonds, NGC Library and Archives
Photo: NGC

it reads: DECLINE OF THE CARIBOU. As Wieland stated, she was in "a panic; an ecological, spiritual panic."[19]

Arctic Day marks Wieland's first use of coloured pencils, the small, round format, and delicate drawings of animals to which she returned nearly a decade later in her *The Bloom of Matter* series.[20] In this work she plays with the simplicity and directness found in schoolbook illustrations to convey the interconnectivity of life in the polar region and communicate her urgent ecological message. "The land which we all count on, that we keep counting on, suddenly we look up and what has happened, it is all churned up, like the James Bay [P]roject."[21] By 1971, Wieland was increasingly aware of the Cree and Nunavik Inuit fight against the Quebec government's plan to build a hydroelectric dam on the east coast of James Bay—the largest construction project in North America—which would devastate the caribou and Indigenous communities. Galvanizing the arts community, Wieland was politically active, participating in raising awareness against the project. In her political poster for a fundraiser featuring Waskaganish Cree chief Billy Diamond (1949–2010), she was unequivocal and incendiary, calling Quebec's plans "a deadly nightmare" and citing "a plot of cultural genocide."

19 Quoted in Magidson and Wright, "Interviews with Canadian Artists," 63.

20 See the "Bloom of Matter" section in this publication, p. 212.

21 Wieland quoted in Magidson and Wright, "Interviews with Canadian Artists," 63.

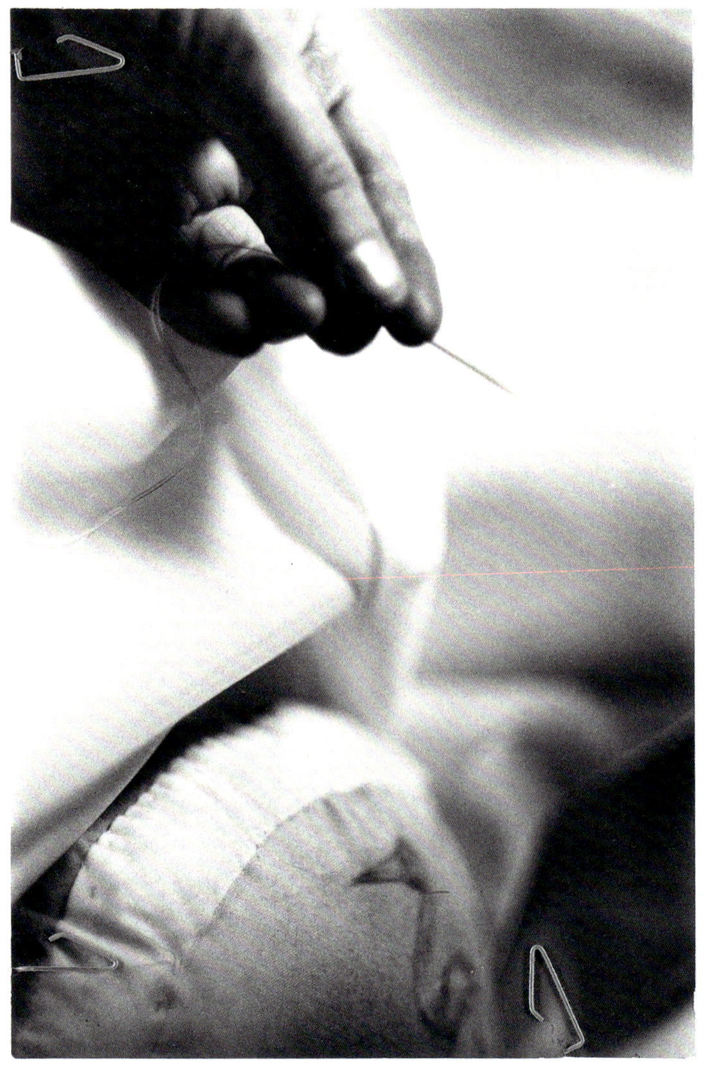

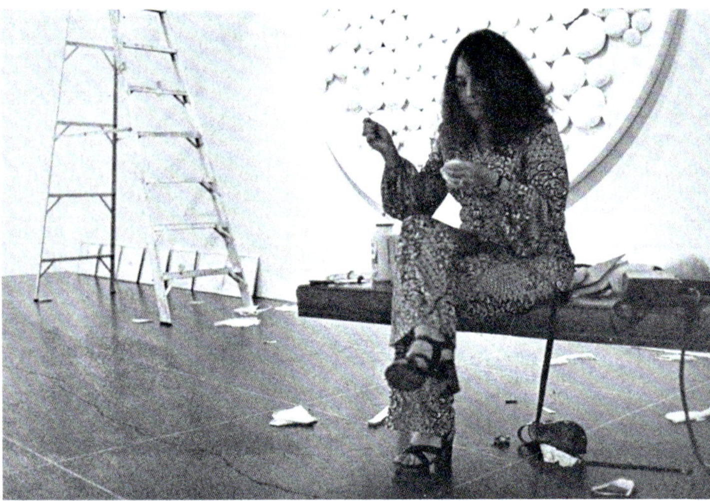

ABOVE
Page from the *True Patriot Love* maquette, 1971
National Gallery of Canada fonds, NGC Library and Archives
Photo: NGC

BELOW
Joyce Wieland working in front of *Arctic Day* at the National Gallery of Canada, 1971
Photo: Arnold Matthews

Through her art, Wieland deftly embedded her politics into her aesthetics. "If you are trying to express something which hasn't been said before, it might require finding other ways—a new form of expression."[22] Her pair of soft Arctic landscapes, *The Water Quilt* and *Arctic Day*—a square grid of embroidered flora and a composite circle of drawn fauna—convey a southern vision of the Arctic without precedent in Western art. As art critic Hugo McPherson (1921–1999) wrote in 1971, "This is Wieland's great pastoral of the north ... it renders lovingly the details of an ecology that is almost unknown in the south."[23] These works are comparable in their ambitious size and scope to the celebrated paintings of icebergs, frozen landscapes, and aurora borealis by Fredric Edwin Church (1826–1900), Rockwell Kent (1882–1971), Lawren S. Harris (1885–1970), and other Group of Seven members, as well as Doris McCarthy (1910–2010), Wieland's teacher and mentor. These artists travelled to the Arctic on government and scientific expeditions and returned to their studios to produce sublime images of empty landscapes and ice. Their paintings shaped a southern notion of the Arctic as mystical and remote.

Wieland absorbed this tradition while growing up, and as an artist. Through her *Arctic Day* drawings and her resolve to glorify embroidery and quiltmaking, she is not defying her artistic

22 Wieland quoted in Magidson and Wright, "Interviews with Canadian Artists," 63.

23 Hugo McPherson, "Wieland: An Epiphany of North," *artscanada*, no. 158–59 (August/September 1971): 17–27.

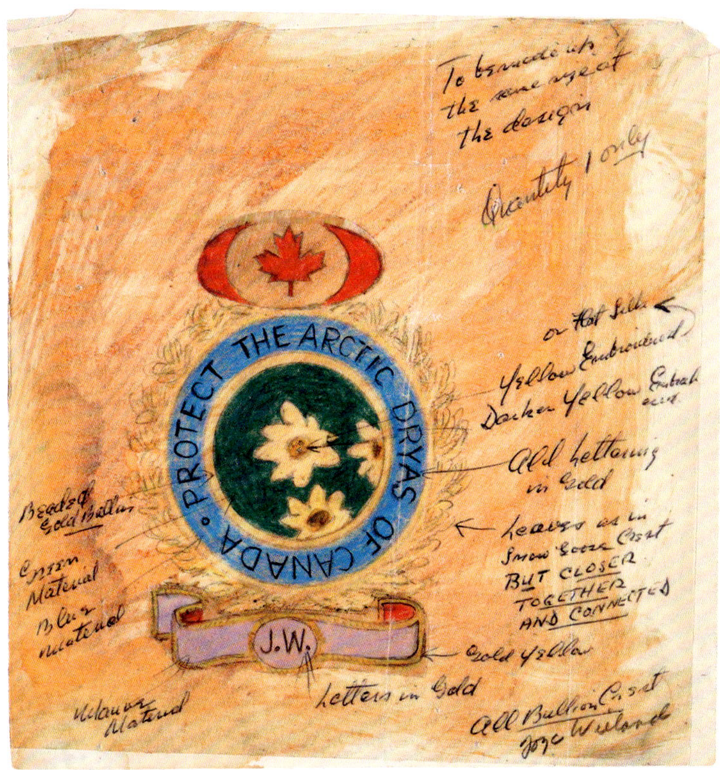

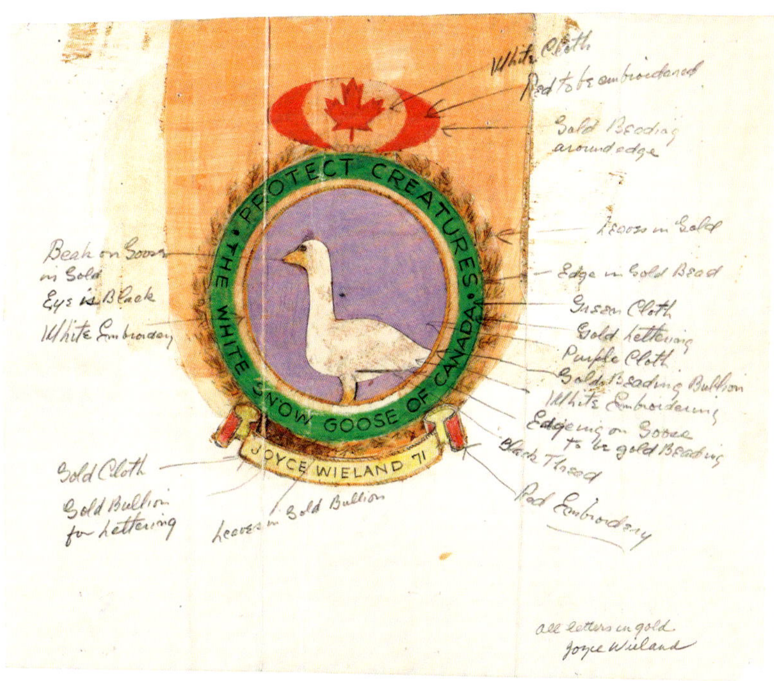

ABOVE
Preparatory sketch for *Protect the Arctic* crest, c. 1971
Graphite and crayon on tracing paper glued to wove paper
25.6 × 21 cm
Joyce Wieland fonds, NGC Library and Archives
Photo: NGC

BELOW
Preparatory sketch for *The White Snow Goose of Canada* crest, 1971
Graphite and crayon on wove paper
21 × 25.6 cm
Joyce Wieland fonds, NGC Library and Archives
Photo: NGC

heritage, rather she is advancing a new "language of emotions," as Leila Sujir calls it—an Arctic imaginary all her own.[24] "You work on your own myth from the very basic things you have around you."[25] Wieland's intention is to awaken southerners to mobilize and defend the environment.

Serving as pendants to her quilted scapes, Wieland produces two small, embroidered crests: *Arctic Dryas* and *The White Snow Goose of Canada* (both 1971).[26] Intended to be sewn on clothes and worn—rather than framed—these arctic emblems call out for their protection: PROTECT THE ARCTIC DRYAS / PROTECT CREATURES. Her ecological appeal culminates a year later in her monumental quilt *Defend the Earth* (1972), commissioned for the National Science Library in Ottawa. Unlike her Canadian modernist predecessors who sought the collaboration of government and corporations in their artistic pursuits,

24 See Leila Sujir's text in this publication, p. 216.

25 Joyce Wieland, "Interview," in *Eclectic Eve*, ed. Janice Cameron, Frances Ferdinands, Sharon Snitman, Madli Tamme, and Annetta Wernick (Toronto: Canadian Women's Educational Press, 1972), unpaginated.

26 The goose is an edition of fifty; however, Wieland had only one dryas crest made, intending to later produce an edition, which she was not able to realize. Wieland, *True Patriot Love*, 209.

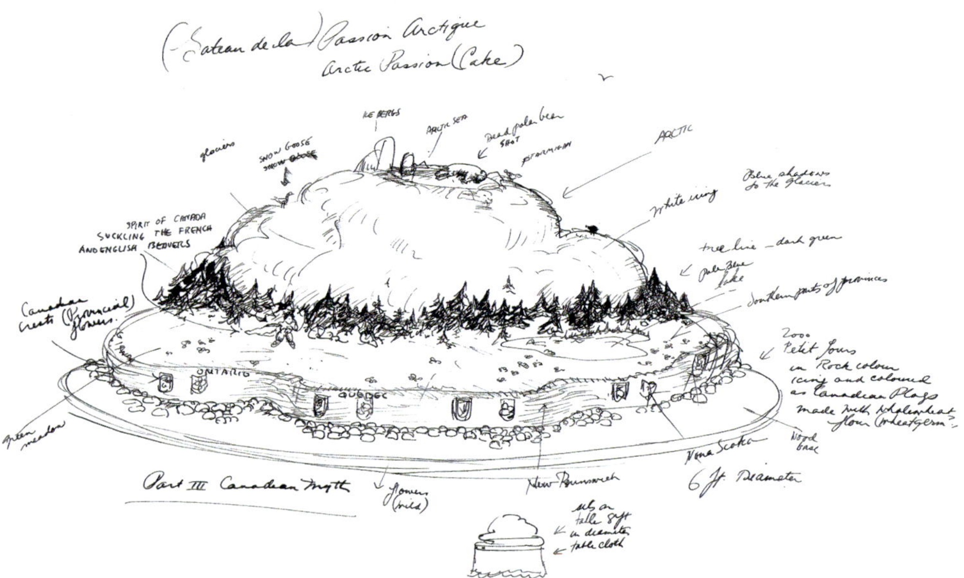

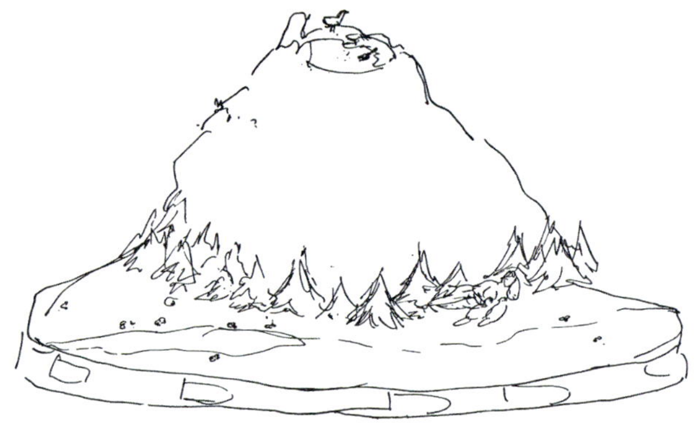

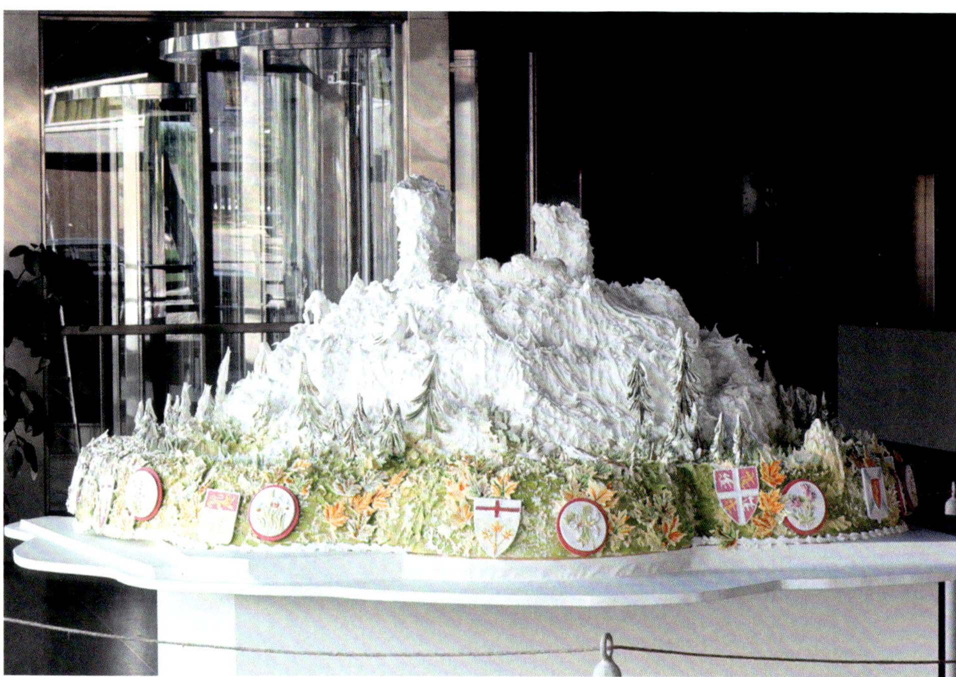

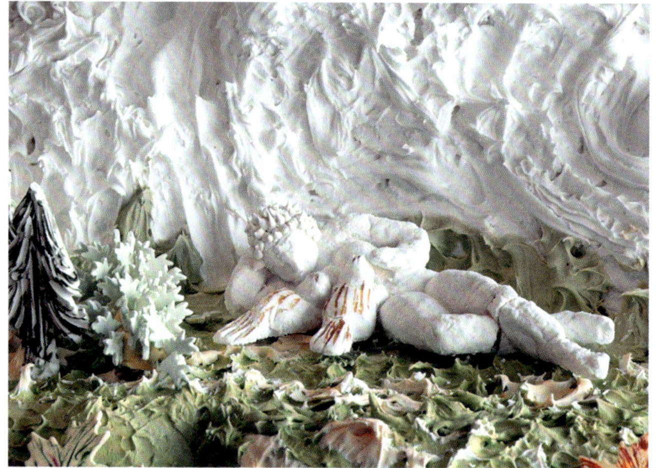

ABOVE, LEFT
Arctic Passion Cake, 1971
Pen and black ink on wove paper
21.9 × 36.4 cm
National Gallery of Canada, Purchased 1973
17162
Photo: NGC

ABOVE, RIGHT
Sketch for Arctic Passion Cake, 1971
Ink on paper
21.6 × 35.6 cm
Courtesy of Ihor Holubizky
Photo: Craig Boyko

BELOW, LEFT
Installation view of *Arctic Passion Cake,* 1971, in *True Patriot Love* exhibition at the National Gallery of Canada, 1971
NGC Library and Archives
Photo: NGC

BELOW, RIGHT
Installation view of *Arctic Passion Cake* (detail), 1971, in *True Patriot Love* exhibition at the National Gallery of Canada, 1971
NGC Library and Archives
Photo: NGC

Page from the *True Patriot Love* maquette, 1971
National Gallery of Canada fonds, NGC Library and Archives
Photo: NGC

ILLUSTRATED FLORA
OF THE CANADIAN ARCTIC ARCHIPELAGO

INTRODUCTION

The present work is intended as a guide or manual to the 340 species and major geographical races of flowering plants and ferns that comprise the vascular flora as it is known at present of the Canadian Arctic Archipelago[1]. Besides conventional keys to families, genera, and species, it contains brief descriptions, line drawings, and maps showing the North American ranges of all species. For each species brief notes are given on local occurrence, soil preferences, economic uses, if any, and on their total or world distribution. A glossary ~~explains~~ the meaning of all special

ᐊᐃ ᐊᐃ

ᐃᒪᕙᐊᒍ ᐊᐅᓚᑎᑕᐅᒐᒪ

ᓴᐯᐅᑎᑕᐅᔨᒐ ᓂᒪᐳᒐᓗ ᑭᑯᐊᑎᑐ ᑯᒥ

ᑕᔨᒍᒐ ᔨᓚᕙᐊᒍ ᐊᒪᓗ ᔨᓚᓂᓗ ᔨᒍᓂᒐᓗ

ᑲᐃᐱᑎᑕᐅᕗᒐ ᐃᓄᑐᓕᕋᒪᓗ

ᓴᕙᒐᓚᔨᒐ ᑯᐱᐊᔨᓂᑯᒍ

Similarly, the reader desiring more detailed information of the flora of the Eastern Canadian Arctic may refer to N. Polunin's "Botany of the Eastern Canadian Arctic", Part I of which (Nat. Mus. Canada, Bull. 92, 1940) deals with the vascular flora; Part II (Nat. Mus. Canada, Bull. 97, 1947) with mosses, lichens, and algae; and Part III (Nat. Mus. Canada, Bull. 104, 1948) with vegetation and ecology. Recent collections of plants from the eastern islands have added materially to the 246 species of vascular plants reported by Polunin from the eastern arctic islands. The more important of these recent collections are in the National Herbarium of Canada and, together with a few published additions to the flora, have been incorporated in the distribution maps at the end of the present work.

[1] Descriptions as well as range and habitat notes (in small print) have been inserted in the text for some 40-odd species that as yet have not been recorded in the flora of the Archipelago but that, for phytogeographic reasons, may be expected to turn up in parts so far incompletely explored.

1

Wieland uses her position as an artist and "cultural activist" to directly address government scientists and enlist them in her environmental cause.

As others have rightly argued, her ideas are circumscribed by her inherited settler colonial notions of land and the North. Nonetheless, Wieland is determined to convey the inextricable interrelation of North and South—our shared responsibility and interdependence among each other and all life on our planet. In her work, she seduces her viewers out of their complacency, perhaps most outlandishly in her *Arctic Passion Cake* (1971), installed centrally in her *True Patriot Love* exhibition. The enormous, six-by-three-foot inedible cake, shaped as an iceberg, was made of about 150 pounds of icing sugar (covering a Styrofoam carcass). At the top was a "blue lake and dead polar bear" whose blood runs down the sides toward Canada's ten provincial crests, which decorate the bottom layer.[27] Among the fir trees circling the iceberg, the "Spirit of Canada" (polar bear's mate) suckles the "French and English Beavers." In *Arctic Passion Cake*, Wieland unveils her Canadian creation myth, a twin nation-form born of interspecies love and ursine sacrifice. This confectionary diorama topples Lawren Harris's notion of the mystic North and proffers Wieland's distinct "new form of expression."[28] A delectable way to face a complicated reality, she might have said.

As the cake was ephemeral and only for display, Wieland made a book anyone could have and hold. The *True Patriot Love / Véritable amour patriotique* (p. 196) publication is a bound, printed collage revealing her complicated relationship to the Arctic. She chose to insert herself and her "photographs of photographs . . . over a Government publication of arctic flora. The pages of

27 The cake was destroyed following the exhibition, but details are available through journalistic accounts and Wieland's sketch, reproduced as the centrefold of her *True Patriot Love* publication (132–33), today part of the National Gallery of Canada collection. Wieland dedicates her book to famous French chef and pâtissier Antonin Carême (1784–1833) on page 217.

28 Quoted in Debbie Magidson and Judy Wright, "Interviews with Canadian Artists: Debbie Magidson and Judy Wright Interview Joyce Wieland," *Canadian Forum* 54 (May/June 1974): 63.

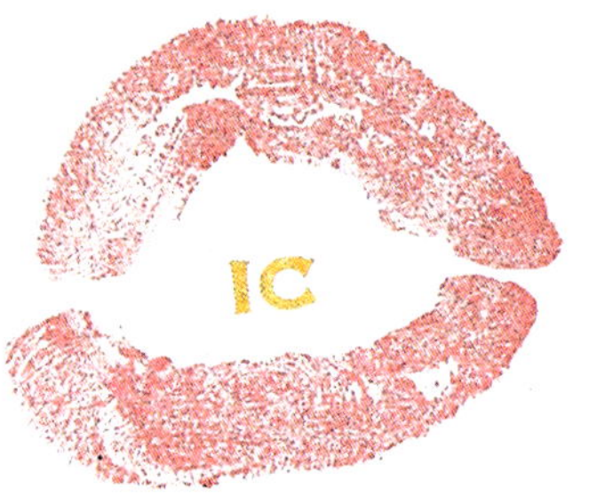

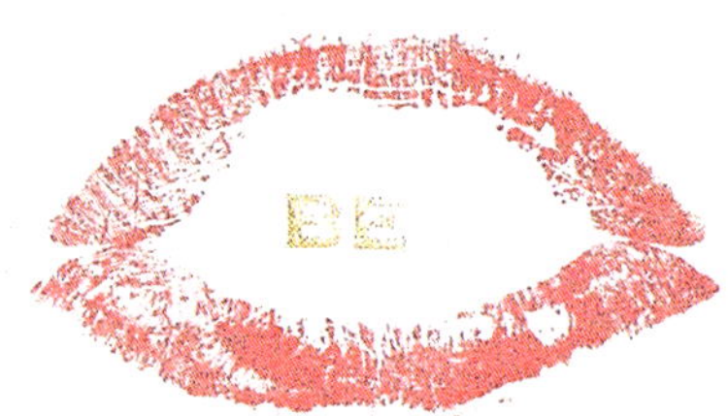

Study for *The Arctic Belongs to Itself* (detail), c. 1973
Lithograph on wove paper
31.2 × 33 cm
Joyce Wieland fonds, NGC Library and Archives
Photo: NGC

the book became the landscape to which I wed the images."[29] The result is an artist book, one of the three editioned works she created for any visitor to purchase, along with the two to be worn, *Snow Goose of Canada*, and *Sweet Beaver* perfume. Her book is not to be read, rather it is to be experienced and absorbed, much like one of her experimental films of the mid-1960s. Wieland's undoing of government sanctioned knowledge, scientific taxonomy, and curatorial writing begins "innocently" with typical Canadian symbols—the flag, the maple leaf, snow, and the words to the national anthem obscuring the opening pages of the book. Then, on page one, she interrupts the English typescript by pinning a text in Inuktitut.[30]

This is a provocative intervention. The act of using a pin—a reference to sewing, mending—to fasten one piece of paper to another is to declare that something—this "glossary"—needs correcting. Right above the pinned Inuktitut, the printed text happens to read "A glossary," while the next word, "explains," is perfectly crossed out by the pin from the verso of the sheet—an effective coincidence. (See TPL maquette, p. 33.) The transformed page presents only the Inuktitut as fully legible, while the English becomes background landscape. The text is an Inuit song, sung by a female shaman named Uvavnuk, about the "trembling" joy of "The Arch of sky / And mightiness of storms."[31] In the next few pages of her book, Wieland pins the French and English versions, as well as their sources, alongside images of the making of her hook rug diptych, *The Great Sea* (1970–1971) (p. 191), a large-scale interpretation of the song.[32] In these few opening pages, she physically and formally reinserts Inuit language, song, and myth, foregrounding the people and their knowledge of the Arctic before and above Western science. Her research reaches into the legendary past as well as contemporary Arctic politics. She includes a newspaper clipping about Jean Chrétien (at the time Canada's minister of Indian Affairs and Northern Development) travelling to Ikaahuk, Inuvialuit (then Sachs Harbour, Northwest Territories), reporting that when an Inuk woman asked Chrétien "What will be left of this island?," he had a politician's evasive answer. The artist suggestively reminds her readers of what government has removed: the Arctic is Inuit homeland and Canadian politics are putting it in danger.

29 The full quote is "I had done some collages. I included this early influence of collage along with photographs of photographs. . . . I also wanted to do a book about Canada; so I collaged over a Government publication of arctic flora. The pages of the book became the landscape to which I wed the images." Wieland in *Women's Bookworks: A Survey Exhibition of Contemporary Artists' Books by Canadian Women, Including Unique Book-Objects and Printed Editions* (Montreal: Centrale Galerie Powerhouse, 1979).

30 It appears Wieland was interested in learning Inuktitut in the late 1970s. See letter from Inuktitut Language Program, phase I, Government of Northwest Territories, February 24, 1978. Joyce Wieland fonds, Clara Thomas Archives and Special Collections, York University, Toronto, 1994-004/001-013.

31 See "The Great Sea" text in this publication, p. 190.

32 Wieland does not use Knud Rasmussen's version of the poem; rather, she selects Inuk poet Tegoodligak's translation published in a pamphlet on Inuit art. See p. 191.

Study for *Facing North – Self Impression*, c. 1973
Lithograph in flesh tone with lipstick on wove paper
29.3 × 35.5 cm
Joyce Wieland fonds, NGC Library and Archives
Photo: NGC

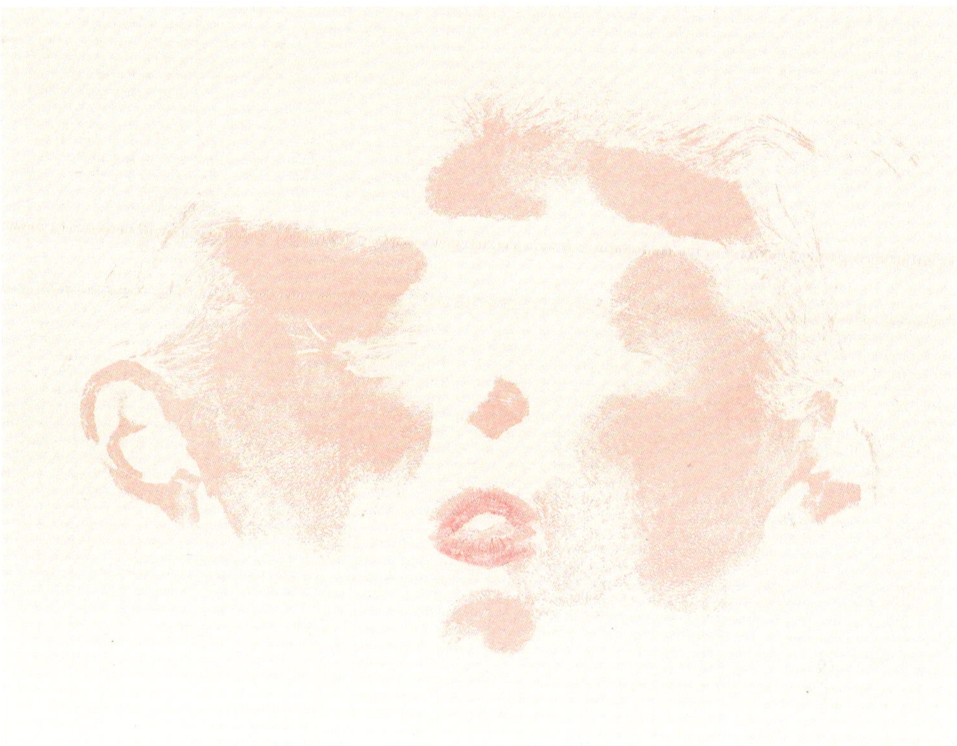

Wieland makes the declarative print *The Arctic Belongs to Itself* (1973) (p. 189) in her signature manner of kissing the lithographic stone, her rouged mouth forming each sound of the phrase indicated below her lips. It is inaccurate to suggest that she is advocating for Inuit sovereignty, no matter her continuing interest in the Inuit fight against the James Bay Project.[33] There are no source materials for this print, and there is no record of Wieland herself talking about it. However, she is neither complacent about nor oblivious to the urgency of disastrous political and ecological developments in the North. On the contrary, as she stated, "By 1967, I was reading a lot of Canadian history and following books and pamphlets coming out by Canadian nationalist economists. Politically involved friends were writing things, and they started to get absorbed in a sense of responsibility toward Canada through art. I wanted to help the situation in Canada."[34] In *The Arctic Belongs to Itself*, she makes her words explicit by stamping them in gold capital letters, tempting us to say them along with her.[35]

Wieland implicates herself further in her other print that year, *Facing North – Self Impression* (1973) (p. 188). Much more than a self-portrait (a rare one for Wieland in the 1970s), the reference to the Arctic is made only indirectly in the title. Yet there she is, pressing her face on the stone, holding the paper down (her fingertips are visible), and making an impression suggestive of the Earth seen from above, with the centre of the print a white space evoking the circumpolar region. She is facing north, pun intended. More to the point, unlike most other Canadians, she is directing her attention to the Arctic. The personal and political

33 For a discussion of Inuit cultural sovereignty, see Heather Igloliorte, "Arctic Culture / Global Indigeneity: Sovereign Nations; Canada and the Inuit of Northern North America," *Negotiations in a Vacant Lot: Studying the Visual in Canada*, ed. Lynda Jessup, Erin Morton, and Kirsty Robertson (Montreal: McGill-Queen's University Press, 2014), 150–70.

34 Quoted in Lauren Rabinovitz, "An Interview with Joyce Wieland," *Afterimage* 8, no. 10 (May 1981): 10.

35 In a test print for this work, she puts the letters inside her mouth. Joyce Wieland fonds, National Gallery of Canada, cat. no. WIEL-2b. See image opposite page.

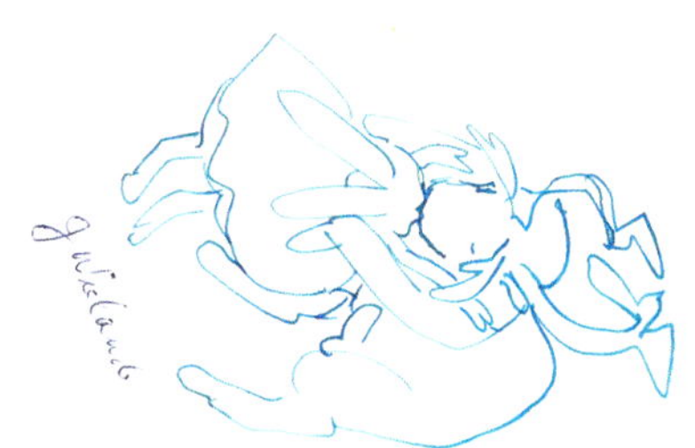

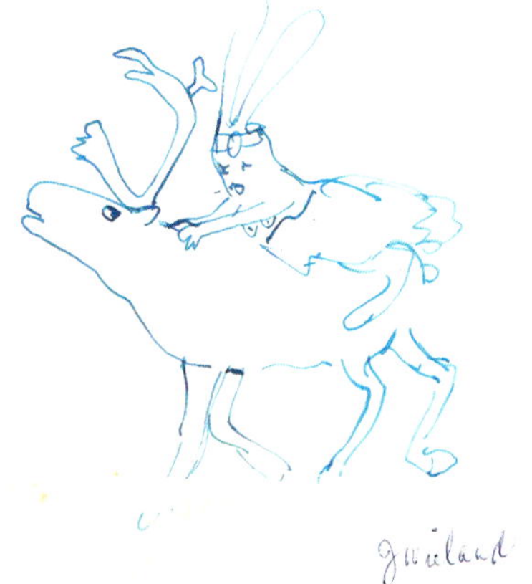

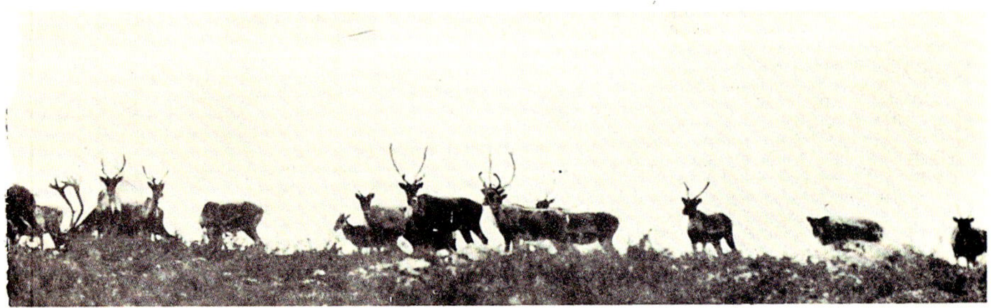

LEFT
Untitled [Tuktu & lapin du Nord], c. 1970
Ink
24.6 × 21.4 cm
The Montreal Museum of Fine Arts
Pierre Théberge bequest in memory of Pauline Talbot Théberge and Pauline Annette Théberge
2019.290
Photo: MMFA, Jean-François Brière

RIGHT
Photograph of caribou by Robert Ruttan in *Tuktu: A Question of Survival; The Caribou of the Northern Mainland* by Fraser Symington, 1965
Print on paper
28.8 × 13 cm
Joyce Wieland fonds, NGC Library and Archives
Photo: NGC

are fused in this tender and tough image. This is Wieland's love of her country: tender and tough.

In November 1975, the James Bay and Northern Quebec Agreement (JBNQA) is signed, considered the first northern comprehensive land claim to be settled in Canada.[36] Around the same time, Wieland has an opportunity to "bring the Arctic south." She wins a prestigious commission to create a permanent work for one of Toronto's newly built subway stations and thus to bring attention to the barren-ground caribou, magnificent northern creatures, to people in the city trying to catch their train. As she said, "it seemed to be that time for the caribou."[37]

The caribou first appeared in Wieland's work in 1970, in a cartoon she published in *Canadian Forum*. Entitled *Aqui Nada*, it is wordplay on "Canada." She valued play with language, considering humour as one of the most potent means of reaching her audience. Wieland would also have been familiar with a theory—espoused in Canadian history textbooks in her day and now highly contested—that the word "Canada" was derived from the Spanish *acá nada*, which translates to "nothing here," the assessment of the place by Iberian explorers in the 1500s. Her caribou was named Tuktu, the Inuktitut word for the animal. *Aqui Nada* is an erotically explicit, political telling of the adventures of Lapin, an arctic hare, and Tuktu, who are in love. Shithead Von Whorehead, "tool of the U.S. Military Industrial Complex," attempts to violate Lapin, but Tuktu destroys the "tool" and they are reunited.[38] "Throughout Wieland's work, eros is a constant and ardent companion," Crean argues, "at

36 Signatories to the James Bay and Northern Quebec Agreement include the Governments of Quebec and Canada, the James Bay Energy Corporation, the James Bay Development Corporation, Hydro-Québec, the Grand Council of the Crees (of Quebec), and the Northern Quebec Inuit Association.

37 Joyce Wieland Interview 4, Jane Lind fonds, National Gallery of Canada (hereafter cited as Jane Lind fonds), box 36, file 28; Joyce Wieland Interview 3, Jane Lind fonds, box 36, file 28, 1–2.

38 Joyce Wieland, "Aqui Nada," *Canadian Forum* 51 (June 1971): 19.

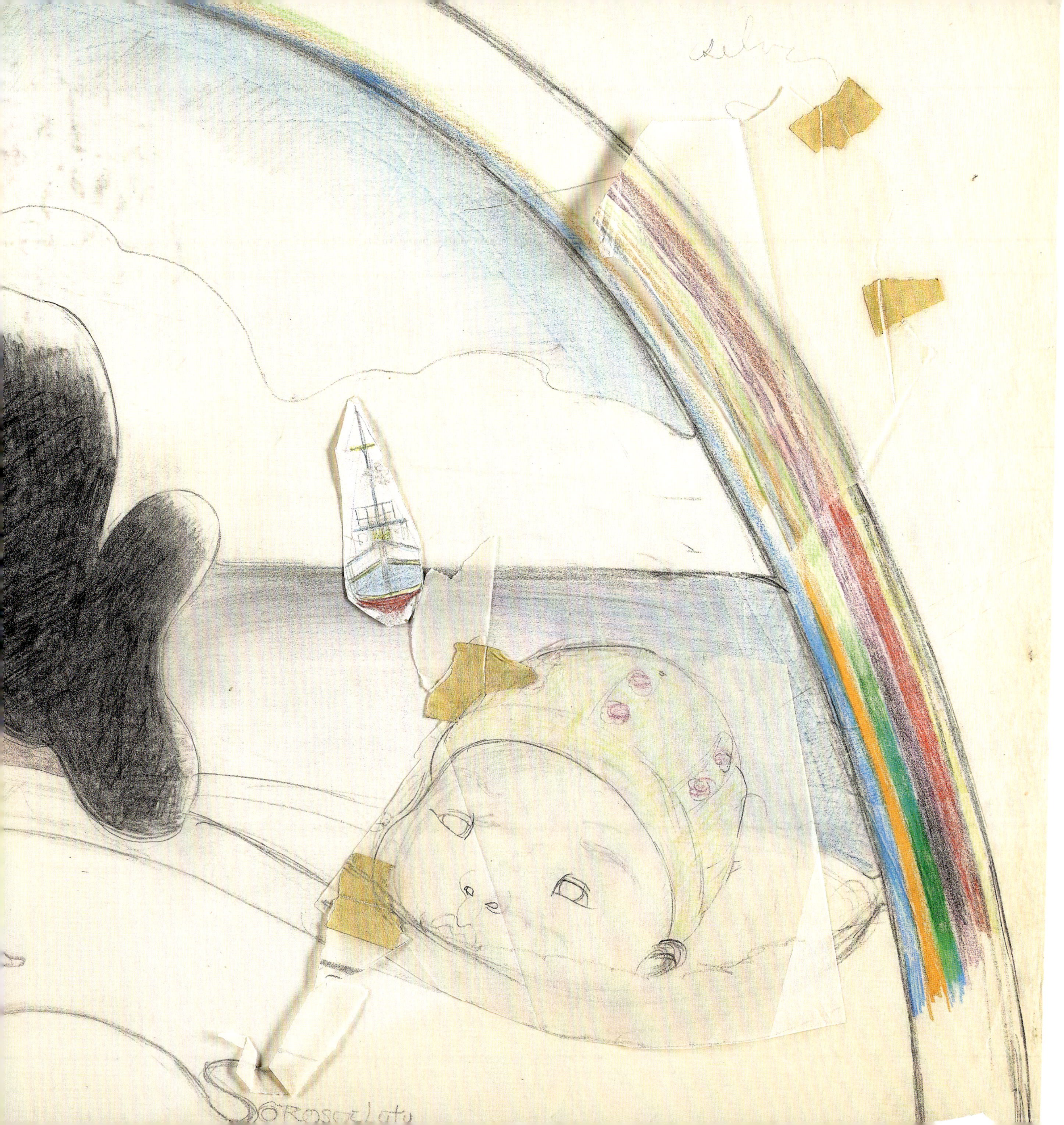

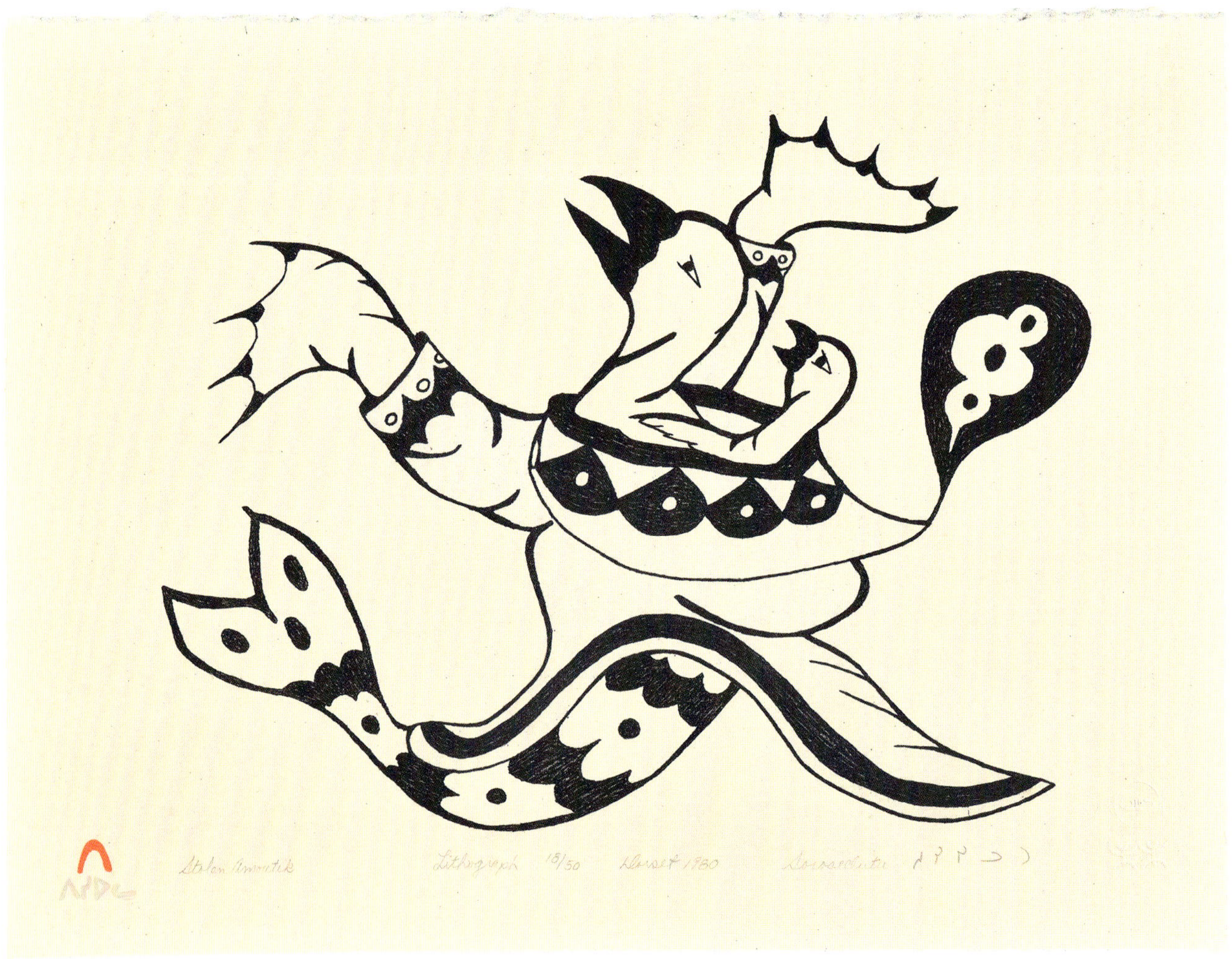

Surusilutu Ashoona
Stolen Amoutik, 1980
Lithograph on paper
28.8 × 38.5 cm
Art Gallery of Ontario
Gift of Samuel and Esther Sarick, Toronto, 2002
2002/9626
© Estate of Surusilutu Ashoona, reproduced with the permission of Dorset Fine Arts
Photo: AGO, Craig Boyko

has collaged a small ship bobbing on the water in the middle ground. It can be read as a reference to Wieland herself, both as a visitor from distant shores and as an artist fascinated by boats that only bring disaster. Surusilutu is poised, beautiful, and monumental, in the style of early Italian Renaissance portraiture. She is carrying a baby on her back, in the hood of her amauti. Most significantly, Surusilutu is active: she is drawing the "cosmos," Uvavnuk's "arch of sky"—a rainbow. Wieland presents Surusilutu as an earthly and cosmic creator and identifies her as an artist. In two other small, signed drawings from 1979, Surusilutu has wings (see p. 211). In one, she is flying to hold up the sky, and in the other she is coming back to Earth.

Wieland spent the last years of her life traversing Earth and sky, finally painting her own rainbow (see p. 244)—an electrifying conduit of energy connecting the two realms.

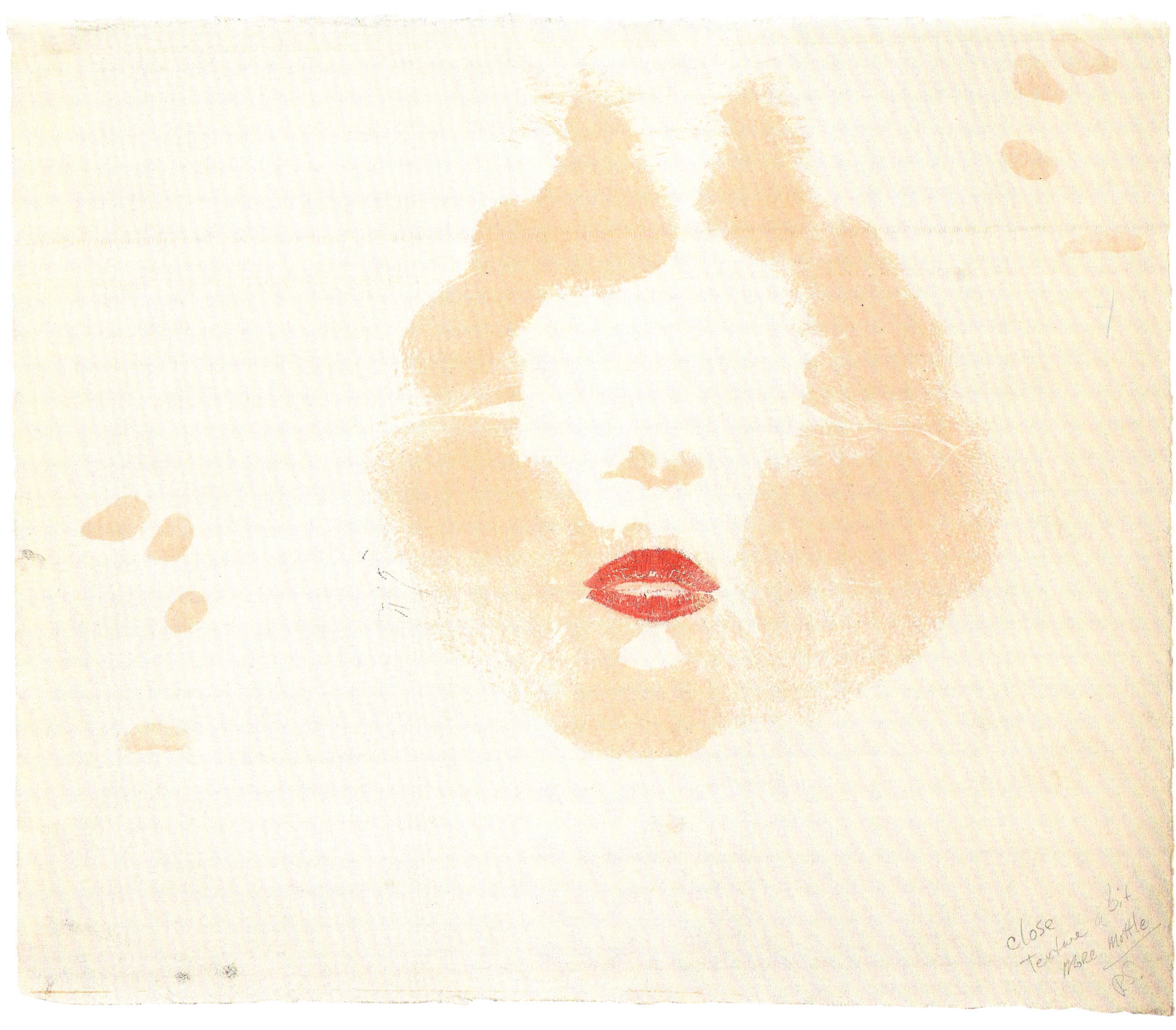

Study for ***Facing North — Self Impression,*** c. 1973
Lithograph in flesh tone with lipstick on wove paper
29.3 × 35.5 cm
Joyce Wieland fonds, NGC Library and Archives
Photo: NGC

MYSELF

Joyce Wieland made drawings all her life—it is what shaped and anchored her practice from the beginning. Encouraged and inspired by her high-school teachers, she found her subject matter early and close at hand in the intimacy of her lived experience, reflecting the directness of the act of drawing itself. From her early twenties, she lived and worked among artists, often the only woman in the circle. By 1956, she was married to an artist who was already gaining notoriety.

Wieland's exploratory ink drawings from the mid-1950s reveal a fascination with her own image and sexual awakening. She found her own expressive line by drawing female figures, examining their femininity as they are entwined in the arms of their lovers. In the late 1950s and early 1960s, her figures dissolve into abstracted erotic shapes, animated by blotches of red ink: the messiness of love and sex. These are daring images, personal and evocative, and they attracted the attention of influential Toronto art dealer Dorothy Cameron (1924–2000), who offered Wieland her first solo show in 1960. It was a remarkable achievement in Toronto's conservative and prudish society of the day. In 1962, Wieland had her first solo show at The Isaacs Gallery, which represented her until the 1980s. "I must show in my work, what it is to love," Wieland wrote in her diary in 1956, and it remained an elemental theme.

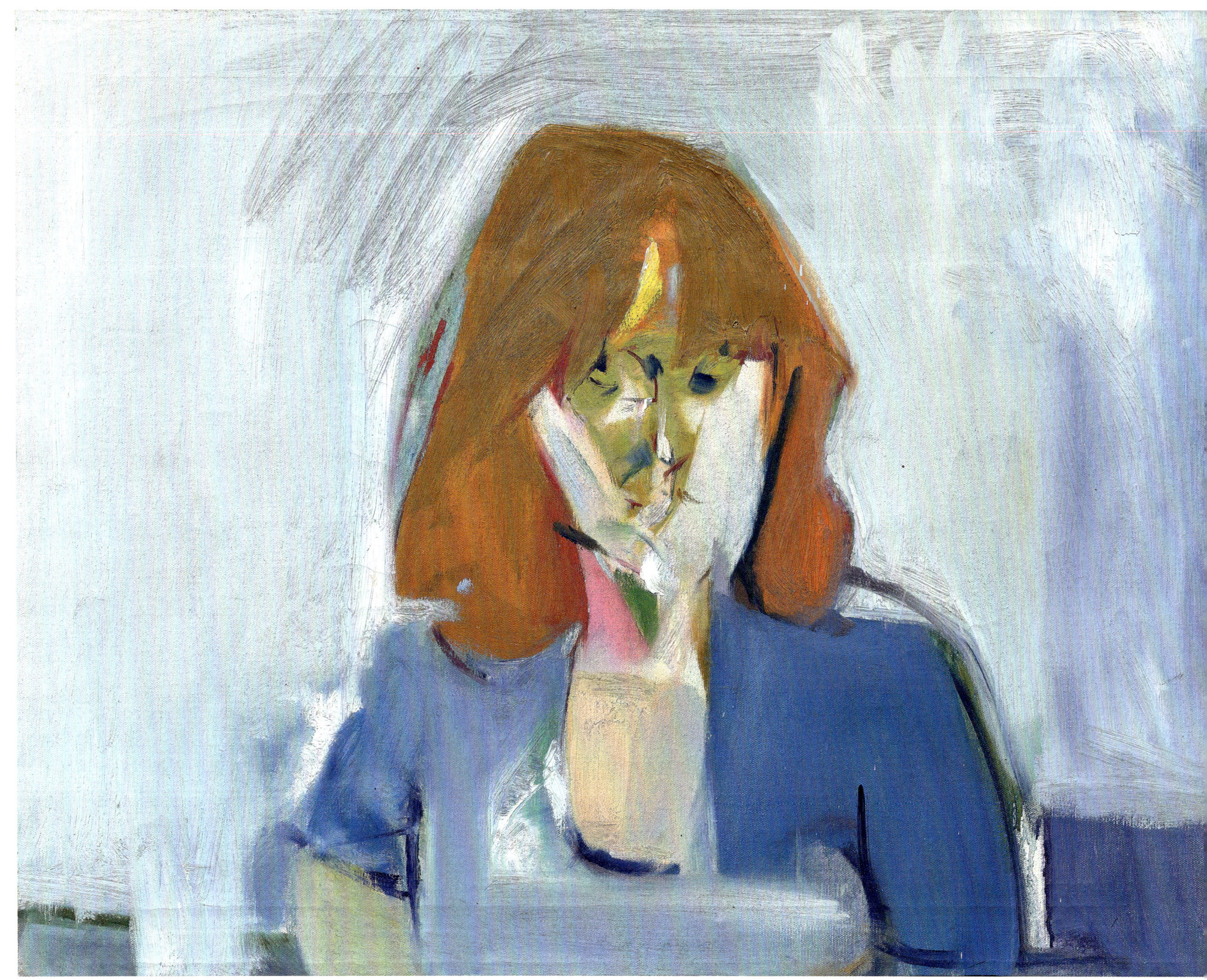

Myself, 1958
Oil on canvas
56 × 71 cm
Collection of Margaret J. Break
Photo: AGO, Craig Boyko

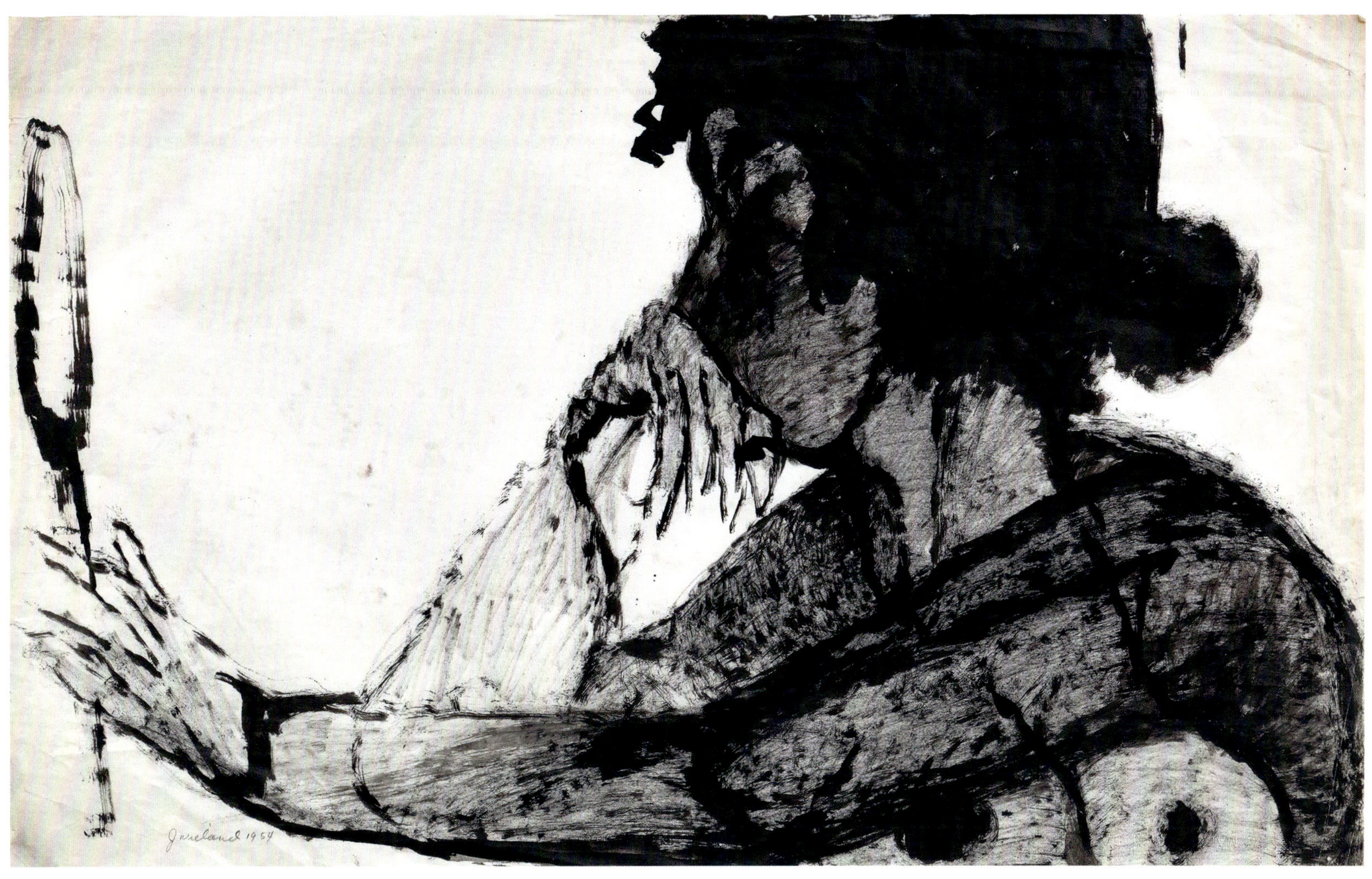

Woman with Mirror, 1954
Ink on paper
43.2 × 71.1 cm
Collection of Doug Watters
Photo: AGO, Craig Boyko

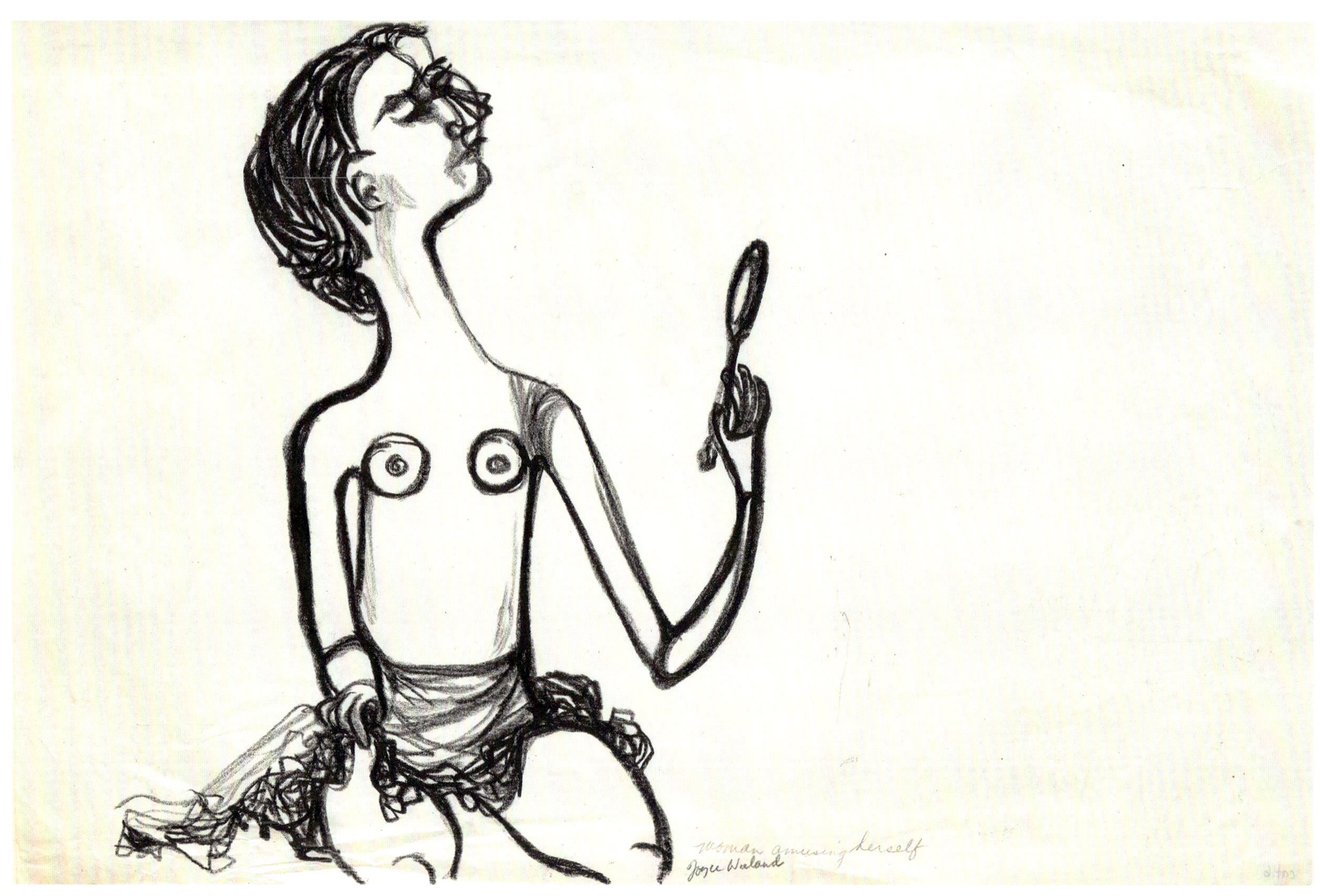

Woman Amusing Herself, c. 1955
Crayon on wove paper
27.9 × 43.4 cm
Art Gallery of Ontario, Gift of Betty Ramsaur Ferguson, Puslinch, ON, 1998
98/633
Photo: AGO, Craig Boyko

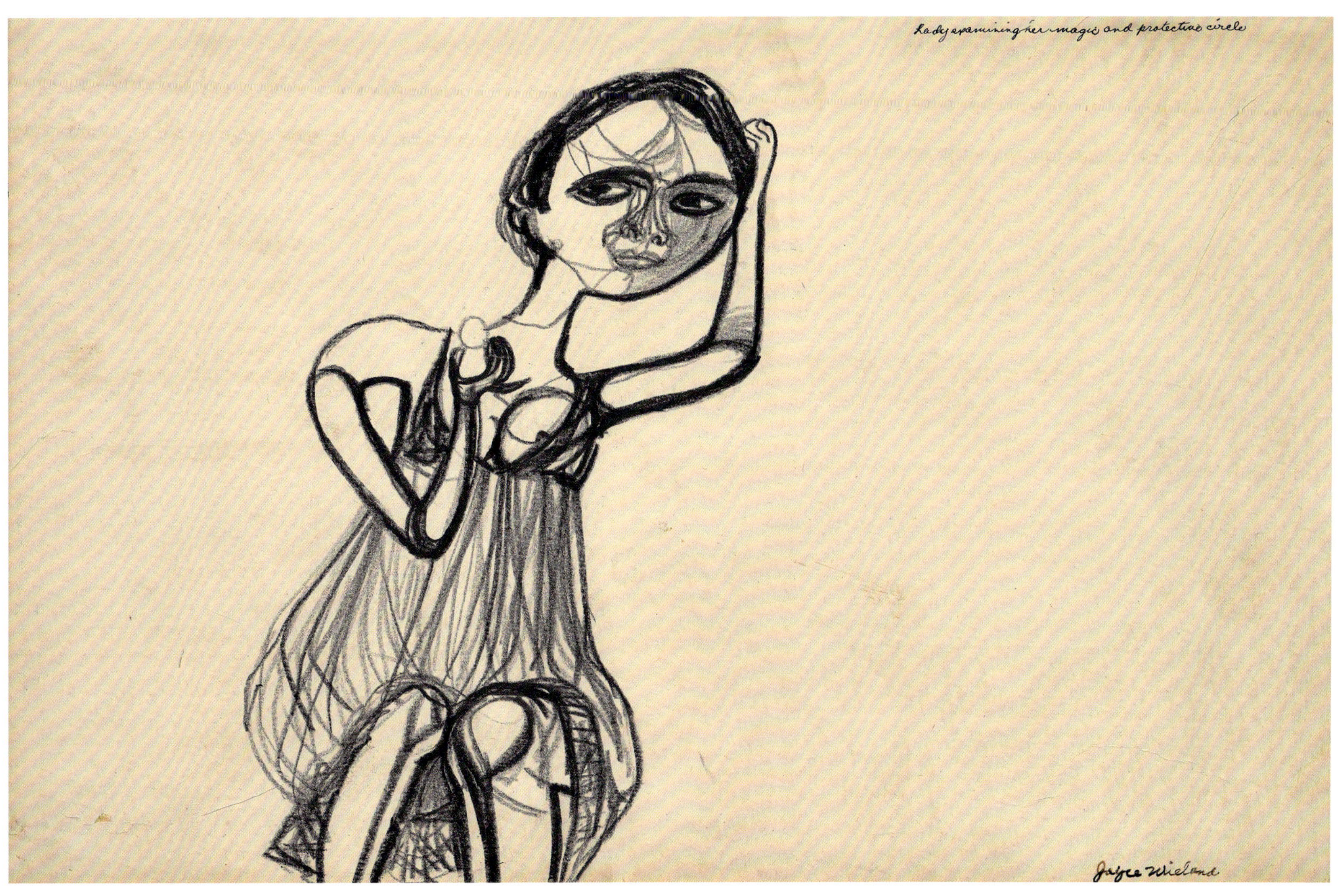

Lady Examining Her Magic and Protective Circle, c. 1955
Crayon on wove paper
27.9 × 44.3 cm
Art Gallery of Ontario, Gift of the Estate of Donald F. Vincent, London, ON, 2000
2000/31
Photo: AGO, Craig Boyko

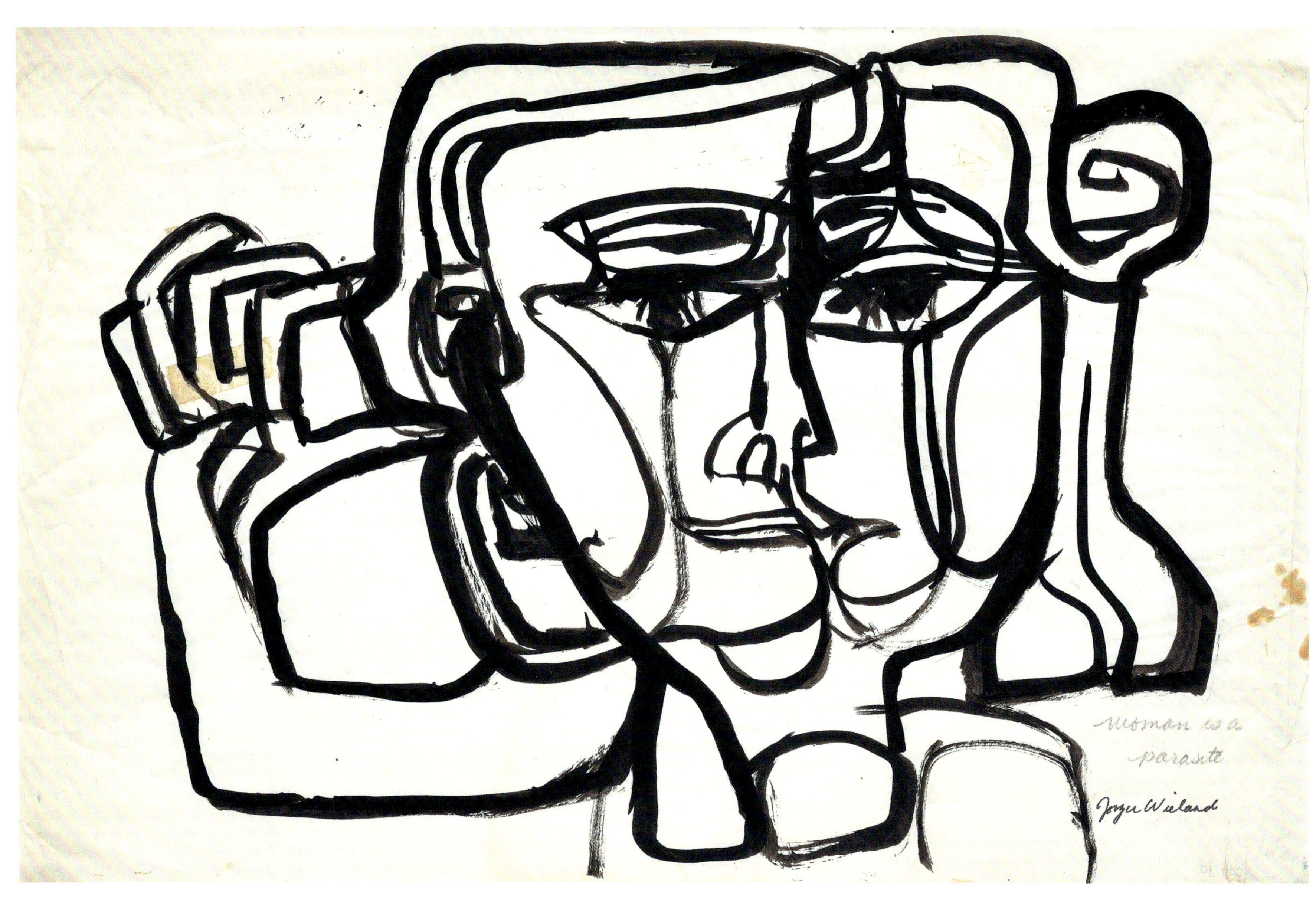

Woman is a Parasite, c. 1958
Ink on wove paper
27.9 × 43.4 cm
Art Gallery of Ontario, Gift of Betty Ramsaur Ferguson, Puslinch, ON, 1998
98/635
Photo: AGO, Craig Boyko

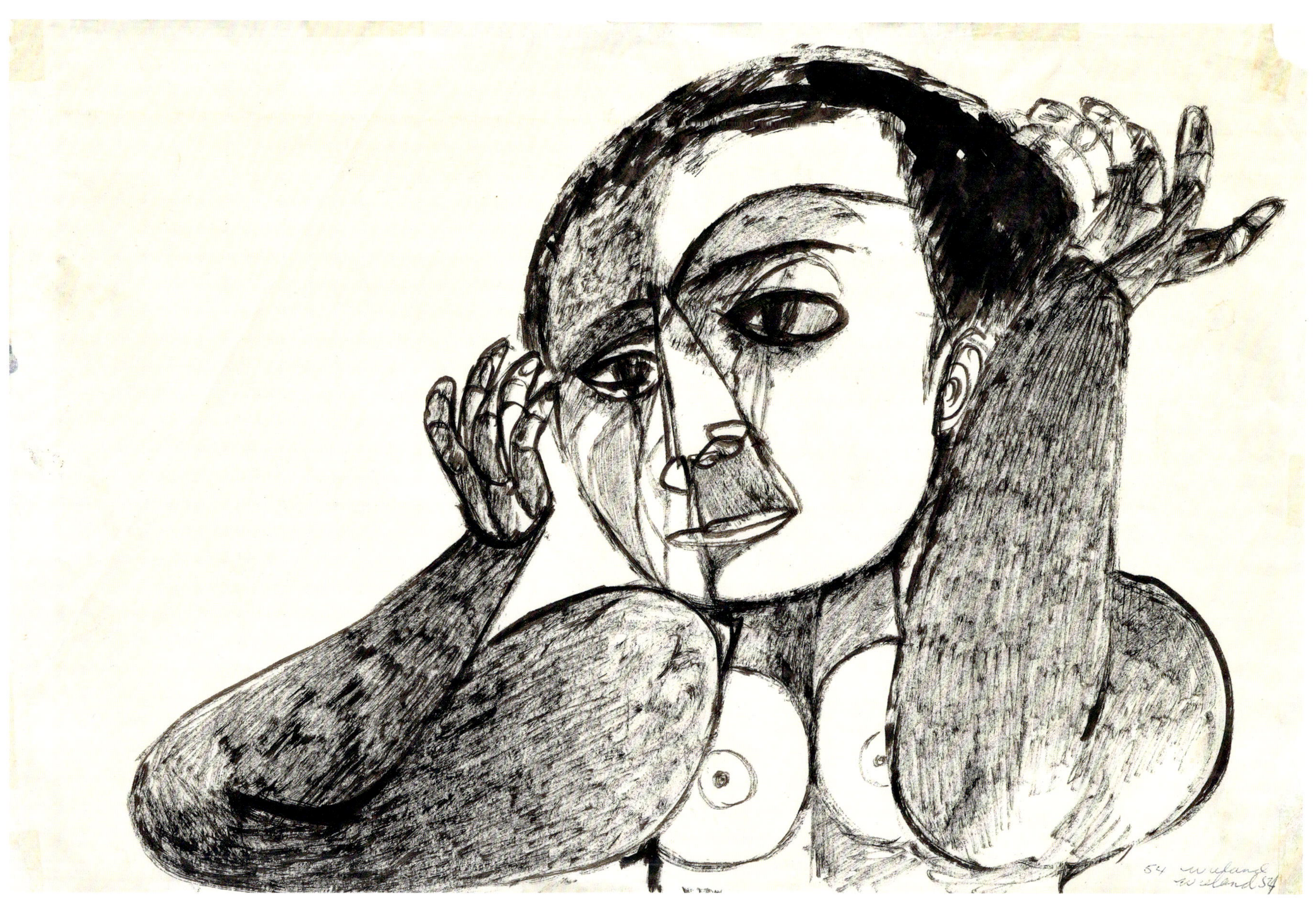

Portrait, 1954
Ink on paper
27.8 × 43.4 cm
Art Gallery of Ontario, In loving memory of Jim Murphy, 2008
2008/442
Photo: AGO, Craig Boyko

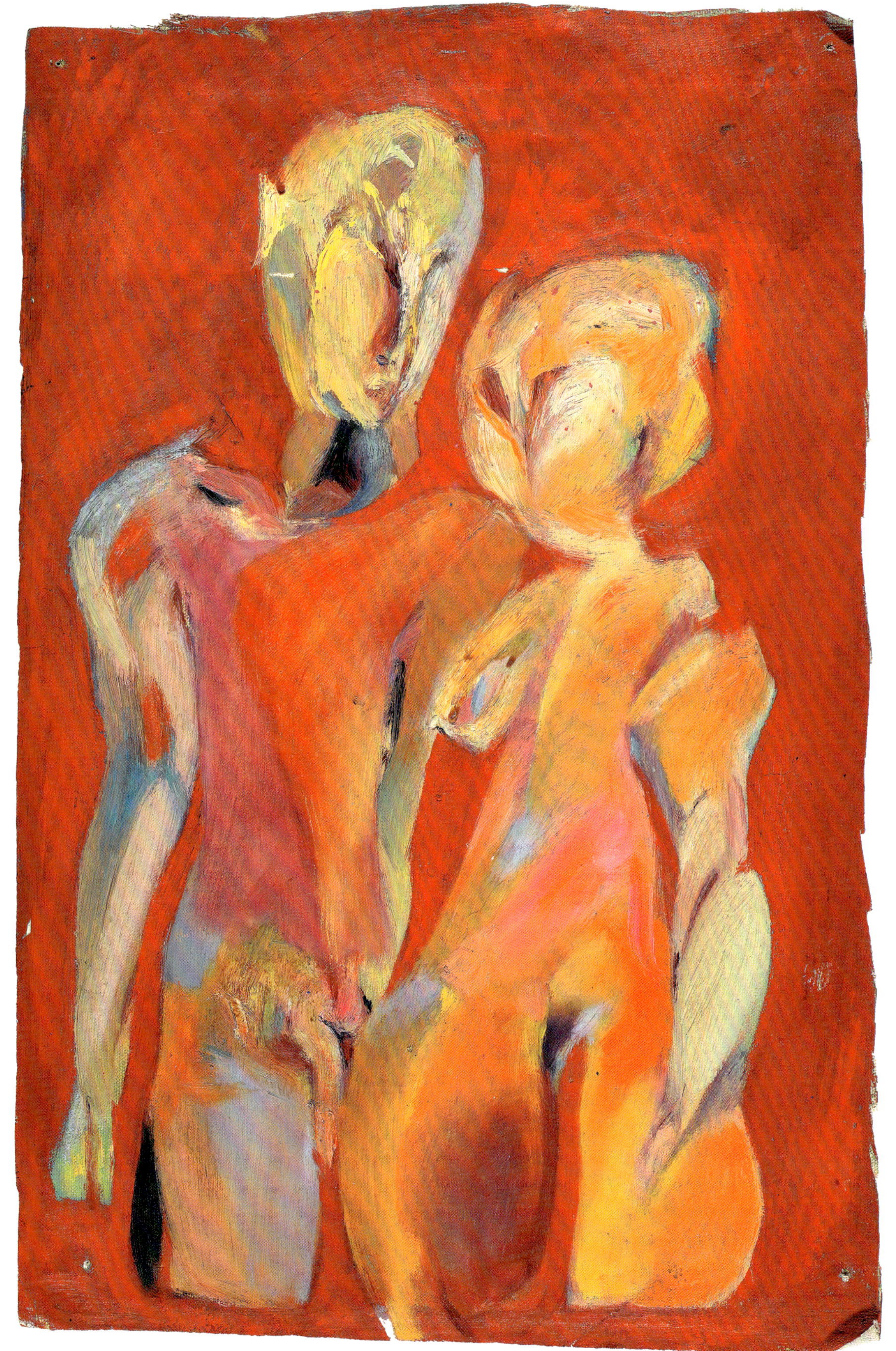

Untitled [Young Couple],
c. 1959
Oil on canvas
47.7 × 32 cm (irregular)
National Gallery of Canada, Gift of Kathy Dain, Brantford, ON, 2010
43295
Photo: NGC

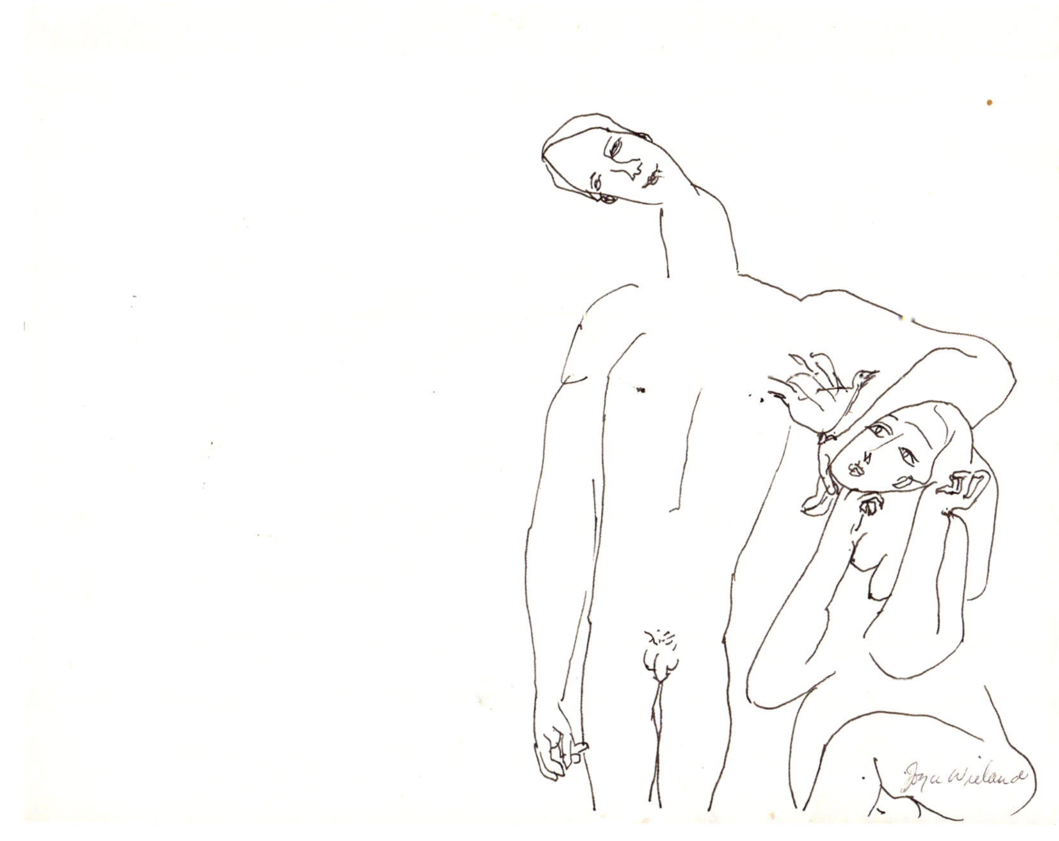

Untitled [Lovers with Dove], c. 1954–1958
Ink on wove paper
21.5 × 28 cm
Art Gallery of Ontario,
Gift of Betty Ramsaur Ferguson, Puslinch, ON, 1998
98/608
Photo: AGO, Craig Boyko

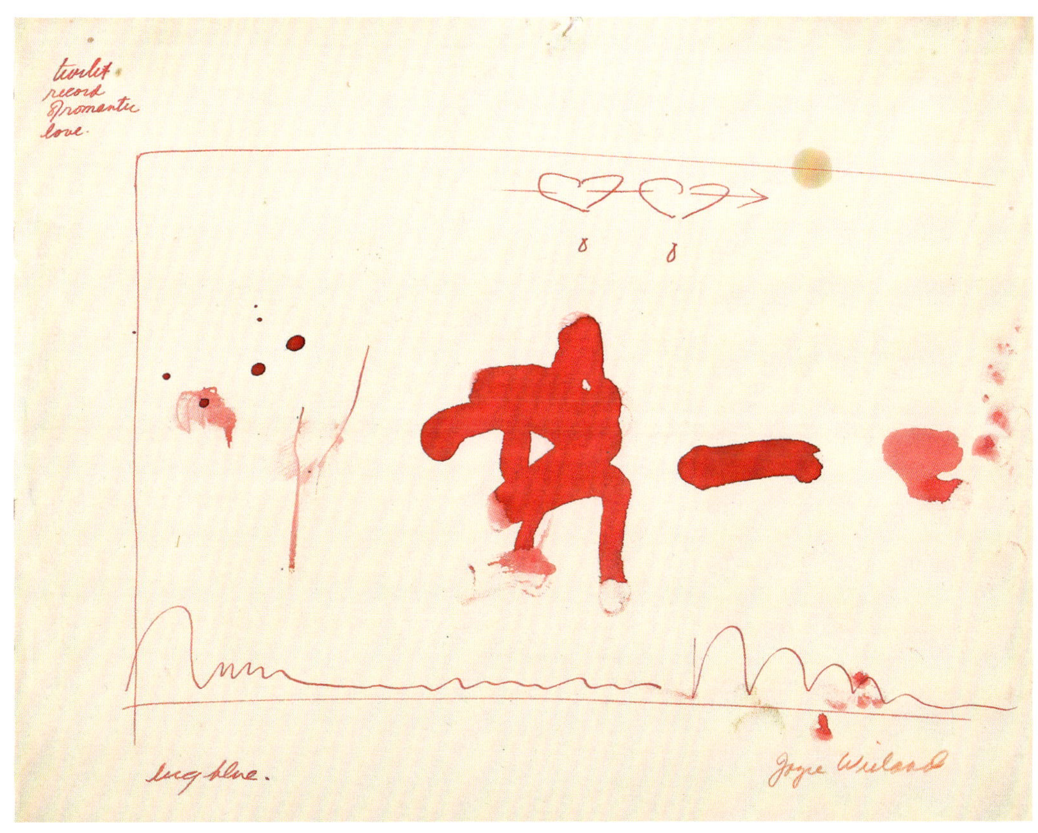

Twilit Record of Romantic Love, 1954–1958
Pen and brush and ink on wove paper
20.2 × 25.4 cm
Art Gallery of Ontario,
Gift of Betty Ramsaur Ferguson, Puslinch, ON, 1998
98/649
Photo: AGO, Craig Boyko

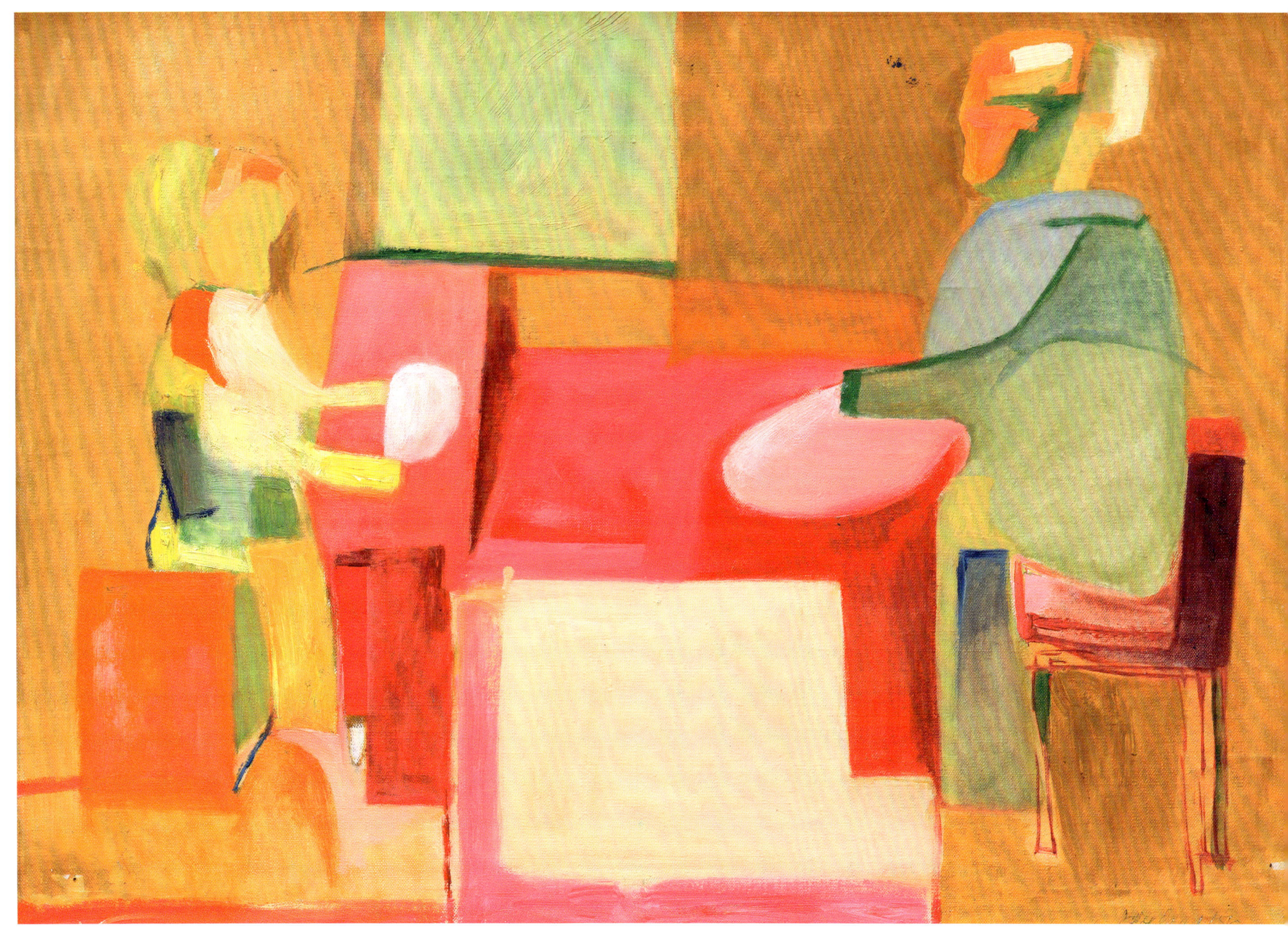

Lunch Time, 1956
Oil on canvas board
34.9 × 49.5 cm
Collection of Katia and John Bianchini
Photo: AGO, Sean Weaver

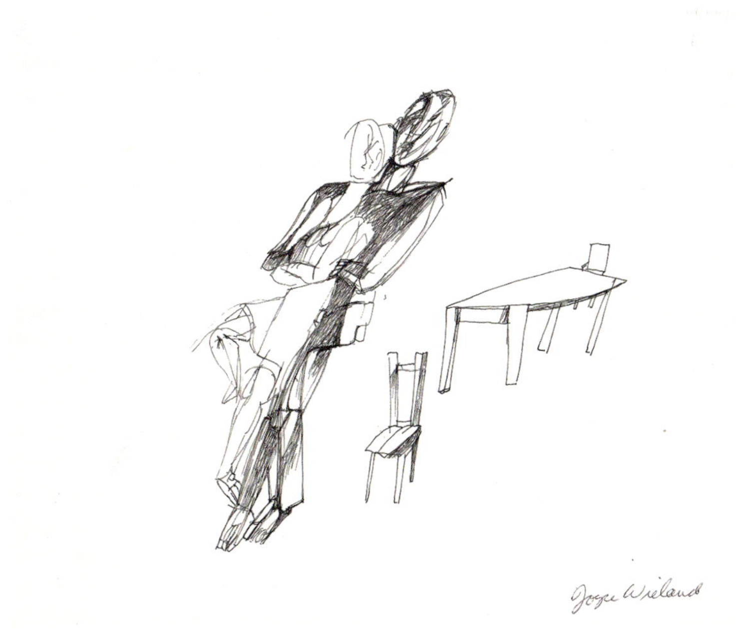

Untitled [In the Kitchen], c. 1954–1958
Ink on wove paper
25.8 × 28 cm
Art Gallery of Ontario, Gift of Betty Ramsaur Ferguson, Puslinch, ON, 1998
98/621
Photo: AGO, Craig Boyko

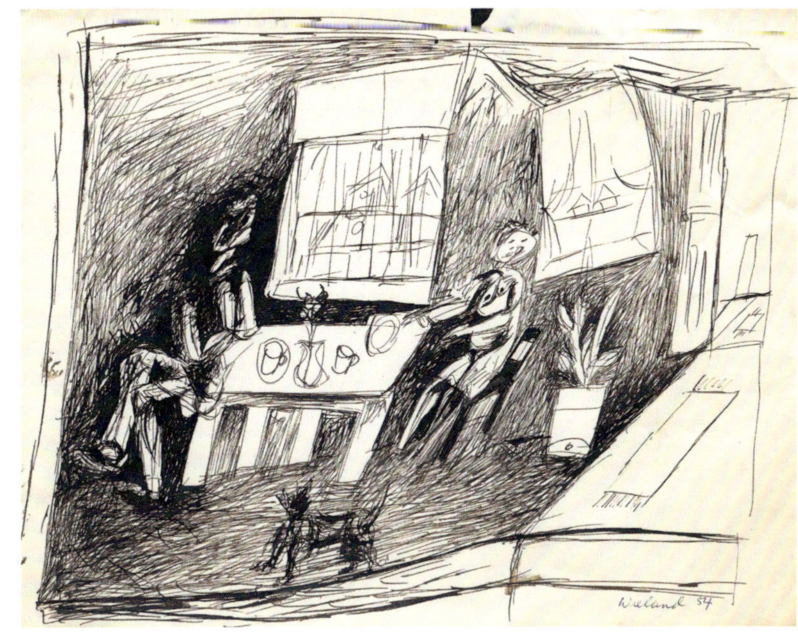

Untitled [Kitchen Conversation], 1954
Ink on wove paper
21.5 × 28 cm
Art Gallery of Ontario, Gift of Betty Ramsaur Ferguson, Puslinch, ON, 1998
98/632
Photo: AGO, Craig Boyko

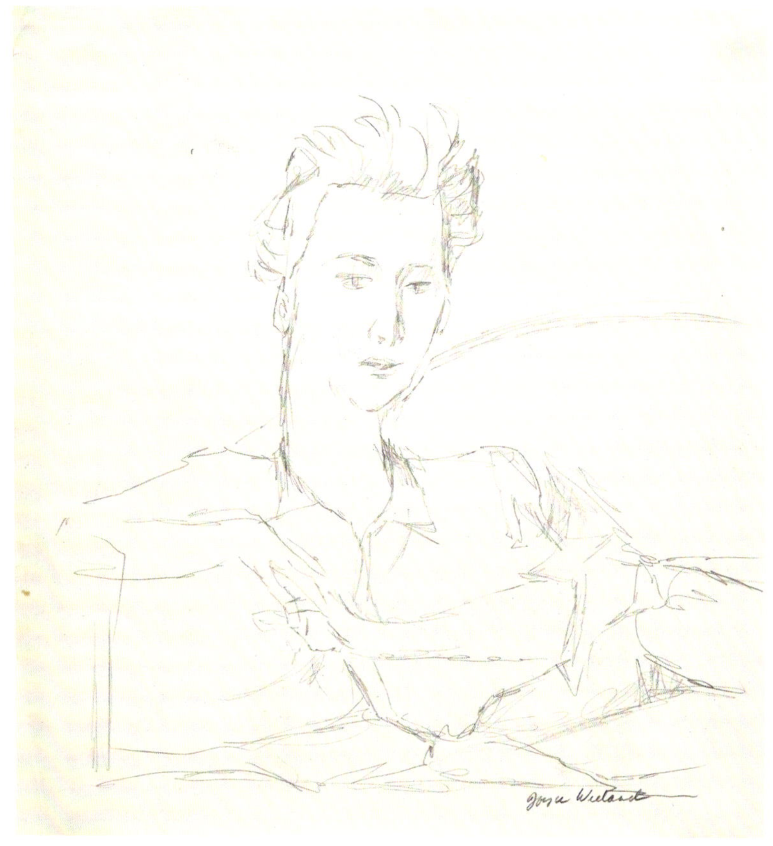

Untitled [Sketch of Mike Snow], 1954–1958
Graphite on wove paper
28 × 25.8 cm
Art Gallery of Ontario,
Gift of Betty Ramsaur Ferguson,
Puslinch, ON, 1998
98/607
Photo: AGO, Craig Boyko

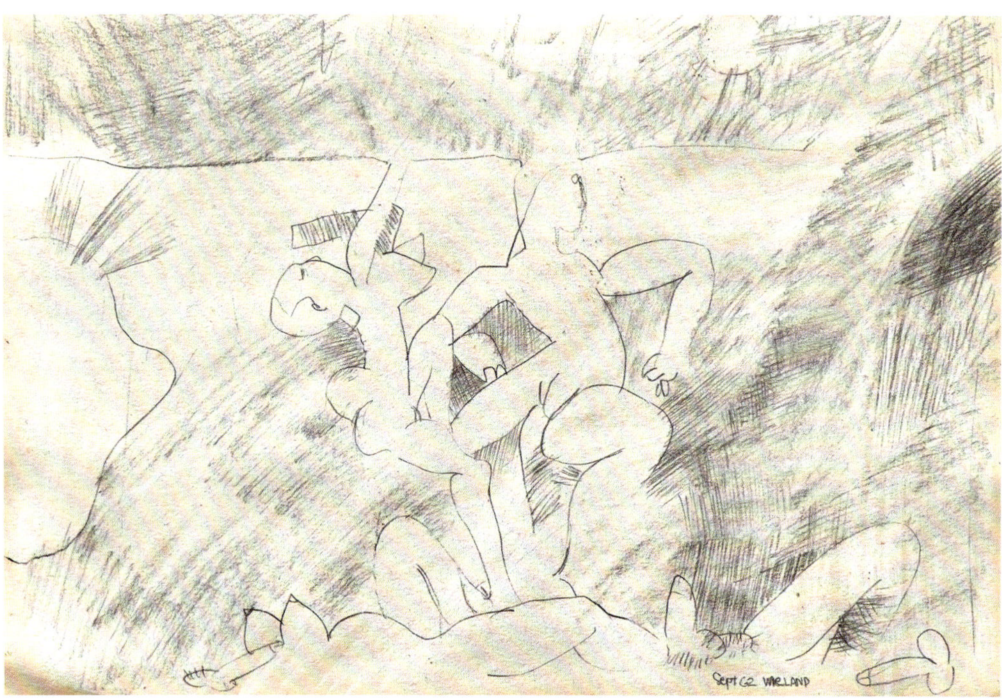

Lovers in the Park, 1962
Pencil and chalk on paper
31.5 × 37.5 cm
Collection of Les G. Lawrence, Toronto
Photo: AGO, Craig Boyko

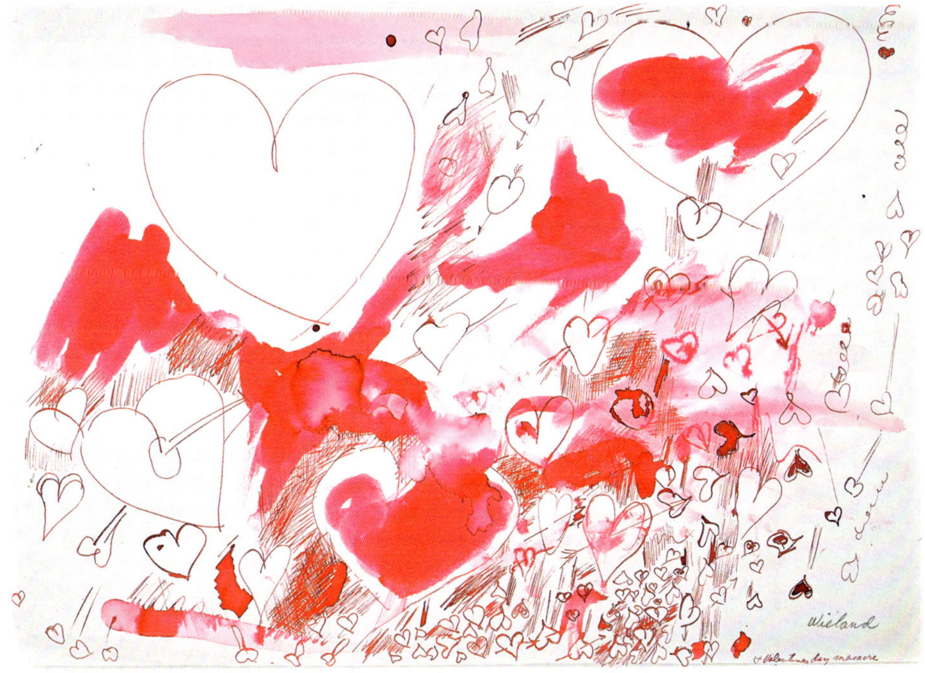

Valentines Day Massacre, c. 1961
Ink on wove paper
28 × 40 cm (irregular)
The Montreal Museum of Fine Arts
Purchased, The Clematis Foundation Fund
2022.142
Photo: MMFA, Jean-François Brière

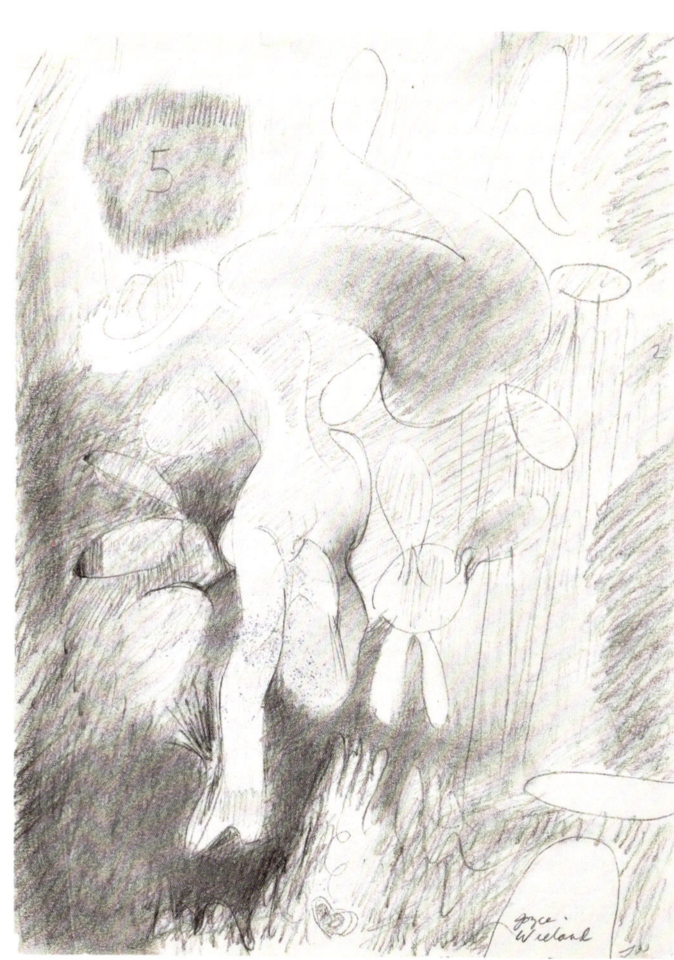

The Lovers #18, 1961
Pencil and chalk on wove paper
27.7 × 20.7 cm
Art Gallery of Ontario,
Gift of Betty Ramsaur Ferguson,
Puslinch, ON, 1998
98/592
Photo: AGO, Craig Boyko

HEART-ON

Joyce Wieland's magnificent works from the early 1960s demonstrate how she distinguished herself as an exceptional colourist. Working for the first time in large scale, she often boldly disrupted the fields of colour by affixing cut-out pieces of fabric to the stained canvas. She further complicated them by adding graffiti-like drawings of arrows, penises, and hearts. Wieland's irreverent approach to her colour-field canvases reflect a broader shift away from the purely formal concerns of painting, while also establishing her unique vocabulary. Conscious of the challenges inherent in navigating a male-dominated art world—initially in Toronto's art scenes, most specifically at The Isaacs Gallery, and later in New York City when confronted by the closed and seemingly paramount art world led by Robert Rauschenberg (1925–2008) and Jasper Johns (b. 1930)—Wieland embraced the untidy elements of domesticity and lived experience, allowing them to seep into her practice. These works brought her institutional recognition and asserted an enduring thematic leitmotif, demonstrating Wieland's audacious use of irony and humour to define her own feminine and feminist imprint.

BLUES SERIES, 1960–1961

The "stuff" at hand—found around the studio, the office, the street, the home—while easily dismissed, can offer the most expressive materials for experimentation and exploration. Wieland was already immersed and practised in modernist collage and its potential for uninhibited creativity and allusive imagery. She believed that "if you turn off your mind in a way, then these things can come through and they wouldn't normally get that opportunity if you're too conscious."[1] By the late 1950s, her distinctive shapes and line were coming into being as an extension of her drawings, transposed onto colour-saturated canvases.

In 1960, Wieland began *Blues Series*.[2] This group of collages combines drawing and painting in service of the tactile three-dimensionality of the cut and crumpled-up "stuff" she assembled and stuck onto flattened cardboard boxes, Masonite, and the backs of placards.[3] They are messy and sensual, casual and lively—even humorous. Wieland's gestures are palpable, traceable; her actions recorded by the manipulation of discarded materials (cardboard, card stock, cardboard tubes, brown paper wrapping, receipts, printed paper), further enhanced by painting and drawing.

Among the first in her series are *Spring Blues* and *Summer Blues* (p. 65), both from 1960. *Spring*—the only truly vertical composition in the series—is delicate and spacious, *Summer* is rough and stuffed, yet both are awash in pastel blues, pinks, and lavender. Wieland emphasizes the coarse texture of *Summer* by smearing deep red patches and marking black lines onto the several layers of torn and glued paper, acting out a feverish collision. In contrast, in *Spring* she uses just a few pieces of paper ripped into rough circles. They float to the top and sink to the bottom edges, revealing an effervescent space, vertical corridors of subtle tonal shifts of blue. In the bottom right, she adds small shards of mirror, adding light and space to the composition.

There is a similar ephemeral quality in 1961's *Summer Blues in the Water* (p. 64) and *Summer Blues Cool* (p. 64), which are the same size as the previous year's works.[4] The torn-up ovoid shapes of . . . *in the Water* float (as they do in *Summer Blues*) in a chalky blue–lavender blend. At the bottom right, Wieland crumples up carbon paper and sticks it on the board, punctuating the composition with a dark stain—a sinking feeling. In contrast, the pale cut-up pages of *Cool* fan out from the bottom into a bright yellow ground—buoyed in a yolky smear. Yellow circles bubble up and travel across the straight edges of office paper. In other compositions, like *Ball* and *The Kiss* (pp. 62–63), her paper forms confront their fragmentary nature in futile attempts at reunification.

With only a few shapes and colours, Wieland invents her own visual vocabulary, transcending language and traversing a wide array of moods and states. Her titles allude to seasons, sex, and weather, hints she offers in her own code. There is movement and energy in the watery sensuality of these arrangements, welling up in the embryonic flux of coming together and multiplying. The scope of this lyrical series, comprised of over twenty works, suggests the fertile nature of these compositions and the freedom of imagination they present in their iterative permutations. Possibly Wieland's most abstract series, *Blues* conjures the elemental stage of cosmic creation—a world coming into being, that morphs twenty years later into the bucolic paradise of her *The Bloom of Matter* pastel drawings.

GEORGIANA UHLYARIK

1 *Artist on Fire* documentary, directed by Kay Armatage, 1987, 54 min, 6mm/DVD, quote at 19:00–19:08.

2 Several works from this series were exhibited in *Joyce Wieland* at The Isaacs Gallery, January 31–February 20, 1962.

3 *Summer Blues in the Water* is created on the back of a printed map of the United States from E.M. Jellinek's "Recent Trends in Alcoholism and in Alcohol Consumption," *Quarterly Journal of Studies on Alcohol* 8, no. 1 (1947): 1–42.

4 The majority of works are 56 × 71 cm; some are 63.5 × 96.5 cm. *Ball* and *Spring* are the largest: 91.5 × 83 cm and 116.3 × 81.3 cm respectively.

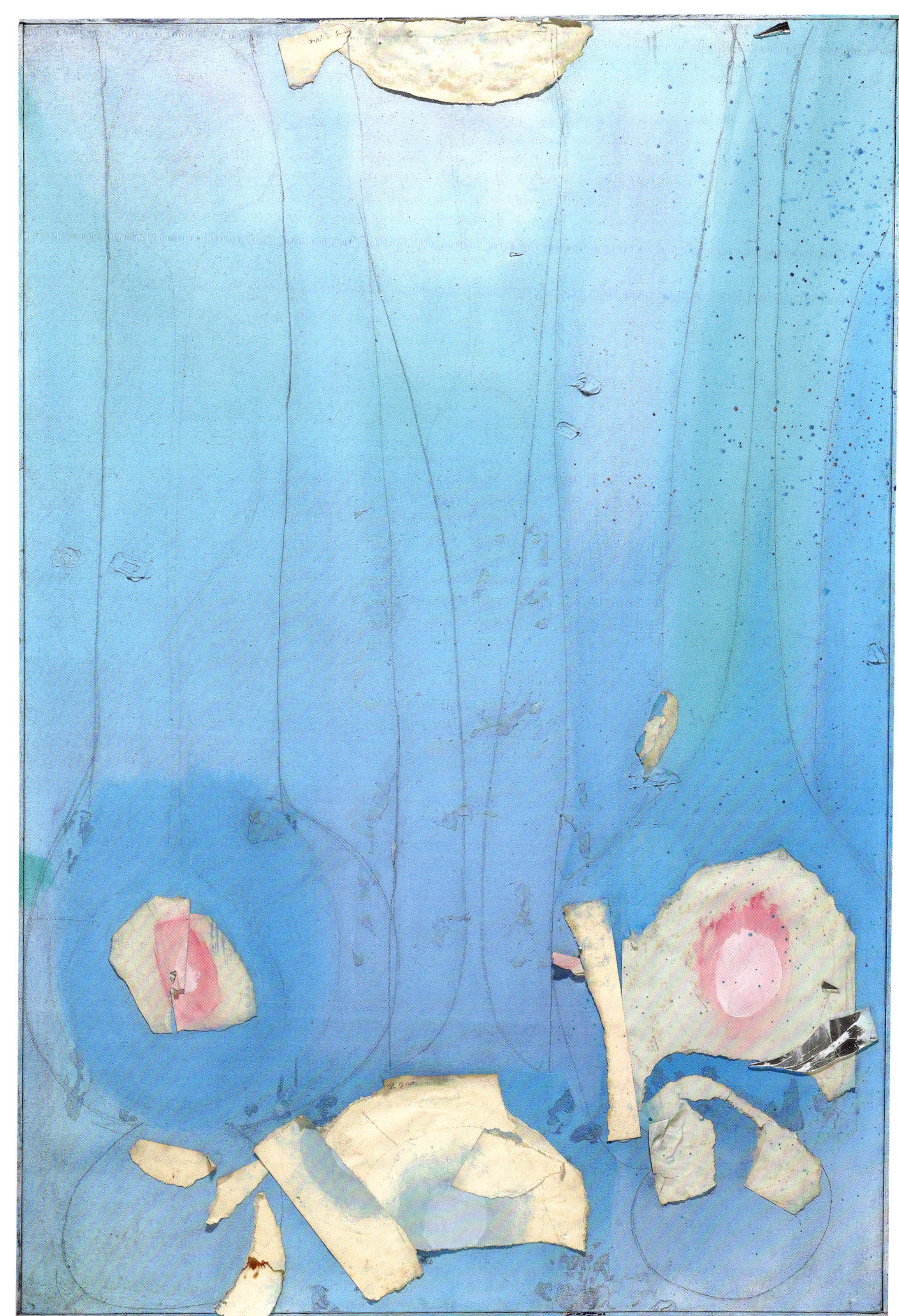

Spring Blues, 1960
Oil, paper, mirror,
and collage on canvas
116.3 × 81.3 cm
National Gallery of Canada,
Gift of Doug MacPherson,
Prince Edward County, ON, 2011
43461
Photo: NGC

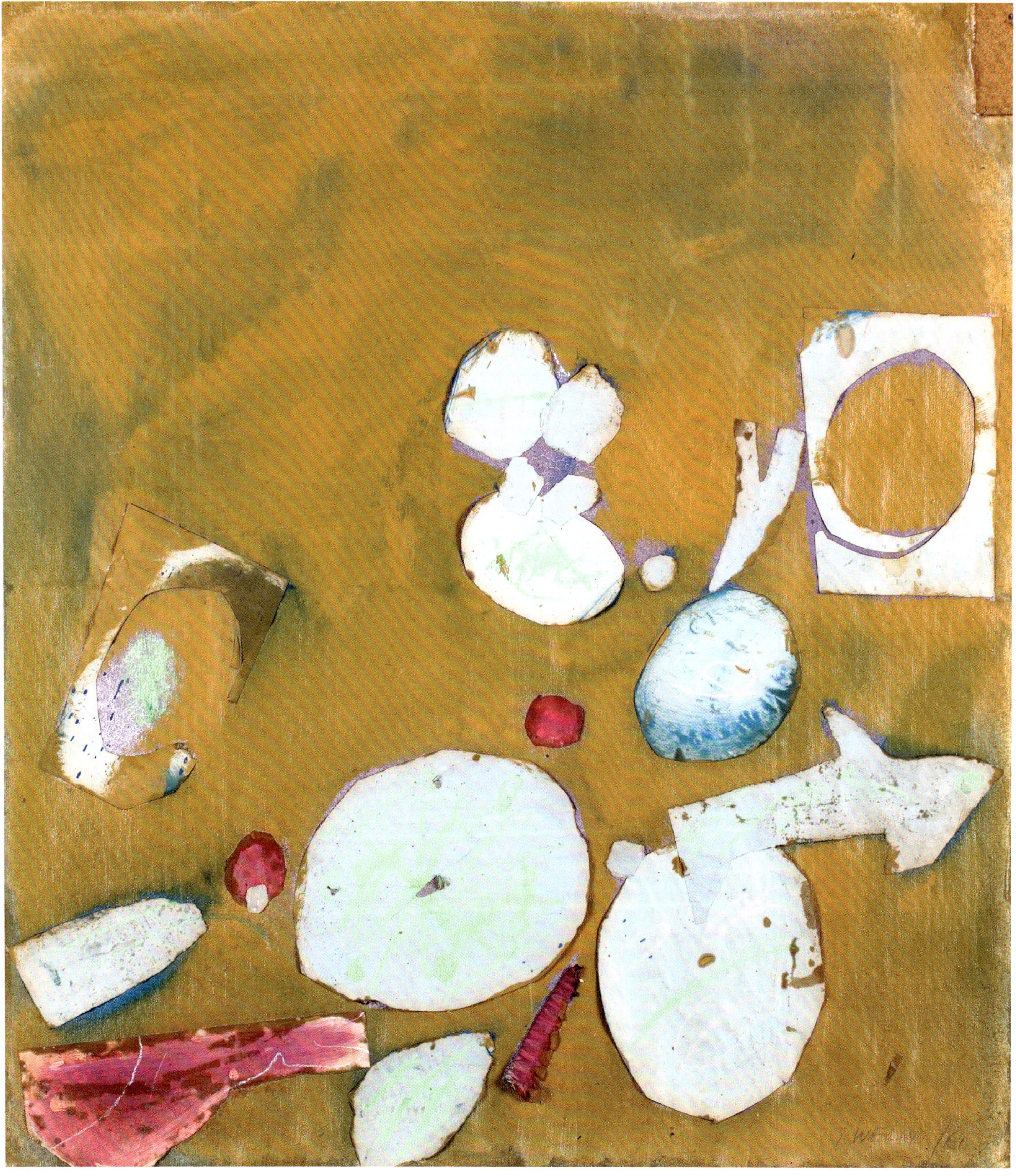

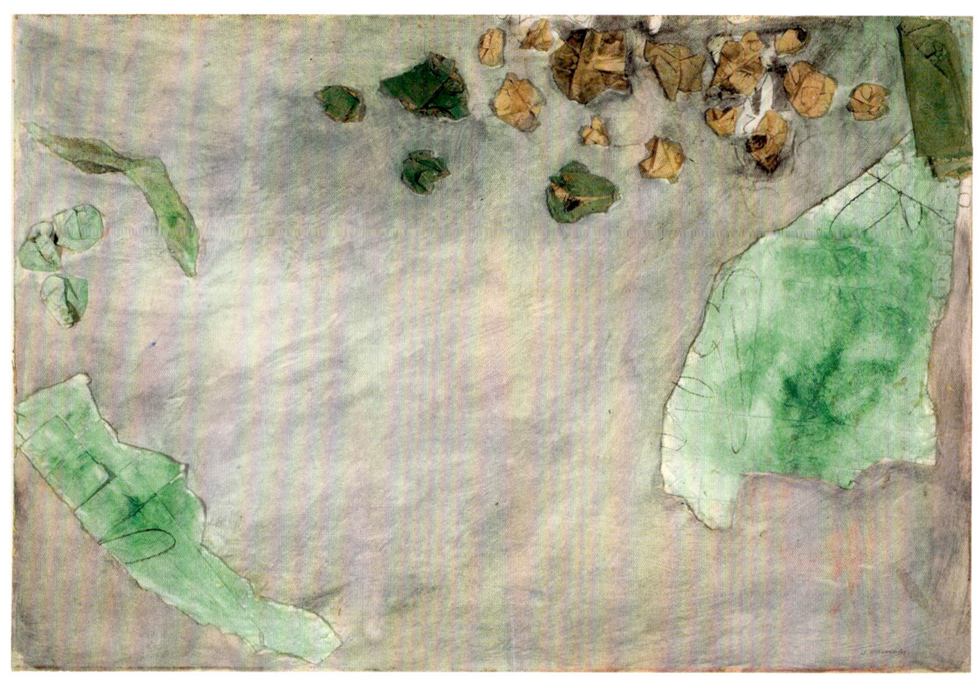

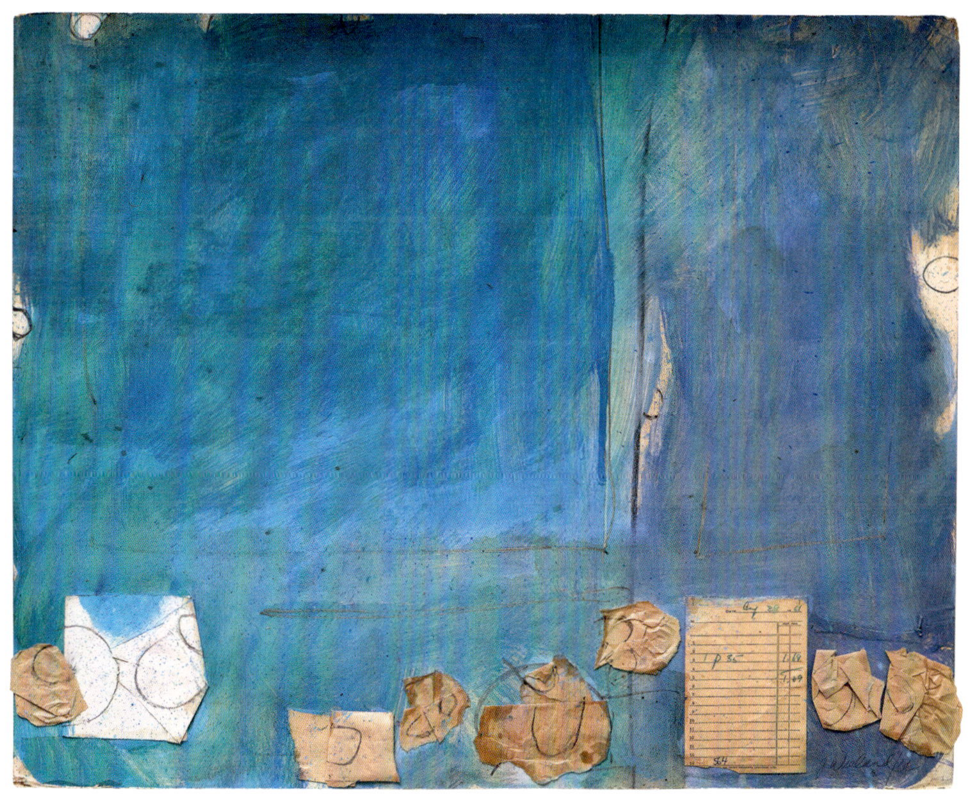

OPPOSITE

Summer Blues — Ball, 1961
Oil, paper, and collage on board
91.5 × 83 cm
Agnes Etherington Art Centre, Queen's University, Kingston, ON, Purchase: Chancellor Richardson Memorial Fund 1992
35-010
Photo: Bernard Clark

ABOVE

Summer Blues — The Kiss, 1961
Watercolour, oil, gouache, and charcoal on wove paper collage mounted on corrugated cardboard
63.5 × 97.2 cm
Collection of Leonard & Bina Ellen Art Gallery, Concordia University, Purchase — Special Purchase Assistance Grant, Canada Council for the Arts, 1983
983.19
Photo: Richard-Max Tremblay

BELOW

Window [Summer Blues], 1961
Acrylic, watercolour, varnish, and collage on paper
55.24 × 71.12 cm
Collection of Susan Rynard
Photo: AGO, Sean Weaver

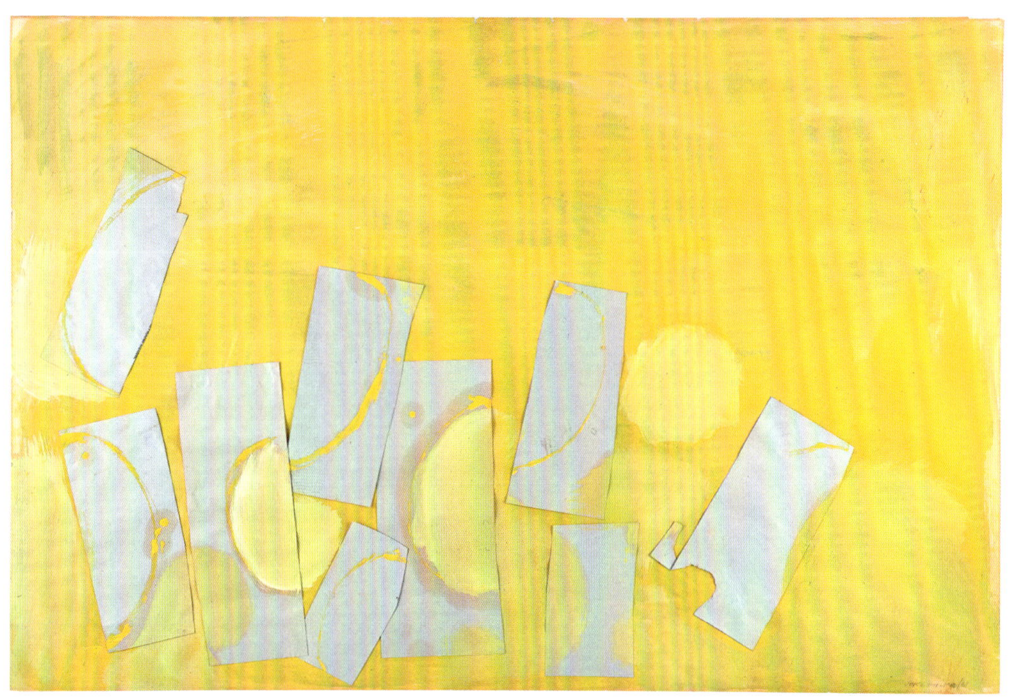

Summer Blues Cool, 1961
Oil, printed type on paper collage elements on paper
63.7 × 96.5 cm
Art Gallery of Ontario, Purchased with funds donated by Susan and Greg Latremoille, Toronto, 2007
2007/65
Photo: AGO, Craig Boyko

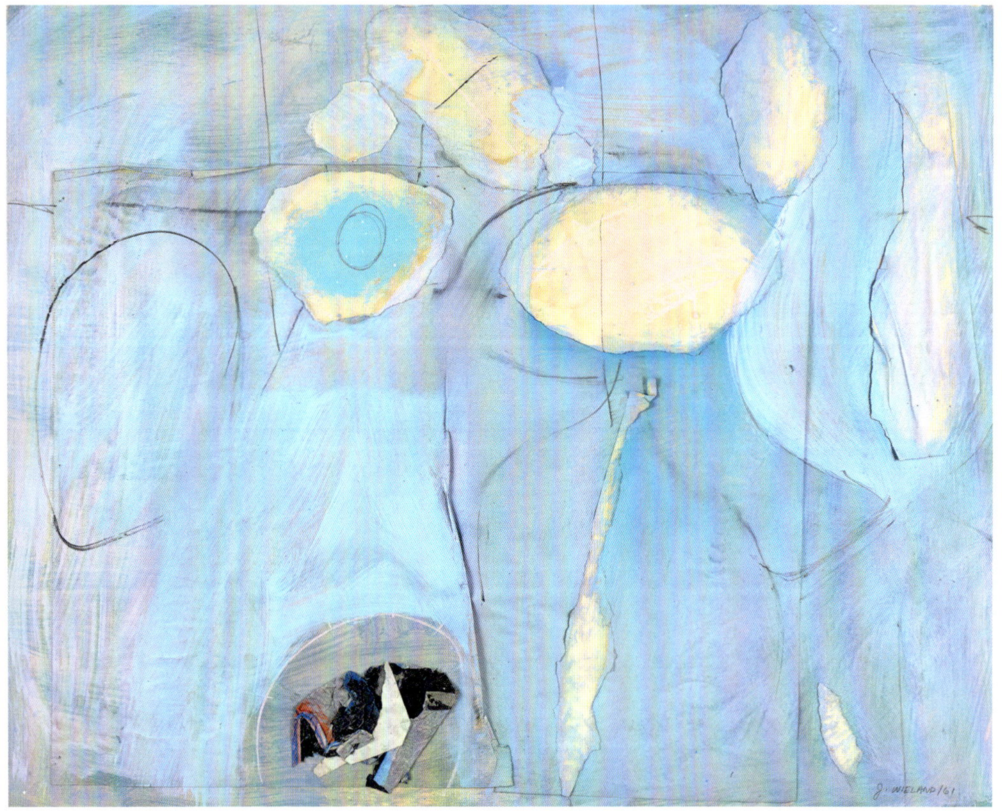

Summer Blues in the Water, 1961
Gouache, graphite, collage on paper
60 × 75 cm
Art Gallery of Ontario, Purchased with funds donated by Susan and Greg Latremoille, Toronto, 2007
2007/64
Photo: AGO, Craig Boyko

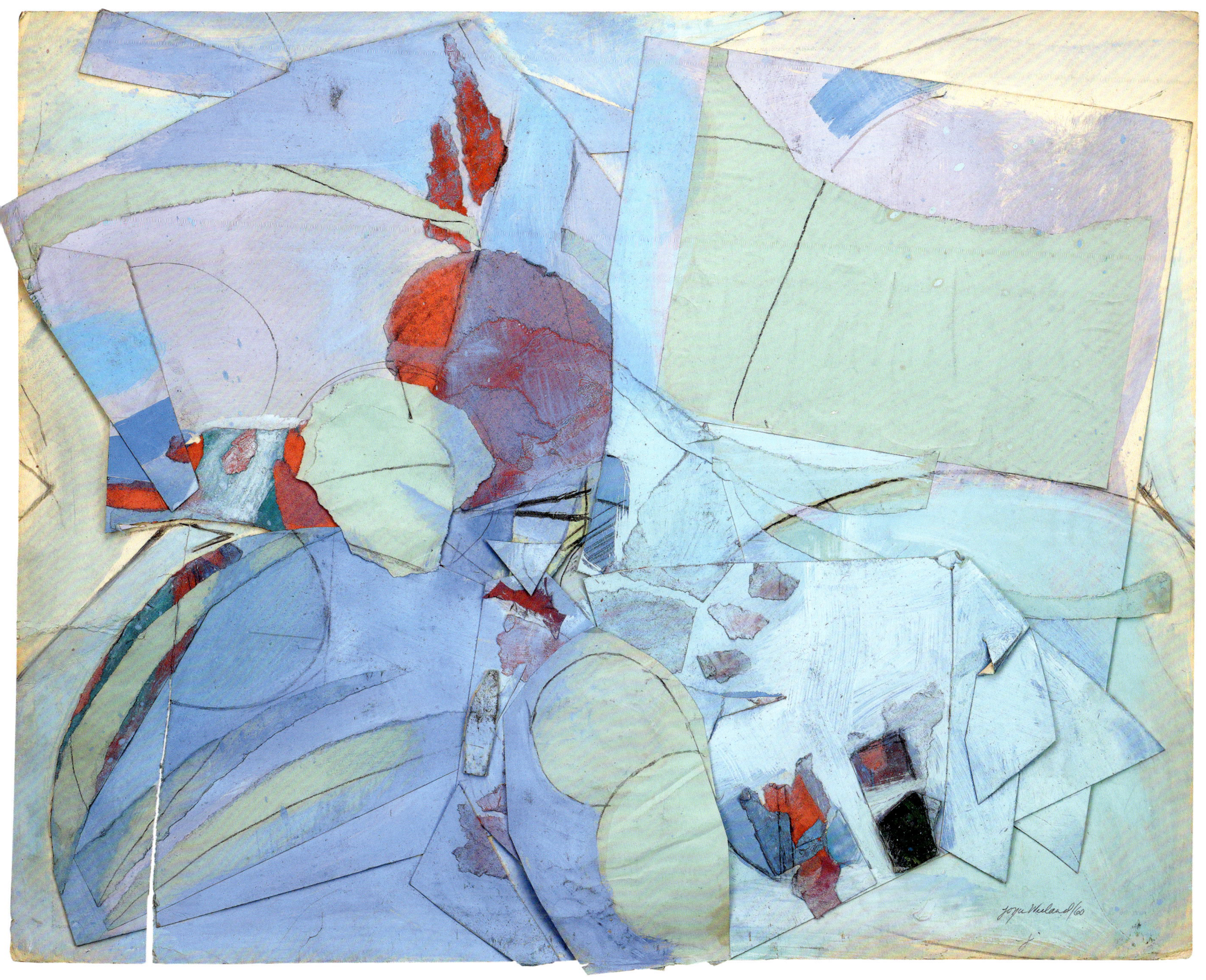

Summer Blues, 1960
Paint, charcoal or pastel, glass, cloth, and collage on paper
56 × 73 cm
Art Windsor-Essex, Purchased 1982
1982.017
Photo: Art Windsor-Essex

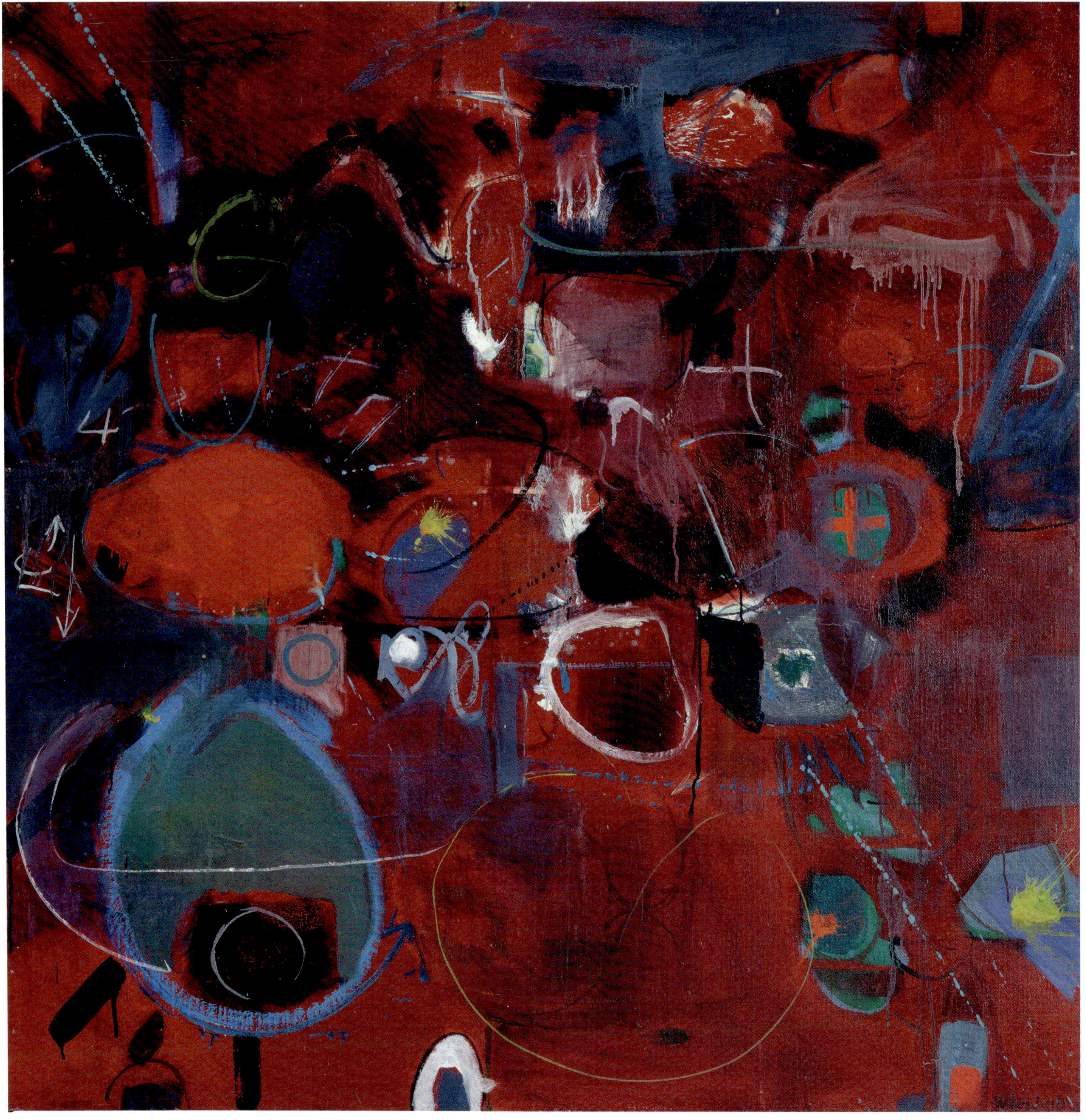

WAR MEMORIES, 1960

This is the battle of Monte Cassino. It's called War Memoir [sic]. *It's the battle of the Canadians in the Second World War. It was stuck in my mind because every day everybody was listening to the radio and my brother was in that battle.*

This painting comes after a year of studying Miró. A conscious decision to be influenced by someone other than the milieu that I was associated with, [most of whom] were men. Very few women survived the years in that particular time to become artists or to be noticed or whatever. It was very difficult and I know people that fell by the wayside. I struggled and I was always with the same group. I didn't want to be a mascot, I didn't want to be my husband's shadow and so I made a conscious decision here to take Miró, whom I loved, and make him my influence.

Joyce Wieland's recollection about making *War Memories* offers a rare insight into the artist's early art-historical influences, as well as the factors at play for women artists in the early 1960s.

Oblique references to the style of Joan Miró (1893–1983) can be observed in the combination of saturated fields of monochrome colour. The variety of painterly marks and a limited palette appear to float on the painting's surface. Parallels between the two exceptional colourists would also later be manifest in their dialogue with other avant-gardes, their use of collage on the paintings' surface, the multidisciplinary character of their works, as well as their collaborative and collective art-making practices.

ANNE GRACE

OPPOSITE
War Memories, 1960
Oil on Masonite
122 × 122 cm
Collection of Munro Ferguson
Photo: MMFA, Julie Ciot

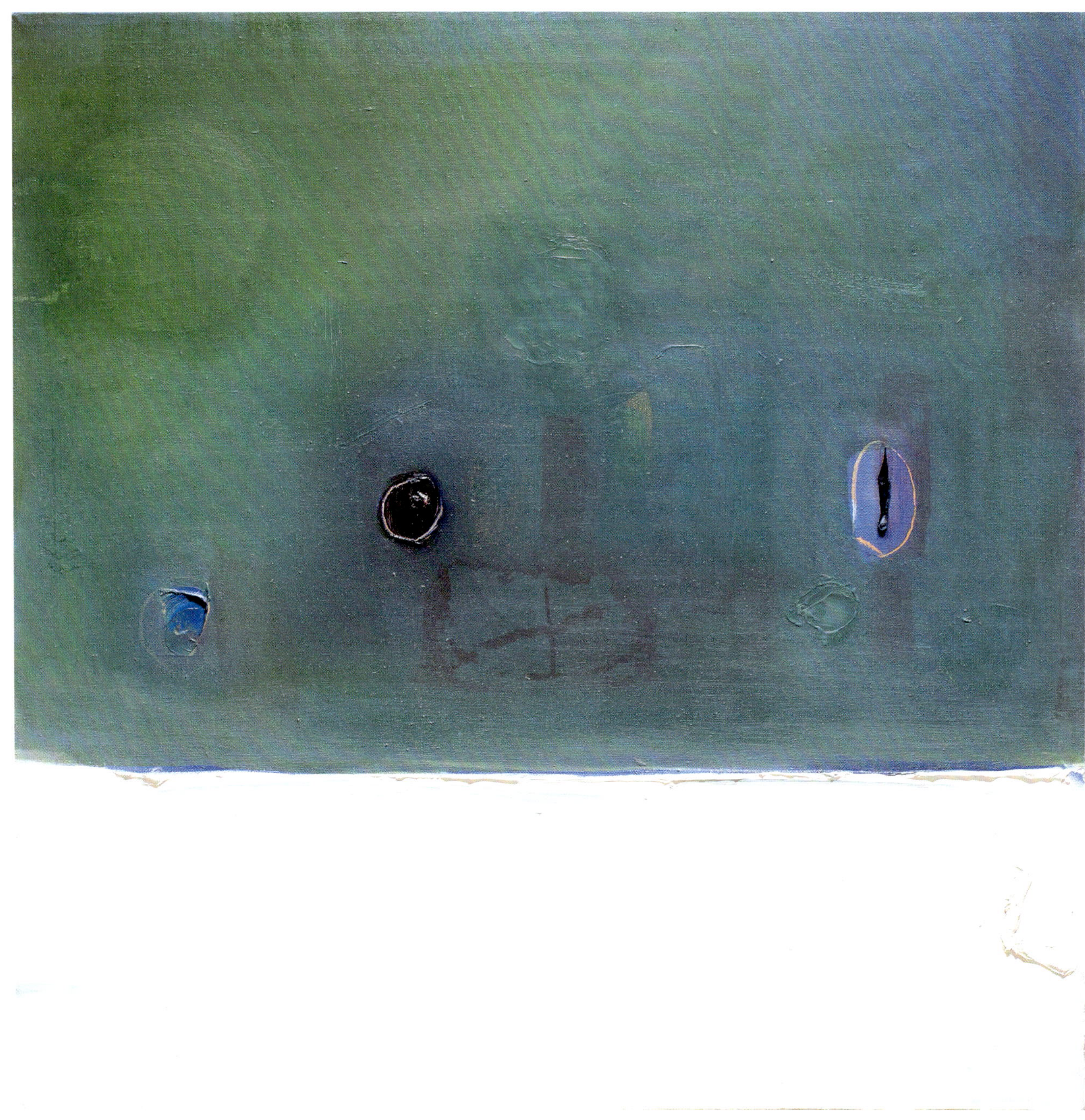

Northern Lights, 1960
Oil on canvas
79.3 × 79.3 cm
Art Gallery of Hamilton, Gift of Irving Zucker, 1992
1992.2.5
Photo: Robert McNair, 2016

The Kiss, 1960
Oil on canvas
81.4 × 63.5 cm
Collection of the
Vancouver Art Gallery,
Gift of Donna Montague
VAG 99.22.6
Photo: Vancouver
Art Gallery

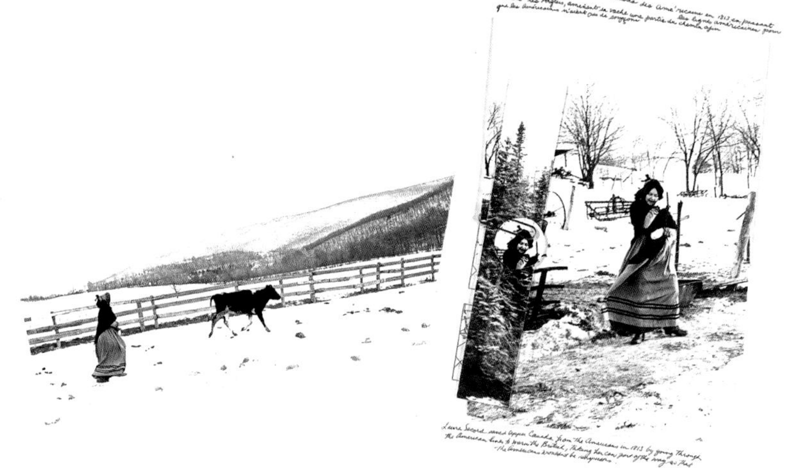

Joyce Wieland as Laura Secord, *True Patriot Love* maquette, 1971
National Gallery of Canada fonds, NGC Library and Archives
Photos: NGC

LAURA SECORD SAVES UPPER CANADA, 1961

In her youth, Joyce Wieland—like many Canadian schoolchildren—was introduced to the figure of Laura Secord (1775–1868). As her teacher described the Canadian heroine's 1813 trek to warn the British of an impending American attack, Wieland, who recalled daydreaming during her other lessons, was captivated.[1] Her studies, typically dominated by the exploits of men, suddenly included the story of a woman who had played a crucial role in the nation's history.

This encounter would inspire Wieland's 1961 collaged painting. A dark orange and green spiral dominate the centre of Wieland's canvas, creating a circular movement in an otherwise chaotic composition. This spiral, and the arrows that lead the viewer's eyes into it, depict Secord's route from her home in US–occupied territory to British lines twenty miles away. Wieland's handling of paint, variously layered, dripped, and sprayed onto the canvas nods to prevalent modes of abstraction. These elements, coupled with her use of found objects—a folded paper airplane, a small Union Jack (Wieland's first incorporation of a flag in her work), and numbers and letters feverishly carved into the paint or drawn in chalk—result in a piece that is textural, kaleidoscopic, and dreamlike, evoking the artist's youthful imagination ignited by her newfound knowledge of Secord's bravery.

Wieland attributed this painting to her search for female role models, or what she called her "female line."[2] Throughout the 1960s, she was disheartened to find that so few women's stories were recorded in Canadian history. She mined the historical record for her foremothers, searching for a "heroine." "Finally," she recalled, "I picked Laura Secord."[3]

One of the artist's earliest explorations of Canada as a subject, *Laura Secord Saves Upper Canada* introduces the feminist and political qualities that came to define Wieland's creative vocabulary, most notably in her 1971 *True Patriot Love* exhibition at the National Gallery of Canada. For the artist's book she created as its catalogue, Wieland photographed herself as Secord, humorously dressing up in a nineteenth-century-style outfit while dragging a cow behind her. In 1973, Wieland would return to her heroine again in the form of a white quilt appliquéd with verse, aptly titled *Laura Secord*. Secord, for Wieland, was proof of women's participation in Canadian history, and, most notably, was a heroine for defending the country from encroachment by the United States. By painting, quilting, and dressing up as Secord, Wieland cast herself in a similar role: a woman charging out to warn other Canadians about what they might lose to American imperialism, and to give Canadian women a sense of their heritage.

SHANNON STRIDE

1 Jane Lind, *Joyce Wieland: Artist on Fire* (Toronto: James Lorimer, 2001), 47, from Lind's interview with Joyce Wieland, August 27, 1986.

2 Wieland interviewed in Barbara K. Stevenson, "The Political and Social Subject Matter in the Art of Joyce Wieland and Greg Curnoe" (master's thesis, Carleton University, 1987), 172.

3 Wieland quoted in Lauren Rabinovitz, "An Interview with Joyce Wieland," *Afterimage* 8, no. 10 (May 1981): 10.

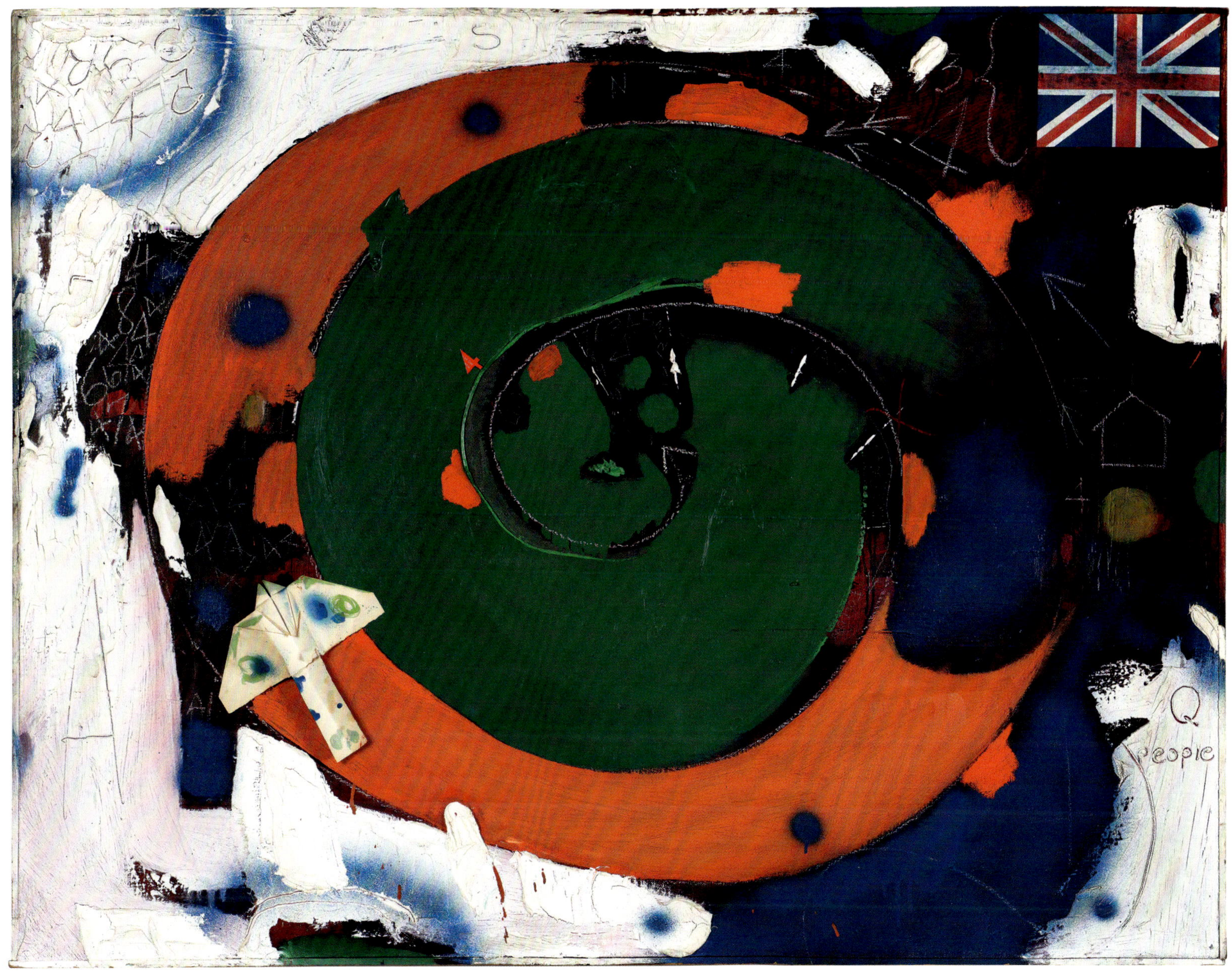

Laura Secord Saves Upper Canada, 1961
Oil, acrylic, spray lacquer paint, white chalk, and collage of cloth and paper elements on canvas
101.6 × 132.1 cm
Collection of the Canada Council Art Bank, Ottawa
76/7-0009
Photo: Brandon Clarida Image Services

"This is one of my first works about Canada. It's called *Laura Secord Saves Upper Canada*, as seen from the air and it's about being in school and being told about Laura Secord and trying to figure out the logistics. Paper airplanes entered, letters, numerals, numbers and so it's a whole theme about being taught in those years when I was in grade four and five and six hearing about this."

"The heart appears . . . in the first cloth work called *Heart-on*. . . . I put [it] onto factory cotton, and it's a strange thing to get it to absorb it. This work is about theatre. The curtains can be changed and there's little secrets inside the pockets. There's always secrets in my work at this period because I felt there should be levels in all works . . . of course, in the greatest works there are many secrets that don't come to you immediately. For instance, say, in Rembrandt's self-portraits it takes years and years and years to see, but then those works are extremely didactic so you are helped along down the line to get some of the roots of the work."

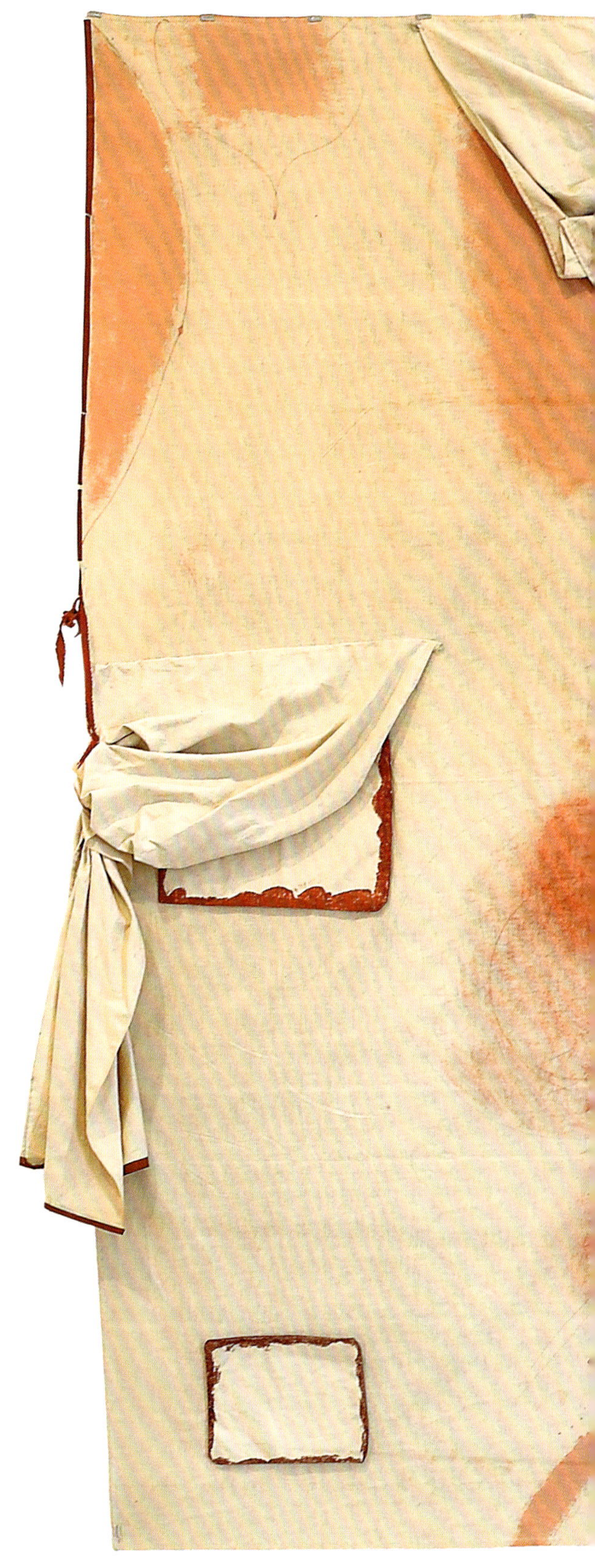

Heart-on, 1962
Red electrical tape, chalk, crayon, and ink,
with linen and wool cut-outs on unstretched linen
177.8 × 251.5 cm
National Gallery of Canada, Purchased 1973
17129
Photo: NGC

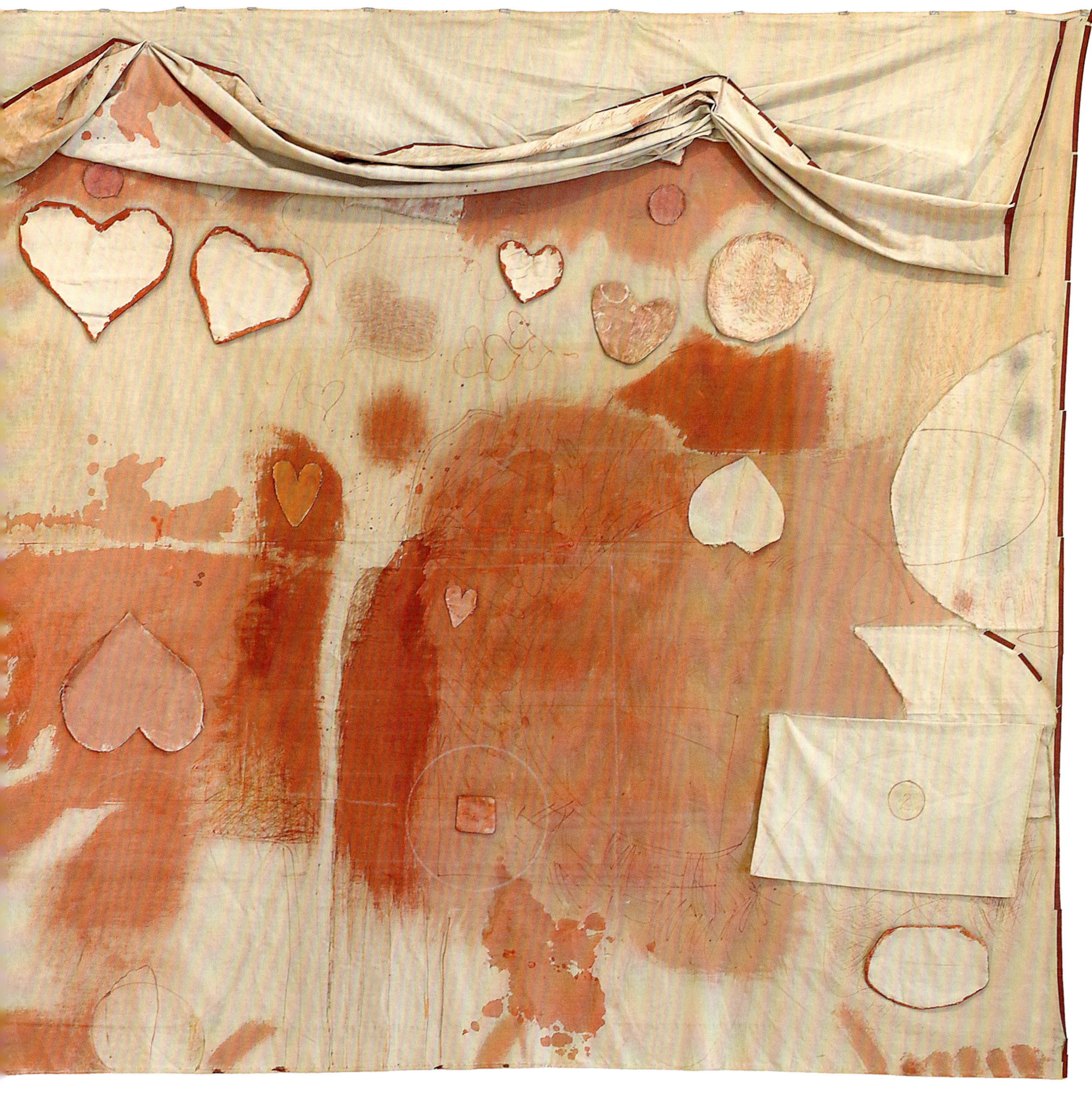

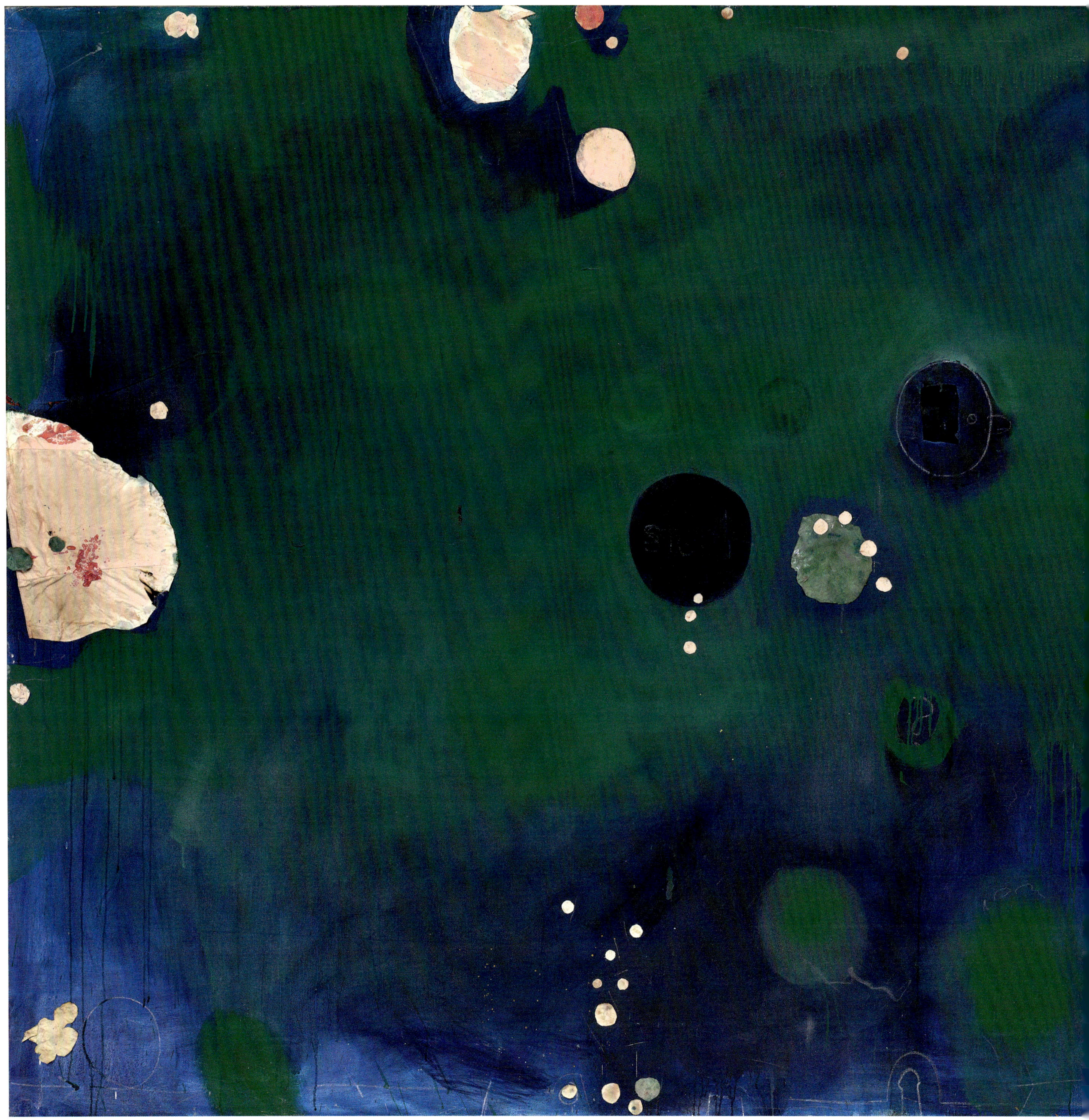

HALLUCINATION, 1961

Working in her friends' spacious coach house in Toronto in 1961, Joyce Wieland painted *Hallucination*, a monumental, deep blue-green aqueous scene with a series of circular fabric forms collaged onto its surface. The various-sized light-pink cloth fragments create an intimacy: the seams indicate that they were once part of a garment. There is a sense of Wieland's presence, a closeness to her.

The artist started using cloth the same year with *Heart-on* while working on costumes at the Toronto Workshop Productions. Her use of fabric may have also been inspired by her sister, Joan Stewart, a quiltmaker. The textile elements in *Heart-on* (p. 72) and *Hallucination* prefigure the quilts Wieland would make with Stewart, as well as the sewn assemblages that follow. Before collaging with cloth, she used paper. The *Blues* series (1960–1961) anticipates this major painting.

"When I started out and was a member of The Isaacs Gallery, I did not want to be influenced by the men," she recounted in 1986. "It was mostly men in that gallery.... I decided to be my own person, and I didn't want to have people say to me, 'Oh, she's a good painter for a woman.'"[1] Wieland established herself with evocative colour field canvases imbued with feminist/feminine imagery—about the body, fertility, sexuality from a woman's perspective—but she maintained a style that shared a formal language with that of her male peers.

Wieland also actively looked beyond Toronto for inspiration, taking in Willem de Kooning's (1904–1997) abstract expressionism and Joan Miró's biomorphic shapes and meandering lines. She embraced spontaneity in her approach, moving freely through her large studio to create gestural marks and loose forms that she would later relate to female reproductive parts. In reference to her paintings from this period, she once said: "When I did those, I never thought—I just felt the urge to make those paintings.... And so, I did them and never thought about them as wombs. And afterwards, sometimes only maybe a year later, you see what a painting is really about. And that's what they seemed to be about: cycles and wombs and eggs."[2]

1 *Artist on Fire* documentary, directed by Kay Armatage, 1987, 54 min, 6mm/DVD, quote at 07:27–07:44.

2 Wieland interviewed in Barbara K. Stevenson, "The Political and Social Subject Matter in the Art of Joyce Wieland and Greg Curnoe" (master's thesis, Carleton University, 1987), 18.

PREVIOUS SPREAD
Hallucination, 1961
Oil, cloth, and paperboard on canvas
193.5 × 259.5 cm
Art Gallery of Ontario, Gift of Milton Winberg, 2016
2017/51
Photo: AGO, Craig Boyko

OPPOSITE
Time Machine Series, 1961
Oil on canvas
203.2 × 269.9 cm
Art Gallery of Ontario,
Gift from the McLean Foundation, 1966
65/25
Photo: AGO, Craig Boyko

Hallucination combines Wieland's colour field painting with graffiti, cartooning, text fragments, and filmic sequencing. The circle is a dominant motif in this work: in addition to the collaged cloth pieces, she draws and paints a variety of circles in blue and green, the dominant hues of the composition. The circles dance over the surface, effervescent, igniting a sense of movement and energy. In a dark-blue circle at the centre of the painting, Wieland has written "STOP," a pictorial interruption that relates formally to a frieze of chalkboard-like line drawings running along the bottom of the canvas that contains two erect penises. The penis motifs, which she later named "sex poetry," are clandestine in this painting. They recur in works throughout the 1960s at varying degrees of covertness, and epitomize her humour and interest in erotic imagery, as well as the element of secrecy. She noted in a 1985 interview: "There are always secrets in my work [during] this period because I felt there should be levels in all works, and of course in the greatest works there are many secrets that don't come to you immediately."[3]

RENÉE VAN DER AVOIRD

3 Transcript of Joyce Wieland artist's talk at the University of Lethbridge, 1985, 3 (edited quote from cassette tape "Joyce Wieland on Her Work"); transcript held at the University of Lethbridge Art Gallery, Alberta.

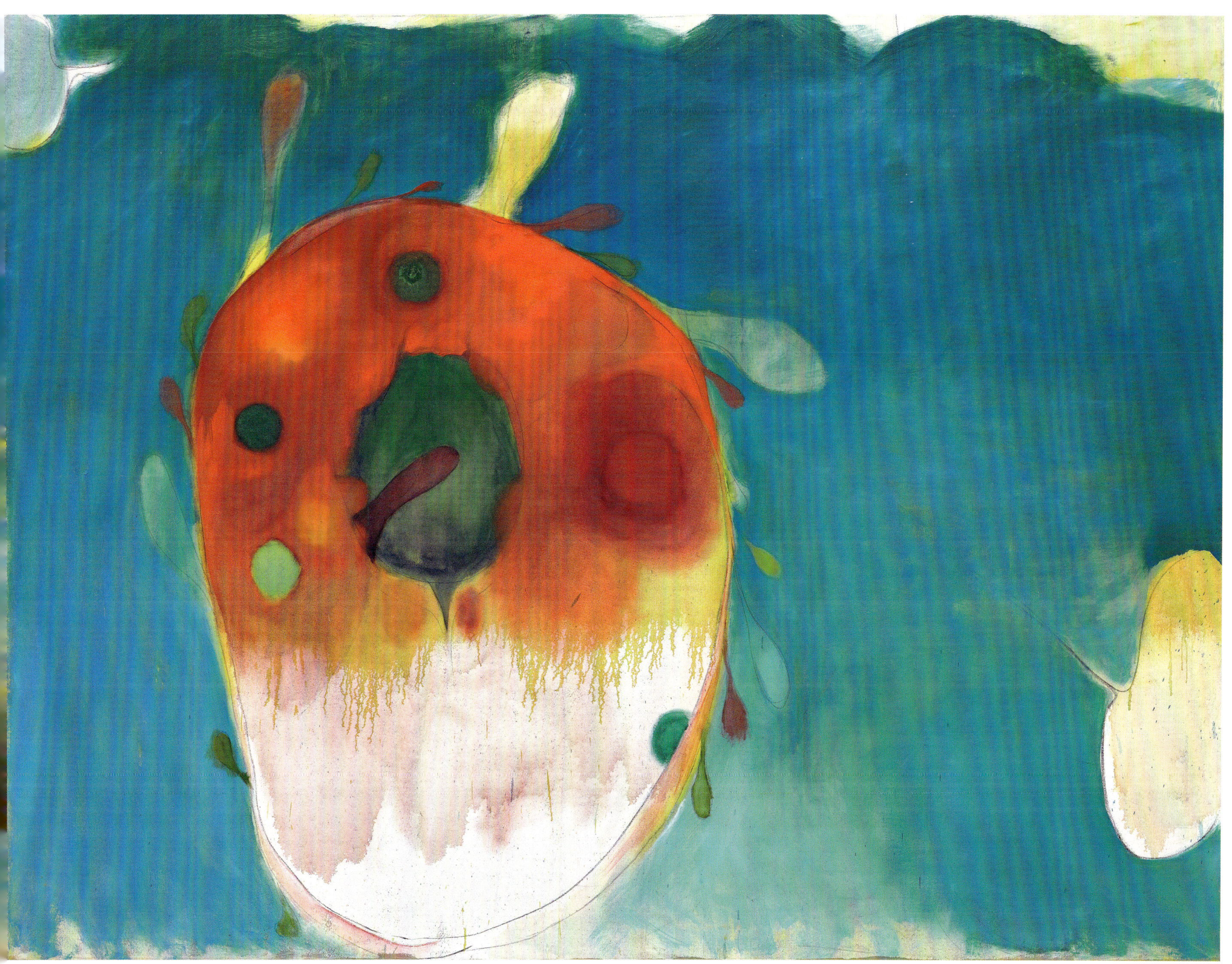

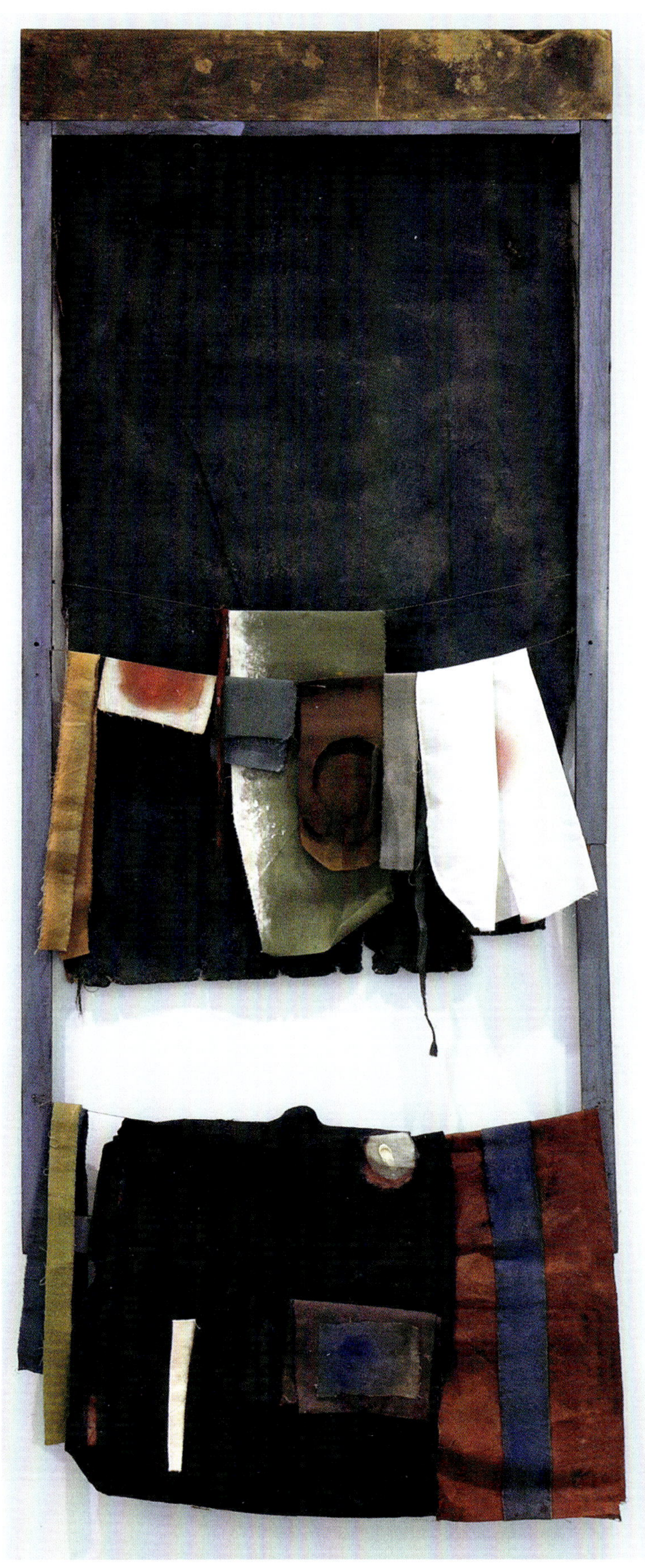

LEFT

The Clothes of Love, 1961
Cloth assemblage
176 × 75 cm
Collection of Rachel Barney

OPPOSITE

Balling, 1961
Oil on canvas
193.2 × 233.6 cm
National Gallery of Canada,
Purchased 1968
15457
Photo: NGC

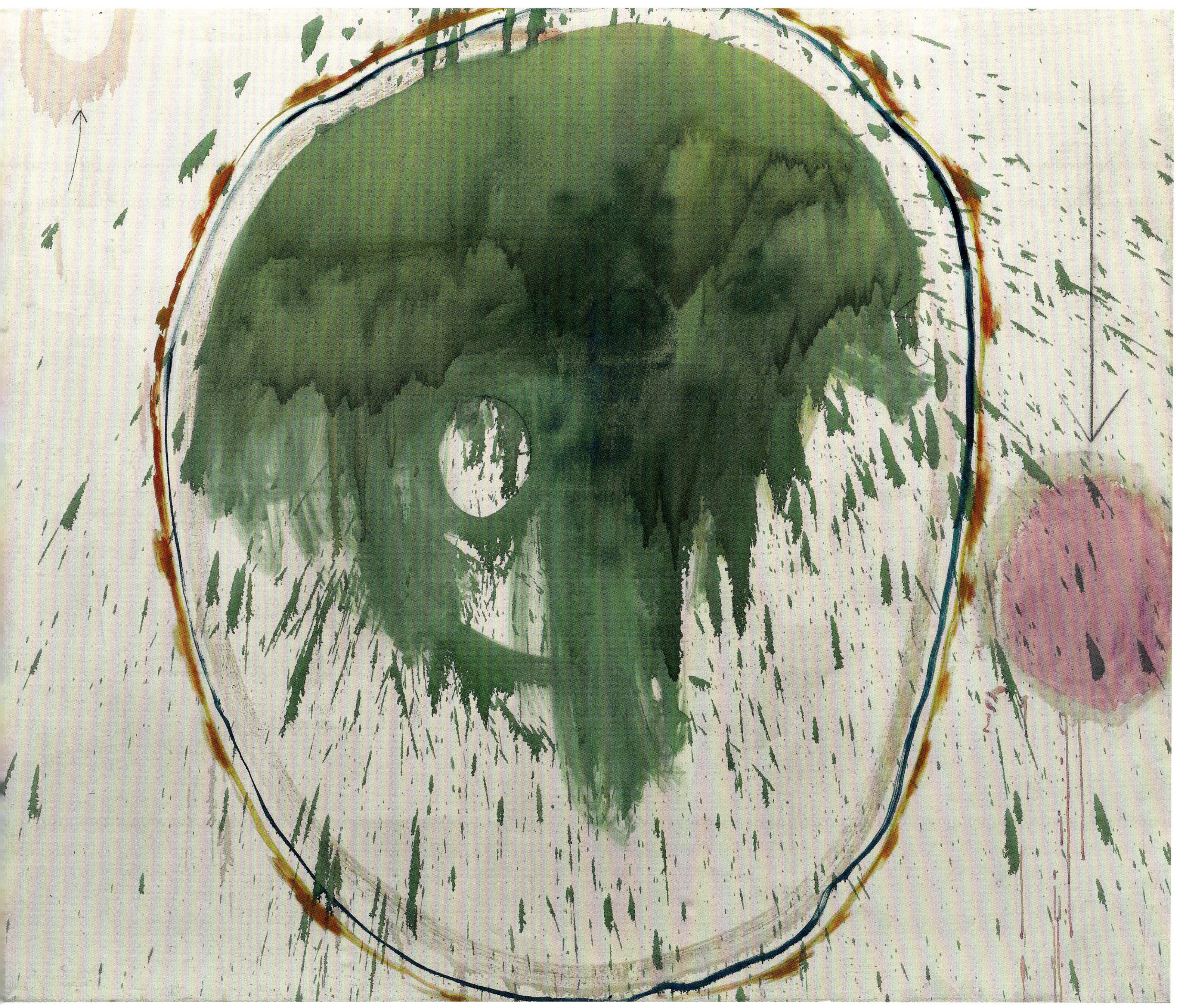

In late 1962, Joyce Wieland and artist Michael Snow (1928–2023) moved to New York City, where they remained until 1971. It would prove to be a crucial decade in Wieland's career, one in which she established her reputation as an avant-garde filmmaker and produced paintings, assemblages, and textiles that she exhibited regularly in Toronto. After devoting her first year in New York primarily to painting, she turned in earnest to film, having already familiarized herself with the medium in Toronto. An analogous relationship developed between Wieland's experimental filmmaking and her visual arts practice during the 1960s.

A recurring motif in her painting was the depiction of sinking boats and crashing airplanes, images from television and newspapers that she considered embodied an American fascination with disasters. The works, which Wieland called "filmic paintings," were characterized by a distinctive formal structure: a grid of sequentially moving images akin to filmstrips or storyboards. Although the artist had already adopted this type of composition before making her first film in New York, she would later transpose it to works in other media as well.

FLICK PICS

Wooden boxes used for packing were among the materials Wieland found on the streets that she repurposed to create sculptural narrative sequences. The disaster theme—evoked by Readymade toy ships and airplanes—also appears in these compartmentalized works, brought into the domestic sphere by their shelf-like construction. Among the objects in the assemblages are a series of coffee cups with lipstick marks, a sugar cube (a nod to Duchamp), a brush, a ring, and a large heart featuring a romantic image of a young woman. Alluding to the passage of time, beauty, love, and death, Wieland offers in these works a contemporary and feminine memento mori.

Her films, paintings, and plastic hangings were permeated by overt political content that reflected a preoccupation with contemporary issues, including her opposition to the war in Vietnam, and marked the beginning of her exploration of national identity.

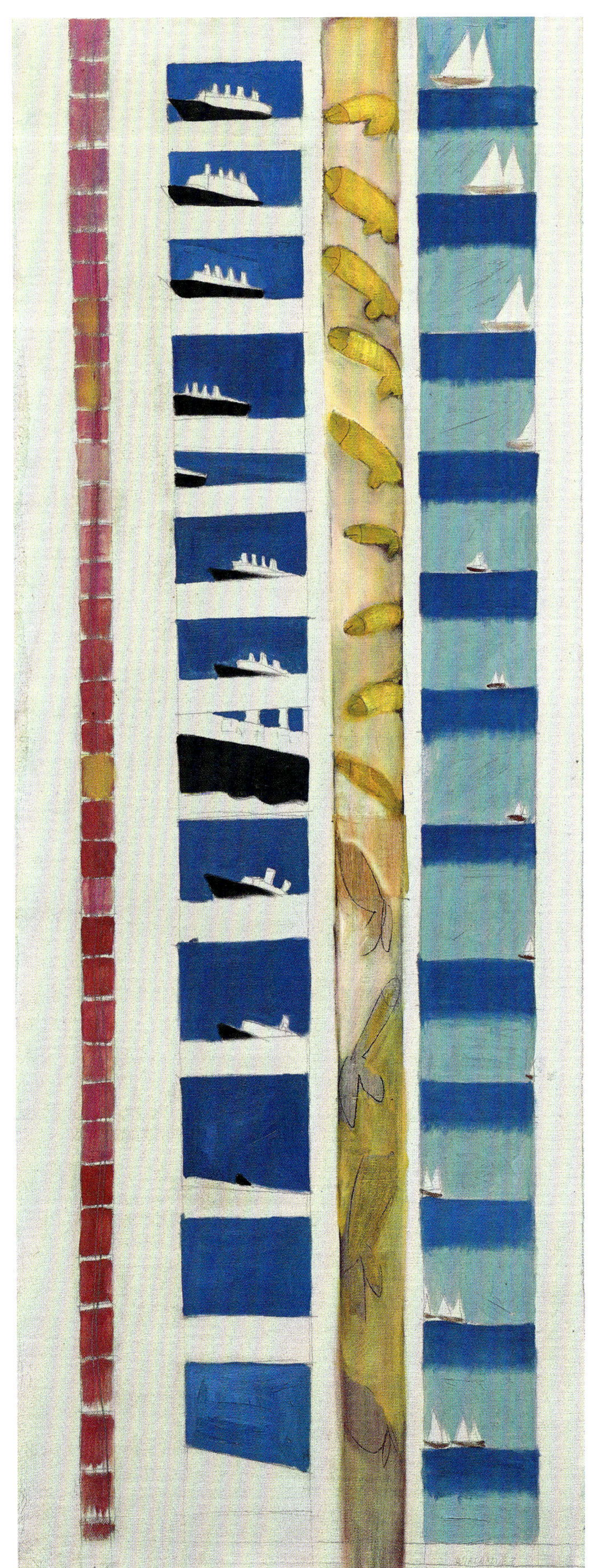

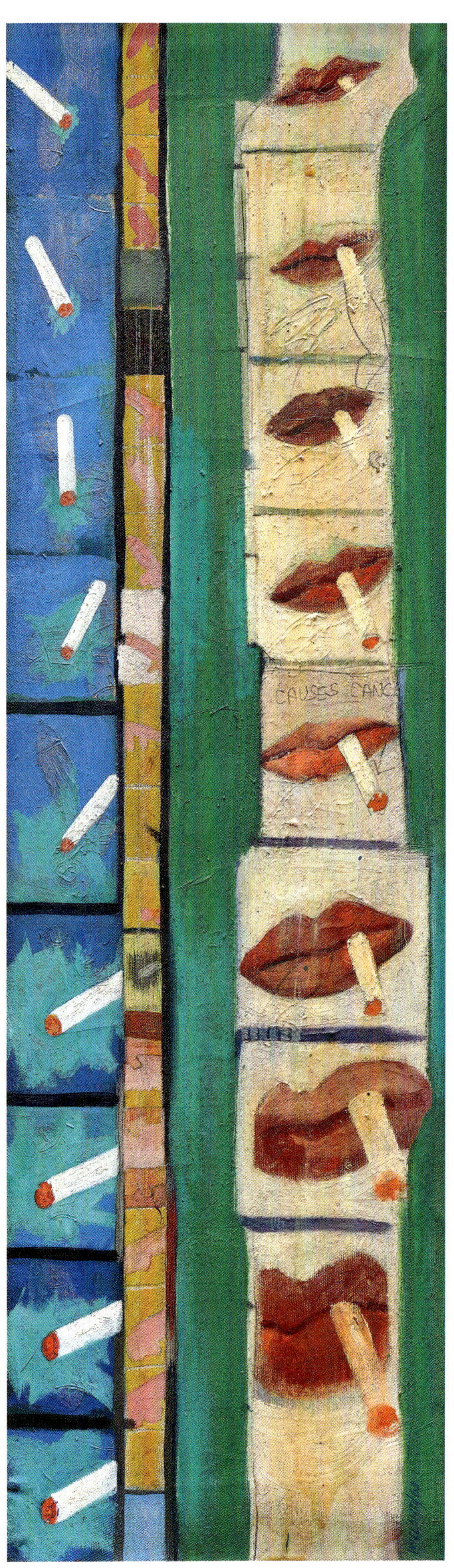

LEFT
Flick Pics #4, 1963
Oil on canvas
106.6 × 40.8 cm
Art Gallery of Ontario, Gift of Morton and Carol Rapp, 2007
2007/429
Photo: AGO, Craig Boyko

RIGHT
West 4th, 1963
Oil on canvas
76.2 × 22.9 cm
Private Collection
Photo: AGO, Craig Boyko

FLICK PICS #4, 1963
WEST 4TH, 1963

There are many resonances between *Flick Pics #4* and *West 4th*, two of Joyce Wieland's filmic paintings from 1963. In *Flick Pics #4*, an ocean liner and a sailboat float in separate vertical sequences. They drift back and forth, coming closer into view and then suddenly disappearing. The jolting animation contrasts with gradual changes in the central image, a cartoon penis in various states of arousal. On the far left, a blurred band of small crimson squares resembling a flickering filmstrip accompanies these nautical and anatomical images.

In *West 4th*, a narrow storyboard similarly shows a metamorphosing penis in the central strip. The phallus is flanked on one side by a lit cigarette falling through the air, and on the other by a set of red-lipsticked lips smoking a cigarette. Wieland has pencilled in the words "causes cancer" above the lips, which come increasingly closer into view midway through the composition. Although this imagery is characteristic of her work—penis, lipsticked mouth—the narrative is less straightforward. The succession of images is ambiguous and can be read in any direction. Like in *Flick Pics #4*, temporality is distorted. The title, *West 4th*, signifies New York City geography: it is a street that bisects Greenwich Village, not far from Wieland's home and studio.

In both paintings there is a potential plight: the falling cigarette in *West 4th* echoes that of the sinking ocean liner in *Flick Pics #4*. Both objects are out of control; however, their dilemmas are not sensationalized. Rather, like the plane crashes and ship disasters in her other paintings from this period, the accidents are presented matter-of-factly. This deadpan response to human tragedy is an expression of Wieland's political awareness while in New York City during the 1960s. "There is the American fascination with disaster and grotesque happenings in the newspaper and on television and it has come out in the work I've been doing."[1] However, she has also noted that her disaster works are based on personal paranoia, dealing with death and loss in her own life.

When Wieland showed these paintings at The Isaacs Gallery in 1963, Toronto critics were astonished by the penis imagery. "For even the initiated, Miss Wieland's work is always a shock: there are parts of the body that one simply doesn't expect to see singled out and painted in such aroused form all over the canvas."[2] It was about more than shock for Wieland, though. She employed the penis as both an emblem of self-awareness—inserting herself into a male's art world—and as a comedic gesture, caricaturing the phallus to a point of mere ornamentation.

RENÉE VAN DER AVOIRD

1 Quoted in Jonathan Holstein, "New York's Vitality Tonic for Canadian Artists," *Canadian Art* 21, no. 5 (September/October 1964): 278.

2 *New Paintings: Joyce Wieland*, Robin Green, *Toronto Daily Star*, November 23, 1963.

COOLING ROOM I, 1964
COOLING ROOM II, 1964

"It's not just painting, not just art," Joyce Wieland told a journalist in 1960. Dadaists "are artistic in a general way ... anti-romantic. They see things whole. Their jokes are about life."[1] Wieland's work in *Dada at The Isaacs Gallery* (December 20, 1961–January 9, 1962) marked her turn toward assemblage. Drawing on deep wells of absurd humour, Wieland channelled the Dada impulse to collapse art and life, making objects with allusions to the everyday. *The Clothes of Love* (1961) (p. 78), included in her first single-artist exhibition with Isaacs, developed this approach further: a wall-mounted open box with fabric elements, some painted, hanging as if on a miniature clothesline.

Wieland's assemblages—of which *Cooling Room I* (p. 84), *Cooling Room II* (p. 86), and *Young Woman's Blues* (p. 90) (all 1964) are paradigmatic examples—come out of these earlier experiments and against this Dadaist background. The boxes allowed Wieland to approximate the same mode of address as painting, while giving her abandon to manipulate objects in real space.[2] Messy and haptic, these multipart sculptures have affinities with Robert Rauschenberg's *Combines* series of the mid-1950s, Joseph Cornell's (1903–1972) boxes from the 1930s, and, earlier still, Kurt Schwitters' (1887–1948) "merz" assemblages beginning in 1918; though, unlike these antecedents, Wieland's constructions are often segmented, with each part given its own frame.

These frames are three-dimensional extrapolations of Wieland's so-called filmic paintings from around 1962–1963 ("compartmented paintings," as Lucy Lippard called them).[3] Each shelf and cubby is seen frontally as a drawn line, a boundary between parts. Wieland gleaned the wooden boxes from a neighbourhood cheese shop in Greenwich Village or along the Hudson River piers, some of them stamped "cooling room," giving rise to the titles.[4]

As well as using common materials, Wieland often devised a recombinant vocabulary within a body of related works. In these three assemblages, the recurring elements include an emblematic red heart; a model plane, crashing in the *Rooms* and taking off in *Blues*; and ships—a tugboat making its way across the top register of *Cooling Room I*, and an ocean liner wedged, immovable, in

1 Sara Bowser, "Joyce Wieland," *Canadian Architect* 5, no. 10 (1960): 69, 71.

2 Box-like constructions have been used by artists as varied as Joseph Cornell, Liz Magor, and Robert Gober, always hanging productively between painting and sculpture.

3 Lucy Lippard, *Pop Art* (London: Thames and Hudson, 1966), 196.

4 Leone Kirkwood, "Canadian Artist in New York Excels in Nameless Art Form," *The Globe and Mail*, March 17, 1965; Marie Fleming, *Joyce Wieland*, exh. cat. (Toronto: Art Gallery of Ontario, 1987): 56.

OPPOSITE
Cooling Room I, 1964
Found objects mounted in painted wooden case
96.5 × 80 × 29.2 cm
The University of Lethbridge Art Collections,
Gift of Vivian and David Campbell, Toronto, 1989
1989.36
Photo: The University of Lethbridge Art Collections

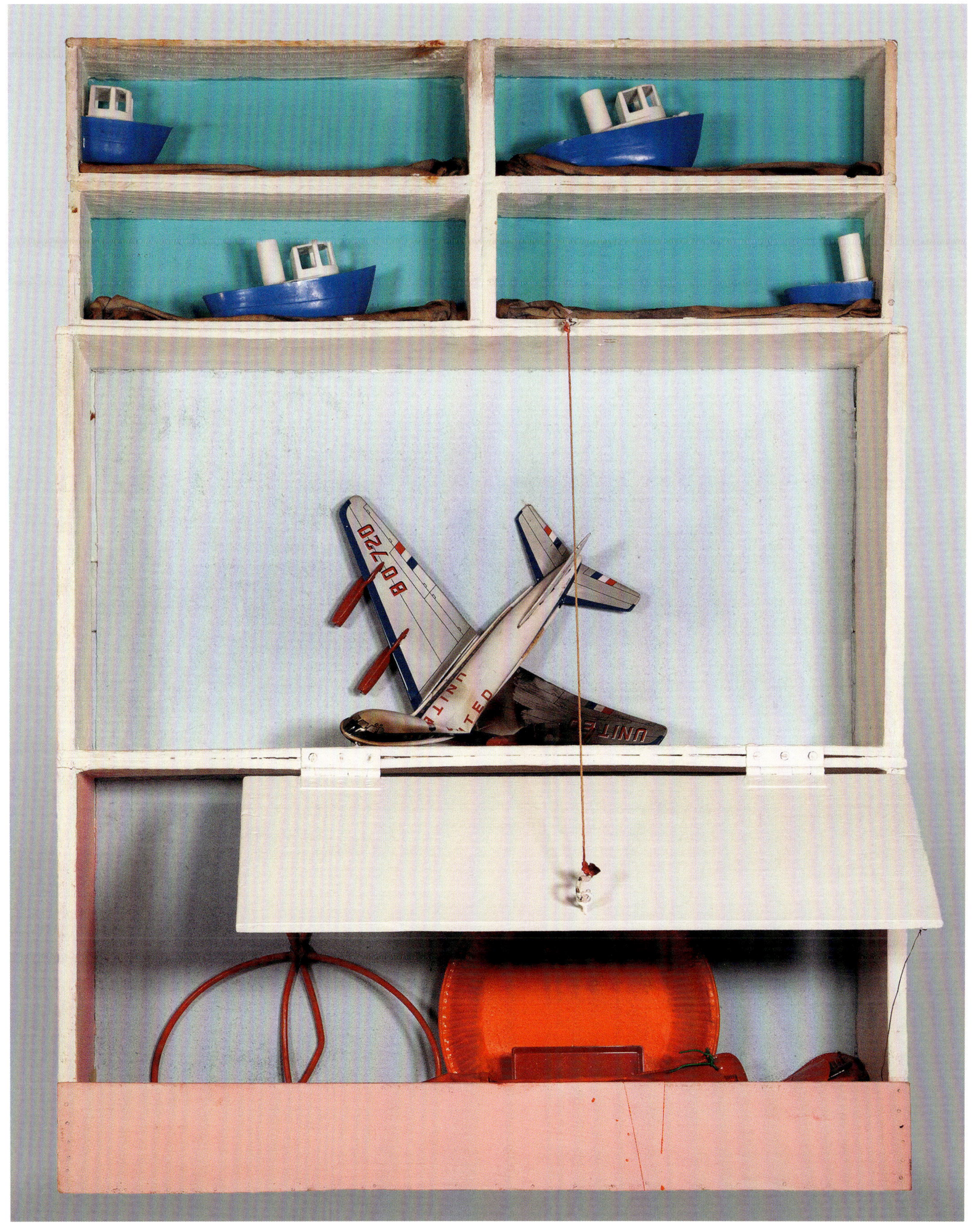
BO 720
UNIT
UNIT

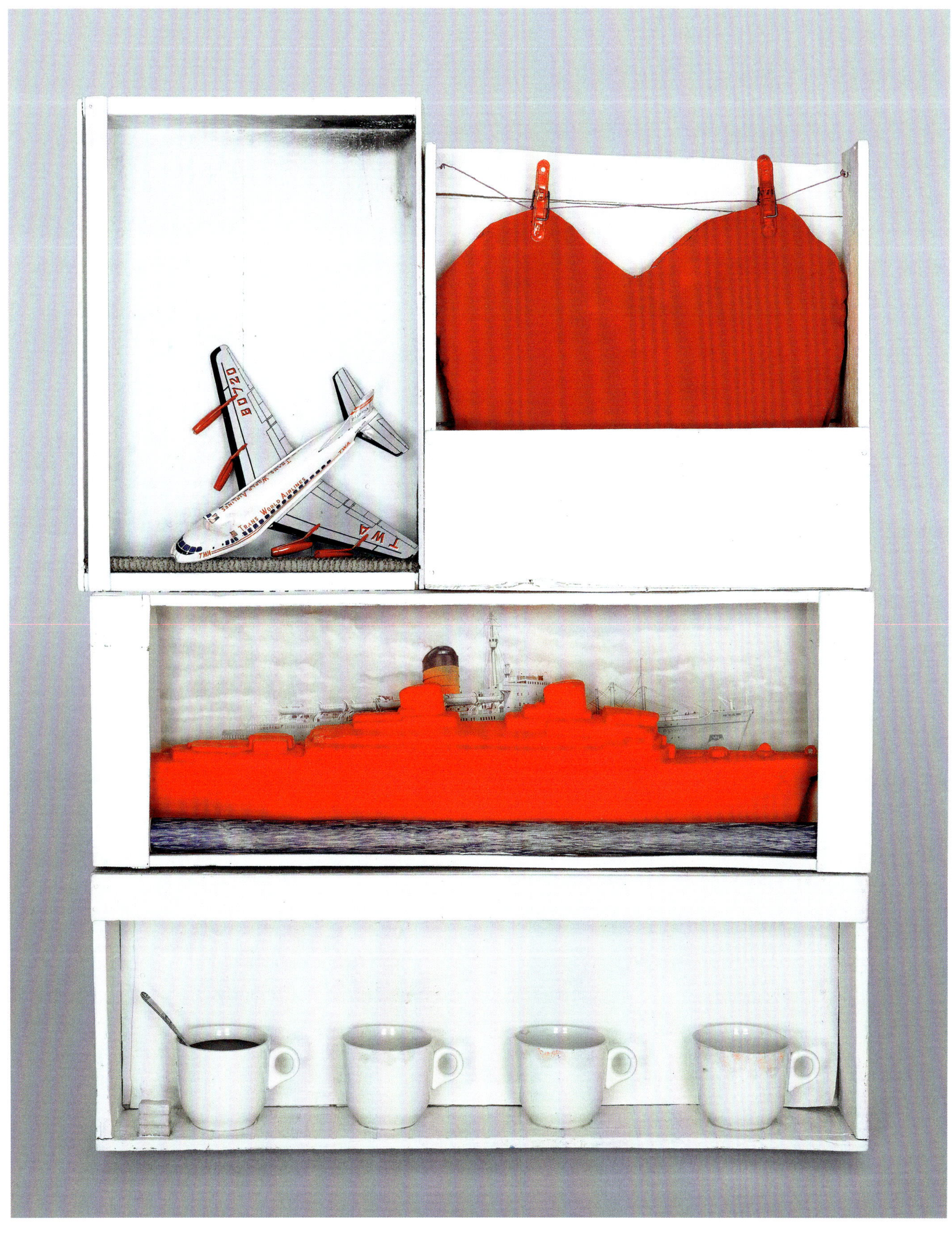
TRANS WORLD AIRLINES
TWA

its frame, doubled against a reproduction of the same in *Cooling Room II*. Wieland builds duration into these boxes, just as she represents time in her filmic paintings.

Though the object varies, the strategy remains the same: the tugboats and coffee cups are analogues, marking time and alluding to daily life. As she described in an artist talk at the University of Lethbridge in 1986, "the animation of . . . the cup with the accumulating lipstick on it [is] sort of reminiscent of being in a studio where there's lots of coffee cups and this sort of thing happened every day."[5] Wieland takes a repeated element and changes its position relative to its frame (the boat) or removes or marks an object (sugar cube, lipstick marks, and coffee). This repetition with difference is the hallmark of her celebrated lithograph *O Canada* (1970) (p. 149), which, not coincidentally, also uses lipsticked lips as indexical marks. Kissing the lithography stone or drinking from a porcelain cup, Wieland makes a shape and then repeats it, describing the passing of time. She sings and she drinks.

ADAM WELCH

OPPOSITE
Cooling Room II, 1964
Wood, paint, metal toy airplane, cloth, metal wire, plastic boat, paper collage, ceramic, cups with lipstick, spoon, mounted in painted wooden case
114.4 × 94 × 18.3 cm
National Gallery of Canada, Purchased 1971
16706
Photo: NGC

5 Transcript of Joyce Wieland artist's talk at the University of Lethbridge, 1985, 4 (edited quote from cassette tape "Joyce Wieland on Her Work"); transcript held at the University of Lethbridge Art Gallery, Alberta.

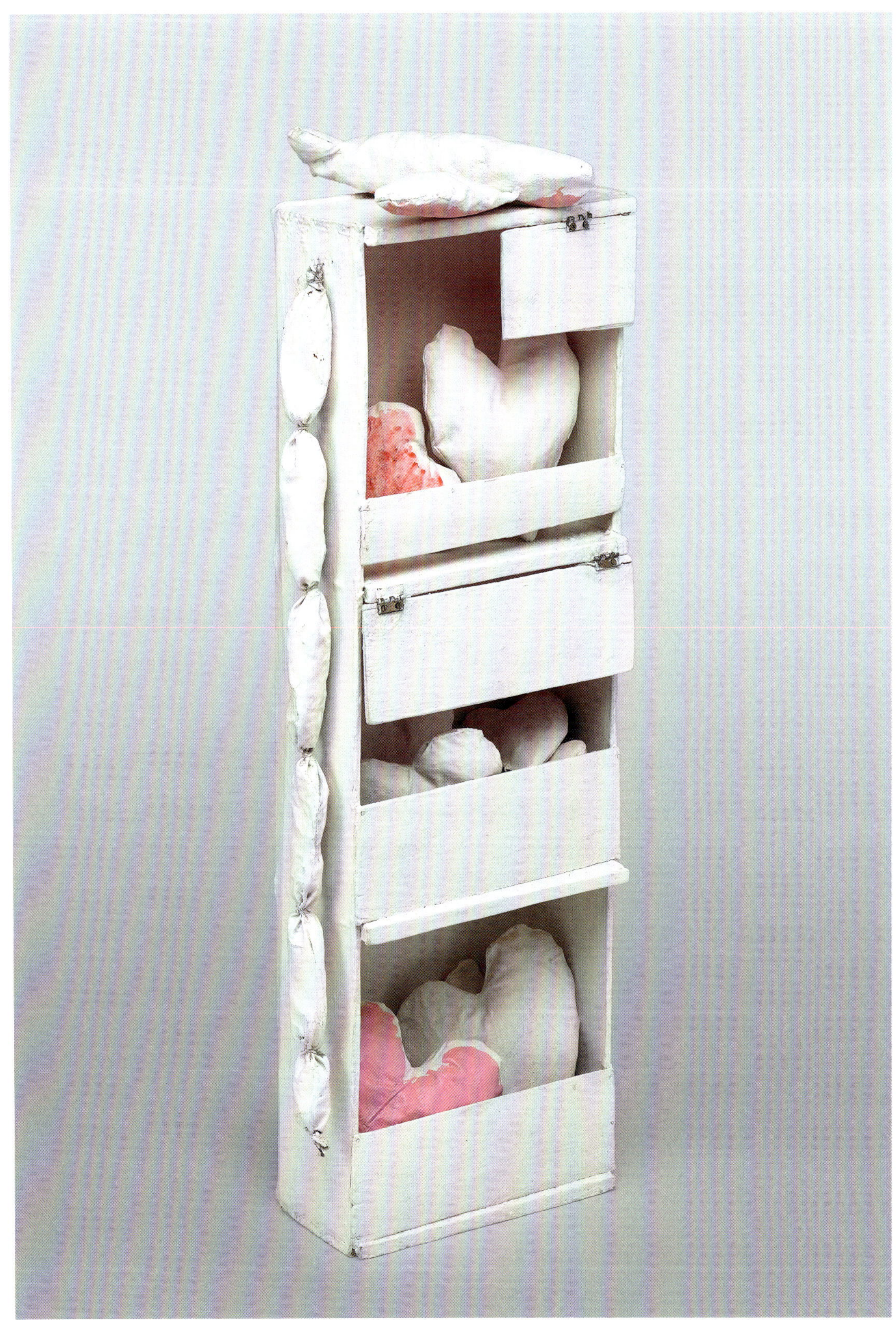

Passengers, 1965
Mixed media construction
67.3 × 22.2 × 11.4 cm
Art Gallery of Ontario, Purchased with funds donated by Susan and Greg Latremoille, Toronto, 2007
2007/62
Photo: AGO, Craig Boyko

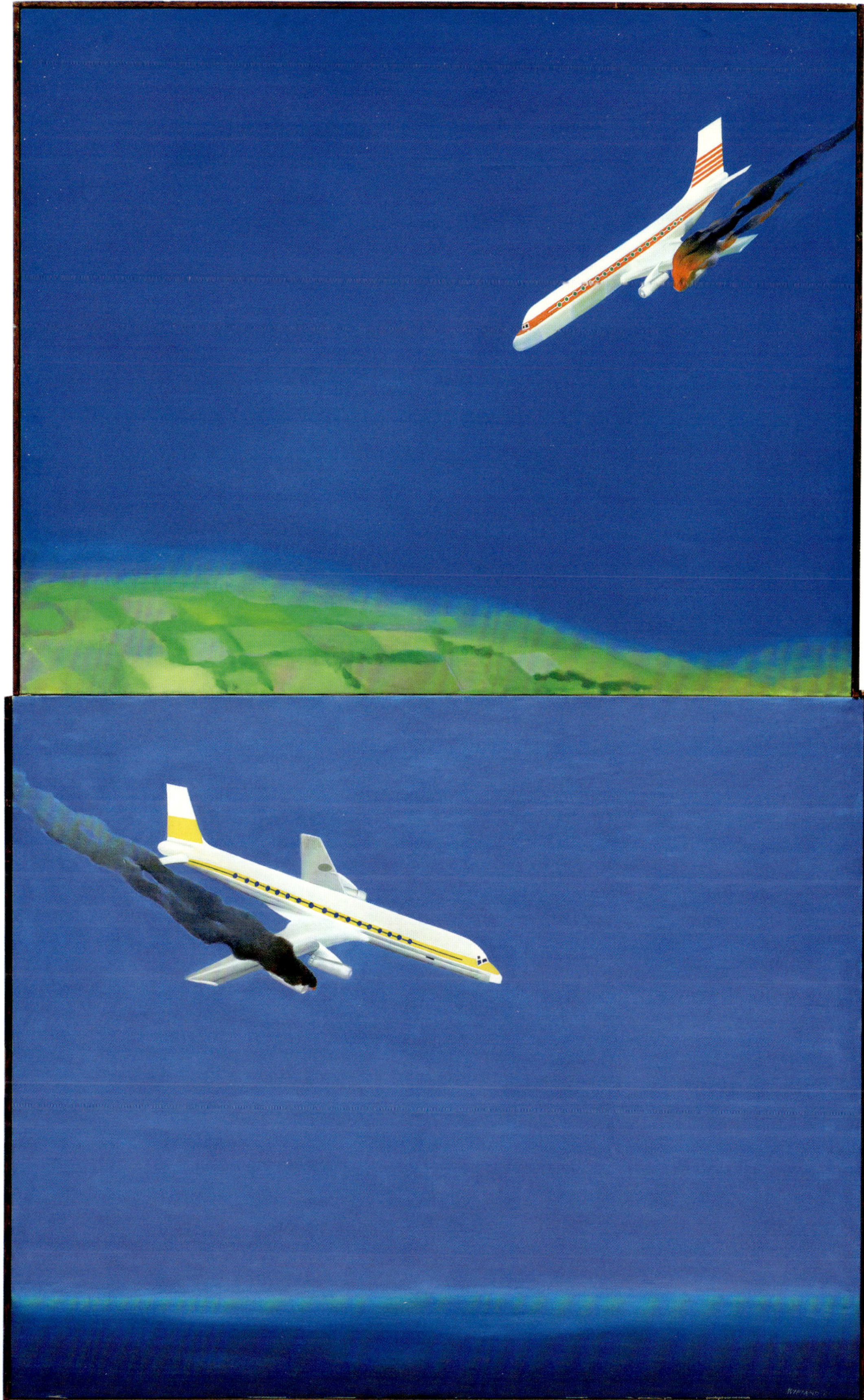

Double-Crash, 1966
Oil on canvas
201.5 × 127.7 cm
Collection of The Robert McLaughlin Gallery, Purchase, 1976
1976WJ57ab
Photo: Laura Findlay

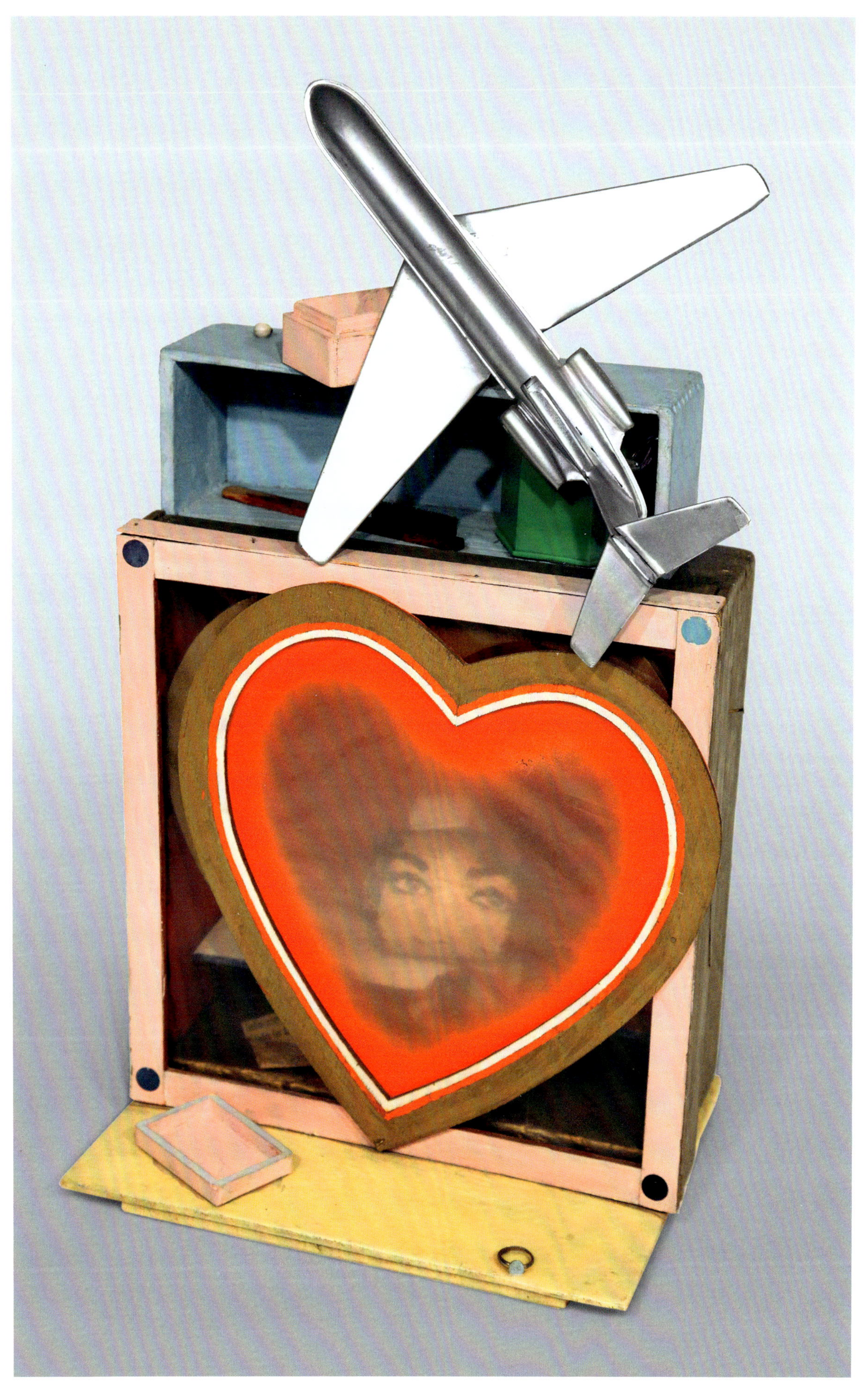

Young Woman's Blues, 1964
Found objects,
painted wooden case
53.3 × 30.5 × 22.2 cm
The University of Lethbridge
Art Collections, Purchased
with funds provided by Canada
Council Special Purchase Grant
1986.72
Photo: The University of
Lethbridge Art Collections

YOUNG WOMAN'S BLUES, 1964

Young Woman's Blues is a box-like construction with familiar elements: a model plane, a red heart, and ready-made printed matter. It privileges a heart-shaped screen through which cut-out illustrations are seen, most prominently a cropped image of a young woman's face. A brush sits incongruously on the ledge above. Together, these impart a sense of domestic labour and confinement that, along with the title, frame the work in gendered terms.

Young Woman's Blues was made while Wieland was living in a loft at 191 Greenwich Street between early 1963 and early 1965—prior to the building being razed to make way for the World Trade Center. Unlike Michael Snow, who maintained a separate studio space, Wieland almost always made her work at home. Both Wieland and Snow scavenged the neighbourhood not only to provide materials for their work but also to adapt their shared living space. As their friend Helen Parmelee wrote in 1963, the loft was furnished "from the streets."[1] For her constructions from this period, Wieland sourced discarded wooden boxes from a Greenwich Village cheese shop. "I just take them. I don't ask permission. Of course it's daylight and people see me. I feel like quite a dope."[2]

Wieland's days were divided between her art and film practice and working as hostess or short-order cook at Phase Two, a coffee house at 302 Bleecker Street. Snow, who had started out as a jazz pianist and was influenced by Greenwich Village fixture Thelonius Monk (1917–1982), began performing there in 1962. Wieland's experiences at Phase Two may appear veiled in the stained coffee cups in *Cooling Room II* (p. 86) or the cleaning brush in *Blues*. Put in stark terms, as Simone de Beauvoir wrote in *The Second Sex* (1949), women's clothes "doom her to impotence": "stockings run; heels wear down; light-coloured blouses and dresses get dirty."[3] To this, add coffee cups that need washing.

A year after making the *Rooms* and *Blues*, Wieland made other box-like assemblages: *Passengers* (p. 88) and *Dad's Dead* (both 1965). They feature, as she told Leone Kirkwood in 1965, "stuffed shapes in boxes." Both works included representations of "hearts and male reproductive organs," made up of underwear, newspapers, bits of fabric and old dresses. "I encase them in cotton. Then I paint them." "It's very female to put things into other things like boxes," Wieland continues, "in a way you could say it's female to limit things."[4]

ADAM WELCH

1 Helen Parmelee, "Joyce Is a Zen Cook," *Toronto Telegram*, November 23, 1963.

2 Quoted in Leone Kirkwood, "Canadian Artist in New York Excels in Nameless Art Form," *The Globe and Mail*, March 17, 1965, 3. Simone de Beauvoir, *The Second Sex*, trans. Constance Borde and Sheila Malovany-Chevalier (1949; repr., London: Jonathan Cape, 2009), 740.

3 Simone de Beauvoir, *The Second Sex (1949)*, trans. Constance Borde and Sheila Malovany-Chevalier (London: Jonathan Cape, 2009), 740.

4 Quoted in Kirkwood, "Canadian Artist in New York."

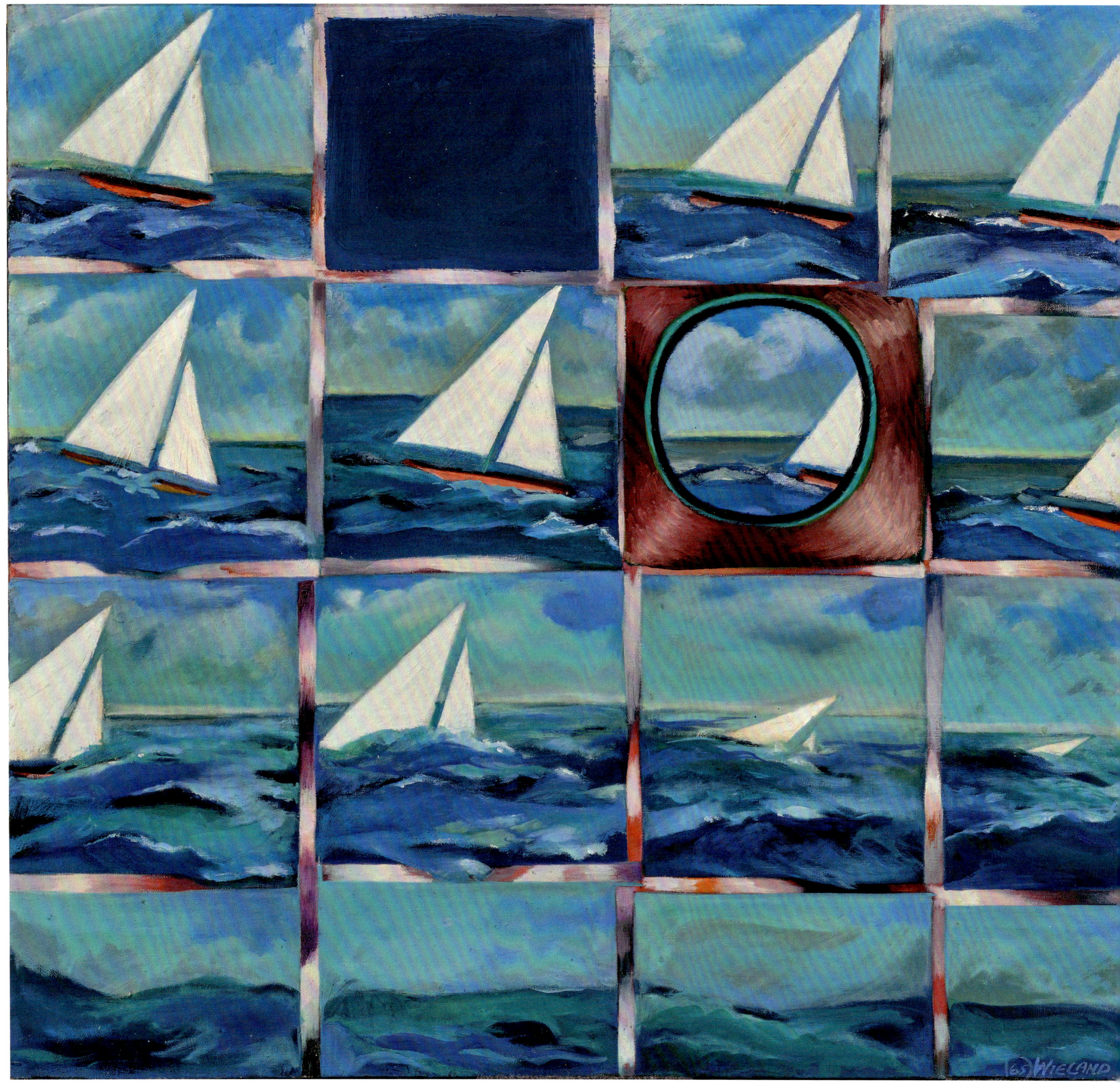
(65) WIELAND

SAILBOAT SINKING, 1965

"There was a tiny downtown museum, The Ships Museum, that I used to go to often. The filmic paintings started to revive then—so much of my work was already influenced by making animated films, doing storyboards and a lot of things that were serial."[1]

Wieland's recollection of her years in New York City during the 1960s reveals the inspiration of her series of paintings of sinking boats and ships, as well as her 1967 short film *Sailboat*. In *Sailboat Sinking*, a cutter navigates choppy waters in a dramatic sequence formed by the appearance, partial disappearance, reappearance, and gradual sinking depicted over the sixteen frames that make up the work. The second square is blocked out completely, the sailboat at sea replaced with opaque black paint. This section of blacked-out canvas interrupting the illusion of the sequential narrative is perhaps a play on the language of structural films, akin to empty acetate or film leader running through the projector with no image, foreshadowing the ship's eventual fate. Wieland often stated her affection for art enriched by layered meanings, a bit of mystery, secrets.

In the second row, a circle is painted within the panel, suggesting the view from a porthole through which we get only a glimpse of the boat as it sails past. The modernist grid organizing the tragic tale contains a painterly pattern within; a close look reveals brushstrokes in shades of pink, blue, and mauve overlapping seamlessly. Wieland allows the churning waves to lick the grid, thus undermining the complete separation between each frame. This is an additional reminder of the materiality of the painting, and the manner in which she sets up playful dialogues between media and interrupts formalist conventions.

ANNE GRACE

Sailboat Sinking, 1965
Oil on canvas
76 × 81 cm
Collection of Munro Ferguson
Photo: MMFA, Jean-François Brière

1 Lauren Rabinovitz, "An Interview with Joyce Wieland," *Afterimage* 8, no. 10 (May 1981): 9.

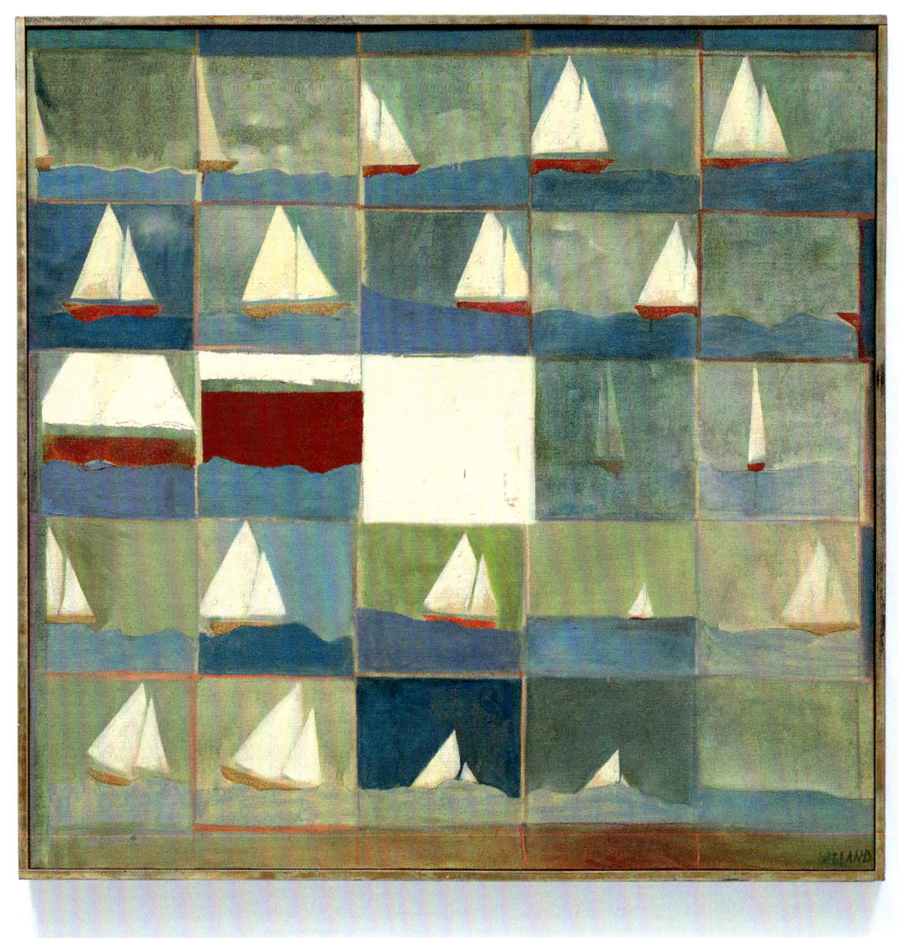

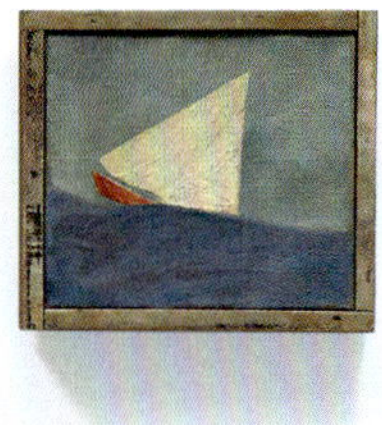

ABOVE
Sailboat Tragedy and Spare Part, 1963
Oil on canvas
151 × 159 cm
Collection of the Vancouver Art Gallery,
Permanent Collection Fund
VAG 78.8 a–b
Photo: Vancouver Art Gallery

RIGHT
Sailing Scene, 1963
Oil on canvas
45.7 × 35.6 cm
Collection of Katia and John Bianchini
Photo: AGO, Sean Weaver

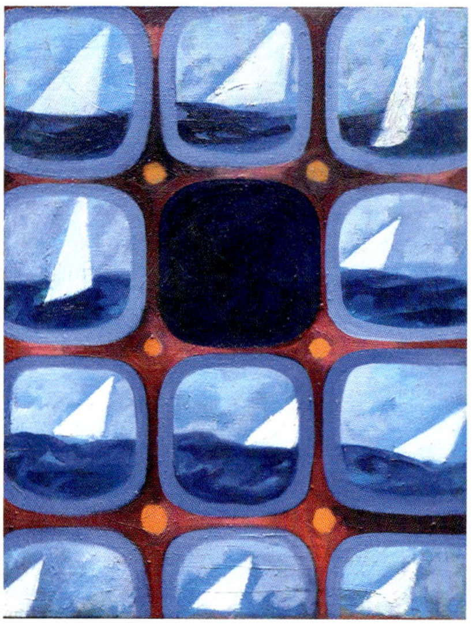

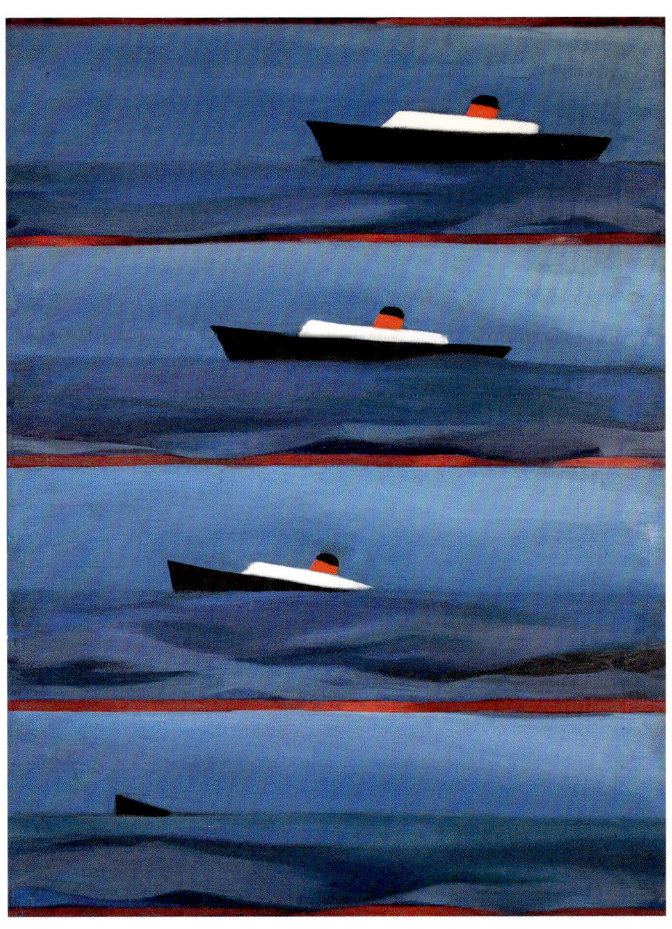

Untitled [Sinking Liner], 1963
Oil on canvas
81 × 61 cm
The University of Lethbridge Art Collections,
Purchased 1985 with funds provided by the Province of Alberta Endowment Fund
1985.28
Photo: The University of Lethbridge Art Collections

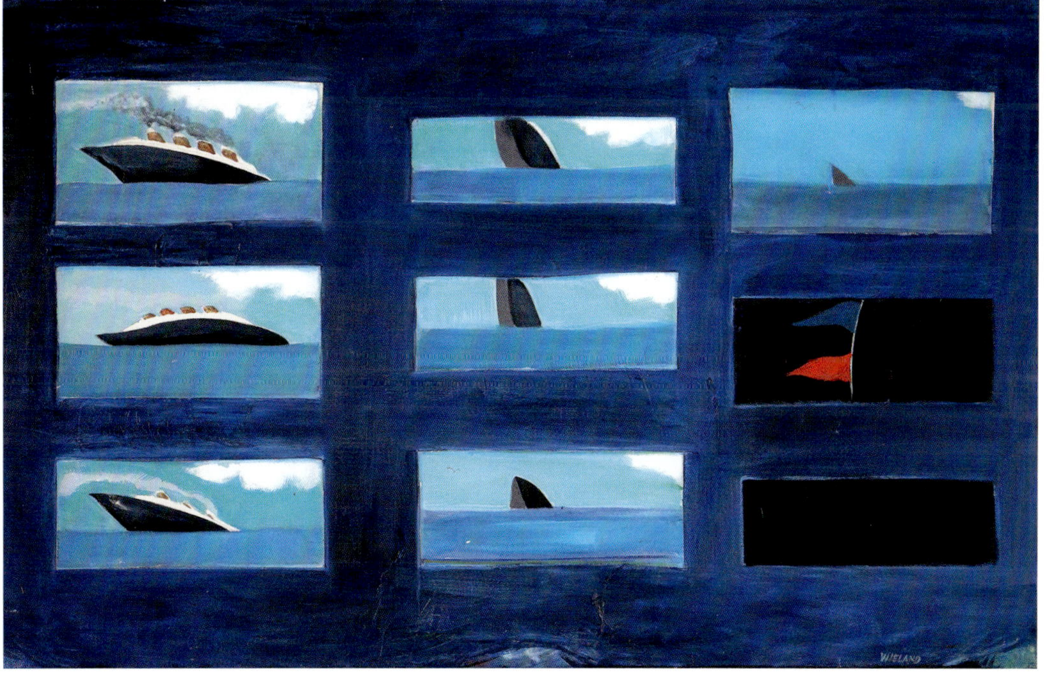

Sinking Liner, 1963
Collage and oil on canvas
63.5 × 101.5 cm
Art Gallery of Hamilton,
Gift of Irving Zucker, 1992
1992.2.6
Photo: Mike Lalich, 2008

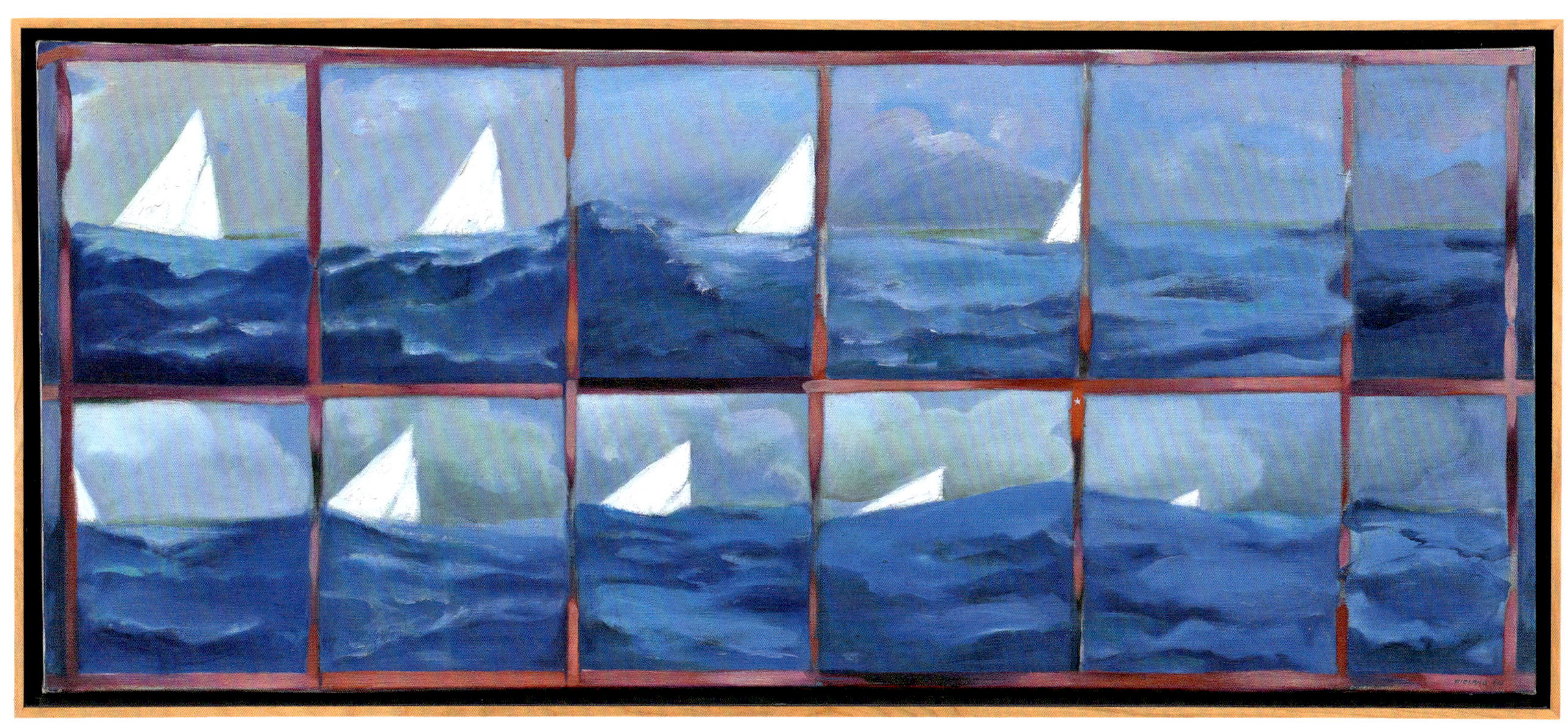

Boat Tragedy, 1964
Oil on canvas
50.2 × 121.9 cm
Art Gallery of Ontario, Gift from the Dominion Bank, 1965
64/23
Photo: AGO, Craig Boyko

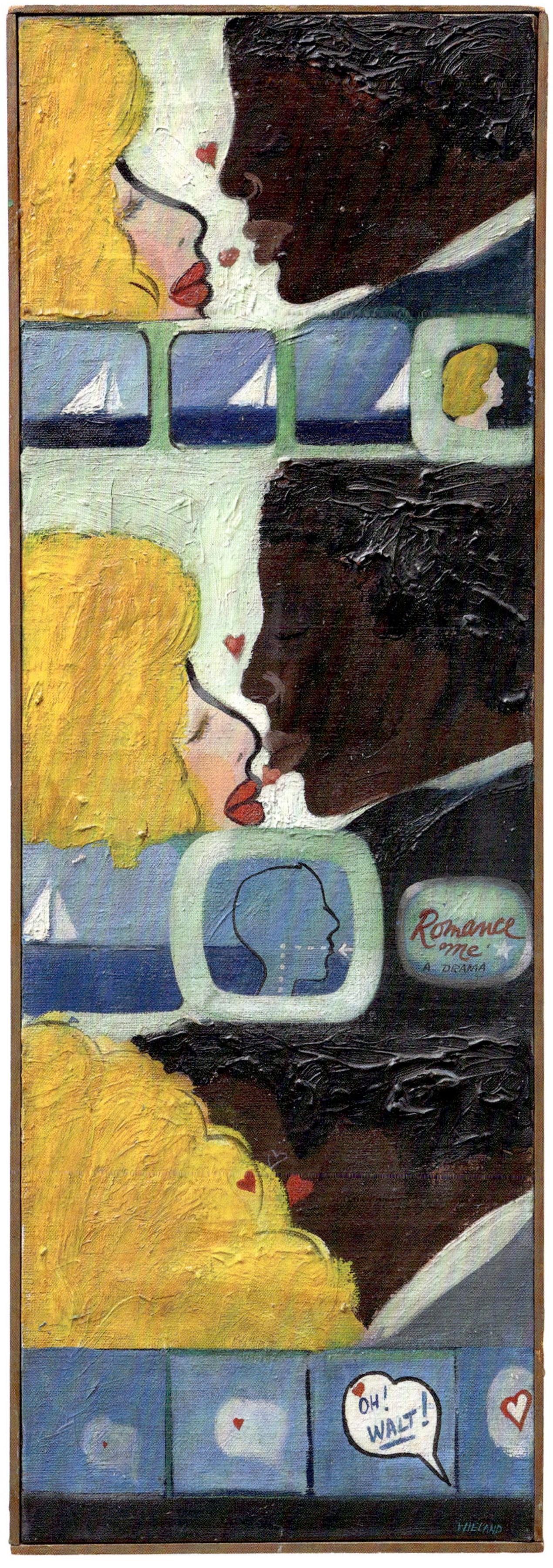

First Integrated Film with a Short on Sailing, 1963
Oil on canvas
66 × 22.7 cm
Collection of Les G. Lawrence, Toronto
Photo: AGO, Craig Boyko

OPPOSITE
March on Washington, 1963
Oil on canvas
37.5 × 42.5 cm
Art Gallery of Hamilton, Gift of Irving Zucker, 1992
1992.2.8
Photo: Mike Lalich, 2008

MARCH ON WASHINGTON, 1963

On August 28, 1963, Joyce Wieland travelled—in the company of Michael Snow and Canadian filmmakers Graeme Ferguson (1929–2021) and Dave Shackman (d. 1965)—from New York City to Washington, DC, in support of the March on Washington for Jobs and Freedom.[1] The event was a turning point in the struggle for American civil rights, bringing together over 250,000 protestors in a loud collective call for congressional passage of the Civil Rights Act, full integration of public schools, and enactment of a bill prohibiting job discrimination. To say the list of official attendees and speakers was remarkable is an understatement. Dr. Martin Luther King Jr. (1929–1968) took to the podium, closing the day with his legendary "I Have a Dream" speech.

Wieland's participation in this momentous event did not go undocumented. She had been living in New York just shy of a year at the time of the march. While her relocation had been somewhat reticent—she stated at the time that she had done so primarily to support Snow's interests—the impact of those early months had a profound effect on her practice. As her contemporary Sylvia Stone (1928–2011), who had been living in New York for nearly two decades, stated in 1964: "New York is simply so fierce."[2] This fierceness, with its attendant art-world misogyny and competition, coupled with an often-deafening political landscape, pushed Wieland to articulate her own vision and voice. She was political, yes, fervently so, but how to express this in a language entirely her own?

She painted *March on Washington* sometime in the months following and sent it to Toronto for her solo exhibition at The Isaacs Gallery in November.[3] At the time, given her increasing interest in filmmaking, she coined the term "filmic painting" to describe a sequential and spatial formal construction. *March on Washington* does not quite fit that bill, but instead presents itself, and its messaging, simultaneously. The signs and symbols include "Freedom Now" on the blue jersey; the Confederate cross and associated stars; and "Wallace" and "Alabama" on the red ribbon clenched tightly between the large, straight white teeth in the upper left.[4] Other symbols are oblique: the lack of readily recognizable flags and banners, the outline of the car.

While Wieland tips her palette to the bright, bold colours and forms of the Pop art movement of the day, the work defies codification. In her deft imagination, the pictorial organization and execution of *March on Washington* mirrors the event itself. While the march was of course temporal in nature, the placards, faces, protest signs, chants, and flags would all have manifested themselves simultaneously in both the experience and memory of that historic day, conflating in a visually and viscerally penetrating reflection. Wieland pays bold homage to this encounter by asking the viewer to adjust accordingly, to make space for the power of her messages, to apprehend and digest instantaneously. As a witness to history, she asks the viewer, in turn, to bear witness to her personal reflection and synthesis of form. In this way, *March on Washington* is part declarative protest, part cautionary tale, and wholly signature Wieland.

TOBI BRUCE

1 Dave Shackman appeared in Wieland's films *Patriotism* (1964) and *Patriotism II* (1965) shortly before his death at an early age.

2 Sylvia Stone in Jonathan Holstein, "New York's Vitality Tonic for Canadian Artists," *Canadian Art* no. 5 (September/October 1964): 271.

3 "Joyce Wieland," The Isaacs Gallery, November 20–December 10, 1963.

4 George Wallace (1919–1998) was elected governor of Alabama in 1962 after campaigning aggressively in favour of racism and segregation. In June 1963, he gained national notoriety when he stood at the entrance of the University of Alabama barring entrance to Black students attempting to register for classes. It took an executive order from President John F. Kennedy (1917–1963), enacted by the general of the Alabama National Guard, for Wallace to move aside.

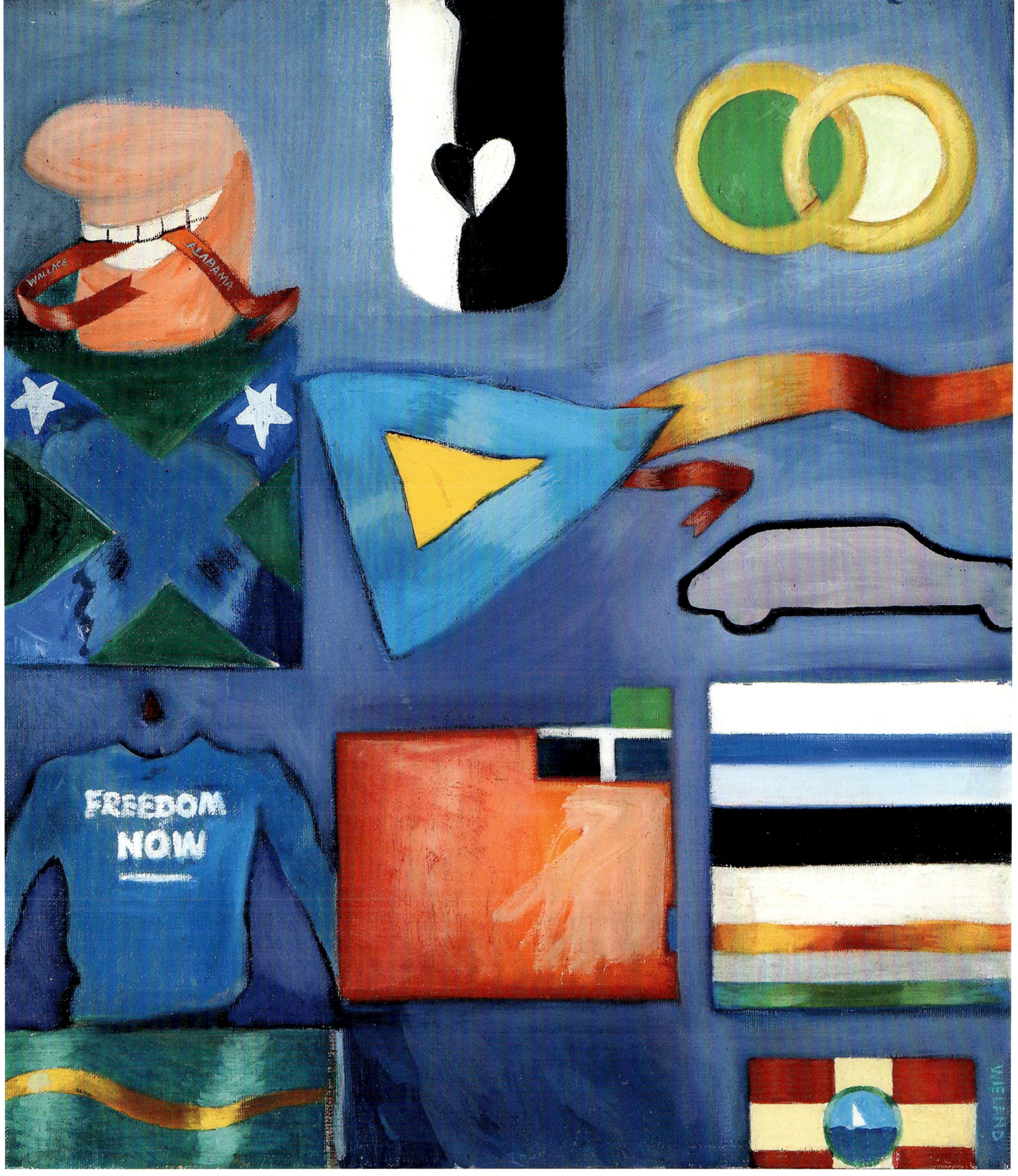
WALLACE
ALABAMA
FREEDOM
NOW
WIELAND

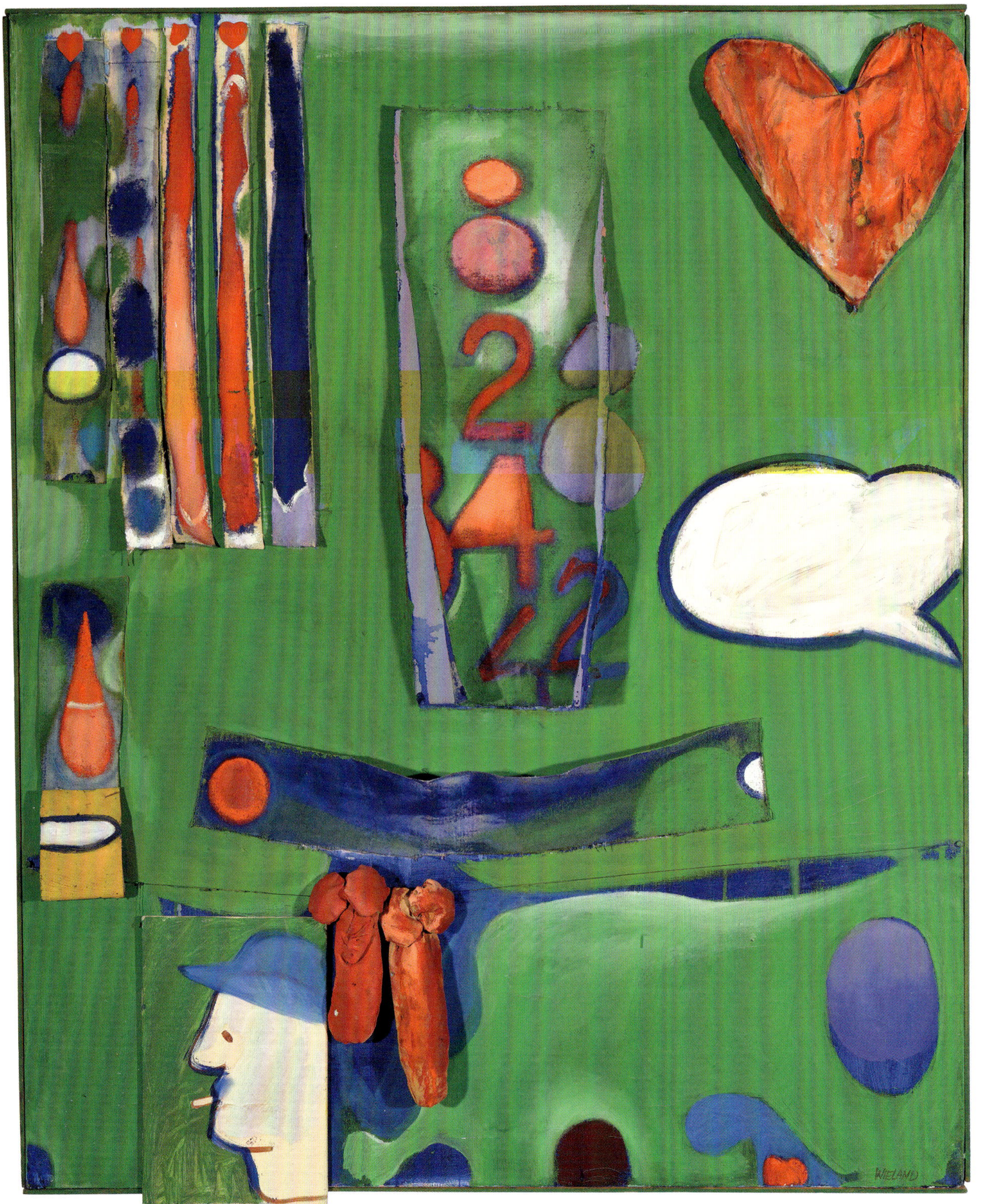

Necktie, 1963
Oil on canvas, cloth, wire, metal
92 × 77 cm
The Montreal Museum of Fine Arts,
Gift of Pierre Théberge in honour of
the Montreal Museum of Fine Arts'
150th anniversary
2009.228
Photo: MMFA, Jean-François Brière

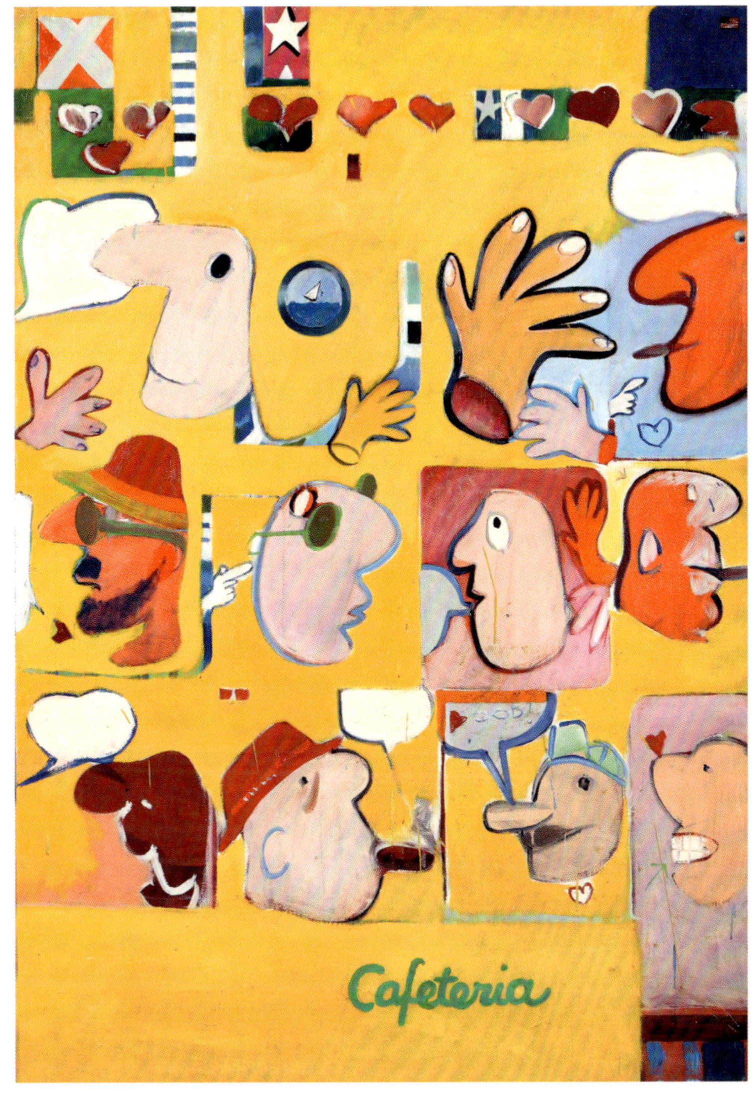

New Yak City, 1963
Oil on canvas
132.1 × 91.4 cm
Agnes Etherington Art Centre, Queen's University, Kingston, ON,
Purchase: Chancellor Richardson Memorial Fund, 1992
35-009
Photo: Bernard Clark

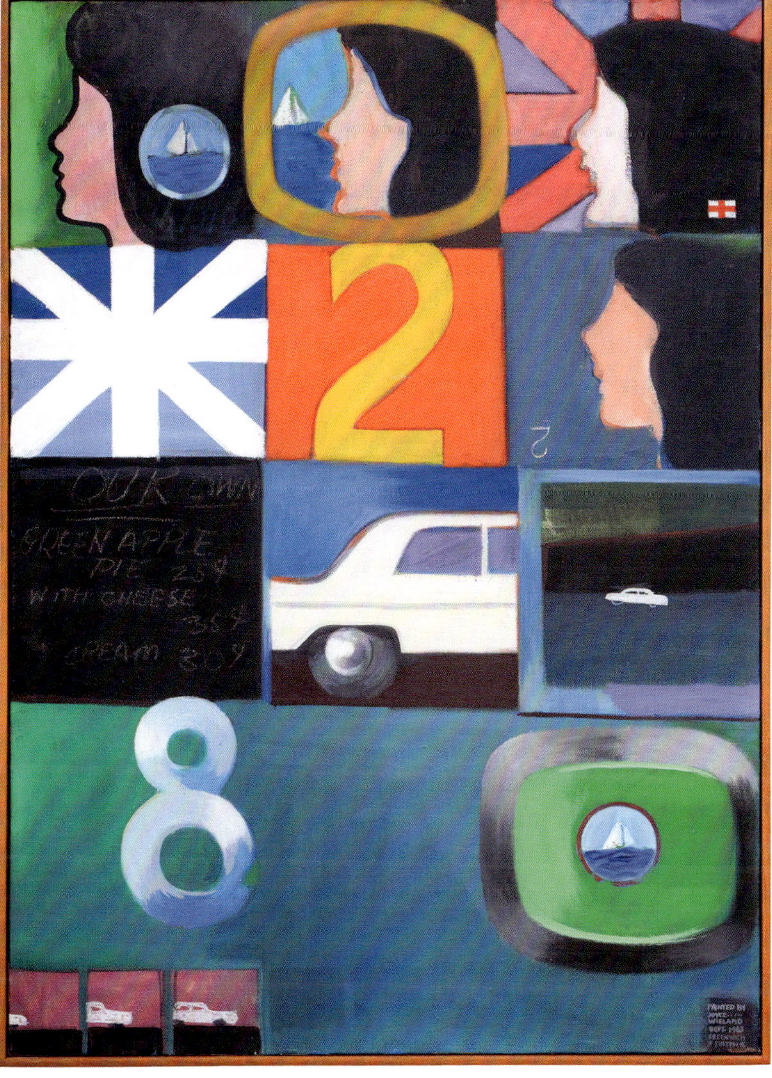

The Battery, 1963
Oil on canvas
81.3 × 58.4 cm
Collection of Katia and John Bianchini
Photo: AGO, Sean Weaver

WATER SARK, 1965

Water Sark begins abruptly with sharp sounds—instruments screeching and squealing—as the film credits, spelled out in colourful hand-cut letters, float superimposed on the image of a swinging white paper globe lantern.[1] A hand emerges to push the light gently, and instantly we drop into the middle of someone else's dream.[2] A dark wedge cuts the image to reveal a bright glimpse of lush pink and green flowers on a table, when suddenly she appears: a woman holding a camera. It is Joyce Wieland close up, her right eye scrunched shut as she points the lens straight out, and with a mirror shard tilts her reflection in and out of the frame. The strident shrills of the soundtrack underscore her image's appearance and disappearance. Oscillating from still life to self-portrait, Wieland fractures space as she reveals herself—in real time—as the creator of her world and of her image.

"*Water Sark* is a desperate self-portrait, photographing myself in those mirrors on the table with all that water and prisms and glasses and cups," she said in 1971. "It resembles the drawings that I did for ten years preceding that film. It was an extension of those drawings. It was a drawing film."[3]

The women in those early drawings, *Woman Amusing Herself* (c. 1955) (p. 48) and *Woman is a Parasite* (c. 1958) (p. 50) for example, may be in the process of awakening consciousness, yet they are still circumscribed by a patriarchal visual vocabulary. They see and know themselves as subjects objectified. In *Water Sark*, Wieland commands the camera as she points it at herself for her own viewing pleasure and knowing—her expanding consciousness. She is her self-possessed, self-reflexive subject, reflected, refracted, magnified, and out of focus through a series of viewing devices, yet most expressively through "innocent rediscovery of water," as she called it.[4] Through water, Wieland creates passages of abstraction, a blur of colours, movement, and translucent shapes that obstruct apprehension or consumption by others. While she offers much to see—the glorious revelation of her breast midway through the film, for example—some images and thoughts are exclusively for her.

The table—"a kind of altar . . . which always has flowers on it"—is the central location of the film and is the artist's studio—a fertile, nourishing, playful space.[5] "The kitchen table has been the core of all my art since I was a child. It was at the table where I drew and I started to make films." In *Water Sark*, "I was trying to make a point about housewife art and wife art and woman's art."[6] Wieland reveals and revels in this newly conceived space, which she calls in her inimitable, spirited way, "the high art of the housewife. . . . 'The housewife is high.'"[7] There are brief moments in the film where the dream feels like a proper visit: there is a red chair, the kitchen stove and the window—she has changed her outfit and done her hair for her invited guest to tea. Yet, she is mouthing words, only for her to hear.

Wieland is able to exist and create both "inside and outside" patriarchy as a tenable, simultaneous position, as cultural theorist Jeanne Randolph (b. 1943) describes her working method. "I do not want to hide the damage, the corrosion, the abnormality, and all the other things that have twisted me into the category called female. I won't hide them; I want to include them. What is broken is as important to me as what is fixed."[8]

In *Water Sark*, Wieland reconstitutes her own image, an "inside" world of colour and desire and imagination, briefly showing glimpses of a room of her own with a view of the grey city in the distance.

GEORGIANA UHLYARIK

1 Regarding the meaning of the title, in 1986 Wieland recounted that "sark" was a word she "loved at that time, a nonsense word which she vaguely associated with an ancient word for boat, and which she playfully substituted for almost anything." Kay Armatage, "The Feminine Body: Joyce Wieland's Water Sark," in *The Films of Joyce Wieland*, ed. Kathryn Elder (Toronto: Cinematheque Ontario, 1999), 144.

2 Joyce Wieland, in a recorded conversation with Hollis Frampton in spring 1971, talks about experimenting with psychedelic drugs (acid) and their importance around the time of making *Water Sark*, saying: "Film is about sound and light really; the acid trips have been about sound and light." Quoted in Hollis Frampton and Joyce Wieland, "I Don't Even Know about the Second Stanza," in Elder, *The Films of Joyce Wieland*, 173.

3 Frampton and Wieland, "Second Stanza," 171–72. Wieland's painting *Hallucination*, 1961, is a poignant precursor as well.

4 Frampton and Wieland, 172. Running water is the only natural sound that interrupts the soundtrack.

5 Frampton and Wieland, 172.

6 Frampton and Wieland, 172. Wieland's gold wedding band is visible in several sequences.

7 Wieland's *Water Sark* filmmaker notes for the Film-Makers' Cooperative catalogue: "I decided to make a film at my kitchen table, there is nothing like knowing my table. The high art of the housewife. You take prisms, glass, lights and myself to it. 'The housewife is high' WATER SARK is a film sculpture, drawing being made while you wait."

8 Dr. Jeanne Randolph, "What Don't Women Want?" in *Femscript: Transcript of the Proceedings of the Symposium on Feminist Art Practice*, January 29, 1995 (Kingston, ON: Organization of Kingston Women Artists, 1996), 7.

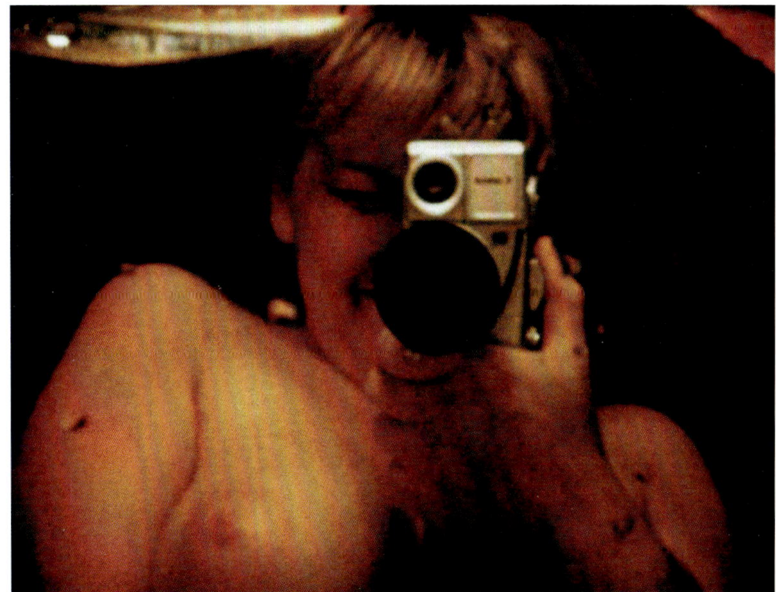

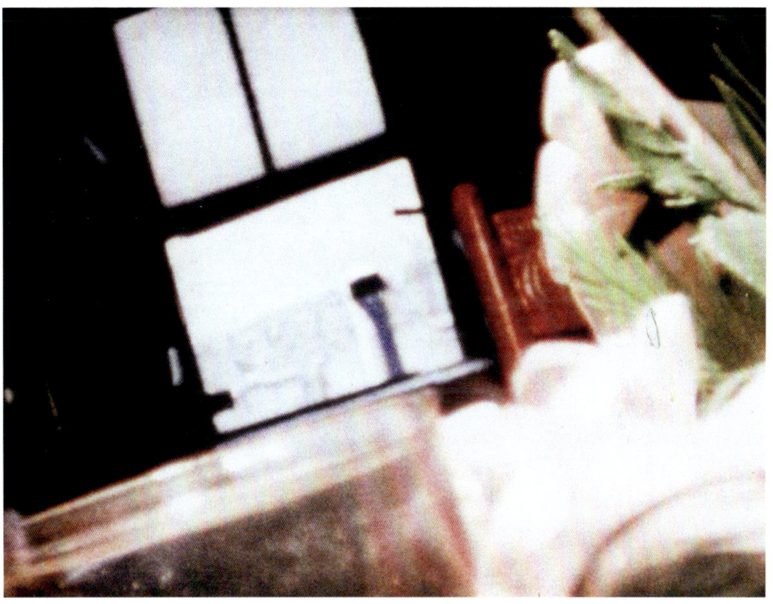

ABOVE
Water Sark (film stills), 1965
Soundtrack: Carla Bley, Mike Mantler, Ray Jessel
Film, 8mm blown up in 16mm, colour, sound
14 min
Joyce Wieland fonds, Cinémathèque québécoise
Photos: Stephen Broomer, courtesy of the CFMDC

FOLLOWING PAGE
Handtinting (film prints), 1967
Film, 16mm, colour, silent
6 min
Joyce Wieland fonds, Cinémathèque québécoise
Photos: Stéphanie Côté, courtesy of Cinémathèque québécoise

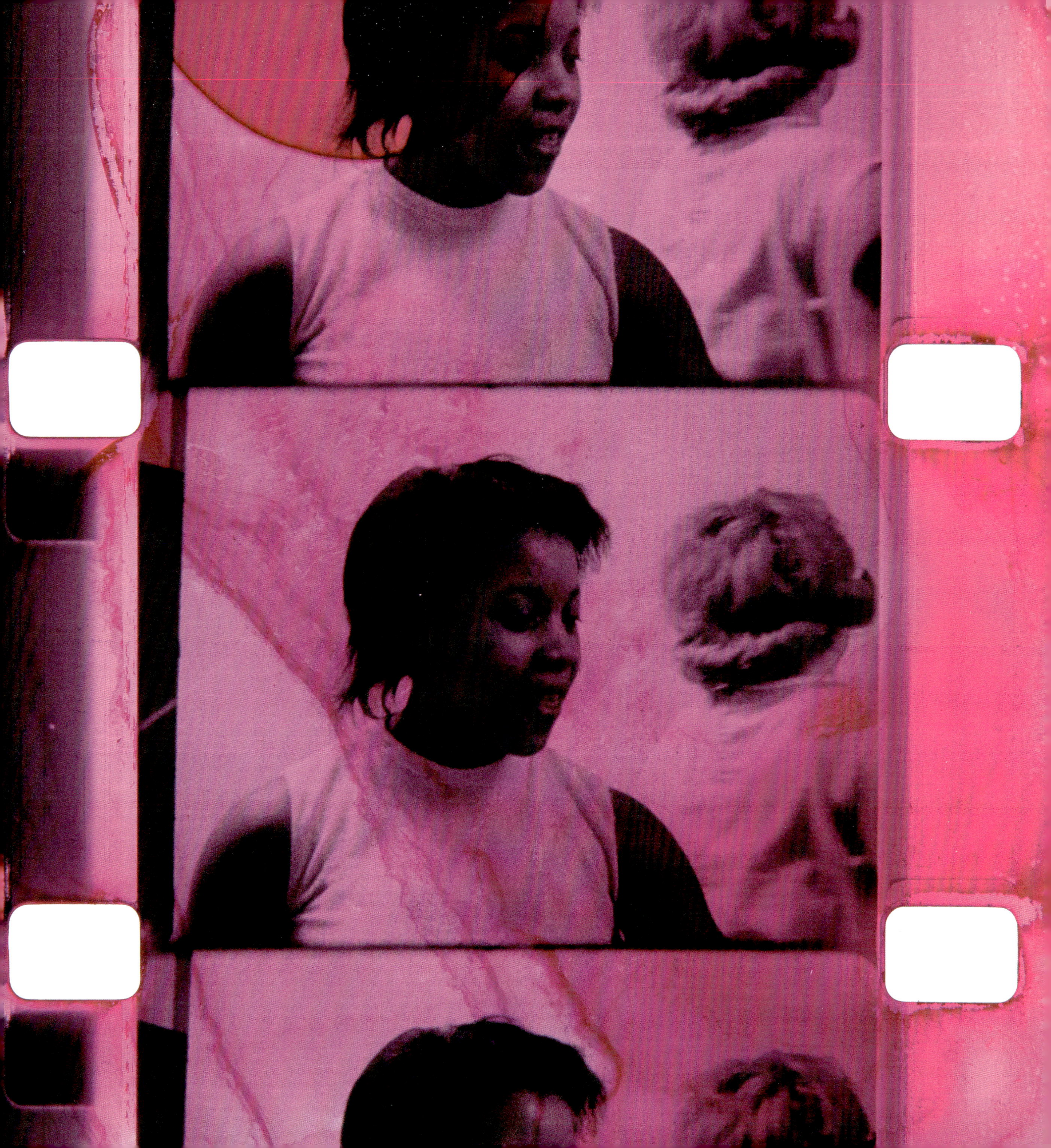

THE EXPERIMENTAL FILMS, 1965–1973

VINCENT BONIN

Joyce Wieland's body of cinematic work ranges from eighteen experimental films to one multi-screen immersive "cinema event" to one narrative feature. This heterogeneity of formats and stylistic categories has given rise to a wealth of critical commentary that often notes the difficulty of associating Wieland with defined avant-garde tendencies.[1] As Kristy A. Holmes suggests, Wieland's 1960s and early 1970s films could be situated in a broader context of the "sensorium" of that period.[2] Yet one of her artistic paths is clear: she was a pivotal figure in the structural film movement during her years in New York, from 1962 to 1971.

In 1969, the film critic P. Adams Sitney proposed the term "structural" to establish formal and theoretical connections among the practices of Tony Conrad (1940–2016), Hollis Frampton (1936–1984), Ernie Gehr (b. 1941), Ken Jacobs (b. 1933), George Landow (1940–2023), Paul Sharits (1943–1993), and Michael Snow (1928–2023), as well as Wieland.[3] However, each filmmaker had individual preoccupations and the group they formed was not united behind a common manifesto. Sitney mentions four films by Wieland: *Sailboat* (1967), *1933* (1967), *Catfood* (1968), and *La raison avant la passion / Reason over Passion* (1969).[4]

Sailboat, Wieland's most emblematic structural film according to Sitney, reprises the boat motif found in her paintings and drawings from the early 1960s. One example of the filmic practice that preceded Wieland's cinematic production is *Flick Pics #4* (1963) (p. 82), which displays the stages of a shipwreck in vertically aligned frames. Squares filled with shapeless red colour appear to occupy the edge area reserved for optical sound on a strip of film. Parallel to this, a second sequence shows sailboats moving from left to right on the horizon. Between the two, a column of

1 Instead, they chose to use loose qualifiers such as "polycentric" (Paul Arthur) and "fluid" (Kay Armatage) to identify a common thread among the works. See Paul Arthur, "Different/ Same/ Both/Neither: The Polycentric Cinema of Joyce Wieland," in *Women's Experimental Cinema: Critical Frameworks*, ed. Robin Blaetz (Durham, NC: Duke University Press, 2007), 45–66; Kay Armatage, "Fluidity: Joyce Wieland's Political Cinema," in *The Gendered Screen: Canadian Women Filmmakers*, ed. George Melnyk and Brenda Austin-Smith (Waterloo, ON: Wilfrid Laurier University Press, 2010), 106–23.

2 The term "sensorium" was proposed by Marshall McLuhan to describe the inextricable interfaces between the body (the senses) and technology. Kristy Holmes-Moss uses this concept along with Gene Youngblood's notion of expanded cinema (1970) to detach Wieland's films from a narrow exegesis of structural film that, she argues, hampers understanding of their political significance. However, Wieland made only one work in this genre of expanded cinema, *Bill's Hat*. See Monika Kin Gagnon, "Into the Archive with Joyce Wieland: Bill's Hat (1967)," *Journal of Canadian Art History* 41, no. 1–2 (2020): 129–44.

3 P. Adams Sitney, "Structural Film," *Film Culture* 47 (1969): 1–10.

4 P. Adams Sitney, "There Is Only One Joyce," *artscanada*, no. 142–43 (April 1970): 43–45.

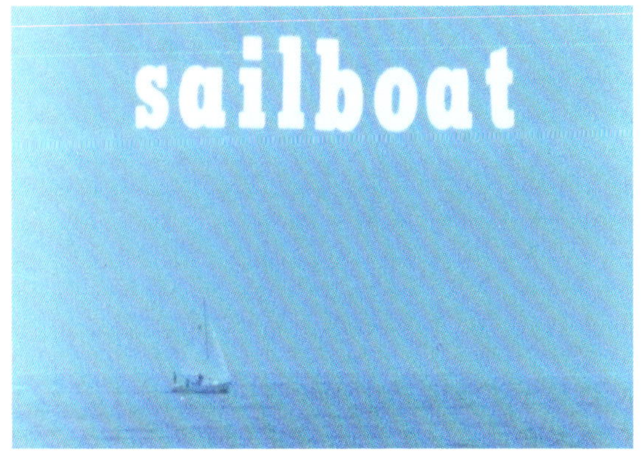

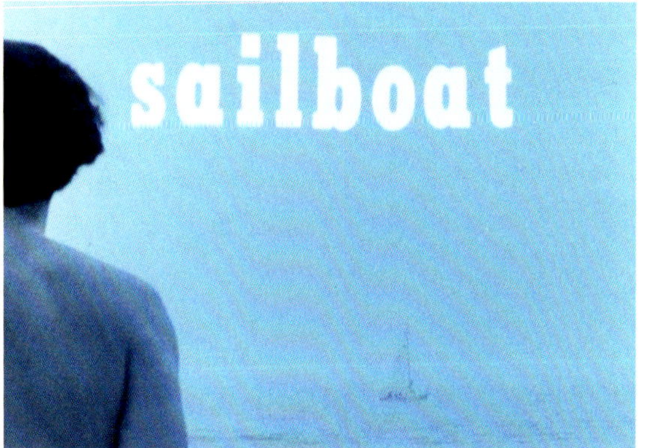

Sailboat (film stills), 1967
Film, 16mm, colour, sound
3 min
Joyce Wieland fonds, Cinémathèque québécoise
Photos: Stephen Broomer, courtesy of the CFMDC

frames decomposes the erection and detumescence of a penis/banana. In the film *Sailboat*, the event is no longer a series of disaster sequences. Almost reprising the action in the second section of the painting, it simply involves a sailboat repeatedly crossing a body of water, with the word "sailboat" superimposed in the upper third of the screen from beginning to end. The repeated views create the illusion of a loop, but the fleeting intrusion of a body indicates that Wieland was tracking the boat as it progressed. With the person (cinematographer Ken Jacobs) passing in front of the camera, the off-screen becomes perceptible. In centring the title and keeping it on screen to the end, Wieland was playing with the tautology of descriptive language, as she later did with greater complexity.

Working with what remains

Wieland's experimental films are characterized by a praxis emanating in part from the economic circumstances of her life in New York. Without taking the path of the documentary genre, she merged her political concerns (her feminism and anti-imperialist nationalism) with cinematic self-reflexivity. Far from a purism claimed by other members of the structural movement, her films can be associated with a materialist approach to form, in which the constraints of production are always considered. The meagre means at her disposal—sometimes she worked with very little money—did not denote deprivation. These limits rather became a possibility for her to always rethink and widen the scope of her agency as an activist, artist, and cultural worker.

In 1968, Wieland published a short text titled "North America's second all-woman film crew" in the periodical *Take One*.[5] In it she recounts her experience putting together technical crews comprised entirely of women. First, she talks about the group formed by the filmmakers Shirley Clarke (1919–1997) and Barbara Rubin (1945–1980), recalling how, in 1967, she and Rubin worked as camerawomen for Clarke's film about the poet Andre Voznesensky. Voznesensky never kept the appointments for the shooting sessions. Without their subject present, they accumulated fill-in material.[6] Wieland later added an anecdote to the account of those days of unsuccessful work.[7] There was unexposed film left over from the shoot in the magazine of the 16mm camera. She used it up by filming Chambers Street through the windows of her loft. At the editing table, she looped the footage and intermittently

5 Joyce Wieland, "North America's second all-woman film crew," *Take One* 1, no. 8 (1967–68): 14–15.

6 The film remained unfinished.

7 Lauren Rabinovitz, "An Interview with Joyce Wieland," *Afterimage* 8, no. 10 (May 1981): 9.

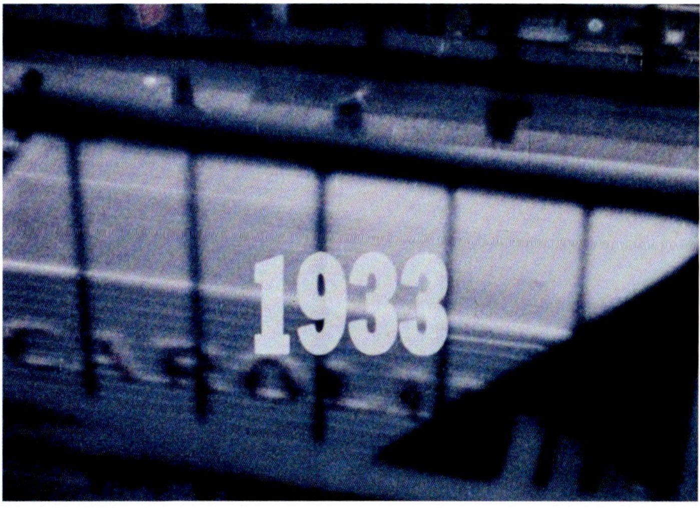

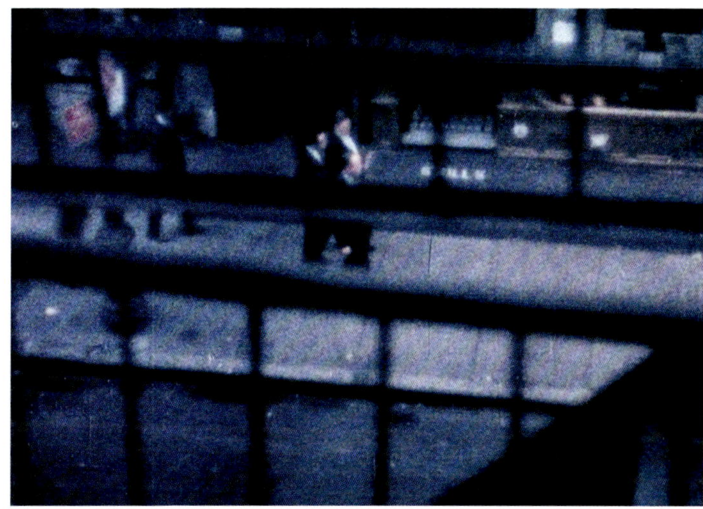

1933 (film stills), 1967
Film, 16mm, colour, sound
4 min
Joyce Wieland fonds, Cinémathèque québécoise
Photos: Stephen Broomer, courtesy of the AGO

superimposed the images of passersby with the word "1933," which became the work's title. As it unfolds, this short narrative cell is interspersed with bits of film leader punctuating the text's appearance and a soundtrack designed to dramatize the accelerated or decelerated trajectories of the bodies.

In the same *Take One* article, Wieland recollects the circumstances of the production of *Handtinting*, in 1967. This time she teamed with Sylvia White (later Davern) and Jane Bryant to produce an industrial film commissioned by Xerox on a retraining session for young women, mostly Black, at a Job Corps vocational centre in West Virginia.[8] After Xerox shelved the project, Wieland was allowed to keep her outtakes. Assembling these fragments allowed her to compile a repertoire of the women's unbridled movements during breaks, away from the grind of regimented training. The resulting work juxtaposes the gestures of the women—still rooted in the context of the original, abandoned documentary—and a new, more abstract, configuration that emphasizes the characteristics of the filmic "medium" through repetition and looping.

Wieland also coloured the film with dye and perforated the leader ends with quilting needles. She described this back and forth of form and content as a matter of equivalence: "The editing and the girls are the subject of *Hand Tinting* [sic]."[9] In 1979, the British theorist and filmmaker Laura Mulvey declared that *Handtinting* was a pioneering work of avant-garde feminist film praxis, pointing to the way the indexical signs (perforations and dyes) on the substrate resonate with the critical resurgence of "women's creative traditions," particularly in Wieland's quilting works.[10] Nearly a decade later, in 1987, film academic Kass Banning saw these layered processes as the filmic equivalent of the feminine

8 Created in the United States in 1964, the program was intended to curb unemployment among disadvantaged youth.

9 Wieland quoted in Kay Armatage, "Kay Armatage Interviews Joyce Wieland," in *Women and the Cinema*, ed. Karyn Kay and Gerlad Peary (New York: Dutton, 1977), 247.

10 Laura Mulvey, "Feminist Film and the Avant-Garde," *Framework* 10 (1979): 9.

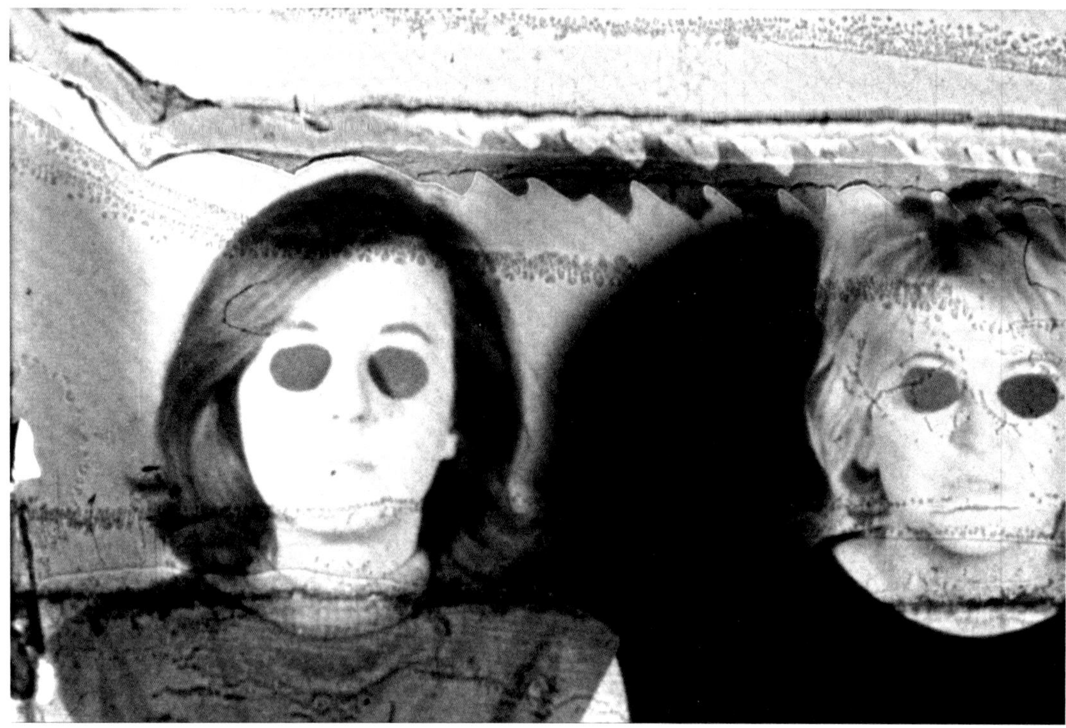

Barbara's Blindness (film still), 1967
Film, 16mm, colour, sound
17 min
Joyce Wieland fonds,
Cinémathèque québécoise
Photo: Stephen Broomer,
courtesy of the CFMDC

writing (*écriture féminine*) theorized by the philosopher Hélène Cixous.[11] As William C. Wees also observes, this film could be categorized under the broad heading of the practice of "found footage" (Wieland had used this technique to make *Barbara's Blindness* with Betty Ferguson in 1965).[12] However, Wees neglects to say that the images come from Wieland. Therefore, the process of recycling could be understood as self-quotation and regaining of agency. Similarly, the section on Pierre Elliott Trudeau in *La raison avant la passion* (1969) (p. 143), with footage shot by Wieland at the 1968 Liberal Party convention and then rephotographed from a Moviola screen, is doubly indebted to improvisation and analytical method (a scrutinization of the fabric of the celluloid itself and, at the same time, the face of Trudeau). Editing became an opportunity to structure images captured on the fly and inscribe different temporalities in the finished film. Wieland employed this approach again in 1984 and 1986, when she used rushes from unfinished films from the 1960s to create new works, both close to and far from their original materials.[13]

Asynchronous sound and image editing

The difficulty in meshing sound and image remained a constraint for Wieland until the 1970s. Nevertheless, the silence of *Handtinting* is an integral part of this work. In the 1965 self-portrait *Water Sark*, she weaves her voice into the fabric of the film without making it heard: in one scene, she is talking through a magnifying glass. Much later, she reprised this motif in *The Far Shore* (1976), where, during one of the many breaks in the narrative, the characters

11 See Kass Banning, "Textual Excess in Joyce Wieland's *Handtinting*," *CineAction* 5 (Spring 1986): 12–14.

12 William C. Wees, "Breaking New Ground: Canada's First Found Footage Films," in *Cinephemera: Archives, Ephemeral Cinema, and New Screen Histories in Canada*, ed. Gerda Cammaer and Zoë Druick (Montreal: McGill-Queen's University Press, 2014), 112–36.

13 The films are *A & B in Ontario* (with Hollis Frampton, 1967–84) and *Birds at Sunrise* (1972–86). In 1984, Kay Armatage and Su Rynard supported Wieland in completing these films. On this subject, see Kay Armatage, "Joyce Wieland, Feminist Documentary, and the Body of the Work," *Canadian Journal of Political Theory* 13, no. 1–2 (1989): 91–100.

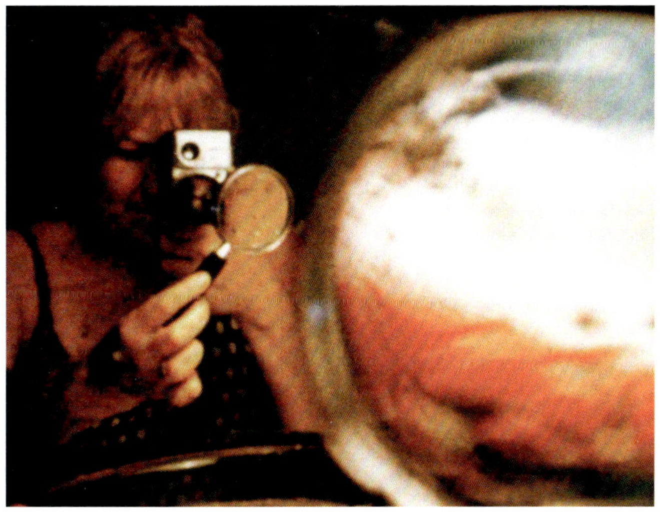

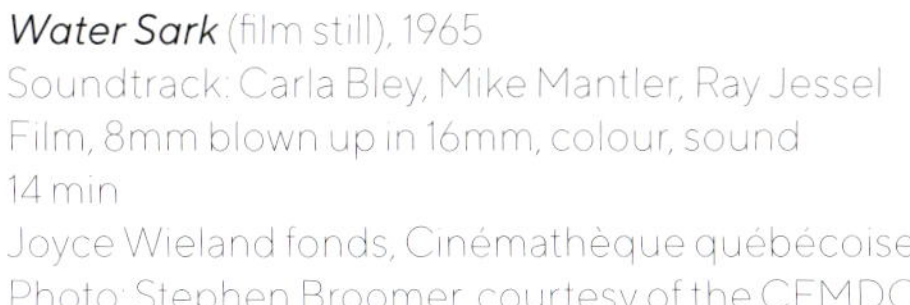

Water Sark (film still), 1965
Soundtrack: Carla Bley, Mike Mantler, Ray Jessel
Film, 8mm blown up in 16mm, colour, sound
14 min
Joyce Wieland fonds, Cinémathèque québécoise
Photo: Stephen Broomer, courtesy of the CFMDC

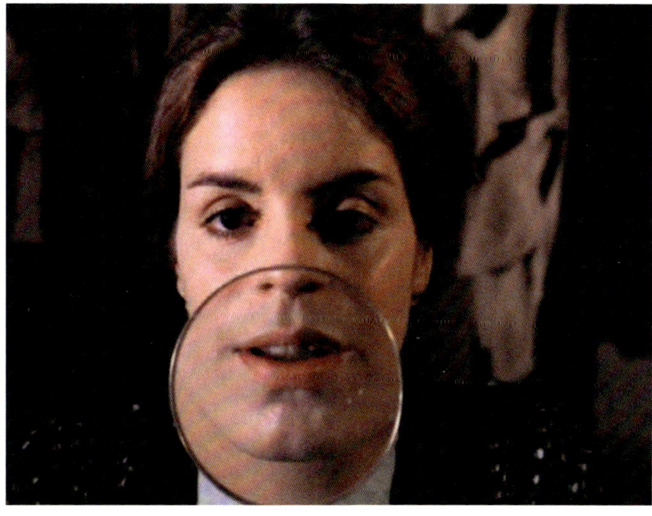

The Far Shore (film still), 1976
Film, 35mm, colour, sound
105 min
Joyce Wieland fonds, Cinémathèque québécoise
Photo: Stephen Broomer, courtesy of the CFMDC

Tom and Eulalie soundlessly recite "secret revolutionary texts" behind a magnifying glass. Set in 1917, the film includes several elements that recall the silent films of that era. Also of note is Wieland's performance of the national anthem "O Canada" in *La raison avant la passion*, clearly mouthed but absent from the soundtrack.

In 1969, Wieland worked with Michael Snow to make *Dripping Water*, in which the illusion of superimposed visual and audio tracks is created and then dispelled. The idea of a loop is suggested by the water steadily dripping into a dish from the top of the frame for ten minutes and returning to its source by means of a hidden hydraulic device. The drips are audible, as is the occasional roar of car engines from the street outside their loft. Snow recorded the sound before the image was shot.[14] As the drips fall, rings form on the water's surface. They are slightly out of sync with Snow's soundtrack, indicating the non-simultaneity of the perceptual registers. *Dripping Water* reduces the frame to its minimal function as a container. However, the presence of the dish makes discreet reference to the film *Water Sark*, which accumulates sequences of water-filled transparent recipients, while, on a separate track, sounds of clinking glass surfaces are heard (with no causal link to the image).

Paracinema

Dripping Water is the only collaborative work attributed to both Snow and Wieland.[15] In 1971, their texts appeared together in issue no. 52 of *Film Culture*. Snow presented the project *La région centrale* (1971), while Wieland published the synopsis of *True Patriot Love*,

14 In an interview with Joe Medjuck, Michael Snow said of *Dripping Water*, "That one came from a tape I'd made." See "The Life and Times of Michael Snow, 1971," in *The Collected Writings of Michael Snow: The Michael Snow Project*, ed. Louise Dompierre (Waterloo, ON: Wilfrid Laurier University Press, 1994), 77.

15 Joint retrospectives of their work were held in 1972 under the title *Films of Michael Snow and Joyce Wieland*, at University Art Museum & Pacific Film Archive at the Pacific Film Archive Theatre / University Art Museum, Berkeley (October 25–December 6, 1972).

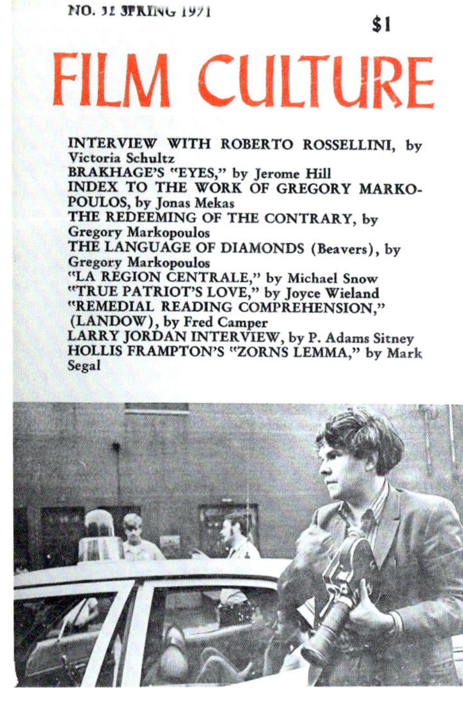

NO. 52 SPRING 1971 $1

FILM CULTURE

INTERVIEW WITH ROBERTO ROSSELLINI, by Victoria Schultz
BRAKHAGE'S "EYES," by Jerome Hill
INDEX TO THE WORK OF GREGORY MARKOPOULOS, by Jonas Mekas
THE REDEEMING OF THE CONTRARY, by Gregory Markopoulos
THE LANGUAGE OF DIAMONDS (Beavers), by Gregory Markopoulos
"LA REGION CENTRALE," by Michael Snow
"TRUE PATRIOT'S LOVE," by Joyce Wieland
"REMEDIAL READING COMPREHENSION," (LANDOW), by Fred Camper
LARRY JORDAN INTERVIEW, by P. Adams Sitney
HOLLIS FRAMPTON'S "ZORNS LEMMA," by Mark Segal

TRUE PATRIOT LOVE

(A Canadian love, technology, leadership and art story)
A movie by Joyce Wieland

This film takes place in the Dominion of Canada in 1919—in a small town near Ottawa, and in Toronto. It is the story of a young French Canadian girl named Eulalie de Chicoutimi and the four men in her life: Jacques Furlough—The Prime Minister of Canada; Claude—a young pilot who was injured in the war; Robert de Chicoutimi—Eulalie's brother, a weak libertine who admires Napoleon; Turner—an English Canadian engineer; and Tom Thomson—the great Canadian painter. Woven into this story is Emily Carr, the great Canadian nature painter, in love with Tom Thomson; Dr. Turner, father of Turner the engineer, also plays a large part, and to some extent his daughter Eunice. Also, Eulalie and Tom have dogs which play a part in the film and add to the visual element.

Characters in "True Patriot Love". . . .

EULALIE de CHICOUTIMI: A young French Canadian girl, twenty, convent educated; her parents are dead and she lives with her brother Robert, who is 19 years older than she. He is a libertine alcoholic. Eulalie is impetuous and slightly crazy, the kind of person who knocks things over when she is in a hurry. She has a large dog who accompanies her everywhere named Marielle. Eulalie loves cars, radios, telephones, pianos, cameras and all sorts of extensions of the "new" technology. As the movie opens she is in love with Jacques Furlough, who has just been made prime minister of Canada. He too has loved her but cannot marry her because of her brother's reputation which would ruin him politically. A young pilot, Claude, is also in love with Eulalie, and an English Canadian engineer, Turner, too, has some strong feelings about her.

TURNER: A bachelor engineer, about 35, from Toronto, who is putting roads and bridges into Quebec. He is completely inhibited and because of this his emotions get expressed in weird ways, suddenly and without warning. He is quite handsome and fair haired . . . he is attracted to Eulalie because she is his opposite and because he has never met anyone like her. He is blinded by her. He comes from a rich Toronto family.

CLAUDE: A young pilot who has recently returned from the war. He is handsome like Clarke Gable but not "all there" 'they say" because of a war injury which caused some brain damage. He spends most of his time up in the air in his plane buzzing Eulalie's

64

house, etc. Some people say he loves her because of her cars and that he tends to overrelate to machines. The remainder of his time is spent in church going (dramatic).

ROBERT is a slob but slightly aristocratic. . . .He has nothing really to rebel against since his parents died. But he continues drinking and screwing old and young women of the town. He is 19 years older than Eulalie; he adores his sister unnaturally and she him.

DR. TURNER is Turner's father, a very successful Toronto doctor and father of a large family. He neglects his sons and prefers his eldest daughter Eunice, (some say his attachment to her is unnatural, and it is). He has helped Tom Thomson for years and loves him more than his own sons. They argue things out about the future of technology, pollution and the relationship between Canada and the United States.

JACQUES FURLOUGH, PRIME MINISTER OF CANADA: Impeccably brilliant and very handsome . . . Furlough has debated some of the best minds in the world. He is a champion skier, swimmer, lover and linguist and a person who is involved with some secret religion. He has left behind a checkered past of broken hearts. He is master of any given situation. People don't like to think of him as ruthless because he looks so good. It's possible that Eulalie is the only woman who has ever really moved him.

EMILY CARR: The foremost woman artist of Canada . . . deeply nature loving . . . who is very much in love with Tom Thomson, the most celebrated Canadian painter. She is eccentric and childish and mystical and resembles the British artist Beatrix Potter.

TOM THOMSON: The most celebrated painter in Canada. Deeply nature-loving; a man similar to Mellors the gamekeeper in *Lady Chatterly's Lover*, only with more sides to him. Thomson in this film is strongly patriotic, and an organic farmer and soil conservationist. He is not really handsome, but has a powerful presence (sexy). He lives for his art but has a tremendous sense of responsibility toward Canada and is against much of the new technology, because he feels man will be unable to control it with sensitivity.

Scene One

Eulalie surrounded by photographs of movie stars and friends in a beautifully designed French style bedroom. She sits at a 17th century desk writing to Jacques who has just been made Prime Minister of Canada . . . guns are firing in the distance and faint cheers are heard . . . mixing with the sound of a low flying airplane

65

the first project of what would become her narrative feature *The Far Shore*, which she completed in 1976.[16] Several elements of the finished film appear in this text, but many almost dreamlike discontinuous scenes were abandoned or modified. It is important to note the existence of this synopsis and, concomitantly, of various preliminary materials for *The Far Shore* that Wieland created and shared with others during the film's conception period, some of which became visible for the public, beyond the artist's circle of peers.

In a conversation with Hollis Frampton in 1971, Wieland described a series of photographs she planned to take to do "character studies ... of the people playing the parts."[17] Excerpts of the synopsis and the script, as well as some of these photos, appear in the companion book to the exhibition *True Patriot Love* held at the National Gallery of Canada in 1971. This artist book (created in lieu of a conventional exhibition catalogue) provides a fragmentary inventory of Wieland's political concerns at the time. The publication could be labelled "paracinematic," to

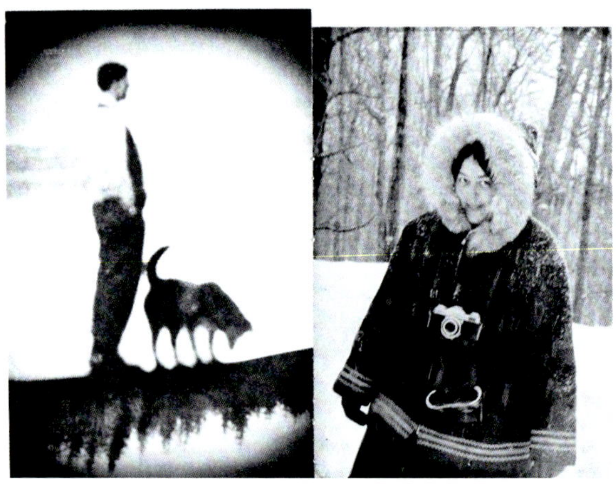

Joyce Wieland's "True Patriot Love" in *Film Culture*, no. 52, spring 1971

16 Joyce Wieland, "True Patriot Love," *Film Culture* 52 (Spring 1971): 64–73.

17 Hollis Frampton and Joyce Wieland: "I Don't Even Know About the Second Stanza," in *The Films of Joyce Wieland*, ed. Kathryn Elder (Toronto: Cinematheque Ontario, 1999), 163.

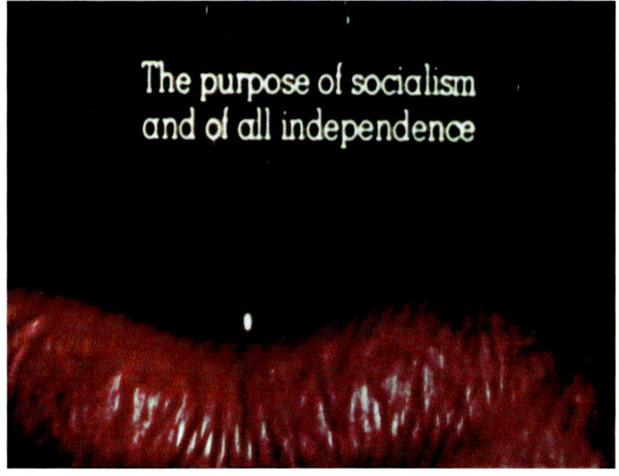

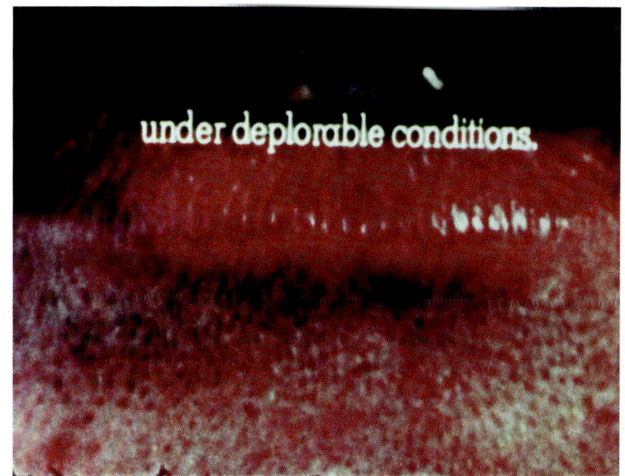

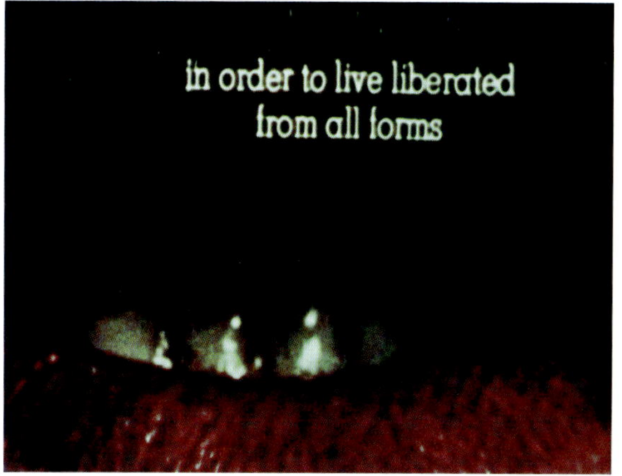

Pierre Vallières (film stills), 1972 • Film, 16mm, colour, sound • 33 min • Joyce Wieland fonds, Cinémathèque québécoise • Photos: Stephen Broomer, courtesy of the CFMDC

borrow the term used by Frampton in the 1971 conversation to describe some of Wieland's artworks.[18] Between 1963 and 1965, she produced hundreds of drawings, paintings, and assemblages based on an analytical approach to cinematic processes and heralding recurrent motifs in works yet to come. In the *True Patriot Love* book, Wieland used the "filmic" dimension conceptually by way of making present a yet unrealized project, without recourse to celluloid or projector. In 1972, Wieland also produced a series of storyboards for the *True Patriot Love / The Far Shore* script, which she was then rewriting.[19] By that time, she had already gathered footage. In her 1972 artist statement "Jigs & Reels," she imagines the opening sequence: "From close-ups of birds shot through a circular black mask we go up into the clouds and from there beam down through the roof of Eulalie's (the heroine) house, and the film gives birth to itself."[20] The images shot for this sequence were set aside and much later edited into her 1986 film *Birds at Sunrise*.

Words are heard

While working on *The Far Shore*, Wieland said she had wanted to return to the use of the close-up to produce a "political report."[21] She was referring indirectly to *Pierre Vallières* (1972), which is composed exclusively of static shots of the Québécois author and militant's mouth, with synchronized sound this time, and translated text. The session in Mont-Laurier, Quebec, called for an ad hoc setup: Wieland's collaborator Judy Steed lay on the ground to record the sound, while Danielle Corbeil, who served as the French interpreter, held Vallières's head to keep his mouth in the centre of the frame (p. 144). Vallières had prepared the content for three speeches whose duration had to more or less match the standard length of three rolls of film (about ten minutes each). Wieland used all the material she filmed,

18 Hollis and Frampton, "Second Stanza," 160. On paracinema and structural film, see also Jonathan Walley, "The Material of Film and the Idea of Cinema: Contrasting Practices in Sixties and Seventies Avant-Garde Film," *October* 103 (Winter 2003): 15–30.

19 On the subject of these drawings, see the exhibition catalogue *Joyce Wieland: Drawings for "The Far Shore" / Dessins pour "The Far Shore,"* ed. Pierre Théberge (Ottawa: National Gallery of Canada, 1978).

20 Joyce Wieland, "Jigs & Reels," in *Form and Structure in Recent Film*, exh. cat., ed. Dennis Wheeler (Vancouver: Vancouver Art Gallery / Talonbooks Books, 1972), n.p. The iris framing was directly inspired by D.W. Griffith's use of circular masks. See p. 145.

21 In unpublished notes, she mentions: "For about a year I have been working on studies of birds in extreme close-up . . . and now felt like using the lense [*sic*] for a political report." Joyce Wieland fonds, CTASC, York University, 1999-004/003, file 3, quoted by Kristy Holmes-Moss in her PhD diss., "Negotiating the Nation: The Work of Joyce Wieland, 1968–1976" (Kingston, ON: Queen's University, 2007): 135.

including false starts, fragments of recorded conversation with her crew, and end-of-reels.

Wieland aimed to give Vallières an occasion to speak, a "platform," and the predetermined editing in which she barely intervenes makes this clear. For her, it was not a matter of adopting the direct cinema protocol (advocated by Shirley Clarke), but of, once again, dialectically linking a mode of address with formal self-reflexivity.[22] After tackling the utopia of bilingualism by fragmenting Trudeau's motto "Reason over passion" to the point of unintelligibility (in *La raison avant la passion*, 1969), Wieland this time was thinking about the role of subtitles. Hypothetically, the translated text would give English speakers access to Vallières's ideas. The words appear in the upper part of the screen, rather than the bottom, and thus are often superimposed on the subject's upper lips. Viewers who do not understand French hear Vallières's voice, with its texture, as a phenomenal, opaque, unfathomable dimension.[23]

In a statement, Wieland gave titles to each section of her film, which do not appear on screen (see pp. 146–147).[24] In the first part, "Mont-Laurier," Vallières starts by describing the economic context of Mont-Laurier, a town where he lived briefly thanks to a job subsidized by the federal government. He mentions the presence of large industries in the region that extracted local natural resources without accountability, often for the sake of US interests. He reports about the case of one factory—a re-education centre—exploiting female workers by giving them very low wages in exchange for long hours of labour ("a true concentration camp"). While he denounces this state-sanctioned capitalism, he also addresses his participation in attempts at co-management of companies to allow the population of the region to take means into their own hands. In the second part, "Women's liberation," he highlights the importance of the women's movement in the socialist revolutionary project aimed at the emancipation of all. In the third part, "Quebec history and race," he establishes a parallel, to a certain extent, between the subjugation of working-poor Québécois in anglophone Canada and the oppression experienced by African Americans in the United States (unacceptable from today's standpoint but reflecting ideological currents of the left at the time). Vallières finally speaks about the need for the people of Quebec to acknowledge their ancestral responsibility, as descendants of the colonies of "Nouvelle France," in the genocide of "the Indians," who were the "true first people." Vallières steps out of the frame before the last roll of film was finished. Wieland did not stop shooting; she used the remainder roll in the magazine to capture two panoramic views of the landscape, back and forth.

Delayed reception

In a 1972 column for the *Village Voice*, the filmmaker and film critic Jonas Mekas wrote that *Pierre Vallières* was one of the most effective political films he had ever seen: "She [Joyce Wieland] eliminated all visual distraction. . . . The purity of her approach, her formal choice, only increases the sharpness of the truth presented in the film."[25] With the exception of this favourable review, *Pierre Vallières* received little notice when it was first shown. Contrary to another political film by Wieland, *Rat Life and Diet in North America* (1968), which had reached a wide audience, its early reception was limited to protagonists in the narrow field of structural film. The work's meagre screening

22 On the ongoing dialogue between Wieland and Shirley Clarke during the 1960s and the documentary portrait in their respective practices, see Bettina Brunner, "What Is a Mouth: Joyce Wieland's *Pierre Vallières* (1972) and the Politics of the Film Portrait," *Moving Image Review & Art Journal* 9, no. 1 (2022): 10–23.

23 Wieland intended to further subvert and complexify the subtitles in her film *True Patriot Love* (ultimately *The Far Shore*), but this aspect of the project did not materialize.

24 These three sections follow each other in the text in an order different from the way they were edited.

25 Jonas Mekas, "Film Journal," *Village Voice*, July 13, 1972.

history and critical attention coincided with a moment of transition in defining avant-garde experimental film when Wieland's comingling of formal decisions with choice of political subject matter were ahead of their time, anticipating the concerns of filmmakers in the late 1970s.

In 1972, *Pierre Vallières* was presented in *Form and Structure in Recent Film*[26] at the Vancouver Art Gallery, along with works by Hollis Frampton, Ernie Gehr, Barry Gerson (b. 1939), Ken Jacobs, George Landow, David Rimmer (1942–2023), Paul Sharits, and Michael Snow. It was also screened during the 1974 survey *New Forms in Film*, including many of the same filmmakers, organized in Montreux, Switzerland, by the film critic Annette Michelson (who had followed Wieland's work closely since the late 1960s). An account from Wieland on the making of *Pierre Vallières*, published in the accompanying catalogue for *New Forms in Film*,[27] is the only reference to the film, since the critics George Lellis and Regina Cornwell, respectively, deal only with her earlier works (*Sailboat*, *1933*, and *La raison avant la passion*).[28] It should be noted that she was the only woman invited to Vancouver and, along with Yvonne Rainer (b. 1934), one of two invited to Montreux.

In 1970, Wieland's work was excluded from the "Essential Cinema" collection of the Anthology Film Archives, whose selection committee was composed of James Broughton, Ken Kelman, Peter Kubelka, Mekas, and Sitney. Despite this ostracism, she nevertheless wanted to be recognized on equal footing with her peers—the members of her affinity group in New York for almost a decade. During a 1974 interview, Wieland expressed her ambivalence about the minor role she had been assigned:

> *I didn't know it [structural film] was a movement until we separated. Now it is thought of historically, and is discussed as a really important movement, like Cubism. . . . We influenced each other, and made wonderful films. However, when it came to my work affecting anyone it was never mentioned. I am forced to talk in terms of influences etc. because that was one of the manifestations of the discrimination. Yet when books have been written to document this movement my work is relegated to a woman's place, small that is.*[29]

Later, several critics and art historians dissociated Wieland's work from the structural movement based on stylistic differences between her and the other filmmakers that they deemed irreconcilable. In her catalogue essay for the Art Gallery of Ontario's Wieland retrospective in 1987, the critic Lucy R. Lippard trivializes this affiliation: "Yet her exposure to and work within the structuralist discipline undoubtedly had a benign effect on her art, rather like Eva Hesse's contemporary response to the minimalism she adopted primarily as an armature for her own emotive expressiveness."[30] Wieland's work was the subject of reappraisal in the field of film studies in the 1980s. During that time, Kass Banning and Kay Armatage proposed methods inspired by post-structural feminist theories for analyzing Wieland's films of the 1960s. Lauren Rabinovitz, for her part, suggested that Wieland's choice to reflexively adopt a conventional narrative genre—melodrama—for *The Far Shore* echoed the critical revisions of experimental film politics by contemporary female directors associated with the "New Talkies."[31]

26 Wieland wrote *Jigs & Reels* for the catalogue that accompanied *Form and Structure in Recent Film*, providing an overview of her practice up to 1972.

27 Joyce Wieland, "'Pierre Vallières': Notes from the Filmmaker," 117.

28 In *Form and Structure in Recent Film*, the essay is "*La raison avant la passion*," by George Lellis, while in *New Forms in Film* it is an excerpt of Regina Cornwell's article "'True Patriot Love.'" The same excerpt of Cornwell's text also appears in *Structural Film Anthology*, ed. Peter Gidal (London: British Film Institute, 1978), 139–40.

29 Debbie Magidson and Judy Wright, "Interviews with Canadian Artists: Debbie Magidson and Judy Wright interview Joyce Wieland," *Canadian Forum* 54 (May–June 1974): 61.

30 Lucy R. Lippard, "Watershed: Contradiction, Communication and Canada in Joyce Wieland's Work," in *Joyce Wieland*, exh. cat., ed. Marie Fleming (Toronto: Art Gallery of Ontario, 1987), 6.

31 Lauren Rabinovitz, "*The Far Shore*: Feminist Family Melodrama," *Jump Cut* 32 (1987): 29–31. In the second half of the 1970s, Chantal Akerman, Lizzie Borden, Betty Gordon, Babette Mangolte, Laura Mulvey, Sally Potter, Yvonne Rainer, and several others opted to employ the codes of narrative fiction feature film without abandoning the critical tropes of experimental film.

In 1999, countering the tendency to exclude Wieland from the community of filmmakers in which she claimed intellectual membership, Catherine Russell included *Pierre Vallières* in a second corpus of "structural films."[32] The theorist then turned her attention to a younger cohort of filmmakers who had assimilated part of the rigorous minimalist vocabulary of Wieland, Frampton, Snow, and other protagonists linked to the original movement, while stripping it away from purism. In the second group, Wieland figures again alongside James Benning and Chantal Akerman, both ten years her junior. Since the sixties, she prefigured a postmodern "experimental ethnography" emerging, according to Russell, between a regained interest in documentary truth and the avant-garde's formalist/materialist preoccupation for surface effects, but *Pierre Vallières* (and, we should add, arguably, *Handtinting* as well as *Solidarity*, 1973) placed her at the cusp of the first and second generation's critical projects.

Praxis

As noted earlier, when Wieland was tackling a political subject, the concordance of the ethics of filming and editing with an awareness of the constraints of production also came from the extension of the structural rubric. *Solidarity*, made in 1973, during the interval between *Pierre Vallières* and *The Far Shore*, constitutes a summation of this practice.

On April 14, accompanied by Judy Steed, Wieland went to Kitchener, Ontario, to film a demonstration by five thousand people marching in support of female workers on strike at the Dare cookie factory. The subject echoes the exploitation of women described by Vallières in one of the three speeches he made in Mont-Laurier. The workers' demands went beyond mere pay equity, denouncing the daily abuse they were subjected to by male bosses. Wieland said of the film: "The subject is the place where ground and feet meet to create solidarity."[33] This sentence condenses one of the definitions of praxis: an action directed toward the possibility of a change in the given social and material conditions of an oppressed community—here, working women.

Wieland placed the scene at ground level, capturing only the feet of the milling picketers, rendering them anonymous. Like *Pierre Vallières*, *Solidarity* redirects perception toward listening by tightly framing the subject. During the march, the demonstrators' voices are heard, in particular a speech by a union spokeswoman. In a few short minutes, the segment provides enough information to convey the struggle the strikers have been waging for months. Distilling all the ways in which Wieland had used language since *Sailboat*, the word "SOLIDARITY" superimposed at the centre of the screen accentuates the here and now while composing an aspirational figure of the common well beyond this circumstance. Leila Sujir observes that through the naming, on the surface of the image, of the wider collectivism of this moment in Kitchener, and by way of metonymical framing, a link is made to "other strikers, other places."[34]

Bearing witness to the social crises and activism of the early 1970s, *Pierre Vallières* and *Solidarity*, seen more than fifty years after their making, remain contemporary. The interest that they still arouse through frequent screenings testifies to the relevance of a conception of political art whose precise form, contingent and tied to events, escapes the grip of fixed didactic genres.

32 Catherine Russell, "Framing People: Structural Film Revisited," in *Experimental Ethnography: The Work of Film in the Age of Video* (Durham, NC: Duke University Press, 1999), 157–90.

33 Statement by Wieland on *Solidarity* (1973) from the program for screenings of her films held in conjunction with the 1987 retrospective at the Art Gallery of Ontario, n.p.

34 Leila Sujir, "A Language of Flesh and of Roses," in *In Search of the Far Shore: The Films of Joyce Wieland* (London: Canada House, 1988), n.p.

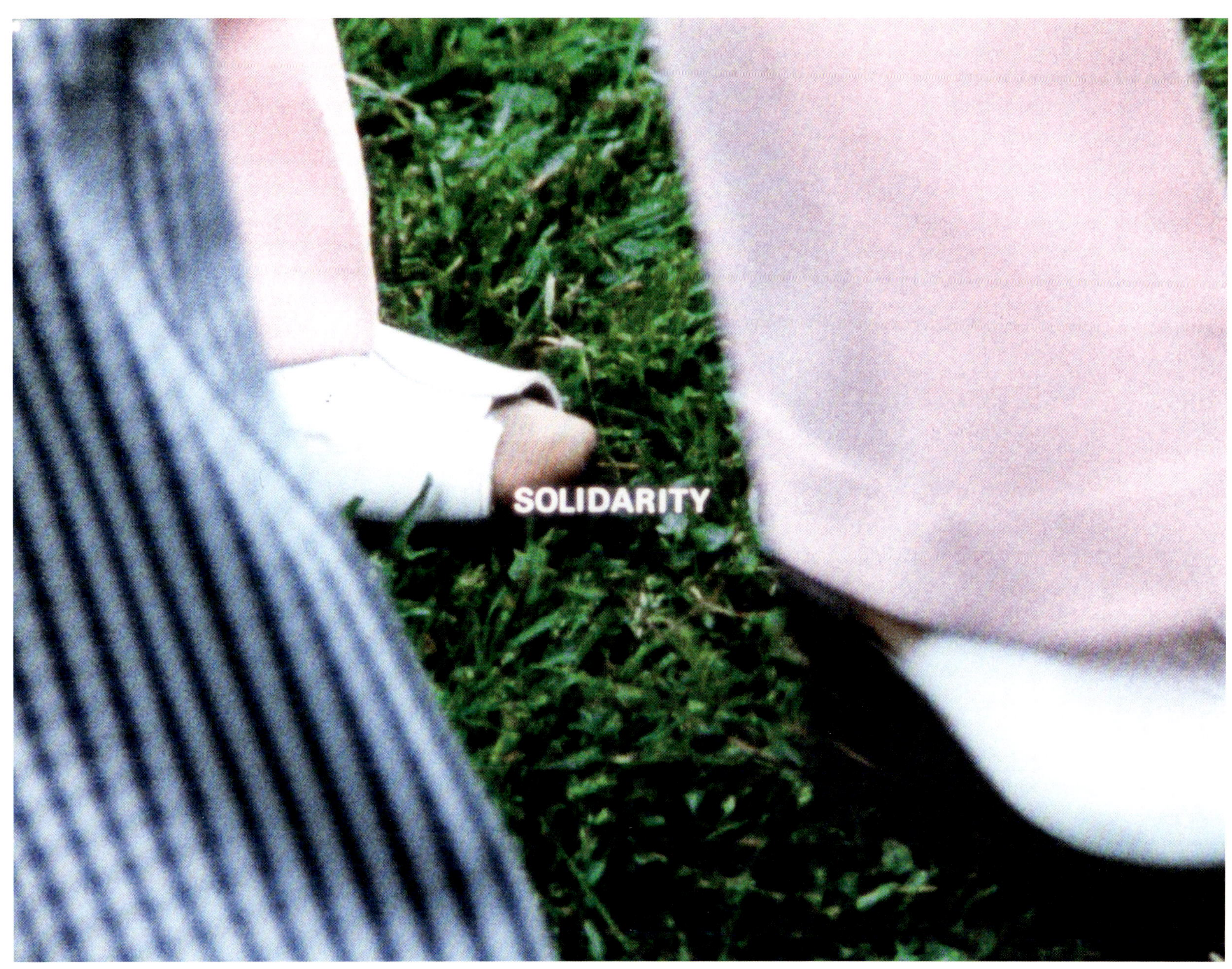

Solidarity (film still), 1973
Film, 16mm, colour, sound
11 min
Joyce Wieland fonds, Cinémathèque québécoise
Photo: Stephen Broomer, courtesy of the CFMDC

In 1966 and 1967, Joyce Wieland produced fifteen plastic works in varying sizes and colours. These vibrant assemblages are made with pieces of translucent plastic in different shapes, which she stitched together using a sewing machine. She stuffed some with traditional quilting batting; into others, she inserted found images and objects. Wieland hung them simply and directly on the gallery wall—showing them publicly for the first time in her exhibition *Hangings* at The Isaacs Gallery in March–April 1967.

Fundamental to the concept of this fantastic series is Wieland's distinctive use of plastic in art, still a relatively novel choice of material at the time. Plastic and stitching came together during the 1960s, when fashion designers exploited the thin, pliable, shiny synthetic material as a means to instill the "new" in a decade of revolution and change. As Wieland sewed the bright hues of plastic together, she made pockets containing an array of images highlighting current affairs and events, as well as personal references, creating a surprisingly clever new format to frame politics for her audience. The plastic also related to her interest in film's formal properties in terms of both its texture and translucency (akin to celluloid), and the possibility of sewing the material allowed her to create assemblages that were sequential in format. The innovative idea of combining elements from a traditionally feminine and artisanal format (quilting and stuffing) with the

STUFFED MOVIE

conspicuously manufactured plastic available in a wide range of vibrant modern hues testifies to the artist's playful challenge of consumerism's mass production and her foregrounding of women's work.

Confedspread—a truncation of "Confederation" and "bedspread"—stands out among Wieland's plastic works for its large scale and its quilt-like construction. Created in anticipation of Canada's 1967 centennial, it reflects her developing interest in Canadian identity while she was living in New York City. Stuffed with two types of quilt batting and featuring maple leaves of different colours—the maple leaf having been adopted as the symbol on Canada's national flag just two years prior—this piece challenges accepted hierarchies through its entanglement of politics, quiltmaking, and modern abstract art.

Wieland was among several artists who embraced plastic as a medium in the late 1960s, yet she was not naive to its detrimental effects, anticipating the problematic relationship we have with the material today.

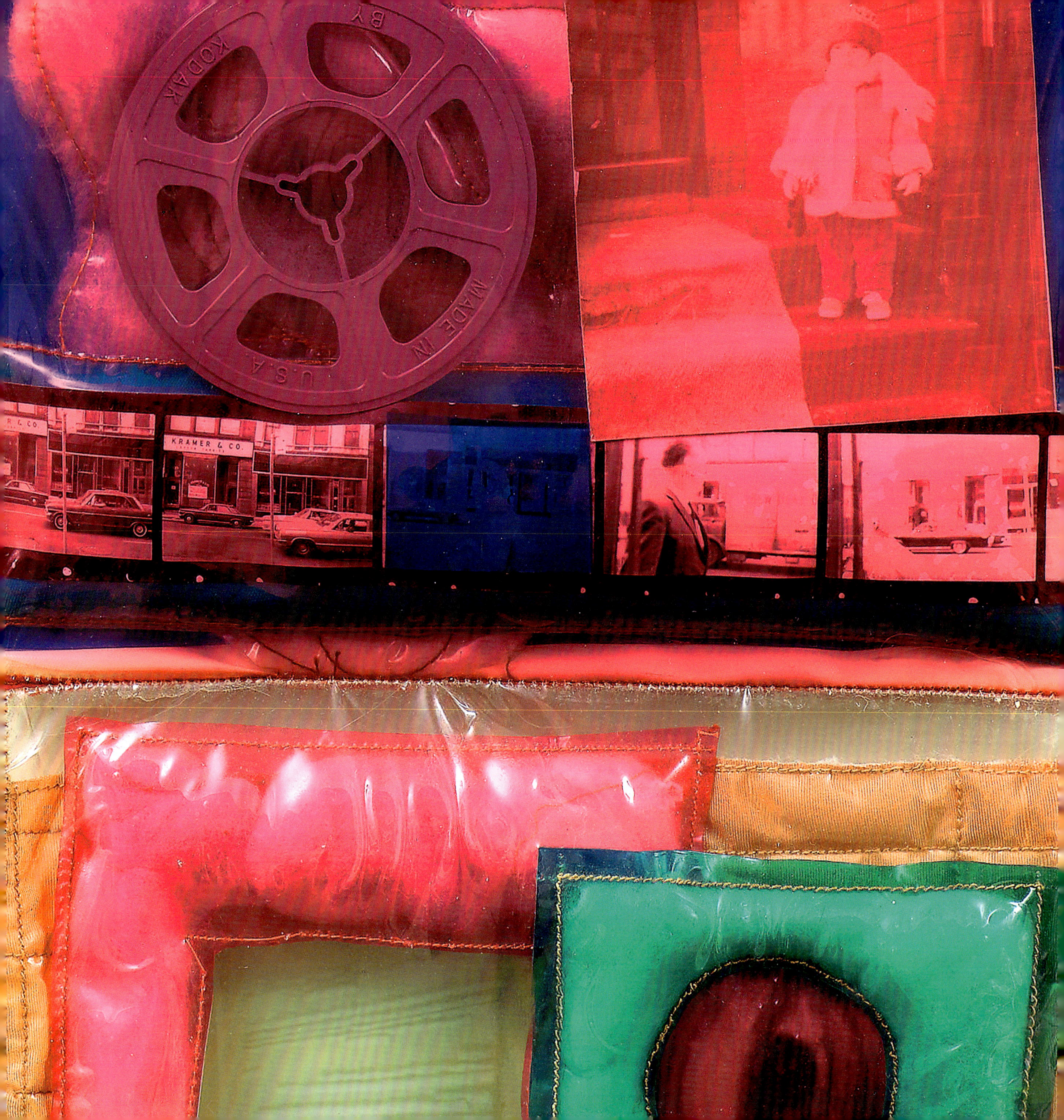
KODAK
BY
MADE IN
U.S.A
KRAMER & CO.

FUN THINGS MADE OF PLASTICS

CONSERVATION INSIGHTS

MARK KEARNEY, STEPHANIE BARNES, RICHARD GAGNIER, RACHEL STARK, SJOUKJE VAN DER LAAN

In the 1960s, when Joyce Wieland was living and creating in New York City, she and many of her contemporaries experimented with a versatile, inexpensive, and widely available synthetic material: plastics. Wieland treated them as she would fabric, cutting pieces and stitching them together into pouches to stuff with quilt batting, found objects, and images. These hangings, as she called them, were placed directly on a nail to be hung on the walls of private homes, where they remained for decades, much admired by collectors. For example, before it was acquired by the AGO in 2017, *The Space of the Lama* (1966) (p. 130) spent much of its life in the kitchen of a friend's country home. Now more than fifty years old, most of Wieland's plastic hangings require conservation treatment.

The conservation of plastics is in the early stages of study. Conservation scientists at the Canadian Conservation Institute (CCI), as well as conservators from the Montreal Museum of Fine Arts, the National Gallery of Canada, and the Art Gallery of Ontario, gathered on several occasions to discuss Wieland's artworks in anticipation of this project. Noting the similarities between plastics used in her pieces and the differences in how well they have been preserved, CCI undertook material analysis to pinpoint the types of plastic and other materials and suggest possible associations. Through collection of this information, and through dialogue and shared observations between conservators

OPPOSITE
Home Movie (detail), 1966
Plastic, thread, paper, batting
104.1 × 20.3 cm
Collection of Robert Fulford and Geraldine Sherman, Toronto
Photo: AGO, Sean Weaver

RIGHT
Patriotism, 1967
Plastic, thread, cloth, photograph, paper, cotton, wood batting
81.7 × 39.6 cm
Collection of the Vancouver Art Gallery, Gift of Donna Montague
VAG 99.22.10
Photo: Vancouver Art Gallery

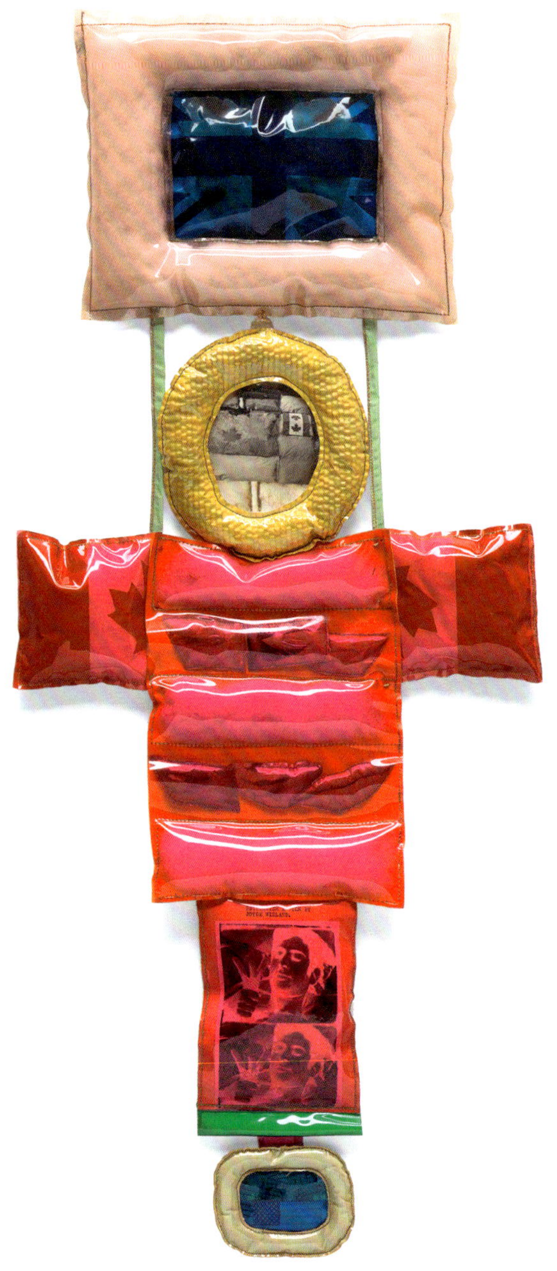

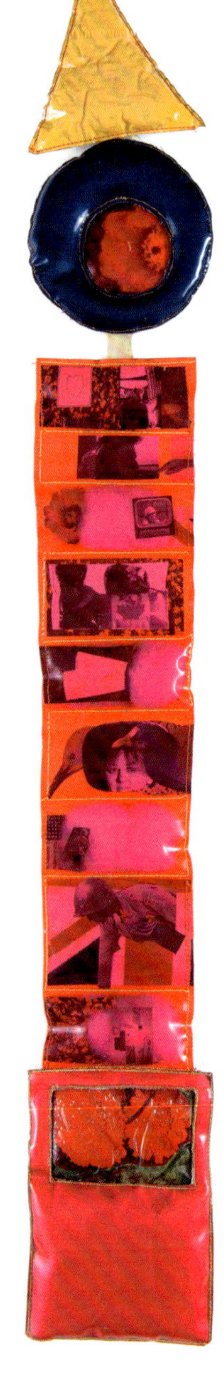

at each institution, developments in the care of Wieland's plastic artwork continues to progress. What follows is a discussion among the team of conservators about the properties and conservation of the plastic assemblages created by the artist in 1966 and 1967.

What is special about the materials Wieland used in her artworks, and the context in which she was using them?

Mark Kearney, Canadian Conservation Institute:
In her plastic assemblages, Wieland incorporates elements made of polyvinyl chloride, commonly known as PVC, which is one of the most important synthetic polymers to have been developed.[1] We now see and interact with it on a daily basis. The material itself is much older than people might assume, having first been developed in the 1870s. However, it was not until World War II that more widespread industrial uses for the material came about. Innovations in manufacturing techniques during this period led to improved and more versatile forms of PVC. By the early 1960s, PVC had become prevalent in commercial use in both the domestic and industrial realms. The use of PVC follows a familiar path in how the public perceives it. Like many other plastics, PVC starts off as an alternative to more traditional materials, but is soon valued for its own unique properties. While it is now challenging to grasp the excitement surrounding these materials at the time, they were once regarded as innovative—teeming with possibilities.

1 Polymers are natural, synthetic, or semi-synthetic substances composed of large molecules formed from smaller chemical units. Initially developed in the late 1800s as an alternative to ivory, synthetic polymers are made from fossil fuels, chemically treated fibres or, most commonly, petroleum. Plastics are formed primarily from synthetic or semi-synthetic polymers. Natural polymers include silk, wool, organic rubber, tar, and cellulose.

OPPOSITE, RIGHT
War and Peace, 8mm Home Movie, 1967
Plastic, thread, found objects, batting
76.2 × 10.2 cm
Macdonald Stewart Art Centre Collection at the Art Gallery of Guelph, Gift of Kathy Dain, 2003
MS2003.085
Photo: Art Gallery of Guelph

RIGHT
Home Movie, 1966
Plastic, thread, paper, batting
104.1 × 20.3 cm
Collection of Robert Fulford and Geraldine Sherman, Toronto
Photo: AGO, Sean Weaver

Wieland's work using plastic as a support for assemblages in the mid-1960s occurred at the height of its popularity among the general public. PVC had become a highly fashionable material to use. Designers like Mary Quant and Pierre Cardin used it in vibrant and exciting colours—a departure from the more subdued monochrome palettes of preceding decades—and introduced the dynamic styles of the swinging '60s. Wieland's art epitomizes this zeitgeist, offering a blend of the familiar and the avant-garde.

Unfortunately, from a conservation perspective, the type of PVC Wieland used is now known to be one of the five problematic plastics we find in museum collections. The same technologies that allowed for its expanded use as a material are now causing harm not only to the artworks themselves but also to other works that come into contact with them. Plasticizers, included in PVC for flexibility, eventually leach out to the surface, trapping dirt and grime and leaving behind a brittle plastic.[2] These processes gradually weaken and alter the visual appearance of the artwork, prompting a reconsideration of our perception of it.

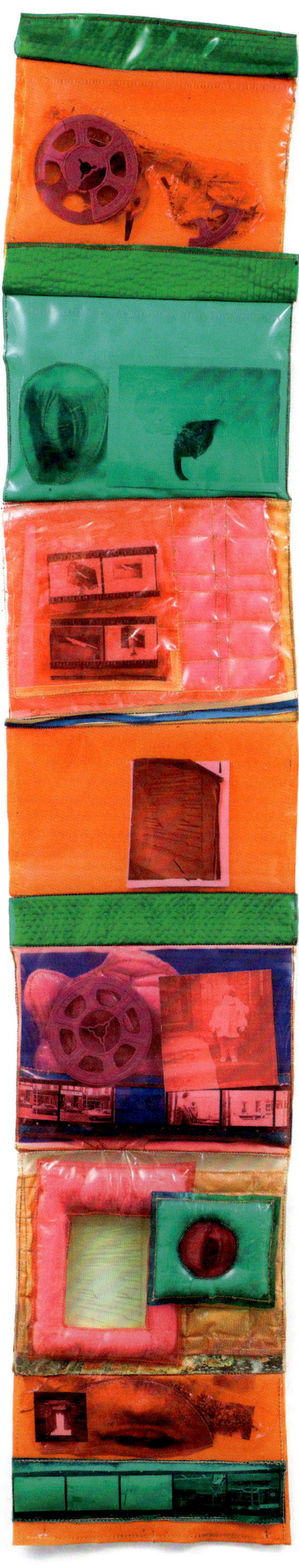

2 Plasticizers are chemical components added to plastic and polymers, especially PVC, to make them softer and more flexible. The first plasticizers, introduced in the mid-to-late nineteenth century, included castor oil and camphor. Synthetic plasticizers, most typically phthalates, were in wide commercial use by the 1930s.

LEFT
D.W. Griffith and His Cameraman Billy Bitzer, 1966
Plastic, thread, photograph, batting
50.5 × 33 cm
Collection of Munro Ferguson
Photo: MMFA, Julie Ciot

RIGHT
Larry's Recent Behaviour, 1966
Plastic, thread, batting, gelatin silver print, offset lithograph
58 × 37 × 6 cm
The Montreal Museum of Fine Arts, Gift of Luc d'Iberville-Moreau
1991.17
Photo: MMFA, Jean-François Brière

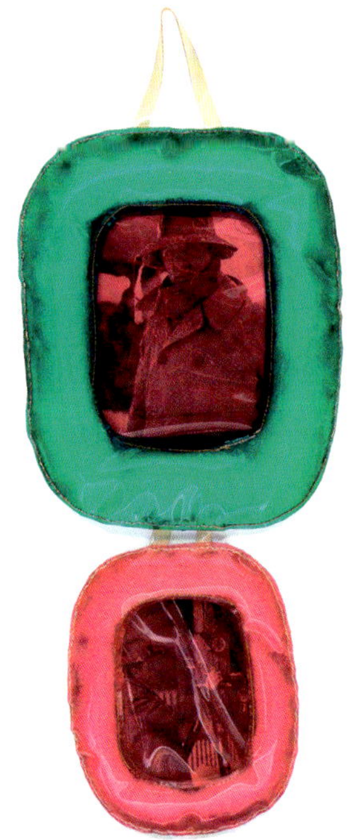

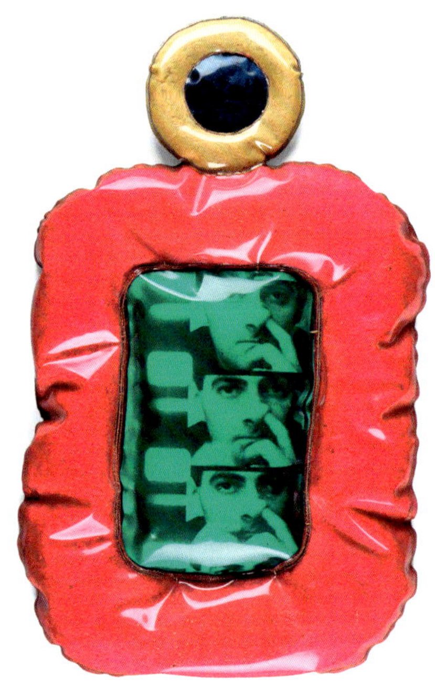

Can you describe the materials found in Wieland's plastic-based pieces, and the manner in which she treats and assembles these elements?

Richard Gagnier, Montreal Museum of Fine Arts:
Wieland was living in New York when she began making wall-hanging assemblages composed of various shapes cut from flexible plastic film, most of it transparent or translucent, but tinted. Plastic of this sort had become widely available and was likely sold at a fabric store—maybe even the one seen in the photo tucked into one of the pockets of *Stuffed Movie* (p. 133).

These objects are configured as assemblages, consisting of vertically arranged units linked by strips of the same material. Even their hangers are fashioned from plastic strips. Most of the plastic is PVC, but there are also opaque polymeric materials such as nylon and polyester. Wieland chose these elements to add not only colour but also texture, often layering them beneath the PVC.

Her assembly method is somewhat unusual in that it borrows from home sewing: all components of the units are machine-stitched with cotton thread matching the colour of each material: pink, red, blue, grey, white. They are fastened with a rather tight straight stitch, frequently in double or triple rows. The pieces were simply placed one on top of the other, with no provision for seam allowance or folding, leaving all of the seams visible. The completed units were handsewn together with stitches repeated over and over. The resulting shapes are similar to cushions or small closed pouches; many are ring-shaped.

More often than not, the units are stuffed with polyester or kapok, a lightweight plant fibre commonly used as filler. Some of the cushions contain only stuffing, but many are embellished with visual elements that pertain as much to the artist's life and her oeuvre as to film, filmmakers, and filmmaking. There are photographs, magazine and newspaper clippings, offset lithographic prints, polaroids, synthetic fabrics such as small Canadian and US flags, strips of 8mm and 16mm film, and even small reels of film. In many cases, photos and images are sewn right into the unit's seam.

Although Wieland used a wide variety of plastic films, the same ones appear repeatedly in her assemblages, suggesting that she bought them by the yard in standard widths. This no doubt explains their use for larger quilt-like pieces, where the units unfold in both width and length, as in *Confedspread* (p. 128) and *Man Has Reached Out and Touched the Tranquil Moon* (p. 161). Atypically, the latter work is composed of small unsealed pouches, each containing a letter of the alphabet made of cotton and stuffed with wool and talcum powder. This "hybrid" textile piece is similar to other of her purely textile works.

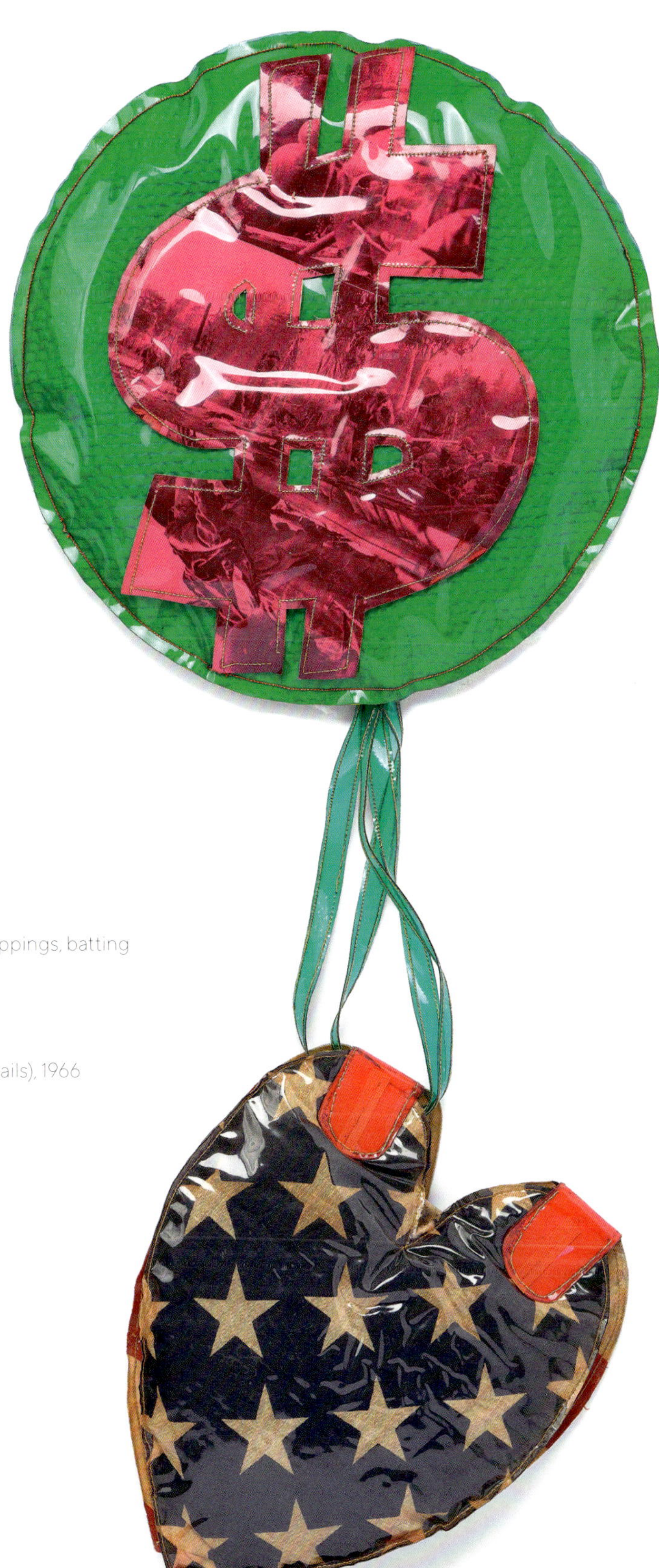

N.U.C., 1966
Plastic, thread, newspaper clippings, batting
63 × 28 cm (various shapes)
Collection of Susan Rynard
Photos: AGO, Craig Boyko

N.U.C. (interior views and details), 1966
Photos: AGO, Craig Boyko

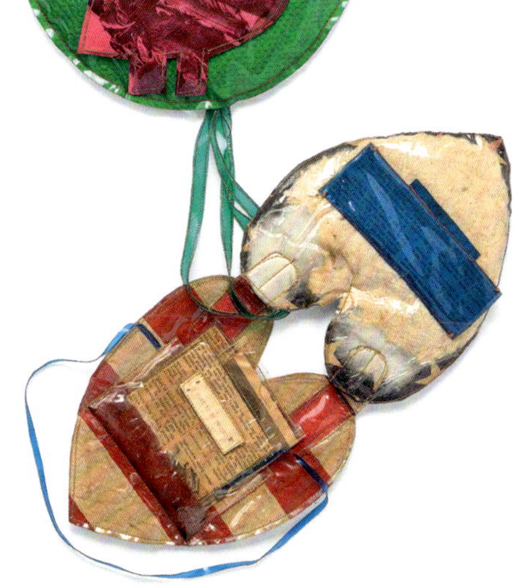

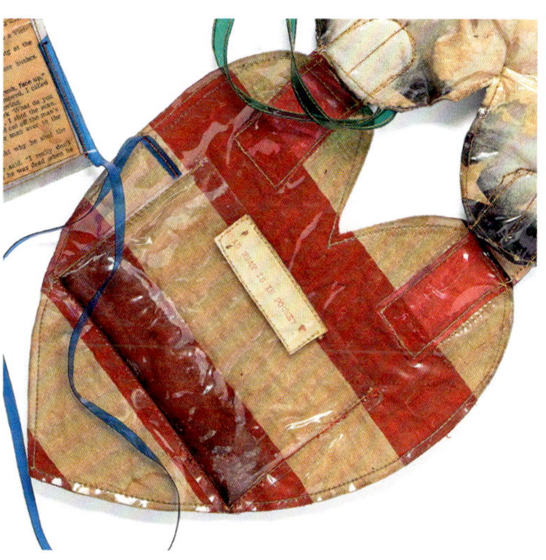

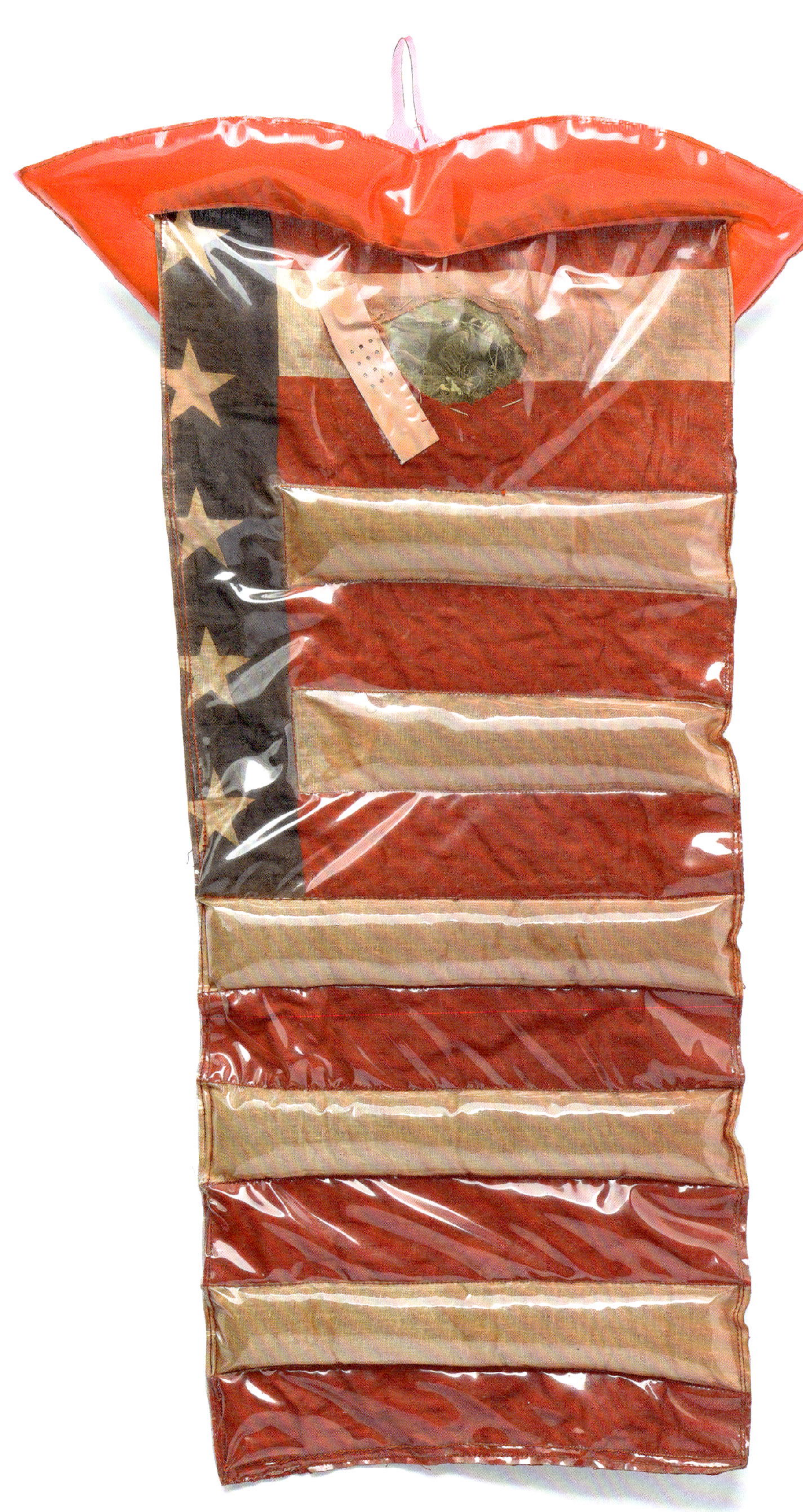

Betsy Ross, Look What They've Done with the Flag that You Made with Such Care, 1966
Plastic, thread, cloth, batting
53.34 × 20.32 × 2.54 cm
Collection of Morden and Edie Yolles
Photo: AGO, Craig Boyko

"THE SAME CORPORATE STRUCTURE
WHICH LEASES NAPALM TO
RESPONSIBLE GROUPS AT
REASONABLE RATES, GIFTS YOU
WITH INEXPENSIVE FUN THINGS
MADE OF PLASTICS. PLASTIC DISHES
ARE KNOWN CARCINOGENS.
UNBACKED VINYL IS MY MEDIUM
THE BLUES WERE CONSIDERED LOW.
I LOVE YOU.
– JOYCE WIELAND"

How are artworks like these analyzed, and what kind of information can we learn from them?

Stephanie Barnes, Canadian Conservation Institute:
The methods we use as conservation scientists (microscopy, vibrational spectroscopy, and separation techniques) are optimized to work with very small samples. The basic plastic type can typically be determined non-invasively, or by using a very small sample about the size of the period at the end of this sentence. With a slightly larger sample of a couple square millimetres, detailed information on the composition of the plastic, plasticizers, and sometimes pigments, can be obtained. Knowing the detailed composition of the plastics can provide information on their intended use, manufacturing process, and degradation pathways. It can help us to predict their long-term stability and make recommendations for conservation, storage, and display.

Most of the samples we have analyzed from Wieland's plastic artworks are composed of PVC, but that is only one small piece of the story. PVC is a highly modifiable material, which can be hard or soft, thick or thin, and is manufactured for a wide range of uses. The plasticizers identified vary between samples and help us to understand the methods of manufacture and intended use.

How does the storage and display environment affect artwork, especially plastics?

Rachel Stark, Art Gallery of Ontario:
Unfortunately, plastic is inherently unstable. Even under the best museum conditions, plastic artworks will fall apart eventually. Different kinds of plastics have different requirements for ideal storage and display conditions, but a basic understanding of environmental factors can go a long way to increase how long a plastic artwork can be enjoyed and viewed as intended.

Both heat and light, especially ultraviolet (UV) wavelengths, break down the polymers that make up plastic on a chemical level. Exposure to light and heat—often combined, like when direct sunshine streams through a window—can cause plastic to become yellowed and brittle. Dyes and colourants in the plastic are also extremely vulnerable to light damage, quickly fading with exposure. Unfortunately, a couple of Wieland's plastic works have already lost most of their original colour.

Water and humidity can cause plastics to swell, shrink, yellow, and discolour, ultimately causing them to be weakened and more sensitive to water as they age. Even oxygen in the air can react with polymers and additives in the plastic material. Oxidation reactions can reduce a material's flexibility and strength, make it crack, reduce glossiness, increase brittleness, and cause discoloration. Other elements also may contribute to the breakdown of plastics. Plasticizers are often unstable and will slowly move out of the bulk material to form a sticky film on the surface. This sticky film can trap dirt and dust, which may exacerbate all the problems mentioned above, as well as create new problems. Well-intentioned attempts to clean the object with commercial cleaning products may do more damage to the plastic.

These factors are often all working together to accelerate the deterioration of the artwork. Removing one or more of these elements and keeping an artwork in a stable environment without large and rapid fluctuations of temperatures and humidity can go a long way toward prolonging its lifespan. The optimal light and temperature levels for storage and display varies depending on the specific materials, but it is generally considered that lowering the temperature and amount of light as much as possible will increase the lifespan of many plastics. The ideal temperature for storing plastic is between 5°C and 10°C. Studies have shown that each 5°C increase in temperature doubles some plastics' deterioration rate.

Will these artworks made with PVC and other synthetic materials be stable enough that future generations can enjoy their meaning and story?

Sjoukje van der Laan, Art Gallery of Ontario:
Despite the "super material" status that plastics had in the 1950s and 1960s, it is now known that most plastics and organic synthetic materials are prone to aging and decay. This is directly noticeable in Wieland's artworks made with plastic.

Scientific research and conservation practices in the last couple of decades have given a better understanding of how all the different existing plastics are likely to "behave" with the passing of time. Through accelerated aging of material samples—a method in which replicated samples are exposed to higher levels of UV light, temperature, relative humidity, and/or atmospheric gases—a prognosis can be given on how synthetic materials like PVC age and what kind of physical and chemical changes are happening to the material. With this knowledge, art conservators know better what kind of deterioration to look for, and how to produce a fitting treatment and preservation plan for the artwork.

The lifespan of an artwork often increases or stabilizes when an artifact is brought into a museum collection, where optimal and stable storage and display conditions are in place and the artifact is closely monitored. In the case of Wieland's plastic works, there are already examples where the plastic is at a more advanced and irreversible level of deterioration. However, through conservation treatment and adjustments of the hanging and display construction, art conservators can stabilize them. The approach in art conservation is to understand how an artwork will look fifty or one-hundred-plus years from now. This also means collecting information on the artist's intent—through archival research, artist interviews, and old photo documentation. In the future, it might be decided to alter the way an artwork is displayed—for example, the point at which a work cannot hang on the wall and must lay flat—or that the exhibition time for a specific artwork is reduced to the minimum. The exposure to light may also be adjusted to the lowest possible measurement (fifty to seventy-five lux); displaying the artwork in a climate-controlled case helps increase its endurance. The goal in art conservation is always the preservation of the artist's intent of storytelling and how this is represented, even when the artwork and its materials are in constant change.

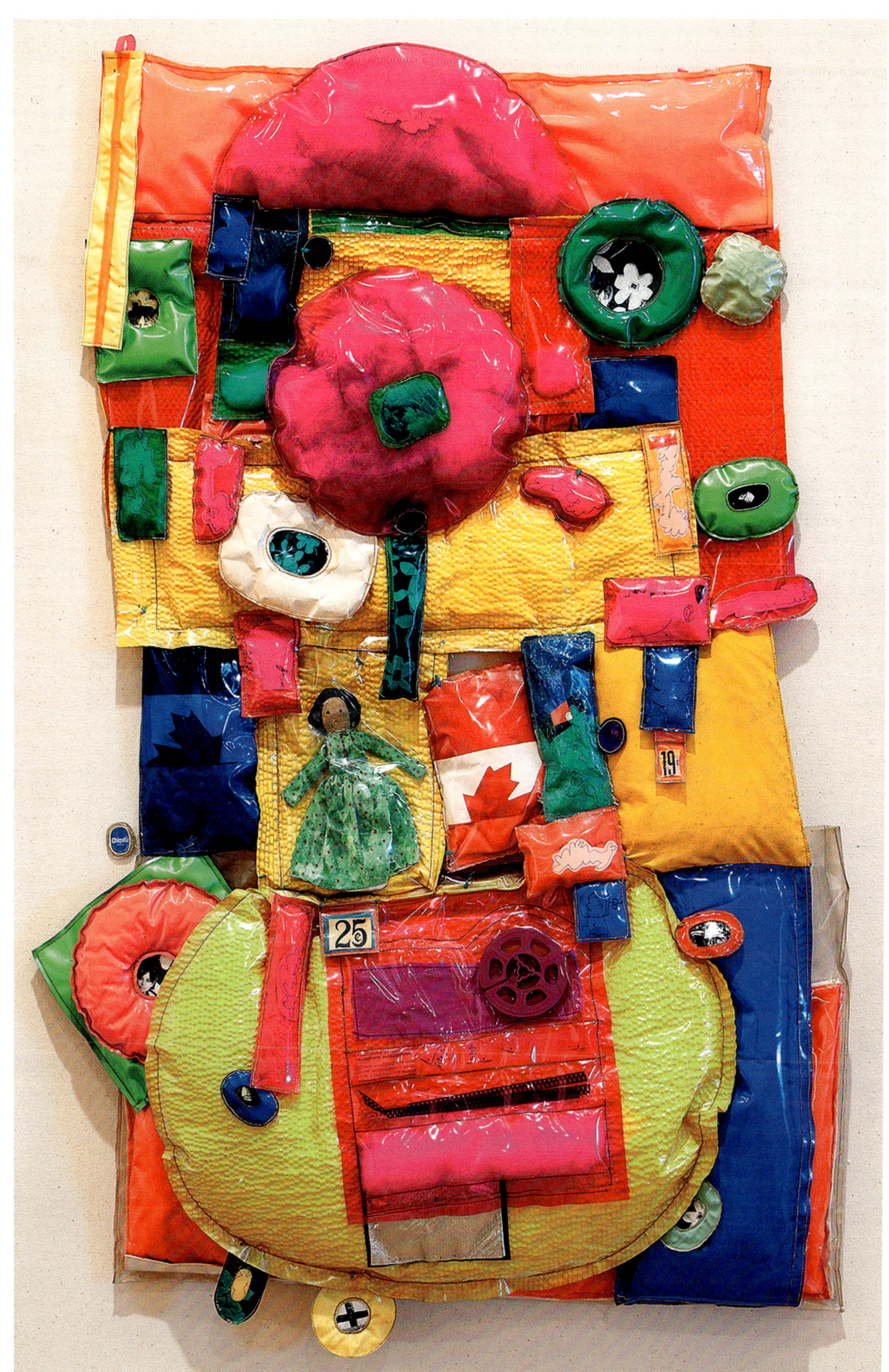

Puerco de Navidad, 1967
Plastic, thread, found objects, paper batting
106.7 × 68.6 cm
The Mendel Art Gallery Collection at Remai Modern, Purchased with funds from the Canada Council Special Purchase Assistance Program 1989
1989.27
Photo: Remai Modern, Troy Mamer

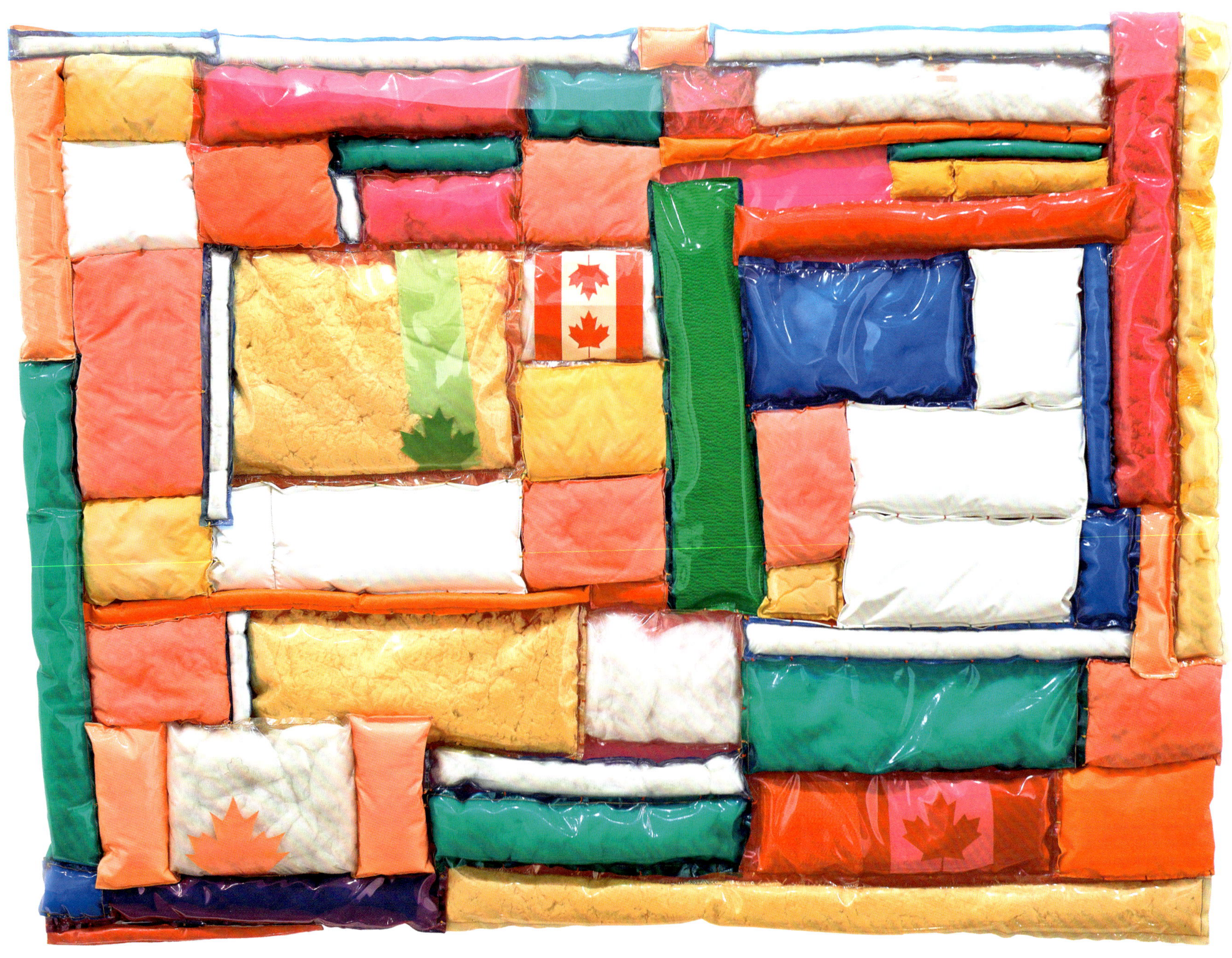

Confedspread, 1967
Plastic, thread, found objects, cloth, batting
146.2 × 200.4 cm
National Gallery of Canada, Purchased 1968
15458
Photo: NGC

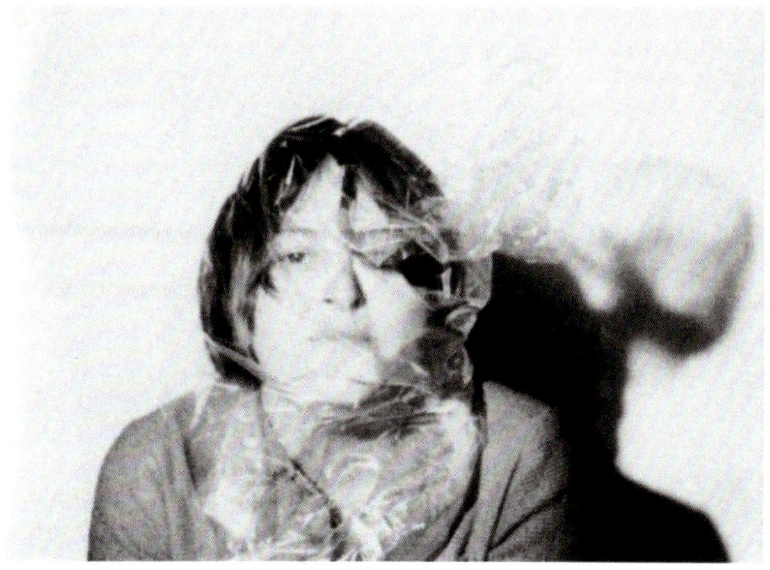

Printed image of Joyce Wieland, part of an invitation to *New Work* exhibition at The Isaacs Gallery, 1967
Joyce Wieland fonds, ASC61828, York University Libraries, Clara Thomas Archives and Special Collections

What is the long-term outlook for these works, and how will it impact the way people can interact with them?

Mark Kearney and Richard Gagnier:
Wieland's plastic works were produced in the mid-to-late 1960s: now almost 60 years old, they are well past the material's conventional lifespan. This means that many of her artworks will continue to undergo significant changes, altering their appearance in an accelerated manner over time.

The analysis and conservation work carried out for this exhibition will prolong the lifespan of these artworks, but not indefinitely. More substantial interventions will be required in the future. Our analysis has found that the general condition of Wieland's plastic artworks is still quite good. Even though the plasticizers have been migrating to the surface of most PVC-based pieces, hence their layer of grime, haziness, and dust accumulation, they still present good flexibility. Structurally they are still sound—although fragile at handling. Tears can be seen at different localized sections, either close to or part of the stitched seams. It might be related to the gradual observed stiffness of the plastic matrix but also to the fact that the short-length stitches associated with their proximity to the edge of the cut shape have created higher tension points, prone to mechanical tear. The observed folds, which are almost permanent now, could be related to poor storage conditions in the past, and the need for flat storage is greater now because of this.

Museum standards stipulate that for every year a light-sensitive object is on display, it must be stored in a cool climate and in the dark for the next three years before it can be exhibited again in public museum conditions. This policy obviously limits public access to the works. As we can only slow down the decay, it also means that in the future it is likely that many of the artworks on display today will require a different display condition: many will no longer be capable of supporting their own weight. It is highly likely that the next time these artworks are brought together for a major exhibition, their physical appearance will be altered compared with how Wieland intended them to appear.

This is the inherent challenge of art conservation: the need to balance the artist's intent, the history of the object, its properties, and its meaning, while at the same time trying to preserve the object for as long as possible.

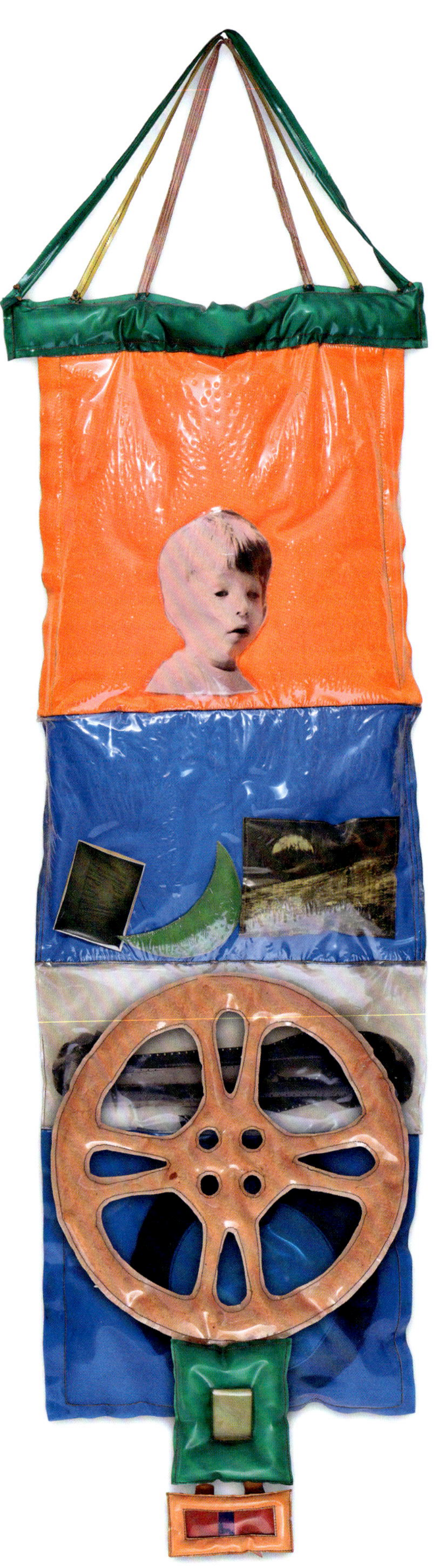

The Space of the Lama, 1966
Plastic, cloth, thread, film, photographs, batting
149.5 × 39.2 × 7.5 cm
Art Gallery of Ontario, Gift of Betty June Ferguson, 2017
2017/79
Photo: AGO, Sean Weaver

THE SPACE OF THE LAMA, 1966

The Space of the Lama was produced during an especially prolific and dynamic period in Wieland's career. Through her plastic hangings—bright, soft, sewn, stuffed, laminated, and easy to transport—she developed her unique blend of layered personal narrative, popular culture references, and heightened social, political, and environmental awareness. As she explained, "[P]lastic was so available; it was all around and it was in the air. I liked the material; I laminated it, I sewed it, I treated it like traditional fabric. I started the idea of putting, of pocketing, of enclosing stuff in it."[1]

The Space of the Lama highlights Wieland's interest in the aesthetic properties of film, and conjures the work's chief cultural reference, the so-called space age. It synthesizes her formal and thematic interests in a vertical sequence of plastic pockets in bright colours: green, orange, blue, and fuchsia, with pale grey and pink. The four rectangular pockets contain mementos: photographs, a green crescent moon, and 16mm and 35mm exposed film. The bottom half of the hanging has an outer layer of shaped stuffed plastic elements: a reproduction of a Goldberg Brothers 16mm film reel, from which two small picture frames dangle.[2]

Suspended in the bright orange fabric stuffed in the top pocket is a large black-and-white photograph of Wieland's godchild,

Munro Ferguson,[3] the son of her close friends Betty and Graeme Ferguson, both filmmakers.[4] Wieland and her husband jokingly nicknamed Munro "Lama," alluding to the reincarnated Dalai Lama, pretending that he was an oracle. She has cut out the shape of the boy's head and placed it centrally, his gaze downward, as though he is looking at the images in the blue pocket below. Stuffed inside are two photographs on each side of the green moon. On the left is a black-and-white image of one of Wieland's first quilted pieces, *Untitled* (1966), a monumental, monochromatic work with a circular central motif.[5] On the right is the first image of Earth captured from the moon. Taken by NASA's Lunar Orbiter 1 on August 23, 1966, the photo was reproduced in *Life* magazine soon after—forever altering humanity's perspective on itself.[6] Wieland takes this iconic image and sews it into its own plastic pocket, giving it the same puffiness and scale as that of her adjacent homemade crescent moon. Munro and this cosmic trio of moons, Earth, and sun lend the piece its title.

GEORGIANA UHLYARIK

1 Quoted in Marie Fleming, *Joyce Wieland*, exh. cat. (Toronto: Art Gallery of Ontario, 1987), 61 — a conversation with Wieland in spring 1986.

2 The polaroid housed in the green frame has since faded.

3 Munro Ferguson (b. 1960) is a filmmaker at the National Film Board of Canada. In 2003, Ferguson made *June*, hand-drawn stereoscopic animation in memory of Wieland. The photograph is likely taken by American photographer Charmian Reading (1931–2014).

4 Wieland and her husband lived with the Fergusons when they first moved to New York City. Betty Ferguson (1933–2022) was an experimental filmmaker and editor who used found footage and montage. Graeme Ferguson (1929–2021) was a cinematographer and filmmaker, and produced the first IMAX film. *The Space of the Lama* was in Betty Ferguson's collection until she donated it to the AGO in 2017.

5 *Untitled*, 1966, quilted cotton, 264.2 × 229.2 cm, Collection of the National Gallery of Canada, Purchased 1967, Acc. 15318. This photograph is also included in the plastic hanging *Home Movie*, 1966. They were all included in Wieland's *Hangings* exhibition at The Isaacs Gallery March 22–April 10, 1967.

6 *Life*, September 9, 1966, 34B–34C.

STUFFED MOVIE, 1966

Stuffed Movie is a filmstrip reimagined and enlarged in bright hues of translucent plastic. In this soft sculpture, Wieland presents a sampling of references from her visual lexicon that unfold vertically like a filmic sequence. Found images and dried plants are encased into custom-sewn plastic pouches, which are held inside five multicoloured pockets. The eclectic contents float in a succession of soft rectangular sleeves, serving as a running list of the artist's ideas, anxieties, and motivations.

Wieland includes several of her classic motifs—the mouth, the film reel, the flag—as well as others that are more singular or surprising, such as the lion and the cowboy. The miscellany of gathered images and objects brings to mind the chaos of mass media and never-ending news cycles that subsumed her at the time. Televisions—especially colour—were new in domestic settings, and people began to receive news and watch movies at home in small formats, evoked by the glowing colourful boxes of this work. By enshrining these sundry images in *Stuffed Movie*, she assigns them prestige, but how important are their referents? Considered collectively, the images could be autonomous; resourcefully selected things from a specific time and place. As such, they relate to the objects in Wieland's 1965 film *Water Sark*, a work that is entirely self-sufficient, comprised of items exclusively from her kitchen: mirrors, water, glasses, and cups.

Some images in *Stuffed Movie* send clear individual messages, though. The word "PESTICIDES" spelled across the bottom section, eerily juxtaposed with a cropped image of a toothy smile, calls out Wieland's profound ecological concerns. Just above, in a fuchsia pocket, she stuffs a photograph of the 1905 massacre of unarmed demonstrators by soldiers of the Imperial Guard in Saint Petersburg. This image, although iconic, has a contested authenticity: it may either be a photograph of the actual event or a still from the 1925 film by Soviet director Vyacheslav Viskovsky (1881–1933) called *Devyatoe Yanvarya (Ninth of January)*. Wieland's inclusion of this image signals her interest in film history, specifically Soviet cinema. It also points to her dedication to political activism. During the 1960s when she was living in New York, she and Michael Snow participated in a number of civil rights protests, including major demonstrations against nuclear proliferation, the Vietnam War, and racial discrimination.

In the central bright orange pocket, Wieland juxtaposes Canadian and US flags, alluding to her cross-border identity. The Canadian flag—barely a year old when she made this piece—sags, folded nearly in half. Another Canadian flag sits directly above it in the yellow pocket. The US flag, smaller and rotated by ninety degrees, holds a central spot in the composition but is flattened in terms of its significance or hierarchy. The flags in this work, like many others, reference Wieland's critical thinking about Canadian identity and nationalism, which deepened while she lived in the United States. In 1965, the red maple leaf design was proclaimed the first official flag of Canada. She subsequently began integrating the new flag into her work, and it became an object of fascination for her as Canada neared its centennial year. ››››

RENÉE VAN DER AVOIRD

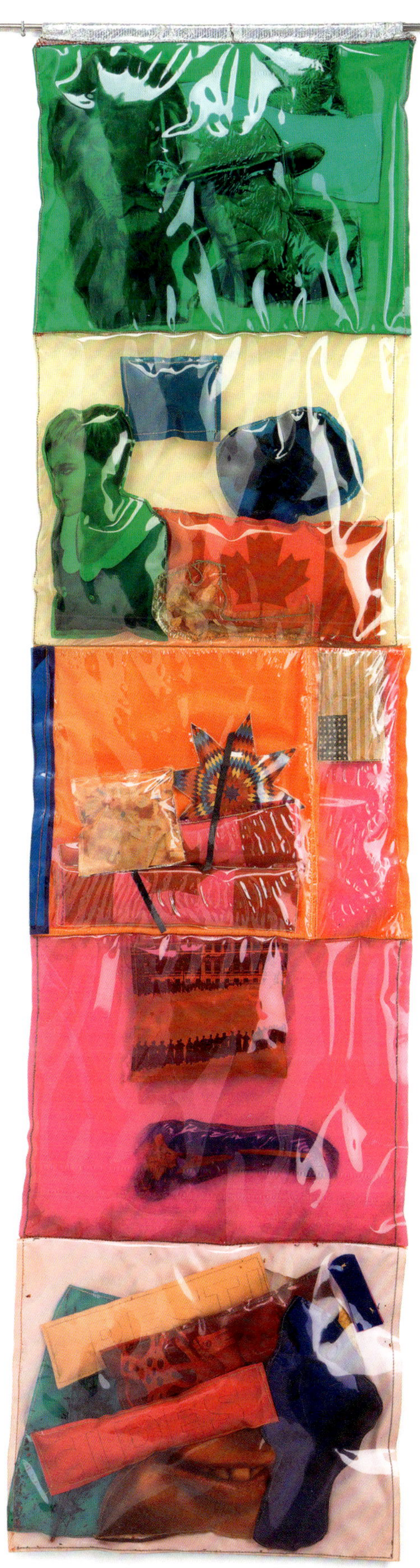

Stuffed Movie, 1966
Plastic, thread, paper, cotton, textile, batting
142.2 × 36.9 × 3 cm
Collection of the Vancouver Art Gallery,
Murrin Estate Funds
VAG 68.6
Photo: Vancouver Art Gallery

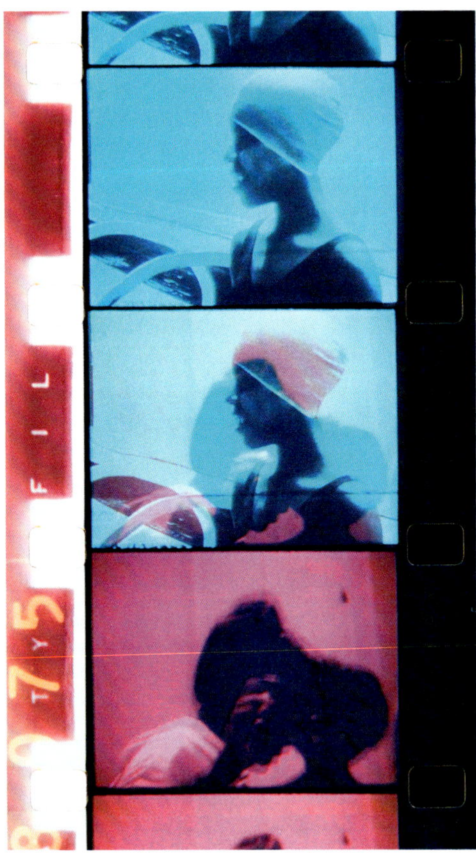

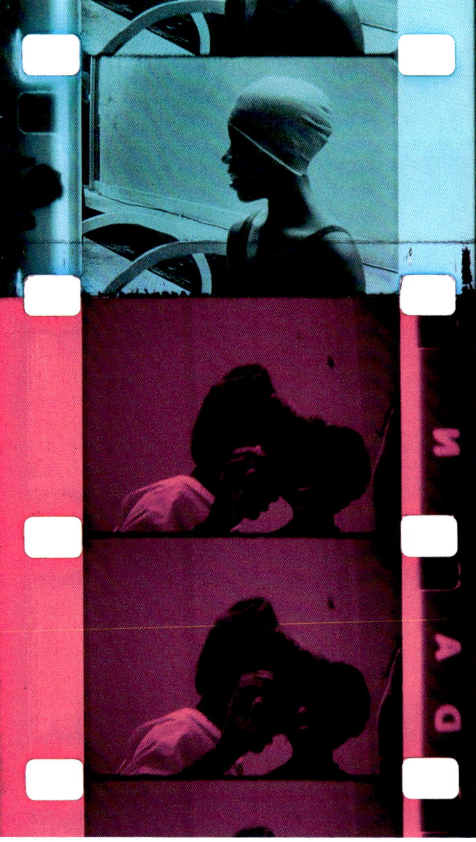

Comparison between the hand-tinted 16 mm original (left)
and the interlaced version (right) of ***Handtinting,*** 1967
Film, 16mm, colour, silent
6 min
Joyce Wieland fonds, Cinémathèque québécoise
Photos: Stéphanie Côté, courtesy of Cinémathèque québécoise

"It was a retraining centre in West Virginia run by Xerox and we made a documentary . . . another Canadian, Sylvia Davern, who was working in animation at the time and two American girls, one doing sound and another shooting. The job came through Sylvia's company. . . . Anyway, I took some of my own outs from the film—some of which were genuine old-fashioned cutaways, and which I felt very strongly about, and began to make *Hand Tinting* [*sic*]. . . . The centre was about 80% Black kids who had come from everywhere. They were lonely, rebellious, funny, restless, and hopelessly poor. What they were offered in the way of education was humiliating to me, some rooms with typewriters, and a machine that spoke to them as they typed. . . . It was a corporate pacification programme. I wanted to do my own film about them. . . .

There's nothing out of the way in it, it has mystery and rhythm and some repetitive portraits of some beautiful faces. The editing and the girls are the subject of *Handtinting*. The editing and the so-called subject matter are equal."

HANDTINTING, 1967

In 2002, the Joyce Wieland estate granted the Cinémathèque québécoise rights to Wieland's cinematic work, extending a bond first forged when the artist entrusted the institution with the safekeeping of her original film prints and other footage. This major museum exhibition devoted to her oeuvre has offered the opportunity to undertake the digitization and restoration of a selection of these films.

Restoring experimental films requires a very different approach compared with more conventional narrative cinema. For instance, apparent "defects"—scratches, stains, dust—may not be defects at all, but instead the result of formal choices or artisanal methods; altering them in such cases would constitute a serious breach of restoration ethics. Therefore, careful study of Wieland's creative process on each film is crucial, which includes tracking down as many references as possible and delving into testimonies from the artist, her collaborators, researchers, and biographers. Restoration is still underway at the time of writing. Bolstered by the inspection of a wide range of material, research continues to uncover surprises and demands constant readjustment.

Among the films restored for the exhibition, *Handtinting* is a striking example of how difficult it can be to determine what does and what does not belong to the original work. The discovery of a 16mm internegative—a colour negative duplicate of the original camera negative, used to make prints for exhibition—with a typical video artifact suggested that Wieland, in an artistic act, may have re-filmed the original copy of her film from a television screen. The subsequent discovery of old distribution copies with no trace of video disproved this hypothesis and led to the decision to use the precious 16mm original, tinted and perforated, as the source for restoration.

The films *Sailboat* and *Pierre Vallières* are concrete examples of the need for close attention to colour and the chromatic elements of Wieland's work—the perception of which can be distorted. In the case of *Sailboat* (p. 106), shot in black and white but printed on colour film with a uniform blue hue, the challenge is to find the right blue. We were lucky enough to locate some early prints still in very good condition despite multiple screenings over the years. These copies serve as a reference for assigning the correct shade to the digitized black-and-white images. For *Pierre Vallières*, however, the search continues for old prints whose colours have not been altered by chemical degradation, so that restoration can do justice to the "Géricault red" of Vallières's lips (p. 111), which Wieland stressed as important.

While an experimental film is usually made by a single person with very few resources, restoring a film of any kind is always a collective endeavour. This project would not have been possible without the enthusiastic help of many individuals and institutions. We want to take this opportunity to thank them. May these restorations allow a wide audience to rediscover the work of an artist who brilliantly redrew the dividing line between cinema and the visual arts.

STÉPHANIE CÔTÉ, GUILLAUME LAFLEUR
WITH APOLLINE CARON-OTTAVI

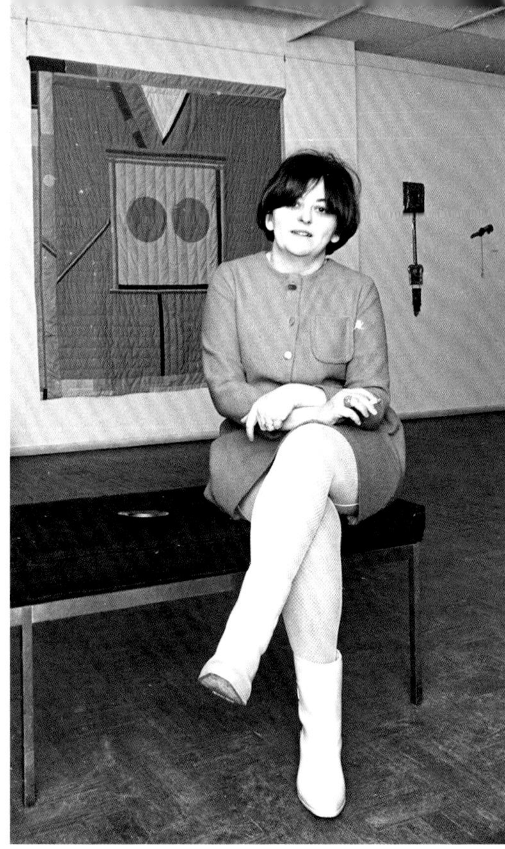

Joyce Wieland in front of *The Camera's Eyes* and *Home Work* at The Isaacs Gallery, 1967
Bill Russell for *Toronto Telegram*
Toronto Telegram fonds, ASC00007,
York University Libraries,
Clara Thomas Archives and Special Collections

FILM MANDALA, 1966
THE CAMERA'S EYES, 1966

A cross-border collaboration with her older sister, Joan Stewart, Joyce Wieland's *Film Mandala* and *The Camera's Eyes* cemented her concept of "women's work." Stewart was living in Desboro, Ontario, near Owen Sound, and Wieland in New York City. "Getting into the making of quilts as a 'woman's' work was a conscious move on my part, particularly when I lived in New York," recalled Wieland. "There was a highly competitive scene with men artists going on there. It polarized my view of life; it made me go right into the whole feminine thing."[1] Her later quilts would carry cheeky political messaging but with these, her earliest quilts, "the first idea of using them was that I was involved with feminine work, things that women had done."[2] Making quilts integral to her artistic practice was Wieland's way of showing "great respect" for "women's work," the kind that her mother had done and that her sister did.[3]

While Wieland had been making textile works since 1959, her first-ever quilt was completed in 1965, commissioned by friends for their child. "Maybe I could design a quilt about a person," Wieland thought, "a quilt for their child that would be about the attributes of the child," like a portrait.[4] Her sister "was making quilts all this time. She needed work. She didn't have any money, and I liked what she was doing."[5] To make quilts, Wieland cut out fabric pieces, basted or pinned them together, and then Stewart finished them. This form of collective labour, like a director making a movie, extended into *Film Mandala* and *The Camera's Eyes*. Both were exhibited in Wieland's solo show *Hangings* at The Isaacs Gallery, Toronto, in spring 1967, alongside other quilt and plastic works. "To meet the deadline for the show," Stewart had further help with quilting from a neighbour, Gladys Chambers, but needed to "find more quilters . . . not an easy matter since this old fashioned craft is not widely known today."[6]

"You were way ahead of everyone saying that quilts were okay," Ardele Lister said to Wieland in 1976.[7] When Wieland turned to quiltmaking in the 1960s, she was on the cusp of a North American "Craze for Quilts."[8] Revival of interest took off in the following decade among scholars, artists, quilters, feminists, collectors, and curators for quilts as women's work, as traditional craft, and as works of art. A "new wave of feminist art" embraced the quilt as "the prime visual metaphor for women's lives, for women's

1 Joyce Wieland, "Interview," in *Eclectic Eve*, ed. Janice Cameron, Frances Ferdinands, Sharon Snitman, Madli Tamme, and Annetta Wernick (Toronto: Canadian Women's Educational Press, 1972), n.p.

2 Joyce Wieland, interview by Ardele Lister, "Joyce Wieland," *Criteria* 2, no. 1 (February 1976): 15.

3 Joyce Wieland, interview by Barbara Stevenson, October 8, 1986, in Kristy A. Holmes-Moss, "Joyce Wieland: Interview and Notes on *Reason over Passion* and *Pierre Vallières*," *Canadian Journal of Film Studies* 15, no. 2 (Fall 2006): 121.

4 Joyce Wieland, interview by Lauren Rabinovitz, "An Interview with Joyce Wieland," *Afterimage* 8, no. 10 (May 1981): 10, and transcript of Joyce Wieland artist's talk at the University of Lethbridge, 1985, 3 (edited quote from cassette tape "Joyce Wieland on Her Work"); transcript held at the University of Lethbridge Art Gallery, Alberta—hereafter cited as Wieland, Lethbridge transcript.

5 Rabinovitz, "An Interview," 10.

6 Elizabeth Kimball, photographs by Michel Lambeth, "Art You Can Use . . . to Keep Warm . . . to Cover a Table . . . to Hang on a Wall," *Star Weekly*, January 14, 1967, 29.

7 Lister, "Joyce Wieland," 15.

8 Title of photo essay in *Life* magazine, May 5, 1972.

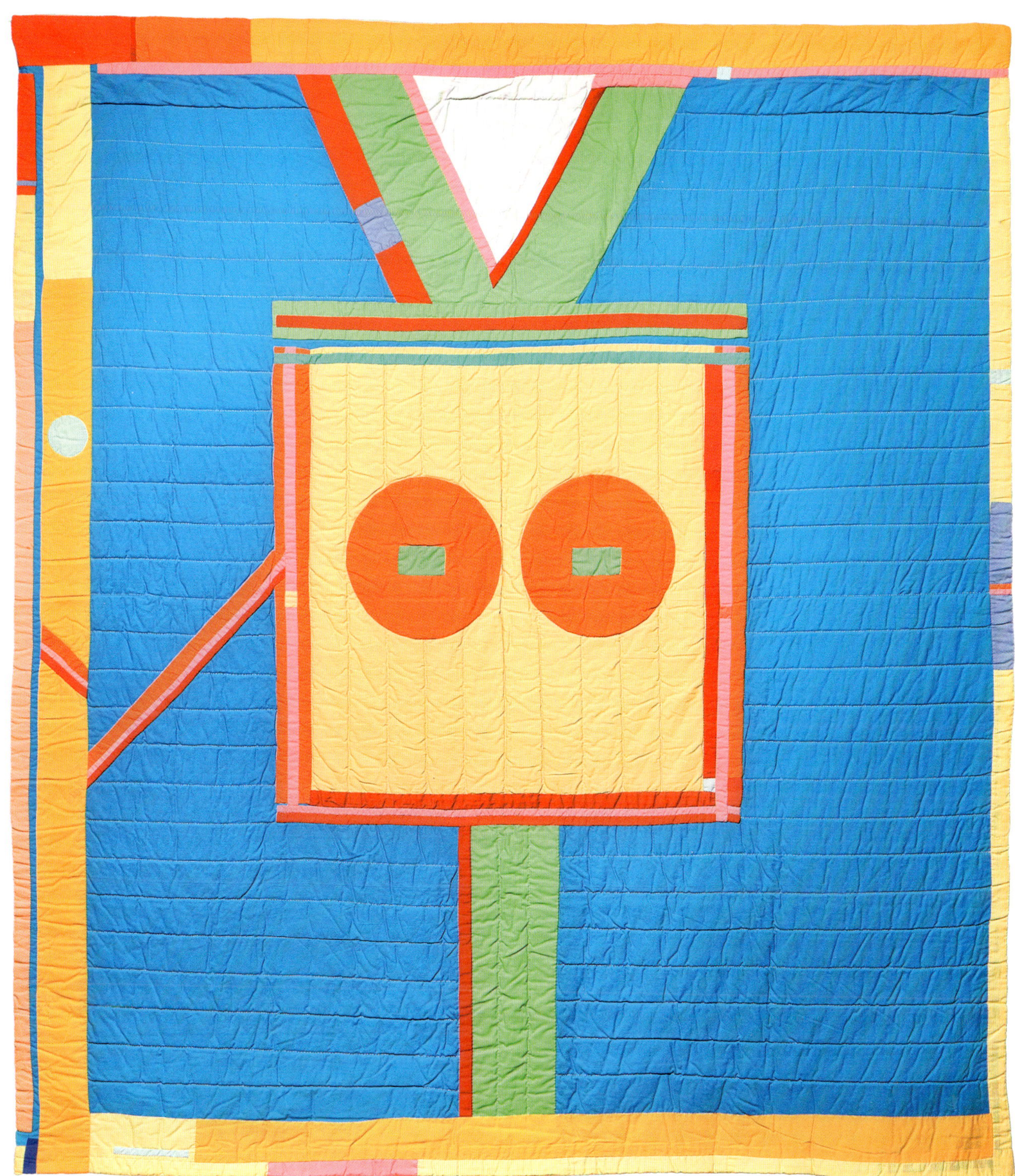

The Camera's Eyes, 1966
Quilting by Joan Stewart
and Gladys Chambers
Cloth, thread, batting
263.8 × 187.6 cm
Art Gallery of Hamilton,
Gift of Irving Zucker, 1992
1992.2.12
Photo: Robert McNair, 2018

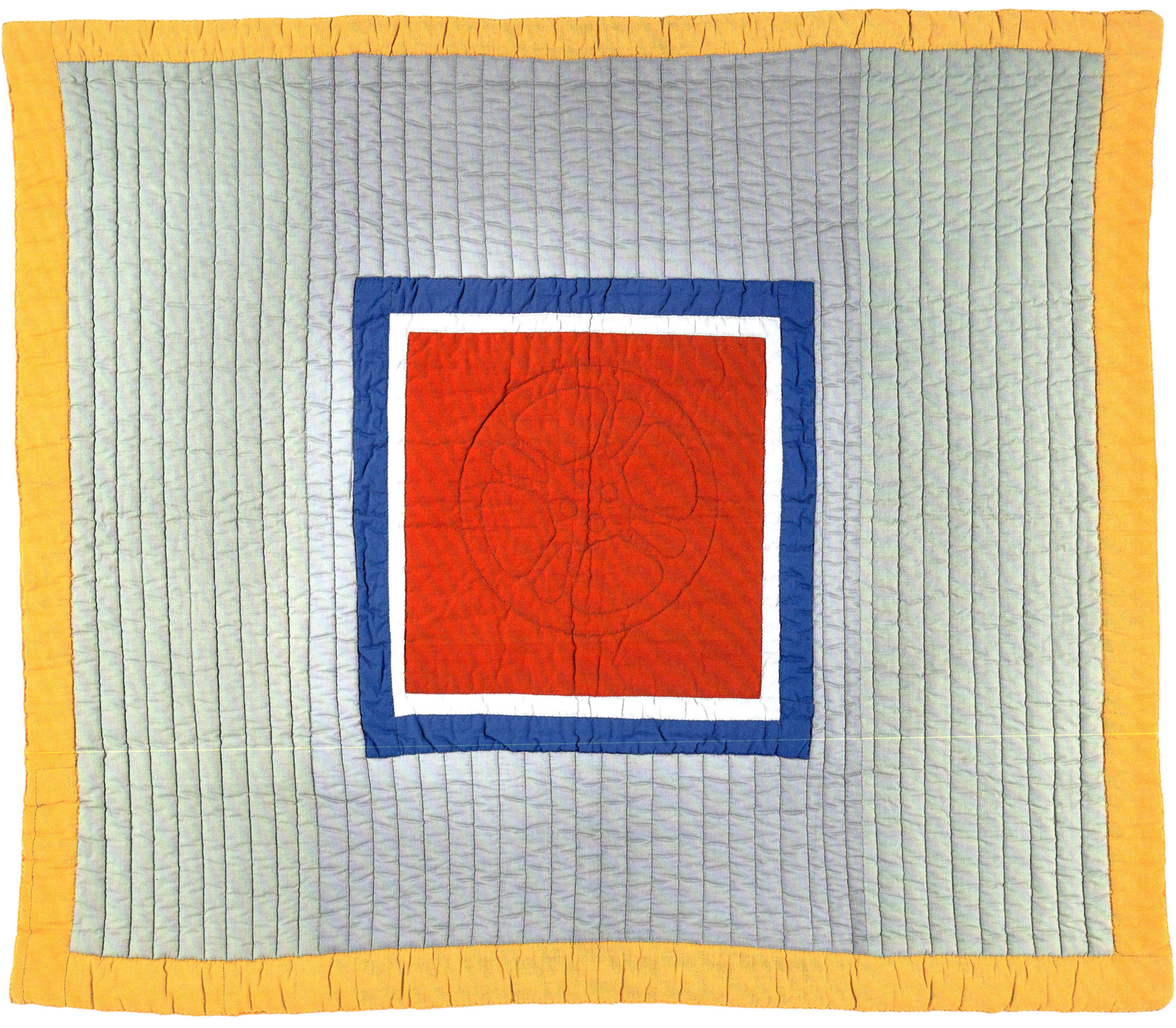

OPPOSITE
Film Mandala, 1966
Quilting by Joan Stewart and Gladys Chambers
Cloth, thread, batting
203 × 202 cm
Macdonald Stewart Art Centre Collection at the Art Gallery of Guelph, Gift of Doug MacPherson, 2006
MS2006.023
Photo: AGO, Craig Boyko

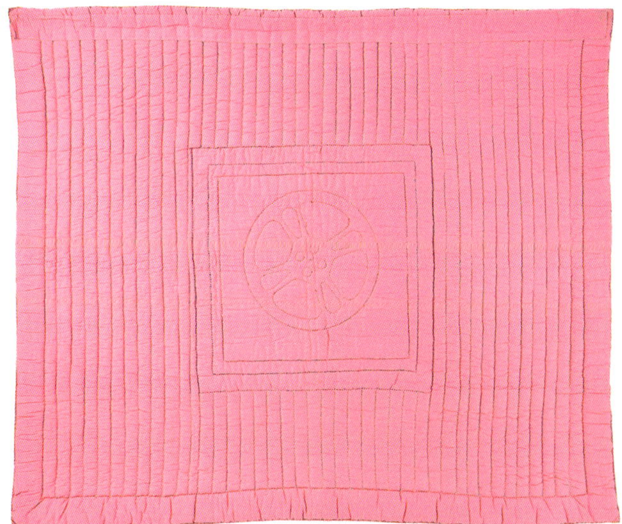

RIGHT
Verso view of *Film Mandala,* 1966
Photo: AGO, Craig Boyko

culture,"[9] while new pattern books, quilter groups, and juried shows satisfied renewed enthusiasm for the craft, fuelled by the colonial nostalgia of nation-marking centennials and bicentennials.[10] Exhibitions at major art institutions were credited for having "recognized" historical quilts as art objects.[11] Feminist response, however, was swift. "Because our female ancestors' pieced quilts bear a superficial resemblance to the work of contemporary formalist artists such as Stella, Noland and Newman (although quilts are richer in color, fabric, design and content)," Patricia Mainardi wrote in 1973, "modern male curators and critics are now capable of 'seeing' the art in them."[12] Wieland was already valuing quilts and making them—to find voice, "to be myself"[13]—within the same male-dominated New York art scene.

"I think my greatest feminist involvement was the creation of the women's work, which I did long before Judy Chicago," Wieland told Barbara Stevenson in 1986.[14]

With *Film Mandala* and *The Camera's Eyes*, Wieland aptly continues "women's work" as a form of fond portraiture. She felt that quilts, true to their tradition, "should be used for special occasions like birthdays, anniversaries, that they should have some celebratory use."[15] Each quilt is an homage to film. Cross-references between two mediums, her film work and her artwork, "began very early in the '60s in New York . . . one thing influencing another from film to art."[16] With bright cheery fabrics pieced just so, Wieland lovingly displays her affection for film's "attributes": the side glance of double spools on an 8mm camera or the "mandala" of a film projection reel, hand-quilted in the centre of whole-cloth red.[17] A secret known only to the artist (or someone who might sleep under the quilt), *Film Mandala* is backed in glowing pink, something she also does in later text quilts. Wieland admired the "radiance" of her sister's stitchwork against the fabric backgrounds she had chosen. With *Film Mandala*, "the light falls on all these lines which in a way are the proportion of 8mm film strips."[18] With *The Camera's Eyes*, "it's like a sea, it's very, very alive and it shows the kind of collaboration between my sister Joan and I here."[19]

ALICIA BOUTILIER

9 Lucy R. Lippard, "Up, Down, and Across: A New Frame for New Quilts," in *The Artist and the Quilt*, ed. Charlotte Robinson (New York: Knopf, 1983), 32.

10 The logo for Canada's centennial in 1967, by Stuart Ash, looked very much like a block quilt design.

11 *Abstract Design in American Quilts*, Whitney Museum of American Art, New York, 1971, and *American Pieced Quilts*, Smithsonian, Washington, DC, 1972. Incidentally, *Abstract Design in American Quilts* opened on the very day that Wieland's *True Patriot Love* opened at the National Gallery of Canada: July 1.

12 Patricia Mainardi, "Quilts: The Great American Art," first published in *Feminist Art Journal* 2, no. 1 (Winter 1973); republished in Norma Broude and Mary D. Garrard, eds., *Feminism and Art History* (New York: Harper and Row, 1982), 343.

13 Lister, "Joyce Wieland," 15.

14 Stevenson, interview, 121.

15 Quoted in Marie Fleming, *Joyce Wieland*, exh. cat. (Toronto: Art Gallery of Ontario, 1987), 68.

16 Wieland, Lethbridge transcript, 4.

17 Mandalas in Wieland's work were also attributed to experiments with LSD, popular in the artistic community at the time. Robert Fulford, "Now, We Get Psychedelic Quilts," *Toronto Daily Star*, March 25, 1967.

18 Wieland, Lethbridge transcript, 3.

19 Wieland, Lethbridge transcript, 4.

The social and political unrest escalating in the United States in the 1960s had a profound impact on Joyce Wieland's political consciousness and artistic expression. As an expatriate living in New York City on the eve of Canada's centenary in 1967, she created a fictitious "cultural activist" movement together with her friend, playwright Mary Mitchell. They staged inventive demonstrations at the Canadian consulate in New York, acting out a Canadian mythology imbued with humorously earnest devotion.

Both Pierre Elliott Trudeau's ascent to power as Canada's charismatic prime minister and the economic dominance of US enterprise and policy stimulated Wieland's imagination and propelled her practice. Her last four years in New York represent her most diverse and expansive artistic production as she worked across many media to create a powerful and insightful multi-sensory expression. Repeating and jumbling the words of Trudeau, Wieland realized her most ambitious experimental film, *La raison avant le passion / Reason over*

FLAG ARRANGEMENT

Passion, in 1969, and puffed up the same words into a pair of quilts, one in English and the other in French. Continuing to scrutinize Trudeaumania, she quotes him again in her largest plastic hanging, *Man Has Reached Out and Touched the Tranquil Moon* (1970), punctuating the phrase with a pocketed Canadian flag that drapes onto the floor. During this highly prolific period, with her distinctive and compelling mixture of wit, fervour, and affection, Wieland created her most celebrated works.

LA RAISON AVANT LA PASSION / REASON OVER PASSION, 1969

Joyce Wieland shot *La raison avant la passion / Reason over Passion* in stages between 1967 and 1968, a period that saw her adopt a strategic nationalism in response to a perceived threat of US imperialism encroaching on Canadian territory, particularly the Arctic.[1] She had taken an allegorical approach for her previous film, *Rat Life and Diet in North America* (1968), filming gerbils on the kitchen table in her loft as stand-ins for political prisoners attempting to flee to Canada.[2] Around this time, Wieland ironically likened her work as an artist to that of a government propaganda agent. This identification is performed in the prelude to *La raison avant la passion*, where she silently mouths the words to Canada's national anthem. Yet much of the film departs from the political focus of *Rat Life* and instead offers views of the the country without making any reference to current events at the time of production.

In the winter of 1967, Wieland journeyed across Canada from Toronto to Vancouver, capturing images of landscapes from the windows of a moving train. That summer, she travelled from Cape Breton to Quebec City to gather more material. The resulting rushes were edited the following year, more or less in the order they were filmed, then superimposed with different permutations of letters from the phrase "Reason over passion," lifted from Prime Minister Pierre Elliott Trudeau's motto.[3] As in her earlier films *Sailboat* and *1933* (both 1967), the title of her work appears again and again, this time at the bottom of the screen, like a subtitle. The scenes of roads, forests, mountains, and the occasional village, all devoid of human presence, accumulate while over 530 possible variations on the letters of Trudeau's three words run their course.

Intercut with the landscape scenes, official templates of the Maple Leaf appear in stroboscopic flashes. Beeps, interspersed with silence, punctuate the shots. In 1972, George Lellis highlighted the parodic aspect of Wieland's use of formal strategies of experimental/structural film along with patriotic iconography, observing that she "give[s] us a sample of just about every possible level of abstraction for the notion of Canada, from the most phenomenal to the most symbolic."[4] For Wieland, one notable aspect of this approach lay in treating Trudeau's ideal of bilingualism with humour. As the cross-country travelogue nears what should be views of Ontario, it is interrupted by an excerpt of a French lesson from a vinyl record bought at a flea market. Flags appear again, alternating with red and white monochromatic frames, while a voiceover instructs the student, "Pierre," to repeat simple French phrases. Next, Wieland includes footage she filmed of Trudeau at the Liberal Party convention in Ottawa on April 6, 1968, when he was elected party leader. By rephotographing the material from the screen of a Moviola (an editing device that magnifies the filmstrip), she keeps the viewer at an analytical distance. The sequence unfolds in slowed-down or sped-up motion; from time to time, Wieland freezes a frame.

Interpretations on this passage abound. Some perceive it as a love letter, while others see it as a sign of Wieland's ambivalence toward Trudeau. The politician's words were not recorded. To replace silence, Wieland assembled a soundtrack with modulations that follow the lead of the processed images, as if reading an abstract optical score. After this sequence, the coast-to-coast journey resumes. The beep motif with the permutating letters continues until a postcard shot of a ship afloat on the Pacific brings the British Columbia segment to a close.

VINCENT BONIN

1 On the evolution of Wieland's political ideas, see Johanne Sloan, "Joyce Wieland at the Border: Nationalism, the New Left, and the Question of Political Art in Canada," *Journal of Canadian Art History* 26 (2005): 80–107.

2 Wieland considered *La raison avant la passion* part of a trilogy about Canada, along with *Rat Life and Diet in North America* and *The Far Shore*, on which she worked from 1971 to 1976.

3 In 1968, Wieland incorporated these words into two quilts titled *Reason over Passion* and *La raison avant la passion*.

4 George Lellis, "La raison avant la passion," in *Form and Structure in Recent Film*, exh. cat., ed. Dennis Wheeler (Vancouver: Vancouver Art Gallery and Talonbooks, 1972), n.p.

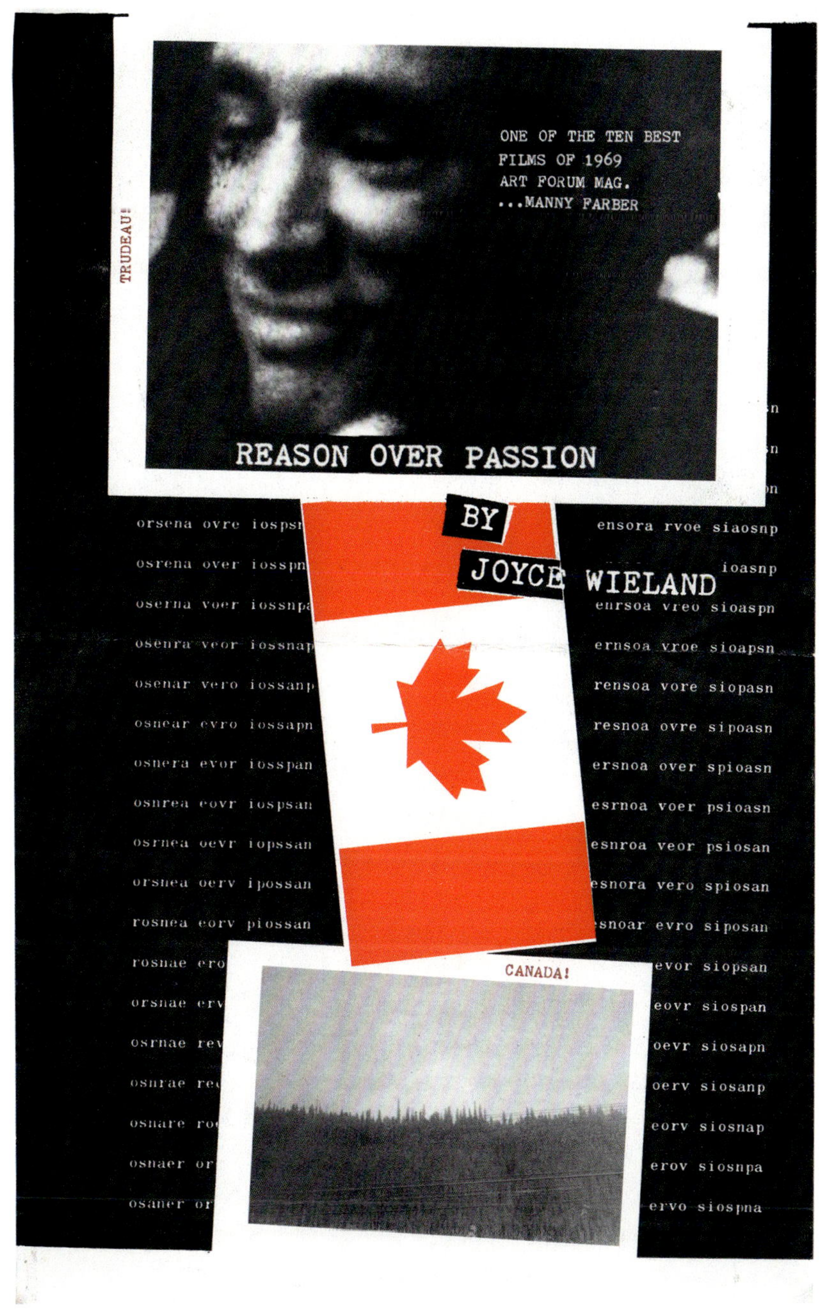

Poster for *La raison avant la passion / Reason over Passion*, 1969
York University Libraries, Clara Thomas Archives & Special Collections, Joyce Wieland fonds, ASC61833

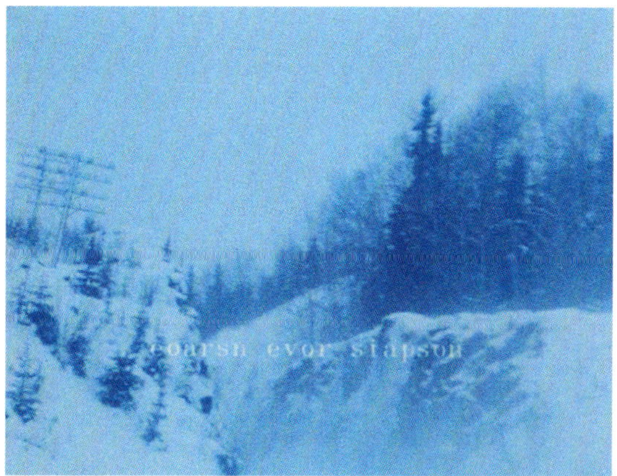

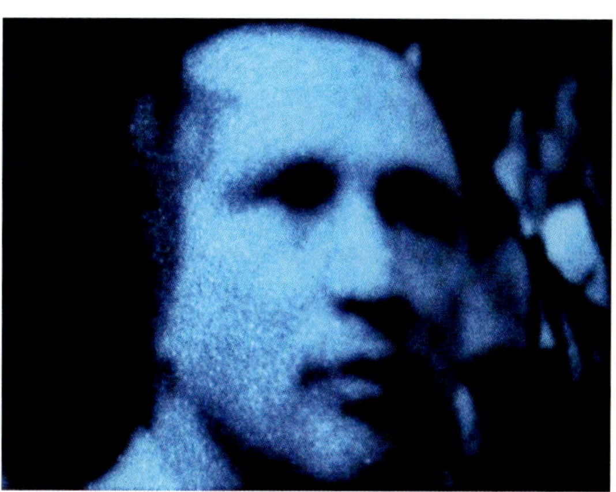

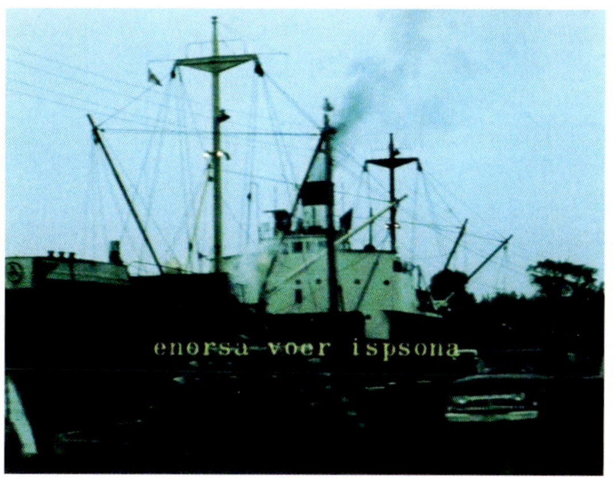

La raison avant la passion / Reason over Passion
(film stills), 1969
Film, 16mm, sound
80 min
Joyce Wieland fonds, Cinémathèque québécoise
Photo: Stephen Broomer, courtesy of the AGO

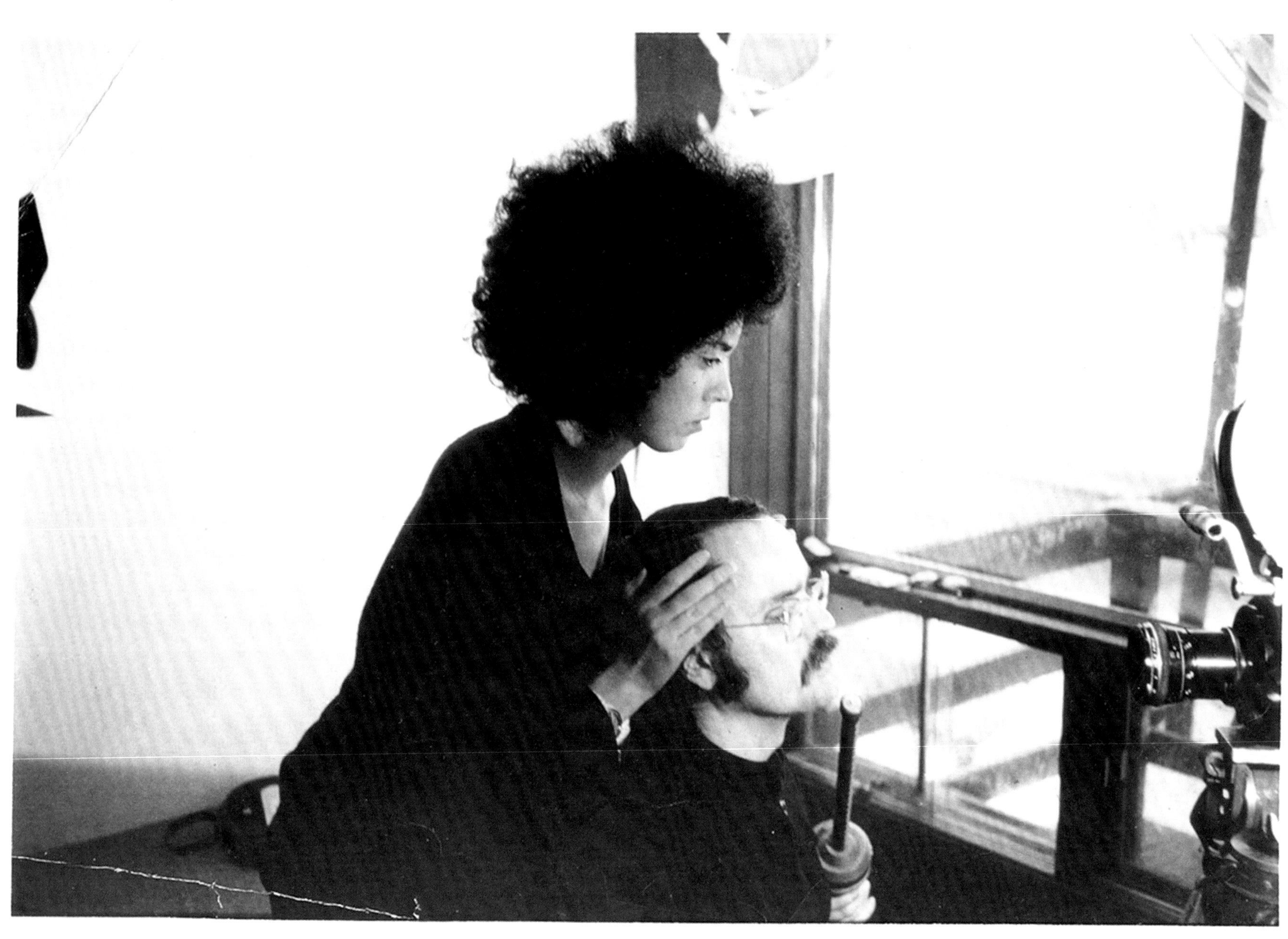

French interpreter Danielle Corbeil holding Pierre Vallières's head during the filming of *Pierre Vallières*, 1972
Photo courtesy of the CFMDC

JIGS & REELS

It was amongst the filmmakers of the "New Cinema" that I first saw the light. They were "Structuralist, "visionary filmmakers," "underground" filmmakers and my friends as well. We were once very intimate in New York, sharing each other's films, tapes, shadows, and conversations. Now the group has dispersed to different places. I doubt whether we shall all see each other that much again, even though we are part of a Movement. I didn't know that I was part of a Movement until for me it was over. I often think of the unique talents of Ken and Flo, Ernie, Hollie, Jonas, Gerson, Andrew, Jack Smith, Sharits, the Kuchars and Bob (not to mention my husband, Mr. Snow).

Now, since I've been back in Canada a lot of things seem in the past which perhaps aren't. Since 1967, all of my work has been about Canada, a country which has been largely sold out to the U.S. multi-national corporations, by visible and invisible Canadians, the American power structure determines the future of this country, by exploitation of our minds and resources.... They would even like to melt the Arctic. All this has disturbed a great many people in Canada, who in the face of this tidal wave, can barely organize to stop or even attempt to humanize some of the catastrophic plans.

In my first exhibition at the National Gallery of Canada 1971, called *True Patriotic Love* [*sic*], I made works such as quilted wall hanging, cartoons, sculpture, sweet beaver perfume, Canadian birthday cake and a book for the show. Most of the pieces were about Canadian nature and land liberation. People from many parts of Canada worked on the exhibit (crafts people, artists, a chef, etc.). This show influenced some artists here and made me feel that I was doing something towards changing things.

In my film *Reason Over Passion* (1969) I was getting used to the idea of making art for someone, a country, a cause. I had already made *Rat Life and Diet in North America* which was a useful film in the direction. *Reason Over Passion* looks at Canada from one coast to another, and the Reason Over Passion of the Prime Minister is permutated, Enrosa Over Ipssona (Beep) Boat Boat Boat—Flag-Fade-Flag—Trees Trees Trees—Enorsa Over Ispsona (Beep). The images let this language speak for them. This is my fourth film to use subtitles in a new way. *1933* (67–68), *Sailboat* (1967), *Rat Life in North America* (1968), and *Pierre Vallieres* [*sic*] (1972), my most recent, making five and finally *True Patriot Love* which will involve a much more complex use of them.

Pierre Valliers [*sic*] (1972) is a mouth-scape film with the voice of a Revolutionary. I chose to do Vallieres [*sic*] lips as a film because I am interested in lips as subject matter. In my art works I have used lip animation ("O Canada Lithograph") and ("O Canada Lip Embroidery") as well as in drawing in past years, my film and art works have influenced one another. The use of lips in this film makes the message clearer (voice, etc.). Here is an extreme close-up of Vallieres [*sic*] mouth (someone is holding his head in an attempt to keep his lips within the skin-deep depth of field). Through his mouth you can meditate on the qualities of voice, the French language, Revolution, French Revolution, Géricault's colour, etc.

Many artists in Canada besides myself (Greg Curnoe and John Boyle, etc.) are trying to make art which will help bind people together, without boring them or dulling them. I have been working on the Tom Thomson myth in a film called *True Patriot Love*. It's a land worship film. Ross Turner, a character in the film depicts one of those Canadians, who without a sigh sold Canada to the American multi-national militarists. That may be a big pill to melt into a poetic film about Canada, Tom Thomson, Eulalie de Chicoutimi, with canoes, birds, animals, moon, star, ice and snow. But it can be done. Three thousand feet of Part One have already been shot. It is called *Birds at Sunrise*. From close-ups of birds shot through a circular black mask we go up into the clouds and from there beam down through the roof of Eulalie's house (the heroine) and the film gives birth to itself. The book "True Patriot Love" which I did for the National Gallery Show includes some of the one hundred or so stills which I did on the theme of Tom Thomson and other characters in the film. Most of the pictures were done by re-photographing existing stills of Tom, etc. These stills investigate photographic qualities which I hope to introduce into the actual body of the film.

JOYCE WIELAND

Excerpts from "Jigs & Reels" by Joyce Wieland, published in *Form and Structure in Recent Film* (Vancouver: Vancouver Art Gallery, 1972), unpaginated.

NEAR THE END OF FEBRUARY 1972, JUDY STEED THE FILMAKER AND MYSELF

DECIDED TO GO TO MONT LAURIER QUEBEC TO WHERE PIERRE VALLIERES WAS WORKING.
JUDY WANTED TO DO A STRAIGHT INTERVIEW ON HIM ~~AND~~ VALLIERE AND I WANTED TO

DO A FILM OF HIS LIPS IN EXTRENE CLOSEUP. FOR ABOUT A YEAR I A HAVE BEEN
WORKING ON STUDIES OF BIRDS IN EXTREME CLOSEUP. .... AND NOW FELT LIKE USING
THIS LENSE FOR A POLITICAL REPORT.
JUDY HAD TRIED TO INTERST CBC AND CFTO IN DOING A FILM ON VALLIERES ~~AT~~ ~~XXXX~~ they said they thought it to be an interesting idea, but it was French.
~~SHEXANDXXXKEETXTHEXAPATHYXXAROUNDXTOORONTOXX~~ AND WE
WE WERE AWARE OF THE GENERAL INDIFFERNCE TOWARD QUEBEC WHICH EXSISTS HERE and
new EXTREME RADICALS CONSIDER HIM ~~XXXX~~ A DECADENT ~~XXXX~~ COP OUT TO PARTI.QUEBEC OIS..ETC.
WE WERE INTERESTED IN HIS WRITINGS AND STRUGGLES TO FIND HIMSELF.HERE WAS A MAN
WHO TRIED TO DO SOMETHING ABOUT ~~XXXXXXXXXXXXXXXXX~~ HIS SOCIETY AND SPENT THREE
YEARS IN JAIL WITHOUT ~~XXXXX~~ TRIAL.....AND WHO HAD BEEN BORN INTO THE EXTREME
POSITION OF FRENCH CANADIAN POVERTY.

AT MONT LAURIER WE WAITED FOR ~~IN~~ VALLIERES IN HIS APARTMENT, WHENHE ARRIVED WE FOUND HE WOULDNT SPEA
K ~~AND~~ ENGLISH WITH US, ~~XX~~ SO THE PROBLEMS OF TRANSLATION FELL TO DANNIELLE CORBEIL
OF THE NATIONAL GALLERY, WHO HAD AGREED TO COME AND HELP AND WHO WANTED TO MEET
VALLIERE . THE MORNING AFTER WE ARRIVED , WE SET ~~XXXX~~ THE CAMERA AND EQUIPMENT
UP INTHE LIVING ROOM AND WAITED FOR HIM TO FINISH BREAKFAST.WHEN HE WAS READINY
HE WALKED IN SAT IN FRONT OF THE CAMERA AND AFFTER A LITTLE PROBLEM OR TWO. (TECH)
HE DELIVERED THREE ESSAYS WITHOUT STOPPING.EXCEPT FOR REEL CHANGE AND CAMERA BREAKDOWN.

1. MONT LAURIER
2. QUEBEC HISTORY AND RACE
3. WOMENS LIBERATION.

EVERYTHING WHICH ~~HAPPENED~~ HAPPENED ~~XXXX~~ IS RECEORDED ON THE FILM.
IT WAS A ONE SHOT AFFAIR.I EITHER GOT HIM ON FILM OR I MISSED. DANNIELLE
HELD HIS HEAD IN POSITION WHILE I LOOKED THROUGH THE LENSE,I HAD TO SIGNAL HER WITH MY
HAND TO BRING HIM INTO FOCUS AND SHE HAD TO HOLD HIM THERE AS BEST SHE COULD , BECAUSE
once the camera rolled ,the shutter action would ~~nearly~~ nearly all but obliterate,
what I could ~~of the focus~~ SEE OF FOCUS. (DEPTH OF FIELD)
~~there for i had the problem of ....light conditions causeing me to shoot fairly~~
~~wide open...depth of fir~~

~~inthe fiel~~

what we see on film is the mouthof a revelutionary,extremely close, his lips,
his teeth,..(and calculous), his spittle streals,his tongue which rolls so
beautifully through his french and finally the reflections in his teeth of the
window behind me.this film mouthscape shows all the process of making the film, CAMERA BREAKDOWN,
~~CAMERA BREAKDOWN~~ , vallieres pulling away after shots , and the final emptying of the CAMERA. I had
over fifty feet in the magazine so i turned the camera around on the tripod and
had it look out the window at the snow ,while it emptied itself.

LEFT AND OPPOSITE
Pierre Vallières: Notes from the Filmmaker,
c. 1972
Photos courtesy of the CFMDC

I CHOSE TO DO THE VALLIERES LIPS AS A FILM XXXXX BECAUSE I AM INTERSTED IN LIPS AS SUBJECT MATTER. IN MY ART WORKS I HAVE USED LIP ANIMATION (O CANADA LITHOGRAPH ANIMATION, AND LIP EMBROIDERY) AS WELL AS IN MANY DRAWINGS A FEW YEARS AGO. MY FILM AND ART WORKS HAVE INFLUENCED ONE ANOTHER. I LIKE THE IDEA OF CONCENTRATING ON ONE SMALL SECTION OF HIS ANATOMY, BECAUSE IT SIMPLIFYS THINGS , HERE IS A CLOSEUP HOLD OF HIS MOUTH ON AND THROUGH WHICH YOU CAN MEDITATE. MEDITATE ON THE QUALITIES OF VOICE , THE FRENCH LANGUAGE, REVOLUTION, FRENCH REVOLUTION, XXXXXXXXXXXXXXXX GERICAULT'S COLOUR, ETC. THESE ARE SOME OF THE THINGS I THINK ABOUT, WHEN I SEE MY FILM.

JOYCE WIELAND

Much of Wieland's correspondence from the 1960s and early 1970s is typed in all caps. In a 1967 letter to journalist Elizabeth Kimball, Wieland adds a postscript: "DONT MIND CAPS, I CANT TYPE IN BOTH CASES FOR THE LIFE OF ME."[1]

Avrom Isaacs fonds, Clara Thomas Archives and Special Collections, York University, Toronto, F0134.1996-036/026, file12.

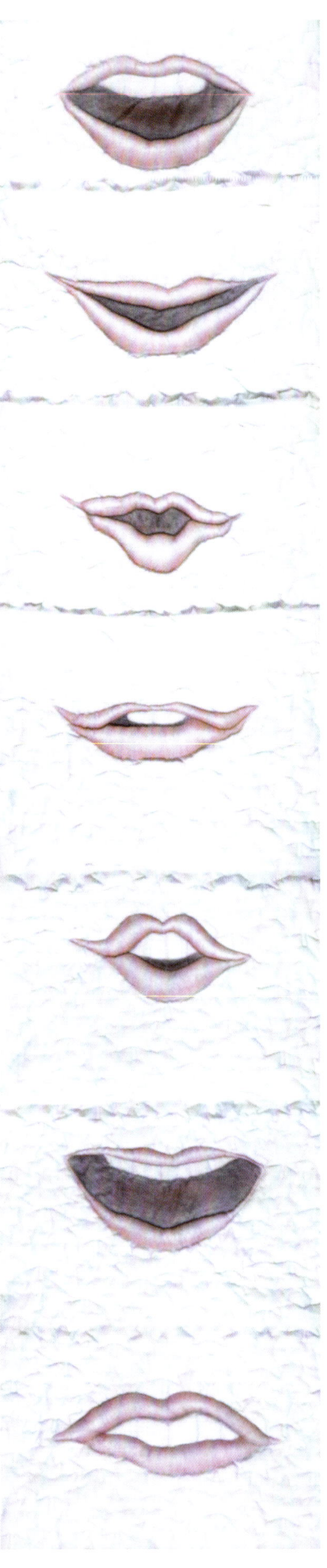

LEFT

The Maple Leaf Forever II, 1972
Coloured pencil on cloth, thread, batting
218.4 × 50.2 cm
Collection of the Canada Council Art Bank, Ottawa
72/3-1097
Photo: Brandon Clarida Image Services

OPPOSITE

O Canada, 1970
Lithograph on paper
Sheet: 57.2 × 76.5 cm
Art Gallery of Ontario, Purchased 1971
70/374
Photo: AGO, Craig Boyko

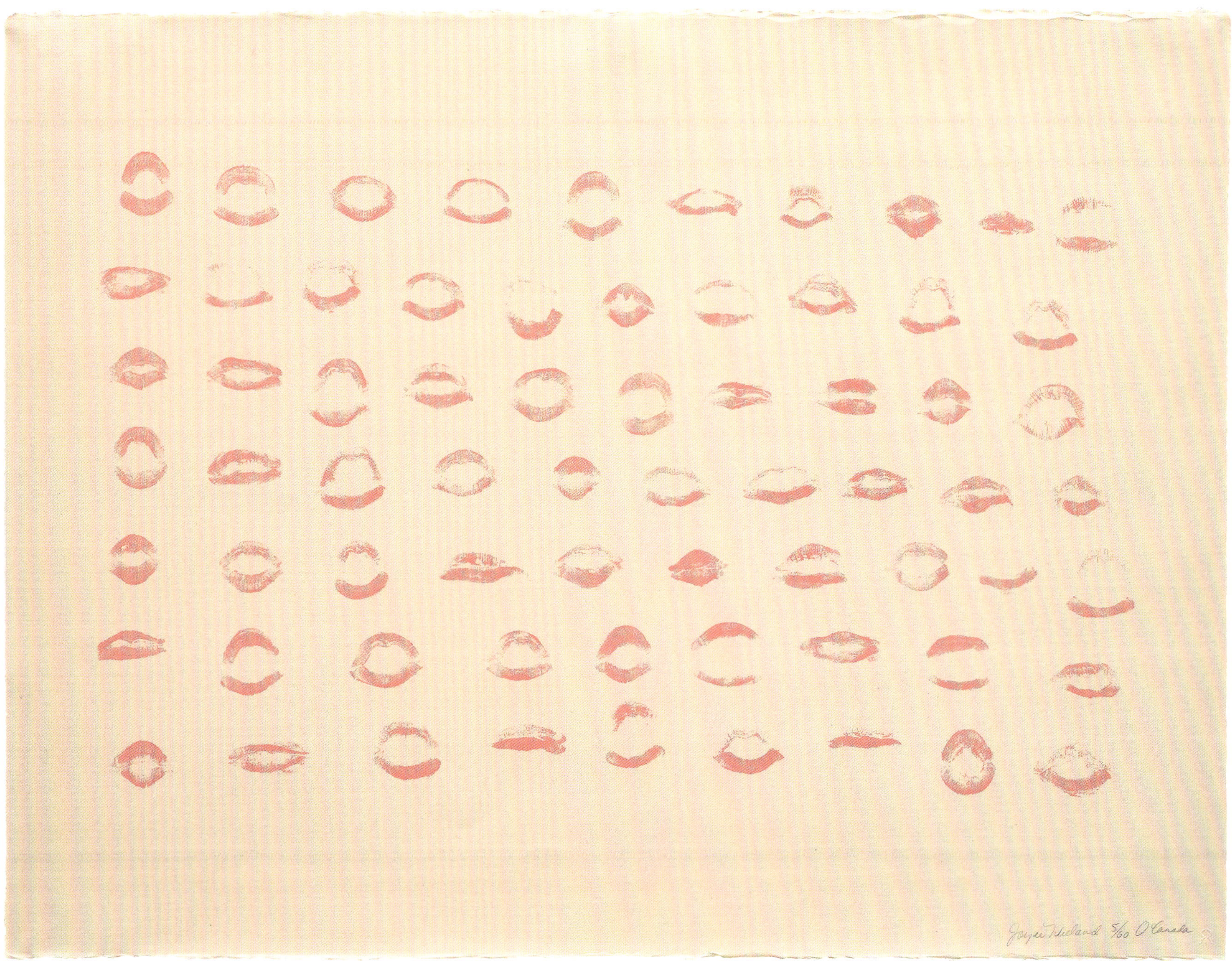

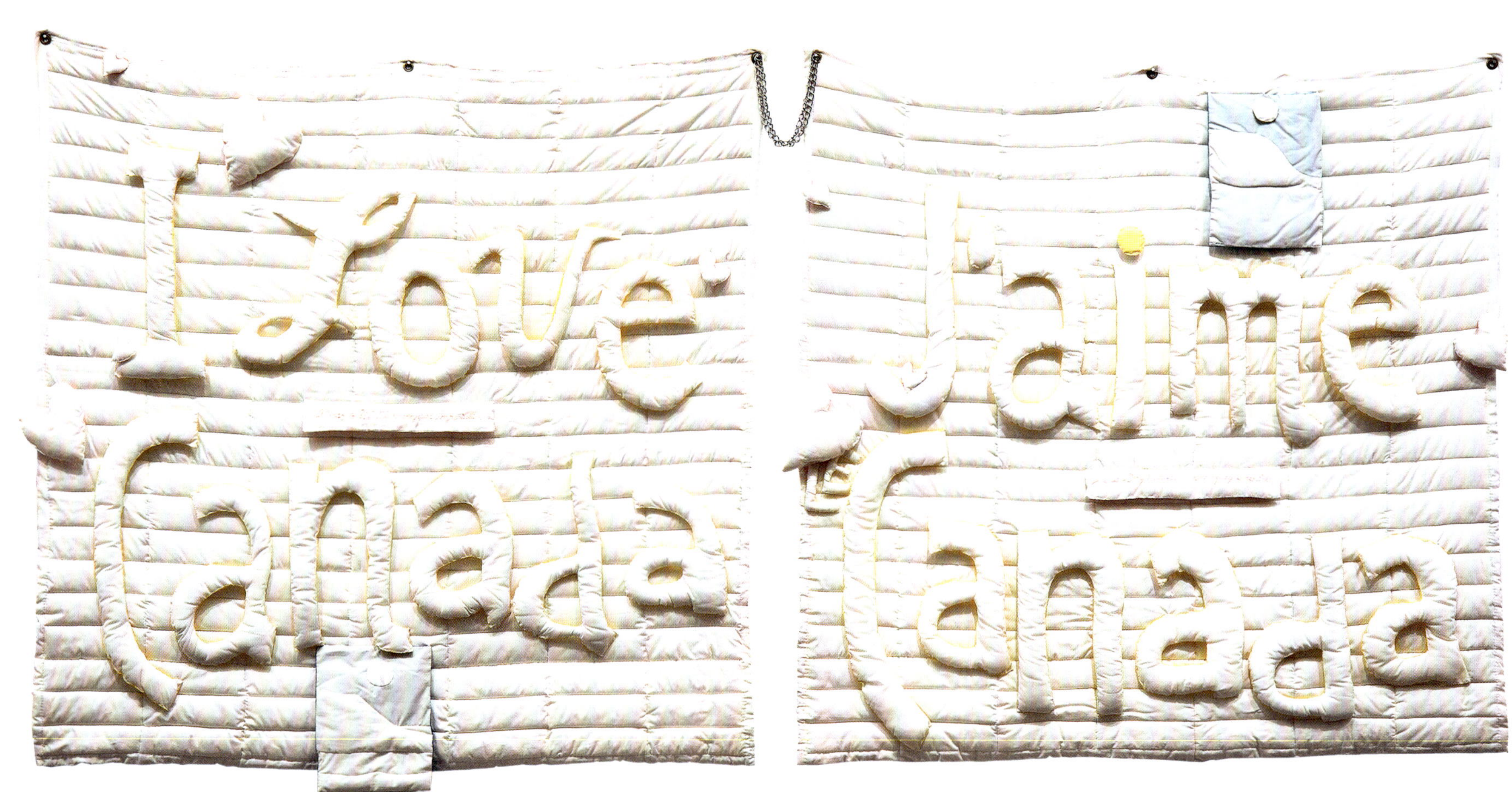

I Love Canada J'aime le Canada, 1970
Cloth, thread, batting, metal
153.1 × 304.7 cm
MacKenzie Art Gallery, University of Regina Collection
1972-21
Photo: Don Hall, courtesy of the MacKenzie Art Gallery

I LOVE CANADA J'AIME LE CANADA, 1970

Like many of her quilted works, *I Love Canada J'aime le Canada* was conceptualized by Joyce Wieland and executed by her sister, Joan Stewart. The two white quilts are joined with a metal chain and feature large stuffed letters, small hearts, and two rectangular panels that include what appears to be an abstracted landscape. Each component is backed with brightly coloured cloth in red, orange, yellow, and blue, which is reflected on the white surface, giving the illusion that the quilt is glowing. What we may not see at first glance—in the middle of each quilt in delicate, cursive embroidery—are the words: "Death to U.S. Technological Imperialism" and "A Bas L'impérialisme Technologicque [*sic*] des E-U." This overt condemnation of American technological expansion, stitched in Canada's recently proclaimed two official languages, is a key aspect of the work. Using quilting and embroidery to engage in political subject matter was a strategy, as Wieland often played with the traditional association these mediums have with femininity and domesticity in order to have her work appear inviting, playful, and non-threatening.

Since the mid-1960s, Wieland had become increasingly interested in the rise of New Left politics developing in Canada.[1] A number of political, economic, and cultural theorists were concerned about the domination of Canada by the United States, leading to the formation of a federal task force, an advocacy group called the Committee for an Independent Canada, a political party called the Waffle, and to numerous books and an important phase for the long-running, widely read political and cultural journal *Canadian Forum*.[2] Wieland was acutely aware of these publications and discussions, and often mentioned her interest in New Left thinking in interviews and notes she made. As she told Anne Wordsworth in 1974: "I used to get all kinds of publications from here [Canada]. One of the first things that really got me going were the things in the *Forum* . . . very deep, really searching things about the economics, I started to wake up then. . . ."[3] In notes she made in 1972, Wieland states, "Since 1967, all of my work has been about Canada, a country which has been largely sold out to the U.S. multinational corporations, by visible and invisible Canadians, the American power structure determines the future of this country, by exploitation of our minds and resources."[4] The New Left's concerns about US control over resource extraction, ownership of multinational corporations, and television programming was perceived as strongly connected to Canada's ability to function effectively as a nation-state. If Canada was going to survive, it was contingent, as Wieland suggests, on the "death" of American technological imperialism.

The New Left was also concerned about national unity and the rise of Quebec separatist sentiments that intensified in the early 1960s. The federal government shared this unease as the separation of Quebec threatened the idea of a unified nation-state. Seeking to ensure unity, the federal government launched a Royal Commission in 1963 to investigate the role of French language and culture, culminating in the Official

1 For further discussion of Joyce Wieland's work and its connection to New Left politics, see Kristy A. Holmes, "Joyce Wieland as Cultural Worker: Ecology, Nation and New Leftism in 'True Patriot Love,'" in *Documentary Protocols (1967–1975) / Protocoles Documentaires (1967–1975)*, ed. Vincent Bonin with Michèle Thériault (Montreal: Leonard and Bina Ellen Art Gallery, 2010), 255–68, and Johanne Sloan, "Joyce Wieland at the Border: Nationalism, the New Left, and the Question of Political Art in Canada," *Journal of Canadian Art History* 26 (2005): 80–107.

2 See, for example, M.H. Watkins, *Foreign Ownership and the Structure of Canadian Industry: Report of the Task Force on the Structure of Canadian Industry* (Ottawa: Privy Council, 1968), and James Laxer, *The Energy Poker Game: The Politics of the Continental Resources Deal* (Toronto: New Press, 1970).

3 Anne Wordsworth, "An Interview with Joyce Wieland," *Descant*, no. 8–9 (Spring/Summer 1974): 110.

4 Joyce Wieland fonds, Clara Thomas Archives and Special Collections, York University, Toronto, 1992-018/007, file 115.

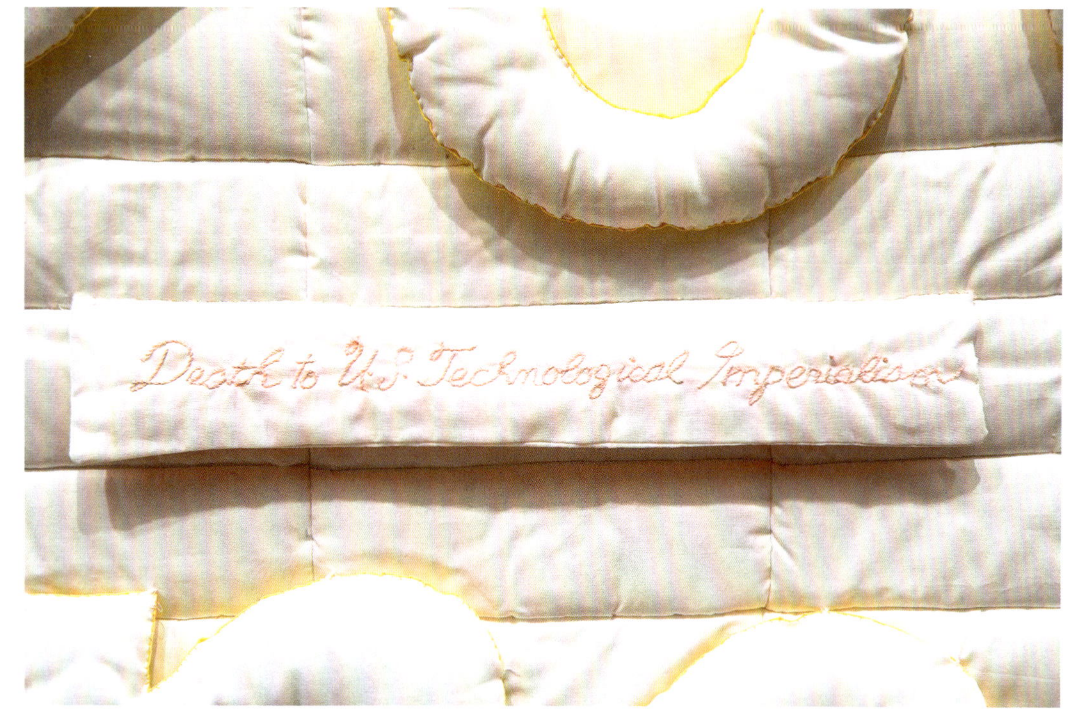

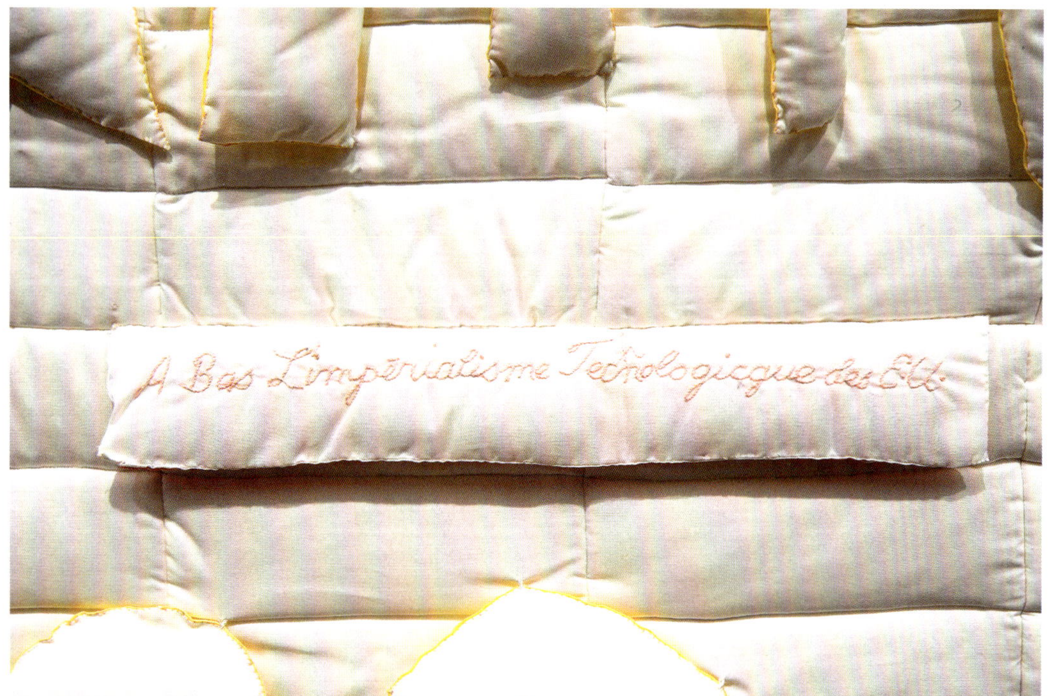

I Love Canada J'aime le Canada (details), 1970
Photos: Don Hall, courtesy of the MacKenzie Art Gallery

Languages Act of 1969. As an artist who was clearly attuned to her political and cultural environment, it is not surprising that Wieland chose to make *I Love Canada J'aime le Canada* in the newly proclaimed official languages joined together, literally and symbolically, with a chain.

While *I Love Canada J'aime le Canada* aesthetically and conceptually explores the rise in New Left thinking around anti-Americanism, national unity, and the importance of bilingualism and biculturalism, it does not account for who and what is erased from this vision of nation. This quilt that boldly and emphatically expresses love for the Canadian nation hits differently than it did fifty-five years ago when Wieland created it.

Displays of devotion or celebration of Canada have come under intense scrutiny in recent years as the historical and ongoing impact of colonization and genocidal practices that have worked to create and sustain the nation-state became pivotal public discussions.[5]

The cultural movements of the late 1960s and early 1970s were the context in which Wieland created a work of art that proclaimed love for a concept of nationhood that is understood today as deeply rooted in colonial violence and genocide.

KRISTY A. HOLMES

5 The Truth and Reconciliation Commission of Canada (TRC) (2008–15) and the National Inquiry into Missing and Murdered Indigenous Women and Girls (National Inquiry into MMIWG) (2016–19) are two significant federal commissions that continue to be widely discussed and debated in Canada. The final reports of both these inquiries clearly state that the residential school system and the historical and ongoing violence and murder of Indigenous women and girls was and is nothing short of genocide. Grassroots social justice movements, such as Idle No More, have also been actively protesting across Canada to protect treaty rights and the environment, and calling to cancel Canada Day celebrations, as "Canada remains a country that has built its foundation on the erasure and genocide of Indigenous nations, including children" (Idle No More media statement, 2021).

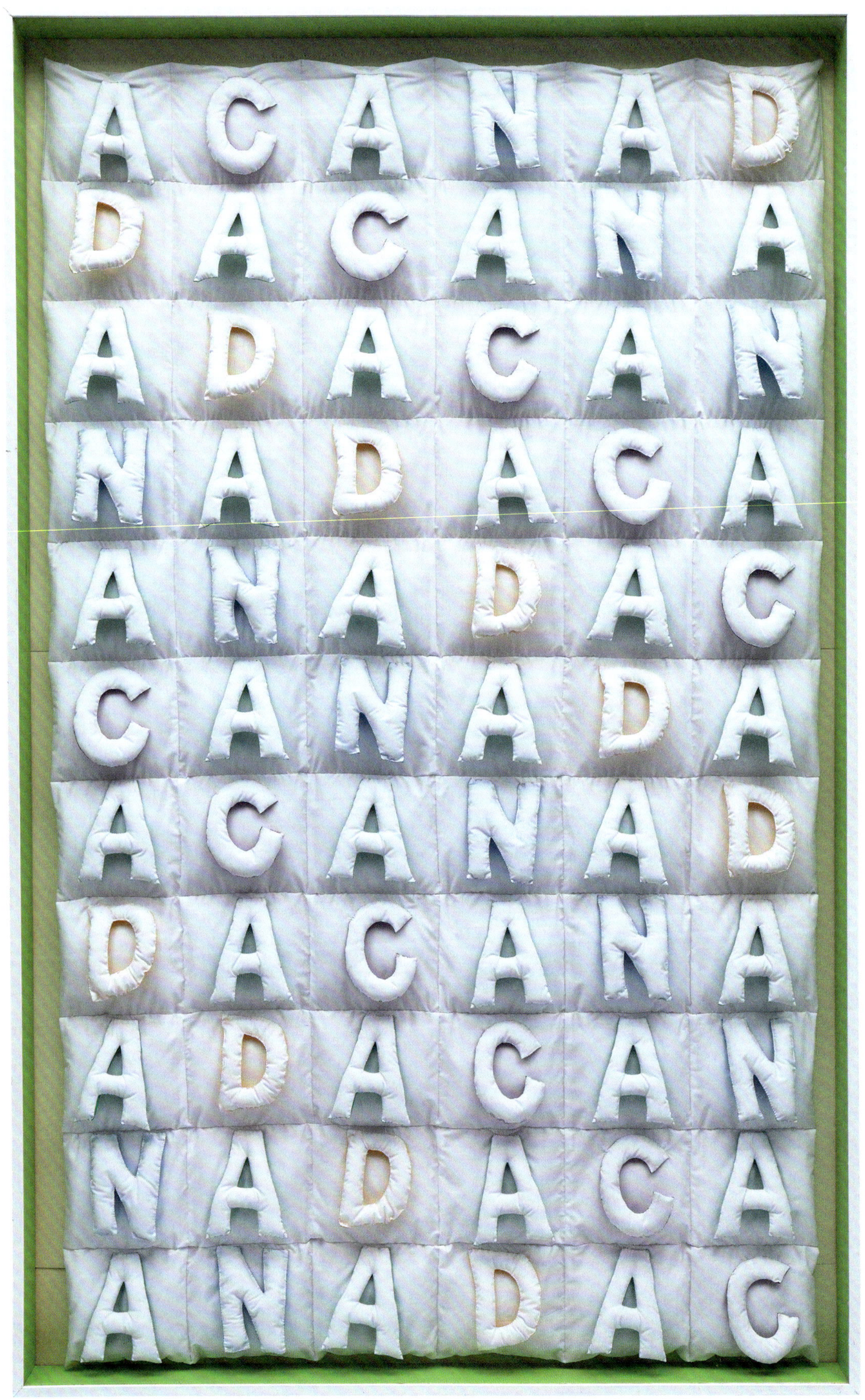

Canada, 1972
Cloth, thread, batting,
original artist frame
223.5 × 140.3 cm
Art Gallery of Ontario,
Gift from the Women's
Committee Fund, 1972
72/56
Photo: AGO, Craig Boyko

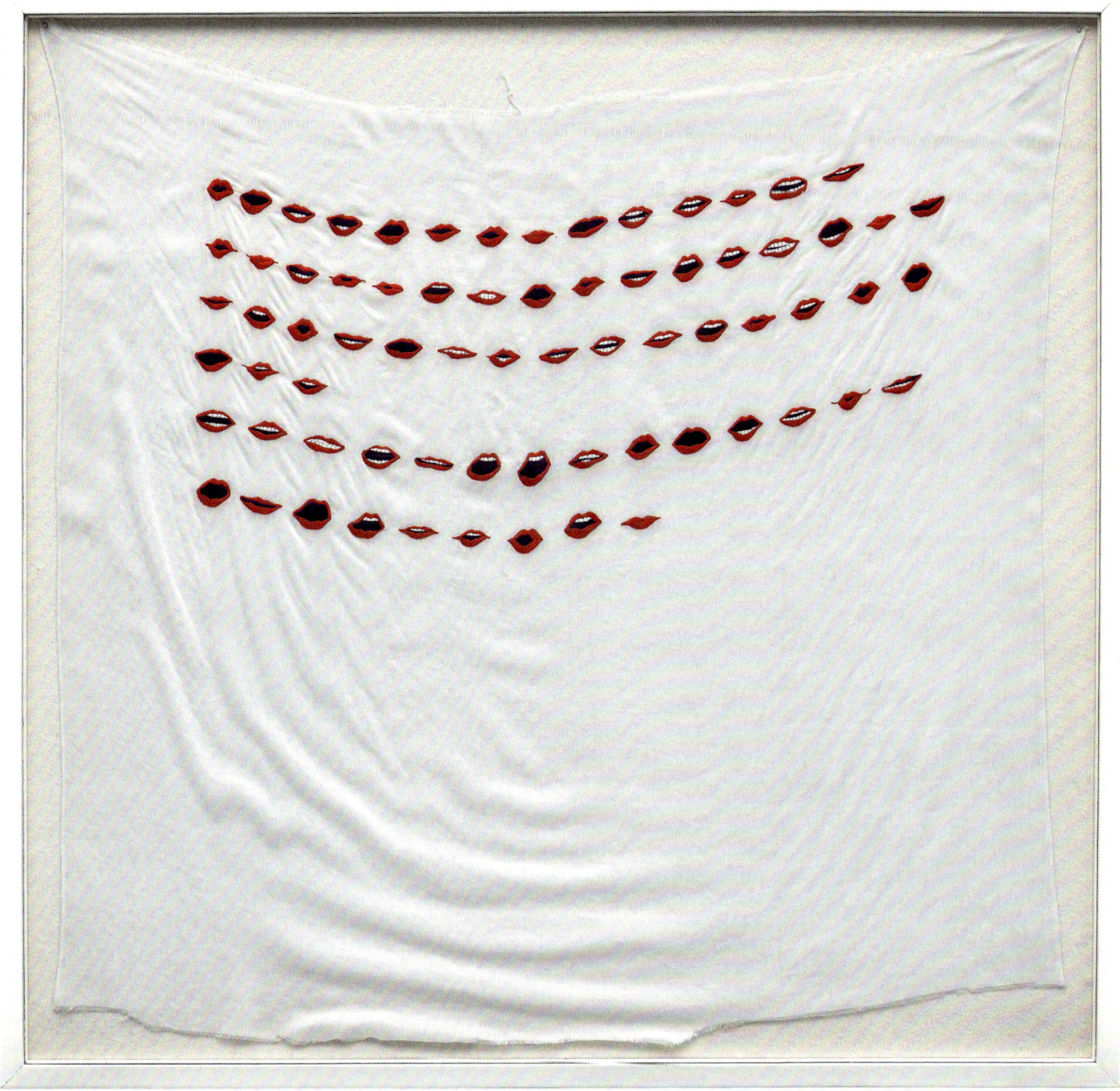

O Canada Animation, 1971
Embroidery by Joan McGregor
Embroidery on cotton
99.06 × 107.31 cm
Collection of Morden and Edie Yolles
Photo: AGO, Craig Boyko

Sir

Genl Monckton is charg'd w^t the first Landing & attack at the Foulon, if he succeeds, you will be pleased to give directions that the Troops afloat be set on shoar w^t the utmost expedition, as they are under your command. and when the 3600 men now in the fleet are landed, I have no manner of doubt, but, that we are able to fight & to beat the French Army; in which I know you will give your best assistance

I have the honour to be

Sir

Your most Obed^t &

most Humble Servant

Jam: Wolfe

Sutherland

8 o'Clock

12th Sep^t 1759.

151

Wolfe's Last Letter, 1971
Embroidery by Joan McGregor
Embroidery thread on cotton
33 × 27.9 cm
Collection of Barry Appleton
BA-0971
Photo: MMFA, Jean-François Brière

Montcalm's Last Letter, 1971
Embroidery by Joan McGregor
Embroidery thread on cotton
33 × 27.9 cm
Collection of Barry Appleton
BA-0971
Photo: MMFA, Jean-François Brière

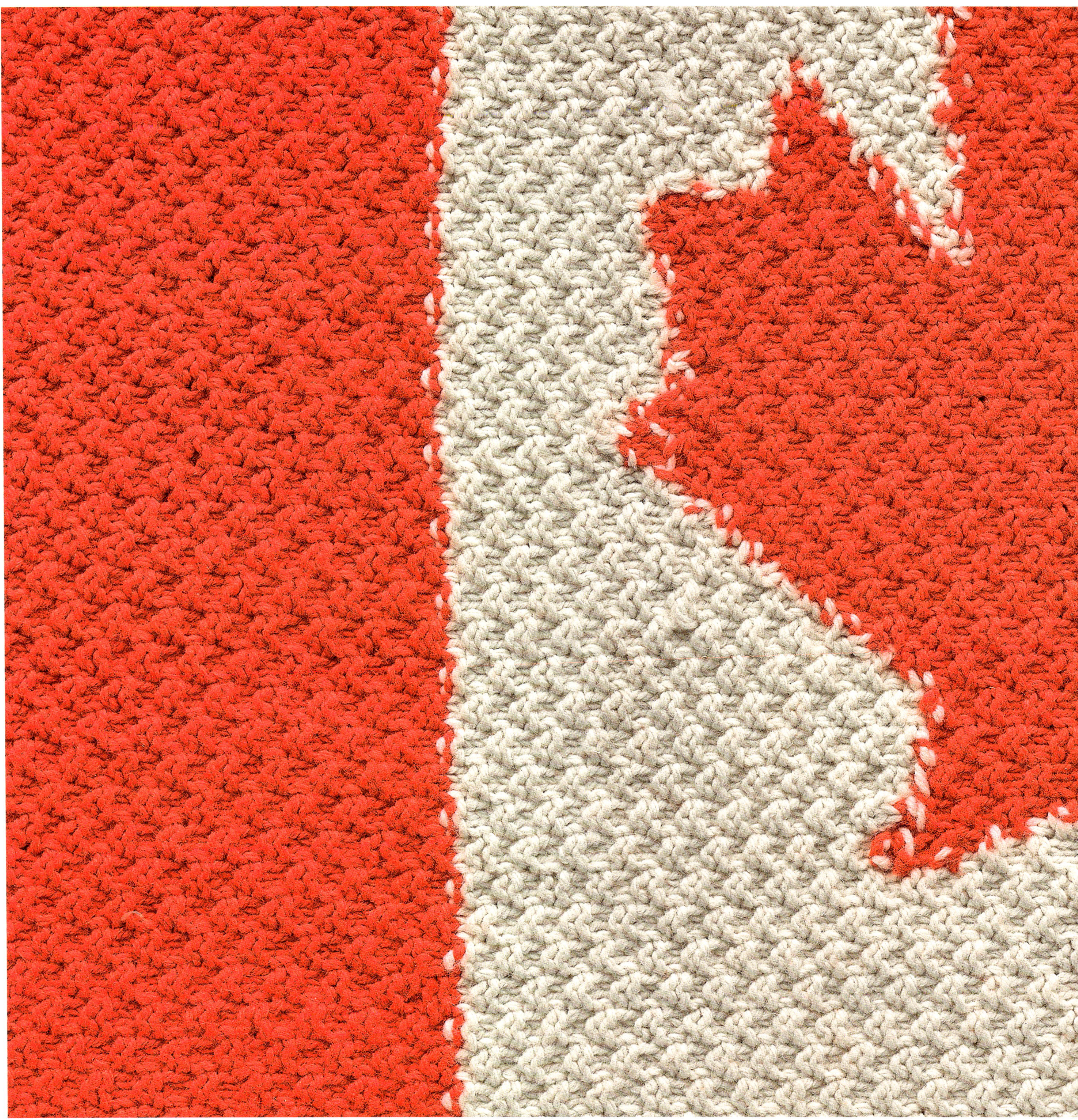

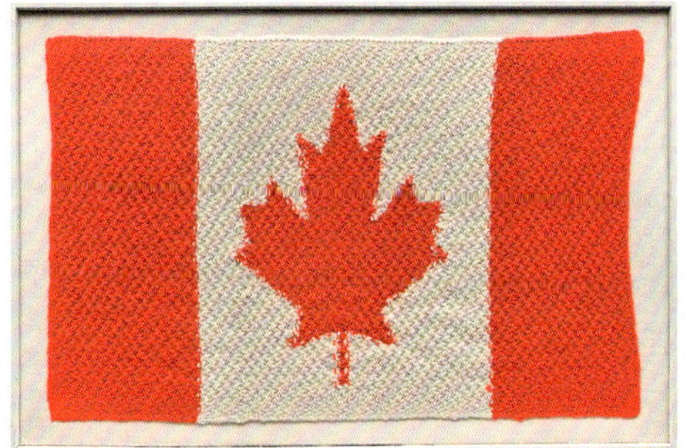
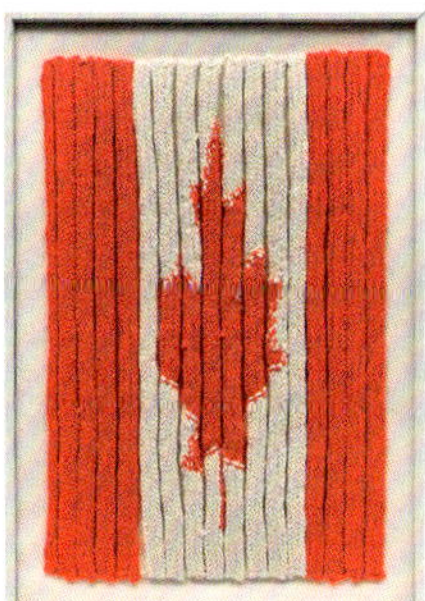
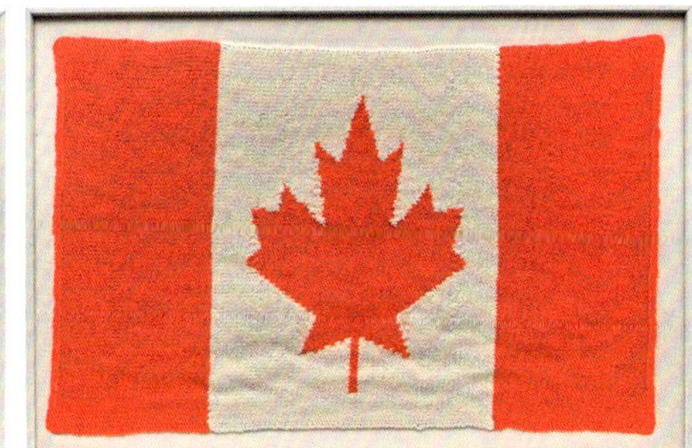
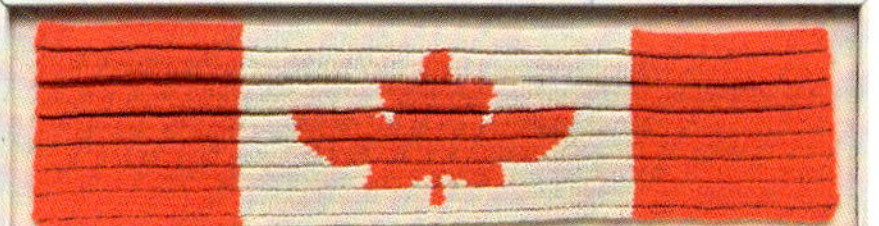

Flag Arrangement, 1970–1971
Knitting by Valerie McMillin
Wool, artist frames
Overall size of four elements: 137 × 285.5 cm (irregular)
Art Gallery of Ontario, Gift of Toronto Star Newspapers Ltd., 2005
2005/20.1 – 2005/20.4
Photo: AGO, Craig Boyko

FLAG ARRANGEMENT, 1970–1971

True Patriot Love / Veritable amour patriotique, Joyce Wieland's 1971 post–Canadian Centennial retrospective held at the National Gallery of Canada, featured *Flag Arrangement,* a knitted work produced between 1970 and 1971. Wieland often collaborated with women who were experts in craft, and for *Flag Arrangement* she hired award-winning Dartmouth, Nova Scotia, knitter Valerie McMillin to use various stitching techniques to knit a Canadian flag series. As McMillin recounted in a 1971 interview with CBC Radio's *As It Happens* host William Ronald, Wieland phoned "out of the clear blue," asking if the flag could be knitted.[1] "You can knit anything if you really make your mind up," McMillin explained, but after completing four of the six pieces Wieland requested, the craftswoman finally protested. "I don't like knitting more than one thing of a thing." She noted that Wieland emphasized the importance of texture over "perfect knitting." McMillin had recoiled at the prospect of them possibly falling out of shape if hung, but when Ronald accompanied her to view *Flag Arrangement* in the gallery for the *As It Happens* feature, she remarked on air: "Oh for heaven's sake, they're wonderful!"

While the same number of stitches comprise each flag, McMillin used rib stitches in the second and fourth flags. As a result, the second flag pulls in like an accordion, with thick vertical ribs ready to be stretched open in a big breathy pull. The rib stitch is used for hats, cuffs, and waistlines to conform to the body, and, if unframed, this piece would stay warmly in place as a comforting shawl. For the fourth flag, McMillin orientated her knitting pattern to start from the side instead of the top, creating thick, uncomfortable-looking horizontal ribs that compress the flag. The ribbing, as Ronald observed, makes the maple leaf look more like the American eagle.

1 William Ronald, a founder of Painters Eleven, hosted CBC's *As It Happens* from 1969 to 1972. Joan Murray, "William Ronald," in *The Canadian Encyclopedia*, Historica Canada, June 4, 2008, last edited July 15, 2015.

OPPOSITE
Man Has Reached Out and Touched the Tranquil Moon, 1970
Plastic, thread, cloth, talcum powder, batting
298.5 × 163.2 cm (irregular)
National Gallery of Canada, Purchased 1971
16708
Photo: NGC

Toronto art critic Robert Fulford described *True Patriot Love / Véritable amour patriotique* as a "specific show," as opposed to a retrospective. When Wieland moved back to Canada in late 1971, she witnessed a national preoccupation with Canadian culture and identity. The question—What is Canada?—had been building since the country's centennial celebrations in 1967 and the Great Canadian Flag Debate that Prime Minister Lester B. Pearson initiated in the House of Commons in 1964. The Maple Leaf, featured in *Flag Arrangement*, replaced the country's de facto flag, the Canadian Red Ensign, as the official national flag in 1965: "bold and clean, and distinctively our own."[2]

"On a cold and damp Friday night in November of 1964," twenty-year-old Joan O'Malley sewed the first fabric version of the Maple Leaf as a favour to her father, Ken Donovan, an assistant director with the Canadian Government Exhibition Commission; Prime Minister Pearson had tasked Donovan with the creation of the first prototypes of the flag concepts. O'Malley has been referred to as "Canada's Betsy Ross," a serendipitous association given that Wieland completed *Betsy Ross, Look What They've Done with the Flag that You Made with Such Care* (p. 124) four years earlier, in 1966.[3]

Wieland led second-wave feminist art production in Canada in opposition to the American cultural chauvinism replete in High Modernism, Pop art, and avant-garde cinema. Characteristically, *Flag Arrangement* is filmic and experimental, combining modernist and activist inspiration in its serial conceptualization of narrative simultaneously through technical process and figurative storyboarding. In the context of *True Patriot Love / Véritable amour patriotique*, Wieland insists on the productive power of women to ground community and belonging in the personal and local, and in embodied care. (○))

ANNA HUDSON

2 "As journalist George Bain wrote the morning after the first flags had flown, Canada's maple leaf emblem 'looked bold and clean, and distinctively our own.'" Norman Hillmer, "Editorial: The Canadian Flag, Distinctively Our Own," in *The Canadian Encyclopedia*, Historica Canada, February 14, 2012, last edited December 11, 2019.

3 Bruce Deachman, "The Story of the Woman Who Sewed Canada's First Maple Leaf Flag," *Ottawa Citizen*, June 30, 2016.

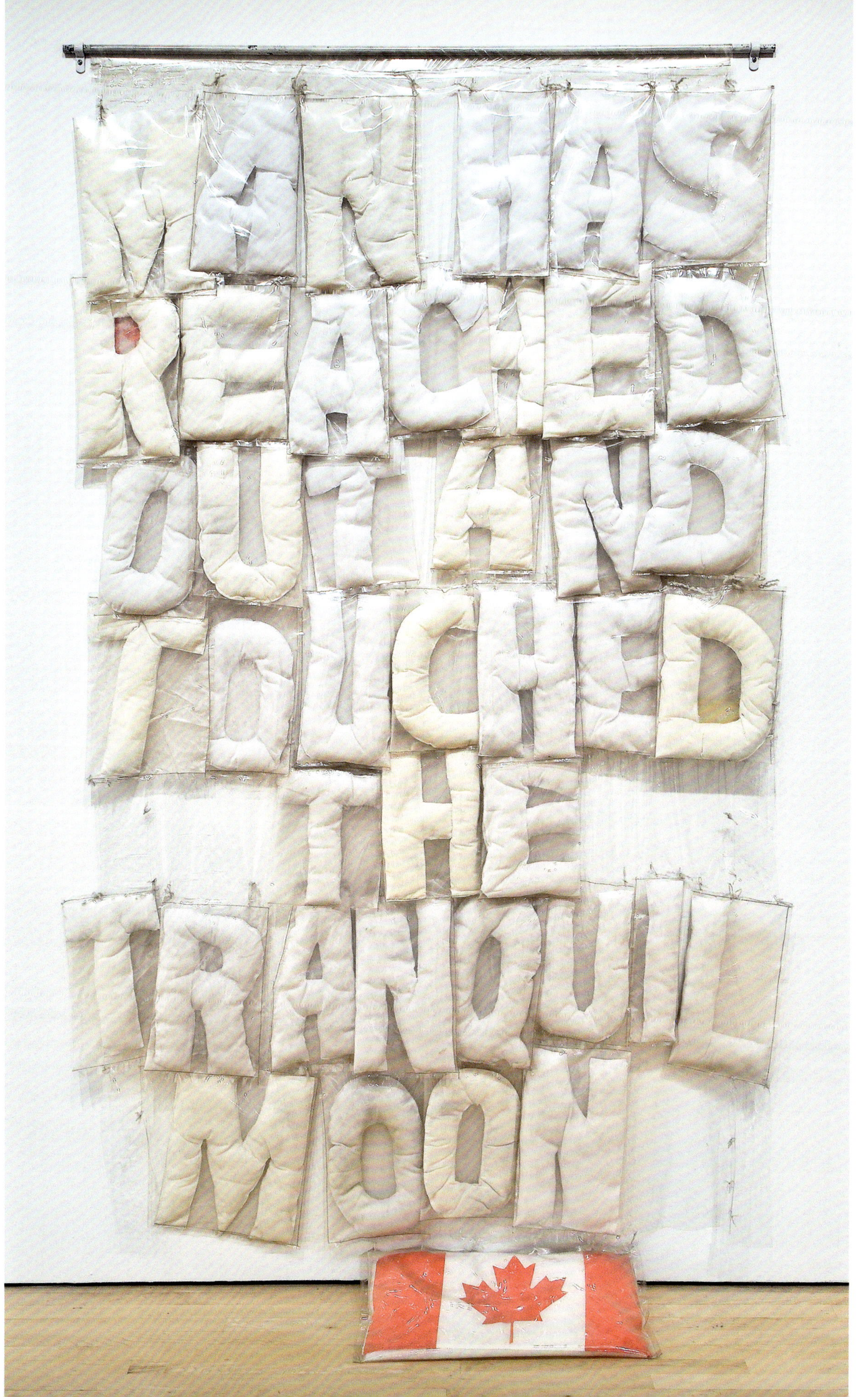
MAN HAS
REACHED
OUT AND
TOUCHED
THE
TRANQUIL
MOON

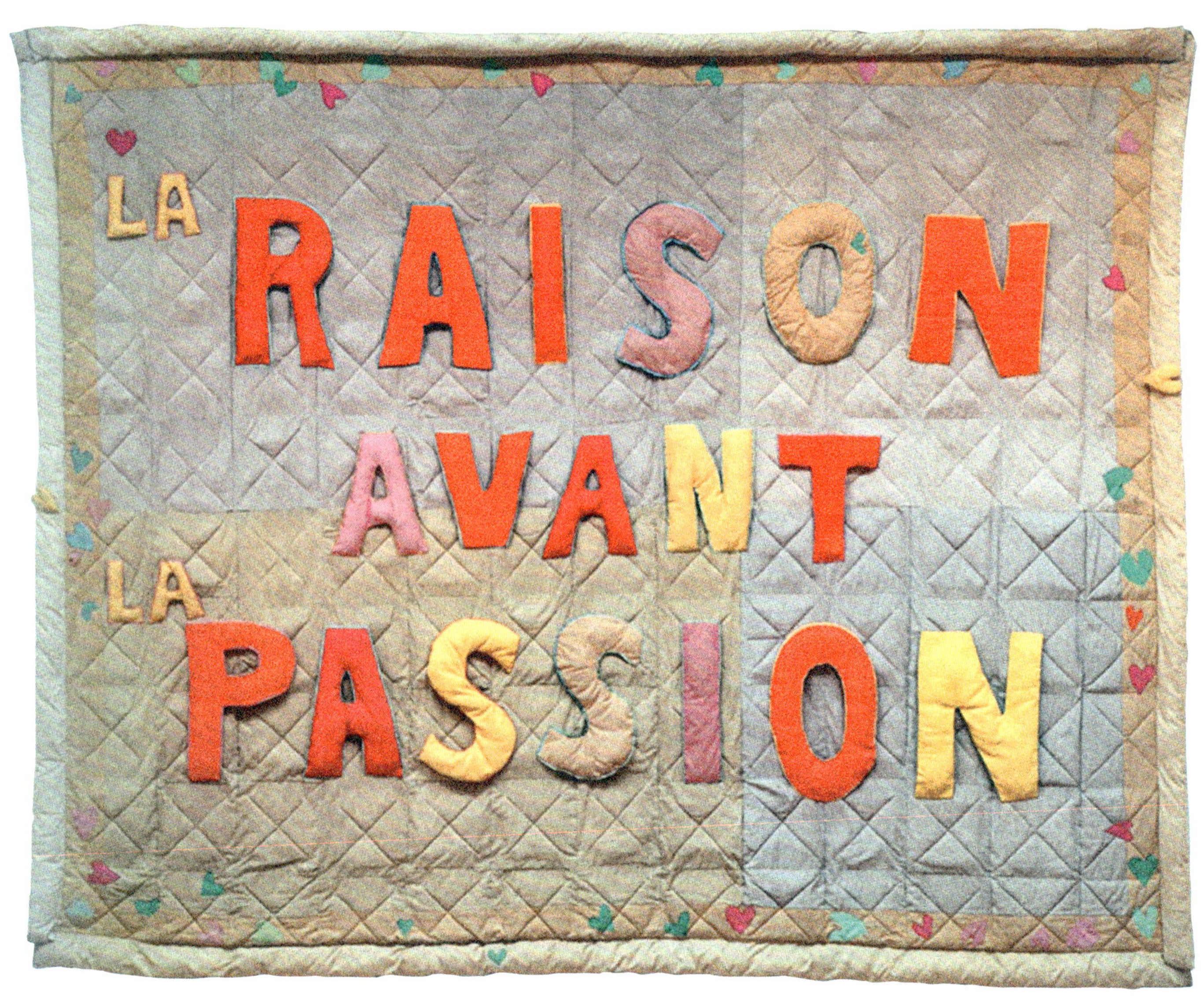

La raison avant la passion
[Reason over Passion], 1968
Cotton, thread, batting
243.8 × 274.3 cm
Private Collection

REASON OVER PASSION, 1968
LA RAISON AVANT LA PASSION, 1968

In the late 1960s United States, amid civil unrest and escalating war in Vietnam, Joyce Wieland believed it was vital to "decolonize" the Canadian nation by extricating it from the United States' orbit.[1] One of her quilted works from this period bears the message "I Love Canada J'aime le Canada," and, stitched in small letters, "Death to U.S. Technological Imperialism / A Bas L'impérialisme Technologicque [*sic*] des E-U."[2] Reengaging with the myth of a peaceful, tolerant, caring, and just Canada, she felt she could perhaps play a part in achieving this progressive vision of Canadian society, in particular by helping to reconcile anglophones and francophones. "I'm a Canadian," she declared. "I believe in Canada. We should work for Canadian unity—English and French—as Canadians, not as anti-Americans. We should be more positive about ourselves."[3]

Wieland succumbed to a certain degree of Trudeaumania of the day, which she would soon disavow.[4] She saw in Canada's future prime minister an answer to increasingly violent and predatory American imperialism.[5] As she approvingly read Pierre Trudeau's speeches in the papers, she was struck by one of his assertions: "For many years, I have been fighting for the triumph of reason over passion."[6] Returning from the Liberal Party convention held in Ottawa in April 1968, she came up with an idea for a film and a quilt entitled *La raison avant la passion / Reason over Passion*.[7] In May of that year, she and Michael Snow held a "quilt-in" in their Manhattan studio apartment.[8] Grouped as Canadians Abroad for Trudeau, a hundred or so people produced a four-by-five-and-a-half-metre quilt. The front of the work bears the words "Reason over Passion" surrounded by little hearts; sewn on the back are small pockets meant to hold private messages for the soon-to-be PM.[9] A year and a half later, in November 1969, at a party in New York where Trudeau was the guest of honour, Wieland and Snow presented him with the French-language version of the quilt as a gift. The Prime Minister was flattered and later sent a letter (p. 268) thanking them for "the magnificent quilt."[10]

In October 1970, after the War Measures Act was invoked, Wieland's enthusiasm for Trudeau waned. She came to see his "reason," which subjugated feelings and compassion, as an instrument of oppression, like any other. She even maintained that her film and quilt were not tributes to Trudeau, but parodies that too many people had taken seriously.[11] She argued for a balance between reason and passion, saying "Of course, 'reason over passion' is the opposite of what I believe: the two should go side by side."[12]

1 "Being a colonized nation, we are generally ashamed of what we are." Betty Ferguson, Garonce Mapleton, Judy Steed, and Joyce Wieland, "Canadian Home Movies," in *Women and Film, 1896–1973 / La femme et le film, 1896–1973* (Toronto: n.p., 1973), 7.

2 Shirley Raphael, "An Artist's Plan for Canada," *Montreal Gazette*, July 10, 1971.

3 Jay Walz, "Canadian Gallery Show Strikes Nationalist Note," *New York Times*, July 16, 1971.

4 Paul Litt, *Trudeaumania* (Vancouver: UBC Press, 2016).

5 Lauren Rabinovitz, "An Interview with Joyce Wieland," *Afterimage* 8, no. 10 (May 1981): 10.

6 Kristy A. Holmes, "Negotiating Citizenship: Joyce Wieland's Reason over Passion," note 2 in *The Sixties: Passion, Politics, and Style*, ed. Dimitry Anastakis (Montreal: McGill-Queen's University Press, 2008), 65.

7 Rabinovitz, "An Interview," 10. See also Holmes, "Negotiating Citizenship," in Anastakis, *The Sixties*, 57–58.

8 "New York Fans Stage Trudeau Quilt-In," *Montreal Gazette*, May 23, 1968.

9 Holmes, "Negotiating Citizenship," in Anastakis, *The Sixties*, 57–58.

10 Joyce Wieland fonds, CTASC, York University, 1992-018/003, file 42. Quoted in Holmes, "Negotiating the Nation," 91.

11 "Eulogizing the leader. I thought it was very funny; but Trudeau, apparently, took it all seriously"; Wieland quoted in Susan M. Crean, "Notes from the Language of Emotion: A Conversation with Joyce Wieland," *Canadian Art* 4, no. 1 (Spring 1987): 65.

12 Crean, ibid.

OPPOSITE
Reason over Passion, 1968
Cloth, thread, batting
256.5 × 302.3 × 8 cm
National Gallery of Canada,
Purchased 1970
15924
Photo: NGC

Interviewing Wieland in 1986, Barbara Stevenson asked, "What message about Trudeau were you conveying in those works?" Wieland's answer was blunt: "I was saying that he had this reason above everything. And it really should be reason *and* passion in a person. But this man is only reason over passion, and ultimately, he's a psychopath." "You'd go that far?" exclaimed Stevenson. "Oh, yes," came the reply.[13]

Perhaps the last word should be left to Margaret Trudeau (b. 1948). In her 1979 autobiography *Beyond Reason*, Trudeau's wife recalls the day when, confronting her unflappable husband, she tore apart Wieland's quilt, which hung prominently on a wall in their home:

"Shaking with rage at my inability to counter his logical, reasoned arguments, I grabbed at the quilt, wrenched off the letters and hurled them down the stairs at him one by one, in an insane desire to reverse the process, to put passion before reason just this once. Pierre was icy. Vandalizing a work of art; how low could I sink? . . . All of it seemed beyond reason to me."[14]

This anecdote shows how important it is, as Wieland insists, that reason and passion go hand in hand.

JEAN-PHILIPPE WARREN

13 Joyce Wieland fonds, CTASC, York University, 1999-003/005, file 05 (hereafter cited as Joyce Wieland fonds, file 05). Quoted in Holmes, "Negotiating the Nation," 93, Wieland's emphasis.

14 Margaret Trudeau, *Beyond Reason* (New York: Paddington Press, 1979), 240.

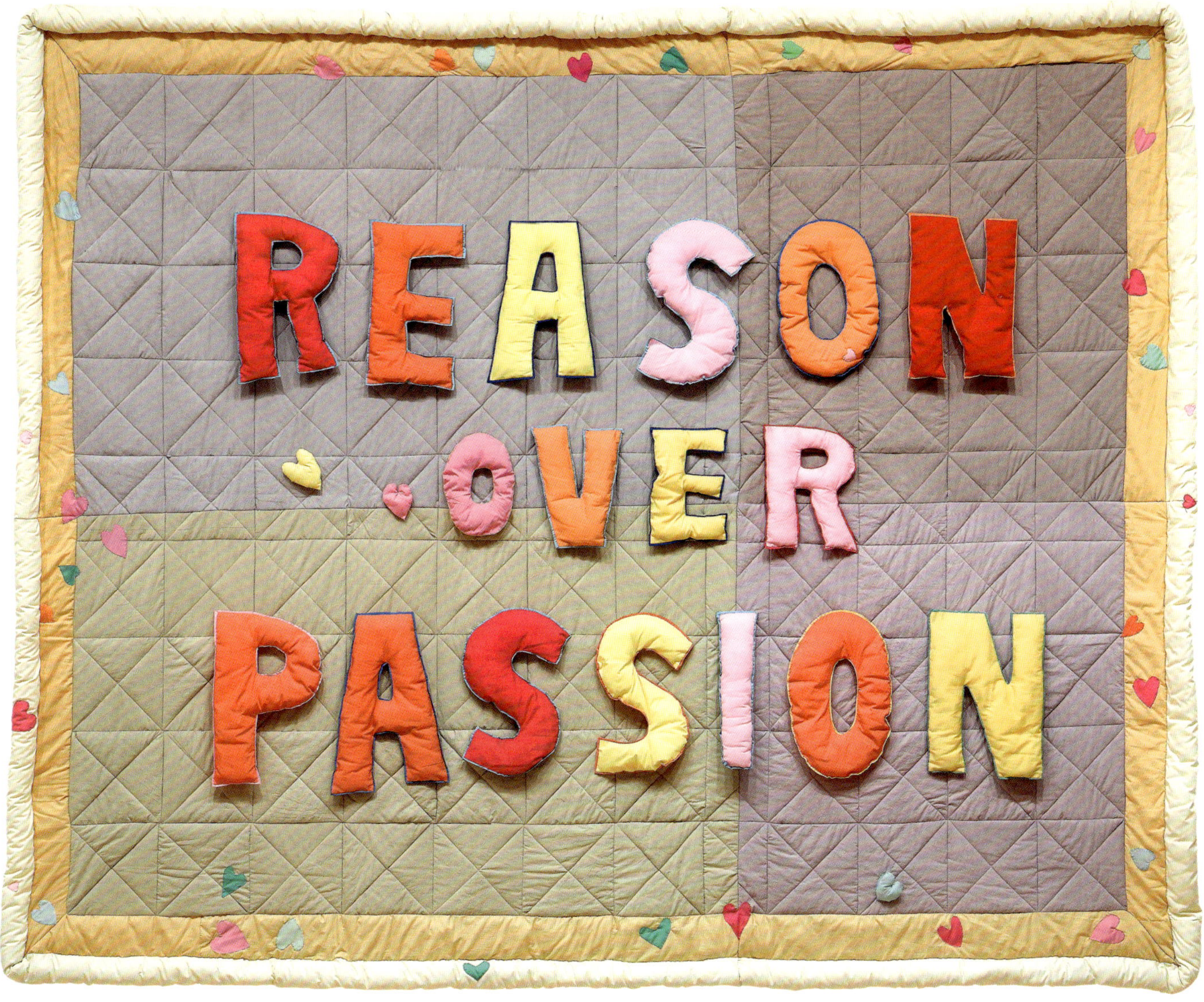

"My friend Mary Mitchell and I had gone to Ottawa to see the 1968 Liberal convention, and coming back on the plane we read what [Pierre] Trudeau had said about 'reason over passion in government' and started laughing. I said, 'I'm going to make a quilt of that,' which I did; we had all these Canadian and famous Americans sewing it. Then we invented this mostly bogus group and sent Trudeau . . . letters on all sorts of letterhead which we made up ourselves. Eventually it got into the papers that there was this huge movement in New York. Trudeau was asked about it and he answered, 'Reason over passion; that's the theme of all my writings.' So we had the second quote! Finally I got this notion that I was a government propagandist . . . I thought it was very funny, but Trudeau, apparently, took it all seriously. Of course, 'reason over passion' is the opposite of what I believe: the two should go side by side."

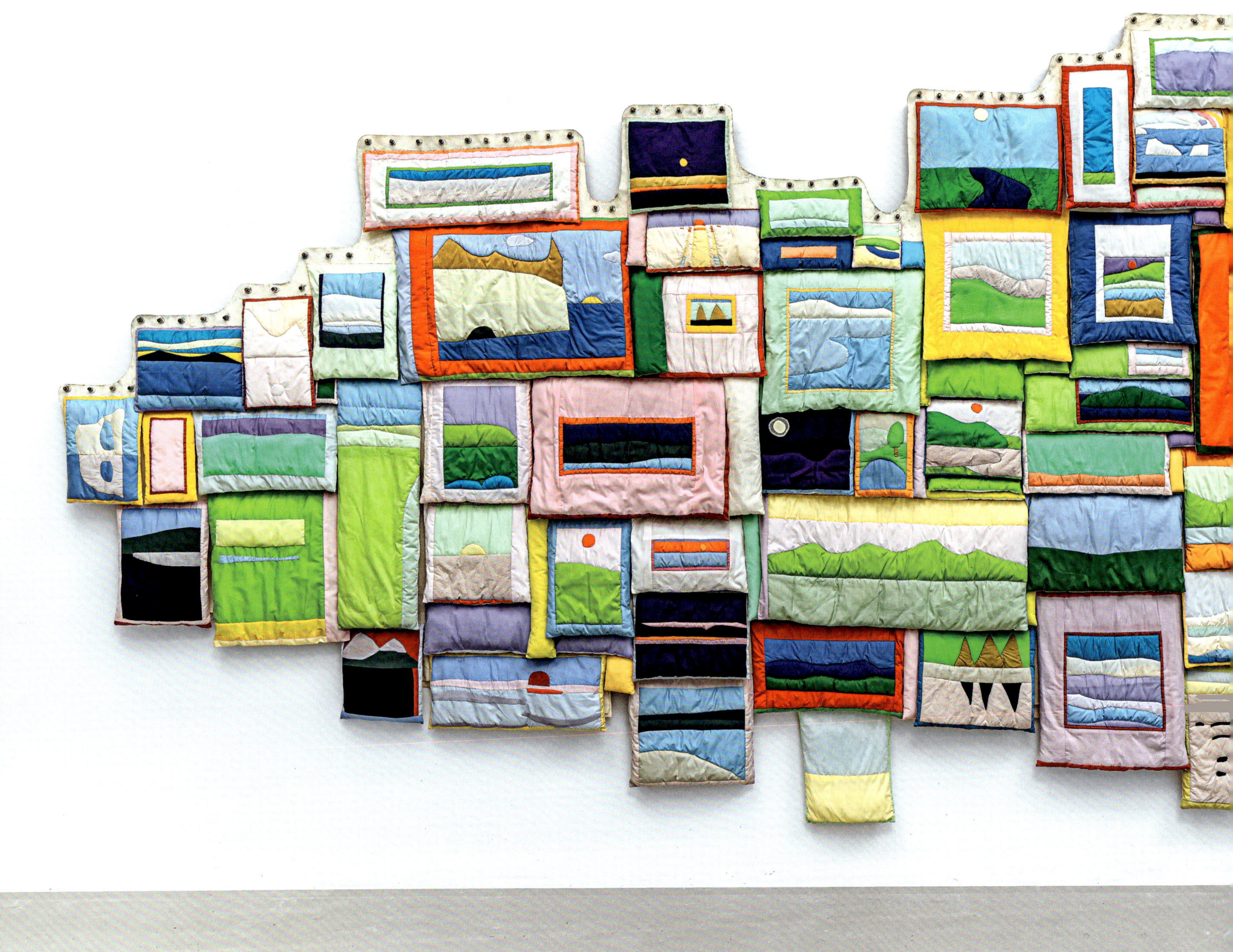

109 Views, 1970
Cloth, thread, batting
243.9 × 786.1 cm
Collection of the Joan and Martin Goldfarb Gallery of York University
A1972.003
Photo: Toni Hafkenscheid

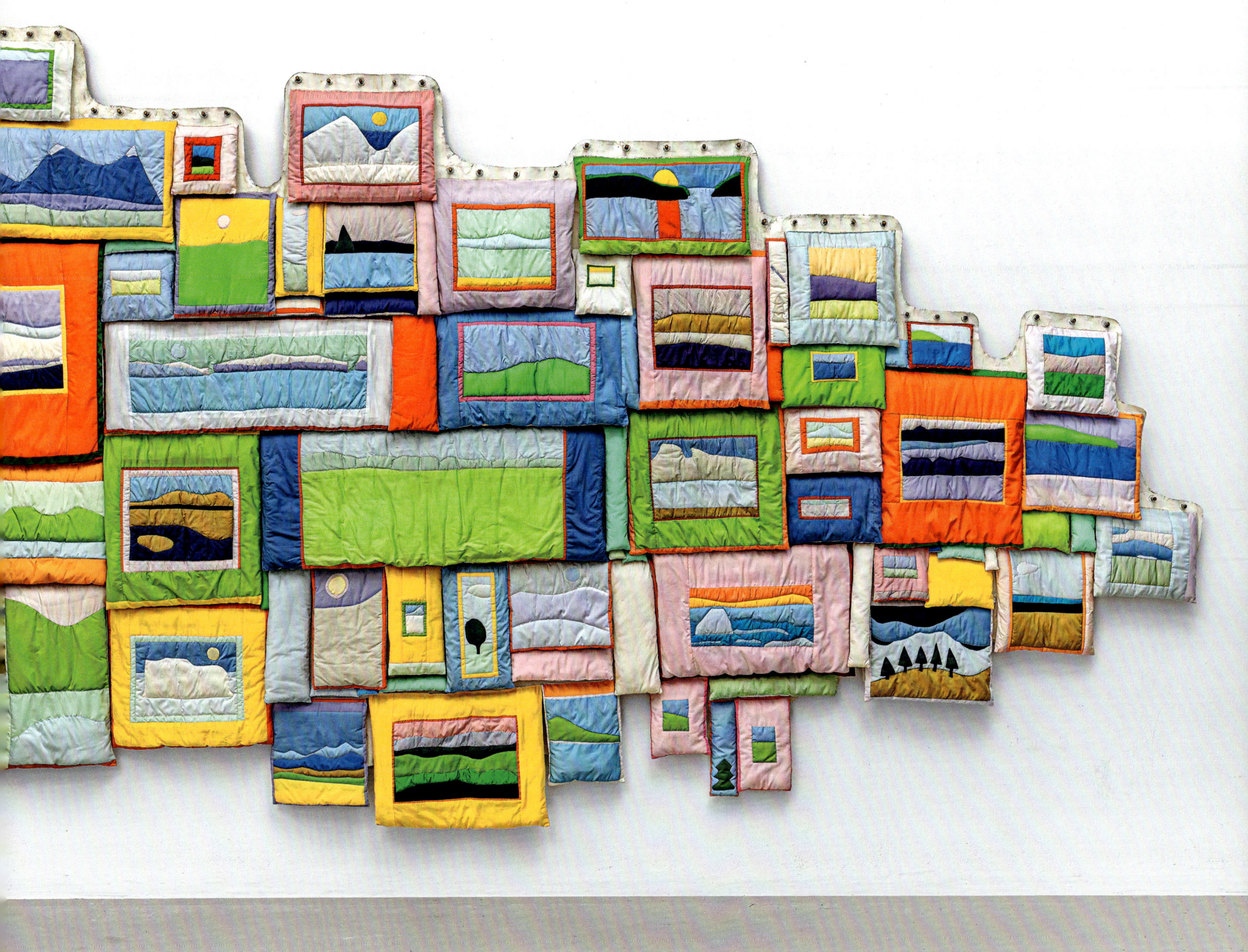

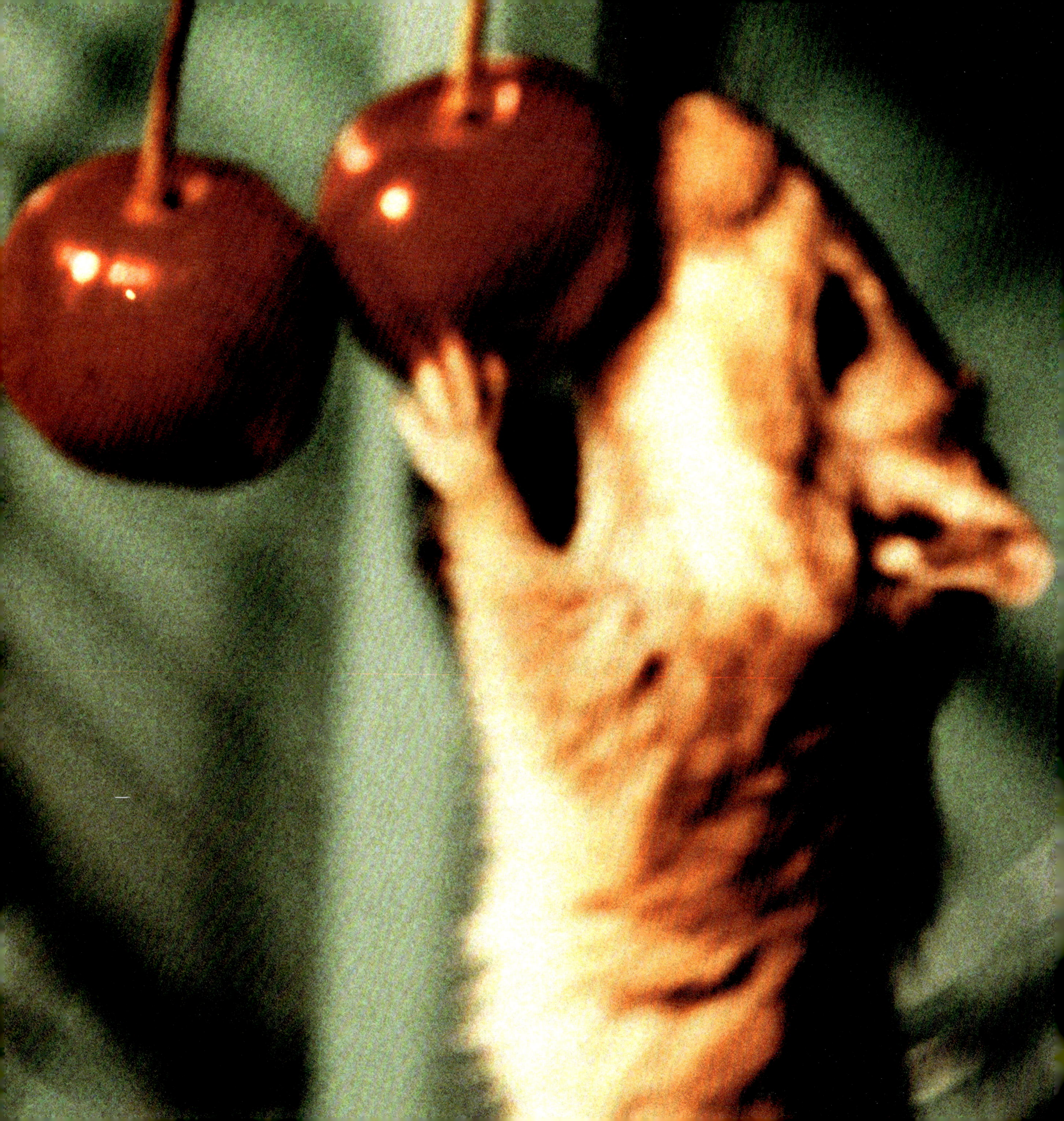

JOYCE WIELAND AND TORONTO FILM CULTURE

JIM SHEDDEN

Though Joyce Wieland made her most celebrated films while she was living in New York City, and has influenced filmmakers and other artists internationally, this essay is concerned with her participation in and influence on film culture in Toronto—the city where she was born and spent the vast majority of her life.[1] Wieland's film work—and visual art in general—is baked into the DNA of that film culture. It continues to have a profound influence on her peers, and on generations of film and media artists who followed in her path. Her influence ranges from being a DIY visionary, to being a woman who created freely in a male-dominated culture, to working outside the system of conventional narrative (and then deciding to work within that system), and in the process developing a deeply original and compelling aesthetic that created new models for other artists working in film. Of primary interest is how the radical heterogeneity of Wieland's film practice has inspired other Toronto film artists across six decades.[2]

"I was struck forcibly by the fact that those early films—*Handtinting, Solidarity, Rat Life and Diet in North America, Pierre Vallières, Sailboat,* and *Water Sark*—were remarkably resistant to any narrow classification, and could not be contained in a cinematic moment that seemed from the perspective of the 1980s to belong largely to the past. Those films spoke, through their variety of formal strategies and subject matter, to concerns being articulated in the most current film theory."

KAY ARMATAGE

1 There is a prevailing notion that Wieland's filmmaking career was happening in New York while the rest of her visual art was happening in Toronto in the 1960s. I am interested in the continuity of her film presence in Toronto, from her early experiments in the late 1950s and her involvement in making the quiet scene of the 1960s a little less quiet, to the shift in her filmmaking when she returns to Toronto in the 1970s.

2 In this essay, I use the imperfect terms "avant-garde film," "experimental film," "underground film," "artists' film," and "documentary cinema" interchangeably. They all refer to the same thing: low-budget or no-budget films made by individuals using small-format film (and video) stocks, without commercial narrative or didactic "baggage," inspired by aesthetic, poetic, and philosophical impulses.

PREVIOUS SPREAD
Rat Life and Diet in North America (film still), 1968
Film, 16mm, colour, sound
16 min
Joyce Wieland fonds, Cinémathèque québécoise
Photo: Stephen Broomer, courtesy of the CFMDC

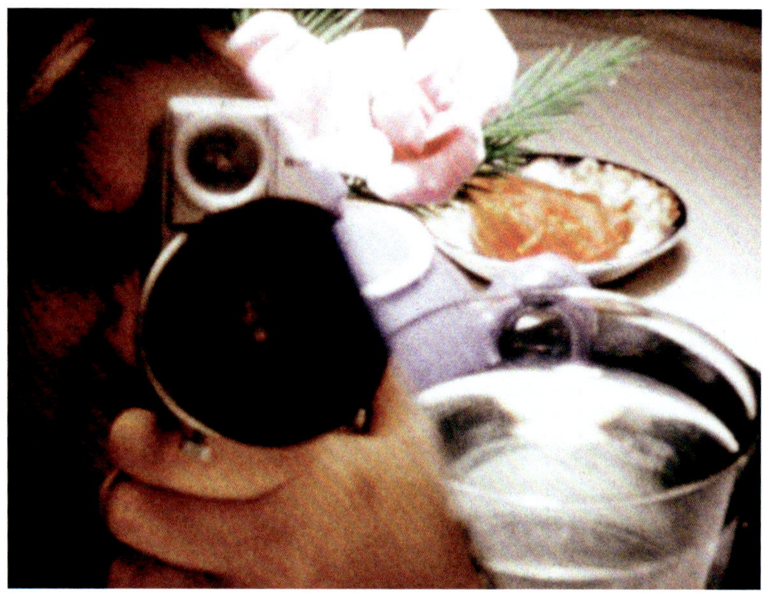

Water Sark (film still), 1965
Soundtrack: Carla Bley, Mike Mantler, Ray Jessel
Film, 8mm blown up in 16mm, colour, sound
14 min
Joyce Wieland fonds, Cinémathèque québécoise
Photo: Stephen Broomer, courtesy of the CFMDC

While pursuing her career as a visual artist in Toronto, Wieland developed a strong interest in cinema through her commercial work at George Dunning's Graphic Associates studio—her day job, as it were—doing animation "fill-ins" and colouring cels, working with cinema at the level of the frame in a tactile manner. There was barely a Toronto filmmakers' scene, so her community in that regard consisted of Michael Snow and other Graphic Associates colleagues such as Warren Collins, Bob Cowan, and Graham Coughtry. In their spare time they made spoof films in 8mm and 16mm, including the lost films that might be considered Wieland's first, *Tea in the Garden* (1956) and *A Salt in the Park* (1958).

"At the age of 16 [Wieland] entered the barren landscape of the Toronto art world and after her initial cold exposure she settled into the secure job of graphic art at E, S & A Robinson. Its weekly drawing classes with live models helped her to endure for four years but there were 15 others there all wanting to be independent artists and with no place to go. 'In 1950 I could walk with my girlfriend Mary from Broadview and Danforth to Keele Street and we wouldn't see anything. We made suicide pacts … and we were considering it because there was fuck-all! There was an art gallery and a few people but no feeling.'"

JOHN PORTER

In 1960, on the occasion of her solo exhibition of drawings at the Dorothy Cameron Gallery in Toronto, Wieland showed seven films by her Graphic Associates colleagues along with Michel Lambeth. Wieland made an invitation by hand that described the September 18 screening as "unusual films realized by a new wave of swell guys."[3]

New York Period, 1963–1971

Wieland's earliest New York films were performance-based works shot on 8mm, *Larry's Recent Behaviour* (1963) and *Patriotism* (1964). She was influenced by friends Ken Jacobs, Jack Smith, and George and Mike Kuchar, as well as Neo-Dada artists like Claes Oldenburg. Yet her unique sense of bawdy humour set her films apart. Without explaining a connection, the film cuts from central figure Larry's body parts to Jackie Kennedy's reaction to John F. Kennedy's assassination, while the soundtrack plays "I Have a Boyfriend," the Chiffons song that was on Dallas radio when the news of the assassination broke.

At the same time Wieland was coming of age in the exciting New York avant-garde film scene, the experimental filmmaking

3 Cameron was not impressed with Wieland's interdisciplinarity, however, and on June 6, 1961, wrote her a letter telling her that she lacked rigour and was not taking her painting seriously; filmmaking and journalism were fragmenting her attention. Jane Lind, *Artist on Fire* (Toronto: James Lorimer, 2001), 124.

"*Water Sark* has been the most important of all her films to me and in several respects. Use of magnifying glass, mirrors, surface water reflections, and other reflections to soften the contours of representation and creating a collage of overlapping and almost seamless visual fragments of spaces (reflected and occupied by her), objects and body parts, and general sense of fluid space or fluidity of environments she creates with her camera. This film resembles the oceanic experience and the fluidity of dream imagery, spilling into one another, not respecting boundaries between self and the world, between self and other, self and objects, and between objects."

IZABELLA PRUSKA-OLDENHOF

scene in Toronto was just being born. Interest in screenings was growing, stirred perhaps by press coverage of Andy Warhol's scandalous Factory films. Presentations began to crop up on university campuses and in galleries, museums, and coffee houses. In 1964, gallerist Avrom Isaacs organized four screenings including works by Wieland, Snow, Coughtry, Cowan, Lipsett, Collins, and others. Wieland's correspondence with Isaacs suggests that his decision to go forward with it had something to do with her urgings: "Just a line to warn you that the Toronto Film Society has made great overtures to Bob Cowan re coming to Toronto and bringing New York avant-garde cinema films," she wrote to him. "They are paying his way too. Now my point is this. You are missing the opportunity of a lifetime. You will be given the greatest credit if you are the first to bring in these films—four of which are truly good films—please do it."[4]

In 1965, Wieland collaborated with her friend Betty Ferguson on *Barbara's Blindness*, a juxtaposition of a found educational film about blindness with seemingly random clips from other sources that challenged viewers' expectations. The same year *Barbara's Blindness* was released, Wieland finished her breakout film, *Water Sark*. Whereas her previous films were rooted in some vestige of narrative, this was, in her words, a self-sufficient work.

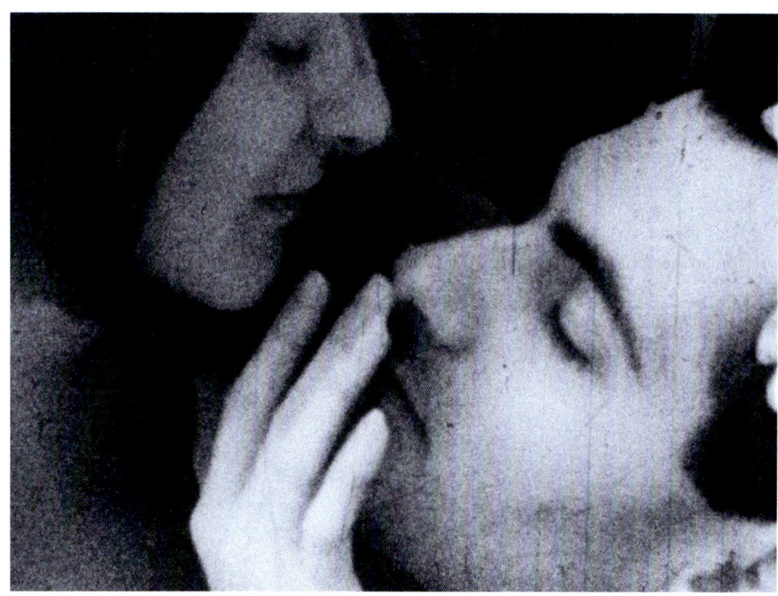

Larry's Recent Behaviour (film still), 1963
Film, 8mm, colour & black and white, sound
17 min
Joyce Wieland fonds, Cinémathèque québécoise
Photo: Stephen Broomer, courtesy of the CFMDC

While still based in New York, in 1966, Wieland was asked to produce an "expanded cinema"[5] piece for Cinethon, a forty-five-hour continuous screening of experimental films, as a kick-off event for a new venue, Cinecity, at the corner of Toronto's Yonge and Charles Streets.[6] Wieland's piece, *Bill's Hat*, was the most

4 Joyce Wieland to Av Isaacs, January 4, 1964, Avrom Isaacs fonds, Clara Thomas Archives and Special Collections, York University, Toronto, 1996-036/002(12).

5 This term was made famous in Gene Youngblood's book of the same name. It was first coined by Jonas Mekas to refer to multi-projector screenings, sometimes involving improvised projection, live music, dance, and other extra-cinematic elements.

6 Cinethon took place June 15 through June 17, 1967, and featured American experimental filmmakers, including Kenneth Anger, Shirley Clarke, George and Mike Kuchar, Ed Emshwiller, and Robert Nelson. The Canadian contributors included David Cronenberg and Robert Fothergill, who were still basically making student skit films, and the idiosyncratic maverick John Hofsess, whose *Palace of Pleasure* represented a polymorphously perverse dialectic informed by Marshall McLuhan and radical Freudo-Marxist theorists like Wilhelm Reich, Herbert Marcuse, and Norman O. Brown.

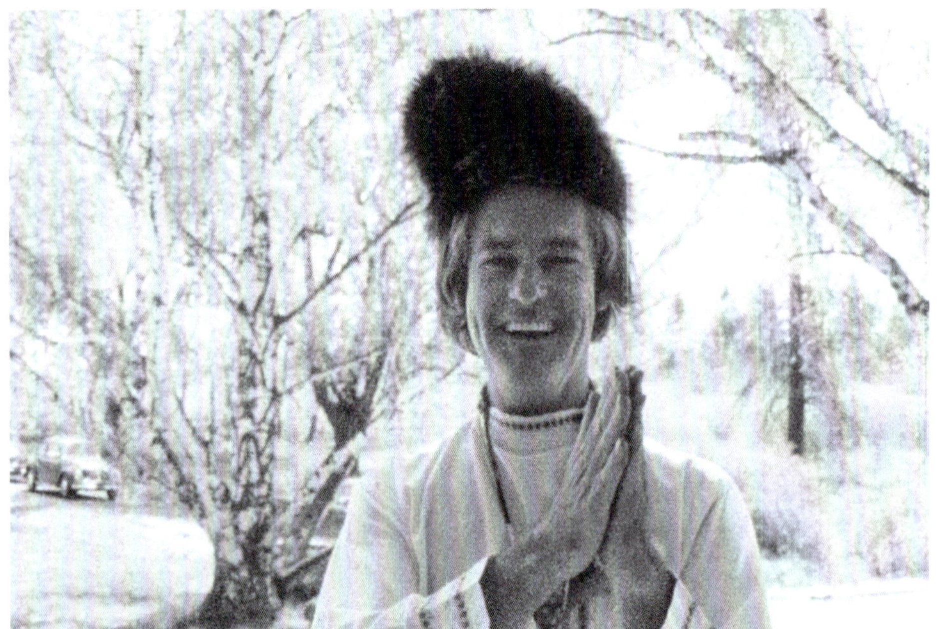

with two of Broomer's collaborators, Eva Kolcze and Cameron Moneo, manipulating both sides of a two-way mirror, using colour gel filters and patterned fabrics, and simply turning the lights off and on. The straightforward, cumulative, collaborative effect resonates with *Bill's Hat*.

The same year the *Bill's Hat* performances took place, Wieland was working on at least five other films that are essential to understanding her oeuvre: *Handtinting* (1967), *Sailboat* (1967), *1933* (1967), *Catfood* (1968), and *Rat Life and Diet in North America* (1968). Wieland also shot *A&B in Ontario* with Hollis Frampton while on a vacation in Toronto in 1967, yet only finished editing it with Su Rynard in 1984. One imagines it resembles the kind of tomfoolery Wieland started during her Graphic Associates amateur filmmaking period.

Rat Life and Diet in North America premiered at the Art Gallery of Ontario in November 1968 as part of a series and competition called Canadian Artists/68, where the works were judged by Jonas Mekas.[10] It was then broadcast on CBC Television in 1969,

vanguard Canadian representation, featuring a triple-screen projection of film and still images of hundreds of people wearing an old raccoon hat that she passed around.[7] The projection was accompanied by a live performance of Stuart Broomer's Kinetic Ensemble. An expansive version of this piece took place a month later, this time at the Art Gallery of Ontario, with two additional screens showing slides (p. 181).

Little attention was paid to *Bill's Hat* by film scholars, biographers, and others documenting Wieland's work until recently. It is hard to say that it had a huge influence on Toronto filmmakers because it is not clear who was in the sold-out audience at Cinethon. In recent years, scholars such as Adam Welch and Monika Kin Gagnon have mined the archive to understand the film/performance better and, in Gagnon's case working with La Cinémathèque québécoise, bring what residual elements there are to the public.[8]

This will doubtless influence filmmakers in Toronto and beyond for years to come. Stephen Broomer, the son of Stuart Broomer, acknowledged that the "family-building" of *Bill's Hat*, for example, was "on my mind when I made *Pepper's Ghost* and *Hang Twelve*."[9] *Pepper's Ghost* is a densely layered work produced

7 Among them A.Y. Jackson, Guido Molinari, Greg Curnoe, Jack Bush, Timothy Leary, Zal Yanovsky, Jackie Burroughs, Roland Michener, and Munro Ferguson.

8 Monika Kin Gagnon, "Into the Archive with Joyce Wieland: *Bill's Hat* (1967)," *Journal of Canadian Art History* 41, no. 1–2 (2020): 129–46.

9 Email to author, January 2024.

10 Wieland did not win; the prize winners in the film category were Jack Chambers, Larry Kardish, Michael Snow, and Keewatin Dewdney.

OPPOSITE
Timothy Leary wearing the beaver hat in *Bill's Hat* (film still), 1967
Film, 60 mm, colour, silent
60 min
Joyce Wieland fonds, Cinémathèque québécoise
Photo: Cinémathèque québécoise

RIGHT
Hollis Frampton (top) and Joyce Wieland (top and bottom) in *A&B in Ontario* (film stills), 1984
Film, 16mm, black and white, sound
16 min
Joyce Wieland fonds, Cinémathèque québécoise
Photos: Stephen Broomer, courtesy of the CFMDC

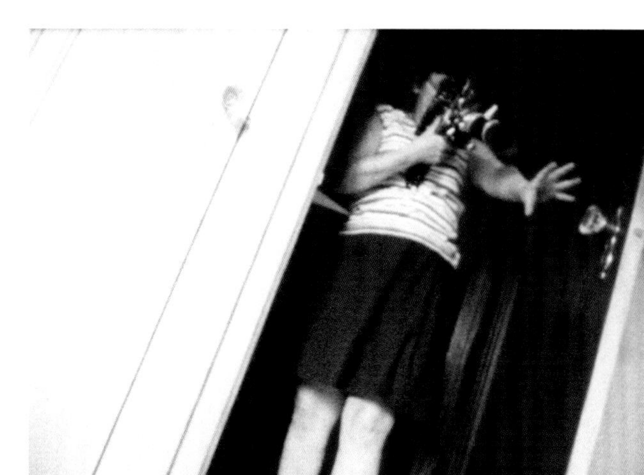

in an episode of the *New Film Makers* series—the kind of programming that is hard to fathom in the present day. Filmmaker Keith Lock recalls seeing *Rat Life and Diet in North America* on TV when he was a teenager; filmmaker and scholar Bruce Elder called it "far and away Wieland's best experimental film."[11] Wieland considered the film a line in the sand: "*Rat Life and Diet in North America* is the first film I made that involved Canada as a subject and had any political reference. It is about coming back to Canada."[12]

"In *Rat Life and Diet in North America* those cherries in the gerbil cage can be almost tasted, sweet and crunchy, and her close-ups of fur in this film and in *Catfood*, create a very tactile and intimate experience, an empathy through proximity to touch. Closeups in *Pierre Vallières* are tactile but also erotic."

IZABELLA PRUSKA-OLDENHOF

Wieland began to develop what could be considered her magnum opus in any medium, *La raison avant la passion / Reason over Passion* (1969), a film that reveals the vastness of her "home" through cinematic landscapes. It employs handheld camerawork and shots from a camera mounted both on the train and a car used during the film's production, along with 537 superimposed nonsensical anagrams of the phrase "Reason over passion," suggesting the instability of language itself.[13]

11 Bruce Elder, *Image and Identity: Reflection on Canadian Film and Culture* (Waterloo, ON: Wilfrid Laurier University Press), 258.

12 Quoted in Debbie Magidson and Judy Wright, "Interviews with Canadian Artists. Debbie Magidson and Judy Wright Interview Joyce Wieland," *Canadian Forum* 54 (May/June 1974): 61.

13 Wieland has said that her film could be called *Passion over Reason*. She recounted an initial fascination with Trudeau, but ultimately felt that "it really should be reason *and* passion in a person. But this man is only reason over passion, and ultimately, he's a psychopath. . . . what happens when people want the kind of power that he achieved in this country[;] . . . . there is a wonderful brain, but when the heart is closed over then it's not much fun anymore." Joyce Wieland, interview by Barbara Stevenson, October 8, 1986, in Kristy A. Holmes-Moss, "Joyce Wieland: Interview and Notes on *Reason over Passion* and *Pierre Vallières*," *Canadian Journal of Film Studies* 15, no. 2 (Fall 2006): 118, 119, Wieland's emphasis.

"Wieland's camera handling, especially in *Water Sark, A and B in Ontario* and in her early films like *Peggy's Blue Skylight* and *Larry's Recent Behaviour* feels more like a pencil than a paintbrush; sketches through which the artist's hand and presence is felt, just as in *Reason Over Passion*, at about the halfway point, where her camera work, handling and catching incredible variances of colour in light when shooting through the train window."

IZABELLA PRUSKA-OLDENHOF

Wieland's sense, after showing the film in New York, was that she "was made to feel in no uncertain terms by a few male filmmakers that I had overstepped my place, that in New York my place was making little films."[14] Wieland felt that the original joyous, anarchic New York scene she had encountered in the early 1960s had become compromised by ambition and the rise of "film theory." Instead, she embraced the suggestion made by Leila Sujir that, in working without a theory herself, "there is a language of emotions."[15]

Return to Toronto 1971 and beyond

Wieland and Snow's return to Toronto in 1971 coincided more or less with the emergence of a local experimental filmmaking scene, with artists like Jim Anderson, David Anderson, Patrick Lee, and Keith Lock, among others.[16] A galvanizing moment for Lock, he says his ambitious diary film about a commune he was part of in Buck Lake, Ontario, *Everything Everywhere Again Alive* (1975), was greatly influenced by Wieland. Lock went on to be the "rehearsal videographer" for her 1976 narrative feature *The Far Shore*.

Wieland and Snow were involved in the ill-fated Toronto Filmmakers Co-op (1971–78), which was intended to be run by and for independent filmmakers like Lock, but eventually attracted commercial filmmakers in the "tax shelter" era. This overreach led to bankruptcy. Along the way, it was the only institution that brought experimental filmmakers together in Toronto. Members showed their films at group screenings. Filmmaker Rick Hancox came to Toronto in 1972 from the United States. He got to know Wieland and Snow when they were on the board of the Co-op together.[17] Hancox was enamoured with the "disarming almost amateur domestic scenes" in Wieland's films and noted *Rat Life and Diet in North America* as particularly influential, though his own *House Movie* (1972) was made before he saw her work. His innovative offscreen sound solutions came to him partly from seeing what Wieland had accomplished with very little budget in *Pierre Vallières* and *Solidarity*, solutions born of economic necessity perhaps, but forming an aesthetic feature as an unintended consequence.

"I first saw *Rat Life and Diet* on CBC after school when I was a teenager, before I met her. In the early '70s, I saw *Solidarity* and [it] had a huge influence on my film *Everything Everywhere Again Alive* [1975]. The camera work on *Solidarity* was very, very shaky and yet the constant title 'Solidarity' reduced eye fatigue. This gave me the seed idea for the superimposed imagery on *Everything Everywhere Again Alive* since it is also entirely handheld."

KEITH LOCK

14 Kay Armatage, "Kay Armatage Interviews Joyce Wieland," *Take One* 3, no. 2 (February 1972): 25.

15 See Leila Suijir, p. 216 in this book.

16 Jim Anderson's *Scream of a Butterfly* (1969) was an animated shot with painting directly on film stock; he also collaborated with Lock on *Work, Bike, and Eat* (1971).

17 Hancox also felt a camaraderie with Wieland and Snow. He was asked to show *Home for Christmas* (1978) at the Grierson Documentary Seminar, where it was almost universally panned. He called Wieland and Snow—almost like calling "his own mother for reassurance"—and they convinced him that he must be doing something right if the (at the time) stodgy Grierson folks disapproved so loudly. This and other references to Hancox were relayed by Hancox to the author in a telephone conversation, January 2024.

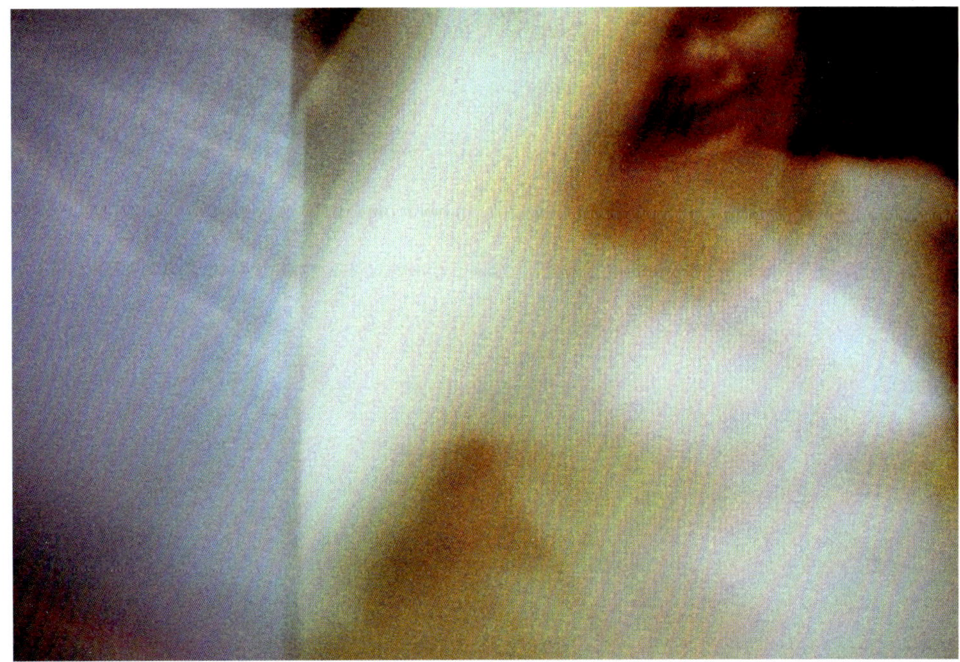

Stan Brakhage
Garden of Earthly Delights
(film still), 1981
Film, 16mm, colour, silent
3 min
Photo: Stephen Broomer, courtesy of the CFMDC

"Both Joyce and Michael were crucial for the Funnel and local movie artists generally. They were a connection between film and art worlds, and between a very, very local scene and New York, and, beyond New York, the other fringe universes. They didn't dig the ditches, hand out the tickets, sweep the floors, but they were conduits, connectors, and both had a lively humour and open-hearted easiness that became models of how an artist might be—and [the idea] that one might dedicate a life to pursuing these marginal concerns."

MIKE HOOLBOOM

Keith Lock and a number of the Buck Lake communards would go on to form the Funnel Experimental Film Theatre, the galvanizing of an experimental film scene in Toronto, in 1977, almost two decades after the explosion of activity in San Francisco and New York. The Funnel was its own thing, true to the Toronto scene, but taking cues from New York underground film organizations like the Millenium Film Workshop, the Collective for Living Cinema, and Anthology Film Archives. Wieland and Snow were founding members of Funnel, part of the "intergenerational sensibility"[18] that defined the organization. According to filmmaker Mike Hoolboom: "Michael Snow and Joyce Wieland … were elders, people to look up to. They made fabulous films, they were famous."[19]

The Funnel community allowed Wieland to play the role of a mentor, having a profound influence on filmmakers like Midi Onodera, Su Rynard, John Price, and Eva Kolcze, among many others. Richard Kerr acknowledged that in his early filmmaking days it was "Snow, Wieland and Chambers [who] sparked my interest and sustained me creatively all my adult life. Wieland, specifically, showed me that it was possible to make a personal film that was political." Kerr cites *Rat Life and Diet in North America*, *Solidarity*, and *La raison avant la passion* as having cleared the way for his films *The Last Days of Contrition* (1988) and *Cruel Rhythm* (1991), where he uses a road-trip approach, perhaps inspired by Wieland, to create impressionistic meditations on America in the Reagan and Bush Sr. eras that ambivalently suggest melancholy, fear, and rage. Hoolboom observes that "*Water Sark* showed me (and more than

18 Dot Tuer in Mike Hoolboom, n.d., mikehoolboom.com/?p=15101.

19 Email to author, January 2024.

a few others) that it was possible to make a 'political' movie without leaving home. It's a movie that gives permission. A feminist film." He calls *Handtinting*[20] "a touchstone miracle. How did she manage to say so much with so little?"[21]

"Joyce opened up the idea that one could be an artist and choose a creative path through life, something that looked quite unusual and appealing when coming from Scarborough. Joyce, by welcoming me into the fold of her life and her eclectic group of women artist friends, opened a portal into a new world. And I learned much about a way of being and doing in the world from these wonderful folks."

SU RYNARD

Just as the "Funnel generation" began to emerge, Wieland completed her most ambitious project: *The Far Shore* (1976) co-produced with her collaborator Judy Steed.[22] Wieland co-wrote the 35mm commercial feature with Bryan Barney. The film reinterprets the figure of Tom Thomson, a personal hero of Wieland's. The main protagonist is a strong female character who challenges societal expectations, her story told through the subversive lens of a melodrama full of pathos and reflection. Wieland explores the complex relationship between humans and the natural world, treating landscape not just as a backdrop but as a plot device and an object of desire for the characters. Critical reception to the film was ambivalent, but negative enough to limit its distribution. The work generated little interest in the experimental film community as well, and it was greeted with hostility in some feminist and political corners.[23]

Though reviews at the time were along the lines of Gary Michael Dault's for the *Toronto Star*—"Movie Looks Gorgeous But the Acting Ruins It"—in the years since it has received positive and serious attention from Toronto writers and critics. Kay Armatage makes the case, following Lauren Rabinovitz, that it should have been seen as an "exploration of parodic reversals of genre elements," and therefore thought about along the same lines as everything from Chantal Akerman's *Golden Eighties* (1986) and Rainer Werner Fassbinder's various Douglas Sirk reworkings to Lawrence Kasdan's *Body Heat* (1981), Neil Jordan's *Mona Lisa* (1986), and Kathryn Bigelow's *The Loveless* (1981). Aside from a few unfinished 1960s projects that she would complete later in the 1980s, *The Far Shore* marked the end of Wieland's filmmaking career.[24]

"Her ecological thinking, [by] which I don't just mean 'the environment' ... I mean ecological consciousness ... an interconnectedness, a way of working that evolves directly out of one's life and living space, through the hands-on process of DIY filmmaking. That is Joyce above all. The Film Farm at its foundation had a feminist influence, and continues to, and of course that is Joyce's perspective, inherently feminist. We screened many of her works at Film Farm. I guess it's hard for me to separate my filmmaking from Film Farm, so all these influences blend."

PHIL HOFFMAN

20 Using footage derived from a professional gig she was doing for the US Job Corps, Wieland depicts young white and Black women in an education centre participating in activities like dancing and swimming. The setting seems restrictive, and the women observe each other's movements. She hand-tints black-and-white footage with uneven fabric dyes, creating a tie-dye effect. Repeated shots and changes in camera speed contribute to a fragmented and disorienting experience, amplified, so to speak, by the melancholy of the silent soundtrack.

21 Email to author, January 2024.

22 CTV reporter Judy Steed met Wieland in 1971 and independently produced the documentary *A Film About Joyce Wieland* (1972). They collaborated on three films: *Pierre Vallières* (1972), *Solidarity* (1973), and *The Far Shore* (1976).

23 See Mike Zryd in "'There Are Many Joyces': Critical Reception of the Films of Joyce Wieland," in *The Films of Joyce Wieland*, ed. Kathryn Elder (Toronto: Cinematheque Ontario, 1999), 201.

24 See Lauren Rabinovitz, "An Interview with Joyce Wieland," *Afterimage* 8, no. 10 (May 1981): 8.

"The films of Carolee Schneemann, Birgit Hein, and Joyce Wieland were all major influences. I have attempted to connect film forms / media forms to *écriture féminine* (Julia Kristeva, Hélène Cixous, Luce Irigaray), proposing a *cinéma féminin*. Wieland's work is radically postmodern, in the sense that while it accepts the visceral/performative aspects of formal experiments with colour, tone, line, and the grain of the voice, pushed beyond modernist art by contaminating the characteristics of one medium with attributes of another—it often turns to folk art, pop culture, language, or politics to vitalize its constructions. What results is a veritable mash-up: hybrid, omnivorous, polymorphously perverse (à la Herbert Marcuse and Norman O. Brown)—indeed, it tends towards an eroticization/spiritualization of all reality, as it attempts to contrive forms that can promiscuously incorporate any and all elements of reality."

BRUCE ELDER

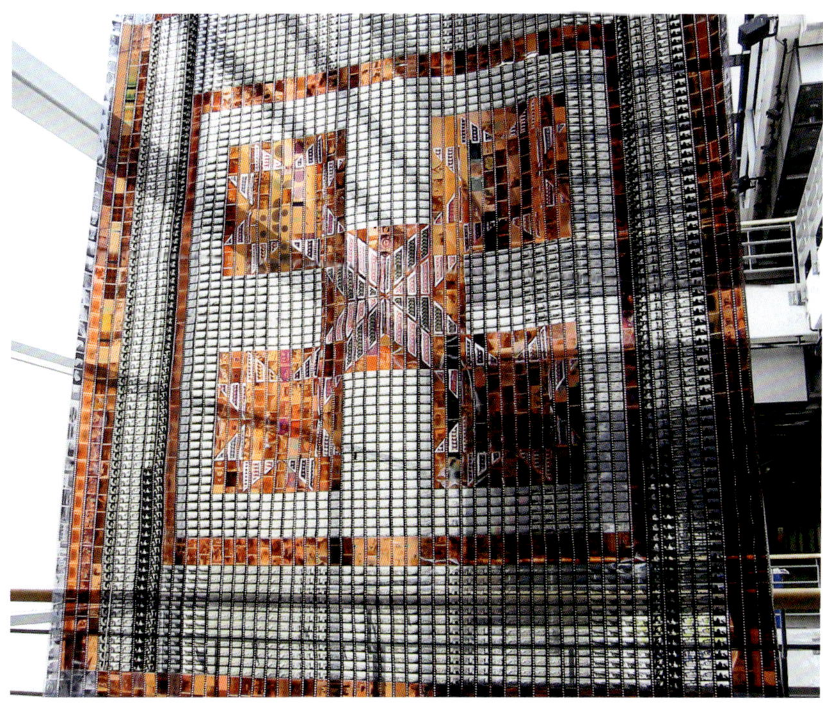

Kelly Egan
c: won eyed jail, 2005
Quilted 35mm film
Courtesy of Kelly Egan

Lasting Legacy

Kay Armatage acknowledges being influenced by *Solidarity*, with its minimalist formal strategies framing political content, in *Speak Body* (1979), a film about abortion that uses both scripted and unscripted voices cut into a "multiple and contradictory voice-over which I hoped would not only challenge the masculine voice of authority that tends to characterize the use of voice-over in documentary cinema, but would also speak from and to feminine subjectivity in a film which deals with female experience and the perception and representation of the female body." Armatage continued this exploration of female voice and identity in *Striptease* (1980) and *Storytelling* (1983). In *Artist on Fire* (1987), Armatage's documentary on Wieland, the artist's voice is clear and uninterrupted, "corporealized" (synced to her lips on the screen), while the other voices—friends, colleagues, critics—are off-screen, more fragmented and unscripted.[25]

"[*In Artist on Fire*,] in contrast to Wieland's voice, which is mixed clearly, completes sentences, speaks alone, and is corporealized (synchronized to her lip movements on screen), the unidentified, disembodied and inter-cut voice-overs are treated with an hallucinatory reverb and embedded in multiple tracks including sounds from Wieland's films, additional sound effects, and music. The intended effect is of contrasting modes of address, identification, and subjectivity."

KAY ARMATAGE

Wieland's filmmaking can be seen as part of a continuum with her coexisting artisanal practices like quiltmaking. Kelly Egan's short *c: won eyed jail* (2005) pays homage to the artist.[26] Egan constructs the work in two parts: a quilt comprised of 35mm still negatives and found film footage, and a 35mm film print made from the same elements. Typically with artists' films, the experience of the projected image is the real work;

25 Kay Armatage, "Joyce Wieland, Feminist Documentary, and the Body of the Work," *Canadian Journal of Political and Social Theory* 13, no. 1–2 (1989): 91–92.

26 Its title is an anagram of Wieland's name.

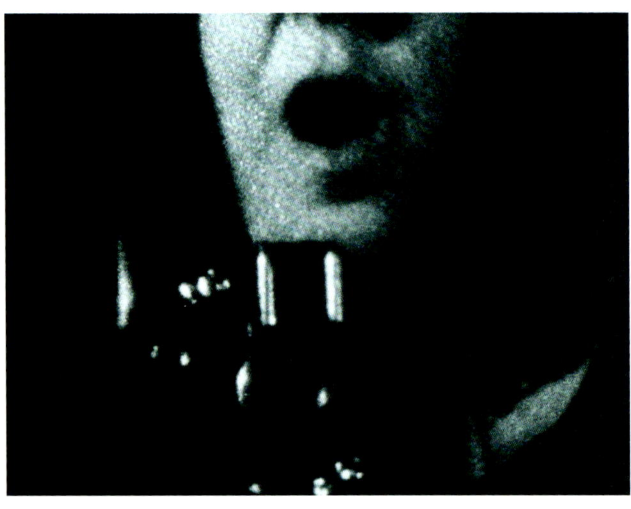

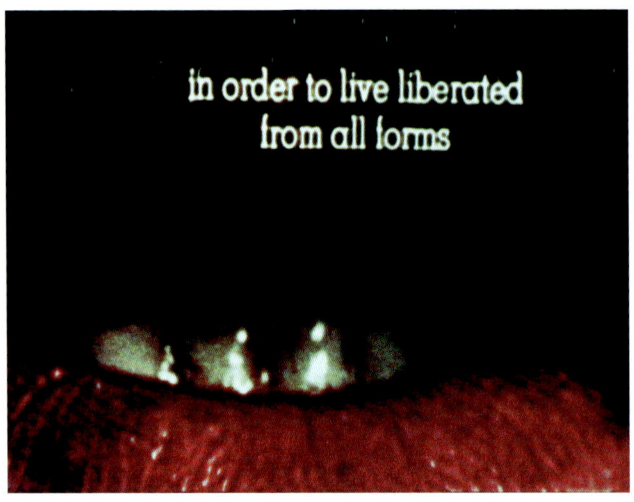

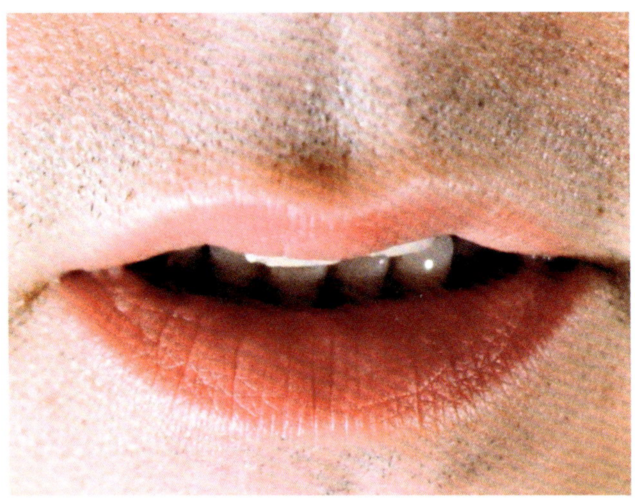

TOP
La raison avant la passion / Reason over Passion (film still), 1969
Film, 16mm, colour, sound
80 min
Joyce Wieland fonds, Cinémathèque québécoise
Photo: Stephen Broomer, courtesy of the AGO

MIDDLE
Pierre Vallières (film still), 1972
Film, 16mm, colour, sound
33 min
Joyce Wieland fonds, Cinémathèque québécoise
Photo: Stephen Broomer, courtesy of the CFMDC

BOTTOM
Bruce Elder
Lamentations: A Monument for the Dead World (film still), 1985
Film, 16mm, colour, sound
437 min
Photo: Stephen Broomer, courtesy of the CFMDC

the film negative and positive are means to this end. For Egan, the woven photo/film quilt is meant to possess the same "art" status as the film.[27]

Bruce Elder's epic within an epic, the seven-hour *Lamentations (Monument to a Dead World)* (1985), contains specific allusions to Wieland's films, including the lips of a film critic and professor, Bart Testa, reading a lecture on St. Augustine, displacing Pierre Vallières's confessions, and Joyce Wieland's silent *O Canada*. More importantly, Wieland, along with Jack Smith and the Kuchar Brothers (in whose films *Knocturne*, 1968, and *Motel Capri*, 1986, Wieland acted) were the direct inspiration for Elder's "broken-down skits," like that with James D. Smith in *Consolations* (1988) as the "Nietzschean Middle Eastern Adventurer" or Franz Liszt in the monastery. Elder has also cited Wieland's bawdy humour during the early Funnel days, and the Neo-Dada spirit, which directly inspired some of his earlier films, like *Permutations and Combinations* (1976).

27 For the past twenty years, Richard Kerr has also been creating lightboxes using 35mm film trailers, which might be seen as film quilts.

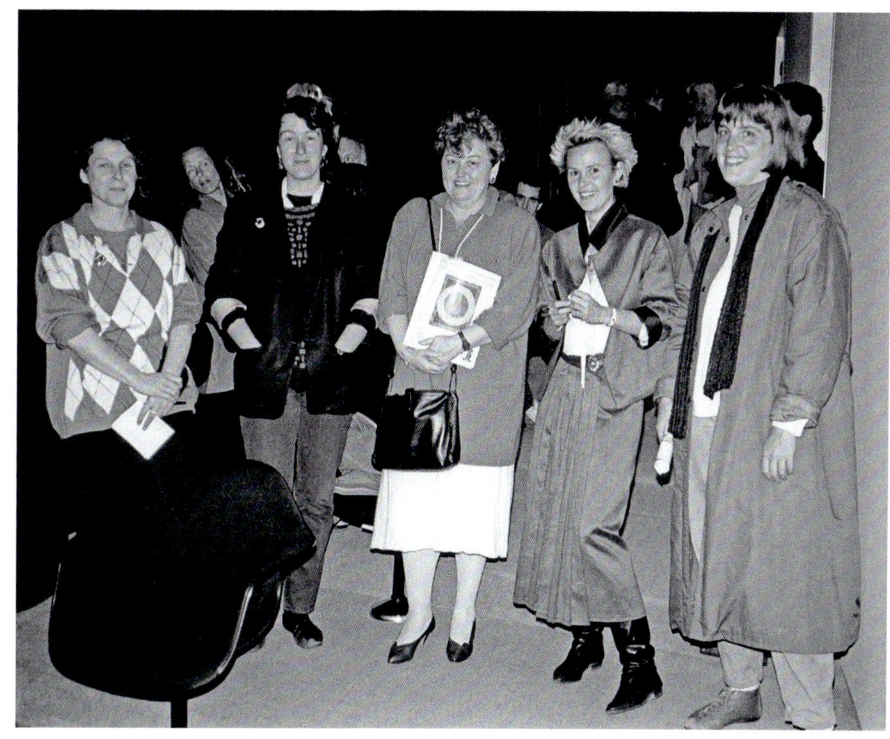

Screening of women's films at the Art Gallery of Ontario's Jackman Hall, May 14, 1986
Left to right: Barbara Sternberg, Cindy Gawel, Joyce Wieland, Annette Mangaard, and Sandra Meigs
Photo © John Porter

Wieland's legacy as a lay ecologist, a feminist, and ultimately an ecofeminist might be her most profound legacy on Toronto film culture. Her foretelling of *l'écriture féminine*, the literary genre called for by writers like Hélène Cixous and Luce Irigaray, which fought to break with masculine stylistic norms in favour of one that embraces female difference through the liberation of the body in culture and text, has been suggested by many scholars and filmmakers. Whether Wieland was living in Toronto or New York, her DIY ethic, her thoughtfulness concerning environmental, feminist, and nationalist politics, her bawdy humour, and ultimately her free-spirited aesthetic influenced Toronto film culture deeply.[28] It is hard to know whether she would appreciate the critical perspective on her work that draws so heavily on the French feminist theories or the philosophy of Maurice Merleau-Ponty. Perhaps she would see how those writers themselves see the word as limiting, each accepting in their individual way that fundamental knowledge comes from the experience of the lived body in the world, more passion than reason, and that the anticipation of *cinéma féminin* is perhaps her deepest gift to Toronto (and world) film culture.

28 Wieland influenced not only filmmakers but also the ethos of a number of independent film and media organizations in Toronto, from TIFF Cinematheque, Liaison of Independent Filmmakers of Toronto, and Innis Film Society to Pleasure Dome, Early Monthly Segments, Images Festival, and ADHOC. The Canadian Filmmakers Distribution Centre's release of *The Complete Works of Joyce Wieland* DVD box set in 2011, and a DVD of Kay Armatage's *Artist on Fire* in 1987 has given new life to her films in the changing media landscape.

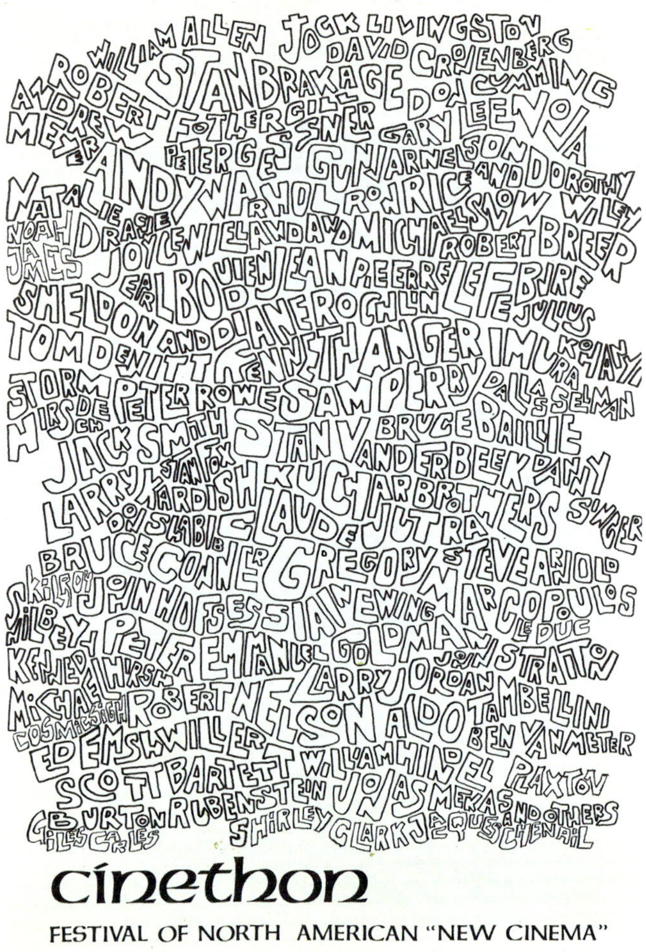

Cinethon brochure, 1967
Published by the Cinethon Festival Committee, Toronto
Edward P. Taylor Library & Archives, Art Gallery of Ontario
Photo: AGO, Craig Boyko

BILL'S HAT, 1967

In June 1967, Cinecity, an underground movie theatre in Toronto, presented Cinethon, a forty-five-hour "Festival of New North American Cinema." The festival featured independent filmmakers ranging from Kenneth Anger to a young David Cronenberg. Wieland's commission was to create "an exercise in Expanded Cinema," defined by the organizers as a "theatre of total sensation," combining multiple superimposed projections, live music, dance, strobe effects, and "programmed sequences of colour and sound ... an assault on the senses, ranging from the horrendous to the irresistably beautiful."[1]

Wieland's piece, *Bill's Hat,* featured film footage and photographs of hundreds of participants whom the artist asked to try on an old raccoon hat. Among those she filmed and photographed over several months were art-world, entertainment, and political luminaries ranging from A.Y. Jackson and Guido Molinari to LSD prophet Timothy Leary. Monika Kin Gagnon's research resurfaced *Bill's Hat* via the Cinémathèque québécoise website. She observes that in the fifty-minute film, at the core of the "Happening," the raccoon hat "takes on an increasingly anthropomorphic character as it moves through [the] cumulative experiences"[2] of the various characters who encounter it in their own settings.

Bill's Hat was performed at Cinethon on June 16, 1967, as a three-screen film projection with live music by Stuart Broomer's Kinetic Ensemble. Later that summer, it was at the Film-Makers Cinematheque in New York City, and at the Art Gallery of Ontario's Walker Court on November 29. Accounts of the three performances vary. The AGO iteration included multiple superimposed 16mm films and slides projected onto three screens and on the audience itself, with an altar of flowerpots, at least sixty burning candles, and two bands—Kinetic Ensemble along with The 25th Hour, a rock band featuring Wieland's nephew Keith Stewart—playing simultaneously over a taped song.

Wieland later announced that she was probably through with the medium of expanded cinema, unless there were proper resources. "I'd like $50,000 [and] six months to prepare a good one."[3] ››››

JIM SHEDDEN

1 *Cinethon: Festival of North American "New Cinema,"* program guide, June 1967.

2 Monika Kin Gagnon, "Into the Archive with Joyce Wieland," *Journal of Art History* 41, no. 1–2 (2020): 131.

3 "Film-maker Casts Dwight Eisenhower Eating Fish." Author unidentified. Joyce Wieland fonds, Clara Thomas Archives and Special Collections, York University, Toronto, ASC33280.

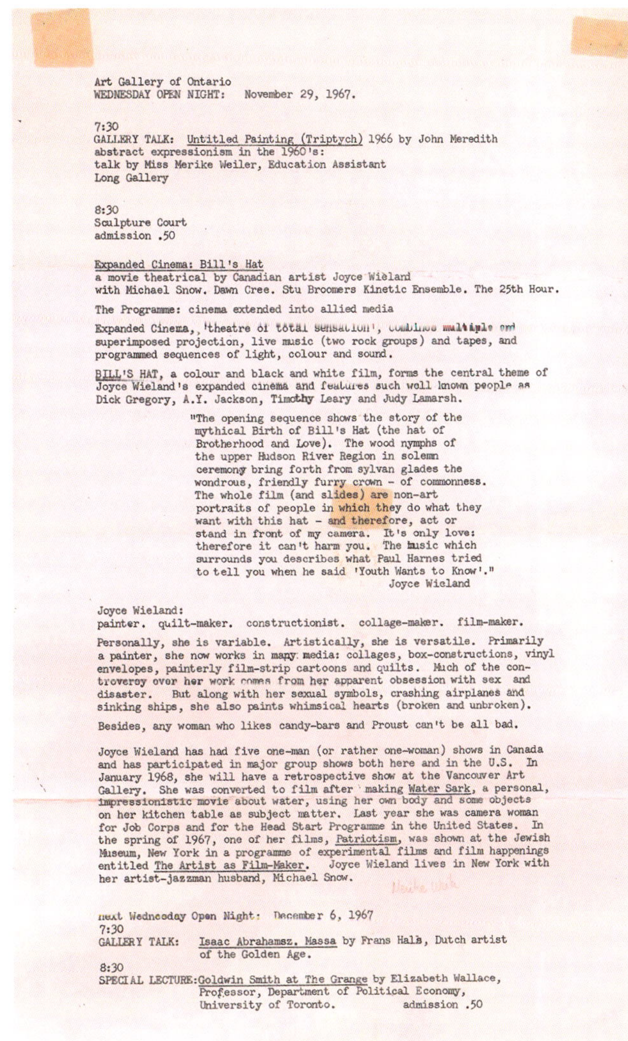

Art Gallery of Ontario
WEDNESDAY OPEN NIGHT: November 29, 1967.

7:30
GALLERY TALK: Untitled Painting (Triptych) 1966 by John Meredith
abstract expressionism in the 1960's:
talk by Miss Merike Weiler, Education Assistant
Long Gallery

8:30
Sculpture Court
admission .50

Expanded Cinema: Bill's Hat
a movie theatrical by Canadian artist Joyce Wieland
with Michael Snow. Dawn Cree. Stu Broomers Kinetic Ensemble. The 25th Hour.

The Programme: cinema extended into allied media

Expanded Cinema, 'theatre of total sensation', combines multiple and superimposed projection, live music (two rock groups) and tapes, and programmed sequences of light, colour and sound.

BILL'S HAT, a colour and black and white film, forms the central theme of Joyce Wieland's expanded cinema and features such well known people as Dick Gregory, A.Y. Jackson, Timothy Leary and Judy Lamarsh.

> "The opening sequence shows the story of the mythical Birth of Bill's Hat (the hat of Brotherhood and Love). The wood nymphs of the upper Hudson River Region in solemn ceremony bring forth from sylvan glades the wondrous, friendly furry crown - of commonness. The whole film (and slides) are non-art portraits of people in which they do what they want with this hat - and therefore, act or stand in front of my camera. It's only love: therefore it can't harm you. The music which surrounds you describes what Paul Harnes tried to tell you when he said 'Youth Wants to Know'."
>
> Joyce Wieland

Joyce Wieland:
painter. quilt-maker. constructionist. collage-maker. film-maker.

Personally, she is variable. Artistically, she is versatile. Primarily a painter, she now works in many media: collages, box-constructions, vinyl envelopes, painterly film-strip cartoons and quilts. Much of the controversy over her work comes from her apparent obsession with sex and disaster. But along with her sexual symbols, crashing airplanes and sinking ships, she also paints whimsical hearts (broken and unbroken).

Besides, any woman who likes candy-bars and Proust can't be all bad.

Joyce Wieland has had five one-man (or rather one-woman) shows in Canada and has participated in major group shows both here and in the U.S. In January 1968, she will have a retrospective show at the Vancouver Art Gallery. She was converted to film after making Water Sark, a personal, impressionistic movie about water, using her own body and some objects on her kitchen table as subject matter. Last year she was camera woman for Job Corps and for the Head Start Programme in the United States. In the spring of 1967, one of her films, Patriotism, was shown at the Jewish Museum, New York in a programme of experimental films and film happenings entitled The Artist as Film-Maker. Joyce Wieland lives in New York with her artist-jazzman husband, Michael Snow.

next Wednesday Open Night: December 6, 1967
7:30
GALLERY TALK: Isaac Abrahamsz. Massa by Frans Hals, Dutch artist of the Golden Age.
8:30
SPECIAL LECTURE: Goldwin Smith at The Grange by Elizabeth Wallace, Professor, Department of Political Economy, University of Toronto. admission .50

Press Release

Art Gallery of Ontario

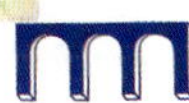

Grange Park,
Toronto 2B, Canada
Telephone: 363-3485

FOR RELEASE PLEASE:

FOR FURTHER INFORMATION:
Miss Janine M. Smiter
Public Relations & Information Officer

WEDNESDAY OPEN NIGHT

EXPANDED CINEMA AT THE ART GALLERY OF ONTARIO

A movie theatrical entitled Expanded Cinema: Bill's Hat by Canadian artist Joyce Wieland will dominate the Art Gallery of Ontario's regular Wednesday Open Night programme on Wednesday, November 29, in the Gallery's sculpture court, at 8.30 p.m.

Noise will be a pre-dominant feature of the evening's event: Bill's Hat, a colour and black and white film which forms the central theme of Miss Wieland's expanded cinema and features such well known people as Miss Judy LaMarsh; artist, A.Y. Jackson and comedians, Dick Gregory and Soupy Sales. A combination of multiple and superimposed projections from two film projectors and two automatic slide projectors onto three large screens will create the basis of Joyce Wieland's 'theatre of sensation'. Sixty candles set in an altar of vinyl and massed flowers will also superimpose diffused images on one of the corner screens.

Two bands, Stu Broomers Kinetic Ensemble of six people, and Keith Stewarts four man rock and roll group The 25th Hour will play simultaneously over taped music; Canadian composer Ray Jessel has written the rock and roll march theme music to Bill's Hat. The twin New York film-makers, George and Mike Kuchar, have said of Miss Wieland's expanded cinema "it makes you want to get up and start dancing in the aisles".

Joyce Wieland was converted to film-making after making Water Sark, a personal impressionistic movie about water, using her own body and some objects on her kitchen table as subject matter. In 1966, she was camera woman on two documentary films for Job Corps and for the Head Start Programme in the United States. In the spring of 1967, one of her films, Patriotism, was shown at the Jewish Museum, New York, in a programme of experimental films and film happenings entitled The Artist as Film-Maker.

Born in Toronto, Joyce Wieland studied art at Central Technical School and first showed her work in a four-man exhibition in 1957. Since then, she has participated in many major group exhibitions in the United States and Canada, including the National Gallery's biennale exhibition in 1965. Galleries that have purchased her work include the Art Gallery of Ontario, the Vancouver Art Gallery, the Montreal Museum of Fine Art, the National Gallery of Canada and the Philadelphia Museum of Art. Joyce Wieland lives in New York with her artist husband, Michael Snow, who also plays a trumpet in the expanded cinema programme.

Wednesday Open Night at the Art Gallery of Ontario on Wednesday, November 29, also includes a gallery talk on the recent accession, John Meredith's Untitled Painting (Triptych), abstract expressionism in the 1960's, at 7.30 p.m.

-30-

November 24, 1967.

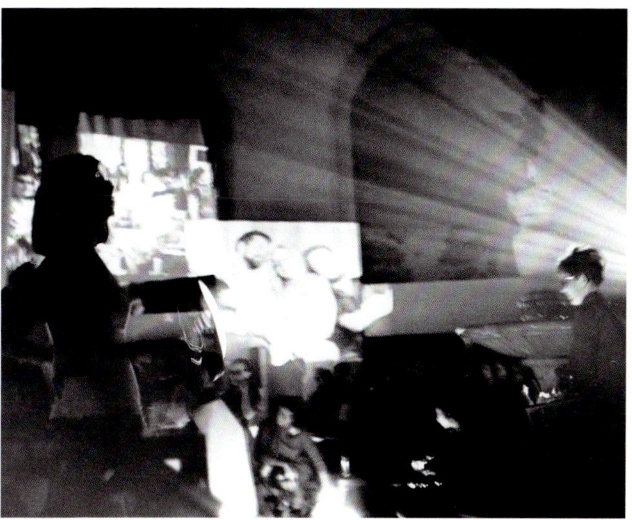

ABOVE, LEFT

Handbill program from the Art Gallery of Ontario, November 29, 1967, regarding events for Wednesday Open Night and mentioning *Bill's Hat* by Joyce Wieland
Avrom Isaacs fonds, ASC33275, York University Libraries, Clara Thomas Archives and Special Collections

ABOVE, RIGHT

Press release from the Art Gallery of Ontario, November 24, 1967, regarding Wednesday Open Night Expanded Cinema at the Art Gallery of Ontario, featuring *Bill's Hat* by Joyce Wieland
Avrom Isaacs fonds, ASC33274, York University Libraries, Clara Thomas Archives and Special Collections

RIGHT

Performance of *Bill's Hat* at Expanded Cinema, Walker Court, Art Gallery of Ontario, 1967
Photo: Denis Robinson

SWEET BEAVER PERFUME BY J. WIELAND, 1971

Symbols of the feminine, nature, and love were abundant in *True Patriot Love*, Joyce Wieland's exhibition at the National Gallery of Canada, which opened on Canada Day (July 1), 1971. The spirited show featured a large number of quilts; the gigantic, iced (inedible) *Arctic Passion Cake*, prepared by the Parliamentary Restaurant chef; twenty-four ducklings and four adult ducks waddling about or paddling in a pond (in fact, a plastic swimming pool); and potted pine trees throughout. Those attending the opening celebration at the Lorne Building on Elgin Street in Ottawa were welcomed by the LaSalle Cadets one-hundred-piece brass band and offered petit fours during the reception.

"I think of Canada as female," Wieland often said. To overtly feminize the symbol of Canada, the industrious beaver, the artist—who revelled in witty conceits—created a "very personal perfume" that she labelled *Sweet Beaver Perfume by J. Wieland*. Sold in different-sized bottles in a limited edition of 125, she described it as an "earthy, woods, sunlit, beaver, animal fragrance," which included Siberian moss as an ingredient. With *Sweet Beaver*, Wieland playfully rendered her Canadian mythmaking a fully sensory experience. (O))

ANNE GRACE

OPPOSITE
Oh Canada!, 1976
Published by London Public Libraries, Galleries and Museums (Ontario)
Book
16 × 11 cm
Edward P. Taylor Library & Archives, Art Gallery of Ontario
Photo: AGO

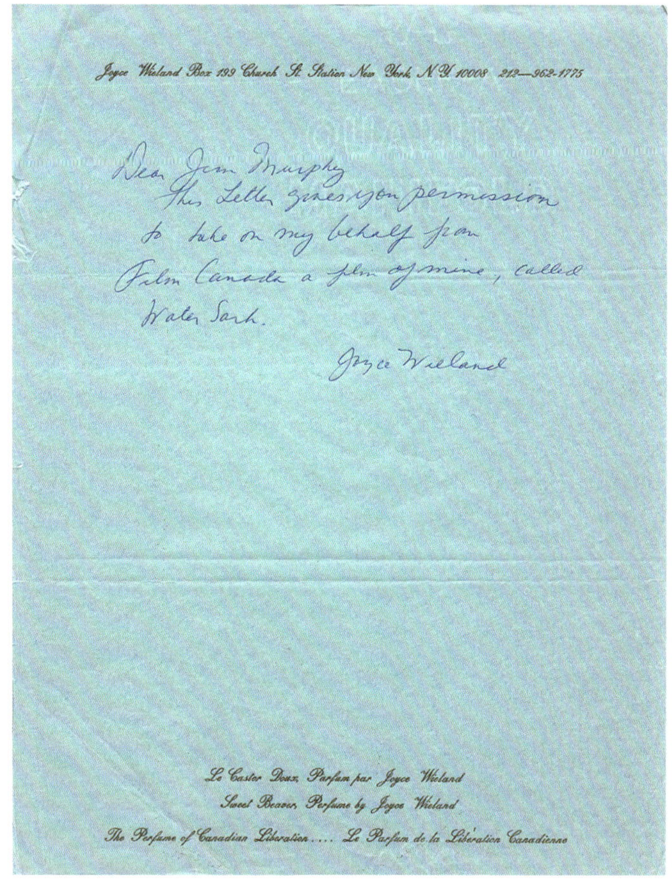

Joyce Wieland Box 199 Church St. Station New York, N.Y. 10008 212—962-1775

Dear Jim Murphy
This letter gives you permission
to take on my behalf from
Film Canada a film of mine, called
Water Sark.

Joyce Wieland

Le Castor Doux, Parfum par Joyce Wieland
Sweet Beaver, Perfume by Joyce Wieland
The Perfume of Canadian Liberation.... Le Parfum de la Libération Canadienne

LEFT
Letterhead printed with "Sweet Beaver Perfume," date unknown
Photo: CFMDC

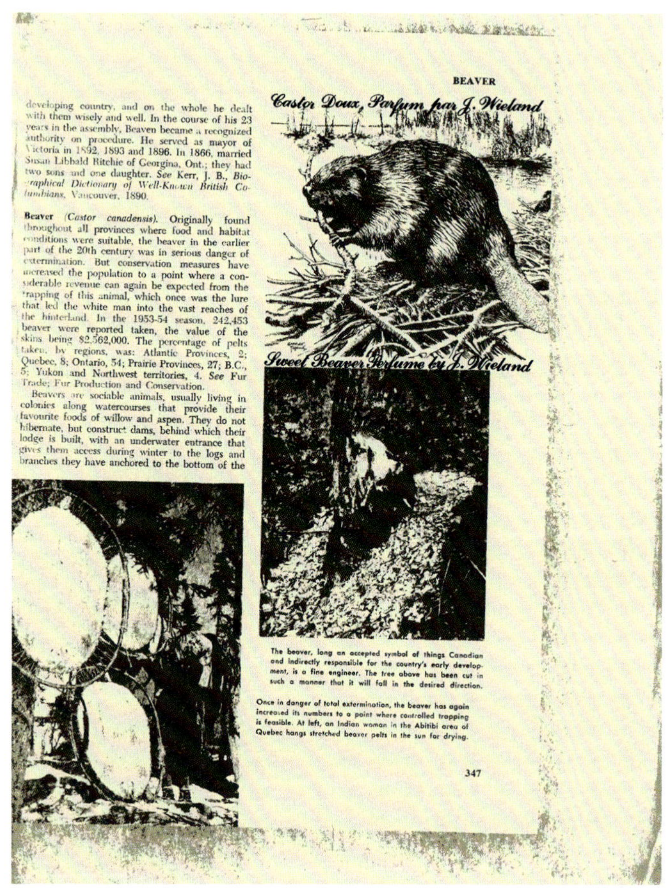

BEAVER

developing country, and on the whole he dealt with them wisely and well. In the course of his 23 years in the assembly, Beaven became a recognized authority on procedure. He served as mayor of Victoria in 1892, 1893 and 1896. In 1866, married Susan Libbald Ritchie of Georgina, Ont.; they had two sons and one daughter. *See* Kerr, J. B., *Biographical Dictionary of Well-Known British Columbians*, Vancouver, 1890.

Beaver (*Castor canadensis*). Originally found throughout all provinces where food and habitat conditions were suitable, the beaver in the earlier part of the 20th century was in serious danger of extermination. But conservation measures have increased the population to a point where a considerable revenue can again be expected from the trapping of this animal, which once was the lure that led the white man into the vast reaches of the hinterland. In the 1953-54 season, 242,453 beaver were reported taken, the value of the skins being $2,562,000. The percentage of pelts taken, by regions, was: Atlantic Provinces, 2; Quebec, 8; Ontario, 54; Prairie Provinces, 27; B.C., 5; Yukon and Northwest territories, 4. *See* Fur Trade; Fur Production and Conservation.

Beavers are sociable animals, usually living in colonies along watercourses that provide their favourite foods of willow and aspen. They do not hibernate, but construct dams, behind which their lodge is built, with an underwater entrance that gives them access during winter to the logs and branches they have anchored to the bottom of the

The beaver, long an accepted symbol of things Canadian and indirectly responsible for the country's early development, is a fine engineer. The tree above has been cut in such a manner that it will fall in the desired direction.

Once in danger of total extermination, the beaver has again increased its numbers to a point where controlled trapping is feasible. At left, an Indian woman in the Abitibi area of Quebec hangs stretched beaver pelts in the sun for drying.

347

Advertisement for *Sweet Beaver* perfume, 1971
Documentation Collection, NGC Library and Archives
Photo: NGC

ARTIST'S STATEMENT
DECLARATIONS DE L'ARTISTE

44

A reminder of a beaver in the summer woods in Canada.
Everyone has a different idea of what that smell might be.
Trying to remember or imagine gives them useful work to do.
Sweet Beaver is a souvenir of Canada.

PHOTOGRAPH OF ARTWORK ·
PHOTGRAPHIE DE TRAVAIL ARTISTIQUE

TITLE · TITRE
SWEET BEAVER

MEDIUM · MATERIEL
perfume/glass (8 synthetic ingredients)

SIZE · DIMENSION
1 oz. bottles/ 1/8 oz. vials

DATE · DATE
1971

ARTIST · ARTISTE
WIELAND, Joyce

FROM · DE
Toronto, Ontario

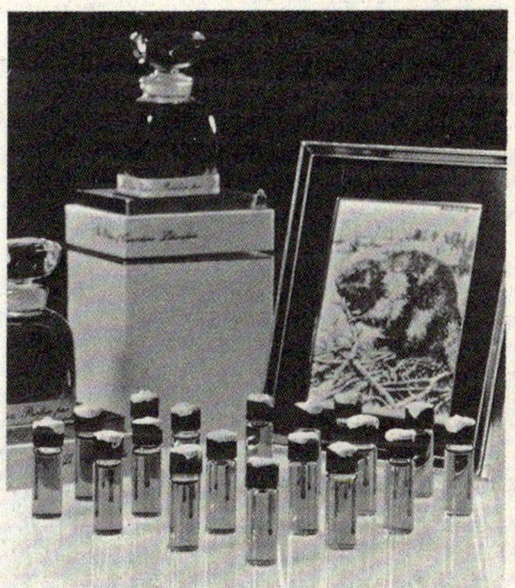

COURTESY OF · GRACE A L'AMABILITE DE
The Isaacs Gallery, Toronto, Ontario

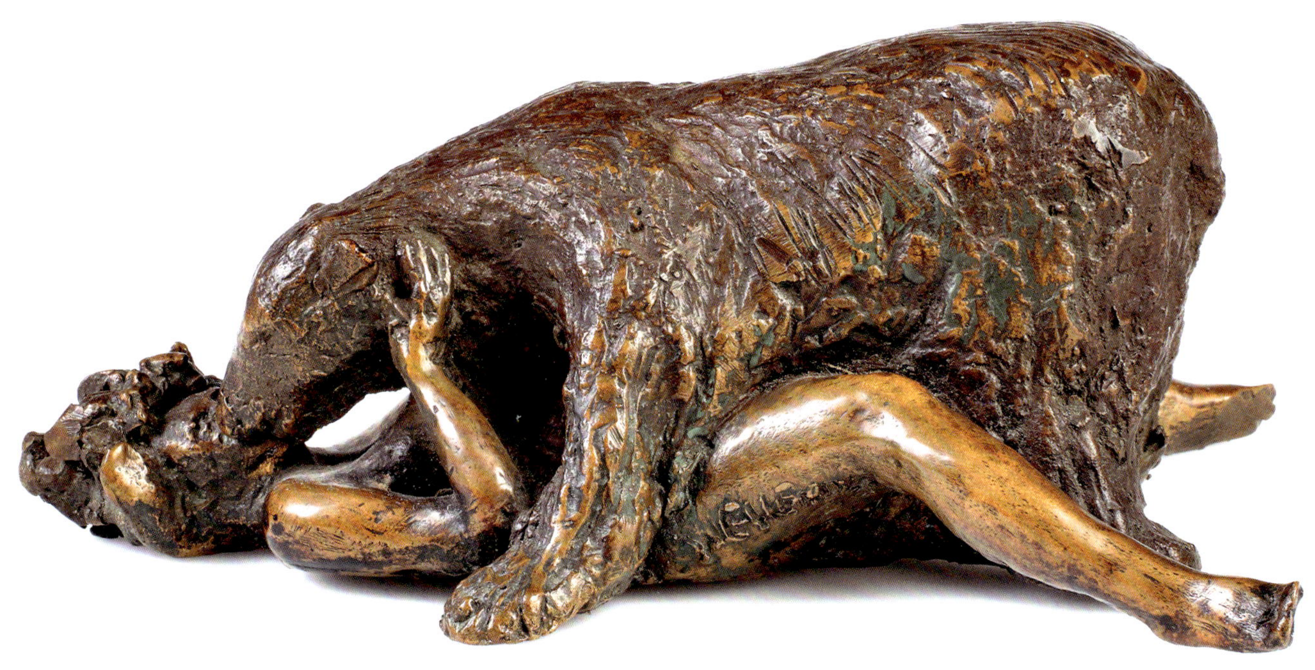

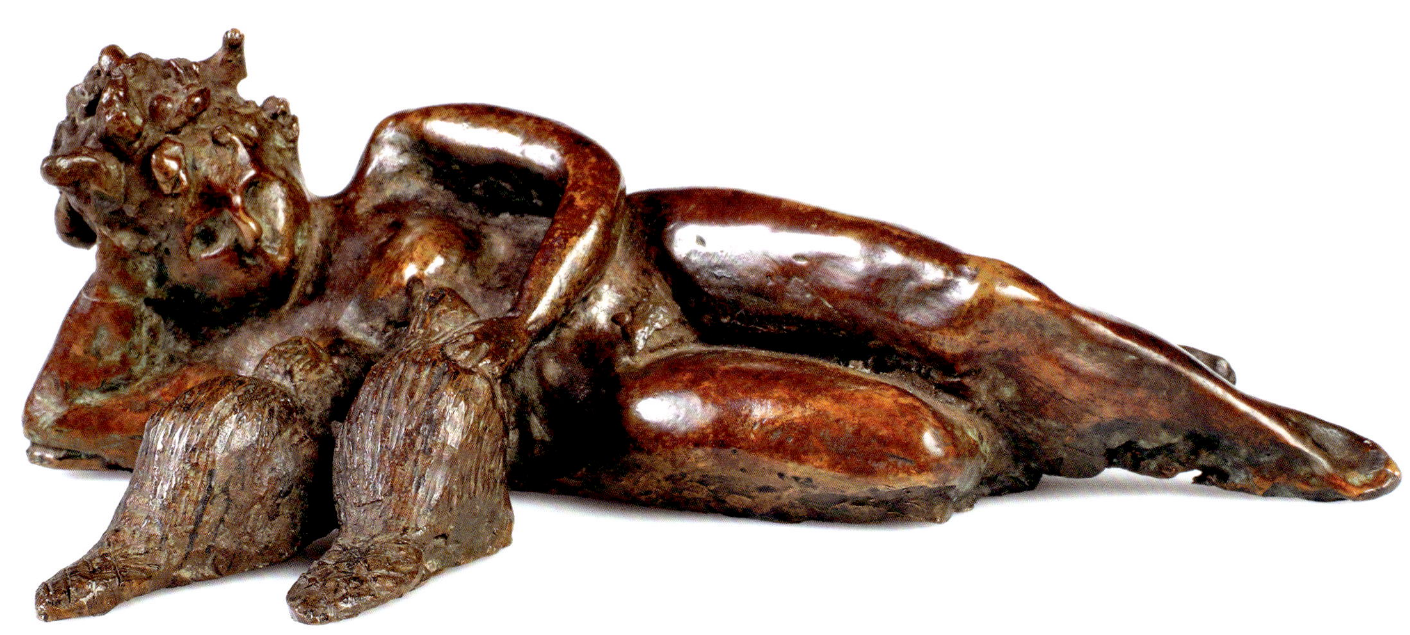

NATURE STUDY, 1970–1971
THE SPIRIT OF CANADA SUCKLES THE FRENCH AND ENGLISH BEAVERS, 1970–1971

In her flurry of personifying Canada as female, Joyce Wieland summoned a lover and a mother. Her partner was a bear; her children were twin beavers. Tender, loving, caring, and, most of all, active, Wieland's "Spirit of Canada" affectionately holds the bear's head just behind the ear while they are kissing, and sweetly caresses her baby beaver to her breast. Her tousled curls bond her to the furry creatures, while her smooth naked skin gleams next to their scruffy bodies. Both fur and females are much desired, much sought after to possess, and yet these beings are far too wild to control, too powerful to be owned. They inhabit their own Arcadian sphere, imbued with the alchemy of "the whole eroticism of nature and landscape, animals and harmony."[1] The couple in *Nature Study* (a.k.a. *Bear and the Spirit of Canada*) has a choice of positions—they are as stable standing up as they are lying down.

Wieland conceived the pair of bronzes as part of her passionate love letter to Canada, her mid-career retrospective *True Patriot Love* in 1971.[2] They are small enough to hold in your hand, and their weight is just right to keep a recipe book open while baking. She blends two sculptural traditions: dainty European figurines that once adorned banquet spreads in the eighteenth century; and grand classical statuary anthropomorphizing continents, ideals, and gods. Wieland's bronzes transgress their lineage by infusing the pastoral and the allegorical with a jolt of convivial interspecies relations, producing a fauna-centric origin story of her country.

GEORGIANA UHLYARIK

OPPOSITE, ABOVE
Nature Study [Bear and the Spirit of Canada], 1970–1971
Bronze
8 × 19.5 × 13.2 cm
Art Gallery of Hamilton, Gift of Irving Zucker, 1992
1992.2.10
Photo: Art Gallery of Hamilton

OPPOSITE, BELOW
The Spirit of Canada Suckles the French and English Beavers, 1970–1971
Bronze
6 × 19.3 × 12.5 cm
Art Gallery of Hamilton, Gift of Irving Zucker, 1992
1992.2.11
Photo: Art Gallery of Hamilton

1 From the documentary film *Artist on Fire*, dir. Kay Armatage, 1987. 54 min, 6mm/DVD. 07:12–08:00.

2 When it was first exhibited in the *True Patriot Love* exhibition at the National Gallery of Canada in 1971, the bear bronze was listed as *Nature Study.* At the AGO 1987 retrospective, it was listed as *Bear and the Spirit of Canada.* Wieland planned to make an edition of seven for both bronze sculptures; to date, it is unknown if more than two of each were fabricated.

Joyce Wieland's interest in the Arctic began in the mid-to-late 1960s, when both the history and contemporary sociopolitical and economic realities of Canada became the main subject matter of her work. Avrom Isaacs (1926–2016), her gallerist in Toronto, had been showing Inuit art in his space, and in 1970 opened the Innuit Gallery [*sic*], the first commercial gallery in the world dedicated exclusively to Inuit art. The world had already come to Montreal for Expo 67, drawn in by the fair's official mascot, the beloved Ookpik (snowy owl), designed in 1962 by Kuujjuaq-based Inuk artist Jeannie Snowball (1906–2002). By 1971, when Wieland first showed her Arctic quilts and cake at the National Gallery of Canada, Inuit art and culture—inukshuks, seal-skin dolls, annual print releases, and soapstone carvings—had become entrenched around the world as symbols of Canada.

Wieland's ideas about the Arctic were filtered through inherited notions of the North as a source of spiritual flow, first articulated by Canadian modernist painter Lawren Harris (1885–1970) in the 1920s and 1930s. Yet her concerns were deeply rooted in the ongoing politicization and co-opting ownership of the North by southern governments, Canadian and US alike. Her two lithographs from 1973, *The Arctic Belongs to Itself* and *Facing North — Self Impression*, express her direct resistance to capitalist forces pillaging the Arctic with no concern for its inhabitants and resultant ecological devastation. While in the southern imagination the region has often been perceived as barren and inhospitable, Wieland's

THE ARCTIC BELONGS TO ITSELF

work about the Arctic is always fully alive and plentiful. It is abundant with flowers—tenderly embroidered in sixty-four panels of *The Water Quilt* (1970–1971). The land is roaming with animals and skies filled with birds—colourfully drawn in over 160 rondel cushions in *Arctic Day* of the same year. The air is filled with song and stories, such as *Great Sea*. The largest quilts she ever produced, *Defend the Earth* (1972) and *Barren Ground Caribou* (1978), are monumental and very public declarations of the ecological urgency to protect the planet and her admiration of the exuberance of the Arctic.

It was a few years later that Wieland would make the trip to Kinngait and experience firsthand the region and its people; a profound part of this was meeting the Inuk artist Surusilutu Ashoona (1941–2011), with whom she felt a special bond. Wieland made two lithographs of Surusilutu, in 1977 and 1979, and at least two drawings of her with wings flying through a luminous sky. It was indeed Wieland's experience of the quality of light in the North that stimulated her to return to drawing with colour pencils, begun that *Arctic Day*, nearly a decade earlier.

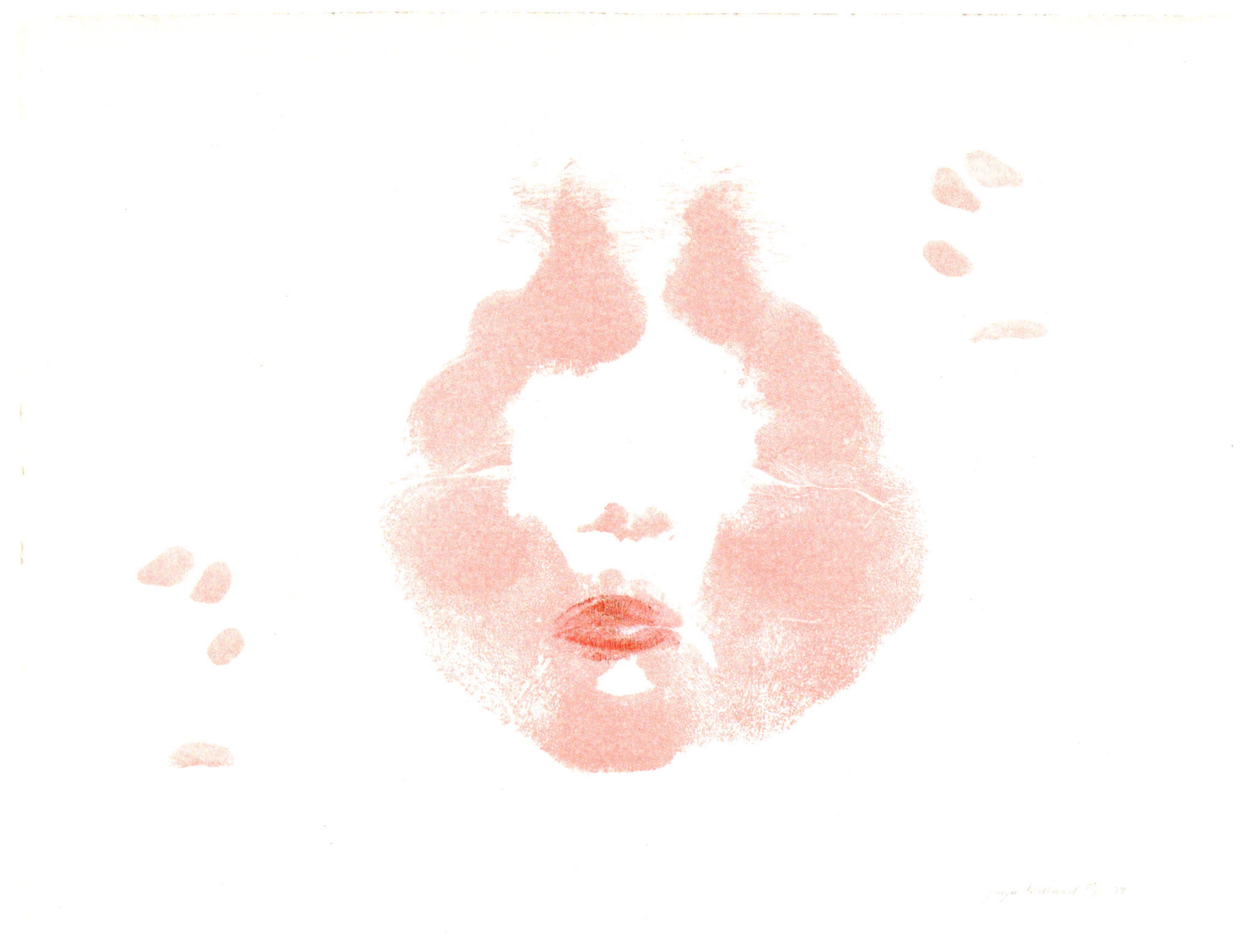

Facing North — Self Impression, 1973
Lithograph on paper
33.1 × 43.6 cm
Art Gallery of Ontario, Purchased 1987
86/286
Photo: AGO, Craig Boyko

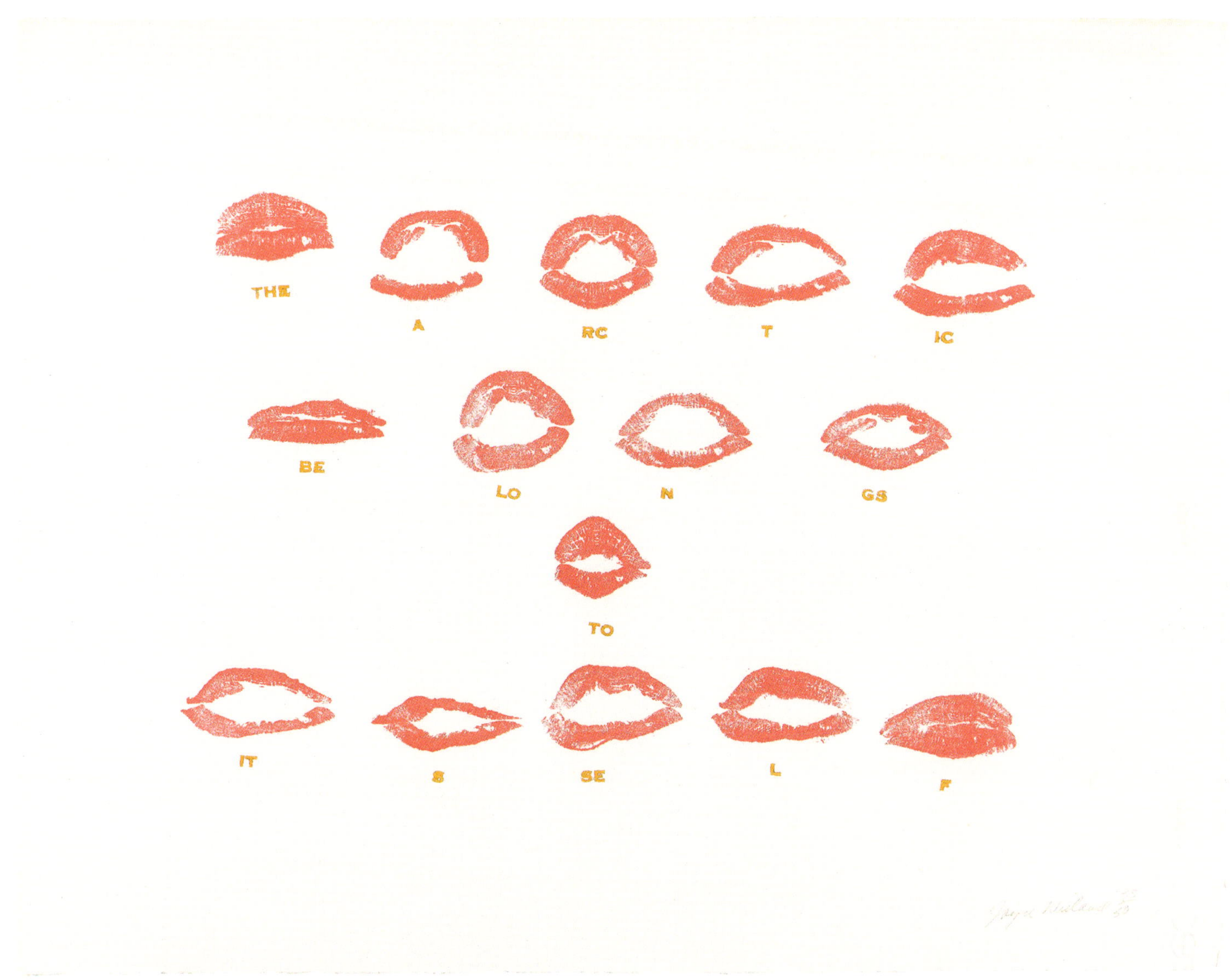

The Arctic Belongs to Itself, 1973
Lithograph on paper
33.2 × 43.4 cm
Art Gallery of Ontario, Purchased 1987
86/285
Photo: AGO, Craig Boyko

THE GREAT SEA, 1970–1971

Wieland intended *The Great Sea* to be a triptych. She engaged Evelyn Mombourquette Aucoin, of Chéticamp, Cape Breton, knowing that in that community "they've been doing this rug hooking for over 125 years at least."[1] They ran out of time after hooking the letters only for the English- and Inuktitut-language burlap panels, and the French version was never realized.

Each letter making up the words of the poem is a small, individual circular hooked rug. The letters are hooked in white wool, with a background of blue, purple, or green. A translucent moiré drapes and gathers at the bottom of each Plexiglass casement covers the words in both panels—as though they are visible through a storm. The fabric has a slightly shimmering, wavy pattern that enhances the effect. The English is in capital letters, arranged in wavy lines suggesting they are bobbing adrift on the waves. The Inuktitut is in syllabics rising up to the top of the vertical panel like bubbles in water. The syllabics are jumbled, forming a pattern rather than legible text. It is an appropriative use of Inuktitut, as is Wieland's adaptation of the Inuit legend itself.

The verse comes from an "Aii Aii" song Wieland found in a booklet on Inuit art published by the Department of Northern Affairs and National Resources in 1954 (republished in 1964 and 1970), which included the translation into English by Inuk poet Tegoodligak.[2] It is from the story of Uvavnuk,[3] who sings this song of a shamanic transformation after a meteor struck her one evening when she went outside to urinate. Her story, "Uvavnuk is struck by a ball of fire," had been collected by Greenlandic-Danish explorer Knud Rasmussen (1879–1933), as told to him by Aua (c. 1880–after 1922) in the early 1920s in the Igloolik region and published in 1929.[4]

Uvavnuk's tale made a deep impression on Wieland. "I made a great quilt from that song," she declared later. "It's called *The Great Sea*."[5] In the first few pages of her *True Patriot Love* book, she includes her research notes for this work, a detail from a letter from Mrs. Aucoin, and photographs documenting the process of its making (p. 197). There are two prominent round photos, a doll of a blindfolded Inuk woman wearing an amauti, and an image evocative of waves—a few stills from Wieland's interpretation of the story.

Wieland connected with the theme of Uvavnuk receiving her song from the fiery ball in the sky, empowering her "to tell the truth to her people."[6] She noted that "many women were shamans," and identified with such "visionaries" who she admired for being "in touch with something that we're no longer in touch with."[7] It is likely that Wieland's bourgeoning interest in Inuit art and culture initiated her trip(s) to Kinngait a few years later. ››››

GEORGIANA UHLYARIK

1 Transcript of Joyce Wieland artist's talk at the University of Lethbridge, 1985, 7 (edited quote from cassette tape "Joyce Wieland on Her Work"); transcript held at the University of Lethbridge Art Gallery, Alberta.

2 The song appears on the first pages of her book *True Patriot Love*, first in Inuktitut, in French on the following page, and then in English (see p. 33). It seems that Wieland photocopied the page, cut the song, and pinned it to pages 1 to 3 of her publication. Source: *Canadian E---o Art* booklet. Design and layout by James A. Houston, photographs by Bert Beaver and the National Film Board.

3 There are various accepted spellings for Uvavnuk; this one is used here for consistency.

4 Wieland includes a typed version of Uvavnuk's tale on page 4 of her book *True Patriot Love*: "A story told to Knud Rasmussen by Aua of Igloolik." Adapted from "Uvavnuk Is Struck by a Ball of Fire," 122–23, in chap. 5, "The Angákut or Shamans," collected by Knud Rasmussen, in *Intellectual Culture of the Iglulik E-----s*, trans. W. Worster (Copenhagen: Gyldendal, 1929), vol. 7, no 1, *Report of the Fifth Thule Expedition, 1921–24: The Danish Expedition to the Arctic North America*, archive.org/details/intellectualcult00rasm/page/122/mode/2up?view=theater.

Wieland's other notes on Uvavnuk's story include uncredited passages from Rasmussen's text. Joyce Wieland fonds, Clara Thomas Archives and Special Collections, York University, Toronto, 1996-036-033-04. She also mentions Rasmussen in her Lethbridge talk of 1985.

5 Kay Armatage, "Interview with Joyce Wieland," in *Women and the Cinema: A Critical Anthology*, ed. Karyn Kay and Gerald Peary (Boston: Dutton, 1977), 261.

6 Armatage, "Interview with Joyce Wieland, 261."

7 Armatage, "Interview with Joyce Wieland, 261."

Aii Aii

The great sea has set me in motion
set me adrift
and I move as a weed in the river
the arch of sky
and mightiness of storms
encompasses me
and I am left
trembling with joy.

translated by **TEGOODLIGAK**

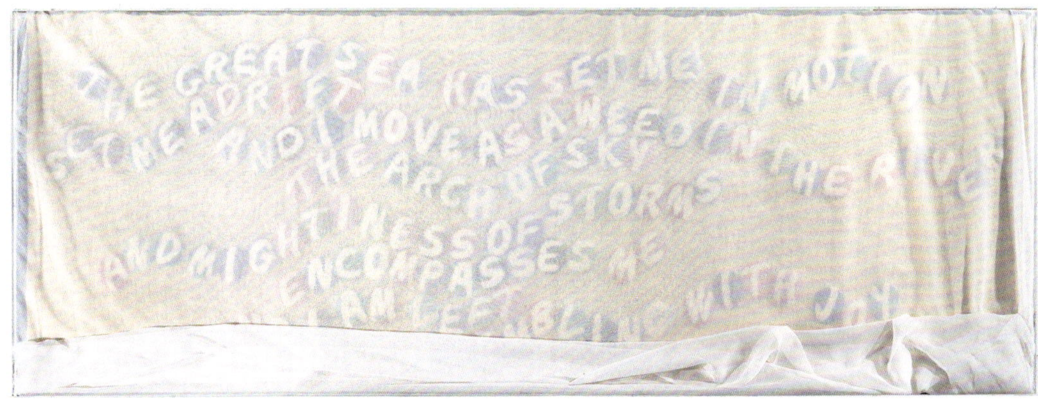

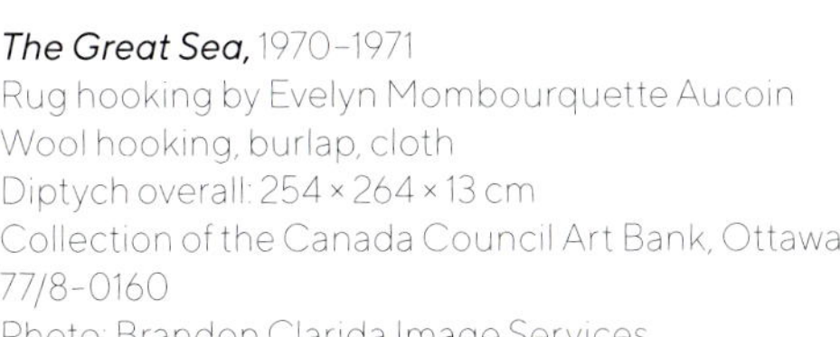

The Great Sea, 1970–1971
Rug hooking by Evelyn Mombourquette Aucoin
Wool hooking, burlap, cloth
Diptych overall: 254 × 264 × 13 cm
Collection of the Canada Council Art Bank, Ottawa
77/8-0160
Photo: Brandon Clarida Image Services

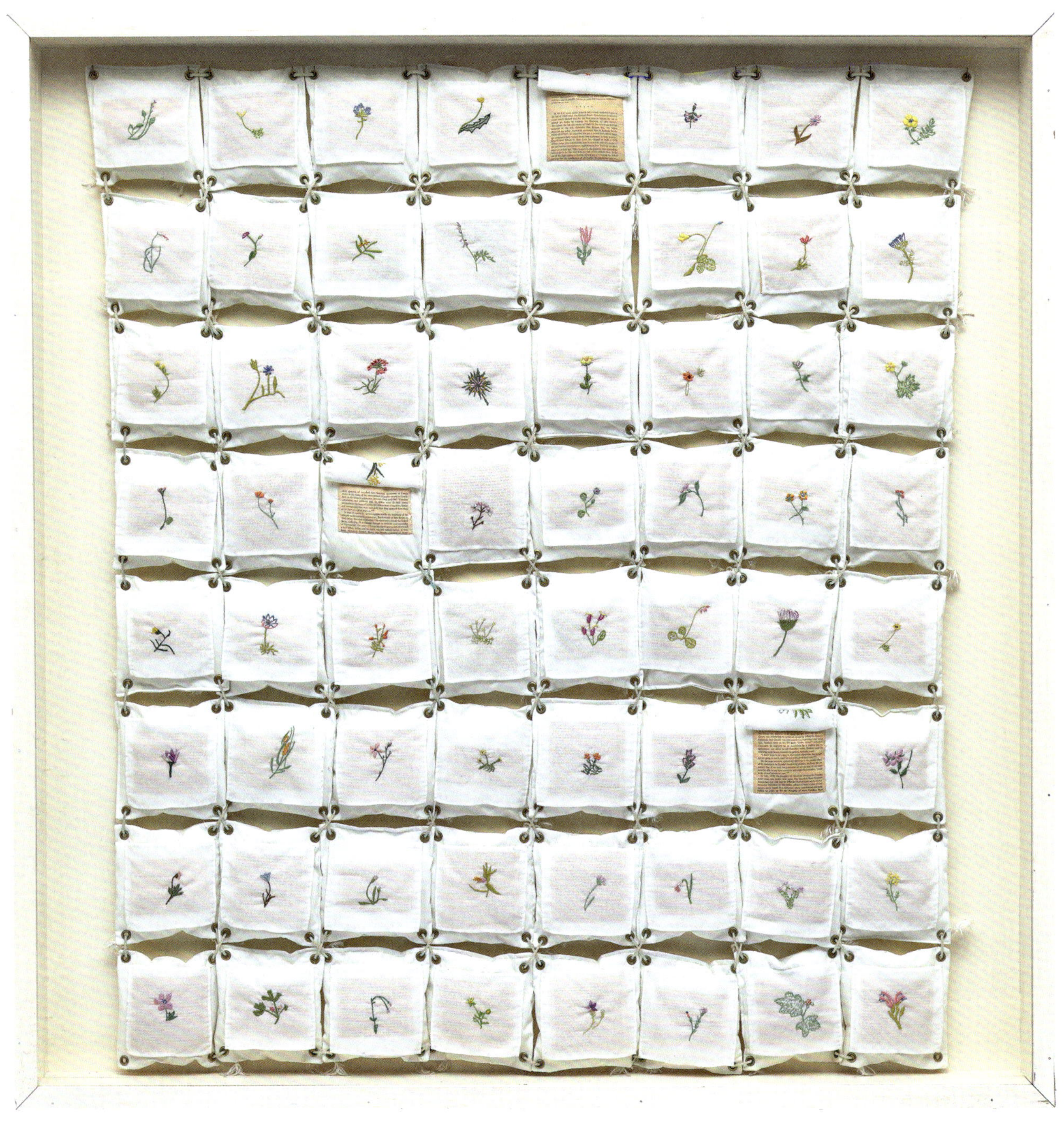

The Water Quilt, 1970–1971
Embroidery by Joan Stewart
Cloth, embroidery thread, thread, metal grommets, braided rope, ink
121.9 × 121.9 cm
Art Gallery of Ontario, Purchase with assistance from Wintario, 1977
76/221
Photo: AGO, Craig Boyko

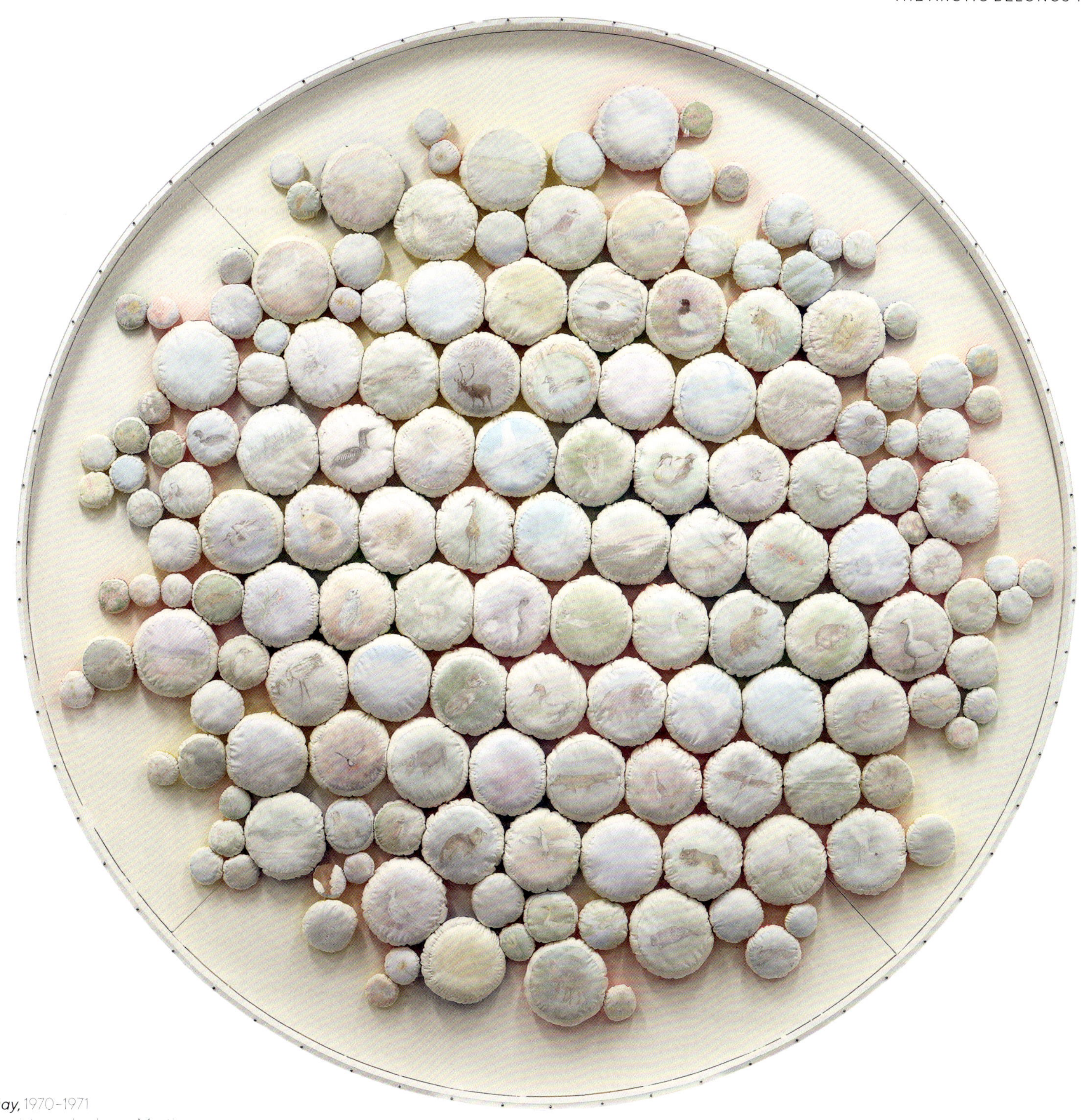

Arctic Day, 1970–1971
Sewing assistance by Joyce Martin
Coloured pencil on cloth cushions, batting
248.6 cm diameter
National Gallery of Canada, Ottawa, Purchased 1971
Photo: NGC

MAQUETTE FOR TRUE PATRIOT LOVE, 1971

The National Gallery of Canada (NGC) invited Joyce Wieland to stage an exhibition opening Canada Day, July 1, 1971. It galvanized Wieland's desire to fully engage with, appropriate, and feminize Canada's official symbols, both newly minted and traditionally entrenched. Wieland was the first living woman artist to have a solo exhibition at the National Gallery. Aware of the project's high profile and wide-reaching platform, she confidently chose to push herself and experiment with all aspects of her artistic practice. Even more bravely, she defied institutional procedures and conventions of exhibition-making, and co-opted the inner workings of political and governmental bureaucracy. In *True Patriot Love*, mouths, hearts, and text fill and expand her imagery to declare love, warn of danger, sing songs, and undo patriarchy.[1] As she wrote (p. 270) to Jean Sutherland Boggs, Director of the NGC, "it's not very often an artist is left free to do whatever he or she wishes to do and is given so much assistance in it. . . . your museum is very rare in the world and . . . your staff is unique and very talented."[2]

Working in collaboration with artisans, fabricators, and museum and government staff, Wieland produced quilted political slogans in both official languages, organizing quilting bees in the NGC's boardroom; knitted flags with sculpted tabletop bronze beavers suckling and a bear frolicking with a female personification of Canada; embroidered 18th-century military letters; made a perfume—*Sweet Beaver, The Perfume of Canadian Liberation*; and baked a cake.[3] In lieu of a conventional exhibition catalogue, she appropriated a government publication, *Bulletin 146, Illustrated Flora of the Arctic Archipelago*.[4] Boggs wrote to Dr. L. Lemieux, Director of the National Museum of Natural Sciences, in March 1971, seeking permission for Wieland to layer the publication with "handwritten statements, photographs and other texts." She explained that Wieland "is very much concerned by what has been happening to the Canadian physical environment as a result of pollution," and assured him that "the original material – both the botanical texts and illustrations – would be visible . . . integrated as sympathetically as possible with her own material." He approved it ten days later.[5]

Wieland took the bulletin apart and pinned, glued, and sewed photographs and clippings; handwrote captions, quotes, and credits and pressed flowers on the majority of the pages. She had it bound back together, creating a limited-edition artist book.[6] The cover design mimics the original, maintaining the same font, size, and layout. Wieland added a few elements, playing with the accessories of an official manual or a guide. On the inside cover, Wieland fixed a small, fabric Canadian flag that flutters when the book is opened. At the back, a paper pocket contains a pink pamphlet that lists the works, and an essay by Regina Cornwell on Wieland's films, along with a map of Canada. There is also a large, folded poster of an unedited conversation—meandering in English and French—between Pierre Théberge (1942–2018), the curator, Wieland, and Michael Snow. The NGC Library and Archives houses her original collaged and reassembled pages.[7]

As Wieland recalled in 1986, she chose *Bulletin 146* "because . . . it had all the flora of the Arctic and . . . as my platform from which to build another work. So that the floor or the earth was the book and then I built up

1 *True Patriot Love*, National Gallery of Canada, Ottawa (July 1–August 8, 1971). A second version of the exhibition was installed at The Isaacs Gallery, October 13–November 1, 1971.

2 Joyce Wieland to Jean Boggs, September 21, 1971, handwritten letter on *Sweet Beaver* perfume letterhead, National Gallery of Canada (hereafter cited as NGC) Library and Archives, NGC3_EX1420_B522_F005.

3 *Arctic Passion Cake*, 1971 (destroyed), 1.67 metres across, resembling the frozen Arctic landscape; it included provincial emblems and allegorical figures. Baked with the assistance of Jan Van Dierendonck, the chef of the parliamentary restaurant. Wieland dedicated the publication to Antonin Carême (1784–1833), credited with being the founder of French gastronomy.

4 Bulletin by A.E. Porsild, Biological Series no. 50 (Ottawa: National Museum of Canada, 1964). It was first published in 1957.

5 NGC Library and Archives, NGC3_EX1420. The NGC was not successful in securing permission from the National Capital Commission (NCC) for the artist to use Confederation Park during the month of July 1971 "to place a flock of sheep in the park. The sheep would of course have to be fenced in, fed, and guarded, etc. but the Gallery would of course be responsible for the fencing and the care of the animals," as curator Pierre Théberge wrote in his request. Within a week, it was declined by the NCC director, despite it being an "interesting and imaginative" use of the park, citing "undesirable features," including "the barnyard odors where people enjoy their lunches, the killing of the grass by the sheep and scattering of hay etc. by wind throughout the park." NGC Library and Archives.

6 A few pages of the original bulletin were not included.

7 "The maquette for *True Patriot Love* by Joyce Wieland = La maquette pour *Véritable amour patriotique* par Joyce Wieland," National Gallery of Canada Library and Archives, EX2187. Some of the original collaged pages are missing from the archives.

things over it and into it."[8] It is a conceptual compendium of the works she was making for the exhibition—expressionistic collages of her work in progress, alongside a variety of photographs that animate the publication and offer a rich texture to Wieland's life and art at that pivotal moment in her creative expression.

GEORGIANA UHLYARIK

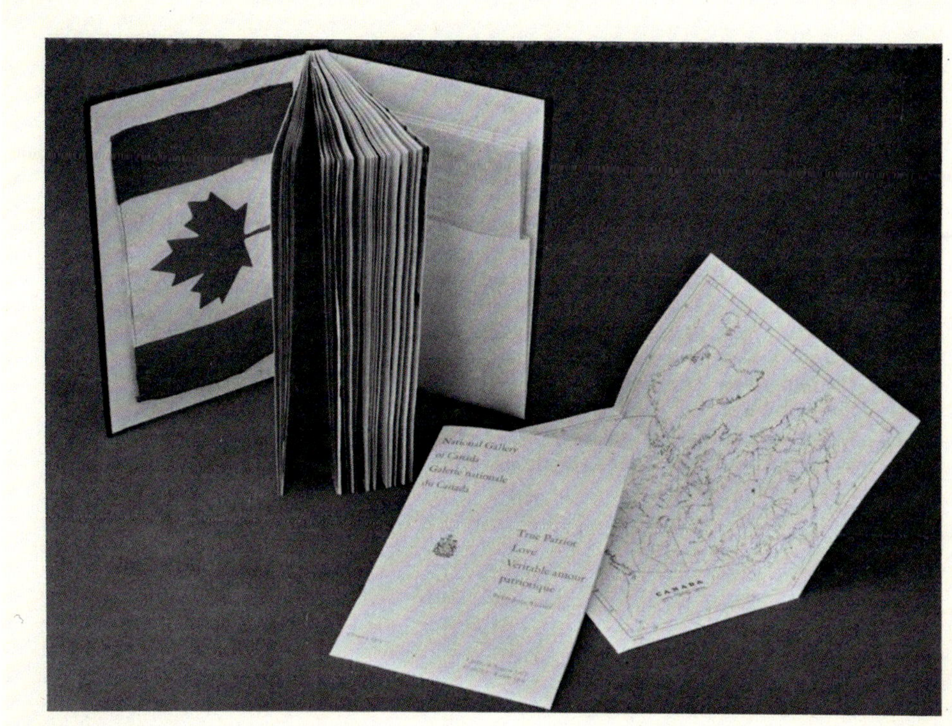

h. WIELAND, Joyce
True Patriot Love. Ottawa: Publications de la Galerie Nationale du Canada, 1971. 2000 exemplaires. Lithographies, drapeau en tissu, 10" x 6¾".

h. WIELAND, Joyce
True Patriot Love. Ottawa: National Gallery of Canada, 1971. Unpaginated. 2000 copies. Lithographed pages with cloth flag, hard cover, 10" x 6¾".

Advertisement for Joyce Wieland's book *True Patriot Love,* published by the National Gallery of Canada, c. 1971
Joyce Wieland fonds, ASC61827, York University Libraries, Clara Thomas Archives and Special Collections

8 Joyce Wieland, interview by Barbara Stevenson, October 8, 1986, in Kristy A. Holmes-Moss, "Joyce Wieland: Interview and Notes on *Reason over Passion* and *Pierre Vallières*," *Canadian Journal of Film Studies* 15, no. 2 (Fall 2006): 117. The full quote is "Because that is an actual government publication, and I found the book and it had all the flora of the Arctic and I chose that as my platform from which to build another work. So that the floor or the earth was the book and then I built up things over it and into it."

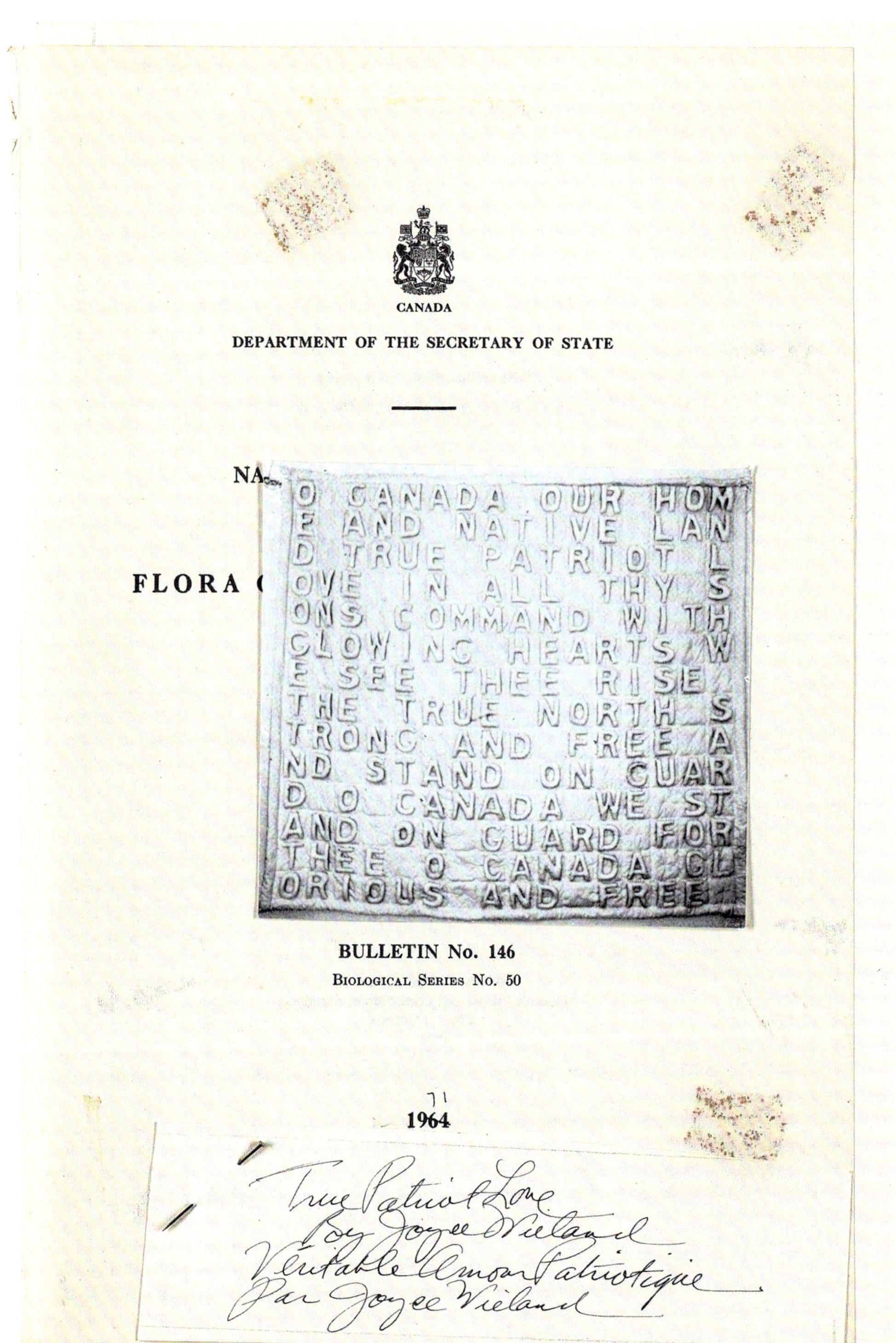

CANADA

DEPARTMENT OF THE SECRETARY OF STATE

NA

FLORA (

BULLETIN No. 146

Biological Series No. 50

71

1964

True Patriot Love
By Joyce Wieland
Véritable Amour Patriotique
Par Joyce Wieland

Pages from the ***True Patriot Love*** maquette, 1971
National Gallery of Canada fonds, NGC Library and Archives
Photos: NGC

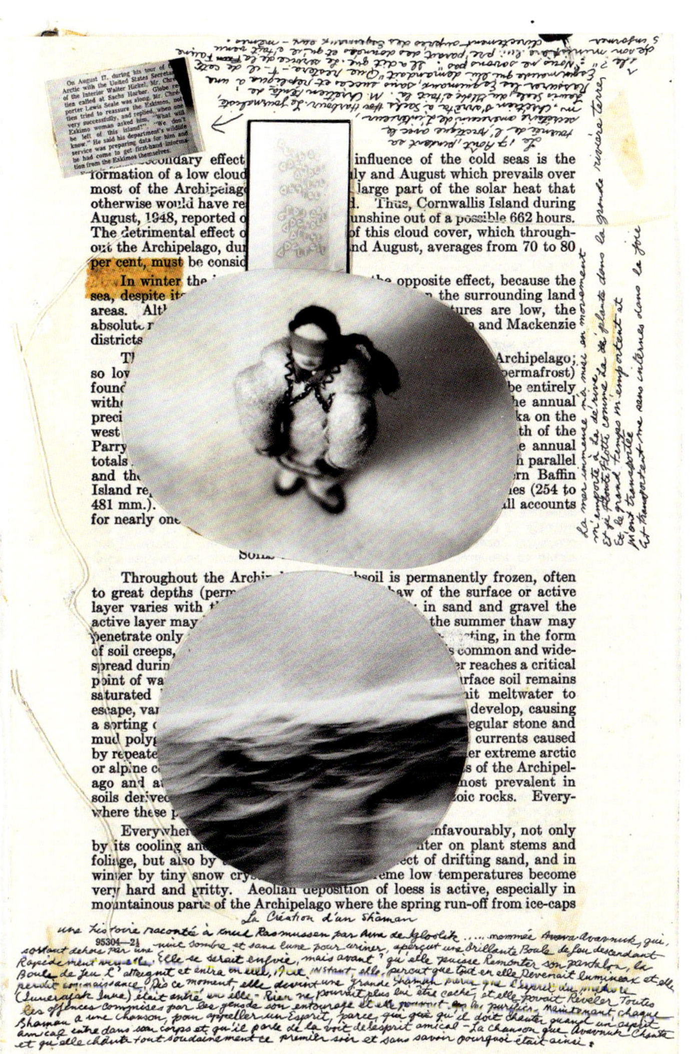
On August 17, during his tour of the Arctic with the United States Secretary of the Interior Walter Hickel, Mr. Chrétien called at Sachs Harbor. Globe reporter Lewis Seale was along. Mr. Chrétien tried to reassure the Eskimos, not very successfully, and replied, when one Eskimo woman asked him, "What will be left of this island?" "We don't know." He said his department's wildlife service was preparing data for him and he had come to get first-hand information from the Eskimos themselves.
secondary effect
influence of the cold seas is the
formation of a low cloud
ly and August which prevails over
most of the Archipelago
large part of the solar heat that
otherwise would have re
d. Thus, Cornwallis Island during
August, 1948, reported o
unshine out of a possible 662 hours.
The detrimental effect o
of this cloud cover, which throughout the Archipelago, du
nd August, averages from 70 to 80
per cent, must be consid
In winter the
the opposite effect, because the
sea, despite it
the surrounding land
areas. Alt
tures are low, the
absolute
and Mackenzie
districts
Archipelago;
permafrost)
be entirely
he annual
ka on the
th of the
e annual
h parallel
rn Baffin
es (254 to
481 mm.).
ll accounts
for nearly one
Throughout the Archi
bsoil is permanently frozen, often
to great depths (perm
haw of the surface or active
layer varies with
in sand and gravel the
active layer may
the summer thaw may
penetrate only
ting, in the form
of soil creeps,
s common and wide-
spread durin
r reaches a critical
point of wa
rface soil remains
saturated
it meltwater to
escape, va
develop, causing
a sorting
egular stone and
mud polyg
currents caused
by repeate
er extreme arctic
or alpine c
s of the Archipel-
ago and a
most prevalent in
soils derive
oic rocks. Every-
where these
Everywhe
nfavourably, not only
by its cooling an
ter on plant stems and
foliage, but also by
ect of drifting sand, and in
winter by tiny snow cry
eme low temperatures become
very hard and gritty. Aeolian deposition of loess is active, especially in
mountainous parts of the Archipelago where the spring run-off from ice-caps
La Création d'un Shâman
95304—21

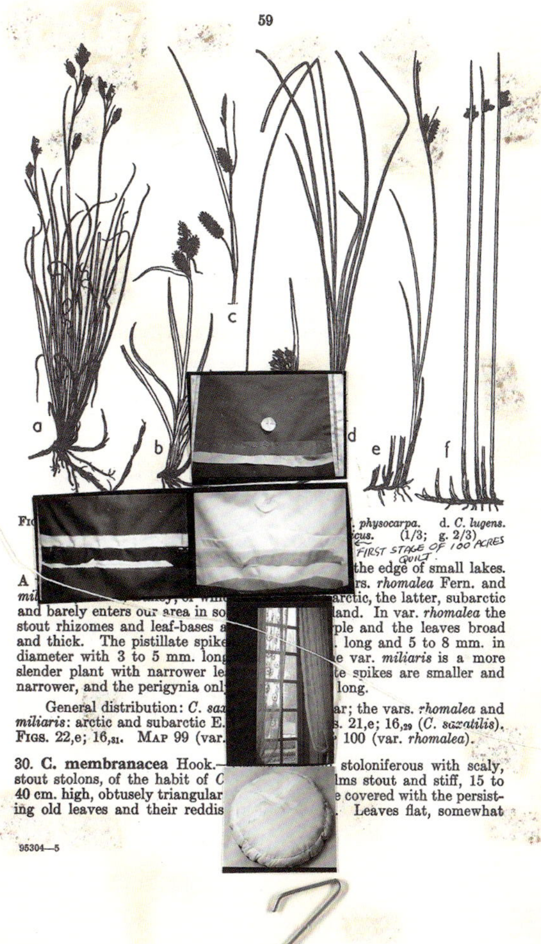
59
a
b
c
d
e
f
physocarpa. d. C. lugens.
(1/3; g. 2/3)
FIRST STAGE OF 100 ACRES QUILT.
the edge of small lakes.
rs. rhomalea Fern. and
arctic, the latter, subarctic
and barely enters our area in so
land. In var. rhomalea the
stout rhizomes and leaf-bases a
ple and the leaves broad
and thick. The pistillate spike
long and 5 to 8 mm. in
diameter with 3 to 5 mm. long
e var. miliaris is a more
slender plant with narrower le
te spikes are smaller and
narrower, and the perigynia onl
long.
General distribution: C. sax
ar; the vars. rhomalea and
miliaris: arctic and subarctic E.
s. 21,e; 16,29 (C. saxatilis).
Figs. 22,e; 16,31. Map 99 (var.
100 (var. rhomalea).
30. C. membranacea Hook.—
stoloniferous with scaly,
stout stolons, of the habit of C
lms stout and stiff, 15 to
40 cm. high, obtusely triangular
e covered with the persist-
ing old leaves and their reddis
Leaves flat, somewhat
95304—5

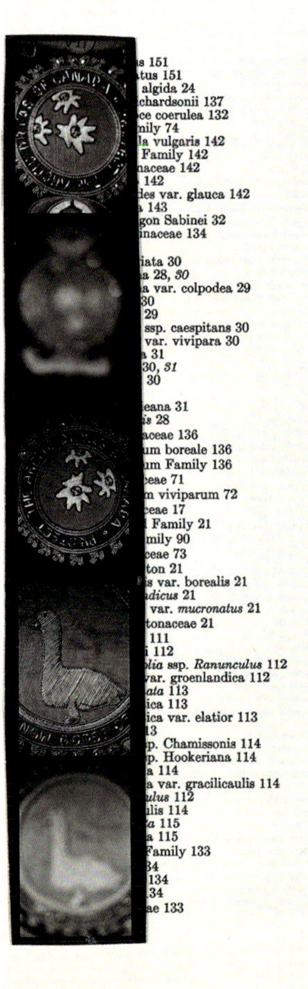

"Pendant que les Americains avaient la frontière... J'ai appris les plans du commandant Américain... Je suis partie tôt le matin, marché 19 milles au mois de juin, sur une partie difficile de la campagne" Laura Secord

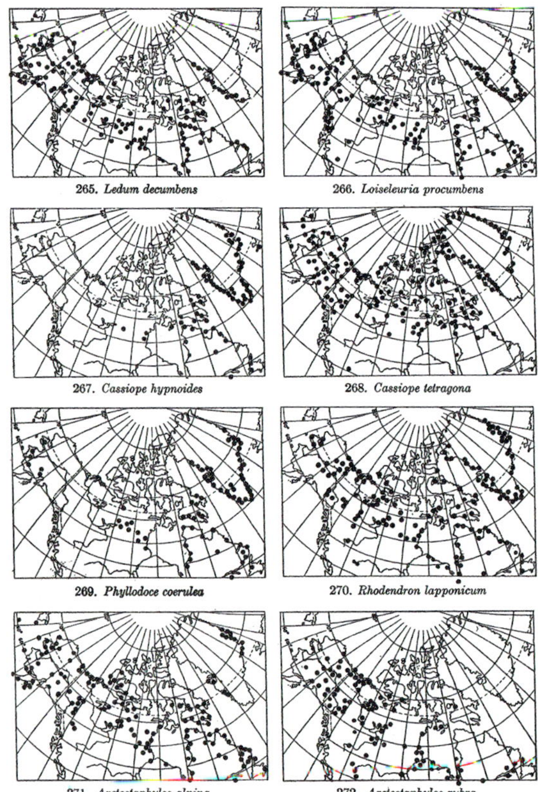

265. *Ledum decumbens*
266. *Loiseleuria procumbens*
267. *Cassiope hypnoides*
268. *Cassiope tetragona*
269. *Phyllodoce coerulea*
270. *Rhodendron lapponicum*
271. *Arctostaphylos alpina*
272. *Arctostaphylos rubra*

"While the Americans had possession of the frontier..... I learned the plans of The American commander..... I left early in the morning, walked 19 miles in the month of June, over a rough and difficult part of the country" Laura Secord

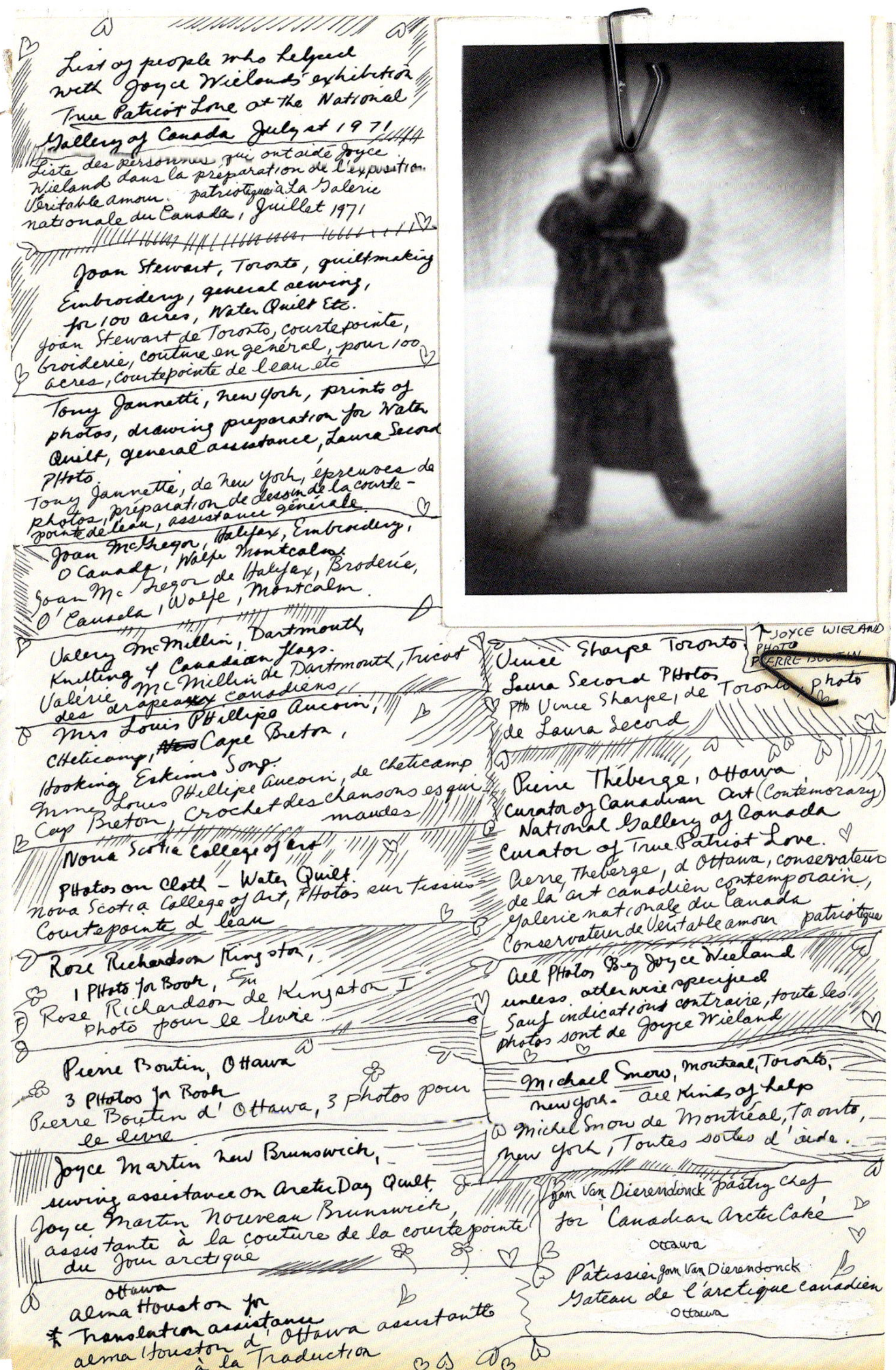

List of people who helped
with Joyce Wieland's exhibition
True Patriot Love at the National
Gallery of Canada July 1st 1971
Liste des personnes qui ont aidé Joyce
Wieland dans la préparation de l'exposition
Véritable amour patriotique à La Galerie
nationale du Canada, Juillet 1971

Joan Stewart, Toronto, quiltmaking
Embroidery, general sewing,
for 100 acres, Water Quilt Etc.
Joan Stewart de Toronto, courtepointe,
broderie, couture en général, pour 100
acres, courtepointe de l'eau etc

Tony Jannetti, New York, prints of
photos, drawing preparation for Water
Quilt, general assistance, Laura Secord
PHoto
Tony Jannetti, de New York, épreuves de
photos, préparation de dessin de la courtepointe de l'eau, assistance générale

Joan McGregor, Halifax, Embroidery,
O Canada, Wolfe Montcalm
Joan McGregor de Halifax, Broderie,
O Canada, Wolfe, Montcalm.

Valery McMillin, Dartmouth,
Knitting of Canadian flags.
Valérie McMillin de Dartmouth, Tricot
des drapeaux canadiens

Mrs Louis PHillipe Aucoin,
Cheticamp, Cape Breton,
Hooking Eskimo Song.
Mme Louis PHillipe Aucoin, de Cheticamp
Cap Breton, Crochet des chansons esquimaudes

Nova Scotia College of Art
PHotos on Cloth - Water Quilt.
Nova Scotia College of Art, PHotos sur tissu-
Courtepointe d'l'eau

Rose Richardson Kingston,
1 PHoto for Book,
Rose Richardson de Kingston 1
photo pour le livre

Pierre Boutin, Ottawa
3 PHotos for Book
Pierre Boutin d'Ottawa, 3 photos pour
le livre

Joyce Martin New Brunswick,
sewing assistance on Arctic Day Quilt
Joyce Martin Nouveau Brunswick,
assistante à la couture de la courtepointe
du Jour arctique

Ottawa
Alma Houston for
translation assistance
Alma Houston d'Ottawa assistante
à la Traduction

JOYCE WIELAND
PHOTO
PIERRE BOUTIN

Vince Sharpe Toronto
Laura Secord PHotos
PHo Vince Sharpe, de Toronto, photo
de Laura Secord

Pierre Théberge, Ottawa
Curator of Canadian Art (Contemporary)
National Gallery of Canada
Curator of True Patriot Love.
Pierre Théberge, d'Ottawa, conservateur
de l'art canadien contemporain,
Galerie nationale du Canada
Conservateur de Véritable amour patriotique

All PHotos by Joyce Wieland
unless otherwise specified
Sauf indications contraire, toutes les
photos sont de Joyce Wieland

Michael Snow, Montreal, Toronto,
New York. All kinds of help
Michel Snow de Montréal, Toronto,
New York, Toutes sortes d'aide.

Jan Van Dierendonck Pastry Chef
for 'Canadian Arctic Cake'
Ottawa
Pâtissier Jan Van Dierendonck
Gateau de l'arctique canadien
Ottawa

DEFEND THE EARTH, 1972

In 1972, Wieland produced *Defend the Earth,* an embroidered and quilted work commissioned by the Canadian government's Department of Public Works. With its round edges, this oversized quilt features the message "DEFEND THE EARTH DÉFENDEZ la TERRE," rendered in stuffed fabric letters and billowy pastel flowers. Wieland was one of seven artists—and the only woman—selected by the Department to create works for the National Research Council Canada's National Science Library in Ottawa. This public art initiative was part of a government program providing up to 1 percent of the building's cost to create works of art—yielding a total of \$130,000 from a construction budget of \$13 million. Wieland's site-specific work, installed in the south entrance lobby of the library—which is one of the most comprehensive facilities of its kind in the world—directs an urgent message to scientists.

The following news release, dated February 5, 1974, was issued to announce the installation of *Defend the Earth*, providing information on the work and insights into Wieland's intentions.

ANNE GRACE

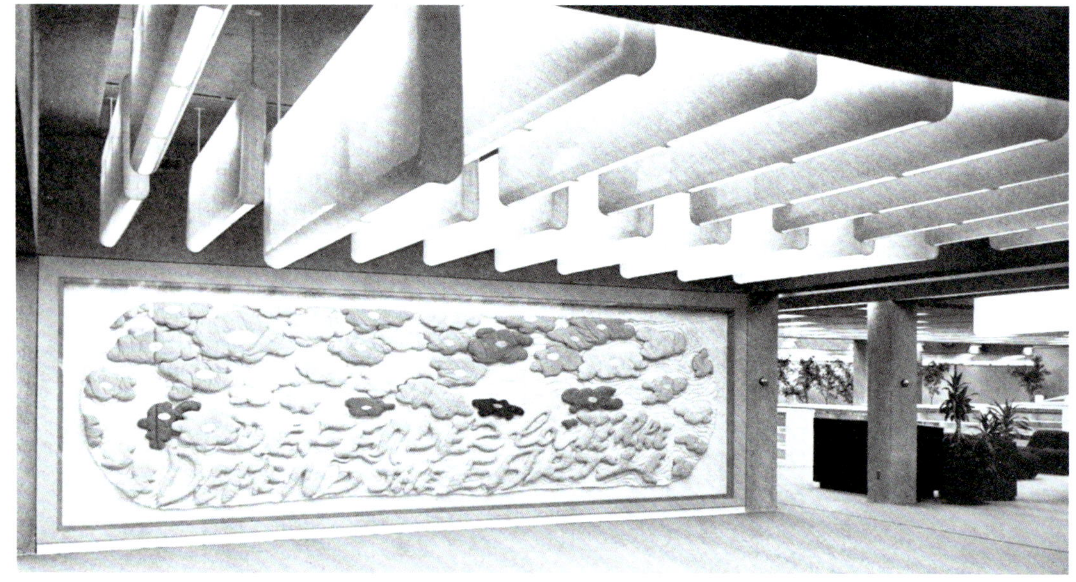

Installation view of *Defend the Earth* in the south entrance lobby of the National Science Library, Ottawa, 1973, published in *artscanada*, Autumn 1974

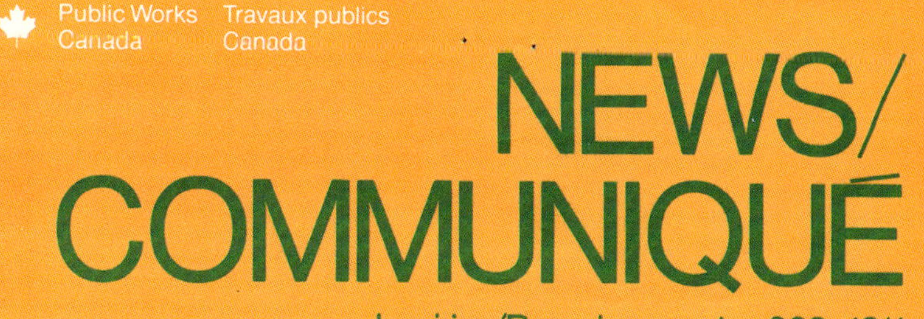

G-592 (B) FOR IMMEDIATE RELEASE

Joyce Wieland's Quilted Wall Hanging

A quilt slightly more than 148 square feet in area has just been hung by Toronto artist Joyce Wieland near the main information desk of the new National Science Library. The library is on the Montreal Road "campus" of the National Research Council.

Well known for the quilted wall hangings, Ms. Wieland feels that the one in the science library represents a new departure in the quilted art form -- it contains the message "Defend the Earth". She chose the theme to express her concern for the need to restore ecological balance in the world.

"For this particular hanging I spent about three months making several preliminary sketches. Finally, I settled on one oval-shaped design. I commissioned a poetess in Toronto, who has worked with me before, to come up with a message which would fit in with the environment of a science library", Ms Wieland explained.

"She came up with Defend the Earth/Défendez la terre, which I have appliqued in nine-inch high letters and stuffed with dacron so they are raised on the hanging.

"But I'm getting ahead of myself", she continued; First, slides were taken of my final designs, projected on the cotton cloth and the designs traced. My sister, Joan Stewart, and I made each flower and letter pattern individually and then stitched them onto the white oval-shaped background.

..2

Communiqué for Joyce Wieland's *Defend the Earth,* released by Public Works Canada, on February 6, 1974
Photo courtesy of the National Research Council

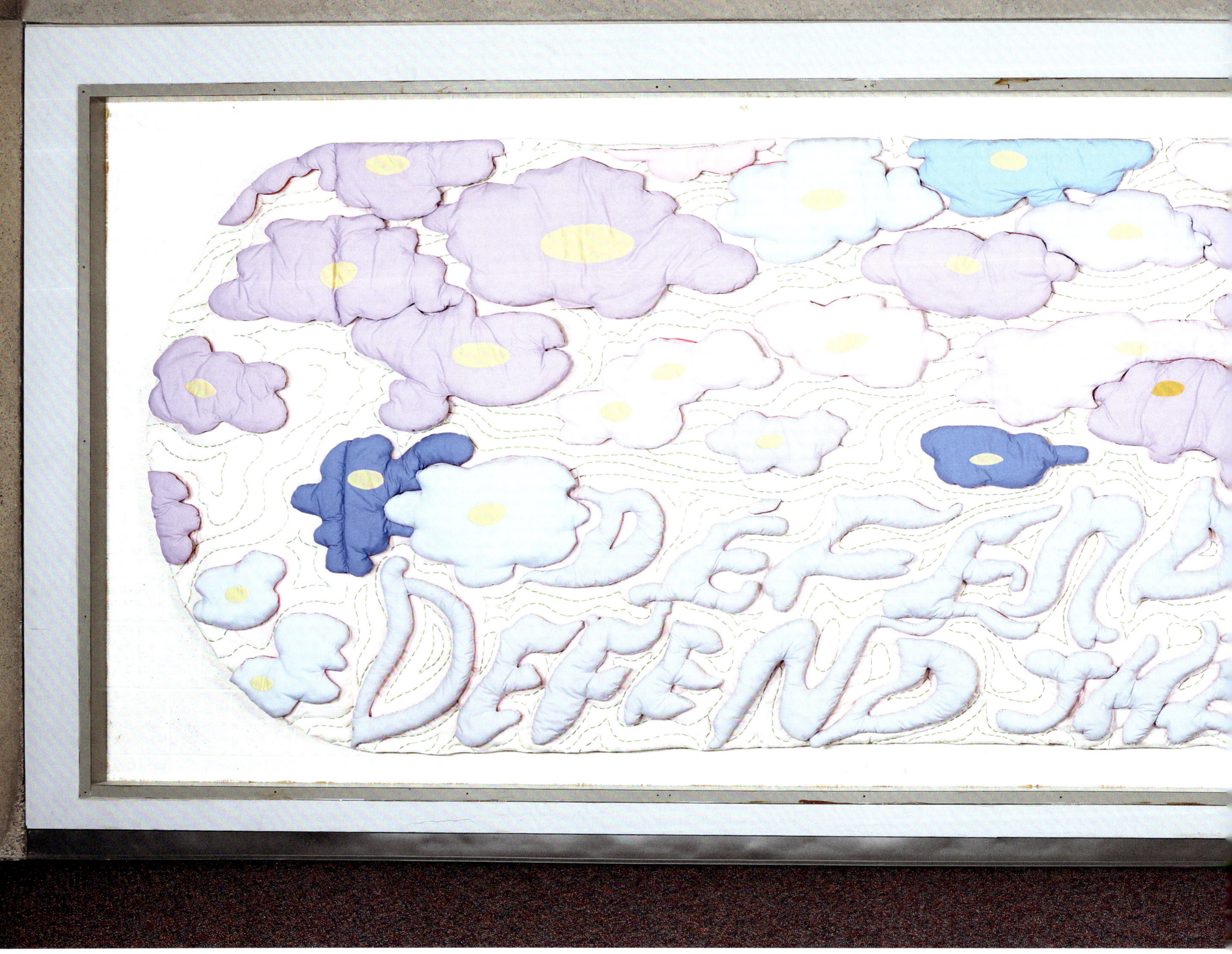

Defend the Earth, 1972
Handwork by Joan Stewart, Quilting and Embroidery Associates
Egyptian cotton, embroidery thread, thread, batting
193 × 716.3 × 12.7 cm
National Research Council Canada, Ottawa, ON, commissioned for the National Science Library
Photo: Rémi Thériault

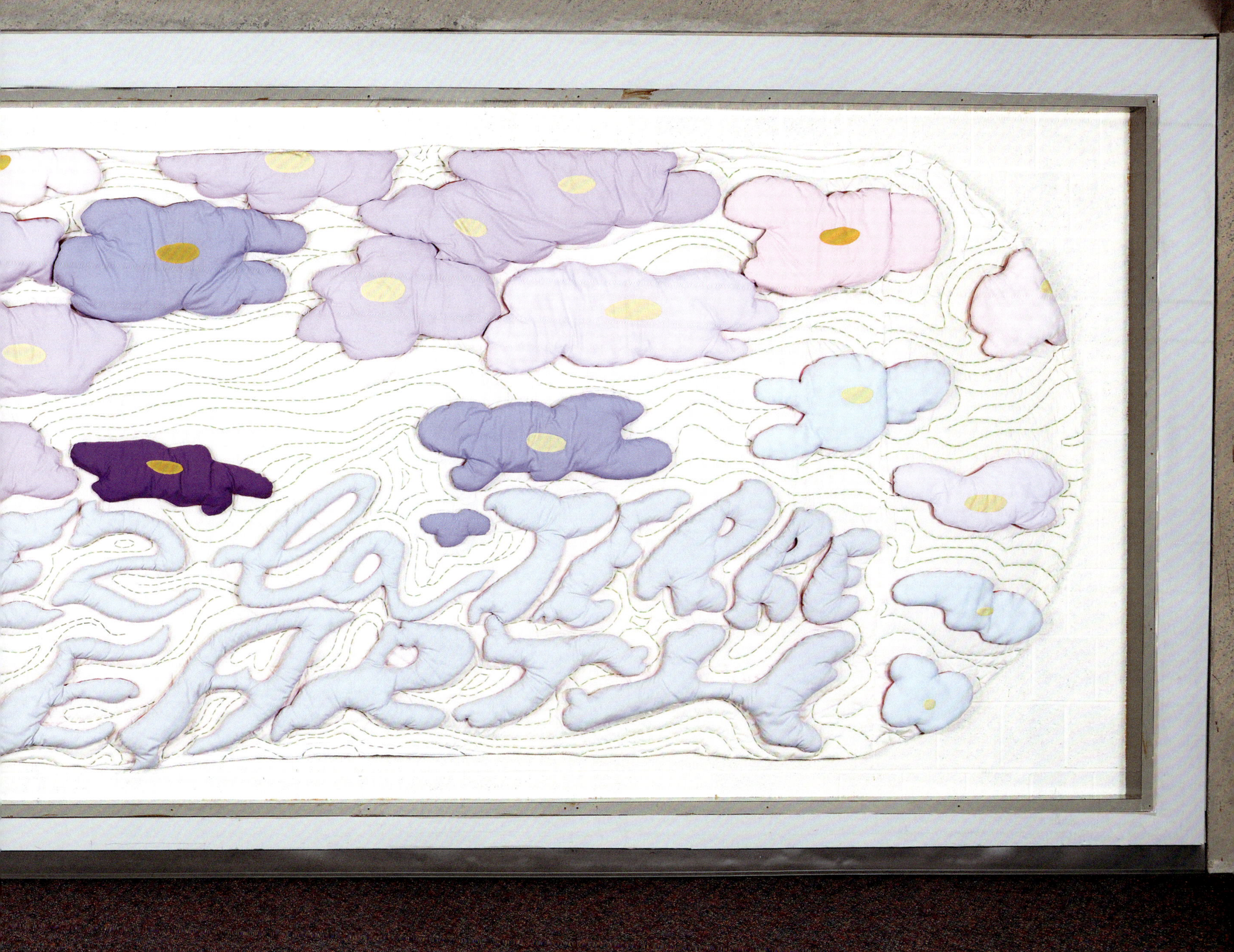

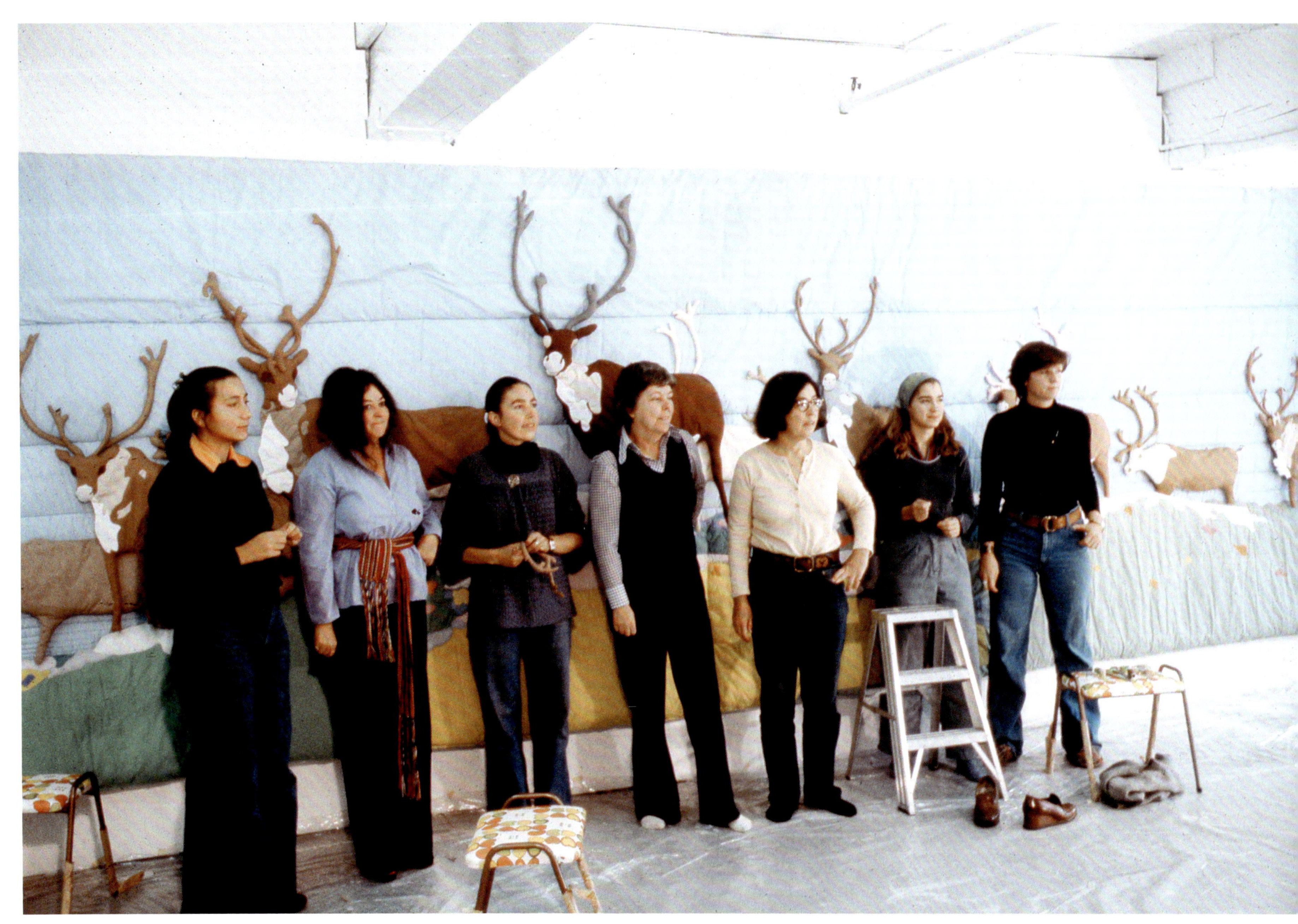

Group photo of quilters and assistants in front of *Barren Ground Caribou* in studio on Ryerson Avenue, Toronto
Joyce Wieland (second from the left), Joan Stewart (centre), Sara Bowser (white sweater), 1977
Avrom Isaacs fonds, ASC05199, York University Libraries, Clara Thomas Archives and Special Collections

BARREN GROUND CARIBOU, 1978

We were brought together by Joyce Wieland to assemble the elements of her quilt for the Spadina TTC station. I was sixteen and, with my friend Esme Hedrick, was one of two teenagers in a disparate group of about twelve women in a large room in an old factory building next to Theatre Passe Muraille, in the west end of downtown Toronto. Joyce's sister, Joan Stewart, was overseeing the project.

There was a large, pale-blue background with horizontal lines quilted into it, representing the sky. It was huge and placed on the floor. There was no furniture in the room. We all worked on our hands and knees, chattering and laughing. Fascinating conversations: how much kissing there should be when lovemaking—before, after, and during. Lots of argument and dissension, and reams of laughter. Very intimate. All of us lolling on the floor. Joan had this huge collection of everything that was to be attached to this vast blueness. Strewn on the floor: pieces of the tundra landscape and the animals and flowers inhabiting it; each had to be attached to the backdrop blue sky. We had a black-and-white, to-scale sketch that we worked from. How each individual item was best attached to the blue was the subject of debate (and much debate there was). Joan was the decision-maker, the encyclopedia of stitches and techniques.

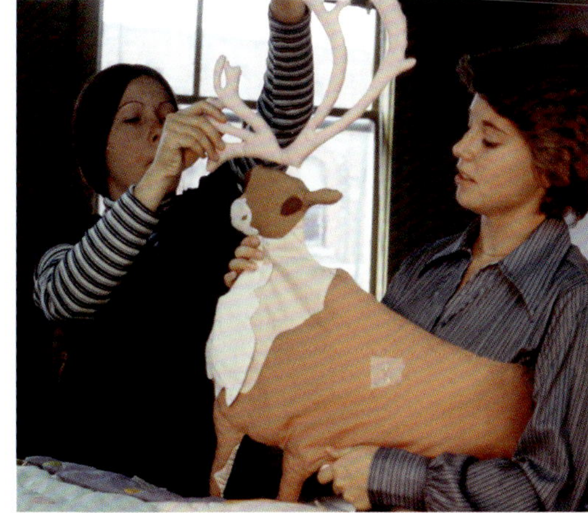

Assembling a caribou for Joyce Wieland's quilt *Barren Ground Caribou,* 1977.
Avrom Isaacs fonds, ASC05207, York University Libraries, Clara Thomas Archives and Special Collections

Joyce was working in another part of the building with Judy Steed. The two of them were in the planning stages for Joyce's film *The Far Shore* (1976) (p. 272). Joyce was both editing the script and fundraising, potential backers were demanding changes to the script, and she was very conflicted. An agitated and stressed Joyce would visit at the end of each morning and afternoon to check in on the quilt. Items were placed for Joyce to OK: a caribou should be moved to the right; the horns on this one were a little wonky—could they be righted? A debate: should this one's hoof be in front of or behind that morsel of tundra? A mad search to find a chair for a despondent Joyce to sit on. A lament that she could not get any distance to see the quilt properly. We would all try and jolly Joyce up, and if we succeeded it was the best: Joyce's wicked sense of humour.

Once it was all assembled, we stood together on a ledge along one long wall and held the quilt up with our hands over our heads. The bottom quarter was still draped on the floor. There was this terrible moment as we realized that the fabric of the entire top horizontal strip of the sky was sagging and drooping over the next horizontal strip below. The entire top seam, 18 metres long, was re-sewn by hand, we pleated a good ten centimetres into the very top edge to stop the drooping. I stayed late; Joan worked from one end and I worked from the other. That night, an exhausted Joyce and a taciturn Mike [Snow] drove me home.

The next time I saw the quilt, it was installed in the subway station.

EO SHARP

BARREN GROUND CARIBOU, 1978

Toronto's urban expansion in the mid-1970s included the construction of the new Spadina subway section, reaching northward from the existing Yonge–University line. From its inception, the Toronto Transit Commission (TTC) extension included an art competition. Each of the new nine stations were to include a major public art commission. Wieland was selected from the thirty-five artists who submitted sketches for assigned locations. Her proposal was for the Spadina subway station's Kendal Avenue entrance, south wall, mezzanine level. She deliberately chose this location "because no natural light will fall on the quilt."[1]

This secondary access to Spadina Station is unlike a typical subway entrance. It is a repurposed house, originally designed in 1899 by architect Robert Ogilvie for barrister Norman B. Gash. The house was acquired by the city in 1972 and community members, along with the Toronto Historical Board, ensured the preservation of its residential character exterior. Proposing a quilt for this location is complementary to Wieland's practice as well as the evocative domesticity of the entrance.

Wieland worked with architects Adamson Associates, who designed the interior of the station, and her sister, Joan Stewart, who oversaw the sewing of the quilt. The quilt was restored in 2018.

GEORGIANA UHLYARIK

1 Avrom Isaacs fonds, Clara Thomas Archives and Special Collections, York University, Toronto, F0134: 1996-036/ box 026, file 14. Transcript on opposite page is located in same file.

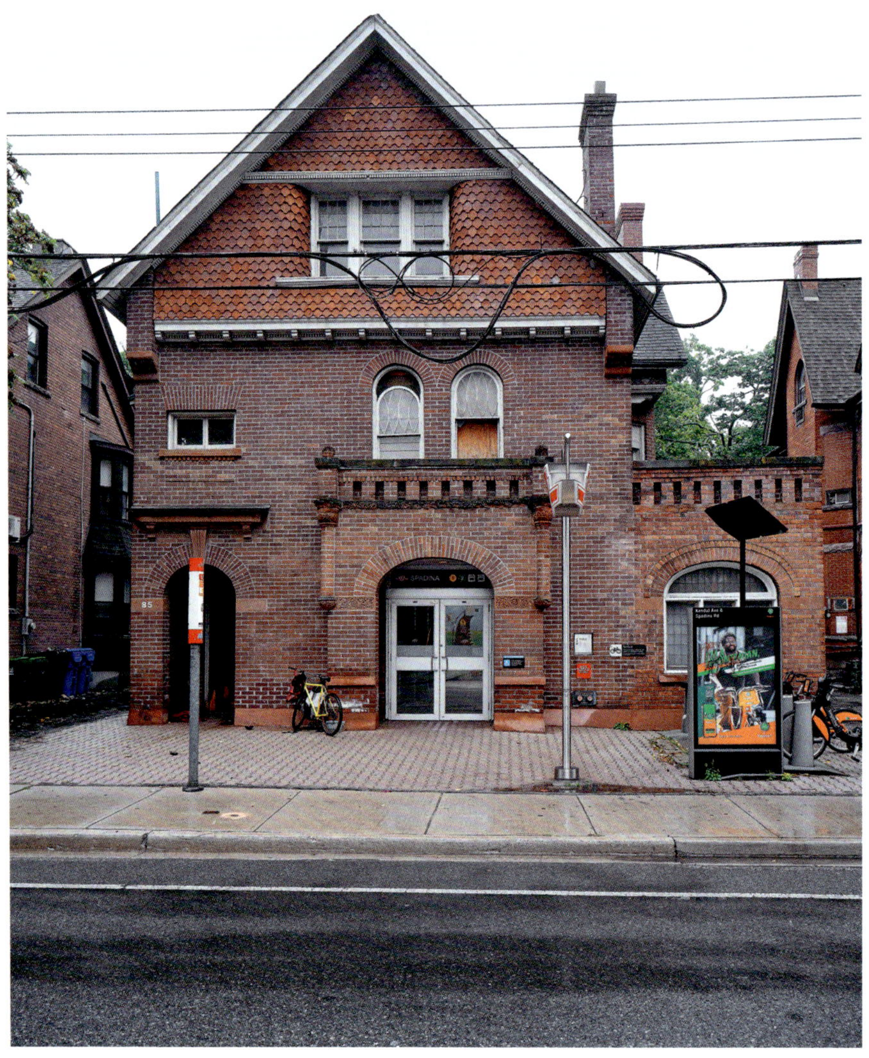

ABOVE
Entrance to the TTC Spadina Station at Kendal Avenue, Toronto, 2024
Photo: AGO, Craig Boyko

NEXT SPREAD
Installation view of *Barren Ground Caribou,* 1978
Cloth, thread, batting
243.8 × 914.4 × 8.68 cm
City of Toronto, Public Art and Monuments Collection
Photo: Laura Findlay

The following is a transcript of Joyce Wieland's proposal, written in 1975:

"Made from 100% cotton: all the components of the piece are stuffed and quilted with Dacron, an inert material which holds its shape permanently.

Hand stitching, applique, and quilting, by Joan Stewart Quilting Associates, Desboro, Ontario.

Barren Ground Caribou is a continuation of the ecological theme in my work. . . . [It] expresses aspects of the public's growing awareness of their environment and its preservation. A subway station is an obvious place to make an offering to nature.

The subject is a favourite ecological theme having to do with the preservation of our Canadian natural heritage. Here the lordly Caribou, those marvelous beasts who roam the barren ground are seen wandering across the Tundra covered with delicate Arctic flora. The quilt is at once intimate and familiar—a very human offering in the purely technological environment of a subway station.

Philosophy

While running towards the lower level to catch a train in a subway, one is confronted with a depiction of a group of Barren Ground Caribou in quilted form. Like prehistoric beasts, they are placed in the modern technological cave of the subway. (Altamira) Let us remember these marvelous beasts before they are no more.

Public Use

The first stuffed, quilted, pillowed work to depict the summer Tundra of the Canadian Arctic in a public place. The depiction of caribou, flora, and rock are designed to be an example of a high point in craft.

The production of this quilt will employ women who have practised their craft for years in Ontario. Through design and craft, this piece could be a true focal point of one of the country's best known cultural expressions—the quilt.

Children will be able to relate to the Arctic landscape, animals, and flowers, in which this quilt abounds. Women, unanimous in their love of this form will find in its techniques a worthy topic of discussion.

I believe that there is something in this work for one and all.

The Quilted Forms:

The quilted form is very affectionate, intimate, a kind of mother love thing, which is as once precious and familiar. (Everyone knows what a quilt is!)

Even though the quilt is protected by glass the viewer feels that the powers—that [w]e have extended to the public, a unique and generous gift. They understand that it is for them and their children.

Glassed Objects:

People go to museums and line up to see all sorts of treasures which are under glass. They are fond of the armour and old weapons. They cannot touch them, still they go back again and again to those objects to view the handcrafted aspects and to fantasize. Every school child returns to the wonder of dioramas of animals and the cases with Egyptian mummies and period clothing.

Therefore I feel to put an art work under glass in a public place is not undemocratic."

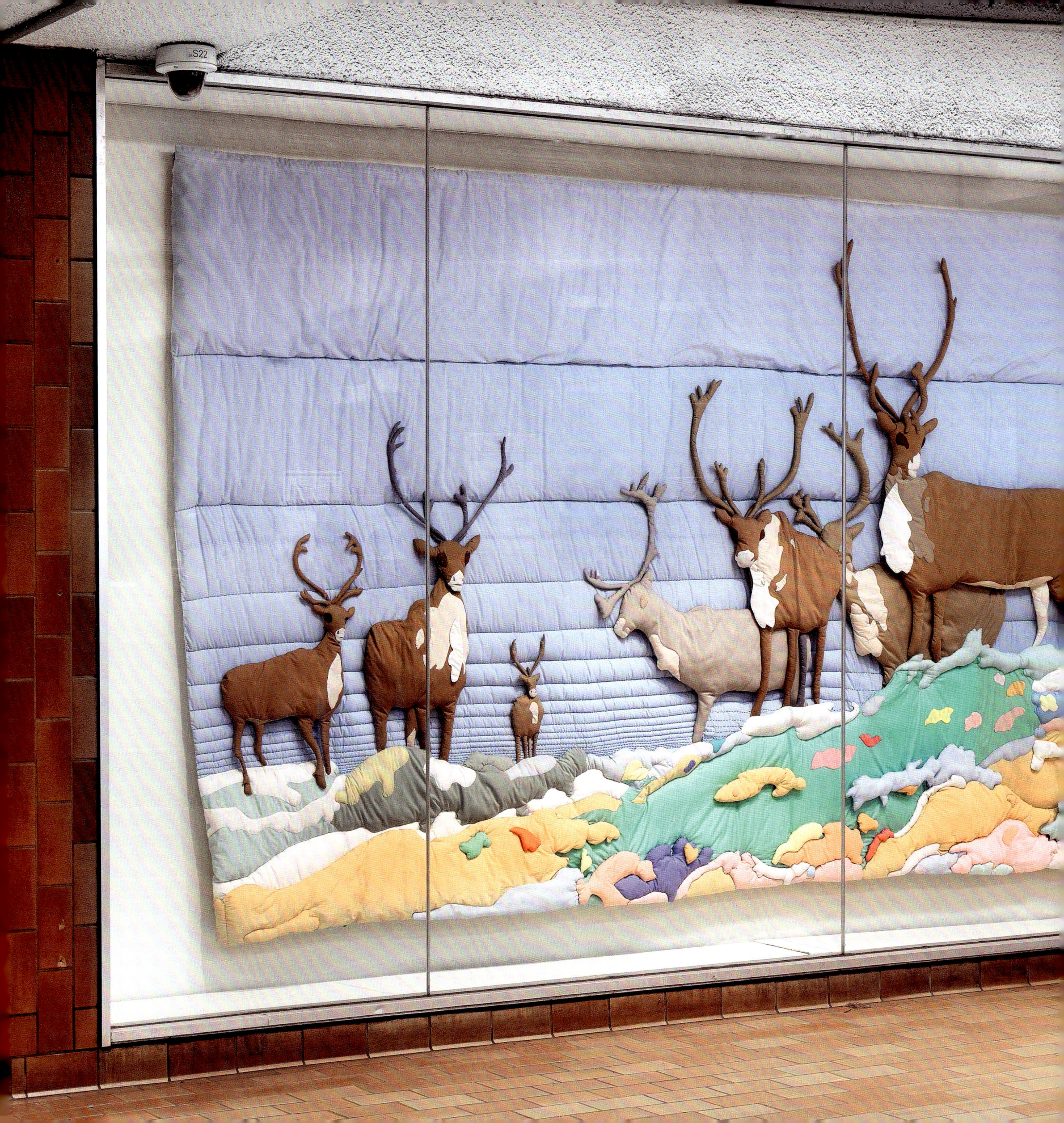
S22

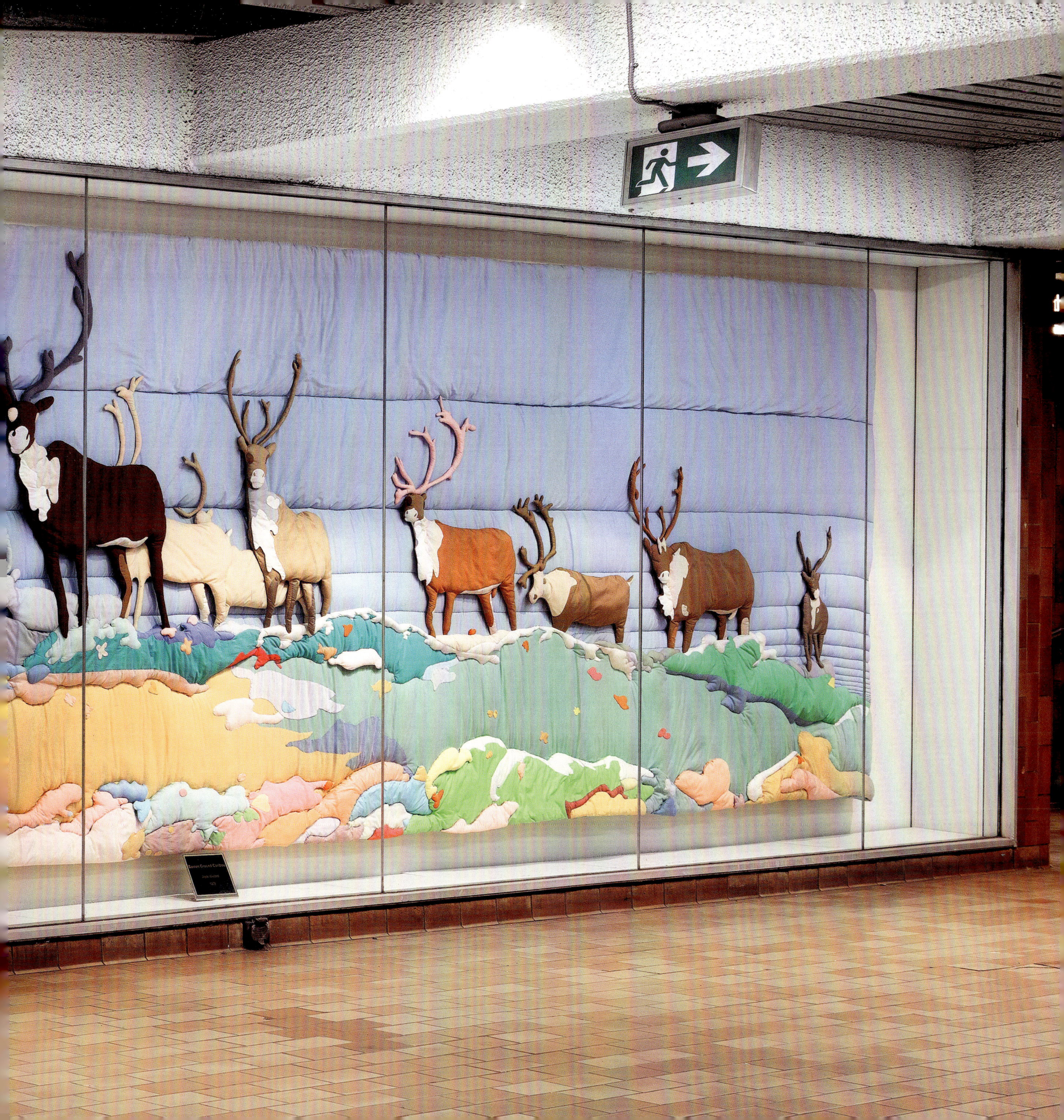

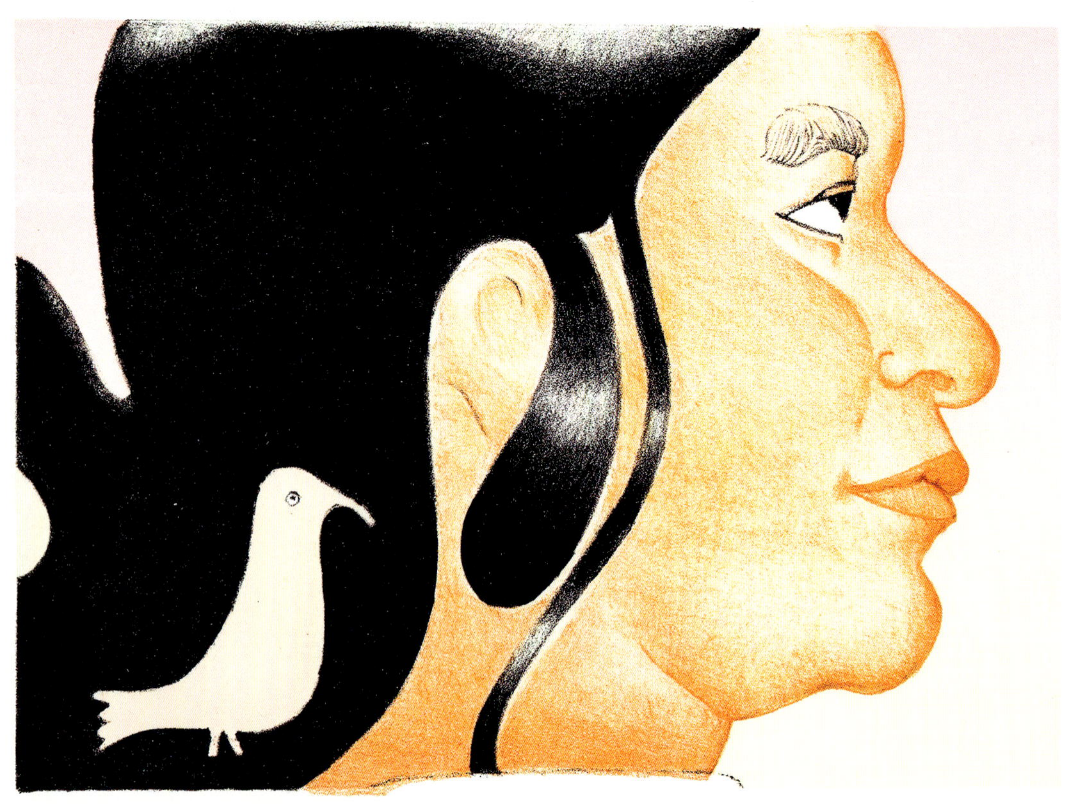

"At the co-op, I looked through stacks and stacks of drawings purchased from the Inuit artists, and the one artist that intrigued me was a woman named Sorseelutu [*sic*], so I hired a translator and asked Sorseelutu to work with me. . . . I realized that I couldn't do my original idea, which was that I would ask an Inuit artist to draw me, and I would draw her so that there would be two points of view. . . . So I drew her. . . . As I drew, other people would step in the house and stand around the wall. When I finished the drawing, they were looking over my shoulder, nodding, and liking it. . . . I only went to Sorseelutu's house once, and when I went back to the lithography studio to compile the prints, I began thinking about the light. Those skies are unphotographable because of the subtleties in colour and light. I realized it would take years to understand Arctic light."

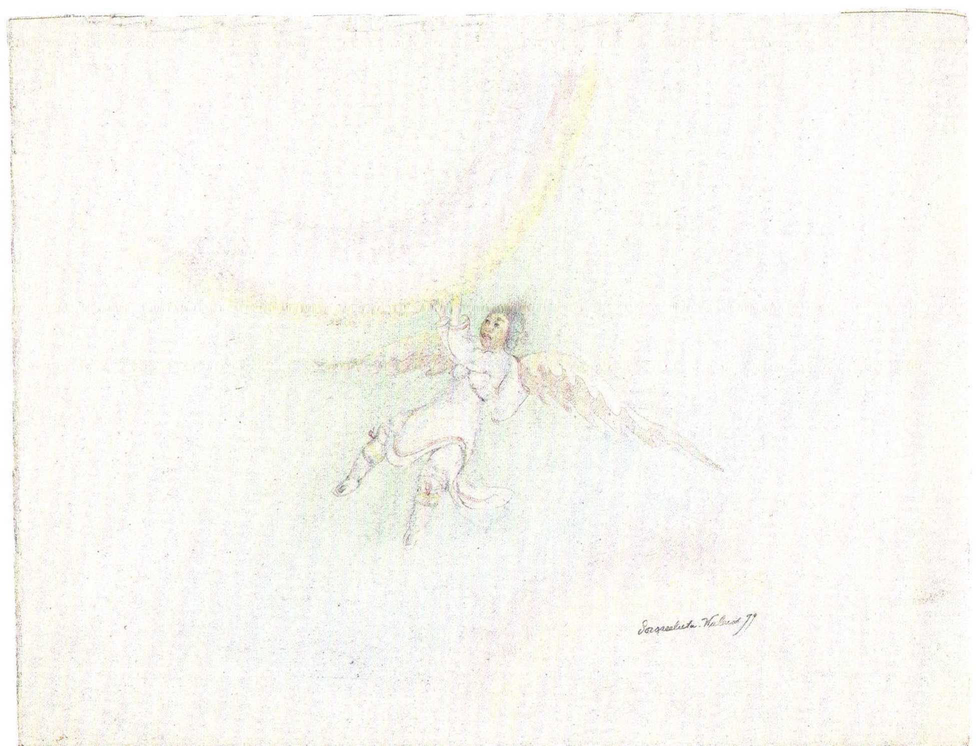

Soroseeluto, 1979
Coloured pencil and graphite on wove paper
28.5 × 37.7 cm
National Gallery of Canada, Ottawa,
Gift of an anonymous donor, 2018,
in honour of Arni and Lydia Hjartarson
Photo: NGC

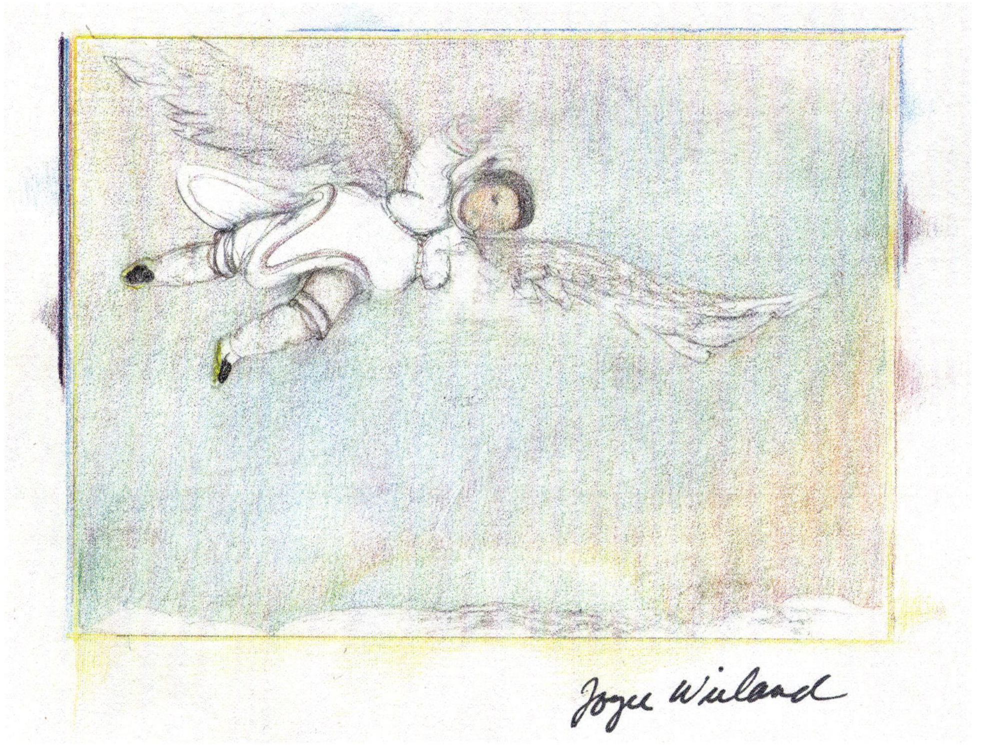

OPPOSITE
Soroseelutu, Cape Dorset, 1977
Lithograph, artist's proof
29.5 × 35.8 cm
The Montreal Museum of Fine Arts, Pierre Théberge bequest in memory of Pauline Talbot Théberge and Pauline Annette Théberge
2019.335
Photo: MMFA, Jean-François Brière

RIGHT
Untitled [Sorosolitu], c. 1979
Pencil crayon, graphite, and possibly chalk on paper
22.86 × 30.48 cm
Collection of Susan Rynard
Photo: AGO, Craig Boyko

For her *The Bloom of Matter* exhibition in the spring of 1981, Joyce Wieland transformed the white cube of The Isaacs Gallery into a Victorian receiving room: peach-coloured walls, house plants, a Persian carpet, a long wooden table, and thirty-two coloured-pencil drawings, mostly tondos, framed in gold and silver. It was the artist's first solo show at the Gallery in over seven years and, for most, an unexpected departure from her signature monumental quilts and experimental films. For Wieland, it was in keeping with her lifelong exploration of the nature of love, ecology, and mythology.

Large public commissions and the production and release of her feature-length film, *The Far Shore* (1976), consumed most of her time in the 1970s. She had made several drawings for the film's storyboards and, most remarkably, designed the poster as a cluster of circular drawings, entwined with Art Nouveau designs announcing it as a "Northern Love Story." It signalled her return to drawing, anticipating her major series *The Bloom of Matter*. This group of delicate, coloured-pencil drawings that she began making in late 1978

THE BLOOM OF MATTER

later developed into tondo paintings and exhibited at her show at Isaacs in 1983. In these intense and highly erotic vignettes, Wieland gives us a glimpse of bucolic splendour with a punch, bathed in pinks, blues, yellows, greens, and browns. Naked figures frolic among deer, hares, birds, fauns, and other fantastic beasts, and swirls of flowers, water, sky, and sunshine. Often, a flower pierces through the edge of the tondo—such fecundity cannot be contained. These drawings, each sensually titled, define the direction the artist would take in her large and final paintings of the 1980s and early 1990s.

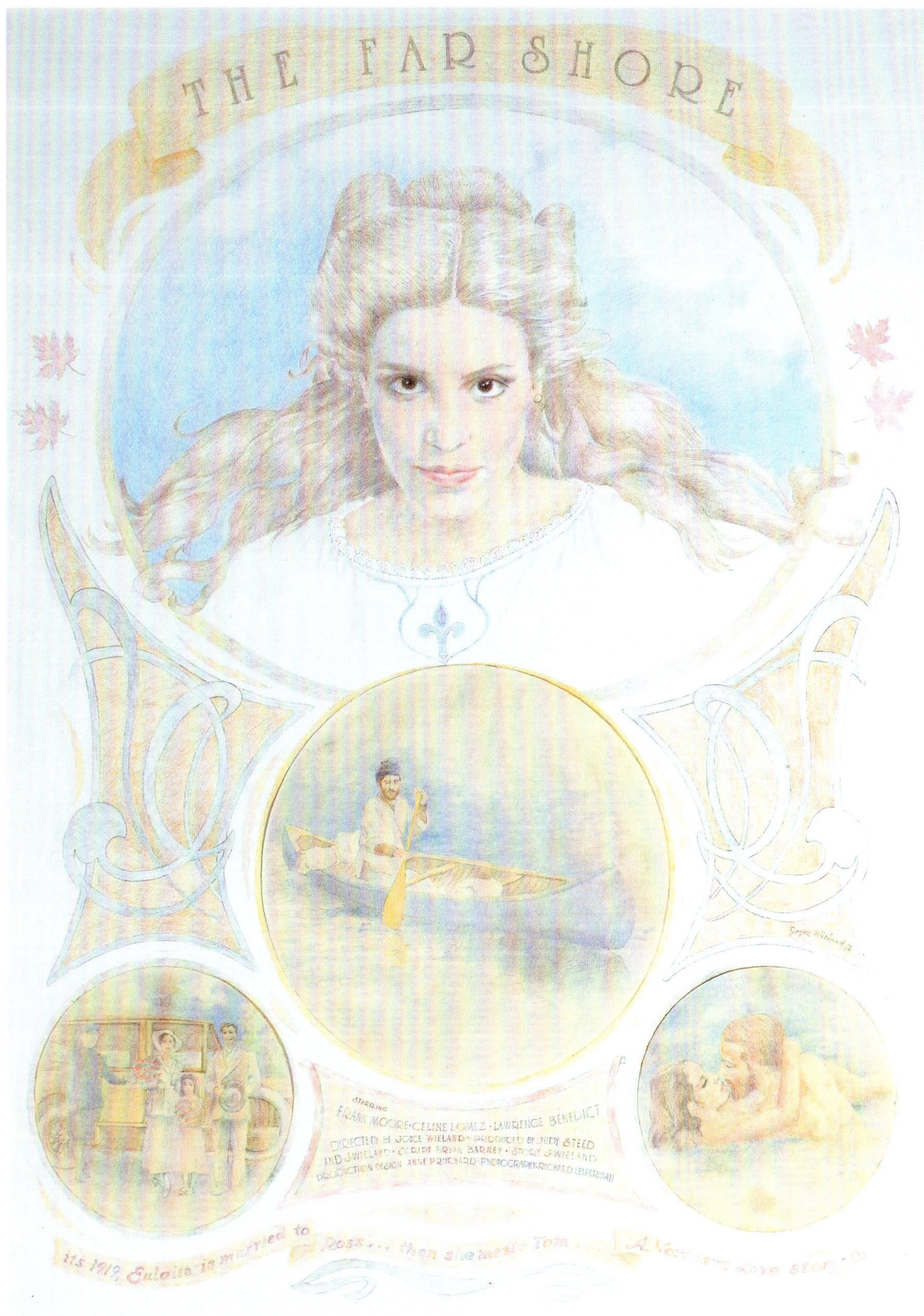

LEFT

Drawing for poster for ***The Far Shore,*** 1976
Graphite and coloured pencil on wove paper and collage on artist illustration board
74.1 × 54 cm
Collection of Museum London,
Gift of Ralph and Rosemary Bull,
London, ON, 1985
85.A.91
Photo: Museum London

OPPOSITE

Detail: Eulalie and Tom tondo

POSTER FOR THE FAR SHORE, 1976

I met Joyce Wieland in 1971, when she and Michael Snow returned to Toronto from New York. She stood out, always—an exciting presence, a feminist, an environmentalist, full of ideas, opinions. Doing things. So when I got involved in "helping" her—I could drive, she could not—the first big adventure was driving my beat-up VW Beetle through a snowstorm to Mont-Laurier, Quebec, to find journalist and writer Pierre Vallières (1938–1998), ardent separatist and intellectual leader of the Front de libération du Québec.

Joyce's camera focused on his lips as he spoke for thirty minutes, in French, about Quebec's history and oppression, women's rights, and Indigenous issues. I sat at his feet with the microphone just under his chin. This was the beginning of the Wieland experience: learning to ride the waves of Joyce's creativity, to support her originality, to not be afraid of controversy. She was full of surprises. When I was helping her raise money to produce her feature-length film *The Far Shore*—an arduous task that took almost six years, with the film premiering in 1976, and for which she generously gave me a co-producer credit—at every step we encountered obstacles.

Potential backers loved the screenplay for *The Far Shore*, loved her idea of imagining a life and death for the legendary painter Tom Thomson (1877–1917), but they did not want Joyce to direct.[1] That was a big fight. It was only in Quebec, with francophone producers and artists, that Joyce found support for her vision of a film that was an authentic expression of her time and place. In Ontario it was the onset of the "tax shelter" era (1974–1982): the films that got made were mostly B-movie tax credit productions with half-baked "stars."

When it came to the poster, Joyce was expected to produce a standard graphic movie poster. Instead she started drawing with soft coloured pencils: a beautiful portrait of lead character Eulalie (played by Québécoise actor Céline Lomez, b. 1953), her eyes strong and determined, fixed on the viewer, and Tom (Frank Moore, b. 1946) beneath her, paddling in his canoe. Below is a smaller image of Tom and Eulalie making love in the lake. I recall some outraged reactions from the movie-business guys to the soft romance, the "old-fashioned" flourishes of Joyce's vision. "That's not a movie poster," they said. "You can't do that."

Of course she could, and she did. Not without a cost to herself. If what she achieved looks easy, it was not. She paid a heavy price for being ahead of her time, going against the grain of the male-dominated art and film world, creating the space to express herself. But she could not help it. Her creativity was a life force within her. It emerged in all the beautiful ways we see endure in her work. Such a gift.

JUDY STEED

1 For an in-depth discussion of *The Far Shore*, see Johanne Sloan, *Joyce Wieland's The Far Shore* (Toronto: University of Toronto Press, 2010).

THE BLOOM OF MATTER, 1979–1981

The drawings in *The Bloom of Matter* bring out the interconnections of all *things*: matter itself blooms and is alive. What Wieland proposes in her representations within the drawings is an ecological (or anti-humanist) model of the universe rather than a humanist one.

The drawings create an intimacy with the viewer both because of their scale (from four inches to fifteen inches) and their surface (like luminous projections, as though light were projected onto paper, the images emerge, disappear and reappear). One must literally be close to the drawings in order for the images to emerge. With the movement of the eye as it travels around the transparent images of plant life, people, goddesses, and places, the drawings become cinematic.

Wieland talking about the drawings recalls, "I was working with paper to create a luminosity. I *found* the drawings in the paper. By looking, I *found* the drawings." The viewer, too, must look for the drawings to emerge, and thus she activates our seeing. Looking becomes bliss.[1]

In terms of influences on the drawings, "Tiepolo's work," Wieland recalls, "was an inspiration along with a trip to the Arctic where I discovered something about the quality of light. I was interested in regional light—a region's light in the Maritimes, the Arctic, Northern Ontario . . ."

Within the drawings, there is a focus on the sensual and the sexual: matter blooms, things touch and grow out of one another, angels (not fairies—note the wings) and goddesses preside, the mythical comes together with the particular. A province is born, *Birth of Newfoundland*. The Roman goddess of love is located in Northern Ontario, *The Venus of Kapuskasing*. Chopin comes to an Ontario lake, *Chopin with Other Polish Patriots at Lake Skootamatta*, and flowers are born, *The Birth Place of Snap Dragons*. In these drawings, the sexual is extended out not only to an other, a lover, but to all matter, which blooms. Sex—regeneration, creation—brings in birth and death, love, and loss.

A language of the emotions is represented within the powerful episodic moments or *glimpses* showing how things grow, how things are born, and how things disappear and die. In *The Death of Love*, "Wieland observed a pig's head, which she had gotten from the market. The drawing shows the pig, a big bruise on its head from a death blow, blood at the corners of its mouth, and life against death, a daffodil in its mouth. This is not a hedonistic representation of emotion, but rather, a powerful *look* at the stuff, the matter—matter in a cycle of sex, birth, and death.

The drawings themselves are gifts, both *for* and *from* Wieland. She says about them: "They came of their own will. They just came one day and two years later, it ended. They were for me, and they healed me." And they are extended out from her, to the viewer, as a gift *for* and *from* love.

LEILA SUJIR

All quotations are from an interview with Joyce Wieland on August 15, 1986, Toronto (Wieland's emphasis).

From an unpublished 1986 essay, from Leila Sujir's fond at Concordia University's Records Management and Archive. Previous drafts can be found in the 1987 Joyce Wieland exhibition files, Edward P. Taylor Library and Archives Special Collections, AGO; text copy edited 2024.

1 See Roland Barthes's discussion of texts of pleasure and bliss in *The Pleasures of the Text* and *Roland Barthes*. Texts of bliss require an active reader, "a mobile, plural reader, who nimbly inserts and removes the quotation marks: who begins to write 'with me'" (*Roland Barthes*, 106).

Roland Barthes, *The Pleasure of the Text*, trans. Richard Miller (New York: Farrar, Straus and Giroux, 1975); Roland Barthes, trans. Richard Howard (New York: Hill and Wang, 1977).

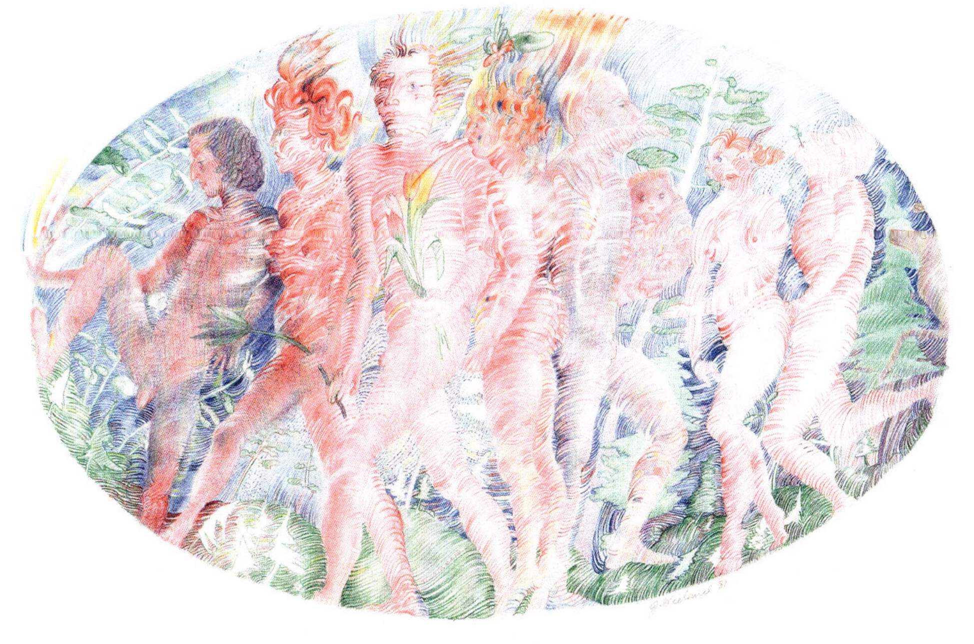

OPPOSITE
Birth of New Foundland, 1980
Graphite and coloured pencil
on wove paper
20.95 × 20.95 cm
MacLaren Art Centre, Barrie, ON,
Gift of Ron McQueen, 2002
2002.7.4
Photo: Andre Beneteau

ABOVE, RIGHT
Chopin with Other Polish Patriots at Lake Skootamatta, 1981
Graphite and coloured pencil
on wove paper
21.6 × 31.1 cm
Collection of Colette Perron-Sharp
Photo: MMFA, Julie Ciot

RIGHT
Victory of Venus, 1981
Coloured pencil on wove paper
48.4 × 61 cm
Art Gallery of Ontario,
Purchased with funds donated
by AGO Members, 2002
2002/47
Photo: AGO, Craig Boyko

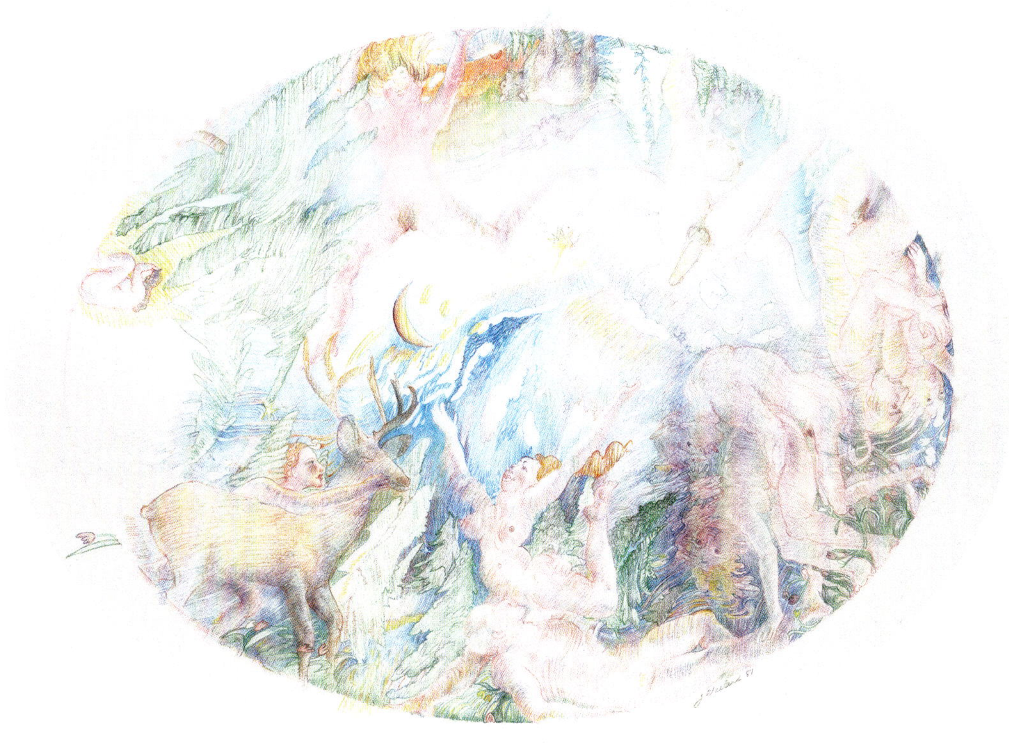

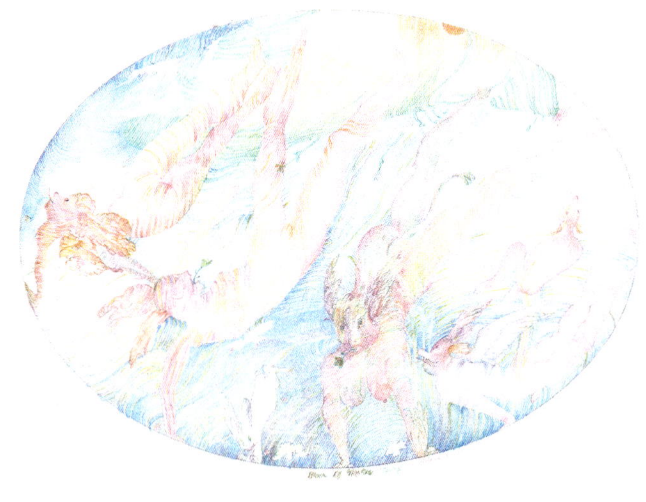

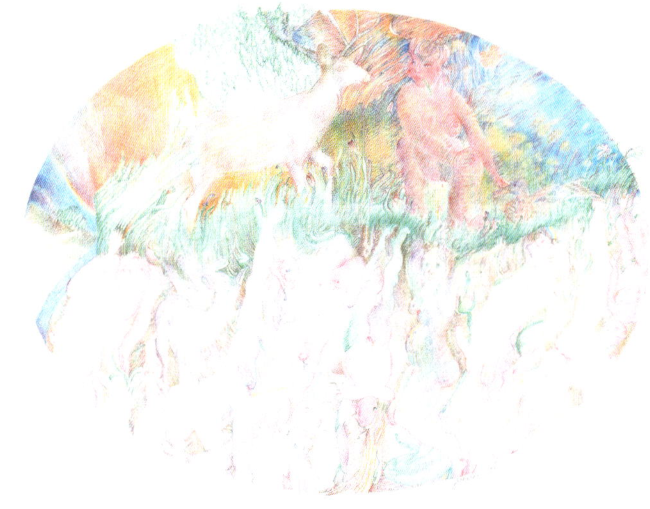

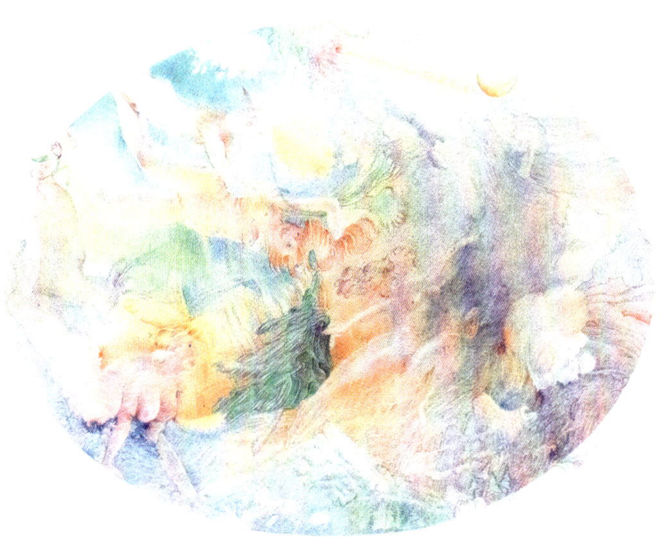

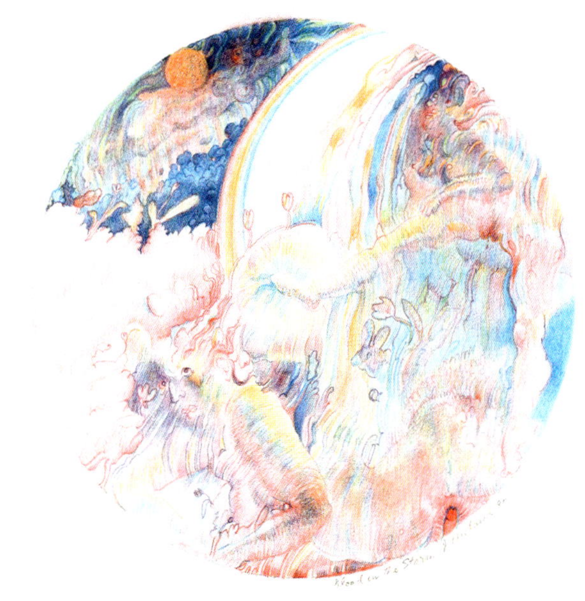

ABOVE, LEFT
Bloom of Matter: Spring, 1980
Coloured pencil on wove paper
27.3 × 38 cm
Art Gallery of Ontario, Purchased 1981
80/192
Photo: AGO, Craig Boyko

ABOVE, RIGHT
The One Above Waits for Those Below, 1981
Coloured pencil on wove paper
36 × 47 cm
Collection of the Canada Council Art Bank, Ottawa
81/2-0542
Photo: Brandon Clarida Image Services

BELOW, LEFT
Goddess of the Earth, Sea and Air, 1981
Graphite and coloured pencil on wove paper
40 × 51.43 cm
Christopher Cutts Gallery, Toronto
7299
Photo: Shayne Cassidy

BELOW, RIGHT
Blood in the Storm, 1980
Graphite and coloured pencil on wove paper
15.8 × 15.8 cm
MacLaren Art Centre, Barrie, ON, Gift of Ron McQueen, 2002
2002.7.3
Photo: Andre Beneteau

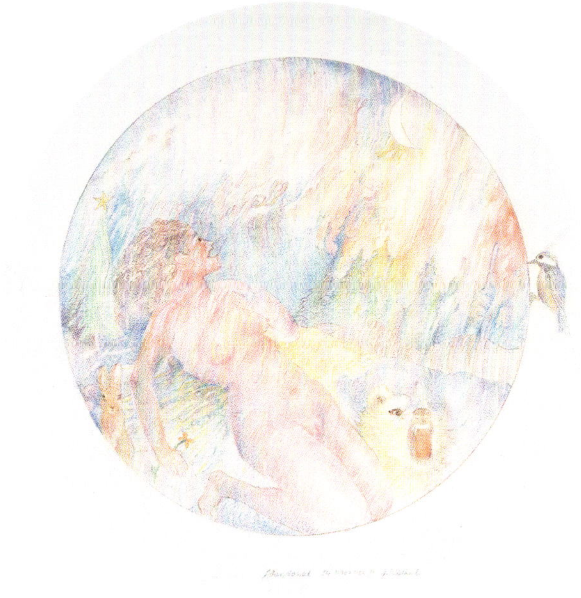

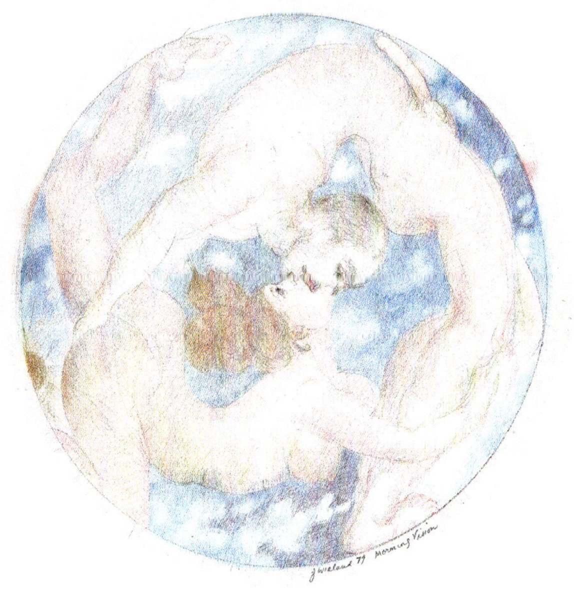

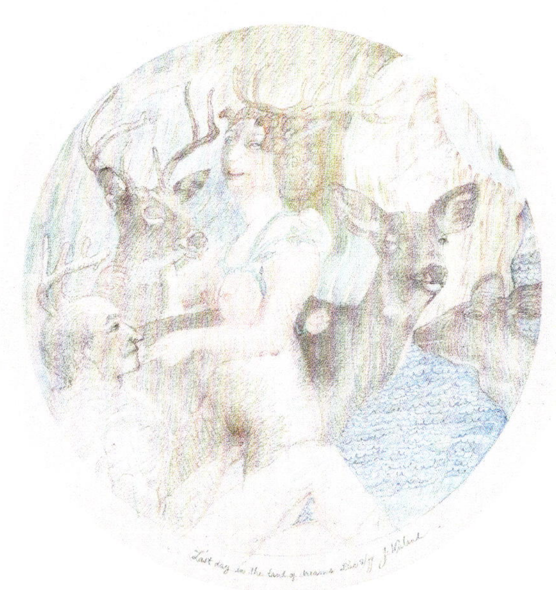

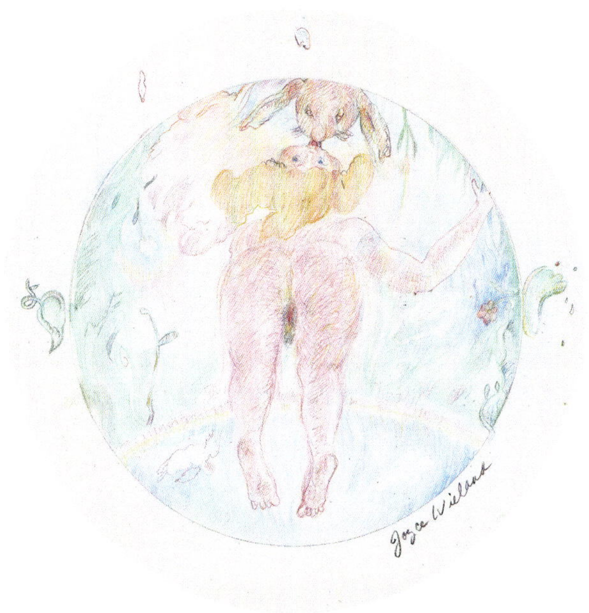

ABOVE, LEFT
Abandoned, 1979
Graphite and coloured pencil on wove paper
27.7 × 35.3 cm
The Montreal Museum of Fine Arts, Purchase, Harry W. Thorpe Bequest and Canada Council Grant
Dr.1980.3
Photo: MMFA, Jean-François Brière

ABOVE, RIGHT
Morning Vision, 1979
Coloured pencil on wove paper
27.9 × 31.9 cm
Art Gallery of Ontario, Gift of Dr. Paul and Joyce Chapnick, 2004
2004/99
Photo: AGO, Craig Boyko

BELOW, LEFT
Last Day in the Land of Dreams, 1979
Coloured pencil on paper
28 × 35.5 cm
Art Gallery of Ontario, Gift of Lisa Balfour Bowen in celebration of husband Walter's seventieth birthday, 2004
2004/70
Photo: AGO, Craig Boyko

BELOW, RIGHT
Untitled [Bather and Hare], c. 1980–1982
Coloured pencil on wove paper
Sheet: 29.5 × 38.8 cm
Art Gallery of Ontario, Gift of Betty Ramsaur Ferguson, Puslinch, ON, 1998
98/642
Photo: AGO, Craig Boyko

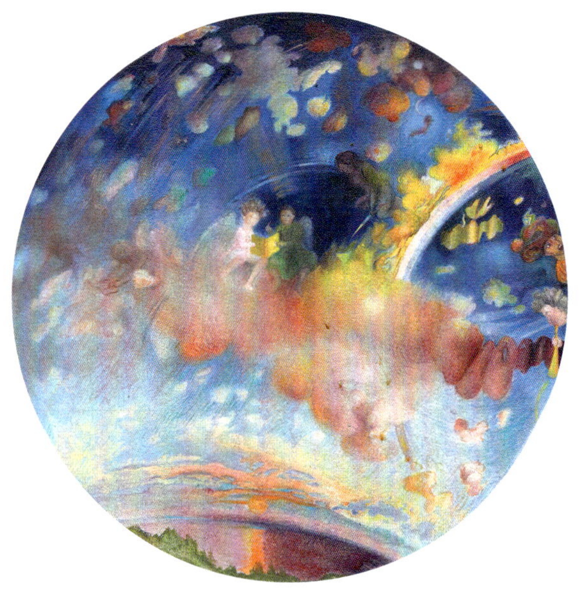

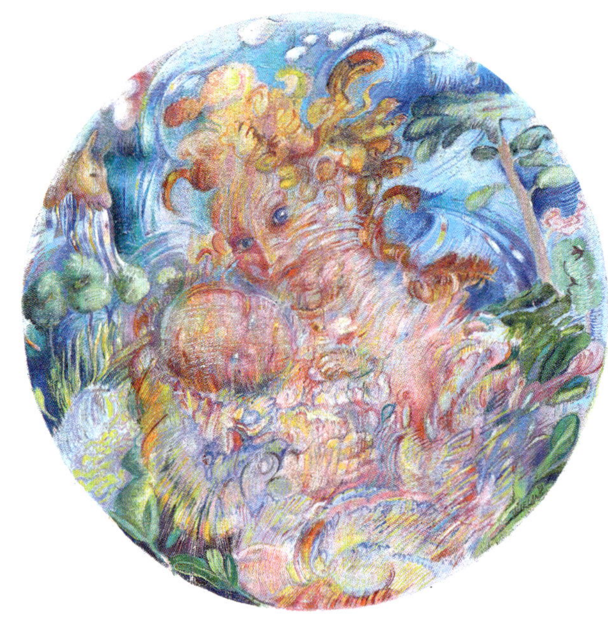

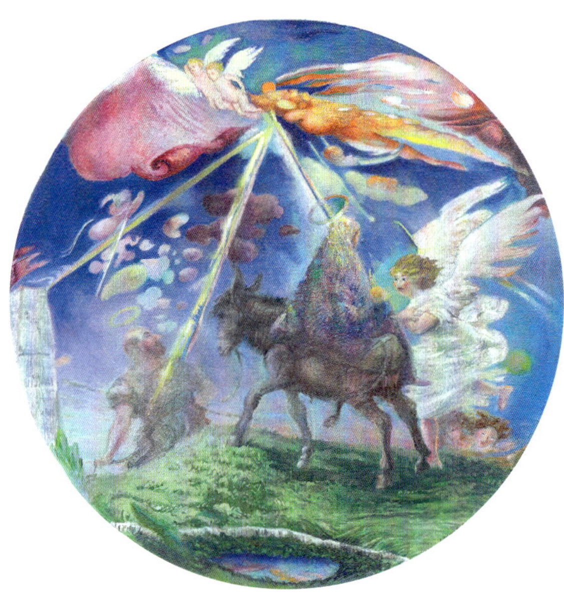

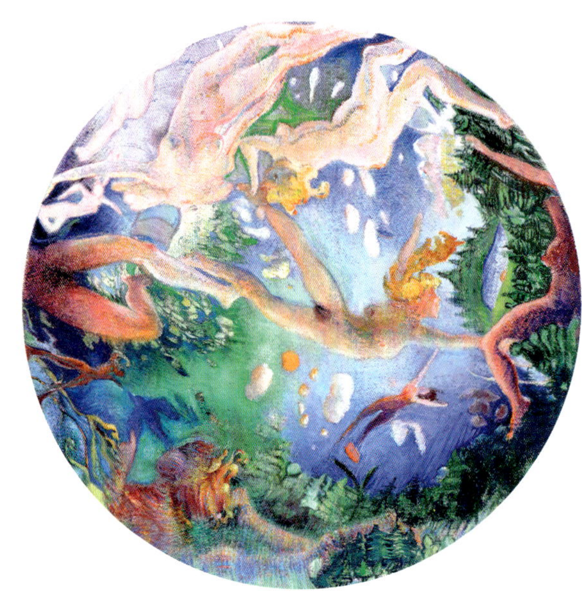

ABOVE, LEFT
The Discussion of Flaubert's Egyptian Journals, 1982
Oil on canvas
56 × 61.3 cm
Art Gallery of Ontario,
Gift of Lynn McDonald, 2020
2020/153
Photo: AGO, Craig Boyko

ABOVE, RIGHT
Mother and Child, 1981
Oil on canvas
41.1 × 38.3 cm
Art Gallery of Ontario,
Gift of Lynn McDonald, 2020
2020/152
Photo: AGO, Craig Boyko

BELOW, LEFT
Flight into Egypt (After Tiepolo), 1981
Oil on canvas
55 × 60 cm
Collection Galeries Bellemare Lambert
Photo: Guy L'Heureux, Courtesy
of Galeries Bellemare Lambert

BELOW, RIGHT
What They Do At Sunrise, 1981
Oil on canvas
33 × 33 cm
Collection of Lucas Ferguson-Sharp
Photo: MMFA, Julie Ciot

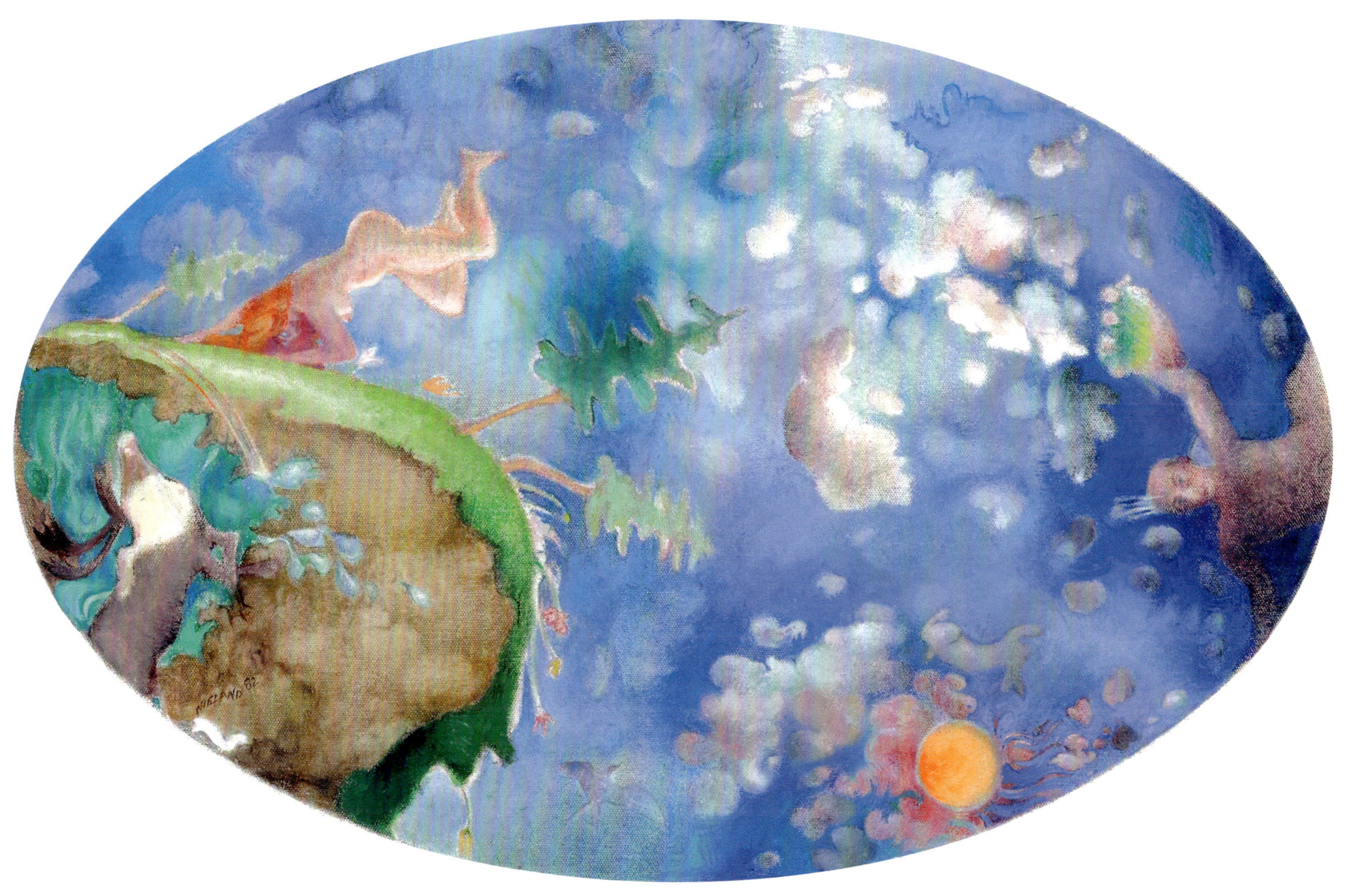

The End of Life as She Knew It, 1982
Oil on canvas
62.23 × 82.92 cm
Private Collection
Photo: MMFA, Julie Ciot

VENUS OF SCARBOROUGH, 1982

In August 1982, Joyce Wieland planted a flower garden in the shape of a goddess. Begonias, aster, and sweet alyssum formed the low relief of *Venus of Scarborough*, who lay on her back in a grassy clearing at the Guild Inn estate, on the eastern edge of Toronto. For three months, the Venus grew near the steep bluffs of Scarborough, overlooking Lake Ontario.[1] Her hair unfurled in profuse beds of orange and yellow chrysanthemums.

Described as "delightful" and the "perfect anniversary piece"[2] in the press, *Venus of Scarborough* was part of a sculpture exhibition commemorating the fiftieth anniversary of The Guild. The exhibition curator, sculptor Sorel Etrog (1933–2014), invited Wieland to participate along with thirty-four other Canadian and international artists. The *Venus*, Wieland's first and only earthwork, was a critical success and reached a level of popularity that pleased her. "I can't tell you how it was so heartwarming to have put something there that they really loved, that everyone liked," she noted. "When they came to the Guild Inn, they would ask: 'where is the lady?'"[3]

Guild Park is an eccentric space. It contains artist studios, a large inn, and a collection of historic architectural remnants retrieved from Toronto demolition sites, including eight Corinthian columns from an old Toronto Dominion bank that have been repurposed as an outdoor theatre. For the 1982 exhibition, Etrog selected many modernist abstract sculptures that neither responded to the surrounding landscape nor the architectural ornaments scattered across the site. However, Wieland used the grounds of The Guild as her very medium. *The Globe and Mail* lauded her and one other artist—New York minimalist Carl Andre (1935–2024)—for their ability to "take the facts of the park, work it through their separate artistic ideologies [. . .] and give it back to the Guild, transmuted into a unique response."[4] Cuban-American artist Ana Mendieta (1948–1985) also had work in the exhibition: *El Laborinto de Venus*, a metre-and-a-half-wide carving in stone—a Venus of her own. Mendieta, however, was not mentioned in the article.

Wieland's idea for this flowering monument came from her particular sense of environmentalism, which valued growth and nourishment. As opposed to excavating land or setting down a monolithic structure, she planted a flowerbed that offered an ephemeral sensory experience. She made *Venus of Scarborough* in her characteristic spirit of generosity. The work therefore embodies her deep concerns for humanity and ecology, as well as her attunement to the cyclic patterns of nature. As Lucy Lippard suggests, the sculpture epitomizes the feminine empathy between earth and body that underpins much feminist art.[5]

Wieland's drawings from the early 1980s embody these ideas, too, notably the works from her *The Bloom of Matter* series. These jewel-like, coloured-pencil drawings represent what has been referred to as the artist's "private mythology."[6] Humorous, erotic, and sensual, they reference historical art, which Wieland once described as "so alive, so full of the tumult of life."[7] Rococo painter Giovanni Battista Tiepolo (1696–1770), known for his grandiose depictions of ancient history and myth, inspired her: like Tiepolo, her drawings depict an array of Venuses in verdant landscapes. Some of her Venuses appear in local scenes, such as the *Venus of Kapuskasing* (1981) and *Goddess in Toronto* (1982). This geographic specificity is a continued form of love for her country. In 1971, she proclaimed, "I think of Canada as female. All the art I've been doing or will be doing is about Canada."[8]

With *Venus of Scarborough*, Wieland engages with Canada, and Scarborough in particular, by physically embedding her work into soil. Flowers appear often in her work: *Nature Mixes* (1962) is a filmic painting that shows the metamorphosis of a flower into

1 *Venus of Scarborough* was situated in a grassy patch between the Clark Centre for the Arts and The Guild Inn, in what is now Guild Park and Gardens in Scarborough, Ontario, approximately twenty kilometres east of downtown Toronto. Guild Park sits along the Scarborough Bluffs, a fifteen-kilometre stretch of white cliffs formed by wind and water erosion from Lake Ontario. The clearing where *Venus of Scarborough* was installed has since been landscaped into an artificial wetland.

2 John Bentley Mays, "A Dizzying Variety of Sculptural Styles: It's a Celebration of The Guild on Its Own Problem-Ridden Site," *The Globe and Mail*, August 7, 1982, E9.

3 Transcript of Joyce Wieland artist's talk at the University of Lethbridge, 1985, 3 (edited quote from cassette tape "Joyce Wieland on Her Work"); transcript held at the University of Lethbridge Art Gallery, Alberta.

4 Mays, "A Dizzying Variety of Sculptural Styles."

5 Lucy Lippard, "Watershed: Contradiction, Communication and Canada in Joyce Wieland's Work," in *Joyce Wieland*, exh. cat., ed. Marie Fleming (Toronto: Art Gallery of Ontario, 1987), 2.

6 Carole Corbeil, "Joyce Wieland Finds Room to Bloom," *The Globe and Mail*, March 2, 1981, 17.

7 Corbeil, "Joyce Wieland Finds Room to Bloom."

8 Lippard, "Watershed," 2.

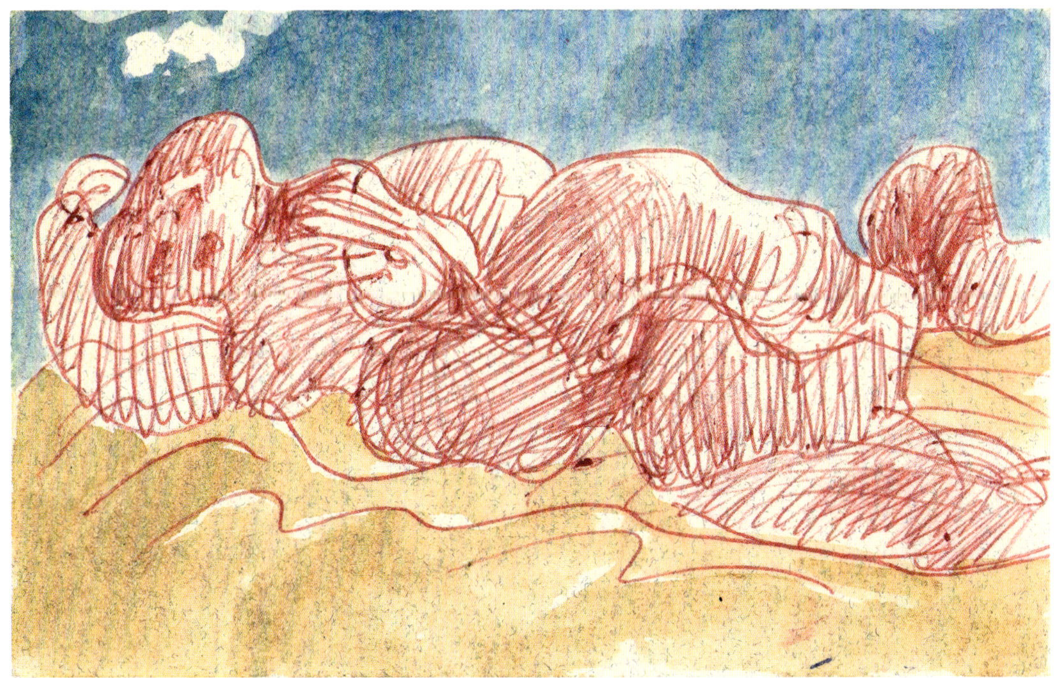

Colour sketch of Venus lying on her side on the back of a Lynn McDonald, Canadian Member of Parliament, business card, c. 1984
Joyce Wieland fonds, ASC61826, York University Libraries, Clara Thomas Archives and Special Collections

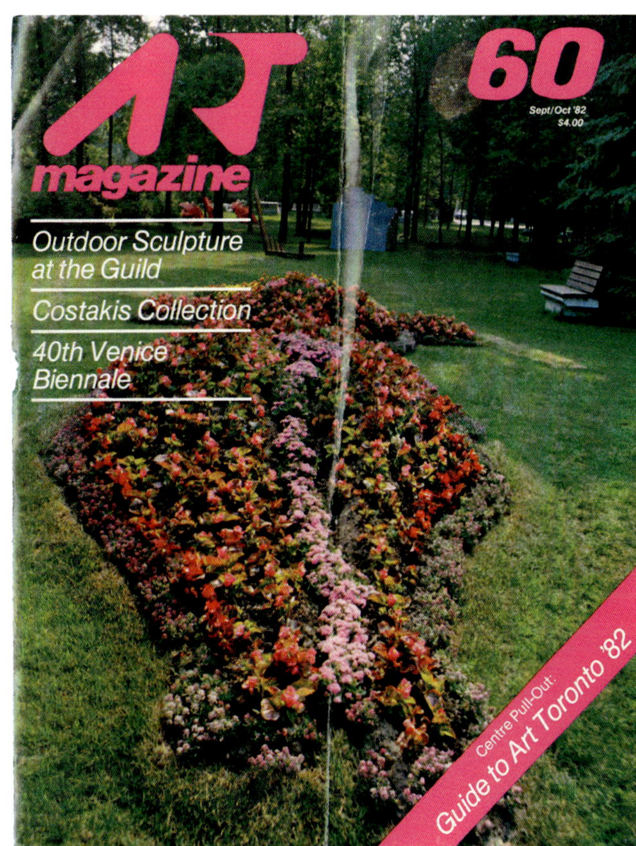

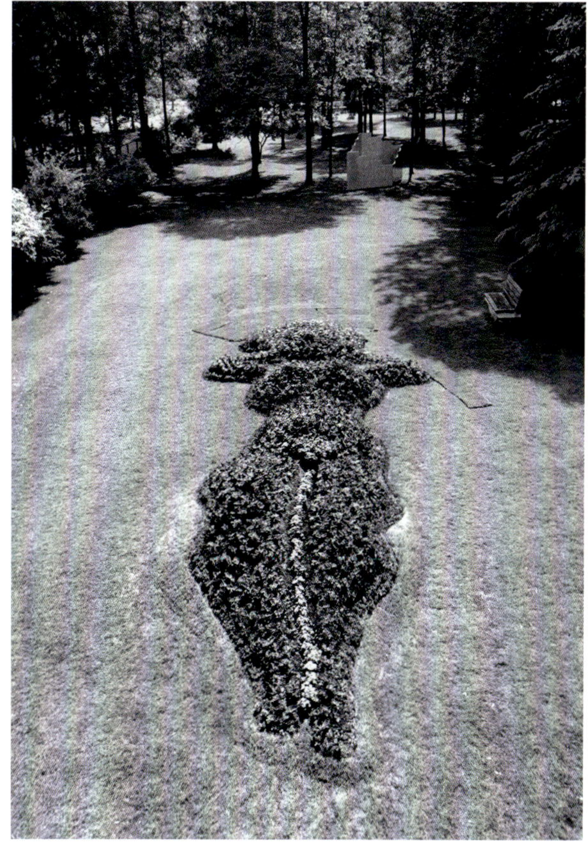

LEFT
Cover of *ART* Magazine (Toronto), September/October 1982
Avrom Isaacs fonds, ASC61414, York University Libraries, Clara Thomas Archives and Special Collections

RIGHT
Venus of Scarborough installed at the *Contemporary Outdoor Sculpture* exhibition at The Guild, curated by Sorel Etrog, 1982
Photo: Jim Chambers

a penis; the film *Water Sark* (1965) features a vase of lush roses in a domestic setting; and *The Water Quilt* (1970–1971) (p. 192) unfolds in an array of endangered arctic blooms. Although *Venus of Scarborough* is her first use of flora as artistic medium, she did include living plants in installations throughout her career, including her retrospectives at the National Gallery of Canada (1971) and the Art Gallery of Ontario (1987). Flowers also appeared in *The Bloom of Matter* at The Isaacs Gallery in Toronto in 1981. For this installation, she created a small archway with a trellis with daffodils above and potted hyacinths and tulips below. Flowers are traditionally rich and varied in symbolism; for Wieland they are loaded with a powerful fecundity that is transgressive, in the vein of Georgia O'Keeffe (1887–1986).

In Wieland's subsequent solo exhibition at The Isaacs Gallery in the spring of 1983, she showed two coloured-pencil studies for *Venus of Scarborough*.[9] In one, the Venus reclines, blue eyes gazing at the sky, arms folded back to support her head, Botticelli curls resplendent, the soft earth supporting her bent legs. In the second study, the Venus lies on her front, long blades of grass brushing up against her flowered skin. She strokes the grass with one hand, and again seems comfortably supported by mounds of green earth in a setting that is symbiotic and harmonious.

Roman goddess of love, beauty, sex, fertility, and victory, the Venus carries strong resonances throughout Wieland's late period, and connects naturally to her earlier practice, too, which consistently dealt with the female experience. While the Venus as a symbol, or character, contains rich meaning—it is an expansive point of reference for Wieland—it also carries a specific personal significance. She once said that the recurring goddess has to do with her mother, who died when Wieland was around ten. It is the lifelong search to reconnect with her mother's lineage.[10] As in all of her work, with *Venus of Scarborough*, Wieland merges personal history with broader concerns, coming full circle and inviting us to consider her worldview as it unifies figure with landscape. ››››

RENÉE VAN DER AVOIRD

Estimation of Plant Species
Identified by Maureen Boles, March 2024

Body, plants for edge moving inward.
Sweet Alyssum (*Lobularis maritima*)
Low-growing mound. Possible varieties based on purple colour:
Royal Carpet
Easter Bonnet Violet
Purple Shades
Begonia
Possible varieties Dragon Wing or Angel Wing.
Fluffy pink at top of mound could be any of these:
Bee Balm (Monarda)
Aster (novae-angliae)
New England cultivar
Plant on the head, orange and yellow: Hardy Garden Chrysanthemums, probably the Anenome classification, which has a round small flower head.

9 Her solo show at Isaacs was April 16, 1982, to March 6, 1983.

10 Wieland quoted in Eimear O'Neill, "Joyce Wieland, 'An Interview,'" *Canadian Woman Studies* 8 (Winter 1987): 35.

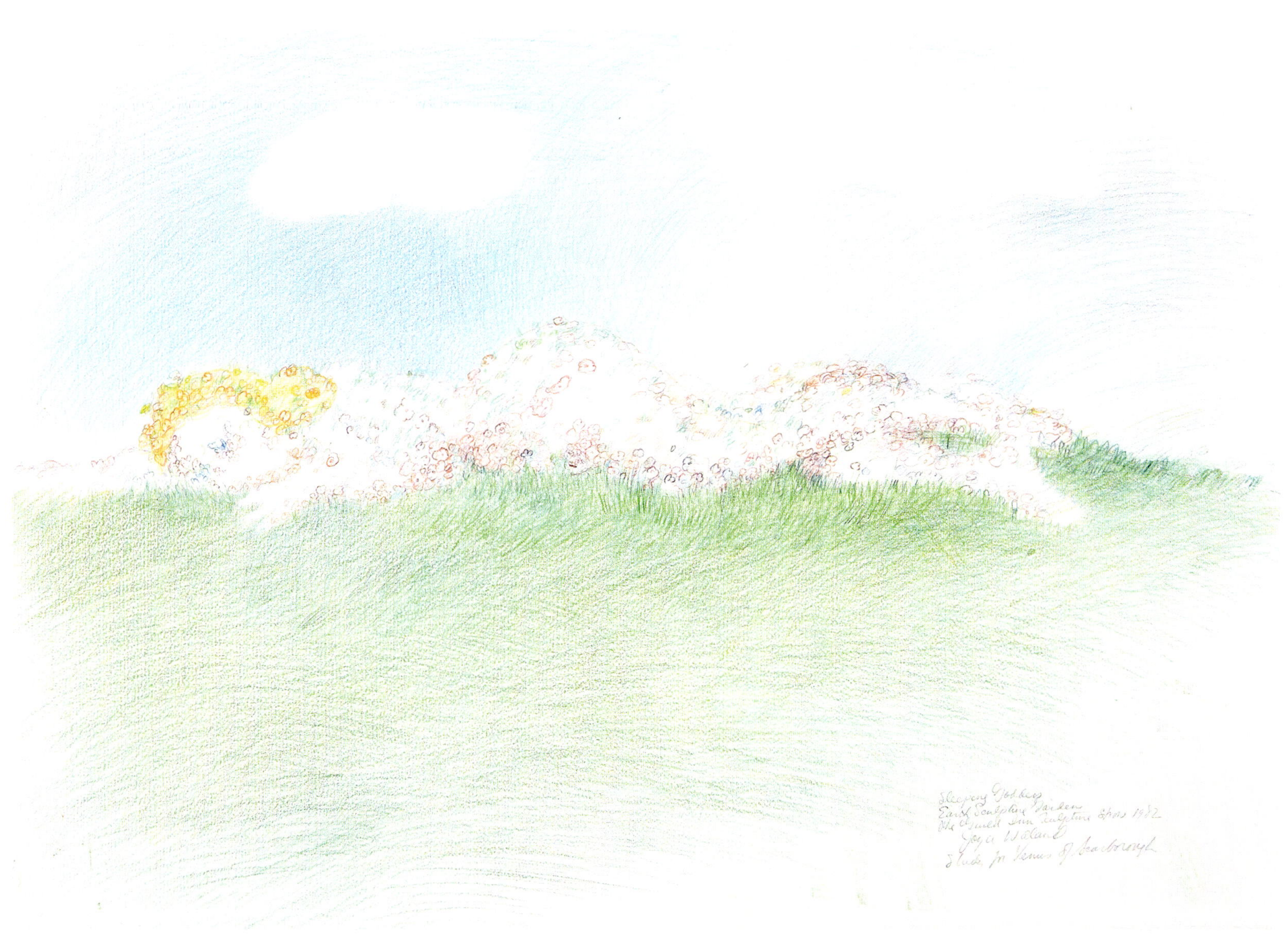

Sleeping Goddess, 1982
Coloured pencil on paper
38.1 × 58.9 cm
Collection of John Cook
Photo: Rémi Thériault

LENS, 1978–1979

Wieland devised ways for elements from one medium to expand into another: drawings into paintings; paintings into film; film into assemblages; assemblages into quilts. With this work, the artist transported the first stanza of the poem "Lens," by Canadian poet Anne Wilkinson (1910–1961), from the page onto a quilt.

Lens marks the last time Wieland would stitch other voices—whether those of poets, politicians, or army generals—into fabric. Wilkinson's poems, praised for their "small, immensely significant details of imagery, music, language and emotion,"[1] resonate with Wieland's own sensibilities. An exploration of perception, *Lens* spoke directly to Wieland as a filmmaker and artist, probing as it does the acuity of the "woman's eye," and magnifying the eloquence of Wilkinson's poem.

ANNE GRACE

Lens

The poet's daily chore
Is my long duty;
To keep and cherish my good lens
For love and war
And wasps about the lilies
And mutiny within.

My woman's eye is weak
And veiled with milk;
My working eye is muscled
With a curious tension,
Stretched and open
As the eyes of children;
Trusting in its vision
Even should it see
The holy holy spirit gambol
Counterheadwise,
Lithe and warm as any animal.

My woman's iris circles
A blind pupil;
The poet's eye is crystal,
Polished to accept the negative,
The contradictions in a proof
And the accidental
Candour of the shadows;

The shutter, oiled and smooth
Clicks on the grace of heroes
Or on some bestial act
When lit with radiance
The afterwords the actors speak
Give depths to violence,
Or if the bull is great
And the matador
And the sword
Itself the metaphor.

II

In my dark room the years
Lie in solution,
Develop film by film.
Slow at first and dim
Their shadows bite
On the fine white pulp of paper.

An early snap of fire
Licking the arms of air
I hold against the light, compare
The details with a prehistoric view
Of land and sea
And cradles of mud that rocked
The wet and sloth of infancy.

A stripe of tiger, curled
And sleeping on the ribs of reason
Prints as clear
As Eve and Adam, pearled
With sweat, staring at an apple core;

And death, in black and white
Or politic in green and Easter film,
Lands on steely points, a dancer
Disciplined to the foolscap stage,
The property of poets
Who command his robes, expose
His moving likeness on the page.

Anne Wilkinson, 1955

1 A.J.M. Smith, "A Reading of Anne Wilkinson," *Canadian Literature*, no. 10 (Autumn 1961), doi.org/10.14288/cl.v0i10.

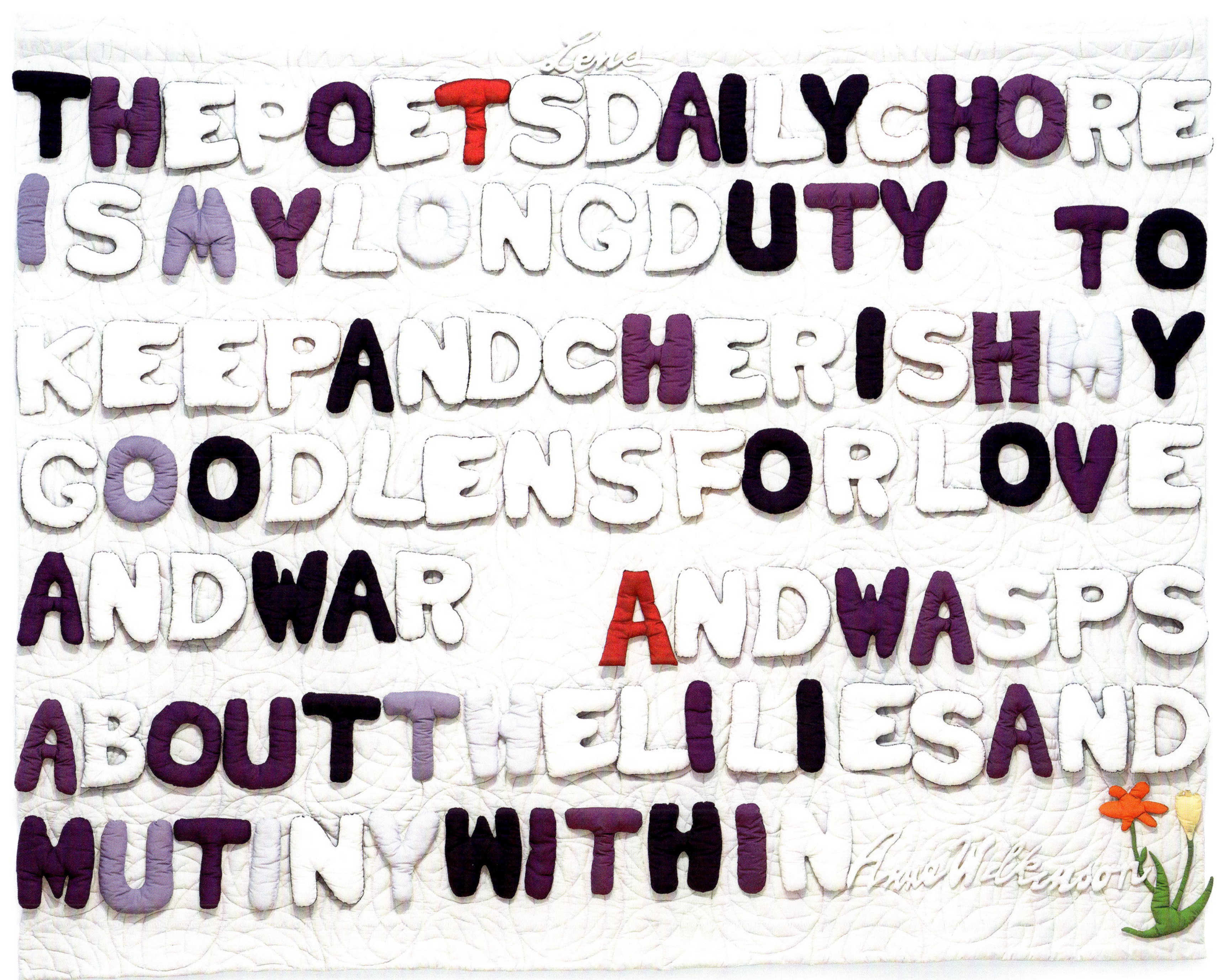

Lens, 1978–1979
Cloth (cotton) with traces of graphite and stainless-steel pins, thread, batting
285.2 × 215.27 × 3.81 cm
Collection of Phyllis Lambert
Photo courtesy Canadian Centre for Architecture

After more than a decade, Joyce Wieland returned at full force to painting in the 1980s. The melodramatic content and formal dynamism of her paintings from this period emerge from the exquisite and intricate *The Bloom of Matter* series. However, the delicacy of the line and the rococo palette of her drawings have given way to fluid brushwork and a saturated palette. Inhabited with women—including the artist herself—these works, many produced for her 1987 retrospective at the Art Gallery of Ontario, continue to puzzle yet fascinate viewers and critics alike.

Paintings such as *Experiment with Life* (1983) and *Paint Phantom* (1983–1984) are fully charged allegories in which the forces of creation and destruction are locked in an eternal, primordial battle. Traditional artist/model, male/female, art/life relationships are reversed, distorted, and delivered with lyrical violence. Wieland's lifelong love of classical music and historic European painting finds its place, revealed in her art-historical references that imbue these paintings with a mannerist quality and heighten the magnitude of the unfolding drama.

EXPERIMENT WITH LIFE

This group of works is among the last Wieland created, before Alzheimer's disease took over her life. Both intimate and large in scale, the romantic, fantastical scenes evoke distant and mythological lands—bucolic lands before time, yet charged with brutality, often set at twilight on hills and in valleys under clouds. They recall Wieland's early stained and colourful canvases, and have the same pulsating inner energy that first established her as a critical painter in Canada.

ARTEMIS, 1983

After three decades filled with paintings, quilts, assemblages, films, bookworks, and bronzes, Wieland trials yet another medium for artistic expression with *Artemis*. Instead of the lithography stone of *O Canada* (1970) (p. 149) or *Facing North — Self Impression* (1973) (p. 188), she presses her face repeatedly against the glass plate of a photocopier. Filmic frames are now standardized sheets of paper. Process colours of cyan, magenta, yellow, and black superpose and pull away from each other in this unique impression.

Non-art technologies quickly gained credibility in the Conceptualism-friendly art world of the late 1960s and early 1970s, and xerography was one. Almost immediately after colour copiers were available as an administrative tool, artists used them.[1] Wieland was well aware of the growing copy industry, having shot footage at a Xerox retraining centre in 1967, which eventually became her film *Handtinting*.[2] When she turned to the "hybrid camera / printing press"[3] technology herself in 1983, it was still freshly receptive to experimentation.

In trying new media, Wieland revisits old genre. A self-portrait multiplied by ten, *Artemis* runs alongside the same year's *Artist on Fire*, in a period that tends to be noted for her return to painting. As Anna Hudson writes, "Early in her career Wieland had fancied the predicament of being a woman and, therefore, the subject of her own artistic gaze."[4] Once again, in what would be the final decade of her career, she re-places herself in that predicament, over and over. "ARTEMIS" in the final frame of this self-portrait identifies the divine persona that Wieland assumes, the most fiercely independent of all the Greek goddesses.

In the first few frames, Artemis/Wieland pushes her way through foliage, collaged or, rather, amassed on the plate. Stuff goes into her mouth or comes out of it like Botticelli's Chloris in *Primavera* (c. 1480). This goddess, however, is in her mid-fifties, putting herself out there, accentuating folds and wrinkles by squishing them. Artemis/Wieland disrupts art-historical imaging of the goddess, and of women in general, while at the same time reinventing the goddess's tenets: vegetation, birth, the hunt, the wild.[5] In later frames, Artemis/Wieland appears to have fashioned the assembled foliage, wearing it on her head and around her neck, smiling and laughing as if at some kind of transposed earthly or godly office party (a friend briefly joins in frame six). Only in the final frame, with just her hands and hair and name written across her forehead, Artemis/Wieland peers at us (we are inside the machine?), assured.

ALICIA BOUTILIER

1 3M launched the first colour copier, Color-in-Color, in 1969, and Xerox the first electrostatic colour copier, Xerox 6500, in 1973. Following a residency at 3M, artist Sonia Sheridan used a Color-in-Color machine in Jack Burnham's exhibition *Software*, at the Jewish Museum, New York, in 1970; a Xerox 6500 was the focus of *Colour Xerography*, curated by Karyn Allen at the Art Gallery of Ontario, Toronto, in 1976; and Ginnie Lloyd opened *Copy Art Exhibition* at La Mamelle, Inc., in San Francisco in 1980, which toured internationally—to name a few.

2 See Canadian Women Film Directors Database, http://femfilm.ca/film_search.php?film=wieland-handtinting&lang=e.

3 To borrow a phrase from *Experiments in Electrostatics: Photocopy Art from the Whitney's Collection, 1966–1986*, curated by Michelle Donnelly, Whitney Art Museum, New York, 2018.

4 Anna Hudson, "Wonder Women and Goddesses," in *Woman as Goddess: Liberated Nudes by Robert Markle and Joyce Wieland*, exh. cat. (Toronto: Art Gallery of Ontario, 2003), 47.

5 The goddess's sacred animal, the deer, is also dear to the artist, who captures them repeatedly in her later work.

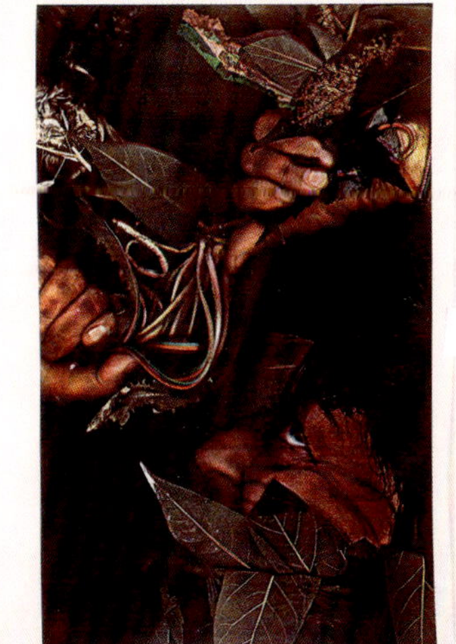
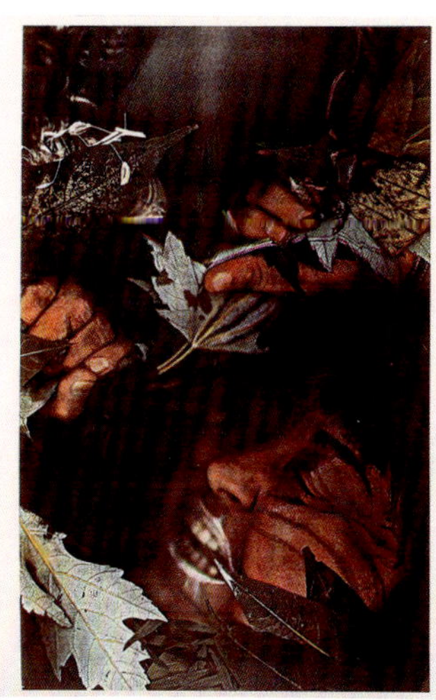
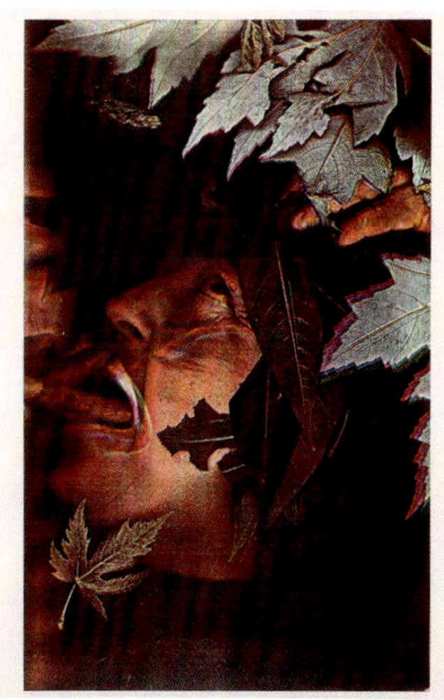
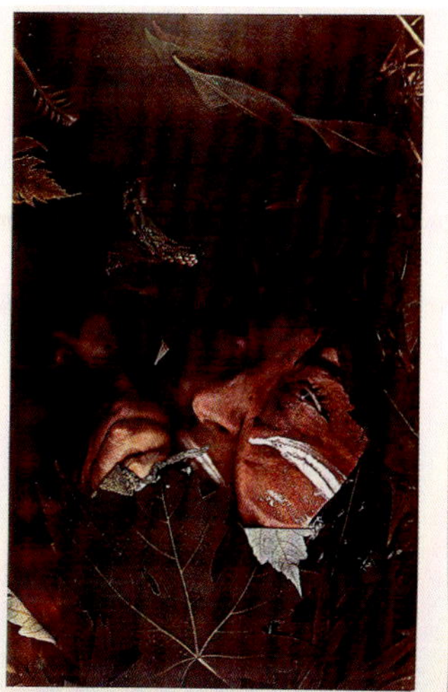
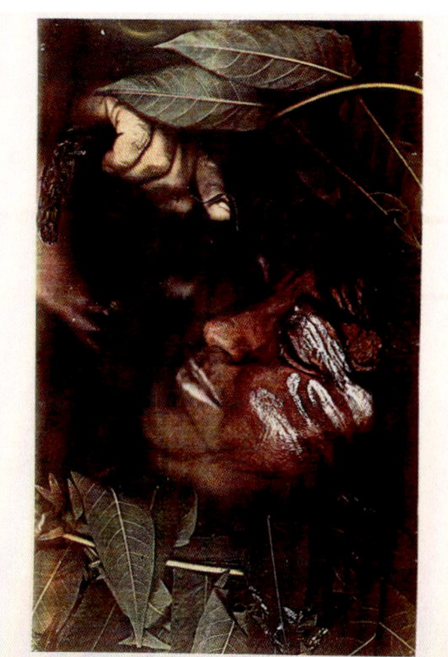
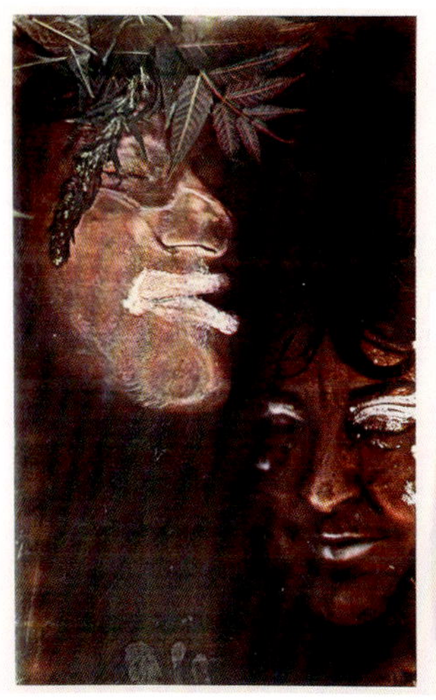
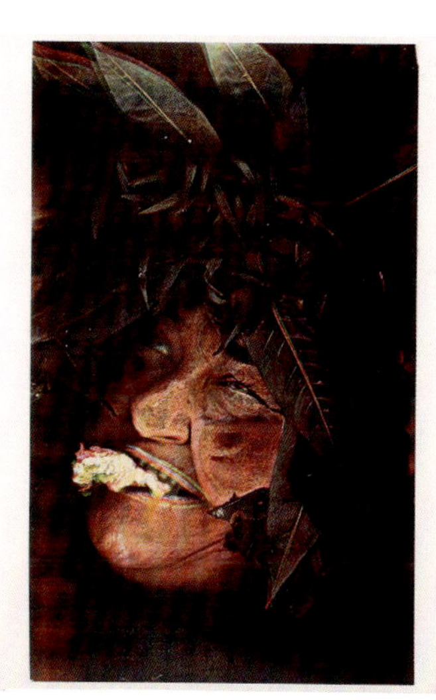
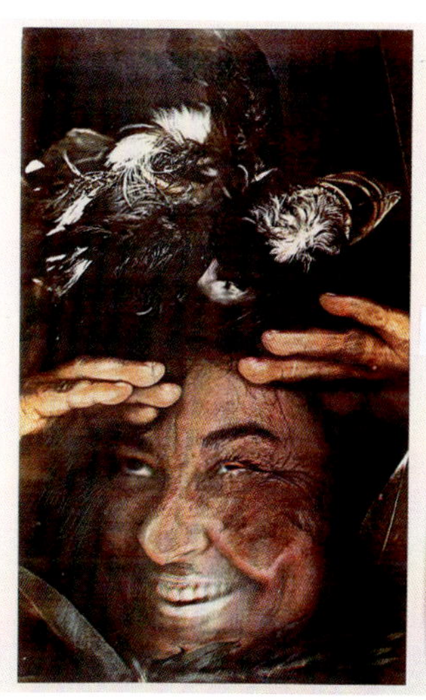
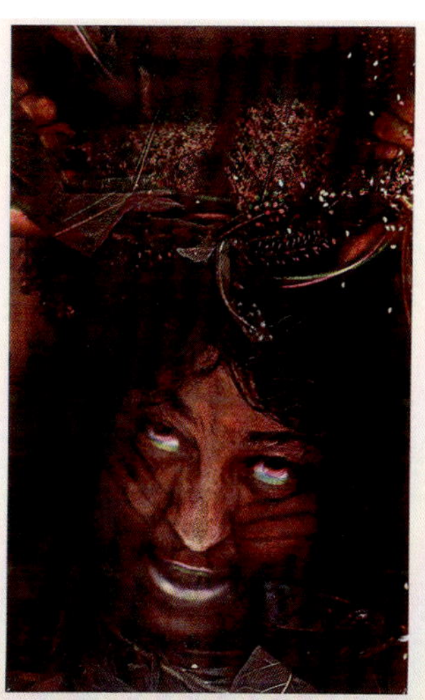
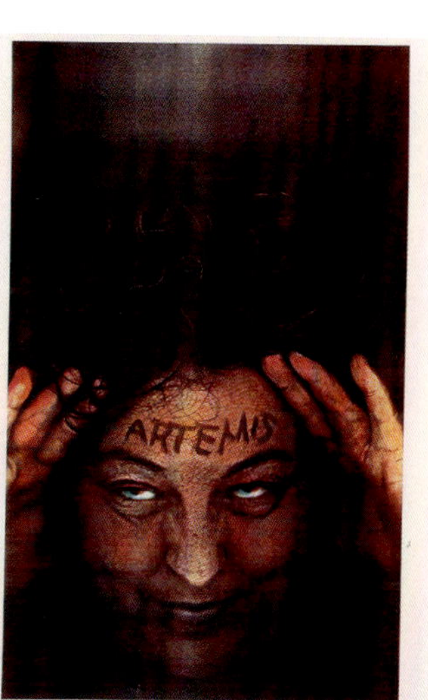

Artemis, 1983
10 colour Xerox photocopies
34.4 × 21 cm (each)
Agnes Etherington Art Centre, Queen's University, Kingston, ON, Purchased 2006, the Elizabeth L. Gordon Art Programme of the Walter and Duncan Gordon Foundation
49-013a-j
Photo: Bernard Clark

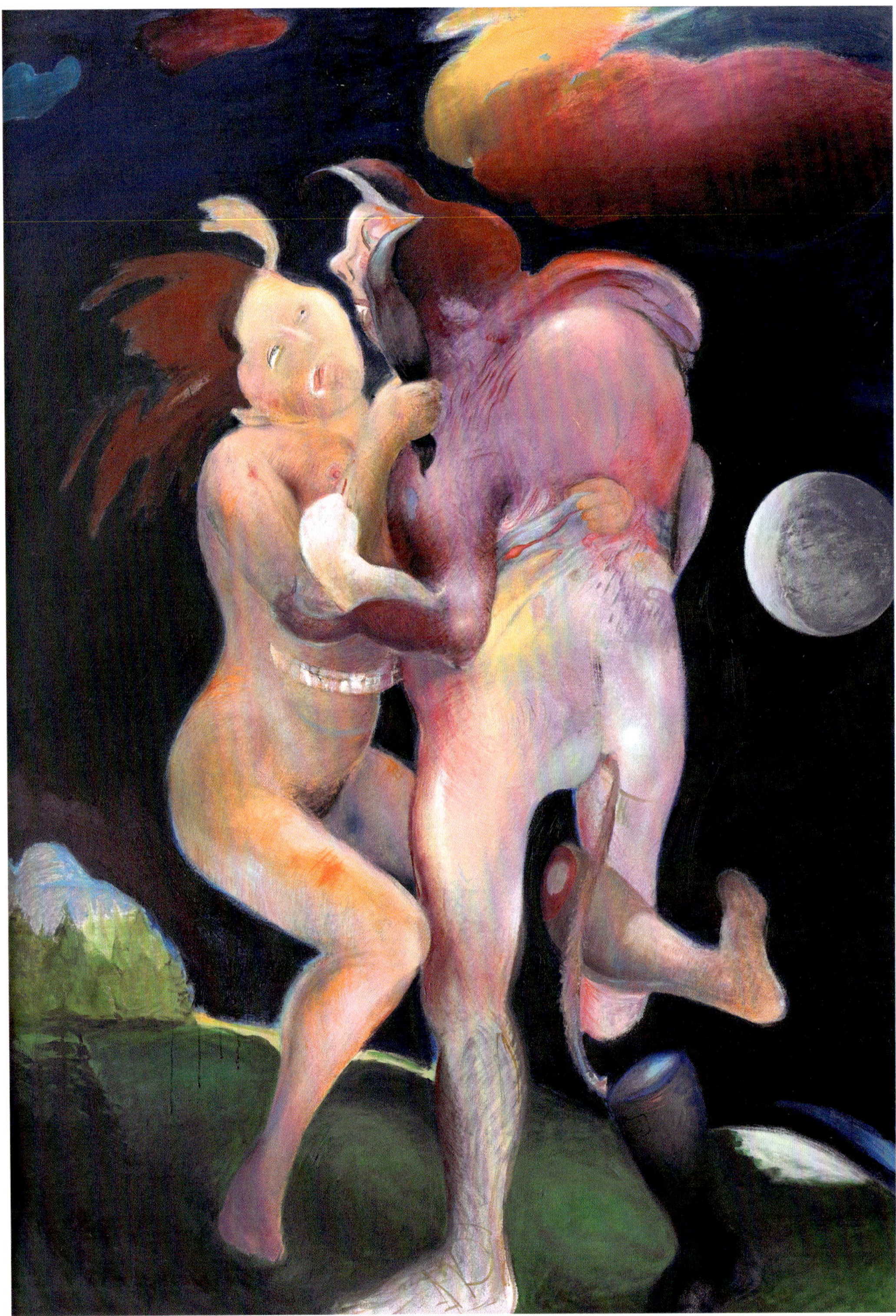

"Then from those [*The Bloom of Matter*] drawings later came the paintings, which didn't exactly reiterate every theme in the coloured drawings, but they started a whole new phase, a different style of painting than I'd ever done. About nature again, about people, about struggles between men and women, about cataclysms. And a knowledge of a certain kind of sky I liked, about trying to paint that. And then, after that, I was able to do very, very shamanistic works that were very deep, about my relationship with my father, being, and all kinds of struggles that were going on, but it took me about two or three years to get to the point of making *Paint Phantom*, say, or *The End of Life as She Knew It*."

LEFT
Paint Phantom, 1983–1984
Oil on canvas
170.2 × 121.9 cm
National Gallery of Canada, Purchased 1985
28803
Photo: NGC

OPPOSITE
Artist on Fire, 1983
Oil on canvas
107.2 × 130 cm
Collection of The Robert McLaughlin Gallery, Purchased 1984
1984WJ8
Photo: Laura Findlay

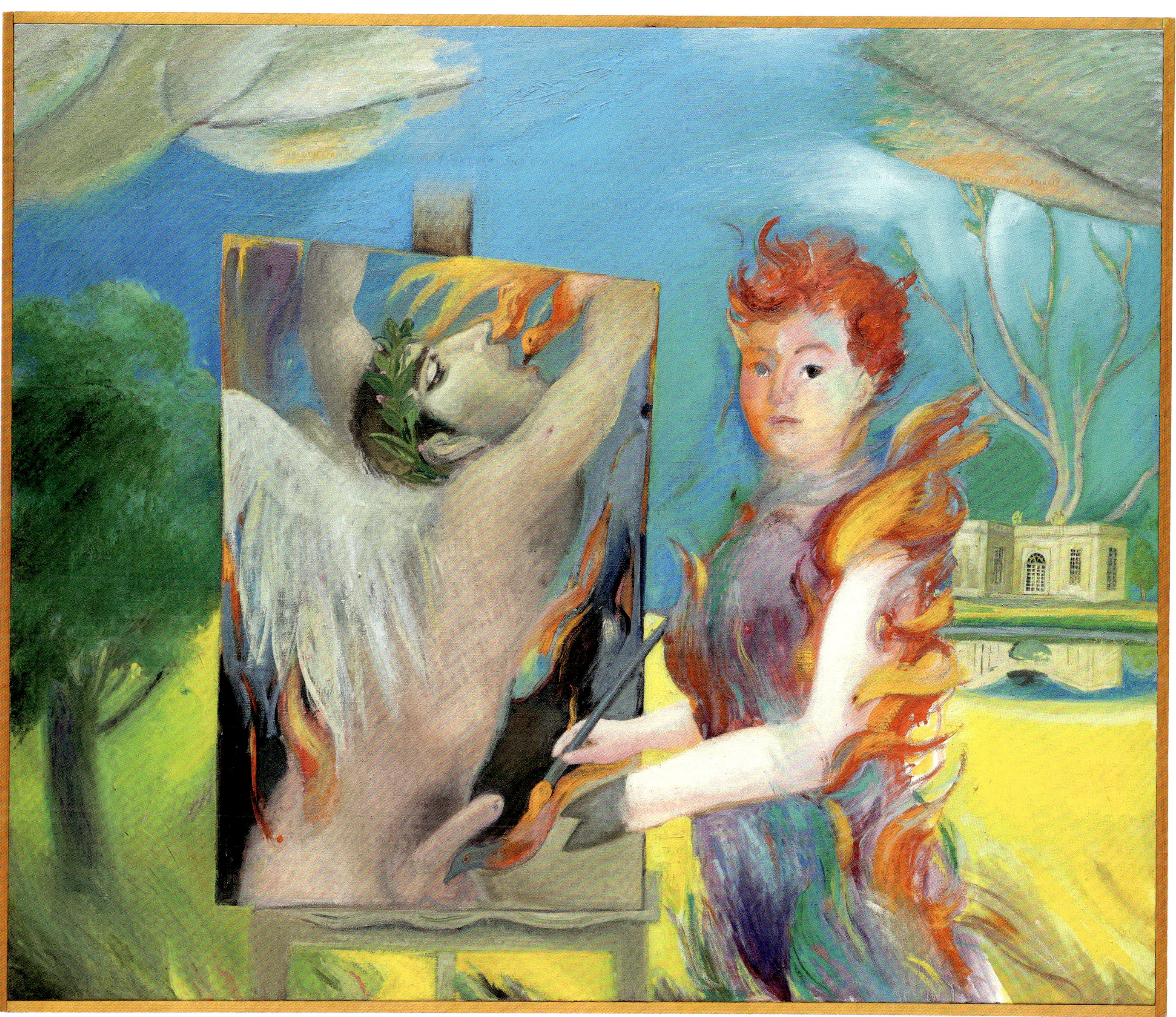

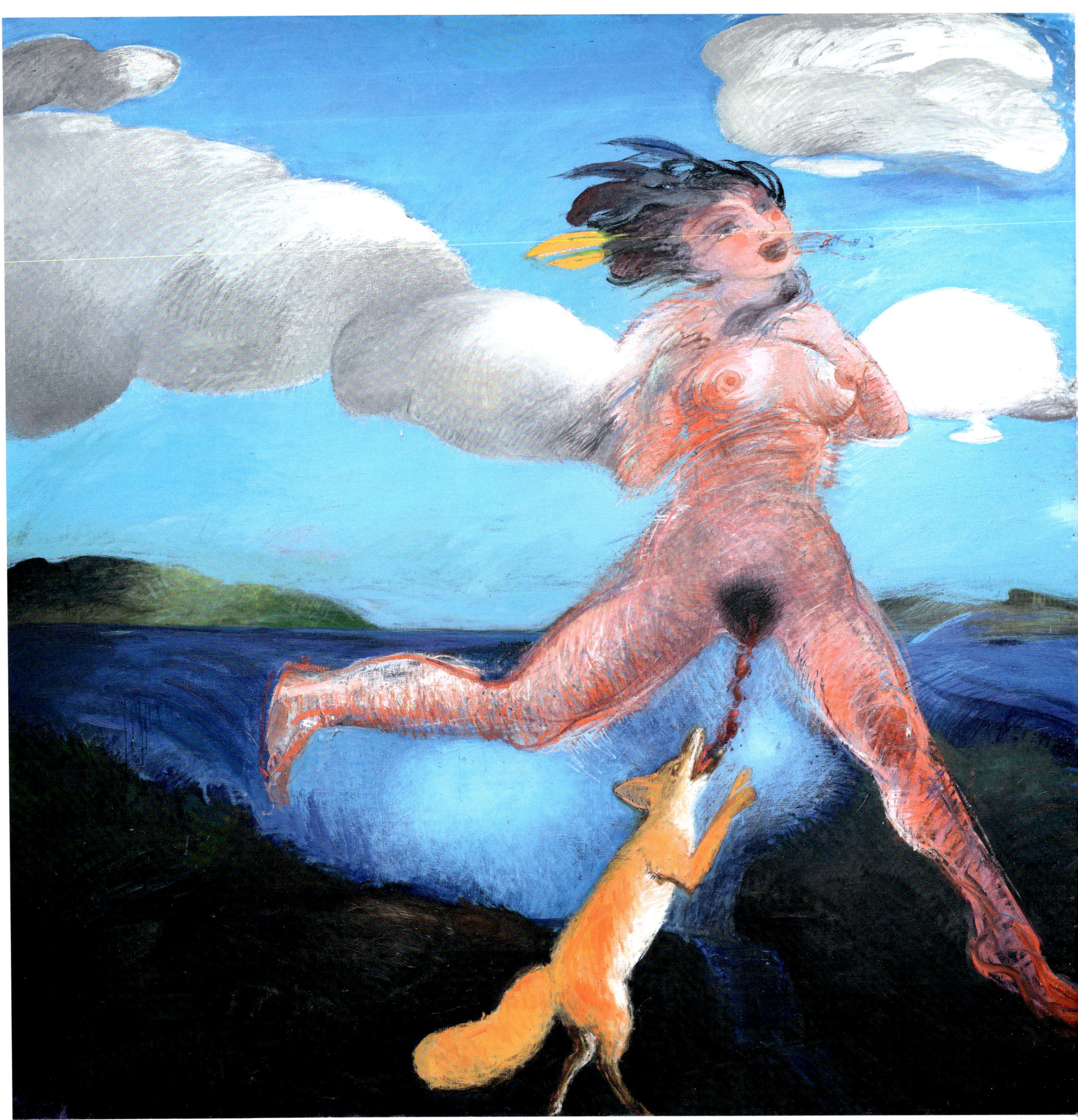

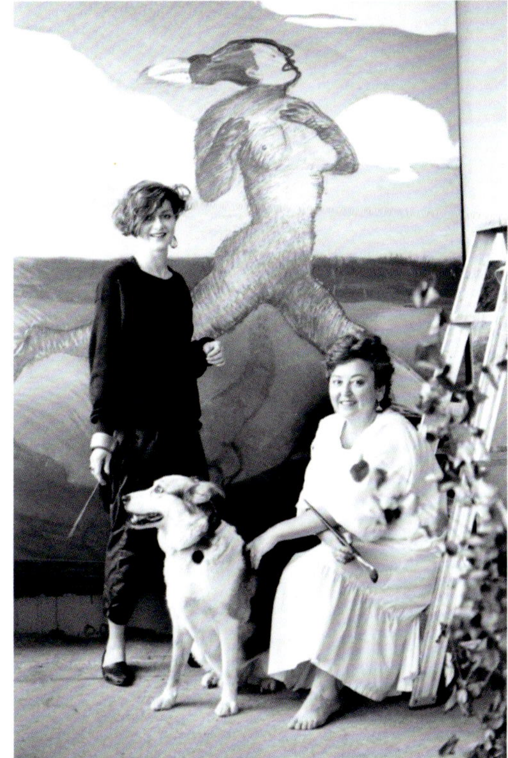

Left to right: Su Rynard, Jordy, and Joyce Wieland at 507 King Street East, 1987
Joyce Wieland fonds, ASC30001, York University Libraries, Clara Thomas Archives and Special Collections

WOMAN AND FOX, 1986

The first time I saw *Woman and Fox* was in 1986 at Joyce's studio at 507 King Street East. Joyce had phoned me—her niece, a student at the time, and occasionally her art and film helper—asking if I would join her and Jordy in a photo session.

When I arrived at the studio, I encountered a huge painting in progress and recognized that this would be no ordinary art-documentation session. I was stepping into a Wieland creation—a tableau depicting the artist at work. Joyce wore a white cotton dress and was barefoot, and I was in my 1980s art-school garb. Jordy, it turned out, was a dog. Paint brushes in hand, we posed in various configurations with our canine companion.

A decade passed before I laid eyes on the finished painting: Against a backdrop of plump clouds and turquoise sky, a naked, rose-coloured woman takes a joyful leap across the canvas. She is airborne—hair feathers flying. Her expression is one of exultation. A song bursts from her mouth. An orange fox laps at a globular stream of blood that flows from between her legs. The landscape is undoubtedly the west coast of Newfoundland, where Joyce spent many summers; a remote and extraordinarily beautiful place where a swath of green meadow meets dramatic rock cliffs that plunge down to a turbulent cerulean sea.

There was a fox there, too.

Animals appear frequently in Joyce's artwork. They are watchful, engaged, and often in an intimate exchange with their human companions. On Joyce's Earth, it is natural for a woman to suckle a beaver, for a fox to drink menstrual blood, for a dog to participate in a photo session. Such entanglements occur in an animate world. They seem pleasant and mutually beneficial. Here, menstruation (the curse) and a taboo exchange with a fox are a positive force.

Had it not been for the photographs taken in the studio that day, I would not have remembered my early encounter with the painting. A mere ten years after this, Joyce would not have remembered either. She was suffering from a cruel disease that slowly took away her spirit, her memory, then her life. We are the lucky ones who benefit from the joy and love that lives on in this work. Forty years on, a first encounter with *Woman and Fox* is still sure to shock.

SU RYNARD

OPPOSITE
Woman and Fox, 1986
Oil on canvas
238.76 × 248.92 cm
Collection of Susan Rynard
Photo: AGO, Craig Boyko

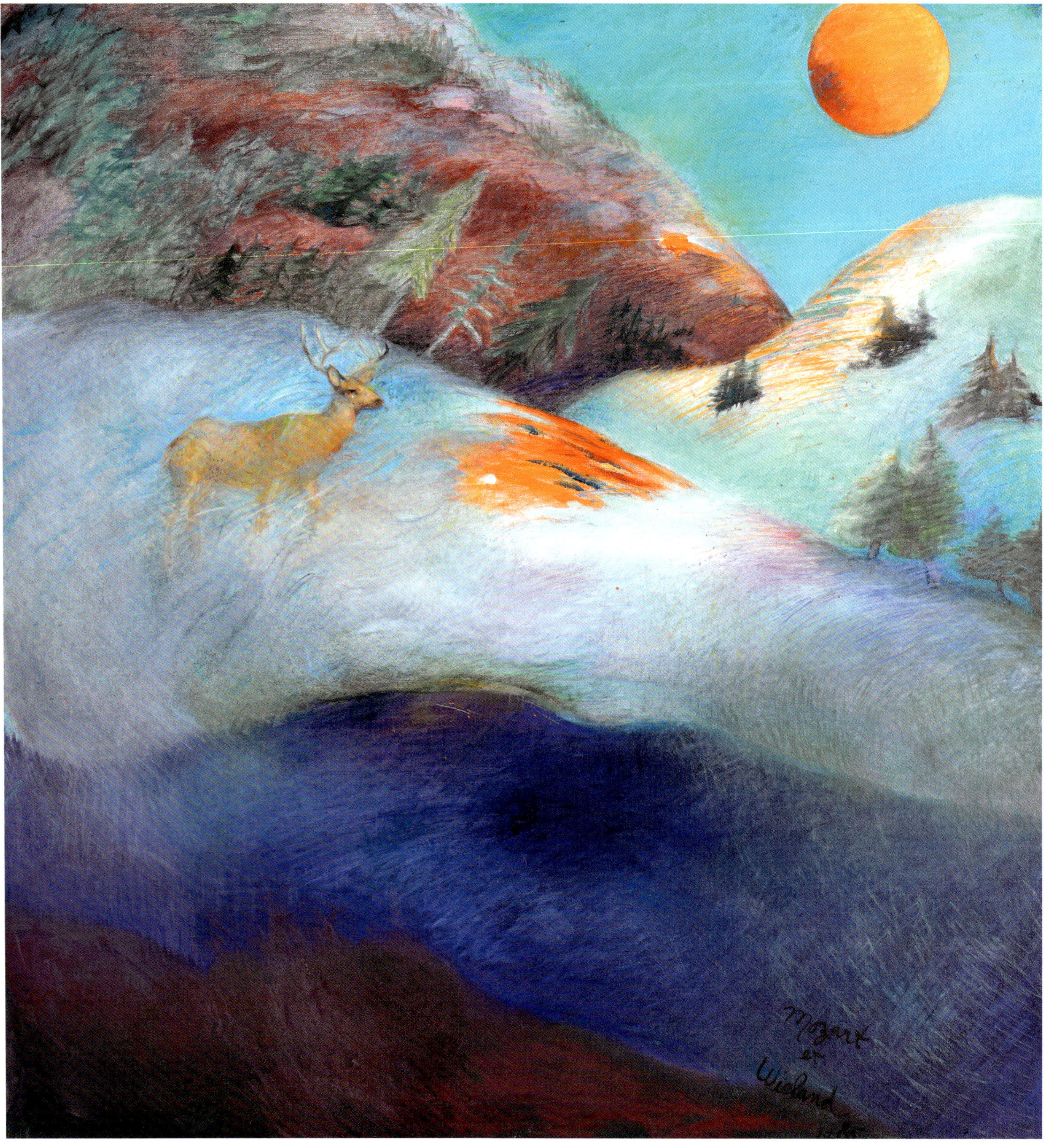
Mozart
et
Wieland

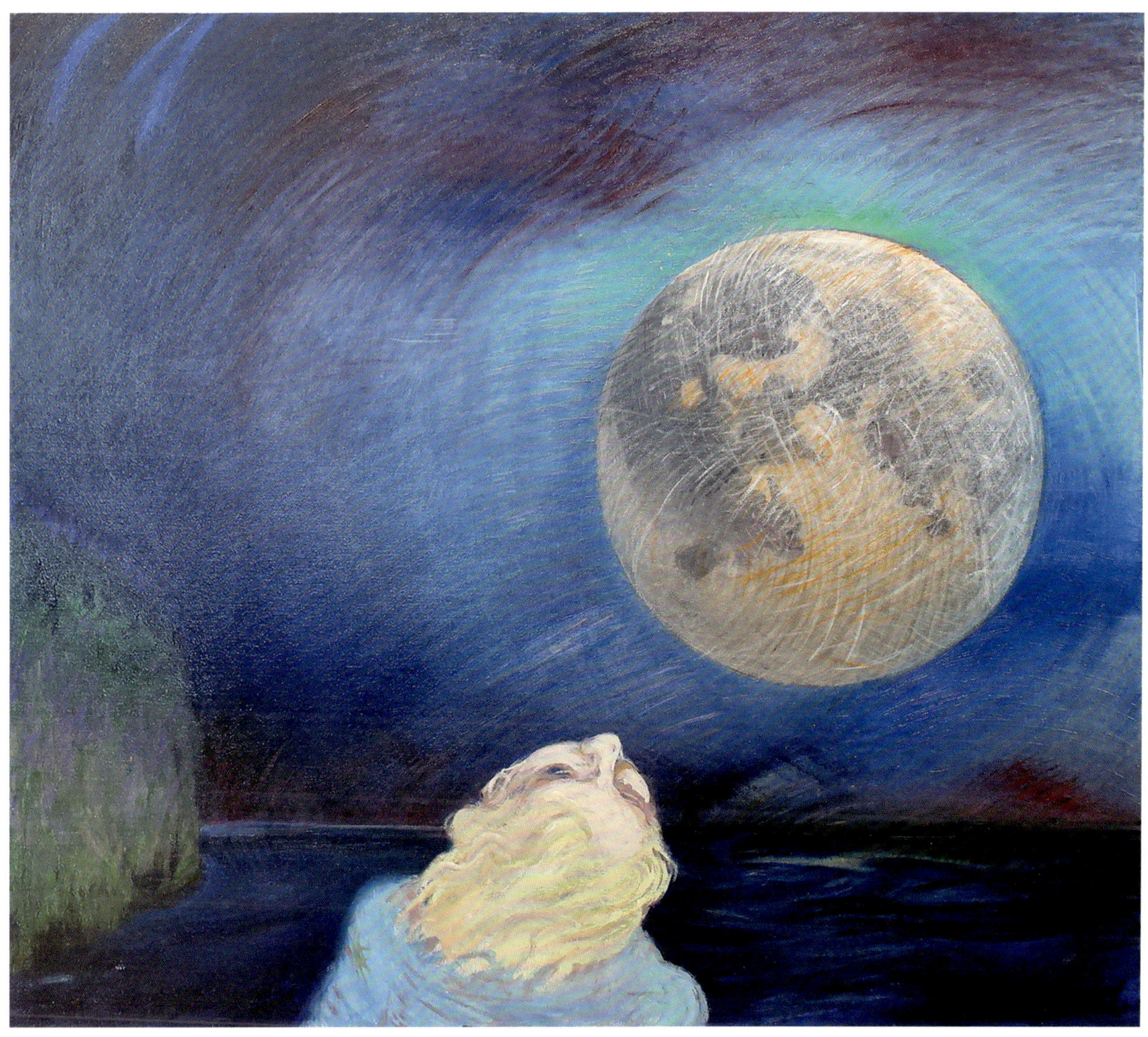

OPPOSITE
Mozart and Wieland, 1985
Oil on canvas
137.2 × 129.6 cm
Art Gallery of Ontario,
Gift of Hyman and Ruth Soloway, 2012
2012/10
Photo: AGO, Craig Boyko

ABOVE
Ann's Moon, 1986
Oil on canvas
81.3 × 94 cm
Private Collection, Mississauga, ON
1780
Photo: The Kalaman Group

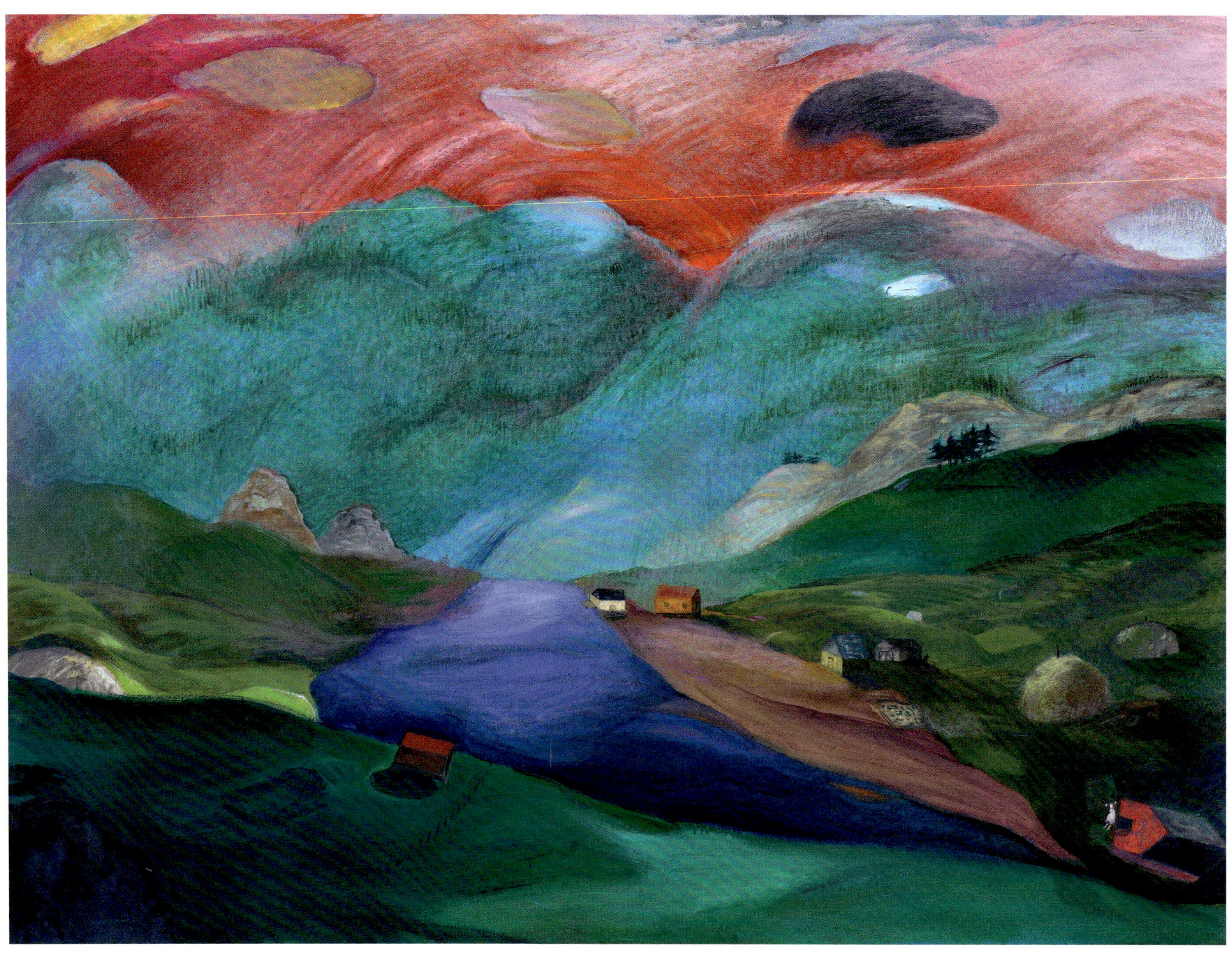

Early One Morning, 1986
Oil on canvas
99.3 × 134.9 cm
Art Gallery of Ontario. Purchased with funds donated by AGO Members, and with funds from the Estate of Mary Eileen Ash and the Estate of Christian Claude, 2008
2008/55
Photo: AGO, Craig Boyko

OPPOSITE
Experiment with Life, 1983
Oil on canvas
62.1 × 82.4 cm
National Gallery of Canada, Purchased 1983
28244
Photo: NGC

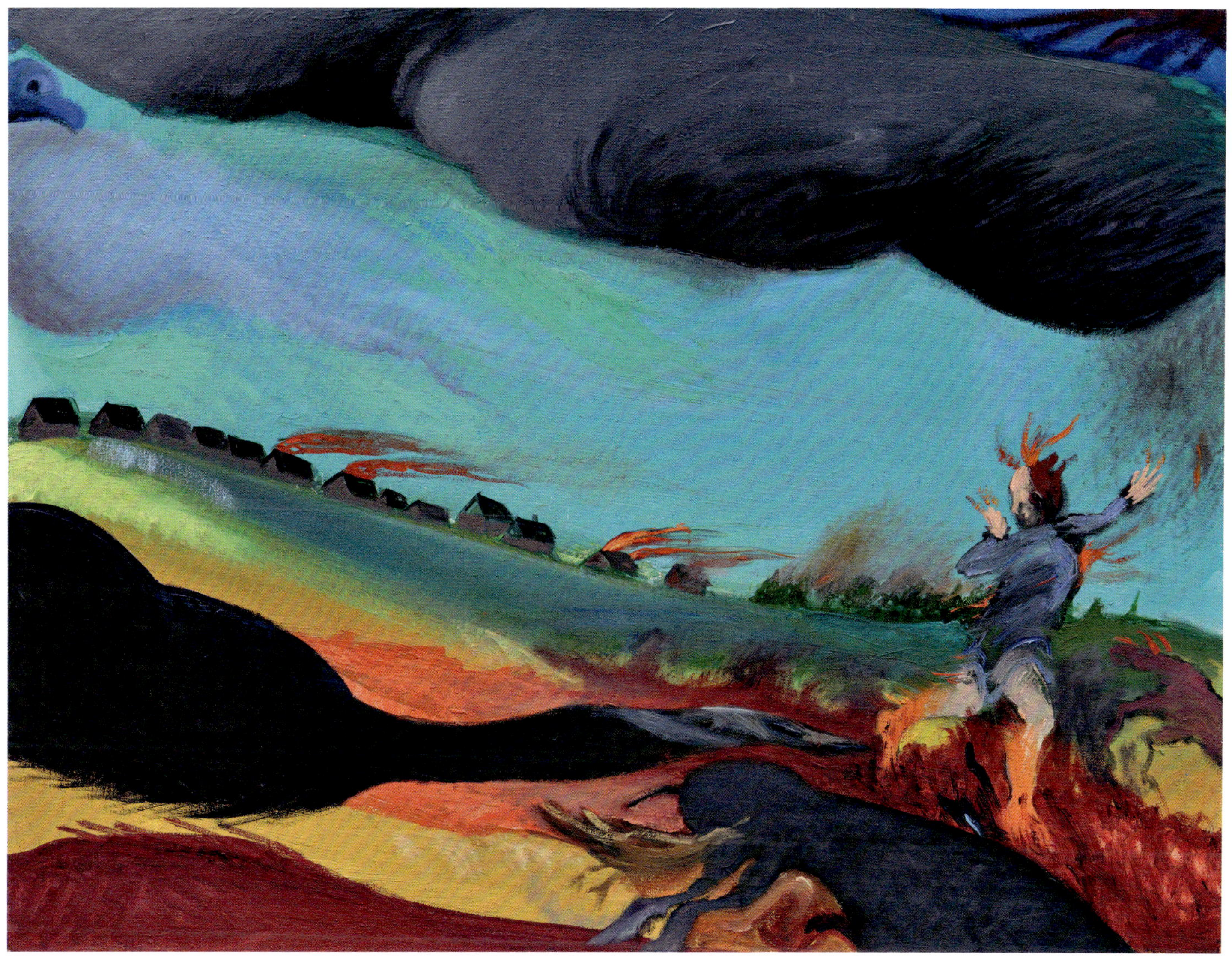

"[*Experiment with Life*] started as a kind of disaster in the suburbs; as though they had bombed Scarborough; and then I left it. The figure hadn't appeared or the flames. It was around for eighteen months. One day I picked it up. I had a very strong feeling [that] I wanted to express something about Vietnam and the thousands of people killed by experiments with chemicals. . . . When I paint something like that, I have a terrible need to do it. The need was so great that it just came out in an hour and a half after waiting eighteen months."

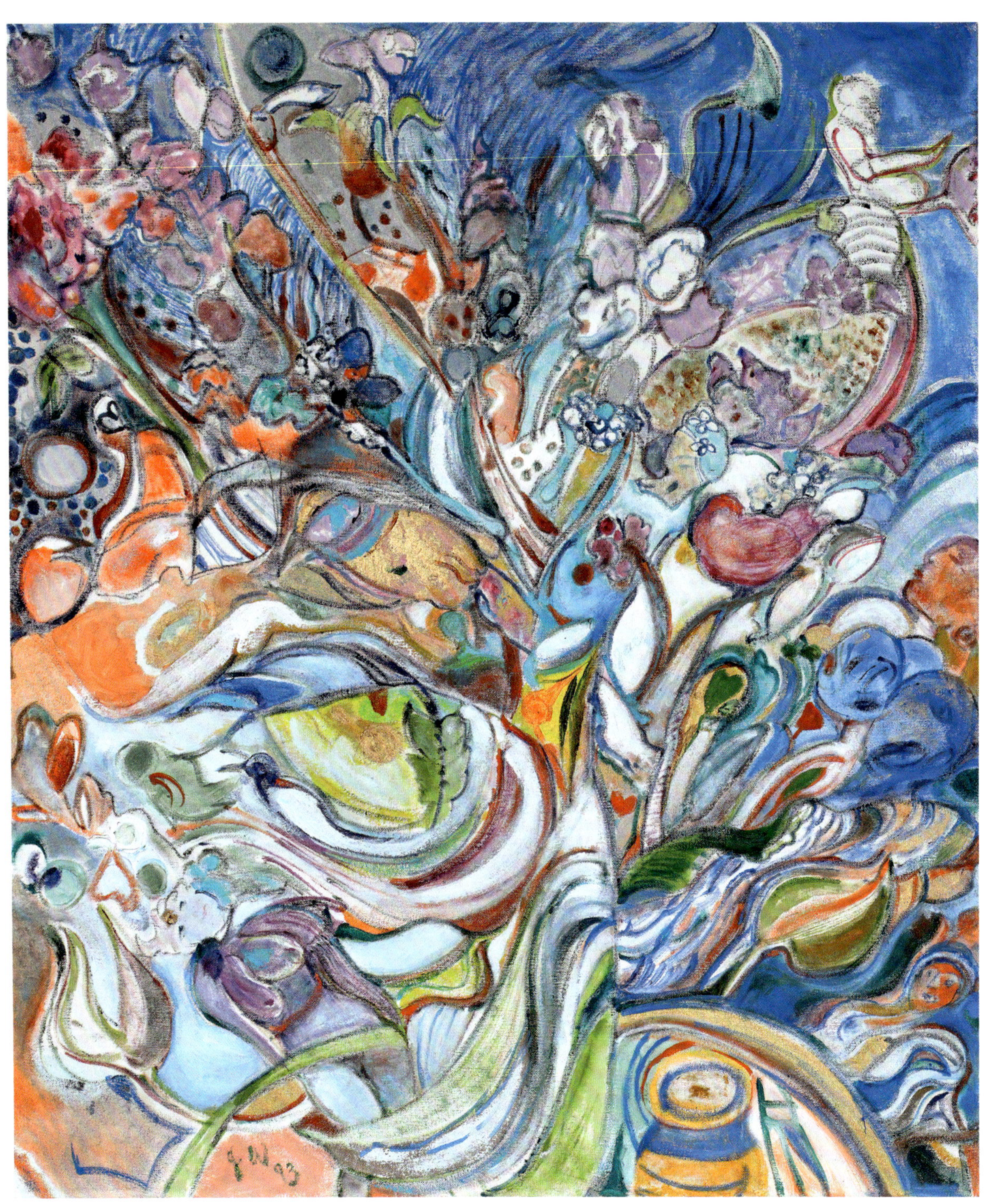

Dreamland, 1983
Oil on canvas
86 × 74 cm
Private Collection, Canada
Photo: AGO, Sean Weaver

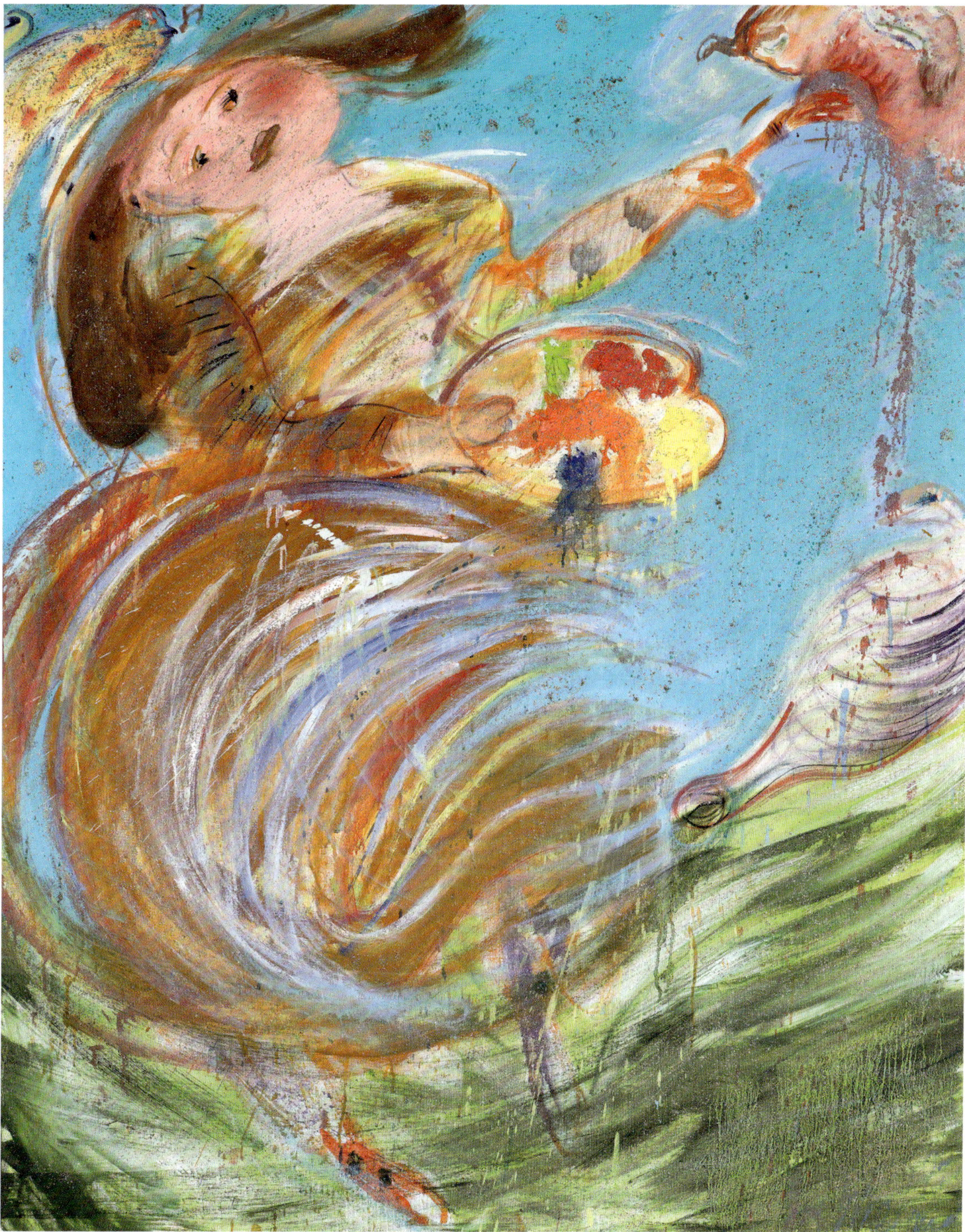

The Peasant Painter, 1987
Oil on canvas
134 × 109 cm
Private Collection, Canada
Photo: AGO, Sean Weaver

CELEBRATION, 1987

Wieland executed her last major commission in 1987, a large painting for the relaunch of the Pantages Theatre in Toronto. *Celebration* radiates the spirit of its title and playfully alludes to aspects of the theatre's history. The lively colours—almost saccharine—rhythms, and figures take on personal significance for Wieland, who had recently travelled to England to trace her genealogy. There she discovered that her father's family comprised three generations of circus and vaudeville performers, including trapeze artists, musicians, and ventriloquists.

The legacy of the Pantages Theatre also ran deep. When it opened in 1920, it was the largest theatre in Canada, with 3,373 seats; it was also touted as the country's most elegant. Owned by Famous Players Canadian Corporation, its management and booking were the responsibility of the Pantages consortia, one of the biggest producers of vaudeville and cinema circuits on the continent. The company was founded in the Yukon by Greek immigrant Alexander Pantages (1867–1936), who had arrived in North America as a deckhand on a merchant ship and, like many others, ended up seeking his fortune in the 1897 Klondike Gold Rush.[1] Wieland would certainly have revelled in the opportunity to bring this fascinating nugget of Canadian history to light, especially because vaudeville, she realized, was now part of her own story. In fact, to the left of the painting is a minute version of herself—mirror in hand, from which flows a rainbow of colours.

ANNE GRACE

Celebration has fresh relevance to contemporary painting: irreverent cartoon playfulness, political subtext, sexuality and Bollywood-like dancing deities whose romances and pleasure play out in various narratives.

At first glance, the painting seems to rush out at the viewer in a blast of colour and movement. Is the exuberance a cover? Beneath it lurks a darker sensibility. Wieland loved to hide secret messages in her paintings. These clues reward the viewer only after repeated scrutiny. As with film, the painting's stories are told in different rhythms and tempos.

A redhead lounges on a globe with "canada" drawn on it. A policeman struggles as he rolls the globe towards the centre of gravity of the painting. Does this moist pink and red vortex represent the seduction of Hollywood, far from the placid Canadian landscape depicted on the right? The starlet may be Fay Wray, a natural redhead. She was one of the most famous movie stars of the 1930s and best known for being abducted by a gorilla in *King Kong*. Wray was born in 1907 on a ranch near Cardston, Alberta.

Among the motifs in the painting are discs, globes, life rings, propellers, spirals of smoke from falling planes, fish and fertility symbols, red lips and hearts, interracial romance, cops and robbers, all found floating, falling, spiralling out of control. There are exits and entrances, survival and tragedy, tiny figures caught up in the swirl of illusion.

A jazz musician holds a trumpet and talkies advance from the silent screen. A band of silver leaf across the top of the canvas suggests the silver screen. A globe in gold leaf—sun or coin?—recalls the original gold leaf in the Pantages Theatre along with the gaudy yellows, blues, and reds of its 1973 renovation.

As with much of Wieland's work, the painting's bravado and orgasmic, unrestrained energy were threatening to some in its time. Yet, with its mastery of intent and scale, *Celebration* can only be viewed as a major work within Wieland's oeuvre.

BARBARA STEINMAN

Edited transcript of an unpublished text on Celebration*, 2009.*

1 In a sordid turn of events, Famous Players renamed the cinema the Imperial Theatre in 1930, after Pantages was convicted in Los Angeles of assaulting a seventeen-year-old dancer and sentenced to fifty years in prison. The conviction was overturned in a 1931 retrial in which Pantages's lawyers sought to discredit his accuser (using evidence that would be inadmissible today), and made claims of a high-level conspiracy against their magnate client.

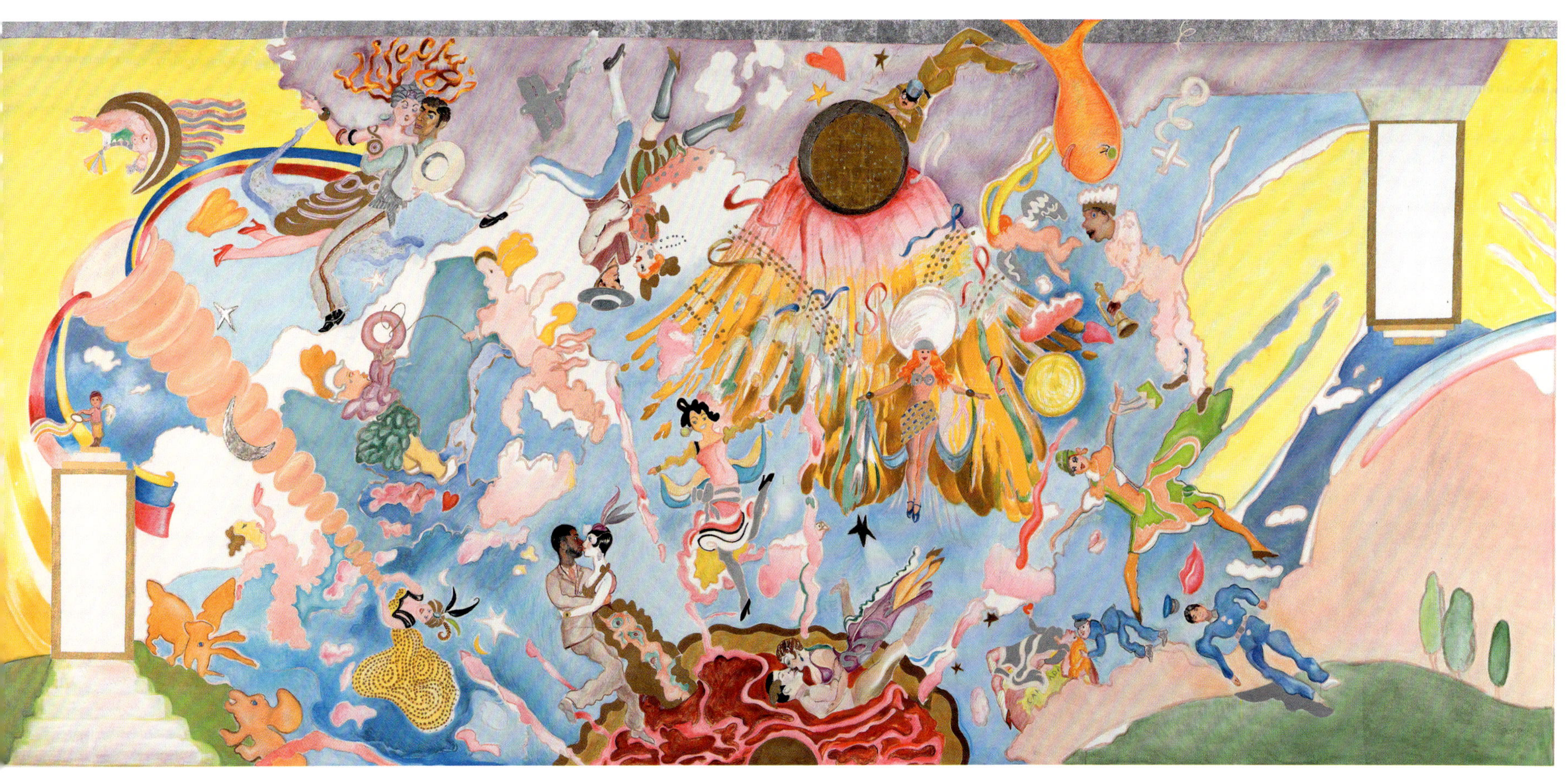

Celebration, 1987
Oil paint, silver and gold leaf, silver and copper metal foil and glitter on canvas
213 × 457 cm
The Montreal Museum of Fine Arts, Anonymous gift
2020.240
Photo: MMFA, Jean-François Brière

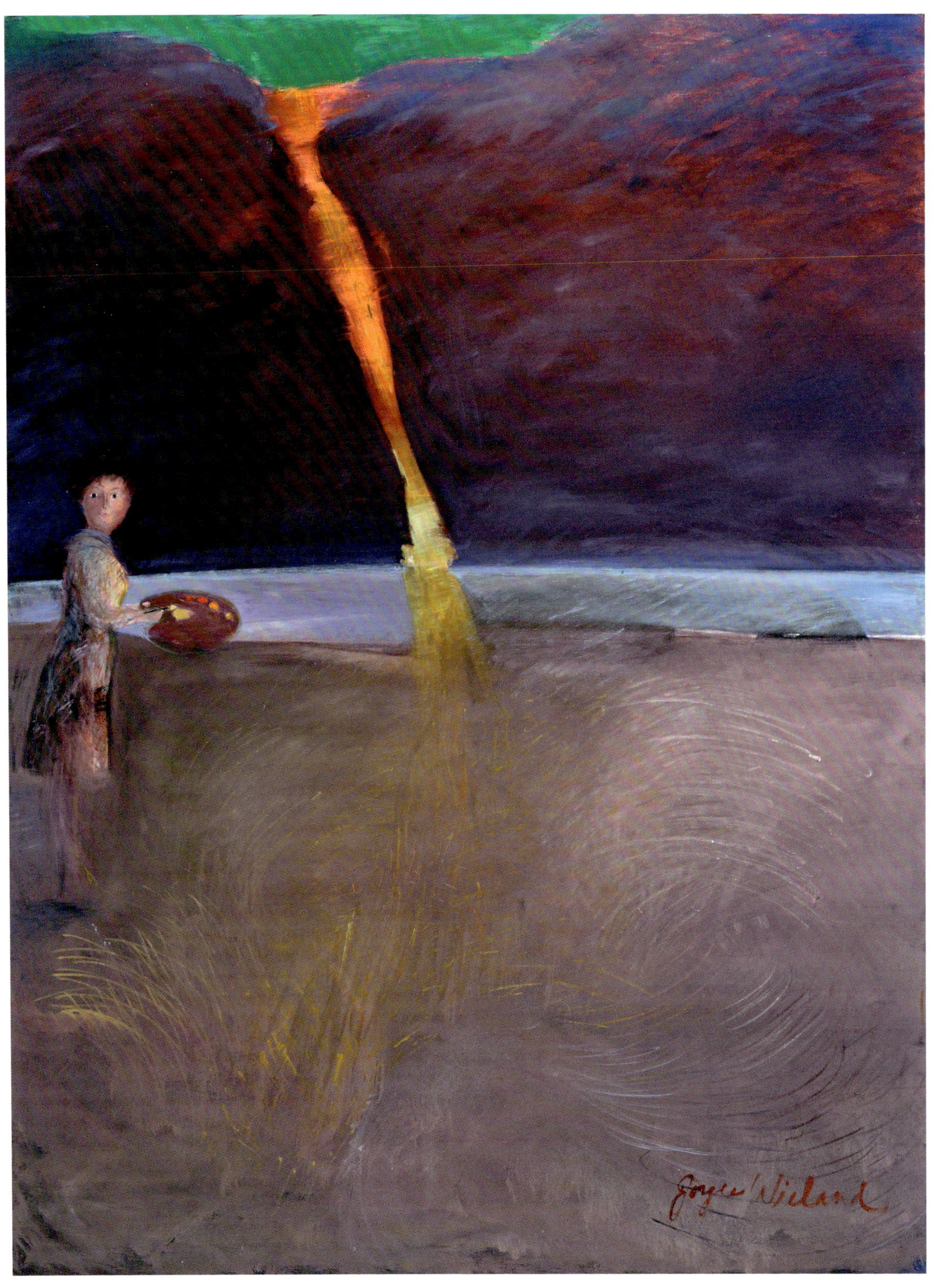

Shaping Matter,
1990–1991
Oil on canvas
180 × 142 cm
Collection of Munro Ferguson
Photo: MMFA, Julie Ciot

SHAPING MATTER, 1990–1991

The "what" itself matters, poet, novelist, and editor Daphne Marlatt emphasizes in her book *What Matters: Writing 1967–70.*[1]

So too with artist Joyce Wieland, the "what" itself matters: plants matter, animals matter, the sky and the ground matter. In her vast body of artwork spanning over three decades, she made sculptures and paintings, prints, artist books, performances, and films. Her approach was shaped by extensive research and her embodied sensibility, making meaning and directing our attention as viewers to "what matters," often humorously. She responsively and passionately indicated again and again that care was needed for the ecosystem and the earth that we are part of, not the owners of, which requires our participation and our protection. She took on the mythologies, the histories, the symbols of nations, regions, and place, playing with meaning through their physical manifestation and details, and took it all both seriously and with a profound humour, conveying a love of life and the world through her artwork.

In Wieland's painting *Shaping Matter*, viewers encounter the scene of a woman, an artist with palette and brush, her head turned toward us, in a landscape that is electrifyingly taking shape: the bolt's movement is central, its orangey-yellow glow flowing, tracing its image in the darkened sky onto the grasses in the ground, onto the artist herself—note the yellow lines of paint mark-making. The artist with her brush strokes is shaping the matter: transformation is taking place. The artist figure is standing, observing, is still, her eyes focused on us: the phenomena of the bolt's trajectory implying movement. The painting gives a moment in time of this occurrence, this possibly visionary experience. The artist figure in *Shaping Matter* has a familial echo from an earlier painting she made: a winged angel, trees around and below her as if she is both grounded and floating in the sky, viewing the flames surrounding the figure of visionary saint and martyr Jeanne d'Arc, in *Purification of Joan* (1983).

Her body of work conveys a gesture extended outward to the world, as gifts to the viewers. Within *Shaping Matter*, the stillness of the figure is notable. She is a grand dame, an extraordinary person, a great artist, an "old mistress" (in a line of old masters), without a place and without her influences or a "school" so that her line in art history would be assured.[2]

Pierre Théberge, who was a curator of contemporary art—and, later, director—of the National Gallery of Canada for her solo exhibition there in 1971, *True Patriot Love*, and then the director of the Montreal Museum of Fine Arts, described our mutual friend Joyce Wieland as

> *one of the great visionary artists of our time, like Paul-Émile Borduas and Emily Carr, who had a sense of things around them—not just isolated personal dramas ... In their work, they look out and see how things are ... Why isn't Joyce better known and appreciated in terms of the art world? Perhaps it is because Joyce isn't macho enough ... because what she shows is so vulnerable, so honest ... It's very real. It punches you. It makes people uneasy. It's not entertaining.*
>
> *I related that to Van Gogh in terms of vulnerability and rawness. He was a very embarrassing person. There is a parallel here between Wieland and Van Gogh.*[3]

Shaping Matter conveys the presence of a great figure: eyes brightly gazing at us, with the sky alight. She is there, with her palette and brush, making a painting, a holder of such knowledge, such awareness, and wisdom, with a capacity for expansiveness.

LEILA SUJIR

1 Daphne Marlatt, Preface, *What Matters: Writing, 1968–70* (Toronto: Coach House, 1980).

2 See Rozsika Parker and Griselda Pollock, *Old Mistresses: Women, Art, and Ideology* (London: Routledge and Kegan Paul, 1981).

3 Pierre Théberge in conversation, March 6, 1987, later published for The Isaacs Gallery exhibition *Joyce Wieland: New Paintings*, April 25–May 15, 1987.

ENTRANCE TO NATURE, 1988

There is the sense both of the prehistoric and of the most contemporary in Joyce's work. Taking from artistic precedent and using it for her own purposes, [Joyce Wieland] looks to artists who have been significant to her in terms of handling of colour or materials. She was able to take from virtually every period in history and [from] many artists and create something unique.

She clearly chose to examine materials and artistic methods that had been classed as crafts—working specifically with female experience, female imagery, and female activities. In the quilts and the embroidery, her oeuvre speaks, at every level, to the feminine experience.

She is emblematic of Kandinsky's dictum about the spiritual role of the artist as prophet or seer—the artist as visionary. There is a quality of seeking to lead.

What is striking is her courage to address issues that others have not been prepared to deal with.

She addresses the feminine presence of the Earth, of the land, of its vulnerability and the artist's role to identify it and to identify with it. She creates free images in the land that come out of a particular experience of growth, nourishment, and future possibilities, as opposed to creating monuments or excavating the land and cutting it.

There are very few women who have confronted femininity, feminism, being a woman, and being an artist directly in their art without becoming literal. Joyce stands with those few women in this century who have done that. ››››

JOYCE ZEMANS

Edited transcript of Joyce Zemans' comments in the documentary film Artist on Fire: Joyce Wieland, *directed by Kay Armatage, 1987.*

OPPOSITE

Entrance to Nature, 1988
Canvas collage with oil, glitter, wire, cardboard, staples, metal pushpins mounted on plywood
193 × 226 cm
Collection of Sally Wright
Photo: AGO, Sean Weaver

NEXT SPREAD

Tess Boudreau Taconis
Joyce Wieland in her studio in the Montague's Home at 19 Prince Arthur Avenue, Toronto (detail), c. 1960
Gelatin silver print
24 × 34 cm
Courtesy of Ihor Holubizky
© Estate of Tess Boudreau Taconis

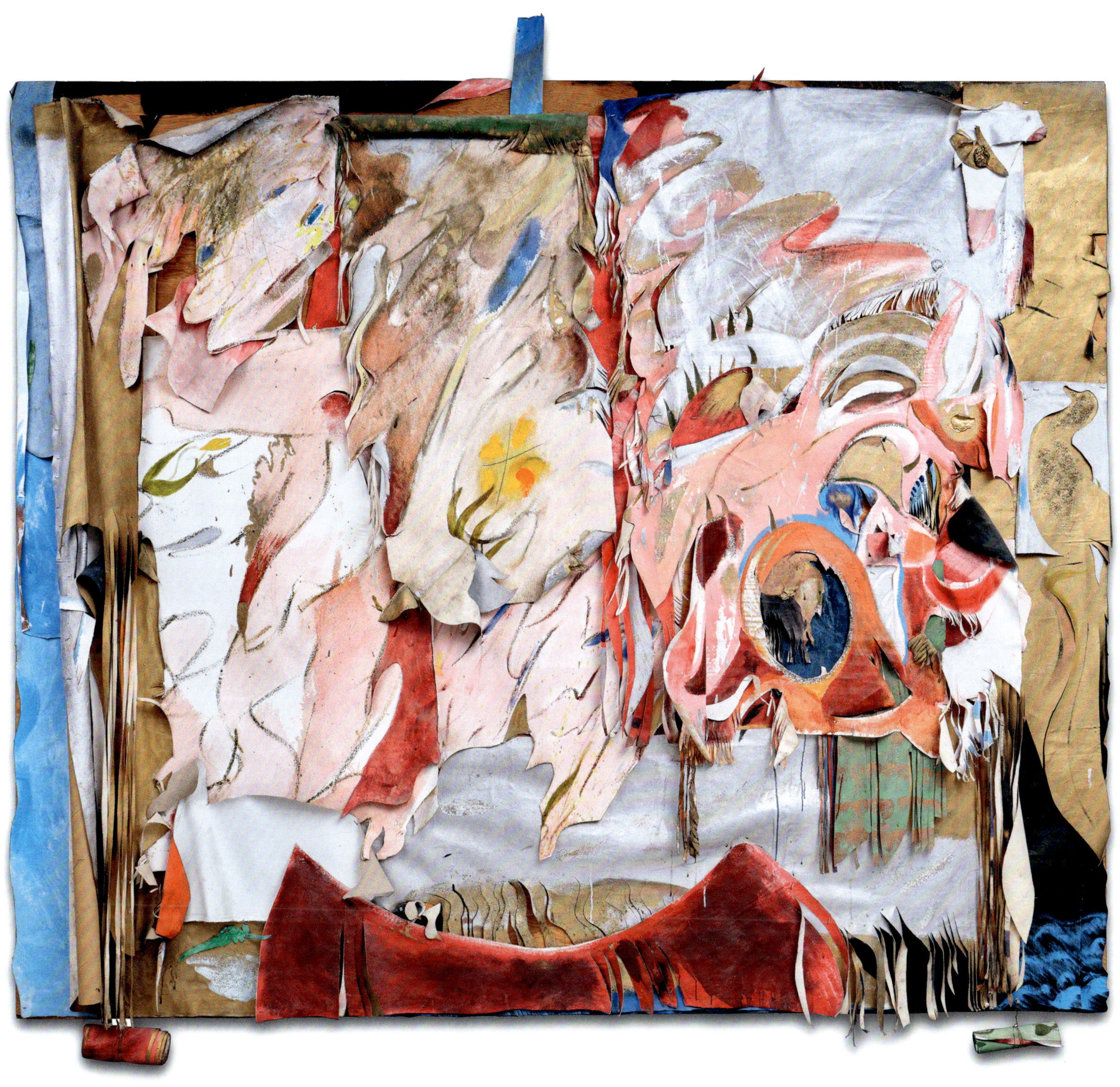

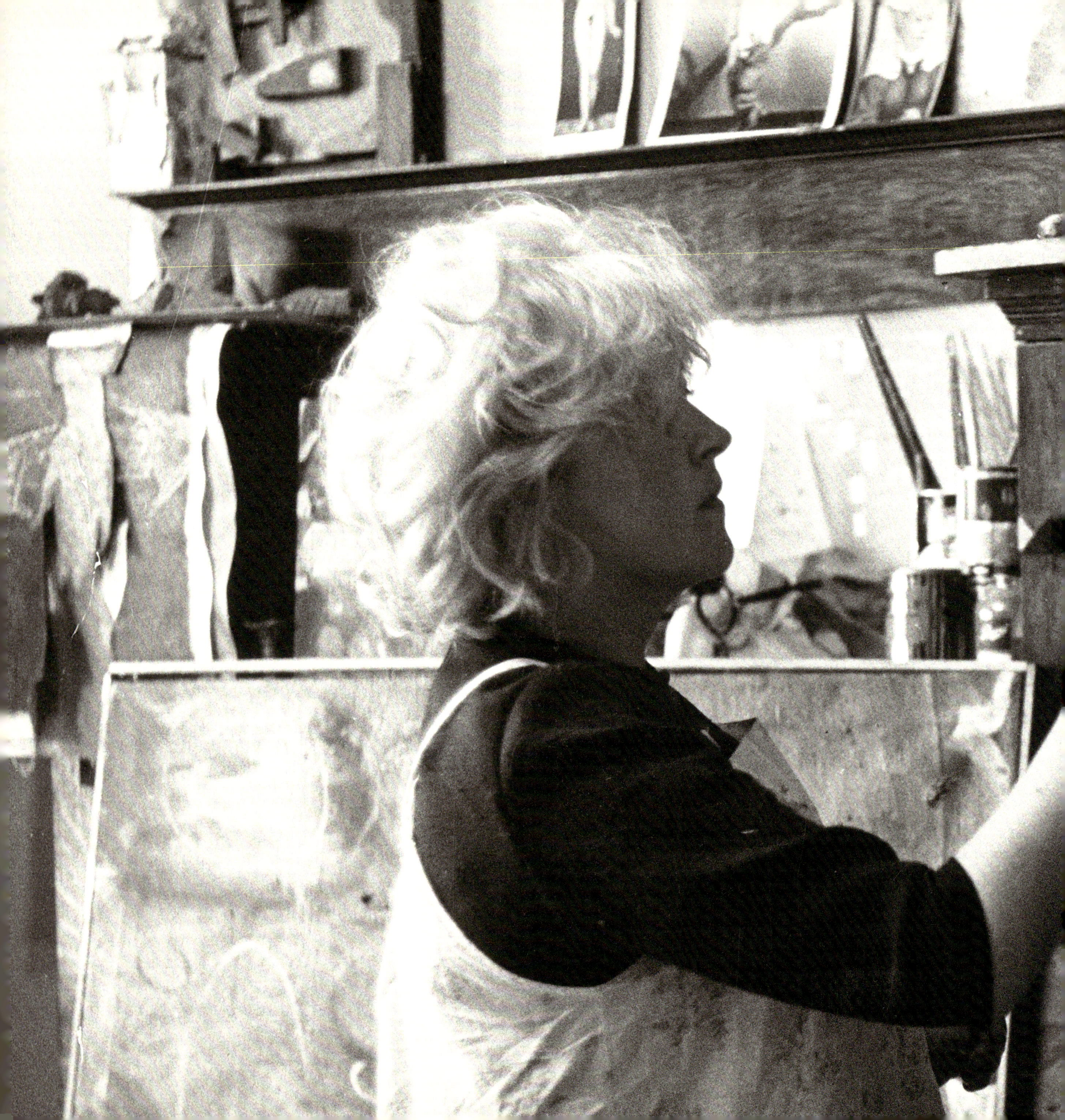

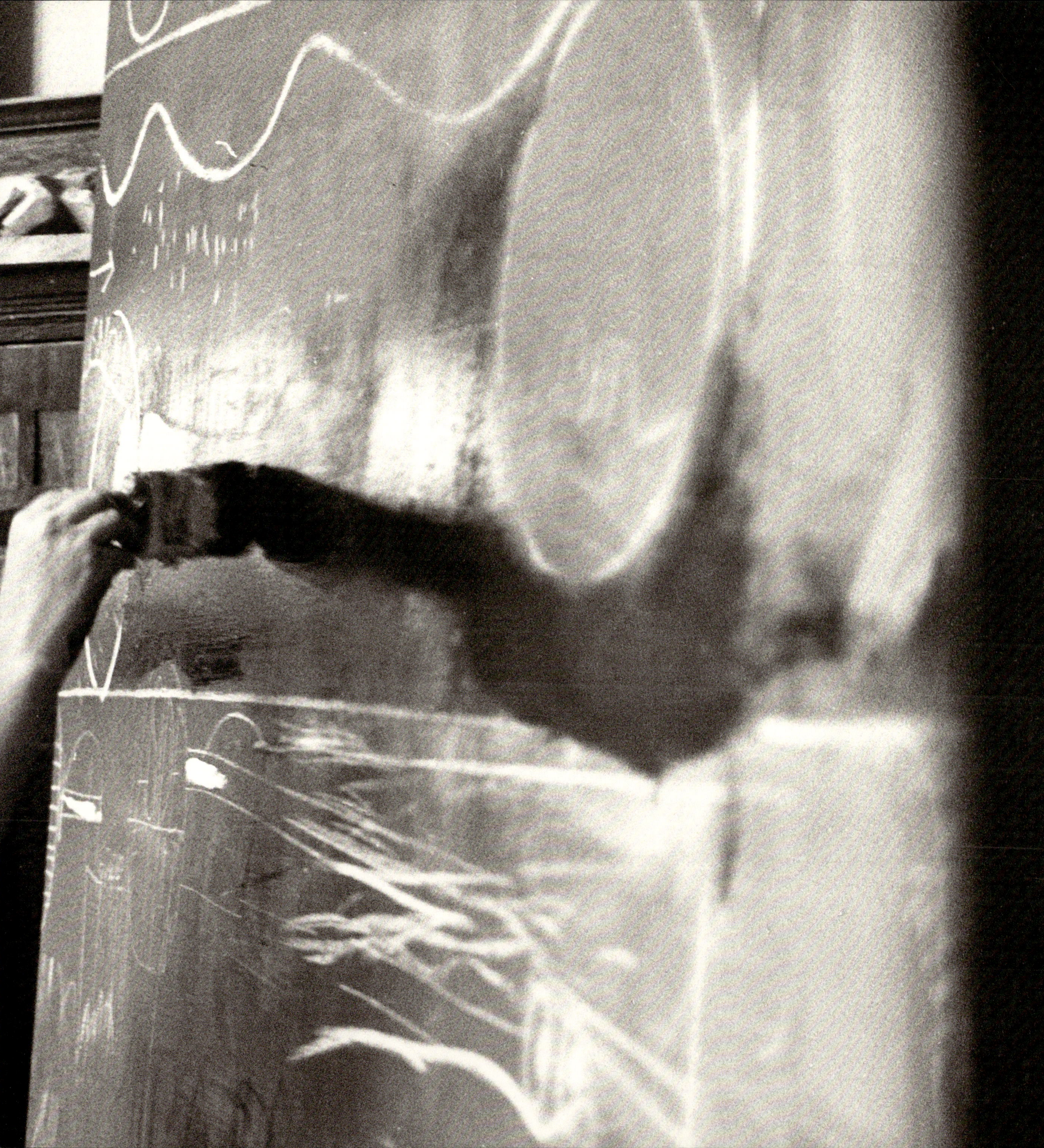

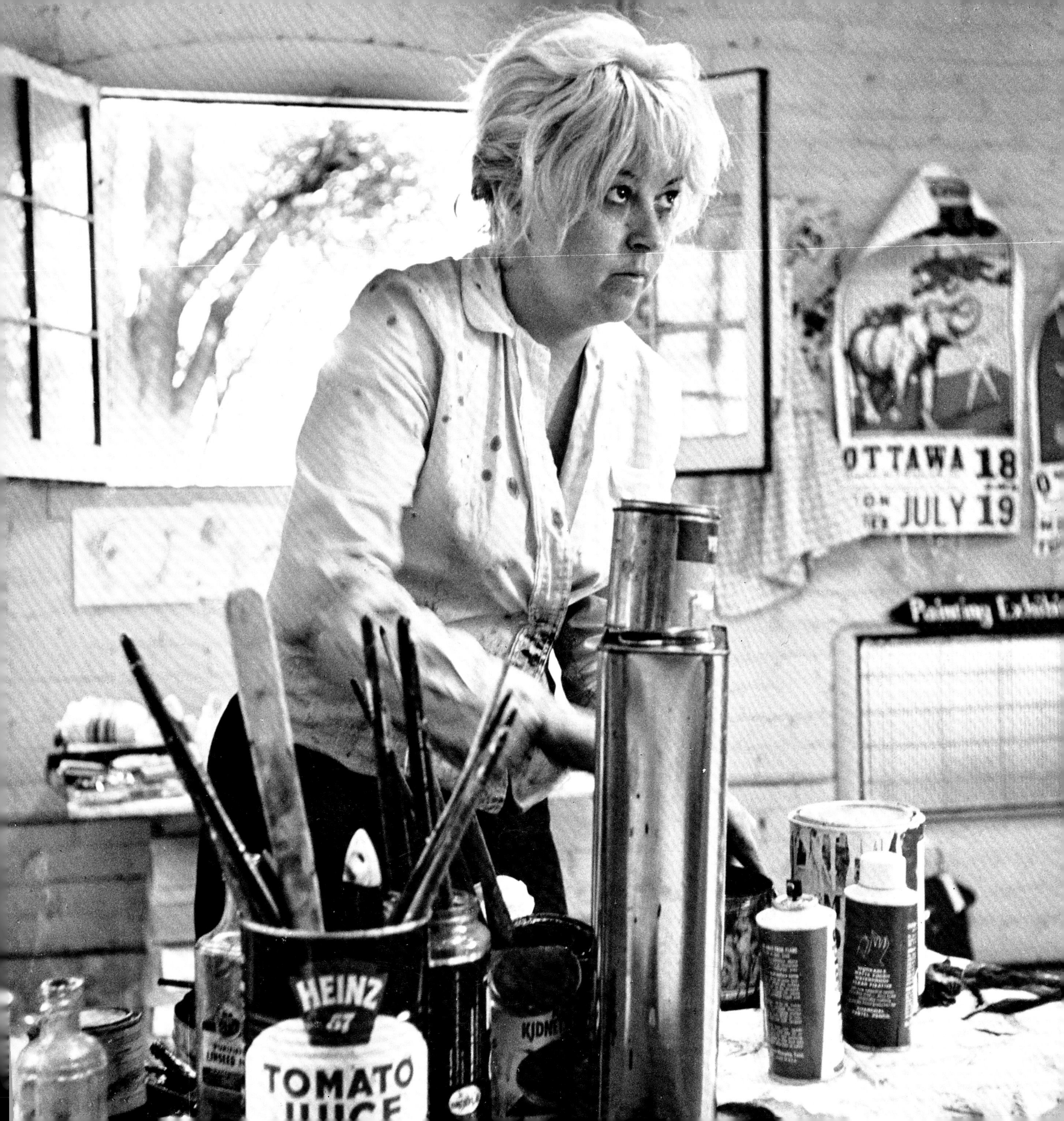

OTTAWA 18
JULY 19
Painting
HEINZ
57
TOMATO

FRAMING WIELAND

SARAH PARSONS

"Personally, she is variable. Artistically, she is versatile."[1]

Shortly before Joyce Wieland decamped for New York City in 1962, she posed for a remarkable photograph by Michel Lambeth (1923–1977) in her Toronto studio.[2] Blond hair tied back and paint speckling her white blouse, she stands behind a crowded worktable, right arm in motion, left hand resting on a can of paint. The table that cuts diagonally across the bottom of the frame is choc-a-block with paint, bottles, jars, rags, spray cans, and tin cans holding worn brushes, many resting at precarious angles and overhanging the edges above the concrete floor. With sun pouring in from an open window behind her, Wieland looks up and to our right, presumably assessing a painting in progress. The mess and Wieland's arrested pose lend the photograph a snapshot quality, while its complex composition suggests expert eyes were involved in the staging and editing. The result frames an artist as she engages in the intense physical and intellectual energy of art practice.

In photographic portraits, we often assume it is the professional photographer who envisions how they want to portray their subject and then directs the shoot as the reigning expert. However, portraiture, and especially photographic portraiture, is necessarily a collaborative undertaking between subject and photographer. Many photographs of Wieland, like the one made in her Toronto studio, are so eclectic, creative, and clever that it is impossible to think they could have been created without her foundational input.[3] Furthermore, given the extent to which Wieland experimented with the act of self-presentation, it would be odd for that experimentation to end when she relinquished the camera. Over the course of her early film *Water*

1 From the handbill program from the Art Gallery of Ontario, November 2, 1967, regarding events for Wednesday Open Night, *Bill's Hat*. Avrom Isaacs fonds, Clara Thomas Archives and Special Collections (hereafter cited as CTASC), York University, Toronto, ASC33275.

2 This was a temporary space for her; she did not have another studio until the 1980s.It was in this coach house–turned-studio, lent to her by Donna and George Montague, where Wieland produced her first major canvases: *Hallucination*, *Balling*, *Time Machine Series*, and *Heart-on*.

3 New approaches to the study of photography have increasingly decentred the role of the photographer as the single creator of photographs, and have demonstrated the value in approaching photography as a medium of collaboration. See Ariella Aisha Azoulay, Wendy Ewald, Susan Meiselas, Leigh Raiford, and Laura Wexler, eds., *Collaboration: A Potential History of Photography* (London: Thames and Hudson, 2024).

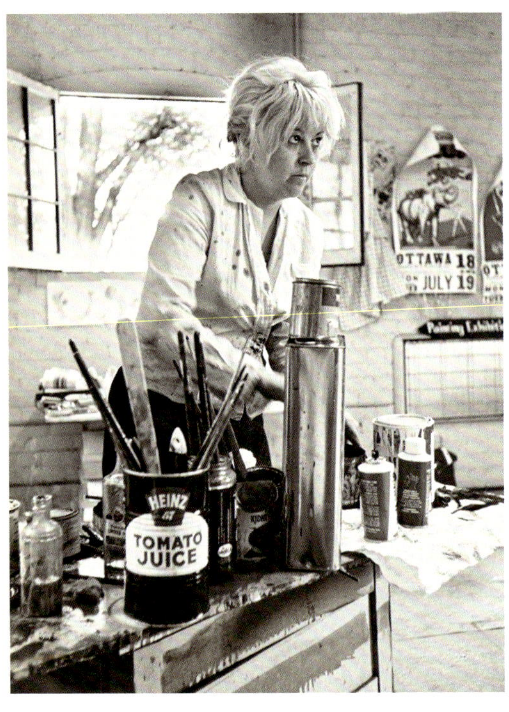

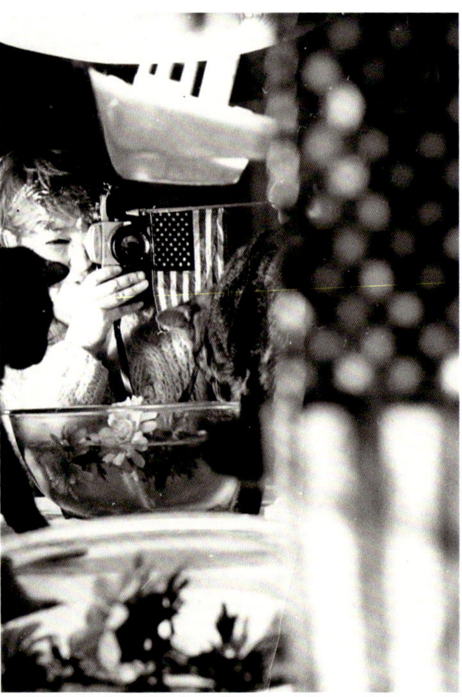

PREVIOUS SPREAD AND FAR LEFT

Michel Lambeth
Joyce Wieland, Toronto (in her studio), 1962
Gelatin silver print
33.7 × 25.5 cm
Art Gallery of Ontario, Gift of Av Isaacs, Toronto, 1994
94/445

Photo: AGO, Craig Boyko

LEFT

Wieland shooting ***Water Sark***, 1965
Joyce Wieland fonds, ASC61832, York University Libraries, Clara Thomas Archives and Special Collections

Sark (1965), we see slices of Wieland's face and body, clothed and nude, reflected through prisms, mirrors, plastic, and glass, and always set behind domestic objects, including flowers, rubber gloves, plastic bath toys, a teapot, and a cat. Wieland described the film as a "desperate self-portrait."[4] Although its impetus may have been fraught, *Water Sark* explored not only the limitation of the domestic sphere but also its possibilities for play, self-expression, and reinvention. In a similar vein of self-exploration, over the course of the 1960s, Wieland made photographs with friends and fellow members of the Toronto art circle, including Lambeth and Tess Boudreau Taconis. Writer and friend Sara Bowser noted that both Wieland and Snow "understood instinctively how to represent themselves to the media ... knew how to be photographed ... how to present their faces to the camera."[5]

Wieland's professional portraits reveal a deep understanding of the various ways in which artists—especially women artists—had been presented photographically. The Toronto studio photograph of Wieland at work deftly draws on several contemporary examples of the artistic portrait genre, including the photographs by German American Hans Namuth. The famous 1949 *LIFE* Magazine article that introduced Jackson Pollock to mainstream America as the greatest living artist was illustrated with Namuth's dramatic black-and-white portraits of Pollock in painterly action. In a Namuth image from 1950, painter Lee Krasner, who was Pollock's wife, perches on a stool at the edge of the frame in the rural barn he used as a studio. She watches Pollock paint, bathed in almost celestial light from the window above. Every detail of the photograph highlights the gendered expectations of their complicated marriage.[6] By contrast, Wieland's studio photograph contrasts and gently satirizes the masculine trope of the genius abstract artist through

4 Wieland to fellow filmmaker Hollis Frampton, quoted in Jane Lind, *Joyce Wieland: Artist on Fire* (Toronto: James Lorimer, 2001), 133.

5 Sara Bowser quoted in Lind, *Joyce Wieland*, 104.

6 Wieland's hair and makeup in this photograph seem very close to that in a photograph made by her friend and photographer Tess Boudreau Taconis, who photographed a number of women artists, including Rita Letendre, and was herself part of an artist couple (Krys Taconis was Dutch and a member of the prestigious international Magnum photography cooperative).

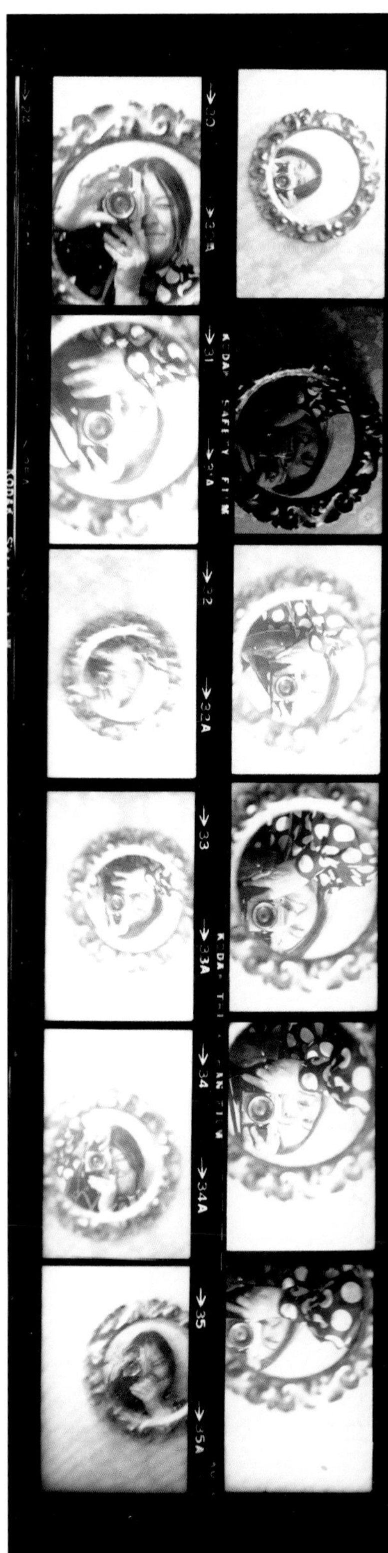

Wieland shooting a camera alongside a round mirror, 1978
Joyce Wieland fonds, ASC61831-cropped, York University Libraries, Clara Thomas Archives and Special Collections

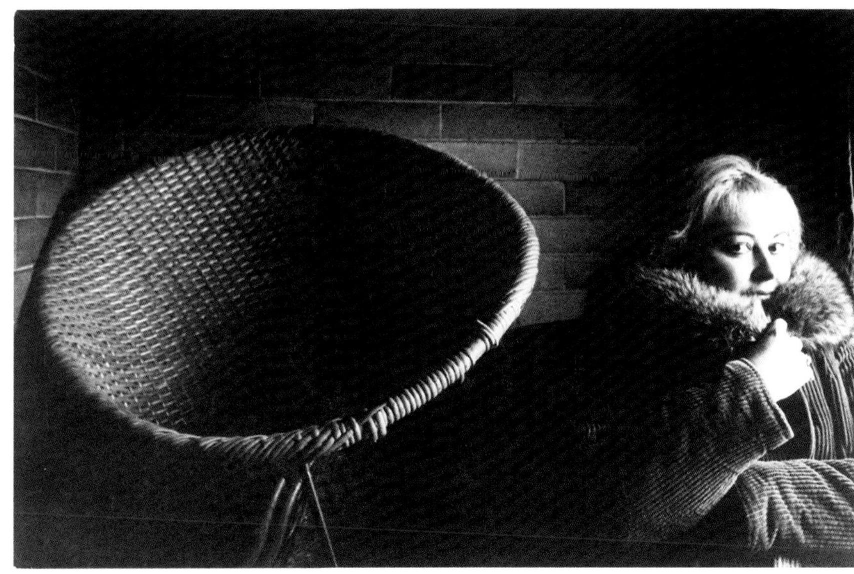

Michel Lambeth
Joyce Wieland (with basket chair), c. 1960
Gelatin silver print
24 × 33.5 cm
Art Gallery of Ontario, Gift of Av Isaacs, Toronto, 1994
94/450
© Estate of Michel Lambeth

the paint stains on her feminine work clothes, the halo of light behind her head, and even her refusal to show us the painting in process. This photograph was made in the summer of 1962 as Wieland prepared to move to New York with more than a little trepidation. If the style of the studio photograph situates her in an older lineage of New York modernism, the looming Heinz tomato juice can in the foreground points to the more recent arrival of Pop and Conceptualism. In May 1962, *Time* magazine published an image of a young Andy Warhol posing in front of his much-discussed *Campbell's Soup Cans* while eating from a can of the real thing. Wieland's photograph counterbalances this familiar symbol of both American consumer culture and contemporary art with two equal-sized posters in the upper right promoting an event in the Canadian capital.

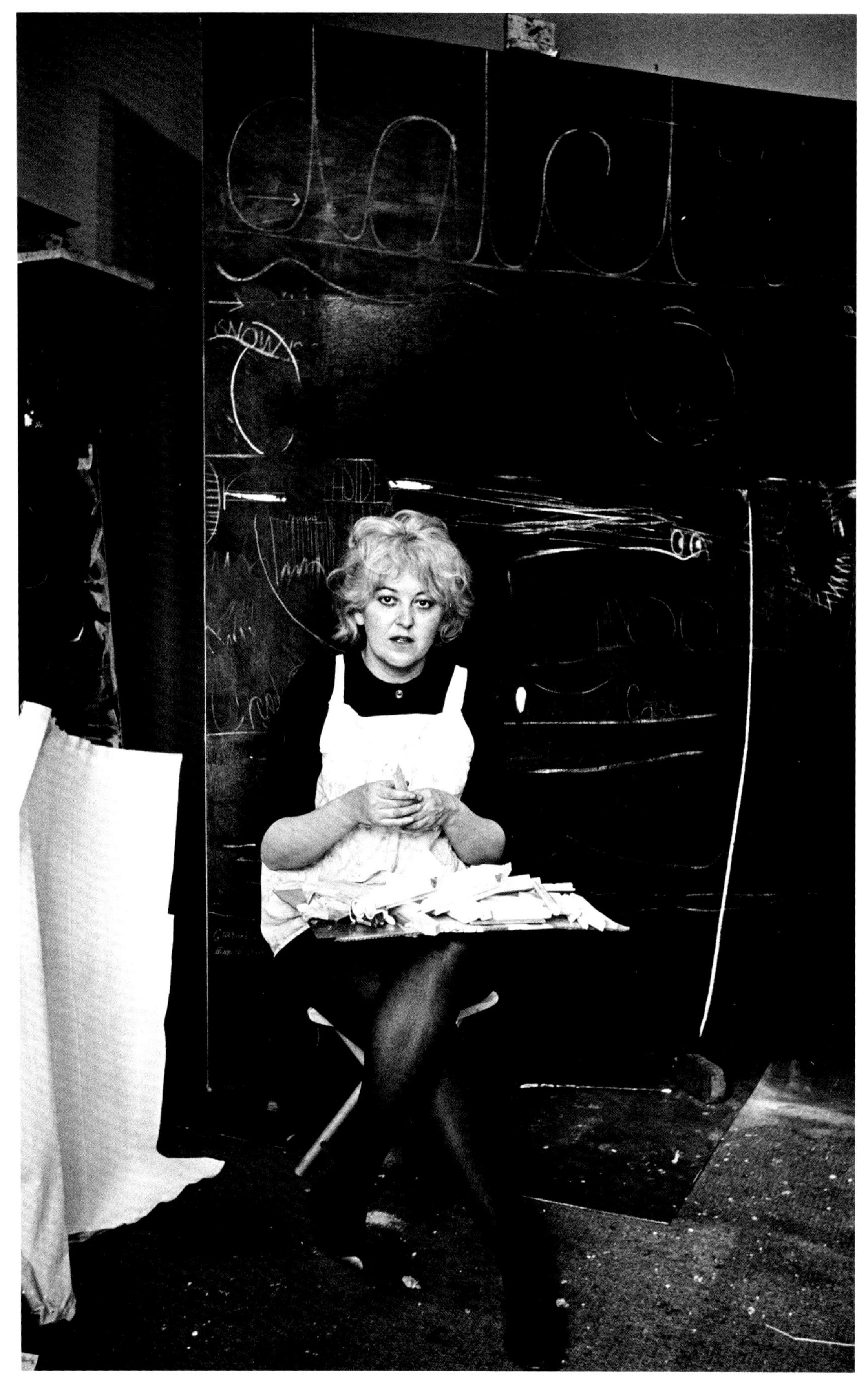

Tess Boudreau Taconis
Joyce Wieland, early 1960s
Gelatin silver print
30.4 × 20.1 cm
Art Gallery of Ontario,
Gift of the artist, 2007
2006/457

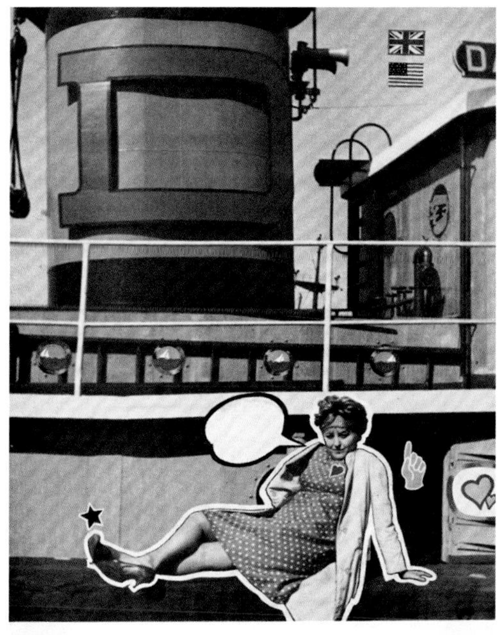

JOYCE WIELAND NEW PAINTINGS

THE ISAACS GALLERY 832 YONGE ST. NOV. 20 – DEC. 10 PREVIEW TUE. NOV. 19 8 to 10 P.M.

Wieland on an invitation to *New Paintings* exhibited at The Isaacs Gallery, 1963
Joyce Wieland fonds, ASC61830, York University Libraries, Clara Thomas Archives and Special Collections

Wieland returned to Toronto in the fall of 1963 to debut a new suite of paintings at The Isaacs Gallery. Again, she leveraged the power of photography to visualize her relationship with the contemporary scene. The exhibition poster featured a playful photograph of the artist reclining nonchalantly in a polka dot dress, trench coat, and heels. Wieland's image had been collaged onto another photograph of what appears to be the deck of a large ship. In this layering of incongruous photographs, the poster echoes British Pop art such as Richard Hamilton's *Just what is it that makes today's homes so different, so appealing?* (1956). The thick white line around Wieland's body and the added elements of a speech bubble, heart, and star further embeds the poster in the style of New York Pop artists like Roy Lichtenstein. Under the headline "Joyce Is a Zen Cook," Wieland recreated the reclining pose for *Toronto Telegram* photographer Charles "Chick" McGregor to illustrate an article about the exhibition. In this compilation, the smiling artist sits atop a chic Saarinen tulip chair (1957) with her discarded stilettos below. Wieland's painting *Sailboat Sinking* (1965) serves as the backdrop, and just below her bare foot is a half-body version of Michael Snow's *Walking Woman* (1963) in silhouette. Arranged altogether, the *Walking Woman*, so long associated with Wieland's role as wifely muse, appears to sink into the floor, perhaps nudged by her foot, which hovers above. Meanwhile, she leans back confidently while the caption tells us her painting has already sold for $400 and on the left is an example of "the work of her artist-husband, Michael Snow."

For Wieland, staging and posing for photographs appears to have offered not only an additional creative outlet, but one that invited and facilitated the spirited collaborations that shaped so much of her feminist practice. A photograph made in late 1964 or January 1965 included another shadowy visual reference to Snow. The long rectangular black-and-white portrait features an unsmiling Wieland dressed in fur, dramatically lit, and posed at a forty-five-degree turn from the lens. The portrait style references the theatrical, earnest celebrity portraits of Ottawa-based photographer Yousuf Karsh. Hovering above Wieland's

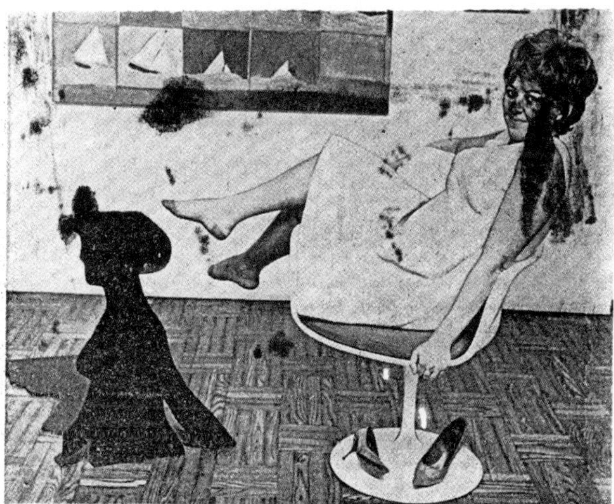

Charles McGregor, Telegram

Joyce Wieland sits in the Isaacs Gallery in front of one of her paintings, Sailboat Sinks, which has been sold for $400. At left is an example of the work of her artist-husband, Michael Snow.

Wieland in a reclining pose in an image for *Toronto Telegram* article "Joyce is a zen cook," November 23, 1963
Photo: Charles McGregor
Avrom Isaacs fonds, ASC61834, York University Libraries, Clara Thomas Archives and Special Collections

fur-capped head is a man's silhouette closely resembling both her husband and his *Walking Woman*.[7] On the panel-backed version of this print in Wieland's archive, the photographer's stamp lists credit to "Chummy" and a studio on the upper west side of Manhattan. In January 1965, Wieland described the photograph's creation in a note to her dealer, Av Isaacs: "Chummy brought [Toronto art critic Harry] Malcolmson over to Mike's studio when Mrs [Elinor] Poindexter [Snow's recently acquired New York gallerist] was there and took pictures."[8] Malcomson recalls Chummy as a tall, exuberant New Yorker who was great company and "made her living as a freelance media events photographer" documenting exhibitions and openings for newspapers and galleries.[9] According to Wieland, this photographic session was a ruckus group effort fuelled by discussions about art in which the women either dressed up and posed or operated the camera. Wieland was at the centre of the maelstrom, reporting to Isaacs that "Mrs P[oindexter] and myself were covered in furs from head to toe, so the pictures should be funny."[10]

The existing photo from the session in Snow's studio is indeed very funny. It plays with forms and ideas on several levels, including inverting the gender of artist and muse. While the lighting and arrangement of the photograph mimics Karsh's honorific style of portraiture, Wieland's slides toward mockery of its pomposity with her incorporation of fur: "Me in racoon and she [Mrs. Poindexter] in beaver." Karsh's portraits almost always integrated a prop or a gesture that signified their subject's unique contribution. Among his artist portraits, Picasso sits pensively behind a vase painted with a nude woman; Georgia O'Keeffe sits beneath a set of antlers; Man Ray holds a mask beside his face.

Wieland casts herself in this formal portrait awash in fur, which fascinated her as a material and symbolic object. Fur would soon become the focus of an expanded cinema installation, *Bill's Hat* (1967), which started with portrait photographs taken by Wieland. In these images made with slide film, a wide range of people, famous and found, take turns trying on Wieland's poofy racoon hat. Beyond her request that they put on that hat and submit to the camera, Wieland does not direct her subjects, creating what she termed "non-art portraits" in which subjects can choose to act or simply stand in front of the camera. The photographs document the exchange with Wieland as much as with the sitter and were often amusing in either their playfulness or their awkward lack thereof. But Wieland, and presumably her collaborators in Snow's studio, also found these fur photographs funny because of the highly erotic resonance of fur.[11] Whether it was Poindexter posing draped in beaver or photographs of various people nestling Wieland's hat on their heads, Wieland clearly revelled in the saucy playfulness and undercover potential of these furry encounters. In an interview with her friend, the journalist Wendy Michener, Wieland hesitates at first, but finally

7 According to a letter in the Avrom Isaacs fonds from May 1965, Chummy also took the photo of Wieland in front of Snow's *Walking Woman* print bought by MoMA that ran as her headshot in the *Toronto Twenty* catalogue.

8 Wieland to Isaacs, on Corrective Film letterhead, January 16, 1965.

9 Email to author, January 26, 2024.

10 On the Poindexter Gallery, see www.aaa.si.edu/collections/poindexter-gallery-records-8940.

11 See Sarah Parsons, "Women in Fur: Empire, Power, and Play in a Victorian Photography Album," *British Art Studies*, no. 18 (November 2020).

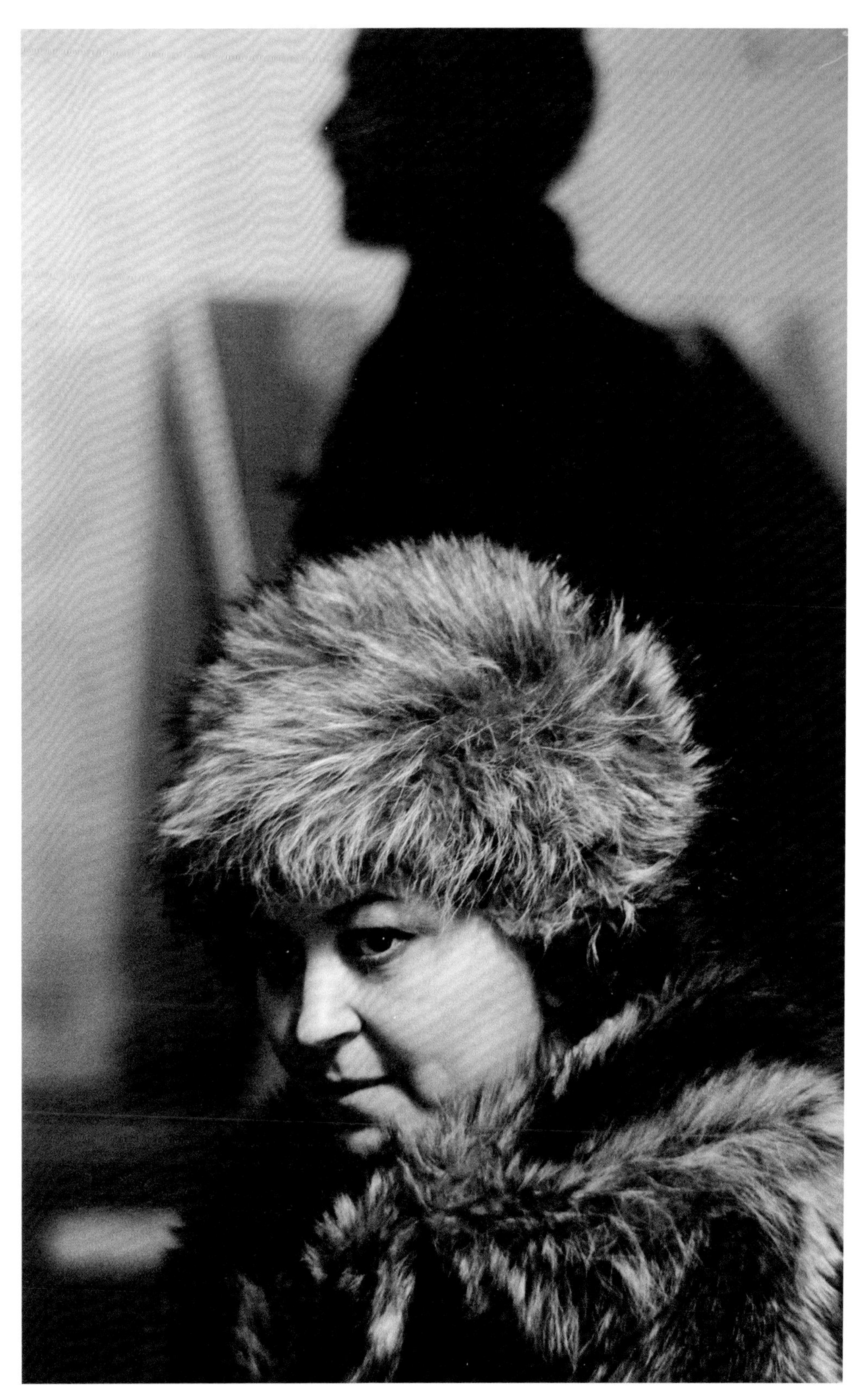

Joyce Wieland wearing a fur hat (likely Michael Snow in the background), c. 1965
Joyce Wieland fonds, ASC33281, York University Libraries, Clara Thomas Archives and Special Collections
Photo: Chummy

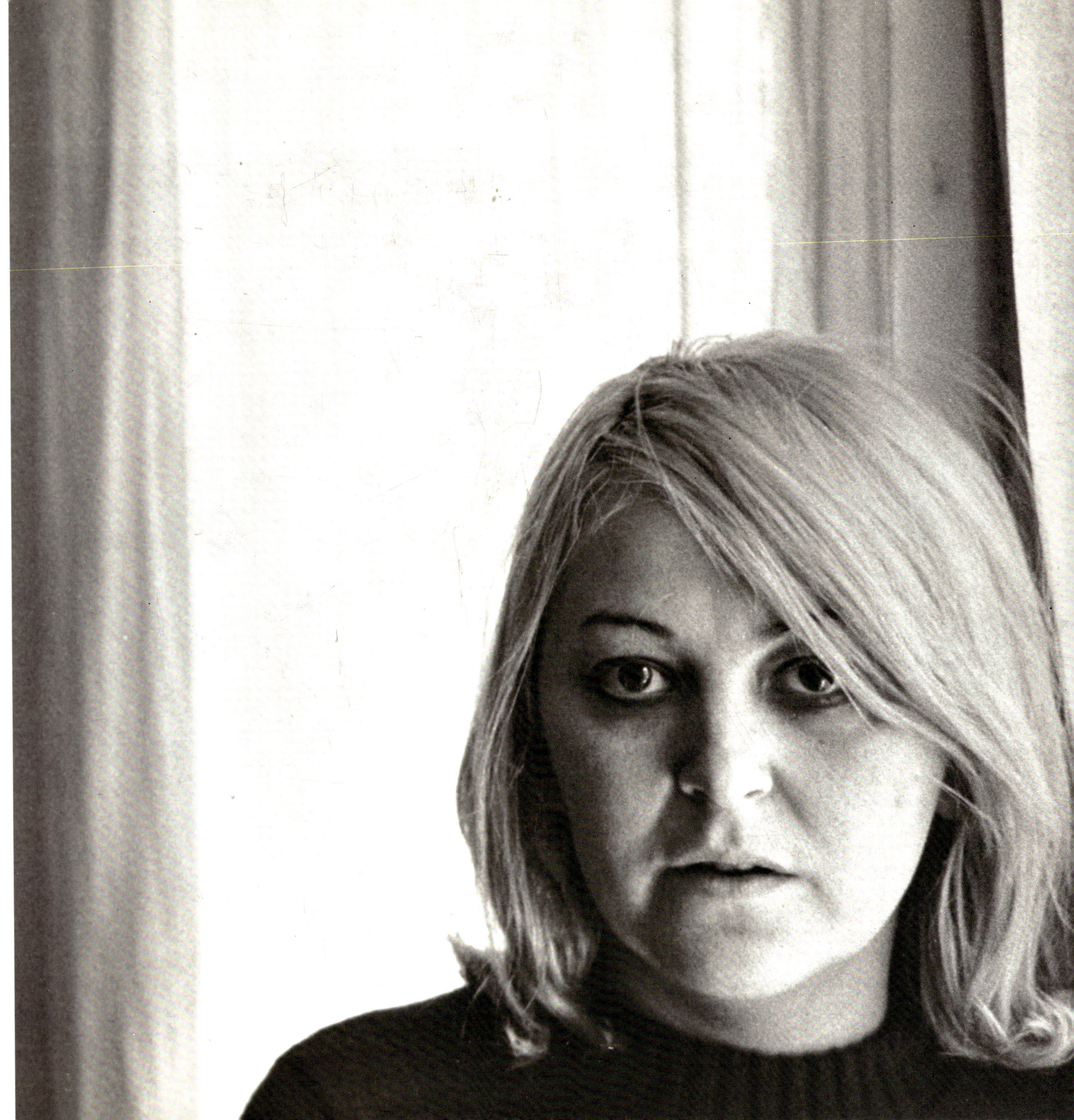

CHRONOLOGY 1930–1998

RHIANNON VOGL

OPPOSITE
Michel Lambeth
Joyce Wieland (by window) (detail), c. 1960
Gelatin silver print
24.5 × 33.7 cm
Art Gallery of Ontario, Gift of Av Isaacs, Toronto, 1994
94/453

Photo: AGO, Craig Boyko

CENTRE COLUMN
Wieland siblings, 1930s
Joyce Wieland fonds, ASC61814, York University Libraries, Clara Thomas Archives and Special Collections

RIGHT COLUMN
Joyce as a child on the beach, 1930s
Joyce Wieland fonds, ASC61812, York University Libraries, Clara Thomas Archives and Special Collections

1930s

1930 Joyce June Wieland is born June 30 in Toronto, the youngest child of Sydney Arthur Wieland (d. 1937) and Rosetta Amelia "Billy" Wieland (née Watson; d. 1941), who emigrated from England in the mid-1920s. The family, which includes Joyce's older brother Sydney (1920–1967) and sister Joan (1921–1993), rents a small house at 99½ Claremont Street in Toronto's West End.

• Early life of poverty exacerbated by her parents' unsteady work during and after the Great Depression.

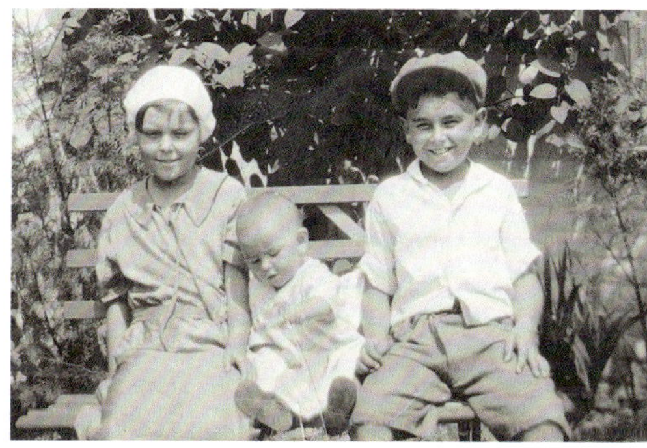

1931 British Parliament passes the Statute of Westminster—an early step toward the patriation of the Canadian constitution.

1933 Family moves just up the street to 101 Claremont.

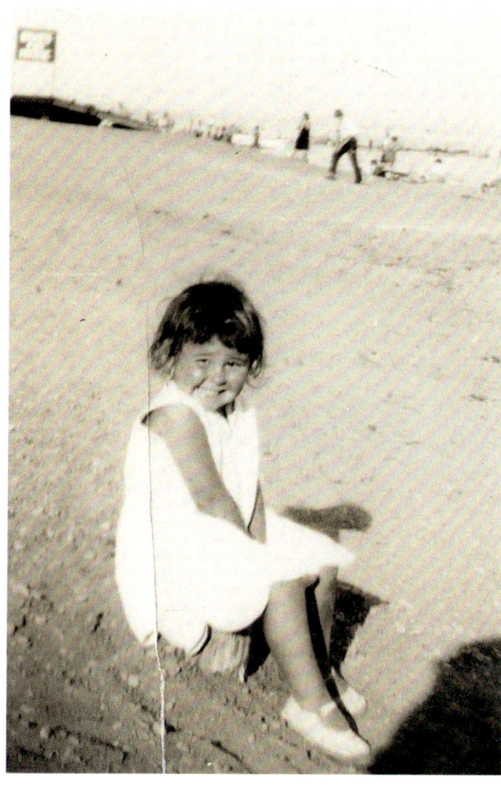

1936 Family moves a few blocks west to 145 Dovercourt Road.

1937 Sydney Wieland Sr. dies, leaving the family in dire financial circumstances. Sid Jr. and Joan work to support the household.

1939 September 3: World War II begins. Canada declares war on Nazi Germany seven days later.

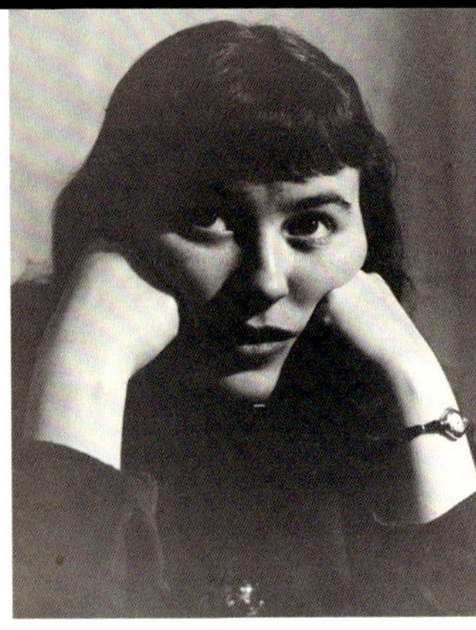

Portrait of Joyce Wieland, c. 1955
Joyce Wieland fonds,
NGC Library and Archives
Photo: NGC

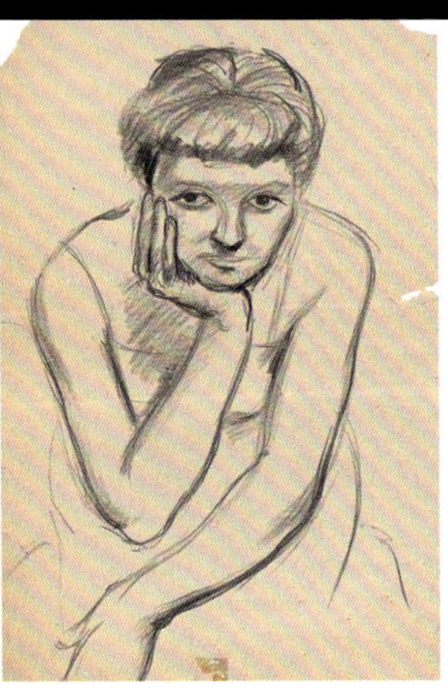

Self-portrait (sketch), 1945
Charcoal on wove paper
59.5 × 43 cm
Joyce Wieland fonds,
NGC Library and Archives
Photo: NGC

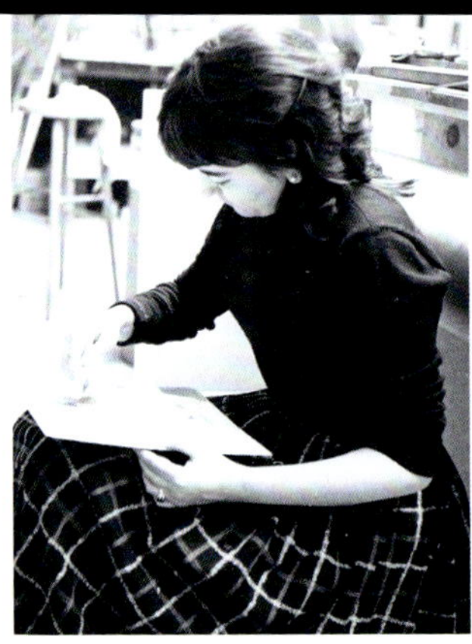

Joyce Wieland sketching,
c. 1955
Joyce Wieland fonds, ASC61444,
York University Libraries,
Clara Thomas Archives and
Special Collections

1940s

1941–42 Discovers the work of Beatrix Potter (1866–1943) and Hugh Lofting (1886–1947).

- Billy dies; Sid Jr. assumes legal guardianship.
- Financial problems prompt the three siblings to move often.

1942 Sid enlists in the Canadian Army, marries Barbara Kerr.

1943–45 The Wieland sisters live with their sister-in-law and her parents. They listen to classical records, visit the public library, and go to the movies at King's Playhouse at Queen Street West and Dovercourt Road.

- Joyce befriends another boarder, Alma, who teaches her to sew.

1944 Enrols at Toronto's Central Technical School, registering in fashion design. She later studies drawing with Doris McCarthy (1910–2010), who encourages her and becomes a mentor, and she joins the high school's fine arts program on McCarthy's advice.

"In public school I used to draw naked [ladies] for the boys. . . . I would get a nickel or a dime, and by the end of the week, I'd made a fortune. It was the age of pinups. . . . I had a really . . . steady market." (Artist on Fire *documentary, dir. Kay Armatage, 1987)*

1945 Joan marries Harvey Stewart.

- Joyce moves in with Sid and Barb in the East End, on Sammon Avenue.
- Among her teachers at Central Tech are Elizabeth Wyn Wood (1903–1966) and Virginia Erskine Luz (1911–2005).
- Meets Barbara King (later Graham); the two women spend time sketching in ravines.
- World War II ends.

1946–47 Joyce Wieland moves residences often, living with various in-laws and friends.

- Attends Communist Party meetings with classmates in grade 12.

1948 Graduates from high school.

- Hired as packaging designer in the E.S. & A. Robinson lithography department.

1949 Newfoundland becomes the last province to join Canadian Confederation.

1950s

1950 Presentation by filmmaker Maya Deren (1917–1961), jointly organized by the Toronto Film Society and the University of Toronto Film Society.

1951 Rents a room at 700 Bathurst Street (across from her old high school) along with other artists, including Chris Yaneff (1938–2004) and Gerald Gladstone (1929–2005).

- Often visits the Art Gallery of Toronto (now the Art Gallery of Ontario).
- Travels by train to Chicago and later to New York City with her friend Mary Karch to visit galleries, attend musicals, and tour the Rockefeller Center.
- Joins political group Canadians for the United Nations; invites Joan to join. Group raises money though art shows and film screenings.
- Buys lithography press and makes drawings using Joan's children as models.

1952–53 Lives with boyfriend Bryan Barney (1930–1996) at 700 Bathurst.

- Begins to freelance for Graphic Associates Film Production Ltd.: "Producers of industrial and educational productions, television commercials and film-ads. Creators of technical animation, cartoons and special effects." Filmmaker and animator George Dunning (1920–1979) was vice president.
- Having saved money, travels to Europe from September to November with Mary Karch; visits Liverpool, London, Brighton, Paris, Vienna, Rome.

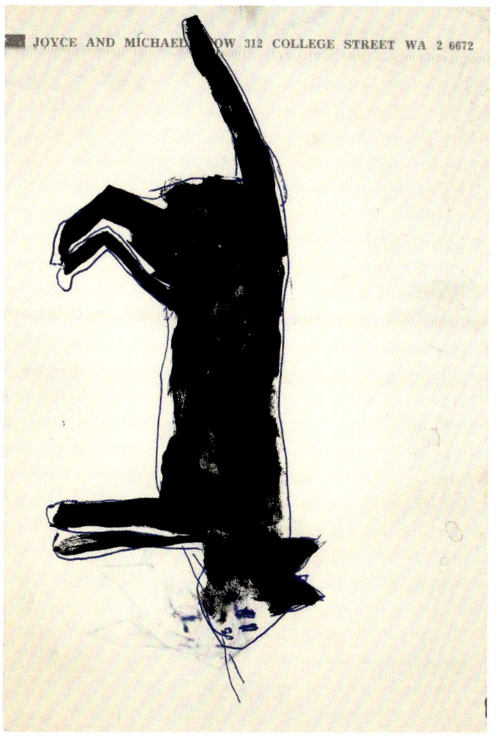

Letterhead with cat sketch, undated
Ink on wove paper, c. 1956
20.2 × 13.7 cm
Joyce Wieland fonds, NGC Library and Archives
Photo: NGC

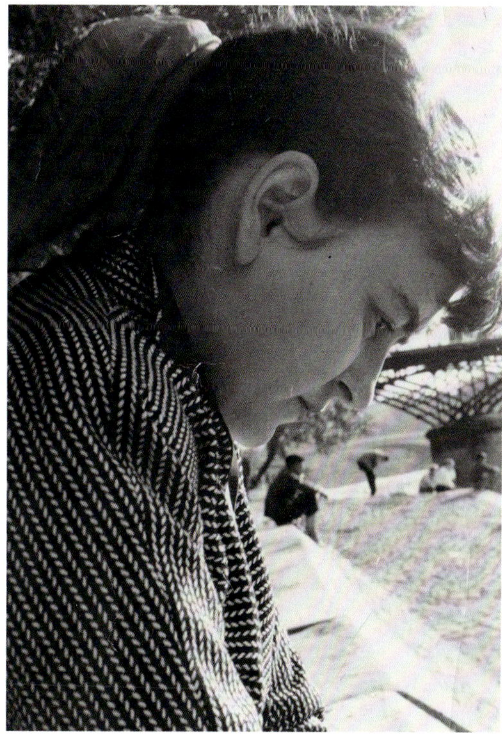

Joyce on her first day in France, early 1950s
Joyce Wieland fonds, ASC61813,
York University Libraries,
Clara Thomas Archives and Special Collections

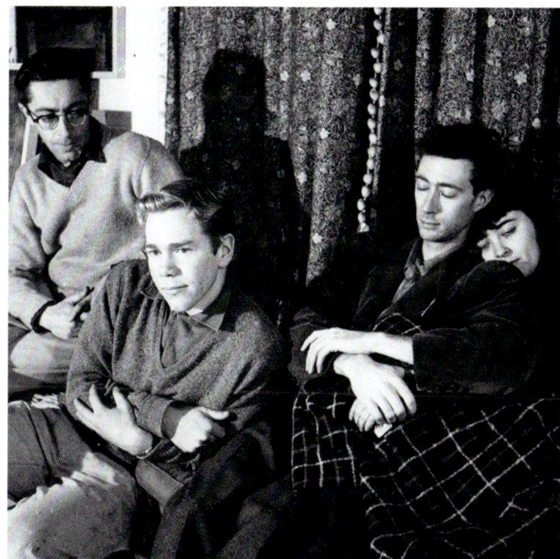

Group photo with Joyce Wieland and
Michael Snow on the right, c. 1956
Joyce Wieland fonds, ASC61811,
York University Libraries,
Clara Thomas Archives and Special Collections

1954 Hired full-time at Graphic Associates.

• Makes early experimental films.

1955 Moves into an apartment across town at 525 Sherbourne Street, with four friends, including Donna Lawson (later Montague).

• Breaks up with Barney; begins relationship with artist Michael Snow (1928–2023), whom she met at Graphic Associates.

• Flies to Buffalo, New York, with Lawson—first airplane ride.

• Graphic Associates closes; Wieland becomes unemployed.

• Late in year, travels to France for several months.

• Avrom Isaacs opens Greenwich Gallery at 736 Bay Street, in the heart of Toronto's bohemian village.

1956 July: Rents apartment with Snow at 312 College Street.

• September: Marries Snow at Toronto City Hall; changes legal surname to Snow but keeps Wieland as artist name.

• Freelances as graphic designer.

• Makes film *Tea in the Garden* (now lost).

• Exhibits for the first time in group exhibition of the Canadian Society of Graphic Art at the Art Gallery of Toronto.

• October: Snow has first solo exhibition at Greenwich Gallery.

1958 Moves with Snow into an apartment at the corner of Charles and Church Streets.

• Works from home studio.

• Travels with Snow to Havana and La Boca, Cuba.

• Makes film *A Salt in the Park* (now lost).

• Late 1950s: reads Emil Ludwig's biography of Napoleon Bonaparte, marking the beginning of her interest in Napoleon and Josephine.

1959 February: Two-person exhibition with Gordon Rayner at Toronto's Greenwich Gallery.

• Two-person drawings exhibition with Snow at the Westdale Gallery, Hamilton.

• August: Greenwich Gallery renamed The Isaacs Gallery.

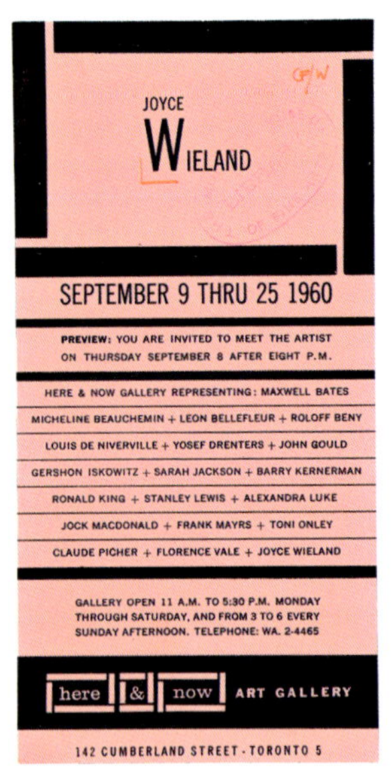

JOYCE
WIELAND

SEPTEMBER 9 THRU 25 1960

PREVIEW: YOU ARE INVITED TO MEET THE ARTIST
ON THURSDAY SEPTEMBER 8 AFTER EIGHT P.M.

HERE & NOW GALLERY REPRESENTING: MAXWELL BATES
MICHELINE BEAUCHEMIN + LEON BELLEFLEUR + ROLOFF BENY
LOUIS DE NIVERVILLE + YOSEF DRENTERS + JOHN GOULD
GERSHON ISKOWITZ + SARAH JACKSON + BARRY KERNERMAN
RONALD KING + STANLEY LEWIS + ALEXANDRA LUKE
JOCK MACDONALD + FRANK MAYRS + TONI ONLEY
CLAUDE PICHER + FLORENCE VALE + JOYCE WIELAND

GALLERY OPEN 11 A.M. TO 5:30 P.M. MONDAY
THROUGH SATURDAY, AND FROM 3 TO 6 EVERY
SUNDAY AFTERNOON. TELEPHONE: WA. 2-4465

here & now ART GALLERY

142 CUMBERLAND STREET · TORONTO 5

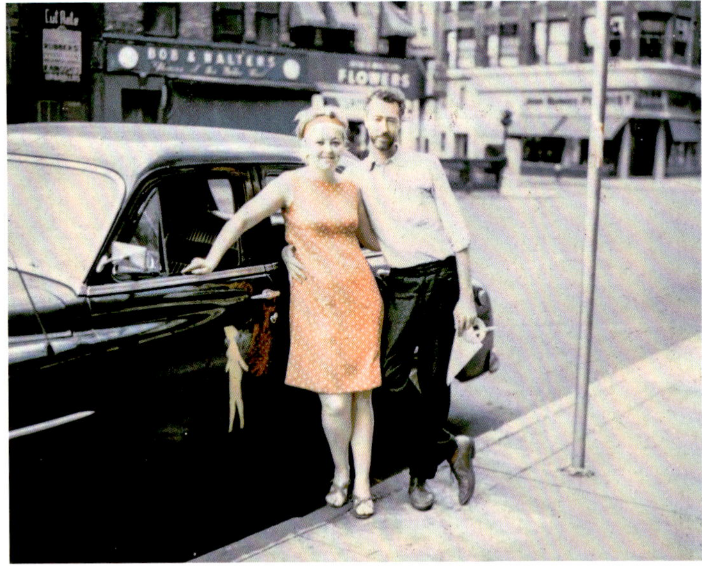

LEFT
Invitation sent by Joyce Wieland to Evan H. Turner, Director of the Montreal Museum of Fine Arts, to her exhibition at the Here and Now Gallery, Toronto, 1960. Photo: MMFA, Julie Ciot

RIGHT
Joyce Wieland and Michael Snow with Graeme Ferguson's car, New York, c. 1963
Photo: Michael Snow Studio

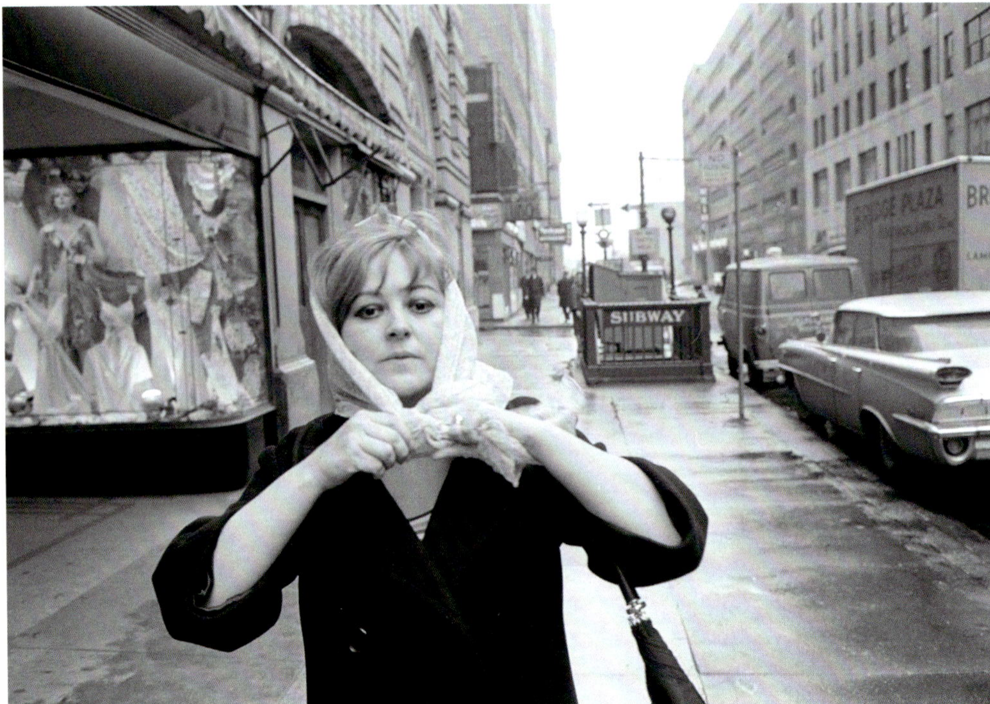

John Reeves
Joyce Wieland in *Canadian Art – Canadian Painters in New York*, 1964
Digitized 35mm black-and-white negative
John Reeves fonds, 2022.004.014071, Media Commons Archives, University of Toronto Libraries
© Estate of John Reeves

1960s

1960 Has temporary studio in the coach house behind Donna and George Montague's home at 19 Prince Arthur Avenue, Toronto.

• Joins the Montagues at summer house in Gatineau, Quebec; they are among her earliest collectors.

• September: First solo exhibition at Dorothy Cameron's Here and Now Gallery, Toronto.

• Writes essay on Napoleon for *evidence magazine*.

1961 Begins work on first large and experimental paintings: *Heart-on* (pp. 72–73); *Time Machine Series* (p. 76); *Hallucination* (p. 74).

• March: The Isaacs Gallery moves to 832 Yonge Street.

1962 February: First solo exhibition at The Isaacs Gallery; one of the few women artists represented by the gallery.

• Summer: Visits NYC with Snow, planning to move there. The couple stays with Betty (1933–2022) and Graeme Ferguson (1929–2021) and their young son Munro Ferguson (b. 1960), until they can find their own place.

• Meets artists Frank Stella (1936–2024), Carl Andre (1935–2024), and Donald Judd (1928–1994).

• October: Travelling exhibition "Drawings by Michael Snow and Joyce Wieland" organized by Hart House Art Gallery at University of Toronto. Hart House, a student activity centre, was restricted to men until 1972.

1963 Settles with Snow in New York. Rents loft at 191 Greenwich Street; poet Paul Haines (1932–2003) and wife Jo Hayward-Haines are neighbours.

- Connects with filmmakers Robert (Bob) Cowan (1930–2011); Hollis Frampton (1936–1984); Shirley Clarke (1919–1997); Kuchar brothers Mike (b. 1942) and George (1942–2011); and couple Ken (b. 1933) and Flo Jacobs (b. 1941). Attends weekly screenings in the Jacobs' loft, and Jonas Mekas's (1922–2019) midnight screenings at the Gramercy Theatre.
- Frequently visits ship museum on South Street; watches ships in Battery Park on Hudson River.
- Makes her first filmic paintings; exhibits at The Isaacs Gallery in November.
- First New York film, *Larry's Recent Behaviour*, screened alongside films by American friends and collaborators.
- Participates with Snow and friends in civil-rights and anti-war protests, including the March on Washington for Jobs and Freedom in August.

1964 Makes films *Patriotism, Patriotism Part II*, staring friend Dave Shackman (d. 1965), who was also Donald Judd's fabricator.

- Using found objects, makes *Cooling Room* constructions (pp. 85–86) and *Young Woman's Blues* (p. 90).
- First public collection acquisitions: *Boat Tragedy* (p. 96), AGO, and *Tragedy in the Air, or Plane Crash*, Vancouver Art Gallery (VAG).
- Features in "New York's Vitality Tonic for Canadian Artists," *Canadian Art*, written by Jonathan Holstein, who co-curated with Gail van der Hoof *Abstract Design in American Quilts* in 1971 at Whitney Museum of American Art.

1965 Makes *Water Sark*; *Barbara's Blindness*, co-directed with Betty Ferguson.

- Acts in *The Sky Socialist* (1965–67) by Ken Jacobs.
- Paints *Sailboat Sinking* (p. 92), last painting until 1980.
- Experiments with psychedelic drugs (legal until 1968).

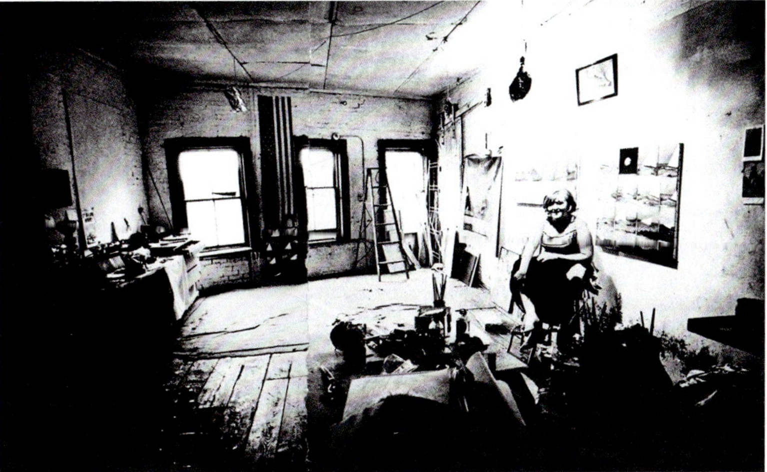

Joyce Wieland in her home and studio, 1964
Published in Jonathan Holstein, "New York's Vitality Tonic for Canadian Artists," *Canadian Art*, September/October 1964
Avrom Isaacs fonds, ASC61412, York University Libraries, Clara Thomas Archives and Special Collections

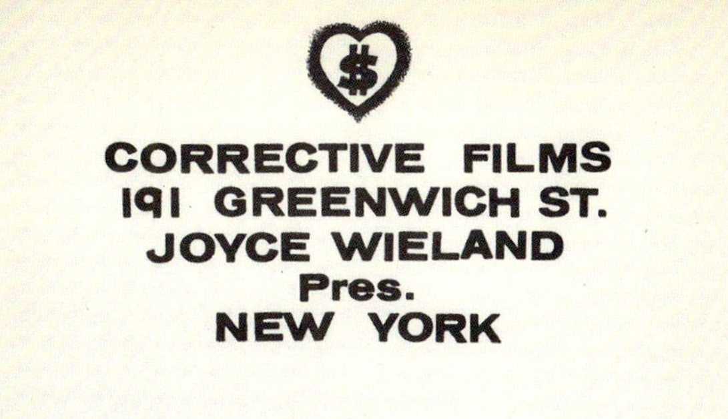

CORRECTIVE FILMS
191 GREENWICH ST.
JOYCE WIELAND
Pres.
NEW YORK

Letterhead, 1965
Joyce Wieland fonds, ASC61822, York University Libraries, Clara Thomas Archives and Special Collections

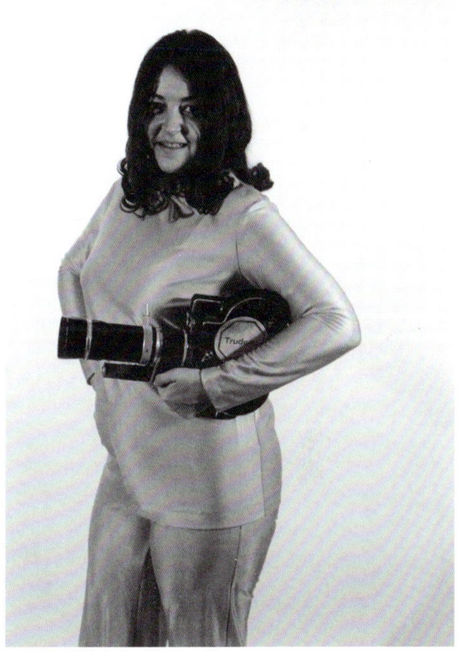

Joyce Wieland, c. 1965
Joyce Wieland fonds, ASC61816, York University Libraries, Clara Thomas Archives and Special Collections

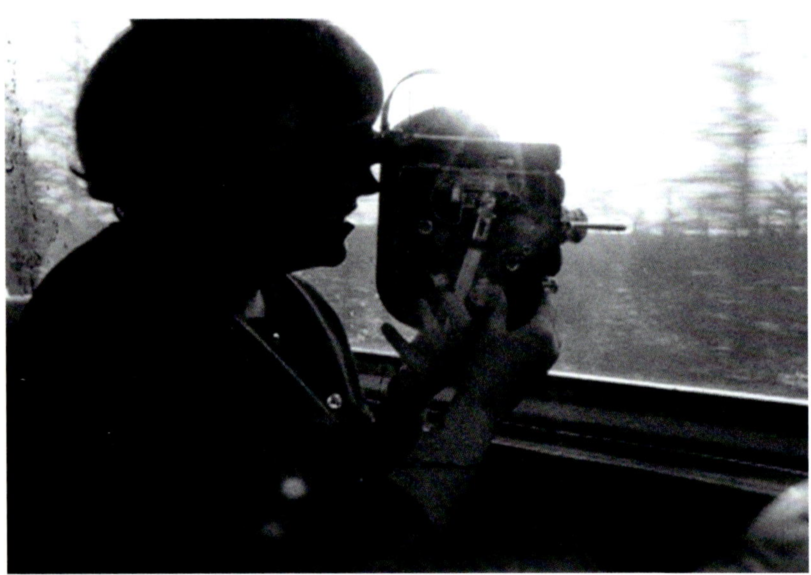

Joyce Wieland in *Wendy and Joyce* (unfinished), 1967
Film, 16mm, colour, silent
Courtesy of Cinémathèque québécoise

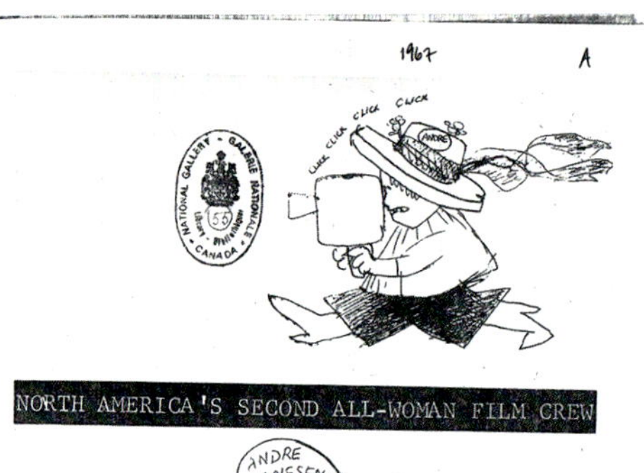

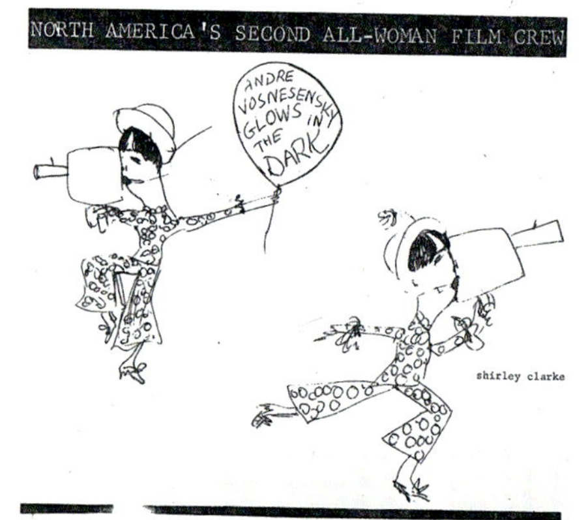

Photocopied page titled "North America's Second All-Woman Film Crew," 1967
Joyce Wieland fonds, ASC61825, York University Libraries, Clara Thomas Archives and Special Collections

Activiste Culturel

PRESS RELEASE ON JOYCE WIELAND ...

THE JEWISH MUSEUM..1109 FIFTH AVENUE.. IS PRESENTING A PROGRAM OF JOYCE WIELAND'S FILMS ON TUESDAY MARCH 25th AT 5:30 AND 7:00 ..films to be shown are SAILBOAT, CATFOOD,1933,AND THE AWARD WINNING,RAT LIFE AND DIET IN NORTH AMERICA....WHICH HAS ALSO RECENTLY BEEN CHOSEN ALONG WITH FIFTEEN OTHER FILMS BY A PRESELECTION COMMITTEE OF WILLARD VAN DYKE OF THE MUSEUM OF MODERN ART AND AMOS VOGEL OF THE LINCOLN FILM FESTIVAL ..TO REPRESENT THE U.S. AT OBERHAUSEN ..THE GERMAN SHORT FILM FESTIVAL.

IN APRIL RAT LIFE AND DIET IN NORTH AMERICA WILL BE PREMIERED ON THE C.B.C.........AND THE FOLLOWING MONTH..MISS WIELAND'S

FILM ON PRIME MINISTER TRUDEAU WILL ALSO HAVE ITS FIRST TELEVISION APPEARANCE.THE PREMIERE OF THIS FILM MARKS THE ANNIVERSARY OF PRIME MINISTER TRUDEAU COMING TO POWER...AND IS TITLED .... REASON OVER PASSION.

THE PUBLIC IS INVITED TO ATTEND THE JEWISH MUSEUM SCREENINGS ADMISSION IS $1.50

Press release on Wieland's letterhead "Activiste Culturel," 1969
Joyce Wieland fonds, ASC61819, York University Libraries, Clara Thomas Archives and Special Collections

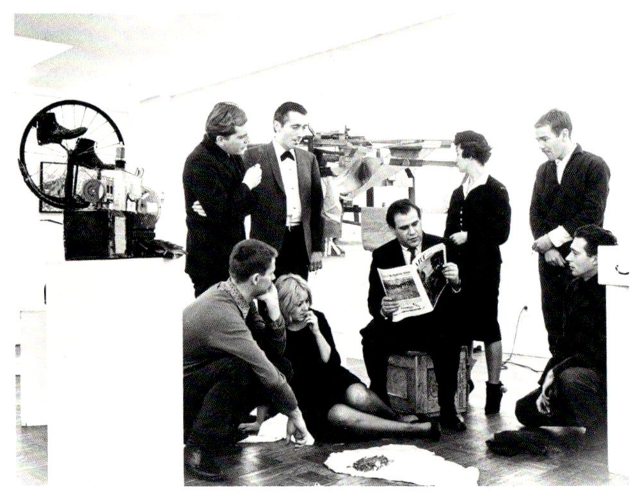

Michel Lambeth
Joyce Wieland (seated on floor), Av Isaacs (reading magazine), Michael Snow (bottom right), with (left to right) Greg Curnoe, Rick Gorman, Dennis Burton, an Air Canada flight attendant, and Graham Coughtry at the Dada exhibit, The Isaacs Gallery, 1962
Gelatin silver print
25 × 33.5 cm
Courtesy of Ihor Holubizky
© Estate of Michel Lambeth

Joyce Wieland .... New Work
The Isaacs Gallery 832 Yonge St.
March 22nd to April 10th, 1967
Preview Tue. March 21, 8 o'clock

The Isaacs Gallery invitation, 1967
Joyce Wieland fonds, ASC61829, York University Libraries, Clara Thomas Archives and Special Collections

1966 Moves to 123 Chambers Street; former Greenwich Street home demolished to make way for World Trade Center construction.

- First plastic assemblages. Includes the new Canadian flag for the first time in plastic hangings *Stuffed Movie* (p. 133) and *Patriotism* (p. 120).
- Designs *The Camera's Eyes* (p. 137) and *Film Mandala* (p. 138), hires Joan Stewart to make the quilts.
- Makes film *Peggy's Blue Skylight*, part of "portrait" trilogy with *Larry's Recent Behaviour* and *Water Sark*.
- Conceives idea for a film about a love affair between a Tom Thomson–like painter and a Québécoise woman, later *The Far Shore* (1976).
- Is awarded first Canada Council for the Arts grant.
- Solo exhibition at artist-run centre 20/20 Gallery in London, Ontario.
- December: First exhibition of Inuit art at The Isaacs Gallery.

1967 March: "Hangings" exhibition at The Isaacs Gallery includes plastic assemblages and quilts.

- Works as a camerawoman on Shirley Clarke's unfinished film *Voznesensky*.
- Travelling exhibition paired with John Meredith, *Wieland and Meredith*, organized by National Gallery of Canada; first textile work acquired by art museum: *Untitled*, 1967, NGC.
- Summer: Included in *Painting in Canada* at Expo 67, the Universal and International Exhibition in Montreal.
- Summer: Travels from Cape Breton, Nova Scotia, to Quebec City, filming footage later used in her first feature-length experimental film, *La raison avant la passion / Reason over Passion* (1969).
- November: Performs and films *Bill's Hat* in Toronto.
- Befriends economics professor Abraham Rotstein and his wife Diane in Toronto, fuelling an interest in Canadian economics, history, and politics.
- Avid reader of *Canadian Forum*; contributes political cartoons to the magazine.

1968 January: First solo exhibition in public art museum: *Joyce Wieland Retrospective, 1957–67*, Vancouver Art Gallery (VAG). Films train ride from Toronto to Vancouver with Wendy Michener (1935–1969) and Rose Richardson, becomes part of *La raison avant la passion / Reason over Passion*.

- April: Attends the Liberal leadership convention in Ottawa; seated in Press Section, films Pierre Elliott Trudeau (1919–2000) for five hours.
- Makes film *Handtinting* using discarded footage from a training film; and *Rat Life and Diet in North America*, first film with Canadian theme.
- Sells *Rat Life* to German television—also to CBC in 1969 and Netherlands TV in 1970.
- Travels with Rose Richardson to film Maritime provinces; visits Chéticamp, Nova Scotia, home of Acadian women cooperative hooking wool rugs.

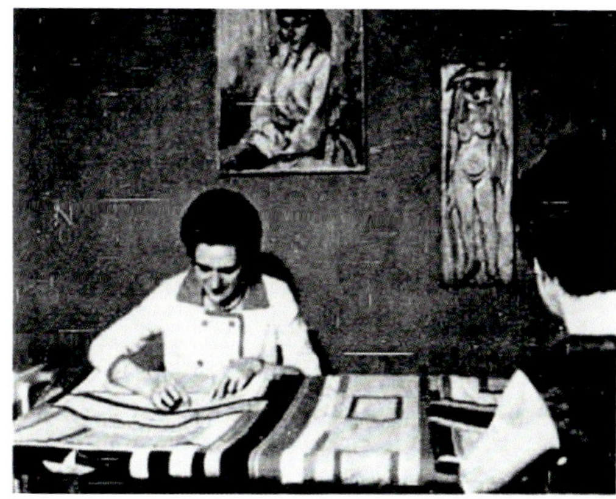

Joan Stewart quilting, 1967
Published in "Art You Can Use," *Toronto Star Weekly*, January 14, 1967

- Museum of Modern Art (MoMA), New York, screens *Five Films by Joyce Wieland*. Her films go on to international film festivals in France, Belgium, Germany, and Lucy Lippard's 995,000 exhibition at VAG (1970).
- First plastic work acquired by art museum: *Stuffed Movie* (1966) (p. 133) VAG.

1969 February: First Toronto retrospective: *Joyce Wieland Retrospective*, Glendon College Art Gallery, York University.

- November: Premiere of *La raison avant la passion / Reason over Passion* at Canada National Arts Centre, Ottawa, to a crowd of 450 people; December: New York premiere at the Elgin Theater.
- November: With Snow, hosts quilt in at New York loft for guest Pierre Trudeau; gifts *La raison avant la passion* quilt to Trudeau, who hangs it in the official residence of the prime minister (24 Sussex Drive, Ottawa).

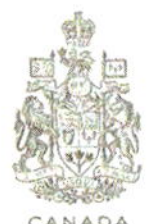

CANADA

PRIME MINISTER · PREMIER MINISTRE

O t t a w a (4)
November 12, 1969.

Dear Mr. and Mrs. Snow:

I think the debt I had to those of you who worked with such enthusiasm almost two years ago, at the time of the Leadership Contest, must be redoubled after your party Saturday night. Your thoughtfulness in putting together an affair of this kind, in a fairly short time and in the midst of busy lives, is something that I appreciated tremendously. More than that, if I may say so, it was a very enjoyable party for me, my only regret being that you had invited so many interesting guests that there was no time to meet them all.

Thank you as well for the magnificent quilt which, if I estimate correctly, must have taken almost as much work as the organization of the party. It is a very sensitive and thoughtful gift and I am honoured to receive it.

In sum, my thanks to you, and through you to all of your colleagues engaged both in the activities of last week-end, and in those of two years ago. The time has been too long, but I am glad that at least now there has been the opportunity to have met them.

With best personal regards, and in the hope of seeing you again, with more films!

Yours sincerely,

Mr. and Mrs. Michael Snow,
123 Chambers Street,
New York, N.Y.

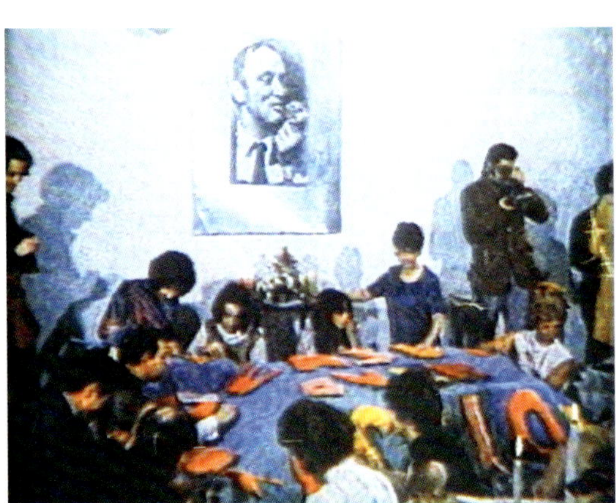

ABOVE

Letter from Prime Minister Pierre Trudeau to Mr. and Mrs. Michael Snow, 1969
Joyce Wieland fonds, ASC61820, York University Libraries, Clara Thomas Archives and Special Collections

BELOW

Quilt-in for the making of *La raison avant la passion* (1968) at Wieland's New York City loft, 1968, shown in "Artist Joyce Wieland in Retrospective in 1987," aired on CBC's *The Journal*, April 24, 1987

1970s

1970 With playwright Mary Mitchell organizes *Les Activistes Culturelles Canadiens*; occupies Canadian Consulate in New York.

• Reads James Laxer's *Energy Poker Game* (1970).

• Teaches for three months at Nova Scotia College of Art and Design (NSCAD), Halifax. Teaches course "Legitimizing Canadian Content in Art"; produces *O Canada* lithograph.

• Visits country fairs in Nova Scotia and Newfoundland seeking knitters and embroiderers to collaborate on textile works for 1971 exhibition at the NGC; hires Valerie McMillin (champion knitter), Joan McGregor (embroiderer), Joyce Martin (quilter), and Evelyn Mombourquette Aucoin (rug hooker).

• Included in *Survey/Sondage 70—Realism(e)s*, curated by Mario Amaya (1933–1986), Chief Curator, AGO at the Montreal Museum of Fine Arts and AGO.

• Submits film outline for *The Far Shore* to the Canadian Film Development Corporation (CFDC); does not receive funding.

• Anthology Film Archives in New York is founded by Jonas Mekas, Jerome Hill, P. Adams Sitney, Peter Kubelka, and Stan Brakhage; Wieland's films excluded from their collection of Essential Cinema Repertory, a deep disappointment for her.

• Avrom Isaacs opens Innuit Art Gallery in Toronto: first commercial gallery dedicated exclusively to Inuit art.

• Travels to Venice with Snow, who represents Canada at the 35th Venice Biennial.

1971 July 1: *True Patriot Love / Véritable Amour Patriotique*, curated by Pierre Théberge (1942–2018), opens at NGC, marking the institution's first solo exhibition of a living woman artist. Extensive media coverage. Hugo McPherson publishes first in-depth article on her work, "Wieland: An Epiphany of North," in *artscanada*.

• Summer: Travels with Snow to Newfoundland; they later build a small cabin there.

• October: Smaller version of NGC show opens at The Isaacs Gallery. Several works purchased by NGC, along with other major public institutions.

• Meets journalist Judy Steed (b. 1943), who makes first documentary, *A Film about Joyce Wieland* (1972).

• Develops lifelong friendship with Jean Sutherland Boggs (1922–2014), NGC's first woman director (1966–1976).

• November: moves back to Toronto with Snow; they purchase house at 137 Summerhill Avenue.

1972 Sets up home office; completes first draft of *The Far Shore*; works with Steed to seek investors.

• Reads Marxist analysis of Quebec history by Pierre Vallières (1938–1998), written while the author was jailed in Manhattan, first published in French in 1967 (English in 1971). Along with Steed and Danielle Corbeil, visits and films Vallières in Mont-Laurier, Quebec, where he recites three texts, at least one of which he has prepared for the film *Pierre Vallières* (1972).

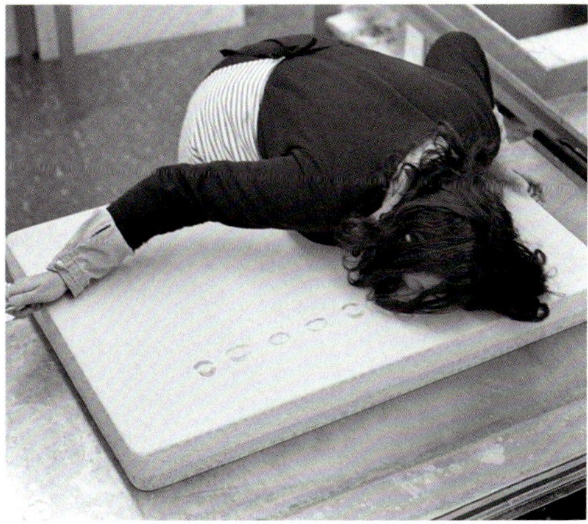

Bob Rogers
Joyce Wieland working on the print *O Canada* at the NSCAD Lithography Workshop, December 1970
Image courtesy of Anna Leonowens Gallery Archive, NSCAD University

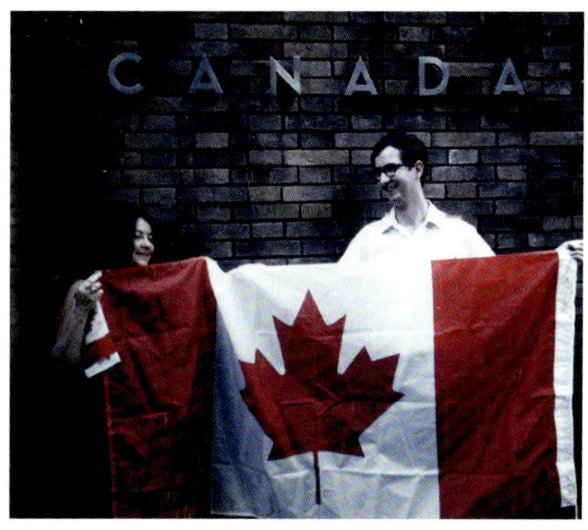

Joyce Wieland and Pierre Théberge at the Canada Pavilion, 35th Venice Biennale, c. 1970
Joyce Wieland fonds, ASC61815,
York University Libraries, Clara Thomas Archives and Special Collections

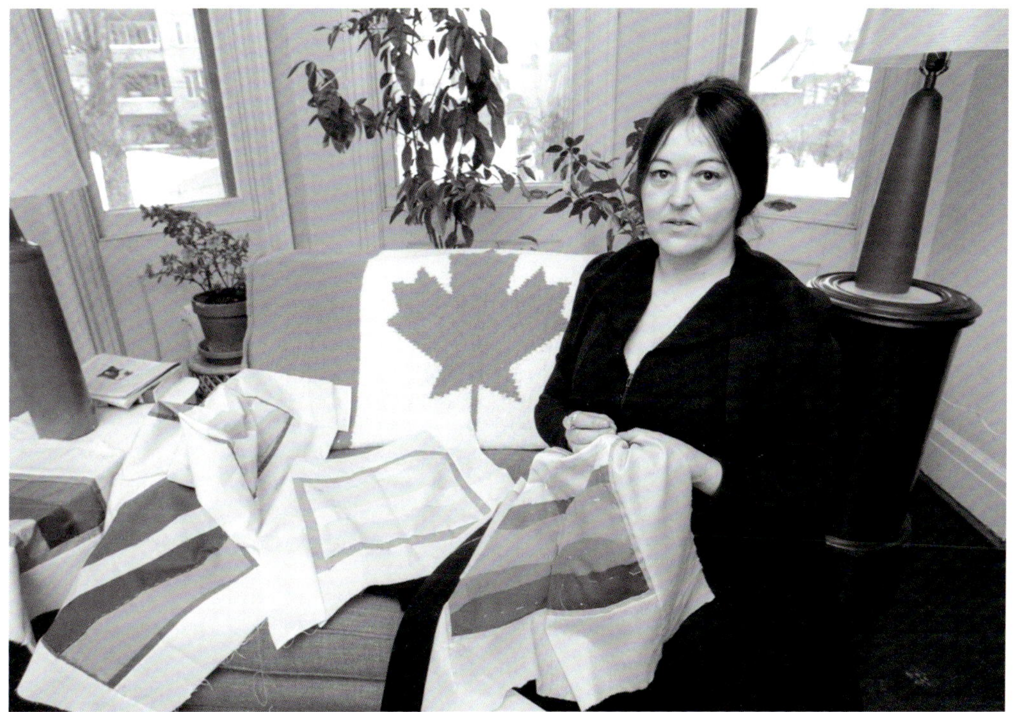

Joyce Wieland at work on pieces for the quilted cloth assemblage *109 Views*, c. 1970
David Davies for *Toronto Telegram*
Toronto Telegram fonds, ASC34390, York University Libraries, Clara Thomas Archives and Special Collections

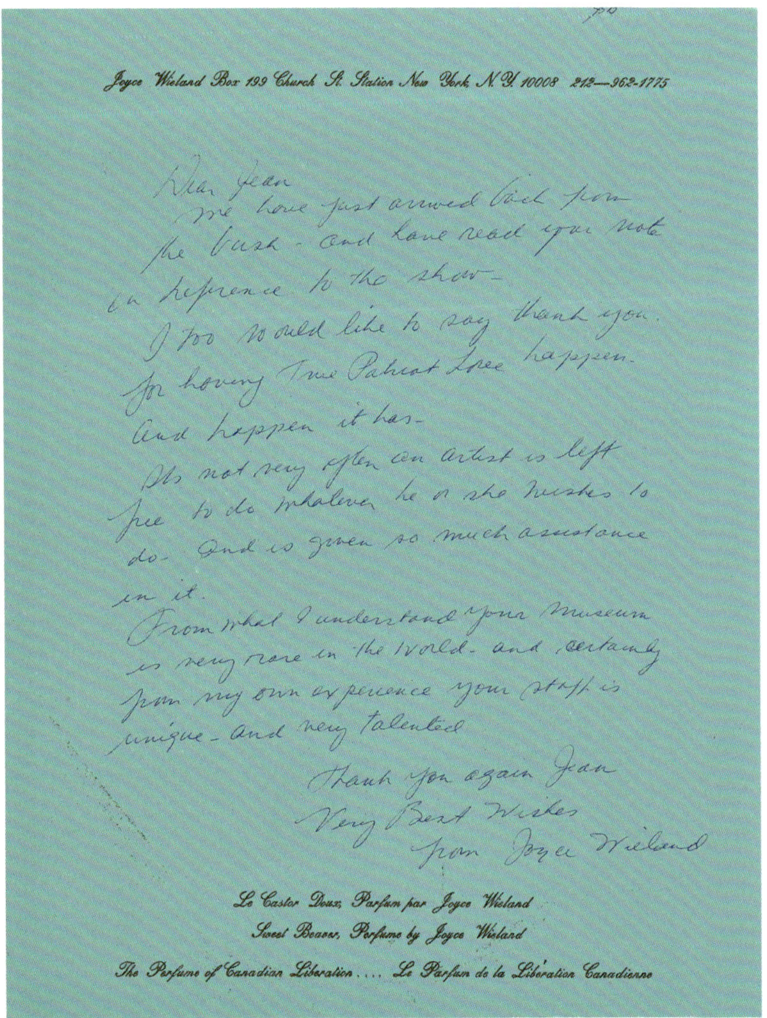

Joyce Wieland Box 199 Church St. Station New York N.Y. 10008 212—962-1775

Dear Jean
we have just arrived back from the bush - and have read your note in reference to the show -
I too would like to say thank you for having True Patriot Love happen.
And happen it has -
Its not very often an artist is left free to do whatever he or she wishes to do - and is given so much assistance in it.
From what I understand your museum is very rare in the world - and certainly from my own experience your staff is unique - and very talented

Thank you again Jean
Very Best Wishes
from Joyce Wieland

Le Castor Doux, Parfum par Joyce Wieland
Sweet Beaver, Perfume by Joyce Wieland
The Perfume of Canadian Liberation .... Le Parfum de la Libération Canadienne

Letter from Joyce Wieland to Jean Boggs, September 1971
National Gallery of Canada fonds, NGC Library and Archives
Photo: NGC

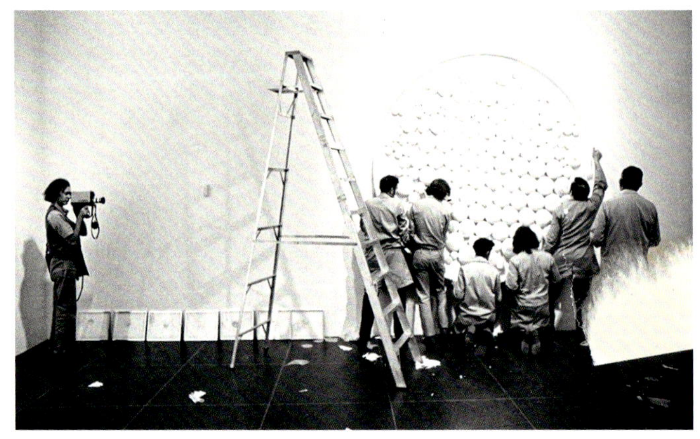

Michael Snow filming the installation of *Arctic Day* for the *True Patriot Love* exhibition at the National Gallery of Canada, 1971
Gelatin silver print
8.7 × 13 cm
Photo: Arnold Matthews

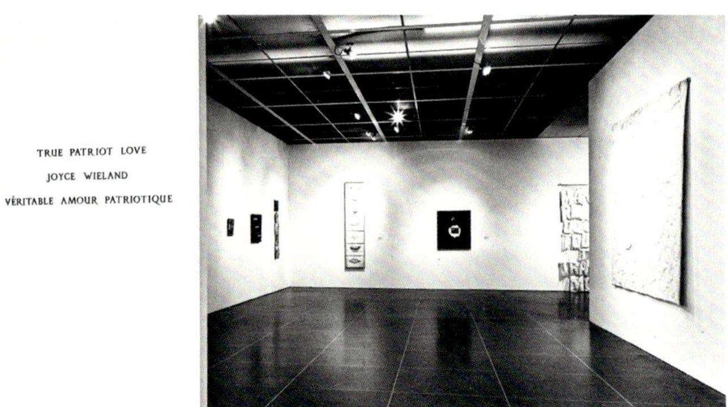

Installation view of the *True Patriot Love* exhibition at the National Gallery of Canada, 1971
Gelatin silver print
8.7 × 13 cm
Courtesy of Ihor Holubizky

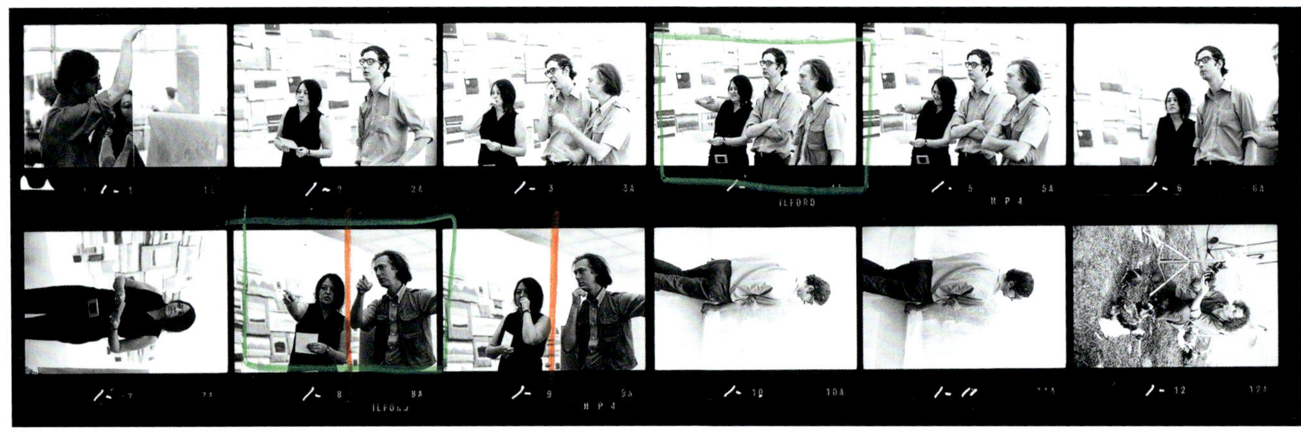

NGC contact sheet with Joyce Wieland, Michael Snow, Pierre Théberge, *True Patriot Love* exhibition, 1971
Photo: NGC

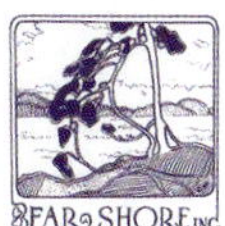
FAR SHORE INC.

PRODUCTION OFFICE TO FEBRUARY 1975: 436 SACKVILLE STREET, TORONTO M4X 1S9 920-0630
HEAD OFFICE: 137 SUMMERHILL AVENUE, TORONTO, ONTARIO M4T 1B1 922-1477 925-2624

Wieland's letterhead printed with "Far Shore Inc.," 1970s
Joyce Wieland fonds, ASC61823,
York University Libraries,
Clara Thomas Archives and Special Collections

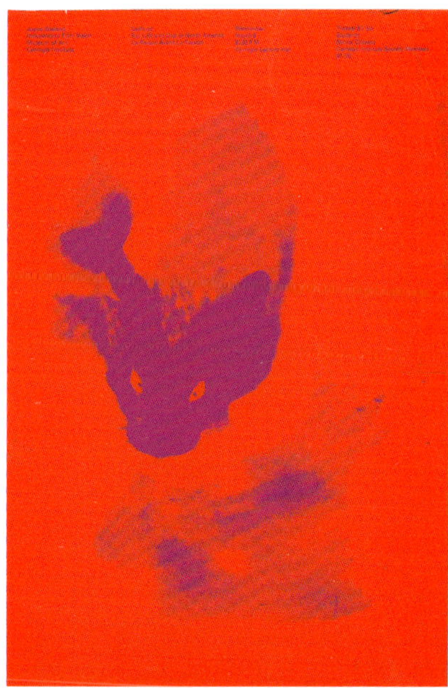

Joyce Wieland Independent Film Maker, Museum of Art, Carnegie Institute, 1972
Photo-serigraph in orange and purple on wove paper, 42.7 × 28.8 cm
National Gallery of Canada, Ottawa, Purchased 1979. 23301. Photo: NGC

Joyce Wieland
137 Summerhill Ave.
Toronto m4t 1b1, Ont.

Phone: 922-1477 or 925-2624 or messages at 923-7301

Letterhead printed with "Joyce Wieland," 1970s
Joyce Wieland fonds, ASC61824, York University Libraries, Clara Thomas Archives and Special Collections

• Writes essay *Jigs & Reels* (p. 145) about her filmmaking. She is the only woman director included in *Form and Structure in Recent Film* exhibition and publication at VAG.

• Screening of *Rat Life and Diet in North America* (1968), *Catfood* (1968), and *La raison avant la passion/Reason over Passion* at Carnegie Museum of Art, Pittsburgh, on March 8.

• The only woman artist commissioned to create a work for the new National Science Library, National Research Council, Ottawa. She designs her first quilted wall mural: *Defend the Earth* (pp. 202–203), unveiled on February 6, 1974.

• *Joyce Wieland: Independent Canadian Art Show*, University of Guelph Art Gallery.

• Wins Victor Martyn Lunch-Staunton Award, Canada Council.

• June 15: Participates along with twenty other artists in one of several demonstrations against appointment of American Richard J. Wattenmaker (1921–2017) as chief curator at the AGO. They chain themselves to the entrance doors.

• Participates in further protest against AGO board membership comprised exclusively of businessmen; later appointed as artist representative on board for a one-year term.

1973 Draws storyboards for *The Far Shore*; hires Bryan Barney to co-write the script; primary focus on fundraising.

• Attends and films workers' march against Dare Foods, Ltd., cookie factory, in Kitchener, Ontario. Makes film *Solidarity*.

• Elected member of the Royal Canadian Academy of Arts.

• Begins to spend summers in Newfoundland.

1974 May: Solo show of works on paper at The Isaacs Gallery; last exhibition until 1981.

• Receives major funding from Canada Film Development Corporation for *The Far Shore*; continues private fundraising.

• Travels to Algonquin Park searching locations; holds rehearsals on Betty Ferguson's farm in Puslinch, Ontario. Pierre Théberge's brother, André (film producer, Productions Magellan Inc.), spends five weeks assisting on filming. Filming begins in November; winter scenes filmed in Rosedale Valley Ravine, Toronto.

1975 Buys small house at 497 Queen Street East, names it Beaver Lodge; house becomes official office for *The Far Shore*.

• Major surgery in May impacts the film production.

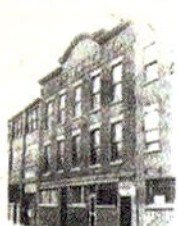

POWERHOUSE

3738 St. Dominique
Montréal, Québec
Canada H2X 2X8

MARCH/APRIL '80

exhibitions/
expositions

du 3 mars au 22 mars 1980
Vernissage: le 3 mars à 20h.

la grande galerie
Exposition de groupe de femmes-sculpteurs
ELISE BERNATCHEZ, LOUISE BOURRET, LINDA COVIT, HANNAH FRANKLIN, SUZANNE MARTEL, LOUISE PAGE, BRIGITTE RADECKI, TATIANA SEGUIN, BARBARA STEINMAN, MANON THIBAULT

Powerhouse propose un projet d'exposition sur la sculpture afin de savoir ce que font les femmes dans ce domain relatif à l'espace.

Le jury a procédé à une sélection retenant finalement 10 propositions considérées comme un éventail des tendances de la sculpture actuelle.

Il sera intéressant de dégager de quelle façon des préoccupations traditionnelles, telles la lumière, relations internes, intégration des éléments (eau, terre...) reviennent à travers des tendances contemporaines.

Cette exposition fait suite dans la lignée et dans l'optique à d'autres expositions de groupe: sur les Fibres et sur le Dessin. On peut noter, depuis deux ans, une nette émergence de la sculpture dans le champ artistique.

Cette exposition regroupera des matériaux aussi divers dans leurs formes, et leurs textures, tels que bois, toile, ciment, papier, carton, polyurétane, plastique, polyester, sable et même vidéo.

Egalement différentes propositions d'utilisation de l'espace: sculptures murales, suspendues, au sol; différentes utilisation de la qualité des matériaux: souple, rigide, massive, aérienne, transparente.

Recoupant diverses démarches/approches: humoristiques, viscérales, conceptuelles et d'équilibre.

L'oeil pourra redéfinir l'espace - d'un parcours autour, de l'intérieur de la pièce - et le corps le sentir - par au-dessus, autour.
- Viviane Prost, Renée Fredette, Linda Covit

la petite galerie
SUZANNE BOURBONNAIS
'Labyrinthe'

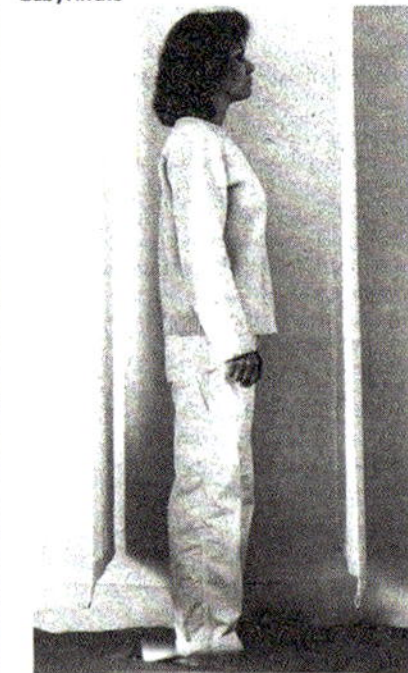

Suzanne Bourbonnais

"Je modifierai l'espace de la petite galerie en construisant avec des matériaux 'souples' un labyrinthe. Ce labyrinthe ne sera pas conçu dans le but de créer de l'angoisse chez le participant, angoisse résultant d'une impression d'isolation et d'emprisonnement. Au contraire, par l'utilisation de matériaux

...ion of elements (water, earth, etc.) resurface in contemporary ideas.

This exhibition groups materials diverse in forms and texture: wood, canvas, cement, paper, cardboard, polyurethane, plastic, polyester, sand and even video; different approaches to the uses of space: sculptures on the wall, on the floor, suspended; qualities of materials: soft, rigid, massive, airy, transparent; orientations/approaches: humourous, visceral, conceptual, centered; a redefining of space - walking around the outside, entering the interior of the piece - the body

Thurs., March 27 at 8:00 p.m.
JOYCE WIELAND

Toronto artist Joyce Wieland will give a lecture/slide presentation on her artwork and her films.

Sunday, March 9, 8:00 p.m.
'An evening with Joyce and Margaret' presented by Ann Pearson

Two sound film strips from the N.F.B. Creative Canadian Series (18 min. each). Joyce Wieland and Margaret Laurence talk about their work, how they got started, the demands of creative work, and what it is to be an artist. The Joyce Wieland presentation includes a short retrospective of her works, and the Margaret Laurence program includes readings from the Manawaka novels.

POETRY READING

Excerpt from the *Powerhouse* newsletter, March/April 1980
Concordia University Library, Special Collections and Archives, P128-HA1727-133

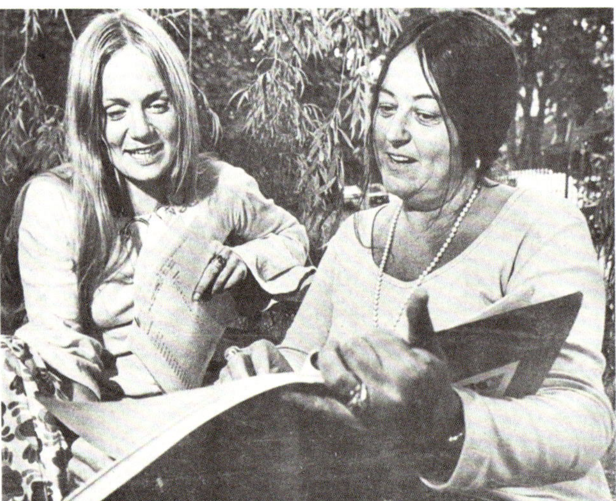

LEFT
Newspaper clipping featuring Judy Steed and Joyce Wieland working on *The Far Shore*, *Toronto Sun*, 1974
Courtesy of Judy Steed

TOP RIGHT
Joan Stewart (on the right) laying out the *Barren Ground Caribou* quilt, 1977
Joyce Wieland fonds, ASC04564, York University Libraries, Clara Thomas Archives and Special Collections

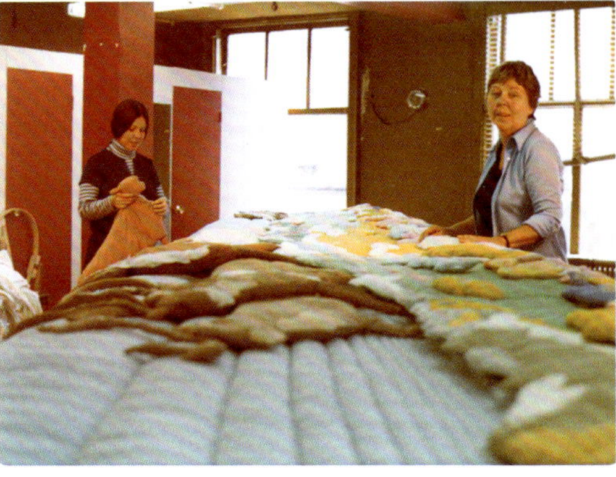

• *The Far Shore* films at Lake Skootamatta, Ontario; the shoot ends in July; rough-cut edit complete in December.

• Wins one of ten Toronto Transit Commission's "art in the subway" contracts for new subway stops; secures use of artist Charles Pachter's (b. 1942) studio to produce second quilted public art-work. *Barren Ground Caribou* (pp. 208–209) is unveiled at Spadina Station, Kendal Avenue entrance, in 1978.

1976 *The Far Shore* premieres August 5 at the National Arts Centre, Ottawa; screens at the Edinburgh Film Festival (August 22–September 11); released on September 23 in Toronto at Towne Cinema, with after-party at the AGO. Film receives poor critical reception yet wins three Canadian Film Awards: Best Supporting Actor (Frank Moore), Best Cinematography (Richard Leiterman), and Best Art Direction (Anne Pritchard).

• With Steed, options Margaret Laurence's (1926–1987) novel *The Diviners* (script by Margaret Atwood, b. 1939); project never realized.

1977 Completes Bata Shoes commission, Eaton Centre, Toronto. (Work later destroyed.)

• Visits Kinngait (Cape Dorset), Northwest Territories (now Nunavut), in 1977 and/or 1979; meets Inuk artist Surusilutu Ashoona (1941–2003); Kinngait co-op produces Wieland's print (p. 210).

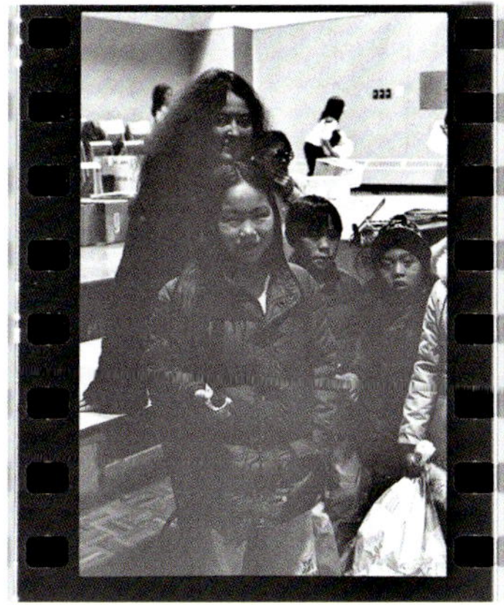

Joyce Wieland and children in Kinngait, c. 1977
Joyce Wieland fonds, NGC Library and Archives
Photo: NGC

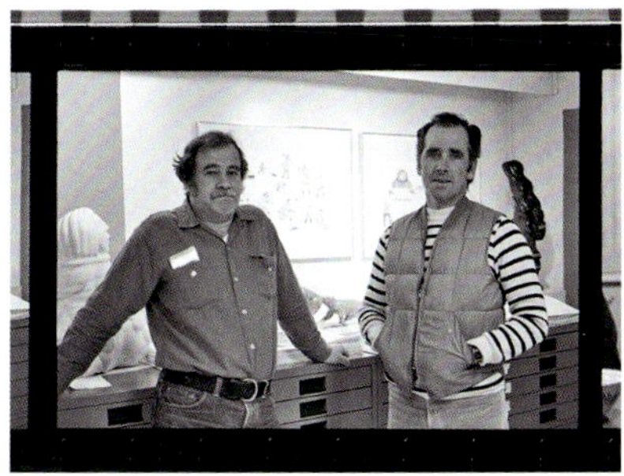

Avrom Isaacs and Terry Ryan in Kinngait printmaking studio, c. 1977
Joyce Wieland fonds, NGC Library and Archives
Photo: NGC

1978 *Joyce Wieland: Drawings from The Far Shore*, National Gallery of Canada (travelling exhibition).

1979 Completes last quilt, *Lens* (p. 277), based on the first stanza of a poem by Anne Wilkinson (1910–1961).

- Kinngait co-op produces Wieland's second print of Surusilutu Ashoona (p. 24).
- Begins a series of figurative coloured-pencil drawings that become *The Bloom of Matter* series.
- Separates from Snow; moves to Beaver Lodge.

1980s

1980 March: Delivers a lecture on her artwork and films at Powerhouse gallery, Montreal.

- Teaches painting; conducts feminist workshop at St. Michael's Printshop in Southern Shore, Newfoundland.
- Attends Buddhist gatherings; explores spirituality and anthroposophy.

1981 Major renovations to Beaver Lodge.

- March: *The Bloom of Matter* at The Isaacs Gallery.
- Returns to painting, *Flight into Egypt (After Tiepolo)* (p. 220), among other tondos.
- July: Cruise with Phyllis Lambert (b. 1927) around Greece and Turkey; makes watercolours later exhibited at Isaacs.
- Interview with Lauren Rabinovitz (b. 1950) published in *Afterimage*. Rabinovitz writes first academic thesis on Wieland, published in 1991 as *Points of Resistance: Women, Power & Politics in the New York Avant-Garde Cinema, 1943–71*

1982 February–March: *Joyce Wieland: New Paintings*, Forest City Gallery, London, Ontario (travelling exhibition).

- April: Solo exhibition at Yajima/Galerie, Montreal.
- Summer: Completes *Venus of Scarborough* (p. 223), an outdoor public commission for Guild Inn, Scarborough.

1983 April: *Turkey Watercolours* exhibition at The Isaacs Gallery.

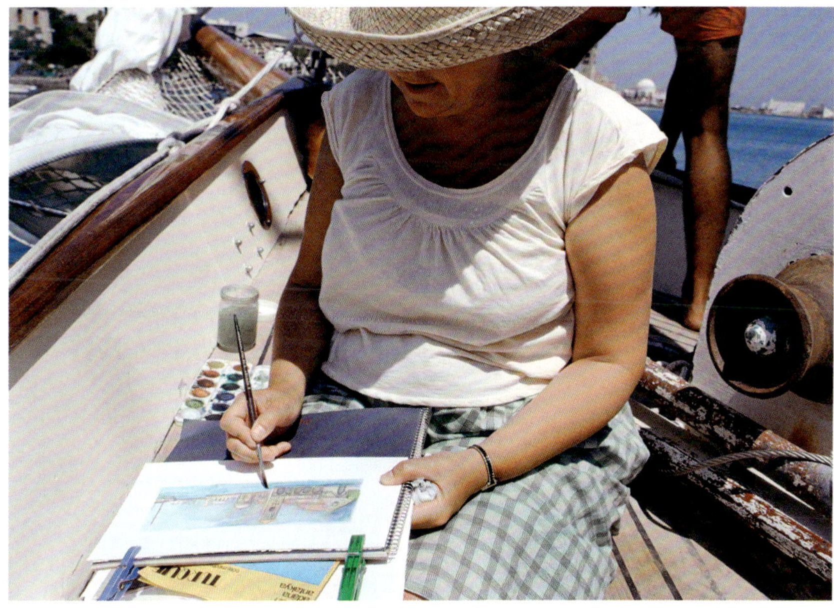

Phyllis Lambert
Joyce Wieland, Mandraki Harbour, Rhodes, Dodecanese, Greece, 1981
Phyllis Lambert fonds, Canadian Centre for Architecture
PL-1586
© Phyllis Lambert

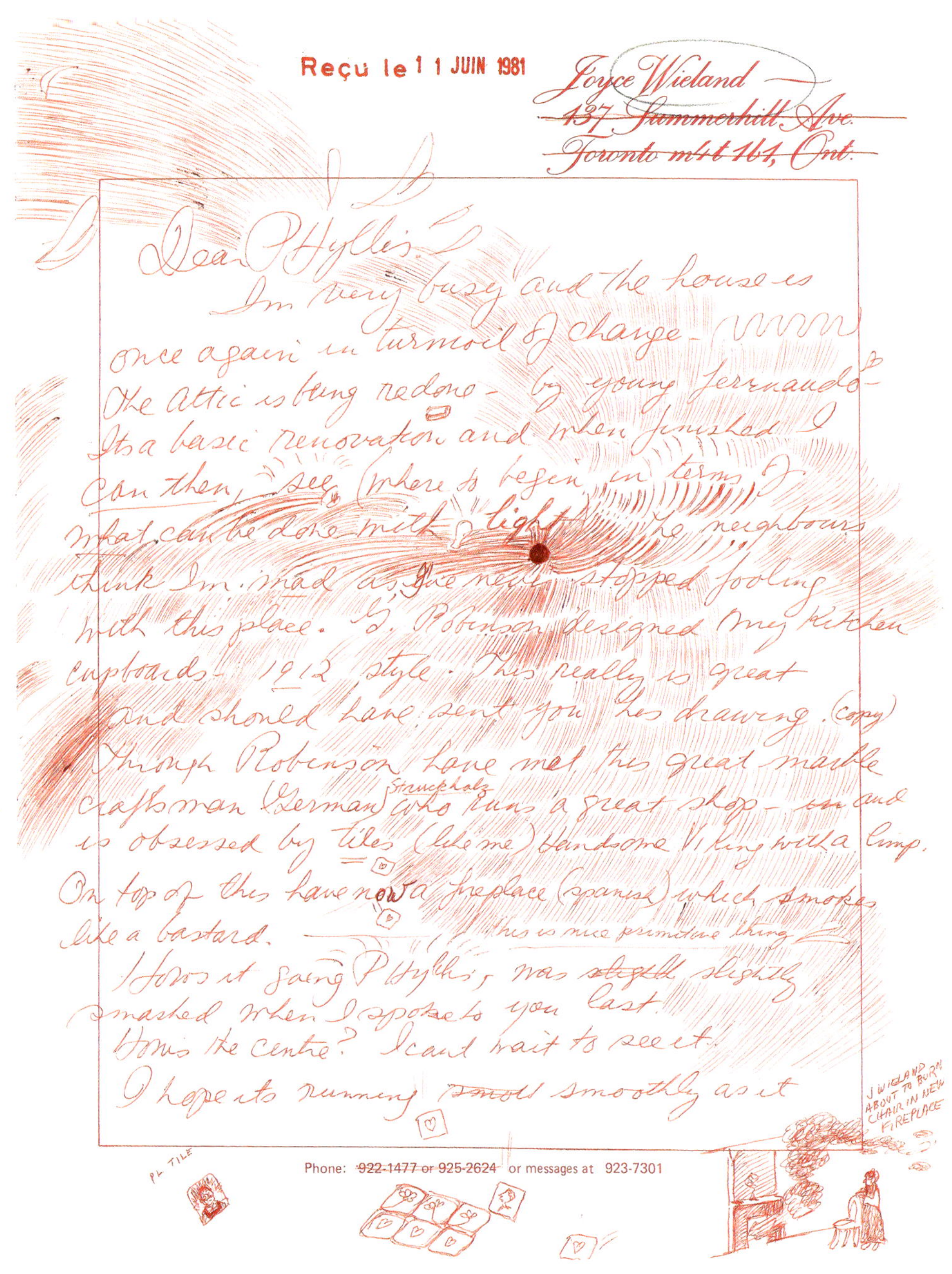

Reçu le 1 1 JUIN 1981

Joyce Wieland
~~137 Summerhill Ave.~~
~~Toronto m4t 1b1, Ont.~~

Dear Phyllis.

I'm very busy and the house is once again in turmoil of change – The attic is being redone – by young Fernando. It's a basic renovation and when finished I can then "see" where to begin in terms of what can be done with light. The neighbours think I'm mad as I've never stopped fooling with this place. G. Robinson designed my kitchen cupboards – 1912 style. This really is great and should have sent you his drawing. (copy) Through Robinson have met this great marble craftsman (German) Strauchholz who runs a great shop – and is obsessed by tiles (like me) Handsome Viking with a limp. On top of this have now a fireplace (spanish) which smokes like a bastard. this is nice primitive thing

How's it going Phyllis, was ~~slightl~~ slightly smashed when I spoke to you last.

How's the centre? I can't wait to see it.

I hope it's running ~~smoo~~ smoothly as it

J WIELAND ABOUT TO BURN CHAIR IN NEW FIREPLACE

PL TILE

Phone: ~~922-1477~~ or 925-2624 or messages at 923-7301

Letter from Joyce Wieland to Phyllis Lambert, 1981
Textual document with sketch in ink on paper
28 × 22.5 cm
Phyllis Lambert fonds, Canadian Centre for Architecture
ARCH288701

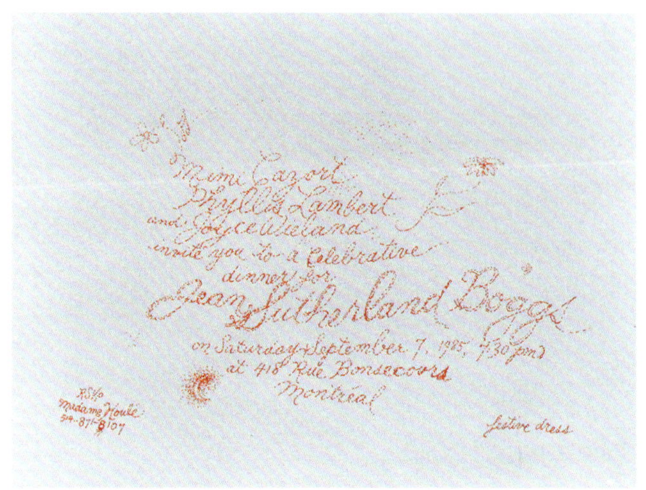

Mimi Cazort
Phyllis Lambert
and Joyce Wieland
invite you to a Celebrative
dinner for
Jean Sutherland Boggs
on Saturday September 7, 1985, 7:30 pm
at 418 Rue Bonsecours
Montreal

RSVP
Madame Houle
514-871-8107

festive dress

Invitation made by Joyce Wieland for a party on rue Bonsecours in honour of Jean Sutherland Boggs, 1985
Ink on paper
Phyllis Lambert fonds, Canadian Centre for Architecture
ARCH289728

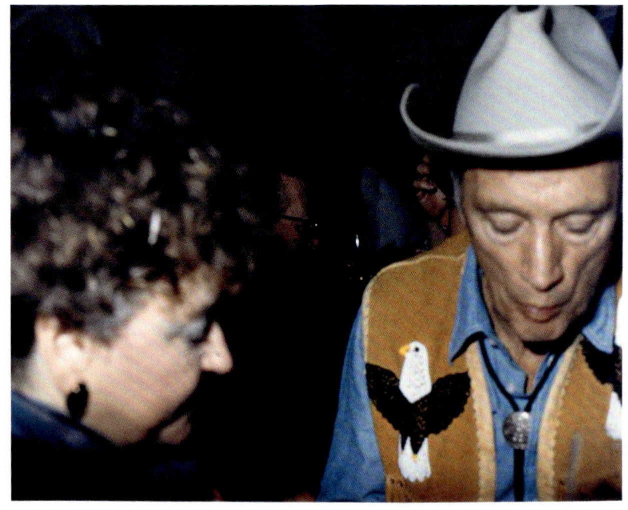

Phyllis Lambert
Joyce Wieland and Pierre Elliott Trudeau at a party organized by Phyllis Lambert and Joyce Wieland on rue Bonsecours in honour of Jean Sutherland Boggs, 1985
Phyllis Lambert fonds, Canadian Centre for Architecture
ARCH289729
© Phyllis Lambert

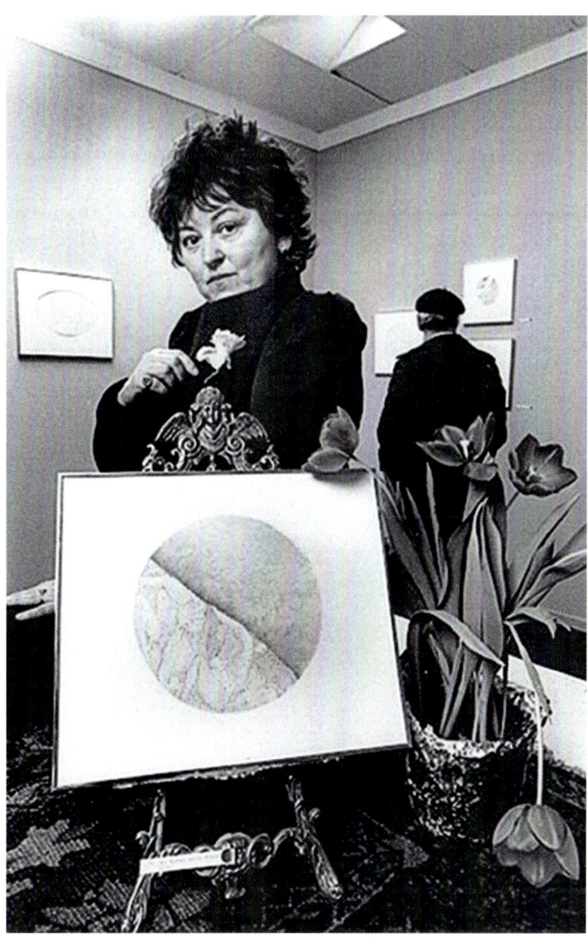

Joyce Wieland at *The Bloom of Matter* exhibition at The Isaacs Gallery, 1981
Photo by Keith Beaty/ Toronto Star via Getty Images

• Begins editing unfinished films from late 1960s with her niece, artist Susan (Su) Rynard: *A and B in Ontario* (co-directed with Hollis Frampton) and *Birds at Sunrise*.

• Meets with AGO director William Withrow (1926–2018), to request retrospective. Once confirmed, she begins to conceive new cycle of paintings.

• Meets film historian Kay Armatage (b. 1943).

• Invested as Officer of the Order of Canada.

• Organizes party with Lambert in Montreal to celebrate retirement of Jean Sutherland Boggs; Pierre Trudeau attends.

1984 Tour of Israel with nine other Canadian artists to develop a cultural exchange with Israeli curators and artists; meets Montreal artist Irene Whittome (b. 1942), and they form an enduring friendship.

1985 *Joyce Wieland: A Decade of Painting* curated by Sandra Paikowsky, Concordia University, Montreal. Exhibition catalogue is the first-ever publication on Wieland's work.

• Invited as visiting artist at San Francisco Art Institute, California.

1986 Armatage begins filming documentary on Wieland.

1987 April: *Joyce Wieland*, AGO (travels across Canada); major publication; film screenings. First exhibition by living woman artist in the history of AGO.

• June: Armatage premieres the documentary *Artist on Fire: The Work of Joyce Wieland* at the International Women's Festival of Film and Video in Montreal; it also screens at the Festival of Festivals (now the Toronto International Film Festival) in September.

• Last show at The Isaacs Gallery, in conjunction with the AGO.

• Completes commission for the Pantages Theatre, a painting titled *Celebration* (p. 243).

• Receives Lifetime Achievement Award from the Toronto Arts Foundation and YMCA Women of Distinction Award.

• Travels to Greece with Lambert.

1988 January: *In Search of the Far Shore: The Films of Joyce Wieland* retrospective as well as inclusion of quilts, paintings, and works on paper is held at Canada House, London, England.

• Makes last textile work, *Entrance to Nature* (p. 247).

• Founds Alma Gallery on Markham Street, Toronto, showcasing women's work (closes spring 1991).

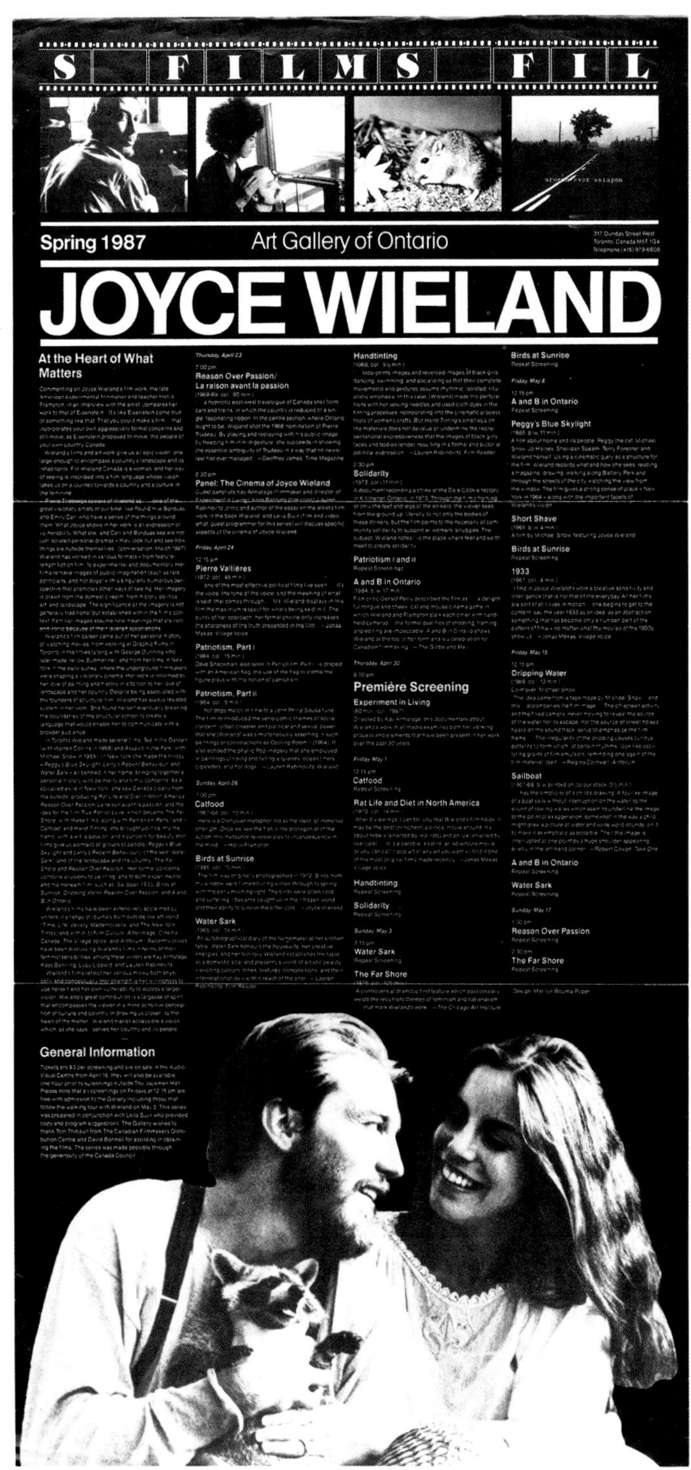

Joyce Wieland films poster, Art Gallery of Ontario, Spring 1987
Joyce Wieland artist's file
Edward P. Taylor Library & Archives, Art Gallery of Ontario
Photo: AGO, Craig Boyko

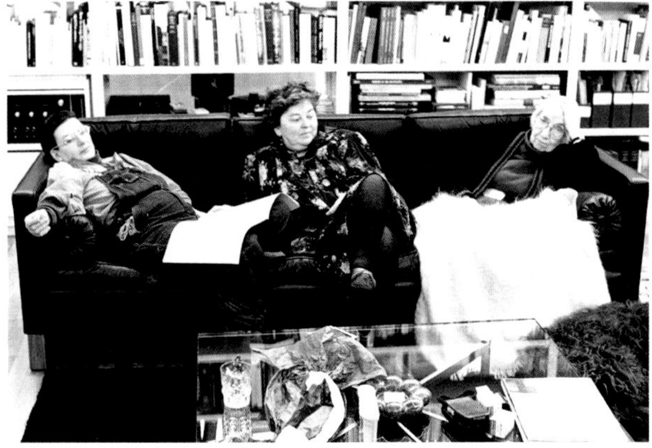

Phyllis Lambert, Joyce Wieland, and Berenice Abbott on New Year's Day, Montreal, 1985
Joyce Wieland fonds, ASC61421, York University Libraries, Clara Thomas Archives and Special Collections

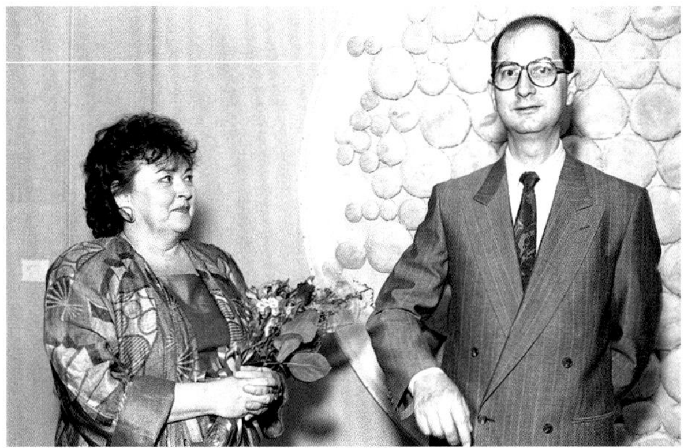

Joyce Wieland and Pierre Théberge at the opening of *Joyce Wieland* at the AGO, 1987
Joyce Wieland artist's file
Edward P. Taylor Library & Archives, Art Gallery of Ontario
Photo: AGO

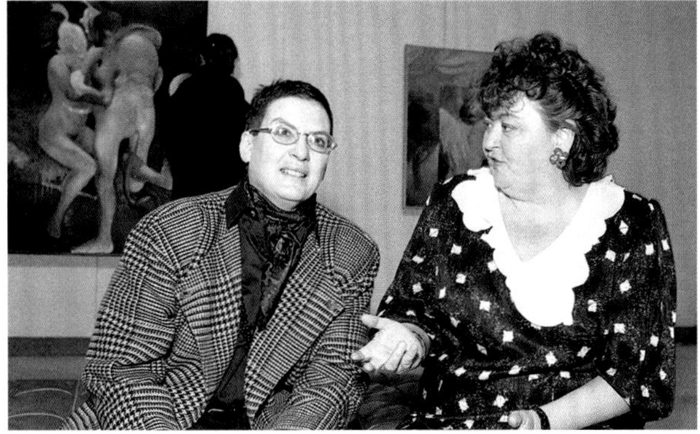

Phyllis Lambert and Joyce Wieland at the AGO, 1987
Joyce Wieland artist's file
Edward P. Taylor Library & Archives, Art Gallery of Ontario
Photo: AGO

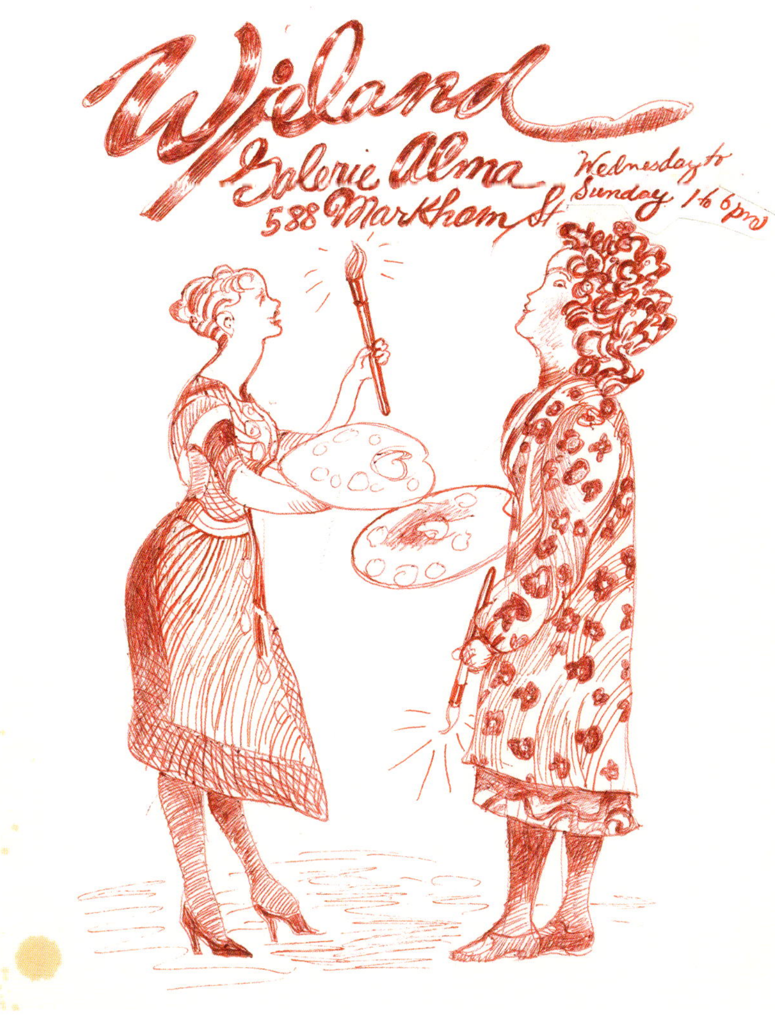

LEFT

Hand-drawn invitation to Wieland exhibition at Galerie Alma, Toronto
Red ink on paper, 1988
Joyce Wieland fonds, ASC61817, York University Libraries, Clara Thomas Archives and Special Collections

NEXT SPREAD

Joyce Wieland in front of the Royal Bank Plaza, Toronto, 1987
Photo: Bernard Weil/ Toronto Star via Getty Images

- Travels across England and to Wales and Scotland with artist Leila Sujir and her mother, Ruth.
- Gives several illustrated lectures across Canada.
- Disagreements with Isaacs lead to severing ties with his gallery after nearly thirty years.
- Artist in residence at University of Toronto School of Architecture, 1988–89.
- First deposit at York University Archives and Special Collections, Toronto; accrual continues until 2001.

1989 Works with sculptor Nikola Wojewoda on *Swan's Cupboard* installation.

1990s

1990 Health deteriorates.

- November–December: *Quilts in Context: The Art of Joyce Wieland*, McMaster Museum of Art, Hamilton; attends public events.

1991 Diagnosed with Alzheimer's disease. Community of women friends care for her during her remaining years.

1994 December: *Twilight Record of Romantic Love*, curated by Jan Allen, Agnes Etherington Art Centre, Kingston, Ontario, including publication; attends public events.

1998 Dies in Toronto on June 27, three days before her sixty-eighth birthday.

- Memorial held at the Art Gallery of Ontario; ashes interred behind the AGO, directly across Grange Park at St. George the Martyr Church.
- Major donation of work from Betty Ferguson to the AGO; Donna Montague donates significant collection to VAG in 1999.
- Films deposited at Cinémathèque québécoise, Montreal; officially acquired in 2002.

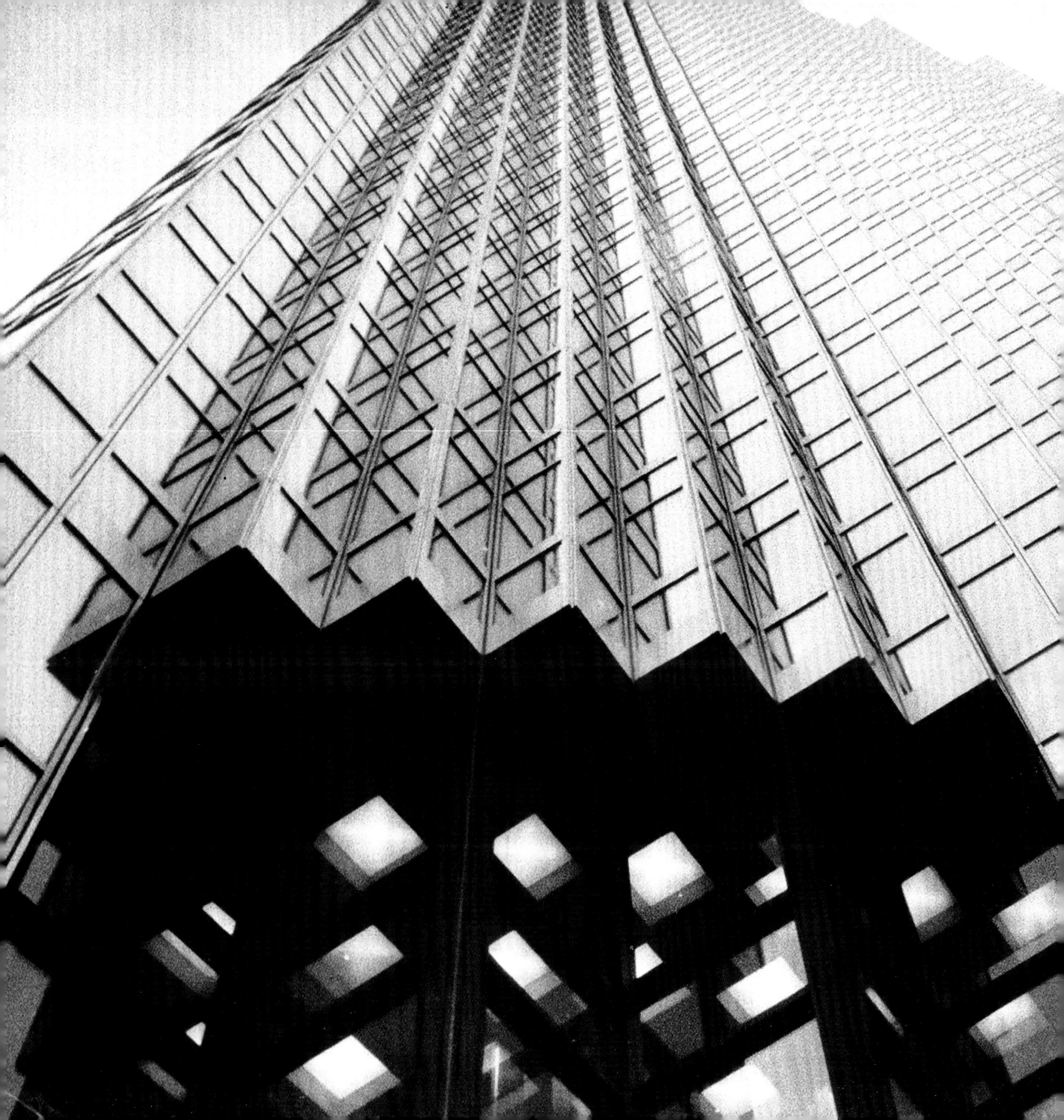

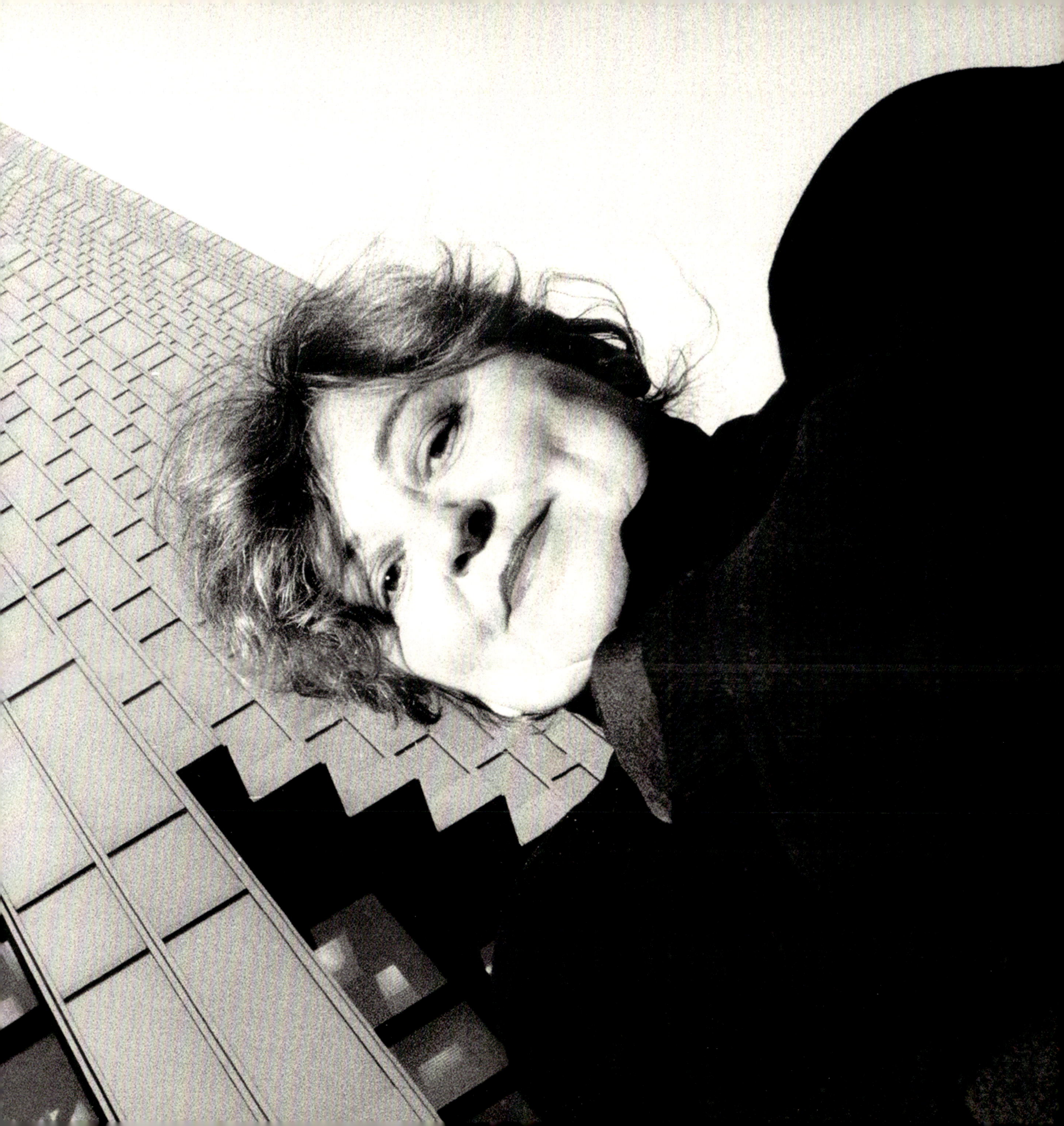

Illustrated Artworks

All works by Joyce Wieland

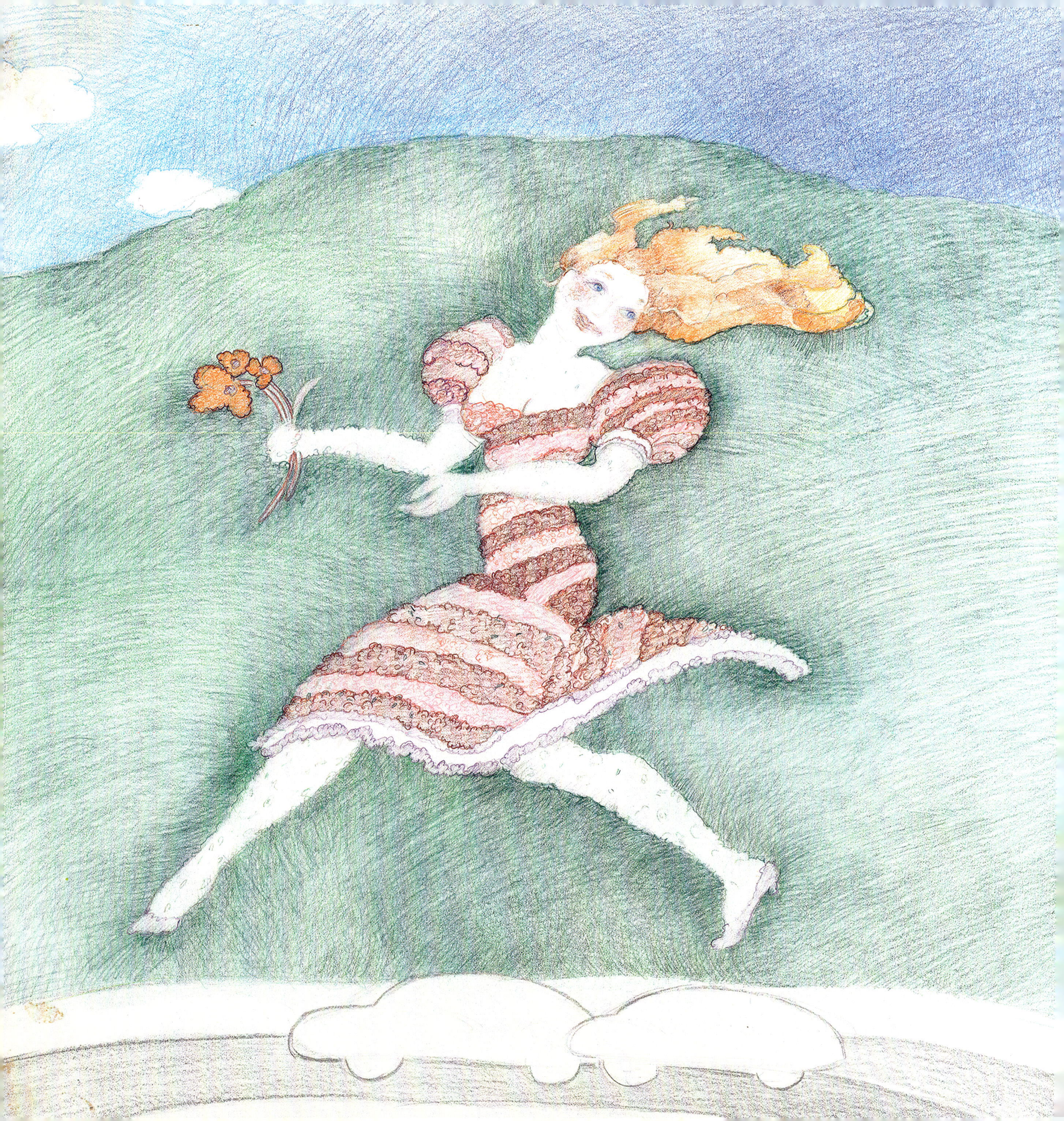

Contributors

Renée van der Avoird is Associate Curator, Canadian Art, at the Art Gallery of Ontario.

Stephanie Barnes is a Conservation Scientist at the Canadian Conservation Institute in Ottawa.

Vincent Bonin is a writer and independent researcher working in Montreal.

Alicia Boutilier is Chief Curator and Curator of Canadian Historical Art at the Agnes Etherington Art Centre in Kingston, Ontario.

Tobi Bruce is Head of Collections and Exhibitions and Chief Curator at the Art Gallery of Hamilton.

Stéphanie Côté is Restoration Projects Manager at the Cinémathèque québécoise, Montreal.

Richard Gagnier is Head of Conservation at the Montreal Museum of Fine Arts (retired October 2024).

Anne Grace is Curator of Modern Art at the Montreal Museum of Fine Arts.

Kristy A. Holmes is Associate Professor of Art History in the Department of Visual Arts at Lakehead University in Thunder Bay, Ontario.

Anna Hudson is a curator and Professor of Art History and Visual Culture at York University in Toronto.

Mark Kearney is a Conservation Scientist at the Canadian Conservation Institute in Ottawa.

Sjoukje van der Laan is Conservator, Contemporary Art, at the Art Gallery of Ontario.

OPPOSITE
Venus of Toronto (detail), 1984
Colour pencil with graphite on paper
45.5 × 58.9 cm
PL-0222
Phyllis Lambert fonds,
Canadian Centre for Architecture

Guillaume Lafleur is Director of Film Programming and Publications at the Cinémathèque québécoise, Montreal.

Sarah Parsons is Professor of Art History and Visual Culture at York University in Toronto.

Su Rynard is a filmmaker and media artist born in Toronto. She collaborated with Joyce Wieland, editing unfinished films.

Eo Sharp is a set and costume designer for theatre in Montreal. She collaborated with Joyce Wieland on *Barren Ground Caribou*.

Jim Shedden is a writer and filmmaker. He is Curator of Special Projects and Director of Publishing at the Art Gallery of Ontario.

Rachel Stark is Assistant Conservator, Contemporary Art, at the Art Gallery of Ontario.

Judy Steed is an award-winning journalist, author, and leadership teacher of mindfulness/meditation. She co-produced Joyce Wieland's 1976 feature film *The Far Shore*.

Barbara Steinman is a Montreal-born video and installation artist.

Shannon Stride is an arts professional and scholar residing in Montreal.

Leila Sujir is a video artist and professor emerita with Concordia University in Montreal.

Tegoodligak was a mid-20th-century Inuk poet, storyteller, and translator from Hivuraa Qikiqtaaluk (South Baffin Island).

Georgiana Uhlyarik is Fredrik S. Eaton Curator, Canadian Art, and co-lead of the Indigenous + Canadian department at the Art Gallery of Ontario.

Rhiannon Vogl is a PhD candidate in the Department of Art History at the University of Toronto.

Jean-Philippe Warren is Professor of Sociology at Concordia University.

Adam Welch is Associate Curator, Modern Art, at the Art Gallery of Ontario.

Anne Wilkinson was a Canadian modernist poet whose work, particularly *Lens* (1955), was a powerful influence on Wieland. She was born and died in Toronto.

Joyce Zemans, CM, Senior Scholar and Professor Emerita, York University, is an art historian, curator, art critic, teacher, and administrator.

Study Days Participants:

Montreal: Adriana Alarcón, Renée van der Avoird, Marie-Eve Beaupré, Vincent Bonin, Eva Crocker, Jacques Des Rochers, Munro Ferguson, Marie Ferron-Desautels, Marc Igloliorte, Monika Kin Gagnon, Martha Langford, Georgia Phillips-Amos, Kirsty Robertson, Denise Ryner, Johanne Sloan, Shannon Stride, Kathleen Vaughan, Jean-Philippe Warren, Adam Welch

Ottawa: Saada El-Akhrass, Renée van der Avoird, Stephanie Barnes, Richard Gagnier, Eric Henderson, Amy Jenkins, Mark Kearney, Christopher MacKay, Kirsty Robertson, Johanne Sloan, Agata Sochon, Shannon Stride, Valerie Tomlinson, Rachel Stark, Geneviève Saulnier, Adam Welch

Toronto: Renée van der Avoird, Shary Boyle, Anjo-Marí Gouws, Kristy Holmes, Tanja Jacobs, Monika Kin Gagnon, Elizabeth Legge, Robyn Lew, Hana Nikčević, Julia Polyck-O'Neill, Su Rynard, Denise Ryner, Eo Sharp, Jim Shedden, Johanne Sloan, Judy Steed, Shannon Stride, Kristen Thomson, Rhiannon Vogl, Adam Welch, Chloe Wittes, Joyce Zemans, Mike Zryd

The AGO would like to acknowledge the support of the Richard and Beryl Ivey Canadian Art Fund for the Joyce Wieland Study Days.

Land Acknowledgement

The Art Gallery of Ontario operates on land that is the territory of the Anishinaabe (Mississauga) Nation and is also the territory of the Wendat and Haudenosaunee. The Dish with One Spoon Wampum Belt Covenant is an agreement between the Haudenosaunee Confederacy and the Anishinaabe Three Fires Confederacy to peaceably share and care for the resources around the Great Lakes. Toronto is also governed by a treaty between the federal government of Canada and the Mississaugas of the New Credit (Anishinaabe Nation). Toronto/Tkaronto has always been a trading centre for First Nations.

The Montreal Museum of Fine Arts is situated in the territory of the Great Peace of 1701, imbued with histories of relation, exchange, and ceremony that have taken place at the centre of the island-metropolis known widely as Montreal. Tiohtià:ke in Kanien'kéha, Mooniyaang in Anishinaabemowin, Molian in Aln8ba8dwaw8gan, and Te ockiai in Wendat are various toponyms that attest to this. With the communities of Kahnawà:ke and Kanehsatà:ke, Tiohtià:ke encompasses the eastern expanse of Kanien'kehá:ka Nation territory, People of the Flint and Keepers of the Eastern Door within the Rotinonshión:ni Confederacy.

Goose Lane Editions is located on the unceded territory of the Wəlastəkwiyik whose ancestors along with the Mi'kmaq and Peskotomuhkati Nations signed Peace and Friendship Treaties with the British Crown in the 1700s.

Thank You

THE AGO GRATEFULLY ACKNOWLEDGES:

Supporting Sponsor

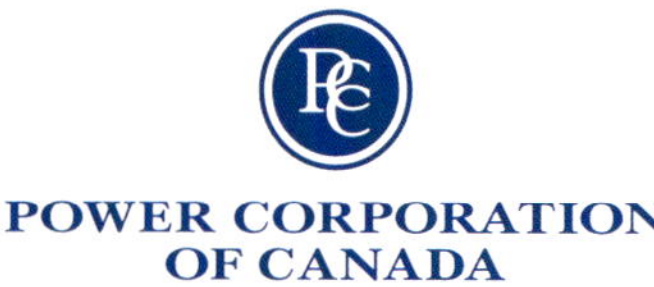

Lead Support

Volunteers of the AGO

Generous Support

Jamie & Patsy Anderson
The Birks Family Foundation
Dr. Ronald M. Haynes
Rosamond Ivey
J.S. McLean Fund
Women's Art Initiative

Additional Assistance

Charles Brindamour & Josée Letarte

The Art Gallery of Ontario is partially funded by the Ontario Ministry of Culture. Additional operating support is received from the City of Toronto, the Department of Canadian Heritage, and the Canada Council for the Arts.

This publication is supported by the Sorel Etrog Publication Fund.

Contemporary programming at the Art Gallery of Ontario is supported by

Canada Council for the Arts Conseil des arts du Canada

Goose Lane Editions acknowledges the generous support of the Government of Canada, the Canada Council for the Arts, and the Government of New Brunswick.

THE MMFA GRATEFULLY ACKNOWLEDGES:

Presenting Sponsor

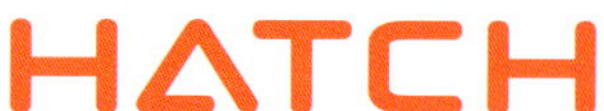

Public Partners

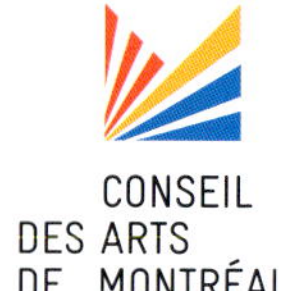

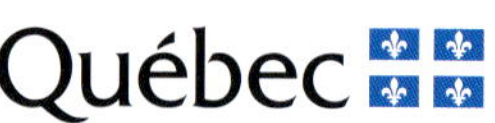

The Montreal Museum of Fine Arts wishes to thank the Canada Council for the Arts for its financial support.

Publication

Editors: Anne Grace and Georgiana Uhlyarik
Publishing Director: Jim Shedden
Publishing Coordinator: Robyn Lew
Production and Content Editor: Kieran Grant
Translator: Jennifer Couëlle
Proofreaders: Laura Kenins, Judy Phillips
Researchers: Charlotte Beyries, Mirra Ianeva, Shannon Stride, Rhiannon Vogl
Designer: Lara Minja of Lime Design
Photographers: Craig Boyko, Sean Weaver
Pre-Press: Paul Jerinkitsch
Printing: Type A, Inc.

AGO EXHIBITION

Deputy Director & Chief Curator: Julian Cox
Curator: Georgiana Uhlyarik
Project Manager: Brittney Sproule
Curatorial Coordinator: Chloé Wittes
Editor: Kieran Grant
Exhibition Designer: Thoeodora Doulamis
Graphic Designer: Evelina Petrauskas
Production: Malene Hjørngaard, Evelyn Quinn

Exhibitions, Collections, and Conservation

Chief, Exhibitions, Collections & Conservation: Jessica Bright
Director, Exhibitions: Laura Comerford
Registration: Donna Austria, Alison Beckett
Collection Information: Liana Radvak, Alexandra Cousins, Tracy Mallon-Jensen
Conservation: Maria Sullivan, Andrew Bugden, Lisa Ellis, Claire Molgat Laurin, Christina McLean, Meaghan Monaghan, Brent Roe, Rachel Stark, Tessa Thomas, Valerie Tomlinson, Sjoukje van der Laan, Joan Weir, Katharine Whitman, John Williams

Logistics and Art Services

Director, Logistics and Art Services: Iain Hoadley
Manager, Art Services: Craig Whiteside
Logistics and Art Services Team: Curtis Amisich, Paul Ayers, Gregory Baszun, Scott Cameron, Colin Campbell, Brian Davis, Andre Ethier, Randal Fedje, Tina Giovinazzo, Ruth Jones, David Kinsman, Jason Laudadio, Paul Mathiesen, Phil Scott, Sasi Sivapalan, Stephanie Vittas, Darin Yorston, Tanya Zhilinsky

Education and Programming

Richard & Elizabeth Currie Chief, Education & Programming: Robert Durocher
Director, Engagement & Learning: Paola Poletto
Director, Strategic Projects & Operations: Deborah Nolan
E&P Team: Charlotte Big Canoe, Maureen DaSilva, Sarah Febbraro, Nathan Huisman, Jesse King, Natalie Lam, Kathleen McLean, Zavette Quadros-Evangelista, Tiana Roebuck, Annie Roper, Bojana Stancic, Joey Suriano

Library and Archives

Rosamond Ivey Special Collections
Archivist and Head, Library and Archives: Amy Furness
Collection Development Librarian: Erin Rutherford
Archivist: Al Stanton-Hagan

Media Production

Manager, Digital Projects: Catherine Thomson
Media: Matthew Scott, Fraser Wrighte
Photographers: Craig Boyko, Leah Maghanoy, Tracey Owusu

Development

Chief Development Officer: Kate Halpenny
Senior Director, Major Gifts and Campaign: Andrea Orr
Philanthropy: Marielle Bryck, Anastasia Hare, Olivia Hsuen-Ferris, Tanika Johnny, Erin Thadani, Teya Vitko
Corporate Partnerships: Aneesa Guerra-Khan, Allison Miller, Taryn Sarkozi
Donor Relations: Michelle Greenspoon, Matt Semansky

MMFA

President: André Dufour
Director: Stéphane Aquin
Deputy Director: Yves Théoret
Chief Curator: Mary-Dailey Desmarais
Director of Learning and Community Engagement: Mélanie Deveault
Director of Communications and Marketing: Michèle Meier
Director General of the MMFA Foundation: Jo-Anne Duchesne
Curator of Modern Art: Anne Grace
Project Coordinator: Chloé Martel

Publications

Head of Publications: Sébastien Hart
Translators-Revisors: Clara Gabriel, Juliette Hérivault
Technicians, Photographic Services and Copyright: Linda-Anne D'Anjou, Marie-Claude Saia

Exhibitions and Collections

Head of Exhibition Administration: Carolina Calle Sandoval

Collection Management and Registration

Head of Collections Management and Registration: Eve Katinoglou
Registrar: Mélissa Bezzi
Logistics Manager: Lilly-Doris Panzou
Cataloguer: Natalie Vanier, Marianne Raymond
Photographers: Jean-François Brière, Julie Ciot
Photographic Services Technician: Claudine Nicol

Design and Production

Head of Design and Production: Nuria Montblanch
Project Manager – Exhibition Design: Carolina Bassani
Exhibition Production Project Coordinator: Mélanie Seibert
Graphic Production Coordinator: Sarah Cousineau
Exhibitions Technicians: Nicolas Cantin, Jean-Benoit Pouliot, Marie-Hélène Rolko, Philippe Chabot, Frank Galiay, Marc Desjardins

Conservation

Interim Head of Conservation: Nathalie Richard
Decorative Arts Conservator: Nathalie Richard
Paper Conservator: Johanne Perron
Paintings Conservator: Valerie Moscato
Framing Technician – Graphic and Photographic Works: Isabelle Goulet
Conservation Technicians: Sacha Marie Levay, Ana Melissa Ramos-Becerra

Learning and Community Engagement

Head of Program Administration and Research: Claire Thiboutot
Cultural Activities Manager: Benoit Jodoin
Head of Regular Programs and Operations: Lisa Traversy
Educational Programs Officers: Patricia Boyer, Laura Delfino, Louise Giroux, Stephen Legari, Karima Ouazar, Kate Walker

This book was published on the occasion of the exhibition *JOYCE WIELAND: HEART ON*, organized by the Art Gallery of Ontario and Montreal Museum of Fine Arts from February 8, 2025, to May 4, 2025 (Montreal), and June 21, 2025, to January 4, 2026 (Toronto).

Published in 2025 by the Art Gallery of Ontario, Montreal Museum of Fine Arts, and Goose Lane Editions.

This book was set in *Dante MT Pro* by Monotype, *TT Norms* by Type Type, *Trade Gothic Next LT* by Linotype and *Typewriter URW* by URW Type Foundry, and printed on 150 gsm Magno Satin paper.

ISBN: 9781773104409

10 9 8 7 6 5 4 3 2 1

Art Gallery of Ontario
317 Dundas Street West
Toronto, Ontario
M5T 1G4
Canada
ago.ca

Montreal Museum
of Fine Arts
2189 Bishop Street,
Montreal, Quebec
H3G 2E8
Canada
mbam.qc.ca

Goose Lane Editions
500 Beaverbrook
Court, Suite 330
Fredericton,
New Brunswick
E3B 5X4
Canada
gooselane.com

Library and Archives Canada Cataloguing in Publication

Title: Joyce Wieland: Heart On / edited by Anne Grace and Georgiana Uhlyarik.
Other titles: Heart on
Names: Wieland, Joyce, 1930–1998. Works. Selections. | Grace, Anne, 1966– editor. | Uhlyarik, Georgiana, editor. | Art Gallery of Ontario, issuing body, host institution. | Montreal Museum of Fine Arts, issuing body, host institution.
Description: Catalogue of an exhibition organized by the Montreal Museum of Fine Arts and the Art Gallery of Ontario. | Includes bibliographical references.
Identifiers: Canadiana 20240437276 | ISBN 9781773104409 (hardcover)
Subjects: LCSH: Wieland, Joyce, 1930–1998. | LCGFT: Exhibition catalogs.
Classification: LCC N6549.W53 A4 2025 | DDC 709.2—dc23

Image credits

Front cover:

Stuffed Movie (detail), 1966
Plastic, thread, paper, cotton, textile, batting
142.2 × 36.9 × 3 cm
Collection of the Vancouver Art Gallery, Murrin Estate Funds
VAG 68.6
Photo: Vancouver Art Gallery, Ian Lefebvre

Back cover:

Water Sark (film still), 1965
Soundtrack: Carla Bley, Mike Mantler, Ray Jessel
Film, 8mm blown up in 16mm, colour, sound
14 min
Joyce Wieland fonds, Cinémathèque québécoise
Photo: Stephen Broomer, courtesy of the CFMDC

Endpapers:

Handtinting (film stills), 1967
Film, 16mm, colour, silent
6 min
Joyce Wieland fonds, Cinémathèque québécoise
Photo: Stéphanie Côté, courtesy of Cinémathèque québécoise

Michel Lambeth
Joyce Wieland (at window) (detail), c. 1960
Gelatin silver print
34 × 26 cm
Art Gallery of Ontario, Gift of Av Isaacs, Toronto, 1994
94/447
© Estate of Michel Lambeth
Photo: AGO, Craig Boyko

Polaroid of Joyce Wieland, c. 1989
Polaroid photograph
11 × 9 cm
ARCH288702
Phyllis Lambert fonds, Canadian Centre for Architecture

Page 1:

Poster (detail) for Joyce Wieland Retrospective, Glendon College Art Gallery, York University, Toronto, 1969
Photo: Art Gallery of Guelph

Page 2:

Hallucination (detail), 1961
Oil, cloth and paperboard on canvas
193.5 × 259.5 cm
Art Gallery of Ontario, Gift of Milton Winberg, 2016
2017/51
Photo: AGO, Craig Boyko

Page 288:

Poster (detail) for an exhibition of Joyce Wieland's work at The Isaacs Gallery, c. February 1962
Avrom Isaacs fonds, ASC61618, York University Libraries, Clara Thomas Archives and Special Collections

PULL-QUOTE REFERENCES

Page 67

Transcript of Joyce Wieland artist's talk at the University of Lethbridge, 1985, 1–2 (edited quote from cassette tape "Joyce Wieland on Her Work"); transcript held at the University of Lethbridge Art Gallery, Alberta.

Page 71

Transcript of Joyce Wieland artist's talk at the University of Lethbridge, 1985, 2 (edited quote from cassette tape "Joyce Wieland on Her Work"); transcript held at the University of Lethbridge Art Gallery, Alberta.

Page 72

Transcript of Joyce Wieland artist's talk at the University of Lethbridge, 1985, 3 (edited quote from cassette tape "Joyce Wieland on Her Work"); transcript held at the University of Lethbridge Art Gallery, Alberta.

Page 124

Joyce Wieland quoted on Plastics Exhibition Poster, Art Gallery of Ontario, October 28–November 14, 1967. AGO archives AGO.162408.

Page 134

Armatage, Kay. "Kay Armatage interviews Joyce Wieland." Interview with Joyce Wieland. *Take One* (Montreal), vol. 3, no. 2 [November–December, 1970; published February 7, 1972], 23.

Page 165

Wieland quoted in Susan M. Crean, "Notes from the Language of Emotion: A Conversation with Joyce Wieland," *Canadian Art* (Spring 1987), 65.

Page 169

Kay Armatage, "Joyce Wieland, Feminist Documentary, and the Body of the Work," *Canadian Journal of Political and Social Theory / Revue canadienne de théorie politique et sociale*, vol. 13, no. 1–2 (1989): 91–2.

Page 170

John Porter, *Vanguard* 13, Summer 1984.

Page 171

Pruska-Oldenhof: Email to author, January 2024.

Page 173

Pruska-Oldenhof: Email to author, January 2024.

Page 174

Pruska-Oldenhof: Email to author, January 2024.
Lock: Email to author, January 2024.

Page 175

Hoolboom: Email to author, January 2024.

Page 176

Rynard: Email to author, January 2024.
Hoffman: Quoted in Kay Armatage, "Joyce Wieland, Feminist Documentary, and the Body of the Work," *Canadian Journal of Political and Social Theory / Revue canadienne de théorie politique et sociale*, vol. 13, no. 1–2 (1989): 99–100.

Page 177

Elder: Email to author, January 2024.
Kay Armatage, "Joyce Wieland, Feminist Documentary, and the Body of the Work," *Canadian Journal of Political and Social Theory / Revue canadienne de théorie politique et sociale*, vol. 13, no. 1–2 (1989): 91–2.

Page 210

Wieland quoted in Lauren Rabinovitz, "An Interview with Joyce Wieland." *Afterimage* 8, no. 10 (May 1981): 12.

Page 232

Wieland quoted in Marie Fleming, *Joyce Wieland*, exh. cat. (Toronto: Art Gallery of Ontario, 1987), 104.

Page 239

Wieland quoted in an interview by Barbara Stevenson, October 8, 1986; Joyce Wieland fonds F0445, Series S00036 1999-003/005, File 5. The Clara Thomas Archives and Special Collections, York University, Toronto. 19–20.

Chartres ✓? 9
Duccio 9½
Titian 10
Tintoretto 11
Fra Angelico 12
Van Meegren 13
Vanderweyden 14
Caravaggio 15
Frans Hals 16
Caravaggio 17
Segnorelli 18
Manpedi 19
Ribera 20
Georges de La Tour 21
Ginteleschi 22
Poussin ♡ ✓ 23
Filippo Lippi 24
Botticelli * ✓✓ 25
Raphael * 26
Ingres ✓✓ 27
Roussillon 28
Leonardo 29
El Greco ✓ ✓ 30

Rouault 89
Van Gogh 90
Delacroix 91
Soutine ✓ 92
Piero de Cosimo 93
Monet ✓✓✓ 94
Fillippo Lippi 95
Uccelo ✓✓✓ 96
Talouse Lautrec 97
✓ David 98
Delaroche 99 ✓
Watteau ✓✓✓ 100
Fragonard 101 ✓✓
Bouche 102 ✓
Rubens 103
Ter Borche 104
Miro ✓✓✓✓✓ 105
Mondrian ✓✓✓ 106 ✓✓✓ xxx
Larry Rivers ✓✓ 107
Elaine de Kooning
Joan Mitchell ✓ 108
Vigee Le Brun ✓✓ 109
Vuillard 110
Mary Cassat 111
Berthe Morisot ✓✓ 112

Hawkins Coleman ✓✓ 48
Duchamp Marcel ✓ ✓✓✓
Picabia ✓ 49
Dali 50
Fra Angelico 51
Ernst ✓ 52
Magritte 53
Homer Watson 54
John Marin ✓ 55
Bilbo Jack
Moore Billy
Reynolds ? 56
Bacon
Arp ✓✓ 57
Arp ✓✓ 58
Delauney ✓ 59
Delauney ✓ 60
Van Doesburg 61
Gris 62
Leger ✓ 63
Moholy Nagy 64
Grace Hartigan 65
Sassetta 66
Durer 67
Cranach 68
Holbein 69
Van Eyck bros 70
Bruegel 72
Bosch 73

Bonnard 126
Carra ✓✓ 127
De Chirico ✓✓✓ 128
Degas *** 129
Goya ✓✓✓✓✓✓✓ * 130
Paul Klee ✓✓✓✓✓✓ 131
Mattisse Pierre ✓✓✓ 132
Monet 133
Picasso 134
Masaccio 135 ✓
T. Baer *
Hans Hoffman ✓ 136
Hoffman
Gorky ✓✓ 137
Pollock * J * 138
Beckman ✓ 139
De Kooning W. 140
La Chaise 141
Rothko Mark * 142
Lipchitz 143
✓ Still Clifford 144
✓ David Smith 145
✓ Newman Barnet 146
Motherwell 14
Jim Dines ✓✓✓
Allan Kaprow
Gottlieb 150
Millet ✓ 151
Kurt Schwitters
Frans Kline
Joyce Wieland
is having a
show of recent
work at the

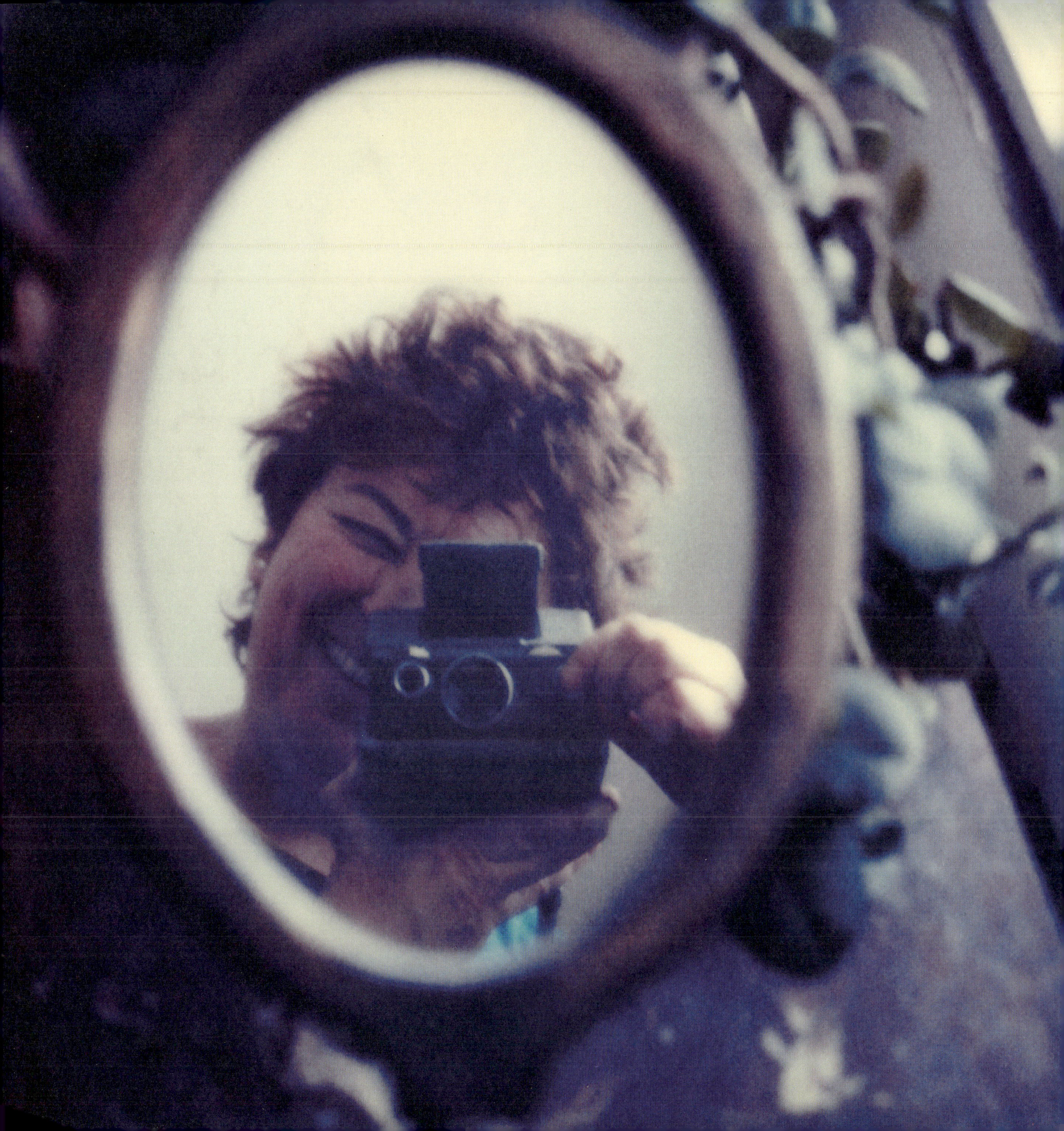

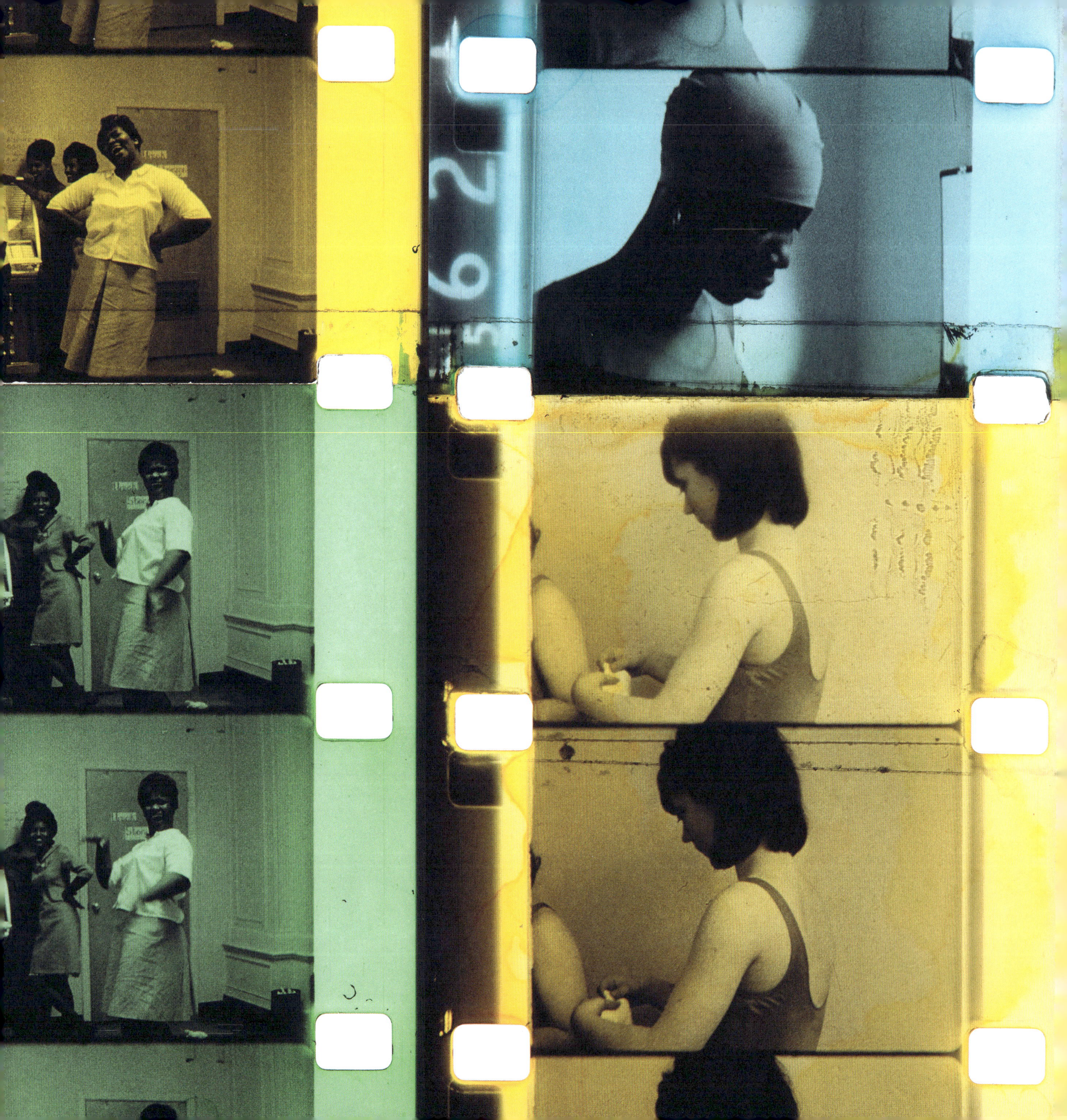